THE HANDBOOK OF ECONOMIC METHODOLOGY

The Handbook of
Economic Methodology

Edited by

John B. Davis

Department of Economics, Marquette University, USA

D. Wade Hands

Department of Economics, University of Puget Sound, USA

Uskali Mäki

Department of Philosophy, Erasmus University, Rotterdam, The Netherlands

Edward Elgar

Cheltenham, UK • Northampton, MA, USA

Published by
Edward Elgar Publishing Limited
8 Lansdown Place
Cheltenham
Glos GL50 2HU
UK

Edward Elgar Publishing, Inc.
6 Market Street
Northampton
Massachusetts 01060
USA

A catalogue record for this book is available from the British Library

Library of Congress Cataloguing in Publication Data
The handbook of economic methodology/edited by John B. Davis,
    D. Wade Hands and Uskali Mäki.
    Includes bibliographical references (p.   ).
    ISBN 1–85278–795–3
    1. Economics—Methodology—Handbooks, manuals, etc. I. Davis,
John Bryan. II. Hands, D. Wade. III. Mäki, Uskali.
HB131.H354   1998
330'.01—dc21   97–29958
                                                                                      CIP

ISBN 1 85898 795 3
Printed and bound in Great Britain by MPG Books Ltd, Bodmin, Cornwall

Contents

Contributors to this volume and their entries

Amariglio, Jack, Economics, Merrimack College, North Andover, US
Poststructuralism
Backhouse, Roger E., Economics, University of Birmingham, UK
Lakatos, Novel Facts, Paradigm/Normal Science, Rhetoric
Balzer, Wolfgang, Institute for Philosophy, Logic and Wissenschaftstheorie Ludwig-Maximilians University, Munich, Germany
Set Theoretic Structuralism
Bausor, Randall, Economics, University of Massachusetts at Amherst, US
Time
Biddle, Jeff E., Economics, Michigan State University, E. Lansing, US
Mitchell
Blaug, Mark, Economics, University of Exeter, UK
Methodology of Scientific Research Programmes, The Positive–Normative Distinction
Boettke, Peter J., Economics, Manhattan College, US
Von Mises
Boland, Lawrence A., Economics, Simon Fraser University, Burnaby, Canada
Conventionalism, Critical Rationalism
Boulier, Bryan L., Economics, George Washington University, Washington, US
Survey Methods
Boumans, Marcel, Economics, University of Amsterdam, The Netherlands
Tinbergen
Boylan, Thomas A., Economics, University College Galway, Ireland
van Fraassen
Bradie, Michael, Philosophy, Bowling Green State University, USA
Evolutionary Epistemology
Caldwell, Bruce, Economics, University of North Carolina, Greensboro, US
Hayek, Hutchison, Situational Analysis
Callari, Antonio, Economics, Franklin and Marshall College, Lancaster, US
Althusser
Cartwright, Nancy, Centre for the Philosophy of the Natural and Social Sciences, London School of Economics and Political Science, UK
Capacities
Coats, A.W., Economics, University of Nottingham, UK
Economic History, Economics as a Profession
Cottrell, Allin, Economics, Wake Forest University, Winston-Salem, US
John Maynard Keynes, Materialism, The Socialist Calculation Debate
Creedy, John, Economics, University of Melbourne, Australia
Edgeworth
Cremaschi, Sergio, Faculty of Letters and Philosophy, University of Turin, Italy
Malthus

Cross, Rod, Economics, University of Strathclyde, UK
The Duhem–Quine Thesis, Hysteresis
Davis, John B., Economics, Marquette University, Milwaukee, US
Conventions, Ontology, Organicism, Ricardo
De Marchi, Neil, Economics, Duke University, US
Mill
Deane, Phyllis, University of Cambridge, UK
John Neville Keynes
Dow, Sheila C., Economics, University of Stirling, UK
Post Keynesianism
Emami, Zohreh, Aererno College, Milwaukee, US
Robinson
Emmett, Ross B., Economics, Augustana University College, Alberta, Canada
De Gustibus Non Est Disputandum, Knight
Evensky, Jerry, Economics, Syracuse University, US
Smith
Gilbert, Christopher L., Economics, Queen Mary and Westfield College, University of London, UK
Econometric Methodology
Goldfarb, Robert S., Economics, George Washington University, Washington, US
Survey Methods
Granger, Clive W.J., Economics, University of California at San Diego, US
Granger Causality
Hamminga, Bert, Philosophy, Tilburg University, The Netherlands
Plausibility, The Poznan Approach
Hammond, J. Daniel, Economics, Wake Forest University, Winston-Salem, US
Friedman
Hands, D. Wade, Economics, University of Puget Sound, Tacoma, US
Positivism, Reflexivity, Relativism, Rorty, Scientific Explanation, The Sociology of Scientific Knowledge
Hargreaves Heap, Shaun, Economics, University of East Anglia, UK
Game Theory, Rational Choice
Henderson, James P., Economics, Valparaiso University, US
Whewell
Henderson, Willie, School of Continuing Studies, University of Birmingham, UK
Metaphor
Hirsch, Abraham, Economics, Brooklyn College, US
Dewey
Hodgson, Geoffrey M., Judge Institute of Management Studies, University of Cambridge, UK
Emergence, Evolutionary Economics, Selectionist Arguments
Hoover, Kevin D., Economics, University of California at Davis, US
Causality, The New Classical Macroeconomics
Janssen, Maarten C.W., Economics, Erasmus University, Rotterdam, The Netherlands
Aggregation, Microfoundations
Jarsulic, Marc, Economics, University of Notre Dame, US
Chaos in Economics

Jennings, Ann L., Economics, Lafayette College, Easton, US
Veblen
Jensen, Hans E., Economics, University of Tennessee, Knoxville, US
Myrdal
Kincaid, Harold, Philosophy, University of Alabama at Birmingham, US
Methodological Individualism/Atomism, Supervenience
Knorr Cetina, Karin, Sociology, University of Bielefeld, Germany
Constructivism
Knudsen, Christian, Copenhagen Business School, Denmark
Functionalism
Lagueux, Maurice, Philosophy, University of Montreal, Canada
A Priorism, Demarcation
Lawson, Tony, Faculty of Economics and Politics, University of Cambridge, UK
Tendencies, Transcendental Realism
Mäki, Uskali, Philosophy, Erasmus University, Rotterdam, The Netherlands
As If, Ceteris Paribus, Coase, Instrumentalism, Realism, Realisticness
Mayer, Thomas, Economics, University of California at Davis, US
Monetarism
Mayer, Tom, Department of Sociology and Institute of Behavioral Sciences, University of Colorado, Boulder, US
Analytical Marxism
Milberg, William S.,Economics, New School for Social Research, New York, US
Ideology
Mirowski, Philip Economics, University of Notre Dame, US
Georgescu-Roegen, Operationalism, Probability
Mongin, Philippe, National Centre of Scientific Research and University of Cergy-Pontoise, France
Expected Utility Theory, The Marginalist Controversy
Mongiovi, Gary, Economics, St. John's University, US
Sraffa
Morgan, Mary S., Economic History, London School of Economics and Political Science, UK
Haavelmo, Models
Nadeau, Robert, Philosophy, University of Quebec, Montreal, Canada
Spontaneous Order
Nelson, Alan, Philosophy, Brandeis University, Waltham, US
Experimental Economics, Natural Kind
Nelson, Julie, A., Economics, University of California at Davis, US
Feminist Economic Methodology
Niiniluoto, Ilkka, Philosophy, University of Helsinki, Finland
Fallibilism, Induction, Truth, Truthlikeness
O'Brien, Denis P., Economics, University of Durham, UK
Robbins
O'Gorman, Paschal F., Economics, University College Galway, Ireland
van Fraassen
Pettit, Philip, Research School of Social Sciences, Australian National University, Canberra, Australia
The Invisible Hand, Verstehen

Piimies, Jukka-Pekka, University of Helsinki, Finland and The European Parliament
Ceteris Paribus
Qin, Duo, Economics, Queen Mary and Westfield College, University of London, UK
Bayesian Econometric Methodology
Redman, Deborah A., George Washington University, US
Feyerabend
Reuten, Geert, Economics, University of Amsterdam, The Netherlands
Dialectical Method, Marx's Method
Rizvi, S. Abu Turab, Economics, University of Vermont, US
Utility
Rosenberg, Alexander, Honors Program, University of Georgia, Athens, US
Folk Psychology
Ruccio, David F., Economics, University of Notre Dame, US
Deconstruction
Runde, Jochen, Girton College, Cambridge, UK
Shackle, Uncertainty
Rutherford, Malcolm, Economics, University of Victoria, Canada
Commons, Institutionalism
Salanti, Andrea, Economics, University of Bergamo, Italy
Falsificationism, Pareto
Samuels, Warren J., Economics, Michigan State University, E. Lansing, US
Methodological Pluralism
Schabas, Margaret, Philosophy, University of York, Canada
Jevons
Sent, Esther-Mirjam, Economics, University of Notre Dame, US
Artificial Intelligence, Bounded Rationality, Simon
Shearmur, Jeremy, Political Science, Australian National University, Canberra, Australia
Popper
Shionoya, Yuichi, Social Development Research Institute, Tokyo, Japan
Schumpeterian Evolutionism
Simon, Herbert A., Psychology, Carnegie Mellon University, Pittsburgh, US
Psychology and Economics, Simulation
Spanos, Aris, Economics, University of Cyprus, Nicosia, Cyprus
Econometric Testing
Stanfield, James R., Economics, Colorado State University, Fort Collins, US
Polanyi
Swedberg, Richard, Sociology, University of Stockholm, Sweden
Economic Sociology, Weber
Tullock, Gordon, Economics, University of Arizona, Tucson, US
Public Choice
Uebel, Thomas E., Philosophy, Logic and Scientific Method, London School of Economics and Political Science, UK
Neurath
Vanberg, Viktor J., University of Freiburg, Germany
Buchanan, Constitutional Political Economy, Rule Following
Vilks, Arnis, Institute for Statistics and Econometrics, University of Hamburg, Germany
Axiomatization

Viskovatoff, Alex, Economics, Central European University, Budapest, Hungary
Holism
Walker, Donald A., Economics, Indiana University of Pennsylvania, US
Walras
Walliser, Bernard, Ecole Nationale des Ponts et Chaussées, Paris, France
Analogy, Generalization
Whitaker, John, Economics, University of Virginia, Charlottesville, US
Marshall
Wible, James R., Economics, University of New Hampshire, Durham, US
Economics of Science, Peirce
Wilber, Charles K., Economics, University of Notre Dame, US
Economics and Ethics
Zamagni, Stefano, Economics, University of Bologna, Italy
Hicks

Introduction

Our goal for the *Handbook of Economic Methodology* was to provide a detailed and comprehensive coverage of the field of economic methodology. Since economic methodology has only become a self-conscious research area during the last decade or two, some readers might wonder why we decided to edit such a volume at this particular time. Why not wait until the field has expanded and gained wider recognition? When we began the *Handbook* project five years ago, we believed there were at least two important reasons for proceeding with the project. These reasons say a great deal about what type of resource the *Handbook* ultimately became. To understand the first, it helps to have a little history of the development of the field of economic methodology.

Economic methodology, at least late twentieth-century economic methodology, developed in part through a process of borrowing from the philosophy of science. Philosophers of science in the 1960s and 1970s were in the midst of abandoning the 'received view' inherited from logical positivism in the 1930s, and the excitement associated with names such as Karl Popper, Thomas Kuhn and Imre Lakatos soon transferred to a small contingent of historians of economic thought interested in the topic of theory appraisal. This historical literature in turn reinvigorated interest in a number of the classic topics in economic methodology, such as the debate between Robbins and Hutchison, Friedman's instrumentalism and Samuelson's operationalism, and it also served to establish economic methodology as a new field closely linked to the history of economic thought. For a number of years, economic methodology travelled along these lines, with continuing application of the postpositivist tradition within the philosophy of science to economics, and with further investigation into important methodological episodes in the history of economic thought back through the marginalist revolution to classical economics. Thus one reason for our feeling the *Handbook of Economic Methodology* would be useful at this particular time was that by the late 1980s economic methodologists had succeeded both in digesting recent developments from the philosophy of science, and in analysing many of the key methodological episodes in the history of economic thought. In effect, there existed a relatively well agreed upon body of metatheoretical research that had been produced during the immediately preceding period.

However, there was another reason for the *Handbook*, and this second reason seems to be somewhat at odds with our first motivation. Simultaneous with the maturing of the field, there appeared a number of altogether new approaches to various topics in economic methodology, and these new approaches challenged the theory appraisal focus that had been economic methodologists' chief preoccupation during the previous decades. The rhetoric of economics and discourse analysis were the first to be recognized, but realism, the sociology of scientific knowledge and postmodernism also offered new strategies. Associated with these new, relatively autonomous, approaches came a range of new issues and topics that were distinct from the type of methodological debates historians of economic thought had already studied: selectionist arguments, hysteresis, holism, metaphor, reflexivity, microfoundations, experimental economics and folk psychology, to name but a few. Along with this development there was also entry into the field by a variety of individuals who had only modest links, or even no links, to the history of economic thought. Most prominently, practising philosophers took up the epistemological, logical, ethical and ontological problems associated with economics (a meeting ground that has been enhanced by the publication of the journal, *Economics and Philosophy*, starting in 1985). In addition, a number of practising economists and econometricians began to write about and comment on the methodology of economics, and more recently contributors from science studies have also added new perspectives. Thus in the last dozen or so years the field of economic methodology has expanded conceptually, in disciplinary focus and in terms of the total number of participants. From being a small and relatively self-contained field examining well-known methodological disputes and using standard postpositivist philosophy of science, methodological discourse has now begun to expand in a variety of different directions and to integrate a wide range of new perspectives.

We felt this more recent development was a very important reason for producing the *Handbook of Economic Methodology* at the present time. Since the field is apparently in a transitional phase, we thought it important to register the relative stability and state of consensus that has been achieved, so that future developments would have a common point of reference. Indeed, if the present proliferation of approaches and strategies continues unabated into the future, having an understanding of the various points of departure will be necessary for understanding what will undoubtedly be a very different, and more diverse, kind of methodological enterprise. Of course, the field may evolve in ways that make its origins of comparatively little interest. Against this are forces operating to establish economic methodology as a distinct field and these forces are likely to ensure some continuity of concern amidst the coming diversity of riches. The emergence of a second journal devoted explicitly to economic methodology – the *Journal of Economic Methodology* – is one indication of this development. Another is the increased acceptance of economic methodology as a legitimate mode of investigation within economics (and other fields, such as the philosophy of science). We hope that this *Handbook* becomes an additional force that sustains the perception of economic methodology as a distinct field with a series of antecedents permitting new developments into the future.

Thus our second reason for producing the *Handbook* at the present time is to lay a foundation (or at least common ground) for the future evolution of the field. Our first reason was to characterize that common ground. How are these two rationales different in practical terms? The answer to this question is important for appreciating the structure of the *Handbook* and the different categories of entries it includes. It is one thing to set forth established understanding of economic methodology with entries on such topics as instrumentalism, Popper, Mill and marginalist controversy, but it is quite another thing to attempt to point beyond these standard topics with entries that focus on debates over more philosophical issues, wider intellectual themes and possible future research. Thus, in addition to ensuring that the *Handbook* has entries on as many as possible of the topics traditionally discussed by methodologists, we also sought to include entries on topics that lay behind these discussions, even if these issues are not always obvious to those engaged in the debate. To this end, we have included entries on such topics as probability, metaphor, aggregation, chaos and emergence. We certainly do not know where the interests of economic methodologists will take the field in the future, but these subjects do seem to have been involved in many of the standard long-standing discussions. In effect, such topics have been employed as foundational materials in the formation of the field of economic methodology. The *Handbook* thus contains two broad categories of entries: those that register where methodology has been, and those that signal where methodology may be going.

Cross-cutting this conceptual breakdown is another, four-way, classification of the volume's entries that has also helped shape the *Handbook*'s final form. With no existing list of entries to which we might refer, we adopted the following four categories to guide the entry selection process.

First, the *Handbook* includes biographical entries meant to introduce important economists, methodologists and (a few) philosophers. Most of these entries concern individuals from the history of economics and economic methodology, but some are individuals whose work is of more recent vintage. It should be noted that we intentionally did not include a number of living individuals who will undoubtedly figure in the future history of economic methodology. Partly this was on account of the difficulty of evaluating contemporaries and partly it was on account of the difficulty of knowing where to stop. There are many talented and accomplished individuals involved in economic methodology today, and many of them are contributors to this volume.

Second, there are a number of entries that focus on issues in economics where methodological controversy has been central. By nature, these entries are mostly on subjects from the less recent history of economic thought, and thus are among the standard topics that one would consider in a course on economic methodology. As the present recedes into the past, there will be other important debates in economics with important methodological implications and overtones. These episodes would be added to the list of entries of future handbooks. Case studies on these episodes constitute an important area of research in economic methodology (as evidenced by the 1996 International Economic Association conference on methodological case studies) and we hope the entries included here will inspire more of this type of research.

Third, there are many entries in this volume that emphasize the philosophical inheritance that economic methodology has received from the philosophy of science. These again, by and large, concern consensus subjects in the field, but they also reflect the fact that economic methodologists are no longer as dependent as they once were on the postpositivist philosophical framework. In addition, there are entries on a number of new areas of philosophical inquiry – both from general philosophy and from more recent philosophy of science – that represent possible future directions for methodological research. Selecting these entries was one of the more difficult tasks involved in editing the *Handbook*, since not only did we have to speculate about the possible significance of different philosophical views, but also we often found ourselves in disagreement about the importance of certain candidates. As a default strategy, a few such candidates were omitted. We leave it to future editors to evaluate the wisdom of our choices on this category of entries.

Fourth, the *Handbook* includes entries on wider intellectual themes that have impinged on the work in economic methodology. These range from general movements in intellectual history to broad philosophical themes that pervade particular points of view in economics and economic methodology. In some instances, the distinction between well-established traditions and possible future developments is relatively easy to discern, since a number of the new programmes are known to most students of economic methodology, but in other cases we have tried to identify recurring themes that have only recently been recovered from the literature of the past. Because of the generality of many of these topics, it was often difficult to know exactly how to delineate entries, how, so to speak, to cut the literature at the relevant joints. Thus a number of the more general entries actually include subthemes that could have been entries themselves. Readers will need to search through them for many of the threads that are woven into larger fabrics.

Finally, we should emphasize that the *Handbook* is aimed at a general readership that includes both those with a research interest in economic methodology and those concerned with learning the basics of the field. Moreover, we believe that the volume will appeal to those interested in orthodox as well as heterodox approaches to economics. This volume, however, is not meant to provide a set of narrow tools that might function as a 'hands-on' or practical guide for the practice of economics. The day-to-day practice of economists enters only indirectly into the literature on the field of economic methodology and correspondingly into this volume. One last caveat: for a variety of reasons connected with the exigencies of the publication process, a number of the entries originally intended for the volume were not able to be included. We apologize to users of this volume for these omissions.

Aggregation

In the economics literature different kind of aggregation issues have been studied, including aggregation over individual behaviours, aggregation over goods and aggregation over time. This entry focuses exclusively on the relation between economic relations of individual behaviour, on one hand, and economic relations of group behaviour, on the other. The entry discusses the more technical literature on this issue and sketches the methodological import of this literature. The entry does *not* have the pretension to say anything on the more general philosophical issues concerning methodological individualism, holism and reductionism.

Although the distinction between individual and aggregate relationships has a long history in economic theory, the first serious investigation into the connection between the two types of relationships stems from 1946. Until that date, economists frequently assumed a straightforward analogy between individual and aggregate relationships. Hicks (1939: 245), for example, wrote that 'the transition [from individual to aggregate level] is made by using the simple principle ... that the behavior of a group of individuals, or a group of firms, obeys the same laws as the behavior of a single unit'.

This state of affairs changed mainly as the result of an article by Klein (1946a). Klein posed what is now understood as the aggregation problem. Suppose the set of individual relationships (functions) can be written as:

$$y_i = f_i(x_{i1}, ..., x_{im}), \qquad i = 1, ..., n, \tag{1}$$

where y_i is the independent variable of interest; x_{ij} is the jth explanatory variable for y_i. Consider further some kind of aggregate relationship (function)

$$Y = F(X_1, ... X_m) \tag{2}$$

and some aggregating functions

$$Y = G(y_1, ..., y_n) \text{ and } X_j = g_j(x_{1j}, ..., x_{nj}) \qquad j = 1, ..., m. \tag{3}$$

From equations (1)–(3) it follows that there are two ways to calculate Y on the basis of all x_{ij}, $i = 1, ..., n$ and $j = 1, ..., m$. First, using (1) and (3),

$$\begin{aligned} Y &= G(f_1(x_{11}, ..., x_{1m}), ..., f_n(x_{n1}, ..., x_{nm})) \\ &= G'(x_{11}, ..., x_{1m}, ..., x_{n1}, ..., x_{nm}) \end{aligned} \tag{4}$$

and second, using (2) and (3),

$$\begin{aligned} Y &= F(g_1(x_{11}, ..., x_{n1}), ..., g_m(x_{1m}, ..., x_{nm})) \\ &= F'(x_{11}, ..., x_{n1}, ..., x_{1m}, ..., x_{nm}) \end{aligned} \tag{5}$$

In equation (4), Y is calculated in two steps: first, the individual relationships in (1) are exploited to calculate all individual values y_i; second, the individual values y_i are aggregated using the first expression in equation (3). In equation (5), Y is also calculated in two steps, but they are different: first, the individual values x_{ij} are aggregated using the second expression in

1

equation (3) to obtain the aggregate values X_j; second the aggregate relationship (2) is used to calculate Y on the basis of the X_j's. It is clear that the two different ways to calculate Y have to yield identical solutions. However, for arbitrary relations (1)–(3), equations (4) and (5) will yield different results. This is the aggregation problem. Two types of approach to the problem have been suggested. Klein (1946a) and (1946b) and Nataf (1948) proposed looking for restrictions on the form of the functions f_i, G, g_j and F. May (1946), (1947) and Pu (1946), on the other hand, imposed certain restrictions on the values the variables x_{ij} may take. In the next two sections these two approaches are discussed, while the third section raises some methodological issues related to the two approaches.

Another issue related to aggregation appeared in the 1970s in the context of general equilibrium theory. As all individuals are assumed to face the same prices, the aggregation problem as discussed above does not arise in the transition from individual to aggregate excess demand functions. However, it was clear that, in order for general equilibrium theory to be useful, that is, for a unique stable equilibrium to exist, some strong conditions had to be imposed on the shape of the aggregate excess demand functions. The question was whether these conditions could be justified on the basis of assumptions on individual maximizing behaviour. This is the subject of the fourth section. A final section offers a brief conclusion.

The Klein/Nataf approach

Klein (1946a) studied the conditions that have to be satisfied in order for aggregation to be feasible if the explanatory variables x_{ij} are free to take on any value. Nataf (1948) proved the theorem that aggregation is feasible if and only if all functions (f_i, G, g_j, F, F' and G') are additively separable. Proofs under different assumptions (continuous functions instead of differentiable ones, or monotonic functions) are provided by Gorman (1953), among others. Nataf's theorem can be illustrated by means of the following example.

Cobb–Douglas production functions

Suppose that there are n firms, each of which has a production function that is given by $q_i = (k_i)^\alpha (l_i)^{1-\alpha}$, $i = 1, \ldots, n$, where q_i, k_i and l_i are the output, the capital input and the labour input of firm i, respectively. By taking the logarithms of both sides, one can see that this set of equations is additively separable. If the aggregating functions are some kind of products, for example, $Q = \Pi_{i=1}^n q_i$, $K = \Pi_{i=1}^n k_i$ and $L = \Pi_{i=1}^n l_i$, then an aggregate relationship exists and it takes the form $Q = \Pi_{i=1}^n (k_i)^\alpha (l_i)^{1-\alpha} = (\Pi_{i=1}^n k_i)(\Pi_{i=1}^n l_i)^{1-\alpha} = K^\alpha L^{1-\alpha}$.

The example demonstrates that, for aggregation to be feasible in the Klein/Nataf approach, it may be necessary to employ aggregating functions that are not easily interpretable from an economics point of view.

The fact that severe restrictions on the functional forms should be imposed may not be so surprising. An aggregate functional relationship can only exist if the aggregate explanatory variables X_j contain all the information that is needed to predict the value of the aggregate variable of interest Y. This means that the way the individual explanatory variables x_{ij} are distributed may not affect the value of Y. It is clear that this can only be the case if some severe restrictions are satisfied.

The May/Pu approach

May (1946) and Pu (1946) take the individual relations and some 'naturally defined' aggregating functions as given. Moreover, they argue that economic theory imposes restrictions on the values the individual explanatory variables x_{ij} may take. To illustrate their approach, suppose that individual production functions and aggregating functions are given by, respectively,

$$q_i = f_i(k_i, l_i) \qquad i = 1, \ldots, n, \tag{6}$$

$$K \equiv \Sigma^n_{i=1} k_i \text{ and } L \equiv \Sigma^n_{i=1} - l_i, \tag{7}$$

Under standard conditions of perfect competition, profit maximization by individual firms implies that

$$\frac{\partial q_i}{\partial l_i} = \frac{w}{p} \text{ and } \frac{\partial q_i}{\partial k_i} = \frac{r}{p} \qquad i = 1, \ldots, n, \tag{8}$$

where prices p, nominal wages w and nominal interest rates r are taken as given. The marginal productivity equations (8) determine the level of the individual production factors k_i and l_i for any level of q_i. Taking (6)–(8) together means that there are $3n + 4$ variables and $3n + 2$ equations. Under some regularity conditions, q_i, k_i and l_i can be expressed in terms of K and L:

$$q_i = h^1_i(K, L), k_i = h^2_i(K, L) \text{ and } l_i = h^3_i(K, L), \qquad i = 1, \ldots, n. \tag{9}$$

Accordingly, an aggregate production function can be defined as $Q \equiv \Sigma^n_{i=1} q_i = \Sigma^n_{i=1} h^1_i](K, L)$ $\equiv F(K, L)$.

The aggregate function defined by the May/Pu approach depends on the model that determines the values of the individual components that make up the aggregate explanatory variables (equation (8)). In other words, the aggregate relationship is context-dependent.

Some methodological considerations
A first question, initially posed by Klein (1946b), is whether equations like (8) are allowed to play a role in the derivation of an aggregate relationship. The issue is especially apparent when considering production functions. Individual production functions are often conceived of as purely technological functions that do not depend on the decisions made by the firms. If the May/Pu approach is adopted, the *aggregate* production function is *not* a purely technological function. Instead, it also depends on the assumption of perfect competition. Klein holds this to be a major objection to the May/Pu approach. May (1947: 63) responds, however, by arguing that even the individual production functions depend upon both technological and non-technological facts such as the organization of the production process.

A second point of difference between the two approaches concerns the way the aggregates should be constructed. May and Pu reject the 'distribution free' approach, because the aggregating functions employed there are 'completely void of any economic significance' (Pu 1946: 299). In response, Klein (1946b: 310), however, states that, 'in constructing scientific theory, we must look for useful results rather than things familiar to the layman'. Furthermore, Klein argues that 'in practice the correlation between these aggregates … and the published ones will be so high that one set can be substituted for the other' (Klein, 1946b: 311). However, this replacement of one set of aggregating functions by another is only legitimate if there is some knowledge that the error one makes in doing so is not too large. This type of knowledge is not provided by the Klein/Nataf approach.

Finally, the choice of one of the two approaches can depend on the aim of the research and the kind of information one disposes of (see Nelson, 1984). Three possibilities are considered. First, Klein thought of his own research in the following terms: 'let us assume the theory of micro and macroeconomics and then construct aggregates which are consistent with the two theories' (Klein 1946a: 94). This view is consistent with the idea that microeconomic theory is well-established and that the aim of research is to study the conditions that are implicitly made by macroeconomists who use models that are based on reasoning by analogy. Nataf's theorem shows that reasoning by analogy is legitimate only if some severe restrictions are met. Second, the Klein/Nataf approach is also the most suitable approach if an aggregate relationship has been observed and the aim of the research is to look for conditions under which this aggregate relationship can be regarded as resulting from some individual relationships and some aggregating functions. Third, the May/Pu approach seems to be the most suitable if the aim of the research is to suggest a new (form of an) aggregate relationship. This approach is useful if one has some knowledge about the form of the individual relationships or if one wants to work out the aggregate implications of assuming certain individual relationships.

Empirical restrictions on aggregate excess demand functions
In the standard theory of consumer demand, individual consumers are supposed to maximize utility subject to a budget constraint. The solution to this problem is the individual (excess) demand function. Under standard conditions, individual and aggregate excess demand functions are continuous and homogeneous of degree zero. Moreover, the sum of the values of individual excess demands is equal to zero. The same holds true for aggregate excess demand (this is known as Walras' Law). The standard model of consumer demand imposes two additional restrictions on the form of the *individual* demand functions. The individual demand functions have to be such that the matrix of substitution effects is symmetric and negative semi-definite. These two conditions have been used to test the applicability of the hypothesis of utility maximization subject to a budget constraint to a particular situation.

An important question is whether utility maximization subject to a budget constraint imposes similar restrictions on the shape of the *aggregate* excess demand functions. Among others, Sonnenschein (1972) and Debreu (1974) showed that the answer is negative: any set of continuous functions that satisfies Walras' Law and that is homogeneous of degree zero can be considered as a set of aggregate excess demand functions. The different proofs of this result employ some rather advanced topology which will not be discussed here (for a good, non-technical, discussion, see Kirman, 1989). The intuition may be grasped as follows. A utility function is a theoretical construct that is attributed to an individual agent by the economist. There is no empirical equivalent of this construct, so that the theorist is not bound to a particular form of the utility function. The difference between individual and aggregate excess demand functions is that in the individual case there is only 'one degree of freedom', while in the aggregate case the theorist is able to choose many different utility functions, one for each individual. Thus the 'degree of freedom' is enlarged considerably and it is no surprise that economic theory imposes fewer restrictions on aggregate excess demand functions than on individual excess demand functions.

Recently, some authors have proposed some solutions for this negative result. The approaches have in common that they restrict the distribution of individual explanatory variables and, in this sense, are in line with the May/Pu approach discussed above. Grandmont (1987) proposes restricting the distribution of preferences over individual agents. The idea is that, although individual preferences are not identical, they are not too dissimilar either. In the different proofs of the negative result referred to above, it may be necessary to assume that the distribution of preferences over individual agents is extremely unequal. If the distribution of preferences is restricted to a certain class, as Grandmont assumes, some further restrictions on the aggregate excess demand functions can be derived.

Hildenbrand (1983) analyses the question why the 'Law of Demand' holds true for many estimated demand curves. He proposes to restrict the distribution of income (endowments) to a certain class. In particular, he shows that the average income effect is negative if the income distribution is independent of the price system and has a decreasing density function. This, together with the negativity of the substitution effect, implies that aggregate demand curves are decreasing in their own price. Thus, by imposing a restriction on the income distribution, Hildenbrand is able to derive an empirically testable restriction that aggregate demand curves must satisfy. Along the same lines, Hildenbrand (1994) analyses properties of market demand that are created when aggregating individual demand relationships.

Methodological lessons

There are two main points made in the literature on aggregation that are of interest from a methodological point of view. The early literature reviewed in the first two sections above shows that in macroeconomics one cannot accept both of the following statements: (a) the structure of aggregate relationships is analogous to the structure of their microeconomic counterpart, and (b) aggregate variables are simply the sum of the individual variables. The aggregation literature has shown that macroeconomists have to remove one of the two statements from their vocabulary. Klein suggests abandoning the first, while May and Pu propose abandoning the second.

The other important point is that there is no *a priori* ground to believe that aggregate excess demand functions satisfy properties that guarantee the stability and unity of the equilibrium point in general equilibrium theory. In this sense the Debreu/Mantel/Sonnenschein result is quite damaging for the potential usefulness of the general equilibrium research program. More recent literature is interesting in the sense that different authors show that by imposing some restrictions on the aggregation procedure some properties of aggregate demand are 'created' that do not have their individual level counterpart.

MAARTEN C.W. JANSSEN

References

Debreu, G. (1974), 'Excess Demand Functions', *Journal of Mathematical Economics*, **1**, 15–21.
Gorman, W. (1953), 'Community Preference Fields', *Econometrica*, **21**, 63–80.
Grandmont, J.-M. (1987), 'Distribution of Preferences and the Law of Demand', *Econometrica*, **55**, 155–61.
Hicks, J. (1939), *Value and Capital*, Oxford: Clarendon Press.
Hildenbrand, W. (1983), 'On the "Law of Demand"', *Econometrica*, **51**, 997–1019.
Hildenbrand, W. (1994), *Market Demand*, Princeton, NJ: Princeton University Press.
Kirman, A. (1989), 'The Intrinsic Limits of Modern Economic Theory: The Emperor has no Clothes', *Economic Journal*, **99**, (supplement), 126–39.
Klein, L. (1946a), 'Macroeconomics and the Theory of Rational Behavior', *Econometrica*, **14**, 93–108.
Klein, L. (1946b), 'Remarks on the Theory of Aggregation', *Econometrica*, **14**, 303–12.
May, K. (1946), 'The Aggregation Problem for a One Industry Model', *Econometrica*, **14**, 285–98.
May, K. (1947), 'Technological Change and Aggregation', *Econometrica*, **15**, 51–63.
Nataf, A. (1948), 'Sur la Possibilité de Construction de Certains Macromodèles', *Econometrica*, **16**, 232–44.

Nelson, A. (1984), 'Some Issues Surrounding the Reduction from Macroeconomics to Microeconomics', *Philosophy of Science*, **51**, 573–94.
Pu, S. (1946), 'A Note on Macroeconomics', *Econometrica*, **14**, 299–302.
Sonnenschein, H. (1972), 'Market Excess Demand Functions', *Econometrica*, **40**, 549–63.

Althusser, Louis

Undoubtedly the most important Marxist philosopher of the second half of the twentieth century, Althusser (1918–90) was moved by an early appreciation of 'the crisis of Marxism' to attempt no less than a complete theoretical and philosophical reconstruction of that system. This reconstruction was quite singular and suggestive, given the philosopher's commitment to remain within Marxism while reshaping its contours in line with the concerns and the imagination of post-World War II French intellectual culture. Of note in this context are his intellectual (in some cases, also personal) relationships with Sartre, Lévi-Strauss, Barthes, Lacan, Foucault and Derrida. Althusser's work influenced (segments within) the Marxist community to accept and even to make significant contributions to a number of trends (structuralism, post-structuralism and deconstruction) that, more recently, seem to have condensed into a general postmodernist revolution. It is thus that Althusser comes to have an important place in the mid-1990s reconfiguration of the methodological environment for economists.

What, in Althusser's work of the 1960s, is most suggestive of more recent intellectual trends is a certain openness and fluidity of the *oeuvre*. His texts are punctuated by bold suggestions (of, for example, an 'epistemological break' between the young and the mature Marx) such as only a worthy philosopher would pose, by limiting and yet heroic concepts (for example, a 'last instance determination by the economy') and by generous, yet studied, acknowledgements of errors and exaggerations (theoreticism). Certainly this fluidity was required by the vicissitudes of post-World War II. Marxism, yet the biographical material that followed Althusser's death suggests that it can also be explained by the transitional epics that punctuated the philosopher's life. A prisoner in Germany during World War II, Althusser first negotiated a personal transformation from a prewar right-wing to a postwar left-wing Catholic. Pushed then by Papal intolerance of left-wing Catholicism, he negotiated a new identity as a member of the French Communist Party, only to face the problem of how to remain institutionally linked with 'the workers' movement' while rescuing it from institutionalized (Stalinist) rigidity. Finally, Althusser had to negotiate his life through the phases of a chronic manic-depression that set in after the war and besieged him, requiring frequent hospitalization, until his death. Given these circumstances, it is reasonable to think that Althusser's renegotiation of Marxism through the prism of psychoanalytic concepts (Freud's 'overdetermination', Lacan's ego–ego mirror) was partially illuminated by his intimate understanding of the exploratory manoeuvres, the excesses and the recoveries of any process of 'character transformation'.

In the 1960s, Althusser tried to develop a rigorous map for Marxist theory. He produced a 'symptomatic reading' through which he tried to remove from Marx's texts the elements of economism and of humanism left by an incomplete break with Hegelian essentialism. Many readers saw in this work (primarily *For Marx* in 1965, and *Reading Capital* in 1968) an attempted theoretical 'purity', and denounced it as a quasi-Stalinist attempt to provide Marxism with an official doctrine. (A number of such criticisms has been compiled in Elliott, 1994, which also contains an extensive bibliography of Althusser's published texts.) But, although he himself acknowledged a certain theoreticism, Althusser explained this work as, rather, an attempt to deStalinize Marxism: the strong anti-essentialism of the work was the premise to an equally strong critique of the teleology (hidden in the form of 'the dialectic') through which official Marxism had justified its statist and totalitarian practices. In this vein, Althusser progressively moved towards rejecting the view that Marxism itself was 'a system' and to replacing it with a view of it as 'an intervention *in* philosophy' (or history, or economics).

This transformation moved Marxism even beyond the modernization of it that Althusser had imagined. Apart from the fact that the recognition of Marxism, and of other theoretical positions, as 'discourse' was an anticipation of the procedures of deconstruction, the idea of Marxism as an intervention – in philosophy, or economics, or historiography – carries the implication that these discursive formations have their (relative) autonomy and are not reducible, as Marxists had once had it, to mere bourgeois manifestations of an underlying reality. If nothing else does, this recognition of the autonomy of discourse(s) by itself represents a significant turn in the Marxist tradition.

Also recognizable in Althusser's attack on essentialism is a postmodernist critique of modernist concepts of science (see Amariglio, 1987, for an early appreciation of this thread). The specific application of this postmodernist anti-essentialism to Marxism produced a re-evaluation of its economics, its concepts of social processes and agents, and its vision of the dynamics of capitalist processes and socialist construction. Central to this re-evaluation was the elaboration, most fully developed in Resnick and Wolff (1987), of Althusser's adaptation of the Freudian concept of 'overdetermination' to social processes. The implication of this concept, that no social process can be in principle abstracted from the theorist's gaze, has given to Marxism a new theoretical impulse to construct concrete analyses of all social process – quite different from the erstwhile theoretical impulse, which only the best Marxist had been able to resist, to eschew the irreducible concreteness of social practices in order to proclaim *presumed* class totalities and historical trajectories.

After more than a decade of relative silence by and on Althusser, a number of texts have more recently given a new voice to Althusser and the Althusserian enterprise. Together with the publication of new material from the Althusser archives, two anthologies (Kaplan and Sprinker, 1993; Callari and Ruccio, 1996) point to a further evolution of the thought of Althusser towards a redefinition of the fundamental category of Marxist philosophy, the very category of materialism. For Althusser, materialism came to stand less as a reference to the traditional 'material' conditions of production and more as a reference to the primacy of the contingent, of the 'aleatory' and of the 'political' in history and society. This last major development in the thought of Althusser parallels well some of the more recent methodological emphases on uncertainty and on the role of identities (race and gender, and others, as well as class) in the constitution of economic processes and of different forms of economic communities.

ANTONIO CALLARI

Bibliography

Althusser, Louis (1965), *For Marx*, trans. Ben Brewster, London: Allen Lane.

Althusser, Louis (1976), *Essays in Self-Criticism*, trans. Grahame Lock, London: New Left Books.

Althusser, Louis (1993), *The Future Lasts Forever. A Memoir*, ed. Olivier Corpet and Yann Moulier Boutang, trans. Richard Veasey, New York: The New Press.

Althusser, Louis and Etienne Balibar (1968), *Lire le capital*, Paris: François Maspero.

Amariglio, Jack (1987), 'Marxism against Economic Science. Althusser's Legacy', *Research in Political Economy*, **10**, 159–94.

Callari, Antonio and David Ruccio (eds) (1996), *Postmodern Materialism and the Future of Marxist Theory. Essays in the Althusserian Tradition*, Hanover/London: Wesleyan University Press.
Elliott, Gregory (ed.) (1994), *Althusser. A Critical Reader*, Oxford/Cambridge, USA: Blackwell.
Kaplan, Ann and Michael Sprinker (eds) (1993), *The Althusserian Legacy*, London/New York: Verso.
Resnick, Stephen and Richard Wolff (1987), *Knowledge and Class: A Marxian Critique of Political Economy*, Chicago: University of Chicago Press.

Analogy

Common language makes use of many loose metaphors, where well-recognized attributes of a given entity are carried over to another entity, in order to suggest for the latter an original and often figurative meaning. Scientific language makes use of more precise analogies, where duly established properties of a given system are transferred to another system, in order to acquire a deeper understanding of its structure and behaviour. Intradisciplinary analogies, developed by comparative sciences, look for a correspondence between characteristics of objects in nearby subfields, and eventually give rise to unified models by identification or reduction of these subfields. Interdisciplinary analogies, developed by theoretical sciences, consider an accepted model in one field and try to adapt it to a foreign field, where it might finally be accepted after some modifications and reinterpretations.

Economics considers intradisciplinary analogies, comparison between different settings like imperfect markets or auctions where several actors are engaged in strategic interactions leading, for instance, to game theory. Economics imports interdisciplinary analogies from physics, where rational mechanics inspired Walras' equilibrium notion, as well as from biology, where physiology influenced the concept of the division of labour. Economics even exports analogies, towards biology where Darwin's natural selection owed to Malthus' population law, as well as towards other social sciences, where market models are applied to 'immaterial' goods. Stressing analogies borrowed by economics from outside, the following considers successively their formal pattern, their validity domain and their practical use, before examining their life cycle.

Formal pattern

An analogy first relates two foreign entities by stating a one-to-one correspondence between some of their respective attributes, then extends that correspondence to respective phenomena which link these attributes. An analogy is 'formalistic' if the modeller just considers that the same analytical structure applies to the corresponding phenomena, expressing a formal invariant of both entities and stressing a precise isomorphism between both fields. An analogy is 'substantive' if the modeller suggests that the same qualitative interpretation holds for the corresponding phenomena, expressing a common understanding of both entities and stressing identical first principles in both fields. Their difference lies in the syntactic role devoted to analogy, either as a way of summarizing foreign phenomena into a synthetic framework or as a way of subsuming unfamiliar phenomena under a unitary meaning.

An analogy is descriptive if the lawlike description of the relation between variables is similar (linear, logarithmic, multiplicative) in the corresponding fields. For instance, the Newtonian law of attraction between two bodies and the Reilly law of road traffic between two towns show the same proportionality to the body masses or town populations and inverse proportionality to the square distance of bodies or towns. An analogy is explanatory if the causal explanation of the behaviour of variables (cycles, hysteresis, chaos) is similar in the corresponding fields.

For instance, in Volterra's predator–prey model and in Goodwin's macroeconomic labour model, out-of-phase cycles concerning two variables are explained by the same underlying structure where the variation of one of two variables is proportional to the level of the other.

In order to control its logical coherence and to assess its structural strength, it is desirable to turn a substantive analogy into a formalistic one, by transforming a verbal interpretation into an analytical explanation. Since an analogy is often available on a restricted subset of magnitudes (two variables varying proportionally can be exhibited in almost any system), formalization helps to check how far the entity correspondence can be extended. Since an analogy is always feasible at a high level of relation genericity (two variables are surely related by a sufficiently general function), formalization helps to check how precisely the entity correspondence can be stated. If an analogy is useful as a means of reasoning by suggesting hidden correspondences between foreign entities, it is only by a rigorous formalization that these correspondences gain some consistency or, on the contrary, vanish away.

When systematizing descriptive analogies, some general rules or principles may be brought out and applied to apparently irrelevant phenomena in natural and social sciences. For instance, the least action principle concerns the minimization of the Hamiltonian of a physical system of bodies submitted to mutual forces, as well as the maximization of the utility of a trader involved in a market animated by mutual exchanges. When specifying explanatory analogies, some general schemes or paradigms may be elicited and illustrated in apparently faraway domains of research. For instance, the evolutionary paradigm concerns the evolution of animals in an ecological network by mutation of genes and selection of organisms, as well as the evolution of firms in an economic market by innovation of routines and competition between organizations.

Validity domain
An analogy asserts that, in spite of the difference of meaning of variables as well as of relations, a model recognized as empirically valid in one field may be considered as valid in another field too. An analogy is 'heuristic', in the context of discovery, if it helps to delineate a newly studied system and to organize its subsystems, stressing the relevance of such a magnitude or the appropriatedness of such a link. An analogy is 'assertive', in the context of proof, if it leads to support for an original system a model already accepted for a well-known one, by some sort of induction process based on sufficiently similar situations. Their difference lies in the semantic role granted to analogy, either as a tool of premodelization which suggests reasonable assumptions, or as a tool of postmodelization which prescribes accepted assumptions.

An analogy is ontological if theoretical models of structural, functional or evolutionary properties which convinced in one field are illuminating in another. For instance, organism models with their blood or nervous networks serve as reference for economic models with their commodities or information networks, as concerns self-regulation by feedback loops, either negative (temperature stabilization, price stabilization) or positive (energy accumulation, Keynesian multiplier). An analogy is methodological if scientific methods of experimentation, testing or simulation which succeeded in one field remain valuable in another. For instance, macroeconomic models are classically compared to meteorological models as concerns the extension and precision of available data, the structure and validity of their basic laws and the horizon and accuracy of their long-term forecasts.

In order to check its empirical validity and to test its potential fecundity, it is wise to avoid using an analogy assertively and to keep it heuristic, by taking it as a question and not as an answer in a scientific debate. Even when a proposition is an exact replica of a recognized one, it may be less testable since it contains some theoretical concepts not directly measurable while the other is composed of observable concepts only. Even when a model is a faithful transcription of an accepted one, it may be less well confirmed since it is tested only in some faraway consequences while the other is tested in its assumptions too. If an analogy is productive as a means of investigation by stressing differences rather than similarities, it is only by a critical discussion that one prevents it from becoming sterilizing and from leading to imperialism.

Any principle which fits well in one field has then to be adapted in its form and its interpretation when it is applied to another field. For instance, contrary to a physical system path derived from a global potential, an economic system path is not derived from a collective utility, even if it stems from actors' behaviour derived from individual utility; moreover, utility is a theoretical concept contrary to energy in physics, which is an observable one. An explanation is even more profoundly transformed when exported to another field, in its underlying mechanisms and validating methods. For instance, the evolution of firms looks more Lamarckian than Darwinian as concerns variation (oriented innovations rather than blind stochastic mutations), transmission (fast cultural imitation rather than slow biological reproduction) and selection (global learning rather than local adaptation).

Practical use

An analogy leans on an image taken from one field in order to make sensible a model proposed in another field, for the sake of other scientists and students or of decision makers and the general public. An analogy is 'pedagogic' if it tries to popularize some model in one field by an appeal to intuition of a phenomenon in another field, especially by borrowing a scientific illustration from a more entrenched discipline. An analogy is 'vindicative' if it pretends to defend a model in one field by an appeal to the authority of a theory in another field, especially by looking for a scientific benchmark from a more advanced discipline. Their difference lies in the pragmatic role attributed to analogy, either as a device for an efficient transmission of unaccustomed knowledge or as a device for a decisive legitimation of uncertain knowledge.

An analogy is positive if it states that some organizational or dynamic property of a system is transferable from one domain to another. For instance, the Boltzmann model of gas kinetics and the Foley model of market kinetics show in a similar way how the macroproperties of the gas or market are related to the most probable configuration of given microproperties of molecules or transactions. An analogy is normative if it asserts that some action or design principle applied to a system can be transposed between already descriptively similar fields. For instance, in the Bernard model of organic sickness as in the Tinbergen model of macroeconomic disturbance, the regulation of an open system is achieved by compensating by an outside medical treatment or economic policy for the inside deviation from normal functioning revealed by certain symptoms.

In order to regulate its social use and to master its ideological influence, it is necessary to limit a vindicative analogy and to favour a pedagogic one, by considering an analogy as a tool and not as a weapon in a social discussion. Taking into account that any concept is always polysemous, a strict demarcation has to be maintained between its technical and its popular sense, especially when the latter is as often value-laden. Taking into account also that any relation has many connotations, the specific point of view concerned with the analogical transfer has to be cautiously singled out, especially when other focuses happen to be more normative. If an analogy is efficient as a means of communication in accelerating the understanding of abstract notions and ideas, it is only by firm relativization that one prevents it from becoming a dogma and from leading to obscurantism.

Any principle is subject to misleading interpretations, especially when applied to more complex and unstable systems than the original ones. For instance, the equilibrium concept suggests that statics is more important than dynamics for mechanical as well as economic systems since steady states are asymptotically obtained by convergence of transitory states; moreover, the term 'equilibrium' is associated with a good state, even if some equilibria are disastrous. It is likely that any explanation is subject to reductive meaning, especially when extended from inert objects to intentional actors. For instance, the evolution theory suggests that outside material or cultural forces are stronger than inside voluntary objectives to guide a social as well as a material system; moreover, the term 'evolution' is correlated to the idea of progress, even if evolution may lead to complete uniformity.

Life cycle

Each specific analogy describes a whole life cycle of several decades, from its initial proposal, when it appears as profoundly illuminating, to its final withdrawal, when it becomes completely disembodied. Its proposal generally follows a preliminary investigation in a field where some properties are first autonomously established before the discovery that similar properties had already been stated in another field. Its discussion consists of a systematic critique of the whole original model when applied to the new domain, with expression of its conceptual content, delineation of its validity domain and evaluation of its practical use. Its dissolution results from the adaptation and partial integration of the model in the reception field, model which finally becomes able to evolve on its own and retains only in its vocabulary the memory of its origin.

Some analogies have ended their life cycles, especially when they correspond to models completely and definitively formalized in the original field. For instance, the Walrasian model inherited from classical mechanics has integrated, in terms of differential equations, the notion of individual optimization associated with a direct causality by reasons and the notion of collective equilibrium associated with a circular causality by actions. Other analogies are still alive, especially when they refer to models again in conceptual evolution in the original field. For instance, the evolutionary model inherited from Darwinian biology is still under discussion with regard to the identification of the concrete support of the reproduction mechanism in economics, or the formalization of the group selection mechanism which is more probable in economics.

Like paradoxes, analogies play a driving role in the history of economic ideas, from past times when they contributed to the scientific status of economics, to modern times when they participate in the unification of science. The classical economists (Smith, Walras, Marshall) all resorted to analogies taken from selected branches of physics and which often originated many years earlier, and even reconstructed physical knowledge in order to have it more easily transposed. The modern economists (Keynes, Samuelson, Friedman) drew analogies from more varied fields of physics and biology and handled them very cautiously, contrary to the practice of minor economists who either feared them or were obsessed by them. The economists of the present day always borrow some analogies rapidly adapted from recent developments of natural sciences (hysteresis, percolation, avalanche), but more often adopt new formal structures by forgetting their disciplinary origin.

The modern form of an analogy is the definition of a general class of models, illustrated in different fields without subordination of one to another. For instance, stochastic processes governed by Fokker–Planck equations or master equations appear in the physical Ising model showing polarization of atoms' magnetic states through neighbouring interactions, as well as in the economic mimetic model showing polarization of agents' expectations through neighbouring imitation. Such a class of models is intermediate between mathematical structures and regional models, in the sense that they are only partially interpreted. For instance, non-linear deterministic dynamics applies at the same time to the evolution of chemical products, animal species, techniques or institutions and are able to explain analogous phenomena such as bifurcations, lock-ins, chaotic attractors or structural instabilities.

BERNARD WALLISER

Bibliography
Amable, B., M. Henry, F. Lordon and R. Topol (1995), 'Hysteresis revisited, a methodological approach', in R. Cross (ed.), *The Natural Rate of Unemployment: reflexions on 25 years of the hypothesis*, Cambridge, MA: Cambridge University Press.
Bak, P., and K. Chen, J. Scheinkman and M. Woodford (1993), 'Aggregate fluctuations from independent sectoral shocks: self-organized criticality in a model of production and inventory dynamics', *Richerche Economiche*, **47**, (1), 3–30.
Bicchieri, C. (1988), 'Should a scientist abstain from a metaphor?', in A. Klamer, D. McCloskey and R. Solow (eds), *The Consequences of Economic Rhetoric*, Cambridge, MA: Cambridge University Press.
Black, M. (1962), *Models and Metaphors*, Ithaca, NY: Cornell University Press.
Cross, R. (1995), 'Metaphors and time reversibility and irreversibility in economic systems', *Journal of Economic Methodology*, **2**, (1), 123–34.
Elster, J. (1977), 'Critique des analogies biologiques, plaidoyer pour l'autonomie des sciences', *Revue Française de Sociologie*, **18**, 369–95.
Foley, D. (1994), 'A statistical equilibrium theory of markets', *Journal of Economic Theory*, **62**, (2), 321–45.
Gutsatz, M. (1985), 'Economie, physique, mathématiques: de l'économie politique à la science économique (1976–1910). Essai sur la constitution d'une science', thesis, University of Aix–Marseilles 2.
Klamer, A. and T.C. Leonard (1994), 'So what's an economic metaphor?', in P. Mirowski (ed.), *Natural Images in Economic Thought*, Cambridge, MA: Cambridge University Press.
Lagueux, M. (1993), 'Natural selection and economics', *Methodus*, **5**, (1), 93–100.
Marshall, A. (1898), 'Distribution and exchange', *Economic Journal*.
Ménard, C. (1981), 'La machine et le cœur. Essai sur les analogies dans le raisonnement économique', in A. Lichnerowicz, F. Perroux and J. Gadoffre (eds), *Analogie et connaissance*, tome 2, Paris: Maloine.
Mirowski, P. (1989), *More Heat than Light*, Cambridge, MA: Cambridge University Press.
Renault, M. (1992), 'Analogie formelle et analogie substantielle en économie: l'économie néo-classique, l'énergétique et la physique des champs', *Economie Appliquée*, **XLV** (3), 55–90.
Théret, B. (1995), 'Du statut des métaphores médicales en économie politique: essai d'approche archéologique', *Cahiers Charles Gide*, 1.

Analytical Marxism

Analytical Marxism is a branch of Marxist thought that uses modern methods of analytical reasoning such as axiomatic logic, mathematical modelling and statistical inference to evaluate and extend Marxist propositions about society. Analytical Marxists view Marxist social analysis as a part of social science rather than as an entirely distinct intellectual endeavour. In contrast to Marxist writers such as Georg Lukács or Louis Althusser, they regard the most important aspect of Marxist social analysis to be its substantive ideas rather than its methodology: Marxists can and should use any legitimate scientific methodology.

Self-conscious analytical Marxism emerges with the publication of Gerald Cohen's, *Karl Marx's Theory of History: A Defence* (1978). This book uses the methods of analytical philosophy to defend a traditional conception of historical materialism that views the decisive trend in history as the development of human productive power. Another important contributor to modern analytical Marxism is John Roemer (1981, 1982) who deploys general equilibrium models to investigate classical Marxist economic problems, reformulate the Marxist theory of exploitation and, most recently, to construct a new conception of market socialism (Roemer, 1994).

Jon Elster (1985) provides a systematic critique of classical Marxism based upon the principles of methodological individualism and rational choice. The most extensive empirical research with an analytical Marxist provenance is Erik Wright's comparative studies of class structure and class consciousness (1985). Wright has also written about the philosophical foundations of analytical Marxism. Adam Przeworski (1985) uses game theory to explore the nature of working class politics under capitalism. An exposition, synthesis and appraisal of the various threads in analytical Marxism is given by Mayer (1994).

Methodology
Analytical Marxists use methods like game theory, causal modelling, optimization theory, mathematical logic and general equilibrium analysis. They find fault with some important propositions of classical Marxism, such as the labour theory of value, the falling rate of profit and the theory of linear social evolution. The social theories and political analyses proposed by analytical Marxists are highly diverse. Whatever unity exists occurs on an abstract metatheoretical plane rather than on the level of social theory or political commitment.

The use of general equilibrium analysis does not require claiming that an economic system is stable or that it approaches an equilibrium. Only a few analytical Marxists actually use general equilibrium analysis. They use it to investigate the joint theoretical consequences of multiple intersecting economic tendencies and how these theoretical consequences change when some of the underlying tendencies are altered. Thus general equilibrium analysis functions as a tool of theoretical elaboration rather than as a means of predicting the trajectory of an economic system.

Methodological individualism has two main functions within analytical Marxism. On the one hand, it guards against forms of reasoning that cannot be developed in a strictly logical manner and/or are not subject to empirical test. Reasoning of this sort has permeated certain forms of Marxism, but analytical Marxists regard it as improper, at least within the domain of science. Methodological individualism also provides a way of connecting macrosocial and microsocial forms of analysis. A scientifically legitimate theory cannot reason exclusively in the domain of social structure. Methodological individualism demands that a scientific theory explain why particular human beings in particular social locations act as they do.

Using a plurality of techniques reflects the self-understanding of analytical Marxism as one scientific approach among many, rather than as an entirely different science with an entirely unique methodology. A scientific approach, no matter how plausible, cannot predict the future development of scientific methodology and should therefore practise all currently reasonable techniques. In the past, many Marxists handicapped themselves by rejecting modern social scientific methodolgy. Analytical Marxists do not want to repeat this mistake.

Theory of history
Analytical Marxists do not have a unified theory of history, but discussion of this topic has revolved around Cohen's conception of historical materialism. This rests upon three main principles: *development thesis*, that the productive forces of society tend to develop throughout history; *primacy thesis*, that the level of development of the productive forces explains the nature of the economic structure; and *superstructure thesis*, that the nature of the economic structure

of society explains the character of its non-economic institutions. These principles imply that the economic structure of society (for example, forms and distribution of property, and organization of work) will vary according to the level of productive development. They also imply that changes in economic structure will be associated with changes in non-economic institutions (for example, law, religion, state and family).

The development thesis has considerable support among analytical Marxists, although there is no consensus about exactly why it holds. Neither the primacy thesis nor the superstructure thesis commands as much agreement. Moreover, most analytical Marxists dispute the functionalist reasoning Cohen uses to support these propositions. Such reasoning, critics maintain, violates the principle of methodological individualism, which requires that individual actors have explanatory priority over social structures.

The most important claim of the classical Marxist theory of history is that capitalism is doomed and, sooner or later, will be replaced by a different mode of production. Analytical Marxists identify structural problems in capitalist economic systems and their work gives greater logical rigour to older Marxist theories of capitalist crisis (Roemer, 1981). The demise of capitalism, they conclude, is conceivable and perhaps desirable, but few, if any, regard it as inevitable or even likely in the foreseeable future.

Exploitation
Exploitation is the most distinctive concept of Marxist social theory. Analytical Marxists, following the lead of John Roemer (1982), have reformulated the concept of exploitation to remove its dependence upon the labour theory of value and to show how it occurs within the framework of general equilibrium theory. Roemer defines exploitation as differential income resulting from differential ownership of productive assets. Thus different kinds of exploitation correspond to different kinds of productive assets. Capitalist exploitation, in particular, results from differential ownership of capital goods.

The first important analytical Marxist result to do with exploitation, sometimes called the Fundamental Marxian Theorem, was proved by Michio Morishima (1973). Given a capitalist economy in equilibrium, this theorem asserts that the rate of profit is positive if and only if exploitation exists. Subsequently, Roemer (1982) established the Class Exploitation Correspondence Principle, a theorem stipulating that people whose optimal economic strategy requires them to hire labour will be exploiters, while people whose optimal strategy requires them to sell labour will be exploited. Roemer also showed that capitalist exploitation does not require wage labour: it occurs equally well through credit relations. In fact, labour and credit markets are exactly equivalent regarding the occurrence of exploitation.

Analytical Marxists have used game theory to generalize and elaborate the concept of exploitation. They have also linked exploitation to the capitalist business cycle and to imperialist relations within the global economy. They have established that several forms of exploitation can occur simultaneously, and that exploitation would exist in a socialist economy or in any other economy characterized by differential ownership of productive assets of any kind. In his recent work, Roemer argues against treating exploitation as a fundamental moral category. Exploitation, he maintains, is not always morally wrong.

Class
What differentiates Marxist from other forms of class analysis is the connection Marxists make between exploitation and class and their use of class analysis to explain historical development.

What differentiates analytical Marxist approaches to class from other varieties of class analysis is (a) the effort to derive a deductive link between exploitation and class, (b) willingness to use all legitimate social scientific methods, including sample surveys and multivariate statistical analysis, to study class relations, (c) use of rational choice concepts to establish a connection between individual and class, and (d) recognition that capitalist societies do not show a pervasive tendency towards polarized class relations.

Among analytical Marxists, the foremost student of class is Erik Wright (1978, 1985). In addition to numerous tightly reasoned and clearly written publications on class, Wright has organized a massive comparative study of class structure and class consciousness that uses a unified concept of class and modern survey methodology to investigate class relations in 11 capitalist countries, including Sweden, England, Germany and Japan.

Wright constructs a general map of class locations in capitalist societies based upon the intersection of three forms of exploitation: capital exploitation (from unequal ownership of capital), organizational exploitation (from unequal control of organizational assets) and skills/credential exploitation (from unequal distribution of skills and credentials). This map defines 12 different capitalist class locations and provides the typological framework for Wright's empirical studies. The results of these studies have illuminated the nature of the middle class, the process of proletarianization, the relation between gender and class, the impact of class on friendship formation and the variations in class structure among different capitalist societies.

Analytical Marxists are themselves divided on whether class is best understood as an aggregate of individuals unified through the possession of similar property or as a structure of positions existing independent of the particular occupants. Although no conceptual convergence seems imminent, dialogue between partisans of these views has already generated notable theoretical innovations and empirical research. Historians sympathetic to analytical Marxist ideas on class have written on topics such as the fall of the Roman Empire, the decline of feudalism, the rise of German fascism and the collapse of European communism.

State
The most distinctive analytical Marxist research on the state is the study, by Adam Przeworski (1985) and his co-workers, on the structural dependence hypothesis. In a capitalist society where the capitalist class controls investments, the structural dependence hypothesis maintains that the state cannot violate the essential interests of the capitalist class without visiting substantial hardships on most citizens.

Przeworski models interaction between the working class, the capitalist class and the state (in the context of a growing economy) as a differential game. He studies what happens over time when all three players act in an optimal way. Przeworski's first formulations sustained the structural dependence hypothesis, using France under socialist rule and Sweden with a social democratic government as examples of its force. Later, he argued that certain methods of taxation would enable the state to redistribute income without curtailing investment, thereby escaping structural dependence. More recently, he has favoured an intermediate position that views the state as dependent upon capital, but not dependent enough to make democracy meaningless.

By adopting a strategic conception of the state, analytical Marxists try to evade the choice between a determinism that makes political action irrelevant and a voluntarism that renders all political outcomes contingent. In this conception, the state is understood as the institutional terrain on which strategic interactions for political power take place. Although it has several attractive features, the strategic conception of the state provides little guidance for either empirical research or theory construction.

Socialism

In recent years, elaborating models of market socialism has been a major activity of analytical Marxists. John Roemer (1994) distinguishes five stages in the development of market socialist theory. The first stage involved recognition that a rational economic system requires use of meaningful prices, while the second stage is defined by attempts to adapt general equilibrium theory for socialist economic calculation. The third stage in the development of market socialist theory brought realization that a rational economic system required the use of actual markets (not merely theoretical simulation of markets). The classical Lange–Lerner model of market socialism, which embodies this realization, was formulated during this stage. Market reforms in communist societies (for example, Yugoslavia, 1949, Hungary, 1968, China, 1977 and the Soviet Union, 1985–91) signalled the advent of the fourth stage. The fifth and current stage in theorizing about market-socialism brings models that eliminate most public ownership of production units and virtually all centralized price setting.

Perhaps the most systematic discussion of market socialist theory is that given by David Miller (1989), who advocates a synthesis of traditional socialism and libertarian philosophy based upon democratically controlled workers' cooperatives and market determined equilibrium prices. Such a system, Miller claims, is preferable not only to capitalism but also to communism (with a small 'c'), traditionally regarded by Marxists as the highest form of social organization.

The model of market socialism proposed by Roemer eschews worker control of production in favour of more traditional management which, he believes, can more readily make major technological innovations. Roemer's model includes three important theoretical innovations: (a) use of a coupon stock market to distribute profits and discipline firm management, (b) use of public banks to monitor performance of production units, and (c) management of investment through government control of interest rates.

Robert van der Veen and Phillipe Van Parijs suggest (Van Parijs, 1992) a different approach to superseding capitalism. They recommend that each adult within a capitalist society receive an unconditional income grant. This basic income grant is gradually expanded until it provides most of a person's income. In this manner society approaches a communist income distribution without an intervening socialist stage.

The examples given above by no means exhaust the models of socialism proposed by analytical Marxists. Despite the theoretical fertility, however, many issues remain controversial. What is the role of markets in a feasible socialism? What is the role of economic planning? Is worker control desirable? How much social and economic planning is feasible? How can a socialist society cope with race and gender inequality? Theoretical analysis alone is not likely to resolve these controversies.

Future directions

Analytical Marxism has made impressive progress over the past two decades, but several improvements are needed to sustain its intellectual momentum. Analytical Marxism must move beyond functionalism and equilibrium analysis to offer a truly dynamic understanding society. In addition to investigating abstract theoretical relationships, its capacity to illuminate specific historical events must be enhanced. Doing empirical research should receive more emphasis, and the intellectual horizons of analytical Marxism should expand to address issues of race, gender, politics and culture. The poor countries of the capitalist world should receive more attention, while efforts to find feasible alternatives to capitalism should continue and even expand.

TOM MAYER

References
Cohen G.A. (1978), *Karl Marx's Theory of History: A Defence*, Princeton: Princeton University Press.
Elster, Jon (1985), *Making Sense of Marx*, Cambridge: Cambridge University Press.
Mayer, Tom (1994), *Analytical Marxism*, Thousand Oaks, CA: Sage Publications.
Miller, David (1989), *Market, State and Community: Theoretical Foundations of Market Socialism*, Oxford: Clarendon, Press.
Morishima, Michio (1973), *Marx's Economics: A Dual Theory of Value and Growth*, Cambridge: Cambridge University Press.
Przeworski, Adam (1985), *Capitalism and Social Democracy*, Cambridge: Cambridge University Press.
Roemer, John E. (1981), A*nalytical Foundations of Marxian Economic Theory*, Cambridge: Cambridge University Press.
Roemer, John E. (1982), *A General Theory of Exploitation and Class*, Cambridge, MA: Harvard University Press.
Roemer, John E. (1994), *A Future for Socialism*, Cambridge, MA: Harvard University Press.
Van Parijs, Philippe (ed.) (1992), *Arguing for Basic Income*, London: Verso.
Wright, Erik Olin (1978), *Class, Crisis and the State*, London: New Left Books.
Wright, Erik Olin (1985), *Classes*, London: Verso.

Apriorism

Apriorism is the philosophical doctrine according to which significant knowledge can be obtained *a priori*, that is, without the help of experience. It is usually opposed to empiricism, according to which sense experience is the source of all knowledge that human beings can acquire about the real world. Two observations must be made to begin with. The first concerns the ambiguity of the term 'experience'. This word often refers to 'sense' experience, but it can also include inner experience (which cannot be so easily defined). Thus, while it is rejected by strict empiricists, the idea that knowledge about the real world can be derived from what is called *inner* experience (by contrast with sense experience) is not sufficient to characterize apriorism *strictu sensu*. The second observation concerns the type of knowledge involved. Most empiricists would readily admit that logical or mathematical truths can be known without resorting to experience, but they will observe that these truths, precisely because they are true in all possible worlds, do not convey any specific knowledge about our actual world. Thus apriorists are those who claim that some knowledge *concerning the real world* can be obtained without resorting to any kind of experience.

   The above distinctions were explicitly made by Immanuel Kant when he was considering the relation between pure and empirical knowledge (1929, Introduction, I). While admitting that 'all our knowledge *begins* with experience', Kant added that it does not follow that all knowledge arises 'out of experience' (41). Consequently, he defined *a priori* knowledge, as opposed to empirical or to *a posteriori* knowledge, as that knowledge which is 'absolutely independent of all experience' (43). As a paradigmatic example of such *a priori* knowledge, Kant repeatedly mentions the knowledge we have that 'every alteration has its cause'. Furthermore, he finds it essential to distinguish between analytic and synthetic judgments (1929, Introduction, IV). The scope of Kant's definition of such judgments is somewhat limited by his old fashioned subject–predicate definition of judgments, but one can consider analytic those statements (like definitions, contradictions and tautologies) whose truth value can be determined only by analysing the meaning of their content and which consequently cannot provide any information about the state of the real world. By contrast, a synthetic statement is a statement whose truth value cannot be determined in such a way and which consequently *provides* some (true or false) information about the world. However, knowledge being conveyed by statements (or judgments), Kant made room *among synthetic judgments*, for the expression of both *a posteriori* and *a priori* knowledge. Now, the idea of a synthetic *a posteriori* judgment does not raise particular difficulty since *a posteriori* knowledge, obtained through experiencing the real world, is necessarily synthetic. But what about *synthetic a priori* judgments? *A priori* knowledge, which is 'absolutely independent of all experience', looks hardly possible if we suppose that it is also synthetic since, by definition, synthetic judgments cannot be grounded – as possibly are definitions and purely logical and mathematical judgments – in an analysis of the meaning of the terms in which they are couched. This had been clearly noted by David Hume when he dramatically claimed that any knowledge which was not the result either of experience or of mathematical analysis should be pitilessly rejected. Thus when Kant claimed that *synthetic a priori* judgments constitute a significant part of our knowledge concerning the state of the world – especially that knowledge implying universal and necessary judgments such as the fundamental principles of Newton's physics – he laid the foundation of a radical apriorism which, in opposition to orthodox empiricism, is the doctrine according to which some statements conveying significant knowledge are both synthetic and *a priori*.

In the nineteenth century, the success of the natural sciences became largely associated with empirical investigations, but it was far less clear that the infant social sciences would have any chance of achieving comparable success on this basis. Indeed, throughout the nineteenth century, economics was considered to be the most successful social science since it had developed a logical apparatus which permitted the explanation of various economic phenomena in a convincing way. However, since experimentation was out of its reach, it was not possible for economists seriously to submit their results to the experimental method which was responsible for the success of the natural sciences, although, this does not mean that the conclusions of economics were considered as *a priori* statements in the sense expressed above. While nineteenth-century economics has often been characterized as an *a priori* science, this was in quite a different sense.

For John Stuart Mill and many of his followers, the goal of all empirical science was to explain specific facts with the help of empirical laws; accordingly, the goal of economics was to explain such specifically economic facts as price movements, levels of output, levels of profits, wages and rents, and so on, with the help of economic laws. In this sense, all such science was deductive and applied an 'a priori method' since specific facts can, *in principle*, be derived from laws. With some natural sciences such as physics, those laws can be tested experimentally through their ability correctly to predict specific facts and, Mill claims, it is this 'accordance' between the results of *a priori* reasoning and 'those of observation *a posteriori*' that is the 'ground of confidence' (1941: 585) we have in such sciences. With the social sciences, however, the multiplicity of 'disturbing' causes which can affect the expected result is such that there is usually no way to predict results with any accuracy. Thus, since disturbing causes can always interfere with the action of the factors analysed by the theory, no observed discrepancy between the theory and the facts can be a good reason to reject this theory, which, occasionally, in the absence of such disturbing causes, can describe perfectly well what is going on in the real world (1941: 585–92; see also 1948: 141–56).

Therefore, the truth of its principles not being affected by contrary results from experience, it was tempting to consider that nineteenth century economics claimed to be *a priori* true. This would be a mistake, however, since methodological views like Mill's are far from implying the systematic rejection of experience as a source of knowledge. According to Mill, economic principles were based on psychological and ethological observation of human behaviour, both through introspective and intersubjective experience. It is true that this is not a specifically economic kind of experience, but it provides the basic principles from which economic theory was, in some sense, derived '*a priori*'. While being untestable through specific economic facts, such a theory was ultimately based on other kinds of facts and could be *verified* by economic facts in some exceptional cases where all the disturbing causes had been taken into account.

This typically nineteenth century economic methodology was later developed by J.E. Cairnes (1965) and by J.N. Keynes (1891) and partially taken over by Lionel Robbins (1935) in the twentieth century. These theorists left no room in their conception of economics for synthetic *a priori* knowledge in the Kantian sense, since they considered experience to be the ultimate source of all knowledge about the real world. In a sense, however, the case of Lionel Robbins is more complex, especially if we consider that the first edition (published in 1932) of his *Nature and Significance* is generally considered more apriorist than the second. According to this final edition, the three main postulates from which the 'propositions of economic theory' can be deduced, namely 'the fact that individuals can arrange their preferences in an order, and in fact do so', 'the fact that there are more than one factor of production' and 'the fact that we are not certain regarding future scarcities' have 'only to be stated to be recognised as obvious' (1935: 78–9). Such a claim can easily be construed as a profession of apriorism, but in the same breath Robbins explains that these postulates are so obvious because they are the very 'stuff of our everyday experience' and, a little further, he adds that these main postulates 'are based upon experience' (80). The point is that neither Robbins nor the nineteenth century economists who made methodological contributions were really anxious to determine whether the fairly evident postulates of economics were established through some kind of experience or otherwise. They tended to think that the content of these postulates does not concern a specifically economic zone of human behaviour and, remaining relatively neutral about the precise nature of the knowledge we have of this zone, they tended to concentrate on the subsequent steps of economic analysis which, by contrast, concern specifically economic matters.

At some points, Frank Knight comes closer to a genuine apriorist position. This is the case, for example, when he claims, not without due precautions, that 'it is not conceivably possible to "verify" any proposition about "economic" behavior by any "empirical" procedure, if the key words of this statement are defined as they must be defined to be used with relevance and precision' (1940: 15). It is mainly with some members of the Austrian school of economics, and more specifically with Ludwig von Mises, however, that we meet a thoroughgoing apriorist theory of economics. By contrast with the above methodological positions, Mises' views refer to laws 'derived *a priori*' (Mises, 1976: 43) that 'permit of no exception' (197) because they belong to a 'universally valid aprioristic theory' (xxvii). These 'laws of human action' (analysed by a basic science that Mises calls 'praxeology') are expressed in statements about which Mises does not hesitate to say: 'No experience can ever be had which would contradict these statements' (1949: 41). In fact, the only common ground between Mises and Mill seems to be what was later called 'verificationism'. Both methodologists admit that the laws of economics can be *verified* by facts in the most favourable cases, but emphasize that they cannot be falsified by any factual observation which would be contrary to theoretical expectations. However, their arguments for rejecting this possibility are different. Mill's main argument is the incompleteness of the set of laws under consideration. According to him, there is no reason to conclude that observation-based laws are contradicted by any facts, since those facts are susceptible to being explained by other (unknown) causes which interfere with the laws in question. Mises' essential argument, on the other hand, is the fact that the laws under consideration have been established *a priori* and are therefore 'universally valid'. Thus, by contrast with other verificationists, Mises claims that the fundamental principles of economics are of a praxeological nature and that, 'like logic and mathematics, praxeological knowledge is in us; it does not come from without' (1949: 64). Naturally, Mises agrees that actual economic science does not cover all the theoretical possibilities open to it and that it has been developed only in some directions (determined by experience) which correspond to the real world; but such a purely restrictive 'reference to experience does not impair the aprioristic character of praxeology and economics' (65). For Mises, the important point is that 'The a priori sciences – logic, mathematics, and praxeology – aim at a knowledge unconditionally valid for all beings endowed with the logical structure of the human mind' (57).

Very few methodologists of economics have followed Mises in adopting such a radical apriorism. The most notable exception among Austrian economists is probably Murray Rothbard, who claimed somewhat ambiguously that the axioms of praxeology, while resting 'on universal inner experience', once enunciated become 'self-evident and hence do not meet the fashionable criterion of "falsifiability"' (Rothbard, 1976: 25). Most modern Austrian economists, such as Israel Kirzner, while acknowledging a debt to Mises, prefer to emphasize the subjectivism (Kirzner, 1986) which is so basic to the Austrian tradition, and tend to avoid referring directly to a highly contested doctrine such as apriorism. Outside the circle of Austrian economists, an 'essentialist' version of apriorism has been defended by Martin Hollis and Edward Nell, who suggested that basic principles of economics (and other truths) can be established by 'logical reasoning' and that economic theory can be based on 'real definitions' which are the expression of an '*a priori* understanding' and which are required to make possible a way out of the circle of interdefined notions (Hollis and Nell, 1975: chs 6 and 7). Even such a strong opponent of apriorism as Karl Popper (1985) has been forced to acknowledge that the principle of rationality, which plays such a fundamental role in economics, should not be rejected whatever the verdict of experience might be. Be that as it may, among most economists and methodologists, especially those anxious to defend the 'positive status' of economics, apriorism has been perceived as a dangerous challenge to empiricism and has been flatly condemned on this ground. Hutchison (1960), Klant (1984: ch.2), Blaug (1980: 93) and Rotwein (1986), who once blamed B. Caldwell for 'flirting with apriorism', are among those who have been the most vehement on this ground. The central objection to apriorism is one which challenges the very idea of 'synthetic *a priori*' statements (for example, Kaufmann, 1937). According to the objectors, the so-called 'synthetic apriori' statements – for example, the statement establishing that marginal utility is decreasing – might be explained in one of two ways: either they are purely definitional and must therefore be considered as analytic and not synthetic at all, or they pretend to say about the real world something which could be false and, in this case, they have to be checked by experience and are not only synthetic but *a posteriori*. Incidentally, the arguments of most opponents of the very idea of a 'synthetic *a priori*' were largely supported by the prevalent ontological view about geometry which Einstein put in a nutshell when he said, 'In so far as the statements of geometry speak about reality, they are not certain, and in so far as they are certain, they do not speak about reality.'

This argument seems to have been decisive in undermining what could otherwise have been an apriorist school in economic methodology. However, one must admit that the existence of synthetic *a priori* statements remains an open philosophical question. The question of the status of mathematical judgments and of their eventual *a priori* character has been the subject of considerable debate in the twentieth century. Even the hard and fast distinction made between 'analytic' and 'synthetic' statements has been somewhat diluted (Quine, 1951; but see Putnam, 1962). Saul Kripke (1972), for his part, questioned the association between '*a priori*' and 'necessary' and insisted on the difference between an epistemological distinction (*a priori – a posteriori*) and a metaphysical one (necessary–contingent), the third relevant distinction (analytic–synthetic) being rather a logical one. In any case, given the ambiguity of the term 'experience', it would not be excessive to conclude that the distinction between '*a priori*' and '*a posteriori*' has never been thoroughly clarified. Be that as it may, it is difficult to accept the idea that the fact that human action is analysed by human beings would be sufficient to provide those human beings with the knowledge of universally valid laws about human action. Yet, on the other hand, it is also difficult to reject the idea that the very intelligibility of human action – whether this action be economic or not – requires some conditions without which human behaviour would be totally unintelligible (see Kirzner, 1986). For example, would it be acceptable to say that increasing marginal utility would fit just as well as decreasing marginal utility as a basic postulate of economics in a hypothetical situation where accurate predictions of observed phenomena could be made with such an odd postulate? Those who would be resistant to answering 'yes' to such a theoretical question, because increasing marginal utility would make human behaviour totally unintelligible to start with, would not necessarily be 'apriorist', but they would agree with the basic world view which has inspired economists sympathetic to apriorism.

MAURICE LAGUEUX

References

Blaug, Mark (1980), *The Methodology of Economics or How Economists Explain*, Cambridge: Cambridge University Press.

Cairnes, J.E. (1965), *The Character and Logical Method of Political Economy*, New York: Augustus M. Kelley.

Dolan, E.G. (ed.) (1976), *The Foundations of Modern Austrian Economics*, Kansas City: Sheed and Ward.

Hollis, M. and E. Nell (1975), *Rational Economic Man*, Cambridge: Cambridge University Press.

Hutchison, T.W. (1960), *The Significance and Basic Postulates of Economic Theory*, New York: Augustus M. Kelley.

Kant Immanuel (1929), *Critique of Pure Reason*, transl. N.K. Smith, London: Macmillan (second impression, 1933; reprinted 1985).

Kaufmann, Felix (1937), 'Do Synthetic Propositions a Priori Exist in Economics? A reply to Dr. Bernardelli', *Economica*, **4**, 337–42.

Keynes, J.N. (1891), *The Scope and Method of Political Economy*, New York: Kelley and Millman (new impression, 1955).

Kirzner, I.M. (ed.) (1986), *Subjectivism, Intelligibility and Economic Understanding*, New York: New York University Press.

Klant Johannes J. (1984), *The Rules of the Game*, Cambridge: Cambridge University Press.

Knight Frank H. (1940), '"What is Truth" in Economics?', the *Journal of Political Economy*, **48**, 1–32.

Kripke, Saul A. (1972), *Naming and Necessity*, Oxford: Basil Blackwell.

Mill J.S. (1941), *A System of Logic, Ratiocinative and Inductive*, book VI, ch.9, London: Longman, Green & Co.

Mill, J.S. (1948), 'On the Definition of Political Economy; and on the Method of Investigation proper to it', *Essays on Some Unsettled Questions of Political Economy*, London: London School of Economics.

Mises, L. von (1949), *Human Action: A Treatise on Economics*, New Haven, CT: Yale University Press.

Mises, L. von (1976), *Epistemological Problems of Economics*, New York: New York University Press.
Popper, Karl (1985), 'The Rationality Principle', in D. Miller (ed.), *Popper Selections*, Princeton, NJ: Princeton University Press.
Putnam, Hilary (1962), 'The analytic and the synthetic', in H. Feigl and G. Maxwell (eds), *Minnesota Studies in the Philosophy of Science, vol. III: Scientific Explanation, Space and Time*, Minneapolis: University of Minnesota Press.
Quine, W.V.O. (1951), 'Two Dogmas of Empiricism', *Philosophical Review*, **60**, 20–43; reprinted in W.V.O. Quine (1953), *From a Logical Point of View*, Cambridge, MA: Harvard University Press.
Robbins, L. (1935), *An Essay on the Nature and Significance of Economic Science*, 2nd edn, London: Macmillan.
Rothbard, M.N. (1976), 'Praxeology: The Methodology of Austrian Economics', in E.G. Dolan (ed.), *The Foundations of Modern Austrian Economics*.
Rotwein, E. (1986), 'Flirting with Apriorism: Caldwell on Mises', *History of Political Economy*, **18**.

Artificial Intelligence

Economics is undergoing profound changes and some of these are inspired by artificial intelligence (AI), the study of making machines do things that would require intelligence if done by human beings. Starting with the view that mental activity can be seen as simply the carrying out of some well-defined sequence of operations, frequently referred to as an algorithm, the objectives of artificial intelligence are to imitate by means of machines, usually digital computers, as much of human mental activity as possible, and perhaps even eventually to improve upon human abilities in these respects. Proponents of strong AI claim that computers can be made to think just like human beings. Advocates of weak AI argue that computers are important tools in the modelling and simulation of human activity.

At least three quite distinct lines of AI-oriented research in economics can be distinguished: applications intended to extend neoclassical economics, applications intended to undermine neoclassical theory and applications that ignore neoclassical theory in the quest for new modelling techniques and fields of analysis (Moss and Rae, 1992). At one extreme, AI systems are being used as a tool for arriving at equilibria, for finding equilibria when direct calculation is intractable and for distinguishing between multiple equilibria. At the other extreme, some researchers are developing AI systems that operate far from equilibrium, continually undergo revisions and improvements, and for which optimality cannot even be defined. Apart from orientation, most applications of AI in economics are concerned with determining courses of action in 'problem spaces' that are too large or complex for the application of constrained-optimization algorithms. AI techniques, then, provide a means of solving difficult optimization problems exhibiting high-dimensional search domains, non-linearities and/or multiple local equilibria, of understanding learning and adaptation among many dispersed economic agents and of modelling evolution, competition and cooperation at the economy-wide level. At least three approaches to AI can be discerned: symbol processing in digital computers, expert systems, and adaptive computing through artificial neural networks, genetic algorithms and classifier systems (Crevier, 1993).

The basic idea of the symbol-processing approach is that intelligence is nothing but the ability to process symbols and that thought consists of expanding symbol structures in a rule-based manner, breaking them up and reforming them, destroying some and creating new ones. The two main processes predominating this theory of thinking are problem solving by heuristic search and problem solving by recognition. This involves (a) putting symbols in, (b) putting symbols out, (c) storing symbols and relational structures of symbols, (d) constructing, modifying and erasing such symbol structures, (e) comparing two symbol structures, and (f) following one course of action or another, depending on the outcome of such a comparison. The result is a step-by-step mental search through a vast 'problem space' of possibilities.

Simon (1969) is one of the main advocates of the symbol-processing approach, not only in computer science but also in economics. The same ideas of 'heuristic' or 'rule-bound' search, 'satisficing' behaviour and 'goal, subgoal' strategy that shape Simon's theory of bounded rationality in economics are also key concepts in his problem space approach to reproducing human-style reasoning in cognitive science. Driven by an interest in exploring the foundations of rationality, Simon analyses the architecture of the mind at the symbolic level without a theory of how these symbolic processes are instantiated at the neural level. Rather than analysing the brain as a predominantly parallel device, Simon settles on a serial system. Starting from these principles, Simon's general purpose computer model of human cognition does seem to capture much of what actually goes on in our heads, since these computers behave efficiently as search engines and can be trained to associate preset responses with appropriate stimulus patterns.

The main limitation of this interpretation of AI stems from the controversial use of symbols with propositional content. A symbol is simply a pattern, made of any substance whatsoever, that is used to denote, or point to, some other symbol, or some object or relation among objects. But where do the symbolic concepts come from? And how do they evolve and grow? Or how are they moulded by feedback from the environment? By themselves, symbols are far too rigid and leave out far too much. If machines could learn, it would be possible to counter the objection that a machine would only be doing what a person had explicitly designed it to do. However, symbol-processing computers cannot come up with useful ideas of their own to make sense of new situations. In response, researchers in symbol processing have put learning on a back burner and are concentrating on the problem of knowledge representation instead.

Expert systems comprise the second major approach to AI and are computer programs based on the idea that one can create systems that capture the decision-making processes of human experts. They automate decision-making processes normally undertaken by a given human expert and assist people in performing a variety of tasks, including diagnosis, planning, scheduling and design. To perform all these tasks, expert systems allow the automatic chaining of rules; that is, following the rules in an order different from the one in which they would function in actual reasoning. As a result, problem solutions do not usually follow from a single string of rules or from a single branch of the tree. Several paths are usually open in the search down the tree. Since they are easy to change or improve, expert systems differ from printed rule books, or even from conventional computer programs, through their flexibility and modularity. Yet another advantage of expert systems is their openness, or self-explanatory character, and their high degree of resiliency in comparison to conventional computer programs. One can usually remove any single rule without grossly affecting the program performance.

There is a broad range of possible applications for expert systems in economics, many of them being at this stage only untested ideas or concepts (Pau, 1986). First, expert systems can be used for project planning and decision support in resource allocation. For example, they can provide commercial customer advice about leasing versus purchasing capital goods. Second, they are being applied to areas in financial and credit analysis such as commercial loan applications. Third, the analysis of games and multiple-criteria policy analysis might benefit from the use of expert systems. These knowledge-based systems can be used to evaluate alternative forecasts with respect to qualitative selection criteria or policy goals. Fourth, efforts are being made to apply expert systems to macroeconomic analysis and modelling. Examples include the configuration of an econometric model prior to estimation. Fifth, expert systems can be applied to public services. In some cases, expert systems are developed to prevent the disclosure of sensitive information at the United States environmental protection agency. Sixth, they are being applied to areas in business management such as multiple criteria budget analysis. Seventh, office automation might be assisted by expert systems such as intelligent word processors with knowledge-based filing and retrieval functions. Finally, planning, scheduling and problem solving in manufacturing might benefit from the use of expert systems.

Since expert systems are constructed using computer languages that can represent and manipulate symbolic information, they are subject to the same limitations as the symbol-processing approach. In particular, basic weaknesses of expert systems involve their problems with time and causality, and their inability to learn, since learning involves the establishment of correspondences and analogies between objects and classes of objects. Expert systems have a tendency to break down when you get to the edge of their knowledge because a given program cannot know the limits of its knowledge and knows even less where missing information might be. Expert systems soon get stuck at points where further improvements can be made only by changing many variables simultaneously. Other drawbacks of expert systems are that they are limited to specialized fields of application and are inferior to the best human experts. Today's expert systems are not much more than sophisticated reminding lists. When know-how is locally unavailable or too expensive, however, expert systems operating in a restricted field can make better decisions than untrained or unconcerned human beings.

The last major division within the AI–economics intersection is the use of adaptive computing systems to simulate intelligence through artificial neural networks, genetic algorithms or classifier systems. Artificial neural networks are being developed mostly by cognitive scientists interested in understanding how computation is performed by the brain. They make use of a general flexible functional form in a process of trial and error. Despite the fact that these models are capable of some kind of rudimentary learning, they are a long way from being realistic models of the brain. Furthermore, they rely completely upon some external supervisor for correcting parameters. A genetic algorithm consists of a set of actions, each of which has a certain strength that depends upon the payoff that would be generated by the action. Through the application of some genetic operators, new actions are created and weak ones are replaced. Although genetic algorithms do not need as much information as supervised artificial neural networks, they still need information concerning the outcome that would be generated for every coded action present in the set. Classifier systems can be combined with genetic algorithms and used to supply the necessary information through an implicit construction of a prediction of the outcomes for all actions in the set. A classifier system is a collection of potential decision rules, together with an accounting system that credits rules generating good outcomes and debits rules generating bad outcomes. Classifier systems have two very desirable efficiency properties: they do not impose heavy memory requirements on the system and much of the processing can be done in parallel.

In economics, the Santa Fe Institute has given a boost to the use of adaptive computing systems for solving complex optimization problems, modelling learning by economic agents and simulating entire economies (Anderson *et al.*, 1988; Lane, 1993a, 1993b). In solving problems, adaptive computing systems can deal with non-linear, noisy, discontinuous and complex/rugged environments. In modelling learning, heterogeneous agents are modelled as responding to an environment that is formed in part by the actions of the other agents and the collection of agents coadapts. Economic simulations by adaptive computing systems give insights into processes of emergent organization, perpetual novelty and incessant evolution. Artificial economies are used to determine whether the trade coalitions that develop are systematically related to system parameters and the characteristics of the constituent agents, and to ascertain whether economic institutions such as money, credit and price systems can develop endogenously. In particular, adaptive computing is being used to derive analytic solutions for double-auction strategies, to select among multiple solutions in repeated prisoner's dilemma games and to analyse the emergence of a medium of exchange, of self-organized markets, of industrial structure, of behavioural norms, of macroeconomic dynamics and of trading rules and patterns in prices and volumes on a stock market. Other applications deal with the systematic exploration of specific learning and imitation rules and their dynamic implications.

The ability to explore a whole range of phenomena very rapidly, to maintain precision and logical consistency, and to balance exploration (acquisition of new information and capabilities) with exploitation (the efficient use of information and capabilities already available) makes adaptive computing a powerful modelling technique. The biggest disadvantages are the general lack of analytic methods – most work is largely computational – and the plethora of possible algorithms for learning and adaptation. While simulations can be an excellent guide to generate intuition, it is always possible that the next simulation will demonstrate dramatically different behaviour. The challenge is to combine the disparate pieces in a theory that explains the pervasiveness of adaptation. Remaining difficulties associated with adaptive computing systems are that they still require the imposition of some centrally choreographed structure, are not open-ended computationally and still lack a clear match between problems and methods.

Some social scientists criticize AI for automating a very limited conception of learning and mental activity (Collins, 1990). They claim that only by conceiving of knowledge as a stable entity that could be acquired and transferred, and by deleting the social and the cultural, are AIers able to render it machine-readable and manipulable by a computer program. While intelligent machines are useful and interesting tools, they are not actors. Machines can mimic us only in those cases where we prefer to do things in a machine-like way. In evaluating the AI–economics intersection and considering this criticism, the differences between the three approaches to AI will have to be kept in mind.

ESTHER-MIRJAM SENT

References

Anderson, P.W., K.J. Arrow and D. Pines (eds) (1988), *The Economy as an Evolving Complex System*, Redwood City: Addison-Wesley.
Collins, H.M. (1990), *Artificial Experts: Social Knowledge and Intelligent Machines*, Cambridge, MA: MIT Press.
Crevier, D. (1993), *AI: The Tumultuous History of the Search for Artificial Intelligence*, New York: Basic Books.
Lane, D.A. (1993a), 'Artificial Worlds and Economics, Part I', *Journal of Evolutionary Economics*, **3**, 89–107.
Lane. D.A. (1993b), 'Artificial Worlds and Economics, Part II', *Journal of Evolutionary Economics*, **3**, 177–97.
Moss, S. and J. Rae (eds) (1992), *Artificial Intelligence and Economic Analysis: Prospects and Problems*, Brookfield, VT: Edward Elgar.
Pau, L.F. (ed.) (1986), *Artificial Intelligence in Economics and Management*, Amsterdam: Elsevier Science.
Simon, H.A. (1969), *The Sciences of the Artificial*, Cambridge, MA: MIT Press.

As if

The view that all human thought and language involves fictions that can be expressed using the 'as if' formulation for our concepts and statements was first consistently defended by Hans Vaihinger in his seminal *Die Philosophie des Als-Ob* (1920). With no explicit connection to

Vaihinger's work, the expression was used and made popular in economics by Milton Friedman's (1953) famous defence of the unrealistic assumptions of the theory of perfect competition.

Friedman's examples are well known. The maximization assumption can be formulated so as to state, 'under a wide range of circumstances, individual firms behave *as if* they were seeking rationally to maximize their expected returns … and had full knowledge of the data needed to succeed in this attempt' (Friedman, 1953: 21). An aspect of Galileo's law can be formulated so as to state, 'under a wide range of circumstances, bodies that fall in the actual atmosphere behave *as if* they were falling in a vacuum' (18). Another example is Friedman's imaginative 'hypothesis that the leaves [around a tree] are positioned as if each leaf deliberately sought to maximize the amount of sunlight it receives' and as if they possessed some other mental capacities (19). Yet another example is concerned with the behaviour of expert billiard players: 'It seems not at all unreasonable that excellent predictions would be yielded by the hypothesis that the billiard player made his shots *as if* he knew the complicated mathematical formulas that would give the optimum directions of travel, could estimate accurately by eye the angles, etc., describing the location of the balls, could make lightning calculations from the formulas, and could then make the balls travel in the direction indicated by the formulas' (21).

Possibly owing to the popularity of Friedman's account amongst economists, the 'as if' formulation of theoretical claims has also gained in popularity within the discipline. It is therefore important to understand what is implied by this formulation. Amongst economists and specialists in economic methodology there seems to be a widely held belief that the use of 'as if' in the formulation of the assumptions of economic theories commits one to an instrumentalist conception of theories. The idea behind this belief is that what follows the 'as if' in one's formulation of a theoretical claim is purely fictional, which implies renouncing the pursuit of representing reality truthfully. This belief is a mistake. The 'as if' formulation can be used to put forth a number of different ideas with either instrumentalist or non-instrumentalist presuppositions and implications. Let us see why this is so.

The popular idea seems to be that the formulation

$$\text{A behaves } as \text{ } if \text{ it were B} \tag{1}$$

may be taken to suggest the attitude that it does not matter whether A is B or not and therefore no truth claims are being made. However, it is obvious that (1) may be true or may be false and, when true, it may successfully serve the purposes of prediction. On the other hand, on many accounts of explanation (1) does not explain, as it does not inform us about why A behaves as it does. It does not say

$$\text{A behaves the way it does because it is B,} \tag{2}$$

where the idea is that (2) explains A's behaviour: it is A's Bness that accounts for A's behaviour. From this perspective, if the theoretician is fully content with (1) without making further questions about why A behaves the way it does, an instrumentalist interpretation suggests itself, while a realist would insist on pursuing something like (2).

On the other hand, the relation between (1) and (2) can be viewed from an epistemological and dynamic perspective which makes (1) perfectly consistent with realism. This interpretation is based on the idea that (1) serves to express epistemic uncertainty concerning why it is that A behaves the way it does. It is suggested by the theoretician that A *might* behave that way because it is B; A's behaviour is consistent with A's being B, and there may be other grounds for believing A is B, but none of these is regarded as sufficient for removing or sufficiently reducing the uncertainty concerning whether A is or is not B. Thus the need is felt to express such epistemic uncertainty explicitly by using (1). Now this is perfectly consistent with an urge to get beyond (1) to something like (2). Indeed, a realist is determined to pursue accounts of form (2) even if much of the time she is forced to be content with using form (1). From this point of view, the 'as if' formulation is a tool in the realist's hands.

At the same time, it must be granted that Friedman's examples do not seem to fit with this non-instrumentalist suggestion. He says that, 'of course, businessmen do not actually and literally solve the system of simultaneous equations' (1953: 22). On his example of the behaviour of billiard players he says that 'our confidence in this hypothesis is not based on the belief that billiard players, even expert ones, can or do go through the process described' (21). On the leaves of a tree hypothesis he says, 'so far as we know, leaves do not "deliberate" or consciously "seek"', nor do they have the other human qualities suggested by the hypothesis (20). While it is obvious that the three examples are different, what they share is that, in each case, it is believed that A is not B even though A behaves as if it were B. Therefore a move from (1) to (2) seems to be excluded in these particular cases. The point is that this situation cannot be generalized: often a move from (1) to (2) is justified.

There is another perspective, an ontological one, from which a similar differentiation of attitudes can be suggested. Consider the following passage by Friedman:

> A meaningful scientific hypothesis or theory typically asserts that certain forces are, and other forces are not, important in understanding a particular class of phenomena. It is frequently convenient to present such a hypothesis by stating that the phenomena it is desired to predict behave in the world of observation as if they occurred in a hypothetical and highly simplified world containing only the forces that the hypothesis asserts to be important. (40)

This passage suggests the idea of theoretical isolation, the idea of theories being about imagined circumstances in which the functioning of only a small set of forces or factors is isolated from that of a vast number of others, in analogy with experimentally closed conditions. The passage says that

> A behaves *as if* it were influenced only by a limited set of significant
> factors C–D, whereas it is actually influenced by a larger set of factors C.   (3)

The passage does not make the more radical claim

> A behaves *as if* factors C–D were real, whereas they are just imaginary.   (4)

The difference between (3) and (4) is that (3) postulates the *isolation* of a few factors as fictional, while (4) postulates those *factors* themselves as fictional. While (4) invites an instrumentalist or fictionalist interpretation, a realist attitude is able to accommodate (3). For example, it is one thing to say that a falling body behaves *as if* it were influenced only by the force of gravitation (and not by other forces) and quite another thing to say that it behaves *as if* gravitation were real. Likewise, to say that firms behave *as if* they were only driven by the profit motive (and not by other motives) is different from saying that the profit motive is an imaginary fiction.

The upshot is that the 'as if' formulation can be used to express a number of different ideas and therefore it alone does not determine one's philosophical outlook.

USKALI MÄKI

Bibliography

Friedman, Milton (1953), 'The methodology of positive economics', *Essays in Positive Economics*, Chicago: University of Chicago Press.

Mäki, Uskali (1992), 'Friedman and realism', *Research in the History of Economic Thought and Methodology*, **10**, 171–95.

Vaihinger, Hans (1920), *Die Philosophie des Als Ob*, Leipzig: Verlag von Felix Meiner.

Axiomatization

In a wide sense, a theory T is said to be axiomatized if some of its statements are singled out as unproved ('first') premises of T, and all the other statements of T are deduced from them. A number of qualifications and further requirements, some of which are discussed below, can be and have been added to this definition in the course of its long history, yielding a multiplicity of (sometimes much) narrower concepts of axiomatization. It must be remarked that terminology varies considerably between authors writing on axiomatization (for example, all of the expressions 'axiomatic theory', 'deductive system', 'formal system', 'formalism', 'calculus', 'syntactical system' and even 'artificial language' are synonymous for some authors, but have distinct meanings for others).

Historically, axiomatization is most certainly an invention of the ancient Greeks, the paradigmatic case being Euclid's axiomatization of geometry around 300 BC. The oldest philosophical analysis of axiomatization can be found in Aristotle's *Posterior Analytics*. According to Aristotle, the first premises (classified into axioms, hypotheses and definitions) cannot themselves be proved, but can be recognized as self-evident by those who are familiar with the theory's subject matter. Consequently, Aristotle regarded all statements of a scientific theory as necessarily true.

In fact, the first premises on which the ancient sciences (such as Aristotle's logic or physics, Euclid's geometry or Ptolemy's astronomy) were erected survived unchallenged for many centuries and seemed beyond reasonable doubt to most mediaeval thinkers. Beginning with the Copernican revolution, however, the old 'necessary truths' were replaced one by one by theories based on quite different first premises. Yet such men as Descartes (1596–1650), Newton (1642–1727) and Leibniz (1646–1716) still firmly held the view that the axioms of mathematics and science should express God's design of the world and Kant (1724–1804) tried to argue that the first premises of what was widely accepted at his time, Aristotle's logic, Euclid's geometry, and Newton's physics, can be ascertained *a priori*. The inclination to view the unproved premises of the established theories as somehow necessarily true was further undermined by the development of non-Euclidean geometries in the nineteenth century and of non-Newtonian physics at the start of the twentieth. By the time of the Vienna Circle (1922–34) it had become perfectly clear that even axioms of the best available scientific theories could still have to be modified in the light of new evidence. Yet even the early logical empiricists believed that at least the axioms of logic and mathematics must be 'true in all possible cases', and although Kant's doctrine of the 'synthetic *a priori*' character of mathematics was repudiated, his distinction between 'analytic' and 'synthetic' truths was used to draw an allegedly sharp distinction: the axioms of logic and mathematics were regarded as 'analytic', but those of 'empirical' theories as 'synthetic'. Consequently, it was believed that only the hypotheses of empirical theories can be refuted, but not the axioms of logic and mathematics (see, for example, Hempel, 1945).

Although the analytic–synthetic distinction itself was soon recognized as a highly questionable dogma (Quine, 1953; cf. also Suppe, 1974), the dichotomy between the 'analytic' axioms of logic and mathematics and the 'empirically meaningful' hypotheses of other theories became a basic tenet of many empiricist accounts of science. Its persuasive power was supported by the emergence of modern formal logic, based on Boole's (1815–64), Peirce's (1839–1914), Peano's (1858–1932) and Frege's (1848–1925) innovations, which immensely extended and made 'rigorous' the relatively loose and limited Aristotelian logic. These developments in logic also prepared the stage for new accounts of axiomatization according to which the 'syntactic' question of whether a statement is provable in a theory must be sharply distinguished from the 'semantic' question of whether the statement is true under some particular interpretation. Although there are common features in the modern conceptualizations of axiomatization, the treatment of both syntactic and semantic aspects varies considerably, depending on whether one looks at specialized literature in logic and the foundations of mathematics, at mathematics other than the philosophically oriented literature on foundations, or at disciplines such as economic theory. Broadly, one can distinguish between *formal axiomatization*, typically used in logic and the foundations of mathematics, and *informal* or *set-theoretic axiomatization*. The latter is typical of both present-day mathematics (excepting foundational studies) and mathematical economics. It has also been repeatedly used to axiomatize parts of physics.

   In logic and the foundations of mathematics, axiomatic theories are today widely regarded as *formal systems*, and formal axiomatization amounts to defining a particular formal system. In order to define formal system *S*, it is required that the following ingredients be specified:

1. the alphabet of *S*, that is, all the signs that appear in *S*;
2. the formation rules of *S*, specifying how the signs from the alphabet of *S* may be combined into 'well-formed' formulas of *S*;
3. the axioms (or 'primitive formulas') of *S*; that is, certain distinguished formulas of *S*;
4. the transformation rules (or 'rules of inference') of *S*, specifying how given (sequences of) formulas may be transformed into new ones.

In general, 'specification' of (1) to (4) is taken to imply that one can decide (by some 'mechanical' procedure) whether a given sign belongs to the alphabet, whether an expression is a well-formed formula, whether a formula is an axiom and whether a given formula results from given other formulas by one of the transformation rules.

   A formula *F* is then said to be *provable in S* (or 'a theorem of *S*', sometimes even 'true in *S*') if a finite sequence of formulas can be written down that ends with *F* and is such that each formula of the sequence is either an axiom of *S* or results from previous formulas of the sequence by one of the transformation rules. (Even if one can decide for any given sequence of formulas whether it is a proof, the formal system *S* need not be *decidable*, in the sense that some mechanical procedure could correctly classify any formula as 'provable' or 'not provable'.)

   A formal system *S* is said to be *inconsistent* if every formula of *S* is provable in *S*. (In particular, every self-contradictory formula is provable in an inconsistent system.) A formal system is (syntactically) *complete* if, for each formula *F*, either *F* or its negation $\neg F$ is provable in *S*. A famous result published by Gödel (1906–78) in 1931 implies that any consistent and sufficiently rich formal system must be incomplete. (As this has sometimes been taken to show the 'limits of formalization', it must be emphasized that Gödel's theorem does *not* say that there are statements which can neither be proved nor disproved in any formal system.)

   A very widespread view of mathematics originates from Hilbert's (1862–1941) philosophy of science which is often labelled 'formalism'. It regards *any* formal system as a legitimate object of mathematics (provided that it is consistent), relegating the problem of whether the axioms of a particular formal system are acceptable in applications to the respective 'applied' science. In fact, however, only very few formal systems are actually studied in mathematics. Beginning in the 1930s, a group of mathematicians writing under the collective pseudonym of Bourbaki attempted to show that 'practically the whole of mathematics' can be derived from *one* particular formal system – a version of what is known as Zermelo-Fraenkel set theory (ZF). Excepting specialized or philosophically oriented investigations in set theory or the foundations of mathematics, some version of ZF is today almost always treated as the unquestioned background of mathematical arguments.

In mathematics (excepting foundational studies), axiomatization thus usually proceeds 'informally' by taking ZF for granted and defining a particular set-theoretic predicate. For example, the following definition is regarded as constituting an informal axiomatization of probability: 'The triple $(\Omega, \mathcal{F}, P)$ is said to be a probability space, if Ω is a set, $\mathcal{F}$ is a σ-algebra in Ω, and P is a mapping from $\mathcal{F}$ to the real numbers such that (a) $P(E) \geq 0$ for all $E \in \mathcal{F}$; (b) $P(\Omega) = 1$, and (c) $P(E_1 U E_2 U...) = P(E_1) + P(E_2) + ...$ for every sequence of disjoint sets $E_1, E_2, ...$ from $\mathcal{F}$'. The conditions (a), (b) and (c) are often called 'axioms of probability', but the word 'axiom' is not meant to suggest that they must hold true for anything except for the set-theoretic entities christened 'probability space' by this definition. Whereas logic and set theory are typically assumed to hold universally, 'axioms' such as the axioms of probability are merely important conditions which hold for some set-theoretic entities, but fail to hold for others.

In economics, axiomatization is of relatively recent origin, and the mathematical economists of this century who have emphasized axiomatization have for the most part followed the practice of 'the working mathematician', not that of the logician. In particular, axioms of logic and set theory are typically *not* made explicit, but are relied upon as background knowledge. Paradigmatic cases are the *Theory of Games and Economic Behavior* (1944) by Hilbert's student, von Neumann (1903–57) and O. Morgenstern, and *Theory of Value: An Axiomatic Analysis of Economic Equilibrium* (1959) by G. Debreu (who was a student of H. Cartan, one of the founders of the Bourbaki group). For example, the latter work contains the following central definition: 'An economy E is defined by: for each $i = 1, ..., m$ a non-empty subset X_i of R^l completely preordered by $\leq_i$; for each $j = 1, ..., n$ a non-empty subset Y_j of R^l, a point ω of R^l. Again, 'standard' logic and set theory are taken for granted, and no specifically economic axioms – unproved first premises beyond those of ZF – are asserted. The superficially strange fact that, in spite of its subtitle, the word 'axiom' does not appear even once in the main text of the *Theory of Value* merely reflects the fact that in mainstream mathematics 'axioms' other than those of logic and set theory are just 'assumptions' or 'conditions' which may or may not be satisfied by an arbitrarily given set-theoretic entity.

Following Debreu, mathematical economists usually distinguish between 'the theory in the strict sense' and its 'interpretations'. The former is, strictly speaking, part of mathematics in the sense that no unproved premises beyond those of ZF are asserted by the 'rigorous' theory, while the interpretations serve to connect it to economic intuition. Interpretations are given informally and are considered as being 'subject to a substantial margin of ambiguity'. It is emphasized (paradigmatically, again, in Debreu, 1959) that one and the same theory admits quite different interpretations. For example, a 'commodity' in general equilibrium theory can be thought of being defined as either by its physical characteristics alone or by its physical characteristics plus date and location of availability, or by its physical characteristics, date, location and the (uncertain) event in which it is made available.

Although interpretations are typically treated very loosely in contemporary economic theory, it must be noted that to some extent semantic questions can be treated with the mathematicians' usual 'standards of rigor'. In fact, 'formal semantics' originating from the work of Tarski (1901–83), Carnap (1891–1970) and others is today a well-established tool of logic and theoretical linguistics. Its basic idea is as follows: while a formal system can be seen as 'uninterpreted', it can be given an interpretation that relates its signs and formulas to something outside the formal system. In particular, an interpretation can assign a 'truth value' (that is, the property of being true or that of being false) to each formula. In general, an interpretation must not be completely arbitrary, but must at least 'respect' the intuitive meaning of some basic signs. (For example, a formula A and B may be interpreted as being true if and only if both A and B are.) A class of admissible interpretations can then be considered as a 'semantics' for the formal system, and various 'semantic' concepts can be formulated: For example, a formal system *S* is said to be *sound* if every formula that is provable in *S* comes out true under each admissible interpretation; a formal system *S* is said to be (semantically) *complete* if all formulas which come out true under each admissible interpretation are also provable in *S*.

In spite of its name, 'formal' semantics of the Tarski–Carnap variety typically proceeds in exactly the same semi-formal manner that characterizes contemporary mainstream mathematics: some version of standard logic and set theory is taken for granted in the semantic 'metatheory'. It must also be emphasized that quite different semantic systems have been suggested in the past decades (notably the 'situation semantics' of Barwise and Perry).

Arguments for and against axiomatization in economics sometimes mainly concern the weight or amount of funding that should be given to axiomatic studies in research and education, but often concern the adequacy of axiomatization in the social sciences as such. Only some of the more fundamental arguments can be mentioned here. Against axiomatization, it is often argued that it induces its practitioners to reduce complex economic problems to – or even to misrepresent them as – what is mathematically tractable. Apparently, many axioms in mathematical economics, such as perfect divisibility of all commodities or transitivity of preferences, have been chosen mainly because they made possible the application of available mathematical knowledge, and the objection that particular axioms are unrealistic has not prevented mathematical economists investigating their logical consequences. Moreover, many important features of economic systems, such as legal norms, conventions, or agents' capacities and modes of information processing, are clearly not captured by concepts such as the set-theoretically defined 'economy'.

As a counterargument to this type of criticism, it can be pointed out that it does not concern axiomatization as such, but only particular choices of axioms. In fact, many developments in mathematical economics are clearly motivated by the wish to replace restrictive and unrealistic assumptions with more realistic ones. For instance, criticism of the transitivity assumption has led to the development of axiomatic equilibrium theories without that assumption.

In favour of axiomatization, it is argued that it facilitates criticism and thus the growth of knowledge in economics, because only axiomatization lays open all the assumptions that are made; thereby it brings out limitations of the theory more clearly than is otherwise possible and facilitates the detection of logical and conceptual errors. It must be said, however, that as long as the interpretation of axiomatic economic theories is treated as loosely as it has been treated in the past, the limitations of any axiomatic theory seem to depend on how it is interpreted, and the interpreted theory inherits all the vagueness of the chosen interpretation. Actually, there are no compelling reasons for limiting formal precision to what can be axiomatized set-theoretically, and interpretations may very well be treated axiomatically: if explicit rules of interpretation are specified for a given formal system *S*, they can be treated as axioms (or axiom schemes) which can be added to those of *S* to form a stronger system *S'*. However, if the rules of interpretation relate the language of *S* to some natural language, the vocabulary of the formal system *S'* would have to include some natural language expressions.

Moreover, the set-theoretic mode of axiomatization commonly used in economics systematically conceals the potential restrictiveness of 'standard' extensional logic and set theory. In fact, it is well known among logicians that some of the basic axioms of this seemingly secure background theory lose their 'self-evident' appearance when applied in the context of 'propositional attitudes', such as beliefs, knowledge, expectations or preference (Quine, 1953; cf. also Vilks, 1995). The problem can be explained by the following example. Standard extensional logic contains the so-called 'axiom of substitutability': (S) If $x = y$, then $P(x)$ implies $P(y)$, where $P(\ldots)$ is any predicate.

If the predicate $P(\ldots)$ is 'Smith does not know whether … is greater than 800 000', and the numbers 7^7 and $823\,543$ are substituted for x and y, respectively, then (S) has the following hardly acceptable consequence. As $7^7 = 823\,543$ is easily verified, it follows that 'Smith does not know whether 7^7 is greater than 800 000' implies 'Smith does not know whether $823\,543$ is greater than 800 000.' But it is perfectly possible that Smith has no idea about the magnitude of 7^7, while he has no difficulty with comparing $823\,543$ with $800\,000$. The problem is closely related to what is known as the 'framing effect' in psychology: an agent's attitude towards a proposition often depends on how the proposition is expressed or 'framed'.

Such examples suggest that 'standard' logic and set theory are much less unproblematic in a social science context than is suggested by the practice of set-theoretic axiomatization. They do not, of course, constitute an argument against *formal* axiomatization.

Arnis Vilks

Bibliography

Barwise, J. and J. Perry (1983), *Situations and Attitudes*, Cambridge, MA: Bradford Books, MIT Press.
Benacerraf, P. and H. Putnam (eds) (1983), *Philosophy of Mathematics: Selected Readings*, Cambridge: Cambridge University Press.
Bourbaki, N. (1968), *Elements of Mathematics: Theory of Sets*, Reading: Addison-Wesley.
Debreu, G. (1959), *Theory of Value: An Axiomatic Analysis of Economic Equilibrium*, New Haven, CT: Yale University Press.
Debreu, G. (1986), 'Theoretical Models: Mathematical Form and Economic Content', *Econometrica*, **54**, 1259–70.
Debreu, G. (1991), 'The Mathematization of Economic Theory', *The American Economic Review*, **81**, 1–7.
Delong, H. (1970), *A Profile of Mathematical Logic*, Reading: Addison-Wesley.
Fraenkel, A., Y. Bar-Hillel and A. Levy (1973), *Foundations of Set Theory*, New York: North–Holland.
Hempel, C.G. (1945), 'On the nature of mathematical truth', *The American Mathematical Monthly*, **52**, 543–56; Reprinted in Benacerraf and Putnam (1983).
Hilbert, D. (1918), 'Axiomatisches Denken', *Mathematische Annalen*, **78**, 405–15; English translation in J. Fang, *Hilbert: Towards a Philosophy of Modern Mathematics II*, New York: Paideia Press, 1970, pp. 187–98.
Hildenbrand, W. (1983), 'Introduction', in G. Debreu, *Mathematical Economics: Twenty papers of Gerard Debreu*, Cambridge: Cambridge University Press.
Kline, M. (1980), *Mathematics: The Loss of Certainty*, Oxford/New York: Oxford University Press.
Mayer, T. (1992), *Truth versus Precision in Economics*, Aldershot: Edward Elgar.
McCloskey, D. (1989), 'Formalism in Economics, Rhetorically Speaking', *Ricerche Economiche*, **43**, 57–75.
Quine, W.V.O. (1953), *From A Logical Point of View*, Cambridge, MA: Harvard University Press.
Stigum, B.P. (1990), *Toward a Formal Science of Economics: The Axiomatic Method in Economics and Econometrics*, Cambridge, MA: MIT Press.
Suppe, F. (1974), 'The Search for Philosophic Understanding of Scientific Theories', in F. Suppe (ed.), *The Structure of Scientific Theories*, Urbana: University of Illinois Press.
Suppes, P. (1957), *Introduction to Logic*, New York: Von Nostrand.
Vilks, A. (1992), 'A Set of Axioms for Neoclassical Economics and the Methodological Status of The Equilibrium Concept', *Economics and Philosophy*, **8**, 51–82.
Vilks, A. (1993), '"Empirical Content" and Formal Economic Theory', *Methodus*, **5**, 47–50.
Vilks, A. (1995), 'On Mathematics and Mathematical Economics', *Greek Economic Review*, **17** (2), 177–204.
Von Neumann, J. and O. Morgenstern (1944), *Theory of Games and Economic Behavior*, Princeton: Princeton University Press.
Woo, H. (1986), *What's Wrong with Formalization in Economics?*, Newark: Victoria Press.

Bayesian Econometric Methodology

Bayesian econometrics refers to the econometric practice which employs Bayesian statistical methods. These methods emanate from Bayes' formula, which relates the inverse conditional probabilities of two sequentially dependent random events/variables, such as D and H_0, in a given complete set of events/variables:

$$P(H_0 / D) = \frac{P(D/H_0)P(H_0)}{\sum_{i=0}^{k} P(H_i)P(D/H_i)} \tag{1}$$

where $H_0, \ldots, H_j, \ldots, H_k$ are mutually exclusive and form an exhaustive set. Expressing any two hypotheses, for example, H_0 and H_j, by equation (1) and taking the ratio of the two lead to Bayes' theorem:

$$\frac{P(H_0 / D)}{P(H_j / D)} = \frac{P(D/H_0)P(H_0)}{P(D/H_j)P(H_j)} \tag{2}$$

Both equations induce philosophically appealing interpretations which have attracted many empirical researchers. Equation (1) shows a systematic and consistent way of revising our confidence in an existing hypothesis H_0 with available data D; equation (2) provides us with a simple criterion for choosing between two mutually exclusive hypotheses by the magnitudes of their probabilities conditioned upon the same data.

In the case of statistical inference where the research objective concerns the unknown values of certain parameters, say θ, of a set of observed variables, say X, equation (1) is transformed into:

$$P(\theta / X) = \kappa P(X / \theta)P(\theta) \tag{3}$$

where κ is known as the normalizing scalar, $P(\theta)$ the prior density function, $P(X/\theta)$ the sampling density function generally approximated by the likelihood function $L(X, \theta)$ and $P(\theta/X)$ the posterior density function. Correspondingly, equation (2) becomes known as the posterior odds test of two differently specified priors, such as $P(\theta_0)$ and $P(\theta_j)$, against the same data sample:

$$\frac{P(\theta_0 / X)}{P(\theta_j / X)} = \frac{L(X,\theta_0)P(\theta_0)}{L(X,\theta_j)P(\theta_j)} \tag{4}$$

The philosophical interpretation of equation (1) and the statistical applicability of equation (3) have formed the main impetus for the development of Bayesian econometrics.

Applications of Bayesian statistical methods appeared in econometrics in the early 1960s, when the paradigm of the structural model approach was being standardized in econometrics.

Within the structural model paradigm, econometricians focused on devising estimation techniques for given structural (economic) models, for example:

$$Y = \beta Z + \varepsilon \tag{5}$$

where $\{Y, Z\} = X$, and ε denotes random disturbance.

However, it was quite common in practice to find a disparity between the sample estimates and the *a priori* expected value ranges of the structural parameter β. Given the strong belief in structural models, econometricians naturally thought of resolving the problem by restricting the parameter estimates within the expected ranges. Since Bayesian inference allows for explicit probability formulation of the expected values into priors, the Bayesian approach was taken as the general solution to the problem of accommodating sample information with *a priori* information within a consistent probability framework.

Under the Bayesian approach, the estimated structural parameter, for example, $\hat{\beta}$ of equation (5), is assumed to take the expected value (called the Bayesian estimator) of the posterior density function $P(\beta/X)$. As the expected value remains invariant to the normalizing scalar κ for most of the distribution types encountered in econometrics, it is generally sufficient to have only the joint density $P(X \cap \beta)$ for the purpose of obtaining the point estimates $\hat{\beta}$. Hence Bayesian econometrics is mainly concerned with formulating the prior $P(\beta)$, and solving various kinds of mathematical problems in deriving its joint density with $L(X, \beta)$ in working out the expectation of the posterior. Mathematically, the imposed prior appears to be the single source of difference in comparison with the classical statistical methods as far as the parameter estimates are concerned. Philosophically, the imposed prior can be regarded as apriorism or even subjectivism. Therefore the use of parameter prior density functions symbolizes Bayesian econometrics, and sometimes even more broadly the Bayesian approach in statistics.

Bayesian econometrics remained within the orthodox structural model paradigm for quite a long time. It was not until the development of extreme bounds by Edward Leamer in the early 1980s that Bayesian econometrics struck and revealed the limits of the structural model paradigm. Extreme bounds analysis basically studies the effects of changing priors on the posterior Bayesian estimate for a given model form, for example the effects of imposing different $P_i(\beta)$, $P_j(\beta)$ on $P_i(\beta/X)$ and $P_j(\beta/X)$ for model (5), following the logic of equation (4). The essential purpose of Leamer's procedure is to make explicit and formalize, under a single principle of Bayesian statistical inference, various ad hoc data-mining activities used to modify given structural models for the results expected by applied modellers. From the viewpoint of econometric modelling procedure, the Leamer school can be regarded as performing model mis-specification analysis by Bayesian methods.

However, it is in general misleading to consider Bayesian econometrics as a separate methodological school in econometrics. Bayesian methods have been applied by all the major methodological schools of econometrics as an alternative, and often mathematically more convenient, statistical route. For example, Bayesian priors have been used by the astructuralist, VAR (vector-autoregression) modelling school as a means of reducing the number of parameters of VAR models; Bayesian methods have been utilized in cointegration analysis of the dynamic modelling school to circumvent certain technical difficulties met by the classical statistics approach in handling non-stationary features of economic variables. An important reason for the wide applicability of Bayesian methods is the identity of the Bayesian estimator with the classical parameter estimator under many situations. The identity is transparent in the case of the specific prior of no *a priori* information. When there is some *a priori* information, the non-Bayesian econometricians would try to specify such information into additional parameter restrictions on the given structural model (or the likelihood function), whereas Bayesian econometricians would simply write it into an informative prior. In the case of updating parameter estimates as sample data increase, for instance, the classical recursive estimation method produces parameter estimates which are identical to the Bayesian estimates, which utilize the estimated parameter density of the original sample as the prior. When the two approaches generate mathematically identical estimators, it seems difficult to accommodate the identity with the difference in interpretation which the Bayesian econometrics attaches to the two types: the classical estimator represents the sample outcome conditioned upon the given hypothesis, $P(\beta/X)$, whereas the Bayesian estimator comes from the inverse conditional state, $P(X/\beta)$. This logical difficulty is, unfortunately, rarely observable owing to the practical inability of the classical approach to specify, into explicit restrictions, those kinds of *a priori* information defined only in vague terms, a situation which has definitely laid the advantage with the Bayesian approach.

Resistance to Bayesian econometrics is therefore mostly based on two arguments: the fragility of the Bayesian parameter estimates due to the arbitrarily specified priors, and the limited role of Bayesian methods in making model choices because of the dependence of the prior specification on given models. These correspond to the broad philosophical criticisms of the general Bayesian approach both for its subjectivity and for the contrasts between the smoothness of the Bayesian learning process and the observed irregularity of the actual process of scientific discovery. These arguments ignore the fact that Bayesian methods can produce results identical to those produced by classical methods.

The key problem with Bayesian econometrics lies in the discrepancy between the mathematical results obtained by means of Bayesian methods and the methodological interpretation of these results. The problem can be traced to a failure to satisfy one or more of the three basic requirements underlying Bayes' formula (1), namely, that the H_i form a closed set, that the H_i are mutually exclusive and that D and H_i are probablistically dependent events. The first requirement is frequently violated when the Bayesian approach is applied to tackle the issue of model choice, or more broadly that of scientific discoveries, since any new non-trivial discoveries tend to open up the originally defined closed set $\{H_i\}$ in such a way as to alter the probability measure assigned on $\{H_i\}$, which has sustained the Bayesian methods. This point is often lost in philosophical discussions of the scientific significance of the Bayesian approach. When Bayesian methods are applied in studies of different priors, the second requirement is frequently forgotten. It is quite common to find cases where Bayesian experiments are carried out with different types of prior density functions for the same set of structural parameters. If we represent these cases by the Bayesian posterior odds test, we get:

$$\frac{P_i(\beta/X)}{P_j(\beta/X)} = \frac{L(X,\beta)P_i(\beta)}{L(X,\beta)P_j(\beta)} = \frac{P_i(\beta)}{P_j(\beta)} \quad \text{for} \ \ i \neq j.$$

This suggests that all the efforts of combining the priors with the likelihood becomes redundant, and that the priors thus defined are in conflict with the third requirement, since the likelihood remains unaffected however the prior is specified. Under such circumstances, the Bayesian principle collapses to a simple multiplication principle, that is, a simple multiplication of the likelihood with the prior. Most of the econometric cases where the Bayesian approach has been applied fall into that category. Unfortunately, the lack of independence has been deeply concealed by the conditional nature of structural models, for example, Y is conditioned upon Z in equation (5), and by the confusion over the nature of the relationship between X and the sample estimator of β: that is, whether it is of a function/mapping induced by the conditioning of Y upon Z, or of a conditional type in its own right.

Because the basic three requirements are seldom met in practical situations where the Bayesian approach has been applied, most Bayesian methods developed in econometrics so far are devoid of Bayes' formula or Bayes' theorem. The term 'Bayesian' is thus a misnomer for 'the prior'. Any philosophical interpretations which have been elaborated from the idea of conditional probabilities of what actually results from the application of the multiplication principle to join two independent probabilities, the likelihood and the prior, can therefore be extremely misleading. The gap between the appealing interpretations evolved from equations (1) and (2) and most of the Bayesian applications in econometrics is yet to be filled.

DUO QIN

Bibliography
Doan, T., R. Litterman and C. Sims (1984), 'Forecasting and Conditional Projection Using Realistic Prior Distributions', *Econometric Reviews*, **3**, 1–100.
Florens, J.-P., M. Mouchart and J.-M. Rolin (1990), *Elements of Bayesian Statistics*, New York: Marcel Dekker.
Howson, C. and P. Urbach (1989), *Scientific Reasoning: The Bayesian Approach*, La Salle, IL: Open Court Publishing Company.
Leamer, E.E. (1978), *Specification Searches*, New York: Wiley.
Leamer, E.E. and H. Leonard (1983), 'Reporting the Fragility of Regression Estimates', *Review of Economics and Statistics*, **65**, 306–17.
Pagan, A. (1987) 'Three Econometric Methodologies: A Critical Appraisal', *Journal of Economic Surveys, 1*, 3–24.
Pagan, A. (1995), 'Three Econometric Methodologies: An Update', in L. Oxley, D.A.R. George, C.L. Roberts and S. Sayer (eds), *Surveys in Econometrics*, Oxford: Blackwell.
Phillips, P.C.B. (ed.) (1994) 'Symposium Double Issue: Bayes Methods and Unit Roots', *Econometric Theory*, **10**, (3/4).
Phillips, P.C.B. and W. Ploberger, (1996) 'An Asymptotic Theory of Bayesian Inference for Time Series', *Econometrica*, **64**, 381–412.
Poirier, D. J. (1988), 'Frequentist and Subjectivist Perspectives on the Problems of Model Building in Economics', *The Journal of Economic Perspectives*, **2**, 121–44.
Qin, D. (1994), 'Has the Bayesian Estimation Principle Ever Used Bayes' Rule?', *Economics Department Discussion Papers*, no. 318, Queen Mary & Westfield College.
Qin, D. (1996), 'Bayesian Econometrics: The First Twenty Years', *Econometric Theory*, **12**, 500–16.
Rothenberg, T.J. (1971), 'The Bayesian Approach and Alternatives in Econometrics -II', in M.D. Intriligator (ed.), *Frontiers of Quantitative Economics*, Amsterdam: North-Holland.
Zellner, A. (1971) *An Introduction to Bayesian Inference in Econometrics*, New York: John Wiley.

Bounded Rationality

Bounded rationality is not a field in itself, but rather an approach to doing economic research. There are many interpretations of bounded rationality and these are not always consistent. Herbert Simon (1987b), the father of bounded rationality, used the term 'bounded rationality' to 'designate rational choice that takes into account the cognitive limitations of the decision-maker – limitations of both knowledge and computational capacity' (266). These bounds affect human cognitive capacity for discovering alternatives, computing their consequences under certainty and uncertainty, and making comparisons among them. Theories of bounded rationality, then, are generated by analysing processes for generating alternatives, procedures such as heuristics for evaluating consequences and strategies such as satisficing for making choices. Decision making is characterized as a selective search in which heuristics are used to determine what paths should be taken and the search halts when a satisfactory solution has been found. In this process, aspiration levels are adapted in response to success or failure.

Early theorists of bounded rationality agreed that the neoclassical model of perfect information, optimal information processing and the utility maximization that results is in severe need of overhaul (see Egidi *et al.*, 1992). They shared the following objections to neoclassical economics: (1) a rejection of positivism as the methodological foundation; (2) a refusal to accept the use of deductive reasoning; (3) a dislike of static analysis of equilibrium outcomes rather than disequilibrium processes; and (4) an objection to the simplistic economic model of rational agents exhibiting optimizing behaviour. In neoclassical economics, choices are assumed to be made: (a) among a given, fixed set of alternatives; (b) with (subjectively) known probability distributions of outcomes for each; and (c) in such a way as to maximize the expected value of a utility function. Instead, theories of bounded rationality can be constructed by modifying the neoclassical assumptions in a variety of ways. In particular, choices are assumed to be made: (a') through a process for generating alternatives; (b') with strategies such as heuristics for dealing with uncertainty; and (c') in such a way as to satisfice. Theories of bounded rationality alter the nature, not only of the conditions and constraints, but also of the given goals.

Theorists of bounded rationality have looked to the accumulated body of knowledge in the behavioural disciplines, cognitive psychology and artificial intelligence for inspiration. Experimental economics has provided one instrument for the development of theories of boundedly rational behaviour (see Davis and Holt, 1993). It has illustrated instances, such as intransitivities in choice behaviour and preference reversal, in which individuals seem to violate some of the axioms underlying neoclassical economics. In the analysis of the sequential processes of search that people use, experimental economists have stressed the fact that aspiration levels change and that the rules of thumb that people use seem to operate at the subconscious level. Another technique that has been used to strengthen bounded rationality economics is computer simulations (see Cyert and March, 1963). One reason is that models of bounded rationality are often too complex to be analysed completely by conventional techniques that lead to closed-form solutions. Simulation studies allow the exploration and analysis of previously inaccessible phenomena. Detailed computational models have been set up to analyse how people, tasks and networks are interrelated in complex, dynamic and adaptive systems.

The original purpose of models of bounded rationality was to characterize the effects of a restricted rational agent on the assumptions (and conclusions) of economic and administrative theory. These models have significantly influenced, directly and indirectly, theories of organizations (see Cyert and March, 1963). Organizations are viewed as devices, alternative to the market, by which individuals acting with incomplete knowledge and information can satisfactorily reduce their uncertainty and make their decisions. At the same time, the bounded rationality of the members of the organization restricts their ability to achieve optimality in the pursuit of their goals. As a result, theories of bounded rationality see organizations as setting targets and looking for alternatives that satisfy those targets, rather than trying to find the best imaginable solution. The typical administrator will follow rules of thumb to consider only those solutions that will satisfy reasonable goals with as few complications as possible. Furthermore, she will attend to goals sequentially, rather than simultaneously. These theories and observations on decision making in organizations have been applied to the systems and techniques of planning, budgeting and control that are used in business and public administration.

Subsequent research has both expanded and distorted the work of the early bounded rationality theorists. Mainly through Williamson's (1975) insistence, the notion of bounded rationality has played a prominent role in transaction cost economics. Williamson sought to link the idea of conflict of interest with the idea of information limitations and saw organizational forms as implicit or explicit solutions to the problems of decision and control created by opportunism and bounded rationality. Opportunism refers to the fact that there is conflict of interest within, as well as between, organizations, and that participants in an organization will lie, cheat and steal in their own self-interest if they can. Bounded rationality makes complete contracting infeasible because not everything can be known and there are limits to the capabilities of decision makers for dealing with information and anticipating the future. However, Williamson was reluctant to accept the notion of satisficing, primarily because he thought it would denote irrational behaviour. At the same time, Simon himself considered satisficing to be a direct implication of bounded rationality. An approach similar in spirit to transaction cost economics, but one that gives much smaller weight to limited rationality, as opposed to conflict, is found in agency theory. As these ideas have been taking shape, attention to bounded rationality has tended to fade into the background, and attention to conflict of interest has become paramount.

Nelson and Winter's (1982) evolutionary theory of business firm growth brought new impulses to the modelling of boundedly rational behaviour in economics. It emphasizes differential survival as a primary basis for changing populations of firms, and sees firms as being selected by virtue of their fit to the environment. Nelson and Winter stressed the inability of firms to carry out the necessary calculations for optimization, because the firm will not 'know' all the things of which it is capable, because all future contingencies cannot be foreseen, because mistakes can be made, and so forth. In Nelson and Winter's view, the notion of satisficing can account for persistence of routines in their evolutionary theory. The theory uses two key concepts: the first is the idea that organizations develop, stabilize and follow routines; the second is a conception of search. Differential outcomes from search result in differential rates of survival and growth in firms. These differences, in turn, affect the distribution of activities and interactions at the industry level. The emphasis on the historical path by which organizational forms are achieved found echoes in a number of other developments such as research on path dependence.

More bounded rationality research has been done in microeconomics than in macroeconomics. Following Radner (1980), game theorists have used bounded rationality ideas to analyse repeated games (see Aumann, 1981). Game theorists have tried to capture bounded rationality by replacing rational players with computing devices such as Turing machines, finite automata or neural network algorithms. Players' rationality is bounded in the sense that they cannot consider strategies other than those that can be played by these computing devices. Rationality is bounded in Turing machines because these machines will sometimes compute forever to give correct answers. In order to come up with a solution, the output follows an arbitrary guessing rule after the machine has been stopped. Bounded rationality in finite automata is captured by imposing constraints on the number of states of the automata or assuming that states are costly. Neural networks, finally, increase the computational capability of a finite automaton by increasing the states of the machine. Whereas Simon saw bounded rationality as an alternative to neoclassical economics, game theorists have used it in an attempt to strengthen it. Bounded rationality permits solutions to be reached which game theorists want to but cannot obtain from fully rational players. In particular, the bounded rationality approach has been applied to the area of refinements of the Nash equilibrium, in the study of the applicability of the Folk Theorem, and on the problem of equilibrium selection.

Both game theorists and macroeconomists have developed models of boundedly rational learning (see Bray and Kreps, 1987). The basic idea in these models is that boundedly rational agents utilize one of three procedures for making and changing their choices on the basis of past outcomes. First, Bayesian learning assumes that players update their subjective probabilities in the face of inconsistencies through the use of Bayes' rule until consistency is achieved. This technique has been used in the problem of equilibrium selection. It has been criticized for not accurately representing 'true' learning. Second, least squares or adaptive control learning assumes that players use standard statistical or econometric procedures for estimation. These procedures are boundedly rational in that economic agents use models that are misspecified and forecasting procedures that are not part of the optimal decision making of these individuals. This approach has been used in the context of rational expectations models. It has been criticized for requiring the agents still to be quite smart. Third, neural network learning assumes that individuals construct explicitly approximate models of their environment which are updated as their information improves. In contrast to least squares or adaptive control learning, agents here know they hold misspecified models of reality. This technique has been used to explore how boundedly rational players can achieve consistent beliefs and, possibly, a Nash equilibrium. As was the case with game theory, the motivation behind the learning literature was different from the interests that drove the original bounded rationality programme. Sargent (1993), for example, developed models of boundedly rational learning in macroeconomics and tried to make connections to Simon's programme. However, whereas Sargent used these models in an attempt to strengthen neoclassical economics, Simon had pointed out in his theory of bounded rationality why the basic assumptions of neoclassical economics did not always work in practice. In particular, Sargent sought to reinforce rational expectations by focusing on convergence to this equilibrium through boundedly rational learning. He also tried to use the concepts developed in the learning literature to deal with some of the problems associated with rational expectations such as multiple equilibria and the computation of equilibria (see Sent, 1997).

While models of bounded rationality have not always appeared as attractive as the axiomatized certainties of neoclassical economics, more and more economists are embracing one form or another of bounded rationality. Models of bounded rationality owe their revival partly to attempts to develop a viable alternative to neoclassical economics and partly to attempts to strengthen neoclassical economics. Whereas the first reason is in the spirit of Simon's contributions, Simon certainly opposes the second.

ESTHER-MIRJAM SENT

Bibliography

Aumann, R. (1981), 'Survey of Repeated Games', *Essays in Game Theory and Mathematical Economics in Honor of Oskar Morgenstern*, Mannheim: Bibliographisches Institut.

Bray, M. and D. Kreps (1987), 'Rational Learning and Rational Expectations', in G. Feiwel (ed.), *Arrow and the Ascent of Modern Economic Theory*, New York: New York University Press.

Cyert, R.M. and J.G. March (1963), *A Behavioral Theory of the Firm*, Englewood Cliffs, NJ: Prentice-Hall.

Davis, D.D. and C.A. Holt (1993), *Experimental Economics*, Princeton: Princeton University Press.

Egidi, M., R. Marris, H.A. Simon and R. Viale (eds), (1992), *Economics, Bounded Rationality and the Cognitive Revolution*, Brookfield, VT, Edward Elgar.

Nelson, R.R. and S.G. Winter (1982), *An Evolutionary Theory of Economic Change*, Cambridge, MA: Harvard University Press.

Radner, R. (1980), 'Collusive Behavior in Noncooperative Epsilon-Equilibria of Oligopolies with Long but Finite Lives', *Journal of Economic Theory*, **22**, 136–54.

Sargent, T.J. (1993), *Bounded Rationality in Macroeconomics*, Oxford: Oxford University Press.

Sent, E.-M. (1997), 'Sargent versus Simon: Bounded Rationality Unbound', *Cambridge Journal of Economics*, **21**, 323–38.

Simon, H.A. (1982), *Models of Bounded Rationality*, 2 vols, Cambridge, MA: MIT Press.

Simon, H.A. (1987a), 'Behavioral Economics', in J. Eatwell, M. Milgate and P. Newman (eds), *The New Palgrave*, New York: W.W. Norton.

Simon, H.A. (1987b), 'Bounded Rationality', in J. Eatwell, M. Milgate and P. Newman (eds), *The New Palgrave*, New York: W.W. Norton.

Williamson, O.E. (1975), *Markets and Hierarchies*, New York: Free Press.

Buchanan, James M.

James M. Buchanan was born (3 October 1919) and grew up in rural Tennessee. He received his BA from Middle Tennessee State College in 1940, and his MS in Economics from the University of Tennessee in 1941. On his return from military service with the US Navy (1941–5), Buchanan entered the economics doctoral programme at the University of Chicago, where he received his PhD in 1948. His academic career began at the University of Tennessee (1948–51). From 1951 to 1956, he taught at Florida State University. After 1956, except for a brief episode at the University of California in Los Angeles (1968–9), Buchanan held appointments at state universities in Virginia, University of Virginia (1956–68), Virginia Polytechnic Institute & State University (1969–83) and from 1983 at George Mason University. Interim appointments in Italy (1955–6), Cambridge University (1961–2) and LSE (1960, 1965, 1967) were important as way stations in Buchanan's academic career. In 1986 Buchanan was awarded the Nobel Memorial Prize in Economic Science for his eminent role as paradigm builder in the fields of Public Choice and Constitutional Economics.

Buchanan's work may appropriately be described as the unfolding of a research programme whose basic contours can already be found in his first main paper, 'The Pure Theory of Government Finance' (1949, reprinted in Buchanan, 1960), namely the systematic and consistent extension of economic analysis into the realm of non-market or collective and, in particular, political decision making. It is this unifying theme that gives his many publications of over four decades a remarkable coherence. This biographical entry is focused on the central elements that distinguish his research programme from that of mainstream economics.

Starting as a public finance economist, Buchanan felt 'intellectual frustration' with orthodox theorizing in his own field as well as in its close neighbour, welfare economics. His dissatisfaction was caused by what he diagnosed as 'methodological confusion', namely an inconsistency between the theoretical perspective that economists applied in their standard field, the study of market processes, and the theoretical perspective that they applied when, in such fields as public finance or welfare economics, they extended their analysis into the realm of politics.

There are, Buchanan argued in his 1949 article, two fundamentally different views of politics or of the state, a collectivist – organicist view considering the state as a supraindividual entity acting for society as a whole, and an individualist view considering the state as the sum of its individual members acting in a collective capacity. Though only the latter view is consistent with the methodological individualism of traditional economic theory, Buchanan found the organicist view of the state to be the tacit theoretical underpinning of public finance and welfare economics. This meant that, in moving between markets and politics, economists were implicitly switching paradigms.

Buchanan pointed out that theoretical consistency should require economists to conduct their study of non-market decision making from within the same analytical framework that they bring to the study of the private economy. And he made it his task to work out an economic theory of politics, and of collective action more generally, that was on the same methodological and conceptual grounds as the economics of market processes, a project that, in his understanding, meant essentially reviving the programme of classical, Smithean political economy.

In Buchanan's view the 'methodological confusion' that he attacked has its roots in an ambiguity inherent in the *maximization paradigm* that dominates so much of theoretical thinking in economics. It is the inappropriate extension of this paradigm from individual units of decision making to social aggregates (Buchanan, 1979: 22f) or, as he puts it, 'the critical methodological error of crossing the bridge from individual maximization to social maximization' (Buchanan, 1977: 237), that has misled economists into abandoning their individualist methodology, both in their explanatory and in their normative accounts of collective decision making.

In essence, the maximization paradigm is based on the notion that there is a 'chooser' who faces a range of alternative options and selects the one that in terms of his own value scale is 'best'. By transferring this notion from the study of individual human choice behaviour to the social aggregate level, Buchanan charges, economists implicitly adopted the supposition that social aggregates or collectives can be understood as choosing entities analogous to individual human decision makers. In doing so, they came to make two assumptions that, while meaningful at the level of individual human choice, are entirely misplaced at the social aggregate level: first, that collectives are entities that choose or maximize and, second, that these entities have their own separate value scales against which alternatives are to be evaluated.

The noted assumptions are, as Buchanan argues, not only inappropriate for aggregates or collectives such as 'the economy' that simply do not exist as organized units capable of concerted action, they are also inappropriate for organized collectives such as 'the state' or private organizations. 'The economy' is not an entity that maximizes anything, nor is 'the state'. Both are institutional arenas in which individuals pursue their interests within the constraints that the respective 'rules of the game' define, and social outcomes emerge from the interaction process that unfolds within these constraints. As Buchanan puts it, 'the economy and the government are parallel sets of institutions', one being that complex of institutions through which individuals pursue their various objectives privately, as opposed to collectively, and the other being that complex of institutions through which individuals make collective decisions, and through which they carry out collective as opposed to private activities (Buchanan, 1979: 144, 146).

If there are no supraindividual collective 'choosers', but only decision-making procedures or institutions through which individual human choices are translated into 'collective choices', there can also be, Buchanan insists, no supraindividual collective value scales against which alternatives could be judged. Apart from the individuals who constitute a collective, there simply is no 'evaluating unit' and it is only to these individuals' subjective evaluations that economists can have recourse in their search for a normative standard.

It is their implicit organicist view of the state, Buchanan presumes, that has led public finance and welfare economists to advance their policy arguments as if their addressee were some benevolent despot, called 'the government', who seeks to advance the 'general' or 'public' interest, and as if it were their own role 'to advise and counsel this despot on, first, the definition of this general interest and, second, the means of furthering it' (ibid.: 145). In his *Finanztheoretische Untersuchungen* of 1896, Knut Wicksell had already directed such criticism at his fellow economists, and it was his reading of Wicksell as well as his study of the classical Italian school of public finance that helped Buchanan to work out his own individualist approach to an economic theory of politics.

The central and straightforward argument in Buchanan's critique is that economists ought to maintain explanatory and normative symmetry between their traditional domain, the study of market interaction, and their approach to political processes, or, in other words, that they ought to build a theoretically consistent bridge between the behaviour of persons who act in the market-place and the behaviour of persons who act in political process.

A primary example of *analytical asymmetry*, and a primary target of Buchanan's criticism, is the *theory of market failure* that emerged from the theoretical welfare economics of the 1950s and 1960s. The basic logic of this theory implied that where markets 'fail', government intervention is called for to rectify such failure. The theory was 'asymmetric' in that it compared real markets with ideal governments. It derived its diagnosis of market failure from measuring the working properties of *factual markets* against the non-attainable *theoretical ideal* of perfect markets. Yet it based its recommendation of government intervention on the implicit assumption that 'the government' would perform its assigned task perfectly, without ever asking whether the working properties of *factual governments* may not also fall short of their supposed ideal. In explicitly posing this question, Buchanan was quite naturally led to become one of the principal founders of the *theory of public choice* as a research programme that sought to establish analytical symmetry by showing that, compared to their respective ideals, real governments 'fail' no less than real markets do, and by insisting that the relevant institutional comparison must be between feasible alternatives: 'if market organization is to be replaced by politicized order, or vice versa, the two institutional structures must be evaluated on the basis of predictions as to how they will actually work' (Buchanan, 1992: 99)

The primary example of the failure to maintain *normative symmetry* Buchanan found in the notion of a *social welfare function*, conceived of as the collective equivalent to individual utility functions. With this notion, he censured, economists departed from the normative individualism that informs their concept of efficiency, as traditionally understood in the context of market interaction. The notion of efficiency in market transactions is based on a *procedural criterion of evaluation*. It takes the preferences of the individual persons involved in such transactions as its normative criterion and is ultimately based on the argument that, because of their voluntary nature, market transactions can be said to make all contracting parties better off – 'better' in terms of their own preferences. In other words, the efficiency criterion looks at the process through which outcomes are generated rather than at any qualities of outcomes that could be judged independently of the process by which they came about.

Buchanan argues that normative symmetry should require that the same criterion, namely the expressed preferences of the individual persons involved, be applied to the realm of politics as well. If 'the state' or 'the government' are nothing but complex sets of institutions through which individuals make collective choices and carry out collective activities, then, he insists, normative judgment has to have the same kind of procedural focus as the traditional concept of efficiency in market transactions. The central normative question becomes how well the institutional structures of politics perform in allowing individuals to engage in mutually beneficial collective endeavours.

The social welfare function approach is an attempt to construct – from within the conceptual framework of the economic paradigm – a normative criterion that would allow for the direct evaluation of outcomes as such, independent of the ways in which they are brought about. In Buchanan's account this attempt has failed, and could not but fail, because it is inconsistent with the individualist normative logic of the traditional notion of efficiency in market transaction. As he put it:

> The whole problem seems best considered as one of the 'either-or' variety. We may adopt the philosophical basis of individualism in which the individual is the only entity possessing ends or values.... A social value scale as such simply does not exist. Alternatively, we may adopt some variant of the organic philosophical assumptions in which the collectivity is an independent entity possessing its own value ordering (Buchanan, 1960: 79)

With his *constitutional economics* approach, Buchanan wants to suggest a *procedural alternative* to the social welfare function approach: 'Whereas the "social welfare function" approach searches for a criterion independent of the choice process itself, ... the alternative approach evaluates results only in terms of the choice process itself' (ibid.: 118). Constitutional economics seeks to identify what, in the realm of collective or political choice, can be considered the appropriate analogue to the notion of voluntary contracting in market transactions. It was in Knut Wicksell's arguments on the *rule of unanimity* as the political counterpart to voluntary market exchange that Buchanan found the clue to the way the ultimate normative benchmark in matters of collective choice has to be defined, namely voluntary consensus of all participating individuals (Buchanan, 1979: 153).

By contrast to the welfare economist, Buchanan's constitutional economist does not consider it his task 'to define goals or objectives of the economy or of the government and then to propose measures designed to implement these goals' (ibid: 146). Instead, he considers his role to be that of an *institutional advisor* who can provide information on potential institutional-constitutional reforms that may help members of polities to pursue their separate and common interests more effectively, whatever these interests may be. In his perspective, 'The "good society" is that which best furthers the interests of its individual members, as expressed by these members, rather than that society that best furthers some independently defined criterion for the 'good'" (Buchanan, 1991: 83).

The theoretical reorientation that Buchanan suggests to his fellow economists is a shift from the *maximization paradigm* to the *contractarian or exchange paradigm* that was constitutive to economics in its Smithean beginnings. To Buchanan, Adam Smith's principal legacy lies in the insight that mutual gains from trade are the essence of the market as 'an institutional framework that facilitates voluntary exchanges among individuals' (Buchanan, 1987: 305). Instead of seeking their discipline's identifying principle in the concept of maximizing choice, Buchanan wants economists to adopt the *gains from trade* perspective as their 'unifying principle' (Buchanan, 1977: 242), a principle that can be applied to the study of non-market or collective social arrangements no less than to the economist's traditional terrain, the study of market exchange. In his view, the economist's distinctive task is the inquiry into how mutual gains may be achieved through voluntary exchange or social cooperation in its various forms, from simple bilateral exchange between two traders to the complex multilateral trade involved in the provision of collective goods, and the exchange of commitments that is the essence of the constitutional choices through which groups of people define the 'rules of the game' under which they are to live.

The gains from trade perspective that Buchanan advocates looks at all human relationships and social institutions, market and non-market alike, from the vantage point of how well they allow individuals to achieve their own interests and to realize mutual benefits from social cooperation. It 'suggests that systems or subsystems be evaluated in terms of the comparative ease or facility with which voluntary exchanges, contracts, or trades may be arranged between and among members of the community' (Buchanan, 1991: 81). And it assigns to the political economist the task of exploring the potential for 'social improvement' through institutional–constitutional reforms that enable persons, in the various realms of human social life, to pursue more effectively their mutually compatible interests.

To Buchanan the ultimate purpose of economic inquiry, a purpose that ought to guide its analytical efforts, must be the contribution it can make in helping to resolve the problem of social order that is 'faced eternally by men who realize that they must live together and that to do so they must impose *upon themselves* social rules, social institutions' (Buchanan, 1979: 208). In his view, economists fail to live up to their proper role if they 'evade their responsibility in the continuing discourse over such rules and institutions by shifting attention to trivialities' (ibid.).

VIKTOR J. VANBERG

References
Buchanan, James M. (1960), *Fiscal Theory and Political Economy*, Chapel Hill: University of North Carolina Press.
Buchanan, James M. (1977), *Freedom in Constitutional Contract*, College Station: Texas A&M University Press.
Buchanan, James M. (1979), *What Should Economists Do?* Indianapolis: Liberty Press.
Buchanan, James M. (1987), *Economics – Between Predictive Science and Moral Philosophy*, College Station: Texas A&M University Press.
Buchanan, James M. (1991), *The Economics and Ethics of Constitutional Order*, Ann Arbor: University of Michigan Press.
Buchanan, James M. (1992), *Better than Plowing and Other Personal Essays*, Chicago: The University of Chicago Press.
Wicksell, Knut (1896), *Finanztheoretische Untersuchungen nebst Darstellung und Kritik des Steuerwesens Schwedens*, Jena: Gustav Fischer.

Capacities

'Capacity' is often used in economics to refer to the extent of capital utilization, but the sense of the term that matters for methodology is different. In methodology, 'capacity' is used to mark out abstract facts about economic factors: what they would produce if unimpeded. For example, does progress in information technology have the capacity to increase income inequality by decreasing workers' bargaining power; that is, does it *tend* to increase income inequality even if that tendency may be offset by countervailing factors? Or how is the capacity of taxes to decrease consumption affected by the operation of other factors with different capacities, such as changes in interest rates, retirement schemes or the rate of inflation?

The notion of capacity has three elements: (1) potentiality (capacities describe what a factor can do in the abstract, not what actually happens in full empirical reality); (2) causality (capacity claims are not claims about coassociation but about what results a factor can *produce*); and (3) stability (the ability to produce the effect in question must persist across some envisaged variation of circumstance). The concept is closely tied to the methodologist's account of analysis and synthesis, to the theorist's idea of structural or autonomous relations and to the econometrician's idea of superexogeneity.

Knowledge of the capacities of proposed changes is critical for policy and forecasting, but it is knowledge that is especially hard to come by. Statistics by themselves can provide neither necessary nor sufficient conditions for any of the three elements implied in a capacity claim. So hardline positivists advise avoiding such claims altogether. Still it is empiricist John Stuart Mill who has argued most clearly and most forcefully for the study of capacities in political economy.

Mill took the features of the economy at any time to be the result of a large number of different causes acting together. The most useful kind of knowledge in economics, he argued, is not that gained by inductive generalization from what few past regularities we may have observed. That is because the background mix of causal factors rarely stays in place long enough for the same effects to be produced repeatedly, and it cannot be relied on to do so. Economics should aim instead, Mill urged, to study the causes severally. We would then be in a position to deduce what should happen for any given combination of causes or for any proposed change in combinations.

In setting out this argument, Mill supposed both that particular effects can be associated with each cause independent of its context and that, when causes act together, there is a rule that computes their joint effect from the effects peculiar to each separately. Mill called the laws connecting each cause with the effect peculiar to it *tendency laws*, since they describe, not what results when the cause is present, but what the cause contributes or tends to produce. Recent philosophical literature substitutes 'capacity' for 'tendency' to separate issues about the stability of causal powers across contexts from any facts relating to dynamics that might be suggested by Mill's own term. Mill was not explicit about what the rules for composing causes in economics might be, but he supposed that they would be simple and universal, in analogy with the law of vector addition for forces in physics.

Mill's view rests on strong methodological assumptions. In particular, it presupposes that it is possible to break the complex precedents of any economic phenomenon into a determinate set of repeatable causal factors each with its characteristic effects, effects that can be recomposed in predictable ways; that is, it presupposes the efficacy of the method of analysis and synthesis. Just as the analytic method of Newtonian physics was challenged by Goethe and others in his particular German tradition, the analytic method of classical economics laid out so clearly in Mill was rejected by the Historical School dominant in German political economy at the end of the nineteenth and beginning of the twentieth century. (England, too, had adherents to the Historical School, including John Kells Ingram, T.E. Cliffe Leslie and Arnold Toynbee.) Gustav Schmoller, in particular, is famous in methodology for his insistence against Carl Menger that history and political economy could not employ exact universal laws as physics does. For Schmoller, as for Mill, economic phenomena are brought about on each occasion by a myriad of interacting causes. But for Schmoller, the role each cause plays depends on the total context in which it is set. So although separate causal factors can be identified and reidentified from one context to another, the separate causes do not have stable capacities.

Views like Schmoller's are often labelled 'holistic'. It is important to distinguish this kind of holism, which rejects the analytic method, from a very different kind of holism that stands in opposition to individualism. The Lucas critique of policy decisions based on observed macroeconomic regularities is a good example to consider since it denies both kinds of holism. As with Mill, Lucas rejects inductive generalization from observed regularities as unreliable. He looks instead for stable principles to describe the behaviour of the basic causes, and from these principles he hopes to derive lessons about what would happen if circumstances were to change. In this he subscribes to the method of analysis and synthesis. In addition, he assumes that the basic causes are the (rational) decisions of individual agents – there are no stable principles relating macroeconomic causes (like inflation) to macroeconomic effects (like unemployment) except those that can be derived from the principles governing individual decisions. In this he subscribes to individualism.[1]

Stability of relations across variations in circumstances matters both to establishing that a factor plays a causal role in a given context and to justifying the elevation of this causal role to the status of a capacity, but in different ways that should not be confused. Consider first just causality. One problem we face when we try to draw causal inferences from statistical data is the problem of the *common cause*. Two factors may covary in a specific context without either one causing the other if they share causal ancestors. In that case we expect (*ceteris paribus*) that the correlation between the two causes will disappear in subpopulations where one factor has a different causal history from the other. One test of causality then is to look to see if the covariation persists regardless of how the putative cause is brought about in that context. A second example where we look for stability across variations is in establishing causal order, as described under 'Causality' in this volume. If A and B are known to be directly causally connected, we can infer that A causes B, as opposed to B causes A, if the distribution of A stays the same across variations in the distributions of other causal factors producing B that are not themselves correlated with A, but not the reverse.

Now consider capacities. Tests for causal relations involve variation over causal histories, keeping the structure fixed. Claims about capacities require stability across more radical variations. A factor may be a genuine cause in a given context – it is truly a good way to produce the effect in that context – even if that role disappears if the context is shifted. This is well illustrated by Trygve Haavelmo (who won the 1989 Nobel Prize in Economics for his work in founding econometrics). Haavelmo uses the example of a car throttle: stepping on the throttle causes the car to accelerate, but only in the context of the properly running car engine. It is one thing to ask, 'Does the relationship between the throttle and the acceleration remain the same across a variety of ways of depressing the accelerator (that is, across a change in causal histories), assuming the structure of the car stays constant?' It is another to ask, 'Will a throttle accelerate a car no matter how the engine is structured?' In the special sense at issue here, the throttle causes the acceleration, but it does not have a basic capacity to do so. The equation that describes its behaviour would not be counted, in the language of Haavelmo and Ragnar Frisch, as *autonomous*. The term *structural*, as used in the Cowles Commission and in the 'Causality' entry in this volume, covers both. A structural equation describes a capacity: a causal relation that stays fixed as changes are imposed on the capacities and the arrangements of other factors.

The Haavelmo example makes clear that claims about capacities are always relative to the range of changes envisaged. In econometrics this point is made explicit in the concept of *superexogeneity* developed by R.F. Engel, D. Hendry and J.F. Richard.[2] Superexogenous factors are not only exogenous to a set of others, but remain so across designated changes in context. 'Exogeneity' has both a causal sense – an exogenous factor may cause effects in the other factors studied but not be caused by them – and a probabilistic sense relevant to procedures of estimation; and the relation between the two is controversial. Engle, Hendry and Richard use 'superexogeneity' only for the latter sense, but the extension to the former is clear.

How do we learn about capacities? Economic theory approaches the problem by the construction of special kinds of idealized models. The criteria for the success of these models are notoriously vague. To pinpoint the capacity of a given factor, the model must isolate it so that it operates unimpeded by interfering or countervailing factors. But no factor does anything in isolation; some specific context must be supplied. For the model to succeed in showing that a factor C has the capacity to produce E, we must be in a position to argue that (a) the specific features incorporated into the model do not interfere with C in its production of E (or do so in a way we know how to calculate away[3]). Beyond that, (b) these features must be detailed enough for it to be determinate whether E occurs or not; and (c) they must be simple enough for us to be able, using accepted principles, to derive E. Finally, and most difficult to formulate, (d) the context must be 'neutral' to the operation of C, allowing E to be displayed 'without distortion'.

Clearly, requirements (b) and (c) pull in opposite directions. So too do (c) and (d). The context is required or there will be no determinate outcome; its characteristics are necessary for the derivation of the effect. Yet there must be a sense in which they can be regarded as inessential: we are justified in assuming that the same (or, more usually, systematically varying) results follow from a range of different backgrounds. We may, for example, study the capacity of skill loss during unemployment to produce persistence in employment shocks by using a model with two overlapping generations of workers of fixed size. The results of the study are only significant to the extent that we can argue that the outcome would be relevantly similar with any reasonable assumptions about workers entering the job market that did not distort the skill-loss mechanism.

The use of the model to establish facts about capacities depends on the appropriateness and applicability of the concepts assumed – those of capacity, interference and distortion – and on the judgments made about them. None of these concepts are operationalizable and there are no strict criteria for their application. Assuming that the judgments are correct, then, in domains where the analytic method is applicable, if conditions (a) to (d) are satisfied we may say that we have a *theoretically grounded* hypothesis about the capacity. The capacity would be expected to be stable across the range of circumstances where the general principles and the assumptions about interference and neutral context are valid.

Empirical support for capacity claims is a further matter. Even controlled experiments that claim to isolate the operation of the factor in question can only show what the factor does in the experimental context. As always with experiments, reasons for expecting that what holds in the experiment will hold elsewhere must come from outside. Alternatively, econometrics can be of help. The direct use of a system of equations estimated from data generated in one context to predict outcomes when the context is shifted clearly supposes that the estimated parameters describe capacities. Any statistical tests that bear on the stability of the parameters are thus relevant, but these obviously require cross-contextual data.

Ideally, for purposes of empirical confirmation we should like the full scheme envisaged by Mill: knowledge of the capacities of all relevant factors present in some particular situation plus the rules of composition. Then we could deduce the expected behaviour and test our hypotheses by the conventional hypothetico-deductive method. Edward Greene argues for a weaker constraint:[4] to entertain seriously a theoretical hypothesis that C has the capacity to produce E, we should find at least one concrete situation in which C *does* produce E. (That it does so can be justified by any methods acceptable to the case at hand.) This is a very weak empirical test, but it seems the least that should be required.

NANCY CARTWRIGHT

Notes
1. This doctrine is sometimes called 'methodological individualism' since it proposes a general prescription for the methods of explaining economic phenomena.
2. See R.F. Engle, D. Hendry and J.F. Richard (1983), 'Exogeneity', *Econometrica*, **51**, 277–304.
3. This caveat will be assumed throughout the rest of the discussion.
4. E.J. Green (1993), 'On the Emergence of Parliamentary Government: The role of Private Information', *Quarterly Review of the Federal Reserve Bank of Minneapolis*, 17, (1), 2–13.

Bibliography
Cartwright, N. (1989), *Nature's Capacities and Their Measurement*, Oxford: Oxford University Press.
Cartwright, N. (1993) 'Aristotelian Natures and the Modern Experimental Method', in J. Earman (ed.), *Inference, Explanation and Other Philosophical Frustrations*, Berkeley, CA: University of California Press.
Cartwright, N. (1995), 'Ceteris Paribus Laws and Socio-Economic Machines', *The Monist*, **78** (3), 276,
Cartwright, N. (1996), 'What is a Causal Structure?', in R. McKim and S.P. Turner (eds), *Causality in Crisis? Statistical Methods and the Search for Causal Knowledge in the Social Sciences*, Notre Dame: University of Notre Dame Press.
Frisch, R., T. Haavelmo, T.C. Koopmans and J. Tinbergen (1948), 'Autonomy of Economic relations', *Memorandum fra Universitetes Socialøkonomiske Institute*, Oslo.
Hausman, D. (1992), *The Inexact and Separate Science of Economics*, Cambridge: Cambridge University Press.
Mill. J.S. (1843), *A System of Logic*, London: Longman, Green & Co.
Woodward, J. (1995), 'Causation and Explanation in Econometrics', in D. Little (ed.), *On the Reliability of Economic Models*, Dordrecht: Kluwer.

Causality

Causality and economics

Classic disputes in economics often turn on causal questions even when causal language is explicitly eschewed. The modern argument over monetarism is really a question of the causal direction between money and prices or nominal income. This debate is ancient, probably predating the clear statements in the eighteenth and early nineteenth centuries in the works of David Hume and David Ricardo, proponents of the view that money causes prices and income, and in Tooke's magisterial *History of Prices*, which argued for the opposite causal order.

Hume not only provides a classic example of causal analysis in economics, but also provides the philosophical account of causality that has defined the issues for 250 years. Three issues arise in any causal analysis. The first is conceptual: what does it mean for one thing to cause another? The second is ontological: what is the essential nature of causes, in Hume's phrase, 'in the objects'? The third is epistemological: how could we infer the existence of causal relations from observations?

For Hume, *A* causes *B*, if *A* and *B* are constantly conjoined, contiguous in space, and *A* precedes *B* in time. *Every time* the explosion of a petrol and air mixture occurs, the piston which is *in direct physical contact* with the explosive mixture *subsequently* descends: this is what we mean when we say, 'The explosion causes the piston to descend.' Beyond this, Hume denies that we know anything about the ontology of causality. If there is some secret connection that accounts for the spatial and temporal pattern of causal relations, we do not know what it is. The epistemological problem for Hume of inferring causes from observations is the same one for inductive inference generally: there is no logical warrant for generalizing from particular instances to a rule.

There are two approaches to causal analysis commonly found in economics. These may be called the *probabilistic approach* and the *structural approach*.

The probabilistic approach
The first thing to notice about economics is that it does not posit relationships that hold without exception, but relationships that tend to hold on average and for the most part. This is reflected in econometric models in the pervasive presence of residual error terms. Modern probabilistic theories of causality (Patrick Suppes provides the classic statement) weaken Hume's condition of constant conjunction. Crudely, *A* causes *B* on probabilistic accounts if $P(B|A) > P(B)$, where '$P(X)$' means 'the probability of *X*' and '$X|Y$' means '*X* conditional on *Y*'. (This simple formulation clearly omits the nuances and qualifications that advocates of probabilistic accounts insist upon.) For example, if the probability that one's headache will end if one takes an aspirin is greater than the probability of its ending unconditionally (that is, whether one takes an aspirin or not), then taking an aspirin is a cause of one's headache ending.

The probabilistic theory of causality in its simplest form is faced with a formidable difficulty: $P(B|A) > P(B)$ implies that $P(A|B) > P(A)$; that is, if *A* causes *B*, then *B* causes *A*. Consider an example: suppose that in a trial for every 100 patients (50 given aspirin, 50 given a placebo) the following average results occur:

		Aspirin	
		No	Yes
Headache	Does not end	40	20
	Ends	10	30

In this case the *P* (headache ending | taking aspirin) = 30/50 = 3/5 > 40/100 = 2/5 = *P* (headache ending). The probabilistic account would therefore conclude that taking aspirin causes headaches to end. But the same data show that *P* (taking aspirin | headache ending) = 30/40 = 3/4 > 1/2 = 50/100 = *P* (taking aspirin). According to the definitions, the headache ending causes patients to take aspirin: but even the advocates of the probabilistic account naturally resist this implication.

The preceding example illustrates an important problem in econometric analysis, known as *observational equivalence*. In probabilistic accounts the problem of observational equivalence is typically solved by following Hume and imposing the condition that causes must precede effects. Thus $P(B_{t+1} | A_t) > P(B_{t+1})$ does not imply that $P(A_{t+1} | B_t) > P(A_{t+1})$, where the subscripts are time indices. We rule out the conclusion that the headache ending causes the patient to receive the aspirin, because in no case does the ending of the headache precede the receiving of the aspirin.

In the probabilistic account, the concept of cause is conflated with method of inferring cause, and issues of ontology are ignored altogether. In economics, the most prominent definition of the causal relation, due to Clive Granger, is based upon such a probabilistic account of causality. A variable *A Granger-causes* a variable *B* if the probability of *B* conditional on its own past history and the past history of *A* does not equal the probability of *B* conditional on its own past history alone. This definition directly supports an inferential procedure since standard statistical tools, such as regression, provide empirical measures of conditional probabilities.

Granger-causality is subject to several paradoxes or puzzles, some of which have analogues in philosophical accounts of probabilistic causality. For example, suppose that there is a mechanism that allows money to control nominal income, and the central bank uses this mechanism optimally to reduce the variance of nominal income as much as possible. To reduce the variation in nominal income, the bank must create appropriately offsetting variations in money. Suppose that, in an extreme case, the central bank is perfectly successful and is able to eliminate *all* of the variation in nominal income. Then, because nominal income is unchanging, there is a zero correlation between past changes in the money supply and nominal income. In reality, nominal income will not be constant, because of unpredictable current shocks from many sources, but an optimally chosen money supply would eliminate that part of the variation in nominal income that was predictable from past information. The variations in the money supply that achieve this control will not be correlated with nominal income because they are chosen precisely to eliminate the predictable variation and they are definitionally uncorrelated with the unpredictable variation. A Granger-causality test, therefore, will fail to indicate causality between money and nominal income, despite the fact that *ex hypothesi* money causes income.

To take another example, economic relations are supposed in many cases to depend critically on people's expectations of the future values of economic variables. In forming these expectations, people often may be better informed about the future course of the variables conditional on current information than an econometrician ever can be. Suppose that the general price level is determined by the interaction of the supply of and demand for money and that the demand for money is inversely related to expected inflation. If people anticipate a future increase in the supply of money, they will expect inflation and thus reduce their current demand for money, which in turn raises the current general price level in order to equilibrate the emergent excess supply of money. Current prices will thus be correlated with future money, so that a Granger-causality test will indicate that prices cause money when *ex hypothesi* money causes prices. This might be regarded simply as a problem of an omitted third cause, so that incorporating the expectations into the relationship would eliminate the problem. The problem arises, however, because people's information is better than the econometrician's information; and, in a complex economy, this is an irreducible fact. To eliminate the information differential completely would require contemporaneous observation of the subjective expectations of every economic agent in the economy – a thing not only impracticable, but impossible in principle.

Another reason to doubt the general usefulness of a probabilistic account of causality in economics is the way in which it uses temporal order to solve the problem of observational equivalence. Properly speaking, a variable measured at time t cannot Granger-cause another variable measured at time t. There are at least two reasons why any concept of causality that depends fundamentally on temporal order will not be generally useful for economics. First, economic data (such as, GNP, consumption or the consumer price index) are collected at fairly wide intervals – years, quarters, months, but rarely weeks, days or hours – but economic activity goes on more or less continuously. Consumption this quarter, for example, is then likely to be related to GNP this quarter: that is, simultaneously. A stock answer to this is that the simultaneous relation is only apparent, and would disappear were data collected at fine enough intervals. However, the conceptual problems of defining, for example, GNP at an interval of a day or an hour are overwhelming, and it would be better to admit simultaneous causation than to be caught in that conceptual morass.

Second, much economic theory is about steady-states, the configurations of economic variables that arise when time is allowed to run notionally to infinity. The relationship between economic variables in long-run steady states may be quite different from what it is in the short-run processes that govern the transitions between steady states, about which little is often known. Yet, while it makes sense to think of one variable in steady state being used asymmetrically to control another, it does not make sense to think of the variables as temporally ordered. Thus a concept of causality that is to capture most of theoretical economic knowledge cannot rely fundamentally on temporal order.

The structural approach
The inadequacy of the probabilistic account of causality is suggested by the strategy of its advocates. Not every A such that $P(B|A) > P(B)$ is regarded as a cause of B. It is recognized that A and B might have common causes, or that third causes might intervene between them, or that probabilities might be calculated with respect to non-homogeneous reference classes, and so forth. In the earlier example, despite the fact that the probabilities indicated that the ending of the headache *prima facie* caused the taking of the aspirin, the advocate of the probabilistic approach rejects the conclusion. Somehow the probabilities got it wrong. But what does that mean? To ask how the approach could go wrong is to have a strong idea of what it is to be right. Certainly, this is partly a matter of causal intuitions. Beyond that there appears to be an implicit notion of causal structure involved in setting the agenda for probabilistic causality.

Structural accounts reject the view that probability relations are useful in defining the concept of cause, although they may grant them a part in the epistemology of inferring causal structure from observations. Structural accounts must define the concept of cause differently. Causes have sometimes been regarded as necessary conditions for their effects. But this is not acceptable in its unadorned form since the same effect might be achieved from different causes – even simultaneously occurring different causes (the case known as *causal over-determination*). Causes have sometimes been regarded as sufficient for their effects. But this will not do in its unadorned form either: for example, the match is the cause of the explosion, but only in conjunction with other necessary factors – the explosive, air, the right humidity conditions and so forth. Many accounts of causation have tried to start either with necessity or sufficiency and add qualifications that would eliminate these obvious, as well as more sophisticated, objections.

J.L. Mackie provides a well-known alternative elucidation of the concept of cause. A cause, says Mackie, is an *INUS* condition, an *i*nsufficient, *n*on-redundant member of a set of *u*nnecessary but *s*ufficient conditions for the effect. The set {match, explosive, air, low humidity} is sufficient for the explosion; there would be no explosion with the match alone, so it is insufficient; there would be no explosion from that particularly complex if the match were missing, so it is non-redundant; but there are other sets of sufficient conditions (explosive, electric ignitor), for example, so the whole complex is unnecessary: the match is, therefore, *a* cause of the explosion.

Whether causation is elucidated principally through INUS conditions or through some variation on a sufficiency or necessity criterion, an appeal is made to the logic of conditional statements ('if *p*, then *q*'). Such conditionals are sometimes known as 'counterfactuals' because 'if *p*, then *q*', may be true even when *p* is false. To assert a counterfactual is to assert the existence of a disposition: the nature of the situation is such that *q* is disposed to occur when *p* does. Such dispositions need not be deterministic; *q* may occur only with some probability. Nevertheless, invariance is implicit in counterfactuals and related dispositional claims. A counterfactual cannot be rightly asserted if, when its antecedents are fulfilled, it no longer entails (probabilistically at least) the same consequence. Invariance of this sort underwrites an intuitively appealing notion: causes are efficacious in bringing about their effects.

A causal structure can then be seen as a network of counterfactual relations that maps out the underlying mechanisms through which one thing is used to control or manipulate another. In effect, the structural account makes the empirical claim that there is something more to causality 'in the objects,' than Humess purely associative notion of causality allows. What more there is needs to be fleshed out in two directions. On the one hand, the appeal to counterfactuals raises ontological issues about the existence of modalities such as necessity or probability. On the other hand, economically satisfactory descriptions of causal mechanisms are needed.

Although economists generally neglect the metaphysical issues, structural accounts of causation have a long history in econometrics. The classic account is due to Herbert Simon. For Simon, the following equations illustrate a case in which x_1 causes x_2:

$$a_{11}x_1 \qquad\qquad = a_{10} \qquad\qquad\qquad (1)$$

$$a_{21}x_1 + a_{22}x_2 = a_{20}, \qquad\qquad\qquad (2)$$

where the a_{ij}s are fixed coefficients and the x_is are variables. In this case the value of x_1 is independent of the value of x_2, but the value of x_2 changes depending upon the value of x_1.

An immediate difficulty with Simon's account of structure, as he himself recognized, is that it is subject to another version of the problem of observational equivalence. There is an infinite number of linear combinations of equations (1) and (2) that have different coefficients, with every possible apparent causal order, each yielding the same values for the x_is. For Simon, the uniquely correct causal structure is the one that is invariant to interventions. On this view, equations (1) and (2) represent a true causal structure only if the a_{ij}s may be treated as parameters that can be selected independently of each other. The invariance of equations (1) and (2) permits them to be treated counterfactually; they represent what would happen to x_2, for example, if x_1 were different, say, because a_{10} were different. Through the notion of invariance, Simon's account of causal structure links the notion – frequently supported by economists and econometricians – that causality is related to (hypothetical controllability) to the conditional analysis of causation well known to philosophers.

Causal inference
The probabilistic account of causality runs the conceptual problem of defining what a cause is together with the epistemological problem of inferring causes from evidence in order to avoid making any ontological commitment to what causes are 'in the objects'. Thus, for example, in Granger's analysis causes are defined by the procedure (that is, conditional probabilities) through which they are inferred.

Structural accounts are appealing in economics partly because they keep the issues of definition, ontology and epistemology distinct. Not defining cause by an inferential procedure, the structural account accommodates a variety of evidence, including, in the right circumstances, the evidence of conditional probabilities. Two inferential questions must be kept distinct. The first is, given A and B, what is the direction of causal influence, if any, between them? The second is, given that A causes B, what is the strength of the causal influence of A on B?

Probabilistic accounts are very appealing in fields in which causal direction is implicitly known. One reason for even the advocates of probabilistic accounts resisting the implication that the ending of headaches causes the receiving of aspirin is that it is a controlled experiment in which the assignment of aspirin or placebo to patients is made independently (temporally, but more importantly) logically prior to the determination of whether their headaches ended. The causal direction is from aspirin to the end of headaches *if there is any causal connection at all*. This situation, for example, is frequent in medical research: with fairly straightforward controls, probabilistic methods can be used to assess the causal efficacy of a pathogen or a treatment (implicit structural understanding, of course, informs the design of those controls). Prior commitment to structure in economics is the basis for the use of probabilistic methods to *measure* causes in *identified* econometric systems of equations that is the legacy of Trygve Haavelmo and the Cowles Commission to econometrics.

Unfortunately, economics does not support implicit structural commitments as well as some other fields, such as medicine, do. It is often the case that more than one causal ordering is consistent with the theoretical and institutional constraints of economics and that alternative causal orderings are observationally equivalent in the sense that they generate the same probability distribution for the data. This is the upshot of the debate over 'explicit causal chain' models or 'process analysis' that raged for 15 years from the late 1940s. One side of this debate (Hermann Wold, Robert Strotz and others) argued that, since causality is both logically and temporally asymmetric, econometrically estimated systems should reflect this asymmetry through the use of recursive systems of equations. The other side (Herbert Simon, Robert Basmann and others) pointed out that, because of observational equivalence, the purely syntactic distinction between recursive and simultaneous systems was not enough to capture the causal asymmetry. Other fields are, of course, not immune from the problem of observational equivalence. Whether the HIV viruses cause AIDS is a question of causal direction no different in principle from whether money causes prices or taxes cause spending. (The heterodox view of the virologist Peter Duesberg is that HIV is simply the most common opportunistic infection of AIDS patients and not the cause of their disease.)

The estimation of identified systems of equations assumes an answer to the question of causal direction in order to pursue the question of measurement. Granger-causality assumes a temporal structure in order to address the question of causal direction using purely probabilistic methods. A third approach is to recognize that the very notion of structure implies that a causal structure must remain invariant in some dimensions to interventions and, indeed, transmit interventions in one part of the structure to other parts of the structure.

In a broad sense, it is this notion that underlies Arnold Zellner's criterion that a causal relation is one that supports 'predictability according to law'. Zellner's criticism of Granger-causality is that it relies on correlations that may not be lawlike, that may not be invariant once used to guide causal production (for example, monetary policy). Unfortunately, Zellner's account is not very helpful because it merely transforms the problem from 'what is a cause and how might one infer it?' to 'what is a law and how might one infer it?' It sets up invariance (lawlikeness) itself as defining the causal relation, where in a richer structural account invariance is a property with a complex relation to causality.

Kevin Hoover's structural approach to causal inference considers competing causal orderings. The causal asymmetries of these orderings is reflected in the asymmetries of alternative conditional probability distributions. The joint probability distribution of A and B may be factored into marginal and conditional distributions in two ways: $D(A, B) = D(A \mid B)D(B) = D(B \mid A)D(A)$. If A causes B, the second of these factorizations is the more stable in the sense that $D(A)$ will remain invariant in the face of structural interventions in the process determining B and (with certain qualifications) $D(B \mid A)$ will remain invariant in the face of interventions in the process determining A. Regressions provide empirically applicable econometric analogues to the conditional probability distributions, and invariance can be evaluated using standard econometric tests for structural stability. The method relies heavily on the identification and assignment of interventions to the A or the B processes typically based on a combination of historical, institutional and statistical knowledge.

In Hoover's analysis, invariance is used instrumentally to reveal underlying causal structure. Recently, other researchers, particularly Clark Glymour and his coworkers and Judea Pearl and his coworkers, have developed other methods of causal inference that are grounded in a structuralist approach. Applications of these methods to economics are only just beginning, so that it is difficult to assess their ultimate importance.

KEVIN D. HOOVER

Bibliography
Basmann, R.L. (1988), 'Causality Tests and Observationally Equivalent Representations of Econometric Models', *Journal of Econometrics*, Annals, **39**, 69–101.
Cartwright, Nancy (1989), *Nature's Capacities and Their Measurement*, Oxford: Clarendon Press.
Granger, C.W.J. (1980), 'Testing for Causality: A Personal Viewpoint', *Journal of Economic Dynamics and Control*, **2** (4), November, 329–52.
Hoover, Kevin D. (1990), 'The Logic of Causal Inference: Econometrics and the Conditional Analysis of Causation', *Economics and Philosophy*, **6** (2), 207–34.
Hume, David (1738), *A Treatise of Human Nature*.
Pearl, Judea (1995), 'Causal Diagrams for Empirical Research', *Biometrika*, **82**, (4), December, 669–88.
Salmon, Wesley C. (1984), *Scientific Explanation and the Causal Structure of the World*, Princeton: Princeton University Press.
Simon, Herbert A. (1953), 'Causal Ordering and Identifiability'; reprinted 1957 in *Models of Man*, New York: Wiley.
Spirtes, Peter, Clark Glymour and Richard Scheines (1993), 'Causation, Prediction and Search', New York/Berlin: Springer-Verlag.
Suppes, Patrick (1970), 'A Probabilistic Theory of Causality', *Acta Philosophica Fennica*, Fasc. XXIV.

Wold, Hermann (1954), 'Causality and Econometrics', *Econometrica*, **22**, 162–77.
Zellner, Arnold (1979), 'Causality and Econometrics', in Karl Brunner and Alan H. Meltzer (eds), *Three Aspects of Policy Making: Knowledge, Data and Institutions*, Carnegie-Rochester Conference Series on Public Policy, vol. 10, Amsterdam: North-Holland.

Ceteris paribus

Ceteris paribus is a Latin expression made up of the flexible words *ceterus* (the other, that which exists besides, the reminder) and *par* (similar, equal in effect). Various translations include 'other things being equal' and 'other things being constant'. Although ubiquitous in economic science since its inception (Piimies, 1997), the expression has received detailed methodological attention in narrow contexts only.

Equivalents of *ceteris paribus* are used by Aristotle in *Posterior Analytics* and by Marcus Tullius Cicero (106–43 BC) in his treatise *On Duties*. The abbreviated expression *ceteris paribus* was subsequently adopted by scholastic authors like Thomas Aquinas (1224/5–74), whose philosophy was strongly influenced by Aristotle. The great mediaeval economic thinker Peter John Olivi (Petrus Iohannis O., *doctor speculativus*, 1247/8–98) employs *ceteris paribus* (CP) clauses in distinctly economic contexts with regard both to value determinants and to intertemporal choice in his set of three treatises on buying and selling, usury and restitution. Olivi, once a suspected heretic, remained for a long time an important but largely uncredited source, whose texts were extensively copied down the centuries by, among others, St Bernardino of Siena (1380–1444) and St Antonio of Florence (1389–1459).

In the late scholastic era, the economic writings of the School of Salamanca integrate the CP clause into monetary doctrines anticipating, for example, the quantity theory of money: *ceteris paribus*, the price level varies inversely with the quantity of money (Martin de Azpilcueta Navarro, 1556; cf. Grice-Hutchinson, 1993). In the English economic literature, CP clauses date back at least to 1662 and the Jesuit-educated William Petty (1623–87; see Persky, 1990) who adds a (labour) cost element to the supply of silver from the Americas in the framework of the quantity theory of money.

The CP clause becomes an object of *methodological* inquiry with John Stuart Mill's (1806–73) definition of political economy as the study of 'the course of action into which mankind, living in a state of society, would be impelled' if acting solely 'from the desire of wealth' and its two permanent countermotives of 'aversion to labour' and positive time preference (Mill, 1836). Mill's distinctions give rise to two kinds of assumptions that could be called *ceteris absentibus* clauses: first, pure economic theory studies economic action in the absence of non-economic motives and, second, it omits minor economic causes that operate in particular circumstances only. The latter, however, can be brought 'within the place of the abstract science' by successive theories of more limited scope. Omitted causes are labelled 'disturbing causes' if they modify the attainment of a state of affairs that would be brought about by major economic causes only.

In *The Principles of Political Economy* (Mill, 1871), explicit CP clauses are rare and fall into several groups, many of which involve (economic) time. The first group covers the constancy – rather than absence – of non-economic causes. That land rents are constantly lower but vary inversely with the money rate of interests, *ceteris paribus*, presupposes the constancy over time of the non-economic desire for 'power and dignity' associated with landed property which drives land prices up relative to agricultural revenue to keep land rents below the money rent (ibid:

649). A second group involves an assumption of normality. Wartime conditions that, exceptionally, keep both land rents and interest rates high are excluded by a CP clause. A third group of CP clauses implicitly defines the appropriate time frame for assertions about supply and demand reactions. Immediate and temporary prices vary with supply and demand shocks. The quantity theory of money is a special case, where the price level temporarily increases with an increase in the quantity of money, *ceteris paribus*, before the supply of money adjusts.

Mill offers no detailed explanation of the relation of the CP clause to disturbing causes, nor is this done by his follower, both in methodology and theory, John Elliot Cairnes (1923–75). The latter, nevertheless, conscientiously points out when and how political economy involves what he understands to be CP clauses. In one of his numerous examples, Cairnes asks how quickly the supply of finished manufacturing, of raw vegetable and of animal products adapts to a demand shift, *ceteris paribus* (Cairnes, 1873: 62).

Alfred Marshall (1842–1924) offers a variation on Cairnes' theme by defining the normal price for each industry both for the short and the long run in terms of a CP clause. According to a famous example (incidentally, of raw animal products) of Marshall's short-run normal price 'for any given daily supply of fish … is the price which will quickly call into the fishing trade capital and labour enough to obtain that supply in a day's fishing of average good fortune'. The normal price brings the market quickly to an equilibrium after a sudden shift, such as a demand shift in the fish market caused by a meat disease (Marshall, 1922: 369–70). Factors that affect supply more slowly are put 'in a pound called *Cæteris Paribus*. The study of some group of tendencies is isolated by the assumption *other things being equal*: the existence of other tendencies is not denied, but their disturbing effect is neglected for a time' (ibid: 366).

After Marshall, the methodological debate on the CP clause tends to concentrate on demand (with the nature of supply curves remaining a substantial economic issue) and its role in partial equilibrium analysis. The emphasis is now on the explicit identification of economic variables of which parity is assumed, and on the grounds of the assumption. In the gradually changing philosophical and theoretical climate, Marshall's intention of isolating tendencies in the economy with CP clauses gives way to discussions of either prediction or theoretical isolation against the backdrop of general equilibrium theory.

A more theoretically laden interpretation of what *ceteris paribus* can mean is offered by Milton Friedman (1949; cf. Yeager, 1960) in his reinterpretation of the Marshallian demand curve. He defines 'the same' as 'same for all points' on a demand curve (in a non-temporal framework), broadens 'other things' to include 'money income' and the 'purchasing power of money', with sameness meaning 'compensating variations' in other prices so as to maintain the purchasing power of money. In other words, no other prices are explicitly arguments of the demand function – they are covered by the CP clause – but their contribution to the purchasing power of money sets a constraint on their aggregate variation. Friedman thus wishes to 'isolate' the substitution effect with the demand curve by *eliminating* (rather than neglecting) variations in income through the CP clause (Friedman, 1949: 474).

In the ensuing debate, Bailey (1958; cf. Yeager 1960) points out that it is technically infeasible to lay down precise constraints on the purchasing power of money. The ambiguities essentially follow from the vagueness of the notion of a general price level or the real quantity of money. In methodological terms, the discussion degenerates into one that is more concerned with the *independent* merits of general equilibrium and partial equilibrium approaches, with less clarification of their mutual *relation* (Buchanan, 1958; Yeager 1960). In a later contribution, Hausman (1990) affords precedence to general equilibrium theory because it provides a *causal ordering* of items which partial equilibrium models adopt, albeit with approximate accuracy. Thus, as income is causally intermediate with regard to general equilibrium primitives and consumption, it inherits an independent role in partial equilibrium explanations. General causal considerations and specific theoretical knowledge may also justify treating demand and supply *functions* of the (relative) price of a good as independent items, in which case such functions have an explanatory status as well. The CP clause then includes a list that 'makes explicit possible disturbances or interferences' which are not 'significantly affected' by the own-price of the good.

Examples like those mentioned above suggest that *ceteris paribus* is a highly ambiguous expression, having a variety of usages. The following outline of a typology should capture many of them. The typology is based on looking separately first at *ceteri* and *par* and then at *ceteris paribus* (Mäki, 1996).

Supposing we translate *ceteri* as 'other things', it is neither the thingness nor the otherness of these other things that gives rise to any serious ambiguity; it is rather the quantification over and further qualifications of the other things. There is a usage according to which only one other thing is picked, such as when calling 'supposing the velocity of money remains constant' a CP clause. Such clauses could be called 'retail' clauses. At the other extreme, *ceteri* may be taken to refer to all other things. In this case we might call the clause a 'wholesale' clause. However, since it is obvious that all other things are never *par* or cannot be known to be so, nor, more importantly, do they need to be, it is customary to restrict the set of other things denoted by '*ceteri*' to other *relevant* things. The relevant sense of 'relevance' in this context is usually left unexplicated, but it seems clear that 'other relevant things' is intended to refer to something like *other potentially causally significant thing*s. Since these things are supposed to be potentially causally significant for the phenomena under examination, it makes sense to neutralize these things with a CP clause; such a clause is not needed for causally insignificant things with a CP clause.

Turning then to an examination of '*par*', we may propose distinguishing at least the following usages. A conventional translation of *par* is 'equal', but this does not yet fix its meaning. Being equal is, of course, a comparative notion, and a further distinction may be suggested by a division between diachronic and synchronic equality. On the diachronic version, 'being equal' means 'being constant', or *remaining* equal over a relevant time period. This gives rise to a diachronic CP clause as in Marshallian time-period analysis. On the synchronic version, 'being equal' means 'being similar', or *being* equal. Here the comparison is between two systems or contexts rather than between two or more points in time of the history of one system. This gives rise to a synchronic CP clause.

Another reading of *par* is to take it as designating the notion of 'being absent'. In this case the impact of some – potentially causally significant – things is neutralized by saying that they are absent altogether in a given situation, rather than constant over time or the same between two or more systems. This version is often called a CP clause, but economists occasionally also call it a *ceteris absentibus* clause. Yet another meaning of *par* is 'being normal'. Thus certain economic lawlike claims may be said to hold only provided the circumstances are somehow normal, such as provided there is no war, political revolution, hyperinflation or natural catastrophe going on in the relevant society. An assumption with such contents might be called a *ceteris normalibus* clause.

We can now focus on the types of claim suggested by the use of a CP qualification in connection with a statement or model in economics. What exactly is being claimed by '*ceteris paribus*, so-and-so'? It is clear that usually no assertion is made to the effect that other things are equal or absent; it is believed that such an assertion would be false. The claim made is about the 'so-and-so'. The question is, how does adding the clause qualify such a claim? At least the following types of modified claim can be distinguished.

First, the qualification suggested by a CP clause may be a transformation of a deterministic claim to a statistical claim, a move from a claim about what happens in all cases to a claim about what happens in most cases. While an unqualified claim will not permit exceptions, a qualified claim will: the so-and-so does not or may not hold in cases where the *ceteris paribus* (or *absentibus* or *normalibus*) clause is false (or radically false).

Second, the clause may be taken to turn a claim that so-and-so into a sufficiently close approximation, given the relevant methodological conventions. It is acknowledged that the clause is not exactly true, and that therefore the implications of the qualified claim or model are not exactly true either. At the same time, it is held that the degree of falsehood of the clause is negligible, in that the degree of approximation of the qualified claim is tolerably good.

Third, the clause may be regarded as suggesting an applicability condition of the unqualified claim: the claim only holds provided the clause holds. The clause is used to describe the domain to which the claim or model can be applied. Obviously, the *ceteris normalibus* version invites this interpretation: a model only applies if the circumstances are somehow normal.

Fourth, the incorporation of the clause into a claim or model may suggest that it has 'gaps' in its picture of the world. These gaps are denoted by the (false) clause and they give rise to divergencies between the picture and the world. It is further suggested that the divergencies are to be explained by resources other than the model itself or its subsequent elaborations, these external resources being adopted either from elsewhere in economics or from other social sciences.

Fifth, the presence of the clause may be taken to suggest a promise or wish or anticipation that the version of a model at hand is only an early step in a sequence of models of increasing richness and refinement. Early versions have 'gaps' in them, but later versions are supposed to fill in at least some such gaps; in other words, later versions will relax some of the 'retail' clauses to incorporate the impact of the formerly neutralized factors.

The ambiguity of *ceteris paribus* can thus be somewhat reduced, even if not fully eliminated. The same can be said about the presence of the clause: in its various forms, it cannot be eliminated even if parts of its contents could be made explicit and controlled. This has major methodological consequences. For example, a model involving the clause is not unproblematically refutable since the blame for failure can easily be put on the falsehood of the clause. It is not surprising, therefore, that Popper and his followers in economic methodology have felt uncomfortable about the clause which has appeared to them a device for hedging hypotheses against critical testing. From another perspective, that of theory and model construction, the role of the clause may be viewed differently: its task is to help theoretically isolate what are believed to be primary or essential factors from the secondary or inessential ones.

USKALI MÄKI

JUKKA-PEKKA PIIMIES

References

Bailey, Martin J. (1954), 'The Marshallian demand curve', *Journal of Political Economy*, **62**, 255–61.
Buchanan, James (1958), 'Ceteris paribus: Some notes on methodology', *Southern Economic Journal*, **24**, 259–70.
Cairnes, J.E. (1873), *Essays in Political Economy – Theoretical and Applied*, London: Macmillan.
Friedman, Milton (1949), 'The Marshallian demand curve', *Journal of Political Economy*, **57**, 463–95.

Grice-Hutchinson, M. (1993), *Economic Thought in Spain: Selected Essays*, ed. L.S. Moss and C.K. Ryan, Aldershot: Edward Elgar.
Hausman, Daniel (1990), 'Supply and demand explanations and their *ceteris paribus* clauses', *Review of Political Economy*, **2**, 168–87.
Mäki, Uskali (1996), '*Ceteris paribus*: Interpretations and implications', unpublished.
Marshall, Alfred (1920), *Principles of Economics*, 8th edn, London: Macmillan.
Mill, John Stuart (1836), 'On the Definition of Political Economy and the Method of Investigation Proper to It'; reprinted in *Collected Works of John Stuart Mill*, vol. 4, Toronto: University of Toronto Press, 1967.
Mill, John Stuart (1871), *The Principles of Political Economy*, 7th edn, ed. W. Ashley; reprinted London: Longmans, Green and Co. 1926.
Olivi, Peter John. *Tractatus de emptionibus et venditionibus, de usuris, de restitutionibus*, ed. G. Todeschini in *Un trattato di economia politica francescana*. Isituto Storico Italiano per il Medio Evo. Studi Storici – Fasc. 125–6. pp. 51–108. Rome 1980.
Persky, Joseph (1990), 'Retrospectives: *Ceteris Paribus*', *Journal of Economic Perspectives*, **4**, (2), 187–93.
Piimies, Jukka-Pekka (1997), 'On the introduction of *ceteris paribus* into economic literature', unpublished.
Yeager, Leland (1990), '*Methodenstreit* over demand curves', *Journal of Political Economy*, **68**, 53–64.

Chaos in Economics

The ideas of chaotic dynamics come to economics from the natural sciences and mathematics. Like economists, scientists in physics, meterology and population biology have long tried to describe and explain phenomena which have very complex behaviour when observed over time. The levels of insect and animal populations, weather patterns and the turbulence of fluid flows all fluctuate in ways that are only approximately captured by the most complicated periodic models. These phenomena are ultimately too erratic and too arbitrarily distributed over their range to make observers happy with periodicity.

Mathematicians such as Poincaré, Kolmogorov and Smale have shown that extremely complex dynamic behaviour can be produced by relatively simple non-linear mathematical models. These insights are somewhat difficult, and they were not immediately disseminated outside a specialist audience. However, with the advent of cheap computing power, applied scientists were led along the non-linear path. Independent, computationally based work in meteorology (Lorenz, 1963) and population biology (May, 1976) demonstrated that extremely complicated behaviour could be produced by empirically relevant mathematical models composed of simple non-linear difference and differential equations. After a time, many scientists saw the potential of non-linear dynamics for explaining phenomena that were otherwise poorly approximated (Gleick, 1987). Mathematicians saw new and promising areas of pure and applied research. The result has been a prodigious flow of research. Thousands of articles and texts on non-linear dynamics are produced annually, and university presses have entire series in 'non-linear science'.

It is easy to see why chaotic dynamics has received such attention. Consider the quadratic difference equation $x_t = \alpha(x_{t-1} - x_{t-1}^2)$, which has been used for some time to describe the growth of biological populations limited by a resource constraint. For lower levels of the parameter α, the variable x will exhibit steady-state or periodic behaviour.[1] However, as α rises through 4.0, the time series behaviour of x becomes much more interesting. Periodic behaviour gives way to extremely complicated dynamics which appear to fill an interval of values of x; and at other values of α periodic behaviour reappears. In other words, periodic and apparently a periodic fluctuations of x can all be produced deterministically, depending on the value of a parameter (cf. Devaney, 1986: 44–51).

In fact, it can be shown that, for particular values of α, the behaviour of x conforms to a now common definition of 'chaos' (ibid.: 50). The most important element of the definition is sensitive dependence on initial conditions. Formally, this means that, given a point on an attractor, there is another arbitrarily close which will separate (locally) at an exponential rate. It implies that any error about the initial state of the dynamical system will cumulate and frustrate computation of the evolution of a trajectory. Even if the deterministic structure of a chaotic economic system is known with complete certainty, a failure to specify initial conditions perfectly, or a failure to make perfect numerical computations of period-to-period dynamics, will mean significant errors of forecast.

A second element in the definition of chaos is the existence of a dense orbit, which means that dynamical behaviour on the system cannot be confined to disjoint subsets on its domain. The system 'mixes' over time. Among other things, this implies that periodic orbits cannot be stable, an additional complication of dynamics.[2] The final characteristic is that the domain of a chaotic system is dense in periodic points, which implies potentially complex behaviour in itself.[3]

After chaotic dynamics was established in science and mathematics, economists began to consider the implications for their subject. Anyone familiar with financial markets, business cycles or commodities futures markets could see that their irregular, turbulent time series were candidates for explanation as chaotic processes. However, the consideration of non-linear dynamics and chaos as explanatory devices has been conditioned by two factors. The first is the newness and difficulty of the mathematics involved, which has made its translation into economic analysis a non-trivial matter. Because of this, much of the economic modelling of chaotic dynamics has relied on the accessible Li–Yorke (1975) theorem.

A second, substantial impediment to the introduction of non-linear dynamics into economic analysis is the existence of an established, if somewhat unsatisfactory, competing explanation of economic dynamics. This explanation derives from the work of Slutsky, and relies on linear–stochastic difference equations. As Slutsky (1927) showed, fairly complicated weighted moving averages of a run of random numbers can produce synthetic time series with a strong similarity to those observed by business cycle researchers. This rediscovery and application of Brownian motion fits easily into a linear framework. If an aggregate economic variable x can be explained by a linear difference equation as simple as $x_t = \alpha x_{t-1} + \varepsilon_t$, where ε_t is a random term, a Slutsky-like process can be produced. Recursive substitution of the equation into itself will produce a moving average of εs, hence a rudimentary cyclical series.

Now this ready-made mechanism has some drawbacks. Even if lags in x can be plausibly justified on economic grounds, they are often insufficient to generate the complexity of observed behaviour. Serial correlation of the error terms is often introduced into economic models with little economic justification. Especially in the case of business cycles, it is also somewhat difficult to explain just what the 'exogenous shocks' are meant to represent. Beyond a short list of plausible examples, such as the 1970s oil shocks, it is not so easy to identify aggregate shocks which can be said to hit entire economies. These difficulties underlie the somewhat uneasy tone of the literature on 'stochastic trends'. They are addressed more frankly by Arrow (1989) in his evalution of the potential contribution of non-linear dynamics to economic theory:

> The general perspective of mainstream (so-called neoclassical) economic theory has certainly had some empirical success. ... But it is clear that many empirical phenomena are not covered well by either the theoretical or the empirical analyses based on linear stochastic systems, sometimes not by either. The

presence and persistence of cyclical fluctuations in the economy as a whole of irregular timing and amplitude are not consistent with a view that an economy returns to equilibrium states after any disturbance. The persistence of unemployment undermines the assumption that prices and wages work to reduce imbalances between supply and demand. Equilibrium theory would tend to suggest that, as technology spreads throughout the world, the per capita national incomes would tend to converge, but any such tendency is very weak indeed. Similarly, different ethnic and class groups and economic regions within a country show only fitful tendencies to converge balanced by the equal likelihood of divergence. Instead of stochastic steady states, we observe that volatility tends to vary greatly over time, quiescent periods with little period-by-period fluctuations alternating with eras of rapid fluctuation. The securities markets have always shown great volatility, while the international financial markets, on which currencies are exchanged, have shown virtual disorganization since exchange rates were allowed to float, although most economists would have regarded free-exchange rate movements as an aid to stabilization.

   These empirical results have given impetus to the closer study of dynamic models and the emphasis on application of new results on nonlinear dynamic models. They have also given rise to criticism of the models themselves, and this tradition goes far back; it suffices to mention the alternative theories of J. M. Keynes.

However, established views and methods have the advantage of familiarity, and are modified with difficulty.

Some economists have ignored these impediments and introduced non-linear dynamics into the discourse of economics. Much of the economic research on chaos has been theoretical, and is frequently concerned with business cycles models. Rather than stimulating new economics, this theoretical effort has for the most part produced a re-examination of existing economic models. The main outcome of this effort is a demonstration that explicit consideration of non-linearity will show the possibility of chaotic behaviour in a wide variety of model settings (cf. Baumol and Behabib, 1989; Behabib, 1991; Bullard and Butler, 1993; Gabisch and Lorenz, 1989; Grandmont, 1987; Lorenz, 1989; Scheinkman, 1990).

The early emphasis on modelling is explicable in terms of the professional hierarchy. Theorists are at the top of the professional ladder, so new ideas must have the approval of high theory before they receive serious consideration. Since economic theorists are oddly averse to computer simulation, which is a central tool in all scientific disciplines concerned with non-linear dynamics, the theoretical work has been almost exclusively deductive. And since economists as a group are hardly adept at mathematics, this theoretical work has been almost exclusively confined to the very limited mathematical territory opened up by Li–Yorke. This theorem establishes sufficient conditions for the existence of chaos on an uncountable subset of the domain of one-dimensional discrete maps. Unfortunately, while the Li–Yorke theorem is tractable to apply, its results are very weak. To show the existence of chaotic behaviour on an uncountable subset of the domain of $x_t = f(x_{t-1})$ may say very little about the dynamics of $f(x)$. An uncountable subset of R^1 can have measure zero, that is, it may be nothing more than a disconnected set of points. Unless a dynamical process begins on one of the points of the chaotic subset, chaos will never be observed. Moreover, perturbations may easily move the dynamical system to non-chaotic behaviour. In computer simulation this situation may manifest itself in chaotic transients, which fade away after the simulation has run for some time. Moreover, discrete one-dimensional maps which produce persistently observable chaotic behaviour also produce time series which are too spiky to correspond easily to observed economic dynamics. Scientists and mathematicians will need to provide simpler mathematical tools if deductive economics is to go much farther in this line.

The emphasis on business cycles derives at least in part from the legacy of dynamic theory and models in Keynesian macroeconomics. Harrod (1939) recognized that the presence of multiplier–accelerator phenomena made macroeconomic stability unlikely. Kaldor (1940) and Goodwin (1951) showed how this instability could produce cycles in non-linear macroeconomic models. Their imaginative early work produced a substantial and continuing line of theoretical effort using non-linear methods. Therefore non-linear Keynesian macro models have been obvious candidates for reconsideration using new techniques. Over time, however, theoretical work has shifted to professionally safer contexts, such as overlapping generations models (Jarsulic, 1993b).

Attempts to test for the presence of chaotic behaviour in economic data, which followed the theoretical initiatives, have drawn on a variety of techniques developed by scientists. Sensitive dependence can be identified by the presence of a positive Lyapunov exponent. This measure can be calculated using simple algorithms and a single time series, and does not require any knowledge of the underlying dynamical system (Wolf, 1986). Accurate estimation requires runs of data several thousand observations long. Since chaotic processes often (but *not* always) operate on sets which have a fractal (that is, non-integer) dimension, it is also common practice to try to estimate the dimension of the dynamical system producing the time series.[4] A fractal estimate is counted as evidence for chaos. This too can be done using easily implemented algorithms (Grassberger and Proccaccia, 1983) and also requires long runs of data for accuracy (cf. Jarsulic, 1993a). Also, since chaotic systems sometimes (but *not* always) exhibit spectral densities which appear to be white noise, spectral densities are sometimes calculated.

Unfortunately for economic researchers, many economic time series have length which ranges from inadequate to just barely sufficient for these tests. At times, economists have behaved as if these data limitations could be ignored. Attempts have been made to estimate set dimension for GNP (Brock, 1986; Frank and Stegnos, 1988; Mullineux *et al.*, 1993), work stoppages (Sayers, 1987), monetary aggregates (Barnett and Chen, 1988; Chen, 1993). Since the series from macroeconomic aggregates are short, it is unreasonable to expect any firm conclusions. Ramsay *et al.* (1990) review the dimension estimates of Barnett and Chen, Sayers, and Scheinkman and Lebaron (1989). They conclude, not surprisingly, that there is little evidence for chaotic behaviour, but some for non-linearity, in the data sets considered. When time series are longer, the dimension results are more believable and have in some cases been more in line with chaos. Frank and Stegnos (1989) find strong evidence of a fractal dimension in gold and silver returns; DeCoster *et al.* (1992) believe their dimension results for commodities futures prices indicate non-linearity. Positive Lyapunov exponents, more closely connected to the definition of chaos, have been estimated for monetary aggregates (Barnett and Chen, 1989).

Since economists have put so much emphasis on dimension estimates, it should be emphasized that drawing conclusions about the existence of non-linearity or chaos on the basis of dimension alone is a problematic procedure. The definition of chaos does not include any notion of a fractal dimension; and as Grassberger and Proccaccia pointed out, not every chaotic system has a fractal dimension. Some economists have also used the BDS statistic (Brock *et al.*, 1991), which utilizes estimates of dimension, and which is actually a test for stochastic dependence against the null hypothesis of stochastic independence, as a device for discriminating between stochastic and chaotic systems. Its usefulness as a test for non-linearity or chaos is controversial (Barnett and Hinich, 1993).

On the basis of the empirical work done so far, there is insufficient evidence to draw firm conclusions about the presence or absence of chaos in economic data. However, when time series are sufficiently long, tests seem to point in the direction of non-linearity and chaos. As in the case of deductive theorizing, progress in the empirical study of economic time series will very likely have to wait for discoveries by scientists and mathematicians. Something along the line of bootstrapping may be necessary to overcome the shortness of macroeconomic time series in which there is so much interest.

The inconclusive results of dimension tests is sometimes given as an explanation for professional wariness about non-linear dynamics in general, and chaotic dynamics in particular. It may also be conjectured that some of this wariness has other sources. Dynamical systems in which local equilibria are unstable, and in which forecasting an infinite future is a ludicrous enterprise, do not fit comfortably into a profession in which perfect foresight and its rational expectations analogue is taken as a preferred reference point. The work of W. Brian Arthur and others has discussed some of this intellectual resistance in detail.

MARC JARSULIC

Notes

1. A dynamical system $x_t = f(x_{t-1})$ exhibits periodic behaviour if $x_{t+T} = x_t$ for some T.
2. A dense orbit is a sequence of values $(x_1, x_2, ...)$ produced by a dynamical system $x_t = f(x_{t-1})$ which comes arbitrarily close to any x_k in the domain of $f(x)$.
3. It can be shown that the last two characteristics, mixing and density of periodic points, imply sensitive dependence (Banks *et al.*, 1992). However, in practice it is sensitive dependence which gives chaotic systems their most interesting features; and it is a characteristic which can be identified in data, independent of knowledge of the underlying dynamical system.
4. For a bounded set A, the capacity dimension is defined as $D = \lim \sup_{e \to \infty} (\log N(e))/(\log(1/e))$, where $N(e)$ is the number of open balls of radius e necessary to cover A. For a straight line segment, which can be assumed to be one unit in length, $D = 1$. As e is reduced from 1, $N(e)$ and $1/e$ are equal and increasing. However, consider the open middle-thirds Cantor set constructed from the same interval. Clearly, when $e = 1/3$, $N < 3$. Hence in this case $0 < D < 1$; and the Cantor set has a fractal dimension. The issue of dimension is discussed in Peitgen *et al.* (1992: 212–19).

References

Arrow, K. (1989), 'Workshop on the Economy as an Evolving Complex System: Summary', in P. Anderson *et al.* (eds), *The Economy as an Evolving Complex System*, New York: Addison-Wesley.
Banks, J., J. Brooks, G. Cairns, G. Davis, and P. Stacey (1992), 'On Devaney's Definition of Chaos', *American Mathematical Monthly*, **99**, (4), 332–4.
Barnett, W. and P. Chen (1988), 'The Aggregation-Theoretical Monetary Aggregates are Chaotic and Have Strange Attractors: An Econometric Interpretation of Mathematical Chaos', in W. Barnett, R. Ernst and W. Halbert (eds), *Dynamic Econometric Modelling*, Cambridge: Cambridge University Press.
Barnett, W. and M. Hinich (1993), 'Has Chaos Been Discovered with Economic Data?', in P. Chen and R. Day (eds), *Nonlinear Dynamics and Evolutionary Economics*, Oxford: Oxford University Press.
Baumol, W. and J. Behabib (1989), 'Chaos: Significance, Mechanism and Economic Application', *Journal of Economic Perspectives*, **3**, 77–105.
Behabib, J. (ed.), (1991), *Cycles and Chaos in Economic Equilibrium*, Princeton: Princeton University Press.
Brock, W. (1986), 'Distinguishing Random and Deterministic Systems', *Journal of Economic Theory*, **40**, (1), 168–96.
Brock, W., D. Hsieh, and B. LeBaron, (1991), *Nonlinear Dynamics, Chaos and Instability*, Cambridge, MA: MIT Press.
Bullard, J. and A. Butler, (1993), 'Nonlinearity and Chaos in Economic Models: Implications for Policy Decisions', *Economic Journal*, **103**, 849–67.
Chen, P. (1993), 'Searching for Economic Chaos: A Challenge to Econometric Practice', in P. Chen and R. Day (eds), *Nonlinear Dynamics and Evolutionary Economics*, Cambridge: Cambridge University Press.
DeCoster, G., W. Labys, and D. Mitchell, (1992), 'Evidence of Chaos in Commodity Futures Prices', *Journal of Futures Markets*, **12**, (3), 291–305.
Devaney, R. (1986), *Chaotic Dynamical Systems*, Boston: Benjamin-Cummins.
Frank, M. and T. Stegnos (1988), 'Some Evidence Concerning Macroeconomic Chaos' *Journal of Monetary Economics*, **22**, 423–38.
Frank, M. and T. Stegnos (1989), 'Measuring the Strangeness of Gold and Silver Rates of Return' *Review of Economic Studies*, **56**, 553–67.

Gabisch, G. and H.-W. Lorenz, (1989), *Business Cycle Theory*, New York: Springer-Verlag.

Gleick, J. (1987), *Chaos*, New York: Vintage

Goodwin, R. (1951), 'The Non-Linear Accelerator and the Persistence of Business Cycles', *Econometrica* **19**, 1–17.

Grandmont, J.-M. (ed.) (1987), *Nonlinear Economic Dynamics*, New York: Academic Press.

Grassberger, P. and I. Proccaccia (1983), 'Characterization of Strange Attractors', *Physical Review Letters*, **50**, 346–9.

Harrod, R. (1939), 'An Essay on Dynamic Economic Theory', *Economic Journal*, **49**, 14–33.

Jarsulic, M. (1993a), 'A Nonlinear Model of the Pure Growth Cycle', *Journal of Economic Behavior and Organization*, **22**, 133–51.

Jarsulic, M. (1993b), *Non–linear Dynamics in Economic Theory*, Aldershot: Edward Elgar.

Kaldor, N. (1940), 'A Model of the Trade Cycle', *Economic Journal*, L, 78–92.

Li, T.-Y. and J. Yorke (1975), 'Period Three Implies Chaos', *American Mathematical Monthly*, **82**, 985–92.

Lorenz, E. (1963), 'Deterministic Nonperiodic Flow', *Journal of Atmospheric Science*, **20**, 130–41.

Lorenz, H.-W. (1989), *Nonlinear Dynamical Economics and Chaotic Motion*, New York: Springer-Verlag.

May, R. (1976), 'Simple Mathematical Models with Very Complicated Dynamics', *Nature*, **261**, 459–67.

Mullineux, A., D. Dickinson and W. Peng (1993), *Business Cycles*, Oxford: Blackwell.

Peitgen, H.-O., H. Jurgens, and D. Saupe (1992), *Chaos and Fractals*, New York: Springer-Verlag.

Ramsay, J., C. Sayers and P. Rothman (1990), 'The Statistical Properties of Dimension Calculations Using Small Data Sets: Some Economic Applications', *International Economic Review*, **31** (4), 991–1020.

Sayers, C. (1987), 'Diagnostic Tests for Nonlinearity in Time Series Data: An Application of the Work Stopping Series', mimeo, University of Houston.

Scheinkman, J. (1990), 'Nonlinearities in Economic Dynamics', *Economic Journal*, **100**, 33–48.

Scheinkman, J. and B. Lebaron (1989), 'Nonlinear Dynamics and Stock Returns', *Journal of Business*, 311–37.

Slutsky, E. (1927), *The Summation of Random Causes as the Source of Cyclic Processes*, vol. III, no. 1, Conjuncture Institute, Moscow; reprinted in *Econometrica*, 1937, **5**, 105–46.

Wolf, A. (1986), 'Quantifying Chaos with Lyapunov Exponents', in A Holden (ed.), *Chaos*, Princeton: Princeton University Press.

Coase, R.H.

Born in 1910 in Britain, Ronald Harry Coase enrolled in 1929 at the London School of Economics. As a student of commerce, he did not formally study economics, which may have contributed to his role as somewhat of an outsider and relatively independent of the disciplinary conventions of the economics profession. He taught at the LSE from 1935 to 1951; at the University of Buffalo from 1951 to 1958; at the University of Virginia from 1959 to 1964; and at the University of Chicago Law School from 1964 to 1981. He was editor of the *Journal of Law and Economics* from 1964 to 1982. Coase was awarded the Nobel Memorial Prize in Economics in 1991 for his work in the theory of the firm and in law and economics; his seminal articles, 'The nature of the firm' (1937) and 'The problem of social cost' (1960) were specifically cited by the Nobel Prize Committee.

Coase's strategy for doing economics is unorthodox. For example, he has been active in doing empirical case studies and he reports his claims and arguments informally rather than by way of formal models. He has also been explicitly critical of the more conventional ways of doing economics. It is not surprising, therefore, that throughout his career Coase has been reflective upon methodological issues. Characteristically, many of his methodological insights are original and deeply challenging.

From his 'The nature of the firm' onwards, Coase has strongly insisted on the importance of developing theories that are more realistic than conventional economic theories tend to be. In a recent statement, he says the following:

> My article ['The nature of the firm'] starts by making a methodological point: it is desirable that the assumptions we make in economics should be realistic. Most readers will pass over these opening

sentences ... and others will excuse what they read as a youthful mistake, believing, as so many modern economists do, that we should choose our theories on the basis of the accuracy of their predictions, the realism of their assumptions being utterly irrelevant. I did not believe this in the 1930s and, as it happens, I still do not.

One way in which Coase thinks conventional economics is unrealistic is that it is too narrow, it excludes from consideration factors in the social world that should be included in the analysis. Among these are factors that characterize the internal organization of the business firm, thus leading to a notion of the firm as a black box: 'What happens in between the purchase of the factors of production and the sale of the goods that are produced by these factors is largely ignored.' This is just one example, as the blame is more general: in standard theory, 'we have consumers without humanity, firms without organization, and even exchange without markets'. As Coase sees the problem with conventional theory, there are 'missing elements' that are to be incorporated into economic theory if it is intended to do its descriptive and explanatory job adequately. Among these neglected elements are positive transaction costs.

Coase is also concerned about the practice amongst economists of examining economic problems separately from the complex context in which they are embedded: 'Any actual situation is complex and a single economic problem does not exist in isolation. Consequently, confusion is liable to result because economists dealing with an actual situation are attempting to solve several problems at once.' He also criticizes much of the conventional theory for being part of 'blackboard economics' and 'without any empirical basis'. What is studied in such economics is 'a system which lives in the minds of economists but not on earth'. He argues that 'when economists find that they are unable to analyze what is happening in the real world, they invent an imaginary world which they are capable of handling. It was not a procedure that I wanted to follow in the 1930s. It explains why I tried to find the reason for the existence of the firm in factories and offices rather than in the writings of economists, which I irreverently labeled as "bilge".' The charge of 'blackboard economics' occurs frequently in Coase's reflections, but it is far from clear what precisely it means. One interpretation would be to link it to Coase's conviction that case studies play an important role in theorizing, an idea which tends not to be shared by those to whom Coase attributes the label 'blackboard economics'.

Coase's crusade for realisticness is not at all his only contribution to methodological reflection. In his 1981 Warren Nutter Lecture, 'How should economists choose?', Coase makes a number of interesting methodological points. For example, he introduces the idea of the rhetoric of economics. Coase argues that economists do not choose theories on the basis of predictivist testing. They 'do not wait to discover whether a theory's predictions are accurate before making up their minds.' Predictivist testing cannot be decisive, because data is malleable: 'if you torture the data enough, nature will always confess'; thus there is 'the tendency of economists to get the result their theory tells them to expect'. Yet, economists appear to practise some sort of predictivist testing. Coase's explanation for this phenomenon represents it as rhetorical persuasion in the market-place of ideas:

These studies, both quantitative and qualitative, perform a function similar to that of advertising and other promotional activities in the normal products market. They do not aim simply at enlarging the understanding of those who believe in the theory but also at attracting those who do not believe in it and at preventing the defection of existing believers. These studies demonstrate the power of the theory, and the definiteness of quantitative studies enables them to make their point in a particularly persuasive form. What we are dealing with is a competitive process in which purveyors of the various theories attempt to sell their wares.

Coase's explanation is thus that empirical tests serve a rhetorical function in a competitive market for economic theories. This move amounts to inviting economists to view economics in economic terms. His metatheory here takes on the form of an economics of economics.

It is clear that Coase has only provided fragments for an economics of economics. For example, he has an idea of the goals and preferences that drive economists in their behaviour. He says that, 'if we have to admit that we are not maximizing our money incomes, we can at least console ourselves by claiming that we are maximizing our self-esteem. It is also true that we value the respect of our colleagues.' Coase's outline for an economics of economics is also a call for an institutionalist economics of theory choice, in analogy with his institutionalist approach to the market for goods and services.

> Instead of confining ourselves to a discussion of the question of how economists ought to choose between theories, developing criteria, and relying on exhortation or perhaps regulation to induce them to use these criteria in making their choices, we should investigate the effect of alternative institutional arrangements for academic studies on the theories that are put into circulation and on the choices that are made. From these investigations we may hope to discover what arrangements governing the competition between theories are most likely to lead economists to make better choices. Paradoxically, the approach to the methodological problem in economics that is likely to be the most useful is to transform it into an economic problem.

Given his advocacy of an economics of economics, it is interesting to note that Coase is also suspicious about expanding the boundaries of the appropriate domain of economics. In an article on 'Economics and contiguous disciplines', he criticizes economic expansionism; he seems to be saying that the expansion of the domain of economics to encompass the domains of neighbouring disciplines – such as political science, sociology, linguistics, education and law – is based on the narrowing of the economic perspective to a logic of choice. He also argues that expansionist victories based on 'techniques' or 'approaches' are going to be short-lived only: they are not based on a common subject matter, the only guarantee of more permanent success.

Coase suggests that there is something specific about the subject matter of economics that imposes limits on its wider applicability. This factor is 'the measuring rod of money'. There are limits to the domain of applicability of economics imposed by the extent to which the 'measuring rod of money' helps constitute the subject matter of inquiry:

> If it is true that the more developed state of economics, as compared to the other social sciences, has been due to the happy chance (for economics) that the important factors determining economic behavior can be measured in money, it suggests that the problems faced by practitioners in these other fields are not likely to be dissipated simply by an infusion of economists since, in moving into these fields, they will commonly have to leave their strength behind them. The analysis developed in economics is not likely to be successfully applied in other subjects without major modifications.

These are some examples of the interesting insights that can be found in Coase's methodological reflections. They are made even more interesting by the fact that it is not clear that they are fully consistent with one another.

USKALI MÄKI

Bibliography
Coase, R.H. (1988), *The Firm, the Marker and the Law*, Chicago: University of Chicago Press.
Coase, R.H. (1994), *Essays on Economics and Economists*, Chicago: University of Chicago Press.
Mäki, Uskali (1998), 'Is Coase a Realist?', *Philosophy of the Social Sciences*, **28**, 5–31.
Mäki, Uskali (forthcoming), 'Against Posner against Coase against theory', *Cambridge Journal of Economics*.
Medema, Steven (1994), *R.H. Coase*, London: Macmillan.
Medema, Steven (ed.) (1998), *Coasean Economics*, Boston: Kluwer.
Posner, Richard A. (1993), 'Ronald Coase and methodology', *Journal of Economic Perspectives*, **7**, 195–210.
Williamson, Oliver E. and Sidney G. Winter (eds) (1993), *The Nature of the Firm. Origins, Evolution and Development*, Oxford: Oxford University Press.

Commons, John R.

John R. Commons was born in Indiana in 1862, and educated at Oberlin College. He embarked on graduate work at Johns Hopkins in 1888, attracted there by the presence of Richard T. Ely, a leading member of the German Historicist-inspired 'new school', but he lost his fellowship after two years and never graduated. Between 1890 and 1899, he held teaching positions at Wesleyan, Oberlin, Indiana and Syracuse, gradually moving from economics to sociology. The last of these positions he lost when his chair in sociology was abolished because of the effect on university fundraising of his 'radical tendencies'. For the next few years Commons remained outside the academic world, working on index numbers and, for the United States Industrial Commission, on immigration. In 1902, he took a position with the National Civic Federation concerning labour relations and conciliation. This experience resulted in Ely offering him a position in the Economics Department at the University of Wisconsin, where he remained for the rest of his career.

In his academic work, Commons is known for his compilation of case studies, as in his *Documentary History of American Industrial Society* (Commons *et al.*, 1910–11) and *History of Labor in the United States* (Commons *et al.*, 1918–35), and for the development of his institutional approach to economics with its emphasis on the integration of law, economics, and ethics (Commons, 1934). Commons was also actively involved in legislative reform, including labour legislation, public utility regulation, industrial safety and workmen's compensation, and unemployment insurance programmes. Allied to these efforts, Commons developed a methodology that, while linked to the general principles of evolutionism, holism and instrumentalism shared by most American institutionalists, was in many respects uniquely his own. Commons often argued as if his methods and theories were developed entirely out of his own observation and experience, but this is an exaggeration. Commons was influenced by the work of his teacher and mentor, Richard T. Ely, by the philosophies of Charles Peirce and John Dewey, and by his extensive reading in law and economics. Nevertheless, Commons' determination that his ideas be useful in resolving concrete social problems, and his many experiences in attempting to put his ideas to practical use, played a significant role in shaping his views.

A number of factors are especially noteworthy about Commons' approach including his fundamental conception of social processes, his basic units of analysis, his concern with whole/part relationships, his instrumentalism and his use of case study and interview techniques. Each of these will be discussed in turn.

Commons' overall conceptualization of social processes was based firmly on three key ideas. First was that social outcomes must be seen as the intended or unintended results of the purposeful acts of individual and collective (corporate) actors. Commons expressed this in terms of what he called his principle of 'willingness'. This principle, he argued, distinguished social science from physical and biological sciences and made mechanical and natural selection analogies inapplicable to economics (Commons, 1934: 94–6). It also formed the basis of his criticism of Veblen's 'elimination of purpose' and emphasis on purely causal argument (ibid.: 654). For Commons, the subject matter of the 'human sciences' is a 'pragmatic being always looking to the future and therefore always motivated by purposes' (ibid.: 655). The second idea was that collective action in the form of organizations such as corporations and unions had, to a significant degree, displaced individual action as characteristic of the economy. The third was that, owing to scarcity of resources, the various purposes or wills of individuals and organizations tended to conflict with each other, particularly over distributional issues. But there is also mutual dependence and a need to resolve conflicts of interest in order to maintain a 'workable mutuality', something that for Commons required political and judicial institutions to decide on and enforce the 'working rules'. Thus Commons' attention was directed to '*intended* or *purposeful* changes, and to a *managed* instead of an *automatic* equilibrium' and on that basis he argued that the correct analogy to apply to social evolution was that of 'artificial selection' (ibid.: 120; see also Biddle, 1990a).

Commons developed two 'units of investigation' (Commons, 1934: 4, 69) related to this overall conception. His basic unit of analysis was the transaction, defined in terms of the transfer of *rights*, and embodying the basic principles of conflict of interest mutual dependence of interest, and the order created by the working rules of society. His second, larger, unit was the going concern, defined as formal and informal organizations from the family, to the corporation, to the state, and even to society, and as a 'joint expectation' of beneficial transactions kept together by the working rules (ibid.: 58). These units replaced the commodities and individuals of orthodox economic analysis.

Commons was concerned to place his analysis of transactions and concerns within the context of the social and institutional whole. He has often been seen as a methodological holist (Ramstad, 1986), but this should not be taken to mean that he argued in terms of supra-individual actors. Commons' concern was to construct what he called 'formulas', formulations of the 'relation of the parts to each other and to the whole' (Commons, 1934: 736). An example can be found in his formulas of the bargaining, rationing and managerial transactions in which the interconnections between transactions and the working rules of society are made clear (ibid.: 59–68). Another example is his discussion of the individual in society: individual actors operate within a social context, and are 'always participants in transactions, members of a concern in which they come and go, citizens of an institution that lived before them and will live after them' (ibid.: 74).

Commons' instrumentalism was derived from Peirce and Dewey. From Peirce he took the conception of the active mind and the pragmatic maxim that 'our idea of anything *is* our idea of its sensible effects' (ibid.: 152). He misinterprets Peirce, however, by defining 'truth' as the existing consensus of scientific opinion. Following Dewey, he applies the pragmatic method to social science to produce an instrumental view of science motivated by social purposes. The various principles and formulas he constructed were, when combined with a social philosophy, designed to be tools for the resolution of specific problems and disputes. They 'allowed the economist to see aspects of a situation' that would not be revealed by conventional theory, and 'provided the insights needed to promote an effective program of social reform' (Biddle, 1990b). Commons conceived of theorizing as 'a complex activity of Analysis, Genesis and

Insight, actively constructed by the mind in order to understand, predict and control the future' (Commons 1934: 102).

In the development and refining of his principles and formulas, Commons made extensive use of case studies and interviews with key players in a situation. Interviewing he called 'the prime method of investigation' (ibid.: 106), but he also made vast compilations of documents recording the details of past developments, most notably in his *Documentary History of American Industrial Society* (Commons *et al.*, 1910–11). In addition, he drew on his own experiences in labour mediation and in drafting legislation to deal with issues such as accident and unemployment insurance. Through such techniques, and the comparative study of cases, he thought that investigators would be able to arrive at reliable generalizations that could provide 'a basis for action in the world as it was' (Biddle, 1990b: 24). This is not to say that Commons wanted to dispense with more abstract theories. *Institutional Economics* (Commons, 1934) is full of discussions of the theories of the major economists from Quesnay onwards, but what Commons was doing in these discussions was to look for what was useful for his own purposes. The theories of other economists were 'raw material to be blended with his own experiential knowledge and shaped into tools for understanding and solving present-day problems' (Biddle, 1991: 87–8).

MALCOLM RUTHERFORD

Bibliography

Biddle, Jeff E. (1990a), 'Purpose and Evolution in Commons's Institutionalism', *History of Political Economy*, **22**, (Spring), 19–47.

Biddle, Jeff E. (1990b), 'The Role of Negotiational Psychology in J.R. Commons's Proposed Reconstruction of Political Economy', *Review of Political Economy*, **2**, (March), 1–25.

Biddle, Jeff E. (1991), 'The Ideas of the Past as Tools for the Present: The Instrumental Presentism of John R. Commons', in JoAnne Brown and David Van Keuren (eds), *The Estate of Social Knowledge*, Baltimore: Johns Hopkins University Press.

Commons, John R. (1934), *Institutional Economics: Its Place in Political Economy*, New Brunswick: Transaction.

Commons, John R. (1950), *The Economics of Collective Action*, New York: Macmillan.

Commons, John R., U.B. Phillips, E.A. Gilmore, H.L. Summer and J.B. Andrews (eds) (1910–11), *A Documentary History of American Industrial Society*, 10 vols, Cleveland: Arthur H. Clark.

Commons, John R., D.J. Saposs, H.L. Summer, E.B. Mittleman, H.E. Hoagland, J.B. Andrews and Selig Perlman (1918–35), *History of Labor in the United States*. 4 vols, New York; Macmillan.

Harter, Lafayette G. (1962), *John R. Commons: His Assault on Laissez-Faire*, Corvallis: Oregon State University.

Ramstad, Yngve (1986), 'A Pragmatist's Quest for Holistic Knowledge: The Scientific Methodology of John R. Commons', *Journal of Economic Issues*, **20**, (December), 1067–1105.

Rutherford, Malcolm (1990), 'Introduction to the Transaction Edition', in John R. Commons, *Institutional Economics: Its Place in Political Economy*, New Brunswick: Transaction.

Vanberg, Viktor (1989), 'Carl Menger's Evolutionary and John R. Commons' Collective Action Approach to Institutions: A Comparison', *Review of Political Economy*, **1**, (November), 334–60.

Constitutional Political Economy

Constitutional Economics or Constitutional Political Economy (CPE) is one of a number of intersecting research programmes in modern economics that seek to revive, in one way or another, the institutional thrust of classical political economy. Common to these research programmes, such as public choice, law and economics, the economics of property rights or the new institutional economics, is the intention to correct for the institutional deficiency of neoclassical mainstream economics without abandoning the essential methodology, especially the methodological individualism, of the received economic paradigm.

What is distinctive about CPE is its focus on the choice of rules and institutions. By contrast to the *choice within constraints* perspective of standard economics, it directs attention to the issue of *choice among constraints*, specifically those constraints that are imposed by the legal–institutional framework within which ordinary economic, social and political activities take place. To use the popular game metaphor, CPE concerns itself with the constitutional issues involved in the *choice of the rules* of the game rather than with the strategic issues involved in the *playing* of the game within given rules. It recognizes, of course, that choices among rules will typically be made in the light of the expected patterns of play that are predicted to emerge from alternative rules of the game. In fact, the systematic study of the causal linkages between what F.A. Hayek (1973: 98ff) has contrasted as the *order of rules* (the constitutional level) and the *order of actions* (the subconstitutional level) is a principal subject of inquiry of CPE. In its study of this subject, CPE can draw on the insights provided by other research programmes within the broader neoinstitutional movement. CPE also recognizes, of course, that choices among constraints are themselves, again, subject to constraints, and that choices among rules most often take place within constraints defined by 'higher-level' rules. That, in ordered society, rule choices are typically embedded in a multi-level system of rules and that, therefore, choices among rules are usually at the same time choices within rules is recognized as an inherent fact of social life. Yet this is not considered to invalidate the claim that, at whatever level they may occur, choices among rules or constraints raise particular kinds of issues that the choice within constraints perspective tends to ignore, issues that constitute the proper domain of CPE.

Another distinct feature of CPE is what one may call its practical or applied orientation, its concern with the issue of how social order may be improved through institutional reform. Because of this concern, CPE has occasionally been described, by advocates and critics alike, as a 'normative science'. This label is, however, potentially misleading. Most CPE practitioners recognize the categorical difference between refutable statements about *what is*, and normative judgments about *what ought to be*, and they are aware of the pitfalls of natural fallacies. They do not consider it the task of CPE to advance value judgments, nor do they want to claim that CPE can provide scientific proof for what may count as 'improvement' in matters of institutional reform. The value orientation that is, no doubt, present in CPE is primarily a matter of its choice of problems, not of its statements about these problems. More specifically, following the individualist orientation of Smithean classical political economy, CPE's principal concern is with the issue of how institutional arrangements can be made to serve the interests of the individual persons that are affected by them. Adam Smith's message had been that what he called 'the simple system of natural liberty' – a competitive market order freed from mercantilist and guild restrictions – would serve the interests of the persons involved better than the then existing mercantilist system. This argument was clearly not meant as a dogmatic claim that such institutional reforms *must* occur. It can, instead, best be understood as a *conditional claim* (what philosophers call a 'hypothetical' as opposed to a 'categorical' imperative) to the effect that, *if* the interests of the individual persons involved are viewed as the standard of evaluation, the proposed institutional reforms promise to lead to an 'order of rules' that works better ('better' in terms of the supposed standard) than its mercantilist counterpart. The arguments that substantiate this claim are not themselves value judgments, they are, instead, refutable 'sociotechnological' conjectures about how, through which kinds of institutional reform, a social rule system can be made to advance better the interests of its individual constituents.

Much of the history of economic thought consists of more or less successful, and some misguided, attempts to develop further our understanding of how 'the market' works as an institutional arena that enables persons to realize mutual 'gains from trade' through voluntary exchange (as well as through voluntary cooperation in team production). CPE builds upon this tradition of inquiry and seeks to generalize and extend the notion of 'gains from trade' from the study of markets to the study of non-market institutions, especially the study of rules and institutions of collective, political choice (Buchanan, 1977: 136ff). Adam Smith signalled his concern with the 'rules of the game' when he described his own subject, political economy, as the 'science of legislation' (Smith, 1981: 468). CPE is the modern counterpart to Smith's enterprise (Brennan and Buchanan, 1985: 2; Hayek, 1973: 4; Vanberg 1994: 5). It seeks to explore the issue of how in general, in all realms of human social life, individuals may be enabled to realize mutual gains from adopting better 'rules of the game'. And the arguments that are advanced in this context are, just as in the case of Adam Smith's 'science of legislation', not themselves normative judgments, but refutable sociotechnological conjectures on how, in the various social realms, the rules of the game may be improved to the benefit of the persons involved.

James M. Buchanan (1977; 1987; 1991; Buchanan and Tullock, 1962), the principal initiator of this research programme, views CPE as an alternative to traditional, utilitarian welfare economics, an alternative that can be claimed to be much more consistent with the essential methodology of the economic paradigm than its established rival. The defining feature of welfare economics, in all its varieties, is the notion of an aggregate measure of 'social welfare', the maximization or advancement of which is considered the task of politics. As John Rawls has described this view, 'The principle of choice for an association of men is interpreted as an extension of the principle of choice for one man' (1971: 24). Buchanan uses the label 'maximization paradigm' to describe such extension of the logic of individual rational maximization to the social aggregate level, an extension that, he charges, amounts to treating collectives or groups as quasi-individuals and, thus, to an implicit departure from the individualist methodological foundations of the economic tradition.

It is not its interest in utilizing theoretical economics as a resource for assisting political reform that makes traditional welfare economics, in Buchanan's eyes, a dubious enterprise. It is the faulty ways by which it goes about this task that leads him to advance his constitutional–contractarian approach as an alternative. Instead of taking its departure from the notion of rational maximizing choice, Buchanan's constitutional political economy builds on the notion of 'gains from trade' as the common denominator that can link the economist's traditional study of market exchange with the practical political project of bettering the human condition. From the constitutional perspective the economist's genuine contribution to this project is that of a specialist in 'gains from trade', of a specialist in exploring the potential for mutual improvement in human social affairs. Accordingly, the natural task of CPE becomes that of generalizing the notion of voluntary contracting from the economist's familiar bilateral *exchange contracts* to the kind of *social contracts* that allow groups of persons to act collectively. This is the reason for the apparent affinity between the CPE research programme and some of the contributions to modern political philosophy, in particular John Rawls's (1971), that revive the tradition of social contract theory (Buchanan, 1987: 31 1). In CPE the concept of the social contract is used to develop for the realm of non-market, collective decision making the analogue to the theory of mutual gains from voluntary trade in markets (Buchanan, 1979: 30ff). It is meant to describe the underlying contractual nature of institutional arrangements that enable individuals to realize mutual gains through collective choice, be it through the kind of complex multilateral trade involved in the production of collective goods or, more relevant for CPE, through the mutuality of commitment that is at stake where groups of persons jointly submit to the constraints of rules.

Compared to the constitutionalist contractarian paradigm, the maximization paradigm appears defective not only in those varieties of welfare economics that commit the naturalist fallacy by presuming the social welfare function to provide a logical bridge between the 'is' and the 'ought'. The maximization paradigm provides poor guidance even if the welfarist argument is interpreted as a hypothetical imperative, that is as an argument about how politics can advance social welfare *if* such welfare is measured by the specified method of aggregation. Not only can the acceptability or relevance of the supposed normative standard be questioned. The entire history of welfare economics is testimony to the failure of attempts to derive from such constructs any *refutable* sociotechnological conjectures that could guide political reforms.

By contrast to received welfare economics, CPE does not seek to identify specific interventions that are supposed to move 'the economy' or 'the society' closer to a conceptual welfare optimum. Instead, it seeks to advance conjectures about potential institutional reforms from which all parties involved could gain and which, therefore, should be able to command general agreement. The addressee of its conjectural advice is the relevant constituency for which the claim of potential mutual improvement is made, and factual agreement among the constituents is the ultimate test of the validity of its conjectures. As Buchanan has put it: 'Normatively, the task for the constitutional political economist is to assist individuals, as citizens who ultimately control their own social order, in their continuing search for those rules of the political game that will best serve their purposes, whatever these might be' (1987:313). This is in contrast to the practice of welfare economics which has been charged with proceeding, implicitly, as if its calling were to advise some imagined benevolent, omniscient and omnipotent government (Buchanan, 1979: 204).

The case for the procedural, rule-focused constitutional approach, and against the interventionist welfarist approach, is supported by an argument that has been stressed notably by Rutledge Vining (1984), namely that outcomes or end results of social, political or economic processes (such as income distribution, concentration of power, employment stability, and the like) 'are not themselves subject to direct alteration', but that it 'is only the system of statutory and administrative rule that is subject to immediate and direct modification' (Vining: 177). Such changes in rules, regulations and administrative procedures, however, typically have unanticipated effects and often produce outcomes quite different from those that were intended. In other words, directly to produce desired outcomes is, as Vining puts it, 'not what a statute does or possibly can do, whatever the political form of the society. ... [The] statute would set forth new "rules of the game"' (ibid.: 174), and it will depend on the strategies chosen by the players under the newly imposed constraints whether and to what extent the intended results will emerge. Accordingly, as Vining concludes, the proper role for the economist as practitioner cannot be that envisaged by the interventionist model of welfare economics, but is, instead, that of 'a specialist advisor to legislators and citizens in a legislative frame of mind' (ibid.: 3) who informs about ways in which changes in the framework of rules will affect the emerging pattern of outcomes.

Rutledge Vining's thoughts on these matters, just like Buchanan's, have been strongly influenced by Frank Knight's (1982: 464ff) reflections on the 'extensive parallelism between play and political and economic life' (ibid.: 466). As Knight had noted, 'All problems of social ethics are like those of play in that they have the two components of obeying the rules and improving the rules, in the interest of a better "game"' (ibid.). There are a number of issues central to the CPE enterprise that Knight has at least touched upon. One concerns the motivational asymmetry that lies in the fact that, while playing a 'given' game successfully is in the immediate self-interest of each player, improving the rules of the game is a collective good for the respective group of players. It is this asymmetry that can explain why the 'capacity to play intelligently, from the standpoint of winning, is much more highly and more commonly developed among human beings than is the capacity to improve the rules or invent better games' (ibid.). It is because of this asymmetry that a special public need can be said to exist for the kind of information that CPE as a 'science of legislation' can provide.

Another issue concerns the differences that have to be considered when the 'gains from trade' paradigm is extended from voluntary market exchange to organized collective activity, both public and private. Of normative significance in free market exchange is the voluntary agreement to the particular transaction. By contrast, of normative significance in organized collective action is the voluntary agreement to the overall arrangement, that is to the respective internal constitution (ibid.: 449), rather than agreement to each and every single transaction or decision made within the ongoing collective enterprise. The constitutional agreement may, and typically will, include the authorization of non-unanimous group decisions and the acceptance of coercion (such as through taxation) at the subconstitutional level of choice. As Knight notes, at the level of constitutional agreement, the direct equivalent to voluntary agreement in market exchange would be voluntary participation in collective arrangements; that is, it would require 'the right and the power to leave the group, hence to join other groups, and eventually to form groupings at will' (ibid.: 465). While these conditions may be largely descriptive for voluntary associations, they can, for intrinsic reasons, never be fully realized for political communities that 'are defined by territorial sovereignty' (ibid.). Where such communities are concerned, 'leaving one group means physical removal to another and is limited by material cost, by cultural differences, and by the laws governing departure and especially entry into other political units, which practically cover the earth' (ibid.). One can conclude that, for political communities, it is, therefore, all the more important that organizational precautions are taken which can make the notion of voluntary agreement to the encompassing constitutional contract as meaningful as the nature of territorial sovereignty will allow (for example, through competitive federalism).

As, again, Knight (1982: 249) has observed, the game metaphor is also instructive in that 'play exhibits in relation to its rules or laws the ubiquitous harmony and conflict of interest' that is inherent in all human social life: 'All the parties to any game have a common interest in the game itself – hence, in general obedience to the rules. But they have conflicting individual interests in winning – consequently, in law-breaking or cheating. Similar considerations apply far more acutely to the improvement of the game by changing the rules' (ibid.). The concept of *constitutional interests* can help to illuminate essential aspects of the 'ubiquitous harmony and conflict of interest' as well as of the two principal problems that Knight alludes to, namely that of the *compliance with* and that of the *improvement of* the rules.

As for the compliance problem, the mixture of 'harmony and conflict of interest' arises from the difference between people's constitutional interests and their strategic interests. The latter concern people's preferences over alternative strategic moves that are available within given rules of the game, the former are about the kinds of rules under which they would prefer to live. The mixture of harmony and conflict between these interests has to do with the fact that, even if within a community there is perfect agreement in constitutional interests, that is, even if all members wish the existing rules to be effective, there may still exist conflict in strategic interests, in that each wants the others to comply with the rules while enjoying for himself the extra benefits that may be had from cheating. If left uncontrolled, such temptation to cheat may undermine the viability of a constitutional order despite the fact that all members may perfectly agree in their constitutional interests. The compliance problem is in essence the problem of how people can make their agreement in constitutional interests effective against the threat of conflicting strategic interests, and this problem can be solved by adopting a workable enforcement scheme in which, again, all parties should share a constitutional interest.

Where the 'improvement of rules' is concerned, the mixture of 'harmony and conflict of interest' results from the tension between *shared* and *partial* constitutional interests, that is, between constitutional interests that people can agree on, and constitutional interests that are biased in their favour. Constitutional rules that favour particular individuals or groups are clearly in the interests of the privileged, but they will not win the voluntary and informed agreement of the non-privileged. People's shared constitutional interests would seem to support only an order without privileges, with genuine equality before the law. Yet, even though their agreed-upon constitutional interests may provide sufficient ground for mutually beneficial cooperation, people may not be able to realize the benefits that could be had from such cooperation if their striving for privileges prevents them from making their shared constitutional interests effective. In CPE, and in modern contractarian political philosophy, this problem is usually dealt with by assuming that constitutional choices are made 'behind a veil' that makes people ignorant or uncertain about their particular position and, thus, eliminates or reduces the problem of differing constitutional interests. Yet there is another way to think about this issue. If people were perfectly free to move costlessly between alternative constitutional regimes, an 'invisible hand' mechanism can be predicted to work that would guide them to rule regimes that command genuine agreement in constitutional interests. Individuals may initially lean towards rule regimes that are biased in their favour, yet such regimes will turn out to be of little benefit to the privileged if nobody else will join in – and why should other people voluntarily opt for regimes that discriminate against them? In the 'real world' of course, people cannot choose in such a frictionless manner among alternative constitutional regimes. Yet if, and to the extent that, there are barriers to mobility, people become exploitable and the striving for privileges becomes a promising constitutional strategy. However, to the extent that this strategy is employed in the process of constitutional change, societies become plagued by what public choice theorists have extensively discussed under the label of 'rent seeking' (Brennan and Buchanan, 1985: 121).

The issue of how the process of constitutional choice and constitutional reform may be organized in such a way that people are enabled effectively to realize their shared constitutional interests and avoid the welfare-decreasing and mutually destructive competition for privileges remains one of the central questions for CPE to investigate. In conclusion, it is worth mentioning that the issue of how to establish and maintain an *economic constitution without privileges* has been a principal concern of the German Ordoliberalism, a research programme that has much in common with the CPE enterprise (Vanberg 1991).

VIKTOR J. VANBERG

References

Brennan, Geoffrey and James M. Buchanan (1985), *The Reason of Rules – Constitutional Political Economy*, Cambridge: Cambridge University Press.
Buchanan, James M. (1977), *Freedom in Constitutional Contract*, College Station: Texas A&M University Press.
Buchanan, James M. (1979), *What Should Economists Do?*, Indianapolis: Liberty Press.
Buchanan, James M. (1987), *Economics – Between Predictive Science and Moral Philosophy*, College Station: Texas A&M University Press.
Buchanan, James M. (1991), *The Economics and the Ethics of Constitutional Order*, Ann Arbor: University of Michigan Press.

Buchanan, James M. and Gordon Tullock (1962), *The Calculus of Consent – Logical Foundations of Constitutional Democracy*, Ann Arbor: University of Michigan Press.
Hayek, Friedrich A. (1973), *Law, Legislation and Liberty*, vol. 1, London: Routledge & Kegan Paul.
Knight, Frank (1982), *Freedom and Reform*, Indianapolis: Liberty Press.
Rawls, John (1971), *A Theory of Justice*, Cambridge, MA: Harvard University Press.
Smith, Adam (1981), *An Inquiry into the Nature and Causes of the Wealth of Nations*, Indianapolis: Liberty Classics.
Vanberg, Viktor J. (1991), 'Review of "Ordo – Jahrbuch für die Ordnung von Wirtschaft und Gesellschaft"', *Constitutional Political Economy*, **2**, 397–402.
Vanberg, Viktor J. (1994), *Rules and Choice in Economics*, London: Routledge.
Vining, Rutledge (1984), *On Appraising the Performance of an Economic System*, Cambridge: Cambridge University Press.

Constructivism

Constructivism is the romance of the social sciences with an 'active' notion of society. It contains various versions of the assumption that the world in which we live and which we experience is in one sense or another (humanly) 'made' and 'created' rather than simply given, that the process of 'world making' is continuous and that this process ought reasonably to be seen as temporally and spatially bounded or situated rather than as structured across indefinite spans of time and space. Such assumptions imply a sense of the inventiveness and creativity of social and economic practice, of the unfolding nature of the contemporary world. There has been a well-nigh meteoric rise of constructivist thinking in various fields since the 1970s in areas ranging from agricultural science (Leeuwis, 1993) and social problems research (Miller and Holstein, 1993) to gender studies (Laws and Schwartz, 1977; Fausto-Sterling, 1985), systems theory and the sociology of knowledge (Knorr Cetina, 1977; 1981; Latour and Woolgar, 1979; Pinch and Bijker, 1984). The shift in historical sensibility implied by the turn towards constructivism is rooted, one assumes, not only in cognition, but in existence, in the eruption of constructive processes in contemporary, transitional scientific and socio economic environments.

What makes a universe 'hot'? The intuitions which motivate constructivism
Two general intuitions motivate most constructivist research. One such intuition is that the world of our experience is structured in terms of human categories and concepts: for Kant, the basic categories of the human mind did the structuring; for the linguist Benjamin L. Whorf it was language; for cognitive anthropologists culture expressed in language; and for those who study symbolic interaction it is meanings infused in negotiations and definitions of the situation. Constructivism, within this agenda, refers to an interest in the way the world is symbolically or conceptually constituted. The vehicles of construction within this kind of constructivism are concepts, symbols, categories or distinctions; the constructors are human institutions (language, culture), biological mechanisms (cognition, perception) or biographical experience. The last two preferences yield forms of perspectivalism.

The second root of constructivism can be seen in the idea that the world is created through human labour. This notion is encapsulated in Marx's famous phrase that 'men make their own history', even though, as Marx added, they do not make it free of constraints. The idea can also be linked to Schütz's notion of 'work' (Wirken) and to the ethnomethodological concept of 'practical accomplishment'. The distinction between the two dimensions of construction resurfaces today in the differences between what Sismondo (1996) calls 'neo-Kantian' constructivism – the notion that representations (causally) shape the material world – and other constructivisms. Nonetheless, in today's empirical versions of constructivism the idea of construction as work/accomplishment has in a sense won; it is closely tied up with constructivism's interactional interpretation and its disaggregational tendencies – the tendency to excavate downwards, to the bedrock of social matter. In current research, this is usually the level at which 'work' is seen to be 'accomplished' by actors pursuing goals and utilizing resources in producing social outcomes; thus, in this line of thinking, the constructors are usually human beings. At the same time, the duration of constructions in current work/accomplishment interpretations tends to be short; the constructivist universe is 'active' on a situation-to-situation basis. Actors are seen as symbol-manipulating, meaning-producing entities. When the work/accomplishment theme is translated into an actorial framework, it becomes fused with the first theme in constructivist thinking, the notion of construction as symbolic/conceptual constitution.

Varieties of current constructivism

Social constructivism
The recent source of the phrase 'social constructivism' is Berger and Luckmann's text on *The Social Construction of Reality* (1967). The authors' central question is, given that, as Marx suggested, social orderings are social conventions, how is it that they are experienced by participants as 'objective' and quasi-natural events? In answering this question, Berger and Luckmann point out different processes; for example, typification in language abstracts from individual experience, habitualization makes habitualized behaviour appear a necessary structure and legitimation processes explain and justify abstract meanings and routines, thus reinforcing their solidity. As these answers suggest, Berger and Luckmann's account is phenomenological/philosophical rather than empirical; the authors do not address the emergence and establishment of concrete social institutions, but rather the conditions of the possibility of institutions in general. Later studies within the social constructivist tradition take their lead from Goffman (1972) and other interactionists, and from the concept of negotiation, rather than from the more macrosociological Marxian, Durkheimian and Mannheimian questions that informed Berger and Luckmann. In other words, later research shifts social constructivism to the symbolic history of outcomes in situations of interaction. It tends to document the social origin of structures and events by pointing out the interactional work accomplished by participants in bringing these events about, and the meanings and definitions with which the respective outcomes and situations are continuously infused.

Constructionism
The second, more recent and radical tradition of constructivist reasoning has sprung up since the late 1970s in the sociology of scientific knowledge and technology (Knorr Cetina, 1977; 1981; 1998; Latour and Woolgar, 1979; Latour, 1987). It derives its relevance from the phenomenon that the very things which we consider the most real in our society are also the most scientific, hence to study the construction of reality today means to study epistemic practice. Constructionism has relocated scientific realism in the empirical analysis of fact production in the natural sciences, as opposed to the philosophical analysis of the logic of fact justification. It is continuous with social constructivism in its tendency to understand construction mainly in terms of individual actors, but there are also important differences. One is the greater challenge constructionism has posed – and the more controversial reception it has met with

(Gieryn, 1982; Giere, 1988; Sismondo, 1996) – owing to the phenomenon that it applies constructivist analyses to an area that we used not to think of as humanly produced but as humanly 'discovered', natural reality.

Some constructionists also depart from social constructivism in dropping the term 'social' from the title of the approach. This may mean a recognition of the phenomenon that social factors are themselves constructed, and hence cannot be unproblematically invoked as independent, explanatory concepts in constructionist studies. It can also mean that construction is seen as construction with objects and entities that are not concurrently social objects: for example, Callon (1986) and Latour and Johnson (1988) include material objects as independent agents with whom the outcome of a construction process may have to be negotiated.

A third way in which constructionism departs from social constructivist ideas is through the emphasis of the original studies on spatializing concepts and on a productive locale, the scientific laboratory (Knorr Cetina, 1992; 1994). There is, finally, a further way in which constructionism in knowledge studies has placed its emphasis differently from social constructivism. This is in showing more affinity for reflexive self-questioning of the form currently prominent in anthropology and postmodernism. Clearly, if one claims, as constructionists do, that scientific findings are (socially) constructed, the analyst's account must be constructed too. This recognition has given rise to an exploration of new literary genres and other means through which the analyst can address reflexivity (Woolgar and Ashmore, 1988; Ashmore, 1989). It also brings this kind of constructionism nearer to the type of perspectival constructivism for which reflexivity – as self-reference – is central in understanding social systems.

Perspectival constructivism
One version of perspectival constructivism derives from work in the biology of cognition and perception by Maturana and Varela (1980). A central idea in this research is that perception is not accomplished by the eye but by the brain and the brain is an informationally closed system that reconstructs an external environment only from memory and interaction with itself. Niklas Luhmann (1984) has extended the analogy from biology to social systems, arguing that these can be seen as closed systems of communication that run on binary codes in terms of which they select and construct outside information. Luhmann also works with the notion that any description or theory of a system rests on binary distinctions made by an observer who, through these distinctions, construes the system. The Luhmannian observer appears to be free to choose her or his standpoint; only function systems run on relatively fixed standpoints (for example, the distinctions between payment and non–payment in the economy). Earlier perspectivalism linked standpoints to class experience (Lukacs, 1971), arguing that workers are in a privileged position to analyse and understand their exploitation. This line of thinking is redressed today by feminist standpoint theory which makes a similar plea for the privileged position of 'women' in analysing discrimination (Hartsock, 1983; Harding, 1991; Giere, 1994). Feminists, however, shy away from the anti-realist implications of constructivist research, turning constructivism on its head: it is not perception/perspective that yields constructions but (perspectival) construction that yields objective descriptions, for example descriptions of the real experience of discrimination.

Implications for economic methodology
The original scandal of recent constructivism derives from the constructionist challenge to our traditional realist and objectivist beliefs regarding knowledge, science and even nature.

Constructionist studies have understood 'the world' as a consequence rather than a cause of scientific representations, scientific representations as constructed rather than as objective renderings of natural facts, and scientific rationality epistemologically indistinguishable from everyday rationality. They have also elevated the role of 'the social' (widely defined; see McMullin, 1992) to a position far beyond that which it has traditionally played in earlier conceptions of science. Such claims are the result of empirical research rather than philosophical argument; the constructionist interpretation of science results from applying the methods of science to itself. Such 're-entries' will need to continue in the future; but already the existing studies raise a number of issues for economic and social methodology.

The first concerns the need to place economists' appreciation for the natural sciences on a new footing, one that relinquishes certain rigid and false assumptions about the way these fields work which are currently held up as models for economic methodology. The second concerns the self-understanding of economics: an empirical observation of economists' procedures would seem to yield valuable insights into what makes economic methodology tick, and provide important comparative material for our understanding of epistemic cultures (see also Mirowski, 1989; McCloskey, 1985; de Marchi, 1992; Mäki, 1992; Knorr Cetina, 1991). A third question can be raised with regard to economic processes: would the analysis of these processes profit from constructivist, less model-oriented approaches (for example, Weintraub, 1991)? Are economic processes not also becoming more constructive and reflexive analogous to social processes and systems? Finally, and coming full circle, should economists not devote more attention to the economics of knowledge and science (Diamond, 1988; Wible, 1991) in ways informed by recent constructionist studies of science, and at the same time make good a sorely felt deficit in these studies (Hands, 1995)?

These issues may not be easy for economists to confront. But the prospects are exciting and, as the last references indicate, the work has already started.

KARIN KNORR CETINA

References

Ashmore, M. (1989), *The Reflexive Thesis*, Chicago: University of Chicago Press.
Berger, P. and T. Luckmann (1967), *The Social Construction of Reality*, London: Allen Lane.
Callon, M. (1986), 'Some Elements of a Sociology of Translation: Domestication of the Scallops and the Fishermen of St. Brieuc Bay', in J. Law (ed.), *Power Action and Belief: a New Sociology of Knowledge?*. London: Routledge & Kegan Paul.
Diamond, A.D. (1988), 'Science as a Rational Enterprise', *Theory and Decision*, **24**, 147–67.
Fausto-Sterling, A. (1985), *Myths of Gender: Biological Theories About Women and Men*, New York: Basic Books.
Giere, R. (1988), *Explaining Science: A Cognitive Approach*, Chicago: University of Chicago Press.
Giere, R. (1994), 'Perspectival Realism', presidential address at the Meeting of the Philosophy of Science Association, New Orleans, October.
Gieryn, T.F. (1982), 'Relativist/Constructivist Programmes in the Sociology of Science: Redundance and Retreat', *Social Studies of Science*, **12**, 279–97.
Goffman, E. (1972), 'The Neglected Situation', in P.P. Giglioli (ed.), *Language and Social Context*, Harmondsworth: Penguin.
Hands, W. (1995), 'The Sociology of Scientific Knowledge and Economics: Some Thoughts on the Possibilities', in R. Backhouse (ed.), *New Directions in Economic Methodology*, London: Routledge.
Harding, S. (1991), *Whose Science? Whose Knowledge? Thinking from Women's Lives*, Ithaca, NY: Cornell University Press.
Hartsock, N.C.M. (1983), 'The Feminist Standpoint: Developing a Ground for a Specifically Feminist Historical Materialism', in S. Harding and M. Hintikka (eds), *Feminist Perspectives on Epistemology, Metaphysics, Methodology and Philosophy of Science*, Dordrecht: Reidel.
Knorr Cetina, K. (1977), 'Producing and Reproducing Knowledge: Descriptive or constructive?', *Social Science Information*, **16**, 669–96.

Knorr Cetina, K. (1981), *The Manufacture of Knowledge: An Essay on the Constructivist and Contextual Nature of Science*, Oxford: Pergamon Press.

Knorr Cetina, K. (1991), 'Epistemic Cultures: Forms of Reason in Science', *History of Political Economy*, **23**, (1), 105–22.

Knorr Cetina, K. (1992), 'The Couch, the Cathedral and the Lab: On the Relationship between Experiment and Laboratory Science', in A. Pickering (ed.), *Science as Practice and Culture*, Chicago: University of Chicago Press.

Knorr Cetina, K. (1994), 'Laboratory Studies: The Cultural Approach to the Study of Science', in J.C. Petersen, G.E. Markle, S. Jasanoff and T.J. Pinch (eds), *Science, Technology and Society Handbook*, Los Angeles: Sage.

Knorr Cetina, K. (1998), *Epistemic Cultures. How Science Makes Sense*, Cambridge, MA: Harvard University Press.

Latour, B. (1987), *Science in Action*, Stony Stratford: Open University Press.

Latour, B. and J. Johnson (1988), 'Mixing Humans with Non-Humans: Sociology of a Door Opener', *Social Problems*, **35**, 298–310, special issue on Sociology of Science, ed. Susan L. Star.

Latour, B. and S. Woolgar (1979), *Laboratory Life: The Social Construction of Scientific Facts*, Beverly Hills: Sage.

Laws, J.L. and P. Schwartz (1977), *Sexual Scripts: The Social Construction of Female Sexuality*, Hinsdale: The Dryden Press.

Leeuwis, C. (1993), *Of Computers. Myths and Modelling: The Social Construction of Diversity, Knowledge, Information and Communication Technologies in Dutch Horticulture and Agriculture Extension*, Wageningen: Wageningen Studies in Sociology.

Luhmann, N. (1984), *Soziale Systeme*, Frankfurt/M.: Suhrkamp.

Lukacs, G. (1971), *History and Class Consciousness: Studies in Marxist Dialectics*, trans. Rodney Livingstone, Cambridge, MA: MIT Press.

Mäki, U. (1992), 'Social Conditioning in Economics', in N. de Marchi (ed.), *Post-Popperian Methodology of Economics: Recovering Practice*, Boston: Kluwer Academic.

Marchi, N. de (ed.), 1992, *Post-Popperian Methodology of Economics: Recovering Practice*, Boston: Kluwer Academic.

Maturana, H. and F. Varela (1980), *Autopoeisis and Cognition: The Realization of the Living*, Dordrecht: Reidel.

McCloskey, D.N. (1985), *The Rhetoric of Economics*, Madison, WI: University of Wisconsin Press.

McMullin, E. (ed.) (1992), *The Social Dimensions of Science*, Notre Dame: University of Notre Dame Press.

Miller, G. and J.A. Holstein (eds) (1993), *Constructionist Controversies*, Hawthorne: Aldine de Gruyter.

Mirowski, P. (1989), *More Heat than Light: Economics as Social Physics: Physics as Nature's Economics*, Cambridge: Cambridge University Press.

Pinch, T. and W.E. Bijker (1984), 'The Social Construction of Facts and Artefacts: or How the Sociology of Science and the Sociology of Technology might Benefit Each Other', *Social Studies of Science*, **14**, 399–441.

Sismondo, S. (1996), *Social Knowledge: Constructivism, Realism and the Politics of Science*, Albany: State University of New York Press.

Weintraub, E.R. (1991), *Stabilizing dynamics: Constructing Economic Knowledge*, Cambridge: Cambridge University Press.

Wible, J.R. (1991), 'Maximization, Replication, and the Economic Rationality of Positive Economic Science', *Review of Political Economy*, **3**, 164–86.

Woolgar, S. and M. Ashmore (1988), 'The Next Step: An Introduction to the Reflexive Project', in S. Woolgar (ed.), *Knowledge and Reflexivity*, London: Sage.

Conventionalism

Conventionalism is a methodological doctrine that constitutes the most common viewpoint adopted by economists to explain the role of theories and models in modern economics. According to this doctrine, theories and models are not claimed to be true but instead are claimed only to be the best available descriptions of the economy. Among economists, conventionalism is a doctrine with many variants and relatives. In one form it is old-fashioned relativism (for example, Shackle 1972: ch. 32; Dow, 1985). In another it is what McCloskey and her followers call 'modernism' (see McCloskey, 1983: 484–5). In yet another it can be seen to be the rationale for so-called 'methodological pluralism' (for example, Caldwell, 1982). The most common form involves the notion that theories are to be evaluated or compared by means of some form of probability calculus (for example, see Hicks, 1979. ch. 8; Poirier, 1988).

Conventionalism is a response to the recognition that neither prior nor subsequent empirical support could ever prove the truth of a theoretical statement whenever that statement is making universal claims. In the case of the prior evidence, there is no form of inductive logic that could ever prove a general statement true using *only* singular observations (for example, observing that the sun has risen every day in the past does not *prove* that it will rise tomorrow). In the case of posterior evidence, to the extent that every theory involves universal statements (for example, '*all* consumers are maximizers') a proof is impossible since it leads to an infinite regress. One has to give a proof of the universal statement but, in the absence of an inductive proof, one must give reasons for the universal statement being true, which opens the proof to questions concerning the truth of the reasons given. And so on. .

Rather than rejecting inductivism (the doctrine presumes all true knowledge must be proven and says that all true knowledge can be proved inductively), conventionalism responds by relaxing the concept of truth status. Conventionalism does this either directly (for example, theories are only 'probably true') or indirectly by relaxing the criteria of sufficient proof (for example, rather than true for 'all consumers' it is enough to show it is true for '*almost* all consumers'). In other words, according to conventionalism, theories ought be viewed, not as 'true' explanations, but as 'good' descriptions. A theory is thus considered to be a descriptive filing system, a way of organizing observation reports.

It can easily be argued that conventionalism is merely the most common response to what Karl Popper calls the 'Problem of Induction' (*how* can we prove the truth of a knowledge claim using *only* singular observations?). According to this argument, the problem of induction is replaced by what might be called a 'problem of conventions' (see Boland, 1980; 1982). Instead of requiring an inductive proof of the truth of a theory, we are to use some notion of conventionally accepted criteria of approximate truth to enable a rational choice between competing theories. So, according to conventionalism, theories are not to be regarded as true or false, but as better or worse. As a result, most of conventionalist methodology is concerned with what might be called the problem of theory choice (for example, see Tarascio and Caldwell, 1979). That is, how and by what criteria can we choose the best theory among competitors?

From the perspective provided by the problem of conventions, most questions of methodology can be reduced to what amount to exercises in economic analysis (see Boland, 1971). Specifically, any choice of a theory or model can be 'explained' as being the result of a maximization process in which the objective function is an accepted measure of 'truthlikeness' and the constraint is the set of available alternative theories or models. To choose the best theory is to choose the one which maximizes the desired attribute. Over the last 50 years, several different criteria or objective functions have been mentioned. The most well defined have been 'simplicity', 'generality', 'verifiability', 'falsifiability', 'confirmability' and 'testability'. Less well defined are 'empirical relevance', 'plausibility' and 'reasonableness'.

Popper has been the leading critic of conventionalism. At root, conventionalism represents one view about the extent to which a theory can be informative (see Agassi, 1963; 1966). Specifically, conventionalism argues that to be informative a theory must be supported by (sense) observations, either by showing how it can be derived from prior observations (that is, by induction) or by showing how it can be confirmed or proved by subsequent empirical evidence (verificationism). In effect, Popper rejects both alternatives and instead claims that a theory can be informative regardless of the extent of its empirical support. Popper's main complaint about conventionalism is that it is too easy to hide behind it in order to avoid criticism (see Popper, 1961; 1965).

The conventionalist ban on the use of the terms 'true' and 'false' in favour of 'better' or 'worse' presents obvious difficulties even for simple discussions. It also complicates the use of other terms such as 'knowing' and 'knowledge', as well as 'explaining' and 'explanation'. Although the terms 'knowledge' and 'explanation' do appear often in economics literature, the ban on using the terms 'true' and 'false' in their literal sense is virtually complete. What needs to be understood, however, is that there is a presumption that, whenever the term 'explanation' is used, one never means literally true explanation. Instead, an 'explanation' only means a true explanation *relative* to some accepted conventional measures of 'approximation'.

While since the early 1950s most methodological debates in economics have been about the criteria to be used in any 'theory choice', there is virtually no discussion of *why* one should ever be required to choose *one* theory! The reason for the lack of discussion of the motivation for 'theory choice' is that the problem of conventions is simply taken for granted. A direct consequence of accepting the need to solve the problem of conventions is the presumption that any article or essay must represent a revealed choice of a theory and that any such choice *can* be justified. The means of justifying the theory choice is to give an argument for the chosen theory being the 'best' as measured by one or more of the conventionalist criteria mentioned above. The problem is to find a set of criteria that everyone can accept. If a set of criteria are accepted, in principle the best theory can always be chosen. For example, many researchers today choose the empirical theoretical statement with the highest R^2 for the given data.

There are advocates and critics for each of the various choice criteria. Those advocates who wish to remain consistent with the dictates of conventionalism will not claim that their explanation of the choice of any particular theory in any way constitutes a proof that the theory is actually true. If by chance the chosen theory is 'best' by all criteria, there could never be an argument. But usually competing theories are best by one criterion and not by another, and in such cases critics, who may also wish to remain consistent with conventionalism, are thus forced to quibble over a choice between criteria (see Boland, 1970).

A different approach is available to those critics who are not bound by the dictates of conventionalism. Conventionalism can be easily criticized by arguing that each criterion is based on a presumed true theory of the nature of any true theory of the phenomena in question. For example, choosing a theory which is the 'simplest' presumes that the real world is inherently simple, thus any true theory of the real world must also be simple; and that, furthermore, although the truth of one's theory may not be provable, the simplicity of competing theories can be established if the measure of simplicity is well defined. A similar argument can be raised against the version of conventionalism which judges theories on the basis of the criterion of generality.

It would seem that conventionalist criteria other than simplicity or generality are less vulnerable. Nevertheless, there are still problems. Verifiability was once the primary conventionalist criterion, but that criterion is no longer taken seriously. Verifiability has not fared well against the logical criticism of Popper and others who argue that all informative, non-tautological theories are unverifiable. For Popper, theories are informative only if they are falsifiable. He seems successfully to have destroyed the belief in verification, as falsifiability and testability are now widely accepted as a minimum condition for the acceptability of any theory or model in economics. This is unfortunate, as theory choice criteria, falsifiability and testability are still quite arbitrary. But worse, those critics *not* bound by conventionalism can also argue that the true theory may not be the most falsifiable or the most testable of the available alternative theories.

For some purists, the acceptance of the criteria of verifiability or falsifiability might seem a little inconsistent if one still accepts conventionalism and its denial of a (non-tautological and non-self-contradictory) theory being literally either true or false. If a theory cannot be false, what does 'falsifiable' mean? These purists find refuge in a set of weaker criteria for the lesser purpose of 'validation'. The most widely used validation criterion is 'confirmability', and rather than seeking to verify a theory or model we are said to be only seeking its confirmation. For example, the universal statement, 'All swans are white', may be said to be confirmed (but not proved) when a very large number of 'white swans' have been observed in the absence of any 'non-white swans'. Alternatively, those who accept Popper's criticism of the purpose for verification may opt for the criterion of 'testability' where the objective is to select only theories which in principle could be 'disconfirmed'.

Validation criteria have their limitations, too: for example, a highly confirmed theory may still be false. But purists can counter with the observation that this is not a problem, since any theory which is logically consistent need not be considered false even in the presence of a reported refutation (that is, of an observed counterexample) because any refuting fact is itself theory-laden. In other words, any proponent of the 'refuted' theory can defend it by questioning the alleged truth of the observed counterexample. This example highlights one of the prominent features of logically consistent conventionalism. In place of the concepts of 'true' and 'false', conventionalism uses 'valid' and 'invalid'. And, furthermore, the only *objective* and non-arbitrary test to be applied to theories or models is that of logical consistency and validity. Even if we cannot prove that a theory or model is true, we know that, at the very minimum, to be true it must be logically consistent.

There are logical problems even with the concept of confirmation. In its simple form it equates a probability of truth with a degree of confirmation. Such a 'degree' concept presumes that a greater quantity of positive evidence implies a higher degree of probability of truth. Unfortunately, with this simple concept one has merely assumed what one wished to establish. Recall that an inductive argument proceeds from particular positive statements – for example, observation reports such as 'A white swan was observed in Hawaii today' – to general statements such as 'All swans in Hawaii today are white.' In the absence of refuting observations, the general statement's probability of truth is measured by the ratio of the number of confirming observations to the unknown but finite number of possible observations, such as the ratio of observed white swans (without double-counting) to the number of all swans in Hawaii today. So long as we specify which day 'today' is, this general statement is both verifiable and refutable.

The only question of empirical significance here is whether subsequent observations of confirming evidence (for example, more white swans) *necessarily* increase the degree of confidence in the general statement *as opposed to its denial* (for example, the statement that there is at least one non-white swan in Hawaii today). Based on the quantity of evidence available, what degree of confidence does one have that the *next* swan observed will be white? Advocates of the confirmability criterion would have us believe that each past observation of a white swan necessarily increases the probability that all future swans observed will be white. This alleged necessity is actually based on a prior, and unsupported, assumption that the general statement is true (or that its ultimate probability is one).

It is not clear why conventionalism is so often taken for granted by economists today. Perhaps it is because conventionalism allows our profession to avoid being destroyed by ideological infighting among dogmatic economists. Perhaps it is because it permits us to find success with a limited objective of constructing models that can be confirmed, rather than trying to find universal 'truths'. Perhaps it merely is, as Popper fears, an all-too-easy way to avoid criticism.

LAWRENCE A. BOLAND

Bibliography
Agassi, J. (1963), *Towards an Historiography of Science, History and Theory, Beiheft 2*, The Hague: Mouton.
Agassi. J. (1966), 'Sensationalism', *Mind*, **75**, 1–24.
Boland, L. (1970), 'Conventionalism and economic theory', *Philosophy of Science*, **37**, 239–48.
Boland, L. (1971), 'Methodology as an exercise in economic analysis', *Philosophy of Science*, **38**, 105–17.
Boland, L. (1980), 'Friedman's methodology vs. conventional empiricism: a reply to Rotwein', *Journal of Economic Literature*, **18**, 1555–7.
Boland, L. (1982), *The Foundations of Economic Method*, London: George Allen & Unwin.
Boland, L. (1989), *The Methodology of Economic Model Building: Methodology after Samuelson*, London: Routledge.
Caldwell, B. (1982), *Beyond Positivism*, London: George Allen & Unwin.
Dow, S. (1985), *Macroeconomic Thought*, Oxford: Basil Blackwell.
Hicks, J. (1979), *Causality in Economics*, Oxford: Basil Blackwell.
McCloskey, D. (1983), 'The rhetoric of economics', *Journal of Economic Literature*, **21**, 481–517.
Poirier, D. (1988), 'Frequentist and subjectivist perspectives on the problems of model building in economics', *Journal of Economic Perspectives*, **2**, 121–44.
Popper, K. (1961), *The Logic of Scientific Discovery*, New York: Science Editions.
Popper, K. (1965), *Conjectures and Refutations: The Growth of Scientific Knowledge*, New York: Basic Books.
Shackle, G. (1972), *Epistemics and Economics*, Cambridge: Cambridge University Press.
Tarascio, V. and B. Caldwell (1979), 'Theory choice in economics: philosophy and practice', *Journal of Economic Issues*, **13**, 983–1006.

Conventions

There are a number of different terms used in economics to characterize social conventions and conventional behaviour: conventions, rules and norms, and sometimes habits, routines, customs and traditions. The vocabulary is not used entirely consistently, but economists tend more often to emphasize rules, norms and conventions, with the latter concept acquiring more interest since the development of game theory.

Perhaps the most remarkable thing about conventions is their ubiquity. In daily life, there are conventions about how to dress, how to speak to others, how to eat, how to wait in line, and so on in truly an endless list. As sociologists note, there are conventions surrounding virtually every activity we engage in. In economic life, innumerable conventions surround market exchange, the forms of which include allowable free-riding, forms of competitive behaviour, expectations about rivals, grounds for trust and mistrust, product quality and fair dealing. Yet until quite recently economists, in their concentration on rational choice theory, have almost entirely ignored the role conventions play in behaviour and decision making. It should come as less of a surprise that the principal issue concerning conventional behaviour in economics is how to accommodate rule and convention following to the theory of instrumental rationality.

The original literature on the subject, stemming from the work of Simon (1982), essentially treats conventions and rules interchangeably, and looks upon them as broad decision strategies alternative to case-by-case decision making. People are procedurally or boundedly rational, not substantively so, and thus they employ rules and conventions to economize on scarce computational resources. Knudsen (1993) traces this to a self-reflexivity, infinite regress problem in traditional rational choice analysis, where to exercise choice we must first decide whether it pays to make a choice, which itself requires that we decide whether it pays to decide whether it pays to make a choice, and so on. Thus conventions and rules are essentially simplifying devices individuals use in decision making.

Yet if rules may be understood as personal means of saving on costly computations, rules in another sense are shared by individuals who are in regular interaction with one another. Here we may also distinguish rules from norms by noting that, whereas shared rules can describe established patterns of behaviour, shared rules in the sense of norms are established patterns of behaviour that individuals believe *ought* to be maintained, either in a moral or pragmatic sense. This normative force some rules have is not explained by seeing them as decision making-simplifying devices. Why is it, that is, that individuals feel compelled to observe conventions?

Lewis (1969), following Hume (1978) and Schelling (1960), has been very influential in this regard by getting economists to think about conventions as patterns of interdependent behaviour, or in game-theoretic terms. On his view, conventions are solutions to coordination problems, where individuals adopt a norm or convention, as in Axelrod's (1984) analysis, tit-for-tat in a repeated game or game with no foreseeable end, to solve prisoner's dilemma-type problems. That the 'cooperate-unless-the-other-doesn't' norm here is in each individual's interest reinforces its observance and thus explains how individuals can come to believe they ought to follow rules and conventions. Lewis's basic definition of convention is thus:

> A regularity R in the behavior of members of a population P when they are agents in a recurrent situation S is a *convention* if and only if, in any instance of S among members of P,
> (1) everyone conforms to R;
> (2) everyone expects everyone else to conform to R;
> (3) everyone prefers to conform to R on condition that others do, since S is a coordination problem and uniform conformity to R is a coordination equilibrium in S. (Lewis, 1969: 42)

A refinement on this is that what has come to be known in game theory as the common knowledge assumption also holds. Gilbert (1989) provides a critical analysis of Lewis and the game-theoretic approach to understanding convention.

An important issue raised by Lewis's approach concerns how conventions come to be established at all. Sugden (1986, 1989) has developed a game-theoretic explanation of the emergence of conventions, not restricted to coordination games, in which individuals first play a symmetrical game in which they do not know the best strategy to adopt and thus repeatedly play a mixed set of strategies until, through trial and error, they learn the proportion between the strategies that maximizes their expected utility. The resulting Nash equilibrium is said to be stable in an evolutionary sense, and the players are said to play evolutionarily stable strategies, or ESSs (a concept which comes from the work of the biologist Maynard Smith (1982) who was concerned with the evolution of patterns of behaviour in animal species). Assuming, however, that more than one stable equilibrium and set of ESSs is available, it can then be shown that, if for any reason whatsoever (say, some 'accident of history') one set of players begins to play asymmetrically, that is, to play one way in certain circumstances and another way in other circumstances, it will be in the interest of all players to adjust to this asymmetrical strategy of play, if the initial number of adherents to the new form of play is significant. This asymmetrical or context-dependent play, when it becomes fully established, constitutes a convention.

Sugden thus takes conventions to be rules or norms regulating social life that obtain in games with more than one ESS, that come about through evolution, that are self-enforcing and that (following Hayek, for example, 1960) reflect anarchic or spontaneous order as the unintended consequences of individuals' acting rationally in terms of their own preferences. The answer to the question of how conventions come to be established is that they are not chosen, but simply evolve without design. Indeed, on Sugden's view, the market as a form of spontaneous order itself depends upon institutions, particularly private property rights and enforceable contracts, which are best understood as conventions resulting from an unintended process of evolution. More generally, Sugden distinguishes three broad categories of conventions: coordination conventions, property rights conventions and reciprocity conventions.

A crucial issue for this view concerns how specific conventions come to evolve rather than others, especially since the initial development of a convention sets in motion a self-reinforcing process that ultimately makes that convention more viable than others. Following Schelling, evolutionary game theorists have appealed to the intuitive idea of prominence and salience, that is, aspects of a situation that stand out in individuals' common experience and serve as focal points around which individuals coordinate their decisions. This raises difficult epistemological issues, however, since it is not easy to say why some things are prominent in our experience and others not so.

Sudgen nonetheless elaborates on Schelling's point to argue that, if prominence is a matter of common experience, conventions may spread by analogy from one context to another. An example is the 'first come, first served' principle of queuing that seems to have many applications. Such an account may be question-begging, however, since it seems the very drawing of an analogy itself presupposes the existence of prior conventions about how we recognize similarities between old and new situations, thus posing the possibility of an infinite regress in the argument. Relevant here, then, is the philosophical literature going back to Quine (1953) on similarity and analytic judgment.

Other researchers in this tradition have emphasized that, just as conventions can come into being, so they can also pass out of being. Hargreaves Heap and Varoufakis (1995) note that the conclusion of an evolutionary process is unlikely to be pure stasis, and that a potential weakness in evolutionary game theory's account of conventions is its failure to explain the subversion of established conventions, or how particular conventions break down and are replaced by others.

An interesting conclusion of the game-theoretic approach to the understanding of conventions is that evolution need not produce conventions that are optimal (as also suggested by the existence of such conventions as the QWERTY keyboard). Sugden's account of the way in which conventions come to be established through accidents of history explains how this is possible, and it is not difficult to produce examples of games in which inefficient conventions in terms of player payoffs become self-perpetuating. This conclusion contrasts with Hume's view that rules and conventions tend to operate in the best interest of society. It also raises questions about the wisdom of seeing the market as an invisible hand process that always works to bring about the greater social good. If conventions evolve spontaneously, and if many of the conventions involved in the market are Pareto-inferior to other conventions we may imagine, then the evolution of the market may be irrational in important respects. This point may be extended by noting that market conventions are sometimes unjust and discriminatory.

These latter conclusions clearly turn on our having standards for evaluating conventions that are independent of the perspectives generated by their evolutionary success. Hume resisted this possibility by arguing in his account of the origin of the principles of justice that the norms of justice are merely long-observed conventions to which we have come to annex the idea of virtue. No higher standard for judgment can thus exist apart from our conventional beliefs and, should some conventions appear inefficient or unjust, we might best attribute this to lags in individuals' acceptance of those conventions.

Needless to say, few moral philosophers today would take such a view seriously. In the first place, it is questionable that moral principles are reducible to conventions and, in the second place, moral principles are not often thought merely a matter of preferences, particularly for those in a more deontological tradition. Perhaps more important for economics, however, is the fact that Sugden does not restrict his analysis of conventions to coordination problems, thus allowing some conventions regarding moral norms to favour some people at the expense of others. Were economists to come to look upon moral norms in this way, Pareto efficiency judgments might lose some of their appeal, and perhaps begin to develop a richer conception of the types of normative judgments appropriate in economics.

John B. Davis

References

Axelrod, R. (1984), *The Evolution of Cooperation*, New York: Basic Books.
Gilbert, M. (1989), *On Social Facts*, London: Routledge.
Hargreaves Heap, S. and Y. Varoufakis, (1995), *Game Theory: A Critical Introduction*, London: Routledge.
Hayek, F. (1960), *The Constitution of Liberty*, London: Routledge & Kegan Paul.
Hume, D. (1978), *A Treatise of Human Nature*, 2nd edn, ed., L. Selby-Bigge, Oxford: Clarendon Press.
Knudsen, C. (1993), 'Equilibrium, Perfect Rationality and the Problem of Self-Reference in Economics', in U. Mäki, B. Gustaffsson, and C. Knudsen, (eds), *Rationality, Institutions and Economic Methodology*, London: Routledge.
Lewis, D. (1969), *Convention: A Philosophical Study*, Cambridge, MA: Harvard University Press.
Maynard Smith, J. (1982), *Evolution and the Theory of Games*, Cambridge: Cambridge University Press.
Quine, W. (1953), *From a Logical Point of View*, Cambridge, MA: Harvard University Press.
Schelling, T. (1960), *The Strategy of Conflict*, Cambridge: Cambridge University Press.
Simon, H. (1982), *Models of Bounded Rationality*, Cambridge: MIT Press.
Sugden, R. (1986), *The Economics of Rights, Co-operation and Welfare*, Oxford: Basil Blackwell.
Sugden, R. (1989), 'Spontaneous Order', *Journal of Economic Perspectives*, **3** (4), 85–97.

Critical Rationalism

A central aspect of Karl Popper's philosophy of science is what he calls 'critical rationalism'. Popper is often credited with explicitly creating critical rationalism in Chapter 24 of his *Open Society and its Enemies*, but to some extent it is also implicit throughout his *Logic of Scientific Discovery*. With the word 'critical' Popper wishes to make clear that his form of rationalism differs from that most closely associated with classical eighteenth-century rationalism that Voltaire satirized in *Candide*. Classical rationalism is based on an optimistic belief that it is possible to be rational about *everything* – and for this reason Popper called this 'comprehensive rationalism'. According to Popper, comprehensive rationalism is part of a more general theory of knowledge which asserts that every knowledge claim must be justified by a proof. Popper and his followers call this theory 'justificationism'.

Whether or not rationalism is comprehensive hinges on whether or not *every* true statement can be proved with a rational argument. According to Willard Van Quine, only tautologies can be proved true (Quine, 1965). Whether this limited notion of comprehensive rationalism is all that one can hope for depends on what one means by a true statement. In one sense, Quine's view may merely constitute an expression of comprehensive rationalism by saying that the only statements that can be true are those that can be proved true. In another sense, to say the only proof is a demonstration of a tautology may form an effective criticism of comprehensive rationalism.

While it might be easy to see that one can criticize comprehensive rationalism, such technical criticisms are not the basis for critical rationalism. Critical rationalism is about the critical use of rational arguments in the context of fallibilism and critical realism: that is, in the context where we seek true knowledge but we admit that our knowledge can be false. In the case of critical rationalism, rationality is identified, 'not with closure, assertion, justification or decision, but with openness, exchange, criticism, debate' (Agassi and Jarvie, 1987b: 438).

Although Popper is credited with creating critical rationalism, it is easy to see that even Aristotle provided the means for a critical view of rationality of arguments with the three axioms of logic often attributed to him. Specifically, every rational argument will satisfy the following three axioms: *the axiom of identity* (any notion or thing referred to in one constituent statement of the argument must be identical to that notion or thing when referred to in any other constituent statement of the argument); *the axiom of excluded middle* (every statement included in the argument is true or false – there is no middle ground such as a 'somewhat true' or 'probably true'); and *the axiom of (non)contradiction* (no statement included in the argument can be both true and false). The critical issue concerns what type of statements are admissible into a rational argument. A statement is admissible into a rational argument only if it satisfies all three conditions. Aristotle's axioms specify the nature of admissible statements such that if any one of the axioms is violated then there is no guarantee that the desired conclusion is true. Obviously, such requirements of admissibility constitute a clear avenue for criticizing anyone's argument. But using the rationality of an argument in this critical manner would not constitute critical rationalism.

Critical rationalism goes farther by denying both the possibility and the necessity of providing arguments to prove any chosen true statement. For Popper, critical rationalism is non-justificationist rationalism because a true statement can be true even if we have not proved it so and because some true statements could never be proved true if by proof we mean an absolute empirical demonstration.

In his *Open Society and its Enemies*, Popper explains his use of the term 'rationalism' to distinguish his view from the classical view. Specifically, he says that his version of rationalism

> is the rationalism of Socrates. It is the awareness of one's limitations, the intellectual modesty of those who know how often they err, and how much they depend on others even for this knowledge. It is the realization that we must not expect too much from reason; that argument rarely settles a question, although it is the only means for learning – not to see clearly, but to see more clearly than before. (Popper, 1966: 227)

Later, in his *Objective Knowledge*, he says, 'The main thing is that for the rationalist *any* criticism is welcome – though he may reply to it by criticizing the criticism' (Popper, 1972: 307).

Critical rationalism is the combination of Socratic fallibilism and a deliberate openness to criticism, both of which are regulated by so-called 'critical realism'. '*Critical Realism* takes the aim of knowledge to be the comprehension and representation of reality ... in opposition to conceptions which take the aim of science to be the construction of systems of signs ... which have no representational function, but which are useful in a certain manner for practical life' (Albert, 1978: 204). Critical rationalism is not just a position on what constitutes a critical argument. It is also about the necessity of a critical attitude. To accept critical rationalism or nonjustificationist rationalism is to 'accept any doctrine which (a) admits the inability to support or justify any belief, and (b) allows any faith on the condition that it be held tentatively, i.e. be left open to criticism and when effectively criticized be relinquished' (Agassi, 1973: 400).

Critical rationalism is most often promoted as an alternative to a failed classical rationalism. The failure follows from justificationist attempts to prove the comprehensiveness of rationalism. The proofs are usually circular, or they lead to an infinite regress (proofs of the argument's assumptions, proofs of the assumptions of the proofs of the argument's assumptions, and so on). To stop the infinite regress it is all too easy to become dogmatic by asserting that certain fundamental assumptions are true and can be used to form the proof of every true statement. This arbitrary stop is called fideism (see Bartley, 1964b) and is sometimes identified with the views of Pierre Duhem (1962). If one does not stop the infinite regress in this way but still insists that all statements which are claimed to be true must be rationally justified, one has the basis of classical scepticism. The problem here, according to Hans Albert, is that

> we need not, indeed cannot, take the demand for an absolute justification for granted. ... If we replace the classical principle of justification by the principle of critical examination, then we can avoid falling back into either dogmatism, as do the defenders of classical rationalism, or into scepticism, as do the disappointed rationalists who see themselves forced into irrationalism, or into those sophisticated blends of dogmatism and scepticism which are so seductive to modern philosophers. (Albert, 1978: 211)

For some reason, Popper in his *Open Society and its Enemies* felt the need to justify his view of rationalism and reached the conclusion that the foundation of any belief in rationalism is an irrational commitment. His student Bartley took him to task by claiming that this was inconsistent. What is needed, according to Bartley, is a comprehensive critical rationalism. Specifically, critical rationalism itself must be open to criticism and be rejected if the criticism is successful. Other students of Popper claim in effect that the mistake Popper made was to try to convince classical rationalists on their own terms (see Agassi, 1973; 1987; Agassi and Jarvie, 1987b). Supposedly, Popper fell into the trap of justificationism and tried to extricate himself by resorting to the dogmatism he purportedly rejects. These other students argue that the critical rationalism of the *Logic of Scientific Discovery* avoids such traps by rejecting the need to justify every claim to knowledge and instead inviting criticism.

In summary, it is important to keep in mind that Popper's critical rationalism is a matter of attitude more than methodology. Critical rationalism says that human knowledge is fallible and thus it is important to welcome criticism. Rationality is not a route to certain knowledge. Rather, rationality is critical debate.

LAWRENCE A. BOLAND

Bibliography
Agassi, J. (1973), 'Rationality and the Tu Quoque argument', *Inquiry*, **16**, 395–406.
Agassi, J. (1987), 'Theories of rationality' in J. Agassi and I. Jarvie, *Rationality*.
Agassi, J. and I. Jarvie (1987a), *Rationality: The Critical View*, Boston: Martinus Nijhoff.
Agassi, J. and I. Jarvie (1987b), The rationality of dogmatism', in J. Agassi and I. Jarvie *Rationality*.
Albert, H. (1978), 'Science and the search for truth: Critical rationalism and the methodology of science', in G. Radnitzky and G. Andersson (eds), *Process and Rationality in Science*, Dordrecht: Reidel.
Bartley, W.W. (1964a), *The Retreat to Commitment*, London: Chatto & Windus.
Bartley, W.W. (1964b), 'Rationality vs the Theory of Rationality' in M. Bunge, (ed.), *The Critical Approach in Science and Philosophy*, London: Collier-Macmillan.
Duhem, P. (1962), *The Aim and Structure of Physical Theory*, New York: Atheneum.
Popper, K. (1961), *The Logic of Scientific Discovery*, New York: Science Editions.
Popper, K. (1966), *The Open Society and Its Enemies, Vol. 2*, London: Routledge & Kegan Paul.
Popper, K. (1972), *Objective Knowledge*, London: Oxford University Press.
Quine, W. (1965), *Elementary Logic*, rev. edn, New York: Harper & Row.

Deconstruction

Why do economists resist the idea that what they do is a kind of writing? In what ways would economics be changed if economists recognized the 'incommensurability' attendant upon the differential structure of language? To what extent has the history of economics been based on a set of hierarchical dichotomies, such as that between certainty and uncertainty? What if such binary oppositions, in which the first term is privileged over the second, were effectively reversed and displaced? What would be the consequences, in short, of 'deconstructing' economics?

The project of deconstruction was initiated by the French philosopher Jacques Derrida who, in a series of highly influential books published in the late 1960s and early 1970s, especially *Speech and Phenomena*, *Of Grammatology*, *Writing and Difference*, *Dissemination* and *Margins of Philosophy*, presented a systematic and original rereading of some of the key texts of western philosophy and social thought, from Plato and Rousseau to Freud and Lévi-Strauss. The protocols and strategies set forth in Derrida's work have since become central to poststructuralism (together with the work of Roland Barthes, Michel Foucault and Jacques Lacan) which, in turn, emerged alongside and has continued to grow in conjunction with postmodernism (as elaborated by Jean-François Lyotard and others). Today deconstruction is a widespread practice of textual interpretation and philosophical argumentation applied to works of philosophy, literature and the 'human sciences', including psychoanalysis, linguistics, politics and, most recently, economics.

From the perspective of deconstruction, western thought has been dominated by a series of attempts to define meaning in terms of truth, rationality, science and objectivity. What unites these various attempts is what Derrida refers to as 'logocentrism', the idea that meaning can or should refer to some transcendent, universal and timeless essence. The problem with logocentrism (or what is often also called the 'metaphysics of presence') is that it can only be said to work to the extent that it marginalizes, sets aside or represses its 'other': all those notions, such as difference, contingency, absence and the like, which threaten to disrupt the possibility of establishing the absolute foundation or essence of meaning.

'Deconstruction' is the term coined by Derrida that refers to a practice of reading which takes as its goal the critique of logocentrism and, thus, a reinterpretation of the concepts and conceptual schemes within western thought for which it has served as the apparent foundation. A deconstructive reading operates as a form of close textual analysis in which 'marginal' elements of a text – elements that other readers might consider less important or even irrelevant, such as the subordinate term of an oppositional hierarchy, a particular metaphor, or the discussion in a footnote – are identified and made to work against the intended or stated logic of that text. The purpose of such a reading is to locate the incongruities or moments of undecidability in the text, not in an attempt to resolve the disunity engendered by such 'aporias' or self-engendered paradoxes but, rather, to keep the text open to what it apparently does not want to say. Deconstruction, then, is an attempt both to recover what logocentric thinking has served to hide or contain and to undermine the protocols and strategies on the basis of which such exclusions have traditionally operated.

A good example of deconstruction, of the way in which a deconstructive approach works both through and against the apparent logic of a text, is Derrida's reading in Part 1 of *Grammatology* of the theory of signs put forward in the early twentieth century by the Swiss linguist Ferdinand de Saussure. According to Derrida, Saussure can be credited with the idea (which, in the 1950s and 1960s, became central to structuralist thought) that linguistic value is not immanent in an individual sign; meaning is not created by relationships of reference or correspondence between signs and their extralinguistic referents but, instead, by relationships of difference between signs. In this sense, meaning is 'arbitrarily' constructed. However, Derrida finds that Saussure attempts to create a 'science of language', first, by deeming language and writing as two different systems of signs and, then, by privileging speech over writing (since Saussure considered words to be associated with the spoken form and writing to be merely a poor copy or representation, and therefore derivative, of speech).

In Derrida's view, Saussure's privileging of speech over writing is indicative of the larger problem of logocentrism: it represents an attempt to find the essence of meaning, to make linguistic meaning singular, present to itself (in the sense that it is uttered between speakers who hear or understand themselves and each other in the moment of speaking) whereas writing (which creates the possibility of a delayed reading, when the author is absent and therefore cannot be interrogated for the meaning of his or her text) is inextricably tied to interpretation and, thus, multiple meanings. Therefore Derrida proceeds to show how, *on the basis of Saussure's own text*, using Saussure's own discussion of writing, the terms of opposition can be reversed – speech (and thus language) can be said to exhibit all the characteristics of writing – and then displaced, since both speech and writing can be subsumed under a larger category of language.

The resulting deconstruction of the hierarchical opposition of speech and writing leads to a new concept of language (what Derrida, in order to distance the term from the specific sense of writing as graphic inscription, calls 'arche-writing' (*archi-écriture*)) which, in turn, is interpreted by extending Saussure's notion of 'difference' (which Derrida refers to as 'différance'). *Différance*, which combines the senses of both 'to differ' and 'to defer' (and with the silence, in spoken French, of the substitution of the 'a' for the 'e' revealing the distinctiveness of writing in relationship to speech), is Derrida's way of raising doubts about the ability of a sign to 'embody', or to correspond to, any essential meaning. It is also the starting point for thinking about meaning as a purely contextual phenomenon, as something that is constituted within specific texts which are themselves infinitely extendible (in time and across space) through other texts. Hence perhaps the most cited of Derrida's pronouncements: 'there is nothing outside of the text' (*il n'y a pas de hors-texte*) (1976: 158).

Not surprisingly, the practice of deconstruction has provoked a great deal of criticism and debate concerning its protocols of textual interpretation and its questioning of central features of western philosophy and social thought. Many of these issues have been posed and discussed in a series of penetrating interviews with Derrida himself (these interviews, especially his 'dialogue' with Richard Kearney, 1984, are perhaps the most accessible introductions to deconstruction). To consider but one of these criticisms, deconstruction is often taken to be a complete denial of reference, an assertion that language refers to nothing but itself – and, therefore, to nothing at all. The interpretation favoured by Derrida and others is that deconstruction serves to problematize traditional (that is, logocentric) theories of reference, to demonstrate that reference is a more complicated or complex process than is usually understood by philosophers and social theorists alike. It attempts to show both that meaning is produced through a network of differences between language and its 'other' (the world, history, reality, and so on) and that such experiences and events outside language are always subject to a movement of interpretation which serves to contextualize them. Therefore deconstruction can be seen not as a denial of reference per se but, rather, as an alternative to traditional notions of reference: it challenges the idea that meaning can be grounded on any kind of linguistic *or* extralinguistic referent; at the same time, it redefines reference in terms of the relations of difference and deferral which create the interpretative contexts within which meanings are produced and disseminated.

The decontructionist focus on the structure of language as writing thus creates the possibility of a different relationship of methodology to economics. On the one hand, it casts doubt on the authority which methodologists often attribute to economics, the idea that economics can best be viewed as (or, alternatively, should be revised so as to conform to the standards of) a science composed of a set of stable meanings and referents. From the point of view of deconstruction, meanings are always unstable to the extent that systems of writing (and thus words) do not refer to and are not governed by immutable essences outside writing. This view of writing undermines the notions of scientificity (together with objectivity, rationality and so on) that have traditionally governed debates in and around economics. On the other hand, the idea that meaning resides in writing opens up methodology to new ways of investigating the discipline of economics. A deconstructive approach seeks to investigate both the kinds of meaning that are produced by economists' writing (by specific instances of writing as well as by the system of writing more generally) and the kinds of meaning that are ascribed by economists and other readers to that writing. What this means is not only that the texts of economics can be analysed in terms of the array of literary devices and forms of rhetoric that economists use to communicate their ideas and to attempt to persuade others of their validity. It also means that the existing languages of economics can be examined in terms of their participation in the logocentric philosophical discourses that have influenced other areas of western thought and, therefore, in terms of the deconstructive moments that Derrida and others have located in those discourses.

One specific implication of understanding economics as writing is that economic concepts are read, not as having general, universal meanings (and, even less, singular meanings that correspond to extratheoretical objects) but, instead, as acquiring different meanings in different, local contexts. This notion of contextual meaning identifies a fundamental incommensurabil-ity in economics, in at least two senses. First, economic theories will differ according to the way they define their respective concepts, and there is no intertheoretical, essential standard according to which one meaning can be said to be prior to or to govern the others. Thus, for example, neoclassical, Keynesian and Marxian economic theories (to name just three) can be said to be incommensurable to the extent that concepts such as value, scarcity, demand and so on literally mean different things in those different theoretical contexts. Second, the concepts of 'academic' economic theory will often differ from those which non-economists use to make sense of economic activity (what traditional methodologists often refer to as 'ersatz' economics). These, too, are incommensurable in the sense that neither group of concepts can be said to capture (or not) any essential meaning. The deconstructive focus on contextual meaning thus leads to a different conversation (among economists as well as between economists and non-economists), one which recognizes the 'play' of meanings associated with the differential structure of economic discourse. It also calls for an analysis of the forces beyond economics, and even beyond language itself (for example, the political and institutional context), in and through which one theory, one set of meanings (such as, today, neoclassical theory), comes to be privileged over all others within economics.

A second implication of viewing economics as writing is that the conceptual oppositions which are often part of economic analysis can be seen to work against or to undermine the apparent logic of that analysis and, thus, to give rise to another logic with which it cannot be resolved. In this sense, economics can be said to deconstruct itself. One example is the dichotomy between certainty and uncertainty, especially as economists have constructed it over the course of the past century. Various notions of certain knowledge (as it has been claimed by economists and attributed to economic agents) have played a central role in economics. At the same time, economists have become aware of the potential for uncertainty (at least on the part of economic agents) and have sought to extend their theories to encompass both forms of knowledge. However, once uncertainty was introduced into economics, it also became clear that there were situations (perhaps many) in which economic agents (and, by implication, economists themselves) may have no knowledge whatsoever. What this notion of 'true uncertainty' has done is to introduce moments of undecidability into economic analysis, for example, by breaking the connections which economists have often presumed between some form of rational decision making and the actions of economic agents. While most economists have attempted to reinstall a hierarchical opposition between certainty and uncertainty (for example, by redefining uncertainty as a form of probabilistic certainty), others have sought to reverse and displace such a hierarchy (for example, by extending uncertainty beyond economic agents to economists themselves). This latter treatment has tended to expose the limits of, and therefore to deconstruct, the very forms of analysis in and through which uncertainty was initially introduced into economics.

Economic methodologists have only begun to explore the rich possibilities opened up by deconstruction. However, the results of Derrida's work indicate that exploring how and why economists resist the idea that what they do is a kind of writing has the potential of opening economics to a different engagement both with itself and with its 'other'.

DAVID F. RUCCIO

Bibliography

Amariglio, J. (1990), 'Economics as a Postmodern Discourse', in W. Samuels (ed.), *Economics as Discourse: An Analysis of the Language of Economists*, Boston: Kluwer.
Amariglio, J., S. Resnick, and R. Wolff (1990), 'Division and Difference in the "Discipline" of Economics', *Critical Inquiry*, **17**, Autumn, 108–37.
Culler, J. (1982), *On Deconstruction: Theory and Criticism after Structuralism*, Ithaca, NY: Cornell University Press.
Derrida, J. (1973), *Speech and Phenomena, and Other Essays on Husserl's Theory of Signs*, trans. D.B. Allison, Evanston: Northwestern University Press.
Derrida, J. (1976), *Of Grammatology*, trans. G.C. Spivak, Baltimore: Johns Hopkins University Press.
Derrida, J. (1978), *Writing and Difference*, trans. A. Bass, Chicago: University of Chicago Press.
Derrida, J. (1981a), *Dissemination*, trans. B. Johnson, Chicago: University of Chicago Press.
Derrida, J. (1981b), *Positions*, trans. A. Bass, Chicago: University of Chicago Press.
Derrida, J. (1982), *Margins of Philosophy*, trans. A. Bass, Chicago: University of Chicago Press.
Derrida, J. (1988), *Limited Inc.*, Trans. S. Weber and J. Mehlman, Evanston: Northwestern University Press.
Derrida, J. (1989), *Edmund Husserl's 'Origin of Geometry': An Introduction*, trans. J.P. Leavey, Jr., Lincoln: University of Nebraska Press.
Kamuf, P. (ed.) (1991), *A Derrida Reader: Between the Blinds*, New York: Columbia University Press.
Kearney, R. (1984), *Dialogues with Contemporary Continental Thinkers: The Phenomenological Heritage*, Manchester: Manchester University Press.
Leitch, V.B. (1983), *Deconstructive Criticism: An Advanced Introduction*, New York: Columbia University Press.
Milberg, W. (1988), 'The Language of Economics: Deconstructing the Neoclassical Text', *Social Concept*, **4**, June, 33–57.
Milberg, W. (1991), 'Marxism, Poststructuralism and the Discourse of Economists', *Rethinking Marxism*, **4**, Summer, 93–104.
Norris, C. (1982), *Deconstruction: Theory and Practice*, New York: Methuen.
Norris, C. (1987), *Derrida*, Cambridge, MA: Harvard University Press.
Rossetti, J. (1990), 'Deconstructing Robert Lucas', in W. Samuels (ed.), *Economics as Discourse: An Analysis of the Language of Economists*, Boston: Kluwer.
Rossetti, J. (1992), 'Deconstruction, Rhetoric and Economics', in N. de Marchi (ed.), *Post-Popperian Methodology of Economics: Recovering Practice*, Boston: Kluwer.

Ruccio, D.F. (1991), 'Postmodernism and Economics', *Journal of Post Keynesian Economics*, **13**, Summer, 495–510.
Ruccio, D.F. and J. Amariglio (1994a), 'Keynes, Postmodernism, Uncertainty', in S. Dow and J. Hillard (eds), *Keynes, Knowledge, and Uncertainty*, Cheltenham: Edward Elgar.
Ruccio, D.F. and J. Amariglio (1994b), 'Postmodernism, Marxism and the Critique of Modern Economic Thought', *Rethinking Marxism*, **7**, Fall, 7–35.
Saussure, F. de. (1966), *Course in General Linguistics*, ed. C. Bally and A. Sechehaye, trans. W. Baskin, New York: McGraw-Hill.
Taylor, M. (ed.) (1986), *Deconstruction in Context: Literature and Philosophy*, Chicago: University of Chicago Press.
Williams, R. (1993), 'Race, Deconstruction and the Emergent Agenda of Feminist Economic Theory', in M.A. Ferber and J.A. Nelson (eds), *Beyond Economic Man*, Chicago: University of Chicago Press.

De Gustibus Non Est Disputandum

Economists regularly provide arguments which take the following form: an increase in the price of good x will lead to a decrease in the price of good y; or a decrease in the cost of producing z will result in an increase in the price of factor w. Such arguments focus our attention on observable phenomenon like prices and incomes. But the explanatory power of the economists' arguments rests upon an assumption about a non-observable phenomenon: economists assume that tastes are given. When questioned about the validity of this assumption, economists often respond with the expression, *de gustibus non est disputandum* – there is no accounting for (or disputing over) tastes.

Prior to the ascendancy of neoclassical economics during the early twentieth century, methodological reliance on an assumption about non-observable phenomena did not pose a serious problem. J.S. Mill (1967) articulated the classical economists' perspective succinctly: economic rationality represents a pervasive aspect of human action, the consequences of which may not be exhibited in actual human conduct because of 'disturbing causes'. Among the latter would be changes in tastes resulting from, for example, education and the acquisition of higher quality preferences. Because economic rationality is only one aspect of human action in Mill's formulation, its explanatory power lies in its relationship to other disciplines which focus on non-economic aspects of human action: the explanation of human action requires investigation by all the human sciences.

In the twentieth century, neoclassical economists have attempted to encompass within economics all the sources of its explanatory power in order to sever their relationship with the other human sciences. Two strategic moves were required to become an independent science. First, the range of human action explained by economics needed to be expanded. In this regard, Frank Knight's (1921) and Lionel Robbins' (1932) reinterpretation of Mill – to say that economics is one aspect of human conduct is to say that every type of human action has its economic aspect – was transformed into a research programme to explain every human action in economic terms (for examples, see Becker, 1976). Second, the treatment of economics' essential assumptions had to be reconfigured to render economic explanations independent of other disciplines. The most important reconfiguration of the assumption that tastes and preferences are given has been Stigler and Becker's (1977) 'De Gustibus Non Est Disputandum'.

Consistent with Stigler's (1961) research on the efficient use of information in the formation of knowledge, and Becker's (1976) research on consumption and the efficient allocation of time in household production, their joint article provided neoclassical economics with a methodological strategy for dealing with the potential arbitrariness of the assumption of given tastes. Central to Stigler and Becker's (1977) strategy is a reinterpretation of the economist's assumption about ends: *de gustibus non est disputandum* is reinterpreted to mean that values and preferences are stable over time and across people. In order to show how the reinterpreted assumption expands the realm of economic explanation, Stigler and Becker provide several examples, among them the problem of explaining music appreciation. Differences in musical tastes have been frequently attributed simply to musical exposure: as Alfred Marshall once said, one does not violate the law of diminishing returns when one says that the more people listen to good music, the stronger their taste for it. Stigler and Becker ask us to suspend our allegiance to this way of thinking for a moment in order to consider an alternative way of analysing the relationship between music appreciation and one's exposure to different musical styles.

Following Becker's (1976) new theory of consumer choice, a person is assumed to maximize a utility function that contains produced commodities (for example, 'health', 'social distinction' or 'music appreciation') rather than purchased goods and services. Keeping things simple, we might consider a utility function that depends on two produced commodities: music appreciation (M) and other commodities (Z): $U = U (M, Z)$. M is a product of both the time allocated to music listening (t_m) and the accumulation of training and techniques which are conducive to appreciating the music heard (music capital $= S_m$); that is, $M = M_m(t_m, S_m)$. Increasing either t_m or S_m will lower the marginal cost of M. Assuming that the marginal cost of producing Z remains the same, we can predict that a person's production and consumption of M will increase. The change in M occurs without implying that the person's musical tastes have changed.

To state the result of Stigler and Becker's strategy more generally: better predictions of human behaviour result from explanations which assign explanatory power to the elements of the production function by which people convert goods and services into the commodities which enter into their utility functions, rather than those which depend upon changes in tastes. Equipped with the assumption of stable preferences, economists are mandated to continue doing what they have always done well: searching for changes in prices or incomes that will explain differences or alterations in conduct. In this sense, Stigler and Becker's reinterpretation of *de gustibus non est disputandum* is consistent with, and an extension of, Milton Friedman's (1953) methodological prescription for neoclassical economics: the empirical adequacy of its predictions, rather than its assumptions, is the distinguishing characteristic of a good theory.

Questions remain, however, and they come from two different directions. On one side are economists who wish to investigate the consequences of one's choices upon preference rankings. For these theorists, Stigler and Becker too easily assume away the phenomena they wish to explain. If choices about preferences and values lie beyond consideration, then economics may not be able to contribute to the explanation of a wide variety of human conduct, including irrational (inconsistent) behaviour, exercises of anticipatory self-control and changing preferences. Famous criticisms of the scientific status of the model of economic rationality by Elster (1984), Knight (1921; 1935) and Schelling (1984) suggest that a model based on the assumption that people know what they want fails to capture the exploratory nature of human action: people may be seeking to satisfy their current preference ranking efficiently while simultaneously evaluating the quality of that ranking against their conception of a 'better' ranking (see also Cowen, 1989). If invoking *de gustibus non est disputandum* makes economic agents 'rational fools' (Sen, 1977), what happens to the scientific status of economics? Economics cannot artificially disentangle its explanatory relationship with the other human sciences, but a mutual exploration can provide a richer and more complex characterization of human action.

On the other side, critics such as Alexander Rosenberg (1979; 1980; 1985) argue that, despite appearances, Stigler and Becker's strategy does not make neoclassical economics into an empirical science because economics continues to rely upon the assumed state of non-observables like utility and preferences. According to this line of criticism, Stigler and Becker do not avoid non-observables (they make an assumption about them) and they actually add a new non-observable into the theoretical framework, Becker's 'produced commodities'. Because there is no scientific theory of preferences which provides a means by which we can distinguish their effects or the effects of a change in price, economic theory in either its traditional or Stigler–Becker form is empirically powerless. Rosenberg's conclusion is that a scientific economics needs to strip away its reliance on non-observables in order to become an empirical science.

These criticisms return us to the basic issues which Stigler and Becker's strategy was supposed to address: namely, what is the scientific status of economics and what relationship does economics bear to other sciences in the explanation of human action?

Ross B. Emmett

References

Becker, Gary S. (1976), *The Economic Approach to Human Behavior*, Chicago: University of Chicago Press.
Cowen, Tyler (1989), 'Are All Tastes Constant and Identical?', *Journal of Economic Behavior and Organization*, **11**, 127–35.
Elster, Jon (1984), *Ulysses and the Sirens: Studies in Rationality and Irrationality*, rev. edn, Cambridge: Cambridge University Press.
Friedman, Milton, (1953), 'The Methodology of Positive Economics', *Essays in Positive Economics*, Chicago: University of Chicago Press.
Knight, Frank H. (1921), *Risk, Uncertainty, and Profit*, Boston: Houghton Mifflin.
Knight, Frank H. (1935), 'Ethics and the Economic Interpretation', *The Ethics of Competition and Other Essays*, New York: Harper & Bros.
Mill, J.S. (1967), 'On the Definition of Political Economy; and on the Method of Investigation Proper to It', *Collected Works of John Stuart Mill*, vol. IV: *Essays on Some Unsettled Questions of Political Economy*, ed. J.M. Robson.
Robbins, Lionel (1932), *An Essay on the Nature and Significance of Economic Science*, London: Macmillan.
Rosenberg, Alexander (1979), 'Does Economics Explain Everything?' *Philosophy of the Social Sciences*, **9**, 509–29.
Rosenberg, Alexander (1980), *Sociobiology and the Preemption of Social Science*, Baltimore: Johns Hopkins University Press.
Rosenberg, Alexander (1985), 'Prospects for the Elimination of Tastes from Economics and Ethics', *Social Philosophy and Policy*, **2**, 48–68.
Schelling, Thomas (1984), *Choice and Consequences*, Cambridge, MA: Harvard University Press.
Sen, Amartya (1977), 'Rational Fools: A Critique of the Behavioral Foundations of Economic Theory', *Philosophy and Public Affairs*, **9**, Summer, 317–44.
Stigler, George J. (1961), 'The Economics of Information', *Journal of Political Economy*, **69**, June, 213–25.
Stigler, George J. and Gary S. Becker (1977), 'De Gustibus Non Est Disputandum', *American Economic Review*, **67**, March, 76–90.

Demarcation

The 'problem of demarcation' is the label Karl Popper gave to the 'problem of drawing a line of demarcation between those statements and systems of statements which could be properly described as belonging to empirical science, and others which might, perhaps, be described as "pseudo-scientific"' (Popper, 1963: 255; see also Popper, 1968a). According to him, it is a mistake to confuse this with problems concerning the truth or acceptability of theories. 'My problem', he wrote, 'was different. *I wished to distinguish between science and pseudo-science*' (Popper, 1968b: 91). By pseudo-sciences, Popper usually meant more or less esoteric doctrines like astrology, but he also frequently had in mind theories like Marxism and psychoanalysis, which many others have considered to be scientific.

This question has also been discussed extensively by economists and philosophers of economics, especially those who were preoccupied with the credibility of neoclassical economics in contrast with more heterodox doctrines. While the label 'demarcation' is rarely used, the problem itself is raised when it comes to deciding whether nonclassical economics, which is considered to be 'scientific' by its defenders, should be put on the same footing as Marxism, neoricardianism or institutionalism. Among methodologists of economics, Mark Blaug heralded a position rather sympathetic to Popper's views (Blaug, 1980). Such a position was strongly contested, however, in the following decade (see, for example, Hausman's and Hands' papers in De Marchi, 1988). Others opted straightforwardly for denying the very existence of any criterion of demarcation. Deirdre McCloskey's rhetorical approach, which is inimical to any methodological demarcationism, is probably the most extreme manifestation of this trend. In other contexts not necessarily related to economics, the need to distinguish scientific results from the multitude of theories which freely pretend to be just as reliable as scientific ones (and to be so for the same reasons) periodically awakens argument about the demarcation problem. For example, the debate which has taken place in various parts of the United States about the academic credibility of 'scientific creationism' nurtured considerable discussion about such a problem (cf. Ruse, 1988: part IV).

While Popper is credited with coining the phrase 'demarcation problem', it is important to observe that the history of endeavours to characterize science, or more precisely, to discriminate between what deserves to be called 'science' and other intellectual achievements, goes back to antiquity and to the Aristotelian characterization of science as infallible or apodictic knowledge. This view, like many of Aristotle's other theses, influenced the perception of science until modern times. But, as Larry Laudan has aptly observed, it became clear in the nineteenth century that science was frequently improved and corrected and that, ipso facto, it could no longer be defined by its alleged infallibility (Laudan, 1983: 114–15). The 'scientific method', rather than any specific characteristic of its content, then started to be considered the hallmark of science. However, none of the various attempts to characterize the scientific method has passed the test of being an unequivocal characterization of science. With the twentieth century and the Vienna Circle, the emphasis turned towards a more radical demarcation between scientific statements – whose meaningfulness was associated with their alleged verifiability – and meaningless or metaphysical statements. Thus, it is mainly with the Vienna Circle that the problem of defining a criterion for demarcating scientific statements from ethical, theological, metaphysical or other unverifiable statements has been formalized as a specific philosophical problem.

It was in this context that Popper offered his own solution to the problem. As is well known, this solution was based on the falsifiability (by contrast with the verifiability) of a theory. A scientific theory 'must be able to clash with facts', as Popper liked to say, whereas a metaphysical theory like psychoanalysis, while perfectly meaningful, is typically compatible with any set of facts and, not being precise enough to exclude any of them, cannot be considered to be scientific. Scientific theories, by contrast, *must* be falsifiable (or refutable) and, in this sense, be bold hypotheses which do not leave room for autoprotective ad hoc stratagems. It was to emphasize the revolutionary character of this criterion that Popper coined one of his favourite quasi-paradoxical phrases: 'irrefutability if not a virtue of a theory ... but a vice' (for example, Popper, 1963: 36).

Given such an uncompromising formulation of the problem, it was tempting to construe it as the problem of finding a litmus test for discriminating between science and pseudo-science. More specifically, one could see it as the problem of defining 'a set of individually necessary and jointly sufficient conditions for deciding whether an activity or set of statements is scientific or unscientific' (Laudan, 1983: 188). It is usually acknowledged today that, construed in such a radical way, this problem has no satisfactory solution. Thomas Kuhn's seminal work (Kuhn, 1962) raised serious doubts about the viability of Popper's answer to this question and other philosophers of science have become more and more sceptical about the reliability of any criteria for demarcating science from pseudo-science. In an influential paper, dramatically entitled 'The Demise of the Demarcation Problem', Larry Laudan made use of various counterexamples systematically to argue that there are no criteria which can provide either necessary or sufficient conditions for declaring a theory to be scientific.

Indeed, the problem with such presumed 'litmus tests' for demarcating science from non-science is that it is always possible to find cases where statements acknowledged to be scientific do not satisfy the criteria and cases where blatantly non-scientific statements fully satisfy them. Indeed, Popper's critics have had no trouble showing that falsifiability as such does not rate better than verifiability and other criteria as a solution to the demarcation problem. On the one hand, there are many pseudo-scientific theories, such as astrology, which contain falsifiable (and usually, falsified) statements. On the other hand, some essential parts of the most respected sciences, namely their most central hypotheses, are generally known to be unfalsifiable. Given this, Laudan's emphatic conclusion was that the whole problem is nothing but a 'pseudo-problem' (Laudan, 1983: 124).

But is it really a pseudo-problem? Some of Popper's critics have endeavoured to devise a more satisfactory criterion. For Imre Lakatos, there is no doubt that the hard core of a science is unfalsifiable and that a criterion like Popper's is inapplicable (Lakatos, 1974; see also Lakatos, 1970). However, he does not consider this a reason to jettison the search for a solution to the demarcation problem; rather, he sees in it a reason to look at research programmes as such, rather than at statements, to decide whether they are scientific or not. In such a framework, a criterion somewhat similar to Popper's is ultimately salvaged, since only 'progressive' research programmes – those programmes which tend to increase their true empirical content – can be considered scientific. Incidentally, it is such a Lakatosian solution to the demarcation problem rather than a strictly Popperian one that Mark Blaug has adopted, even though he almost dissolves the very idea of demarcation by reducing it to a 'continuous spectrum' going from physics to poetry with economics somewhere in between (Blaug, 1980:13).

Be that as it may, Lakatos' sophisticated theory was received as a kind of treason by Popper – as was the attempt of W.W. Batley, who emphasized criticizability and rationality rather than sheer falsifiability (Bartley, 1968) – even though Popper admitted that the falsification of a theory *does not* necessarily mean its rejection by scientists (cf. Schilpp, 1974: 250, 1009). But such more 'tolerant' approaches to the demarcation problem were not really successful in satisfying the sceptics, who were able to find other troublesome counterexamples to their claims. After all, many sciences have experienced long periods of relative degeneration, while pseudo-sciences are sometimes progressive. Thus, when Laudan suggested that the demarcation problem should be relegated to the class of pseudo-problems (1983: 124) and even that we should 'drop terms like "pseudo-science" and "unscientific" from our vocabulary' (ibid.: 125), relatively few people objected to such a radical dismantlement of the problem, the solution of which Popper took to be 'the key to most of the fundamental problems of the philosophy of science' (Popper, 1963: 42).

But what are the consequences of dropping terms like 'pseudo-science' and 'unscientific'? Perhaps that, instead of attempting to disqualify incriminated theories as 'unscientific' or as 'pseudo-scientific', we should simply discriminate between 'bad science' and 'good science'. But, if someone is unable to set out the criteria for determining what should be *counted* as a science, how could he or she pretend to be able to assess the *value* of any piece of science? To say that a theory which looks more valuable (more verified, more falsifiable, more progressive or whatever else) than another is a better piece of science is very close to saying that what characterizes a science is the criterion which is adopted to substantiate this claim. In short, it is difficult to drop the terms 'pseudo-science' and 'unscientific' from our vocabulary without also dropping the terms 'science' and 'scientific'. And what about the alternative attitude, which would consist of jettisoning the very notion of science and caring only for the well-groundedness of statements? The question to be raised in this case would concern the basis on which statements would be declared well grounded. But, on the one hand, according to the Duhem–Quine thesis, any criterion concerning the status of scientific statements has to be applied to *sets* of interrelated statements and, on the other hand, when dealing with such sets of interrelated statements, any attempt to specify criteria in the systematic way which is required to avoid ambiguity would reintroduce problems quite similar to those that confront the rejected demarcation problem. Thus the prospects for this alternative do not seem very bright.

However, to conclude that the demarcation problem remains unsolved and possibly unsolvable when construed in a way which requires the search for a 'litmus test' or criterion does not imply that it is a 'pseudo-problem'. Indeed, if we were to drop from our vocabulary every opposing pair of terms the referents of which cannot be separated from one another by specifying necessary and sufficient conditions, it is doubtful that we would be left with a very substantial vocabulary. For example, the problem of distinguishing art from non-art is not considered to be a pseudo-problem, even though the chances of finding necessary and sufficient conditions for singling out artworks are pretty thin. This does not eliminate the significance of a demarcation problem in art (or in science); it rather forces us to construe this problem as one of determining which features are normally characteristic of art (or of science) and of explaining why those features do not amount to unequivocal criteria. The problem is almost unavoidable since practising artists and practising scientists would hardly accept the idea that 'anything goes' in the practice of art or of science. After all, the very arguments which were decisive in rejecting demarcation criteria as satisfactory implied the recognition of some working distinction between science and pseudo-science. Indeed, to show that falsifiability is not an acceptable criterion, Popper's critics have usually underscored that it does not discriminate between *what is known to be science* (typically physics) and *what is known to be pseudo-science* (typically astrology). (See, for example, Laudan, 1983; 121; Lakatos, 1974: 246). Thus those who strongly object to any alleged solution to the demarcation problem do not seem ready to abandon a workable distinction between science and pseudo-science, even though this distinction clearly cannot be regarded as laying down an unequivocal line of demarcation.

In this context, one attractive option has been to forget methodological considerations and turn instead to a purely sociological approach to the demarcation problem. Instead of cultivating unsolvable epistemic questions, why not consider science to be nothing but the activity of those who claim to do science in institutions which are generally associated with science? This approach looks upon any demarcation criterion more as the result of a successful 'negotiation' than as an epistemic norm (Pinch, 1979: 341–3). Transposed into a language more familiar to economists, this approach would solve the demarcation problem by appealing to a 'market for ideas' in which only theories persuasive enough to be 'bought' by the academic community deserve to be called 'scientific'. While such sociological approaches are more pervasive than one would expect, methodological attempts to characterize the kind of ideas which tend to persuade scientific communities (in contrast to those which tend to persuade other communities) still refuse to disappear completely.

Philosophical attempts to stigmatize pseudo-science did not fail to reappear here and there. With or without explicit references to 'demarcation' as such, various other specific characteristics of science (such as progress in the precision of predictions, improbability of successful predictions, systematicness, repeatability and so on) have been invoked in recent decades. Each of these has been extensively debated. Some philosophers have insisted that, instead of a single criterion, a set of interrelated features might have to be invoked on a case-by-case basis to demarcate science from pseudo-science. For example, Andrew Lugg has argued that a careful analysis of their various forms would show that, while they might not be identified with the help of a single criterion, the pseudo-sciences differ from the sciences by being, in one sense or other, either flawed or pointless (Lugg, 1987; 1992).

Thus demarcating science from pseudo-science is an ideal which has been strongly contested during recent decades, but ironically a typical consequence of this contestation has been to force those who consider any kind of laxism about science to be damaging to the very meaning of scientific activity to give a new attention to the question of the nature of science. In this context, philosophers of economics whose views have been challenged by the rhetorical approach could hardly avoid giving a central place in their methodological analyses to the question of the nature and specificity of scientific activity. It seems that, one way or another, the demarcation problem is destined to rise from its own ashes even long after its 'demise'.

MAURICE LAGUEUX

Bibliography

Bartley, W.W. (1968), 'Theories of Demarcation between Science and Metaphysics', in I. Lakatos and A. Musgrave (eds), *Problems in the Philosophy of Science*.
Blaug, Mark (1980), *The Methodology of Economics*, Cambridge: Cambridge University Press.
Cohen, Robert S. and Larry Laudan (eds) (1983), *Physical, Philosophy and Psychoanalysis, Essays in Honor of Adolf Grünbaum*, Dordrecht: D. Reidel.
De Marchi, Neil (1988), *The Popperian Legacy in Economics*, Cambridge: Cambridge University Press.
Kuhn, Thomas (1962), *The Structure of Scientific Revolutions*, Chicago: University of Chicago Press.
Lakatos, Imre (1970), 'Falsification and the Methodology of Scientific Research Programmes', in I. Lakatos and A. Musgrave (eds), *Criticism and the Growth of Knowledge*.
Lakatos, Imre (1974), 'Popper on Demarcation and Induction', in P.A. Schilpp (ed.), *The Philosophy of Karl Popper*.
Lakatos, Imre and Alan Musgrave (eds) (1968), *Problems in the Philosophy of Science*, Proceedings of the International Colloquium in the Philosophy of Science, London, 1965, vol. 3 of *Studies in Logic and the Foundation of Mathematics*, Amsterdam: North-Holland.
Lakatos, Imre and Alan Musgrave (eds) (1970), *Criticism and the Growth of Knowledge*, Cambridge: Cambridge University Press.
Laudan, Larry (1983), 'The Demise of the Demarcation Problem', in R.S. Cohen and L. Laudan (eds), *Physics, Philosophy and Psychoanalysis*.
Lugg, Andrew (1987), 'Bunkum, Flim-Flam and Quackery: Pseudoscience as a Philosophical Problem', *Dialectica*, **41**, 221–30.
Lugg, Andrew (1992), 'Pseudoscience as Nonsense', *Methodology and Science*, **25**, 91–101.
Pinch, Trevor J. (1979), 'Normal Explanations of the Paranormal: The Demarcation Problem and Fraud in Parapsychology', *Social Studies of Science*, **9**, 329–48.
Popper, Karl (1963), *Conjectures and Refutations: The Growth of Scientific Knowledge*, New York: Harper Torchbooks.
Popper Karl (1968a), *The Logic of Scientific Discovery*, New York: Harper Torchbooks.

Popper, Karl (1968b), 'Remarks on the problems of demarcation and of rationality' in I. Lakatos and A. Musgrave (eds), *Problems in the Philosophy of Science*.
Popper Karl (1974), 'Replies to My Critics', in P.A. Schilpp (ed.) *The Philosophy of Karl Popper*.
Ruse, Michael (ed.), (1988), *But Is It Science? The Philosophical Question in the Creation/Evolution Controversy*, Buffalo, NY: Prometheus Books.
Schilpp, Paul Arthur (ed.) (1974), *The Philosophy of Karl Popper*, 2 vols, La Salle, IL: Open Court.

Dewey, John

The American philosopher John Dewey started his career as a Hegelian but gradually, with some help from Charles Peirce, evolved into the leading pragmatist in America. He became well known while at the University of Chicago, both as philosopher and educator, and later while at Columbia gained a reputation as the leading American philosopher. Even during Dewey's heyday, mainstream economists paid little attention to him; in recent times he has been cited, but primarily for the purpose of showing that his pragmatic ideas are unacceptable when viewed within the context of the more fashionable notions of present-day philosophers. (Compare, for example, Blaug, 1980; Machlup, 1978; Caldwell, 1982; Boland, 1982; for a rare instance of a dissenting view, see Hirsch and de Marchi, 1990.)

Institutional or evolutionary economists and methodologists cite Dewey as a source of inspiration for their approach to economics, but Dewey seems to have inspired different members of the group in different ways and it is not easy to determine from their comments the specifics on the way his ideas have contributed to their various approaches to economics. What is true of all of them, however, is that they find Dewey's philosophy generally attractive because it suggests a critique of the mainstream approach. In this critique, and in the more positive suggestions that could be derived from Dewey's basic notions, can be found ideas which are highly relevant for economic methodology.

In his *Logic: The Theory of Inquiry* (1938), John Dewey tells us:

> Classical political economy, with respect to its logical form, claimed to be a science in virtue, first, of certain ultimate first truths, and secondly, in virtue of the possibility of rigorous 'deduction' of actual economic phenomena from these truths. From these 'premises', it followed, in the third place, that the first truths provided the norms of policy activity in the field of economic phenomena; or that actual measures were right or wrong, and actual economic phenomena normal or abnormal, in the degree of their correspondence with deductions made from the systems of conceptions forming the premises ... once arrived at [the premises] were regarded as unquestionable truths, or as axioms with respect to any further truths, since the latter should be deductively derived from them. (Dewey, 1938: 504–5).

Dewey's criticism, succinctly put, is as follows:

> From the standpoint of logical method, the conceptions involved were not regarded as *hypotheses* to be employed in observation and ordering of phenomena, and hence to be tested by the consequences produced by acting upon them. They were regarded as *truths* already established and therefore unquestionable (Ibid., 505)

On the face of it, it is not readily apparent how applying Deweyan logic to economics would make much of a difference. After all, 'verification' is an ingredient of mainstream economic methodology as it is of Dewey's logic. What, then, is the difference? It consists in the way the notion of 'verification' is conceived. In mainstream economic methodology, 'verification' (call it 'verification 2') has little bearing on the validity of a theory. The usual conception of validity (call it 'verification 1'), the process whereby light is shed on the validity of theory, is determined in mainstream methodology before 'verification 2' is done, when axioms (or assumptions) of the theory are chosen.

For example, John Stuart Mill – who better than anyone before or since has reported on how mainstream economists do economics and will therefore be used here to illustrate the mainstream position – argued that 'to verify the hypothesis itself *a posteriori* … is no part of the business of science at all'. Here the term 'verify' is used in the first sense. Mill also argues 'the latter methods [that is, *a posteriori*] is nothwithstanding of great value … not as a means of discovering truth, but of verifying it and reducing to the lowest point [the] uncertainty … arising from the complexity of every particular case' (Mill, 1967: 431). In this instance, of course, Mill is using the term 'verification' in the second sense. The validity of the *theory* Mill was concerned with had already been established. What remained in a practical context was to gauge whether a hypothesis designed for policy purposes could be relied on. It is in *this* sense that 'verification' finds a role in mainstream methodology as it does in mainstream practice.

The 'verification' Dewey is talking about is verification in the first sense. It is not that in this instance Dewey is revealing his pre-Popper naïveté, mistaking verification for falsification, but rather that for him 'verification' is a key part of the inquiry process which connects theorizing at an earlier and a later stage. This kind of verification is anathema in mainstream economic methodology. Thus, even though Mill, again typically here, accepted 'this twofold logical process and reciprocal' for sociology (Mill, 1973, bk 6, ch. 5, s. 6), where acceptable observation is not limited by a tightly formulated model, he rejected it for economics. He did this because 'Such is undoubtedly its character as it has been understood and taught by all its most distinguished teachers' (Mill, 1967: 325). Things have not changed much since, except the gap that has widened considerably between methodology and practice.

It follows from what has been said that observation plays a very different role in Deweyan thinking than it does in the mainstream tradition. In the latter, observation must be constrained by a model resting on plausible premises; it is therefore limited. The kind of extensive observation of specific experience that was done by Wesley Mitchell, for example, or Milton Friedman at the (old) National Bureau, is ruled out. In mainstream methodology it has a considerably more limited rationale. Since such work as was done at the Bureau is as unlikely to create tightly-formulated form models as is mainstream modelling to create models whose implications accord with what happens in the world in any substantive way, it lead to the charge that it is 'facts without theory'. 'Theory' in this sense does not apply to formulations whose implications accord with what actually happens, but rather refers to formal models which are either an end in themselves or are used to find 'disturbing causes' (illustrated by Mill, 1967: 330) in the data of experience, for the purpose of making the theory practically useful. Data are fitted to the theory; theory is not fitted to the data but is prior to them.

The rationale of Dewey's logic is different. It encourages extensive observation, using whatever theoretical frameworks are available or seem to be called for by the observations. Such extensive observation is considered desirable in this way of thinking because Dewey encouraged reasoning from observed facts to formulated theoretical concepts (and thence to further observation) for economics as for other disciplines. In mainstream economic methodology, and even more in actual practice, very extensive observation is ruled out – as Mill put it (Mill, 1967: 329) and is still embedded in the mainstream way of thinking – because of the belief that 'sufficiently ample grounds are not afforded [in economics] for a satisfactory induction by a comparison of the effects'; one must instead try *first* to discover true causes. Since economic phenomena 'do *mainly* depend, at least in the first resort, on one class of circumstances' (that is, the economic motive) (Mill, 1973, bk 6, ch. 9, s. 3), and we know what this motive is from introspection, we do not need any extensive observation to discover the cause. If the search for truth in economics involves any observation, it is primarily at the periphery of the science. For example, in the mainstream view, to be an excellent professor of economics, as Mill here again so well put it (Mill, 1967: 333), does not require one to have undertaken detailed investigations of what goes on in real economies.

From what has been said, it may appear that an economist with a Deweyan orientation would have to jettison the mainstream contribution and begin afresh. Some institutional or evolutionary economists who appeal to Dewey have in fact made such a recommendation, though different institutionalists seem to have had different conceptions of Dewey's philosophy and some have been ambivalent, supporting revolution in one place and counselling moderation in another. Actually, Dewey himself was rather moderate in his recommendations. He observes:

> A strong case might be made out for the position that if [mainstream economic theory] had been framed and interpreted on the ground of applicability to existing conditions under specific spatio–temporal conditions ... they were to a considerable extent directive operational hypotheses relevant to those historical conditions. (Dewey, 1938: 506)

But then what relevance does Dewey have for economics? One way Dewey can be useful is in bringing to the fore the *a priori/a posteriori* issue which comes up through the ages (illustrated again very well by Mill (1967: 324). What has hampered meaningful discussion of this issue is that apriorists generally give a distorted picture of aposteriorism and those inclined in an aprioristic direction have not done very much to make a case. Dewey can help us to see the shortcomings in the aposteriorist picture as formulated by apriorists (the methodologists of the traditional approach) as well as to formulate the rationale of aposteriorism in a way which makes sense even to those who are not disciples of aposteriorism. The questions that arise in such discussion are interesting and significant and can help make more meaningful the arguments that often arise in economic discussion (such as Keynesianism v. monetarism).

Another way Dewey can be useful is in helping us to focus on aspects of the formulations of the more insightful mainstream methodologists which are generally overlooked because they are near its outer edges. Again using Mill as an example, we note that in his *Logic* (bk 6, ch. 9, s. 3) Mill gives as a major argument that it is necessary in economics to formulate a model of narrow economic behaviour *a priori* because this task is so difficult that it would be disruptive to keep stopping in the course of research to work out bits and pieces of it necessary in working on particular problems. But this makes economic science, when limited to this task, not only a *separate* science, as has been observed (Hausman, 1992), but also, in a more important sense, a *preliminary* or *incomplete* one. To go beyond this preliminary stage and thereby make full contact with the real world, it is necessary, as was admitted by Mill (*Logic*, bk 6, ch. 9, s. 4; 1967), again typically, to call in the sociologist in order to add non-economic motives to the analysis. It is further necessary, in any serious practical inquiry, to call on the 'practical man', a figure considered by Mill, as he is still today, especially by the theoretically minded, to be unscientific in his attitude towards inquiry, but who has a great deal of knowledge about the details of specific economic experience.

If we stop to ponder the implications of all of this, a process which Deweyan thinking suggests that we do, it is difficult to avoid the conclusion that the methodology of economic science as conceived by mainstream methodologists, which concentrates on the logic of narrowly focused economic behaviour, is far too narrow. How can it be broadened? If, as Mill, a good guide here again, suggests, we call in the sociologist and the 'practical man', the approach of both of which is very different from that of mainstream economic science methodology, we need a logic which makes their work meaningful for our purposes. Ideas developed by Dewey might be helpful in this regard.

What has been said suggests still another way in which Dewey's ideas can be helpful. In the field of economics, one finds research programmes the results of which are generally taken to be of value in the profession but whose rationale radically violates the tenants of mainstream methodology. Such, for example, is the work of Wesley Mitchell and members of the (old) National Bureau of Economic Research, including Milton Friedman, whose most important work falls within this research programme. (The attempt is made, in Hirsch and de Marchi (1990), to use Dewey to try to understand the non-mainstream 'facts without theory' aspects of Friedman's work.) To this might be added the work of researchers today (a research programme discussed in Simpkins, 1994; cf. also Hoover, 1994), who are attempting to carry on work in business cycles and macroeconomics in a spirit related to that of the (old) National Bureau. This presents us with something of a problem in economic methodology. How, for example, are we to understand the place of someone like Milton Friedman, winner of every mainstream honour, the rationale of whose work is characterized by leaders of the profession as unacceptable in basic conception because it is 'facts without theory' (Hammond, 1996)? This problem is, or should be, troubling to anyone who wishes to understand what economists do and why they do it. Dewey can help us to understand the nature of this problem. (For an example of such analysis, see Hirsch and de Marchi, 1990).

ABRAHAM HIRSCH

Bibliography
Blaug, Mark (1980), *The Methodology of Economics*, Cambridge: Cambridge University Press.
Boland, Lawrence A. (1982), *The Foundations of Economic Method*, London: Allen & Unwin.
Caldwell, Bruce J. (1982), *Beyond Positivism: Economic Methodology in the Twentieth Century*, London: Allen & Unwin.
Dewey, John (1938), *Logic: The Theory of Inquiry*, New York; Henry Holt.
Hausman, Daniel M. (1992), *The Inexact and Separate Science of Economics*, Cambridge: Cambridge University Press.
Hirsch, Abraham and Neil de Marchi (1990), *Milton Friedman: Economics in Theory and Practice*, Ann Arbor: University of Michigan Press.
Hoover, Kevin D. (1994), 'Econometrics as Observation: The Lucas Critique and the Nature of Econometric Inference', *The Journal of Economics Methodology*, June
Machlup, Fritz (1978), *Metholdogy of Economic and Other Social Science*, New York: Academic Press.
Mill, John Stuart (1967), *Essays on Economy and Society, Collected Works*, vol 4, Toronto: University of Toronto Press.
Mill, John Stuart (1973), *A System of Logic Ratiocinative and Inductive, The Collected Works*, ed. J.M. Robson, Toronto: University of Toronto Press.
Simpkin, Scott (1995), 'The Rebirth of Empiricism in Macroeconomics', a revised version of a paper delivered at the Southern Economic Association meetings in November (mimeo).

Dialectical Method

Of the main philosophical traditions, the dialectical has been only modestly influential in the economics methodology. With few exceptions, the applications of dialectics to economics are restricted to scholars that have in some way been influenced by the work of Marx (1818–83).

There is, however, no *a priori* reason why a dialectical method should be restricted to a Marxian orientation.

The dialectical method, in the modern sense, derives from the work of Hegel (1770–1831) who aimed at critically synthesizing rationalism and empiricism. Both rationalism and empiricism conceive the world in terms of a subject–object or thought–reality dualism, and both reduce the foundation of knowledge to one of these poles. Hegel's project was to transcend the one-sidedness of these philosophies; that is, to overcome them without losing sight of them. This aim Hegel shares with Kant (1724–1804). However, the latter's philosophy is considered insufficient, in that it does not overcome dualism: it separates the form from the content of knowledge, it poses a conceptual apriorism and it postulates a 'thing in itself' which we cannot know.

Today, dialectics is in fact a family name for a variety of strands, as are rationalism and empiricism. Two main strands are *historical dialectic* and *systematic dialectic*. The first applies to the study of society and its philosophy, arts and science – or, more specifically, an economy and its economics – in their historical emergence. Popular accounts of dialectics often stress this first strand, owing to the two circumstances that Marx is often introduced by way of an historical materialist view of society (see entry, 'Marx's Method'), and Hegel by way of his work on the philosophy of history (Hegel, 1837). (Note that this dialectic also figures prominently in Popper's depiction of Hegel and Marx.) In what follows I emphasize the systematic dialectics. The primary sources for this dialectic are Hegel's two works on logic (see particularly Hegel, 1817). Below I merely highlight a few elements of it in so far as they relate to some of the problems that face the mainstream philosophy of economics.

I start by outlining an economic example, so as to bring to the fore some of the issues that systematic dialectics aims to deal with. Consider a simple model of investment (I), which is dependent on consumption (C), the money supply (M) and government expenditure on education (G). So we have $I = aC + bM + cG$. Suppose that the model is made operational, and particular values for the parameters a, b and c are estimated. A relevant question would then be: are these variables equally 'important'? In the usual economic models approach this would be answered by pointing out their *quantitative* difference, by the size of the variables times their parameters. But a prior question is: can a *qualitative* order of significance be assigned to these variables? Then at least one such ascription would be in terms of their *necessity* or their *contingency* with respect to the economic system that we are theorizing. Suppose that qualitative analysis has shown that both consumption and banking are necessary to investment – that is, they are a condition of the existence of investment – whereas we could still have investment without government expenditure on education. Then the latter's qualitative importance would not be reflected in its quantitative significance. Although the government expenditure may thus quantitatively codetermine the level of investment, the question would be: to what extent does this determine the *concept* of investment – that is, what investment *is* conceived as something that is systematically interconnected with other phenomena?

Although these and similar questions seem very relevant to our theorizing as regards the economy and society, they appear difficult to answer within the discourse of a mainstream economics framework. The main problem is that, in contradistinction to systematic dialectics, it lacks a systemic hierarchy of determinations. More specifically, first, it lacks systematically related conceptual layers or levels of abstraction: once defined within an argument, a concept retains its meaning – it is fixed and cannot be developed (although concepts may change over the history of a discourse). For the dialectician, on the other hand, definitions are merely useful as an initial starting point; processes of reconceptualization are the kernel of a dialectical argument. Second, it lacks the notion of a system as determined by interconnected *necessary* entities, as opposed to merely contingent aspects, that is, necessary to the very existence of the system as a self-reproducing entity as a whole. Indeed, one aim of dialectical research is to differentiate the necessary from the contingent. Here the notions of 'system' and 'whole' depend much on our perspective. While the aim is to widen the perspective from all possible angles – that is, those necessary to the object of inquiry – we may still want to restrict the analysis *pro tempore* to more narrow points of view (the jargon for which is 'a moment'), as long as we are *explicitly* aware of the ties of these to greater wholes. (Cf. Ollman, 1993.)

In general, a systematic dialectical presentation (*Darstellung*) can be characterized as a movement from an abstract–universal starting point to the concrete–empirical, gradually concretizing the starting point in successive stages, thus ultimately aiming to grasp the empirical phenomena in their systemic interconnectedness. We cannot fruitfully proceed from the starting point by immediately subsuming single empirical phenomena – things, human relations, processes and so on – as particulars under this universal since this provides merely empty truth. Such subsumption might indicate what these phenomena have in common, but not what, if anything, *unites* them systemically: how they are interconnected. Further, it is the *difference* between phenomena which determines them; but this difference also fails to say what, if anything, unites them systemically. As long as we have not specified both differentiation and unification of related phenomena, we have provided no concrete determination. It is this double determination (*difference in unity*) that systematic dialectics seeks. As Hegel expresses it, 'The truth of the differentiated is its being in unity. And only through this movement is the unity truly concrete.' At the starting point: 'difference is still sunk in the unity, not yet set forth as different' (Hegel, 1833: 83). I will briefly expand on the starting point and the way to proceed from it.

For any dialectical presentation the starting point, or point of entry, is crucial (as it is for any theory). The starting point of its presentation is a universal, all-embracing abstract concept which is proposed as rendering the comprehension of the object totality (in Hegel's *Logic*, the ubiquitous starting point is 'being'). Such an all-embracing concept seems in a way hopelessly true (everything is a being). So why seek more when we have the all-embracing concept in our hand? Notwithstanding that we have posited a putatively all-embracing concept, we clearly need to seek more concrete content.

Further reflection reveals that such a concept does not represent the truth in its full, mundane richness. Remaining at the same all-embracing *level* of abstraction ('flatly', as in a conventional economic model), the category from which we started is seen to contain its *negation* or its opposite, a category contrary to it ('nothing' at the beginning of Hegel's *Logic*). But this differing contrast is equally hopelessly omnipotent and true: insufficient. This apparent negative result may have a positive outcome if we find a category uniting as well as concretizing both of our earlier concepts ('becoming' at the beginning of Hegel's *Logic*).

In either case (negation and concretization) opposed concepts are applied to the *same* entity, and in this specific sense Hegel calls these opposites 'contradictions'. It is the purpose of the dialectical presentation to resolve the contradiction (opposition) from which we start ('the essence of philosophy consists precisely in resolving the contradiction of the Understanding': Hegel, 1833: 71).

Next to the differentiation of the systemically necessary from the contingent, negation and concretization are two important principles that drive the dialectical presentation forward towards ever more empirically concrete levels so as to arrive at the concrete comprehension of the object of inquiry. Thus the presentation moves forward by the transcendence of contradiction and by providing the ever more concrete *grounds* – the conditions of existence – of the earlier determination. This forward movement does not ignore the earlier determination, rather, it overcomes the opposite moments (identity–difference, universal–particular) of the earlier determination, so as to posit them at a conceptually more concrete level: the ground provides the unity of the opposed moments. But, at the same time, that is a further, more concrete determination of the *difference*, a difference previously posited only in itself (*an sich*, potentially, implicitly) as it now appears. So the differences that were previously not set forth as such now come into existence (that is, a more concrete existence, yet still abstract in the sense of not being fully developed). The ground at this new level itself then gains momentum; it is itself an abstract existent showing the contradiction that it cannot exist for itself (*für sich*, actually), whence the presentation has to move on in order to ground it in its turn, so as to provide *its* conditions of existence (Hegel, 1817: ss. 120–24; 1833: 81–3). And so on, until the presentation claims to have reached the stage where it comprehends the existent as actual, as actuality (*Wirklichkeit*), in the sense that its conditions of existence have now been determined such that it is indeed actual, concrete, self-sufficient or endogenous existence, which requires no external or exogenous determinants for its systemic reproduction. (Note that, in many mainstream economic models, some of the essential determinants are treated as exogenous.)

By having reconstituted the empirical 'facts' which were at the base of the initial inquiry, the dialectical presentation then is a conceptualization of the concrete in successive steps (levels of abstraction) ultimately gaining full comprehension. If successful, the presentation is able to grasp the concrete as an interconnected self-sufficient system (and ideally it is also a self-determining system).

Returning to our earlier economic model example, one category of mainstream economic models ('rationalist') is indeed devised for conceptual exploration. However, the aim here is the exploration of the implications of (axiomatic) definitions: they are not devised for an internal conceptually layered *development*, even less so in the perspective of systemic necessity (interconnection) or contingency. The other category of models ('empirical') is generally not devised to set up an empirically concrete self-sufficient system. The 'endogeneity' or the 'exogeneity' of variables does not pertain to their systemic necessity or contingency.

This article ends with a few remarks on a controversial issue: Hegel's idealism (see for example, Norman, 1976: ch. 6; Forster, 1993). It was said at the beginning of this article that Hegel's dialectic aims to transcend the subject–object dualism of both rationalism and empiricism. Dualisms and oppositions, consequently, play a major role in his dialectic. Hegel often refers to dualisms and oppositions in terms of contradictions. From the point of view of mainstream methodology (rationalist or empiricist), it is tempting either to see Hegel advancing a rationalist logic or to see him describing oppositions in empirical reality.

From the point of view of rationalism, it is the interdependence of opposed concepts (such as buyer and seller, or truth and error) that is highlighted: they necessarily form a unity in the sense that one concept can have no existence without the other (the concept of buyer just by itself would then be a contradiction). From the point of view of empiricism, real entities in conflict are characterized by interdependent opposed concepts (master–slave, bourgeoisie–proletariat); again, the one entity can have no real existence without the other (when there are no subjects, there are no kings). Even if (one of) these two senses of opposition may make sense to many, Hegel holds that the two can be shown to be the same: the activity of consciousness posits the object of knowledge *as* an object of knowledge. Since he develops this insight from the Idea as a union of subjectivity and objectivity, his philosophy is termed 'Absolute Idealism'.

GEERT REUTEN

Reader's guide

Hegel (1817) is the primary source for systematic dialectics: most difficult, yet most fruitful. Hegel (1812) covers the same structure in more detail. Hegel (1833) is a somewhat easier primary source; pages 53–86 of the English translation provide a nice gist of Hegel's logic.

Norman (1976) provides a lucid critical introduction to Hegel's thought in 125 pages (recommended). Forster (1993) introduces Hegel's method in 40 pages. Ollman (1993) is a lucid account of how the dialectical method may be deployed in practice, first at an introductory and then at a more advanced level. The book finishes with a number of illuminating case studies. Reuten and Williams (1989) Part One, pp. 3–49, sets out a systematic dialectical method; the other parts apply this to the capitalist economy, state and economic policy. Smith (1990) provides a systematic dialectical account of Marx's *Capital*; Chapter 1 gives a good outline of Hegel's dialectical method; Chapter 3 sets out Hegelian, objections to Marx's *Capital*.

References

Forster, Michael (1993), 'Hegel's dialectical method', in F.C. Beiser (ed.), *The Cambridge Companion to Hegel*, Cambridge: Cambridge University Press.

Hegel, G.W.F. (1812), *Wissenschaft der Logik*, Engl. transl. (1969) of the 1923 Lasson edition, A.V. Miller, *Hegel's Science of Logic*, Atlantic Highlands, NJ: Humanities Press, 1989.

Hegel, G.W.F. (1817), *Enzyklopädie der Philosophischen Wissenschaften im Grundrisse 1, Die Wissenschaft der Logik*, Engl. transl. of the third edition (of 1830), T.F. Geraets, W.A. Suchting and H.S. Harris, *The Encyclopaedia of Logic*, Indianapolis/Cambridge: Hackett Publishing Company, 1991.

Hegel, G.W.F. (1833), *Einleitung in die Geschichte der Philosophie* ed. J. Hoffmeister, 1940; Engl. transl. T.M. Knox and A.V. Miller *Introduction to the Lectures on the History of Philosophy*, Oxford: Clarendon Press, 1985.

Hegel, G.W.F. (1837), *Vorlesungen über die Philosophie der Geschichte*, 3rd edn, ed. J. Hoffmeister, 1955; Engl. transl. selections, H.B. Nisbet (1975), *Lectures on the Philosophy of World History, Introduction: Reason in History*, Cambridge: Cambridge University Press, 1984.

Norman, Richard (1976), *Hegel's Phenomenology; A philosophical introduction*, Atlantic Highlands, NJ/Brighton: Humanities Press/Harvester Press.

Ollman, Bertil (1993), *Dialectical Investigations*, London/New York: Routledge.

Reuten, Geert and Michael Williams (1989), *Value-Form and the State*, London/New York: Routledge.

Smith, Tony (1990), *The Logic of Marx's Capital; Replies to Hegelian Criticisms*, Albany: State University of New York Press.

Duhem–Quine Thesis, The

This thesis refers to a set of ideas that have been associated with the French physicist and historian of science, Pierre Duhem, and the American philosopher, Willard Van Orman Quine. At the core of the thesis are two related ideas that can be attributed to both Duhem and Quine: *non-separability*, meaning that the empirical claims of hypotheses arise from conjunctions of hypotheses and background knowledge rather than from individual hypotheses taken in isolation; and *unfocused refutation*, in the sense that anomalous empirical evidence implies falsity somewhere in the conjunction of hypotheses and background knowledge under consideration, rather than necessarily implying that any particular hypothesis is false.

A stronger version of the thesis, to be found in Quine (1953) but not in Duhem, is often distinguished. This can be described as *tenacity*: 'any statement can be held true come what may, if we make drastic enough adjustments elsewhere in the system' (Quine, 1953: 43). Grünbaum (1960) pointed out that this strong version of the thesis is invalid: it cannot be guaranteed that a non-trivial revision of auxiliary hypotheses will reconcile a particular target hypothesis with otherwise anomalous empirical evidence. This strong version of the thesis is not to be found in Quine's later restatements of his position (Quine, 1980: viii).

Other ideas which have been attributed, spuriously, to the Duhem–Quine thesis include *under-determination* and *relativism*. Underdetermination is the notion that 'there are in principle always an indefinite number of theories that fit the observed facts more or less adequately' (Hesse, 1980: viii). This is a logical possibility, but only in the sense that trivially different versions of the same theories could be invented. More pertinently, the history of science has not been characterized by indefinitely large numbers of rival theories. The related idea of relativism is that social factors need to be invoked to explain why scientists adopt particular theories (Bloor, 1981, for example). This claim is not evident in Duhem or Quine, and does not necessarily follow from the ideas of non-separability and unfocused refutation which are at the core of the Duhem–Quine thesis.

Duhem
An early statement of the thesis can be found in Duhem (1892), though the classic text is Duhem's *La Théorie Physique: Son Objet, Sa Structure* (1906, 2nd edn 1914), the English translation of which appeared in 1954 as *The Aim and Structure of Physical Theory*. The core notion of *non-separability*, and an extended discussion of how physicists can proceed in the face of the *unfocused* nature of tests of their individual hypotheses, are both contained in Duhem's text. Most of the objections raised against what has come to be known as the Duhem–Quine thesis do not apply to Duhem's original thesis. The subsequent confusion could have been avoided if an English language translation of Dubem's text had been available earlier. Instead, British and American philosophers tended to be exposed to the extended or stronger variant of Duhem's thesis expressed in Quine's (1951) essay, 'Two Dogmas of Empiricism', reprinted in Quine's *From a Logical Point of View* (1953). This essay contains just one reference to Duhem (1914: 303–28), backed by a reference to Lowinger's (1941) account of Duhem's methodological position (Quine, 1953: 41). Ironically enough, given the subsequent confusion, Quine's reference to Duhem involves only the notion of *non-separability*: 'our statements about the external world face the tribunal of sense experience not individually but only as a corporate body' (Quine 1953: 41).

Duhem's concern in *The Aim and Structure of Physical Theory* was to establish that the Newtonian method, whereby 'in a sound physics every proposition should be drawn from phenomena and generalised by induction' (Duhem, 1954: 191), did not provide a tenable account of contemporary physics (see Ariew, 1984). Instead, an experiment in physics consists of 'precise observation of phenomena accompanied by an *interpretation* of these phenomena; this interpretation substitutes for the concrete data really gathered by observation abstract and symbolic representations which correspond to them by virtue of the theories admitted by the observer' (Duhem, 1954: 147). This means that 'the prediction of the phenomenon ... does not derive from the proposition challenged if taken by itself, but from the proposition at issue joined to that whole group of theories ... if the predicted phenomenon is not produced, not only is the proposition questioned at fault, but so is the whole theoretical scaffolding used by the physicist' (ibid.: 185).

This reasoning yields the Duhem or Duhem–Quine thesis: 'the physicist can never subject an isolated hypothesis to experimental test, but only a whole group of hypotheses: when the experiment is in disagreement with his predictions, what he learns is that at least one of the hypotheses constituting this group is unacceptable and ought to be modified: but the experiment does not designate which one should be changed' (ibid.: 187).

Quine

The marriage of Duhem to Quine to form a thesis sprang from Quine's reference to Duhem in his 'Two Dogmas of Empiricism'. The two dogmas in question were the *analytic–synthetic* distinction between statements grounded independently of matters of fact, and those grounded in fact; and *reductionism*, 'the belief that each meaningful statement is equivalent to some logical construct upon terms which refer to immediate experience' (Quine, 1980: 20).

The two dogmas, which are 'at root identical' (ibid.: 41), are debunked using a field of force metaphor that involves a stronger, extended version of Duhem's account of *non-separability*:

> total science is like a field of force whose boundary conditions are experience … a conflict with experience at the periphery occasions readjustments in the interior of the field … the total is so undetermined by its boundary conditions, experience, that there is much latitude of choice as to what statements to re-evaluate in the light of any single contrary experience …no particular experiences are linked with any particular statements in the interior of the field, except indirectly.' (Ibid.: 43).

Quine has subsequently dissociated himself from this extreme version of holism: 'all we really need in the way of holism … is to appreciate that empirical content is shared by the statements of science in clusters and cannot for the most part be sorted out among them … practically the relevant cluster is indeed never the whole of science … there is a grading off' (ibid.: viii).

Challenges

Various attempts have been made to challenge the Duhem–Quine thesis, but the challenges have succeeded only against extended or stronger versions of the thesis that go beyond the notions of non-separability and unfocused refutation which lie at the core of the thesis. Popper's challenges are instructive in this respect. A first argument (Popper, 1963: 238) is that, in axiomatized systems, counter examples can be found that satisfy all of the axioms except one, therefore serving to refute the axiom thus isolated: this point fails because Duhem is not referring to purely axiomatic systems, but to scientific theories in which theories are linked, in some way, to observational evidence.

A second challenge (ibid.: 239) is that scientists can take background knowledge and auxiliary assumptions as given, and regard anomalous evidence as refuting one or other of the hypotheses which are the targets for testing: this fails because the 'refutation' would still remain inconclusive in that the fault may lie in the background knowledge or auxiliary hypotheses taken as given (see Duhem, 1954: 216–18).

A third challenge (Popper, 1963: 242) is that scientists do invoke good reasons for changing specific components of their theoretical systems when confronted by refutations: this is not denied by the Duhem–Quine thesis, but 'these reasons of good sense do not impose themselves with the same implacable rigour that the prescriptions of logic do … there is something vague and uncertain about them … they do not reveal themselves at the same time and with the same degree of clarity to all minds … hence the possibility of lengthy quarrels between the adherents of an old system and the partisans of a new doctrine' (Duhem, 1954: 217).

Illustration

An obvious example of the Duhem–Quine thesis at work arises in fishing. The person fishing has to choose a type of fly or lure, a strength and colour of fishing line, a depth and location at which to fish, and so on. The choices made, for any particular cast, are *non-separable*. If a fish is not caught, the lack of success is *unfocused*, in the sense that it could, in principle, be any of the choices made that was inappropriate.

Similarly, testing any particular hypothesis in economics against the evidence requires the invocation of a substantial number of supportive hypotheses. Testing the hypothesis of stability in the demand for money, for example, requires the employment of auxiliary hypotheses which specify the variables affecting the demand for money, say how these variables are determined, specify how the supply of money is generated, say how to measure money and the other variables, specify the functional forms and time lag structures involved, and so on (see Cross, 1982). In any particular test, the target and auxiliary hypotheses are *non-separable*, so in the event of money holdings being significantly different from the levels expected on the basis of the theory the refutation is *unfocused*: it could be the target hypothesis of stability or one or more of the auxiliary hypotheses that are to blame for the refutation. In such circumstances, there can be 'reasons of good sense', as Duhem argued, for changing particular components of the theory, but there is 'something vague and uncertain about them – hence the possibility of lengthy quarrels'.

ROD CROSS

References

Ariew, R. (1984), 'The Duhem Thesis', *British Journal of the Philosophy of Science*, **35**, 313–25.
Bloor, D. (1981), 'The Strengths of the Strong Programme', *Philosophy and Social Criticism*, **11**, 199–213.
Cross, R. (1982), 'The Duhem–Quine Thesis, Lakatos and the Appraisal of Theories in Macroeconomics', *Economic Journal*, **92**, 320–40.
Duhem, P. (1892), 'Quelques Réflexions au Subjet des Théories Physiques', *Revue des Questions Scientifiques*, 2nd series, (1), 139–77.
Duhem. P. (1906), *La Théorie Physique: Son Objet. Sa Structure*, Paris: Marcel Rivière and Cie, 2nd edn 1914.
Duhem, P. (1954), *The Aim and Structure of Physical Theory*, translation of Duhem (1914), Princeton: Princeton University Press.
Grünbaum, A. (1960), 'The Duhemian Argument', *Philosophy of Science*, **27**, 75–87.
Harding, S.G. (ed.) (1976), *Can Theories be Refuted?*, Dordrecht: Reidel.
Hesse, M. (1980), *Revolutions and Reconstructions in the Philosophy of Science*, Bloomington, IN: Indiana University Press.
Lowinger, A. (1941), *The Methodology of Pierre Duhem*, New York: Columbia University Press.
Popper, K. (1963), *Conjectures and Refutations*, London: Routledge & Kegan Paul.
Quine, W.V.O. (1951), 'Two Dogmas of Empiricism', *Philosophical Review*, January; reprinted in Quine (1953).
Quine, W.V.O. (1953), *From a Logical Point of View*, Cambridge, MA: Harvard University Press, 2nd rev. edn 1980.

Econometric Methodology

As the new century approaches, econometric methodology has become as diverse as the contexts in which it is applied and the purposes for which it is used. This was not the case even 20 years ago, and indeed will not even now be appreciated by the novice econometrician sitting through a standard graduate econometrics programme. These programmes, like the textbooks they follow, are almost invariably based upon a particular paradigm, which we will refer to as *standard econometrics*, which became accepted in the 1950s and 1960s as 'the way to do econometrics'.

The fundamental tool in standard econometrics is the linear single equation regression $y = X\beta + u$. Here β is a set of constants (the coefficients) to be estimated. A set of well-known assumptions about the regressor variables X and the disturbance term u guarantee that the ordinary least squares (OLS) estimator b of β will be best linear unbiased (BLU). Critical among these assumptions is that the disturbances are mutually (and therefore, in time series applications, serially) independent. Weaker but more reasonable assumptions, which nevertheless require independence, ensure consistency and asymptotic efficiency of b but leave its finite sample properties unclear. More generally, when the regressor variables are such as will not sustain even this weaker set of assumptions, estimation is by two stage least squares (TSLS), justified as the asymptotically efficient instrumental variables (IV) estimator.

In the standard econometrics paradigm, the *structure* reflected in the equation $y = X\beta + u$ is taken as known. Hypothesis testing is relative to this structure (in the linear case, tests of the form $H_0: R\beta = r$) but the structure itself cannot be questioned. Equivalently, only those hypotheses nested within the maintained hypothesis $y = X\beta + u$ may be tested. It is standard practice to report equation diagnostics: the R^2 measure of fit, in time series data the Durbin–Watson residual serial correlation test, and perhaps also more general serial correlation, heteroscedasticity and functional form tests. Rejection of serial independence forces re-estimation using an autoregressive least squares (ALS) procedure, of which the Cochrane-Orcutt (CORC) procedure is the best known. This is the pathology of the regression model: equation diagnostics indicate the presence of a disease (residual serial correlation and so on), the symptoms of which are inefficiency and biased inference (in extreme cases, inconsistency) and for which the prescribed treatment is substitution of a more appropriate estimator.

The premise which underlies this approach is that of a known structure. This has the implication that the econometrician is solely concerned with quantification. As with theories in all other sciences, economic theories specify *ceteris paribus* or boundary conditions. Because economic data are predominantly non-experimental, these conditions will not hold in the data. In certain instances, perhaps in microeconometric applications using large data-sets, it may be possible to control adequately for these factors by including a large set of additional regressors relating to individual (firm or household) characteristics. In other instances, perhaps certain theories in finance, the effects of non-controlled factors may be negligibly small relative to those specified by the theory. In these cases, econometricians continue to play traditional games, elaborating estimators to deal with departures from the standard assumptions (non-randomness of the sample in microeconometrics, more general distributional assumptions in finance). But elsewhere the starting point of a known and constant model was found untenable, in particular as faith in the old Keynesian certainties diminished, and in response to the Lucas Critique, which suggested that macroeconomic relationships would mutate under the influence of policy (Lucas, 1976).

Of course, many macroeconometricians have pressed on regardless, asking their readers to suspend disbelief. To do econometrics in this way is to use data to *illustrate* the theory, very much as calibration is used in general equilibrium modelling. If the reader believes the author's model, these are the numbers she must use to turn it into a description of the US economy over the specified sample period. Otherwise, there are two possible responses. The first is to remain within a structural framework but to expand the econometrician's task to that of simultaneously searching for the appropriate structure and quantifying it, while the second is to abandon structural pretensions, reverting to a model of sufficient generality to embrace all reasonable structures.

The search problem in macroeconometrics consists of selecting a subset of variables and lag lengths for inclusion in a linear regression estimated on a relatively small number of observations (40–100 is typical). However, this will generally allow so many possibilities that exhaustive search will be practically impossible. It is therefore quite likely that different investigators will arrive at different final specifications even if they share the same objective. Even more problematic is the fact that, since any investigator's final specification has been selected on the basis of fit, good fit can no longer be claimed as evidence for the plausibility of the model. If the selection criteria further include high, 'correctly-signed' t statistics, then those statistics cannot be used to test hypotheses. Indeed, all standard inferences are invalidated since we now need to consider any test statistic as conditioned on exactly this specification being selected. This is the so-called 'pre-test problem' (Judge and Bock, 1978).

Ed Leamer highlighted the role of specification search in econometric practice (Leamer, 1978, 1983). He viewed the combination of iterative estimation and specification search in conjunction with classical statistical methodology as arbitrary and as yielding invalid inferences. He proposed *extreme bounds analysis* (EBA) as a means of circumventing these difficulties. EBA replaces point coefficient estimates with ranges defined by the maximum and minimum estimates across specifications. This runs into the objection that absurdly extreme bounds can be generated by specifications that would be clearly rejected within the standard paradigm (McAleer *et al.*, 1985).

In practice, Leamer's advocacy of an explicitly Bayesian approach has won greater support, particularly in North America (Leamer, 1986; Zellner, 1988). The econometrician specifies her prior distribution over the joint density of a complete list of parameters unconstrained by paucity of degrees of freedom. Confrontation with the data modulates this into the posterior distribution. In practice, this is equivalent to supposing a degree of presample information (Qin, 1996). Valid inference is re-established but the search is now introspective and pre-sample. A major non-Bayesian worry is that this procedure does not allow the possibility of the data suggesting radically different alternatives from those anticipated in the prior. However, acknowledging that at least at an informal level we are all Bayesian, there is merit in formalizing these intuitions in those situations in which theory and data are insufficient to tie down relationships.

An alternative, searching, methodology has been developed by a school of British econometricians under the influence of Denis Sargan. David Hendry is the best-known expositor of this approach which is often characterized as *general-to-simple* (GtoS) modelling (Sargan, 1980; Gilbert, 1986; Hendry, 1994). In this approach, one starts with a very general specification, limited only by available degrees of freedom, and then searches for simplifications which are 'congruent' with the data (that is, which satisfy classical F or χ^2 tests). The contrast is with the simple-to-general approach implicit in the standard paradigm where one starts with the simple $y = X\beta + u$ and then augments the model, for example by supposing that the disturbance u follows an AR(1), to obtain a more general and better-fitting equation.

GtoS has the advantage that one only considers specifications that are not rejected by the data, but does not, by itself, overcome the problem that a large number of alternative specifications might meet this criterion. This is dealt with by the second plank in the programme, *encompassing* (Mizon, 1984). One model is said to encompass a second if it can explain the second model's lack of fit. Given two models, A and B, there are four possibilities: A encompasses B, B encompasses A, neither model encompasses the other (the data are indecisive) and the models both encompass each other (both are too simple). Encompassing is implemented through non-nested hypothesis testing, in principle either within a classical or a Bayesian framework. It should in principle result in different econometricians being able to agree about the preferred simplifications of a common general starting model. Despite this, the pre-test problem still remains, and hypothesis testing relative to the simplified specification is necessarily conditioned on that simplification being valid.

The more radical alternative is to eschew the search for simple structure, at least in so far as it is reflected in the imposition of zero or equality restrictions on general autoregressive distributed lag (ADL) models. Christopher Sims argued that these restrictions are often 'incredible' and reflect naively simple views of the operation of economic processes (Sims, 1980). He suggested instead the estimation of vector autoregressions (VARs). If y_t is now a vector of m variables, a VAR(p) model would represent this as an unrestricted pth order autoregression $A(L)y_t = \varepsilon_t$ where L is the lag operator such that $Ly_t = y_{t-1}$ and $A_0 = I$. Note that VAR models are closed, in the sense that every component of y is explained within the model. Of course, with mp coefficients in each equation, many (often most) will be individually poorly determined, but this is not of itself a problem since the coefficients are not parameters of interest. Instead, VAR modellers are typically interested in the moving average representation of the model (the MAR) obtained by inverting $A(L)$. Noting that this requires that each component of y is stationary (see below), the MAR $y_t = A(L)^{-1}\varepsilon_t = B(L)\varepsilon_t$ expresses y as a vector of infinite backward moving averages of the disturbances. The MAR lag polynomials $B(L)$ can be quite smooth even when the VAR polynomials $A(L)$ are poorly determined and spiky (as the consequence of collinearity). But in any case, when degrees of freedom are short, it is open to VAR modellers to adopt Bayesian estimation procedures, for example by specifying priors which show distributed lag weights declining smoothly (Litterman, 1986).

Interest in the MAR polynomials derives from the fact that they may be used to analyse the impact and transmission of shocks. Because the $A(L)$ coefficients are not structural, the lag length p may be selected as sufficiently long for the VAR residuals to be serially independent. Then, by shocking each equation in turn, the econometrician may examine the impulse response functions of each component of y with respect to that shock. The difficulty is that the shocks on the different equations will in general not be independent. However, if it is possible to impose a 'causal ordering' on y, independence can be achieved. Write $E(\varepsilon_t\varepsilon_t') = \Sigma$. Relative to any ordering of the variables, there exists a unique lower triangular matrix Q such that $\Sigma = QQ'$. This allows us to write $\varepsilon_t = Qv_t$ where the latent disturbances v_t are mutually as well as serially independent (they also have unit variance). Because Q is lower triangular, ε_{1t} is simply a resealed version of v_{1t} but ε_{2t} depends on both v_{1t} end v_{2t} and so on. This transformation allows the econometrician to examine the response of any component of y as the set of responses to each of the m impulses v, and to decompose the variance accordingly (Lütkepohl, 1991).

The original VAR specification $A(L)y_t = \varepsilon_t$ was deliberately atheoretical. Theory enters only in the choice of variables to by analysed. However, theory is required to interpret impulse response functions and variance decompositions. A variable ordering which puts, say, the money supply as the first component of y invites the reader to think that money supply innovations are independent of any other shocks to the economy. A shock to the money supply will result in a shock to, say, GDP, but not the reverse. The economist therefore needs to impose structure in order to interpret an estimated VAR. Typically, the identification required to interpret structural VARs (SVARs) comes from informational considerations (Canova, 1995).

Perhaps the most important development in time series econometrics over the past 15 years has been the increased awareness of the consequences of non-stationarity in macroeconomic variables. The random walk is the most simple non-stationary process. Economic aggregates are closer to random walks with drift, as the result of trend growth, although generally they will have more complicated time series properties than this. Differencing these real variables will give stationarity. Since price levels are also invariably non-stationary, nominal variables inherit this property from both their real and their nominal components and, indeed, typically need to be differenced twice to give stationarity. The *nonsense regression* problem (Yule, 1926) poses a major difficulty in the analysis of nonstationary variables: regression of one non-stationary variable on another will often give an apparently good but entirely spurious fit, even when the variables are completely independent, simply through the chance matching of ex post trends. This has induced a preference for analysis in terms of stationary (appropriately differenced) variables.

At the same time, non-stationarity provides new opportunities. The logarithms of real (personal) consumption lnC and (personal disposable) income lnY are, for example, non-stationary, but in most countries the savings ratio, which to a first order approximation is $-(lnC - lnY)$, is stationary. This implies that consumption and income are *cointegrated*, that is, they have a common stochastic trend. Within a VAR framework, this suggests modelling in terms of ΔlnY and $ln(C/Y)$ rather than ΔlnY and ΔlnC in order to impose stationarity of the savings ratio. Within the British tradition, cointegration motivates the so-called *equilibrium correction* model (ECM) specification in which an ADL(p) model of a non-stationary variable is reformulated as an ADL($p - 1$) model in terms of the differenced variables (to achieve stationarity) plus level terms lagged p periods with the cointegrating restrictions imposed. The ECM specification, which was a feature of British econometrics prior to the modern analysis of cointegration (see Gilbert, 1989), is rationalized by the Granger Representation Theorem. This states that, if two variables are cointegrated, one must be linked to the other through an equation which can be represented in this form (Engle and Granger, 1987). Thus an ADL(2) of lnC_t on lnY_t would be reformulated as an ADL(1) of ΔlnC_t on ΔlnY_t augmented by a term in $(lnC_{t-2} - lnY_{t-2})$ where the implied restriction that the coefficients on the two lagged levels terms sum to zero derives from the cointegration result.

Cointegration has therefore resulted in a degree of convergence between VAR modelling and the British tradition, in that the apparent arbitrariness of the ECM is rationalized while, by exploiting cointegration in specifying structural VARs, VAR modellers essentially arrive at the same point. VARs may be seen as unrestricted forms of more parsimonious structural models, against which these must be tested (Clements and Mizon, 1991). At the same time, a new tendency has emerged which regards the long run constancies, that is, the cointegrating relationships themselves, as the objects of theoretical interest, while the short run dynamics, which are the focus of VAR models, are simply nuisance noise (Park and Phillips, 1988). This forces attention onto estimation of the static long run equations, the disturbances on which incorporate the short-term dynamics and are therefore serially dependent. From this perspective, cointegration brings econometrics right back to the standard econometrics paradigm from which we started.

A common empirical finding is that equations which apparently fit well within a particular sample, and indeed which encompass rival specifications, nevertheless break down dramatically as soon as new data are available. One can control for this to some extent by looking at stability within the sample, in particular by the use of recursive estimators which are now standard in most estimation software, but it nevertheless remains true that good sample fit does not guarantee post-sample performance. The only reasonable position is that equations which fit poorly within a sample are unlikely to do better out of sample. This experience counsels humility in making claims on the basis of time series data and raises the issue of the extent to which time series econometrics can be informative about structure.

Unsurprisingly, structure means different things to different economists. There is a view, seldom stated explicitly, that aggregate macroeconomic data can never be informative about structural parameters, but, if true at all, this is only true of so-called 'deep structural' parameters of preferences and technology – the conditions for representative agent aggregation are clearly not met in practice (Gorman, 1953; Kirman, 1992). If structural parameters are located entirely at the microeconomic level, inference about them can only be securely carried out from micro-econometric data. However, there are also broad constancies evident in aggregate data, and these relate both to long-run cointegrating relationships and, in many cases to short-term responses. The parameters of these aggregate relationships cannot be inferred directly from the deep structural microeconomic parameters since they also depend on the distribution of shocks across agents. But even after allowing for this extra informational requirement, the view that modelling must be entirely micro-based is both excessively optimistic about the possibility of complete state description and likely to require huge resources to answer often fairly simple questions. The more reasonable position is that structure exists at both the aggregate and disaggregate levels and that microeconometrics and macroeconometrics are complementary in understanding the functioning of the economy (see, for example, Stoker, 1993). Econometricians will increasingly look at aggregation as an empirical rather than an ideological issue, a development which will be facilitated by the availability of long panel data sets (that is, panels of repeated observations on a common sample of firms or individuals over a number of time periods).

CHRISTOPHER L. GILBERT

References

Canova, F. (1995), 'Vector autoregressive models: specification, estimation, inference and forecasting', in M.H. Pesaran and M. Wickens (eds), *Handbook of Applied Econometrics*, Oxford: Blackwell.
Clements, M.P. and G.E. Mizon (1991), 'Empirical analysis of macroeconomic time series: VAR and structural models', *European Economic Review*, **35**, 887–932.
Engle, R.F. and C.W.J. Granger (1987), 'Cointegration and error correction: representation, estimation and testing', *Econometrica*, **55**, 251–76.
Gilbert, C.L. (1986), 'Professor Hendry's econometric methodology', *Oxford Bulletin of Economics and Statistics*, **48**, 283–307.
Gilbert, C.L. (1989), 'LSE and the British approach to time series econometrics', *Oxford Economic Papers*, **41**, 108–28.
Gorman, W.M. (1953), 'Community preference fields', *Econometrica*, **21**, 63–80.
Hendry, D.F. (1994), *Dynamic Econometrics*, Oxford: Oxford University Press.
Judge, G.G. and M.E. Bock (1978), *The Statistical Implications of Pre-test and Stein-Rule Estimators in Econometrics*, New York: Wiley.
Kirman, A.P. (1992), 'Whom or what does the representative individual represent?', *Journal of Economic Perspectives*, **6**, 117–36.
Leamer, E.E. (1978), *Specification Searches: Ad Hoc Inference With Non-Experimental Data*, New York: Wiley.
Leamer, E.E. (1983); 'Let's take the con out of econometrics', *American Economic Review*, **73**, 31–43.

Leamer, E.E. (1986), 'A Bayesian analysis of the determinants of inflation', in D.A. Belsley and E. Kuh (eds), *Model Reliability*, Cambridge, MA: MIT Press.

Litterman, R.B. (1986), 'Forecasting with Bayesian vector autoregressions – five years of experience', *Journal of Business and Economic Statistics*, **4**, 25–38.

Lucas, R.E. (1976), 'Econometric policy analysis: a critique', in K. Brunner and A.H. Meltzer (eds), *The Phillips Curve and Labor Economics* (supplement to *Journal of Monetary Economics*, **1**), 19–46.

Lütkepohl, H. (1991), *Introduction to Multiple Time Series*, Berlin: Springer-Verlag.

McAleer, M., A.R. Pagan and P.A. Volker (1985), 'What will take the con out of econometrics?', *American Economic Review*, **75**, 293–307.

Mizon, G.E. (1984), 'The encompassing principle in econometrics', in D.F. Hendry and K.F. Wallis (eds), *Econometrics and Quantitative Economics*, Oxford: Blackwell.

Park, J.Y. and P.C.B. Phillips (1988), 'Statistical inference in regressions with integrated processes: I', *Econometric Theory*, **4**, 468–97.

Qin, D. (1996), 'Bayesian econometrics: the first twenty years', *Econometric Theory*, **12**, 500–516.

Sargan, J.D. (1980), 'Some tests of dynamic specification', *Econometrics*, **48**, 879–97.

Sims, C.A. (1980), 'Macroeconomics and reality', *Econometrica*, **48**, 1–48.

Stoker, T.M. (1993), 'Empirical approaches to the problem of aggregation over individuals', *Journal of Economic Literature*, **31**, 1827–74.

Yule, G.U. (1926), 'Why do we sometimes get nonsense correlations between time-series?', *Journal of the Royal Statistical Society*, **89**, 2–9, 30–41.

Zellner, A. (1988), 'Bayesian analysis in econometrics', *Journal of Econometrics*, **37**, 27–50.

Econometric Testing

Introduction

Econometric testing refers to statistical testing as applied to econometric modelling. In this sense it differs from traditional hypothesis testing in so far as it is applied to a whole spectrum of activities with regard to confronting theories with data: 'One approach which to my knowledge has been completely ignored is the integration of economic methodology and philosophy with econometrics' (Caldwall, 1982: 216). The situation described by Caldwell has not changed significantly over the last decade or so and we still need to integrate economic methodology with econometrics and philosophy of science. The thesis adopted in this entry is that some of the difficulties experienced by econometrics in attempting to confront theories with observed data can be explained by the lack of a systematic framework for dealing with the different facets of empirical modelling and theory testing: whether the modeller tests for error autocorrelation or the demand for food is income-inelastic, the test procedure is the same. It is argued below that the two testing situations are fundamentally different and require different testing procedures. Unfortunately, the basic framework for all types of testing in econometrics is currently basically the same: the Neyman–Pearson framework (see Lehmann 1986, sprinkled with some elements from the Fisher approach such as p-values. Gigerezer (1987) argued persuasively that the current textbook version of hypothesis testing constitutes a monstrous hybrid of two fundamentally different approaches to testing: Fisher's and Neyman–Pearson's.

In view of the fact that testing lies at the heart of most issues concerning the theory appraisal question, it is imperative to formulate a coherent methodological framework for theory appraisal where the role of testing is clear. Simplistic views which use categorizations of assumptions into primary (economic theoretical) and secondary (statistical), or subscribe to the view that the modeller should use statistical procedures which rely on as few statistical assumptions as possible, and the like, are grossly inadequate to deal with the problem. Their major weakness is in conflating theoretical and statistical issues and as a result the theory is often blamed for an inept choice of probabilistic assumptions and statistical inference is often blamed for insufficient theory formulations. What is needed is a clear separation of the statistical from the purely theoretical issues. A major consideration in this context is that of *statistical adequacy*.

The thesis adopted in this entry is that the methodological framework in Spanos (1986; 1989) can be used to provide a coherent framework for theory appraisal where the statistical and theoretical issues are considered separately and the testing procedures are different in nature and follow a certain logical sequence. In a nutshell, the probabilistic reduction framework distinguishes between the statistical and the theoretical models, interpreting the former in an instrumentalist light; it uses the Fisher approach for testing the adequacy of the statistical model and the Neyman–Pearson approach for testing the empirical validity of the theory. In the next section we consider the basic elements of the probabilistic reduction approach as a prelude to the discussion that follows. In the third section, the Fisher and Neyman–Pearson approaches are considered separately and then compared. The main conclusion is that, from the methodological viewpoint, the distinction that matters is that between two types of testing we might call *testing within* and *testing without*: (a) testing within the boundaries demarcated by the postulated statistical model and (b) testing outside the boundaries demarcated by the postulated statistical model. The Fisher approach is germane to testing without, but the Neyman–Pearson approach is appropriate for testing within. The final section brings together the requirement for these different types of testing and how the two approaches to testing can meet these needs.

The reduction approach: a brief introduction

A statistical model is viewed as a consistent set of probabilistic assumptions pertaining to certain random variables giving rise to the observed data in question. The quintessential statistical model in econometrics is the linear regression model shown in Table 1 (see Spanos, 1986). As we can see, the model itself is a set of probabilistic assumptions.

A statistical model constitutes a summarization of the sample information viewed in a relativist/anti-realist light. In this sense, a statistical model can be very useful as a basis of empirical modelling, depending on whether the postulated assumptions are appropriate (statistically adequate) for the data in question. In cases where the assumptions of the model are not valid for the data in question, the statistical model is not merely useless, it can lead to misleading conclusions. This is because in statistical inference we postulate a statistical model *a priori* and the inference results are valid only if the postulated statistical model is adequate. 'Statistical adequacy' refers to *validity* of the assumption underlying the postulated statistical model. It is an issue of paramount importance because all the statistical inference results relating to estimation, testing and prediction depend crucially on the statistical adequacy of the model. When some of these assumptions are invalid, the statistical inference results are, in general, invalid. The first step in ensuring statistical adequacy is to specify explicitly the assumptions of the statistical model in order to be able to assess their validity. The list of assumptions defining the linear regression model in Table 1 purports to provide a complete and consistent set of assumptions; there are no hidden or redundant assumptions.

The problem of statistical adequacy in the context of the reduction approach as three interrelated facets: specification, misspecification and respecification. 'Specification' refers to actual choice of the statistical model based on the information provided by the theoretical model and the features of the observed data in question. Understanding what assumptions are entailed and how they relate to the information available (data plots and so on) is imperative if the modeller aspires to use valid statistical inference to address theoretical questions of interest.

Table 1   The linear regression model

I   Statistical GM: $y_t = \beta_0 + \beta'_1 x_t + u_t, t \in \mathbb{T}.$

1   $D_t = \{X_t = x_t\}$ is the relevant conditioning information set with
    $\mu_t = E(y_t | X_t = x_t) = \beta_0 + \beta'_1 x_t$: the systematic component, and
    $u_t = y_t - E(y_t | X_t = x_t)$: the non-systematic component.
2   θ: $(\beta_0, \beta_1, \sigma^2) \in \mathbb{R}^k \times \mathbb{R}_+$, are the statistical parameters of interest,
    $\beta_0 = E(y_t) - \beta'_1 E(X_t), \beta_1 = [Var(X_t)]^{-1} Cov(X_t, y_t).$
3   X_t is weakly exogenous with respect to θ.
4. No *a priori* restrictions on $\theta := (\beta_0, \beta_1, \sigma^2)$.
5. *Rank* $(X) = k$, for $T > k$.

II Probability model:
    $\Phi = \{D(y_t | X_t; \theta), \theta := (\beta_0, \beta_1, \sigma^2) \in \mathbb{R}^\neg \times \mathbb{R}_+, y_t \in \mathbb{R}\}.$
    (i) $D(y_t | X_t; \theta)$, is normal,
6   (ii) $E(y_t | X_t = x_t) = \beta_0 + \beta'_1 x_t$: is linear in x_t,
    (iii) $Var(y_t | X_t = x_t)] = \sigma^2$ is homoskedastic (free of x_t),
7. The parameters $\theta := (\beta_0, \beta_1, \sigma^2)$ are *t*-invariant.

III Sampling Model:

8   $(y_1, y_2, \dots y_T)$ is an independent sample drawn sequentially from $D(y_t | X_t; \theta), t = 1, \dots, T.$

'Misspecification' refers to informal graphical checks and the formal testing of the assumptions underlying the statistical model. Misspecification testing has been one of the most important developments in econometric modelling over the last two decades. It began with the Durbin–Watson test in the early 1950s, but it was not until the 1970s that the problem of statistical adequacy and misspecification became of interest. Probably the first textbook in econometrics, at any level, to consider the problem of misspecification testing as an integral part of empirical modelling is Spanos (1986). After more than a decade of important contributions (see, for example, Ramsey, 1969; Newey, 1985; Tauchen, 1985) it is imperative to collect the various results and provide a systematic framework for misspecification testing.

'Respecification' refers to the choice of an alternative statistical model when the original choice is found to be inappropriate for the data in question. This process of respecification will continue until a statistically adequate model is found. Ideally, we would like to deal with the statistical adequacy issue at the specification stage, so as to avoid wasting a lot of time searching for an adequate statistical model or drawing misleading conclusions based on an inadequate model. An efficient utilization of the information available at the outset, using graphical techniques, will often minimize the effort at the misspecification and respecification stages. An adequate statistical model is only a means to an end: confronting economic theories with observed data.

Identification constitutes the next stage in empirical modelling where the theoretical model is related to the statistically adequate summary of the information in the observed data (the end result of the previous stages). If the assumptions of the estimated statistical model are not data-acceptable, any testing of the theory will be misleading. In the context of the above framework, testing comes into the procedure at two important stages. At the misspecification stage, testing takes the form of 'assessing' the validity of the postulated statistical model against the observed data. Once a statistically adequate model is established, testing returns at the identification stage, during which the theory can be confronted with the data via its adequate summary. The nature of testing at the misspecification stage is very different from testing at the identification stage. In both cases the testing is based on the postulated statistical model, such as the linear regression model, but misspecification testing constitutes testing beyond the boundaries of the postulated model and identification testing constitutes testing within the boundaries of the postulated model. In misspecification testing, the question is whether the data lend credence to the postulated statistical model, but in identification testing the aim is to accept or reject the theory in question.

The development of testing
Hypothesis testing during the early nineteenth century amounted to nothing more than an informal comparison between the values of the parameters specified by the hypothesis in question and the corresponding estimates. The model era of hypothesis testing begins with Pearson (1900) who proposed the well known *chi-square test* as a way to measure the 'goodness of fit' in the case of fitting the Pearsons family to a set of data. Using the first four 'sample' moments, Pearson would select a member of the Pearson family that best describes the data and then compare the theoretical frequency (f_i) with the estimated frequency $(\hat{f})$ by measuring the distance:

$$\eta = \sum_{i=1}^{m} \frac{\left(\hat{f_i} - f_i\right)^2}{f_i} \underset{\alpha}{\sim} \chi^2(m-1), \tag{1}$$

where f_i denotes the theoretical frequency associated with the ith interval ($i = 1, 2, \ldots, m$ and the intervals are mutually exclusive and cover the range of values of the random variable in question) and $\hat{f_i}$ the relative frequency of the interval i, based on the observed data; '$\underset{\alpha}{\sim}$' reads 'asymptotically distributed' and χ^2 $(m-1)$ denotes a chi-square distribution with $m-1$ degrees of freedom. Intuitively, the larger the value of η the worse the fit. Hence, for a given value of η (based on the observed data), say $\bar{\eta}$, the modeller would decide whether the distance was large enough to indicate 'bad fit' using the tail probability of $\chi^2(m-1)$:

$$Pr\,(\eta > \bar{\eta}) = p. \tag{2}$$

A small value of p corresponds to a large value of η, and thus the smaller the value of p the less convincing the fit was considered to be. The use of the tail probability of the (asymptotic) distribution of the distance function is first formalized by Pearson.

In the Pearson formulation we can see the following features: (a) a primitive notion of null hypothesis $H_0 : f(x; \theta) \in \mathscr{P}\,(b_0, b_1, b_2, b_3)$, (b) a discrepancy function η, (c) the distribution

(1) of a distance function, and (d) the tail probability (2), where $\mathscr{P}(b_0, b_1, b_2, b_3)$ denotes the Pearson family of densities characterized by the four parameters. Implicit in the above formulation is also a decision to accept or reject H_0 based on (2).

Fisher's approach

The new era in hypothesis testing begins with Gosset's 1908 seminal paper where he 'showed' that, in the case of the normal model (see Table 2), the asymptotic result:

$$\tau(X) = \left(\frac{\sqrt{n}\left(\hat{\mu}_n - \mu\right)}{s}\right) \underset{\alpha}{\approx} N(0,1),$$

used during the preceding period, where '$\underset{\alpha}{\approx}$' reads 'asymptotically distributed', $\hat{\mu}_n = \frac{1}{n}\Sigma_{i=1}^n X_i$ and $s = \frac{1}{n-1}\Sigma_{i=1}^n (X_i - \hat{\mu}_n)^2$ was inaccurate for small n because the finite sample result is:

$$\tau(X) := \left(\frac{\sqrt{n}\left(\hat{\mu}_n - \mu\right)}{s}\right) \sim St(n-1), \tag{3}$$

where $St\,(n-1)$ denotes a Student's t distribution with $(n-1)$ degrees of freedom. This result was formally proved and extended by Fisher (1915) and used subsequently as a basis for several tests of hypotheses associated with a number of different statistical models in a series of papers, culminating with his 1925 book.

Table 2   Normal statistical model

I	Statistical GM: $X_i = E(X_i) + \varepsilon_i,\ i \in \mathbb{N}$.
II	Probability model:

$$\Phi = \left\{ f(x;\theta) = \frac{1}{\sigma\sqrt{2\pi}}\exp\left\{-\frac{1}{2\sigma^2}(x-\mu)^2\right\}, \theta := \left(\mu,\sigma^2\right) \in \mathbb{R} \times \mathbb{R}_+, x \in R \right\},$$

III   Sampling Model: $X := (X_1, X_2, \ldots, X_n)$ is a random sample.

Fisher used the result (3) to derive a test for what he called the *null hypothesis*: $H_0: \mu = \mu_0$, by arguing that even though (3) holds for the 'true' value of μ, under the assumption that H_0 is valid, the true value is μ_0 and one can infer that:

$$\tau(X) := \left(\frac{\sqrt{n}\left(\hat{\mu}_n - \mu_0\right)}{s}\right) \overset{H_0}{\sim} St(n-1), \tag{4}$$

where '$\overset{H_0}{\sim}$' reads 'under H_0 is distributed as'. The essence of this result is that $\tau(X)$ constitutes a *pivotal function*: a distance function of the sample whose distribution is known and does not depend on any unknown parameters θ. Using this result, Fisher proceeded to derive a measure of 'how much a particular sample realization deviates from H_0', based on the probability of the tail area of the distribution (4) beyond the observed value $\tau(x)$ of the statistic $\tau(X)$. This measure, known as the 'p-value' takes the form

$$Pr\ (\tau(X) \geq \tau(x); H_0 \text{ is valid}) = p, \qquad (5)$$

and denotes the probability of observing a sample realization that would produce a statistic value equal to or greater than the one we already observed. In view of the fact that, the greater the value of $\tau(x)$, the more serious the indications against H_0, we can interpret small values of p as evidence against H_0; the smaller the value of p, the less plausible H_0 is. In a certain sense, a high p-value might be interpreted as *a measure of how much credence the observed data lent to the null*. In the early stages of his work, Fisher suggested p-values of 0.05 and 0.01 to be used as intuitive thresholds. Later on, however, he insisted that one should separate the p-value from the decision to accept or reject H_0 (see Fisher, 1956).

As we can see (Table 3), Fisher built on the previous work of Pearson but provided more structure to the hypothesis-testing procedure by introducing the notion of a null hypothesis, its finite sample distributed under H_0 and formalizing the notion of a p-value and its inferential role in connection with the data.

Table 3   Elements of a Fisher test: $\{\tau(X), p\}$

(F1)   a null hypothesis (H_0),
(F2)   a pivotal function $\tau(X)$
(F3)   the distribution of $\tau(X)$ under H_0,
(F4)   the p-value $P(\tau(X) \geq \tau(x); H_0 \text{ valid}) = p$.

An important limitation of the Fisher approach is the problem of choosing the pivotal function $\tau(X)$. This provided the motivation for Neyman and Pearson (1928) whose stated purpose was to deal with this limitation of the Fisher approach, something that Fisher never accepted and which led to numerous heated exchanges between Neyman and Fisher (see, for example, Fisher, 1956).

The Neyman–Pearson framework
Neyman and Pearson (1928; 1933) argued that Fisher had no logical basis for (a) his choice of test statistics such as (4), and (b) his use of the p-value as a measure of how much a sample realization deviates from the null hypothesis. It was clear that for each null hypothesis one could construct several pivotal functions and the Fisher approach did not provide a way of deciding which one is the most appropriate among these functions. Their solution to this problem was to view hypothesis testing as *a choice between rival hypotheses* and, thus, change the focus of hypothesis testing from providing a measure of how much credence the observed data lend to the null to deciding whether to accept or reject the null hypothesis on the basis of the observed data. The key to their approach was the introduction of the notion of an *alternative hypothesis* to supplement the notion of the null hypothesis and thus transform testing into a choice among different hypotheses.

The general specification of a hypothesis in the Neyman–Pearson formulation takes the form:

$$H_0 : \theta \in \Theta_0 \quad \text{against} \quad H_1 : \theta \in \Theta_1 := \Theta - \Theta_0. \tag{6}$$

The thing to note about this formulation is that it limits itself to hypotheses which can be expressed in terms of the parameters of the postulated statistical model in question. It turns out that a number of interesting hypotheses do not lend themselves naturally to this formulation.

The introduction of the alternative hypothesis and the fact that $\Theta_0 \cup \Theta - \Theta_1 = \Theta$ implies that one of the two hypotheses is implicitly assumed to be valid, leading naturally to the realization that there are two types of errors one can commit in this framework: type I error, reject H_0 when in fact it is valid; type II error, accept H_0 when in fact it is invalid. It is interesting to note that Neyman and Pearson (1928) criticized Fisher for recognizing only the type I error and ignoring the type II error. This criticism, however, was rather misplaced because Fisher did not see hypothesis testing as a decision problem (see Fisher, 1956). By evaluating the probabilities of the two types of error, Neyman and Pearson realized that there is an inevitable tradeoff between them. The Neyman–Pearson (1928; 1933) solution to this tradeoff was to treat the null hypothesis as more important than the alternative. This led to the argument that the modeller would rather ensure that the probability of rejecting the null when valid (type I error) is small, and then choose a test which minimizes the probability of type II error. The test is defined by separating the sample space χ into two mutually exclusive regions $\chi = C_0 \cup C_1$ and $C_0 \cap C_1 = \emptyset$ where:

$$C_0 := \{x : \tau(x) \le c_\alpha\}, \ C_1 := \{x : \tau(x) > c_\alpha\},$$

which in effect correspond to the partition of the parameter space into: $\Theta_0 - \Theta_1 = \Theta$.

The *decision rule* takes the form: if $x \in C_0$, accept H_0, if $x \in C_1$, reject H_0. Using the *power function* defined by:

$$\mathcal{P}(\theta) = Pr \ (x \in C_1) \text{ for } \theta \in \Theta, \tag{7}$$

the pivotal function $\tau(X)$ is chosen so as to ensure that:

$$\max_{\theta \in \Theta_1} \mathcal{P}(\theta) \quad \text{such that} \quad \max_{\theta \in \Theta_1} \mathcal{P}(\theta) \le \alpha, \tag{8}$$

where α denotes the *size* of the test.

A Neyman–Pearson (N–P) test is summarized in Table 4. A test, defined by the rejection region $C_1^* := \{x : \tau(x) > c_\alpha\}$, is optimal in this context if it is *uniformly most powerful* in the sense that:

$$\mathcal{P}^* \ (\theta) = Pr \ (x \in C_1^*) \ge P(\theta) = Pr \ (x \in C_1) \text{ for } \theta \in \Theta_1,$$

where C_1 is the rejection region of any other α-size test.

The major result on which the whole approach was founded was the *Neyman–Pearson lemma*. Consider the case where the statistical hypothesis is specified in terms of a simple H_0 and a simple H_1, as follows:

$$H_0 : \theta = \theta_0 \quad \text{against} \quad H_1 : \theta = \theta_1. \tag{9}$$

Table 4   Elements of an N–P test: $\{\tau(X), C_1\}$

(NP1)   a null (H_0) and an alternative (H_2) hypothesis,
(NP2)   a pivotal function $\tau(X)$
(NP3)   the distribution of $\tau(X)$ under H_0,
(NP4)   the significance level (or size) α, and.
(NP5)   the rejection region C_1.

Then, the size α test defined by:

$$C_1 = \left\{ x : \frac{f(x;\theta_1)}{f(x;\theta_0)} > k \right\}, \quad \text{where} \quad Pr\left(\left[\frac{f(x;\theta_1)}{f(x;\theta_0)} \right] > k; H_0 \text{ valid} \right) = \alpha, \tag{10}$$

is a uniformly most powerful (UMP) test of size α for (9). In practice, UMP tests constitute the exception rather than the rule. Beyond the simple hypotheses case, there is no single method which will yield an optimal test. A method which can be viewed as a generalization of the Neyman–Pearson lemma, in the sense that when the simple and/or alternative are not simple the test uses the maximum likelihood estimators, is the likelihood ratio procedure.

Likelihood-based procedures   These include the *likelihood ratio test*, for hypotheses of the form:

$$H_0 : \theta \in \Theta_0 \quad \text{against} \quad H_1 : \theta \in \Theta_1.$$

The pivotal function of the likelihood ratio test is defined in terms of the ratio:

$$\lambda_n(X) = \frac{\max\limits_{\theta \in \Theta_0} L(\theta; X)}{\max\limits_{\theta \in \Theta} L(\theta; X)}, C_1 = \{x : \tau(X) = \lambda_n(X) \le k\}, \tag{11}$$

where $L(\theta; x)$ denotes the likelihood function.
   Another procedure is the *asymptotic likelihood ratio test*. It is often the case in practice that, for a given sample size n, sensible distance functions do not give rise to pivotal functions. In such cases we need to resort to asymptotic theory, which states that 'under certain restrictions' (see Wilks, 1938),

$$-2 \ln \lambda_n(X) \cong n\left(\tilde{\theta} - \hat{\theta}\right)' \left(\mathcal{I}_\infty(\theta)\right)^{-1}\left(\tilde{\theta} - \hat{\theta}\right)_{\tilde{\alpha}}^{H_0} \chi^2(r),$$

where r denotes the number of restrictions. Note that $\tilde{\theta} = \max_{h(\theta)=0} (L(\theta; X))$ and $\hat{\theta} = \max_{\theta \in \Theta} (L(\theta; X))$ denote the *restricted* and *unrestricted* maximum likelihood estimators (MLE) of θ, respectively and $\mathcal{I}_\infty(\theta) = \lim_{n\to\infty} \frac{1}{n}\mathcal{I}_n(\theta)$ where $\mathcal{I}_n(\theta) = E(\partial \ln L(\theta;X)/\partial\theta)^2$ denotes the Fisher information matrix for a sample of size n.

The *asymptotic efficient score test*, introduced by Rao (1947), is a test based on the score function:

$$s(\theta; X) := \frac{\partial \ln L(\theta; X)}{\partial \theta}, \quad \text{with} \quad E\left(\frac{\partial \ln L(\theta; X)}{\partial \theta}\right) = 0 \quad \text{and} \quad Var\frac{\partial \ln L(\theta; X)}{\partial \theta} = \mathcal{I}_n(\theta).$$

In the general case where the hypothesis of interest is composite and comes in the form of r (possibly) non-linear restriction:

$$H_0 : h(\theta) = 0, \quad \text{against} \quad H_1 : h(\theta) \neq 0,$$

the score test's asymptotic pivotal function takes the form:

$$s(X) = \frac{1}{n}\left(s\left(\tilde{\theta}; X\right)\right)'\left(\mathcal{I}_\infty\left(\tilde{\theta}\right)\right)^{-1}\left(s\left(\tilde{\theta}; X\right)\right)_{\tilde{\alpha}}^{H_0} \chi^2(r), \tag{12}$$

This procedure is also known as the Lagrange multipler (LM) test procedure.

Another asymptotically equivalent test procedure, the *Wald test procedure*, based on the asymptotic pivotal function:

$$w(X) = \left(h\left(\hat{\theta}\right)\right)'\left(Cov\left[h\left(\hat{\theta}\right)\right]\right)^{-1}\left(h\left(\hat{\theta}\right)\right)_{\tilde{\alpha}}^{H_0} \chi^2(r), \tag{13}$$

was proposed by Wald (1943).

It can be shown that all three types of test procedure are asymptotically equivalent in the sense that asymptotically they share the same properties (see Serfling, 1980); it should be emphasized that the asymptotic equivalence is up to second order. The likelihood ratio (LR) test is based on both the restricted and unrestricted MLEs, the efficient score (ES) test is based only on the restricted MLE and the Wald test is based only on the unrestricted MLE. Taking this difference into consideration, it is inevitable that the LR test will have superior finite sample properties in general. The Wald test has a very important drawback in so far as the distance on which it is based $h(\hat{\theta})$ is ad hoc and cannot be compared with that of either the likelihood ratio or the efficient score distances $\| \tilde{\theta} - \hat{\theta} \|$ and $\| s(\tilde{\theta}; X) \|$, which constitute natural metrics as normalized by Fisher's information. Hence it is likely that the Wald test will be sensitive to the way one formulates the hypotheses, and any changes in the formulation might lead to different decisions. For an extensive discussion of these asymptotic test procedures in econometrics, see Engle (1984).

Fisher versus Neyman–Pearson

It is generally accepted that the Neyman–Pearson formulation has added some rigour and coherence to the Fisher formulation, but it is not obvious whether it has superseded the latter. The line of argument adopted in this entry is that the Neyman–Pearson method constitutes a different approach to hypothesis testing which can be utilized to improve on some aspects of the Fisher approach, but that the intended scope of the latter is much broader. In particular, the Fisher approach is more germane to misspecification testing.

In comparing the two approaches, it is important to emphasize that the point of departure of both is a postulated statistical model, such as the linear regression specified above. The first important difference between the two approaches is in terms of the basic objective. The main objective of the Fisher approach is to use the data as evidence to bear upon the validity of the null hypothesis. That is, the focus is *inferential* regarding the extent to which the sample realization lends credence to the null hypothesis. On the other hand, the main purpose of the Neyman–Pearson approach is *prescriptive*: make a decision to accept or reject the null hypothesis by comparing its data-based support with that of the alternative hypothesis.

Looking more closely at the two formulations we observe that the Neyman–Pearson approach supplements (F1) with an alternative hypothesis (H_1) and replaces (F4) with the power function defined in terms of the parameter space Θ. Using the latter in conjunction with a pre-specified significance level α, an optimal test (when it exists!) can be determined. That is, the whole Neyman–Pearson approach revolves around the parameter space of the postulated statistical model. It is generally accepted that, in cases where the null the alternative hypothesis of interest can be specified in terms of the parameter space Θ of a given statistical model, and the aim is to choose among the values in Θ, the Newman–Pearson approach provides a more satisfactory solution to the problem of choosing an optimal test $\{\tau(X), C_1\}$. The modus operandi of the Neyman–Pearson approach is the *power function* which ensures that the test chosen has maximum power in the direction of the specified alternative. The key to defining the power function is the *alternative hypothesis* which takes a parametric form within Θ.

In view of the above, two things become apparent. First, the argument that the main difference between the Fisher and the Neyman–Pearson approaches is the presence of the alternative hypothesis is nothing but a red herring. The Neyman–Pearson specification of the null and the alternative hypotheses in (6) constitute a partition of the parameter space of the postulated model. Moreover, whether the hypotheses H_0 and H_1 are simple or composite, as well as the optimality of the test, depend crucially on the particular Θ. Secondly, an N–P test depends crucially on the validity of the postulated model and in particular on the implicit assumption that Θ includes a statistically adequate model. Both the Neyman–Pearson and the likelihood ratio statistics are defined in terms of the distribution of the sample and the likelihood function, both of which utilize the assumptions of the postulated statistical model. For example, the validity of a *t*-test depends crucially on the validity of probabilistic assumptions such as normality, identically distributed, and independence, underlying the simple normal model (see Table 2). This suggest that the Neyman–Pearson theory is appropriate for testing within the boundaries demarcated by the postulated model. In this sense, if indeed the simple normal model turns out to be statistically adequate in a particular case, testing a theory restriction within its boundaries using the Neyman–Pearson procedure will be the appropriate procedure.

In contrast, the Fisher approach specifies only a null hypothesis. However, even Fisher could not deny the fact that to every null hypothesis in his approach there corresponds the alternative hypothesis, the negation of the null:

$$H_0 : \theta \in \Theta_0 \quad \text{against} \quad H_1 : \theta \notin \Theta_0. \tag{14}$$

A direct comparison between (6) and (14) reveals that the real difference (as opposed to the apparent) between the two approaches is that the Fisher approach does not necessitate a parameterization for the alternative hypothesis within the postulated parameter space Θ. That is, for a Fisher test the parameter space is not necessarily the complement of Θ_0, relative to Θ. Hence a Fisher hypothesis can be non-parametric in the sense that it can be formulated in terms of other distributional features beyond the parameters in Θ, moments, quantiles and so on. A cursory look at Fisher's three books (see Fisher, 1925; 1935; 1956) reveals that a number of tests favoured by Fisher, such as goodness of fit, independence and homogeneity tests, belong to the latter category.

Having pinpointed the real difference between the two approaches to the formulation of the alternative hypothesis, the question which arises is to what extend the notion of power is relevant in the context of the Fisher approach. Even Fisher could not exorcize the notion of power from his approach to testing. In an unguarded moment, he conceded the relevance of the power function 'for comparing the sensitiveness, in some chosen respect, of different possible tests of significance' (Fisher, 1925: 11). This is hardly surprising, given that the presence of an alternative hypothesis (the invalidity of the null) in the Fisher approach constitutes an important dimension. As a result, a more general notion, which measures the *sensitivity of a test statistic in detecting departures from the null*, is both relevant and desirable. The sensitivity notion, however, should be definable also in terms of non-parametric formulations of the type alluded to above.

In conclusion, the above discussion has made it clear that the Fisher approach differs from that of Neyman–Pearson in two important respects: its basic objective and how the hypotheses relate to the postulated parameter space Θ.

Testing within versus testing without
Having discussed the two different approaches to hypothesis testing, let us return to the problem of testing in the context of the reduction approach, as summarized in the second section. We remind the reader that in the preliminary discussion we raised the difference between two types of testing: misspecification and identification testing. Let us discuss the latter first.

Assuming that the statistical model chosen (perhaps after several rounds of specification, misspecification testing and respecification) is statistically adequate, identification takes the form of restrictions $h(\alpha, \theta) = 0$, relating the statistical ($\theta \in \Theta$) and theoretical parameters ($\alpha \in A$) of the form:

$$g(.) : \Theta \to A,$$

where α is of lower dimensionality than θ. The idea is to relate the theoretical parameters of interest (elasticities and so on), as suggested by the theory in question, to the statistical parameters (moments) in order to bestow a theoretical interpretation to some functions of the latter. The traditional econometric textbook identification is concerned with whether the implicit function $h(\alpha, \theta) = 0$ has a *unique solution* of the form:

$$\alpha = g(\theta).$$

Here we interpret identification in a broader context and of course we view it in conjunction with a statistically adequate model (see Spanos, 1990). This type of testing we called *testing within*, because it can be interpreted as testing within the boundaries as demarcated by the postulated statistical model.

The above form of testing should be contrasted to misspecification testing, which, by its very nature, is concerned with assessing the validity of the postulated statistical model with regard to the observed data. Its basic aim is to utilize the data information to bear upon the empirical validity of the postulated model and not to accept or reject individual assumptions defining the model. In the case of the linear regression model given in Table 1, the modeller can assess its statistical adequacy by testing the validity of assumptions 1–8 defining the model. A moment's reflection suggests that any attempt to test such assumptions will have two important implications with regard to the original parameter space $\theta := (\beta_0, \beta_1, \sigma^2) \in \mathbb{R}^k \times \mathbb{R}_+$. First, it is obvious that testing such assumptions will take us beyond the parameter space $\Theta := \mathbb{R}^k \times \mathbb{R}_+$. For instance, the use the skewness-kurtosis statistic to test the normality assumption involves the parameters α_3 and α_4 (the skewness and kurtosis coefficients) which do not belong to the original model parameter space Θ. The same is true in the case of a non-parametric test such as the Kolmogorov test based on the null hypothesis.

$$H_0 : F(y_t \mid x_t; \theta) = \Phi_0(y_t \mid x_t; \theta), \, y_t \in \mathbb{R}, \tag{15}$$

where $F(.)$ denotes a general cumulative distribution function (cdf) and $\Phi_0(.)$ the cdf of the normal distribution. Second, there is usually no unique way to specify the negation of the null hypothesis: non-normality, non-independence and t-variance can take numerous forms. For the reasons mentioned above, misspecification testing amounts to searching outwards (*testing without*) from the boundaries of the postulated statistical model.

Having discussed the nature of the two types of testing, we turn to the question whether the Fisher and Neyman–Pearson approaches are up to the task.

The Neyman–Pearson formulation

The thesis to be argued in what follows is that the Neyman–Pearson approach is tailor-made for testing within but inappropriate for testing without. Noticing that, in identification testing, A is a restricted version of Θ, we can see that the Neyman–Pearson framework can be utilized as it stands to test these restrictions because they constitute testing within the boundaries demarcated by the postulated statistical model. Moreover, the validity of this test is assured by the statistical adequacy of the postulated statistical model. What is more, the purpose of identification testing is prescriptive: to accept or reject a certain theory. All in all, we conclude that the Neyman–Pearson formulation is ideal for this type of testing; by the same token, Fisher's formulation is inappropriate.

If we turn now to misspecification testing, we conclude that, in view of the above discussion and the fact that the Neyman–Pearson approach presupposes that the postulated statistical model includes a statistically adequate summary of the data, the approach, as it stands, is inappropriate for misspecification testing purposes. The question which naturally arises at this stage is, 'Given the above limitations, how has this framework been used for misspecification testing purposes thus far?' The answer is that the procedure has been greatly misused by implicitly augmenting the parameter space in an ad hoc fashion every time a misspecification test is designed. Hence, by attaching all the enlargements to the original statistical model's parameter space (one enlargement for each assumption), the modeller creates an implicit statistical model which plays the role of a comprehensive (all-encompassing) mishmash which will be a coherent and a consistent model only by accident.

A much better way to deal with this enlargement is to embed the postulated statistical model in a broader *comprehensive statistical model* (with an extended parameter space Ω), specified in order to ensure that (a) it is both consistent and statistically adequate (but possibly overparameterized), and (b) the hypotheses take the form of restrictions on Ω whose null reduces it to the Θ.

These conditions are not easy to ensure in practice because such comprehensive models are not readily available; they do require some imagination and general families of joint distributions. Even in cases where they are available, however, the Neyman–Pearson approach needs to be modified because the objective in misspecification testing is not quite to accept or reject a null hypothesis but to utilize the data information to bear upon the validity of the statistical model. Hence the conclusion one can draw from the above discussion is that even a modified Neyman–Pearson formulation needs to be reinterpreted in the direction of Fisher's *p*-values in order to be used in the context of misspecification testing.

The Fisher formulation

In Fisher's approach, the modeller confronts a null hypothesis (which is not necessarily parametric) with the data to assess whether the value of a chosen pivotal function suggests probabilistically that the hypothesis in question deviates enough to permit the conclusion that the null is not supported by the data in hand. In view of this objective and the nature of the 'alternative' (the negation of the null) in misspecification, as discussed above, we conclude that the Fisher approach seems to be better suited for misspecification testing purposes. Indeed, the choice of non-parametric 'alternatives' provides a very useful tool in the Fisher formulation. The term 'non-parametrics' is used to denote formulations of the negation of the null hypothesis in terms of any features of the distribution (moments, percentiles, quantiles and so on) in question other than the parameters $\theta \in \Theta$ of the postulated statistical model.

The obvious question that is likely to be raised by an econometrician trained in Neyman–Pearson tradition with respect to the utilization of the Fisher approach for misspecification testing purposes is: 'What about the optimality of such tests?' Obviously, one cannot talk about power in the strict sense because that requires parameterizing the negation of the null hypothesis, which is often an impossible task. By the same token, one cannot avoid the question of the 'sensitivity' of a given Fisher test with respect to certain directions of departures. Specifying such directions without utilizing explicit parameterizations is made possible by using features of distributions other than the parameters of the postulated model. However, unless the modeller has *a priori* information with regard to the likely direction of departures and thus can utilize a directional test, the only choice is searching for broader forms of departures around the boundary of the null: what we might call *local directions*. It must be noted that the majority of the supposedly Neyman–Pearson misspecification tests proposed in the literature, such as the Lagrange multiplier tests (see Engle, 1984, for a survey) and the information matrix tests (see White, 1982), belong to this category. The reason is that, when the test involves only the estimation of the statistical model under the null, it is in general a local test. Hence, by reinterpreting such tests in the Fisher formulation, we can utilize them as proper misspecification tests. The same applies to the so-called 'non-parametric tests' such as Kolmogorov's test based on the empirical cumulative distribution function and Pearson's chi-square test. For an extensive discussion on misspecification testing, see Spanos (1996).

Returning to the question of optimality in the context of misspecification testing, one can say that the optimal test, in a given situation, is the test that can detect any departure from the postulated null that is present in the observed data. This, however, begs the question because, unless one has *a priori* information (see Cox and Hinkley, 1974), the possible departure directions are not known. Moreover, the question of optimality in this context is always relative to a given data set. As a result of this, the apparent choice facing the modeller involves the inevitable tradeoff between less sensitive but broad tests in local directions and more sensitive directional tests with respect to specific directions. The latter is a real choice only in cases where there is *a priori* information with respect to the possible departures. However, the involvement of the observed data in the optimality question raises another promising possibility. The judicious use of smoothing techniques, known also as non-parametric methods (see Hardle, 1990), is likely to lead to misspecification tests which will allow the data to point towards the direction of departures (see Hidalgo, 1995).

The above discussion has left unexplored two possibilities: using (a) comprehensive statistical models and (b) *a priori* information in order to employ directional tests in the context of misspecification testing. These possibilities arise naturally in the context of the reduction approach (see Spanos, 1995; 1996). In conclusion, it is worth exorcising the ghost of pre-test bias that seems to hover above any attempt to use misspecification testing to assess the adequacy of statistical models. As argued in Spanos (1995), the pre-test bias problem arises when a misspecification test is used to choose an optimal estimator. No such thing arises in the above context because, first, the data are often observational and, second, the aim is to choose not estimators but statistical models. In the case of observational data, as opposed to experimental data (design of experiments and sample surveys), the modeller has nothing to do with the structure of the observed data and no amount of preliminary data analysis or misspecification testing is likely to have any effect on the systematic information contained in such data. As for the charge of 'data mining', it is clear from the above discussion that the aim is to summarize the information in the data in such a way as to bring out all forms of systematic information. Utilizing data plots and misspecification tests helps the modeller to discern effectively most forms of systematic information present in the data. If that is called 'data mining' then we consider the term tantamount to careful statistical analysis of observed data. In this context it is worth reminding ourselves that the father of modern statistical inference defined the objective of statistics as the *reduction of data*: 'A quantity of data, which by its mere bulk is incapable of entering the mind, is replaced by relatively few quantities which shall adequate represent [ideally] the whole ... of the relevant information contained in the original data.' (Fisher, 1922: 311).

ARIS SPANOS

Bibliography
Caldwell, B. (1982), *Beyond Positivism: Economic Methodology in the Twentieth Century*, London: George Allen & Unwin.
Cox, D.R. and D.V. Hinkley (1974), *Theoretical Statistics*, London: Chapman & Hall.
Engle, R.F. (1984), 'Wald, Likelihood ratio, and Lagrange multiplier tests in Econometrics', in Z. Griliches and M.D. Intriligator (eds), *Handbook of Econometrics II*, Amsterdam: North-Holland.
Fisher, R.A. (1915), 'Frequency distribution of the values of the correlation coefficient in samples from an indefinitely large population', *Biometrika*, **10**, 597–21.
Fisher, R.A. (1922), 'On the mathematical foundations of theoretical statistics', *Philosophical Transactions of the Royal Society*, A, 222, 309–68.
Fisher, R.A. (1925), *Statistical Methods for Research Workers*, Edinburgh: Oliver & Boyd.
Fisher, R.A. (1935), *The Design of Experiments*, Edinburgh: Oliver & Boyd.
Fisher, R.A. (1956), *Statistical Methods and Scientific Inference*, Edinburgh: Oliver & Boyd.
Gigerenzer, G. (1987), 'Probabilistic thinking and the fight against subjectivity', in L. Krurger, G. Gigerenzer and M.S. Morgan (eds), *The Probabilistic Revolution, vol. 2: Ideas in the Sciences*, Cambridge, MA: MIT Press.

Gosset, W.S. (1908), 'On the probable error of the mean', *Biometrika*, **6**, 1–25.

Hardle, W. (1990), *Applied Non-parametric Regression*, Cambridge: Cambridge University Press.

Hidalgo, J. (1995), 'A nonparametric conditional moment test for structural stability', *Econometric Theory*, **11**, 671–98.

Lehmann, E.L. (1986), *Testing Statistical Hypotheses*, New York: Wiley.

Neyman, J. and E.S. Pearson (1928), 'On the use and interpretation of certain test criteria for purposes of statistical inference', *Biometrika*, **20A**, 175–250, 263–94.

Neyman, J. and E.S. Pearson (1933), 'On the problem of the most efficient tests of statistical hypotheses', *Philosophical Transactions of the Royal Society of London*, A, 231, 289–337.

Newey, W.K. (1985), 'Maximum likelihood specification testing and conditional moment tests', *Econometrica*, **53**, 1047–70.

Pearson, K. (1900), 'On the criterion that a given system of deviations from the probable in the case of a correlated system of variables is such that it can be reasonably supposed to have arisen from random sampling', *Philosophical Magazine*, **50**, 157–72.

Rao, C.R. (1947), 'Large sample tests of statistical hypotheses concerning several parameters with application to problems of estimation', *Proceedings of the Cambridge Philosophical Society*, **43**, 40–57.

Ramsey, J.B. (1969), 'Tests for specification errors in classical linear least squares regression analysis', *Journal of the Royal Statistical Society*, **B**, 350–71.

Serfling, R.J. (1980), *Approximation Theorems of Mathematical Statistics*, New York: Wiley.

Spanos, A. (1986), *Statistical Foundations of Econometric Modelling*, Cambridge: Cambridge University Press.

Spanos, A. (1989), 'On re-reading Haavelmo: a retrospective view of econometric modelling', *Econometric Theory*, **5**, 405–29.

Spanos, A. (1990), 'The Simultaneous Equations Model revisited: statistical adequacy and identification', *Journal of Econometrics*, **44**, 87–108.

Spanos, A. (1995), 'On theory testing in Econometrics: Modeling with nonexperimental data', *Journal of Econometrics*, **67**, 189–226.

Spanos, A. (1996), 'Misspecification Testing in Econometrics', mimeo, University of Cyprus.

Spanos, A. (1997), *An Introduction to Econometrics*, Cambridge: Cambridge University Press.

Tauchen, G. (1985), 'Diagnostic testing and evaluation of maximum likelihood models', *Journal of Econometrics*, **30**, 286–315.

Wald, A. (1943), 'Tests of statistical hypotheses concerning several parameters when the number of observations is large', *Transactions of the American Mathematical Society*, **54**, 426–81.

White, H. (1982), 'Maximum Likelihood Estimation of misspecified models', *Econometrica*, **50**, 1–26.

Wilks, S.S. (1938), 'The large sample distribution of the likelihood ratio for testing composite hypotheses', *Annals of Mathematical Statistics*, **9**, 60–62.

Economic History

Economic history is an inescapably hybrid discipline and, notwithstanding the more strident and partisan claims of some of its more strident and partisan devotees, it has no single correct relationship with either of its academic parents, economics and history. In the past century or so the actual relationships have varied markedly over time and from place to place. It will therefore be helpful to give some indication of these variations by sketching the history of economic history in Britain and the United States, rather than plunging immediately into the murky methodological issues that have aroused such intense controversy since the early 1960s, much of it futile.

Economic history's 'take-off' into sustained academic growth in Britain occurred from 1882 to 1904, following the publication of the first comprehensive textbook by William Cunningham. Prior to that time there had been innumerable separate publications on trade, industry, agriculture, wages and poverty, and so on, but they had lacked a general disciplinary or intellectual framework. The new movement was chiefly inspired by opposition to classical economics, which had been 'an ahistorical subject, not to say an anti-historical one, while history was not conceived as being concerned with things economic.' (Harte, 1971: xxv). There had in fact been an English *Methodenstreit* during the 1870s and 1880s, which covered much the same ground as its German and American counterparts, including 'a dispute over the appropriate use of an inductive or deductive methodology in economic study, the role of the scientist in society, competition over academic posts and intellectual territory within the universities, and, perhaps, most importantly, broadly dissimilar social and political ideals'. (Koot, 1987: 4).

Nevertheless, the combined influence of the Cambridge economists, H. Sidgwick, A. Marshall and J.N. Keynes, brought about a compromise, as a result of which economic history became recognized as an independent academic subject in the United Kingdom, and later throughout most of the British Empire. Any hopes of converting economics into a historical subject were effectively dashed by the publication of Marshall's *Principles of Economics*, in 1890. By 1926, one of the leading pioneer economic historians, W.J. Ashley (who, in 1892, had been appointed to the first designated chair in the subject in the English-speaking world, at Harvard) summed up the situation by saying that: 'the theoretical economists are ready to keep us quiet by giving us a little garden plot of our own; and we humble historians [*sic*] are so thankful for a little undisputed territory that we are inclined to leave the economists to their own devices' (quoted in Koot, 1987: 1). Ashley became the first president of the newly founded Economic History Society in 1926, and the following year the *Economic History Review* began publication, marking a phase of limited but solid academic growth up to the end of World War II. In the postwar period, economic history enjoyed an unprecedented expansion, so that by 1970 it was 'established in practically every British university; there are nearly thirty professors of the subject and almost as many departments offering teaching for degrees in it. It is the only branch of history to have attained this status' (Harte, 1971: xi). More recently, however, there has been a serious contraction, the reasons for which will be considered later.

The history of economic history has been very different in the USA, where there have never been independent departments in the subject (or, as in Britain, in economic and social history). This is largely attributable to the influence of the German Historical School of economics, which was much deeper and more lasting in America than in Britain. Lacking a strong predilection for economic theory, many American economists took the historical dimensions of their subject for granted, and while focusing on 'applied' or policy-oriented topics they incorporated sizeable chunks of historical background and analysis into their courses on such subjects as money and banking, labour, transport, international trade, public utilities and business. Specialization and compartmentalization were facilitated by the extraordinarily rapid late nineteenth and twentieth-century expansion in American higher education, and there seemed little room for independent departments of economic history. This helps to explain why the founding of the Economic History Association was delayed until 1941, 15 years after its British counterpart, despite the fact that the potential membership was much greater in the USA.

Unlike most of their British counterparts, American historians recognized the role of economic forces in the nation's development and saw no need to create a separate academic domain for the study of such matters. While some espoused an explicit economic interpretation of history – even in a deterministic, though rarely Marxist form – a larger number sought to construct a coherent synthesis of political, economic, social, legal and environmental elements. Around the turn of the century the so-called 'progressive' historians, F.J. Turner, C. Beard, V. Parrington and J.H. Robinson, discouraged the study of 'any single department of life in its own terms', so that 'they neglected economic history in pursuing the undifferentiated flux of life'. As a result, 'of the forty leading colleges and universities that had offered economic history in 1902, nine had dropped the course by 1920' (Higham *et al.*, 1965: 190, 191n). Thereafter, despite the rise of business history, general economic history stagnated during the inter-war years, both pedagogically and intellectually.

After World War II, there was a dramatic internal (were the term not anachronistic, one might even say 'palace') revolution in American economic history, led by an able, energetic and ambitious group of young scholars who attacked their elders with relentless missionary fervour. Their 'new' economic history, or 'cliometrics' as it was lightheartedly dubbed, provoked innumerable commentaries, manifestos and critiques of the movement's nature, methods and limitations, potentialities and achievements, that cannot be reviewed here. One primary aim was to put American economic history on a 'sound quantitative foundation', an objective wholly compatible with the long-standing emphasis on empirical work in American economics. This dates back at least to the original platform of the American Economic Association in 1885, and forward through the multi-volume Carnegie Institution studies of American economic and legislative experience in the early 1900s (all of which were written by economists), to the massive output of the National Bureau of Economic Research from the 1920s to the present. In addition to the accumulation of new and better quantitative data and the utilization of state-of-the-art statistical methods, the new economic historians also stressed the explicit use of economic theory (in practice, static neoclassical microeconomic analysis) in studying historical problems, in contrast to the loose and implicit theorizing so often found in the old economic history. The first two pioneers, A. Conrad and J.H. Meyer, emphasized the desirability of a *combination* of theory, statistical inference and economic history, and doubtless the combined effect was greater than the sum of its parts.

There was, indeed, substantial justification for the younger generation's criticisms of the inherited corpus of American economic history writings, which various earlier commentators had described as lacking distinguished treatises, new schools of thought, manifest ideology, active research and controversy. In the new movement, especially from the early 1960s, there was certainly no dearth of controversy, and the cliometricians' excessive claims to radical novelty in the interpretation of the American past, reinforced by their aggressive polemics – some of which sought to write off all the work of earlier generations as useless – raised fundamental questions about the respective roles of economics and history in the discipline. Most of the cliometricians were economists wielding the concepts and techniques they had recently acquired in graduate school. Many of the older economic historians could not fully understand the new techniques being utilized in their fields, and some did not try to. They felt threatened, were resentful at the destruction of their accumulated intellectual capital, and protested at the wave of what they called 'quantomania', 'metrophilia' and other species of 'methodolotry'. Some of the cliometricians demonstrated little or no interest in the sources and quality of their data, or the historical context of the topics they were investigating – in other words, they seriously neglected the historical dimensions of their subject.

However, it would be quite wrong to give the impression that the cliometricians were a homogeneous group employing uniform methods, and adopting the same negative attitude to their predecessors. The initial phase of missionary enthusiasm and overstatement of aims and achievements soon gave way to a more sober and balanced view of the tasks of economic history. Moreover, it would be quite wrong to regard the work of Robert Fogel, by far the most brilliant, imaginative and ambitious new economic historian, as typical (cf. Coats, 1995). Fogel went far beyond his colleagues in deploying large-scale counterfactual models, the most dramatic but least plausible of that controversial species. He demonstrated a capacity to produce outstanding conventional historical research and analysis, but what one critic called his 'daredevil impulse' attracted far more attention. In 1974, together with Stanley Engerman, he published *Time on the Cross*, a remarkably ambitious and assertive study of ante-bellum American slavery. This is the most controversial economic history book ever produced, and it has no close rivals even in the cliometric canon. The authors made extraordinarily bold claims, extending their quantitative analytical history into hitherto untouched realms. As it transpired, their claims for the novelty, objectivity and scientific validity of their findings were quickly and effectively challenged by competent critics, who uncovered serious flaws. Nevertheless, this did not prevent both authors from subsequently being elected President of the Economic History Association, or Fogel being awarded the Nobel Prize in Economics, jointly with Douglas North, another but in many respects very different member of the first cohort of cliometrician's.

Fogel's earlier work on American railroads and *Time on the Cross* (and the various supplementary volumes that followed) constituted landmarks in American historiography, but by the mid-1970s cliometrics was coming of age. A bitter phase of internecine warfare, in which some new economic historians turned away from their predecessors to attack their brethren, proved to be brief, for they turned to the constructive work of developing their subject in accordance with the long-standing theoretical–quantitative tradition in American economics.

Sad to relate, neither the British practice of establishing independent departments of economic history nor the cliometricians' policy of clinging firmly to the economists' coattails has served to protect economic history from significant decline in the 1980s and 1990s (Coleman, 1987; Field, 1987). The British structure afforded ample opportunities for collaboration with academic neighbours, and it seemed entirely logical for a hybrid subject. But, unfortunately, neither the economists nor the historians have proved to be valuable allies or co-workers; and too many British economic historians have been content to continue to cultivate Ashley's 'garden plot', with the inevitable consequence that teaching and research have been insular, generated mainly by intradisciplinary interests. The new economic history did not shake this complacency, partly because many British economic historians reacted negatively to the cliometricians' claims, but also, and probably more seriously, because so few of them have had the intellectual equipment needed for cliometric work.

In the USA, cliometrics was initially welcomed by economists as a stimulating new approach, especially when it had a direct bearing on problems of interest to them, such as the processes of long-run growth and fluctuations. But in time, owing to the fact that the new economic history had a generally constricting effect on its practitioners, the cliometricians came to be regarded as much the same as other properly trained economists, distinguished solely by the fact that they were working on earlier periods. In most cases they lacked the vision, breadth and depth of learning to be found among the leading 'old' economic historians.

At this time the future of economic history as an academic discipline seems to be in some doubt, or at least seriously troubled. On both sides of the Atlantic there have been advocates of a rapprochement with history, though the prospects of a major shift in that direction seem poor. Opportunities for collaboration with sociologists, social historians and demographers offer some hope. But this is not the appropriate place for speculation on such matters.

A.W. COATS

Bibliography
Coats, A.W. (1980), 'The Historical Context of the New Economic History', *Journal of European Economic History*, 9, 185–207.
Coats, A.W. (1990), 'Disciplinary Self-Examination, Departments and Research Traditions in Economic History: The Anglo-American Story', *Scandinavian Economic History Review*, **38**, 3–18.

Coats, A.W. (1995), 'Comments on Schabas's: The Nature and Significance of the New Economic History. A Response to "Parmenides and the Cliometricians"', in D. Little (ed.), *On the Reliability of Economic Models*, Dordrecht: Kluwer.

Coleman, D.C. (1987), *History and the Economic Past. An Account of the Rise and Decline of Economic History in Britain*, Oxford: Clarendon Press.

Field, A.J. (ed.) (1987), *The Future of Economic History*, Boston: Kluwer Nijhoff.

Harte, N.B. (ed.) (1971), *The Study of Economic History: Collected Inaugural Lectures*, London: Cass.

Higham, J., with L. Krieger and F. Gilbert (1965), *History*, Englewood Cliffs, NJ: Prentice Hall.

Koot, Gerard (1987), *English Historical Economics. 1870–1926, The Rise of Economic History and Neomercantilism*, Cambridge: Cambridge University Press.

Economic Sociology

In a very general way one can define 'economic sociology' as the analysis of 'economic institutions'. This is, for example, more or less what Schumpeter does (Schumpeter, 1954: 20). There also exists, however, another way of defining economic sociology, namely as the application of the sociological perspective to economic phenomena. This latter definition means, in all brevity, that one applies the various concepts of sociology – such as gender, network, social structure, and so on – to economic phenomena. That the sociological perspective differs on a number of methodological points from the one that can be found in mainstream economics is clear from Table 1.

It would not be correct to say that only sociologists have contributed to the growth of 'economic sociology' (a concept, incidentally, that emerged during the second half of the nineteenth century in France, England and Germany). Indeed, as Schumpeter makes clear in *History of Economic Analysis*, a number of economists have made outstanding contributions to our understanding of 'economic institutions', as opposed to 'economic mechanisms'. This includes not only Marx but also the German historical economists, such as Wilhelm Roscher, Gustav Schmoller and Werner Sombart (see Schumpeter, 1954: 807–20). There are also the three original institutionalists: Thorstein Veblen, Wesley Clair Mitchell and John R. Commons.

Since the mid-1970s, there existed in addition something called 'New Institutional Economics', to which such people as Ronald Coase and Oliver Williamson have made key contributions. What separates this new institutional economics from old institutionalism is basically its positive attitude to microeconomics and strict adherence to rational choice: economic institutions, it is argued, can be explained through an extension of microeconomics, especially through the concept of transaction costs. Agency theory, property rights and cooperative game theory have a similar approach.

The history of the attempt by sociologists to develop economic sociology has not been written, but it is nonetheless clear that three major attempts have been made to put this topic on the map (see Swedberg, 1987). The first of these was made around the turn of the century (Weber, Durkheim and Simmel); the second took place in the 1950s (Parsons, Smelser and Polanyi); and the third began in the early 1980s and is still going on ('new economic sociology': Harrison White, Mark Granovetter, Viviana Zelizer and others).

Sociology was founded during the years 1890–1920, and each of its three founders – Max Weber, Emile Durkheim and Georg Simmel – produced major works in economic sociology. Simmel's most important study in this respect is *The Philosophy of Money*, first published in 1900, in which the role of money in modern culture is analysed with great subtlety. Simmel is also famous for his suggestive portraits of various economic types, such as the spendthrift and the miser (see Simmel, 1978).

Table 1   Economic sociology and mainstream economics: a comparison

	Economic sociology	Mainstream economics
Concept of the actor	The actor is connected to other actors and is part of groups and society	The actor is not connected to other actors ('methodological individualism')
Economic action	Many different types of economic action are used, including rational ones; rationality as *variable*	All economic actions are assumed to be rational; rationality as *assumption*
Constraints on the action	Economic actions are constrained by the scarcity of resources, by the social structure and by meaning structures	Economic actions are constrained by the scarcity of resources, including technology
The economy in relation to society	The economy is seen as an integral part of society; society is always the basic reference	The market and the economy are the basic references; society is 'out there'
Goal of the analysis	Description and explanation; rarely prediction	Prediction and explanation; rarely description
Methods used	Many different methods are used, including historical and comparative ones; the data are often produced by the analyst ('dirty hands')	Formal, especially mathematical model building; no data or official data are often used ('clean models')
Intellectual tradition	Marx, Weber, Durkheim, Schumpeter, Polanyi, Parsons/Smelser; the classics are constantly reinterpreted and taught	Smith, Ricardo, Mill, Marshall, Keynes, Samuelson; the classics belong to the past; emphasis is on current theory and achievements

Source: Neil J. Smelser and Richard Swedberg, 'The Sociological Perspective on the Economy', in N.J. Smelser and R. Swedberg (eds), *Handbook of Economic Sociology*, Princeton: Princeton University Press, 1994.

Durkheim started out his career with a work in which he criticized Adam Smith for thinking that the only function of the division of labour was to produce wealth (Durkheim [1893] 1984). What Smith had missed, Durkheim argued, was that the division of labour also puts people together by making them more dependent on one another; it produces the potential for 'organic solidarity'. Another important theme in Durkheim's work was that certain forces in the modern economy may disturb society's cohesion and thereby create 'anomie' or a lack of rules for the way to behave. Durkheim was much more active than Simmel in having economic sociology established as a distinct area of study and he also encouraged several of his students to devote themselves to this new field. Marcel Mauss' imaginative study, *The Gift*, was, for example, written under Durkheim's influence (Mauss [1925] 1969).

The one who was to make the most sustained effort to establish economic sociology was, however, Max Weber. Educated in the tradition of the German Historical School, Weber was nonetheless also positive towards theoretical economics of Menger's type. As opposed to Durkheim, who detested economics and wanted to replace it with economic sociology, Weber saw economic sociology as a complement to mainstream economics. Of Weber's many and multifaceted works, three in particular are of relevance to economic sociology: *The Protestant Ethic and the Spirit of Capitalism* (1904–5), *Economy and Society* (1921–2) and *General Economic History* (1923). It was especially in *Economy and Society*, more precisely in its second chapter, 'Sociological Categories of Economic Action', that Weber outlined what a true *Wirtschaftssoziologie* might look like. Starting from the individual, Weber first discussed 'social economic action', then proceeded to 'economic organizations' and ended with 'market economies' and 'planned economies'. Throughout the famous Chapter 2, Weber also emphasized the absolutely crucial role that *meaning* and *struggle* play in the sociological perspective on the economy.

For reasons that are not clear, the efforts by the founding fathers to launch economic sociology did not catch on, and after 1930 few works were produced. In the 1950s, however, economic sociology experienced something of a renaissance through the works of Karl Polanyi, Talcott Parsons and Neil Smelser. In 1944, Polanyi had written an imaginative work on the triumph of the market economy in England – *The Great Transformation* – but it was not until he and a couple of collaborators in 1957 put together *Trade and Markets in the Early Empires* that his work became widely noticed. In particular, it was Polanyi's notion that the economy had been 'embedded' in various institutions in pre-industrial society that caught on. Polanyi's work set off a long and heated debate between those who believed that economic theory could be useful in the analysis of pre-industrial societies ('formalists') and those who rejected this idea ('substantivists') see Orlove, 1986).

Talcott Parsons, in cooperation with his young colleague, Neil Smelser, produced a heavily theoretical work in 1956 entitled *Economy and Society*. The main idea was that society can be conceptualized as a social system, consisting of several subsystems, of which the economy is one. The economic subsystem interacts with the other subsystems and all have important functions in maintaining the social system as a whole. Neil Smelser later attempted to use the same theoretical approach in a study of the Industrial Revolution in England; he also produced the first textbook in economic sociology (Smeller, 1959; 1963).

The attempt to relaunch economic sociology in the 1950s was followed by a new silence, which was not broken until the late 1970s. A pioneering effort to apply sociology to the study of markets was made around this time by Harvard's Harrison White (see, for example, White, 1981). By the mid-1980s, a number of White's students had begun to produce works in economic sociology, especially with the help of the networks approach that he had taught them (see also Burt, 1982; Baker, 1984). In 1985, one of these, Mark Granovetter, published a programmatic article about economic sociology in the *American Journal of Sociology* (Granovetter, 1985). He here made a frontal attack on new institutional economics, arguing that

Oliver Williamson and others basically analyse economic institutions in a non-social manner; they were 'sociological babes in the woods' (Granovetter, 1985: 502).

Granovetter has remained the key figure in 'New Economic Sociology' (a term that he coined around this time), not least through his argument that all economic institutions are 'socially constructed'. Using the electrical utility industry in the United States as his example, Granovetter suggests that economic institutions are typically created via networks and that these later 'congeal' into more resistant social structures (Granovetter, 1992).

New economic sociology has attracted a number of competent sociologists, mainly in the United States but also in Europe and elsewhere. The influence of organization theory and cultural sociology on new economic sociology has been very strong and resulted in many creative studies. Viviana Zelizer, for example, has analysed the way children's economic value has changed during the last century (Zelizer, 1985); Nicole Biggart has studied the structure and evolution of women's door-to-door sales organizations (Biggart, 1989); and Neil Fligstein has reinterpreted the history of the modern corporation in the United States from a sociological perspective (Fligstein, 1990). In 1992 a new reader in economic sociology appeared (Granovetter and Swedberg, 1992) and in 1994 a giant *Handbook of Economic Sociology* was published (Smelser and Swedberg, 1994) . In the last work, many of the most prominent proponents of new economic sociology are represented and its more than 30 chapters cover the full range of economic life.

RICHARD SWEDBERG

References
Baker, Wayne (1984), 'The Social Structure of a National Securities Market', *American Journal of Sociology*, **89**, 775–811.
Biggart, Nicole (1989), *Charismatic Capitalism: Direct Selling Organizations in America*, Chicago: University of Chicago Press.
Burt, Ronald (1982), *Toward A Structural Theory*, New York: Academic Press.
Durkheim, Emile (1984), *The Division of Labor in Society*, trans W.D. Halls, New York: The Free Press; first published 1893.
Fligstein, Neil (1990), *The Transformation of Corporate Control*, Cambridge, MA: Harvard University Press.
Granovetter, Mark (1985), 'Economic Action and Social Structure: The Problem of Embeddedness', *American Journal of Sociology*, **91**, 481–510.
Granovetter, Mark (1992), 'Economic Institutions as Social Constructions: A Framework for Analysis', *Acta Sociologica*, **35**, 3–12.
Granovetter, Mark and Richard Swedberg (eds) (1992), *The Sociology of Economic Life*, Boulder, CO: Westview Press.
Mauss, Marcel (1969), *The Gift: Forms and Functions of Exchange in Archaic Societies*, trans. Ian Cunnison, London: Cohen & West; first published 1925.
Orlove, Benjamin (1986), 'Barter and Cash Sale on Lake Titicaca: A Test of Competing Approaches', *Current Anthropology*, **27**, 85–106.
Parsons, Talcott and Neil Smelser (1956), *Economy and Society: A Study in the Integration of Economic and Sociological Theory*, London: Routledge & Kegan Paul.
Polanyi, Karl (1957), *The Great Transformation*, Boston: Beacon Press, first published 1944.
Polanyi, Karl, Conrad Arensberg and Harry Pearson (eds) (1971), *Trade and Markets in the Early Empires: Economies in History and in Theory*, Chicago: Henry Regnery Company; first published 1957.
Schumpeter, Joseph A. (1954), *History of Economic Analysis*, New York: Oxford University Press.
Simmel, Georg (1978), *The Philosophy of Money*, 2nd edn, trans. Tom Bottomore and David Frisby, Boston: Routledge & Kegan Paul.
Smelser, Neil (1959), *Social Change in the Industrial Revolution: An Application of Theory to the British Cotton Industry*, Chicago: University of Chicago Press.
Smelser, Neil (1963), *The Sociology of Economic Life*, Englewood Cliffs, NJ: Prentice-Hall.
Smelser, Neil and Richard Swedberg (eds) (1994), *Handbook of Economic Sociology*, Princeton: Princeton University Press.
Swedberg, Richard (1987), 'Economic Sociology: Past and Present', *Current Sociology*, **35**, (1),1–221.
Weber, Max (1988), *The Protestant Ethic and the Spirit of Capitalism*, trans. Talcott Parsons. Gloucester, MA: Peter Smith; first published 1904–5.

Weber, Max (1979), *Economy and Society: An Outline of Interpretive Sociology*, 2 vols, Trans. Ephraim Fischoff *et al.* Berkeley: University of California Press; first published 1921–2.

Weber, Max (1981), *General Economic History*, trans. Frank Knight, New Brunswick: Transaction; first published 1923.

White, Harrison (1981), 'Where Do Markets Come From?', *American Journal of Sociology*, **87**, 514–41.

Zelizer, Viviana (1985), *Pricing the Priceless Child: The Changing Social Value of Children*, New York: Basic Books.

Economics and Ethics

There are three ways in which ethics enters economics. First, economists have ethical values that help shape the way they do economics. This builds into the core of economic theory a particular view of how the economy does work and how it should work. Second, economic actors (consumers, workers, business owners) have ethical values that help shape their behaviour. Third, economic institutions and policies affect people in different ways and thus ethical evaluations, in addition to economic evaluations, are important.

Economists have ethical Values

The issue of ethical value judgments in economics is at least as old as the John Neville Keynes argument which divided economics into three areas: positive (economic theory), normative (welfare economics) and practical (economic policy). The first deals with 'what is', the second with 'what ought to be', and the third with how to get from one to the other. Although the majority of economists admit that ethical values permeate welfare economics and economic policy, they proceed with some confidence in the belief that their work in pure and applied economic theory is ethically neutral. Methodologists studying the question are more cautious.

In recent years there has been a flurry of literature calling into question economics' scientific character. Part of that literature deals explicitly with the impact of ethical value judgments on economics as a science: value neutrality versus value permeation. There are two pervasive tenets to the value neutrality argument. The first is a reliance on the Human guillotine which categorically separates fact ('what is') from value ('what ought to be'); the second basic tenet strongly supports the first by claiming that, since we have objective access to the empirical world through our sense experience, scientists need not concern themselves with 'what ought to be'. This second tenet is the crucial point and the one which critics have sought to undermine.

One of the recent criticisms of the value neutrality thesis, Kuhnian (Kuhn, 1970) in character, is convincing to many. Kuhn's rejection of the second tenet – that we have objective access to the empirical world through our sense experience – is important for those opposed to the value neutrality position. He argues that the empirical world can be known only through the filter of a theory; thus facts are theory-laden. A major argument of those who build on Kuhn's approach runs as follows: a world view greatly influences the scientific paradigm out of which one works; value judgments are closely associated with the world view; theories must remain coherent with the world view; facts themselves are theory-laden; therefore the whole scientific venture is permeated by value judgments from the start. This world view, or *Weltanschauung*, shapes the interests of the scientist and determines the questions asked, the problems considered important, the answers deemed acceptable, the axioms of the theory, the choice of 'relevant facts', the hypotheses proposed to account for such facts, the criteria used to assess the fruitfulness of competing theories, the language in which results are to be formulated, and so on (see Wilber and Hoksbergen, 1986).

Thus it is argued, the paradigm or research programme of *any* scientific community is circumscribed by boundaries laid out in a world view which, while not perhaps individually subjective, is nevertheless empirically untestable, or metaphysical, as Boland and others would say (see Boland, 1981; McCloskey, 1985; Piderit, 1993). The defence of value-neutrality still stands, but the pillars seem to be weakening. Blaug concedes that both 'factual', and 'moral' arguments rest 'at bottom' 'on certain definite techniques of persuasion, which in turn depend for their effectiveness on shared values of one kind or another' (Blaug, 1992: 115).

Economic actors have ethical Values

Economists recently have been thinking through the implications of one of Adam Smith's key insights: self-interest leads to the common good if there is sufficient competition *and* if most people in society have internalized a general moral law as a guide for their behaviour (see Evensky, 1993). Smith believed most people, most of the time, did act within the guidelines of an internalized moral law and that those who did not could be dealt with by the police power of the state. One result of this rethinking is the recognition that (a) people act on the basis of embodied moral values as well as from self-interest and (b) the economy needs that ethical behaviour to be efficient.

Hausman and McPherson recount an experiment in which wallets containing cash and identification were left in the streets of New York. Nearly half were returned to their owners intact, despite the trouble and expense of doing so to their discoverers (Hausman and McPherson, 1996: 58). The effort expended and apparently unselfish behaviour demonstrated by those who returned the lost goods may, as Hausman and McPherson assert, reflect a manifest commitment to societal norms over egoistic desires. Many researchers have found the same phenomenon (Dawes and Thaler, 1988; Elster, 1990; Frank, 1988).

It is not solely for the sake of accuracy that economists should pay attention to evidence that human actions are guided by concerns not solely self-interested, but also because there are real economic consequences. Self-interest in a competitive environment is not sufficient to yield the common good. Pushed to its logical extreme, individual self-interest suggests that it would usually be in the interest of an individual to evade the rules by which other players are guided.

Under conditions of interdependence and imperfect information, rational self-interest frequently leads to socially irrational results unless that self-interest is constrained by an internalized moral code. A classic example is that of an employer and a worker, each of whom suspects that the other cannot be trusted to honour their explicit or implicit contract. For example, the employer thinks the worker will take too many coffee breaks, spend too much time talking with other workers and generally work less than the employer thinks is owed. The worker, on the other hand, thinks the employer will try to speed up the pace of work, fire her unjustly if given the chance and generally behave arbitrarily. When this is the case the worker may tend to shirk and the employer to increase supervision to stop the expected shirking. If the worker supervises herself, production costs would be lower. Thus this distrust between employer and worker reduces efficiency.

What constrains individuals from seeking solely their self-interest? One answer is that our tendency to maximize our material welfare at the expense of others is inhibited by a deeply ingrained set of moral values. There are a number of approaches used to represent formally the relation between moral values and the standard utility framework of economic theory. We must distinguish between altruistic desires and moral norms, the former being more readily incorporated into an individual's utility function. The latter might better be modelled as metapreferences or conceived of as constraints on maximization. There are difficulties with each of these approaches, which leaves the subject an unsettled one.

One approach to formally incorporating moral values is to treat them as preferences comparable to preferences for goods and services. An individual's compliance with a moral norm generates a sense of satisfaction adding to the agent's welfare. Concurrently, defying a norm held as important creates disutility for the individual. This formulation appears more appropriate in modelling altruistic behaviour, such as purchasing a gift for one's child, than it does for an ethical norm like honesty or a commitment like duty.

Amartya Sen (See, 1987) has proposed an approach in which rational individuals would have both metapreferences and ordinary preferences. Moral values regarding fairness, liberty and honesty, among others, make up the metapreference function and it in turn shapes the ordering of ordinary preferences. So, for example, a person who has a strong preference for consuming grapes still does not buy any because of a commitment to justice for farm workers. This approach is also helpful in capturing in formal terms the internal conflict surrounding such personal choices as whether or not to smoke. An individual may simultaneously desire a cigarette (ordinary preference) and desire not to smoke (metapreference) in the first place.

Rather than conceiving of ethical values as preferences included among others in a standard utility function, or as metapreferences guiding the preference rankings of common goods, norms might also be seen as constraints on choices. As in a budget constraint, norms could be seen as externally imposing (presumably from the conscience or superego) limits on available choices. However, unlike their fiscal counterpart, norms may be violated; therefore the limits they impose are not rigid. Also attempts to distinguish norms-as-constraints from norms-as-preferences is often a muddy task.

Economic policies and ethical outcomes

In measuring economic success by a policy's ability to satisfy individual consumers' preferences, several important issues must be dealt with (see Cowen, 1993). Welfare economics plays down issues of distribution to varying degrees, depending on the proposed criteria for policy making. Sometimes it is argued that only those policy changes should be made that represent Pareto improvements. The Pareto rule is of limited use, however, for policy evaluation. Since interpersonal comparisons of utility are ruled out, the only thing that can be said is that a policy which benefits someone without hurting anyone is an unambiguous gain for society. Because this type of policy is almost never possible, economists have been forced to fall back on the concept of potential Pareto improvements, for instance, in cost–benefit analysis. This is where winners gain more than losers lose and therefore, potentially, are able to make compensation so that no one loses. Compensation schemes are very difficult to design, however, because it is so hard to identify the winners and losers. If the losers are not compensated by the winners then interpersonal comparisons of utility have been made, violating the foundational position of welfare economics. The result is that the ethical guideline becomes a straightforward consequentialist utilitarianism – the greatest good for the greatest number.

One possible definition of consequentialism is the belief that the morally relevant features of an action are its consequences, the events which result from it. Potential Pareto optimality is a special case of consequentialism, because it restricts its attention to one particular set of consequences: effects on the utility of agents (in practice, income becomes a proxy for utility). However, it is widely recognized by moral philosophers that a wide variety of potentially important considerations are inappropriately excluded by consequentialism. Here we note only one, agent-centred restrictions. The importance of agent-centred restrictions can be seen in the means–ends controversy. First, focusing only on the consequences ignores the fact that the means used might be morally unacceptable. A reduction of consumer goods prices by the use of child labour cannot be evaluated only by looking at consequences. Also arguing that the consequences will not change does not justify the agent's actions. For example, in the mid-1980s, many colleges and universities were considering divesting their portfolios of securities of companies that did business in South Africa. Many economists argued that this well-intentioned effort would be ineffectual, since other investors from around the world would provide any needed capital. This argument clearly neglected the possible relevance of agent-centred restrictions.

Another kind of problem overlooked by the focus on individual preference satisfaction concerns what Anderson has called the social conditions of delivery of a good (Anderson, 1993: ch. 7). Economists look at the economy as instrumental for obtaining other goods, such as utility. Thus, for example, one can evaluate the desirability of free market arrangements by examining their impact on the utility of individual agents. The market itself, in this view, has no intrinsic value or disvalue, but in some cases this may be an erroneous assumption. There may be cases in which agents have a preference not just for certain commodities but over whether those commodities are provided by a market or by some other means. The supply of blood is one example (see Titmus, 1993). Another example is commercial surrogate motherhood. Anderson argues that this practice of putting motherhood on the market in effect treats children as commodities, with possibly baleful psychological effects on both the parents and the children. Such arguments counter the notion that we can determine whether the market is best simply by checking to see if it allocates goods efficiently; the market itself may be the object of preferences and norms, which must be taken into account.

Another problem of individual preference satisfaction is seen where preferences are in some way based on error. Desires can spring from erroneous belief, a sense of resignation, acculturation that leads to the repression of actual needs, or a lack of information. Economists attempt to come to grips with only the last of these. They claim that it is paternalistic to argue that people make wrong choices. However, they are beginning to understand that the appeal to individual preferences has its limits. It begs the question of how these preferences are formed and it also sidesteps the reality that preferences are dependent on unreliable beliefs. People may believe that a new steel mill will not damage the health of those downwind, but if they are mistaken should their preferences still guide policy? Finally, there is a gap between what I prefer and what I actually do. I prefer not to smoke but my addiction leads me to buy cigarettes anyway. The question must be dealt with: should individually and socially undesirable preferences guide policy decisions?

CHARLES K. WILBER

References
Anderson, Elizabeth (1993), *Value in Ethics and Economics*, Cambridge, MA: Harvard University Press.
Blaug, Mark (1992), *The Methodology of Economics: Or How Economists Explain*, 2nd edn, Cambridge: Cambridge University Press.
Boland, Lawrence (1982), *The Foundations of Economic Method*, London: Allen & Unwin.
Cowen, Tyler (1993), 'The Scope and Limit of Preference Sovereignty', *Economics and Philosophy*, **9**, (2), October, 253–69.
Dawes, Robyn M. and Richard H. Thaler (1988), 'Cooperation', *Journal of Economic Perspectives*, **2**, (3), 187–97.
Elster, Jon (1990), 'Selfishness and Altruism', in Jane J. Mansbridge (ed.), *Beyond Self-Interest*, Chicago: University of Chicago Press.

Frank, Robert H. (1988), 'Beyond Self-Interest', *Passions Within Reason: The Strategic Role of the Emotions*, New York: W.W. Norton.
Evensky, Jerry (1993), 'Ethics and the Invisible Hand,' *Journal of Economic Perspectives*, **7**, (2), Spring, 197–205.
Hausman, Daniel M. and Michael S. McPherson (1996), *Economic Analysis and Moral Philosophy*, Cambridge: Cambridge University Press.
Kuhn, Thomas S (1970), T*he Structure of Scientific Revolutions*, 2nd edn, Chicago: Chicago University Press.
McCloskey, Donald N. (1985), *The Rhetoric of Economics*, Madison: University of Wisconsin Press.
Piderit, John J., SJ. (1993), *The Ethical Foundations of Economics*, Washington, DC: Georgetown University Press.
Sen, Amartya (1987), *On Ethics and Economics*, Oxford: Basil Blackwell.
Titmus, Richard M. (1993), *The Gift Relationship*, London: Allen & Unwin.
Wilber, Charles K. and Roland Hoksbergen (1986), 'Ethical Values and Economic Theory: A Survey', *Religious Studies Review*, **12**, (3/4), July/October, 205–14.

Economics as a Profession

Generally speaking, economists regard themselves and are regarded by others as professionals, although it is difficult to say precisely what this means in practice. Any profession necessarily has both internal and external dimensions: that is, its members must be subjectively aware of themselves as professionals and also be recognized as such by those who use their services, and by the general public. Recognition is based on the possession of degrees, diplomas or other qualifications not readily accessible to laymen, which testify to the professionals' expertise and lead to above-average remuneration, specialized appointments, delegation of authority and responsibility, and/or social esteem. Any definition of a profession must incorporate both static and dynamic elements: that is, a set of characteristics that differentiate the professionals from non-professionals, and an account of the process whereby this differentiation was achieved and has been sustained.

Economics is not one of the traditional status professions, such as law or medicine, whose practitioners have effective controls over entry, membership and occupational conditions (often backed by legal sanctions, which enhance the inelasticity of supply). Rather, it is one of the modern type of professions based on the command of a specialized body of knowledge, intellectual skill or technique, acquired through a protracted period of training or apprenticeship. This species 'remains closer to the academic conditions of proof ... gives less protection to the individual member ... [and] concerns itself less with official certificates of competence than the traditional professions' (Goode, 1960; see also Millerson, 1964). Its members' organizations are learned societies rather than vested interest guilds or labour unions, and their allegiance is primarily to the substantive field, not the guild. Although their functions are often performed in a bureaucratic context, 'the science, not the bureaucracy, determines employment standards, and because the work is largely science, not art, it can be evaluated with some precision. Competence can be tested, and thus there is less need for either certification or licensure or guild protection' (Goode, 1960).

These requirements are too stringent to be fully applicable in the case of economics, especially the testing of competence and the evaluation of performance. Moreover, there has long been an intermittent, but ultimately fruitless, debate as to whether economics is a science. Some of the problems in defining the economics profession stem from the fact that economics is a vocationally non-specific discipline: that is, it is difficult to specify what economists actually do and to identify the limits of their expertise. In large organizations, other than universities, people with academic qualifications in economics can be found at many different levels in the hierarchy, often working alongside statisticians, mathematicians, operations researchers, accountants and other categories of specialists. Their functions and skills interact and overlap to some extent, especially now that training in economics places such heavy emphasis on quantification and technique. And it must be borne in mind that basic economics is not so esoteric and arcane a field that it cannot be grasped by intelligent laymen. This means that the economist's expertise is liable to be questioned, especially when policy matters are under consideration.

Earlier definitions of economics (or political economy) such as the provision of financial advice to a sovereign, or the study of material welfare, or the production, distribution and exchange of goods and services, have latterly been considered too restrictive. On the other hand, Lionel Robbins' famous 'aspect' definition of economics as 'the science which studies the relationship between ends and scarce means which have alternative uses' is too permissive, for it prescribes no boundaries whatsoever. In recent decades there has been an aggressive movement – not, however, inspired by Robbins' definition – known as 'economics imperialism', whose practitioners are busily engaged in colonizing territories hitherto regarded as non-economic. This movement is based on an exaggerated belief in the value of elementary economic theory as an explanatory device. While these imperialists have sometimes provided stimulating new insights into various subjects, they too often fail to appreciate that a general theory which purports to explain everything ultimately explains nothing. The theory needs to be adapted to the subject matter and buttressed by substantial empirical research before it will yield much fruit; and even then important non-economic aspects of the subject matter may be slighted or ignored. So far, although economic analysis is nowadays taken much more seriously by specialists in some cognate subjects, such as politics and law, economics imperialism has not significantly increased economists' employment opportunities in those fields. Most economists prefer to remain on an exalted theoretical plane, rather than doing the work required to achieve mastery in those domains.

As noted earlier, the raison d'être of the professional economist's employment, whether in academia or elsewhere, is the command of specialized knowledge, and in a *Handbook of Economic Methodology* it is appropriate to consider briefly the relationship between professionalism and methodology. Methodology has two distinct, but interrelated dimensions: the cognitive and the regulative. The former is concerned with such questions as what is valid knowledge in the discipline? How can it be attained? How can its validity be demonstrated or tested (confirmed or falsified)? What are its limitations, for example with respect to problem solving or policy making? The regulative dimension, on the other hand, includes such questions as how can sound or correct standards of scientific knowledge or professional practice be established, taught and maintained? Indeed, are there such standards, other than the consensus of the professional community or the scientific establishment? How are knowledge-seeking processes most effectively organized and/or controlled? And how is economic knowledge most effectively advanced, disseminated and applied in practice?

Methodological discussion has an ineradicably prescriptive aspect. Whether as pedagogues or as practitioners, professional economists applaud outstanding exemplars – both individuals and specific performances – and criticize errors and failures. Methodological controversy presupposes that good (that is, sound or acceptable) practices should be adopted, and inferior ones corrected or abandoned; and it will be implied, or even explicitly stated, that those who violate recognized professional (or scientific) procedures will suffer loss of credibility or even professional recognition. But as economics lacks a recognized code of professional ethics, formal exclusion from the 'community of the competent' is not an available option.

Controls over entry into the profession (other than meeting degree requirements), status differentiations within the profession (such as the election of Fellows) and systems of accreditation have been proposed from time to time, but economists as a body have been ideologically strongly opposed to monopoly, both within their own ranks and more generally (Johnson, 1972). Cynics maintain that the essence of professionalism is power – a species of conspiracy against the laity – and that professionalization is a dynamic process involving 'an attempt to translate one order of scarce resources – specialized knowledge and skills – into another – social and economic rewards.' (Larson, 1978). Economists may indeed be ideologically hostile to monopoly, but it has been suggested that their customary attachment to competition and free trade would soon be abandoned were they to be faced with the prospect of a large influx of foreign economists offering their services at bargain prices! Opposition to professional controls may be attributable less to ideology than to the realization that such restrictions could not be specified in an acceptable form, or be enforceable.

Similar problems arise with a code of professional ethics. While economists generally recognize, if only implicitly, that they have obligations to their clients, and to society at large, they seem to consider it sufficient to rely on the familiar notion that economics is a 'positive' not a 'normative' science, and that the economist *qua* economist, is a detached, neutral, non-partisan expert or technocrat. (Presumably they would accept the Victorian dictum that gentlemen need no code of ethics, whereas no code of ethics will make gentlemen out of a bunch of crooks – or 'kept cats', or 'hired guns', to use more up-to-date terminology). Unfortunately, matters are not as simple as this. Few economists confine themselves to 'pure' theory, in an effort to avoid normative commitments; and especially in non-academic situations their professional ideology often takes the form of partisan advocacy of market methods. Unlike most, especially traditional, professionals, they do not seek detachment from the market-place (Herman, 1982). However, as Richard Nelson and others have emphasized, the constraints of bureaucratic and political life mean that economists in government cannot function merely as undeviating partisan advocates of efficiency. In practice they

> must also tailor their advocacy of market methods, efficient resource use, and other approaches to the political environment ... modify proposals to make them attractive in terms of equity, or to avoid infringing on real or perceived 'rights' ... recognize that they are members of an organization with which they must conform to some degree ... [and] develop and exercise skills in bureaucratic and political tactics, which are necessarily interwoven with their exercise of economic experience. (Nelson, 1987)

Adherence to a strict form of professionalism, which assumes the omnipresence of rationality, will inevitably limit economists' effectiveness. Indeed, some conservative economists believe that government work is necessarily corrupting, even if only mildly so, because of the unavoidable compromises involved. Others claim that if good (that is, competent) economists go into government, they do not stay good for long, since they rapidly suffer from professional obsolescence.

Whatever the difficulties of living up to the professional (or scientific) ideal, there has been an enormous increase in the number of academically trained economists in non-academic employment in this century. They can be found throughout business, banking, not-for-profit organizations, parastatal bodies, international agencies and in local, regional and national governments throughout the world. This expansion began in many countries after the great depression of the 1930s, and accelerated remarkably during and after World War II. To a considerable extent it resulted from the increase in government activities and responsibilities, and has been sustained in part by the growing internationalization of political and economic affairs (Coats, 1997). A strict laissez-faire regime would, presumably, reduce the demand for economists in government. Yet, curiously enough, in the 1980s, during the campaign to reduce the role of government and deregulate certain government bodies in the United States, economists were often called upon to devise methods of deregulation and to study and predict the effects of such policies.

However, this does not mean that economists can always be guaranteed an expanding market for their services. Recent studies in the United States, Britain and Australia suggest that there is a significant growth of feeling that the current academic training of economists does not equip them for non-academic work, owing to excessive emphasis on a high level of abstraction, mathematization and formalization, much of which is irrelevant to contemporary economic problems, and especially policy issues. Certainly, the leading centres of graduate education do not make serious efforts to distinguish between those destined for academic careers and those destined for employment in the so-called 'real world', and to provide appropriate education for both categories. Failure to do so may in the future prove crippling to a profession that has enjoyed a remarkable sustained boom over the past six or seven decades.

A.W. COATS

Bibliography
Coats, A.W. (1978), 'Methodology and Professionalism in Economics. A Subordinate Theme in Fritz Machlup's Writings', in J. Dreyer (ed.), *Breadth and Depth in Economics*, New York: D.C. Heath.
Coats, A.W. Bob (1993), *The Sociology and Professionalization of Economics. British and American Economic Essays*, vol. II, London: Routledge; see especially Part III: *The economics profession and the role of economists in government*.
Coats, Bob (ed.) (1997), *The Post-1945 Internationalization of Economics*, Durham, NC: Duke University Press.
Goode, W. (1960), 'Encroachment, Charlatanism, and the Emerging Professions: Psychology, Sociology, Medicine', *American Sociological Review*, **25**, 902–14.
Hansen, W.L. (1991), 'Education and Training of Economics Doctorates: Major Findings of the American Economic Association's Commission on Graduate Education in Economics', *Journal of Economic Literature*, **29**, 1054–87.
Herman, E.S. (1982), 'The Institutionalization of Bias in Economics', *Media Culture and Society*, **4**, 275–91.
Johnson, T.J. (1972), *Professions and Power*, London: Macmillan.
Krueger, A.O. *et al.* (1991), 'Report of the Commission on Graduate Education in Economics', *Journal of Economic Literature*, **29**, 1035–53.
Larson, M.S. (1978), *The Rise of Professionalism: A Sociological Analysis*, Berkeley: University of California Press.
Millerson, Geoffrey (1964), *The Qualifying Associations. A Study in Professionalization*, London: Routledge & Kegan Paul.
Nelson, R.H. (1987), 'The Economics Profession and the Making of Public Policy', *Journal of Economic Literature*, **25**, 45–91.
Towse, R. and M. Blaug (1990), 'The Current State of the British Economics Profession', *Economic Journal*, **100**, 227–36.

Economics of Science

An economics of science is just beginning to emerge in the economics literature. At present, the theoretical tools of microeconomics are being applied to science.[1] The assumption made is that science, among other things, is an economic phenomenon. Without a doubt, an economic approach to understanding science faces inherent limits. There may be no better way to study the limitations of an economic view of the world than to focus on science and see how much of scientific conduct and practice can be understood from an economic point of view.

Most other approaches to science have ignored economic factors. The vast bulk of the sociological, psychological, historical and philosophical literature regarding the nature of scientific inquiry and progress has ignored the role of economic constraints and market processes in science. Typically, economic factors are classified as an external influence on science and thereafter disregarded. Mostly, science is studied as though resources are available infinitely at zero cost. Scientists are assumed to follow the norms of rational scientific conduct without regard to the material incentives within science and the opportunity cost of being a scientist relative to some other occupational opportunity.

While most economists have not considered the economics of science, they have practised a methodology of economics. Most economists claim to practise something they call 'positive economics'. The surprising fact about this 'positive economic methodology' is that it ostensibly disregards economic ideas. Like philosophers, economists have theorized as though science and economics can be done without paying attention to scarcity and resource costs. Furthermore, another economic idea, an economic metaphor – the competitive market-place of ideas – plays no role in positive economic methodology. Positive economics as typically conceived is a non-economic methodology of economic science. For example, Milton Friedman's widely read essay, The 'Methodology of Positive Economics', and the many articles and books interpreting the essay, mention little, if any, economics. In one passage in the essay, it is striking that economic issues are excluded from those considered relevant to progress in economic science:[2]

> Progress in positive economics will require not only the testing and elaboration of existing hypotheses but also the construction of new hypotheses. On this problem there is little to say on a formal level. The construction of hypotheses is a creative act of inspiration, intuition, invention; its essence is the vision of something new in familiar material. The process must be discussed in psychological, not logical categories; studied in autobiographies and biographies, not treatises on scientific method; and promoted by maxim and example, not syllogism or theorem. (Friedman, 1953: 42–3)

It may be that Friedman is merely restating the familiar positivist distinction between the context of justification and the context of discovery and that he has no intention of excluding economics as an approach to understanding science. While it has been argued that Friedman is not a positivist (Boland, 1979; Hirsch and de Marchi, 1990), the tacit limited acceptance of such a positivist distinction is merely one way of excluding economic aspects of science. If economic analysis is associated with Friedman's 'logical categories', it is quite clear that a view such as Friedman's would tend to retard the exploration of science from an economic point of view. Most other economic methodologists have followed the same path as Friedman and ignored the economic dimensions of science and economic science. The most important exceptions are noted below.

At present there is a small band of individuals whose research has coalesced to form an economics of science. While there are a few scholars in economics and other disciplines who have paid particular attention to economic aspects of science, and they will be mentioned below, attention here is focused on those economists who are now advocating an economics of science.[3] In this small core group there are several prominent individuals. Two of these, Arthur Diamond and David Levy, have been students of George Stigler and trace their interest in an economics of science to Stigler's interest in economic aspects of science. Two others, James Wible and Wade Hands, root their interest most generally in economic issues found in the philosophy and sociology of science and more specifically in economic issues and aspects of science raised by philosophers Charles Sanders Peirce and Karl Popper and their philosophies. And Philip Mirowski has authored or co-authored several important contributions.

Arthur Diamond, trained as a philosopher, has spent most of his career investigating the economic aspects of science. In his work he attributes the idea of an economics of science to Stigler, and he often quotes this passage:

> The history of science provides the information to investigate the behavior of sciences. For insufficient reasons the study of the behavior of sciences is labeled the sociology of science. The behavior of sciences has been investigated by sociologists – of whom the foremost is Robert Merton – but it has also been investigated by physicists such as Thomas Kuhn, by psychologists such as Edwin Boring, and in fact by a member or two of almost every discipline. One must be a mathematician to understand the evolution of mathematics and an economist to study the evolution of economics, and sociology puts its imperialistic title on this area of study only on the ground that sciences are practiced by human beings and therefore involve social behavior. In the same sense it would be possible and equally meritorious to describe as *the economics of science the economic organization and evolution of science.* (Stigler, 1982b: 112); emphasis added.

Stigler has contributed pieces that clearly bring the Mertonian approach to the economics profession.[4] These have been collected into two volumes of selected works (Stigler, 1982a; 1984). Stigler has also authored several pieces that, retrospectively, one might want to include in an economics of science (Stigler, 1963; 1982b; 1986). The general point that a great deal of Stigler's research on the economics profession can be interpreted as an economics of science must be attributed to Diamond (1995). Diamond (1988; 1994) has fashioned a Stiglerian approach to economic aspects of science and has authored many more essays than could be cited here and a long survey of the field of the economics of science (Diamond, 1996).

David Levy, another student of Stigler's, has written several pieces on the economics of science. Levy (1988) has analysed the scientist's tradeoff between fame and fortune using a utility function approach to scientific choice. In his other contributions, Levy and Susan Feigenbaum (1993a; 1993b) have used econometrics to explore many aspects of the replication of scientific research. One contribution of Levy and Feigenbaum (1993a) drew 15 commentaries in the journal in which it appeared, *Social Epistemology*.

Hands and Wible have been influenced more by Popper and Peirce than by Stigler. Hands has noted that Popper's approach to the social sciences, his situational determinism, is a generalization of the logic of neoclassical microeconomics to other social settings: 'Popper's entire philosophy of science is simply *an application of the method of neoclassical economic theory.* The possibility of such an incredible conclusion only exemplifies the problems which await anyone interpreting Popper's writings on the topic' (Hands, 1985: 85–6, emphasis added). Furthermore, Hands has noted many of the economic themes in philosophy of science and the sociology of science. Hands' (1994a; 1994b; 1995) recent research draws connections between an economics of science and other approaches to science. Wible's interest in an economics of science stems from three influences: an interest in Peirce's (1879) long-neglected essay on the economics of research project selection, Lawrence Boland's (1971) essay on methodology as an exercise in economics analysis, and an interest in the issue of self-reference, also known as the reflexive question.[5] Taking Popper, Peirce and Boland as sources of inspiration, Wible (1998) has written a monograph on the economics of science which relies on the microeconomics of Chicago economists such as Becker, Ehrlich and Coase and the evolutionary perspectives of Hayek, Kuhn and Polanyi. The monograph also addresses the issue of self-reference.

Mirowski's contributions are somewhat eclectic. He has co-authored a piece on the problem of replication failure in the field of econometrics which uses a game-theoretic extension of the incentive structures faced by scientists (Mirowski and Sklivas, 1991). In another contribution, Mirowski (1994) is concerned with precision in economic and scientific research. This contribution is quite compatible with Peirce's (1879) emphasis on the economic aspects of precision in empirical research. Most recently, Mirowski (1995) has written a long review of philosopher Philip Kitcher's *Advancement of Science* in which many of the problems and prospects for an economics of science are raised.

Theoretically, four basic economic approaches can be applied to the general question of an economics of science: (1) a utility-theoretic approach to science and misconduct in science, (2) a cost–benefit approach to the normal, legitimate activities of science, (3) an economics-of-organizations approach to the institutional structure of science, and (4) inquiry into the notion of science as a competitive market-place of ideas.[6] Because an economics of science must include economics, a concern with self-reference must also be addressed.

First, the traditional utility-maximizing model of economic rationality has been adopted to explain many of the economic aspects of science. Diamond (1996: 5) makes it clear that such an approach is 'necessary for anyone who hopes to have a complete understanding of the advance of science and the behavior of scientists'. Levy (1988) also presents a formal utility model suggesting a tradeoff between fame and fortune. Wible has used the indirect utility approach found in the work of Gary Becker and Isaac Ehrlich to analyse problems with misconduct in science such as fraud and replication failure. Wible (1991) has analysed replication failure as a consequence of the rational allocation of time in the context of an implicit incentive system rewarding innovation more highly than replication. In another piece, Wible (1992) has created an explanation of fraud in science as an optimizing decision under conditions of uncertainty.[7]

Second, the normal legitimate activities of the scientist can also be explained with an economic, cost–benefit approach. A cost–benefit approach builds on the contribution of Charles S. Peirce (1879) and can be found in the works of philosophers Nicholas Rescher (1978a; 1978b; Wible, 1994b) and Gerard Radnitzky (1987a; 1987b). Their work implies that scientists choose theories, facts and research programmes which maximize the net present value of their careers. Much of the data which enter such a cost–benefit decision comes from judgmental substitutes for more desirable quantitative information. This allows significant room for disagreement and theoretical and paradigmatic pluralism.

Third, the institutional structure of science can be analysed with the emerging economics-of-organizations literature. Wible (1995) has argued that a dual economy of market and non-market processes characterizes science. This analysis is rooted in Ronald Coase's (1937) theory of the firm, the transactions cost theory of Oliver Williamson (1985) and the theory of a dual economy in Okun (1981). Commercial markets and firms are not the primary institutional structures of science. Many of the organizational structures of science such as journal publishing, peer review, research groups, research programmes and invisible colleges are unique. These structures solve many of the economic problems of science that could not be resolved within the governance structures of commercial firms and markets. Economic and methodological aspects of the institutional structure of science have also been explored by Uskali Mäki (1993a; 1993b). In one paper he explores the thesis that the institutions of science have methodological significance and in the other he views science as a social institution. Mäki seems to refrain from advocating the use of neoclassical microeconomics for the more patterned, behavioural aspects of science.

Fourth, since both the cost–benefit and economics-of-organizations approaches to science raise questions about science and markets, an economics of science invites exploration of the history and meaning of the widely used metaphor that science is a competitive market-place of ideas. A conception of a competitive market-place of ideas is most developed in the works of Karl Polanyi (1962a; 1962b) and Friedrich Hayek (1948; 1978) and to a lesser extent in Ronald Coase (1974) and Stigler (1963; 1986). If the market-place of ideas actually functioned as a commercial market where ideas were bought and sold in the same fashion as goods and services, the metaphor would be redundant. There would be no difference between commercial markets and the so-called market-place of ideas. If 'market-place of ideas' is really a metaphor, it suggests the irrelevance of real commercial markets to science. Science is not a market, but in some ways functions as markets do. Science, like markets, tends to be self-corrective. Much of the self-correctability of science is located in evidential considerations rather than in economic or market processes. Any self-correctability of science is quite remarkable when it is realized that, to the extent it does so, science must make progress in the face of pervasive market failure. A similar point is made by Thomas Mayer (1993) when he argues that academic researchers are not disciplined by the 'demand' side of the market. In the context of an economics of science, the self-correctability of science is made more difficult because of market failure.

The application of the economics of science to the discipline of economics raises the question of reflexivity or self-referentiality. The reflexivity issue has been discussed by Wade Hands (1994a) and Wible (1998).[8] Hands argues that an economics of science leads to the reflexivity or self-reference problem. The reflexivity problem has been much investigated in recent sociology of science. In sociology, it has been realized that the sociology of science applies to itself and to the rest of sociology. Similarly, an economics of science invites an application to itself and the rest of economics. An economics of science explicitly addresses a potential inconsistency: if the laws of economics are in any sense universal, the discipline of economics should not be an exception to those laws.

Although an economic approach to science is just in its beginning stages, there are important precursors. Perhaps the first to see the importance of economic dimensions of science was none other than Charles Sanders Peirce (1879). Peirce created a mathematical model analysing the economics of research project selection. A key concept in Peirce's analysis was the notion that the accuracy of statistical inference was dependent on resources available for measurement.[9] Peirce's economics of research has inspired philosopher Nicholas Rescher to take an economic approach to understanding science. Rescher (1978a; 1989) maintains that many aspects of the problem of induction can be resolved once economic considerations are taken into account. One of these aspects of induction takes the form of an economic critique of Karl Popper's notion of falsification. Rescher (1978b) also argues the thesis that, owing to cost escalation, scientific progress will be subject to logarithmic retardation. Scientific progress depends on new technologies of observation. As observation becomes complex and costly, research projects become more and more expensive. Given a constant stream of resources to science, progress must inevitably slow down. Rescher presents an economic critique of scepticism and anarchism. Both positions are criticized as being economically irrational because each wastes either information or attention.

Two other contemporary philosophers, Gerard Radnitzky and William Bartley, are worthy of note in regard to an economics of science. Radnitzky (1987a, 1987b) has maintained that a cost–benefit logic is implicit in scientific reasoning and also in Popper's falsificationist methodology of science. Radnitzky asserts that the recognition of data as 'fact' and the selection of a theory by the scientist are economic problems. The scientist makes the choice of facts and theories on the basis of an implicit, subjective net–benefit calculation. The selection of a research topic within a scientific discipline involves selection subject to relative incentives and disincentives which either encourage or discourage certain lines of inquiry. It is interesting that Rescher and Radnitzky have independently developed a cost–benefit approach to science. Whereas Radnitzky has sympathetically interpreted Popper from a cost–benefit perspective, Rescher has criticized Popper's notion of falsification from a cost–benefit conception inspired by the ideas of Peirce. Rescher has suggested that, because of limited resources in science, the number of falsifiable hypotheses must be reduced using the sort of economic criteria imagined by Peirce.

Besides Radnitzky, the late William Bartley (1990) authored a monograph which is an economic critique of science, philosophy and universities. Bartley maintains that there is market failure in the market-place of ideas. Such failure presents the occasion for one ideology to dominate another. Apparently, Karl Popper's philosophy of science has not been accepted within the professional community of philosophers and philosophers of science. Bartley unequivocally believes that Popper's contributions are intellectually superior to those of his rivals. The only reason for these inferior ideas dominating is failure in the market-place of ideas. Similar arguments are advanced against universities. Bartley asserts that science done in universities is stagnating at a depressed level because of the lack of competition. Universities must be restructured if they are to be more competitive and creative locations for basic research and innovative teaching.

Other than those philosophers mentioned above, Michael Ghiselin (1987) has argued for a bioeconomic view of knowledge and scientific discovery; Philip Kitcher (1993) has conceived of scientific rationality in a means–ends framework and provided a long analysis of the division of cognitive labour; and Alvin Goldman and Moshe Shaked (1992) have created an economic model of scientific activity and the acquisition of truth. The sociologist of science, Robert Merton (1973) has written several pieces on the reward structure of science. Furthermore, an entire issue of *Science in Context* was given to the issue of science and economic calculation (Power, 1994).

Among economists, there are several pieces that are noteworthy precursors to an economics of science. In 1971, Lawrence Boland published an essay, 'Methodology as an Exercise in Economic Analysis', in which he conceives of the choices that confront the scientist as an economic problem in welfare economics. Among many things, theories can be ranked according to criteria of generality and simplicity. What is needed is a truth or verisimilitude function to select the best of all of the theories. In welfare economics, what is needed for such a choice is a social welfare function. According to Arrow, it is impossible to construct such a welfare function. By analogy, Boland argues that it is impossible to construct what amounts to a meta-level truth or social welfare function for competing theories. In this application, what is known about a theoretical impossibility in economics is extended to the problem of theory choice in philosophy of science.

There are several papers that place scientists, professors or economists in a formal or informal optimizing framework. W.E. Becker (1975) has created a model of the university professor as a utility maximizer. Robert Tollison has argued that the activities of economists as scientists should be the subject of economic analysis: 'Economists are not outside the economy ... The economist is a rational, maximizing individual, subject to the predictions of economic science' (Tollison, 1986: 911). In a review of research on the economics profession, David Colander (1989) has asserted that the economics profession should make an excellent case study for the application of economic theory.[10]

It can be argued that economics needs an economics of science. Studies of the discipline carried out by economists are mostly ranking studies done with a great deal of apparent, if not blatant, self-interest. Theoretically and scientifically, thinking about the economics profession by economists appears to be unsystematic, ad hoc and biased. It would seem that systematic inquiry into the conduct of economic science from an economic perspective could teach economists as much about professional economics as all of the essays on positive economic method and all of the ranking studies which have ever been produced. The same point can be made about science in general. Many approaches to understanding science suffer from a general lack of concern and awareness of the complex economic issues involved in a non-commercial market process like science. An economics of science could change the situation. An economics of science would no doubt direct a great deal of scholarly attention to the economic aspects of science, epistemology and the economics profession that have been neglected for much too long.

JAMES R. WIBLE

Notes

1. What has motivated my work on the economics of science is a search for a growth of knowledge microfoundation for both macroeconomics and money as a substantive alternative to rational expectations. An economics of science implies that scientists use all available information and are forward looking in ways that simply cannot be formulated with the rational expectations hypothesis.
2. Tollison (1986) has quoted this passage from Friedman to make a similar point about the absence of economics from positive economic methodology.
3. An older piece on the economics of science is Nelson (1959).
4. Another important figure in the sociology of the economics profession has been A.W. Coats (1984).
5. Of course, Boland has a reputation as one of the foremost proponents of Popperian ideas among contemporary economic methodologists.
6. Of course, game theory may be used to extend these basic results to strategic situations.
7. Some scientists deliberately take advantage of their accumulated reputation and skill and then deliberately and grossly violate well-known standards of scientific conduct. The biomedical area has been particularly vulnerable because of the extraordinary funds funnelled into this type of research. The piece on fraud is an application of the Chicago approach to the economics of crime.
8. Mäki (1992) has written a long survey of contemporary sociology of science which considers the problem of reflexivity.
9. See Wible (1994a) for a detailed treatment of Peirce's essay.
10. Peter Earl (1983) created a behavioural theory of economists' behaviour, treating them as workers and consumers. But Earl rejects the possibility of a neoclassical microeconomic approach to science.

References

Bartley, W.W. (1990), *Unfathomed Knowledge, Unmeasured Wealth: On Universities and the Wealth of Nations*, La Salle, IL: Open Court.
Becker, W.E. Jr. (1975), 'The University Professor as a Utility Maximizer and Producer of Learning, Research and Income', *Journal of Human Resources*, **10**, 107–15.
Boland, L.A. (1971), 'Methodology as an Exercise in Economic Analysis', *Philosophy of Science*, **38**, 105–17.
Boland, L.A. (1979), 'A Critique of Friedman's Critics', *Journal of Economic Literature*, **17**, 503–22.
Coase, R.H. (1937), 'The Nature of the Firm', *Economica*, **4**, 366–405.
Coase, R.H. (1974), 'The Market for Goods and the Market for Ideas', *American Economic Review*, **64**, 384–91.
Coats, A.W. (1984), 'The Sociology of Knowledge and the History of Economics', *Research in the History of Economic Thought and Methodology*, a research annual, vol. 2.
Colander, David (1989), 'Research on the Economics Profession', *Journal of Economic Perspectives*, **3**, (4), 137–48.
Diamond, Arthur (1988), 'Science as a Rational Enterprise', *Theory and Decision*, **24**, 147–67.
Diamond, Arthur (1996), 'The Economics of Science', *The International Journal of Knowledge Transfer and Utilization*, **9**, Summer/Fall, 6–49.

Diamond, Arthur (1994), 'The Determinants of a Scientist's Choice of Research Projects', in T. Horowitz and A.I. Janis (eds), *Scientific Failure*, London: Rowman & Littlefield.

Diamond, Arthur (1995), 'George Stigler's Contributions to the Economics of Science', University of Nebraska, paper presented to the History of Economics Society at Notre Dame, 4 June.

Earl, Peter E. (1983), 'A Behavioral Theory of Economists' Behavior', in A.S. Eichner (ed.), *Why Economics is not Yet a Science*, Arkmonk, NY: M.E. Sharpe.

Friedman, Milton (1953), 'The Methodology of Positive Economics', *Essays in Positive Economics*, Chicago: University of Chicago Press.

Ghiselin, M.T. (1987), 'The Economics of Scientific Discovery', in G. Radnitzky and P. Bernholz (eds), *Economic Imperialism: The Economic Approach Applied Outside the Field of Economics*, New York: Paragon House Publishers.

Goldman, Alvin I. and Mose Shaked (1992), 'An Economic Model of Scientific Activity and Truth Acquisition', *Liaisons: Philosophy Meets the Cognitive Sciences*, Cambridge, MA: MIT Press.

Hands, D. Wade (1985), 'Karl Popper and Economic Methodology: A New Look', *Economics and Philosophy*, **1**, 83–99.

Hands, D. Wade (1994a), 'The Sociology of Scientific Knowledge and Economics: Some Thoughts on the Possibilities', in Roger Backhouse (ed.), *New Perspectives in Economic Methodology*, London: Routledge.

Hands, D. Wade (1994b), 'Economics and Laudan's Normative Naturalism: Bad News from Instrumental Rationality's Front Line', University of Puget Sound, December.

Hands, D. Wade (1995), 'Blurred Boundaries: Recent Changes in the Relationship Between Economics and the Philosophy of Natural Science', *Studies in the History and Philosophy of Science*, **26**, 1–22.

Hayek, F.A. (1948), 'The Use of Knowledge in Society', in *Individualism and Economic Order*, Chicago: University of Chicago Press.

Hayek, F.A. (1978), 'Competition as a Discovery Procedure', in *New Studies in Philosophy, Politics, Economics and the History of Ideas*, Chicago: University of Chicago Press.

Hirsch, Abraham and Neil de Marchi (1990), *Milton Friedman: Economics in Theory and Practice*, Ann Arbor: University of Michigan Press.

Kitcher, Philip (1993), *The Advancement of Science: Science without Legend. Objectivity without Illusions*, New York: Oxford University Press.

Levy, David (1988), 'The Market for Fame and Fortune', *History of Political Economy*, **20**, 615–25.

Levy, David and Susan Feigenbaum (1993a), 'The Market for (Ir)Reproducible Econometrics', *Social Epistemology*, **7**, 215–32.

Levy, David and Susan Feigenbaum (1993b), 'Testing the Replication Hypothesis When the Data Set is Subject to Gross Error', *Economic Letters*, **34**, 49–53.

Mäki, Uskali (1992), 'Social Conditioning of Economics', in Neil de Marchi (ed.), *Post-Popperian Methodology of Science*, Boston: Kluwer Academic Publishers.

Mäki, Uskali (1993a), 'Economics with Institutions: Agenda for Methodological Inquiry', in U. Mäki, B. Gustafsson and C. Knudsen (eds), *Rationality, Institutions and Economic Methodology*, London: Routledge.

Mäki, Uskali (1993b), 'Social Theories of Science and the Fate of Institutionalism in Economics,' in U. Mäki, B. Gustafsson and C. Knudsen (eds), *Rationality, Institutions and Economic Methodology*, London: Routledge.

Mayer, Thomas (1993), *Truth versus Precision in Economics*, Brookfield, VT: Edward Elgar.

Merton, Robert K. (1973), *The Sociology of Science: Theoretical and Empirical Investigations*, (ed.), N.W. Storer Chicago: University of Chicago Press.

Mirowski, Philip (1994), 'A Visible Hand in the Marketplace of Ideas: Precision Measurement as Arbitrage', *Science in Context*, **3**, 563–89.

Mirowski, Philip (1995), 'Philip Kitcher's *Advancement of Science*: A Review Article', *Review of Political Economy*, **7**, 227–41.

Mirowski, Philip and Steven Sklivas (1991), 'Why Econometricians Don't Replicate (Although They Do Reproduce)', *Review of Political Economy*, **3**, 146–63.

Nelson, Richard R. (1959), 'The Simple Economics of Basic Scientific Research', *Journal of Political Economy*, **67**, 297–306.

Okun, Arthur M. (1981), *Prices and Quantities: A Macroeconomic Analysis*, Washington, DC: Brookings.

Peirce, C.S. (1879), 'Note on the Theory of the Economy of Research', *United States Coast Survey* for the fiscal year ending June 1876, US Government Printing Office 1879; reprinted in *Operations Research*, **XV**, 1967, 642–8; also reprinted in *The Collected Papers of Charles Sanders Peirce*, Vol. VII, ed. A.W. Burks, Cambridge, 1958, 76–83; and in *The Writings of Charles S. Peirce: A Chronological Edition*, Vol. 4, 1879–1884, (ed.), C.J.W. Kloesel 1986, 72–8.

Polanyi, Michael (1962a), *Personal Knowledge: Towards a Post-Critical Philosophy*, Chicago: The University of Chicago Press.

Polanyi, Michael (1962b), 'The Republic of Science: Its Political and Economic Theory', *Minerva*, **1**, 54–73.

Power, Michael (ed.) (1994), 'Science and Economic Calculation', issue of *Science in Context*, **7**, Autumn.

Radnitzky, Gerard (1987a), 'Cost–Benefit Thinking in the Methodology of Research: The "Economic Approach" Applied to Key Problems of the Philosophy of Science', in G. Radnitzky and P. Bernholz (eds), *Economic Imperialism: The Economic Approach Applied Outside the Field of Economics*, New York: Paragon House Publishers.

Radnitzky, Gerard (1987b), 'The "Economic" Approach to the Philosophy of Science', *British Journal for the Philosophy of Science*, **38**, 159–79.

Rescher, Nicholas (1978a), *Peirce's Philosophy of Science*, Notre Dame: University of Notre Dame Press

Rescher, Nicholas (1978b), *Scientific Progress: A Philosophical Essay on the Economics of the Natural Sciences*, Oxford: Basil Blackwell.

Rescher, Nicholas (1989), *Cognitive Economy: The Economic Dimension of the Theory of Knowledge*, Pittsburgh: University of Pittsburgh Press.

Stigler, George, J. (1963), 'The Intellectual and the Market Place', Occasional Paper No. 11 of IEA.

Stigler, George, J. (1982a), *The Economist as Preacher and Other Essays*, Chicago: University of Chicago Press.

Stigler, George, J. (1982b), 'Does Economics Have a Useful Past?', in G.J. Stigler *The Economist as Preacher*.

Stigler, George, J. (1984), *The Intellectual and the Marketplace*, Cambridge, MA: Harvard University Press.

Stigler, George, J. (1986), 'The Process and Progress of Economics', Nobel Memorial Lecture 8 December in K.R. Leube and T.G. Moore (eds), *The Essence of Stigler*, Chicago: University of Chicago Press.

Tollison, Robert D. (1986), 'Economists as the Subject of Economic Inquiry', *Southern Economic Journal*, **52**, 909–22.

Wible, James R. (1991), 'Maximization, Replication, and the Economic Rationality of Positive Economic Science', *Review of Political Economy*, **3**, 164–86.

Wible, James R. (1992), 'Fraud in Science: An Economic Approach', *Philosophy of the Social Sciences*, **22**, 5–27.

Wible, James R. (1994a), 'Charles Sanders Peirce's Economy of Research', *Journal of Economic Methodology*, **1**, 135–60.

Wible, James R. (1994b), 'Rescher's Economic Philosophy of Science', *Journal of Economic Methodology*, **1**, 314–29.

Wible, James R. (1995), 'The Economic Organization of Science, the Firm, and the Marketplace', *Philosophy of the Social Sciences*, **25**, March, 35–68.

Wible, James R. (1998), *The Economics of Science: Methodology and Epistemology as if Economics Really Mattered*, London: Routledge.

Williamson, Oliver (1985), *The Economic Institutions of Capitalism*, New York: Free Press.

Edgeworth, Francis Y.

Francis Ysidro Edgeworth (1845–1926) was born in Ireland into a very large Anglo-Irish family, with many scientific, literary and educational connections. He was educated at home by tutors until entering Trinity College Dublin (1862) to study languages, and eventually moved to Balliol College Oxford (1868), taking a first in *Literae Humaniares* (1873). He was called to the bar in 1877, although it is unlikely that he intended to follow a legal career, and the same year saw the publication of his first book, *New and Old Methods of Ethics*. After a varied period lecturing on English language and literature, and philosophy, and even applying for a professorship of Greek, Edgeworth obtained the Tooke Chair of Economic Science and Statistics at King's College London in 1890. In the next year he became Drummond Professor at All Soul's College Oxford, a position he held until retirement in 1922.

During the 1880s, Edgeworth also published *Mathematical Psychics* (1881), his most important work in economics, and *Metretike: or the Method of Measuring Probability and Utility* (1887), acted as secretary to the British Association Report on Index Numbers (producing three volumes) and served as President of Section F of the British Association (1889). He was later a Guy Medalist (gold) of the Royal Statistical Society (1907) and was president of the society during 1912–14. He served as editor or co-editor (with Keynes) of the *Economic Journal* from its beginning in 1890 until his death. In 1925, he edited, for the Royal Economic Society, his three volumes of *Papers Relating to Political Economy*. For further details of Edgeworth's background and career, see Creedy (1986).

Probably the single most dominant characteristic of Edgeworth's approach to economics is that it is mathematical. Although Walras and Jevons had both used elementary mathematics as an important part of their work, Edgeworth's writings were characterized by a considerably deeper knowledge and a much more original use of techniques. He argued that mathematics provides powerful assistance to 'unaided' reason, and could check the conclusions reached by other methods, 'bringing the ingots of common sense to be assayed and coined at the mint of the sovereign science' (Edgeworth, 1881: 3). Edgeworth thus considered it his duty to point to any fallacies, so that his work often seems driven by criticism of others. In order to justify the use of very complex mathematics to generate what often seemed very narrow results, Edgeworth argued that the 'road, though short, is so slippery as to require every precaution' (Edgeworth, 1925, ii: 286).

The contrast between Edgeworth and Marshall in their attitude to mathematics is just one aspect of a more general difference between their approaches. Although both men turned to economics from mathematics and moral philosophy, their backgrounds in these subjects were very different. Marshall generally used biological analogies and was concerned with developing maxims. In contrast, Edgeworth's interest was intellectual; he generally used mechanical analogies and was more concerned with developing theorems, although he stressed 'the conduciveness of good-feeling to wisdom' (Edgeworth, 1925, i: 10). Marshall, the trained mathematician, who began his economic studies by 'translating' J.S. Mill into mathematics and working on Cournot's *Recherches*, later had an 'obsession for hiding his tools', whereas Edgeworth, the self-taught but more creative mathematician, 'gloried in his tools' (Pigou, in Pigou and Robertson, 1931: 3). In moral philosophy, only Edgeworth could be described as a thoroughgoing Utilitarian, whereas Marshall had more sympathy for the German Idealists and the work of Kant and Hegel.

Edgeworth regularly stressed the importance of the 'interposing chasms' between theoretical results and their application to policy problems. His outlook was not simply one of caution, but is more accurately described as being negative. The negative attitude is also linked to his view, mentioned above, of the role of mathematics in exposing errors, whereby 'an effort is required to remove prejudices worse than ignorance; a great part of the career of our science has consisted in surmounting preliminary fallacies' (Edgeworth, 1925, i: 5). His attitude may be illustrated by his comment on the maximum sacrifice principle in public finance:

> the premises, however inadequate to the deduction of a definite formula, may suffice for a certain negative conclusion. The ground which will not serve as the foundation of the elaborate edifice designed may yet be solid enough to support a battering-ram capable of being directed against simpler edifices in the neighbourhood. (Edgeworth, 1925, ii: 261)

This feature of Edgeworth's work reflects an attitude which extended to many other aspects of his life; indeed Price (1946: 33) mentioned that he could hardly ever obtain from his 'balancing friend' a definite conclusion on any matter, 'except occasionally the damnation of an outrageous fallacy'.

His basic methodological position can be described as strongly deductive and *a priori*, and during his early career such a position faced much criticism from the Historical School. Edgeworth felt obliged to provide many defences of the deductive method, and these often took the form of showing how other economists had advocated its use (his appeal to authority will be discussed later). However, he argued that, 'like the cultivated Athenians, we should eschew the invidious disparagement of each others' pursuits' (Edgeworth, 1925, i: 11). His interest in the natural sciences often led him to make comparisons with scientific laws, especially to show that the physical sciences also relied on abstraction and approximation. For example, after discussing the fact that an engineer making a tunnel may assume that gravel is a 'continuous substance', but that in considering the progress of a worm through the same substance, the same assumption cannot be made, he commented, 'it cannot be considered as paradoxical that a less exact science should rest in part on similarly inexact axioms' (Edgeworth, 1925, ii: 390). However, Edgeworth was not simply attempting to reproduce natural science methodology in economics. He stressed rather the 'congruity between the theory of political economy and ... *literae humaniores*' and argued that 'many of the difficulties which beset political economy are common to morals and metaphysics' (Edgeworth, 1925, i: 4, 5).

Edgeworth carefully argued that the assumptions used in economics are very often untestable and he therefore took precautions against the accusation of 'plucking assumptions from the air'. He was conscious of the fact that the difficulty is in making the crucial abstractions which make the particular problem under consideration tractable, but which are not question begging. His attitude to many *a priori* assumptions was directly related to his approach to statistical inference, with reference to 'the first principle of probabilities, according to which cases about which we are equally undecided ... count as equal' (Edgeworth, 1881: 99). Hence all feasible values, say of elasticities, were regarded as equally likely until evidence is obtained. The importance of equal *a priori* probabilities was also crucial to his justification of utilitarianism as a principle of distributive justice. Edgeworth argued that, for individuals faced with a range of indeterminacy along the contract curve, 'it may seem to each that as he cannot have his own way, in the absence of any definite principle of selection, he has about as good a chance of one of the arrangements as another ... both parties may agree to commute their chance of any of the arrangements for ... the utilitarian arrangement' (ibid.: 55; see also Edgeworth, 1925, i: 57; ii: 102, 322). In the 1950s, this idea was reformulated using the expected utility approach to produce a utilitarian social welfare function, and is now referred to as 'contractarian neo-utilitarianism'.

The presumption in favour of equal *a priori* probabilities was, however, 'liable to be superseded by specific evidence ... There is required, I think, ... in order to override the a priori probability, either very definite specific evidence, or the consensus of high authorities' (Edgeworth, 1925, ii: 391). This quotation helps to illustrate Edgeworth's attitude to authority and his many allusions to the views of other leading economists, though he was not 'tongue-tied by authority'. One method of showing that an assumption is sensible for the problem at hand is to show that other authorities made similar assumptions. Price (1946: 38) refers to Edgeworth's books, which were 'copiously interleaved ... with slips of paper, inserted, characteristically, I suppose, to facilitate prompt reference to authority for ... support of tentative opinion waveringly advanced'. Keynes suggested that 'his ostensible reverence for authority and disinclination to say anything on his own responsibility led him to waste an abundance of time' (Keynes, 1972: 265). However, Edgeworth stressed that, in a 'speculative and controversial science, a certain multiplication of authorities is desirable'. He also urged that the history of economic analysis is very important, partly to 'correct our estimates of authority' (Edgeworth, 1925, i: 6).

Edgeworth's attitude to authority can also be related to his utilitarianism. An important issue which concerned early utilitarians, for whom happiness was the ultimate end, involves the nature of evidence about the consequences of acts. The problem is that most people cannot know the full consequences of their acts, so that certain rules of moral conduct must be accepted and followed. This contrasts with intuitionism, where individuals are assumed to have immediate consciousness of moral rules. For utilitarians, the opinions of special highly regarded individuals about the appropriate rules to follow are taken to be credible though it may not be possible to show conclusively that they are 'correct'. Edgeworth extended this to economics and argued, for example, that 'we ought to defer even to the undemonstrated dicta and opinions of the wise, who have a power of mental vision acquired by experience' (Edgeworth, 1925, ii: 149). Furthermore, he argued that authority 'may afford more than commonplace advice to common man' (1877: 27).

In questions of moral philosophy Edgeworth regarded Sidgwick as the highest authority (see Edgeworth, 1925, ii: 147–52) and he came to regard Marshall as the highest authority in economics. Edgeworth's views on the necessity of authority, which derived from this particular utilitarian concern, are in line with those of John Austin and George Cornewall Lewis, both of whom are mentioned by him (Edgeworth, 1881: 103, 126). In his economic and statistical work, he was very conscious of the fact that it is often necessary to make *a priori* assumptions which are not capable of being tested. Edgeworth appealed to authority as almost equivalent to more conventional types of evidence. He wished to show that his abstractions were sensible for the problem at hand, and one way of doing this was to show that others had made similar assumptions. This attitude is still followed by many economists today.

JOHN CREEDY

References

Creedy, J. (1986), *Edgeworth and the Development of Neoclassical Economics*, Oxford: Basil Blackwell.
Edgeworth, F.Y. (1877), *New and Old Methods of Ethics*, Oxford: Parker.
Edgeworth, F.Y. (1881), *Mathematical Psychics*, London: Kegan Paul.
Edgeworth, F.Y. (1887), *Metretike: or the Method of Measuring Probability and Utility*, London: Temple.
Edgeworth, F.Y. (1925), *Papers Relating to Political Economy*, 3 vols, London: Macmillan.
Keynes, J.M. (1972), *Essays in Biography*, London: Macmillan
Pigou, A.C. and D.H. Robertson (1931), *Economic Essays and Addresses*, London: P.S. King.
Price, L.L. (1946), 'Memoirs and Notes on British Economists 1881–1946', Brothertan Library, University of Leeds.

Emergence

The notion of emergence has an established history in biology and other disciplines and has made infrequent appearances in economics. Emergence refers to the idea that novel properties may 'emerge' in a complex system that are not reducible to constituent microelements at a 'lower level'. The concept of emergent properties is typically prominent in critiques of reductionism: the idea that all aspects of a complex phenomenon must be explained in terms of one level, or type of unit. In particular, concepts like consciousness and purposeful behaviour may be regarded as an emergent property of the complex human nervous system (Sperry, 1991).

The philosopher of science Paul Feyerabend (1965: 223) has provided another useful example. Consider the relationship between the movements of molecules, at one level, and the concept of temperature, on another. Feyerabend asserts that, although the concept of temperature can be associated with statistical mechanics and the movements of molecules, the kinetic theory cannot 'give us such a concept' as temperature, which relates to an interactive level above and beyond the combined movements of molecules.

The concept of self-organization in complex systems is also related to the concept of emergence. Prigogine and Stengers (1984) developed the idea of order emerging from chaos some time ago. They showed that order and structure can develop through the interaction of elements such as cells or molecules. This idea has been developed by Kauffman (1993; 1995) and his co-workers at the Santa Fe Institute in the United States.

An emergent property may be defined as a feature of a complex system that (a) can be described in terms of macro- or aggregate-level concepts, without reference to the attributes of specific micro-level entities, (b) persists for time periods significantly greater than those required for describing the underlying microinteractions, and (c) is not explicable entirely in terms of the microproperties of elemental components of the system (adapted from Lane, 1993: 91).

The emergence of emergence
The idea of emergence was hinted at by John Stuart Mill (1843: bk. 3, ch. 6, para. 2) with his idea of 'heteropathetic' causation. The word 'emergent' in this context was first suggested by the philosopher George Lewes (1875: ch. 3, 412). Subsequently, the philosopher of biology C. Lloyd Morgan (1927; 1933) wrote extensively on the topic. Following Mill and Lewes, Morgan (1927: 3–4) defines emergent properties as 'unpredictable' and 'non-additive' results of complex processes. He saw such properties as crucial to evolution in its most meaningful sense, where 'the emphasis is not on the unfolding of something already in being but on the outspringing of something that has hitherto not been in being. It is in this sense only that the noun may carry the adjective "emergent"' (ibid.: 112). For Morgan, evolution creates a hierarchy of increasing richness and complexity in integral systems 'as new kinds of relatedness' successively emerge (ibid.: 203) and the 'non-additive' character of complex systems must involve a shift from mechanistic to organic metaphors: 'precedence should now be given to organism rather than to mechanism – to organization rather than aggregation' (Morgan, 1933: 58).

One of the few economists to take note of the concept of emergence in the inter-war period was John A. Hobson. In his book on Veblen, Hobson (1936: 216) wrote: 'Emergent evolution brings unpredictable novelties into the processes of history, and disorder, hazard, chance, are brought into the play of energetic action.' Despite Morgan and Hobson, the idea of emergence was largely submerged in the positivistic and reductionist phase of Anglo-American science in the inter-war period (Ross, 1991). The idea of emergent properties was rediscovered by Sir Karl Popper and others after World War II. As Popper (1974: 281) has remarked: 'We live in a universe of emergent novelty', a novelty which is as a rule 'not completely reducible to any of its preceding stages' (Popper, 1982: 162).

The existence of emergent properties at each level means that explanations at that tier cannot be reduced entirely to phenomena at lower levels. As the biologist Ernst Mayr (1985: 58) puts it:

> Systems at each hierarchical level have two characteristics. They act as wholes (as if they were a homogeneous entity), and their characteristics cannot (not even in theory) be deduced from the most complete knowledge of the components, taken separately or in other partial combinations. In other words, when such systems are assembled from their components, new characteristics of the new whole emerge that could not have been predicted from a knowledge of the components. ... Recognition of the importance of emergence demonstrates, of course, the invalidity of extreme reductionism. By the time we have dissected an organism down to atoms and elementary particles we have lost everything that is characteristic of a living system.

Although reductionism is still prominent, both in biology and in the social sciences, in biology strong and influential voices can be found against it, reflecting the history of the concept of emergence in that subject.

Methodological individualism and macroeconomics

The notions of emergence and downward causation are used in critiques of methodological individualism and of the reductionist idea that macroeconomics can only be built on 'sound microfoundations'. If socioeconomic systems have emergent properties – by definition not entirely explicable of constituent elements at a basic level – then the ideas of explaining the macrobehaviour of socioeconomic systems level completely in terms of individuals and individual actions (methodological individualism) or, more generally, completely in terms of microeconomic postulates (the microfoundations project) are confounded. Furthermore, in explaining complex systems we may be *forced* to rely on emergent properties at a macro level. There are strong arguments to suggest that neither methodological individualism (Udéhn, 1987) nor the microfoundations project (Rizvi, 1994) can ever be successful in reducing all features of the system to its micro components.

By reference to the concept of emergence, the relative autonomy of macroeconomics and the idea of the workability of aggregates can be asserted. Decades ago, the institutional economist Wesley Mitchell (1937: 26) argued that economists should begin, not with a theory of individual behaviour, but with the statistical observation of 'mass phenomena'. Mitchell and his colleagues in the US National Bureau for Economic Research in the 1920s and 1930s played a vital role in the development of national income accounting and suggested that aggregate, macroeconomic phenomena have an ontological and empirical legitimacy. Arguably, this important incursion against reductionism in economics created space for the Keynesian revolution. Through the development of national income accounting, the work of Mitchell and his colleagues helped to establish modern macroeconomics and in particular influenced and inspired the macroeconomics of Keynes (Mirowski, 1989: 307).

Chaos theory and 'artificial world' simulations

Emergence has been related to chaos theory. Working on non-linear mathematical systems, chaos theorists have shown that tiny changes in crucial parameters can lead to dramatic consequences, known as the 'Butterfly Effect – the notion that a butterfly stirring the air today in Peking can transform storm systems next month in New York' (Gleick, 1988: 8). There are parallels here with the account of 'bifurcation points' in the work of Prigogine and Stengers (1984). After behaving deterministically, a system may reach a bifurcation point where it is inherently impossible to determine which direction change may take; a small and imperceptible disturbance could lead the system into one direction rather than another.

Chaos theory suggests that apparent novelty may arise from a deterministic non-linear system. From an apparently deterministic starting point, we are led to novelty and quasi-randomness. Accordingly, even if we knew the basic equations governing the system we would not necessarily be able to predict reliably the outcome. The estimation of 'initial conditions' can never be accurate enough. This does not simply undermine the possibility of prediction: in addition, the idea of a reductionist explanation of the whole in terms of the behaviour of its component parts is challenged. As a result, the system can be seen to have emergent properties that are not reducible to those of its constituent parts. Chaos theory thus undermines the idea that science is largely about prediction and reductionism. Furthermore, it can sustain a concept of emergence.

In recent years, much work has been done with complex, non-linear computer systems, attempting to simulate the emergence of order and other 'higher-level' properties. Reviewing the modelling of such 'artificial worlds', Lane (1993: 90) writes that a main thrust 'is to discover whether (and under what conditions) histories exhibit interesting *emergent properties*'. His extensive review of the literature in the area suggests that there are many examples of artificial worlds displaying such attributes. This lends credence to the idea that emergence is important in the real world.

Emergence distinguished from supervenience

Finally, it may be useful to compare the concept of emergence with that of supervenience, as developed by Rosenberg (1976; 1985) in both economics and biology. Supervenience applies to the situation where the identity of two or more entities at the macro level does not assume identity at the constituent micro level, but identity at the micro level does guarantee identity at the macro level. In this case the macro level can be said to be supervenient. Accordingly, similar properties at the macro level cannot all be explained by a single set of micro-level components, but identical configurations of micro-level components all give rise to identical macro-level phenomena. The concept of supervenience is used to defend a qualified form of reductionism. Supervenience retains ontological reductionism and the priority of the micro level over other, higher levels.

By contrast, modern concepts of emergence suggest that different outcomes are possible with near-identical configurations and interactions of micro-level elements. As chaos theory suggests, tiny, seemingly insignificant, differences can lead to quite different systemic outcomes. It may be noted that the supervenience concept was developed before chaos theory was seen to pose a severe challenge to reductionism. In chaotic systems, almost exact identity at the micro level does not guarantee identity at the macro level, and supervenience is eluded.

GEOFFREY M. HODGSON

References

Feyerabend, Paul K. (1965), 'Reply to Criticism', in Robert S. Cohen and Max W. Wartofsky (eds), *Boston Studies in the Philosophy of Science*, New York: Humanities Press.

Gleick, James (1988), *Chaos: Making a New Science*, London: Heinemann.

Hobson, John A. (1936), *Veblen*, London: Chapman and Hall; reprinted 1991 by Augustus M. Kelley.

Kauffman, Stuart A. (1993), *The Origins of Order: Self-Organization and Selection in Evolution*, Oxford/New York: Oxford University Press.

Kauffman, Stuart A. (1995), *At Home in the Universe: The Search for Laws of Self-Organization and Complexity*, Oxford/New York: Oxford University Press.

Lane, David A. (1993) 'Artificial Worlds and Economics', parts I and II, *Journal of Evolutionary Economics*, **3**, (2), May, 89–107; **3**, (3), August, 177–97.

Lewes, George Henry (1875), *Problems of Life and Mind*, vol. 2, London.

Mayr, Ernst (1985), 'How Biology Differs from the Physical Sciences', in David J. Depew and Bruce H. Weber (eds) *Evolution at a Crossroads: The New Biology and the New Philosophy of Science*, Cambridge, MA: MIT Press.

Mill, John Stuart (1843), *A System of Logic: Ratiocinative and Inductive, Being a Connected View of the Principles of Evidence and the Methods of Scientific Investigation*, 1st edn, 2 vols, London: Longman.

Mirowski, Philip (1989), *More Heat Than Light: Economics as Social Physics, Physics as Nature's Economics*, Cambridge: Cambridge University Press.

Mitchell, Wesley C. (1937), *The Backward Art of Spending Money and Other Essays*, New York: McGraw-Hill.

Morgan, C. Lloyd (1927), *Emergent Evolution*, 2nd edn, London: Williams and Norgate.

Morgan, C. Lloyd (1933), *The Emergence of Novelty*, London: Williams and Norgate.

Popper, Sir Karl R. (1974), 'Scientific Reduction and the Essential Incompleteness of All Science', in Francisco J. Ayala and Theodosius Dobzhansky, (eds), *Studies in the Philosophy of Biology*, Berkeley/Los Angeles: University of California Press.

Popper, Sir Karl R. (1982), *The Open Universe: An Argument for Indeterminism*, from the *Postscript to the Logic of Scientific Discovery*, ed. W.W. Bartley, London: Hutchinson.

Prigogine, Ilya and Isabelle Stengers (1984), *Order Out of Chaos: Man's New Dialogue With Nature*, London: Heinemann.

Rizvi, S. Abu Turab (1994), 'The Microfoundations Project in General Equilibrium Theory', *Cambridge Journal of Economics*, **18**, (4), August, 357–77.

Rosenberg, Alexander (1976), *Microeconomic Laws: A Philosophical Analysis*, Pittsburg: University of Pittsburg Press.

Rosenberg, Alexander (1985), *The Structure of Biological Science*, Cambridge: Cambridge University Press.

Ross, Dorothy (1991), *The Origins of American Social Science*, Cambridge: Cambridge University Press.

Sperry, Roger W. (1991) 'In Defense of Mentalism and Emergent Interaction', *Journal of Mind and Behavior*, **12**, (2), 221–46.

Udéhn, Lars (1987), *Methodological Individualism: A Critical Appraisal*, Uppsala: Uppsala University Reprographics Centre.

Evolutionary Economics

The term 'evolutionary economics' is currently applied to a variety of approaches and heterodox groupings within the subject. In its broadest sense it signifies a concern with economic change and development, in some cases in opposition to equilibrating or to static models. A narrower definition would relate it to the use in economics of a Darwinian or Lamarckian metaphor taken from biology. A number of usages of the label are evident today.

1. Recognizing the early plea by Thorstein Veblen for an 'evolutionary' and 'post-Darwinian' science of economics, followers of Veblen and John Commons frequently describe their approach as 'evolutionary economics', often using the terms 'institutional' and 'evolutionary' as virtual synonyms, as exemplified in the title of the Association for Evolutionary Economics, the USA-based association of institutional economists.
2. Work influenced by Joseph Schumpeter is also described as 'evolutionary economics', as evidenced by the title of the *Journal of Evolutionary Economics*, published by the International Joseph Schumpeter Association.
3. The approach of the Austrian School of economists is often described as 'evolutionary', as portrayed in Carl Menger's theory of the evolution of money and other institutions, and by the extensive use of an evolutionary metaphor from biology in the later works of Friedrich Hayek, especially in relation to the concept of spontaneous order.
4. In addition, the economics of assorted writers such as Adam Smith, Karl Marx, Alfred Marshall and others is also sometimes described as 'evolutionary' in character.
5. Evolutionary game theory is a prominent recent development in mathematical economics.
6. The word 'evolutionary' is sometimes attached to work in what is also described as 'complexity theory', typically that associated with the Santa Fe Institute in the United States, involving applications of chaos theory and various other types of computer simulation. In this and allied simulation work, the use of replicator dynamics, genetic algorithms, genetic programming and so on can be found.

Apart from the important earlier influences, the increasingly fashionable use of the term 'evolutionary economics' today can be largely traced to the impact of Richard Nelson and Sidney Winter's classic (1982) work, *An Evolutionary Theory of Economic Change*, although other recent developments in both orthodox and heterodox economics are also important. Despite the early debate on evolutionary analogies following Armen Alchian's famous 1950 article (Alchian, 1950; Penrose, 1952), the use of the word 'evolutionary' did not become widespread in economics until after 1982.

In fact, the term 'evolutionary economics' is now put to a number of varied and even contradictory uses. There is no established consensus on what it should mean and many use the term while wrongly taking it for granted that a common and obvious meaning is implied. As the biologist Jacques Monod is reported to have said in a lecture on biological evolution, 'Another curious aspect of the theory of evolution is that everybody thinks that he understands it!' Likewise, a curious aspect of 'evolutionary economics' is that many people use the term as if it required little further explanation and that everyone knows what it means. Probe further and the falsity of this is revealed. Clearly, nothing is more guaranteed to generate confusion and to stultify intellectual progress than to raise a muddled term to the centrepiece of economic research, while simultaneously suggesting that a clear and well-defined approach to scientific enquiry is implied. In fact 'evolution' can be used to describe varied approaches in contemporary economics. Elsewhere (Hodgson, 1993: 3), a taxonomy of relevant meanings has been attempted. But the topic is so complex that alternative classifications are possible and a different one is attempted here. This pays particular attention to the varied ontological and methodological foundations of the theories involved.

Varieties of evolutionary economics': a possible classification scheme
Approaches to 'evolutionary economics' are here classified with regard to the following four philosophical criteria.

1. *The ontological criterion (novelty)*: whether or not substantial emphasis is given to the assumption that 'evolutionary' processes in economics involve recurrent or periodic novelty and creativity, thus generating and maintaining a variety of institutions, rules, commodities and technologies. Conceptions of 'economic evolution' which stress novelty typically highlight indeterminacy and the possibility of cumulative divergence, in contrast to convergence and equilibria (Foss, 1994; Hodgson, 1993). For example, the Austrian School of economists, and those influenced by them, give pronounced stress both to the indeterminacy and the potential novelty of human imagination, action and choice (Lachmann, 1977; Loasby, 1976; Shackle, 1955). Another possible source of inspiration is the writings of Sir Karl Popper, in which indeterminacy, novelty and emergent properties are stressed (Popper, 1982). However, novelty does not necessarily involve indeterminacy. For instance, chaos theory highlights potential novelty and divergence, and does this using unpredictable but essentially deterministic systems (Gleick, 1988).
2. *The methodological criterion (reductionism)*: whether explanations in 'evolutionary economics' are reductionist (typically invoking the tenet of methodological individualism that explanations of socioeconomic phenomena must be in terms of constituent individuals and relations between them) or non-reductionist (emphasizing emergent properties at higher levels of analysis, group selection, group knowledge, and so on). Although by far the most common form of reductionism in social science is methodological individualism (suitably defined), this popular term is sometimes used in additional, ambiguous and contradictory ways (for example, Winter, 1988) and is thus avoided here. (See Hodgson, 1993: chs 11–12, 15.)

3. *The temporal criterion (gradualism)*: whether the alleged gradualism of economic 'evolution' or, by contrast, the possibility of intervening periods of rapid change and disruption, is stressed. A notable appearance of this dichotomy is in the controversy between gradualistic and punctuated – or saltationist – theories of technological evolution in particular (Basalla, 1989; Mokyr, 1991) and economic evolution in general (Loasby, 1991; Marshall, 1890; Schumpeter, 1942).

4. *The metaphorical criterion (biology)*: whether extensive use is made of metaphors from biology or not. A motivation for the use of biological metaphors is to replace the mechanistic paradigm which dominates mainstream economics. It has been frequently argued that economies are closer in their constitution to biotic than to mechanical systems, and that a biological metaphor is thus more appropriate in economics (Georgescu-Roegen, 1971; Hodgson, 1995; Marshall, 1890). Others have distanced themselves in varying degrees from biological metaphors (Schumpeter, 1954; Witt, 1992).

These four binary criteria give 16 possible classifications, which are portrayed in Figure 1. Of course, the ordering of the criteria is largely arbitrary, but it could be argued that the ontological criterion is the most fundamental. However, space does not permit a detailed justification of the classification system and the individual classifications. In addition, some of the variants evade precise classification because of ambiguities in the works of the authors involved. An important example here is Friedrich Hayek, who is placed in two boxes because of the ambiguity of his attachment to reductionism and methodological individualism. Despite claiming allegiance to this methodological imperative, especially in his later works he has championed group selection and a departure from strict reductionism and methodological individualism has thus been identified (Vanberg, 1986).

Furthermore, the precise application of the criteria is difficult and in some cases must be tentative, for example with the criterion of 'extensive use' of the biological metaphor. For this reason this – arguably important – criterion is given the lowest implicit ranking of the four in Figure 1. As well as a judgment as to what is and is not 'extensive', there is a further judgment required on the nature and degree of the 'use' of the metaphor. Is it explicit or implicit, for instance? For example, although allusions to the biological metaphor are found in the work of John Commons, unlike the case of Veblen the use of it is not here deemed to be extensive. Accordingly, there is an important difference on this question within the 'old' institutionalist tradition. Commons is put with Ulrich Witt, who has criticized the use of the biological metaphor (Witt, 1992: 7), along with Giovanni Dosi, who like Commons has made no such criticism but does not in practice apply the metaphor explicitly and extensively.

Similar problems of classification arise with Smith, Marx, Menger, Marshall and Walras. They all recognized invention and innovation in economic processes, but their stress on determinism or unilinear development (Smith), or on a teleological view of history as a progression towards a given end (Marx), or on equilibrium outcomes (Menger, Marshall, Walras) means that they pay less attention than others to novelty and creativity.

In addition to the evident lack of unanimity in the 'old' institutionalist camp, there may be several surprises in this classificatory schema. The biggest and most significant one might be Joseph Schumpeter. However, the classification can be defended. First, it was Schumpeter himself who coined the term 'methodological individualism' and repeatedly tried to emulate and develop reductionist approaches in economics, particularly Léon Walras' attempt to base explanations of systemic economic phenomena on the 'microfoundations' of individual actors.

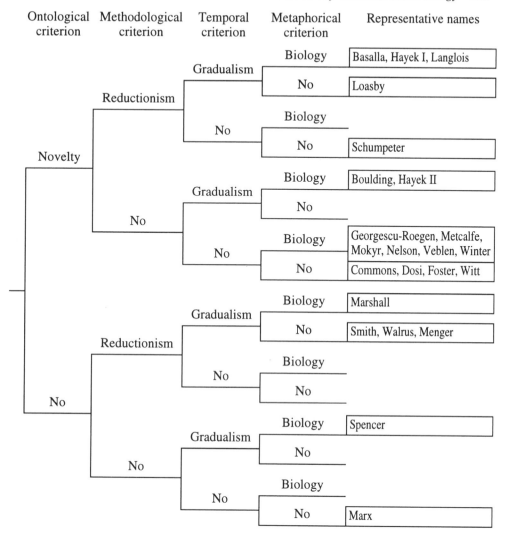

Ontological criterion	Methodological criterion	Temporal criterion	Metaphorical criterion	Representative names
Novelty	Reductionism	Gradualism	Biology	Basalla, Hayek I, Langlois
			No	Loasby
		No	Biology	
			No	Schumpeter
	No	Gradualism	Biology	Boulding, Hayek II
			No	
		No	Biology	Georgescu-Roegen, Metcalfe, Mokyr, Nelson, Veblen, Winter
			No	Commons, Dosi, Foster, Witt
No	Reductionism	Gradualism	Biology	Marshall
			No	Smith, Walrus, Menger
		No	Biology	
			No	
	No	Gradualism	Biology	Spencer
			No	
		No	Biology	
			No	Marx

Figure 1   Possible classifications of 'evolutionary economics'

Second, Schumpeter expressed an uneasiness with the extensive use of metaphors from the natural and physical sciences. He defined the word 'evolution' in broad developmental terms, making no reference to biology (for example, Schumpeter, 1954: 964). In particular, he proclaimed that, in general in economics, 'no appeal to biology would be of the slightest use' (ibid: 789).

The metaphor of natural selection: Veblen, Nelson, Winter

By contrast, we now consider an important group of 'evolutionary economists' who have made a much more direct and explicit appeal to an evolutionary metaphor from biology. In post-Darwinian biology, evolution requires three essential components. First, there must be sustained variation among the members of a species or population. Variations may be blind, random or purposive in character, but without them, as Darwin insisted, natural selection cannot operate.

Second, there must be some principle of heredity or continuity through which offspring have to resemble their parents more than they resemble other members of their species. In other words, there has to be some mechanism through which individual characteristics are passed on through the generations. Third, natural selection itself operates either because better adapted organisms leave increased numbers of offspring or because the variations or gene combinations that are preserved are those bestowing advantage in struggling to survive. This is known as the principle of the struggle for existence.

Veblen stands out as the very first economist to apply the evolutionary analogy in the strict terms of the aforementioned three principles. For instance, we can find the notion of the relative durability of habits or routines and their role as heritable traits in his writings (Veblen, 1899: 190–1). Likewise, Veblen (1914: 86–9) recognized the role of creativity and novelty with his concept of 'idle curiosity'. Veblen's recognition of the open-endedness of the evolutionary process is evidenced in his conception of 'change, realized to be self-continuing or self-propagating and to have no final term' (Veblen, 1919: 37). Finally, Veblen (1899: 188) subscribed to a notion of evolutionary selection in the socioeconomic sphere.

Much more recently, Nelson and Winter (1982) explicitly appropriated and amended these ideas from biology to build their evolutionary theory. Sensibly, an exact correspondence between the ideas in the two sciences is not claimed. Nevertheless, this biological triad of ideas demarcates their own 'evolutionary' approach from different and contending uses of the term. Yet there is a close parallel in their use of the triad in the earlier work of Veblen. Although Nelson and Winter failed to acknowledge his influence, Veblen is a more appropriate precedent than Schumpeter for the rediscovery and development of the biological analogy in the 1980s and 1990s.

There are further parallels, particularly on the question of reductionism. Veblen's stress on institutions as units of analysis and evolutionary selection is evidence of an anti-reductionist strain in his work. Similarly, Nelson and Winter have emphasized the group-based character of knowledge and learning in their work. Information stored by each individual member of an organization is not fully meaningful or effective except in the context provided by the fragments stored by other members (Winter, 1982). However, reductionist strains of evolutionary theory are possible and the use of a biological metaphor is not necessarily an antidote to them. Indeed, there is a strongly reductionist strain in modern biology, particularly in the view that explanations of organism behaviour can be entirely in terms of constituent genes. A prominent example of such 'genetic reductionism' in biology is the work of Richard Dawkins (1976). However, other biologists take a different view, arguing that complete reductionism is not possible and that different levels of analysis are appropriate (Depew and Weber, 1985, Eldredge, 1985; Gould, 1982).

Mutations of evolutionary economics
The challenge provided by evolutionary economics is not only theoretical but ontological, epistemological and methodological. The stress on ontology coincides with a general movement in philosophy back towards matters of ontological grounding that were dismissed as 'metaphysical' in the era of logical positivism. In finding their inspiration in philosophers such as Charles Sanders Peirce and Alfred North Whitehead, the very early institutionalists (for example, Commons, 1934) had ontological concerns. The works of Whitehead, and more recent philosophers such as Roy Bhaskar (1979), promote an organicist ontology involving a stratified universe with emergent properties at each level. Several philosophers have also criticized the

application to biology of reductionism or of the atomist ontology of classical mechanics (Mayr, 1985; Murphy, 1994; Ruse, 1986; Sober, 1984).

Foss (1994) argues forcefully for an ontological characterization of the divergence between evolutionary and neoclassical thinking in economics. He maintains that evolutionary economics of the type developed by Giovanni Dosi, Richard Nelson, Sidney Winter, Ulrich Witt and others is concerned with 'the transformation of already existing structures and the emergence and possible spread of novelties' (Foss, 1994: 21). Indeed, whereas evolutionary economics theorizes on the basis of a universe that is open, in the sense that the emergence of novelties is allowed, neoclassical economics addresses closed systems and suppresses novelty. In short, evolutionary and neoclassical economics start from very different ontological assumptions about the social world. In this manner, Foss also forges explicit links between evolutionary economics and the philosophical realism of Bhaskar (1979).

There are a number of implications in this argument. The quite different ontological grounding of evolutionary economics on Whiteheadian or Bhaskarian foundations has a number of implications, as elaborated elsewhere: for example, a rejection of 'typological essentialism' in favour of 'population thinking' (Foss, 1994; Hodgson, 1993: 47, 68–9, 102, 114, 263; Mayr, 1985; Metcalfe, 1988) the recognition of the openness of socioeconomic systems, the creativity and indeterminacy of human agency, the potentiality for novelty, the possibility of emergent properties and the resultant undermining of reductionist methodologies. However, it should be emphasized that such specific ontological and methodological dispositions are far from universal within biology itself.

Notably, the adoption of an organicist ontology implies that the reductionist and methodological individualist project to explain all social and economic phenomena in terms of given individuals and the relations between them is confounded. The adoption of an organicist ontology means precisely that the individual is not given (Winslow, 1989). Organicism obstructs the treatment of individuals as elemental or immutable building blocks of analysis. Prominent exponents of organicism, such as Whitehead and Bhaskar, argue further that *both* the explanatory reduction of wholes to parts *and* parts to wholes should be rejected. Just as society cannot exist without individuals, the individual does not exist prior to the social reality. Individuals both constitute, and are constituted by, society. Unidirectional modes of explanation, such as from parts to wholes (and vice versa) are thus thwarted.

Just as biology contains a divergence of views, promoted by differences between atomist and organicist ontologies and, consequently, different attitudes to reductionism, strands of evolutionary economics are likely to mutate and differentiate in the future. Some are more concerned to give the mathematical models of mainstream economic theory a slight 'evolutionary' flavour, while typically retaining methodological individualism. Others are less warmly disposed towards formal methods and are concerned more with the genesis of creativity and novelty, with the empirical grounding of evolutionary ideas and with applications to economic policy.

GEOFFREY M. HODGSON

Bibliography

Alchian, Armen A. (1950), 'Uncertainty, Evolution and Economic Theory', *Journal of Political Economy*, **58**, June, 211–22.
Andersen, Esben Sloth (1994), Evolutionary Economics: Post-Schumpeterian Contributions, London: Pinter.
Basalla, George (1989), *The Evolution of Technology*, Cambridge: Cambridge University Press.

Bhaskar, Roy (1979), *The Possibility of Naturalism: A Philosophic Critique of the Contemporary Human Sciences*, Brighton: Harvester.

Boulding, Kenneth E. (1981), *Evolutionary Economics*, Beverly Hills, CA: Sage Publications.

Clark, Norman G. and Calestous Juma (1987), *Long-Run Economics: An Evolutionary Approach to Economic Growth*, London: Pinter.

Commons, John R. (1934), *Institutional Economics – Its Place in Political Economy*, New York: Macmillan; reprinted 1990 with a new introduction by M. Rutherford, New Brunswick: Transaction.

Dawkins, Richard (1976), *The Selfish Gene*, Oxford: Oxford University Press.

Depew, David J. and Bruce H. Weber (eds) (1985), *Evolution at a Crossroads: The New Biology and the New Philosophy of Science*, Cambridge, MA: MIT Press.

Dosi, Giovanni, Christopher Freeman, Richard Nelson, Gerald Silverberg and Luc Soete (eds) (1988), *Technical Change and Economic Theory*, London: Pinter.

Eldredge, Niles (1985), *Unfinished Synthesis: Biological Hierarchies and Modern Evolutionary Thought*, Oxford: Oxford University Press.

England, Richard W. (ed.) (1994), *Evolutionary Concepts in Contemporary Economics*, Ann Arbor: University of Michigan Press.

Foss, Nicolai Juul (1994), 'Realism and Evolutionary Economics', *Journal of Social and Evolutionary Systems*, **17** (1), 21–40.

Foster, John (1987), *Evolutionary Macroeconomics*, London: George Allen & Unwin.

Georgescu-Roegen, Nicholas (1971), *The Entropy Law and the Economic Process*, Cambridge, MA: Harvard University Press.

Gleick, James (1988), *Chaos: Making a New Science*, London: Heinemann.

Gould, Stephen Jay (1982), 'The Meaning of Punctuated Equilibrium and its Role in Validating a Hierarchical Approach to Macroevolution', in Roger Milkman (ed.), *Perspectives on Evolution*, Sunderland, MA: Sinauer Associates.

Hanusch, Horst (ed.) (1988), *Evolutionary Economics: Applications of Schumpeter's Ideas*, Cambridge: Cambridge University Press.

Hayek, Friedrich A. (1988), *The Fatal Conceit: The Errors of Socialism, the Collected Works of Friedrich August Hayek*, vol. I, ed. W.W. Bartley, London: Routledge.

Hodgson, Geoffrey M. (1993), *Economics and Evolution: Bringing Life Back Into Economics*, Cambridge/Ann Arbor, MI: Polity Press/University of Michigan Press.

Hodgson, Geoffrey M. (ed.) (1995), *Economics and Biology*, Aldershot: Edward Elgar.

Hodgson, Geoffrey M., Warren J. Samuels and Marc R. Tool (eds) (1994), *The Elgar Companion to Institutional and Evolutionary Economics*, Aldershot: Edward Elgar.

Lachmann, Ludwig M. (1977), *Capital, Expectations and the Market Process*, ed. with an introduction by W.E. Grinder, Kansas City: Sheed Andrews and McMeel.

Langlois, Richard N. and Michael J. Everett, (1994), 'What is Evolutionary Economics?' in L. Magnusson (ed.), *Evolutionary and Neo-Schumpeterian Approaches to Economics*.

Loasby, Brian J. (1976), *Choice, Complexity and Ignorance: An Enquiry into Economic Theory and the Practice of Decision Making*, Cambridge: Cambridge University Press.

Loasby, Brian J. (1991), *Equilibrium and Evolution: An Exploration of Connecting Principles in Economics*, Manchester: Manchester University Press.

Magnusson, Lars (ed.) (1994), *Evolutionary and Neo-Schumpeterian Approaches to Economics*, Boston: Kluwer.

Marshall, Alfred (1890), *Principles of Economics: An Introductory Volume*, London: Macmillan.

Mayr, Ernst (1985), 'How Biology Differs from the Physical Sciences', in D.J. Depew and B.H. Weber, *Evolution at a Crossroads*.

Metcalfe, J. Stanley (1988), 'Evolution and Economic Change', in Aubrey Silberston (ed.), *Technology and Economic Progress*, Basingstoke: Macmillan; reprinted in Witt (ed.) (1993b) *Evolutionary Economics*.

Mokyr, Joel (1991), 'Evolutionary Biology, Technical Change and Economic History', *Bulletin of Economic Research*, **43**, (2), April, 127–49.

Murphy, James Bernard (1994), 'The Kinds of Order in Society', in Philip Mirowski (ed.), *Natural Images in Economic Thought: Markets Read in Tooth and Claw*, Cambridge/New York: Cambridge University Press.

Nelson, Richard R. and Sidney G. Winter (1982), *An Evolutionary Theory of Economic Change*, Cambridge, MA: Harvard University Press.

Penrose, Edith T. (1952), 'Biological Analogies in the Theory of the Firm', *American Economic Review*, **42**, (4), December, 804–19.

Popper, Sir Karl R. (1982), *The Open Universe: An Argument for Indeterminism*, from the *Postscript to the Logic of Scientific Discovery*, ed. W.W. Bartley, London: Hutchinson.

Ruse, Michael (1986), *Taking Darwin Seriously: A Naturalistic Approach to Philosophy*, Oxford: Blackwell.

Saviotti, Pier Paolo and J. Stanley Metcalfe (eds) (1991), *Evolutionary Theories of Economic and Technological Change: Present Status and Future Prospects*, Reading: Harwood.

Schumpeter, Joseph A. (1942), *Capitalism, Socialism and Democracy*, London: George Allen & Unwin.

Schumpeter, Joseph A. (1954), *History of Economic Analysis*, New York: Oxford University Press.

Shackle, George L.S. (1955), *Uncertainty in Economics*, Cambridge: Cambridge University Press.

Sober, Elliott (1984), *The Nature of Selection: Evolutionary Theory in Philosophical Focus*, Cambridge, MA; MIT Press.

Vanberg, Victor J. (1986), 'Spontaneous Market Order and Social Rules: A Critique of F.A. Hayek's Theory of Cultural Evolution', *Economics and Philosophy*, **2**, (1), April, 75–100; reprinted in Witt (ed.) (1993b), *Evolutionary Economics*.

Veblen, Thorstein B. (1898), 'Why is Economics Not an Evolutionary Science?', *Quarterly Journal of Economics*, **12**, (3), July, 373–97; reprinted in Veblen (1919), *The Peace of Science*.

Veblen, Thorstein B. (1899), *The Theory of the Leisure Class: An Economic Study of Institutions*, New York: Macmillan.

Veblen, Thorstein B. (1914), *The Instinct of Workmanship, and the State of the Industrial Arts*, New York: Augustus Kelley; reprinted 1990 with a new introduction by M.G. Murphey and a 1964 introductory note by J. Dorfman, New Brunswick: Transaction.

Veblen, Thorstein B. (1919), *The Place of Science in Modern Civilisation and Other Essays*, New York: Huebsch; reprinted 1990 with a new introduction by W.J. Samuels, New Brunswick: Transaction.

Winslow, Edward A. (1989), 'Organic Interdependence, Uncertainty and Economic Analysis', *Economic Journal*, **99**, (4), December, 1173–82.

Winter Jr, Sidney G. (1982), 'An Essay on the Theory of Production', in S.H. Hymans (ed.), *Economics and the World Around It*, Ann Arbor: University of Michigan Press.

Winter Jr, Sidney G. (1988), 'On Coase, Competence and the Corporation', *Journal of Law, Economics and Organization*, **4** (1), Spring, 163–80; reprinted in O.E. Williamson and S.G. Winter (eds) (1991), *The Nature of the Firm: Origins, Evolution and Development*, Oxford. Oxford University Press.

Witt, Ulrich (1987), *Individualistische Grundlagen der evolutorishen Ökonomie*, Tübingen: Mohr.

Witt, Ulrich (ed.) (1992), *Explaining Process and Change: Approaches to Evolutionary Economics*, Ann Arbor: University of Michigan Press.

Witt, Ulrich (ed.) (1993a), *Evolution in Markets and Institutions*, Heidelberg: Physica-Verlag.

Witt, Ulrich (ed.) (1993b), *Evolutionary Economics*, Aldershot: Edward Elgar.

Evolutionary Epistemology

Evolutionary epistemology is the attempt to address questions in the theory of knowledge from an evolutionary point of view. Evolutionary epistemology involves, in part, deploying models and metaphors drawn from evolutionary biology in the attempt to characterize and resolve issues arising in epistemology and conceptual change. As disciplines coevolve, models are traded back and forth. Thus evolutionary epistemology also involves attempts to understand how biological evolution proceeds by interpreting it through models drawn from our understanding of conceptual change and the development of theories. The term 'evolutionary epistemology' was coined by Donald Campbell (1974) although the fundamental projects collected under that designation go back to Darwin.

The evolution of epistemological mechanisms (EEM) versus the evolution of epistemological theories (EET)

There are two interrelated but distinct programs which go by the name 'evolutionary epistemology'. One focuses on the development of cognitive mechanisms in animals and humans. This involves a straightforward extension of the biological theory of evolution to those aspects or traits of animals which are the biological substrates of cognitive activity, for example, their brains, sensory systems and motor systems. The other programme attempts to account for the evolution of ideas, scientific theories, epistemic norms and culture in general by using models and metaphors drawn from evolutionary biology. Both programmes have their roots in nineteenth century biology and social philosophy, in the work of Darwin, Spencer, James and others. There have been a number of attempts in the intervening years to develop the programmes in detail (see the bibliography and review in Campbell, 1974). Much of the contemporary work in evolutionary epistemology derives from the work of Konrad Lorenz (1977), Donald Campbell (for example, 1974), Karl Popper (1972, 1984) and Stephen Toulmin (1967, 1972). These two programmes have been labelled EEM and EET (Bradie, 1986). EEM is the label for the programme which attempts to provide an evolutionary account of the development of cognitive structures; EET is the label for the programme which attempts to analyse the development of human knowledge and epistemological norms by appealing to relevant biological considerations. Some of these attempts involve analysing the growth of human knowledge in terms of selectionist models and metaphors (for example, Popper, 1972; Toulmin, 1972; Hull, 1988). Others argue for a biological grounding of epistemological norms and methodologies but eschew *selectionist* models of the growth of human knowledge as such (for example, Ruse, 1986; Rescher, 1990). It is important to keep the EEM and EET programmes distinct. A successful selectionist explanation of the development of cognitive brain structures provides no warrant, in itself, for extrapolating such models to understand the development of human knowledge systems. Similarly, endorsing a selectionist account of the way human knowledge systems grow does not, in itself, warrant concluding that specific or general brain structures involved in cognition are the result of natural selection for enhanced cognitive capacities. The two programmes, though similar in design and drawing upon the same models and metaphors, do not stand or fall together.

Ontogeny versus phylogeny
Biological development involves both ontogenetic and phylogenetic considerations. Thus the development of specific traits, such as the opposable thumb in humans, can be viewed from the point of view both of the development of that trait in individual organisms (ontogeny) and of the development of that trait in the human lineage (phylogeny). The development of knowledge and knowing mechanisms exhibits a parallel distinction. The growth of an individual's knowledge corpus and the development of her appreciation of epistemological norms, as well as the neural development of her brain, are all ontogenetic processes. The growth of human knowledge and development of epistemological norms across generations are phylogenetic processes, as is the evolution of brains in the human lineage. The EEM/EET distinction applies to both sorts of process. We may be concerned either with the ontogenetic or phylogenetic development of, for example, the brain or the ontogenetic or phylogenetic development of norms and knowledge corpora. One might expect that, since current orthodoxy maintains that biological processes of ontogenesis proceed differently from the selectionist processes of phylogenesis, evolutionary epistemologies would reflect this difference, but curiously enough, for the most part they do not. For example, the theory of 'neural Darwinism' as put forth by Edelman (1987) and Changeux (1985) offers a selectionist account of the ontogenetic development of the neural structures of the brain. Karl Popper's conjectures and refutations model of the development of human knowledge is a well-known example of a selectionist account which has been applied both to the ontogenetic growth of knowledge in individuals and to the transgenerational (phylogenetic) evolution of scientific knowledge. B.F. Skinner's theory of operant conditioning, which deals with the ontogenesis of individual behaviour, is explicitly based upon the Darwinian selectionist model. (Skinner, 1981).

Descriptive versus prescriptive approaches
A third distinction concerns descriptive versus prescriptive approaches to epistemology and the growth of human knowledge. Many have argued that neither the EEM programmes nor the

EET programmes have anything at all to do with epistemology properly (that is, traditionally) understood. The basis for this contention is that epistemology, properly understood, is a normative discipline, whereas the EEM and EET programmes are concerned with the construction of causal and genetic (that is, descriptive) models of the evolution of cognitive capacities or knowledge systems. No such models, it is alleged, can have anything important to contribute to normative epistemology. The force of this complaint depends upon how one construes the relationship between evolutionary epistemology and the tradition.

There are three possible configurations of the relationship between descriptive and traditional epistemologies. First, descriptive epistemologies can be construed as competitors to traditional normative epistemologies. On this view, they are trying to address the same concerns and offering competing solutions. Riedl (1984) defends this position. A standard objection to such approaches is that descriptive accounts are not adequate to do justice to the prescriptive elements of normative methodologies. Second, descriptive epistemology might be seen as a successor discipline to traditional epistemology. On this reading, descriptive epistemology does not address the questions of traditional epistemology because it deems them irrelevant or unanswerable or uninteresting. Many defenders of naturalized epistemologies fall into this camp (for example, Munz 1993). Third, descriptive epistemology might be seen as complementary to traditional epistemology. This appears to be Campbell's view. On this analysis, the function of the evolutionary approach is to provide a descriptive account of knowing mechanisms while leaving the prescriptive aspects of epistemology to more traditional approaches. At best, the evolutionary analyses serve to rule out normative approaches which are either implausible or inconsistent with an evolutionary origin of human understanding.

The extent to which an evolutionary approach contributes to the resolution of traditional epistemological and philosophical problems is a function of which approach one adopts. (cf. Bradie, 1986; Ruse, 1986; Radnitzky and Bartley, 1987).

Future prospects
EEM programmes are saddled with the typical uncertainties of phylogenetic reconstructions: is this or that organ or structure an adaptation and, if so, for what? In addition, there are the uncertainties which result from the necessarily sparse fossil record of brain and sensory organ development. The EET programmes are even more problematic. While it is plausible enough to think that the evolutionary imprint on our organs of thought influences what and how we do think, it is not at all clear that the influence is direct, significant or detectable. Selectionist epistemologies which endorse a 'trial and error' methodology as an appropriate model for understanding scientific change are not analytic consequences of accepting that the brain and other ancillary organs are adaptations which have evolved primarily under the influence of natural selection. The viability of such selectionist models is an empirical question which rests on the development of adequate models. Hull's (1988) contribution is, as he himself admits, but the first step in that direction. Much hard empirical work needs to be done to sustain this line of research. Non-selectionist evolutionary epistemologies, along the lines of Ruse (1986), face a different range of difficulties. It remains to be shown that any biological considerations are sufficiently restrictive to narrow down the range of potential methodologies in any meaningful way.

Nevertheless, the emergence in the latter quarter of the twentieth century of serious efforts to provide an evolutionary account of human understanding has potentially radical consequences. The application of selectionist models to the development of human knowledge, for example, creates an immediate tension. Standard traditional accounts of the emergence and growth of scientific knowledge see science as a progressive enterprise which, under the appropriate conditions of rational and free inquiry, generates a body of knowledge which progressively converges on the truth. Selectionist models of biological evolution, on the other hand, are generally construed to be non-progressive or, at most, locally so. Rather than generating convergence, biological evolution produces diversity. Popper's evolutionary epistemology attempts to embrace both, but does so uneasily. Kuhn's 'scientific revolutions' account draws tentatively upon a Darwinian model but, when criticized, Kuhn has retreated (compare Kuhn, 1962: 172f with Lakatos and Musgrave, 1970: 264). Toulmin (1972) is a noteworthy exception. On his account, concepts of rationality are purely 'local' and subject themselves to evolution. The net result is the need to abandon any sense of 'goal directedness' in scientific inquiry. This is a radical consequence. Pursuing the evolutionary approach to its logical conclusion raises fundamental questions about the concepts of knowledge, truth, realism, justification and rationality.

Disciplines often borrow each other's metaphors. For example, economics, evolutionary theory and epistemology trade concepts of competition back and forth. The 'struggle for existence', which Darwin borrowed from Malthus, was reappropriated by the Social Darwinists in the latter part of the nineteenth century and used as a justification for laissez-faire capitalism. In the selectionist epistemological models of Popper (1968), Toulmin (1972) and Hull (1988), there is a struggle for existence in the 'market-place of ideas'. Economic considerations of costs and benefits are appropriate here (cf. Rescher, 1978; 1989; Wible, 1994). This has obvious implications for the advancement of knowledge, and more subtle implications for the concept of knowledge.

The gathering and dissemination of information involves costs. Who controls the purse strings controls the direction of research and the flow of information. If there is a *market-place* of ideas, should it be regulated? If so, how and to what end? Here both epistemic and economic considerations come into play. If the growth of knowledge is truly evolutionary, there is no guarantee that convergence on Truth or a Final Theory will occur. Indeed, if that evolution is governed by market forces that include economic factors intermixed with epistemic factors, a fundamental reassessment of the concepts of truth and knowledge seems in order.

Taking Darwin seriously demands a fundamental re-examination of the human epistemological condition in the light of our understanding of biological evolution. This task is not one that can or should be consigned to philosophers or biologists alone. Rather, it is one that invites and demands interdisciplinary efforts from a range of specialists in philosophy, biology and the social sciences.

MICHAEL BRADIE

Bibliography
Bradie, M. (1986), 'Assessing Evolutionary Epistemology', *Biology & Philosophy*, 1, 401–59.
Campbell, D.T. (1974), 'Evolutionary Epistemology', in P.A. Schilpp (ed.), *The Philosophy of Karl Popper. I*, La Salle, IL: Open Court.
Changeux, Jean-Pierre (1985), *Neuronal Man*, New York: Pantheon.
Edelman, G.M. (1987), *Neural Darwinism: The Theory of Neuronal Group Selection*, New York: Basic Books.
Hull, D. (1988), *Science as a Process: An Evolutionary Account of the Social and Conceptual Development of Science*, Chicago: University of Chicago Press.
Kuhn, T. (1962), *The Structure of Scientific Revolutions*, Chicago: University of Chicago Press.
Lakatos, I. and A. Musgrave (eds) (1970), *Criticism and the Growth of Knowledge*, Cambridge: Cambridge University Press.

Lorenz, Konrad (1977), *Behind the Mirror*, London: Methuen.
Munz, Peter (1993), *Philosophical Darwinism: On the Origin of Knowledge by Means of Natural Selection*, London: Routledge.
Plotkin, H.C. (ed.) (1982), *Learning, Development, and Culture: Essays in Evolutionary Epistemology*, New York: John Wiley & Sons.
Popper, K.R. (1968), *The Logic of Scientific Discovery*, New York: Harper.
Popper, K.R. (1972), *Objective Knowledge: An Evolutionary Approach*, Oxford: The Clarendon Press.
Popper, K.R. (1984), 'Evolutionary Epistemology', in J.W. Polland (ed.), *Evolutionary Theory: Paths into the Future*, London: John Wiley.
Radnitzky, G. and W.W. Bartley (1987), *Evolutionary Epistemology, Theory of Rationality and the Sociology of Knowledge*, LaSalle, IL: Open Court.
Rescher, N. (1978), *Scientific Progress: A Philosophical Essay on the Economics of Research in Natural Science*, Oxford: Basil Blackwell.
Rescher, N. (1989), *Cognitive Economy: The Economic Dimension of the Theory of Knowledge*, Pittsburgh: University of Pittsburgh Press.
Rescher, Nicholas (1990), *A Useful Inheritance: Evolutionary Aspects of the Theory of Knowledge*, Lanham, MD: Rowman.
Riedl, Rupert (1984), *Biology of Knowledge: The Evolutionary Basis of Reason*, Chichester: John Wiley.
Ruse, M. (1986), *Taking Darwin Seriously: A Naturalistic Approach to Philosophy*, Oxford: Blackwell.
Skinner, B.F. (1981), 'Selection by Consequences', *Science*, **213**, 501–4.
Toulmin, Stephen (1967), 'The Evolutionary Development of Natural Science', *American Scientist*, **55**, 4.
Toulmin, Stephen (1972), *Human Understanding: The Collective Use and Evolution of Concepts*, Princeton: Princeton University Press.
Wible, J.R. (1994), 'Rescher's Economic Philosophy of Science: A Review of Nicholas Rescher's *Cognitive Economy*, *Scientific Progress*, and Peirce's *Philosophy of Science*', *The Journal of Economic Methodology*, **1/2**, 314–29.

Expected Utility Theory

Expected Utility Theory (EUT) states that the decision maker (DM) chooses between risky or uncertain prospects by comparing their expected utility values, that is, the weighted sums obtained by adding the utility values of outcomes multiplied by their respective probabilities. This elementary and seemingly commonsensical decision rule raises at once some of the most important questions in contemporary decision theory. We will focus here on two of these questions. First, what do the utility numbers in the formula refer to, and in particular do they belong to the same value scale as do the utility numbers that represent the DM's choices under certainty? Second, is the weighted sum procedure of combining probability and utility values the only one to be considered, and if there are indeed alternative modellings, how will the theorist choose? Most of this entry is concerned with risk as opposed to uncertainty, that is, with choice contexts in which probabilities are *given*, be they objective or not. Corresponding to the standard distinction between risk and uncertainty, there are two received versions of the theory, Von Neumann–Morgenstern theory (VNMT) and subjective expected utility theory (SEUT), respectively. We will only touch on the latter. Before examining the two questions in turn, we restate the sources and basic axiomatic structure of EUT. It has been used as both a positive and normative (or prescriptive) theory. Methodological discussions are primarily concerned with the theory in its positive role, and with the second question, which in effect concerns the relaxation of the 'VNM independence axiom'.

The history of EUT is often construed in terms of the following smooth generalization process: the principle of maximizing expected monetary values antedates EUT, which is now in the process of being generalized in two directions, by either non-additive or non-probabilistic decision theories. The highlights in this sequence are Bernoulli's (1738) resolution of the St Petersburg paradox, and Allais' (1953) invention of a thought-provoking problem widely referred to as

the Allais paradox. In the St Petersburg game, people were asked how much they would pay
for the following prospect: if tails comes out of the first toss of a fair coin, to receive nothing
and stop the game and, in the complementary case, to receive two guilders and stay in the game;
if tails comes out of the second toss of the coin, to receive nothing and stop the game and in
the complementary case, to receive four guilders and stay in the game; and so on ad infinitum.
The expected monetary value of this prospect is $\Sigma_n(2^n \times 1/2^n) =$ infinite. Since the people always
set a definite, possibly quite small upper value on the St Petersburg prospect, it follows that
they do not price it in terms of its expected monetary value. Bernoulli argued in effect that they
estimate it in terms of the utility of money outcomes, and defended the log function as a plausible
idealization, given its property of quickly decreasing marginal utilities. Because the resulting
series, $\Sigma_n(\log 2^n \times 1/2^n)$, is convergent, Bernoulli's hypothesis was supposed to deliver a
solution to the paradox; more on the history of this problem in Todhunter (1865).

Bernoulli's hypothesis counts as the first systematic occurrence of EUT theory. Two
centuries later, Allais questioned the naturalness of EU-based choices by devising t h e
following questionnaire.

Question 1: which prospect would you choose of $x_1 =$ to receive 100 million FF with probability
1, and $y_1 =$ to receive 500 million FF with probability 0.10, 100 million FF with probability
0.89, and nothing with probability 0.01?
Question 2: which prospect would you choose of $x_2 =$ to receive 100 million FF with probability
0.11, and nothing with probability 0.89, and $y_2 =$ to receive 500 million FF with probability
0.10, and nothing with probability 0.90?

Allais found that the majority answers were x_1 to question 1 and y_2 to question 2, and argued
that this pair of prospects could indeed be chosen for good reasons. But it violates EUT, since
there is no function U that would satisfy both:

$$U(100) > 10/100\ U(500) + 89/100\ U(100) + 1/100\ U(0)$$

and

$$11/100\ U(100) + 89/100\ U(0) < 10/100\ U(500) + 90/100\ U(0).$$

Although the word 'paradox' is frequently used in the history of EUT, it should be clear from
this and the previous examples that it does not refer to deeply ingrained conceptual difficulties,
such as Russell's paradox in set theory, or the EPR paradox in physics, but rather just to problems
or anomalies for the theory that is currently taken for granted: expected monetary value theory
in the St Petersburg case and EUT in the Allais case.

There are few explicit EU calculations in economics before von Neumann and Morgenstern
(1944), who chose to determine the utility value of a randomized strategy in this mathematically
convenient way. Their theoretical choice has proved to be of long-lasting influence. Not only
is current game theory (including its branch specializing in incomplete information games, which
dates back to Harsanyi's work in the late 1960s) still heavily dependent on EU calculations,
but the same can be said, although to a lesser degree, of today's microeconomics of imperfect
information, as textbooks will confirm. Like Bernoulli, von Neumann and Morgenstern are
concerned with the case in which the probabilities are part of the decision problem. Their work

did not yet amount to an axiomatization in the sense decision theorists and economists have become accustomed to. It is only with Marschak and with Herstein and Milnor, in the early 1950s, that the EU formula was derived as the numerical counterpart of a qualitatively defined preference structure subjected to various axiomatic constraints. In honour of the founders, this derivation was named the VNM theorem, and the crucial axiom in the construction VNM independence. This terminology might hide the historical fact that the very axiom which was to arouse innumerable discussions is not even stated in von Neumann and Morgenstern's account! Fishburn (1989) and Fishburn and Wakker (1995) discuss this fact while surveying the work of the formative years.

All available axiomatizations assume that there is a binary relation ≤ on the set X of all risky prospects, called also lotteries, and subject this relation to the *preordering* (that is, transitivity and completeness), *continuity* and *independence* properties. Little will be said here about the first axiom, not because it lacks empirical content, but because it is not specific to the theory of risky or uncertain choices. (However, the transitivity condition has come to be discussed widely in the EUT context, in particular because of the 'preference reversal' phenomenon, on which the reader is referred to Hausman, 1992.) The second axiom typically says that if, x is strictly preferred to z, which is strictly preferred to y, then a suitable mixture of x and y will be strictly preferred to z, and z will be strictly preferred to another suitable mixture of x and y. In the presence of the first, this axiom makes it possible to 'represent' the qualitative datum ≤ by some, yet unspecific, numerical function $u(x)$. It has some empirical content but plays mostly a technical role. The third axiom (VNM independence) can be stated in the following easy form, due to Samuelson: for all x, y and z in X, and any number α such that $0 < \alpha < 1$, $x \leq y$ if and only if $\alpha x + (1 - \alpha)z \leq \alpha y + (1 - \alpha)z$.

Expressed in words, preference inequalities are preserved when the initial two lotteries are mixed in a given proportion with a third lottery. This axiom is responsible for the specific, expectational form of the function $u(x)$ provided by the VNM theorem. A few constructions also involve a compound lottery axiom, which says in effect that any lottery having further lotteries as its outcomes can be reduced to a one-stage lottery. This further axiom has a definite empirical content and is now regarded as being responsible for some cases of violation of EUT. Notice that it is automatically satisfied by the standard formalization of lotteries in terms of probability functions (since a mixture, that is, convex combination, of probabilities is again a probability).

Historically, SEUT can be said to result from two distinct traditions, one the Bernoulli–VNM tradition of decision theory, the other the mathematical and philosophical tradition of subjective probability, which can be traced back to the British empiricists and Bayes, and which was revived in the 1930s by Ramsey and de Finetti. (The contrast between 'objective' and 'subjective' schools of probability is surveyed in Fine, 1973; see also Fishburn's 1986 introduction to subjective probability.) De Finetti was particularly emphatic in claiming that probability does not exist in any substantial sense. As he conceived of it, probability does not even necessarily exist in the subject's mind; it might just be the numerical expression, as defined by an outside observer, of the property that the subject behaves coherently when choosing between uncertain prospects. This interpretation elaborates on the Dutch book theorem, which was first sketched by Ramsey: a Dutch book is a list of bets on all possible events which leads to a net loss of money whichever state of the world is realized; the theorem shows that to avoid Dutch books is equivalent to choosing among prospects according to the expectation of their monetary values, where the expectation is taken with respect to some well-defined probability. Leaving aside the strong anti-realist stand taken by de Finetti, as well as (though to a lesser degree) Ramsey, these authors were the first to bridge the analysis of probability with a (rudimentary) decision theory. Savage (1954) consolidated and enlarged the bridge by showing that to satisfy certain behavioural requirements in the style of, but more abstract and general than, the no-Dutch-book assumption is equivalent to choosing among prospects according to the expectation of their utility values, where the expectation is taken with respect to some well-defined pair of probability and utility function. The non-trivial step in Savage's contribution is to reveal these two items simultaneously from the axiomatically constrained preference behaviour. To do so, he made implicit use of VNM theory. While two of his axioms (P3 and P4) are reminiscent of the Dutch book scheme, his postulate P2, or 'sure-thing principle', is the counterpart of VNM independence in the subjective probability framework. Unsurprisingly, VNM independence and the 'sure-thing principle' have been criticized in broadly similar ways, and have led to parallel generalizations. Savage's axiomatization has also induced a specific 'paradox', Ellsberg's (1954), which is usually understood as contradicting the existence of subjective probabilities and constitutes the starting point of another generalization trend.

To make precise the first question raised at the outset, a formal statement of the VNM theorem is needed. Denoting by $c_1, ..., c_k$ the outcomes of lottery x, and by $p_1, ..., p_k$ the attached probability values, the theorem says that if the three axioms of preordering, continuity and independence hold, there is a representation of the preference relation in terms of the expectation of some utility function U on the outcomes, that is, $\Sigma_i p_i U(c_i)$ and that the U function in this representation is 'unique up to a positive linear transformation'. Now, the question is, does U refer to the same quantities as does the utility function of non-stochastic theories, such as consumer theory in microeconomics? The 'measurability controversy' in which Baumol, Friedman and Savage, Ellsberg, Luce and Raiffa were involved in the 1950s, was mostly concerned with this problem. The participants agreed that, for a given individual, the *ordinal* properties of $U(c)$ should be the same as those of any alternative index $V(c)$ provided by the non-stochastic theory of preferences among outcomes. However, there were severe disagreements on what added properties the VNM theorem delivered. A view shared by some prominent economists, including perhaps von Neumann and Morgenstern themselves, was that the $U(c)$ index succeeded where earlier indexes from non-stochastic theory had failed; that is, it had *cardinal* properties in the sense of measuring the individual's preference differences or intensities over the outcome set. This conclusion was supported by the following argument: take three outcomes c, c' and c'' such that $U(c) > U(c') > U(c'')$, and suppose that: $1/2U(c) + 1/2U(c'') > U(c')$ holds. Then $U(c) - U(c') > U(c') - U(c'')$ trivially follows; because the last inequality does not depend on the particular representation U (see the uniqueness part of the VNM theorem), it would seem natural to interpret it as implying that the individual's intensity of preference of c over c' is stronger than the intensity of his preference of c' over c''. Hence the conclusion that VNM had gone beyond the purely ordinalist stand at which the Paretian school had stopped. By and large, the 'measurability controversy' resulted in the rejection of this optimistic interpretation. It was shown to rely on a superficial understanding of the uniqueness part of the VNM theorem. To make sense of a cardinal index in the desired sense, one should first of all impose a special axiom on the preference relation on outcomes, to the effect that preference differences or intensities are meaningful. In the presence of suitably strengthened versions of the preordering and continuity axioms, this added axiom will have the effect of determining another utility function W on outcomes, which is itself 'unique up to a linear transformation'. But unless this is explicitly required by adding still another axiom, there is no reason why W should be a linear transformation of the VNM index, U. In other words, the uniqueness part of the theorem does provide a formal method for comparing utility differences but the numbers derived in this way might be unrelated to the measurement of preference differences on the outcome set. The refutation sketched here is in accord with Fishburn's (1989) and further clarified by Bouyssou and Vansnick (1990).

Although the negative point just made might now count as standard doctrine, it is not universally recognized. Harsanyi is prominent among those who interpret the VNM index as measuring the individual's true preference differences. He actually needs this interpretation in order to tighten up and clarify the important work he pursued in the 1950s to connect EU theory with utilitarianism. Because of Harsanyi's influence on current welfare economics, the 'measurability controversy' is not yet closed; for further details, see Mongin and d'Aspremont (forthcoming). Allais' notion of cardinality is also at variance with the standard doctrine, although for reasons of his own.

The second of the two questions mentioned at the outset is concerned with the VNM independence axiom and has led to a host of competing answers. Among the many available generalizations of this axiom, two will be singled out here. Machina's proposed theory directly generalizes the EU representation without investigating the corresponding properties of the preference relation. The first step is to replace the linearity-in-the-probabilities property of the EU representation by the weaker property of differentiability with respect to the probabilities. It can be checked that EUT then holds as a local approximation of the new theory: there are as many EU representations as there are lotteries (formally, probability distributions) and these many representations can be used to approximate relevant properties of the global, differentiable representation in the neighbourhood of the lottery x they are associated with. Each of them gives rise to a function on outcomes which will be denoted by $U_x(c)$. (Note the difference from VNM theory, which deduced a function $U(c)$ independent of the particular lottery x.) Clearly, the U_x may exhibit widely differing curvature properties. The second step in Machina's theory precisely consists in determining how the curvature of U_x varies with x: following the 'fanning out' hypothesis, it should satisfy a condition of increasing risk aversion (as measured in terms of concavity) when x varies in the direction of increasing stochastic dominance (roughly speaking, in the direction of lotteries that move probabilistic weight towards the better outcomes). The whole of this technical construction can be illustrated elegantly in terms of indifference curves: step 1 then means that the agent's indifference curves are of any smooth shape, instead of being parallel straight lines, as in the VNM particular case; and step 2 simply means that they become steeper when one looks in the direction defined by the best outcome. As Machina (1983) explains, it becomes possible to account for the common, systematic pattern underlying a number of well-established anomalies of EUT: not only the 'common consequence effect' (which is Allais' paradox in more abstract form), but also the 'common ratio effect' (a related anomaly, which was investigated by Kahneman and Tversky), the 'utility evaluation effect' (an anomaly which emerged from the attempts at numerically estimating the $U(c)$ function), and a lesser known effect, called 'oversensitivity to changes in small probability-outlying events'.

Another generalization of EUT which has perhaps become more popular than any other among decision theorists is the so-called rank-dependent or anticipated utility theory (AUT). It is now endowed with an axiomatic version which clarifies the sense in which VNM independence is weakened, but is easier to discuss in terms of functional representations. Assuming that the outcomes $c_1, \ldots, c_k$ of lottery x are ranked in increasing preference order, AUT evaluates x as follows:

$$f(p_1)\, U(c_1) + \{f(p_1 + p_2) - f(p_1)\}\, U(c_2) + \ldots + \{f(p_1 + p_2 + \ldots + p_k)$$
$$- f(p_1 + p_2 + \ldots + p_{k-1})\}\, U(c_k)$$

where $f: [0, 1] \to [0, 1]$ and $f(0) = 0, f(1) = 1$ and f is weakly increasing.

This added function is intended to capture the agent's distortion of probability values. When f is the identity function, the formula collapses into EUT. If f satisfies $f(p) \geq p$ for all p, and in particular is concave throughout, it expresses a psychological attitude akin to risk aversion: think of a lottery with two distant monetary outcomes and compare it with the lottery giving its expected monetary value for sure. Conversely, $f(p) \leq p$ for all p expresses a kind of risk-seeking attitude. The case of a S-shaped f has also been explored; it involves a strong tendency to overweight small probability values. Various shapes can be invoked to account for the Allais paradox and the other related effects.

Conceptually, there are two important connections between AUT and earlier work. First, the idea of enriching EUT with a probability distortion element is very natural, and indeed emerged at an early stage of the empirical psychologists' work. For instance, Kahneman and Tversky's 'prospect theory' involved generalizing EUT in terms of the following formula:

$$g(p_1)\, U(c_1) + g(p_2)\, U(c_2) + \ldots + g(p_k)\, U(c_k).$$

Natural though it seems, this formula leads to an unwelcome consequence. Decision theorists were willing to give up the linearity-in-the-probabilities property of EUT, but not this further, much weaker implication of VNM independence: if lottery x stochastically dominates lottery y, the agent prefers x to y. The stochastic dominance property can be violated in Kahneman and Tversky's generalization of EUT. Importantly, it is always satisfied by the AUT formula, in which cumulative distribution values, rather than probability values irrespective of the order of prospects, are assumed to be distorted. Following Quiggin's (1993) interpretation, this is indeed the decisive contribution of AUT: it salvaged the psychologists' intuition in the only way compatible with a hard core postulate of decision theory. Second, AUT connects with the 'measurability controversy'. As explained above, one of the results of this controversy was that the VNM cardinalization should not be confused with the cardinalization relevant to the measurement of preference differences in the certainty case. A closely related conclusion is that the property of risk aversion, as measured by the concavity of the VNM index, should not be confused with the property of diminishing marginal utility of money, which belongs to the certainty context. A richer theory than EUT is needed to express this conceptual distinction formally. According to many decision theorists, AUT is the theory needed: the added function f has the role of expressing risk attitudes, so that U can be reserved for the altogether different use of conveying certainty-related properties, such as diminishing marginal utility.

Perhaps the most important methodological question raised by EUT is whether the process of successful generalization sketched above can be interpreted as evidence of scientific progress. Mongin (1988) gives some perspective on this issue by investigating EUT in the context of Duhem's problem: the problem of choosing which part of a compound hypothesis should be sacrificed when that hypothesis is faced with unfavourable evidence. This paper emphasizes the Duhem problem raised by the axiomatic structure of VNM theory and, using standard philosophy of science arguments, claims that this problem was solved satisfactorily when – after many hesitations – decision theorists agreed to follow Allais' suggestion of sacrificing VNM independence while retaining the weaker property of stochastic dominance and the other axioms. Another, perhaps equally important, Duhem problem of EUT has to do with the structure of evidence. Even leaving aside thought experiments, introspection and stylized facts, which play a role in decision-theoretic discussions as they do elsewhere in economics, truly experimental evidence can be interpreted as telling only against the background of delicate auxiliary hypotheses. The crucial ones relate to the subject's cognitive abilities (typically, his understanding of probability and expectation), his financial motivations (rewards should be neither too small nor too large) and to the subject's consistency from one set of answers to another (for example, when data on different gambles are matched against each other, or gambling data are matched against market data). The only existing discussions of auxiliary hypotheses are by experimenters themselves, who have invented further experiments to assess their hidden role: see the continuing work around the widely used 'Becker–De Groot–Marschak procedure', as reported in, for example, Camerer (1995). The experimenters' assessments of their own methods rarely lead to clear-cut conclusions. However, there is some reason for believing that the Duhem problem, in the second of the two senses distinguished here, was at least sometimes resolved satisfactorily: it would seem as if the four effects listed by Machina were correctly interpreted as telling evidence against EUT, rather than against auxiliary hypotheses, because they follow a highly systematic pattern of mutually supporting evidence.

To solve the Duhem problem in the theory of risky choice would be an important negative step, but it would not yet provide a positive guarantee of scientific progress. Mongin noted that Machina's generalized expected utility theory (GEUT) satisfies neither Popper's nor Lakatos criteria of progressivity; the same could probably be said of AUT. Leaving aside the refutationist context in which this conclusion is phrased, the underlying philosophical problem appears to be that both GEUT and AUT are generalizations of EUT in the sense of being logically weaker than EUT. As a result, they account for violations of EUT in a loose way: they are compatible with these violations whereas EUT was not, but they do not *imply* them; hence, on a standard construal, they do not *explain* them. Similarly, neither GEUT nor AUT really explain the occasional empirical success of EUT. When philosophers of physics say that relativity theory is more general than Newtonian mechanics, they do not mean to suggest that the former is a logical weakening of the latter; rather the contrary: they mean to say that, for some values of relevant parameters, the former implies the latter. The theory of risky choices is far from this stage, even if both Machina's discussion of 'fanning out' and the investigation of the f function in AUT can be construed as coarse attempts to identify the parameters whose special values would turn the more general theories into the particular case of EUT. It is at least a reassuring feature of recent experimental work that the logical structure of the test problem is fully taken into account, and that methods are being devised to compare not only EUT with alternatives but also these alternatives among themselves (for example, Hey and Orme, 1994).

The previous assessment was concerned with EUT viewed as a positive theory of individual behaviour, but part of the current discussion of VNM independence is normative in character. Friedman and Savage (1952) had claimed for this axiom the normative force of the stochastic dominance principle; the flaw in their argument is blatant. A more important defence revolves around a restatement of independence in terms of temporal consistency; it has gained wide acquiescence. To explain why Allais' solution might be irrational, some authors reformulate the lotteries in the Allais paradox by using decision trees and assuming that the agent's and nature's choices follow each other in a specific order. Hammond axiomatized the underlying structure of this argument under the name 'consequentialism'; his theory also provides a defence of Savage's sure-thing principle; see McClennen's (1990) critical account.

By and large, the still lively discussion around dynamic rationality does not interact with experimental work. The specialists' wisdom is that these are completely separate areas, since one belongs to positive decision theory and the other to normative decision theory, which allegedly do not communicate with each other. Methodologists should be impressed by this application of Hume's thesis. There are several reasons for believing that the cleavage between two groups of investigations is inappropriate. First, any piece of axiomatic decision theory is *prima facie* open to both positive and normative interpretations, so that the cleavage cannot be a material one but at most a distinction between two vantage points. For instance, Hammond's axioms could be discussed also at the experimental level, even it is not obvious how to test them. Second, it can be argued that the positive vantage point is not entirely self-contained. One way of controlling for experimental data is simply to attempt to reproduce them in different circumstances; another, which was used in the context of the Allais paradox, is to check verbally whether subjects acquiesce in the (normative) principles of choice they spontaneously apply. Third, some decisions theorists are primarily interested in applying EUT and its variants to actual decisions, typically in business and medicine. Their *prescriptive* use of the theory implies that they have to face, and in some sense supersede, the positive–normative dichotomy. For instance, the parameter values in the prescriptive model derive from data obtained from the subject, which data can be obtained only by assuming, that the subject obeys some theory. Incoherences will result if the (normative) theory which underlies the prescriptions is too distant from the (positive) theory assumed in order to collect the data.

Methodologists have hardly begun to explore the developments of EUT. The above shows that they constitute a rich vein of case studies. Actually, a stronger suggestion can be made. Over the years, EUT assumptions have strengthened their grip on economic theorizing: today, they are no longer reserved for a particular department that is, the economics of risk and uncertainty, but in a sense channelled everywhere by game-theoretic reasoning (which we said earlier heavily relies on VNMT and SEUT). We believe that every attempt at constructing a general economic methodology should be subjected to the test of whether or not it delivers a coherent account of EUT. A famous precedent here is Friedman, whose articles with Savage anticipate his methodological themes.

PHILIPPE MONGIN

References

Allais, M. (1953), 'Le comportement de l'homme rationnel devant le risque', *Econometrica*, **21**, 503–46.

Bernoulli, D. (1738), 'Specimen theoriae novae de mensura sortie', *Commentarii Academiae Scientiarum Imperialis Petropolitanae*, **5**, 175–92.

Bouyssou, D. and J.C. Vansnick (1990), 'Utilité cardinale dans le certain et choix dans le risque', *Revue économique*, **6**, 979–1000.

Camerer, C. (1995), 'Individual Decision Making', in J.K. Kagel and A.E. Roth, *The Handbook of Experimental Economics*, Princeton: Princeton University Press.

Ellsberg, D. (1954), 'Classic and Current Notions of "Measurable Utility"', *Economic Journal*, **64**, 528–56.

Fine, T.L. (1973), *Theories of Probabilities*, New York: Academic Press.

Fishburn, P.C. (1986), 'The Axioms of Subjective Probability', *Statistical Science*, **1**, 335–58.

Fishburn, P.C. (1989), 'Retrospective on the Utility Theory of von Neumann and Morgenstern', *Journal of Risk and Uncertainty*, **2**, 127–58.

Fishburn, P.C. and P. Wakker (1995), 'The Invention of the Independence Condition', *Management Science*, **41**, 1130–1144.

Friedman, M. and L. Savage (1952), 'The Expected Utility Hypothesis and the Measurability of Utility', *Journal of Political Economy*, **60**, 463–74.

Hausman, D. (1992), *The Inexact and Separate Science of Economics*, Cambridge: Cambridge University Press.

Hey J. and C. Orme (1994), 'Investigating Generalizations of Expected Utility Theory Using Experimental Data', *Econometrica*, **62**, 1291–1326.

Machina, M. (1983), 'Generalized Expected Utility Analysis and the Nature of Observed Violations of the Independence Axiom', in B.P. Stigum and F. Wenstop (eds), *Foundations of Utility and Risk Theory with Applications*, Dordrecht: Reidel.

McClennen, E.F. (1990), *Rationality and Dynamic Choice*, Cambridge: Cambridge University Press.

Mongin, P. (1988), 'Problèmes de Duhem en théorie de l'utilité espérée', *Fundamenta Scientiae*, **9**, 299–327.

Mongin, P. and C. D'Aspremont (forthcoming), 'Utility Theory and Ethics', in S. Barbera, P. Hammond and C. Seidl (eds), *Handbook of Utility Theory*, Dordrecht: Reidel.

Quiggin, J. (1993), *Generalized Expected Utility. The Rank-Dependent Model*, Boston: Kluwer.

Savage, L.J. (1954), *The Foundations of Statics*, New York: Dover; 2nd rev. edn, 1972.

Todhunter, I. (1865), *A History of the Mathematical Theory of Probability*, Cambridge; reprinted, Bronx, NY: Chelsea Publishers.

Von Neumann, J. and O. Morgenstern (1944), *Theory of Games and Economic Behavior*, Princeton: Princeton University Press.

Experimental Economics

Methodologists have often found social sciences, including economics, problematic because of their relationship to experiment. The worry is that experiment is sometimes thought an integral feature of scientific inquiry, but experiment, especially controlled, repeatable laboratory experiment, has been almost non-existent in the practice of social science. It might be argued that there are subdisciplines of physics that are similarly impoverished; astrophysics and seismology come to mind as fields in which scientists hungry for data must often wait for Nature's cooperation. But this argument involves a gross exaggeration. Many of the phenomena studied in astrophysics and seismology are independently confirmed on a different scale in laboratories. And many celestial objects of interest are constantly emitting radiation, while seismologists have been known to use explosives to generate data. There is no analogy for the social sciences, especially for such theories as historical materialism where the whole thing can happen only once, so to speak.

There is, however, a growing literature that reports on the quite new practice of laboratory experimentation in economics. Some of this work attempts to study the behaviour of individual responses to lotteries, or two-person bargaining situations. Probably the most well developed experimental paradigms deal instead with market behaviour. These experiments, pioneered by Vernon Smith and his associates, all place experimental subjects at computer terminals where they make entries which they are to interpret as buying and selling. Each subject thus interacts only with the terminal and never face-to-face with the other agents in the market.

An enormous obstacle to investigating the market behaviour of economic agents in this way is ensuring that the subjects behave as economic agents. If the hypothesis being experimentally tested is, for example, that a market consisting of economic agents in specified conditions will reach equilibrium according to some piece of theory, it is necessary that the subjects' behaviour conform to the theory's description of them. Only in this way can the theory's implications for such agents be tested. The obstacle is removed by putting in place a schedule of incentives for the subjects that 'induces' an appropriate utility function. In other words, the subject will leave the laboratory well off if he behaves as though he were maximizing the utility function that the experimenter wishes. On the whole, the results of these experiments appear to confirm standard economic theory. Occasionally, however, some interesting anomalies do appear; for example, equilibrium is sometimes reached more quickly when information is less perfect.

Since these experiments use subjects performing artificially constructed tasks, they are *simulations*. They do not directly create the phenomena the scientist is interested in studying, as so often (but not always) happens in the physical sciences. This means that very interesting methodological questions remain to be answered before we can be confident that the simulations are realistic enough to count as experimentally confirming existing theories or as providing a source of phenomena for new ones.

ALAN NELSON

Further reading

Nelson, Alan (1986), 'New Individualistic Foundations for Economics', *Nous*, 469–90.
Roth, Alvin (1986), 'Laboratory Experiments in Economics', *Economics and Philosophy*, 245–73.
Smith, Vernon (1988), 'Theory, Experiment and Economics', *The Journal of Economic Perspectives*, 151–69.

Fallibilism

'Fallibilism' is a term derived from the Latin verb *fallere*, to deceive, to err. It was introduced by Charles Peirce in the 1890s to express the epistemological doctrine that 'people cannot attain absolute certainty concerning questions of fact'. Later it was used by Karl Popper in connection with his falsificationist methodology.

Epistemology is the study of the possibility, nature and limits of knowledge. Plato's dialogue 'Theaetetos' formulated the classical definition: knowledge (Gr. *epïsteme*) is justified true belief. As a rationalist, Plato argued that such genuine knowledge can be obtained by reason concerning the eternal immutable realm of ideas, while we can have only opinions (Gr. *doxa*) about the ever-changing sensible world. Aristotle claimed that scientific knowledge (Latin *scientia*) consists of necessarily true propositions about the essences of things. Many later proponents of rationalist and empiricist epistemologies have urged that at least the best parts of human knowledge are infallibly true, incorrigible or absolutely certain: there are situations where it is impossible that the knowing subject is mistaken. The foundationalist epistemologies have claimed that no knowledge would be possible unless there were some indubitable privileged statements (such as the clear and distinct axioms of Descartes, or the reports of immediate sense experience of the positivists) (Chisholm, 1977). In this sense, the traditional epistemology has been dominated by the 'quest for certainty', as John Dewey put it.

However, philosophers as early as the ancient Sceptics – the school of Pyrrho of Elis and the later leaders of Plato's Academy – presented forceful arguments against the certainty and even the possibility of knowledge: our ideas may be confused and our senses may deceive us. Therefore they recommended that the 'wise man' never assent to anything: to avoid the risk of error, it is better to withhold judgment on all issues. The most radical sceptics extended this thesis from everyday experience and science to morality and religion as well. But when the Pyrrhonian scepticism was reborn in the Renaissance, it was often employed as a 'war machine' against science to restore faith (Popkin, 1979).

Fallibilism as an epistemological programme was born as a middle way between dogmatism and scepticism. The Stoic philosophers argued that a man cannot act unless he believes something. Carneades, the leader of the Academic sceptics, replied that it is sufficient to rely upon 'verisimilitude'. This term, used in Latin by Cicero, is usually translated as 'probability'. The interpretation of this view leads to two variants that may be called weak and strong versions of fallibilism (Niiniluoto, 1984). According to weak fallibilism, all human knowledge is hypothetical or uncertain. There is no absolute certainty or infallibility even in our most reliable beliefs. There is always a risk or a possibility that we are mistaken and, therefore, as Peirce said, 'any scientific proposition whatsoever is always liable to be refuted and dropped at a short notice'. However, Peirce added, this does not preclude our having most likely actually attained truth 'in numberless cases, although we can never be absolutely certain of doing so in any special case'. Weak fallibilism thus differs from scepticism, since it admits that our knowledge claims are associated with probability.

Peirce himself understood inductive probabilities in terms of truth-frequencies associated with methods of reasoning. Thereby he anticipated such long-run characteristics as levels of significance in testing hypotheses and in confidence intervals of the Neyman–Pearson statistics. The Bayesian probabilists, on the other hand, understand probabilities of the form $P(H/E)$ as rational degrees of belief in the truth of a hypothesis H on the basis of the available evidence E. Thus $P(H/E) = 1$ if H is completely certain on E, and $P(H/E) = 0$ if E refutes H. The values of probability between 0 and 1 represent various degrees of uncertainty or incomplete conviction. For J.M. Keynes (1921), such inductive probabilities are uniquely determined degrees of partial entailment, while the subjectivist school (F.P. Ramsey, B. de Finetti, L.J. Savage) takes them to be relative to a person or a decision maker. Bayesian degrees of belief can be used in decision making, so that, following Cicero's advice, probability becomes 'the guide of life'. Similarly, Peirce argued that belief should guide our actions; if it fails, the task of inquiry is to lead us from the irritation of doubt to a new state of belief.

Weak fallibilism is the background philosophy of many of the contemporary methodological programmes, such as subjective Bayesianism, inductive logic, the hypothetico-deductive conception of science and statistical inference.

Strong fallibilism asserts that human knowledge is liable to error in the strict sense that even our best claims are false. Human errors are actual, not only possible, as in weak fallibilism. This idea has its roots in the idealist metaphysics and theology: as Cardinal Cusanus said in the fifteenth century, God is infinite, and finite human knowledge can only approximate Him as a regular polygon approximates a circle. A similar view was supported in the tradition of Hegelian dialectics, with doctrines about 'degrees of truth' and 'degrees of reality'. In modern science, Robert Boyle in the seventeenth century compared the search for the truth with the mathematical method of finding the roots of equations through false guesses. Later a similar comparison was made with the iterative methods which approach the true solution indefinitely or asymptotically without ever reaching it (Laudan, 1981).

Peirce combined these metaphysical and methodological ideas in his pragmatist theory of truth and reality, where truth is defined as 'the opinion which is fated to be ultimately agreed to by all who investigate'; that is, the ultimate limit of endless inquiry within the scientific community using the scientific method. Hence scientific claims are not only uncertain, as weak fallibilism asserts; also absolute exactitude and absolute universality are unattainable. Strong fallibilism thus urges that all of our scientific claims are, strictly speaking, false. As scientific theories are intentionally based on idealizations and simplifications, they are in many cases even known to be false. Therefore science is not concerned with belief, since the probability of theories is zero. Strong fallibilism still differs from scepticism, since it takes it to be possible that the results of science make progress towards the truth as an asymptotic limit.

Popper's falsificationism shares many elements with strong fallibilism (Popper, 1962, 1979). The defining character of scientific statements is their falsifiability. A scientist should follow the method of 'conjectures and refutations' by proposing bold hypotheses and putting them to severe tests. A hypothesis that survives a test is thereby corroborated – and worthy of further tests – until it is proved false by observational evidence. The growth of scientific knowledge thus follows the pattern of Darwinian evolution. Popper rejects the idea that scientific hypotheses could ever be shown to be true or even probable. Instead, theories are more or less truthlike, and scientific progress means increasing truthlikeness; that is, better correspondence with reality. Popper's proposed concept of truthlikeness measures the distance of a theory from the whole truth and thus combines the goals of truth and information – without excluding the possibility of true theories.

Fallibilism denies that there is a steady rock bottom of human knowledge. Therefore its views are naturally supported by coherentist epistemologies which take the justification of a belief to depend on its connections with other beliefs (Lehrer, 1990; Haack, 1993). Any part of the 'web of belief' can be questioned, but not all of its elements at the same time. This view is expressed by Otto Neurath's and W.V.O. Quine's famous simile of the reconstruction of a boat on the sea (Quine, 1960). Some fallibilists in the camps of pragmatism and logical empiricism have taken the further step of advocating the coherence theory of truth, but, as the examples of Peirce and Popper show, fallibilism can also be developed on the basis of a realist correspondence view of truth.

Often logic and mathematics are accepted as exceptions to the principle of fallibility, since their truths are regarded as conceptual or analytic and, hence, *a priori* and certain. In this sense, it is possible to restrict fallibilism to empirical knowledge and maintain infallibilism for mathematical knowledge.

The division of analytic and synthetic, or conceptual and factual, truths was severely criticized by Quine. The recent recovery of empiricist and quasi-empiricist views of mathematics has vitalized claims that mathematical statements are factual and empirical (Lakatos, 1976; Kitcher, 1983). This seems to be correct only on the condition that mathematics is interpreted as a theory of some things or aspects of the physical reality: arithmetic speaks of pebbles, geometry of the structure of the physical space. Moreover, it has been convincingly shown by George Polya that induction and analogy are powerful methods of discovery in mathematics, and even the evidence for some well-known mathematical theorems (such as, Goldbach's conjecture) is so far only inductive. The use of computers to verify steps of mathematical proof (for example, the four colour theorem) implies that the conception of a proof can involve fallible elements.

ILKKA NIINILUOTO

Bibliography
Chisholm, R. (1977), *Theory of Knowledge*, 2nd edn, Englewood Cliffs, NJ: Prentice-Hall.
Haack, S. (1993), *Evidence and Inquiry*, Oxford: Blackwell.
Keynes, J.M. (1921), *A Treatise on Probability*, London: Macmillan.
Kitcher, P. (1983), *The Nature of Mathematical Knowledge*, Oxford: Oxford University Press.
Lakatos, I. (1976), *Proofs and Refutations*, Cambridge: Cambridge University Press.
Laudan, L. (1981), *Science and Hypothesis*, Dordrecht: D. Reidel.
Lehrer, K. (1990), *Theory of Knowledge*, Boulder, Westview Press.
Niiniluoto, I. (1984), *Is Science Progressive?*, Dordrecht: D. Reidel.
Popkin, R.H. (1979), *The History of Scepticism from Erasmus to Spinoza*, Berkeley: University of California Press.
Popper, K. (1962), *Conjectures and Refutations*, London: Routledge & Kegan Paul.
Popper, K.R. (1979), *Objective Knowledge*, 2nd rev. edn, Oxford: Oxford University Press.
Quine, W.V.O. (1960), *Word and Object*, Cambridge, MA: MIT Press.

Falsificationism

Karl Popper launched the falsificationist crusade in his *Logic of Scientific Discovery*, whose first German edition appeared in 1934 (the English edition was published only in 1959, but in the meantime Popper's ideas spread among English scholars through his teaching at LSE from 1946 and his publications of 1944–5 and 1945). In the first chapter(s) of this classic treatise the author starts from a simple point of logic: if we take for granted the Humean problem of induction (that is, the impossibility of 'proving' a universal statement by means of observations 'confirming' it, no matter how numerous), a fundamental asymmetry resulting from the logical form of universal statements becomes apparent: 'For these are never derivable from singular statements, but can be contradicted by singular statements. Consequently it is possible by means of purely deductive inference (with the help of *modus tollens* of classical logic) to argue from the truth of singular statements to the falsity of universal statements' (Popper, 1959: 41; see also Popper, 1983, s. 22). In contrast, singular statements may be confirmed by the report of a single observation but never 'falsified', because contrary observations, no matter how numerous, cannot confirm the impossibility of different empirical evidence appearing in the future.

This point was of course by no means new. Indeed, *modus tollens* and *modus ponens* as rules of correct deductive reasoning were already known in mediaeval logic (and, under the form of the falsity of a conditional sentence with a true antecedent and a false consequent, *modus tollens* had already been known among the Megarians and the Stoics in ancient Greece: cf. Kneale and Kneale, 1962: ch. 3). In Popper's hand, however, the falsificationist principle becomes the founding block of a whole new methodological and epistemological perspective (further developed in Popper, 1963; 1972; 1983) whose main features can be summarized as follows.

First, the problem of induction is 'solved' by denying either the possibility of inductively inferring general 'laws' from a collection of single observations (as claimed by traditional naive empiricism) or the prospect of finding a satisfactory solution to the problem of confirmation (as maintained by logical empiricists) and by showing that the only meaningful use of single observations is that of considering them as possible cases of falsification of a theory or of a 'conjecture'.

Therefore, second, the falsifiability of a theory is taken as the main necessary condition for appraising theories against empirical evidence. In other words, falsifiability constitutes the true criterion of *demarcation* of 'scientific' propositions. The importance Popper attributed to this demarcation criterion can be seen in several passages of his intellectual autobiography, where we are told, among other things, that since the early 1920s Popper developed his own ideas 'about the *demarcation between scientific theories* (like Einstein's) *and pseudoscientific theories* (like Marx's, Freud's and Adler's)', having been 'shocked by the fact that the Marxists (whose central claim was that they were social scientists) and the psychoanalysts of all schools were able to interpret any conceivable event as a verification of their theories' (Popper, 1976a: 41–2, emphasis in the original);

Consequently, third, the possibility of pursuing a *justificationist* account of scientific knowledge is denied, in favour of a *fallibilist* account (because we can never be sure of having reached the 'truth' owing to the possibility of future falsifications and, moreover, even if we could attain such a 'truth', we would not be able to recognize and conclusively demonstrate such an attainment, so that – according to Popper – we should regard our knowledge as always provisional and potentially fallible).

Fourth, at the methodological level, the most important thing to be explained is thus the *growth of knowledge*; that is, how we may have 'progress' in scientific knowledge in spite of its fallibilist character.

Fifth, at the epistemological level *critical rationalism* emerges as a conception according to which:

In the development of science, observations and experiments play only the role of critical arguments. And they play this role alongside other, non-observational arguments. It is an important role; but the significance of observations and experiments depends *entirely* upon the question whether or not they may be used to *criticize theories*. ... There is only one element of rationality in our attempts to know the world: it is the critical examination of our theories. (Popper, 1963: 152, emphasis in the original)

Such a conception is also defended on ethical and political grounds. In this respect, Popper went so far as to claim that, differently from other species,

> Man has achieved the possibility of being *critical of his own tentative trials, of his own theories*. These theories … can be critically discussed, and shown to be erroneous, without killing any authors or burning any books. … If the method of rational critical discussion should establish itself, then this should make the use of violence obsolete: *critical reason is the only alternative to violence so far discovered*. It seems to me clear that it is the obvious duty of all intellectuals to work for *this* revolution – for the replacement of the eliminative function of rational criticism. (Popper, 1976b: 292, emphasis in the original)

The main problems with falsificationist methodology, never completely solved by Popper himself or by his followers, concern (a) the characterization of the notion of truthlikeness and the conditions under which we may speak of increasing verisimilitude of our theories (absolutely necessary in order to support Popper's fallibilist account of scientific activity); (b) the specification of a possible measure of the 'degree of corroboration' (that is, a measure of the severity of the tests passed by the theory under scrutiny and, therefore, how 'rational' is our belief in the truthlikeness of a certain theory); (c) the related issue of how to detect possible 'immunizing stratagems' introduced 'ad hoc' in order to save the concerned theory from falsification; and (d) the possibility of finding a convincing answer to the objection contained in the Duhem–Quine thesis (asserting the impossibility of identifying the specific assumption responsible for a falsifying instance among an overly complex and heterogeneous set of explicit theoretical conjectures, auxiliary hypotheses, initial conditions, implicitly assumed background knowledge, and so on). All these points might seem technicalities, but they are also signals of a more fundamental problem: on the one hand, indeed, Popper retained from logical empiricism the hypothetical–deductive model of scientific explanation, together with the idea that the subject of appraisal could be a single scientific theory (considered in isolation), but on the other hand he identified the 'growth of knowledge' as the central issue of methodological and epistemological inquiries. In a sense it might be said that he ultimately failed to bridge completely the gap between these two very different conceptions of the outcome of scientific activity: the former involving a static description of the deductive skeleton of a collection of single theories and the latter requiring a much more articulated account of how possible directions in scientific research come to the attention of scientists and are further pursued or eventually discarded according to some notion of scientific rationality. Surely, Kuhn's proposal to distinguish between a normal science worked out within the secure borders of commonly accepted 'paradigms' and a revolutionary science attempting to change the guiding 'paradigm', or Lakatos' restatement of falsificationism within his methodology of scientific 'research programmes' were attempts to address precisely this problem (whether successful or not is another story, a suitable subject for other entries in the present volume).

Turning to economics, we may first note that for some decades the Popperian tradition was kept alive among historians of economic thought and economic methodologists by Terence Hutchison (1938; 1964; 1976; 1977; 1978; 1981; 1988), who has been joined more recently by Mark Blaug (1976; 1980), Lawrence Boland (1982) and Johannes Klant (1984; 1994), while among economists the falsificationist creed was probably diffused through the introductory chapters in the various editions of Richard Lipsey's famous textbook (see, for instance, Lipsey, 1989). Popper's influence on economists at LSE during the late 1950s and early 1960s is interestingly reconstructed in de Marchi (1988a). The interest of historians in Popperian methodology and the subsequent debate on the 'growth of knowledge' is hardly surprising.

Indeed, as is noted by Caldwell (1991: 9), 'For intellectual historians, the ability of a methodology to make sense of the past history of their discipline is understandably an important and desirable characteristic.'

All this, however, would not suffice in itself to explain why a substantial portion of the literature on economic methodology of the last two decades has been concerned with the adequacy of falsificationism with respect to a number of issues, raising many highly controversial and still unsolved questions (space constraints prevent even a brief survey here of all the issues at stake in that debate, but compare, for instance, the harsh dismissal in Hausman, 1988, with the passionate defence in Blaug, 1994, or the variously dubitative conclusions in Backhouse, 1994a; Caldwell, 1991; Hands, 1993a; de Marchi, 1988b). The area of consensus among economic methodologists on such matters may be reduced to the following theses:

> (1) Falsificationism – the methodology of bold conjectures and severe tests – is often preached in economics but it is almost never practised. ... (2) Though 'hard cores' and 'positive heuristics' abound, 'novel facts' as defined by the Lakatosian school have been few and far between in the history of economic thought. ... (3) The 'Duhemian problem' is particularly difficult in economics: the complexity of economic phenomena and questions about the empirical basis of the discipline make empirical testing an extremely complex affair. (Hands, 1990: 73)

Such a minimalist account, however, should not lead the reader to conclude that the whole debate is 'much ado about nothing'. On the contrary, the attention devoted to falsificationism in economic methodology appears to be fully justified if we pay due attention to the fact that it is thanks to Popperian methodology that, in one way or another, economic methodologists have approached in new ways some of the most important issues in their field. Three significant examples may be briefly mentioned here. The first is offered by Friedman's (1953) famous plea for 'as if' methodology for economics and the debate which followed this. Until the late 1970s, this influential essay was the point of reference for almost all investigations in economic methodology and contributed to spreading among economists Friedman's peculiar version of falsificationism (contained in two incidental passages which nevertheless communicate his tendency to conflate the degree of corroboration with that of verisimilitude and therefore, as argued in Salanti, 1987, to muddle falsificationism with induction by elimination). The actual instrumentalist nature of Friedman's methodological position became clear (see, for instance, Coddington, 1972; Wong, 1973; Caldwell, 1980; Musgrave, 1981; Frazer and Boland, 1983; Hirsch and de Marchi, 1990) only when the critics approached it with a better cognizance of Popper's works.

A second example is given by some methodological analysis of the epistemological status of general equilibrium theory: all those who are unwilling to surrender to the formalist justifications advanced by the advocates of modern general equilibrium analysis have had to resort, in one way or another, to some sort of Popperian arguments (this claim cannot be adequately documented here, but compare Backhouse, 1991; 1993; Coddington, 1975; Hausman, 1981; Ingrao and Israel, 1990; Rosenberg, 1986; Salanti, 1991; 1993a; 1993b; Weintraub, 1985; 1993).

A final relevant illustration of Popperian influence concerns the issue of the epistemological status of methodological individualism (undoubtedly a major theme for any serious approach to the methodology of economics). As is well known, when Popper considered the case of the social sciences he generalized the method usually followed in (micro)economics as the method of situational logic or situational analysis (Popper, 1944–5: part 4; 1976c; 1985; there are interesting exegeses in Agassi, 1960; 1975; Latsis, 1972; 1983; Koertge, 1975; 1979) and advocated its adoption by all the other social sciences wishing to reach the same standard of rigour. It is not clear whether situational analysis is compatible with falsificationism or not, because it would shelter the rationality principle within a misleading appearance of methodological invulnerability (cf. Hands, 1985; Caldwell, 1991), but it is indisputable that Popper's defence of the rationality principle is more appealing than more traditional aprioristic approaches to its justification.

To sum up: it may well be that in economics falsificationism is often preached but almost never practised and that normative principles which cannot be observed even with the best of intentions are plainly useless and/or misleading, but this does not mean, as the examples above are meant to show, that Popper's books can be put on the highest shelves in our bookcases. After all, even a post-Popperian methodology of economics (to use the title of de Marchi, 1992) might rediscover one day that the traditional epistemological problem of explaining how scientists' fallible and self-interested endeavours can produce (objective?) knowledge and (progressive?) scientific attainments does merit some further reflection.

ANDREA SALANTI

Readers guide

Popper's most important books and collections have been quoted in the text, while a good introductory anthology of Popper's thought can be found in Miller (1985). The secondary literature on Popper, as may be expected for one of the greatest philosophers of the twentieth century, is enormous. A good starting point is Schilpp (1974). For a clear account of the debate on the 'growth of knowledge', a survey of which may be found in Lakatos and Musgrave (1970), see Suppe (1977). Even the debate among economists on Popper's methodology has produced a substantial amount of literature. See, for instance, Blaug (1980), Boland (1982), Caldwell (1982; 1991), de Marchi (1988c), Hausman (1992), Hands (1992; 1993b) and Backhouse (1994b).

Bibliography

Agassi, J. (1960), 'Methodological individualism', *British Journal of Sociology*, **11**, 244–70.
Agassi, J. (1975), 'Institutional individualism', *British Journal of Sociology*, **26**, 144–55.
Backhouse R. (1991), 'The neo-Walrasian research programme in macroeconomics', in N. de Marchi and M. Blaug (eds), *Appraising Economic Theories: Studies in the Methodology of Scientific Research Programmes*, Aldershot: Edward Elgar.
Backhouse R. (1993), 'Lakatosian perspectives on general equilibrium analysis', *Economics and Philosophy*, **9**, 271–82.
Backhouse, R. (1994a), 'The Lakatosian legacy in economic methodology', in R. Backhouse (ed.), *New Directions in Economic Methodology*, London: Routledge.
Backhouse, R. (ed.) (1994b), *New Directions in Economic Methodology*, London: Routledge.
Blaug, M. (1976), 'Kuhn versus Lakatos or paradigms versus research programmes in the history of economics', in S. Latsis (ed.), *Method and Appraisal in Economics*, Cambridge: Cambridge University Press.
Blaug, M. (1980), *The Methodology of Economics. Or How Economists Explain*, Cambridge: Cambridge University Press.
Blaug, M. (1994) 'Why I am not a constructivist: Confessions of an unrepentant Popperian', in R. Backhouse (ed.), *New Directions in Economic Methodology*, London: Routledge.
Boland, L. (1982), *The Foundation of Economic Method*, London: Allen & Unwin.
Caldwell, B. (1980), 'A critique of Friedman's methodological instrumentalism', *Southern Economic Journal*, **48**, 363–73.
Caldwell, B. (1982), *Beyond Positivism: Economic Methodology in the Twentieth Century*, London: Allen & Unwin.
Caldwell, B. (1991), 'Clarifying Popper', *Journal of Economic Literature*, **29**, 1–33.
Coddington, A. (1972), 'Positive economics', *Canadian Journal of Economics*, **5**, 1–15.
Coddington A. (1975) 'The rationale of general equilibrium analysis', *Economic Inquiry*, **13**, 539–58.
Frazer W.J. and L. Boland (1983), 'An essay on the foundations of Friedman's methodology', *American Economic Review*, **73**, 129–44.
Friedman M. (1953), 'The methodology of positive economics', *Essays in Positive Economics*, Chicago: University of Chicago Press.
Hands, D.W. (1985), 'Karl Popper and economic methodology: A new look', *Economics and Philosophy*, **1**, 83–99.

Hands, D.W. (1990), 'Thirteen theses on progress in economic methodology', *Finnish Economic Papers*, **3**, 72–6.

Hands, D.W. (1992), 'Falsification, situational analysis and scientific research programs: The Popperian tradition in economic methodology', in N. de Marchi (ed.), *Post-Popperian Methodology of Economics. Recovering Practice*, Dordrecht: Kluwer.

Hands, D.W. (1993a), 'The Popperian tradition in economic methodology: Should it be saved?', *Testing Rationality and Progress. Essays on the Popperian Tradition in Economic Methodology*, Lanham, MD: Rowman & Littlefield.

Hands, D.W. (1993b), *Testing, Rationality and Progress. Essays on the Popperian Tradition in Economic Methodology*, Lanham, MD: Rowman & Littlefield.

Hausman, D.M. (1981), 'Are general equilibrium theories explanatory?', in J.C. Pitt (ed.), *Philosophy in Economics*, Dordrecht: D. Reidel.

Hausman, D.M. (1988), 'An appraisal of Popperian methodology', in N. de Marchi (ed.), *The Popperian Legacy in Economics*, Cambridge: Cambridge University Press.

Hausman, D.M. (1992), *The Inexact and Separate Science of Economics*, Cambridge: Cambridge University Press.

Hirsch, A. and N. de Marchi (1990), *Milton Friedman. Economics in Theory and Practice*, Ann Arbor: University of Michigan Press.

Hutchison, T. (1938), *The Significance and Basic Postulates of Economic Theory*, London: Macmillan.

Hutchison, T. (1964), *'Positive' Economics and Policy Objectives*, London: Allen & Unwin.

Hutchison, T. (1976), 'On the history and philosophy of science and economics', in S. Latsis (ed.), *Method and Appraisal in Economics*. Cambridge: Cambridge University Press.

Hutchison, T. (1977), *Knowledge and Ignorance in Economics*, Chicago: University of Chicago Press.

Hutchison, T. (1978), *On Revolutions and Progress in Economic Knowledge*. Cambridge: Cambridge University Press.

Hutchison, T. (1981), *The Politics and Philosophy of Economics*. Oxford: Basil Blackwell.

Hutchison, T. (1988), 'The case for falsificationism', in N. de Marchi (ed.), *The Popperian Legacy in Economics*, Cambridge: Cambridge University Press.

Ingrao, B. and G. Israel (1990), *The Invisible Hand*, Cambridge, MA: MIT Press.

Klant, J.J. (1984), *The Rules of the Game*, Cambridge: Cambridge University Press.

Klant, J.J. (1994), *The Nature of Economic Thought*, Aldershot: Edward Elgar.

Kneale, W. and M. Kneale (1962), *The Development of Logic*, Oxford: Oxford University Press.

Koertge, N. (1975), 'Popper's metaphysical research program for the human sciences', *Inquiry*, **19**, 437–62.

Koertge, N. (1979), 'The methodological status of Popper's rationality principle', *Theory and Decision*, **10**, 83–95.

Lakatos, I. and A. Musgrave (eds) (1970), *Criticism and the Growth of Knowledge*, Cambridge: Cambridge University Press.

Latsis, S.J. (1972) 'Situational determinism in economics', *British Journal for the Philosophy of Science*, **23**, 207–45.

Latsis, S.J. (1983), 'The role and status of the rationality principle in the social sciences', in R.S. Cohen and M.W. Wartowsky (eds), *Epistemology, Methodology, and the Social Sciences*, Dordrecht: D. Reidel.

Lipsey, R.G. (1989), *Introduction to Positive Economics*, 7th edn, Oxford: Oxford University Press.

de Marchi, N. (1988a), 'Popper and the LSE economists', in N. de Marchi (ed.), *The Popperian Legacy in Economics*, Cambridge: Cambridge University Press.

de Marchi, N. (1988b), 'Introduction', in N. de Marchi (ed.), *The Popperian Legacy in Economics*, Cambridge: Cambridge University Press.

de Marchi, N. (ed.) (1988c), *The Popperian Legacy in Economics*, Cambridge: Cambridge University Press.

de Marchi, N. (ed.) (1992), *Post-Popperian Methodology of Economics. Recovering Practice*, Dordrecht: Kluwer.

Miller, D. (ed.) (1985), *Popper Selections*, Princeton: Princeton University Press.

Musgrave, A. (1981) '"Unreal assumptions" in economic theory: The F-twist untwisted', *Kyklos*, **34**, 377–87.

Popper, K. (1944–5) 'The poverty of historicism', *Economica*, **11**, 86–103; 119–37; **12**: 69–89 (reprinted as *The Poverty of Historicism*, London: Routledge & Kegan Paul, 1957).

Popper, K. (1945), *The Open Society and Its Enemies*, 2 vols, London: G. Routledge & Sons.

Popper, K. (1959), *The Logic of Scientific Discovery*, London: Hutchinson (originally published as *Logik der Forschung*, Vienna: Springer, 1934; last English reprint, London: Routledge, 1992).

Popper, K. (1963), *Conjectures and Refutations*, London: Routledge & Kegan Paul (5th English edn, London: Routledge, 1989).

Popper, K. (1972), *Objective Knowledge*, Oxford: Clarendon Press.

Popper, K. (1976a), *Unended Quest. An Intellectual Autobiography*, Glasgow: Fontana/Collins.

Popper, K. (1976b), 'Reason or revolution?', in T.W. Adorno *et al.* (eds), *The Positivist Dispute in German Sociology*, London: Heinemann.

Popper, K. (1976c), 'The logic of the social sciences', in T.W. Adorno *et al.* (eds), *The Positivist Dispute in German Sociology*, London: Heinemann.

Popper, K (1983), *Realism and the Aim of Science*, London: Routledge.

Popper, K (1985), 'The rationality principle', in D. Miller (ed.), *Popper Selections*, Princeton: Princeton University Press.

Rosenberg, A. (1986), 'Lakatosian consolations for economics', *Economics and Philosophy*, **2**, 127–39.

Salanti, A. (1987), 'Falsificationism and fallibilism as epistemic foundations of economics: A critical view', *Kyklos*, **40**: 368–91.

Salanti, A. (1991) 'Roy Weintraub's "studies in appraisal": Lakatosian consolations or something else?', *Economics and Philosophy*, **7**, 221–34.

Salanti, A. (1993a), 'A reply to Professor Weintraub', *Economics and Philosophy*, **9**, 139–44.

Salanti, A. (1993b), 'Lakatosian perspectives on general equilibrium analysis: A reply', *Economics and Philosophy*, **9**, 283–7.

Schilpp, P.A. (ed.) (1974), *The Philosophy of Karl Popper*, La Salle, IL: Open Court.

Suppe, F. (ed.) (1977), *The Structure of Scientific Theories*, Urbana, IL: University of Illinois Press.

Weintraub, E.R. (1985), *General Equilibrium Analysis. Studies in Appraisal*, New York: Cambridge University Press.

Weintraub, E.R. (1993) 'But Doctor Salanti, bumblebees really do fly', *Economics and Philosophy*, **9**, 135–8.

Wong, S. (1973), 'The F-twist and the methodology of Paul Samuelson', *American Economic Review*, **63**, 312–25.

Feminist Economic Methodology

Feminist economic methodology is not, at the point of this writing, one specific body of methodological prescriptions. What practitioners of economics who take a feminist view on methodology share, however, is a notion that current methodological practice is biased by being built around values and concerns which have historically been, in Euro-American culture, associated with a particular conception of masculinity. The feminist methodological programme is to expose these biases in non-mainstream as well as mainstream economic methods and to explore less biased, and thus more adequate, alternatives.

While the more general feminist initiative in economics involves more than an analysis of method (including, for example, concern with the neglect of subject areas traditionally of concern to women), this entry will describe only the methodological implications of feminist thought. It must be clarified from the outset, however, that most scholars in this area do *not* see the methodological enterprise as developing a 'female' economic methodology, in which women economists would use different methods from men economists, or a 'feminine' methodology, in which only 'soft' techniques meet approval. The methodological insights, while of course applying to work: on issues of particular concern for women, are not seen as limited to such applications. Feminist methodological insights are seen as applying to men and women practitioners alike, and to all areas of economic study.

One may trace two streams feeding into this developing enterprise. First, for some economists the interest in feminist economic methodology has arisen from dissatisfaction with standard economic treatment of women and families. Starting in the 1970s, for example, in reaction to Gary Becker and the 'new home economics', several (feminist) economists including Bell (1974), Ferber and Birnbaum (1977) and Sawhill (1977) suggested that economics as traditionally construed provides too narrow a framework for analysis of certain phenomena. Standard economics has no vocabulary with which adequately to analyse phenomena fraught with connection to other people, such as responsibility for children; phenomena tightly linked to tradition and socialization, as for example the division of household tasks; phenomena driven by relations of domination, like labour market discrimination; or the phenomenon of marked changes in world view, as in the women's liberation movement. Treatment of these issues using only the language of individual agency, markets, choice and unchanging preferences left these scholars with a 'gnawing feeling of dissatisfaction' (Ferber and Birnbaum, 1977: 19) – a feeling that what was most important had been left out. Sawhill (1977) suggested that standard methods of analysis may have become a Procrustean bed, distorting rather than facilitating good analysis. Feminist analysis in the 1980s and early 1990s has continued to question the adequacy of standard concepts in analysing women and households, subjecting to critique neoclassical explanations of labour market discrimination (for example, Bergmann, 1983) and Marxist, bargaining and Beckerian models of the household (for example, Sen, 1983; Folbre, 1986; Folbre and Hartmann, 1985; Seiz, 1991). By the late 1980s, noted feminist economists were also taking part in methodological discussions that went beyond questions of women and households (Bergmann, 1987; Strober, 1987).

The other root of feminist economic methodology does not come from within economics itself, but rather from feminist work on the social construction of science. Feminist scholars have used techniques of literary criticism, historical interpretation, and psychoanalysis 'to "read science as a text" in order to reveal the social meanings – the hidden symbolic and structural agendas – of purportedly value-neutral claims and practices.' (Harding, 1986: 23). Works published in the mid-1980s by E.F. Keller (1985), Bordo (1937), Harding (1986) and others put the abstract, general, detached, emotionless, 'masculine' approach taken to represent scientific thinking, into historical and psychosexual context. Science was identified with masculinity, detachment and domination (and femininity with nature, subjectivity and submission) in the language of some seventeenth century scientists, according to research done by Keller (1985). Bordo (1987) interpreted the Cartesian model of objectivity, based on dispassion and detachment, as related to anxiety created by the loss of the mediaeval feeling of connection to nature (identified as feminine) during the period of the rise of modern science. Some scholars have found further enrichment in work in psychology and philosophy which has shown how a 'connected' way of being in the world – a way of being that, in contrast to the 'masculine' image of science noted above, is characterized by being concrete, particular, embodied and passionate – has been both culturally inscribed with the 'feminine' gender and held in very low esteem (Chodorow, 1978; C. Keller, 1986). The feminist concern with the social construction of dualisms such as science/nature, separated/connected and masculine/feminine has also led some feminist scholars to search out commonalities with postmodernist thought (Nicholson, 1990).

In the early 1990s, these two streams of scholarship came together in an explosion of research, conferences and publications (for example, England and Kilbourne, 1990; Nelson, 1992; Seiz, 1992; Ferber and Nelson, 1993a; Kuiper *et. al.*, 1995). The central theme, again, has been the exposing of the particularity, bias and unspoken purposes of notions of economic methodology which have been supposed to be universal, objective and value-free.

The main (though not exclusive) target of feminist criticism has been mainstream Euro-American economics. One might characterize mainstream economics as being built around the neoclassical model of autonomous, rational agents, whose preferences are fully formed, who make choices freely and who interact through markets. Work which mathematically elaborates the implications of such a model is often considered to add to economic knowledge (as evidenced by acceptance in professional journals), whether or not any empirical checking is attempted. To many economists, economics is in fact *defined* by its model and method: economics and the application of the mathematical rational choice model are one and the same. To the extent that empirical work is undertaken, emphasis is placed on sophisticated statistical analysis and formal testing of hypotheses. Some differences between feminist economic methodology and mainstream practice may be outlined as follows:

First, humans are seen as connected, as well as individuated. Human beings are not, as portrayed in the rational choice model, entirely autonomous. Humans begin life as dependent infants, and often end life dependent from age or illness as well. In between, humans spend their life in intimate connection with their parents, partners, children and close friends. The masculine myth of detachment has only been sustained by making 'invisible' all the work traditionally done by women in caring for dependants and maintaining emotional ties. While autonomy (of women or men) may be a useful assumption upon occasion, theories of human behaviour based on 'separateness' alone are playing with only half a deck (England, 1993; Strassmann, 1993).

Second, choice is seen as only one among many facets of economic allocation. While choice may be useful in explaining many economic allocations, restricting inquiry to choice-based explanations means that the influences of coercion, tradition and socialization are pushed into the shadows (Bergmann, 1983). While human agency as expressed in choices should not be ignored, a definition of economics around the subject matter of providing for human needs would allow for a less distorted science (Nelson, 1993a).

Third, the use of a broader range of methods is supported. Formal, abstract reasoning is often seen by mainstream economists as the only way to 'rigorous' knowledge, since according to the Cartesian epistemological position only that which can be proved thorough logic can be known. Such a view of knowledge is extremely narrow, ruling out all contextually based, verbally reasoned, analogy-related, experiential or empirically informed ways of knowing. While such formal methods may be hard, logical, 'scientific' and precise, they are also, on their own, rigid, inattentive to context, inhuman and thin. The feminist analysis suggests that these methods have been given high prestige at least in part because they form a bulwark against those sorts of reasoning (for example, verbal, qualitative) that are perceived as 'soft' or 'feminine'. A feminist approach to knowledge, in addition to valuing being hard, logical, and so on (so as not to fall into the traps of being weak, illogical, unscientific and vague) would also put high value on forms of reasoning that are flexible, humanistic, attentive to context and rich (Nelson, 1992).

Fourth, objectivity is seen as based in the scientific community. The notion that objective results can be obtained simply by adhering strictly to defined methods is seen by feminist scholars of science as an emotionally loaded, culturally created construct in and of itself. Refusing the artificial detachment of the 'masculinist' world view, objectivity may be seen instead as the outcome of the critical discussion of open scientific communities (Ferber and Nelson, 1993b; Nelson, 1993b).

Finally, closer contact with the 'real world' is encouraged. The high value given to abstract and formal reasoning has led to a denigration of applied or policy-oriented research, concrete data gathering and active explorations of 'how the world actually works'. Compared to other social and natural scientists, economists are woefully lacking in skills of observation and woefully uninformed about the most basic characteristics of their supposed subject matter. While not overlooking the benefits of adequate theorizing and appropriate econometric technique, feminist economists are urging that more attention be paid to real-world issues and data gathering of the qualitative and experiential as well as the quantitative sort (Bergmann, 1987; Strober, l987).

The definition of economics around the mathematical elaboration of the rational choice model reflects masculinist bias. Using model and method rather than subject matter to define economics has served an important political function, in excluding from 'serious' discourse all those who might hold alternative views about economics and economic methodology (Strassmann, 1993). Current work in feminist economic methodology serves to push those boundaries. Feminist economic methodology is not for investigation of 'women's issues' alone, nor is it for use only by female economists. It seeks, rather, to rid judgments about methodological adequacy from sexist biases.

JULIE A. NELSON

References

Bell, Carolyn Shaw (1974), 'Economics, Sex and Gender', *Social Science Quarterly*, **55**, (3), 615–31.

Bergmann, Barbara R. (1983), 'Feminism and Economics', *Academe: Bulletin of the American Association of University Professors*, **69**, (5), September–October, 22–5.

Bergmann, Barbara R. (1987), '"Measurement" or Finding Things Out in Economics', *Journal of Economic Education*, **18**, (2), 191–203.

Bordo, Susan (1987), *The Flight to Objectivity: Essays on Cartesianism and Culture*, Albany: State University of New York Press.

Chodorow, Nancy Julia (1978), *The Reproduction of Mothering: Psychoanalysis and the Sociology of Gender*, Berkeley: University of California Press.

England, Paula (1993), 'The Separative Self: Androcentric Bias in Neoclassical Assumptions', in M. Ferber and J. Nelson (eds) *Beyond Economic Man*, Chicago: University of Chicago Press.

England, Paula and Barbara Stanek Kilbourne (1990), 'Feminist Critiques of the Separative Model of Self: Some Implications for Rational Choice Theory', *Rationality and Society*, **2**, (2), 156–71.

Ferber, Marianne A. and Bonnie G. Birnbaum (1977), 'The "New Home Economics": Retrospects and Prospects', *Journal of Consumer Research*, **4**, June, 19–28.

Ferber, Marianne A. and Julie A. Nelson (eds) (1993a), *Beyond Economic Man: Feminist Theory and Economics*, Chicago: University of Chicago Press.

Ferber, Marianne A. and Julie A. Nelson (1993b), 'Introduction: The Social Construction of Economics and the Social Construction of Gender', in *Beyond Economic Man*, Chicago: University of Chicago Press.

Folbre, Nancy (1986), 'Hearts and Spades: Paradigms of Household Economics', *World Development*, **14**, (2), 245–55.

Folbre, Nancy and Heidi Hartmann (1988), 'The Rhetoric of Self-Interest: Ideology and Gender in Economic Theory', in Arjo Klamer, Donald N. McCloskey and Robert M. Solow (eds), *The Consequences of Economic Rhetoric*, Cambridge: Cambridge University Press.

Harding, Sandra (1986), *The Science Question in Feminism*, Ithaca, NY: Cornell University Press.

Keller, Catherine (1986), *From a Broken Web: Separation, Sexism, and Self*, Boston: Beacon Press.

Keller, Evelyn Fox (1985), *Reflections on Gender and Science*, New Haven: Yale University Press.

Kuiper, Edith and Jolande Sap (eds) (1995), *Out of the Margin: Feminist Perspectives on Economic Theory*, London: Routledge.

Nelson, Julie A. (1992), 'Gender, Metaphor and the Definition of Economics', *Economics and Philosophy*, **8**, (l), 103–25.

Nelson, Julie A. (1993a), 'The Study of Choice or the Study of Provisioning? Gender and the Definition of Economics', in M. Ferber, and J. Nelson (eds), *Beyond Economic Man*, Chicago: University of Chicago Press.

Nelson, Julie A. (1993b), 'Value-Free or Valueless? Notes on the Pursuit of Detachment in Economics,' *History of Political Economy*, **25**, (1), 121–45.

Nicholson, Linda J. (ed.) (1990), *Feminism/Postmodernism*, London: Routledge.

Sawhill, Isabel V. (1977), 'Economic Perspectives on the Family', *Daedalus*, **106**, (2), 115–25.

Seiz, Janet A. (1991), 'The Bargaining Approach and Feminist Methodology', *Review of Radical Political Economics*, **23**, 22–9.

Seiz, Janet A. (1992), 'Gender and Economic Research', in Neil de Marchi, (ed.), *Post-Popperian Methodology of Economics: Recovering Practice*, Boston: Kluwer-Nijhoff.

Sen, Amartya (1983), 'Economics and the Family', *Asian Development Review*, **1**, 14–26.

Strassmann, Diana (1993), 'Not a Free Market: The Rhetoric of Disciplinary Authority in Economics', in M. Ferber and J. Nelson (eds), *Beyond Economic Man*, Chicago: University of Chicago Press.

Strober, Myra H. (1987), 'The Scope of Microeconomics: Implications for Economic Education', *Journal of Economic Education*, **18**, 135–49.

Feyerabend, Paul K.

A philosopher and historian of science, Feyerabend was born in 1924 in Vienna, where he would later study theatre at the Weimar Institute and then history, physics, mathematics and astronomy at the University of Vienna. Just as Feyerabend was about to begin his university studies Germany occupied Austria; he was subsequently conscripted into the army, to be released after being wounded shortly before the German capitulation. On crutches and still recuperating, he took voice lessons at the music academy in Weimar, rejoined the theatre scene, and decided to study history and sociology instead of physics because he thought it would help him understand the war. When his course plan failed to meet his expectations, he could not resist the attraction of physics and philosophy, joining the 'Kraft Circle' (led by Viktor Kraft) and studying under the physicists Hans Thirring, Karl Przibram and Felix Ehrenhaft. Later, the notes he took from the Kraft Circle were condensed into a dissertation; he received his doctorate in 1951, after which he immediately applied for a scholarship to study with Wittgenstein at Cambridge. When Wittgenstein died, Karl Popper became his second choice; hence for a limited time he joined Popper's group at the London School of Economics. At first an enthusiastic follower of Popper and an intellectual clearly situated in analytic philosophy's mainstream, Feyerabend later parted ways on significant issues, becoming one of Popper's greatest critics and more than a bit of an iconoclast. It is the iconoclastic character of his philosophy that is responsible for his never having gained a popular following, as was the case with his colleagues Popper and Lakatos. While economists know his name, his philosophy of science has never caught on for two reasons: it does not lend itself to appropriation and continues today to be misunderstood, his 'anarchism' and attacks on 'rationalism' ranking foremost on the list of misunderstandings that make Feyerabend suspect to the economist.

From 1958 to his retirement in 1990, Feyerabend was professor of philosophy at the University of California at Berkeley. For a short time in the 1960s he had tenure at four universities: Berkeley, Yale, Berlin and London. At the end of his career he held concurrent posts at Berkeley and at the Federal Institute of Technology in Zurich. Feyerabend just managed to complete his autobiography, *Killing Time*, before he died of a brain tumour in February 1994 at the age of 70.

Feyerabend enjoys the distinction of being the great flamboyant among philosophers of science and is best known for his work *Against Method*, where his crusade against methodological rules is given its fullest expression. He makes a case against the formulation of and adherence to methodological rules, subsequently declaring himself an 'epistemological anarchist', or, for those who prefer an alternative label, a 'flippant dadaist', an appellation that prompted Hans Lenk (1982) to coin the word 'Dadasoph' in his honour. But beneath Feyerabend's humorous labels is a rejection of the once popular belief that scientists do and should rely on methodological rules to do good science. According to Feyerabend, the adoption of methodological rules causes science to become rigid and dogmatic. He warns that, not only do they make science too simple, but adherence to them would in fact inhibit science, and he provides numerous examples to show how the adherence to methodological rules would have arrested scientific discovery. He reminds us that creativity and genius cannot be squeezed into epistemological prescriptions. But if scientists insist on devising rules, Feyerabend grants them one rule to fall back on: 'anything goes'.

Besides the view that methodologies do not provide rules adequate to guide science, three other fundamental methodological messages run through all of Feyerabend's works: theories are incommensurable, science is not necessarily rational or superior to other types of knowledge, and the removal of methodological constraints enhances individual freedom and creativity. Feyerabend has not been alone in showing that the facts used by scientists to judge theories are based on theoretical assumptions and are therefore also theoretical. Once one recognizes that the concepts and observation statements embedded in a theory are theory-dependent, it becomes clear that the basic concepts of one theory cannot be formulated completely in terms of another. With this acknowledgement the old distinction between theory and facts breaks down: if facts are also theoretical, scientists' assumption that a fact clashing with theory will ultimately be resolved in favour of the fact has to be abandoned, as does the yardstick for measuring two theories. And so theories become incommensurable, an uncomfortable situation for philosophers of science trying to show that science progresses. The loss of a common standard for comparing theories, reasons Feyerabend, makes theory comparison subjective and underscores the fact that one source of knowledge may not be better than another. In view of all this, Feyerabend (1995: 90) warns against 'the promise of a method that enables individuals to free themselves from prejudice'. And so Feyerabend comes to advocate a pluralism similar to the position taken by John Stuart Mill in his essay *On Liberty*. The proliferation of scientific traditions, theories and methods, he insists, prevents science from becoming indoctrination. A pluralistic environment promotes competition between theories and methods, the most favourable environment for exposing bad theories and cranks.

A careful study of Feyerabend's work reveals that his criticism of the contemporary philosophy of science goes beyond methodology to a critique of the institution of higher learning. Among his points of contention: higher education is no longer training students to think; well-informed persons need to know both sides of an argument; science should not be treated as an ahistorical enterprise; there is no clean line dividing science and non-science; and the scientific community takes itself far too seriously or, put another way, scientists are not particularly self-critical or modest. He pokes fun at the filiopietistic, always-agree-with-your-supervisors academic tradition. The best education, Feyerabend wryly concludes, is one that immunizes people against systematic attempts at education.

The merits of Feyerabend's work are only now coming to light. His work has gone unappreciated for several reasons. His sense of humour and use of irony, rhetorical jabs, choice of extreme terminology such as 'epistemological anarchism' and 'anything goes' – in short, his dadaistic approach – have put off most readers. There is the additional problem that Feyerabend is a disquieting philosopher: his aim is to expose the failings of his contemporaries and to counteract the negative effects of science such as dogmatism, scholasticism, scientism and the ideology of science. One of the reasons for writing *Against Method*, Feyerabend (1995: 179) tells us in his autobiography, was 'to free people from the tyranny of philosophical obfuscations and abstract concepts such as "truths", "reality", or "objectivity", which narrow people's vision and ways of being in the world'. He, moreover, never adhered to a school or stooped to hagiographical philosophy of science. While the first reason is a justified criticism of Feyerabend's style, the latter reasons for ignoring him tend to confirm Feyerabend's own criticisms of the institutions of science and education.

DEBORAH A. REDMAN

Bibliography

Feyerabend, Paul K. (1975a), 'How to Defend Society Against Science', *Radical Philosophy*, **11**, 3–8.
Feyerabend, Paul K. (1975b), '"Science". The Myth and Its Role in Society', *Inquiry*, **18**, (2), Summer, 167–81.
Feyerabend, Paul K. (1978a), *Against Method*, London: Verso.
Feyerabend, Paul K. (1978b), *Science in a Free Society*, London: New Left Books.
Feyerabend, Paul K. (1979), *Erkenntnis für freie Menschen*, Frankfurt am Main: Suhrkamp.
Feyerabend, Paul K. (1995), *Killing Time: The Autobiography of Paul Feyerabend*, Chicago/London: University of Chicago Press.
Lenk, Hans (1982), 'Die "Feyerabendglocke" des Szientismus', *Conceptus*, **16**, 3–11.
Munévar, Gonzalo (ed.) (1991), *Beyond Reason: Essays on the Philosophy of Paul Feyerabend*, Dordrecht/Boston/London: Kluwer Academic.
Redman, Deborah A. (1990), *Economics and the Philosophy of Science*, New York/Oxford: Oxford University Press.

Folk Psychology

The theory implicit in everyday explanations and predictions of human behaviour, folk psychology embodies a large number of generalizations so well established as to be stigmatized as truisms: for instance, that burns cause pain sensations, that under normal daylight conditions people with their eyes open can see medium-sized objects in front of them, and so on. Folk psychological theory is also employed without explicit recognition in all the social sciences which purport to explain and/or predict human behaviour as action caused by the joint operation of beliefs and desires. Economics differs from the other social sciences only in the degree to which microeconomics employs a self-conscious formalization of the folk psychological theory of the causes of human action: the theory of rational choice. Thus controversies about the folk psychological theory of human behaviour vex economic theory as well.

Folk psychology explains human action as the effect of our desires working together with our beliefs about matters relevant to their attainment. It explains action by bringing it under some such a generalization as the following:

[L] If an agent desires goal *g*, and believes that action *a* is the best available way of attaining *g*, then, *ceteris paribus*, the agent will do action *a*.

A little reflection will reveal that each of us is committed to this schema both in explaining the behaviour of others to ourselves and in predicting the behaviour of others with whom we interact. What is more, we infer the beliefs and/or desires of individuals from observation of their actions and their environment in accordance with [L], though we are rarely aware of our reliance on it. Similarly, history, biography and the social sciences which seek to provide understanding of human action by showing its meaning, intelligibility or rationality make implicit appeal to [L]. Some social scientists and philosophers have held that this understanding is not causal, and that [L] or whatever underwrites the intelligibility of human action is not therefore a scientific theory. This approach has had little impact on the philosophy of economics.

Microeconomic theory makes explicit appeal to [L], or rather to a formalization of it. The theory of rational choice substitutes the terms 'expectation' and 'preference' for the commonsense terms 'belief' and 'desire', and translates [L] into the claim that economic agents choose those actions which maximize preference subject to their expectations. For a preference structure simply represents a cardinal or ordinal ranking of desires by their objects, and expectations are beliefs relevant to future actions – the only ones we need concern ourselves with in explaining these actions. Beliefs are sometimes invisible in economic theory, when the assumption of perfect information fixes them and so renders them irrelevant to explanation of differences among agents' choices. And some have supposed wrongly that revealed preference theory (Samuelson, 1947) has shown how to exclude desires – tastes and preferences – from economic theory (see below).

The character of rational choice theory as formalized folk psychology is reflected with particular clarity in Von Neumann and Morgenstern's elaboration of the theory under conditions of uncertainty. Von Neumann–Morgenstern theory enables us to infer an agent's set of expectations – beliefs about various probabilities – by offering a series of wagers and observing the agents' actions, that is their choices, provided we hold the agents' preferences constant: *mutatis mutandis*, we can infer agents' preferences from the agents' choices, but only if we hold expectations constant. But this is in essence what we do in everyday life when we infer beliefs from actions, by holding desires constant, and vice versa.

General statements like [L] have been repeatedly subjected to philosophical scrutiny (see Christensen and Turner, 1993; McIntyre and Martin, 1993), largely because they are the focus of accounts of the differences between the aims and methods of the human sciences and the natural ones. It is widely accepted that the social sciences lack the predictive power of the natural sciences. Many writers identify the source of this weakness as the complexity of social phenomena, and its recalcitrance to experiment. Most of these writers accept [L] or something like it as at least the first approximation to a causal law which governs individual choice and so has a role in explaining individual choices and their aggregate effects. But some identify the source of the failure of social sciences to attain the aims of natural science as [L]'s failure as a law. Others deny that the social sciences have failed, identifying a different aim from that of predictive power and arguing that [L] contributes to the successful attainment of that aim, but not as a causal law or the first approximation to it. These philosophers and social scientists defend the methodological autonomy of the social sciences by claiming that [L] is not meant to be a law, but is a conceptual device for interpreting, rendering intelligible and otherwise making meaningful human actions. So understood, [L] and other principles of folk psychology are not to be understood as putative causal laws to be tested by observation, but rather as normative or semantic claims that reveal the significance of the actions they are called upon to explain.

The debate surrounding the cognitive status of [L] – and its formalization in rational choice theory as well – has long turned on the 'intentionality' or propositional content of states of belief and desire that cause action. Thus the belief that wheat prices are rising contains the proposition that 'wheat prices are rising', and the desire to acquire wheat contains the statement that 'wheat is acquired'. The trouble with treating these beliefs and desires as the causes of choice is that they are not empirically observable, and their existence can only be inferred from observation of the very phenomenon – actual choices – that they are called upon to explain. This threatens the status of beliefs and desires as causal variables and of [L] as an empirical generalization: if the occurrence of these causes can only be inferred from the occurrence of their effect, an explanation that cites them to explain an effect cannot be empirically tested and confirmed independently of the effect it explains. Similarly, a putative law, connecting preferences and expectations on the one hand with their effects in choice on the other, cannot be tested. Because we cannot establish that its antecedent obtains except where we already know that its consequent has obtained, the putative law is unfalsifiable.

This problem is at the root of criticisms of rational choice theory, and the theory of the consumer, as being without predictive power. Of course such criticisms are exaggerated. The problem is not that these theories are completely without predictive power. Rather, their power extends no farther than that of folk psychology, and this theory has seen no uncontroversial increase in its predictive precision in several millennia at least.

The empirical problem of establishing with precision the content of agents' psychological states spawned behaviourism in psychology, and revealed preference theory in economics. Behaviourism held that the causes of action were non-mental and that statements about beliefs and desires when explanatory were disguised descriptions of these causes. Revealed preference theory treated preferences attributions as inferable from actual choices so long as these were transitive.

Behaviourism failed as a research programme because its explanations of behaviour were no more powerful and accurate than folk psychology's explanations, and revealed preference theory requires strong mentalistic assumptions holding beliefs constant in the construction of preference maps, as the Von Neumann–Morgenstern (1947) theory of uncertain choice reflects. This requirement makes evident economic theory's reliance on psychological states as explanatory variables. A more thoroughgoing attempt to escape economic theory's dependence on folk psychology proceeds from the recognition that the main explanatory and predictive objective of economics is the behaviour of markets and other aggregates. The trouble with this stratagem is that these explanations usually proceed by aggregating individual choices and, where they do not, as in macroeconomic theory, the chief theoretical criticism has been that macrotheories fail to have adequate microfoundations: that is, they fail to incorporate a theory of rational choice.

The alternative view according to which [L] and its formalization are principles which enable us to render human behaviour intelligible as action, but have no causal or empirical role, has never been a popular one in economics. As noted above, except for proponents of Austrian economics, economic theories have uniformly embraced the obligation to provide a predictively useful, policy-relevant theory of economic phenomena. As such they cannot adopt an interpretation of their theory that secures the cogency of the theory in exchange for surrendering its causal relevance for predicting and controlling behaviour. This, however, has been the strategy among other non-quantitative social sciences. The divergent attitudes of the varying social sciences towards folk psychology and its cognitive status are a litmus test for whether they aim to provide a predictively powerful science of human behaviour or a humanistic appreciation of the meaning of human action.

ALEXANDER ROSENBERG

Bibliography

Christensen, S. and D. Turner (1993), *Folk Psychology and the Philosophy of Mind*, Hillsdale, NJ: Erlbaum.
McIntyre, Lee and M. Martin (1993), *Readings in the Philosophy of Social Science*, Cambridge, MA: MIT Press.
Rosenberg, A. (1992), *Economics – Mathematical Politics or Science of Diminishing Returns*, Chicago: University of Chicago Press.
Samuelson, P. (1947) *Foundations of Economic Analysis*, Cambridge, MA: MIT Press.
Von Neumann, J. and O. Morgenstern (1947), *Theory of Games and Economic Behavior*, Princeton, NJ: Princeton University Press.

Friedman, Milton

Friedman was born in Brooklyn, New York on 31 July 1912. He was introduced to the ideas of the great neoclassical economist Alfred Marshall as a Rutgers University undergraduate by the young Arthur Burns. His studies of Marshall's *Principles of Economics* continued under Jacob Viner as a University of Chicago graduate student in 1932–3. A fellowship pulled Friedman away from Chicago to Columbia University in 1933, where he studied business cycle analysis with Wesley C. Mitchell. After an interruption of his dissertation work by World War II, Friedman took his PhD from Columbia in 1946, and the same year joined the University of Chicago faculty.

At Chicago, where he taught until his retirement in 1977, Friedman became the leader of the Chicago School of Economics. Among his many publications that gave shape to that school are *Price Theory: A Provisional Text* (1962a), *A Monetary History of the United States, 1867–1960* (with Anna J. Schwartz, 1963) and *Capitalism and Freedom* (1962b). Friedman was awarded the John Bates Clark Medal by the American Economic Association in 1951. He served as president of the Association in 1967. He is a fellow of the American Statistical Association and the Econometric Society. Friedman was awarded the Nobel Prize in Economic Science in 1976.

'The Methodology of Positive Economics' (1953) is the most prominent of Friedman's many distinguished contributions to economic methodology. From this essay two generations of economists have learned that it is important to separate positive economics from normative economics, and that the goal of positive economics is to obtain hypotheses that yield predictions about phenomena not yet observed. They have learned that predictions provide the only means of testing hypotheses; they cannot be tested by the realisticness of the theories' assumptions. Furthermore, theories that predict well are likely to have less realistic assumptions than their counterparts that predict less well.

Friedman's essay became the most widely read and cited work in economic methodology. Its influence was due, not only to its persuasiveness, but also to the stature Friedman gained as an economist. The ideas in the essay underlay much of the distinctive Chicago School economics. It proved to be a trove of material for methodologists, rich as it is with illustrations from economics and analogies from the physical world. These include the formula for the distance travelled by a ball dropped in a vacuum, the relationship between light and the density of leaves around a tree, and a billiards player who makes shots 'as if' he was aided by complicated mathematical calculations (the latter first presented in Friedman and Savage, 1948). Friedman used these to illustrate the folly of attempting to test a theory by the realisticness of its assumptions.

Methodologists were primarily interested in typecasting the essay philosophically in order to evaluate it. However, typecasting proved not to be an easy task, for Friedman gave few hints indicating which philosophical school the essay might represent. Among the more popular candidates are, in broad terms, Popperianism, positivism and instrumentalism. Numerous interpretations were more finely drawn, such as positivist instrumentalism, Deweyian instrumentalism and predictivist instrumentalism. Some methodologists have found elements of several, often incompatible, philosophical doctrines.

There is a good reason for Friedman's essay not fitting neatly into philosophy of science taxonomy. Philosophy of science had a scant role in the formation of Friedman's ideas on methodology and his writing the essay. He was only casually familiar with the philosophy of science literature. In two important senses, Friedman drew his methodology from economics. First, his interest in methodological issues derived from economic issues, such as how to evaluate competing theories of market behaviour. Second, the literary source for Friedman was not the work of philosophers of science but of an economist, Alfred Marshall. Indeed, the key economic issue for which Friedman sought methodological guidance in the 1940s, when he was forming the ideas that culminated in the essay, was the Walrasian challenge to Marshallian value theory. Thus the only label Friedman used for his methodology, though consequentially *not* in the famous essay, was 'Marshallian'. He used this label throughout his career in contradistinction to 'Walrasian'. Friedman's view of the essential difference between the methodologies was that Marshallians regard theory as an 'engine for the discovery of concrete truth', valuing the ability to explain facts more highly than mathematical elegance and generality. Walrasians reverse the order, placing greater value on mathematical elegance and generality.

If the various philosophical identifications of Friedman's methodology do not fit very well because Friedman developed his ideas at a considerable distance from the philosophy of science literature, the Marshallian label fits much better for just the opposite reason. The historical record makes clear Friedman's allegiance to the economic theory of Marshall's *Principles of Economics* and his use of Marshall's methodological commentary in development and support of his own ideas. Also the key ideas in 'The Methodology of Positive Economics', where he did not use the Marshallian label, are found in his writings where he did, and vice versa.

The seeds of Friedman's use of the Marshallian and Walrasian categories to frame methodological questions are found in a brief book review that Friedman published in 1941 and in the book that was the subject of the review. Robert Triffin's aim in *Monopolistic Competition and General Equilibrium Theory* (1940) was to reorient E.H. Chamberlin's theory of monopolistic competition from a Marshallian to a Walrasian framework. This involved a shift in the unit of analysis from the industry to the firm, set within the 'whole economic collectivity'. Triffin thought the methodological gains from Walrasian monopolistic competition were twofold. Monopolistic competition provided greater realisticness in the choice of assumptions than perfect competition and monopoly. It made theory descriptively more accurate. Also Walrasian general equilibrium provided 'purification and formalization of economic theory' in comparison with Marshallian particular equilibrium. The core idea of Friedman's methodology is a rejection of these two developments in economic theory as progress.

In the review, Friedman accepted Triffin's judgment that for a theory whose focus is product differentiation there is no logical role for Marshallian industries. Therefore monopolistic competition presented economists with the necessity of making a choice between Marshallian demand and supply curves for the products of industries and the new theory which had no logical stopping place between the individual firm and the economic system in its entirety. Friedman argued that the most important problems in the real world concern industries rather than firms; therefore monopolistic competition has little usefulness. Even though real-world firms do not produce undifferentiated products in perfectly competitive or purely monopolistic industries, Marshall's theory has more analytical relevance to real-world problems. 'The fact that we state a problem in terms of a particular "industry" is likely to mean that the differences among the products of the members of the industry are less important, *so far as the specific problem is concerned*, than the similarities' (Friedman, 1941: 390, emphasis in original). This book review was the first instance of Friedman arguing that the realisticness of assumptions is of limited importance in and of itself.

Friedman developed criticism of formalized economic theory in another review (1946), of Oscar Lange's *Price Flexibility and Employment*. He argued that Lange's 'taxonomic theorizing', with its emphasis on formal structure and logical interrelations, was an approach used all too often in economics. Theoretical categories were selected with little regard to their amenability to practical application or empirical testing. Friedman first presented a detailed methodological discussion framed in terms of the Marshallian and Walrasian approaches to economic theory in 'The Marshallian Demand Curve' (1949). He argued that the difference was not partial versus general equilibrium. Rather, Marshallians, whom he thought were a minority at the time, were faithful to Marshall's vision of economics providing hypotheses based on factual evidence and tested by their ability to predict the consequences of changes. Walrasians placed factual evidence and empirical testing in secondary roles; they made abstractness, generality and mathematical elegance ends in themselves. They shifted the emphasis from explanation to description, from testing by the correctness of predictions to testing by the realisticness of assumptions.

In a review (1955) of William Jaffé's translation of Walras's *Elements of Pure Economics*, Friedman likened Cournot to Marshall, contrasting both to Walras:

> Economics not only requires a framework for organizing our ideas, it requires also ideas to be organized. We need the right kind of language; we also need something to say. Substantive hypotheses about economic phenomena of the kind that were the goal of Cournot are an essential ingredient of a fruitful and meaningful economic theory. Walras has little to contribute in this direction; for this we must turn to other economists, notably, of course, to Alfred Marshall. (1955: 908)

J. DANIEL HAMMOND

Bibliography
Friedman, Milton (1941), 'Review of *Monopolistic Competition and General Equilibrium Theory* by R. Triffin', *Journal of Farm Economics*, **23**, February, 389–91.
Friedman, Milton (1946), 'Lange on Price Flexibility and Employment: A Methodological Criticism', *American Economic Review*, **36**, September, 613–31; reprinted in *Essays in Positive Economics*.
Friedman, Milton (1949), 'The Marshallian Demand Curve', *Journal of Political Economy*, **57**, December, 463–95; reprinted in *Essays in Positive Economics*.
Friedman, Milton (1953), 'The Methodology of Positive Economics', *Essays in Positive Economics*, Chicago: University of Chicago Press.
Friedman, Milton (1955), 'Léon Walras and His Economic System', *American Economic Review*, **45**, December, 900–909.
Friedman, Milton (1962a), *Price Theory: A Provisional Text*, Chicago: Aldine.
Friedman, Milton (1962b), *Capitalism and Freedom*, Chicago: University of Chicago Press.
Friedman, Milton and L.J. Savage (1948), 'The Utility Analysis of Choices Involving Risk', *Journal of Political Economy*, **56**, August, 270–304.
Friedman, Milton and Anna J. Schwartz (1963), *A Monetary History of the United States, 1867–1960*, Princeton: Princeton University Press.
Hirsch, Abraham and Neil de Marchi (1990), *Milton Friedman: Economics in Theory and Practice*, Ann Arbor: University of Michigan Press.
Marshall, Alfred (1920), *Principles of Economics*, 8th edn, London: Macmillan.
Triffin, Robert (1940), *Monopolistic Competition and General Equilibrium Theory*, Cambridge, MA: Harvard University Press.

Functionalism

> As economics expands beyond its hard core of price theory, and its central concern with quantities of commodities and money, we observe in it this same shift from a highly quantitative analysis, in which equilibrium at the margin plays a central role, to a much more qualitative institutional analysis, in which discrete structural alternatives are compared. (Herbert Simon, 1978: 6)

Introduction
Since the 1960s, economics has continuously expanded beyond its boundaries. Many phenomena earlier viewed as outside the domain of the field are now considered natural explananda. The first step towards this imperialistic expansion of traditional market and price theory attempted to incorporate or assimilate non-economic domains to the paradigm of maximization. In recent years, however, the imperialist expansion strategy seems to be replaced by a more modest and adaptive research strategy, implying greater openness to explanations traditionally central to the other social science disciplines. This applies particularly to the functionalist type of explanations in sociology and anthropology. Functionalist explanations originally stem from biology, explaining a certain species or organism as an adaptation to its specific environment. Similarly, the social sciences have attempted to explain structural phenomena such as

institutions, norms, conventions and organizations as efficient adaptations to the environments. This interest in functionalist explanations within economics primarily seems to be a consequence of the increasing attention devoted to institutions in explaining economic phenomena.

From orthodox equilibrium analysis to functionalist explanations
Since the late 1960s, a series of new schools have emerged in economics, such as the property right tradition, agency theory, transaction cost theory, game theoretical institutionalism and constitutional political economy. Common to these schools is that they are not primarily interested in applying the comparative–static method to explain/predict specific *empirical events*, but rather they seek to analyse what Simon, quoted above, calls 'discrete structural alternatives': that is, to explain the existence of *sustained* and *structural* phenomena, such as social institutions, norms, and behavioural rules. Thus functionalist and adaptive explanations go a step further than equilibrium explanations in explaining the structure which the latter usually view as exogenous. The latter typically lead to more quantitatively oriented prediction by comparing two states of equilibrium within the *same* system before and after a parameter shift, whereas functionalist and adaptive explanations are more structural and qualitative, taking as their point of departure that social systems have been confronted by some repeated problem of interaction of the coordination or collaboration type. This problem is subsequently resolved by the emergence of a social institution, norm or behavioural rule.

The existence of an institution, norm or behavioural rule is explained by its function or 'beneficial consequences' in resolving the given problem of coordination or collaboration. However, contrary to the purely intentional or rational choice type of explanation, the possible 'beneficial consequences' of an institution are not anticipated, and in some cases not even recognized, by the agents involved (compare P. van Parijs, 1981). If the agents do not recognize the beneficial consequences of an institution, the explanation is referred to as latent functional, whereas an explanation based on the actors recognizing, but not anticipating, the beneficial consequences is referred to as a manifest functional explanation.

Some historical notes
The functionalist type of explanation in economics was introduced by Armen Alchian in his article 'Uncertainty, Evolution and Economic Theory' (1950) as an alternative to the rational choice model. The fact that firms in a certain industry followed certain rules-of-thumb, or behavioural rules, was not necessarily the result of deliberate choices based on rational considerations, but might as well be the result of a selection process. Or, in the words of Alchian, the traditional individual rationality perspective of economics was exchanged for a population perspective:

> By backing away from trees – the optimization calculus by individual units – we can better discern the forest of impersonal market forces. This approach directs attention to the interrelationships of the environment and the prevailing types of economic behaviour which appear through a process of economic natural selection. (1950: 19)

Alchian demonstrated that many economic phenomena might just as well be explained by a functional–evolutionary as an intentional–rational model, and his ideas were soon adopted as an important ingredient of the basic methodology of the Chicago School. Milton Friedman (1953) used Alchian's thesis as his point of departure in his classic defence of the hypothesis of profit maximization. The basis was the philosophical thesis of underdetermination: in principle, a series of different, and possibly conflicting, theoretical mechanisms may exist, explaining the very same empirical phenomena. Therefore, according to Friedman, we will never find the true mechanism or 'explanation' because all theories based on stochastic behaviour and market selection will predict exactly the same empirical phenomena as orthodox theory of profit maximization. Thus, since it is impossible empirically to indicate one explanation as being better than other explanations, Friedman concludes that we will never be able to discover the 'true' explanation. Consequently, our theories can only be interpreted as instruments for deducing predictions and not as more or less true explanations of reality. Therefore the assumptions of a theory, such as the hypothesis of profit maximization in neoclassical theory, must never be interpreted literally but always subject to an 'as if' proviso.

The structure of functionalist explanations
As it appears from the examples above, the existence of a norm or an institution is explained by its 'beneficial consequences', that is, its ability to economize on some costs. Thus the existence of a norm or an institution is explained by referring to its unanticipated but realized beneficial consequences. However, such an explanation presents a problem in that the temporal order of explanans and explanandum have been reversed as compared to a causal explanation. Here explanans is always assumed to exist before or simultaneously with explanandum. From functionalist models we seem to be able to explain the existence of an institution (explanandum) in the same way as we explain the giraffe's long neck by referring to its (explanans) 'beneficial consequences', or function. However, this implies that temporally explanadum comes before explanans. Is that acceptable?

Within biology the reverse temporal order does not necessarily appear to be a problem. For example, when we explain the giraffe's long neck by referring to its beneficial effects in terms of getting food and so on, we know that we can always assume Darwin's mechanism of natural selection to have been active and produced the given phenomenon. That is, we can refer to a causal mechanism which makes the teleological nature of functionalism unproblematic. The functionalist explanation is merely an 'as-if' explanation of a different and more complex causal explanation based on Darwin's mutation and selection mechanism. However, according to Jon Elster (1983) this position will not be acceptable within the social sciences. The moment we attempt to explain an institution or a behavioural pattern X by its function or beneficial consequence Y for a group Z, the explanation is only legitimate, according to Elster, if it fulfils the following five criteria: (1) Y is an effect of X; (2) Y is beneficial for Z; (3) Y is unintended by the actors producing X; (4) Y, or at least the causal relation between X and Y, is unrecognized by the actors in Z; and (5) Y maintains X by a causal feedback loop passing through Z. Elster's main argument, in regard to functionalist explanations in the social sciences, is that in each single case the mechanism or feedback loop by which an institution is maintained must be specified. Or, as Elster formulates it:

> I want to argue that many purported cases of functional explanation fail because the feedback loop of criterion (5) is postulated rather than demonstrated ... Functionalist sociologists argue *as if* (which is not to argue *that*) criterion (5) is automatically fulfilled whenever the other criteria are. Since the demonstration that a phenomenon has unintended, unperceived and beneficial consequences seem to bestow some kind of meaning on it, and since to bestow meaning is to explain, the sociologist tends to assume that his job is over when the first four criteria are shown to be satisfied. (Elster, 1983: 58–9).

More specifically, Elster recommends both a natural selection mechanism and a reinforcement mechanism as two possible examples of feedback loops legitimizing the use of functionalist explanations. The first form of mechanism was used by Armen Alchian (1959) as an argument explaining why apparently adaptive or teleological behavioural patterns do not necessarily involve any form of foresight or 'intention', but can emerge from a market selection process. While this selection mechanism takes place at the population or industry level, the reinforcement mechanism takes place at the level of the single decision maker. The reinforcement mechanism means that rewarded behaviour is reinforced, whereas punished behaviour is discouraged. The individual 'becomes aware' of the relationship between a certain behaviour and its 'beneficial consequences', and from this learning process works out rules.

Functionalism, Panglossianism, and the demand for falsification

When introducing the functionalist explanation into economics, Armen Alchian (1950) was careful to stress that the selection mechanism, and thus the environment's ability to 'shape' economic behaviour, usually only led to 'better', but not necessarily the best or most efficient institutions, decision rules and so on. This was quite in keeping with the views of the founder of the theory of evolution, Charles Darwin, who had emphasized that the selection mechanism only ensured 'survival of the fitter', not necessarily 'survival of the fittest'. (The latter term is not Darwin's, but was introduced by the sociologist and philosopher Herbert Spencer.) However, Alchian's more sophisticated point was soon forgotten, when Milton Friedman used his selection argument to defend the profit-maximizing hypothesis. Consequently, many adopted the position that optimization and adaptation were basically identical. Existing institutions were explained in terms of optimal adaptations to environments, with the presumption that a perfectly functioning selection mechanism was active. Against this background, it is reasonable to criticize many of the Chicago School's contributions for taking to what the biologists Gould and Lewontin (1984) called 'Panglossianism'. This term is borrowed from Voltaire's *Candide*. The comic Doctor Pangloss continuously argues that 'things cannot be other than they are … everything is made for the best purposes. Our noses were made to carry spectacles, so we have spectacles. Legs were clearly intended for breeches, and we wear them' and so on. At certain times economics has shown similar tendencies to explain (rationalize) existing institutions, decision rules and so on as the most efficient.

Elster (1983) had only criticized the use of functionalism within the social sciences, whereas Gould and Lewontin's criticism was more general. They claimed that it would be unreasonable to view the selection mechanism as an 'optimizing' agent, not only within the social sciences but also within of biology. According to Gould and Lewontin, this involved the danger of being able to construct a 'problem' ex post to which the social rule or institution that one wanted to explain was an 'optimal' solution. This is always possible owing to the thesis of underdetermination referred to earlier, which says that we can always construct several – and potentially infinite – 'optimization-as-selection' stories to explain the same phenomenon. If something implies that we must reject one 'optimization-as-selection' story, we can always construct another, arguing that our social institution actually is the most 'efficient' solution to a slightly different problem.

Gould and Lewontin (1984) claim that the damage of Panglossianism, and the 'adaptive' research programme, was that basically one demonstrated the will to immunize the 'optimization assumption' against any imaginable empirical data. This was done by avoiding falsification by constructing new 'selection stories' based on previous 'falsified instances'. Without explicitly referring to Popper, Gould and Lewontin argued that this research strategy did not comply with the falsificationist rule not to apply 'conventionalist strategies'. There was also no compliance with the rule against using ad hoc hypotheses that were not independently testable. As a result, the adaptionist programme did not meet Lakatos' criterion of progressivity. It offered no 'new' or 'excess' contents. It was merely an adaptation of existing empirical data.

CHRISTIAN KNUDSEN

References

Alchian, Armen (1950), 'Uncertainty, Evolution and Economic Theory', *Journal of Political Economy*, **58**, (3), 211–21.

Elster, Jon (1983), *Explaining Technical Change. A Case Study in the Philosophy of Science*, Cambridge: Cambridge University Press.

Gould, S.J. and R. Lewontin (1984), 'The Spandrels of San Marcos and the Panglossian Paradigm: A Critique of the Adaptionist Programme', in E. Sober (ed.), *Conceptual Issues in Evolutionary Biology*, Cambridge, MA:

Parijs, P. van (1981), *Evolutionary Explanation in the Social Sciences. An Emerging Paradigm*, Totowa, NJ: Rowman and Littlefield.

Simon, Herbert (1978), 'Rationality as Process and as Product of Thought', *American Economic Review*, Papers and Proceedings, May, 1–16.

Game Theory

When people interact, the consequences associated with any individual's action often depend on the actions of others. For example, when two motorists drive towards each other on the same road, each has a choice between driving on the right and driving on the left and the outcome associated with each possible action depends critically on the other's decision. Thus a (left, right) combination yields a crash while a (left, left) or (right, right) selection means they pass without incident. Such interdependence between individual decisions is the essence of social life and game theory promises an analysis of what rational agents will do in such circumstances. In short. it is concerned with interactive or strategic decision making.

Formally, a 'game' is any interaction that is governed by a set of rules specifying the possible actions for each participant and a set of outcomes for each combination of actions. And the distinctive approach of game theory is to assume that (a) the agents know these rules, (b) they are instrumentally rational (that is, their preferences satisfy the axioms of rational choice theory and so they can be regarded as subjective expected utility maximizers, see 'Rational choice' in this volume) and (c) they have common knowledge of their rationality and the rules of the game. In addition it is sometimes assumed that agents have common priors.

All assumptions have methodological significance. Assumption (b) combines with (a) here to model interactive decision making in a very particular way. They establish, so as to speak, the ontology of social interactions in game theory. The rules supply a 'structure' to the social interaction which establishes the available actions and how they combine to yield the possible outcomes. The object of the analysis is then to explain how rational agents select (or should select) an action or actions and it seems natural to draw on the instrumental sense of reason for this purpose as it offers an account of how people choose between actions in terms of the way the likely outcomes contribute to that agent's preference satisfaction. Thus 'action' and 'structure' are separated with individual decisions with respect to action playing a distinct role in determining outcomes, albeit within a framework supplied by the rules of the game.

This is not an uncommon view of the relation between action and structure, but it is controversial to those like Giddens (1979) who regard action and structure as being mutually constituted. The key source for this alternative view is Wittgenstein and the contrast is between his notion of a language game and game theory's games. Nevertheless, the great virtue of the game theoretic separation for the western tradition of individualism is that it allows a clear and distinct part to be played by individual decision making in determining outcomes. Indeed, in so far as the structure (the 'rules') can itself be explained in terms of the deposits of previous social interactions of this sort, the way remains open in game theory to a thoroughgoing methodological individualist account of social outcomes.

The assumption that agents are subjective expected utility maximizers may seem natural once the rules of the game have established the nexus between actions and outcomes, but it is not obvious that this will explain by itself how an agent selects what action to undertake. In settings where there is a dominant strategy/action (that is, an action which is the best response to all possible actions that the other person might undertake), it will suffice. Instrumental reason here directs the agent to the use of the dominant strategy (as in the case of the prisoner's dilemma game, where cheating is a dominant strategy). But in many settings there is no dominant strategy as the action which best satisfies an agent's preferences varies with the choice of action by the other agent. Thus the best strategy for a motorist travelling along the road in our example is to drive on the left if the other motorist drives on the left and it is to drive on the right if the other motorist drives on the right. In such cases, the instrumental calculation of what to do for the best seems to require an account of how agents form expectations regarding what the other will do before it can go to work. This is where assumption (c) comes into play. There is no way to state the common knowledge of rationality assumption compactly. It literally means that each person knows they are rational each knows that each person knows they are rational, each knows that each knows that each person is rational, each knows that each knows that each knows that each person is rational, and so on in an infinite chain of knowing what was known in the link before.

At first glance, this may not seem a very helpful way of fixing agents' expectations since it seems in a two-person game to make your expectation of what the other person will do depend on what they expect you to do (as they too are rational and so will choose the action which is best relative to the expectation they hold regarding your action). Thus it seems merely to send the problem back to its starting point as you now reflect that what they expect you will do must depend on what they expect that you expect they will do and so on. However, since a rational person will not play a dominated strategy, it can in some games lead through the iterative deletion of dominated strategies to a narrowing of strategies which will be rationally pursued: any strategy which remains after such a process is called 'rationalizable' (see Bernheim. 1984; Pearce, 1984).

Unfortunately, many games have either no dominated strategies (as is the case in the motoring example) or the process of iterative deletion of dominated strategies leaves several 'rationalizable' strategies for each player. Thus game theory often draws on the further assumption of common priors, either directly or more controversially as an implication of the common knowledge of rationality assumption (see Aumann, 1976). This assumption (sometimes also known as the Harsanyi doctrine) holds that rational agents will draw the same inferences when faced with the same information. Thus, when agents share the same information set which comprises a game, its rules and the common knowledge of the players' rationality, they should draw the same inference regarding how the game will be played by rational agents. In short, there should be a unique (even if probabilistic) way for rational agents to play the game. This may not be known at first, but, if there is a unique way for rational players to act in the game, then what is known is that this way of playing the game must entail a combination of actions which are best replies to each other. To see this, notice that, when there is a unique way of playing which is inferred by both players and this involves an action which is not a best reply, there is an inconsistency since a non-best reply by an agent would not be consistent with that agent being an expected utility maximizer.

The Nash equilibrium of a game comprises strategies which are best replies to each other and the use of the common priors assumption is the most usual, recent way in which this equilibrium concept is justified. (Earlier lines of argument in support of the Nash equilibrium concept were more informal relying for instance on the task of reflecting on what a book on how games should be played would say about play if it was not to be undermined by being read by all potential rational players.) The common priors assumption, however, is not without controversy as it is not obvious that rational agents must always draw the same inference from the same information. Rational belief may simply be underdetermined by the information. For example, if rational belief formation involves applying some algorithm to the information, then even when agents share the same algorithm there seems bound to be scope for differing interpretations of how to apply the rules since it is well known that no set of rules can supply the rules for their own application. Indeed, unless there was scope for such differences, it would be difficult to understand, for example, why many trades took place in financial markets unless one wished to claim that there were surprising differences in the information available to agents in those markets.

Despite such doubts over its justification, the Nash equilibrium concept has achieved an unrivalled status and as a result much recent research has focused on the tricky issue of explaining equilibrium selection in games with multiple Nash equilibria (in the earlier motoring example there are two Nash equilibria in pure strategies: (left, left) and (right, right)). This is the object of the so-called Nash refinement project. This has many strands. Two are worth mentioning in this context.

One focuses on games where there is an explicit dynamic structure and appeals to the logic of backward induction. This principle involves considering what rational players would do in the last stage of the game (if it is reached) and then uses this to figure out what rational players would do in the penultimate stage of the game (if this is reached) and so on until the first stage. Thus the equilibrium of the game is deduced, in effect, backwards by starting at the last possible point in the game and working backwards. The difficulty which can arise with applying this logic is that it sometimes leads to the conclusion that rational players will not take the actions which lead to the later stages of the game. Why is this a problem? Notice that, on this account, such an equilibrium set of actions is supported by reflection on what rational agents would do in the later, and now out-of-equilibrium, stages of the game. The difficulty then is simply how to reconcile the presumption that both agents are rational, and there is common knowledge of this, with the agents using a reflective process which considers what rational agents will do in out-of-equilibrium parts of the game, since surely rational agents will not find themselves in out-of-equilibrium parts of the game (see Binmore, 1987). Or to put this worry the other way round, if you find yourself in what is for rational players an out-of-equilibrium part of the game, would it not seem sensible to doubt the rationality of your opponent? The response to such worries is to introduce the possibility of 'trembles' (execution errors which lead agents to play a strategy which they have not chosen to undertake). Thus a person may find themselves at an out-of-equilibrium part of the game, but this is not grounds for doubting their rationality since a 'tremble' could be responsible.

This is a pleasing line of argument for game theory since it does not threaten any of the fundamental assumptions, but it is not obvious that it will dissolve the worries in all circumstances. For example, suppose there are a large number of potential stages to the game, say a hundred, and the logic of backward induction yields the conclusion that rational agents will end the game at the first stage. Is it plausible to imagine in support of this conclusion that the hundredth stage is reached as a result of a sequence of trembles which mistakenly lead the agents to select non-rational action in each of the previous 99 stages?

A second noteworthy approach to Nash equilibrium selection appeals to the notion of 'salience' or focal points found in Schelling (1960). For example, when Schelling set his students a problem of meeting a friend in New York without being told the location, a majority replied they would go to Grand Central Station. In short, Grand Central Station was the 'salient' meeting point. In such cases it seems that agents are able to draw on information which is extraneous to the strict game-theoretic description of the interaction and so coordinate their decisions on a particular outcome. For this reason, it is a line of argument which is potentially worrying for traditional game theory. In particular, it begins to breach the neat division between action and structure, since action in the game is now to be explained by something outside the game itself. Indeed, it is tempting to argue that 'structure' in the form of these shared sources of extraneous information now influences action and so set the stage for a more Wittgensteinian approach to games.

SHAUN HARGREAVES HEAP

References

Aumann, R. (1976), 'Agreeing to disagree', *Annals of Statistics*, **4**, 1236–9.
Bernheim, D. (1984), 'Rationalisable strategic behaviour', *Econometrica*, **52**, 1007–28.
Binmore, K. (1987), 'Modeling rational players: part I', *Economics and Philosophy*, **3**, 179–214.
Giddens, A. (1979), *Central Problems in Social Theory*, London: Macmillan.
Pearce, D. (1984), 'Rationalisable strategic behaviour and the problem of perfection', *Econometrica*, **52**, 1029–50.
Schelling, T. (1960), *Strategy of Conflict*, Cambridge, MA: Harvard University Press.

Generalization

When looking at historical development of economic theory, two syntactic operations are at work in building (usually formalized) models, inducing their semantic and pragmatic properties. At certain times, a seminal article puts forward an original model, whether it be imported from the natural sciences eventually through mathematics, or elaborated directly in economics with classical formal tools. Subsequently, consolidation articles try to generalize this model, making its assumptions more universal, generic and profound, in order to have consequences dealing with an always larger class of phenomena. For instance, the 'correspondence principle' asserts that a new theory contains the old one as a special case, valid under restrictive conditions, and revives profoundly the interpretation of its concepts and structures.

A formalized model may be defined by a set of fundamental assumptions, a set of auxiliary assumptions which specify the preceding ones and a set of field assumptions which delineate its validity domain. According to what set of assumptions is modified (in an appropriate way), three basic generalization processes are conveniently distinguished, called enlarging, weakening and rooting. Although formally independent, the three processes are connected when one studies the empirical validity and operational use of a model, in order to choose among its many variants. Each process will be described and illustrated separately, from a structural as well as a functional point of view, before one considers the complementarity and substitutability of all the processes.

Enlarging

The enlarging process extends the field assumptions of a model, without modifying its fundamental and auxiliary assumptions, the model gaining in universality by a wider extensional definition. The inverse process called 'narrowing' keeps the formal structure of the model, but applies it to a restricted set of configurations, each characterized by the application domain of its entity and property variables. Enlarging and narrowing are combined in an analogical transfer, where a model is shifted from one specific domain to another, through a one-to-one correspondence between associated magnitudes. Such an analogy is substantial if the respective interpretations of variables extend to the interpretations of relations, and formal if the respective interpretations of relations are disconnected.

In physics, the law of ideal gas which relates its pressure, volume and temperature, is applied to other fluids provided with the same property variables, such as plasmas and even liquids. In decision theory, the expected utility choice model for a decision maker in a risky environment is applied to symbolic as well as material actions (Pascal's wager argument) or to pigeons as well as humans. In game theory, the Nash equilibrium is applied to two countries involved in international trade, to state and economy where macroeconomic policy is concerned, or to two firms in the duopoly context. In economics, the demand function is defined for physical goods such as oil, cars or toys, more immaterial goods such as labour, money or information, and even 'non-physical' goods such as marriage, crime or worship.

The enlarging process can be more ambitious, leading finally to classes of partially interpreted models, applied in economics as well as in physics or biology and gathered by 'systemic thinking'. It first extends only the spatiotemporal location of basic entities, for instance the simplified Keynesian model considered as relevant for any (modern) period and for any (developed) country. It further generalizes some attributes of a given entity, for instance the discounting factor of a player in an infinite game, alternatively interpreted as the subjective probability that the game ends at each period. It finally relates different entities with corresponding attributes, for instance the choice of a producer maximizing his profit under a technical constraint similar to the choice of a consumer minimizing his expenditure under a utility constraint.

The role of enlarging is to derive from analogous assumptions analogous conclusions, by using a common formal framework whose properties are studied once for ever. For example, by substituting for usual goods contingent goods (available in the future under uncertain events), the desirable properties of a competitive equilibrium (existence and uniqueness, Pareto-optimality) are preserved. Conversely, this makes it possible to justify similar conclusions with similar assumptions, hence to explain a similar phenomenon in different fields with the same formal mechanisms. For example, in order to allow for cycles in various systems, it is always possible to explain them either by outside influences (cyclical, stochastic) or by inside structures (two-period delays, non-linearities).

Weakening

The weakening process keeps the fundamental assumptions of a model, but relaxes its auxiliary assumptions for given field assumptions, the model gaining in genericity by a less restricted specification. The inverse process called 'strengthening' imposes a logically stronger formal structure on the model, especially in fixing the value of a given parameter, and even in pushing this parameter to zero, as in 'idealization' (Nowak, 1980) Weakening and strengthening are combined in sensitivity analysis, where some propositions of a model get alternative specifications, in order to test the robustness of consequences derived from such variants. When a model is weakened, its interpretation is modified since old concepts receive an extended meaning, usual relations allow a renewed reading and innovative notions receive an original signification.

In physics, the law of ideal gas is weakened under the form of the van der Wals law introducing two (formerly nil) unspecified parameters (or non-zero specified in the case of a variant law). In decision theory, the expected utility model gets different extensions, especially the 'anticipated utility model' bringing in a (formerly an identity) deformation function of cumulative probability of events. In game theory, the Nash equilibrium is generalized to games with incomplete information ('Bayesian equilibrium'), but also to weaker notions with complete information ('rationalizable equilibrium'). In economics, the demand function is weakened by introducing other explaining variables than prices and revenue, or by abandoning all restrictions imposed on its form, such as the Slutsky conditions.

The weakening process can be more ambitious, leading finally to qualitative models (such as interaction graphs) characterized by structural properties (such as loops) especially studied by 'qualitative economics'. It first assigns a more general analytical form to a parametric relation, for instance by transforming a linear cost function (with constant unitary cost) into an affine one (with additional fixed cost) or a quadratic one (with increasing marginal cost). It further introduces new explanatory variables in a given relation, for instance by letting the utility function of a consumer depend on others' consumption (fashion, congestion) or others' utility (altruism, envy). It finally brings a whole new dimension into a model, for instance by extending the duopoly model from statics to dynamics, from certainty to uncertainty or from two firms to any number of firms.

The role of weakening is to infer from weaker assumptions weaker conclusions, which may allow for phenomena previously excluded but readily observable. For example, in consumer theory, when the utility function is no longer separable, but allows substitution between goods, some goods may become inferior, that is, their demand lessens when revenue increases. Symmetrically, it is possible to deduce weaker conclusions from weaker assumptions and especially to avoid 'negative' results which are considered undesirable on positive or normative grounds. For example, in social choice theory, the impossibility of drawing a collective preference relation from individual ones under general conditions is alleviated when considering individual preferences as single-peaked rather than unrestricted.

Rooting
The rooting process searches for a set of postulates which logically justify the fundamental assumptions of a model without bothering about auxiliary and field assumptions, the model thus gaining in profoundness. The inverse process called 'blooming' tries to find a model compatible with some occurrence of grounding postulates, each postulate giving rise to a finite number of alternative expressions. Rooting and blooming are combined in the 'comparative principle' which reduces the difference between two models in the same field to differences in such and such postulates explaining them, the others being identical. When a model is rooted, its significance is enriched, since new 'hidden factors' are introduced in the postulates and original 'causal links' relate the hidden and observable magnitudes.

In physics, the law of ideal gas is a macro law which stems from micro properties of molecules, a statistical distribution of these molecules together with relations between macro variables and micro distributions. In decision theory, the expected utility model is grounded on a set of axioms concerned with the decision maker's preferences over lotteries, namely weak order, continuity and independence. In game theory, the Nash equilibrium is justified by players' cognitive processes involving common knowledge of rationality, of independence of play and of common prior, but is justified as well by learning or evolutionary processes. In economics, the decreasing demand function of a consumer may be deduced from his optimizing behaviour, but may stem alike from a conservative behaviour or a stochastic behaviour.

The rooting process can be more and more ambitious, leading finally to a few basic principles concerning individual behaviour and social interaction, especially studied by decision theory and game theory. First, it may only derive a reduced relation from structural ones, for instance a consumption function depending on past revenue from a consumption function depending on future revenue and from an (extrapolative) expectation function for revenue. Second, it infers a relation from a whole set of underlying assumptions, for instance an aggregate production function from individual production functions associated with assumptions on the distribution of firms and the competition among firms. Third, it gives to some relation or rule axiomatic foundations, for instance by grounding the Nash solution for bargaining in cooperative games on axioms such as individual and collective rationality, independence and symmetry.

The role of rooting is to suggest one or several explanations for a given phenomenon, since it is always possible to justify a finite number of facts with an infinite number of contrasted models. For example, the proportionality of real wage to labour productivity stems from the neoclassical model (productivity adjusted to exogenous wage), the efficient wage model (worker's effort induced by wage) and the signalling model (wage adapted to education linked to productivity). Rooting is even able to exhibit reciprocal explanations of two models, in so far as one model correctly specified is able to justify the other, and conversely. For example, the optimizing behaviour rule is justified by a dynamic satisficing model when the aspiration levels are adjusted to past results, and the satisficing behaviour rule is justified by a meta-optimization model trading off direct utility and processing costs.

Links

As far as empirical validity is concerned, the enlarging process makes a model more refutable (for a given interpretation of its entity variables) since its set of testable consequences is increased to new fields. However an 'immunizing stratagem' transforms a validation test into an application test, which only delineates the domain where the model is empirically valid, without trying to falsify it. On the contrary, the weakening process makes a model less refutable since, by acquiring more degrees of freedom, the set of testable propositions contradicting it gets smaller. As before, an immunizing stratagem transforms a validation test into an estimation test, where the best specification of the model compatible with the data is simply singled out, without concern for falsification.

Applied to the same model, enlarging and weakening must be considered as correlated processes, since the weakened model is associated with a field of application potentially more extended. For instance, the 'augmented' Phillips curve, where price expectations are introduced to explain wages in addition to price observations and unemployment, naturally applies to a wider spatiotemporal domain. When a model is refuted, the modeller may at a first stage weaken it, and hence enlarge it in order to incorporate the controversial field, but at a second stage he has to strengthen it again without excluding the controversial field. For instance, as the expected utility model is refuted in Allais' experiment, it is possible to generalize it by the anticipated utility model, but this last should be strengthened again by specifying the probability deformation function.

Where operationality is concerned, the weakening process makes a model more synthetical since it summarizes a class of models, and this can be pursued hierarchically from the completely numerical models to the most generic ones. However, it is hard to deduce by analytical calculus non-trivial conclusions from assumptions which are too generic, and numerical simulation with more specific models is needed to infer more precise consequences. In the same way, the rooting process makes a model more comprehensive since it is justified by hidden assumptions, and this can be pursued sequentially from the observable phenomena to very first principles. As indicated above, if it is rather easy to justify an empirical fact with a shrewd combination of elementary laws, it is much harder to state basic postulates able to ground an already theoretical model.

Applied to the same model, weakening and rooting must be considered as complementary pragmatic processes, since a weakened model is often obtained by weakening one or more of its founding assumptions. For instance, if the Stone demand function of a consumer is derived from a Cobb–Douglas utility function, a generalized demand function stems from a CES (constant elasticity of substitution) utility function. Moreover, the modeller can combine the two processes in order to construct a whole system of neighbouring models in two orthogonal directions, deducing horizontally and specifying vertically, as tried by the 'structuralist school' (Stegmuller *et al.* 1982). For instance, the expected utility model lies in the middle of a network going horizontally from basic axioms to applied choice models and vertically from the most general maximizing criterion on lotteries to the expected payoff maximization rule.

BERNARD WALLISER

Bibliography

Nowak, L. (1980), *The Structure of Idealization*, Dordrecht: Reidel.
Stegmuller W., W. Balzer and W. Spohn (1982), *Philosophy of Economics*, Berlin: Springer Verlag
Walliser B. (1994), 'Three generalization processes for economic models', in B. Hamminga and N. de Marchi (eds), *Idealization VI: Idealization in Economics*, Poznan: Rodopi.

Georgescu-Roegen, Nicholas

Nicholas Georgescu-Roegen (1906–94) belonged to that small but select group of economists who helped shape the neoclassical mathematical orthodoxy in America in the 1930s and 1940s, but then turned against it in later life, having observed the fruits of his labours. Although he was well known amongst postwar economists for his contributions to theoretical areas such as the non-substitution theorems, integrability conditions in utility theory and the treatment of stochastic choice, his later heretical turn is his most significant bequest to economic methodology. In his magnum opus, *The Entropy Law and the Economic Process*, and, to a lesser extent, his papers collected in *Analytical Economics* and *Energy and Economic Myths*, he sought to reorient economics away from a rather outdated fascination with mechanics in favour of something which he called 'bioeconomics'. Although the outlines of this transformed discipline were still left vague at his death, he can be seen in retrospect as heralding the biological turn so prevalent in economics at the end of the twentieth century.

Georgescu-Roegen displayed something more than an amateur grasp of the philosophy of science from the 1960s onwards, and this facility is one of the definitive hallmarks of his later work, though it was not much appreciated by his fellow economists. While others might make superficial references to Popper or Kuhn, he was busy citing technical work by Poincaré on determinism, Cantor on the continuum, David Bohm on causality and Whitehead on holism, as well as much else. In the case of an author who felt confident passing from the non-algorithmic character of thought to the weaknesses of statistical mechanics to the texture of the arithmetical continuum in a text ostensibly concerned with economics, the quest to provide a capsule summary of his thought may seem vain or perverse. Nevertheless, it is possible to identify three major themes to which he repeatedly returned in his writings: the nature of probability in a world of stochastic laws; the problem of the similarities and differences in the uses of mathematics in the sciences; and the importance of thermodynamics for value theory.

Georgescu-Roegen's early training was in statistics in the Pearsonian tradition; thus it is all the more noteworthy that he became a rather strident critic of the Cowles econometric orthodoxy. Beginning with the observation that neoclassicism had made little headway in accommodating stochastic considerations in price theory, he felt that none of the standard justifications for the error term were at all persuasive in regression analysis. He believed the problem lay deeper than the usual 'adjustments' to the standard linear model, and this led him to examine the various philosophical schools of probability, all of which he found wanting. Towards the end of his career, he believed that the way out of the impasse was to admit that probability as used in economics was a dialectical rather than a numerical concept. As he put it, the Borel–Cantelli definition of probability 'is a complete thought in the Hegelian sense because it defines probability by probability'. Thus he came to a conviction that, to the extent that economic laws were intrinsically stochastic, economics had to be a dialectical science.

Georgescu differed from the other protagonists of the mathematical revolution of the 1930s, in that his theoretical concerns increasingly raised doubts in his own mind about the adequacy of the formalisms used in economics. In addition to the dialectical character of probability cited above, there was a dissatisfaction with conventional functional representations of choice theory and production theory. Later in his career, he insisted that economics was beset by the vice of 'arithmomorphism', which he defined as the projection of the characteristics of sets of discrete numbers upon an essentially dialectical reality. The fetishism of the attachment to specific inappropriate mathematical representations was traced to a dynamic where economists tended to mimic the physical sciences without adequate understanding of the demands of the respective subject matters: 'Time and again, we can see the drawbacks of importing a gospel from physics into economics and interpreting it in a more catholic way than the consistory of physicists.'

Nevertheless, far from repudiating physics, Georgescu believed that economics should pay more attention to it, especially to the speciality of thermodynamics. Indeed, he maintained that 'of all physical concepts only those of Thermodynamics have their roots in economic value' for without the constraint of the entropy law there would be no primal scarcity in the world. Thermodynamics not only dictated a thoroughgoing stochastic approach to the phenomenon; it also served to indict neoclassical production theory for ignoring the fundamental irreversibility of time; and after the OPEC embargo he seemed to believe it was the source of fundamental conflicts in capitalist development. From the 1970s onwards, Georgescu's dire predictions were largely ignored by economists, but did gain a hearing amongst ecologists (of the energetics school of Howard Odum) and people concerned with environmental issues. Because of this shift in audience, Georgescu was often misunderstood as advocating an energetics theory of value, a charge he went to great lengths to refute in some of his final essays.

One would search in vain for a 'school' of thought inspired by Georgescu-Roegen; his own ambivalence about total renunciation of utility theory made him neither fully an orthodox insider nor a stauch outsider to the profession. Furthermore, the assertion that the incorporation of biological themes would adequately counteract the anthropomorphism and physics envy of neoclassicism was never sufficiently motivated in his work. However, it is difficult to identify another economist in the twentieth century whose depth of insight into the intricate interplay of physics, mathematics and economics surpassed his own.

PHILIP MIROWSKI

Bibliography
Georgescu-Roegen, Nicholas (1971), *The Entropy Law and the Economic Process*, Cambridge, MA: Harvard University Press.
Georgescu-Roegen, Nicholas (1976), *Energy and Economic Myths*, Oxford: Pergamon Press.
Mirowski, Philip (1992), 'Nicholas Georgescu-Roegen', in Warren Samuels (ed.), *New Horizons in Economic Thought*, Aldershot: Edward Elgar.

Granger Causality

Causality is a concept that occurs often in economic theory, hypotheses and discussions. As economics is a decision science, the direct cause is often a piece of information received by a decision maker that effects the decision about to be made, which is then reflected in the outcome from the decision. For example, the information could be about the quality or price of a consumption good, the decision is whether or not to buy and the outcome is the observed consumption by the economic agent. It follows that the cause need not be temporally or spatially adjacent to the effect, as sometimes assumed by philosophers more used to the physical sciences. It also follows that causality in economics is likely to be of a stochastic rather than a deterministic nature; there is a probability that a price change leads to a change in sales, for example. Similar ideas occur elsewhere; see, for instance, Good (1988), Suppes (1979) and Skyrms and Harper (1988). The obvious example is that, if one smokes, one does not necessarily get cancer but the probability of getting cancer increases. For the econometrician, the task of finding a plausible definition of causation is rather different to that facing the philosopher, as the definition has to be operational; that is, statistical tests using actual data need to be based on it, rather than the thought experiment type of tests often used by philosophers. It is obviously impossible to use a statistical device to test causality in a unique event, but economic time series provide essentially a repetition of many events and so are plausible candidates for such tests.

It would be interesting to try to compare modern concepts of causality, used by present-day philosophers such as Skyrms and Harper (1988) and Gärdenfors (1988), and the classical thinkers on the topic, such as David Hume. However, the developments have been so significant that a comparison is difficult, going from deterministic, physical relationships and contiguity to stochastic, decision-based relationships and non-contiguity. It is like trying to compare a clockwork watch with a quartz watch; the objective is the same, but little else. A problem with the literature is that some writers appreciate the developments, while others do not accept them and continue debates along ancient lines.

The definition of causality discussed here is based on two premises, that the cause occurs temporally before the effect and that the cause contains information about the effect that is not available elsewhere. The second premise indicates that there will be a statistical relationship between a measurable cause and effect, but that this relationship will be a deep one in some sense, not merely a significant correlation or regression coefficient (a discussion can be found in Granger, 1980). The pair of premises imply immediately that the cause will help forecast the effect, whatever information set is used. To express this more formally, consider the question of whether or not a series Y_n caused another series X_{n+1}, one step ahead. Let Ω_n denote the universal information set and $\Omega_n - Y_n$ be this set except for the information in the Y series. The universal information set comprises all information available at time n, but contains no redundant information, so that if a pair of series are perfectly functionally related they are not both in Ω. The general definition is that Y_n causes X_{n+1} if

$$prob\ (X_{n+1} \in A \mid \Omega_n) \neq prob\ (X_{n+1} \in A \mid \Omega_n - Y_n)$$

for some sets A. Thus knowing the series Y_n alters our knowledge of the next X_{n+1} extra to all the other information available. The definition is not practical, of course, as Ω_n is never available. To make it operational one has to go to a less general definition. Suppose that $\underline{W}_n$ is a vector of variables, including X_n but not Y_n, presumably mostly economic series that are thought to be possibly related to X_n, and let J_n be an information set available at time n consisting of $\underline{W}_{n-j}$, $j \geq 0$. Let J'_n be J_n plus Y_{n-j}, $j \geq 0$, and $F(X_{n+1} \mid J_n)$ be the conditional distribution of X_{n+1} given the information in J_n. If $F(X_{n+1} \mid J_n) \neq F(X_{n+1} \mid J'_n)$ then Y_n is said to be a '*prima facie* cause of X_{n+1} with respect to the information set J'_n'. Presumably, there is a specific reason to ask if Y_n does cause X_{n+1}; perhaps it is suggested by some theory, rather than Y and X just being chosen at random from a long list of variables. Thus one may start with an *a priori* probability or belief of a causality being found and the '*prima facie*' phrase is used to indicate that this belief is at least still maintained from this conditional probability test. Naturally, it is not a full test as J'_n is used rather than Ω_n. If $\underline{W}_n$ is expanded to include further series, then Y_n may no longer be found to cause X_{n+1}. It is difficult to perform actual tests on whole distribution functions; it is rather easier to consider specific moments, such as means. A necessary condition for prima facie causality is if

$$E[X_{n+1} \mid J_n] \neq E[X_n \mid J'_n]$$

in which case Y_n is a '*prima facie* cause of X_{n+1} in mean with respect to J'_n'. It follows that, if $\sigma^2 (I_n)$ is the variance of the one-step forecast errors of X_{n+1} given the information set I_n, assuming forecasts are optimum and thus unbiased, then $\sigma^2 (J'_n) < \sigma^2 (J_n)$ if one has *prima facie* causality in mean. Thus a test of this causality is quite easily based on this improved forecastability of X_{n+1} if the information in Y_{n-j} is utilized. Here the quality of forecasts is measured by a squared error cost function; other cost functions could be used. It should be noted that the definitions do not assume that variables are stationary or that only linear forecasts are used, although practical tests of them sometimes do add these extra assumptions. The definition was introduced by Norbert Wiener (1956) and made specific in Granger (1969; 1980), although some earlier writers had discussed related ideas, as in Bunge (1963). A recent viewpoint on it by a philosopher is given by Gärdenfors (1988).

Any definition will have properties and consequentially difficulties. Amongst the properties of the definition discussed above are the following:

1. If Y_n causes X_{n+1}, X_n causes Z_{n+1} then Y_n may or may not cause Z_{n+k}, some $k > 0$.
2. If Y_n causes X_{n+1} then X_n may or may not cause Y_{n+1}. If both causes are found, then one can say that feedback is occurring.
3. If Y_n causes X_{n+1}, then one can apply different lag polynomial backward filters $a_1 (B)$, $a_2 (B)$, where B is the lag operator such that $a_1 (0)$, $a_2 (0)$ are both non-zero and have $a_1 (B) Y_n$ cause $a_2 (B) X_{n+1}$.
4. One cannot discuss causation of deterministic series X_n, that is one that is perfectly forecastable from its own past.

Some problems can occur when variables are measured with error, the errors having temporal memory, or when an important variable is missing from the information set or if the variables are recorded when they are observed rather than when they occur. As an example of the latter problem, clearly the January New York unemployment figure will be recorded for January even though it becomes available in March, say. However, if thunder and lightning are recorded when they are observed, lightning will always precede thunder, because light travels faster than sound, even though they are produced at the same, identical moment of time.

The actual testing procedure that is recommended is to construct a linear model relating X_{n+1} to $\underline{W}_n$, and then to construct a second model relating X_{n+1} to $\underline{W}_n$, Y_n. One test is to see if the

Y_{n-j} term enters the second model significantly or, equivalently, to see if the second model fits better than the first. However, model construction techniques often involve a certain amount of manipulation and 'data mining' and neither of these tests is based strictly on the definition which calls for extra forecasting. A better test is to compare the out-of-sample forecasting abilities of the two models; if there is *prima facie* causality, the second model should produce forecast errors with significantly lower variance. An example of the use of this procedure is given in Ashley *et al.* (1980) relating US aggregate advertising and consumption levels. It is found, using quarterly data, that consumption causes advertising but that advertising does not cause consumption. The result may seem surprising to macroeconomists but is not to economists in the area of marketing. There are many tests of causality, based on the definition, which are usually tests of fit rather than forecasting ability and they have been widely applied.

Non-causality has been confused with the concept of (complete) exogeneity but a clarifying discussion has been given by Engle *et al.* (1983), who also define various forms of exogeneity useful for statistical inference, conditional forecasting and policy determination, some of which are based on the causality definition. There have been attempts to generalize the definition to produce tests of 'instantaneous causality', in which current Y_{n+1} causes X_{n+1}, but they are of limited usefulness as they seem to have the property that if Y causes X then necessarily X causes Y, so that the idea of a clear-cut direction of causality is lost. Various attempts have also been made to generalize the definition to continuous time but they seem to be non-operational and to lose the premise that cause precedes effect.

The definition makes no statement about controllability, although some writers take this to be the characterizing property of causality, believing that, if there is a cause, it can be used to control. There seems to be no necessity for this belief, but Hoover and Sheffrin (1992) have based a definition on it and have attempted to make it operational.

In general, applied papers have used the definition uncritically or have merely commented that it is the best operational definition available to them. A useful critical discussion has been given by Zellner (1979) who prefers definitions depending on economic theory. Although this definition will probably not be the one eventually accepted, as it is too simplistic and statistically based, it will likely be a component of whatever definition eventually evolves. At the very least it has proved to be a useful methodological device, forcing empirical modellers to condition on the past of the series under consideration before asking if other information is useful.

CLIVE W.J. GRANGER

References

Ashley, R., C.W.J. Granger and R. Schmalansee (1980), 'Advertising and aggregate consumption: an analysis of causality', *Econometrica*, **48**, 1149–68.

Bunge, Mario (1963), *Causality*, Cleveland: World Publishing Co.

Engle, R.F., D.F. Hendry and J.F. Richard (1983), 'Exogeneity', *Econometrica*, **51**, 277–304.

Gärdenfors, P. (1988), *Knowledge in Flux*, Cambridge, MA: MIT Press.

Good, I.J. (1988), 'Causal Tendency: A Survey', in B. Skyrms and W.L. Harper (eds), *Causation, Chance and Credence*.

Granger, C.W.J. (1969), 'Investigating causal relationships by econometric models and cross-spectral methods', *Econometrica*, **37**, 424–38.

Granger, C.W.J. (1980), 'Testing for causality: a personal viewpoint', *Journal of Economic Dymamics and Control*, **2**, 329–52.

Hoover, K.D. and S.M. Sheffrin (1992), 'Causation, spending and taxes: sand in the sandbox or tax collector for the welfare state?', *American Economic Review*, **82**, 225–48.

Skyrms, B. and W.L. Harper (eds) (1988), *Causation, Chance and Credence*, Dordrecht: Kluwer.

Suppes, P. (1970), *A Probabilistic Theory of Causality*, Amsterdam: North-Holland.

Wiener, N. (1956), 'The Theory of Prediction', *Modern Mathematics for Engineers*, series 1, ed. E.F. Beckerbeck.

Zellner, A. (1979), 'Causality and Econometrics', *Carnegie–Rochester Conference on Public Policy*, **10**, 4–56.

Haavelmo, Trygve M.

'This year's laureate in economics showed how economic theories can be tested', read the 1989 press release headline when Trygve Magnus Haavelmo was awarded the Nobel Prize in Economic Sciences. This headline might be construed as misleading, for Haavelmo did not write a rule book on how to test theories, but provided the much more difficult foundational analysis to justify economic theory testing using econometrics.

Born in Norway in 1911, Haavelmo graduated from the University of Oslo in 1933 and then worked as research assistant to Ragnar Frisch. When war broke out he travelled to the United States, drafting his pathbreaking essay on the foundations of econometrics in 1941; this was published as a supplement to *Econometrica* under the title 'The Probability Approach in Econometrics' during the wartime shortage of publishable material in 1944. (He had already abstracted his famous results on simultaneous equations models (1943a) while recovering from appendicitis in the Norwegian hospital for sailors.) Haavelmo was associated with the Cowles Commission under Jacob Marschak's direction in the mid-1940s, and in 1947 returned to the University of Oslo, where he quickly became a professor and remains a researcher.

In the early 1940s, econometrics was a well-established, though not widely used, method of applied economics. Haavelmo clearly drew on the developments of these earlier years for his essay, which formed the basis for a fundamental revision, if not revolution, in econometrics. His work provided the theoretical basis for the explosion of applied econometrics after the 1950s, though his programme was not immediately adopted in its entirety (see Spanos, 1989; Morgan 1990; Qin, 1993). His conceptual foundations also formed the basis of many subsequent developments in theoretical econometrics. Despite all this, his role was almost forgotten until he was awarded the Nobel Prize. Even after 50 years (and many rereadings) Haavelmo's essay still impresses with its combination of breadth of coverage, depth of understanding of the problems involved and wealth of helpful concepts employed to help solve these problems. His ideas continue to inform and guide the philosophical analysis of econometrics (as is evident from the secondary literature in the Bibliography below). Haavelmo's essay has justly become known as the most important individual methodological document in econometrics.

The possibility of testing economic theories against statistical economic data depended, Haavelmo stated, on building a strong 'bridge' between the two sides (theory and data) to replace the casual arguments and ad hoc practices of his predecessors. The bridge has two main foundations: (1) a redefinition of economic data so that probability-based methods of statistical inference could be legitimately applied to them, and (2) a constructive account of econometric models as intervening devices between theory and data to provide solutions to a series of knotty correspondence problems.

As regards *probability thinking*, Haavelmo wrote his text at a time when it was usual to understand statistical social science as some kind of not-yet-too-successful substitute for the controlled experiment of physical sciences. Indeed the main developments of mathematical statistics from the 1890s to the 1930s had been in those fields where laboratory experiments were impossible, but where some kind of control was exerted through new measurement techniques (for example, by Yule in social theory) or through careful experimental design (for example, R.A. Fisher in genetics) so that the resulting statistical measurements provided the basis for probability inferences. In taking a pro-probability starting point, Haavelmo was arguing against the beliefs of most econometricians of the period, including his mentor, Frisch, who had tried to develop a general non-probabilistic approach to econometrics (see Morgan,

1987). Haavelmo in fact developed the views of Koopmans (1937), who had already argued that economic data (even the single point realizations of time-series data) could be regarded as a random sample from a hypothetical probability distribution (see Hendry and Morgan, 1995). Adopting this position opened the door for estimating economic relationships using multivariate techniques (developed in the inter-war period by R.A. Fisher and others) and then for applying rigorous statistical inference based on either Neyman–Pearson testing procedures or those of Wald (both Neyman and Wald had played a part in Haavelmo's conversion to probability thinking; see Qin, 1993). Haavelmo showed how these various ideas and methods could be combined, developed and consistently applied in the specific subject domain of economics.

He found the probability approach attractive because it allowed both for uncertainty in the economic world (and he later came to the conclusion that 'the "laws" of economics are not very accurate' (Haavelmo, 1958: 355)) and for ignorance in economists' knowledge of the world. The probability approach was, for Haavelmo, the obvious logical way to deal with this double uncertainty and to formalize the measurement and testing of economic theories. Thus the rigorous application of the probability approach formed the basis of Haavelmo's defence (1943b) of Tinbergen against Keynes' famous methodological attack. Haavelmo's beliefs about probability theory and probabilities appear to have been primarily instrumental in character. Although he discussed both the subjectivist and the frequentist account of probabilities (and recently Le Gall, 1994, has suggested a propensity interpretation), he remained uncommitted to either, for he found that, whenever and however probability thinking was fully formalized, it inevitably abstracted away from the problems you wanted it to solve and the material to which you thought it applied.

Econometric models were to form the second foundation. Whether the door to statistical testing of economic theories could be properly opened depended not just on new ways of thinking about data, but also, Haavelmo argued, on a new view of economic theories. It is in this area that his work is truly innovative and original. Since economics did not lend itself to experiments (at that time, at any rate), the statistical data that economists had were the result of 'passive observation' of Nature's experiments: the people, firms and economies at work in their uncontrolled environment. The only way to test theories was therefore to build models to match that data, so that economists could become 'master of reality, by passive agreement' (Haavelmo: 1944: 15). For Haavelmo, theoretical models are merely mathematically defined restrictions on the variations of a system, and they have no economic meaning until they are accompanied by 'a design of experiments' 'rules for choosing the facts to which the theoretical model is to be applied' (ibid.: 4, 6).

'Experimental design' involved a twofold injunction: to adapt the theoretical model so that it was about what could in principle be observed; and to incorporate a probabilistic format such that the model becomes a hypothesis about statistical data. For example, a theoretical model might be concerned with the potential consumption choices of households with given income and prices. To turn this into a testable hypothesis, the model needed to be reformulated as a statistical hypothesis about the actual consumption decisions taken by one household, or a set of households, with the same given income and facing similar prices over a particular period of years. The statistical data on the actual decisions from such households would constitute a sample from the hypothetical population of possible decisions (the original theoretical level). The 'design of experiments' mentality advocated by Haavelmo invites the economist to rewrite his model in terms of the behaviour and circumstances which would operate as a test of the theory, and to give a probability formulation of that model to enable such a test to be carried out by the application of statistical inference procedures.

Haavelmo's essay not only constructed these two foundations, but provided an immensely detailed account of the entire set of correspondence problems between economic theory and data and the bridging principles to solve these in econometrics. His ideas and solutions grew out of a sophisticated understanding of the fundamental practical problems of applied economics. The subtlety of detail in his account is highly rewarding and cannot be caught in this brief description, but one short example will give something of the flavour. It is in Haavelmo's discussion of economic laws that we gain our first full understanding of Frisch's (1938) concept of autonomy. Haavelmo shows why autonomous structural relations are more fundamental for our understanding and for describing the behaviour of the economic system than the superficial phenomenological (or, in Frisch's language, 'confluent') relations derived from the underlying structural relations (see Aldrich, 1989; Cartwright, 1989). By contrast, 'constancy' is defined by Haavelmo as an empirical characteristic of estimated economic relations, which he stresses is essential not only for the inferential project (measurement and testing require homogeneity within the time period), but also for prediction and policy purposes. Haavelmo surprises us here: he points out that many econometric relations are unbelievably simple, much simpler than the laws we think we are measuring. But these simple relations often turn out to be non-constant and so he argues against using simplicity as a criterion in applied economics. An understanding of both of these concepts, along with the more traditional identification problem (of separating out individual relations in a system of mutually dependent relationships: see Morgan, 1990), is required for an analysis of causality and thus policy intervention using econometric models (see Qin, 1993; Aldrich, 1994).

It is difficult to categorize Haavelmo in terms of any standard methodological label. For example, consider a brief conjunction of two statements: theoretical models are 'necessary tools in our attempt to understand and "explain" events in real life' (Haavelmo, 1944: 1); but the 'explanations' they offer are 'our own artificial inventions ... not hidden truths to be discovered' (ibid.: 3). He is neither a naive operationalist, nor pure instrumentalist, nor strict logical positivist. Nevertheless, his essay provides a consistent and comprehensive methodological programme for econometrics. It is based on an analysis which is critical of past methods, but is primarily a constructive attempt to provide a set of correspondence instructions for applied economics. These are not mechanical rules based on a philosophy of science, or on logic or mathematics. Rather, these are generic practical instructions (despite their philosophical sophistication). Their successful prosecution, however, turns out to be far from easy. As Haavelmo warns at every turn, applied econometrics is a difficult art requiring both wisdom and experience.

MARY S. MORGAN

Bibliography

Aldrich, John (1989), 'Autonomy', *Oxford Economic Papers*, **41**, 15–34.
Aldrich, John (1994), 'Haavelmo's Identification Theory', *Econometric Theory*, **10**, 198–219.
Cartwright, Nancy (1989), *Nature's Capacities and Their Measurement*, Oxford: Clarendon Press.
Epstein, Roy J. (1987), *A History of Econometrics*, Amsterdam: North-Holland.
Frisch, Ragnar K. (1938), 'Statistical versus Theoretical Relations in Economic Macrodynamics'; (reprinted 1995, in D.F. Hendry and M.S. Morgan (eds), *The Foundations of Econometric Analysis*, Cambridge: Cambridge University Press.
Haavelmo, Trygve M. (1943a), 'The Statistical Implications of a System of Simultaneous Equations', *Econometrica*, **11**, 1–12.
Haavelmo, Trygve M. (1943b), 'Statistical Testing of Business-Cycle Theories', *Review of Economic Statistics*, **25**, 13–18.

Haavelmo, Trygve M. (1944), 'The Probability Approach in Econometrics', *Econometrica*, **12** (supplement), i–viii, 1–118.
Haavelmo, Trygve M. (1958), 'The Role of the Econometrician and the Advancement of Economic Theory', *Econometrica*, **26**, 351–7.
'Bibliography of Trygve Haavelmo's Publications (1938–1987)', *Scandinavian Journal of Economics*, (1990), **92**, 25–30.
'The Nobel Memorial Prize in Economics, 1989, Press Release', *Scandinavian Journal of Economics*, (1990), **92**, 11–15.
Hendry, David F. and Mary S. Morgan (1995), *The Foundations of Econometric Analysis*, Cambridge: Cambridge University Press.
Koopmans, Tjalling C. (1937), *Linear Regression Analysis of Economic Time Series*, Publication no. 20, of the Netherlands Economic Institute, Haarlem.
Le Gall, Philippe (1994), *L'Histoire de l'Econométrie: l'Erosion du Déterminisme*, thesis, Université de Paris I Panthéon–Sorbonne; published 1996, Paris: Editions de-la Decouverte.
Morgan, Mary S. (1987), 'Statistics without Probability and Haavelmo's Revolution in Econometrics', in L. Krüger, G. Gigerenzer and M.S. Morgan (eds), *The Probabilistic Revolution. Vol I: Ideas in the Sciences*, Cambridge, MA: MIT Press.
Morgan, Mary S. (1990), *The History of Econometric Ideas*, Cambridge: Cambridge University Press.
Morgan, Mary S. (1991), 'The Stamping Out of Process Analysis in Econometrics', in N. de Marchi and M. Blaug (eds), *Appraising Economic Theories*, Aldershot: Edward Elgar.
Nerlove, Marc (1990), 'Trygve Haavelmo: A critical appreciation', *Scandinavian Journal of Economics*, **92**, 17–24.
Qin, Duo (1993), *The Formation of Econometrics*, Oxford: Clarendon Press.
Spanos, Aris (1989), 'On rereading Haavelmo: A retrospective view of econometric modelling', *Econometric Theory*, **5**, 405–29.

Hayek, Friedrich A.

Friedrich August Hayek was born in Vienna on 8 May 1899 and died in Freiburg, Germany on 23 March 1992. Educated at the University of Vienna, Hayek studied psychology as well as economics, and in 1920 wrote a paper on theoretical psychology that formed the basis for the book, *The Sensory Order* (1952b). His major professor in economics was Friedrich von Wieser. Wieser and Eugen Böhm von Bawerk were the most famous of the 'second generation' members of the Austrian School of Economics founded by Carl Menger. Hayek's contemporaries among the students included Oskar Morgenstern, Gottfried Haberler and Fritz Machlup. His ultimate degrees were in law (1921) and political science (1923).

After receiving his first degree, Hayek worked at a temporary government agency set up to clear war debts. Ludwig von Mises, already famous for work on monetary theory and soon to publish a critical work on socialism, was one of the directors and soon became Hayek's mentor. On graduating, Hayek left for a 15-month visit to the United States. Armed with letters of introduction from Joseph Schumpeter, he met most of the major American economists. As a research assistant at New York University he also studied the Federal Reserve System and picked up some statistical techniques that would later qualify him for a job as director of a business cycle institute. Upon returning to Austria, Hayek worked principally in monetary theory and prepared for university teaching, passing his *Habilitation* in 1929. During these years he was a regular participant in Mises' famous *Privatseminar*.

Methodology in the early writings
Methodological themes appear occasionally in Hayek's writings in the 1920s and early 1930s. During his visit to the United States, he was surprised and dismayed to find that institutionalism was all the rage. While praising the institutionalists for amassing the data that any adequate business cycle theory must explain, he was critical of the notion that data could be used either to construct or to test a theory (1984: 5–6).

The fullest statement of Hayek's early methodological beliefs can be found in the opening chapter of his *Monetary Theory and the Trade Cycle* (1966). Hayek's first claim is that the use of theory is the distinguishing characteristic of all scientific investigation. Empirical studies provide the data to be explained, and may be useful for pragmatic purposes such as forecasting, but theory always takes precedence over empirical work. The specific theory used within economics he dubbed 'equilibrium theory'. Hayek apparently meant by this supply and demand analysis, and praised the Walrasian formulation of it (ibid.: 42). Science, then, employs theory and any adequate economic theory of the trade cycle must both explain the facts and be consistent with supply and demand analysis.

A central feature of equilibrium theory is that markets clear. During the trade cycle something prevents the market-clearing mechanism from working, so discovering what that 'something' might be was viewed by Hayek as the major task of trade cycle theory. His answer was *money*:

> Money being a commodity which, unlike all others, is incapable of finally satisfying demand, its introduction does away with the rigid interdependence and self-sufficiency of the 'closed' system of equilibrium, and makes possible movements which would have been excluded from the latter. (Ibid.: 44)

Having argued for a monetary theory of the *origins* of the cycle, Hayek's final move was to claim that, in order to trace the *effects* of a monetary disturbance, one had to be able to show its impact on relative prices within the system. Other monetary theories of the cycle focused on the impact of changes in the money supply on other aggregates (for example, the price level), so were unable to do this. Fortunately, Hayek's own theory of the cycle, which included a capital goods sector as well as a consumption goods sector, was available to remedy the deficiency. Methodological arguments (such as that theories must be used in science; new theories in economics must be consistent with 'equilibrium theory') clearly play a role in Hayek's defence of the Austrian theory of the cycle, but what comes out most strongly is his theoretical argument that any adequate model of the cycle must include capital-theoretic foundations and that the absence of such foundations in other accounts had led to both theoretical misunderstanding and policy error.

Lionel Robbins, newly appointed head of the Economics Department at the London School of Economics, invited Hayek to London in the spring of 1931 to deliver a series of lectures on his theory of the cycle. Published later that year as *Prices and Production*, the lectures ultimately resulted in Hayek's appointment in 1932 to the Tooke Chair of Economic Science and Statistics at the LSE. He held this position until his departure for the University of Chicago in 1950.

Soon after arriving in London, Hayek became embroiled in a dispute with John Maynard Keynes and some of his disciples at Cambridge. Hayek published a two-part review of Keynes' 1930 book, *A Treatise on Money*, scoring Keynes' model for lacking an adequate theory of capital. In a notorious reply, Keynes spent most of his energies not in defending his own theory but in attacking the model found in *Prices and Production*. This was quickly followed by an equally critical review of Hayek's book by Piero Sraffa. The battle helped spur both of the major protagonists to rethink their theories. Keynes' next book was *The General Theory of Employment, Interest and Money*, published in 1936, while Hayek's was *The Pure Theory of Capital* (1941a); the latter turned out to be his last major theoretical work in economics. A still unresolved mystery is why Hayek chose not to review *The General Theory*. Though he offered a number of explanations over the years for this sin of omission (see, for example, the editor's introduction and final three chapters in Caldwell, 1995), none seems completely satisfying.

Hayek's transformation
In 1964 Hayek wrote:

> Though at one time a very pure and narrow economic theorist, I was led from technical economics into all kinds of questions usually regarded as philosophical. When I look back, it seems to have all begun, nearly thirty years ago, with an essay on 'Economics and Knowledge'. (1964a: 91)

The essay mentioned was Hayek's 1936 Presidential Address delivered before the London Economics Club, published as 'Economics and Knowledge' in *Economica* in 1937. That the article marked the beginning of a change in the direction of Hayek's thought is today widely accepted. There has been some debate, however, over the exact nature of the transformation (for example, Hutchison, 1981; 1992; Caldwell, 1988; 1992a; 1992b.)

In the paper, Hayek examined the concept of equilibrium. He argued that the notion when applied to an individual is unproblematical: individual agents are *always* in equilibrium, given their own subjective perceptions and beliefs (which may of course be wrong) concerning external reality, and including beliefs about the actions of others. Societal equilibrium is a different matter. For society to be in equilibrium, the individual subjective beliefs of agents about the world and the actions of others must be in some sense *correct*. What is required of agents is that they have correct foresight. As Hayek put it: 'Correct foresight is then not, as it has sometimes been understood, a precondition which must exist in order that equilibrium may be arrived at. It is rather the defining characteristic of a state of equilibrium' (Hayek, 1937: 42). This is obviously a very strong condition. In Hayek's opinion, economic theory should be able to show how such a state of equilibrium might be brought about. Unfortunately, the whole question is avoided within standard analysis because it is assumed that all agents have the same *objectively correct* perceptions. Equilibrium theory assumes that coordination has already been achieved, whereas for Hayek 'the question why the data in the subjective sense of the word should ever come to correspond to the objective data is one of the main problems we have to answer' (ibid.: 39).

In my opinion, Hayek's transformation consisted of his ultimate rejection of standard economic analysis (that is, the 'equilibrium theory' that he once praised so highly) as a tool for shedding light on the central question of how agents' plans are coordinated. Hayek recommended that a 'market process' view be put in its place, a view that gives a prominent role to freely adjusting market prices in bringing about whatever coordination we might find existing in the world. Exploring this issue led Hayek away from economic theory proper and towards an examination of institutions, in search of the institutional framework that might best promote the coordination of plans. A market order in a democratic state with strong constitutional safeguards against majoritarian or special interest redistributive legislation was the ideal that he eventually came to endorse in such works as *The Constitution of Liberty* (1960) and *Law, Legislation and Liberty* (1973–9).

Terence Hutchison argues, alternatively, that 'Economics and Knowledge' marks Hayek's break with the apriorism of his mentor Ludwig von Mises, and the beginning of Hayek's adherence to the methodological precepts of Karl Popper. Without going into the details of the disagreement between Hutchison and Caldwell, it can certainly be acknowledged that Hayek's argument that one cannot move easily from equilibrium of the individual to societal equilibrium can be viewed as a challenge to some of Mises' writings. Hayek himself saw the article as signalling a demurral from Mises' views. Our major disagreements concern whether Hayek *ever* endorsed Mises' apriorism, and both the timing and extent of his endorsement of Popperian ideas.

The scientism essay
During the war years, Hayek increasingly focused on questions of methodology. First came 'The Counter-Revolution of Science' (1941b), an historical piece in which the evolution and intermingling of socialist and positivist doctrines, particularly in their French variants, were examined. In his next essay, 'Scientism and the Study of Society' Hayek defined 'Scientism' as 'the slavish imitation of the method and language of Science … an attitude which is decidedly unscientific in the true sense of the word, since it involves the mechanical and uncritical application of habits of thought to fields different from those in which they have been formed' (1942–4: 24). The paper contains both a critique of scientistic ideas and his own prescriptions regarding the proper methods for the social sciences.

For Hayek, scientism was revealed in such pernicious doctrines as objectivism (the view that true sciences only make reference to observable, objective reality: behaviourism in psychology is a prime example), collectivism (the tendency to treat aggregate concepts, like 'society' or 'the economy', as actual objects of study) and historicism (the attempt to find historical laws that govern the evolution of the collective entities). Such doctrines are ill-suited for shedding light on the actual subject matter of the social sciences, which Hayek then describes.

Hayek's first premise is that the structure of all human minds is the same. We all have what he calls 'opinions' – perceptions and beliefs – on the basis of which we act. Since these 'opinions' are the foundations for our actions, they are properly the starting point, they constitute the 'data' or 'facts', of the social sciences. What can be said about them? First, the opinions of agents are *subjective*, and hence not observable. Next, their existence is *independent* of the beliefs of the social scientist. Third, agents *differ* in what they believe and what they know. Fourth, some of the opinions held by agents are *true*, and some are *false*. Finally, whether true or false, these opinions are the *basis for actions*.

Given this description of reality, what is the proper method of the social sciences? In the 'Scientism' essay, Hayek insists that the proper starting point is the opinions of individual agents. From there, the social scientist 'builds up' to the level of more complex social phenomena. Hayek dubs this the 'compositive method', a term used by Carl Menger to describe his own approach. Of great interest are those social phenomena which are the result of human action but not of human design, the so-called 'unintended consequences' of human action, and particularly spontaneous social orders. The task is to show how individual human action leads to such aggregate phenomena.

The task is not an easy one. Because the complexity of the subject matter of the social sciences limits our ability to understand them, the social scientist is hardly ever in a position 'to predict the precise outcome of a particular situation; and he could never confirm them by controlled experiment – although they might be disproved by the observation of events which according to his theory are impossible' (ibid: 73). Often the best that one can do is to 'explain the principle on which certain phenomena are produced' (ibid: 74).

Given the discussion above, it should be clear how Hayek reached the conclusion that neither objectivism (since 'opinions' are subjective and non-observable) nor collectivism (since he was committed to methodological individualism) is appropriate within the social sciences. But what of historicism: could one not trace the evolution of various complex social phenomena through time? Again, the importance of methodological individualism within the 'causal-genetic' approach of the Austrians comes to the fore. Following Menger, Hayek insisted that one should seek the genesis of institutions in the self-seeking behaviour of individual agents. Menger's *Principles of Economics* (1976) still provides what are perhaps the best examples of the application of this doctrine. The emergence of markets, of market prices, of competition and of money are all shown to occur naturally as a result of the self-seeking behaviour of individuals in a world of scarcity. Because they lacked these methodologically individualist 'microfoundations', the explanations of historicists were viewed by the Austrians as theoretically ungrounded.[1]

The Sensory Order and later essays
Hayek's 'Scientism' essay contains all the essential elements of his methodological programme; what came later principally filled in the gaps. The most important of the later works is Hayek's exploration of the foundations of theoretical psychology, *The Sensory Order*. Here Hayek describes how the neural connections of the human brain establish an 'order' which governs how an individual perceives the world. Though this may sound Kantian, it is not, for Hayek also asserts that the neural connections are themselves changeable and affected by past perceptions. It made sense for Hayek to resuscitate his work on psychology when he did: *The Sensory Order* was his way of fleshing out the notions, first enunciated in the 'Scientism' essay, that the structure of the human mind is the same, but the perceptions and beliefs that agents hold differ.

Further elaborations are contained in Hayek's essays 'Degrees of Explanation' (1955), 'The Theory of Complex Phenomena' (1964b) and 'The Pretence of Knowledge' (1975), the last his Nobel lecture. The major themes of these articles are that (a) economics qualifies as a science, but (b) it is a science that studies complex phenomena, and (c) as such, it faces limitations, particularly in its ability to yield testable predictions. It is in these later articles that Hayek's enthusiasm for Karl Popper's philosophical views is most evident. Indeed, the 1967 collection, *Studies in Philosophy, Politics and Economics* was dedicated to Popper, just as Popper's own *Conjectures and Refutations* (1965) had been dedicated to Hayek. Hayek thanks Popper for providing a criterion for demarcating science from non-science, and also for showing him that even the natural sciences never really followed the objectionable methods of scientism, that in fact the differences between the natural and social sciences are only differences of degree.

But there is also a tension in this later work. For example, though he praises Popper's emphasis on falsifiability, Hayek also writes:

> The advance of science will thus have to proceed in two different directions: while it is certainly desirable to make our theories as falsifiable as possible, we must also push forward into fields where, as we advance, the degree of falsifiability necessarily decreases. This is the price we have to pay for an advance into the field of complex phenomena. (Hayek, 1964b: 29)

In his Nobel address he raises the concerns again:

> We cannot be grateful enough to such modern philosophers as Sir Karl Popper for giving us a test by which we can distinguish between what we may accept as scientific and what not – a test which I am

sure that some doctrines now widely accepted as scientific would not pass. There are some special problems, however, in connection with those essentially complex phenomena of which social structures are so important an instance, which makes me wish to restate in conclusion in more general terms the reasons why in these fields not only are there absolute obstacles to the prediction of specific events, but why to act as if we possessed scientific knowledge enabling us to transcend them may itself become a serious obstacle to the advance of the human intellect. (Hayek, 1975: 31–2)

The tension between the ideas of Hayek and Popper is a real one. It is not, however, altogether surprising. Though Hayek never accepted Ludwig von Mises' variant of apriorism, he did fully endorse his mentor's subjectivism, a position that would not sit well with Popper. And though Hayek was quite happy to accept Popper's apparent demonstration that economics 'qualified' as a legitimate science, he always retained the standard Austrian suspicion, evident in his earliest writings, about the uses of empirical work.

Those eager to discover 'what Hayek really thought' about methodology would be wise to bear in mind that two of his lifelong friends were Ludwig von Mises and Karl Popper, men whose views on methodology could not be more opposed. Hayek never publicly disagreed with either of them.

BRUCE CALDWELL

Note

1. Methodological individualism is clearly present in Hayek's early work, particularly in the 'Scientism' essay, but by the 1950s and 1960s he begins modifying his emphasis. For example, 'individuals' are still important, but, depending on the problem, the 'individuals' need not be human agents. The extent to which Hayek may have moved away from methodological individualism, and whether such a move creates tension in his work, are still matters of debate in the secondary literature.

References

Caldwell, Bruce (1988), 'Hayek's Transformation', *History of Political Economy*, **20**, 513–41.
Caldwell, Bruce (1992a), 'Hayek the Falsificationist? A Refutation', *Research in the History of Economic Thought and Methodology*, **10**, 1–15.
Caldwell, Bruce (1992b), 'Reply to Hutchison', *Research in the History of Economic Thought and Methodology*, **10**, 33–42.
Caldwell, Bruce (ed.) (1995), *Contra Keynes and Cambridge: Essays and Correspondence*, Vol. 9 of *The Collected Writings of F.A. Hayek*, Chicago: University of Chicago Press/London: Routledge.
Hayek, Friedrich A. (1931), *Prices and Production*, London: Routledge.
Hayek, Friedrich A. (1937), 'Economics and Knowledge'; reprinted in F.A. Hayek (1948), *Individualism and Economic Order*, Chicago: University of Chicago Press.
Hayek, Friedrich A. (1941a), *The Pure Theory of Capital*, Chicago: University of Chicago Press.
Hayek, Friedrich A. (1941b), 'The Counter-Revolution of Science'; reprinted in F.A. Hayek (1952a).
Hayek, Friedrich A. (1942–4), 'Scientism and the Study of Society'; reprinted in F.A. Hayek (1952a).
Hayek, Friedrich A. (1952a), *The Counter-Revolution of Science: Studies on the Abuse of Reason*, Glencoe, IL: Free Press.
Hayek, Friedrich A. (1952b), *The Sensory Order: An Inquiry into the Foundations of Theoretical Psychology*, Chicago: University of Chicago Press.
Hayek, Friedrich A. (1955), 'Degrees of Explanation'; reprinted in F.A. Hayek (1967).
Hayek, Friedrich A. (1960), *The Constitution of Liberty*, Chicago: University of Chicago Press.
Hayek, Friedrich A. (1964a), 'Kinds of Rationalism'; reprinted in F.A. Hayek (1967).
Hayek, Friedrich A. (1964b), 'The Theory of Complex Phenomena'; reprinted in F.A. Hayek (1967).
Hayek, Friedrich A. (1966), *Monetary Theory and the Trade Cycle*, trans N. Kaldor and H.M. Croome, New York: A.M. Kelley.
Hayek, Friedrich A. (1967), *Studies in Philosophy, Politics and Economics*, Chicago: University of Chicago Press.
Hayek, Friedrich A. (1973–9), *Law, Legislation and Liberty*, Chicago: University of Chicago Press.
Hayek, Friedrich A. (1975), 'The Pretence of Knowledge'; reprinted in F.A. Hayek (1978), *New Studies in Philosophy, Politics. Economics and the History of Ideas*, Chicago: University of Chicago Press.
Hayek, Friedrich A. (1984), *Money, Capital and Fluctuations: Early Essays*, ed. R. McCloughry, Chicago: University of Chicago Press.

Hutchison, T.W. (1981), *The Politics and Philosophy of Economics: Marxians, Keynesians and Austrians*, New York: New York University Press.

Hutchison, T.W. (1992), 'Hayek and "Modern Austrian" Methodology: Comment on a Non-Refuting Refutation,' *Research in the History of Economic Thought and Methodology*, **10**, 17–32.

Keynes, John Maynard (1971) *A Treatise on Money*, reprinted as volumes 5 and 6 in *The Collected Writings of John Maynard Keynes*, London: Macmillan.

Keynes, John Maynard (1973), *The General Theory of Employment, Interest and Money*, reprinted as volume 7 in *The Collected Writings of John Maynard Keynes*, London: Macmillan.

Menger, Carl (1976), *Principles of Economics*, trans. J. Dingwall and B. Hoselitz, New York: New York University Press.

Popper, Karl (1965), *Conjectures and Refutations: The Growth of Scientific Knowledge*, 2nd edn, New York: Harper.

Hicks, John R.

John Richard Hicks was born in Warwick, England on 8 April 1904. A pupil at Clifton College from 1917 to 1922, he was admitted to Balliol College, Oxford, as a student of mathematics. In 1923, he switched to the newly instituted PPE (Philosophy, Politics and Economics). In 1925, he took his MLitt submitting a thesis on 'Wages differentials in mechanical and building sectors'. In 1926, he moved to the London School of Economics (LSE), first as a visiting scholar, at the invitation of Lionel Robbins, and immediately thereafter and until 1935 as a teacher.

At LSE, Hicks learned his 'job' as an economist. According to his own recollections, 'In those nine years I went from an initial condition of appalling ignorance, to the first theoretical realizations.' Here began his brilliant academic career, a career that brought him a fellowship at Gonville and Caius College, Cambridge, from 1935 to 1938 (the interviewers for this position were Pigou and Keynes); from 1938 to 1945 he held the Jevons Chair of Political Economy in Manchester; from 1945 to 1952 he was co-founder and fellow of Nuffield College at Oxford; finally, he occupied the Drummond Chair of Political Economy at All Souls College, Oxford. In 1965, he left Oxford before the expiry of his term to concentrate on his research work. Over half of his whole scientific production originated in the time following his retirement. In 1964, he was knighted for his scientific prowess, the following year he was appointed emeritus fellow of All Souls College; finally, in 1972, he shared with Kenneth Arrow the Nobel Prize for Economics. He was the first British economist to be awarded this honour and was to donate the whole of the prize money to the LSE library. His last book, A *Market Theory of Money*, appeared posthumously in August 1989 – he died in May of the same year - and his last essay, 'The Unification of Macro-economics' was read, *in absentia*, on July 1989 in Siena at a seminar to which he had been invited. This shows better than anything else Hicks' devotion to scientific work, his reluctance in the face of any frivolity and the serene consciousness of his intellectual and spiritual adventure.

A fundamental feature of Hicks' way of doing economic research, a feature which most clearly reveals his style of thinking and his independence, is his refusal of any form of methodological dogmatism. This refusal is accompanied by the pressing advice to revise traditional opinion regarding the neutrality of method with respect to the cognitive targets of the theoretical system to which the method has to be applied. Especially in his later contributions, those after the publication of *Economic Perspectives* (1977), and more particularly in the essays 'A discipline, not a science' (1983) and 'Is economics a science?' (1983), Hicks skilfully demonstrates that the two essential features of scientific knowledge (the progressive correction of errors and the adoption within a single theoretical system of the notions acquired) cannot be achieved by applying externally to research a general methodology. Rather, these features result from a method that each science develops by itself, in relation to its own object. The method has to be reinvented each time by the researcher and is the most typical product of his or her ingeniousness. This confutes the neopositivist principle that the sense and truth of a proposition depend on the method of its verification. Just as new disciplines are born without having to wait for someone to formulate their method, it is the task of economists to set their own rules for a sound methodological behaviour.

Hicks' reader is struck by the extraordinary range and variety of subjects and even the structure of arguments treated in his writings. Yet at the same time all his writings share a distinctive aspect, which is the tendency always to search for a new perspective or to discover some neglected aspect of a phenomenon. According to Hicks, theories are not discovered in the way that an explorer discovers a new land. They are inventions of the human mind, whence the importance of intuition, of the 'view' in theoretical inquiry. To Hicks, the 'view' is not merely an expository service, it is of fundamental use, if the task is to construct a new edifice, not just to refurbish an old one.

The essence of the Hicksian vision is the belief that pluralism and variety are fundamental aspects of scientific development within which no unitary plan or scheme can be discovered. There are certain continuities, even uniform sequences of ideas – the schools of thought – but none of these continuities remains unchanged and what marks the end of a 'continuous' story is so totally different from what marked its beginning as to make the latter not easily recognizable. Hence Hicks' typically tolerant attitude towards the most diverse theoretical positions and his convinced acceptance of both theoretical and methodological pluralism. It is remarkable in this respect that Hicks never permitted himself to be involved in disputes or controversies between diverging schools: 'I am too open to be an Austrian, for I am an open Marshallian, and Ricardian, and Keynesian, perhaps even Lausannian, as well' (Hicks, 1983: 128).

Hicks reacted to the crisis of normative methodologies in economics (both the rationalist and the empiricist ones) with a research programme open to variety, well aware of the fact that results of great relevance are continually obtained even if one starts from differing methodological positions not compatible among themselves. A remarkable test of such a disposition is represented by Hicks' 'conversion' around the middle of the 1960s, a conversion that induced the great neoclassical economist to judge as 'a piece of rubbish' the theses on the functional distribution of income which he had himself formulated in 1932 in the *Theory of Wages*. That same conversion led him to reconsider the general theoretical significance of methodological individualism and the hypothesis of individual maximizing behaviour, besides inducing him to reject the interpretation of Keynes based on his 1937 IS–LM model.

Especially in 'Some questions of time in economics' (1976) and in *Causality in Economics* (1979), Hicks confutes the neopositivist principle that the sense and truth of a proposition depend on the method of its verification. He also confutes the statement that science has nothing to do with truth for the reason that what science produces is only propositions which are exact, that is, 'obtained from' (*ex-actu*) premises derived hypothetically. The empirical confirmation of the hypothesis would only mean that the operational validity of that hypothesis has been proved. But this is insufficient, according to Hicks, for discovering the actual nature of the object studied with that hypothesis.

The fundamental question Hicks poses in *Capital and Time* (1973), a book specifically written to elaborate the intuition anticipated in *A Theory of Economic History* (1969), and in *Methods of Dynamic Economics* (1985) is the following: which model should be used to describe the functioning of an economic system, a system that, in order to function properly, absorbs and eliminates disturbances, or rather, an open system, out-of-equilibrium, exposed to a continuous flow of disturbances but capable of living off them? In other words, are external and internal shocks to be considered mere inconveniences to be minimized and restrained, or are they to be seen as elements that serve to foster the development of the system? This is essentially the problem of the 'traverse' of a heterogeneous capital stock from one growth equilibrium to another, a problem which defeated the late Hicks but which reveals his attitude towards theoretical inquiry: the openness to all that has not yet been seen.

In his *Collected Essays*, Hicks says: 'Anyone who has been through these three volumes of essays ... can be forgiven for thinking that the position to which I have come is distinctly sceptical. I would not altogether deny that this is so, though *critical* is the adjective I would myself prefer' (Hicks, 1983: 365). Indeed, scepticism is an inappropriate word: in any case we are faced by a constructive, not nihilistic, scepticism. To admit a plurality of levels within the scientific adventure implies the acknowledgement that the sphere of 'economic science' is larger than a certain methodology of positivist origin had led us to believe. This does not entail that the abandonment of old dreams should coincide with the desire for regress or with the adoption of nihilistic diagnoses.

In an almost unknown paper, written two years after the publication of his *Value and Capital*, Hicks writes:

> In the field of economics, over-specialisation is doubly disastrous. A man who is a mathematician may live a stunted life, but he does not do any harm. An economist who is nothing but an economist is a danger to his neighbours. Economics is not a thing in itself; it is a study of one aspect of the life of man in society. ... The economist of tomorrow (sometimes of today) will also know what to advise, on economic grounds; but if, through increasing specialisation, his economics is divorced from any background of social philosophy, he will be in real danger of becoming a dodgemerchant, full of ingenious devices for getting out of particular difficulties, but losing contact with the plain root-virtues, even the plain economic virtues, on which a healthy society must be based. Modern economics is subject to a real danger of Machiavellism – the treatment of social problems as matters of technique, not as facets of the general search for the Good Life. (Hicks, 1941: 6)

It is this very lesson on method which makes Hicks' work so influential with so many authors of different schools and methodological stances.

STEFANO ZAMAGNI

Bibliography
Hamouda, O.F.(1993), *John R. Hicks – The Economist's Economist*, Oxford: Basil Blackwell.
Hicks, J.R. (1941), 'Education in Economics', *Manchester Statistical Society*, April, 1–20.
Hicks, J.R. (1969), *A Theory of Economic History*, Oxford: Oxford University Press.
Hicks, J.R. (1973), *Capital and Time*, Oxford: Oxford University Press.
Hicks, J.R. (1976), 'Some questions of time in economics', in A.M. Tang, F.M. Westfield and J.S. Worley (eds), *Evolution, Welfare and Time in Economics*, New York: D.C. Heath.
Hicks, J.R. (1977), *Economic Perspectives*, Oxford: Oxford University Press.
Hicks, J.R. (1979), *Causality in Economics*, Oxford: Basil Blackwell.
Hicks, J.R. (1983), *Collected Essays on Economic Theory*, vol. III, Oxford: Basil Blackwell.
Hicks, J.R. (1985), *Methods of Dynamic Economics*, Oxford: Oxford University Press.
Hicks, J.R. (1989), *A Market Theory of Money*, Oxford: Oxford University Press.

McKenzie, L.W. and S. Zamagni (eds) (1991), *Value and Capital Fifty Years Later*, London: Macmillan.
Zamagni, S. (1997), 'John Richard Hicks and his School', in *Commentaries to J.R. Hicks' Value and Capital*, Klassiker der National-Ökonomie, Düsseldorf: Verlag Wirtschaft und Finanzen.

Holism

Holism is any of a set of views according to which the parts forming a whole cannot be adequately understood or described individually but only by considering their relation to the whole. Although one can be an adherent of holism on one set of issues – such as how society is constituted, how knowledge is justified or how meaning is determined – and not another, it is nevertheless true that holism brings with it a cast of mind that tends to exert its influence across issues. In general, holism has been more popular in continental and especially German philosophy, while Anglo-American thought, with some exceptions, has tended to be hostile to it: the uncompromising individualism of British liberal thought and classical as well as neoclassical economics are good examples. Nevertheless, holism has become considerably more respectable in analytic philosophy in the past two decades. While there are many different holisms, there are three that seem to be most significant in the philosophical literature relating to economic methodology: methodological holism (as opposed to methodological individualism), coherentism (as opposed to foundationalism) and semantic holism (as opposed to semantic atomism). Each of these will be discussed briefly in what follows.

The distinction between *methodological individualism* and *methodological holism* constitutes a principal dividing line between approaches to the study of society, with the extreme individualism of neoclassical economics serving as an example of the former and the sociological views of society of Durkhein and Marx as examples of the latter. According to the methodological individualist, the proper way to study social phenomena is to study the beliefs, preferences, and choices of individuals, and any social phenomenon, no matter how apparently far removed it is from the intentions of individuals, is still reducible to them. (The term 'methodological' is inherited from the logical positivists' distinction between methodological individualism and what they called metaphysical holism, providing a good illustration of how a writer's attitude about holism tends to remain constant across problem areas: logical positivists tended to be anti-holists in all respects.) The holist holds, in contrast, that some macro-level social phenomena are not reducible even in principle to the individual level. This may be because they fulfil 'latent functions' which by their very nature must remain unknown to individuals (thus one may hold that, in addition to advertising a product, an advertisement is reinforcing a consumptive attitude in general) or simply because the phenomenon in question is so complex and has such a long history that it is out of individuals' control purely as a practical matter: thus, social contract theory notwithstanding, it is hard to see by means of what set of voting rules a society could define from scratch, and go on to adopt, a language in which it will henceforth communicate. One can thus see that the methodological question of how best to study society relates to the substantive question of to what degree society actually is the product of individual choice and indeed of whether social pressures and constraints are so strong that the commonsense picture of the rational actor free to make his choices is undermined altogether, with the actor's choices being explained, not by his intentions, but by high-level social processes unknown to him.

Recently, Philip Pettit has argued that the debate between holism and individualism actually amounts to two debates, about the horizontal issue of the relationship between an individual and other individuals in a society (atomism v. holism) and the vertical issue of the relationship between individuals and society (individualism v. collectivism). The former is concerned with the extent to which human beings depend upon their social relationships for the possession of their ability to think or for some other fundamental human capacity. The latter is concerned with whether the existence of aggregate social entities, such as the obtaining of aggregate-level regularities, means that human beings do not conform to the common-sense view of them as autonomous, rational creatures. It is possible to be a holist while also being an individualist: that is, one can, against liberal individualism, accept that embeddedness in a community is constitutive of being human and rational, and at the same time hold that the existence of the kind of high-level regularities uncovered by social scientists does not undermine human beings' fundamental freedom.

With respect to the problem of the justification of knowledge, holism takes the form of *coherentism* and is opposed to *foundationalism*. There are two main questions that need to be answered by any theory of justification. First, are all our beliefs equivalent in terms of how they are justified, or are some beliefs 'more basic' than others, so that our non-basic beliefs are justified by being inferrable from our basic beliefs, but our basic beliefs do not depend on our other beliefs? Second, what grounds have we for holding our beliefs to be true? According to foundationalism, we do have a class of beliefs that serve as a bedrock for our other beliefs. The reason we have for holding these beliefs to be true usually takes the form of *empiricism*: we can be confident in our basic beliefs because they in some way directly correspond to experience. (The reason we hold our non-basic beliefs to be true is presumably that we validly infer them from our basic beliefs.) In the context of the justification of *scientific* knowledge, this set of doctrines comes down to the idea that theories are verified by a discrete set of experiments which test them: the experiments, being direct tests of empirical reality, serve as the bedrock upon which theory rests. The most famous assault upon this view is the Duhem–Quine thesis, according to which theories cannot be tested independently of each other, but only together with science taken as a whole. The reason advanced for this position is that, in practice, to test any given theory one must combine it with other theories in order to get a definite prediction; if this prediction is falsified, one can never be sure that is because the theory one wants to test, rather than one of the 'auxiliary' theories, is false.

The task faced by coherentism is to explicate in what way 'knowledge is confirmed as a corporate body', to use Quine's phrase. Several problems are involved. First, since beliefs support each other, a view must be developed according to which this support does not amount to a species of circular reasoning, but does involve sources of knowledge which are in some sense independent of each other. Second, one must provide an account of inference which will inevitably be more complicated than one sufficient for foundationalism. According to the latter, all that is required for a non-basic belief to be acceptable is that it deductively follow from basic beliefs. But how is one to decide between two propositions, both of which seem more or less supported by empirical observations, on the basis of how well they 'cohere' with the rest of knowledge? Various solutions have been proposed, prominent among which, in the case of scientific theories, is the ability of a theory to unify fields of knowledge previously considered to be unrelated. Third, one must avoid falling into the trap of concluding from the idea that beliefs support each other, that there is nothing 'outside' our beliefs which serves as a 'source' of knowledge (as is held for instance by Donald Davidson). In other words, despite one's having abandoned the position that empirical beliefs are basic, one must nevertheless find a way of incorporating an empirical input coming from 'outside' into one's web of belief.

According to the theory of meaning directly opposed to holism, *semantic atomism*, the meaning of a representation is given solely by that representation, independently of all others. Thus the logical positivists, for example, held that the meaning of a sentence is given by its conditions of verification. According to *semantic holism*, in contrast, the meaning of a representation can be understood only in the context of the whole of the language of which it forms a part. If taken at face value, semantic holism, of which present-day adherents include Donald Davidson, W.V. Quine and John Searle, has some unpalatable consequences. For example, as Thomas Kuhn has argued in a historical rather than philosophical context, since the physics of Newton and that of Einstein comprise distinct, closed systems, when one speaks of mass or momentum in one theory, one is referring to something completely different from what one refers to when using the other theory – since these terms are embedded in different theories, and since (following Frege) meaning determines reference. This consequence, according to which competing scientific theories are *incommensurable*, goes against the intuition that there is a continuity between the concepts of Newtonian and relativistic mass and momentum, so that the theories can be compared on some rational basis transcending the two theories. (This consequence also makes it unclear in what way two theories can even be said to compete: if classical and modern physics are about two completely unrelated sets of phenomena, why can the two not simply stand side by side?)

There are several responses to this problem. One is to stand by semantic atomism. This position now tends to be favoured mainly by philosophers of mind such as Jerry Fodor, intent on maintaining the analogy between the human mind and the computer, according to which thought is produced by nothing more than the syntax of a language. (Since syntax is essentially what is left of a language once meaning has been abstracted from it, the only candidate for the 'carrier' of meaning remaining is the individual words themselves.) This has problems of its own, since if one wants to explain how meaning actually *works*, one is forced to maintain that we are able to entertain concepts such as 'neutrino' or 'microprocessor' through the lucky circumstance that we acquired the ability to represent specifically those kinds of objects at some time in our evolutionary history. Another response is to adopt the intermediate position of *semantic molecularism*, according to which the meaning of a term is determined, not by the whole language, but only by other terms directly related to that term. A third is to abandon the notion of meaning altogether and adopt *semantic nihilism*: words have no meanings. In philosophy, this position is embraced by philosophers such as Daniel Dennett and Paul and Patricia Churchland, convinced that cognitive science is poised for a revolution in how we understand the mind (or to realize that there is no such thing); more generally, it is associated with deconstructionism and poststructuralism. A fourth response is to make use of the distinction between meaning and reference by allowing that corresponding terms in two different theories have different meanings, but providing an account by means of the 'true' theory of how the 'false' theory, despite being false, nevertheless is able to refer successfully to real entities.

In the heyday of logical positivism, the term 'holism' carried with it associations of eerie *Weltgeist* and the charming, if not very productive, idea that everything is connected to everything else; however as the difficulties of the verification theory of meaning and other positivist orthodoxies became increasingly apparent, holist doctrines gradually came to gain acceptance by some and toleration by others as a kind of necessary evil. More recently, however, there have appeared attempts to avoid the extremes of both atomism and holism by developing positions incorporating ideas from both. Thus, while it is recognized that a satisfactory account of mind cannot be delivered without considering the interpersonal dimension, it is argued that individual autonomy is still a perfectly tenable concept. Similarly, while scientific frameworks that serve as what Kuhn called paradigms appear to be justified and compared with each other in a holistic manner, the day-to-day testing of hypotheses and models with restricted implications characteristic of 'normal science' can still be held to be carried out essentially in the straightforward manner described in college textbooks. And while to understand a given word, it is necessary to understand a number of related words, all of which mutually determine each others' meanings, it is nevertheless true that once the overall 'interpretative framework' is in place, words often can be defined in an atomistic manner, as 'tiger' for example can be defined simply by pointing at a tiger.

ALEX VISKOVATOFF

Bibliography

Haack, Susan (1993), *Evidence and Inquiry: Towards reconstruction in epistemology*, Oxford: Blackwell.
Mandelbaum, Maurice (1957), 'Societal laws', *British Journal for the Philosophy of Science*, **8**, 211–24.
Pettit, Philip (1993), *The Common Mind: An essay on psychology, society, and politics*, New York: Oxford University Press.
Putnam, Hilary (1978), *Meaning and the Moral Sciences*, London: Routledge & Kegan Paul.
Quine, W.V. (1953), 'Two dogmas of empiricism', *From a Logical Point of View*, 2nd edn, Cambridge, MA: Harvard University Press.
Searle, John R. (1983), *Intentionality: An essay in the philosophy of mind*, Cambridge: Cambridge University Press.

Hutchison, Terence W.

Terence Wilmot Hutchison was born in 1912 in Bournemouth, Hampshire. He studied economics at Cambridge, achieving a 'first' in 1934. Joan Robinson was an undergraduate tutor and an apparent early influence. Hutchison went to Germany in 1935 and lectured for a time at the University of Bonn. He received his MA from Cambridge in 1937. In later years his principal academic affiliation was with the University of Birmingham, where he was Mitsui Professor of Economics from 1956 to 1978 (Blaug and Sturges, 1983: 180; Coats, 1983a; 1983b).

Though he published a note on methodology soon after finishing his undergraduate degree (Hutchison, 1935), his first substantial contribution was *The Significance and Basic Postulates of Economic Theory* (1938). The book may be read as a sustained response, well informed by the philosophy of science of his day, to Lionel Robbins' *An Essay on the Nature and Significance of Economic Science* (1932), which defined economics as the science that studies the allocation of scarce means among multiple competing ends. Robbins argued that the fundamental generalizations of economics are all self-evident propositions about reality. These are combined with simplifying assumptions (such as, the rationality postulate) as well as with subsidiary empirical hypotheses to yield the deductions of economic theory. Empirical studies cannot produce economic laws. Rather, their functions are to suggest plausible subsidiary hypotheses and to serve as checks on the applicability of a given theory.

Robbins' essay was widely viewed as an apology for deductive theory at a time when the ability of standard theory to make sense of the world was under question, and as a defence of the non-interventionist strictures of the Austrian School at a time when interventionist sympathies were escalating. The book elicited criticisms from many quarters (for example,

Cannan, 1932; Fraser, 1932; Souter, 1933), but Hutchison's was the most methodologically sophisticated.

Hutchison's arguments may be summarized as follows.

1. The 'propositions of pure theory' consist of relations that are defined within some formal system, but are themselves independent of all facts.
2. To gain empirical content, 'these propositions must *conceivably* be capable of empirical testing or *be reducible to such propositions* by logical or mathematical deduction ... their truth or falsity, that is, must make some conceivable empirically noticeable difference' (Hutchison, 1935: 9–10, emphasis in the original).
3. This can be done by turning the premises of economic theory into empirical synthetic statements, and by making sure that *ceteris paribus* clauses are fully specified.
4. The 'fundamental assumption' of economic theory is that agents maximize, but their ability to do so depends crucially on a further assumption, that agents have correct foresight or perfect knowledge. But the future is uncertain, so this assumption is typically violated.
5. Hutchison concludes that, owing to the presence of 'the uncertainty factor ... the method of deduction from some "Fundamental Assumption" or "principle" of economic conduct is more or less useless' (ibid.: 118). He recommends instead that empirical investigations, over a wide range of possible conditions of actual choice behaviour, be undertaken.

That dependence on the assumption of full knowledge undermined the results of standard theory became a theme that Hutchison would repeat throughout his later writings. His proposal that economists should investigate actual choice behaviour makes him the twentieth-century methodological godfather of the 'psychology of economics' movement.

In the middle 1950s Hutchison debated with Fritz Machlup in the pages of the *Southern Economic Journal*. Machlup raised the question: must all economic propositions be testable? For 'the sake of a clear exposition' (Machlup, 1955: 5) Machlup divided the views of economists into two categories, labelled 'extreme apriorism' and 'ultra-empiricism'. Those who endorse the former view, and this despite the appearance of provocativeness their contentions might sometimes have had, typically object only to 'verifying the basic assumptions in isolation' (ibid.: 7). The ultra-empiricist, on the other hand, 'insists on the independent verification of all the assumptions, hypothetical as well as factual, perhaps even of each intermediate step in the analysis' (ibid.: 8). Machlup portrays his own position as occupying a sensible middle ground. He advocates 'indirect testability': fundamental assumptions (and, in particular, the 'Assumed Type of Action') are 'high-level generalizations' and need not be independently 'verified' (ibid.: 8–11). Rather, they are tested when the 'lower-level hypotheses' or predictions of the system as a whole are checked against reality. Machlup cites contemporary philosophers of science in support of his position, and provides a diagrammatic model of the way testing takes place. Interestingly, though he lists a number of economists as falling into the apriorist group, only Hutchison is mentioned as an exemplar of ultra-empiricism.

Machlup's article drew responses from both camps (Rothbard, 1957; Hutchison, 1956). Hutchison argued that Machlup's dichotomy was unhelpful in dividing up the many positions in the literature on testing, and denied in any case that he was an ultra-empiricist, since in his book he had only called for the 'conceivable testability' of fundamental assumptions. Hutchison summarizes his differences with Machlup as follows: 'while admitting the principle of indirect verification, we cannot agree to the kind of loose and sweeping appeal to it which Professor

Machlup seems to be making' (Hutchison, 1956: 482). In a reply Machlup (1956) characterizes Hutchison's final position as one of *reluctant* ultra-empiricism.

Hutchison took up another perennial methodological problem, that of value judgments, in '*Positive' Economics and Policy Objectives* (1964). First, he reviews the literature on the positive–normative distinction from the classical period onwards. He then provides a comprehensive statement of the sources of value judgments in economics. In the second half of the book, he reviews the objectives of economic policies, showing how they have grown more complex through time. This state of affairs, he concludes, demands that economists try all the harder to be clear about where values enter into their analyses. In this careful and nuanced study, Hutchison demonstrates his skills as a historian and a methodologist. It is also the first work (but also see the 1960 preface to Hutchison, 1938) in which the ideas of Karl Popper begin to appear as a clear influence.

In Hutchison's writings from the 1970s to the present, a number of recurring themes may be identified.

1. There are no laws in economics, only trends. These trends provide the bases for whatever predictive power economics might possess (Hutchison, 1977: ch. 2).
2. The pervasiveness of trends implies that testing will be very difficult in economics. But this is joined with the invocation that economists should nonetheless do all that they can to formulate testable theories, to submit them to repeated tests and to take the results seriously. Hutchison believes (and at times expresses the belief passionately) that such procedures are necessary if we are to avoid dogmatism (ibid.; Hutchison, 1981: ch. 7).
3. There is frequent invocation of the work of Popper in support of his programme. Unlike Mark Blaug, whose views are closest to his among modern methodologists, Hutchison is decidedly lukewarm towards Lakatos (Hutchison, 1977, ch. 3; 1988a). He has also defended the view, contra Caldwell (1992a; 1992b), that Hayek moved from a Misesian to a Popperian position in methodology (Hutchison, 1981: ch. 7; 1992a).
4. In the postwar period, there has been a 'formalist revolution' which has caused mainstream economics to become increasingly policy-irrelevant; because of its consequences, Hutchison also calls this a 'crisis of abstraction' (1977, ch. 4; 1992b: chs 3–5).
5. In recent work, Hutchison has criticized a number of contemporary positions, decrying, for example, both pluralism, which is 'a recipe for obscurantism and chaos' (1992b: 50) and the rhetoric of economics, in which 'incoherence is more or less systematic' (ibid.: 139).

Hutchison also made a number of contributions to the history of economic thought, in articles and essays (for example, 1978; 1981; 1994) and two books (1953; 1988b). Assessments of Hutchison's methodological work include Blaug (1980) and Caldwell (1982); for his work as a historian, see Coats (1983a).

References

Blaug, Mark (1980), T*he Methodology of Economics: Or How Economists Explain*, Cambridge: Cambridge University Press.

Blaug, Mark and Paul Sturges (eds) (1983), *Who's Who in Economics: A Biographical Dictionary of Major Economists, 1700–1981*, Cambridge, MA: MIT Press.

Caldwell, Bruce (1982), *Beyond Positivism: Economic Methodology in the Twentieth Century*, London: Allen & Unwin; reprinted, with a new preface, London: Routledge, 1994.

Caldwell, Bruce (1992a), 'Hayek the Falsificationist? A Refutation', *Research in the History of Economic Thought and Methodology*, **10**, 1–15.

Caldwell, Bruce (1992b), 'Reply to Hutchison', *Research in the History of Economic Thought and Methodology*, **10**, 33–42.

Cannan, Edwin (1932), 'Review: Robbins' *Essay ...*', *Economic Journal*, **42**, (167), September, 424–7.

Coats, A.W. (1983a), 'T.W. Hutchison as a Historian of Thought', *Research in the History of Economic Thought and Methodology*, **1**, Greenwich, CT: JAI Press.

Coats, A.W. (1983b), 'Half a Century of Methodological Controversy in Economics: As Reflected in the Writings of T.W. Hutchison', in A.W. Coats (ed.), *Methodological Controversy in Economics: Historical Essays in Honor of T.W. Hutchison*. Greenwich, CT: JAI Press.

Fraser, L.M. (1932), 'How Do We Want Economists to Behave?,' *Economic Journal*, **42**, (168), December, 555–70.

Hutchison, T.W. (1935), 'A Note on Tautologies and the Nature of Economic Theory', *Review of Economic Studies*, **2**, (2), February, 159–61.

Hutchison, T.W. (1938), *The Significance and Basic Postulates of Economic Theory*, London: Macmillan; reprinted, with a new preface, New York: Kelley, 1960.

Hutchison, T.W. (1953), *A Review of Economic Doctrines: 1870–1929*, Oxford: Clarendon Press.

Hutchison, T.W. (1956), 'Professor Machlup on Verification in Economics', *Southern Economic Journal*, **22**, (4), April, 476–83.

Hutchison, T.W. (1964), *'Positive' Economics and Policy Objectives*, London: Allen & Unwin.

Hutchison, T.W. (1977), *Knowledge and Ignorance in Economics*, Oxford: Blackwell.

Hutchison, T.W. (1978), *On Revolutions and Progress in Economic Knowledge*, Cambridge: Cambridge University Press.

Hutchison, T.W. (1981), T*he Politics and Philosophy of Economics: Marxians, Keynesians and Austrians*, New York: New York University Press.

Hutchison, T.W. (1988a), 'The Case for Falsification', in Neil de Marchi (ed.), *The Popperian Legacy in Economics*, Cambridge: Cambridge University Press.

Hutchison, T.W. (1988b), *Before Adam Smith: The Emergence of Political Economy, 1662–1776*, Oxford: Blackwell.

Hutchison, T.W. (1992a), 'Hayek and "Modern Austrian" Methodology: Comment on a Non-Refuting Refutation', *Research in the History of Economic Thought and Methodology*, **10**, 17–32.

Hutchison, T.W. (1992b), *Changing Aims in Economics*, Oxford: Blackwell.

Hutchison, T.W. (1994), *The Uses and Abuses of Economics: Contentious Essays on History and Method*, London: Routledge.

Machlup, Fritz (1955), 'The Problem of Verification in Economics', *Southern Economic Journal*, **22**, (1), July, 1–21.

Machlup, Fritz (1956), 'Rejoinder to a Reluctant Ultra-Empiricist', *Southern Economic Journal*, **22**, (4), April, 483–93.

Robbins, Lionel (1932), *An Essay on the Nature and Significance of Economic Science*, London: Macmillan; 2nd rev. edn, 1935.

Rothbard, Murray (1957), 'In Defense of "Extreme Apriorism"', *Southern Economic Journal*, **23**, (3), January, 314–20.

Souter, R.W. (1933), '"The Nature and Significance of Economic Science" in Recent Discussion', *Quarterly Journal of Economics*, **47**, (3), May, 377–413.

Hysteresis

Hysteresis means 'that which comes later', being derived from the Greek. The Scottish physicist–engineer James Alfred Ewing coined the term in 1881 to refer to phenomena that display a persistence of their previous state (Ewing, 1881a; 1881b). A broad definition is that hysteresis effects are those which remain once the initial causes giving rise to the effects are removed. The presence of such effects violates the standard presumption that physical systems are reversible, and revert to the status quo ante if some temporary cause or disturbance is removed. With hysteresis this is not the case: the processes are not reversed and the system does not revert to the status quo ante once a temporary disturbance is removed.

Conservative fields of force and neoclassical economics
The immediate background to the coining of the term 'hysteresis' was the emergence of the idea, associated with Faraday and Maxwell, of physical reality as consisting of fields of force

(see Hesse, 1980). The preceding Newtonian account of physical reality, in terms of forces acting reciprocally between material points or bodies. was replaced by an image of continuous fields of force, which are not explicable mechanically, this image being formalized in Maxwell's differential equations for electromagnetic fields (Maxwell 1861–2).

From the 1870s onwards, neoclassical economists carried over to economics metaphors drawn from physics, the implication being that economic systems behave, at least in some respects, like the physical systems described by Newtonian mechanics. or by Maxwellian fields of force (see Mirowski, 1989). When neoclassical economics was reformulated in axiomatic terms in the 1930s, 1940s and 1950s (see Ingrao and Israel, 1990), the conservative field of force metaphor was retained, the use of Lyapunov methods of stability analysis, for example, introducing an account of dynamics appropriate to a conservative field of force (Weintraub, 1991: 76). The resulting neoclassical equilibria display *homeostasis*, or self-maintenance (see Arrow, 1988: 278), returning to the status quo ante after temporary disturbances abate.

Ewing and hysteresis in fields of force

Shortly after the concept of a field of force was formalized by Maxwell, violations of the properties of homeostasis and reversibility were observed by Kohlrausch, who termed the effect *elastische Nachwirkung* (elastic after-effect), and others including Fromme, Warburg and Ewing (see Glazebrook, 1935). Ewing observed this effect in electromagnetic fields in ferric metals, the fields not reverting to their original characteristics once a temporary magnetizing force was removed: 'these curves exhibit, in a striking manner, a persistence of previous state … to this action … the author now gives the term Hysteresis' (Ewing, 1881b: 22). Ewing's assessor for this Royal Society paper, William Thompson (later Lord Kelvin), objected to Ewing's coining of the term 'hysteresis', suggesting that the phrase 'effects of retentiveness' be used instead (see A.W. Ewing, 1939). Ewing stuck to his guns, arguing that the term would have wider relevance than just to the thermoelectric and electromagnetic effects initially considered:

> I have ... found it convenient and even necessary to employ a new term, which merely designates this peculiar action without implying any theory as to its cause ... Hysteresis [occurs] when there are two qualities [y] and [x] such that cyclic variations of [x] cause cyclic variations of [y] [and] the changes of [y] lag behind those of [x] ... the value of [y] at any point of the operation depends not only on the actual value of [x], but on all the preceding changes (and particularly on the immediately preceding changes) of [x], and by properly manipulating these changes any value of y within more or less wide limits may be associated with any given value of [x]. (Ewing, 1885: 524–6, with y and x replacing the M and N of the original)

The contrasting cases of homeostasis and hysteresis in a force field are illustrated in Figure 1. In the case of a conservative field of force, as described by Maxwell's equations, the application of a temporary magnetizing force changes the field characteristics along the trajectory *AB*, and the removal of the force leads to a retracing of the original path along the trajectory *BA*, restoring the original field characteristics at *A*. With hysteresis, the initial trajectory *AB* is not retraced on removal of the magnetizing force, the trajectory *BC* being followed instead. Hence the trajectories are not reversed and the system does not return to its original state, returning instead to a new state of rest at *C*. The original field characteristics can be restored, but only by applying the coercive force indicated at point *D*. The system thus does not conserve energy, energy being dissipated over the magnetizing cycle. Instead the system displays *remanence*; that is, the application of successive disturbances of opposite magnitude does not lead to reversion to the original state.

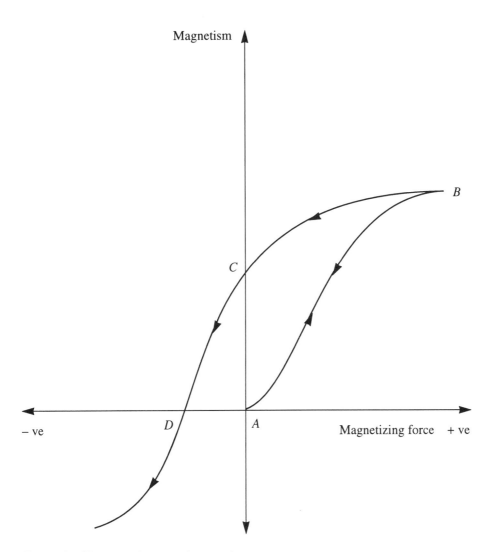

Figure 1   Homeostasis versus hysteresis

Ontological and epistemological hysteresis

Hysteresis involves the idea that causes can have effects at a temporal distance. The implied notion of action at a distance presents ontological problems: how is it possible, in the nature of phenomena, for action to be exerted at a temporal distance? Leibniz summarized this ontological objection:

> for since this command in the past no longer exists at present, it can accomplish nothing unless it has left some subsistent effect behind which has lasted and operated until now, and whoever thinks otherwise renounces any distinct explanation of things, if I am any judge, for if that which is remote in time and space can operate here and now without any intermediary, anything can be said to follow from anything else with equal right. (Leibniz, 1668, cited in Elster 1976: 372).

Consider the example of how past experience affects human behaviour: ontologically it is implausible to argue that there could be such an influence without past experience having left traces in neurons and neural networks inside the brain. Ontologically speaking, there is no hysteresis 'over and above the influence that is mediated by the traces left by the past in the present' (Elster, 1976: 373).

At the epistemological level, however, the question is whether explanations that involve merely 'the traces left by the past in the present' are more informative than hysteretic ones invoking causes from the past. In terms of explaining human behaviour, it is reasonably clear that invoking past experiences or mental states is more informative than the purely neurological explanations to be derived from dissecting neurons (see Jackson and Pettit, 1992). To invoke neurons or neural activity requires an explanation of their own behaviour. As outlined in what follows, systems with hysteresis have an erasable property of selective memory, which in itself might provide an explanation for the neurological conduits whereby past events influence present behaviour.

Krasnosel'skii

Ewing's hysteresis loops. which are partially illustrated in Figure 1, were based on experimental results concerning the behaviour of electromagnetic fields in ferric metals. A general framework for explaining such phenomena was proposed in Preisach (1938). Since the late 1960s, the Russian mathematician Mark Krasnosel'skii and associates have abstracted this approach from the specific context of magnetization and developed general mathematical models of systems with hysteresis (Krasnosel'skii and Pokrovskii, 1983; English translation 1989).

The two key elements responsible for producing hysteresis are *non-linearities* in the way input shocks affect the outputs of a system and *heterogeneity* in the elements that make up the system. The analysis applies to non-linear relationships in general, and to the case where the heterogeneity arises from individual elements changing over time (Krasnosel'skii and Pokrovskii, 1989). In the following illustration, a specific type of non-linearity, in the form of discrete switching points, and a specific type of heterogeneity, in the form of the cross-section of elements having different switching points, is employed (see Mayergoyz, 1991).

Consider how an aggregate demand shock ε affects the number of firms in production, P, and the number remaining latent, or having become bankrupt, L/B. A particular firm requires aggregate demand to take a value of a or more to make production viable, and a value of b or less to induce bankruptcy. There is thus a range of values of aggregate demand, $b < \varepsilon < a$, which leads to inertia; that is, the firm remains in production, or remains latent or bankrupt according to its acquired propensity. Then introduce heterogeneity by allowing different firms to have different a and b switching points, forming a set of hysteresis operators F_{ab} across the cross-sectional distribution of firms. The question is then one of how a particular history of aggregate demand shocks affects the number of firms in (P) and out (L/B) of production. It turns out that such a system has two key properties: *remanence* and *selective memory* (see Amable *et al.*, 1991; 1995; Cross, 1993; 1994; 1997; for demonstrations of the way these properties arise in the context of economic systems).

To see how these properties arise, consider the effects of the sequence of aggregate demand shocks represented in Figure 2. The expansionary shock ε_1 leads firms with $a \leq \varepsilon_1$ to enter production, firms with $a > \varepsilon_1$ remaining latent or bankrupt. The subsequent contractionary shock ε_2 leads firms with $b \geq \varepsilon_2$ into bankruptcy, firms with $b < \varepsilon_2$ remaining in production. And

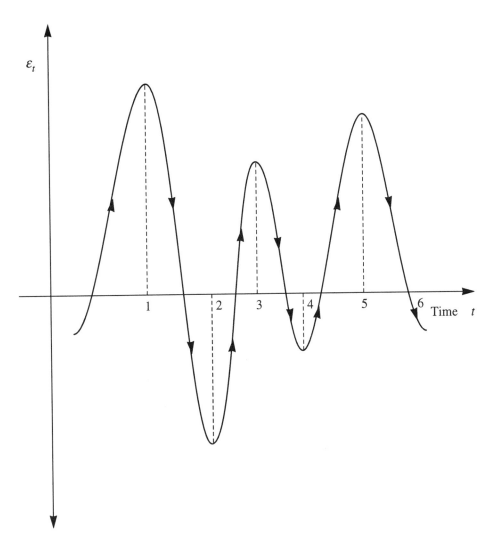

Figure 2   Aggregate demand shocks

similarly for the subsequent expansionary shock ε_3 and contractionary shock ε_4. Figure 3 uses the Mayergoyz (1991) half-plane diagram to show how these shocks affect the balance between firms in (*P*) and out (*L/B*) of production. Each point on the half-plane $a \geq b$ represents a particular firm by way of its a and b switching values. The sequence of aggregate demand shocks ε_1, ε_2, ε_3, ε_4 traces out the staircase partition on Figure 3 with vertices $(\varepsilon_1, \varepsilon_2)$, $(\varepsilon_3, \varepsilon_2)$ and $(\varepsilon_3, \varepsilon_4)$. The area above the partition represents firms out of production (*L/B*), the area below firms in production (*P*). The selective memory property can be seen by considering the effects of the demand shock ε_5. This serves to erase the memory of the ε_3 and ε_4 shocks, which become dominated, the new staircase partition between firms out of (*L/B*) and in (*P*) production having vertices $(\varepsilon_1, \varepsilon_2)$ and $(\varepsilon_5, \varepsilon_2)$. Thus the hysteresis memory is selective, only the non-dominated extrema of the shocks experienced having effects that remain once the shocks disappear. Aggregate output can be expressed as:

$$y_t = \iint_{a \geq b} g(a,b) F_{ab} \varepsilon_t \, da \, db \qquad (1)$$

where $g(a, b)$ is a weight function indicating the contribution to total output of particular firms.

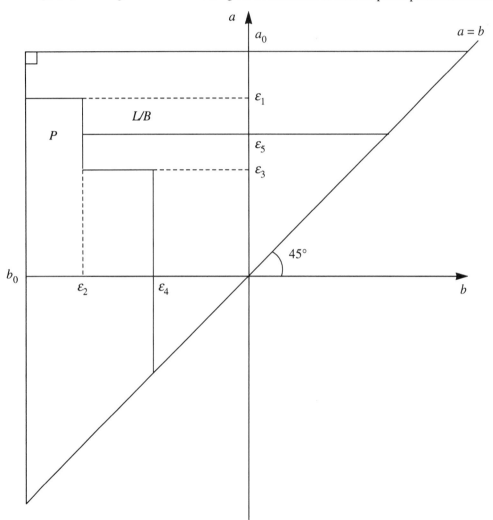

Figure 3   The selective memory property

Hysteresis is a non-linear phenomenon
Since the 1980s, the term 'hysteresis' has been hijacked in the economics literature to refer to zero/unit root solutions to economic models specified in terms of *linear* differential/difference

equations (Giavazzi and Wyplosz, 1985; Wyplosz, 1987, for example). For example, the reduced form for a model of output might be:

$$y_t = \alpha + \beta y_{t-1} + \gamma z_t + \delta_t. \tag{2}$$

where y is output, z is a vector of 'structural' factors determining the 'natural rate' of output, δ is a stochastic disturbance and α, β and γ are parameters, with $0 < \beta \leq 1$. In the standard homeostatic equilibrium case, $\beta \neq 1$, the equilibrium conditions $y_t = y_{t-1}$ and $\delta_t = 0$ yield:

$$y^* = \frac{\alpha + \gamma z^*}{1 - \beta} \tag{3}$$

and so past disturbances to output have no effect on equilibrium output y^*. In the unit root case of $\beta = 1$, however, equilibrium output is no longer uniquely defined by expression (3), evolving instead as:

$$y_T^* = y_0 + \alpha T + \gamma \sum_{i=0} z_{T-1} + \sum_{i-1} \delta_{T-i} \tag{4}$$

Thus equilibrium output depends on *all* of the history of the deterministic and stochastic influences on output.

In the above unit root case, output is determined by 'the whole shape of behaviour at previous times', which presents 'an uncomfortable feeling' (Samuelson, 1972: 441). This is implausible. It also involves a misuse of the term 'hysteresis' (see Amable *et al.*, 1995; Cross, 1993). As indicated in the earlier discussion, hysteresis is a property which arises in *non-linear* systems with *heterogeneous* elements. In such systems only a selected subset of past disturbances have continuing effects on the output of, in this case, economic systems.

Hysteresis in economic systems

Although used occasionally since the 1940s, by economists such as Schumpeter, Georgescu-Roegen, Samuelson and Phelps (see Cross and Allan, 1988), the term 'hysteresis' only came into widespread use in economics in the 1980s. Arguably, however, the term refers to a wide range of effects that have long been postulated, albeit informally, to characterize the behaviour of economic systems. Marshall, for example, pointed out that 'if the normal production of a commodity increases and afterwards diminishes to its old amount, the demand price and supply price are not likely to return, as pure theory assumes they will, to their old position for that amount' (Marshall, 1890: 425–6). To take a further example, Keynes' *General Theory* shares with hysteretic models the property that a range of equilibria are consistent with any given set of exogenous conditions (see Summers, 1988). Tobin puts the point forcefully: 'for many years I and others have argued that prolonged actual unemployment will become "natural" ... but no one paid heed until the label "hysteresis-effect" came into vogue' (cited in Cross, 1993: 68).

Thinking of economic systems as being haunted by hysteresis involves a shift away from the homeostatic models of reversible processes that form the mainstream of economic analysis. Such a shift involves substituting non-linear for linear models of economic processes and allowing for heterogeneity in the elements that make up economic systems. Various aspects of economic behaviour, such as self-reinforcement (Arthur, 1988), no longer appear as anomalies once irreversible processes are admitted. If economies are seen as evolving complex systems (Anderson *et al.*, 1988; Waldrop, 1994; Day and Chen, 1993), hysteresis models provide an account of the way the memory of past disturbances is organized within such systems.

ROD CROSS

References

Amable, B., J. Henry, F. Lordon and R. Topol (1991), 'Strong Hysteresis: an Application to Foreign Trade', *OFCE Working Paper 91-03*, Paris: OFCE.

Amable, B., J. Henry, F. Lordon and R. Topol (1995), 'Hysteresis Revisited: a Methodological Approach', in R. Cross (ed.), *The Natural Rate of Unemployment: Reflections on 25 Years of the Hypothesis*, Cambridge: Cambridge University Press.

Anderson, P.W., K.J. Arrow and D. Pines (eds) (1988), *The Economy as an Evolving Complex System*, Redwood City: Addison-Wesley.

Arrow, K.J. (1988), 'Workshop on the Economy as an Evolving Complex System: Summary', in P.W. Anderson *et al.* (eds), *The Economy as an Evolving Complex System*.

Arthur, W.B. (1988), 'Self-Reinforcing Mechanisms in Economics', in P.W. Anderson *et al.* (eds), *The Economy as an Evolving Complex System*.

Cross, R. (1993), 'On the Foundations of Hysteresis in Economic Systems', *Economics and Philosophy*, **9**, (1), 53–74.

Cross, R. (1994), 'The Macroeconomic Consequences of Discontinuous Adjustment', *Scottish Journal of Political Economy*, **41**, (2), 212–21.

Cross. R. (1997), 'Force Fields, Hysteresis and Economic Equilibria', *Journal of Economic Studies*, **24**, (4), 258–67.

Cross. R. and A.C. Allan (1988), 'On the History of Hysteresis', in R. Cross (ed.), *Unemployment, Hysteresis and the Natural Rate Hypothesis*, Oxford: Blackwell.

Day, R.H. and P. Chen, (1993), *Non-Linear Dynamics and Evolutionary Economics*, New York: Oxford University Press.

Elster. J. (1976), 'A Note on Hysteresis in the Social Sciences', *Synthèse*, **33**, 371–91.

Ewing, A.W. (1939), *The Man of Room 40: The Life of Sir Alfred Ewing*, London: Hutchinson.

Ewing. J.A. (1881a), 'The Effects of Stress on the Thermoelectric Quality of Metals', *Proceedings of the Royal Society of London*, **32**, 399–402.

Ewing. J.A. (1881b), 'On the Production of Transient Electric Currents in Iron and Steel Conductors by Twisting them when Magnetised or by Magnetising them when Twisted', *Proceedings of the Royal Society of London*, **33**, 21–3.

Ewing, J.A. (1985), 'Experimental Researches in Magnetism', *Philosophical Transactions of the Royal Society of London*, **176**, (II), 523–640.

Giavazzi, F. and C. Wyplosz, (1985), 'The Zero Root Problem: A Note on the Dynamic Determination of the Stationary Equilibrium in Linear Models', *Review of Economic Studies*, **52**, 353–7.

Glazebrook, R.T. (1935), 'James Alfred Ewing 1855–1935', *Obituary Notices of the Royal Society of London*, **I**, 475–92.

Hesse, M. (1980), *Revolutions and Reconstructions in the History of Science*, Brighton: Harvester.

Ingrao, B. and G. Israel, (1990), *The Invisible Hand Equilibrium in the History of Science*, Cambridge, MA: MIT Press.

Jackson, F. and P. Pettit (1992), 'In Defence of Explanatory Ecumenism', *Economics and Philosophy*, **8**, 1–21.

Krasnosel'skii, M.A. and A.V. Pokrovskii (1983), *Sistemy s Gisteresisom*, Moscow: Nauka.

Krasnosel'skii, M.A. and A.V. Pokrovskii (1989), *Systems with Hysteresis*, Berlin: Springer-Verlag.

Marshall, A. (1890), *Principles of Economics*, 1st edn, London: Macmillan.

Maxwell, J.C. (1861–2), 'On Physical Lines of Force', reprinted in W.D. Niven (ed.), *The Scientific Papers of James Clerk Maxwell*, Cambridge: Cambridge University Press.

Mayergoyz, I.D. (1991), *Mathematical Models of Hysteresis*, Berlin: Springer-Verlag.

Mirowski, P. (1989), *More Heat than Light*, New York: Cambridge University Press.

Preisach, P. (1938), 'Über die Magnetische Nachwirkung', *Zeitschrift für Physik*, **94**, 277–302.

Samuelson. P.A. (1972), *The Collected Scientific Papers of Paul A. Samuelson*, Vol. III, ed. R.C. Merton, Cambridge, MA: MIT Press.

Summers. L.H. (1988), 'Should Keynesian Economics Dispense with the Phillips Curve?', in R. Cross (ed.), *Unemployment, Hysteresis and the Natural Rate Hypothesis*, Oxford: Blackwell.

Waldrop, M.M. (1994), *Complexity: The Emerging Science at the Edge of Order and Chaos*, London: Penguin Books.

Weintraub, E.R. (1991), *Stabilising Dynamics: Constructing Economic Knowledge*, New York: Cambridge University Press.

Wyplosz, C. (1987), 'Comments', in R. Layard and L. Calmfors (eds), *The Fight Against Unemployment*, Cambridge, MA: MIT Press.

Ideology

The term 'ideological' has been used at various times in the history of economic thought to mean biased, non-objective, false, value-laden, illusory, normative, political, bourgeois, moralistic, particular and even cosmological and metaphysical. Is economics a 'science' or is it merely 'ideology'? This question, in one form or another, has dogged the pursuit of economic knowledge since at least the time of Adam Smith. The ideological has always been construed as the opposite of the scientific, suggesting an ideal of objective economic inquiry.

The history of economic thought can in fact be read as a series of efforts to distance knowledge claims from the taint of ideology, a continuing struggle to establish the field's scientific merit. At the same time, the criticism that an economic theory is 'ideological' has often served as a way of establishing the superiority of one theory over another (Meek, 1967). The search for a natural economic order has been an important dimension of the struggle to establish economics as science: From Smith's pursuit of Newtonian laws of economic motion, to Ricardo's exposition of the natural laws of distribution, Jevons' mechanical analogies, Marshall's extensive use of biological metaphors and, finally, to Samuelson's use of the techniques of optimization and dynamics borrowed from physics, economic phenomena have been represented as natural, subject to natural laws. This has linked economics to natural science – a sort of legitimation by association. But the naturalization tendency can also be seen as a manifestation of the more general quest for objectivity in social inquiry, an attempt to purge the influence of ideology.

Until Marx, the methodological struggle for economists was to distinguish political economy from ethics. It is with Marx that the methodological problem in political economy became the demarcation of economic science from ideology. Ideology, as part of the superstructure, reflects the class relations of society, since 'The mode of production of material life conditions the social, political and intellectual life process in general' Marx (1981: 20–21) Accordingly, the dominant ideology supports the interests of the dominant class: hence the term 'vulgar' or 'bourgeois' economics to describe the marginalists as serving to legitimate or apologize for the status quo (Robinson, 1962: 52).

The nineteenth-century conception of ideology as an interpretive frame, dependent on the individual's or group's social position in relation to the 'objective' social relations, is embedded in a theory of consciousness, encompassing epistemology, ethics and aesthetics. With the rise of science in the twentieth century, the issue of ideological bias became focused on the epistemological aspect, and 'the ideological' became associated with anything that was not scientific or objective. This shifted the focus to the question of 'value-ladenness'; that is, the degree to which the very concepts and categories of social analysis are imbued with beliefs and norms, despite a veneer of objectivity. According to Gunnar Myrdal,

> There is no way of studying social reality other than from the viewpoint of human ideals. A 'disinterested social science' has never existed and, for logical reasons, cannot exist. The value connotation of our main concepts represents our interest in a matter, gives direction to our thoughts and significance to our inferences ... The recognition that our very concepts are value-loaded implies that they cannot be defined except in terms of political valuations. (Myrdal, 1958: 1–2)

Myrdal argued, furthermore, that as economists rely increasingly on the use of mathematics and econometrics the value-ladenness of its main concepts is not reduced but simply 'easier to disregard' (Myrdal, 1954).

Schumpeter's (1954) distinction between 'vision' and 'analysis' boldly and cleverly circumvented the Myrdal critique. Vision is defined as the prior beliefs and world views that necessarily precede and imbue all economic analysis – what Schumpeter describes as 'the pre-analytic cognitive act'. Analysis is the working out of the systematic aspects of vision-imbued posits. According to Schumpeter (1954: 42), 'Analytic work begins with material provided by our vision of things, and this vision is ideological almost by definition.' But, while vision precedes analysis, Schumpeter argued that it is possible to separate the two and thus to focus exclusively on analysis. Not only is purely analytical progress possible, but such progress is the very essence of science.

As economics moved from its Marshallian to its Samuelsonian mode in the 1950s and 1960s, analysis so dominated the field that vision seemed to have disappeared entirely. The technique of constrained optimization came not only to define the proper scope of economics, but to offer, as John Hicks (1946: 24) wrote, 'a unifying principle for the whole of economics'. The concern with ideological bias was reduced to the much milder and cleaner problem of distinguishing between positive and normative analysis.

Despite the enormous advances in economic analysis since the 1950s, the discipline has not successfully immunized itself against the critique of ideological bias, even while the Schumpeterian distinction between vision and analysis has remained in use. Maurice Dobb (1973: 5–7) criticizes efforts to separate the two in the study of the history of economic ideas. Robert Heilbroner asserts that economic thought is firmly rooted in vision, and thus 'ideological' (that is value-laden) by nature. He writes, 'All systems of thought that describe or examine societies must contain their political character, knowingly and explicitly, or unknowingly and in disguise' (Heilbroner, 1990: 109). But Heilbroner does not draw the usual negative conclusion from this state of affairs. To the contrary, he argues (similar to the later writings of Myrdal) that it is vision – including its value-laden aspect – that provides much of the creative impetus for understanding social life. Consequently, vision should be the subject of open debate. It is not the presence of, but the persistent denial of vision that robs economics of social validity and that leaves contemporary economics so limited as a tool for understanding social life (Heilbroner and Milberg, 1995). Harding (1995), from a feminist perspective, goes one step further, claiming that value-explicit work is more 'objective' than that which claims to be value-free.

The other recent source of doubt about the ability of economics to distinguish its scientific from its non-scientific claims is McCloskey's (1983) rhetorical approach to economic methodology. McCloskey's position is that economic discourse of any sort – verbal, mathematical, econometric – is rhetoric; that is, an effort to persuade. None of these discursive forms should necessarily be privileged over the others unless it is agreed by the community of scholars to be more compelling. Moreover, objective truth drops out as a goal of social inquiry, since 'We have no way to get outside our own human conversations and get in the mind of God in order to tell whether such and such an argument is True' (McCloskey, 1988: 277). McCloskey's views are closely tied to those of postmodernism that have been influential across the social sciences and humanities. While McCloskey (1994: 339) herself has argued that the rhetoric approach has no particular implication for the role of ideology in economics, others have used this approach precisely to unveil the ideological nature of economic argument.

Ideology, in this view, is a particular discourse that is put forth as universal or absolute (Milberg, 1988; Rosetti, 1990).

McCloskey's critique of objectivity in economics has also opened up a rich discussion of the ideology of subjectivity itself. As in the political readings of economic rhetoric, the critical evaluations of the economic subject – *homo economicus* – have emphasized the particularity and narrowness of the various conceptions, and especially of their gender and race bias (Williams, 1993; Hartman and Folbre, 1988). It is the suppression of the contradictory and social aspects of individual identity that reveal the ideology of both the neoclassical and Marxian conceptions of 'man'. The rhetorical approach thus adds a new twist to the critique of the tendency to represent economic phenomena as natural. In sum, a postmodern perspective calls into question both the nineteenth-century efforts to discover natural economic laws and the twentieth-century concern with objective, scientific inquiry (Milberg, 1993).

Is economics a science or is it merely ideology? The answer to this question of course requires a definition of terms. All discourse – even that which we call 'scientific' – is ideological when that term is defined as the portrayal of a particular system of meaning as universal. In language we can intentionally distort, be crudely political in claiming access to absolute truth, or openly admit that social 'constructs' embody our interpretation of social life. The key term in the question posed above is neither science nor ideology, but the pejorative term 'merely'. Ideology, seen as the underlying vision of society and subjectivity, becomes not just an unavoidable component of the process of creating social knowledge, but a necessary element in the creative process of making sense of social life. Only when economists move away from the pursuit of universal knowledge of 'the economy' and towards an acceptance of the necessity of vision and the historical and spatial contingency of knowledge will the concern over ideological 'bias' begin to fade. Such a turn would have important implications for economic method as well, as knowledge claims would increasingly find support, not in models of constrained optimization, but with such techniques as case studies and historical analyses of social institutions and politics.

WILLIAM S. MILBERG

References
Dobb, Maurice (1973), *Theories of Value and Distribution since Adam Smith: Ideology and Economic Theory*, Cambridge: Cambridge University Press.
Harding, Sandra (1995), 'Can Feminist Thought Make Economics More Objective?', *Feminist Economics*, **1**, (1), 7–32.
Hartman, Heidi and Nancy Folbre (1988), 'The rhetoric of self-interest: Ideology of gender in economic theory', in Arjo Klamer *et al.* (eds), *The Consequences of Economic Rhetoric*, New York: Cambridge University Press.
Heilbroner, Robert (1990), 'Economics as Ideology', in W. Samuels (ed.), *Economics as Discourse*, Boston: Kluwer Academic.
Heilbroner, Robert and William Milberg (1995), *The Crisis of Vision in Modern Economic Thought*, New York: Cambridge University Press.
Hicks, J.R, (1946), *Value and Capital*, 2nd edn, London: Oxford University Press.
Marx, Karl (1981), *A Contribution to the Critique of Political Economy*, ed. Maurice Dobb, New York: International Publishers.
McCloskey, Donald (1983), 'The Rhetoric of Economics', *Journal of Economic Literature*.
McCloskey, Donald (1988), 'The Consequences of Economic Rhetoric', in Arjo Klamer *et al.* (eds), *The Consequences of Economic Rhetoric*, New York: Cambridge University Press.
McCloskey, Donald (1994), *Knowledge and Persuasion in Economics*, New York: Cambridge University Press.
Meek, Ronald L. (1967), *Economics and Ideology and Other Essays*, London.
Milberg, William (1988), 'The Language of Economics: Deconstructing the Neoclassical Text', *Social Concept*, **4**, (2).
Milberg, William (1993), 'Natural Order and Postmodernism in Economic Thought', *Social Research*, **60**, (2), Summer, 255–77.

Myrdal, Gunnar (1954), *The Political Element in the Development of Economic Thought*, Cambridge, MA: Harvard University Press.
Myrdal, Gunnar (1958), *Value in Social Theory: A Selection of Essays on Methodology*, ed. Paul Streeten, London: Routledge & Kegan Paul
Myrdal, Gunnar (1972), 'How Scientific Are the Social Sciences', *Against the Stream: Critical Essays on Economics*, New York: Random House.
Robinson, Joan (1962), *Economic Philosophy*, Chicago: Aldine.
Rosetti, Jane (1990), 'Deconstructing Robert Lucas', in W. Samuels (ed.), *Economics as Discourse*, Boston: Kluwer Academic.
Schumpeter, Joseph (1954), *History of Economic Analysis*, New York: Cambridge University Press.
Williams, Rhonda (1993), 'Race, Deconstruction and the Emergent Agenda of Feminist Economic Theory', in Marianne Ferber and Julie Nelson (eds), *Beyond Economic Man: Feminist Thought and Economics*, Chicago: University of Chicago Press.

Induction

Induction is a mode of inference which has a central place in the methodology of the empirical sciences. It is weaker than logical deduction, since it is not necessarily truth-preserving. But it is also ampliative or knowledge-increasing, since the content of its conclusion is not explicitly or implicitly present in the premises. Thus induction may allow us to expand the domain of our rationally warranted or probable beliefs.

Deductive inference is characterized by the condition that the conclusion is a logical consequence of the premises: whenever the premises are true, the conclusion must be true as well. The first formal system of deductive logic was presented by Aristotle in his theory of syllogistic. Aristotle required that the theorems of special sciences be demonstrated by deductive syllogisms, but he realized that the first premises or axioms cannot be established in this way. The process of reaching these general axioms he called *epagoge*. This term was translated as *inductio* by the Latin commentators. The standard (but nowadays not unchallenged) interpretation has assumed that Aristotle had two conceptions of induction. First, in intuitive induction, a universal generalization is grasped by a psychological process involving the perception of some particular instances of the generalization. Second, in complete induction, a generalization is obtained by enumerating all of its instances. The latter idea is preserved in the term 'mathematical induction', which refers to a demonstrative method of proving arithmetical generalizations for all natural numbers.

In the theories of enumerative induction, inductive generalization is taken to proceed from an incomplete part to a whole, from a finite sample to a population. For example, all of the ravens observed until now have been black, hence all ravens are black. Statistical generalization goes from a sample to a statistical statement about a population. For example, 10 per cent in a random sample of the citizens of Paris are left-handed, hence 10 per cent of the Parisians are left-handed. Singular inductive inference proceeds from a sample to a new individual from the population. For example, all of the swans observed so far have been white, hence also the next swan to be examined will be white.

Enumerative induction is fallible, since it is possible that the conclusion is false even when the premises are true The classical example illustrating this was the discovery of black swans in Australia. If this contrast to truth-preserving deduction is taken as the characteristic of induction, the scope of inductive inference includes also the argument that Charles Peirce called 'statistical deduction', which applies an inference from a statistical statement about a population to an individual or a sample. For example, 90 per cent of the Parisians are Catholic, hence probably this randomly selected Parisian is a Catholic. In the context of statistical prediction and explanation, this mode of argument is also called direct inference. Another non-deductive argument, which often is treated as a species of induction, is analogy: from observed similarities between two objects it is inferred that they share some further property. For example, argument by analogy is used when the results of medical experiment with animals are emended to cover human beings.

Francis Bacon in the early seventeenth century thought that induction by simple enumeration is 'childish'. He argued that induction should involve a systematic tabular method of excluding putative but false connections between the examined variables, so that the finally remaining only alternative is established with certainty. This idea has been called 'eliminative induction' or 'demonstrative induction'. It was further developed in John Stuart Mill's 'Rules of Experimentation' (Mill, 1843; Blake *et al.*, 1960).

David Hume, in his *Enquiry concerning Human Understanding* (1748), raised serious doubts about the possibility of justifying induction. He argued that all of our beliefs, which go beyond the immediately certain domain of our knowledge about our present sensations, are in some way based upon inductive inference. These beliefs are reliable only if the world is uniform, that is, the future resembles the past. But this principle of the uniformity of nature is itself a general statement which can be justified only by induction. Therefore the attempt to justify induction seems to be viciously circular. Hume himself concluded that there are no necessary connexions between causes and effects in nature: induction is only a habit of our mind to expect regular successions between ideas. Hume's challenge has been met in three basically different ways (von Wright, 1957). First, Immanuel Kant claimed that the laws of nature are necessary truths imposed by our mind on the phenomenal world. Second, Karl Popper's falsificationism accepts Hume's message: induction is impossible. General statements or laws of nature cannot be proved true or even probable, but they can be shown to be false by counterexamples. Thus science does not employ, nor does it need, induction at all (Popper, 1959). The third approach is to accept the fallibility of induction, and to analyse the relation between its presises and conclusion in terms of probability.

The classical theory of probability, as formulated by Laplace in the early nineteenth century, calculated probabilities of hypotheses by means of Bayes' theorem. In this Bayesian tradition, probability $P(H/E)$ is interpreted as a rational degree of belief in the truth of hypothesis H on the basis of evidence E. This degree of belief is usually taken to be a subjective or personal probability of an agent or a scientist whose behaviour satisfies some rationality or coherence conditions (Howson and Urbach, 1989; Earman, 1992). The work of Frank Ramsey, Bruno de Finetti, L.J. Savage and Patrick Suppes has shown in detail under what conditions degrees of belief satisfy the axioms of probability theory (Kyburg and Smokler, 1964; Skyrms, 1975). In Rudolf Carnap's inductive logic, inductive probabilities are determined by symmetry assumptions concerning the underlying language (Carnap, 1962). Jaakko Hintikka's systems differ from Carnap's in their ability to assign non-zero probabilities to universal generalizations (Hintikka and Suppes, 1966).

Some Bayesians (like Carnap and Richard Jeffrey) think that the theory of induction only tells how the probabilities of hypotheses are determined; these probabilities can then be employed in rational decision making (Jeffrey, 1965). Moreover, the concept of confirmation (of H on E) can be defined as increase of probability, that is, $P(H/E) > P(H)$. Others (like Hintikka and Isaac Levi) have formulated inductive rules for the tentative acceptance of hypotheses on the basis of evidence. One variant of inductive acceptance is the so-called 'inference to the best explanation': among rival hypotheses, it recommends the acceptance of the hypothesis that gives the best explanation of the given data.

A powerful reformulation of the problem of induction has been given in cognitive decision theory by Isaac Levi (1967) and Jaakko Hintikka. If the aim of our inquiry is truth, and nothing but the truth, then the epistemic utility of accepting a hypothesis H on evidence E can be taken to be equal to its truth value (1 for truth, 0 for falsity). Then the expected utility of accepting H is simply $P(H/E).1 + P(\text{not-}H/E).0 = P(H/E)$. The rule of maximizing expected epistemic utility leads then to the conservative principle of accepting only trivially true tautologies or hypotheses logically entailed by the evidence. But if our aim is truthful information, where the information content of H is measured by $\text{cont}(H) = 1 - P(H)$, so that our gain is $\text{cont}(H)$ when H is true and our loss is $\text{cont}(\text{not-}H)$ when H is false, the expected utility is $P(H/E) - P(H)$.

The frequentist school analyses probability in terms of statistical relative frequencies in hypothetical populations or in repeated experiments. Peirce defined the probability of induction as the relative frequency with which this mode of inference carries truth with it. Valid deduction has thus the truth-frequency one. Peirce's ideas anticipate the frequentist treatments of induction in the twentieth century: Hans Reichenbach's probability logic and the Neyman–Pearson theory of statistics (Salmon, 1966).

In the Bacon–Mill tradition, induction was assumed to be both a method of discovery and a method of proof of scientific laws. Today the doctrine that scientific hypotheses are discovered by induction is known as inductivism. This view is opposed by the hypothetico-deductive (HD) conception of science: scientific statements and theories are free creations, hypotheses, that are tested by deducing empirical predictions from them. According to Popper, the HD method has no inductive element. But, as positive test results E cannot logically prove general theories H, the relation of a hypothesis H and the supporting evidence E is usually taken to be inductive (Salmon, 1966). Thus most theorists of induction would distinguish the discovery of hypotheses (or abduction, as Peirce called it) from the testing of hypotheses (Hempel, 1966) and they contend that probabilistic theories of induction concern only the latter methodological task of supporting (confirming, corroborating) or refuting hypotheses. A middle position between inductivism and the HD method is advocated by the 'friends of discovery', who argue that there are non-inductive logics of discovery (Nickles, 1980).

The Popperian approach would exclude induction from economic methodology. The rival view contends that induction plays an important role in economics in the testing of theoretical hypotheses, in making economic predictions and in describing the behaviour of rational agents making decisions under uncertainty and risk.

ILKKA NIINILUOTO

Bibliography

Blake, R.M., C.J. Ducasse, and E.H. Madden (1960), *Theories of Scientific Method: The Renaissance Through the Nineteenth Century*, Seattle: University of Washington Press.
Carnap, R. (1962), *The Logical Foundations of Probability*, 2nd edn, Chicago: University of Chicago Press.
Earman, J. (1992), *Bayes or Bust?*, Cambridge, MA: MIT Press.
Hempel, C.G. (1966), *The Philosophy of Natural Science*, Englewood Cliffs: Prentice-Hall.
Hintikka, J. and P. Suppes (eds) (1966), *Aspects of Inductive Logic*, Amsterdam: North-Holland.
Howson, C. and P. Urbach, *Scientific Reasoning: The Bayesian Approach*, La Salle: Open Court Publishing Co.
Jeffrey, R. (1965), *The Logic of Decision*, New York: McGraw-Hill.
Kyburg, H.E. and H. Smokler (eds), *Studies in Subjective Probability*, New York: John Wiley.
Levi, I. (1967), *Gambling With Truth*, New York: Alfred A. Knopf.

Mill, J.S. (1843), *A System of Logic*, London.
Nickles, T. (ed.) (1980), *Scientific Discovery, Logic and Rationality*, Dordrecht: D. Reidel.
Popper, K. (1959), *The Logic of Scientific Discovery*, London: Hutchinson.
Salmon, W. (1966), *The Foundations of Scientific Inference*, Pittsburgh: University of Pittsburgh Press.
Skyrms, B. (1975), *Choice and Chance*, 2nd edn, Belmont: Dickenson.
von Wright, G.H. (1957), *The Logical Problem of Induction*, 2nd edn, Oxford: Blackwell.

Institutionalism

The methodology of American (old) institutional economics has always been the subject of debate and disagreement, sometimes within the movement but more often between those within and those outside it. Institutionalists themselves have frequently attempted to distinguish themselves from other traditions of thought, and neoclassical economics in particular, on methodological grounds (Gruchy, 1947; Dugger, 1979), but the diversity of the specific methods utilized by the major figures in the movement (Veblen, Mitchell and Commons) has meant that such characterizations have been necessarily confined to only the most general of principles. Moreover, institutionalists have had to cope with the widespread (although inaccurate) opinion that the only distinguishing mark of institutionalist methodology is its misguided descriptivism and disdain of theory. Koopmans' (1947) critique of Burns and Mitchell as 'measurement without theory' echoes in Coase's (1984) remark that all the institutionalists produced was 'a mass of descriptive material waiting for a theory, or a fire'. Perhaps because of this hostile attitude on the outside, institutionalists have shown a reluctance to engage in any very critical examination of their own methodological conventions and practices and a tendency to exaggerate the methodological unity of their movement. This is unfortunate, as a proper discussion of institutionalist methodology raises issues of central importance for the methodology of all social science. Space constraints mean that only the briefest of outlines can be given here. The discussion will be divided into two parts, the first dealing with the general methodological principles that guide institutional economics, and the second dealing with more specific methods and techniques of investigation.

Methodological principles
The methodological principles of most importance in the institutionalist tradition are to be found in the evolutionary and holistic (in a particular sense) view of the social and economic world, combined with the instrumentalist theory of knowledge taken from the work of John Dewey. It is as a result of these principles that institutionalists reject the formalism, rationalism, positive/normative distinction and testing procedures generally associated with neoclassical economics, and have instead sought to develop methods linked to their own stress on the institutional basis of behaviour, the complex and evolving nature of the social whole and the testing of theories as instruments for the solution of social problems. However, even at this level of generality, differences between institutionalists can be found, and statements about what is accepted by everyone within the tradition have to be made with care. This section will examine in turn the principles of evolutionism, holism and instrumentalism.

Evolutionism
Institutionalism was founded upon an evolutionary conception of economics, as is obvious in Veblen's distinction between the pre-Darwinian character of orthodox economics and the post-Darwinian nature of the 'modern science' he wished to emulate (Veblen, 1898). Veblen's

references to Darwinism involve a number of methodological points, most of which are contained within his notion of 'cumulative causation'. Cumulative causation involves the rejection of both static equilibrium analysis and the idea that economic change is to be explained in the teleological terms of purpose of intent, and the substitution of an analysis of economic evolution that emphasizes its continuous, sequential and cumulative character, and which runs in purely causal terms. Veblen was, of course, aware that individuals are intentional actors, but his point was that individuals take their objectives from the surrounding social conventions and norms, and that fundamental changes to institutions come about, not as the result of a choice to shift the institutional base in order to achieve better some given end, but as a result of accumulated economic and technological developments that lead to new patterns of life and new ways of thinking that come to displace the old. For example, capitalism evolved out of feudalism with the gradual development of larger-scale production, markets and the subsequent emergence of production for profit and money making as the accepted end of economic activity. Institutional evolution, here, is an adaptive process, but one that is unintentional and operates via habituation to new conditions of life. This idea of cumulative causation lies at the heart of a great deal of institutionalist writing, but many institutionalists, most notably J.R. Commons, have sought to give intentional processes a greater role.

Commons argued that the correct evolutionary metaphor to apply to institutions was that of the artificial selection of the plant or animal breeder rather than that of natural selection (Commons, 1934: 657). For Commons, the key selective processes in society were judicial and legislative, both of which operated according to the purposes of the decision makers and in response to the need to resolve conflicts as they arose and to maintain the workability of the system over time. The instrumentalist perspective adopted by virtually all institutionalists since Veblen, and discussed below, is also something that implies that intentional processes can, at least potentially, play a significant role.

Holism

The term 'holism' is not used within institutionalism to impute agential power to any holistic entity. It is sometimes suggested that Commons' references to the 'collective will' do involve the notion of the social whole as an actor, but all Commons intended to convey in such language was the outcome of political and judicial processes of decision making. The term 'holism' is used to indicate that society is more than just a group of independent actors, that individuals operate within sets of social conventions and norms that define acceptable objectives and established roles and that these social conventions and roles cannot themselves be fully explained in purely individualistic terms – in other words, to reject reductionist versions of methodological individualism. It is true that American institutionalists have not always provided adequate treatments of the behaviour of individual actors that results in institutions becoming established or being changed (Ayres, for example, insisted on keeping his analysis at the cultural level), but a great deal of the work of both Veblen and Commons does provide an analysis of the way individual and corporate actors, operating within given institutional structures, can create new institutions, and is not inconsistent with positions such as Agassi's 'institutional individualism' (Rutherford, 1994).

The holistic perspective of American institutionalists is also responsible for their rejection of highly abstract and formal types of theorizing. Their emphasis on the institutional basis of behaviour leads to a rejection of the maximizing assumption that is the basis of most neoclassical formalism. They complain that the influence of institutions on individuals is difficult to capture in highly abstract and formal models, with the result that in formal models the institutional context is either eliminated altogether or treated as epiphenomenal. Furthermore, the institutional system is complex and evolving, characteristics that are not captured in the standard formal models. Instead institutionalists utilize less formal types of theorizing, sometimes in what are termed 'pattern models' (Wilber and Harrison 1978) that are relatively concrete and retain an emphasis on the interconnections between the parts and the whole system and on its 'holistic quality'. In a pattern model the behaviour of any part is explained by being related to the whole system of which it is a part and by its particular place within the whole.

Instrumentalism

The instrumentalist theory of knowledge as developed in the work of John Dewey quickly became incorporated within the institutionalist tradition. Put briefly, Dewey's version of instrumentalism views theories as instruments or tools for the betterment of human life. Theories are both developed and judged as tools, they arise out of attempts to modify the world and are judged on the basis of the consequences of their implementation. What is sought is not truth or certainty, but effectiveness in application. For most institutionalists, then, the test of their ideas is to be found in their application to the solution of social problems. This approach to knowledge also removes the traditional dichotomy between science and metaphysics. Obviously, theories can be judged effective or ineffective only when some objective or goal is specified, but more than this. Instrumentalism treats ideas concerning appropriate objectives in the same way as 'scientific' theories. Objectives (that may take the form of a set of values) are not ultimates but 'ends-in-view' and are themselves subject to appraisal and reappraisal on the basis of the consequences of the attempt to achieve them.

The exception to the above approach is Veblen, who was perhaps more influenced by Charles Peirce than by Dewey. For Peirce, the 'pragmatic maxim', with its focus on the practical consequences of an idea, was a way to establish the *meaning* of an idea, and not a test of acceptability. Indeed, Peirce was deeply opposed to the use of science for social engineering purposes. Although Veblen's detachment is sometimes exaggerated, he did see science as something to provide critical insight into the course of social evolution rather than as a tool to be used to control it (Ross, 1991). This, of course, is consistent with his emphasis on the unintended nature of fundamental institutional change.

Techniques of investigation

The more particular techniques of investigation developed by institutionalists can be seen as attempts to implement the general methodological principles outlined above. This does not mean that there is no diversity in the techniques utilized by different individuals. On the contrary, a variety of techniques can be found in the institutionalist literature, some still in use, some not. One can also find attempts to associate institutionalism with certain techniques that have never been adopted by institutionalists!

Each of the three founding figures of the institutionalist tradition used different approaches. Veblen's technique was to build a narrative account of institutions, their economic impact and evolution, out of available sources. For example, he made extensive use of the information contained within the *Report of the Industrial Commission*, but conducted few empirical investigations or case studies himself. Veblen's literary form of theorizing was, of course, common throughout the social sciences, but his lack of empirical investigation and checking of his conclusions was a factor that disturbed Wesley Mitchell. Mitchell saw the regularities in aggregate economic data as reflecting the standardizing influence of institutions on the behaviour of masses of individuals, and wished to utilize empirical data to examine the strengths and weaknesses of alternative hypotheses and define the explanatory task remaining to the theorist. In this he developed his notion of 'analytic description' which was designed to keep theorizing and concrete empirical investigation in the closest possible contact. These ideas are well displayed in Mitchell's work on business cycles, work that was also connected to his advocacy of national planning. Commons developed and refined his concepts and principles through a combination of wide reading in both law and economics, extensive case studies (including his monumental studies on American industrial society and trade union history) and practical involvement in mediation and in the drafting of legislation. He also pioneered the use of interview techniques in the attempt to understand the position of key players in a dispute or policy debate, and to help him to bring to bear his own considerable powers of 'negotiational psychology' in creating a resolution.

In the postwar period, Mitchell's quantitative techniques came under attack by Koopmans (1947) and others, and rapidly lost out, at least among more mainstream economists, to the techniques of econometric estimation being put forward by the Cowles Commission. Commons produced few followers in the academic world, but his particular blend of methods would, in any case, have been difficult to emulate. The tradition of literary theorizing continues, as does the use of case studies, but these are not unique to institutionalism. It has been claimed that institutionalists utilize especially the technique of 'participant observation' (Wilber and Harrison, 1978), but this is a claim that seems to confuse the broad institutionalist participation in efforts at social reform with the very specific technique of participatory field observation in sociology and anthropology, in which an observer joins and becomes an accepted member of a small social group in order to absorb and understand the group's norms and outlook. A survey of articles in the *Journal of Economic Issues* (Lind, 1993) found no significant use of interviews or surveys or of any other techniques not 'allowed' in mainstream economics, including participant observation. What has distinguished the work of institutionalists in the recent past is rather the rejection of formal mathematical modelling and econometrics in favour of informal pattern models and a more descriptive use of data. Whether this will continue as new methods of modelling evolutionary and dynamic processes are developed remains to be seen.

MALCOLM RUTHERFORD

Bibliography
Coase, Ronald H. (1984), 'The New Institutional Economics', *Journal of Institutional and Theoretical Economics*, **140**, March, 229–31.
Coats, A.W. (1954), 'The Influence of Veblen's Methodology', *Journal of Political Economy*, **62**, December, 529–37.
Commons, John R. (1934), *Institutional Economics: Its Place in Political Economy*, New Brunswick: Transaction.
Dugger, William M. (1979), 'Methodological Differences Between Institutional and Neoclassical Economics', *Journal of Economic Issues*, **13**, December, 899–909.
Gruchy, Allan G. (1947), *Modern Economic Thought: The American Contribution*, New York: Prentice-Hall.
Koopmans, Tjalling C. (1947), 'Measurement Without Theory', *Review of Economics and Statistics*, **29**, August, 161–72.
Lind, Hans (1993), 'The Myth of Institutionalist Method', *Journal of Economic Issues*, **27**, March, 1–17.
Mirowski, Philip (1987), 'The Philosophical Bases of Institutionalist Economics', *Journal of Economic Issues*, **21**, September, 1001–38.
Ramstad, Yngve (1986), 'A Pragmatist's Quest for Holistic Knowledge: The Scientific Methodology of John R. Commons', *Journal of Economic Issues*, **20**, December, 1067–1105.
Ross, Dorothy (1991), *The Origins of American Social Science*, Cambridge: Cambridge University Press.
Rutherford, Malcolm (1994), *Institutions in Economics: The Old and the New Institutionalism*, Cambridge: Cambridge University Press.

Veblen, Thorstein (1898), 'Why is Economics not an Evolutionary Science?', *The Place of Science in Modern Civilisation*, New York: Russell and Russell.
Wilber, Charles K. and Robert S. Harrison (1978), 'The Methodological Basis of Institutional Economics: Pattern Model, Storytelling and Holism', *Journal of Economic Issues*, **12**, March, 61–89.

Instrumentalism

In the philosophy of science, instrumentalism is usually understood as a view about the character of theories and the goals of theorizing. It is conventionally presented as the opponent of realism on these matters. This opposition has been variously put as one between theoretical concepts as fictions versus theoretical concepts as factually referential; theoretical claims as tools devoid of truth value versus theoretical claims as true or false assertions of the world; prediction versus explanation as the goal of theorizing; acceptance of a theory without belief in it versus acceptance of a theory presupposing belief; or merely entertaining a theory versus asserting its truth.

The concept itself – instrumentalism – derives from the concept of instrument. Hence theories are regarded as instruments for attaining a goal or a set of goals. On a very broad definition, we are all instrumentalists, since we all agree that theories are instruments for pursuing some goal or another. The ordinary notions of instrumentalism found in philosophy of science and economic methodology are more narrow as they impose restrictions upon the set of relevant goals. Typically, the excluded set of goals includes that of true representation by the theory itself (not to be confused with the hope that the predictive implications of the theory will be true representations of phenomena). Thus one is not an instrumentalist if one thinks that theories are or should be, among other things, true descriptions of the world.

Instrumentalism has a long history in the sciences and their philosophical commentaries. The ancient Greek distinction between physical and mathematical astronomy is a classical example, representatively put by Germinus in the first century BC: the task of physical astronomy is to give an account of the real substance of heavenly bodies and the causes of their movements, while mathematical astronomy is content with saving the phenomena by using expedient assumptions and providing calculations consistent with the data. Another example is Osiander's introduction to Copernicus' *Revolutionibus* (1543) which characterizes the theory as a calculation device, although most Copernicans are supposed to have held a realist interpretation of the theoretical claim that the earth revolves around the sun rather than vice versa. It should be added that all such examples taken from the history of science are subject to rival interpretations.

In economics, the label of instrumentalism has been used when characterizing the methodological positions of Milton Friedman and Fritz Machlup. It is also not uncommon to see the whole or a major part of neoclassical economics described in these terms. On the other hand, one tradition hostile to conventional neoclassical theory identifies itself as holding an instrumentalist position. This is a major strand of North American institutionalism, inspired by John Dewey's pragmatist instrumentalism. In order to see the differences between such positions, we have to be more specific about the various goals or purposes with respect to which scientific theories can serve as instruments and also about the alternative characterizations of these theory instruments themselves.

An instrumentalist characterizes scientific theories variously as tools, rules of inference, calculation devices and 'inference tickets', among other things. The relevant properties of theories then are pragmatic rather than semantic. Thus we are invited to assess theories as to their usefulness, convenience, tractability, fruitfulness, applicability and efficiency rather than their truth and falsehood. In consequence, in an empirical test, one tests the usefulness and applicability of scientific theories, not their truth.

To say that the relevant properties of theories are pragmatic rather than semantic is not to imply that theories do not have semantic properties. On this question, two versions suggest themselves. A more radical version of instrumentalism says that theories indeed do not have semantic properties at all. It say that theories and their terms do not – because they cannot – refer to anything real, nor do they have truth values: they are neither true nor false. For example, the term 'photon' does not have a real (non-fictional) referent and therefore apparent claims about photons cannot be true or false. Yet theories involving the term may be useful for certain purposes. One variety of this view subscribes to a dichotomy between observational and theoretical terms in the language of a science and suggests that theoretical terms – the building blocks of theories – do not refer because they do not refer to anything observable (and one can only refer to observables), while observational terms – not constituting theories – do refer. Within this framework, it may be held that, in so far as predictions are phrased in terms of the observational language, they do have truth values.

A more moderate version of instrumentalism says that theories do possess such semantic properties, but that these properties are irrelevant, the relevant properties being pragmatic. According to this version, it does not matter even if the terms of a theory fail to refer to anything real (even though they might so refer) or if the claims of a theory are false (even though they might be true). Referential and veristic success – even if possible – does not add to the value of a theory. Only the pragmatic virtues of theories matter. Methodological instrumentalism of this sort incorporates semantic realism about reference and truth.

Once these two versions have been distinguished from one another, it can be argued that Friedman's and Machlup's views (at least in so far as their commentaries on the theory of the perfectly competitive firms are concerned) can be distinguished in just these terms. Friedman's formulations imply that the assumptions of economic theory describe the world but, when taken as such descriptions, they are false. Machlup's formulations suggest that certain economic theories involve theoretical terms which do not refer to anything real – but only to imaginary fictions – and thus such theories are neither true nor false.

One of the benefits of instrumentalism is that it facilities dealing with theories or assumptions which are somehow puzzling, such as being counterintuitive, or as being contradicted by experiments or by other theories. The instrumentalist solution is to recommend a relaxed attitude towards such theories: it does not matter that theories appear to include such puzzling features; once we understand that theories are not intended as factual claims about reality, those features no longer appear as puzzling. Thus instrumentalism played a liberating role in the controversy over the Copernican suggestion: one can accept the heliocentric theory without violating the Scripture by denying the theory any factual status. Likewise, one may defend an economic theory whose assumptions appear to be at odds with experimental results or psychological theories by arguing that the theory or its assumptions were never intended to assert anything about the world.

One of the problems with some of the conventional notions of instrumentalism is that they tend to phrase the issue as dealing with theories and their properties without paying sufficient attention to different types of elements in theories, with such elements playing different roles. Of course, one of the traditional versions of instrumentalism was based on dividing the language of science into theoretical and observational parts and treating them differently: the theoretical part fictionalistically, the observational part realistically. One may argue that this is not the relevant or sound distinction, and that some other distinction is needed, such as one between major and minor elements in theories. It can then be suggested that considerations of truth are relevant mainly in regard to the major elements. This suggestion might be able to accommodate the fact that good scientific theories typically involve false elements. In other words, a sound realism might have to accommodate an element of moderate instrumentalism.

Consider, then, the goals with regard to which theories are taken to serve as instruments. Two distinctions among the set of possible goals seem relevant for understanding different types of instrumentalism. The first is between epistemic and non-epistemic goals. The second is between scientific and extrascientific goals. Not surprisingly, the sharpness of both distinctions can be easily challenged.

One major form of instrumentalism is usually defined in terms of goals which are epistemic and scientific. This is the view that theories are instruments for predicting phenomena. The idea can be put more generally in terms of systematization (organization, summary) of data, including both prediction and retrodiction. The goal here is epistemic in that it consists in predictive knowledge, for example. The goal is scientific in that its pursuit is part of scientific practice. It is important to understand that putting an emphasis on prediction does not define instrumentalism: it is neither necessary nor sufficient for an instrumentalist position. Holding the view that good theories are predictively powerful and that theories are to be assessed in terms of their predictive power does not yet make one an instrumentalist. A non-realist view of the character of theory instruments is also needed. Within economics and economic methodology, this predictivist form of instrumentalism is customarily attributed to the metatheoretical formulations of Friedman and Machlup.

The goals can also be non-epistemic and scientific. To take an extreme example, if scientific theories are taken to be instruments for generating aesthetic pleasure for scientists, one holds a peculiar form of non-epistemic instrumentalism. Another form would hold that theories are problem-solving tools, instruments for solving scientific problems of various sorts. Sometimes aspects of theorizing in economic research practice are characterized in ways which may be translated in such terms.

Some forms of instrumentalism are based on the idea that the goals with respect to which theories are instruments are non-epistemic and extrascientific. Darwinian versions of this idea may straightforwardly hold that scientific theories are instruments of survival – not of scientists but of the species of humans. The goals may also be variously specified as maximum happiness or well-being, or minimum suffering of people at large, effective control or management, or simply extrascientific problem solving. In the context of economics, an obvious view is that it is the task of theories to help reach whatever goals have been set for economic policy. A variation of the Darwinian form of instrumentalism has gained popularity within the North American tradition of institutionalist economics through John Dewey's philosophy. Ideas – theories and values – are here conceived as evolving and context-dependent instruments for social problem solving.

Holding the view that it is the task of theories to help attain non-epistemic goals does not as such make one an epistemic instrumentalist. In other words, one may insist that good theories are good tools for scientific or extrascientific problem solving without accepting the view that theories do not have semantic properties or that whatever semantic properties they have is irrelevant. It is possible to combine epistemic realism and non-epistemic instrumentalism by suggesting that, the more truthful a theory, the more reliable it is in problem solving.

One of the problems of standard forms of instrumentalism is that they discourage scientists from raising certain kinds of questions, namely questions about the reasons why a given theory either possesses or fails to possess certain pragmatic virtues, why it either serves or fails to serve the attainment of certain goals. In contrast, a realist would encourage scientists not to stop asking such questions, and would suggest that considerations of the semantic properties of a theory – its referential status and truthfulness – might be relevant for accounting for pragmatic success and failure (even though the link is far from unambiguous).

USKALI MÄKI

Bibliography

Boland, Lawrence (1979), 'A critique of Friedman's critics', *Journal of Economic Literature*, **17**, 503–22.
Caldwell, Bruce (1992), 'Friedman's predictivist instrumentalism – A modification', *Research in the History of Economic Thought and Methodology*, **10**, 119–28.
Dennis, Ken (1986), 'Boland on Friedman: A rebuttal', *Journal of Economic Issues*, **20**, 633–60.
Friedman, Milton (1953), *Essays in Positive Economics*, Chicago, University of Chicago Press.
Machlup, Fritz (1955), 'The Problem of Verification in Economics', *Southern Economic Journal*, **22**, 1–21.
Mäki, Uskali (1992), 'Friedman and realism', *Research in the History of Economic Thought and Methodology*, **10**, 171–95.
Morgenbesser, Sidney (1969), 'The realist–instrumentalist controversy', in S. Morgenbesser *et al.* (eds), *Philosophy, Science, and Method: Essays in Honor of Ernest Nagel*, New York: St Martin's Press.
Nagel, Ernest (1961), *The Structure of Science*, New York: Harcourt Brace.
Popper, Karl (1963), *Conjectures and Refutations*, London: Routledge & Kegan Paul.

Invisible Hand, The

The notion of the invisible hand enjoys great prominence in economic thought, particularly in more popular presentations. The best way to introduce it may be to go back to the first presentation of the idea in Adam Smith, to identify the main features of the invisible hand in that presentation, and then to examine how far those features are found both in current paradigms of the invisible hand and in current variations on those paradigms.

Adam Smith (1982: 184–5) first spoke of the invisible hand in his comment on 'the proud and unfeeling landlord':

> The capacity of his stomach bears no proportion to the immensity of his desires, and will receive no more than that of the meanest peasant. The rest he is obliged to distribute among those, who prepare, in the nicest manner, that little which he himself makes use of, among those who fit up the palace in which this little is to be consumed, among those who provide and keep in order all the different baubles and trinkets, which are employed in the economy of greatness; all of whom thus derive from his luxury and caprice, that share of the necessaries of life, which they would in vain have expected from his humanity or his justice. … [The rich] are led by an invisible hand to make nearly the same distribution of the necessaries of life, which would have been made, had the earth been divided into equal proportions among all its inhabitants, and thus without intending it, without knowing it, advance the interest of the society, and afford means to the multiplication of the species.

This example displays three features which distinguish the central cases of invisible hand organisation (Nozick, 1974; Ullmann-Margalit, 1978; Elster, 1983). An aggregate pattern is collectively produced by the efforts of certain agents: here the rich man and his employees. But the product and mode of production are highly distinctive. First, the pattern produced is presumed to be socially desirable: the equal distribution of necessaries is associated, in Smith's words, with the cause of humanity and justice. Second, the agents collectively produce that pattern despite being each individually oriented towards quite a different end: the rich man towards his gratification, the employees towards a means of making their living. And third, the orientation of the agents to that end has high explanatory potential; it explains not just the continuation of that pattern but also its emergence: we are told how an equal distribution of necessaries must have begun to materialize, not just why it may be expected to continue.

The three features mentioned involve, respectively, desirability, non-intentionality and explanatory power. Those features are replicated in other examples that are often taken as paradigms of the invisible hand. Take the case of bargaining among two or more parties. As each bargainer tries to get others to do what they want, at the least concession possible from themselves, they collectively produce an aggregate pattern of redistribution. And the process involved satisfies the invisible hand features. It is socially desirable, at least by Paretian standards: some people have their preferences further satisfied – perhaps this is true of all – while none have their preferences further frustrated. The parties produce the pattern despite the fact that they are each oriented towards something other than an overall Pareto-improvement: namely, their own advantage. And this orientation is powerfully explanatory: it serves to explain not just why they stick by that pattern but how it came about in the first place.

For a second example, consider how politicians rely on electoral support to continue in office and how they allegedly respond to lobbying pressures from various interest groups. Interest group pluralism suggests that, as the different interest groups each form their own lobby and as politicians try to respond to lobbying pressures in a way that does most for the prospect of their re-election, they combine to produce a result under which lobbying interests are satisfied in roughly the proportion of their social presence. If the theory is correct, again we see an invisible hand at work. The pattern of interest satisfaction produced is socially desirable to the extent that it represents a sort of fairness. The parties involved produce it despite the fact of each being oriented towards a different end: their own re-election or the representation of their particular interest; and that orientation can explain, not just the continuity of the pattern, but the fact of its emergence.

The three features are also found in perhaps the best-known example of the invisible hand: the competitive market mechanism whereby producers are drawn, so it is alleged, to sell at the competitive level where price equals marginal cost of production. The assumption is that each producer is self-interested and rational and that in any area of production new producers are free to enter at any time. This means that in each area of production everyone will be better off if all cooperate in fixing a price than if all defect, but that defection will always be better for each than sticking with any agreed non-competitive price: defection will promise to increase that individual's share of the market more than is sufficient to compensate for the lower price they charge. Each area of production will involve a free-rider problem and, as the individual purchasers seek to free-ride on the fidelity of others to any agreed price, they will force the price down to the lowest at which producers can stay in business. The idea is that in a competitive market the price of every good produced will be forced down to marginal cost and everyone will share in that assumed public benefit.

It is clear that the three features of desirablity, non-intentionality and explanatory power are as much in evidence here as in our earlier examples of the invisible hand. The pattern of pricing produced is socially desirable by criteria accepted on all sides of economics. The pattern is produced in a non-intentional way, with each of the agents involved being oriented to something quite distinct from the good of competitive pricing. And the way in which that pattern is produced is supposed to be able to explain, not just the continuation of the pattern, but its emergence in the first place.

But if we are to understand the invisible hand, it is important to recognize that, as the paradigm examples satisfy the three constraints associated with desirability, non-intentionality and explanatory power, so there are peripheral cases where one or more of the constraints are not properly fulfilled. When desirability fails, we have a mechanism that is sometimes described, not as an invisible hand, but as an invisible backhand (Hardin, 1982). The most prominent general case of this phenomenon is the unsolved collective action problem: most notably, the *n*-person prisoner's dilemma. For a particularly telling case, consider T.C. Schelling's story as to how total residential segregation – something we may take to be socially undesirable – can come about, whether between blacks and whites, Catholics and Protestants, or whatever other groups (Schelling, 1969). Each party in a mixed neighbourhood has eight neighbours, as a square on a draughtsboard has eight adjacent squares. Suppose that each comes to be dissatisfied with a situation where there are fewer than four of their kind among their immediate neighbours. A little experiment on a draughtsboard shows that, if each party assumes this not particularly bigoted motivation then, as by an invisible backhand, a short sequence of moves will lead to total segregation. Those parties in unsatisfactory situations will move and by moving they will make the situations of other parties unsatisfactory, so that they move too: and so on, to the point where there is nearly total segregation.

The second constraint on the invisible hand is non-intentionality: the parties are each oriented towards a different end from the pattern that they collectively produce. It is because of this different orientation that they do not have to be aware of the pattern involved: that the pattern is not necessarily visible, even if it fails to be necessarily not visible: even if it fails to be strictly invisible. How can this constraint be violated, given that it is tied up with what earns its name for the invisible hand? Standard invisible hand mechanisms require agents to do something intentionally – say, to pursue their own private ends – and in doing that to help non-intentionally to bring about the relevant collective pattern; the actions pursued in the name of their own intentional ends serve, accidentally as it were, to produce that pattern. But not only may people bring about a collective pattern in virtue of actions that are non-intentional in relation to that end, intentional in relation to another, they may also bring about a collective pattern in virtue of responses that are entirely unintentional: responses, such as the formation of an opinion, that involve nothing like an action.

This way of varying the non-intentionality constraint points us towards what has been described as 'the intangible hand' (Brennan and Pettit, 1993; Pettit, 1993). Suppose that it is a matter of common belief among people that they subscribe to certain standards of behaviour, and suppose that it is also a matter of common belief among them that, if they comply, they are likely to be noticed complying and if they deviate, they are likely to be noticed deviating. On the assumption that people care about the good opinion of others, there is every reason to expect in such a situation that they will police one another into complying with the behaviour that attracts approval. Create situations in which people know what is expected, and know that it will be obvious whether or not they satisfy those expectations, and you will have created a situation where people may satisfy expectations out of a desire to attain a good opinion in the minds of others (Pettit, 1990).

The third constraint on the paradigm invisible hand is associated with the fact that it makes it possible to explain both the emergence and the continuation of the behaviour in question. But here, too, variation is possible. There are many cases of invisible hand mechanisms that serve to explain, not how a pattern of behaviour emerged, but why it is sustained. Consider those explanations for a pattern like universal truth-telling stabilizing which suppose that people follow a strategy like tit-for-tat: tell the truth in the first round of any encounter with another and after that do whatever they did in the previous round (see Taylor, 1987; Hardin, 1982; Axelrod, 1984; Sugden, 1986). Such accounts will not explain why universal truth-telling emerged but they may explain why it persists: if everyone follows the tit-for-tat strategy, then, under plausible assumptions, no one can expect to gain a benefit by unilaterally departing from that strategy.

Not only can invisible hand mechanisms explain persistence but fail to explain emergence. They may be weaker still in explaining only the resilience or robustness of a certain pattern: only the capacity of the pattern to survive various more or less likely contingencies. Consider the explanatory import of David Lewis' (1969) observation that conventions often serve people well in enabling them to solve coordination predicaments: they lead people to act in complementary ways in situations where no one minds what they do, provided their behaviour is complementary to others'; no one minds which side of the road they drive on, provided all drive on the right or all on the left, and so on. This story would retain explanatory relevance even in cases where people actually developed conventional behaviour, and actually sustained conventional behaviour, without reference to such predicaments: even in cases, for example, where they sustain the behaviour in a wholly unthinking, habitual way. For it directs us to the fact that under any of those contingencies where individuals might be tempted to deviate they would soon see their mistake and return to the pattern involved; that pattern has an important resilience over the contingencies in question (Pettit, 1995).

PHILIP PETTIT

References
Axelrod, Robert (1984), *The Evolution of Cooperation*, New York: Basic Books.
Brennan, Geoffrey and Philip Pettit (1993), 'Hands Invisible and Intangible', *Synthèse*, **94**, 191–225.
Elster, Jon (1983), *Sour Grapes*, Cambridge: Cambridge University Press.
Hardin, Russell (1982), *Collective Action*, London: Johns Hopkins University Press.
Lewis, David (1969), *Convention*, Cambridge, MA.: Harvard University Press.
Nozick, Robert (1974), *Anarchy, State and Utopia*, New York: Basic Books.
Pettit, Philip (1990), '*Virtus Normativa*: Rational Choice Perspectives', *Ethics*, **100**, 725–55.
Pettit, Philip (1993), *The Common Mind: An Essay on Psychology, Society and Politics*, New York: Oxford University Press.
Pettit, Philip (1995), 'The Economic Mind: *Homo Economicus* as Virtual Reality', *Monist*, **78**, 308–29
Schelling, T.C. (1969), 'Models of Segregation', *American Economic Review*, **59**, 488–93.
Smith, Adam (1982), *The Theory of the Moral Sentiments*, ed. D.D. Raphael and A.L. Macfie, Indianapolis: Liberty Classics.
Sugden, Robert (1986), *The Economics of Rights. Cooperation and Welfare*, Oxford: Blackwell.
Taylor, Michael (1987), *The Possibility of Cooperation*, Cambridge: Cambridge University Press.
Ullmann-Margalit, Edna (1978), 'Invisible-hand Explanations', *Synthèse*, **39**, 262–91.

Jevons, William Stanley

It is difficult to think of a major economist more versatile and original than Jevons (1835–82). In addition to significant contributions in theoretical and applied economics, logic and the philosophy of science, he wrote frequently on the social debates of his time and published numerous scientific articles, some of which contained fundamental breakthroughs, on meteorology, mechanics, astronomy, biology, geology and mathematics. Born in Liverpool, he studied mathematics and the natural sciences at University College London. After five years of work as an assayer in Sydney, Australia, Jevons returned to London to study political economy. His academic career took him first to Owens College Manchester, where he worked his way up from tutor to professor, and then, in 1876, to London as Professor of Political Economy at University College. Poor health led him to resign in 1881 and he died the following year in a drowning accident.

Jevons is best known for his *Theory of Political Economy* (1871) which, together with the works of Carl Menger and Léon Walras, unleashed the Marginal Revolution in economic thought. He considered his *Principles of Science* (1874), however, to be the most important of his dozen books. Although it contains very little on economics per se, its insights into logic and scientific methodology had direct bearing on his programme to mathematize the subject.

Jevons was one of the first to advance the logicist view, later associated with Bertrand Russell and A.N. Whitehead, that mathematics could be reduced via the concept of number to logic. One of his first books, *Pure Logic* (1863), assimilated and revised the formal sentential logic set out by Augustus De Morgan and George Boole. Jevons devised his own system of notation and interpretation of the main operations, some of which, the inclusive reading of the disjunctive for example, became orthodox. His subsequent textbooks, *Elementary Lessons in Logic: Deductive and Inductive* (1870), *Primer of Logic* (1876) and *Studies in Deductive Logic* (1880), were widely translated and extensively used well into the early part of the twentieth century. Jevons' mechanistic approach to logic also inspired him to construct a logical piano, now viewed as an early progenitor of the electronic computer.

Jevons was a strict empiricist in the tradition of Bacon, Locke and Hume: scientific inquiry begins and ends with observation, guided by analogies. Nevertheless, he was much more sceptical about the ability of scientists to comprehend physical nature than many of his predecessors. He challenged J.S. Mill's faith in the uniformity of nature and echoed Hume's caveats about induction: nature is simply too mysterious and complex for our feeble methods of investigation and we can never do more than treat a small fraction of its phenomena. While Jevons never really questioned the belief that scientific knowledge had progressed, he kept in view its fragility. Apprised of non-Euclidean geometry, for example, Jevons emphasized that even mathematics was no longer the royal road to certainty.

In economics, Jevons was a self-proclaimed revolutionary who sought to overturn the classical doctrine of Ricardo and Mill and put in its place a mathematical theory predicated on a utility theory of value. To motivate these changes, he argued that, in so far as economics deals with quantitative phenomena, prices and the like, it is necessarily mathematical. Previous economists had reasoned mathematically without realizing it, but the time had come to make explicit the proper language of the discipline and to use it to generate new insights. Jevons could proudly point to the principle of diminishing marginal utility, which he among others at the time independently discovered and which introduced the differential calculus to economics.

Like Mill, Jevons maintained that what is now termed the hypothetico-deductive method of Newtonian physics was best suited to economics. He recognized that, as a species of induction, however, this method did not preclude subsequent revisions of a given hypothesis. Hope that one was working in the right direction lay in the overarching unity of science and in the eventual reduction of the world we experience to atomic configurations. Jevons drew not only methodological analogies between physics and economics, but conceptual ones as well, for example the distinction between statics and dynamics in price movements and the notion of the mind as a pendulum or a lever in equilibrium. One highly original foray was his work on dimensions for economic variables, the equivalents to mass and time in physics. These analogies might be viewed as unwarranted attempts to dress economics up in the garb of physics and thereby purchase greater certainty and exactitude, but for Jevons there was a deep conviction that the mind ultimately was mechanistic and mathematical in its operations.

Jevons was a strong proponent of probability and statistics and sought applications of these methods in his economics. He defined probability as a process of forming rational expectations of future events, although he steered away from the frequentist approach because of its overly contingent character. In this respect, his views accord with the rationalist line later developed by John Maynard Keynes. His work on devising an index for the value of gold was pathbreaking, and his efforts to link the business cycle to the cycle of sunspots, while often ridiculed, nonetheless exemplify his strong bent for statistical inference. Jevons also undertook the construction of demand curves, although he had doubts about their linearity. He firmly believed that, once the mathematical theory of economics was fully developed, the abundant data to be found in the accountant's office would amply verify its basic principles. Of critical importance to his programme was the view that mathematics per se did nothing to augment the certainty or exactitude of the theoretical claims: mathematical functions served to highlight the quantitative degree of approximation between fact and theory, but only by obtaining more empirical evidence itself could one enhance the veracity of a given claim.

In sum, Jevons offers us a radically new conception of economics (and was one of the first to insist on dropping the adjective 'political'). His economic theory is grounded in methodological individualism and Benthamite psychology; even capital and labour are construed subjectively. And every effort should be made to render explicit the mathematical character of economic theory. This would also serve to highlight the universal and ahistorical nature of the central problem of economics, namely the maximization of utility subject to given physical constraints.

MARGARET SCHABAS

Bibliography

Aldrich, John (1987), 'Jevons as Statistician: The Role of Probability', *Manchester School*, **40**, 233–57.
Bostaph, Samuel and Yeung-Nan Shieh (1987), 'Jevons's Demand Curve', *History of Political Economy*, **19**, 107–26.
Peart, Sandra J. (1993), 'W.S. Jevons's Methodology of Economics: Some Implications of the Procedures for "Inductive Quantification"', *History of Political Economy*, **25**, 435–60.
Schabas, Margaret (1990), *A World Ruled by Number: William Stanley Jevons and the Rise of Mathematical Economics*, Princeton: Princeton University Press.
Stigler, Stephen M. (1982), 'Jevons as Statistician', *The Manchester School*, **50**, 354–65.
White, Michael (1989), 'Why are there no supply and Demand Curves in Jevons?', *History of Political Economy*, **21**, 425–56.

Keynes, John Maynard

J.M. Keynes (1883–1946) was the best known economist of the twentieth century, and for good reason. His 'struggle to escape' the confines of what he called classical economics did not simply parallel, but rather actively promoted, the transition of the major industrial economies from the Depression and malaise of the 1930s to the brave new postwar world of full employment and opportunity. Keynes' scholarly career began in earnest in 1921 with the publication of his *Treatise on Probability*; other milestones were his *Treatise on Money* of 1930 and his magnum opus of 1936, *The General Theory of Employment, Interest and Money*. But besides his academic works, strictly so called, Keynes' fame and influence rested on a long series of writings designed to educate and persuade the more general reader on the burning topics of the day – from his brilliant account of *The Economic Consequences of the Peace* following World War I to his incisive analysis of *How to Pay for the War* in the course of World War II – as well, of course, as his tireless personal involvement in public life. More than for any other economist, a thumbnail sketch must completely fail to do justice to the many facets of Keynes' life and work, but fortunately he has been well served by his biographers (most notably Roy Harrod, Robert Skidelsky and Donald Moggridge).

   Keynes' work provides a perennial source of fascination for methodologists and philosophers of economics, for two main reasons. First, Keynes thought he was making a revolution in economic theory with his *General Theory*, yet even before his book was published there began an intense debate over the nature and significance of this putative revolution. Having passed through many phases, this debate remains alive. Economists are still divided on the validity of Keynes' claims; and among those who accept them as broadly valid, there is still disagreement over which aspect of his theory is, so to speak, the 'active ingredient', primarily responsible for justifying his view that, in the absence of intelligent government intervention, capitalist economies tend typically to operate in a state of underemployment equilibrium (candidates include wage- or price-stickiness, fundamental uncertainty and the 'essential properties of interest and money'). Second, as the literature of the last decade has reminded us, Keynes began his academic career as a philosopher of probability. It is plausible that there may be a connection between his economics and his distinctive philosophical views, and some have argued that the key to a proper understanding of the former lies in the latter. For these reasons the discussion of Keynes' economics has a natural tendency to run into 'foundational' issues.

   In the interest of carving out a manageable topic, a threefold distinction will be made below between method, methodology and philosophy. By Keynes' method is meant the sorts of arguments and reasoning used in his economic writings; by his methodology, his explicit statements regarding how economics should be done and why; and by his philosophy, (primarily) his general conception of probability and uncertainty and their role in economic life. The three fields so demarcated are highly interconnected, but we will concentrate on the second – Keynes' methodology as such – after offering a few brief remarks on the third. (A good bibliography on the first field is found in Littleboy, 1990.)

   Unlike his father, Neville, Maynard Keynes did not leave us a substantial treatise on economic philosophy or methodology. Compounding both the problem and the interest of interpretation is the fact that, although Keynes made several allusions, in his later writings, to his earlier work on probability, he never returned to a systematic reworking of those ideas, while he did indicate that he recognized the force of Frank Ramsey's critique of his *Treatise on Probability*, and in the memoir *My Early Beliefs* gave the impression of distancing himself quite substantially from his early philosophical positions. There has therefore been a vigorous debate over the degree of continuity in Keynes' philosophical conceptions. Anna Carabelli (1988) and Rod O'Donnell (1989) have both argued for a substantial continuity, claiming that Keynes' concession to Ramsey should not be taken at face value. Bradley Bateman (1987) and John Davis (1994) have made, in somewhat different ways, the contrary claim that Keynes came to abandon a good deal of what was most distinctive in his early philosophy. Bateman has Keynes coming to accept an empiricist philosophy (as opposed to his early rationalism), while Davis argues that the Platonistic strand in Keynes' early philosophy was replaced by socially informed conceptions of 'intuition' and 'convention' that display some similarity with the later Wittgenstein. Runde (1994) takes the view that Keynes abandoned the ontology of logical probability relations between propositions, perceptible via the faculty of intuition, but continued to regard qualitative (non-quantifiable) probability comparisons as basic to epistemic probability.

Whatever position one takes on these debates, it seems clear that Keynes' economics does carry a particular philosophical charge. One of his central objections to 'classical economics' concerned its dichotomy between the 'real' and the 'monetary' sides of the economy; for Keynes money was not a veil, but rather a fully integral aspect of a market economy. Keynes (1936: 293) took his stand in favour of a theory of 'shifting equilibrium – meaning by the latter the theory of a system in which changing views about the future are capable of influencing the present situation. *For the importance of money essentially flows from its being a link between the present and the future.*' He insisted that economic analysis be directed towards a 'real world in which our previous expectations are liable to disappointment and expectations concerning the future affect what we do to-day' (ibid.: 293–4). However the link may be explicated in detail, these statements clearly echo, in a broad sense, his early concern with matters of probability and uncertainty and their centrality to the human condition.

The continuity of Keynes' philosophical views may be in question, but in at least one important respect there is substantial continuity in his methodological views: his marked scepticism regarding quantification and formalization, mathematics and statistics. From the early drafts of the *Treatise on Probability*, via the methodological remarks in *The General Theory*, to his critique of Tinbergen's econometric studies in the late 1930s, Keynes consistently criticizes what he regards as inappropriate attempts to quantify or formalize domains of study whose inherent nature makes such procedures problematic. With regard to probability relations, he insisted that these can be assigned numerical values only in special cases, common in the statistics textbooks but uncommon in the real world. Worse, in many cases probabilities cannot even be compared in terms of lesser or greater – this, too, demands particular conditions which are not always met. Carabelli (1992) has argued that the same principles underlie Keynes' refusal (announced in Chapter 4 of *The General Theory*) to employ a conception of aggregate real output as such, and his decision to restrict himself to the two basic units, namely employment and sums of money, which he considered genuinely quantifiable.

As for mathematical formalism, Keynes' scepticism may be partly attributed to his Marshallian heritage (see his memorial of Marshall in Keynes, 1972), but he provided a more fully articulated objection to the overuse of mathematics than his one-time mentor, notably in *The General Theory* (Keynes, 1936: 297–8) and his remarks to Roy Harrod on economics as a moral science (Keynes, 1973: 295–300). Keynes tells us that economics is a 'science of thinking in terms of models joined to the art of choosing models which are relevant to the contemporary world. It is compelled to be this, because, unlike the typical natural science, the material to which it is applied is, in too many respects, not homogeneous through time' (ibid.: 296). He goes on to say that economics necessarily deals with 'introspection and with values', with 'motives, expectations, psychological uncertainties. One has to be constantly on guard against treating the material as constant and homogeneous' (ibid.: 300). Keynes evidently believed that algebraic and statistical methods, while they are powerful tools where properly applicable, inherently bias the economist toward suppressing the essential complexity of his subject matter.

In Keynes' own economic work, there is some mathematics (in Chapters 20 and 21 of *The General Theory*, for instance), but for the most part this is restricted to the manipulation of identities. While willing to write down equations (in general function form) by way of illustration of some of the behavioural relationships he posited, he stopped short of working these up into a system of simultaneous equations. Consistent with the foregoing, Keynes' critique of Tinbergen (for contrasting views on the merits of which see Tony Lawson, 1989; Mary Morgan, 1990) makes it clear that he did not believe that the material of economics exhibits enough stability and homogeneity over time to license the application of formal statistical methods. In his own economic work, he cites tables of data for various purposes but never does any formal statistics: as his remarks to Harrod indicate, this was not just a matter of personal preference, or a case of division of intellectual labour, but a matter of theoretical principle.

It is noteworthy that, even in the heyday of Keynesian economics in the postwar period, very few economists accepted these distinctive methodological proscriptions. Rather, they busied themselves with constructing formal models based on what they took to be the central substantive insights of *The General Theory* – mostly variants of Hicks' SI–LL system (now better known as IS–LM) – and, before long, with the building of Keynesian macroeconometric models for forecasting and policy evaluation purposes. Neither has any prominent postwar Keynesian shared Keynes' scruples regarding the aggregation of 'real output' in the context of short-run macrotheory; at most, theorists have wanted to distinguish between the output of consumer goods in general and that of investment goods in general. And few have found Keynes' procedure of working in terms of 'wage-units' particularly attractive. On the first of these points, there has, of course, been considerable debate. Members of the Post Keynesian school (for example, Paul Davidson, 1991) have argued that the temptations of formalization have been to the detriment of the Keynesian heritage, resulting in the effacement of important substantive elements of his theory – particularly those relating to the role of incalculable uncertainty in economic life, as stressed by Keynes in his post-*General Theory* writings. From the same viewpoint, the store set by Keynesian macroeconometric models may be seen as hubris, whose nemesis came in the form of the widespread rejection of Keynesian economics in general following the breakdown of the predictive ability of such models in the 1970s.

At any rate, amidst the incalculable uncertainties of intellectual life, we can be sure that the debate over Keynes' methodological views, as over his economics and philosophy, will continue for a long time to come.

ALLIN COTTRELL

References

Bateman, Bradley (1987), 'Keynes's Changing Conception of Probability', *Economics and Philosophy*, **3**, 97–119.
Carabelli, Anna (1988), *On Keynes's Method*, New York: St Martin's Press.
Carabelli, Anna (1992), 'Organic Interdependence and the Choice of Units in the General Theory,' in B. Gerrard and K. Hillard (eds), *The Philosophy and Economics of J.M. Keynes*, Aldershot: Edward Elgar.
Davidson, Paul (1991), *Money and Employment, Collected Writings*, vol. 1, New York: New York University Press.
Davis, John B. (1994), *Keynes's Philosophical Development*, Cambridge: Cambridge University Press.

Keynes, J.M. (1936), *The General Theory of Employment, Interest and Money*, London: Macmillan.
Keynes, J.M. (1972), *Essays in Biography, Collected Writings*, vol. X, ed. D.E. Moggridge, London: Macmillan for the Royal Economic Society.
Keynes, J.M. (1973), *The General Theory and After: Part II, Defence and Development, Collected Writings*, vol. XIV, ed. D.E. Moggridge, London: Macmillan for the Royal Economic Society.
Lawson, Tony (1989), 'Realism and Instrumentalism in the Development of Econometrics', *Oxford Economic Papers*, **41**, (1), 236–58.
Littleboy, Bruce (1990), *On Interpreting Keynes*, London/New York: Routledge.
Morgan, Mary (1990), *The History of Econometric Ideas*, Cambridge: Cambridge University Press.
O'Donnell, Rod (1989), *Keynes: Philosophy, Economics and Politics*, New York: St Martin's Press.
Runde, Jochen (1994), 'Keynes After Ramsey: In Defence of *A Treatise on Probability*', *Studies in History and Philosophy of Science*, **25**, 1–25.

Keynes, John Neville

In 1876, when Neville Keynes (1852–1949) graduated in moral sciences at the University of Cambridge, and began to teach logic and political economy there, the latter subject had acquired a dismal academic reputation. Its leading student text was still J.S. Mill (1848), which synthesized doctrines drawn from Smith, Malthus and Ricardo and presented the mix as an established orthodoxy; but that orthodoxy came under wide-ranging attack in England in the 1860s and 1870s. Policy makers and social reformers, for example, criticized its doctrinaire allegiance to the principles of laissez-faire and its failure to address the ethical problems posed by industrialization. Academics concerned to advance their scientific understanding of changing economic systems had begun to question the basic premises and analytical techniques of classical political economy. Mill (1869) had himself opened the first serious breach in its methodological foundations by recanting the classical wage-fund doctrine in the course of a book review published in a reputable periodical. Even J.E. Cairnes (often described as 'the last of the classical economists') began a definitive statement of economic methods by lamenting 'the present oscillating and unscientific condition of the science in respect of fundamental principles' (Cairnes, 1875).

The methodological critique of classical political economy polarized in the 1870s as the proponents of diametrically opposite approaches claimed ultimate scientific validity for their analytical techniques. On the one hand, there were the historical economists who claimed to be following the method of the natural sciences in adopting a strictly inductive approach to the pursuit of economic truth and condemned Ricardo's hypothetico-deductive theorizing. On the other hand there were the mathematical economists such as Jevons (a natural scientist by training) who spurned 'the noxious influence of authority' (Jevons, 1871) and set out to reconstruct economic theory on appropriate mathematical foundations.

By the 1880s, however, a new generation of political economists – of whom J.N. Keynes was one – was emerging into international prominence and bypassing the current *Methodenstreit*. They shared a conviction that they had inherited a logical system of economic ideas which was still advancing in explanatory power. Economists such as Wagner in Germany, Cossa in Italy, Menger in Austria and Ely in the United States all advocated a judicious blend of empirical and theoretical, inductive and deductive, techniques of analysis as the proper foundation for a progressive scientific economics. In England, Alfred Marshall was the acknowledged leader of the self-styled 'new school of political economy' (Foxwell, 1887). He had taught Keynes as an undergraduate and, before returning to Cambridge as its professor of political economy in 1885, was regularly sending him draft chapters of his forthcoming magnum opus (Marshall,

1890) for comment and criticism. Keynes himself had already published a textbook on logic (Keynes, 1884) when he began to work on what he then called the 'logic of political economy' or the 'true principles of economic method'. His second book (Keynes, 1891) developed out of a course of lectures on the scope and method of political economy that he had delivered at Oxford in 1885, to the class which Marshall had just abandoned in order to take up the Cambridge chair. With this carefully researched monograph, Keynes effectively laid to rest the confused, long-running debate between the critics of, and the apologists for, classical political economy by writing a definitive methodological text for the new political economy that assumed the mantle of economic science in the 1890s.

Keynes began his monograph by reviewing the recent methodological debates in terms of two polar views of the scope and method of the discipline – one seeing it as a positive, abstract and deductive science, the other as an ethical, realistic and inductive science – and by claiming that it was all of these things. He then set out to demonstrate in systematic detail that the appropriate method of analysis could be either abstract or realistic, deductive or inductive, mathematical or statistical, hypothetical or historical according to the object of the investigation. In defining the hard core of economic theory as a pure science and in distinguishing it from applications of theory, which came closer to art than to science, Keynes was following Mill (for example, Mill, 1843) among others. He went further than his predecessors, however, by dividing political economy into three separate compartments: (1) 'a positive science', that is 'a body of systematized knowledge concerning what is'; (2) 'a normative or regulative science', that is 'a body of systematized knowledge relating to criteria of what ought to be and concerned therefore with the ideal as distinguished from the actual'; and (3) 'an art as a system of rules for the attainment of a given end' (Keynes, 1930: 34–5).

From this perspective, the economist's policy prescriptions are seen to be shaped by his knowledge of the economic laws derived from positive science and of moral laws or ideals derived from normative science, without being wholly dependent on either. In effect, this system of classification permitted the theoretical economist to insulate his fundamental theorems from accusations of ideological bias, or immorality or relativity, as well as from the failures of practical economic policies.

Keynes went on to explain and defend, with the authority that comes from consensus, the method which the new generation of economists regarded as central to scientific political economy, that is the hypothetico-deductive technique of analysis. After arguing, for example, that 'all sciences of causation and pre-eminently sciences employing the deductive method – including political economy and astronomy – contain a hypothetical element' (Keynes, 1930: 218), he insisted that the real strength of the hypothetico-deductive technique lay in its inductive element, and that political economy 'must both begin with observation and end with observation'. As Keynes showed, this broad methodological approach enabled the new political economy, on the one hand, to embody the latest research results of economic historians, and, on the other, to take advantage both of the growing mass of economic statistics produced to inform governmental agencies and of new statistical techniques devised in response to the needs of other developing scientific disciplines.

Keynes' *Scope and Method of Political Economy* attracted generally favourable reviews both at home and abroad. In his own country, the consensus among leading theorists rapidly insulated it from controversy so that it was read only by those who needed to recall exactly where the neoclassical orthodoxy scored over its classical predecessors. The next methodological treatise to attract attention in England was Robbins' *Nature and Significance of Economic Science* (1932), which related to a different era in the development of economic ideas, when Neville Keynes' son, Maynard, was leading current debates on alternative techniques of economic analysis.

PHYLLIS DEANE

Bibliography
Cairnes, J.E. (1875), *The Character and Logical Method of Political Economy*, 2nd edn, London: Macmillan.
Cossa, L. (1876), *Guide to the Study of Political Economy*, edited and introduced by W.S. Jevons in an English translation of 2nd Italian edn, London: Macmillan, 1880.
Ely, R.T. (1884), *The Past and Present of Political Economy*, Baltimore: N. Murray for Johns Hopkins.
Foxwell, H.S. (1887), 'The economic movement in England', *Quarterly Journal of Economics*, October.
Jevons, W.S. (1871), *The Theory of Political Economy*, London: Macmillan.
Keynes, J.N. (1884), *Studies and Exercises in Formal Logic*, London: Macmillan.
Keynes, J.N. (1891), *The Scope and Method of Political Economy*, London; 4th edn 1917 reprinted 1930 in LSE Economic Classics.
Marshall, A. (1890), *Principles of Economics*, London: Macmillan.
Mill, J.S. (1843), *A System of Logic, Ratiocinative and Inductive*, London: Parker.
Mill, J.S. (1848), *Principles of Political Economy with some of their Applications to Social Philosophy*, London: Parker
Mill, J.S. (1869) 'Thornton on labour and its claims', *Fortnightly Review*, May.
Robbins, L. (1932), *An Essay on the Nature and Significance of Economic Science*, London: Macmillan.
Wagner, A. (1886), 'On the present state of political economy', *Quarterly Journal of Economics*, October.

Knight, Frank H.

Frank H. Knight (1885–1972) is best known today for his treatment of profit and the theory of the firm in *Risk, Uncertainty and Profit* (1921). His other major theoretical contributions include his modifications of Alfred Marshall's time period analysis, his critique of Albert Pigou's theory of social cost (which foreshadowed Coase's (1960) famous essay), his capital theory arguments with the Austrians in the 1930s and his role as the leading anti-Keynesian theorist in the United States from the late 1930s to the 1950s. Knight also made a significant contribution to the development of American economics as a teacher: he taught Edward Chamberlin and Henry Simons at the University of Iowa during the early 1920s, before moving in 1928 to the University of Chicago, where, as co-founder of the Chicago School tradition with Jacob Viner, he counted among his students eventual Nobel laureates George Stigler, Milton Friedman, Gary Becker and James Buchanan.

Knight wrote extensively on economic method and economic philosophy generally. From the opening words of his first major publication, *Risk, Uncertainty and Profit* (written in 1916) to the last words of his posthumous essay on the history of economics (Knight 1973: 61), he produced a steady stream of articles and book reviews dealing with questions of method in economics and the social sciences, and the relation of economics to ethics, religion and other areas of intellectual inquiry (the most notable essays are collected in Knight, 1935; 1947; 1956). Apart from their interest to economic methodologists, Knight's writings on economic philosophy are significant because they played a role in almost all the major twentieth-century debates regarding the nature, method and role of the social sciences in America (see Ross, 1991: 420–27; Emmett, 1991).

The method Knight advocated for economics *as a science* can be described as analysis and abstraction: 'We have given us the task of reducing to order a complex mass of interrelated changes, which is to say, of analyzing them into uniformities of sequence or behaviour, called laws, and the isolation of the different elementary sequences for separate study' (Knight,

1921: 3). Although he recognized the difficulties which analysing the complexities of social interaction presented, Knight nevertheless defended the theoretical framework of neoclassical economics on the grounds that it constituted a legitimate exercise of analysis and abstraction. Against those who argued that economic theory was not rooted in empirical reality, Knight defended the importance of abstraction, and the impossibility of empirically verifying the abstractions (Knight, 1935: 105–47; 1956: 151–78). Against those who contended that neoclassical economics had the wrong set of assumptions, Knight argued that intentionality was central to human action and therefore that neoclassical economics started at the right place (Knight, 1935: 76–104; 1925). And against those who wanted economics to be either more historical or more policy-oriented Knight argued that, as necessary as historical and public policy emphases are, there is still room for an independent scientific economics rooted in abstraction and analysis (Knight, 1935: 277–359).

Throughout these debates, Knight stood at odds with the dominant modes of methodological thinking in American social science: the objectivist, behaviouristic approaches common to the other social sciences and to the American institutionalist tradition (see Samuels, 1977) and the positivistic approach that emerged with the American neoclassical tradition between the wars (see Hammond, 1991). At the same time, however, Knight was conscious of the limitations which the scientific process of analysis and abstraction placed on economics. For one thing, the necessity to abstract in order to analyse and understand meant for Knight that economic theory was far removed from the concrete reality of everyday life and therefore required great care in its application to the problems of modern society. In the tradition of J.S. Mill, Knight argued that economic laws can, at best, be viewed as tendencies. Making prediction the touchstone of economics' scientific status, as his student Milton Friedman did, was a mistake in Knight's estimation (see Knight, 1921: 3–18; 1935, 105–47).

The limitations Knight was most interested in were those set up by the interaction between economics and ethics. For Knight, social discourse was simultaneously a public process of deciding about the means of accomplishing our goals and a conversation about the nature of the goals we want to have (see Knight, 1935: 19–40, 277–359; 1956: 121–34). Ascribing to an ethical theory which placed priority on the search for better values rather than our adherence to established values, Knight argued that no human decision (about public policy or even consumer purchases) could be evaluated simply as a technical means–end (that is, economic) decision: 'Social action … is group-determination. … As directive of social action, discussion has for its objective the solution of … ethical problems, the establishment of agreement upon ethical ideals or values, for the reconciliation of conflicting interests' (Knight, 1956: 133). The social task which the economist could play (that of helping to determine the best means to any given end), therefore, was circumscribed by the larger social task of self-determination: 'But the social problem is not … one of means and end. It is a problem of values. And the content of social science must correspond with the problem of action in character and scope' (Knight, 1956: 134).

Because these limitations distanced the scientific task of economic theory from the social/moral task of creating public policy, Knight wanted economic theorists *qua* scientists to give up the quest for a public voice on economic policy. He imagined a cadre of economic theorists who would take a '"consecrated" attitude toward their common work [as scientists], "devoting" themselves to a truly cooperative quest of the right or "best" solutions to problems, absolutely renouncing interest in individual prominence and power, and going to the public only with dispassionate statements of fairly established results' (Knight, 1935: 358). At the same time, he understood all of us as citizens to have a role in social discussion about the kind of people we want to be. Knight's work can perhaps best be seen as emerging from the tension he saw between his role as a scientific economist and his role as a citizen.

ROSS B. EMMETT

References

Coase, Ronald (1960), 'The problem of social cost', *Journal of Law and Economics*, **3**, 1–44.
Emmett, Ross (1991), 'The economist as philosopher: Frank Knight and American social science during the twenties and early thirties', PhD dissertation, University of Manitoba.
Hammond, J. Daniel (1991), 'Frank Knight's antipositivism', *History of Political Economy*, **23**, 359–81.
Knight, Frank H. (1921), *Risk, Uncertainty and Profit*, Boston: Houghton Mifflin Co.; reprint, Chicago: University of Chicago Press, 1971.
Knight, Frank H. (1925), 'Fact and metaphysics in economic psychology', *American Economic Review*, **15**, 247–66.
Knight, Frank H. (1935), *The Ethics of Competition and Other Essays*. New York: Harper & Bros.; reprint, Chicago: University of Chicago Press, 1980.
Knight, Frank H. (1947), *Freedom & Reform: Essays in economics and social philosophy*, New York: Harper & Bros.; reprint, Westport, CT: Greenwood Press, 1979.
Knight, Frank H. (1956), *On the History and Method of Economics. Selected Essays*, Chicago: University of Chicago Press.
Knight, Frank H. (1973), 'Economic history', in Philip Wiener (ed.), *Dictionary of the History of Ideas: Studies of selected pivotal ideas*, vol. 2, New York: Charles Scribner's Sons.
Ross, Dorothy (1991), *The Origins of American Social Science*, Cambridge: Cambridge University Press.
Samuels, Warren J. (1977), 'The Knight–Ayres correspondence: The grounds of knowledge and social action', *Journal of Economic Issues*, **11**, 485–525.

Lakatos, Imre

Born in Hungary in 1922, Lakatos worked in the Hungarian Ministry of Education, but though a Communist, he was imprisoned for three years because of his revisionist views. To avoid further imprisonment, he left the country after the 1956 uprising. After a period in Cambridge, where he wrote the doctoral thesis on which *Proofs and Refutations* (1976, originally published in 1963–4) is based, he taught at LSE from 1960 until his death in 1974. Though strongly influenced by Popper, he parted company with him in important respects (notably believing that a 'whiff of inductivism' was essential in order to avoid the pitfall of scepticism). He is best known for his methodology of scientific research programmes (MSRP) which, he believed, strengthened Popper's falsificationism to the extent that it could stand up to the criticisms levelled against it by Kuhn. Lakatos' MSRP was first applied to economics by Spiro Latsis, who used it to analyse the theory of the firm (Latsis, 1972). Partly as a result of a conference at Napflion in 1974 (Latsis, 1976), the MSRP came to dominate discussions of economic methodology until the late 1980s. As a conference in Capri (De Marchi and Blaug, 1991) revealed, however, by the end of the 1980s there was considerable scepticism about the usefulness of such ideas for understanding developments in economics.

Though often perceived as an attempt to integrate the ideas of Kuhn and Popper, Lakatos' philosophy of science was an extension of his earlier philosophy of mathematics, regarded by many philosophers as his most original and important work. Because MSRP is discussed in a separate entry (and also under 'Novel Facts' in the present volume), it is more useful to focus on this earlier, and still relatively underexplored, work.

In *Proofs and Refutations*, Lakatos' main target is the 'Euclidian' view of mathematics (whether Hilbert's formalism or the logicism of Frege and Russell) that seems to provide secure foundations for mathematical truth. According to this view, mathematical knowledge is justified by showing how it can be deduced, using infallible deductive logic, from an initial set of self-evidently true statements containing only perfectly clear terms. But this, Lakatos argued, is achieved only by stretching the meaning of such terms so as to ensure success (Lakatos, 1978, II: 3–23). In *Proofs and Refutations* he provided a brilliant illustration of this in the form of a study of the history of the Descartes/Euler conjecture: the conjecture that, for a polyhedron, $V - E + F = 2$, where V is the number of vertices, E the number of edges and F the number of faces. Several conclusions can be drawn from this history.

1. Mathematical knowledge, like scientific knowledge, grows through a series of proofs and refutations, the latter being achieved by counterexamples.
2. As mathematical knowledge grows, concepts stretch and evolve. For example, the initial definition of a polyhedron is as a solid, the faces of which are polygons. As the theorem evolves, new definitions are created: a polygon becomes, amongst other things, (a) a surface that, after removal of a plane, can be stretched onto a plane and (b) a network of vertices and edges.
3. Proofs are important in the generation of theorems and concepts. They are not the final stage in the process, but the basis for proof analysis which, through the discovery of counterexamples, leads to new definitions of concepts, new proofs and new theorems.
4. Rigorous proof is achieved by analytifying a theorem. Suitably narrowing the definitions of concepts makes a theorem true; broadening them makes it false. Lakatos thus writes of the content-*decreasing* power of rigour.

Lakatos' history is of 'informal' mathematics. It deals with proofs that, because not all the lemmas on which they depend are explicit, and not all the concepts involved are totally clear, are not completely rigorous, and with the way in which assumptions and concepts evolve. His purpose is to show that there is a logic to the way mathematicians respond to counterexamples. When confronted with a counterexample, the strategies which may be pursued include monster barring, exception barring, lemma incorporation and concept stretching. For example, suppose we are working with a version of the theorem that defines a polygon as a solid with polygonal faces, and we encounter the counterexample of two tetrahedra joined together along one edge (for which $V - E + F = 6 - 11 + 8 \neq 2$).

1. This can be dismissed as a pathological case (a monster), not a genuine counterexample.
2. It can be admitted that there are exceptions to the theorem.
3. A 'hidden' lemma can be discovered and incorporated into the theorem.
4. 'Polyhedron' can be redefined, for example as a surface, or as a system of edges and vertices.

His conclusion was that some strategies for coping with counterexamples were better than others. Finding hidden lemmas, and thus explaining counterexamples, was better than the method of monster barring. The mark of a good theory is that it 'not only *explains* but *produces* its refutations' (Lakatos, 1976: 94).

Lakatos is thus concerned with the logic of *discovery*, his contention being that the distinction between discovery and justification is blurred. This is a consequence of his rejection of formalism. In a formal system there are only two sorts of thing that can be discovered: solutions to problems that a suitably programmed Turing machine could solve in finite time; and solutions to problems where one can be guided 'only by the "method" of "unregimented insight and good fortune"' (ibid.: 4). He continues,

> Now this bleak alternative between the irrationalism of a machine and the irrationalism of blind guessing does not hold for live mathematics: an investigation of *informal* mathematics will yield a rich situational logic for working mathematicians, a situational logic which is neither mechanical nor irrational, but which cannot be recognised and, still less, stimulated, by formalist philosophy. (Ibid.: 4)

A footnote to this passage accuses formalists of using the term 'mathematics' as though it could be identified with formal systems, and then 'with a surreptitious shift in meaning, using the term "mathematics" in the ordinary sense'.

Lakatos' concern, both here and in his later methodology of scientific research programmes, was with methodology. If we see it simply as a method of theory appraisal, asking it to tell us what will be successful in the future, it fails. However, Lakatos had a different aim. He wished to argue that mathematical (and later, scientific) knowledge was objective. Being unable to ground mathematical knowledge in truth, he sought to ground it in the *growth* of knowledge: even if we cannot know that mathematical knowledge is true, we can start from the assumption that it grows. In *Proofs and Refutations* he was looking for a methodology that was both a theory-neutral heuristic and a standard of objectivity. In 'The methodology of scientific research programmes' (Lakatos, 1978, I: 8–101), however, this changed. Heuristics became local – specific to individual research programmes – reflecting acceptance of the fact that there are no general rules of how to increase knowledge, merely ones that work in particular areas (the rules of the MSRP, of course, were put forward as universally valid). The purpose of 'methodology' was not to provide rules for science, but to provide a theory of objectivity. It was thus perfectly acceptable for it to be backward-looking. Like Charles Sanders Peirce, Lakatos used growth of knowledge as a surrogate for truth.

Lakatos' philosophy of mathematics is important as the background from which his methodology of scientific research programmes emerged, but its importance for economic methodology extends beyond this. The main reason is that much economics is 'informal' mathematics in the sense in which Lakatos uses the term. *Proofs and Refutations* may provide insights into the way such mathematics evolves. For example, proofs of the 'invisible hand' theorem have become more rigorous, but only through becoming analytified, with concepts such as 'competition', 'market' and 'price' being changed in the process (see Backhouse, 1997).

ROGER E. BACKHOUSE

Bibliography

Backhouse, Roger E. (1997), *Truth and Progress in Economic Knowledge*, Cheltenham/Lyme, NH: Edward Elgar.

Cohen, R.S., P.K. Feyerabend and M.W. Wartofsky (eds) (1976), *Essays in Memory of Imre Lakatos*, Boston Studies in the Philosophy of Science, Vol. XXXIX. Dordrecht/Boston: Reidel.

Hacking, Ian (1981), 'Lakatos's philosophy of science', in Ian Hacking (ed.), *Scientific Revolutions*, Oxford/New York: Oxford University Press. (revised and abridged version of 'Imre Lakatos's philosophy of science', *British Journal for the Philosophy of Science*, **30**, 1979, 38–410).

Lakatos, Imre (1976), *Proofs and Refutations: the Logic of Mathematical Discovery*, ed. John Worrall and Elie Zahar, Cambridge/New York: Cambridge University Press.

Lakatos, Imre (1978), *Philosophical Papers, Volume 1: The Methodology of Scientific Research Programmes; Volume 2: Mathematics, Science and Epistemology*, Cambridge/New York: Cambridge University Press.

Latsis, Spiro J. (1972) 'Situational determinism in economics', *British Journal for the Philosophy of Science*, **23**, 207–45.

Latsis, Spiro J. (1976), *Method and Appraisal in Economics*, Cambridge/New York: Cambridge University Press.

De Marchi, Neil and Mark Blaug (eds) (1991), *Appraising Economic Theories: Studies in the Methodology of Research Programmes*, Aldershot/Brookfield, VT: Edward Elgar.

Malthus, Thomas Robert

Thomas Robert Malthus (1766–1834) was educated at Cambridge; although the education he received was aimed at preparing clergymen, 'this was tantamount, in the circumstances of the day, to producing a Newtonian natural and moral philosopher' (Winch, 1987: 18). The bequest of his education included, first, the calculus of fluxions and MacLaurin's version of Newtonianism (see James, 1979: 25–30) and second, a distinctive Cambridge cast of mind the *via media*, best exemplified by the theologian William Paley, embracing theological utilitarianism, philosophical whiggism, empiricized natural law and an obsession with 'middles' (see Waterman, 1991b).

Malthus won notoriety with his *Essay on the Principle of Population* (1798), deeply revised in the 1803 edition. His systematic treatise on the *Principles of Political Economy* (1820) resulted partly from his teaching at the East India College and partly from his sustained controversy with Ricardo. The Scottish tradition of moral Newtonianism, exemplified by Hume, Smith and Dugald Stewart, was the main source for his methodological considerations. In fact, he describes Smith as the Newton of political economy (Malthus, 1824, VII: 257) and contrasts the 'consistent theory of Newton' with the 'eccentric hypotheses of Descartes', an example of the old mode of philosophizing, that makes 'facts bend to systems' (Malthus, 1798: 59), while the new mode fosters 'patient investigation, and well authenticated proofs' (ibid.: 60n).

In this mood, the *Essay* starts with two 'postulates' (indispensability of food and ineliminability of sexual drive) and then proceeds to derive consequences from them, subsequently to be confirmed by 'experience, the true source and foundation of all knowledge' (ibid.: 10). Postulates, so understood, are contrasted with 'mere conjectures' (ibid.: 8).

In the *Principles* he contends that, on the one hand, moral and political sciences enjoy a privileged status vis-à-vis natural science, in so far as their subject matter is more directly accessible; on the other, the study of 'the laws which regulate the movements of human society' is made less easy by obstacles unknown to the natural sciences, namely the impossibility of reducing human needs and tastes to mathematical figures (Malthus, 1820, I: 1–16). In the 1803 edition of the *Essay*, from Hume's warning that 'of all sciences there is none where first appearances are more deceitful than in politics' (Hume, 1752: 397) he derives a mistrust of so-called 'practice': the 'practical men' draw rash generalizations on the basis of a too limited experience (Malthus, 1803, II: 185). He notes the backwardness of 'the science of moral and political philosophy' but believes that 'the brilliant career of physical discovery' may provide an example to be followed, so that social science will partake in the success of natural science (ibid.: 203).

Yet the proofs political economy can afford cannot compete in certainty with 'those which relate to figure and number' in so far as the practical results of its proposition depend upon 'so variable a being as man' and 'so variable a compound as the soil' (Malthus, 1820, I: 1); thus political economy is closer 'to the science of morals and politics than to that of mathematics' (ibid.: 2). What makes 'the laws which regulate the movements of human society' different from physical laws is the fact that the former are 'continually modified by human interference' (ibid.: 13), or the existence of feedbacks, 'the operations of that circle of causes and effects ... which are acting and re-acting on each other' (ibid.: 16). Thus 'great general principles' may be said to 'partake ... of the certainty of the stricter sciences', while other propositions of political economy 'absolutely require limitations and exceptions' (ibid.: 8).

Hence, there are two main sources of error. The first is 'a precipitate attempt to simplify and generalize' instead of acknowledging 'the operation of more causes than one in the production of particular effects' (ibid.: 6); this goes hand-in-hand with an identification of the moral sciences with mathematics (ibid.: 355). In his correspondence with Ricardo this is the main methodological issue (see Ricardo, 1951–73, VI: 28–9; 82; 139–40). The second source is the temptation, into which the 'practical men' fall, to mistake 'appearances, which are merely co-existent and incidental ... for causes' (Malthus, 1820, I: 21). This is even more damaging, in so far as it yields theories 'both complex and incorrect' (ibid.: 21). In a word, he threads a middle way between apriorism and hyperempiricism (see Wrigley, 1986: 35; Würgler, 1957: 197). A further third source is the unwillingness to bring theories to the test of experience: an 'isolated fact' cannot refute a 'consistent theory, which would account for the great mass of phenomena observable' (Malthus, 1820, I: 10); principles should 'be carefully founded on an experience sufficiently extended' (ibid.: 518); instead, the practical men back their claims with limited experience, and apriorist theorists like Ricardo stick to a theory even if it proves 'inconsistent with general experience' (ibid.: 10–11).

Talk of laws of nature was not unusual with Malthus: the two postulates of the first *Essay* express two 'fixed laws of our nature' (Malthus, 1798: 8, 59); in the second *Essay*, occasional mention is made of 'the laws of nature' (Malthus, 1803, I: 10; II: 87–8); in the *Principles*, besides 'general laws' and usual 'propositions of political economy' 'laws of nature' are mentioned, meaning laws of *physical* nature constantly at work 'in the production of necessaries' (Malthus, 1820, I: 147–8). In short, Malthus draws a distinction between three kinds of scientific laws: (1) the usual propositions of political economy, which are only probable and always admit of exceptions, (2) the most general principles, which are almost certain, being based on the most basic human passions, and (3) the fixed laws of nature, which admit of no exception.

Analogy is a key idea for Malthus, also inherited from Newton via the Scottish philosophers and Paley. In both the first *Essay* and the *Principles*, analogy is appealed to as a methodological criterion intended to rule out unnecessary extravagant hypotheses. In the *Essay*, he appeals to it to argue against Condorcet that it is 'unphilosophical to expect any specific event that was not indicated by some kind of analogy in the past ... For instance, man has discovered many of the laws of nature: analogy seems to indicate that he will discover many more; but no analogy seems to indicate that he will discover a sixth sense, or a new species of power in the human mind, entirely beyond the train of our present observation' (Malthus, 1798: 86). In the *Principles*, he appeals to what he calls the 'rule of analogy' in the context of the familiar iatropolitical simile, for example in support of laissez-faire. He writes: 'The ablest physicians are the most sparing in the use of medicine, and the most inclined to trust to the healing power of nature' (Malthus, 1820, I: 20). Thus rulers should refrain from intervening in their subjects' business unless it has been proved with overwhelming evidence that they should do so. At another place, the iatropolitical simile is used in order to limit a conclusion that may be drawn from Malthus' principle of population, stressing the importance of what happens in the course of 'intervals' between two permanent states. He writes:

> If the human body had been subjected to a very powerful stimulus, we should surely be cautious not to remove it too suddenly. And, if the country had been unfortunately subjected to the excitement of a long continuance of excessive expenditure, it surely must be against all analogy and all general principle, to look for the immediate remedy of it in a great and sudden contraction of consumption. (ibid.: 520–21)

The doctrine of proportions is an intriguing one. The 'law of population' in the *Essay* states: 'Population, when unchecked, increases in geometrical ratio. Subsistence increases only in an arithmetical ratio' (Malthus, 1798: 9). The law is presented here as a *self-evident* truth; the second *Essay* adds some empirical evidence (Malthus, 1803, I: 12). In both formulations the problem is like the problem of the composition of forces in dynamics: a third factor, 'the strong law of necessity' will be brought in, 'acting as a check upon the greater power' of population, so that the rates of increase of the two factors be kept equal (ibid.: 15; cf. Malthus, 1798: 14–17). It is probably the case that later considerations on the role of proportions in political economy were suggested to Malthus by his 'diagram' of the rates of increase of means of subsistence and population. The *Principles* state that 'all the great results in political economy ... depend upon *proportions*' (Malthus, 1820, I: 432). This doctrine prompts an aversion to the 'tendency to extremes' (ibid.: 352n), one of the great sources of error in political economy, 'where so much depends upon proportions' (ibid.: 252; added in the 1836 edition). This doctrine 'necessarily opens the way to differences of opinion' concerning the optimal proportions, 'and thus throws a kind of uncertainty over the science of political economy' (ibid.: 515).

The Corn Laws (1814) states that many problems in morals and politics 'seem to be of the nature of the problems *de maximis* and *minimis* in fluxions; in which there is always a point where a certain effect is the greatest, while on either side of this point it gradually diminishes' (Malthus, 1814, VII: 102). A letter to Whewell of 1829 contains the same statement (de Marchi and Sturges, 1973: 387), adding that mathematical calculations may *in some cases* be introduced with advantage into political economy, 'particularly with a view to determining the different *degrees* in which certain objects are affected, under different hypotheses', but adding also that the main difficulty 'is getting data ... sufficiently near the truth; and such as can be stated distinctly in mathematical language' (ibid.: 386–7).

Malthus also wrote an essay on *Definitions in political economy* (1827) in which he draws a threefold partition: (1) *mathematics* which offers fewer problems, since, even if 'words may vary ... the meaning ... is always the same', (2) *natural history*, where the problem may arise of assigning one individual to one of two 'adjoining classes', and (3) *morals and politics*, where one more source of complication arises, since terms may be 'understood differently by different persons, according to their different habits and opinions' (Malthus, 1827, VIII: 5). Projects of radical reform in the language of morals and politics are unpractical, since the terms 'are of constant application in the daily concerns of life' (ibid.: 6). He suggests that in political economy two authorities be followed, namely, the 'conversation of educated persons' and 'the most celebrated writers in the science'. Deviations from ordinary usage may be introduced, with prudence, only for clarity's and consistency's sake (ibid.: 7). In the *Principles*, Malthus criticizes Ricardo for departing from 'the ordinary and most correct language of society' (Malthus, 1820, II: 217) and yet he refuses to follow Whewell in his carelessness about definitions, for scientific definitions are hypotheses to be confirmed and 'new definitions of terms' and 'our advances in knowledge ... act and react upon each other' (de Marchi and Sturges, 1973: 184–5).

To sum up, the main philosophical influences on Malthus' work were Scottish Newtonianism as instantiated by MacLaurin's *Account* and Hume's *Essays* in a former phase, and by Dugald Stewart's *Elements* in a latter phase; and Paley's theological utilitarianism, as illustrated in his *Principles of Moral and Political Philosophy*, and the overall intellectual attitude of Cambridge *via media* in politics, morals, theology and epistemology. The two influences overlapped at several points. These influences carried a version of the Newtonian legacy centred on anti-essentialism and antideductivism, a preoccupation with the peculiarity of social studies, a concern with the role of scientific language and, besides a peculiar way of establishing a partial autonomy while keeping some interaction between descriptive social science and moral discourse.

Malthus' population theory and his political economy have much in common, both in terms of positive contents and in terms of methodological inspiration, but it must be said that there was an evolution in Malthus' attitude, besides his positive doctrines, and that the turning point came about 1803. In 1798, Malthus' own 'experimental' attitude in moral subjects did not lead him any further than Hume's thought experiments. In the second *Essay* and in the *Principles*, he became increasingly aware of the role of multicausality, of the existence of feedback loops, of the approximate character of any mathematical 'model', of our inability to ascertain the right proportion of factors that should be at work in one given circumstance and of the virtues of realism of hypotheses as an antidote to the perennial risk of drawing extravagant inferences at some stage of our inferential chains as a result of some hidden (and at that stage irrelevant) error in our starting point assumptions.

One may say in conclusion that Malthus was no 'inductive and intuitive investigator' (Keynes), nor was he an 'unclassical' economist (Wurgler), or a follower of Edmund Burke's 'traditionalism' (Paglin); even less did he suffer from 'mental imbecility', as was proclaimed by Marx; he was indeed as classical as Ricardo was, provided that classicism is not reduced to a dogmatic belief in a ready-made set of unchanging economic laws, and his friend Ricardo owed him more than received wisdom admits.

SERGIO CREMASCHI

Bibliography
Cremaschi, Sergio and Marcelo Dascal (1996), 'Malthus and Ricardo on Economic Methodology', *HOPE*, **28**, (3), 475–511.
Hume, David (1752), 'Of the Populousness of Ancient Nations', reprinted in T.H. Green and Th.H. Grose (eds), *The Philosophical Works*. vol. III, Aalen: Scientia Verla, 1964.
James, Patricia (1979), *Population Malthus. His Life and Time*: London: Routledge.
Keynes, John M. (1972), 'Thomas Robert Malthus', *Essays in Biography*, London/New York: Macmillan/St Martin's Press.
Malthus, Thomas R. (1798), *An Essay on the Principle of Population*, in Malthus, 1986, vol. I.
Malthus, Thomas R. (1803), *An Essay on the Principle of Population*, 2 vols, ed. P. James, Cambridge: Cambridge University Press, 1989.
Malthus, Thomas R. (1814), *Observations on the Effect of the Corn Laws*, in Malthus, 1986, vol. VII.
Malthus, Thomas R. (1827), *Definitions in Political Economy*, Malthus, 1986, vol. VIII.
Malthus, Thomas R. (1820, 1836), *Principles of Political Economy*, 2 vols, ed. J. Pullen, Cambridge: Cambridge University Press, 1989.
Malthus, Thomas R. (1824), *On Political Economy*, in Malthus, 1986, vol. VII. (1986), *The Works of Thomas Robert Malthus*, 8 vols, ed. E.A. Wrigley and D. Souden, London: Pickering.
de Marchi, Neil B. and R.P. Sturges, (1973), 'Malthus and Ricardo's Inductivist Critics: Four Letters to William Whewell', *Economica*, **40**, 379–93.
Paglin, Morton (1973), *Malthus and Lauderdale. The Anti-Ricardian Tradition*, Clifton, NJ: Kelley.
Pullen, John (1982), 'Malthus on the Doctrine of Proportions and the Concept of the Optimum', *Australian Economic Papers*, **21**, 270–85.
Ricardo, David (1951–73), *The Works and Correspondence*, 11 vols, ed. P. Sraffa, Cambridge: Cambridge University Press.
Waterman, A.M.C. (1991a), *Revolution. Economics and Religion. Christian Political Economy, 1798–1833*, Cambridge: Cambridge University Press.
Waterman, A.M.C. (1991b), 'A Cambridge "Via Media" in Late Georgian Anglicanism', *Journal of Ecclesiastical History*, **42** (3), 419–36.
Winch, Donald (1987), *Malthus*, Oxford/New York: Oxford University Press.
Wrigley E.A. (1986), 'Introduction', in Malthus, 1986, vol., I.
Würgler, Hans (1957), *Malthus als Kritiker der Klassik. Ein Beitrag zur Geschichte der klassischen Wirtschaftstheorie*, Winterthur: Keller.

Marginalist Controversy, The

Between 1946 and 1953, the *American Economic Review* (AER) published several papers on the relevance or otherwise of the 'marginalist' theory of the firm (the term 'neoclassical' was not yet in popular use). The leading articles were by Lester (1946) and Machlup (1946), who took aggressively opposite stands. This collection of papers constitutes the 'marginalist controversy' *stricto sensu*. In a broader sense, which will be the sense considered here, the expression 'marginalist controversy' also refers to closely related discussions of the theory of the firm that took place for a longer span of time (from 1939 to around 1955) and in a variety of English and American journals and conferences. The 'full-cost pricing' (FCP) controversy, which was started by the Oxford economists Hall and Hitch (1939), is the single most important of these related discussions. Although the economics involved in the 'marginalist controversy' antedates modern industrial organization and will strike one as both rudimentary and outdated, there are at least two reasons why not only historians, but also methodologists and philosophers of science, should be interested in them. First, they influenced the thinking of those writers, like Machlup and Friedman, who reorganized the methodological defence of orthodox economics around 'irrealism of assumptions'. Second, and more importantly, these debates provide for illuminating case studies: they illustrate the economists' decisions about the content and boundaries of the received theory when the latter is faced with unfavourable evidence.

The 1940s and 1950s witnessed extensive research on the price-setting behaviour of individual firms. It was pursued partly with a view to giving a more factual basis to the then prevailing theories of imperfect competition (notably, Joan Robinson's marginalist theory in *The Economics of Imperfect Competition*, 1933), partly in the hope of clarifying macroeconomic and economic policy issues (such as price rigidity in the face of low output, as evidenced in the 1930s). The leading study in the field of industrial prices was by Hall and Hitch (1939). It was published along with other findings by Oxford economists and, as Harrod pointed out, shared with them a disquieting feature: all the results of the Oxford surveys appeared to conflict with the received doctrine of the time. Hall and Hitch had used the questionnaire method and gathered an unrepresentative sample of 38 firms; they had found that a high proportion of these firms set their prices in a 'full-cost' way. Typically, the company would make an ex ante estimate of average cost, as determined by some notion of its 'normal' output, and then add to it one or more percentage margins (the 'mark-up'). Hall and Hitch said little on how margins vary with demand conditions. They insisted that this pricing mechanism is a 'rule of thumb' and could result in maximum profits by accident only; hence the clash with Robinson's theory of imperfect competition. Hall and Hitch justified FCP on the grounds that 'producers cannot know their demand or marginal revenue curves'. Despite their heterodox pronouncements, they were ambivalent towards existing theory and sketched an alternative account of industrial pricing. That alternative argument is based on the 'kinked demand curve', a minor but interesting case of simultaneous discovery in economics. The 'kinked demand curve' was independently introduced by Sweezy in 1939 and might already have been in Chamberlin. It formalizes the following peculiarity of oligopolistic markets: a price rise will not be followed by competitors and should thus be accompanied by a heavy fall in demand; a price cut will be followed by competitors and can then bring about only a limited rise in demand; accordingly, the demand to the firm exhibits a kink at the prevailing market price. This piece of doctrine can be used to account for price rigidity on oligopolistic markets; it was one of the many answers given to the riddle of the 1930s: falling output instead of falling prices. It did not belong to Robinson's 'box of tools' but was consistent with her profit-maximization assumption; actually, profit-maximization was required together with the kinked demand curve to derive an account of price rigidity. Hall and Hitch used it that way, in flat contradiction of their claim that firms know nothing about demand.

Various inquiries followed Hall and Hitch's. Part of this work, notably Andrews' *Manufacturing Business* (1949) and Harrod's non-optimizing model in his *Economic Essays* (1952), carries with it the heterodox suggestion that profit maximization should be replaced by the 'full-cost principle', to be understood as a novel theoretical construct. However, the more widespread view of the 1940s and 1950s was that FCP referred to an empirical datum rather than a theoretical principle: it was a well-evidenced piece of behaviour which raised a problem for the profit-maximizing theory of the firm but was not necessarily in contradiction with that theory. The marginalist respondents, in particular Austin Robinson, Machlup and Heflebower, simultaneously debased the claim that FCP was the starting point of an alternative theory and argued that FCP as a datum could be reconciled with (sophisticated) marginalism. In retrospect, they were successful in both strategies. The discussion in America came to a halt after 1953, when the conference 'Business Concentration and Price Policy' took place and Heflebower read a carefully designed report which impressed the attendants. On the theoretical side, he argued that the 'full-costers' work 'short-cuts a deep understanding of the market'. On the empirical side, he concluded that FCP evidence is not incompatible with profit maximization. Although Heflebower had just sketched a reconciling model, the issue was regarded as settled to the benefit of marginalism by the majority of the profession in America. The British story is not so easy to tell, owing to the persisting heterodoxy of Andrews and part of the Oxford group, but it is best seen as culminating in A. Robinson's devastating review (1950) of Andrews' *Manufacturing Business* and the ensuing controversy in the *Economic Journal*. Around 1955, a majority of British economists had probably reached a conclusion no different from that of their American colleagues, but they had seen the matter slightly differently – more as a contest between two principles than as an empirical test of marginalism. Elsewhere than in America and England, the FCP controversy was derivative.

The FCP controversy came to be intermingled with the 'marginalist controversy' in the narrow sense when Machlup (1946) attempted to answer in the same breath both Hall and Hitch and the American economist Lester, who had attacked the received theory for reasons of his own. Lester (1946) had been intrigued by the paradoxical consequences of a change in the north–south wage differential in the United States: the employment in some relevant industries had increased more in the south than in the north *after* a minimum wage had been established in the south around 1940, a decision which of course changed relative labour costs unfavourably. Using a questionnaire, he found that the companies' most frequent reactions to increased relative costs were, in this order, (1) to increase production efficiency, (2) to implement labour-saving devices, (3) to make increased sales efforts, (4) to change the price or quality of products, and finally (5) to reduce output and employment. Lester was struck by the fact that adjustment (5), which is the competitive adjustment par excellence, came last in the list, and that adjustments (3) and (4), which are predicted by the imperfect or monopolistic competition models, fared just a little better. He interpreted (1), and ambiguously (2), as indicating unexploited profit possibilities before the relative cost change. He concluded that his data shook confidence in marginalism as a whole.

Machlup's first answer was to cast doubts on questionnaire data in general, on the grounds that questionnaires lead to unrepresentative samples, unnoticed manipulation and semantically ambiguous conclusions. Then he proceeded to argue that Lester's data, exactly as Hall and Hitch's, established only that the textbook model of short-run profit maximization under perfect competition was inadequate, but that virtually any other model in the marginalist toolkit could be reconciled with the evidence. He clearly took Hall and Hitch's work more seriously than Lester's and made some effort to explain how FCP can be reconstructed as a 'cartel device' in some cases and a 'clue to demand elasticity' in other oligopolistic contexts. A controversy ensued in the 1946–1948 issues of the *American Economic Review*. Some of the participants attempted to arbitrate the initial conflict, in particular Oliver, who noted in 1947 that the antimarginalists had at least shaken the marginalists' caricature of a businessman in a continuous state of alert, ready to adjust to any exogenous change. The Lester–Machlup debate contributed to popularizing the notion of the company as making infrequent decisions that are primarily influenced by expectations of its competitors' policies. This is an important insight but little was done to formalize it beyond Machlup's hints. Although no contribution to the AER controversy can be said to be decisive, it can be conjectured that it influenced American economists into thinking that Robinson's and Chamberlin's initial models had to be refined, but that the profit-maximizing framework was flexible enough to accommodate the available evidence.

It is difficult to keep the FCP and AER controversies separate from a continuing discussion in the 1940s and 1950s on the shape of cost curves. Most of the literature on FCP either argues on the basis of evidence or just takes for granted that the average cost curve was flat on the normal operating interval. This explains why 'full-costers' were vague about the output level at which average costs were computed in the FCP formula: it simply did not matter. Interestingly, some marginalists, such as Stigler, accepted the empirical claim that average costs are approximately constant. A curious dissenter from this view is Eiteman (1947), who published the results of a questionnaire on average cost curves and concluded that the businessmen's typical perceived curve is decreasing throughout, that is, up to the point of full capacity. From this finding and other assumptions, it was possible to argue that profit maximization was refuted. A discussion on Eiteman took place in the AER from 1947 to 1953. It casts light on Lester's related point that reserve capacity might be difficult to reconcile with profit maximization.

Besides disputing the relevance of questionnaire data and attempting to account for the evidence in marginalist terms, Machlup had sketched a third, primarily methodological defence of the received doctrine. Using the metaphor of the automobile driver, he had claimed that the economist's concepts are helpful only to predict 'the probable effect of change', by which he meant 'in what direction output, prices and employment are likely to be altered'. Since part of Lester's and Hall and Hitch's work was critically concerned with just that sort of prediction, Machlup's claim in itself did not carry much force. At best, it could serve to reject outside the boundaries of economics, that other part of Hall and Hitch's work which was concerned with 'rules of thumb' and the procedural side of business decisions. However limited its relevance in the present context, Machlup's (1946) methodological pronouncement is important because it is perhaps the first dramatic occurrence of a doctrine which has since become influential throughout economics. In 1955, Machlup formulated it more precisely: economics aims at deriving observable changes in prices and quantities from observable changes in exogenous variables (for example, demand or technology); theoretical assumptions really act as an 'engine of analysis' by making it possible to derive such predictions; and there are two kinds of theoretical assumptions in the marginalist theory of the firm – one is fixed and truly fundamental (profit-maximization), the other can be freely modified depending on the context (the firm's competitive time, its cost curve and time horizon). Machlup's delineation of the aim and scope of economics in 1955 is sometimes wrongly attributed to Friedman, who was never as precise about what counts as a consequence and what counts as an assumption. On the other hand, Machlup's wording in 1955 reveals the strong influence of Friedman's 1953 essay. The paper has an instrumentalist undertone that was absent from the eclectic piece against Lester. It makes a spectacular application of the 'irrealism of assumptions' thesis by suggesting that the economist should check empirically neither his fundamental assumption *nor even his auxiliary assumptions*: the firm's competitive type is a matter for theoretical decision rather than empirical investigation.

We have shown above that the 'marginalist controversy' constituted one of the sources of an influential methodology, a connection particularly stressed in Mongin (1986). There have been other interpretations. Lee (1984) emphasized the connection with the 'reformist' theories of the firm that flourished from the late 1950s onwards: Baumol's sales maximization hypothesis, Marris' 'managerial' conception, Cyert and March's 'behavioural theory of the firm', to cite a few. It is correct to note that these writers were acquainted with, and to a significant extent influenced by, the discussions just reviewed. However, it would be a mistake to believe that these writers were representative of the majority of the economics profession. Such drastic adjustments in the theory of the firm were not *needed* to resolve the 'marginalist controversy'. Current textbooks sometimes emphasize the connection between the latter and the early work on oligopoly by Bain, Modigliani and Sylos-Labini, around 1960, which directly anticipates today's 'theories of industrial organization'. Again, it is a fact that these writers learnt something from the 'marginalist controversy', but it would be incorrect to think that they provided it with its final episode. As emphasized in Mongin (1992), the controversy had been resolved earlier and in terms of standard prewar marginalism.

To illustrate, consider Heflebower's account of FCP. He showed that this pricing mechanism was not acknowledged beyond doubt outside the following contexts: (a) oligopoly with a leading firm whose cost figures are borrowed by followers, (b) oligopoly with explicit agreement to use conventional cost figures, and (c) oligopoly with implicit agreement such as was involved in cases brought to the courts. He also effectively summarized the scattered evidence on margins: he showed that they varied through time, roughly in agreement with demand conditions as reflected by the business cycle. He also found that *actual* selling prices departed from full-cost computations in a cyclical way. All this is truly good empirical work given the standard of the time and the available industrial statistics. What is surprising is that Heflebower made so little of his findings. He made no serious effort to tighten the connection between FCP and collusive oligopoly. His view of demand was influenced by a famous formula in Joan Robinson's analysis of monopoly: $(P - MC) / P = 1/e$, where P is price, MC marginal cost and e the price-elasticity of demand. The left-hand side defines a concept of margin, which the right-hand side says is influenced by demand in a certain way. It would have been possible to subject this very precise formula to a test. Heflebower did not even make a rough attempt at such a test. He was satisfied with the comment that contrary to some of the 'full-costers' predictions, the received doctrine *somehow* took demand into account: hence the former were refuted and the latter was borne out! These were the conclusions that, roughly speaking, emerged from the 1953 conference. The FCP debate is a fascinating example of inconsistent application of empirical methods to economics.

Philippe Mongin

References

Eiteman, W.J. (1947), 'Factors Determining the Locations of the Least Cost Price', *American Economic Review*, **37**, 910–18.

Friedman, M. (1953), 'The Methodology of Positive Economics', *Essays in Positive Economics*, Chicago: University of Chicago Press.

Hall, R.L. and C.J. Hitch (1939), 'Price Theory and Business Behaviour', *Oxford Economic Papers*, **2**, 12–45; reprinted in T. Wilson and P.W.S. Andrews (eds), *Oxford Studies in the Price Mechanism*, Oxford: Clarendon, 1951.

Heflebower, R.B. (1955), 'Full-Cost, Cost Changes and Prices', in *Business Concentration and Price Policy*, A Conference of the Universities–National Bureau Committee for Economic Research, Princeton: Princeton University Press.

Lee F.S. (1984), 'The Marginalist Controversy and the Demise of Full-Cost Pricing', *Journal of Economic Issues*, **18**, 1107–32.

Lester, R.A. (1946), 'Shortcomings of Marginal Analysis for Wage–Unemployment Problems', *American Economic Review*, **36**, 63–82.

Machlup, F. (1946), 'Marginal Analysis and Empirical Research', *American Economic Review*, **36**, 519–54.

Machlup, F. (1955), 'The Problem of Verification in Economics', *Southern Economic Journal*, **22**, 1–21.

Mongin, P. (1986), 'La controverse sur l'entreprise (1940–1950) et la formation de l'irréalisme méthodologique', *Economies et Sociétés*, **20**, 95–151.

Mongin, P. (1992), 'The "Full-Cost" Controversy of the 1940s and 1950s: A Methodological Assessment', *History of Political Economy*, **24**, 311–56.

Robinson, J. (1933), *The Economics of Imperfect Competition*, London: Macmillan.

Marshall, Alfred

Founder of the Cambridge School of Economics, which rose to world eminence in the inter-war years, and teacher of A.C. Pigou and J.M. Keynes, Marshall (1842–1924) embarked upon an academic career in 1865 after success in Cambridge University's competitive Mathematical Tripos. Turning from mathematics to the philosophy of mind, alias 'psychology', he was appointed in 1868 as lecturer in moral science at his college, St John's, teaching for Cambridge's Moral Science Tripos, then in its golden age under Sidgwick's leadership. Marshall's teaching responsibilities included 'political economy', for which he soon revealed a strong aptitude. By 1870, he had elected the subject as his life's work, convinced that viable schemes for social amelioration or reform must rest on a sound grasp of economic possibilities. Political economy was ripe in 1870 for transformation into a new science of economics, and Marshall's distinctive approach to economic theory had been well formed by the early 1870s, although little was to appear in print before 1879 and it was 1890 before his masterwork, *Principles of Economics*, appeared to cement his international reputation.

Marriage in 1877 to Mary Paley, his one-time student, forced Marshall to leave Cambridge for positions in Bristol and Oxford, but he returned to Cambridge as Professor of Political Economy in 1885, holding the chair until voluntary retirement in 1908. As professor he struggled doggedly to expand the scope for his subject in Cambridge, attaining partial success in 1903 with the creation of a new Economics Tripos. But resources and enrolments remained scant and it was only after his retirement that the new Cambridge School of Economics began to flower. Prolonged efforts to complete *Principles* with a second volume came to nothing, but the initial volume was extensively revised (see Guillebaud, 1961, for details and for the text of the eighth and final edition). In 1903, the British tariff controversy turned Marshall's efforts to international aspects of industrial and commercial policy, a project realized only partly when *Industry and Trade* at last appeared in 1919. His final work, *Money Credit and Commerce* (1923), mainly reassembled earlier fragments. Marshall's occasional writings are largely reproduced in Pigou (1925) and his contributions to government enquiries in J.M. Keynes (1926). Early economic writings and manuscripts are reproduced in Whitaker (1975) and early 'philosophical' manuscripts in Raffaelli (1994), which illuminates the philosophical backdrop.

Marshall's early philosophical speculations soon gave way to a general distaste for extended abstract reasoning and a preference for close contact with the texture of the real world and reliance on common sense. There is considerable truth to Coase's remark (1975: 27) that Marshall 'had little interest in what he termed "philosophical economics". And in a sense ... he held no views on method.' Nevertheless, the early absorption of a heady mix of utilitarianism, idealism and evolutionism (Mill, Kant, Hegel, Spencer, Sidgwick, W.K. Clifford and T.H. Green being among the important influences) must have shaped Marshall's persisting world view.

Hammond (1991) gives a useful conspectus of Marshall's views on 'scope and method'. The principal statement of these is in *Principles* (Book I and Appendices C, D in later editions: Book I in the first four editions; see also his 1885 inaugural lecture (Pigou 1925: 152–74), his 1902 'Plea' for a new Tripos (Guillebaud, 1961, II: 161–78) and *Industry and Trade*, Appendix A). The treatment of scope and method in the first five editions of *Principles* shows significant rewriting and shifts of emphasis, perhaps associated with the exigencies of academic politics over curricular reform in Cambridge, as Kadish (1991) suggests. In any case, it must be borne in mind when assessing Marshall's pronouncements on method that he was anxious to enhance the public standing of economics by stressing both its scientific character and the fundamental harmony of its disputatious exponents. This led him to emphasize measurement, the establishment of stable empirical laws, and the complementarity and mutual necessity of both induction and deduction. In practice, however, he was unsympathetic to any approach that failed to employ and cumulatively refine a well-defined analytical structure of deductively connected propositions. He thus remained in the Mill–Cairnes tradition broadly conceived, although *Industry and Trade* was to become more case-oriented. J.N. Keynes (one of Marshall's early students and father of J.M.) described Marshall's practice as 'deductive political economy guided by observation' (1891: 216–17n). Keynes, while writing his book, received many letters about it from Marshall. These reveal little difference on substantive issues of method, although much chivvying on matters of attribution and undiplomatic exposition.

Despite its centrality for Marshall, deductive argument was to be chastened and constrained from building airy castles on shaky empirical foundations by remaining always in close contact with the observable and verifiable. Assumptions, both overt and tacit, must conform to the real situation being analysed, calling for restricted scope and frequent reality checks. Economics is 'a study of mankind in the ordinary business of life', as the opening sentence of his *Principles* emphasizes. On one point Marshall differed conspicuously from Mill by replacing hypothetical wealth-pursuing 'economic man' with complex actual man who, while occasionally constrained by conscience or propriety, faced widespread potential tradeoffs between wealth and other goals. This appears to invite latter-day economic imperialism. But only those persistent behaviour patterns sufficiently regular to be discernible at the group level were to be brought into the economists' analysis, other aspects of behaviour being handled ad hoc by commonsense judgment as 'disturbing causes'. This narrows the difference between Marshall and Mill to one more of exposition than substance (see Guillebaud, 1961, I: 783), although Marshall's treatment gains sharpness from his fuller treatment of consumption.

Various aspects of Marshall's thought have methodological resonance: his concept of an 'organon' of enquiry and his related distinction between 'analysis' and 'theory'; his motto, 'The many in the one and the one in the many'; his distrust of formal statistical methods; his notion of continuity – in the development of human knowledge, institutions and character, in the transitions underlying conceptual categories, in the web of social and economic life. The last continuity underlies his reliance on partial-equilibrium reasoning. Variables endogenous on a wider view are provisionally deemed exogenous in the analysis of some portion of the web where their role is minor, rough workability being preferred over precise but useless comprehensiveness. Despite its close association with his name, Marshall gave surprisingly little attention to the formal justification of this style of analysis, regarding it as an entrenched feature of most scientific and practical reasoning. His 'time analysis', with its distinction between short- and long-run equilibria, was perhaps his most ingenious and influential application, but it was for him no more than a first step in grappling with the complexities due to the passage of time.

Marshall's ambition to model economics on biology rather than mechanics was hardly realized and its importance to him is easily exaggerated. He did draw clear distinctions between individual and collective experience, whether of persons or businesses. More importantly, he stressed the moulding by experience of human character, wants and abilities, the intergenerational transmission of acquired traits and the role of individual enterprise as the source of variation, driving by natural selection the evolution of technology, custom and institutions. Plasticity of the human element complicates both judgment of social welfare and the democratic determination of public policy. This imposes on the far-seeing, among whom Marshall obviously includes himself, a special duty to lead and educate in the evolutionary version of 'pushpin versus poetry'.

JOHN WHITAKER

References
Coase, R.H. (1975), 'Marshall on Method', *Journal of Law and Economics*, **18**, April, 25–31.
Guillebaud, C.W. (1961), *Alfred Marshall, Principles of Economics: Ninth (Variorum) Edition*, 2 vols, London: Macmillan.
Hammond, J.D. (1991), 'Alfred Marshall's Methodology', *Methodus*, **3**, June, 95–101.
Kadish, A. (1991), 'University Reform and the Principles', *Quaderni di Storia dell'Economia Politica*, **9** (2–3), 289–309.
Keynes, J.M. (ed.) (1926), *Official Papers of Alfred Marshall*, London: Macmillan.
Keynes, J.N. (1891), *The Scope and Method of Political Economy*, London: Macmillan.
Marshall, A. (1919), *Industry and Trade*, London: Macmillan.
Marshall, A. (1923), *Money Credit and Commerce*, London: Macmillan.
Pigou, A.C. (1925), *Memorials of Alfred Marshall*, London: Macmillan.
Raffaelli, T. (1994), 'Alfred Marshall's Early Philosophical Writings', *Research in the History of Economic Thought and Methodology – Archival Supplement*, vol. 4, pp. 53–159.
Whitaker, J.K. (1975), *The Early Economic Writings of Alfred Marshall, 1867–1890*, 2 vols, London: Macmillan.

Marx's Method

Karl Marx (1818–1883) was not only an economist but also a sociologist, philosopher and political activist. Although he is perhaps best known for a political pamphlet, *The Communist Manifesto*, written in 1848 jointly with Friedrich Engels, his main scientific work is an economic analysis of capitalism, as laid down in *Das Kapital*, a treatise of 2200 pages in three volumes (1867, 1885, 1894 – the latter two posthumously edited by Engels). The method of the latter work will be the main focus of this article.

Marx's *Capital* is an investigation of the characteristic form of the capitalist mode of production. It proceeds by presenting a movement from abstract to concrete (complex) categories. Starting with an analysis of the commodity, exchange and money, he develops the social forms of capital and capitalist production, showing how these are reproduced by definite social relations (Volume I). Having constituted capital as a social form distinct to this mode of production he traces its internal structure of circulation and reproduction (Volume II), and moves on to the dynamics of the market and production, the connection between the industrial and the financial system and distribution (Volume III). What is the method adopted by Marx in this presentation?

Before explicating key terms such as 'mode of production', 'social form' and 'abstract–concrete', let us first consider Marx's view on the study of history: 'historical materialism'. A brief pronouncement of it is to be found in the Preface to his *Critique of Political Economy* (1859), where Marx states that legal relations and political institutions are to be comprehended from 'the material conditions of life', and that the 'anatomy' of the latter 'has to be sought in political economy'. Thus

> in the social production of their existence, men inevitably enter into definite relations, which are independent of their will, namely relations of production appropriate to a given stage in the development of their material forces of production. The totality of these relations of production constitutes the economic structure of society, the real foundation, on which arises a legal and political superstructure and to which correspond definite forms of social consciousness. The mode of production of material life conditions the general process of social, political and intellectual life. (Marx, 1859: 20–21)

If we turn to Marx's main work, *Capital*, the text quoted above seems hardly helpful. We can see *why* Marx undertook the study of 'the economic structure' of capitalist society, but not *how*. However, from Marx's writings, especially the critiques of his political economic predecessors, three main methodological principles can be discerned. First is the difference between general and determinate categories, the former applying to societies – or more particularly, to productive activity – generally, the latter to historically specific 'modes' or 'social forms' of production (Murray, 1988: ch. 10). Thus capitalism is regarded as a particular social form of production with specific determinate categories applicable to it. In this context Marx criticizes, for example, Smith and Ricardo for applying determinate 'capitalist' economic categories to other (previous) social formations, thus muddling the understanding of their specificity. The concept of 'social form' is indeed a key to Marx's work. In capitalism, human labour and its products necessarily take the 'value-form' (money), and this form begets so much a life of its own that it dominates the content (even if the latter – labour, production, the product – remains a necessity). The form, money, has become the subject and object of this mode of production. From this springs Marx's famous account of alienation and money-fetishism: human relations have become (like) relations between things (*Capital*, I: ch.1; *Economico-philosophical Manuscripts of 1844*).

This takes us to the second methodological principle: immanent exposition and critique. Whereas 'mere criticism' takes some prescriptivist stand, external to the object of inquiry, an immanent critique takes its stand from within the object of inquiry, showing its internal inconsistencies and contradictions. This 'method of critique' considers that its object of inquiry is reflexive; it conceives that what is investigated is already a social reality which has its own self-interpretation. Marx's *Capital*, then, is an immanent exposition and critique of a social reality (capitalism) as well as of the theoretical expression of capitalist social relations in the discourse of political economy. This aspect of Marx's method, brilliantly set out in Benhabib (1986: chs 1–4), is indicated in the subtitle of *Capital*, 'A critique of political economy', as well as by the appearance of the term 'critique' in many other titles of Marx's writings.

A third methodological principle is the requirement for a hierarchy of determinations within the set of determinate categories, although this also applies to those general categories that remain at work along the determinate ones. Since in Marx's presentation the capitalist mode of production is shown to be an organic unity, 'knowledge of it must take the form of a *system of related categories* rather than a series of discrete investigations' (Arthur, 1992: x; cf. Marx's Introduction, 1953). More specifically Marx sets out, as already indicated, a system of categories layered from abstract to concrete and complex. Thus in the course of *Capital* we are gradually led into ever more concrete levels of abstraction, each made explicit by a conceptual 'transformation' (*Verwandlung*). (The famous value-price transformation (conversion) is merely one of many; whilst one can apply quantitative operations at some definite level of abstraction, some scholars doubt if it makes sense at all to apply them between levels of abstraction: see, for example, T. Smith, 1990: 169–71).

Most commentators agree that Marx's method in *Capital* is indeed a movement in stages from abstract to concrete categories. There is, however, disagreement on the status of each of the levels, as well as on the mode of progression from one level to the other. For a long time the method has been looked upon as a logical–historical approach (an interpretation propagated by Engels), or as a method of successive approximation where one starts with simplifying assumptions that are gradually being dropped (propagated by Sweezy, 1942). Other interpretations have focused on the particular dialectic adopted by Marx (see, for example, the contributions and references in Moseley, 1993; Moseley and Campbell, 1997; Arthur and Reuten, 1998; Norman and Sayers, 1980) and which some argue to be a systematic dialectic. The former two interpretations do not deny Marx adopting a dialectic; it is, however, de-emphasized in their accounts.

Anyway, it should be stressed that the presentation in *Capital* is not a deductive argument, nor does the movement from abstract to concrete mean that the former is non-empirical. Indeed, Volume III seems to get to an empirical level – as it is commonly understood – and mainstream economists therefore have always felt more at ease commenting on this rather than the earlier two volumes. However, the 'abstract' Volume I is loaded with often very detailed empirical descriptions and references to statistical reports. How are we to account for this?

Consider the abstract categories of *Capital I* that refer to relations *within* a historically determinate mode of production, that is, the capitalist. Take for example 'surplus-value'. Then the *phenomenal empirical* expressions of such a category may be visible (for example, struggle over the length of the working day), to the extent that the *categorical* development to the concrete is a simple expression of that abstract category; not, however, to the extent that the categorical development is a complex one, especially where the totality of the system inverts its appearances (as with interest or 'productivity of capital') or reverses its dynamic (as in the case of tendencies and countertendencies). The empirical references at each stage, then, must be carefully selected accordingly. Now of course, at first sight, this seems to have a circular flavour (note, though, that such empirical references are not meant to be a proof: they are, at that stage, illustrations). However, and this is the important point, for Marx it is, at any stage, the apparent *insufficiency* in comprehending more complex empirical phenomena that must drive the presentation forward to the more complex concrete categories.

But cannot we then dispense with the abstract categories once we have reached their concretization? No, the point is that the concrete categories derive meaning from their *interconnection* with the abstract categories, their 'inner structure'. At the end of the movement from abstract to concrete, 'the concrete is concrete because it is the concentration of many determinants'. (These issues are elaborated upon in Marx's Introduction to the *Grundrisse*, 1953, written in 1857, from which the last sentence has been quoted.)

Regarding Marx's method there are, as indicated, three strands of interpretation, and the extent to which Marx may be considered an heir of Hegel's dialectic has always been controversial. Two factors have contributed to this controversy. The first is the order of and delay in the appearance in print of Marx's work, both in the original German and in English translation. For brevity, I will merely give two examples. In 1932, two philosophically and anthropologically important works of Marx appeared in German: *The German Ideology* (with Engels) and the *Economico-philosophical Manuscripts* of 1844 (English translation 1938–63). A key 1857/8 manuscript, the *Grundrisse*, drafting *Capital* in a rather dialectical style, received its full German publication in 1953 and its English version only in 1973 (its Introduction had appeared in a German journal in 1903). Thus several times a new Marx seems to be on the stage, and in particular the 1932 and 1953 works quite changed the dialectical interpretation.

The second factor is that, throughout his writings over a period of 40 years, Marx was not consistent in his appreciation of Hegel's dialectic (he in fact reread some of Hegel's work several times). For some authors (for example, Althusser, 1965) there appears to be 'an epistemological break' in Marx's work: later on in his life he is supposed to have taken a radical break from the human, anthropological and Hegelian orientation of his youth. Arthur (1986) convincingly argues for a continuity both in terms of method and general problematic of the research programme. With this, Arthur does not deny Marx's radical critique of Hegel. As Murray (1988: 221) expresses it in an important study of Marx's method, 'Hegel was Marx's chief mentor and antagonist'. Whereas Murray de-emphasizes the Hegelian dialectic for Marx's method (similarly, for example, Mattick, 1993), T. Smith (1990) in a most original contribution has shown how the whole of *Capital* can be read as a systematic dialectic (see the entry, 'Dialectical Method'). Still others take the position that *Capital* provides important systematic dialectical and form-theoretical outlines that need, however, reconstruction and further development (Backhaus, 1969; Reuten and Williams, 1989; Arthur, 1993; Reuten, 1995).

This takes us, finally, into the issue that Marx's method and theory cannot not be equated with Marxian method and Marxian theory. Marx laid the foundations for a particular tradition of several methodological styles of research. However much these styles may diverge, they have in common the three general methodological characteristics set out earlier on: (1) the difference between general and historically determinate categories, (2) the method of immanent exposition and critique, and (3) setting out a system of determinate interconnected layers of categories for concretely grasping empirical reality. For better or worse, this distinguishes the Marxian tradition from mainstream approaches to methodology.

Reader's guide
Marx's texts on method have been collected in Carver (1975). Marx's method must of course be judged from his own work. The first chapters of *Capital* especially are difficult, but they are essential to the appreciation of the method. Arthur (1992) provides in 15 pages a good and accessible introduction to the work, emphasizing various methodological aspects. Some recent methodological assessments are in the collections edited by Moseley (1993), Bellofiore (1998), Moseley and Campbell (1997) and Arthur and Reuten (1998); earlier ones are Mepham and Ruben (1979) and Schmidt (1969), the latter with by now 'classical' contributions from, for example, Backhaus, Iljenkow and Zeleny. Bonefeld *et al.* (1992) extends from Marx to recent Marxian theory.

GEERT REUTEN

Bibliography

Althusser, Louis and Etienne Balibar (1965), *Lire le Capital*, vols I and II, Paris: Maspero; Engl. trans, Ben Brewster: Louis Althusser and Etienne Balibar, *Reading Capital*, London: New Left Books, 1970.

Arthur, Christopher J. (1986), *Dialectics of Labour; Marx and his relation to Hegel*, Oxford/New York: Basil Blackwell.

Arthur, Christopher J. (1992), 'Introduction', in C.J. Arthur (ed.), *Marx's Capital, a student edition*, London: Lawrence & Wishart.

Arthur, Christopher J. (1993), 'Hegel's *Logic* and Marx's *Capital*', in F. Moseley (ed.), *Marx's Method in 'Capital'*.

Arthur, Christopher J. and Geert Reuten (eds) (1998), *The Circulation of Capital: Essays on Volume Two of Marx's 'Capital'*, London/New York: Macmillan/St Martin.

Backhaus, Hans-Georg (1969), 'Zur Dialektik der Wertform', in A. Schmidt (ed.), Beiträge zur marxistischen Erkenntnistheorie; Engl. transl M. Eldred and M. Roth, 'On the Dialectics of the Value-form', *Thesis Eleven*, **1**, 1980, 99–120.

Bellofiore, Riccardo (ed.) (1998), *Marxian Economics: A Reappraisal, Volumes I and II*, London/New York: Macmillan/St Martin.

Benhabib, Seyla (1986), *Critique, Norm and Utopia*, New York: Columbia University Press.

Bonefeld, W., R. Gunn and K. Psychopedis (eds) (1992), *Open Marxism, Volume I and II*, London/Boulder: Pluto Press.

Carver, Terrell (ed.) (1975), *Karl Marx Texts on Method*, Oxford/New York, Blackwell/Barnes & Noble.

Likitkijsomboon, Pichit (1992), 'The Hegelian Dialectic and Marx's *Capital*', *Cambridge Journal of Economics*, **16**, (4), 405–19.

Marx, Karl (1859), *Zur Kritik der Politischen Ökonomie*, MEW 13, Berlin: Dietz Verlag, 1974; Engl. edn Maurice Dobb, transl. S.W. Ryazanskaya, *A Contribution to the Critique of Political Economy*, London: Lawrence & Wishart, 1971.

Marx, Karl (1867, 1885, 1894), *Capital; A Critique of Political Economy*, vols I–III (German originals I:1867, 1890; II: 1885; III: 1894), trans. Ben Fowkes (I) and David Fernbach (II and III), Harmondsworth: Penguin Books, 1976, 1978, 1981.

Marx, Karl (1932), *Economico-philosophical Manuscripts* in *Early Writings*, trans. Rodney Livingstone and Ted Benton, Harmondsworth: Penguin Books, 1975 (includes 'Critique of Hegel's Doctrine of the State', the 'Theses on Feuerbach' and the 1859 Preface mentioned in the text).

Marx, Karl (1953), *Grundrisse; Foundations of the critique of political economy (Rough Draft)*, trans. Martin Nicolaus, Harmondsworth: Penguin Books, 1973.

Mattick, Paul (1993), 'Marx's Dialectic', in F. Moseley (ed.), *Marx's Method in 'Capital'*.

Mepham, John and D-H. Ruben (eds) (1979), *Issues in Marxist Philosophy, Volume I, Dialectics and Method*, Brighton: Harvester.

Moseley, Fred (ed.) (1993), *Marx's Method in 'Capital'; A reexamination*, Atlantic Highlands, NJ: Humanities Press.

Moseley, Fred and Martha Campbell (eds) (1997), *New Investigations of Marx's Method*, Atlantic Highlands, NJ: Humanities Press.

Murray, Patrick (1988), *Marx's Theory of Scientific Knowledge*, Atlantic Highlands, NJ/London: Humanities Press.

Norman, Richard and Sean Sayers (1980), *Hegel, Marx and Dialectic; A Debate*, Brighton/Atlantic Highlands, NJ: Harvester/Humanities Press.

Reuten, Geert (1993), 'The difficult labour of a theory of social value; metaphors and systematic dialectics at the beginning of Marx's *Capital*', in F. Moseley (ed.), *Marx's Method in 'Capital'*.

Reuten, Geert (1995), 'Conceptual collapses; a note on value-form theory', *Review of Radical Political Economics*, **27** (3), 104–10.

Reuten, Geert and Michael Williams (1989), *Value-Form and the State*, London/New York, Routledge.

Schmidt, Alfred (ed.) (1969), *Beiträge zur marxistischen Erkenntnistheorie*, Frankfurt a.M.: Suhrkamp.

Smith, Tony (1990), *The Logic of Marx's Capital; Replies to Hegelian Criticisms*, Albany: State University of New York Press.

Sweezy, Paul A. (1942), *The Theory of Capitalist Development*, New York/London: Modern Reader Paperbacks

Materialism

The term 'materialism' has had several meanings in the history of philosophy, often associated with a particular accompanying adjective. Thus 'historical materialism' refers us to Karl Marx's theory of history as a process of class struggle, 'dialetical materialism' denotes Marx's inversion of Hegel's dialectic and 'mechanical materialism' calls to mind the early modern temptation to see simple machinery behind all phenomena (while of course crass materialism is mere acquisitiveness, a different animal altogether).

This entry, however, is concerned with materialism in the sense of the modern philosophy of mind, namely, the doctrine that 'no thought or feeling occurs without an impulse or twitch of some nerve or fiber as its bodily implementation' and that in consequence it is best to 'recognize mental activity as part of the activity of the body' rather than 'to admit mind as a second substance' (Quine, 1987: 132). This doctrine is now more or less uncontroversial among philosophers (although see Madell, 1988, for a spirited defence of Cartesian-style dualism). What, one may ask, does this have to do with economics? Economists would seem to be committed to the existence of various sorts of mental objects (most notably expectations and preferences) but it might also seem that they have no particular commitment regarding the ontological character of these objects. Why should it make any relevant difference whether they have their being in a Cartesian immaterial medium or in a set of neural states?

To see why it might make a difference, we need to examine a little more closely the varieties of philosophical materialism (for a useful summary of which, see Paul Churchland, 1984). The *identity theory*, as the name implies, makes mental states identical with neural states – nothing more nor less than the latter. *Functionalism* is the doctrine that, while mental states are implemented by specific brain states, they can be identified only by reference to their functional roles, in relation to both behaviour and other mental states. On this view, a given mental state might be implemented by an indefinite disjunction of particular brain states, or computing machine states for that matter. According to *eliminativism*, however, these theories do not pursue the radical implications of materialism with sufficient rigour. Eliminativists argue that, although *some* sorts of mental states may be susceptible to an identity theory or functionalist analysis, many are not; and those that are not must be regarded as in poor ontological standing: they are elements of a primitive 'folk psychology' that will ultimately be eliminated as our understanding of neuroscience progresses. (The term 'folk psychology' is not the exclusive property of the eliminativists, but the latter give it a particularly dismissive charge.)

A connection between eliminative materialism and economics has been made by Alexander Rosenberg (1992). What if the economists' expectations and preferences turn out to be variants of questionable folk psychological notions, rather than mental objects that may be explicated in rigorous materialist terms? Rosenberg argues that this is indeed the case, and that as a result economics cannot hope to do substantially better than common sense in predicting economic behaviour. The economists' basic categories fail to latch onto real, distinct aspects of the world (in the philosophical jargon, to 'carve nature at the joints') and the best we can hope for in a theory based on such categories is the sort of hedged, imprecise and heuristic 'explanation' of behaviour offered by folk psychology. If expectations and preferences were objective and independently measurable phenomena, then the theory which explains and predicts behaviour on the basis of these categories would be open to progressive refinement as a result of improvement in the technology of measurement (as has been the case with many physical theories). But there can be no independent measurement in the case at issue: in fact, the ascription to people of particular expectations and preferences is, Rosenberg argues, bound up in a circular relationship with the observable behaviour that is supposedly being explained.

Rosenberg's argument poses an interesting challenge for economists. Cottrell (1995) tries to turn at least part of the force of his objection by reference to Dennett's broadly functionalist version of materialism, in particular what he calls 'intentional system theory' (see Dennett, 1987). Dennett argues that prediction of behaviour on the basis of intentional states (such as expectations and preferences) is, in relation to certain sorts of complex systems that have been 'well designed' by evolutionary processes, far from vacuous, and that the circularity in question is not truly vicious. Economics (or part of the subject, at any rate) may perhaps be conceived as applied intentional system theory, in Dennett's sense. Other responses to Rosenberg are possible. For instance, one might argue that certain sorts of economic theory are able to generate valid predictions on a basis other than the expectations/preferences couple. One interesting example in point is the work of Farjoun and Machover (1983), who justify some of the predictions of Marxian economics using little more than the idea that an economy – somewhat like a gas, in the theory of statistical mechanics – is a system with very large degrees of freedom. On this basis certain important regularities can be expected to emerge (in Marx's phrase) 'behind the backs of' the human participants in the economy, and more or less independently of their beliefs and volition.

A further potential implication of materialism for economics may be noted in closing. The human brain is an admirable calculating engine: it is nonetheless the finite material product of a process of biological evolution, which implies certain limitations. Thorstein Veblen (1961: 73) famously ridiculed what he called the 'hedonistic' conception of the economic agent as 'a lightning calculator of pleasures and pains, who oscillates like a homogeneous globule of desire of happiness under the impulse of stimuli that shift him about the area, but leave him intact'. From a materialist perspective, Veblen was right enough. In order to develop an adequate conception of the human economic agent it is necessary to pay attention to the materially determined limits of our ability to 'calculate pleasures and pains' – perhaps along the lines indicated by Simon (for example, 1992), Heiner (1983) and Sargent (1993).

ALLIN COTTRELL

References

Churchland, Paul (1984), *Matter and Consciousness*, Cambridge, MA: MIT Press.
Cottrell, Allin (1995), 'Intentionality and Economics', *Economics and Philosophy*, **11** (1).
Dennett, Daniel C. (1987), *The Intentional Stance*, Cambridge, MA: MIT Press.
Farjoun, Emmanuel and Moshe Machover (1983), *Laws of Chaos*, London: Verso.
Heiner, Ronald (1983), 'The Origin of Predictable Behavior', *American Economic Review*, **73**, (4), September, 560–95.
Madell, Geoffrey (1988), *Mind and Materialism*, Edinburgh: Edinburgh University Press.
Quine, W.V. (1987), *Quiddities*, Cambridge, MA: Harvard University Press.
Rosenberg, Alexander (1992), *Economics – Mathematical Politics or Science of Diminishing Returns?*, Chicago: University of Chicago Press.
Sargent, Thomas J. (1993), *Bounded Rationality in Macroeconomics*, Oxford: Oxford University Press.
Simon, Herbert (1992), *Economics, Bounded Rationality and the Cognitive Revolution*, Aldershot: Edward Elgar.
Veblen, Thorstein (1961), 'Why is Economics not an Evolutionary Science?', *The Place of Science in Modern Civilization, and Other Essays*, New York: Russell and Russell (originally published in the *Quarterly Journal of Economics*, **XII**, July 1898).

Metaphor

Metaphor, a figure of speech in which one thing is talked about in terms of language and attributes drawn from another, was brought to the attention of economists in the context of a wider set of issues associated with the rhetoric of economics (McCloskey, 1983; 1986; Henderson, 1982). Earlier, there had been some historical study of particular metaphors such as the development of notions of the 'wheel of wealth', or the links between the circulation of blood and of money (Patinkin, 1973, Viner, 1937). McCloskey, however, chose to weave the notion of particular economic metaphors with literature on the theory of metaphor, as developed by scholars engaged in literary and philosophical discussions. Such discussions challenged 'glassy metaphors of the mind' in which an external world is reflected by language and thought and returned to a much earlier idea, associated with the historian Vico. Vico held that, by working in the world, people create it anew. Metaphors are neither reflections of some 'real world', nor merely 'textual decoration', but rather a means whereby a world is constructed. Innovative metaphors disrupt established ideas, extend economic theory and develop the language of economics.

There are problems to be encountered in making a systematic analysis of the role of metaphor in economics discourse. If we are dealing with metaphor as (primarily) a phenomenon of language, it is not self-evident what meaning is to be attached to 'the language of economics'. There are different schools of economic thought, engaged in differing problems and practices, and the possibility of a series of economic languages, differing in significant detail, but carrying a 'family resemblance' amongst them, must be considered (see below). Language use in formal economics is evidenced by text types, or genres, such as textbooks, economic reports and innovative research articles. Speech acts associated with the face-to-face discussion of economics may work in ways that are different from the formal written discourse of academic economics (Klamer, 1983). In principle, the more widely the discursive net is cast, the more the catch will resemble contemporary features of standard language development.

Recognizing and defining metaphor can also be problematic. Various figures of speech, accompanied by exemplification from economics texts, can be found in the literature on the rhetoric of economics. Metaphor, other significant tropes and figures such as personification, hyperbole, paradox and the analytical device known as analogy are included (McCloskey, 1983; 1986; Henderson, 1994). These can assist in the textual identification of metaphor and so raise the awareness of economists to its nature. A useful generic definition is that metaphor is a situation in which what is said or written is not literally what is meant. Exemplifications of this sense of metaphor are necessary, especially if the aim is to undertake text analysis. Such exemplifications, however interesting, can hardly be ends in themselves, for what is of interest is not each example but a methodological evaluation of the complex role of metaphor in the promotion and extension of economic argument. Given that the notion of metaphor covers just about every feature of language use, systematic discussion requires a specification of a theory of metaphor.

Although Aristotle's notion of transference of meanings between two nouns, 'Achilles is a lion', is no longer sufficient to encapsulate all aspects of the contemporary understanding of metaphor, it remains useful as a starting point. We know that 'Achilles' is not a 'lion'. By a process of negotiation, we are supposed to be able to work out, unambiguously, the terms in which transference can take place. This can be done by developing a series of positive and negative analogies of the senses in which 'Achilles' 'is' and 'is not' a 'lion'. The nouns are not synonyms and the phrase is not a definition. Readers of poetry are, however, unlikely to process a metaphor in this way. Given wider textual relationships, something more impressionistic or cumulative might do. Poetic extension is often between two radically unlike entities, and it is the linguistic displacement which creates the similarity. Reducing the poetic metaphor to literal comparisons, in the manner of Aristotle, may not be possible.

A consideration of a simple example illustrates the ways in which economists call imaginatively upon the ordinary resources of language to develop economic terminology. In the British National Concordance, the terms 'clean' and 'dirty' associated with the term 'price' is found only in a single financial economics source held as part of the wider collection of sources.[1] Here we have an adjective, rather than, as in Aristotle's example, a noun, carrying the transfer of meaning. If we come across a 'clean price', we are expected to determine meaning: the price has not been 'washed' or 'dusted' but it may have been 'contaminated' in some way. The conclusion may be that something has been removed to make it more acceptable. We would be unlikely to get any further on the basis of comparison. But the definition of the process of 'price cleaning' is entirely technical and a larger unit of text is required to make this apparent. The terms of the metaphor only partially apply, but the vocabulary item supplied is useful and any ambiguity of meaning is resolved by a definition. The living 'clean' is effectively, and in this case rapidly, neutralized by the technical definition. The technical process itself did not require an insight into the concept of 'cleaning' in order to come into being. Given this use of 'clean', adjusting prices in other situations then requires an alternative metaphor, as in 'shadow' prices as used in neoclassical project appraisal analyses. The metaphor is, in each case, descriptive, rather than generative. Metaphor in this sense 'extends what we can say … with the vocabulary we have' (Loewenberg, 1973: 44). This process of language development, can either be ad hoc, as in this case, or *extended*. Ad hoc developments may have little to tell us about systematic economic thought, other than that, in minor ways, the vocabulary is continually adjusting. The development of an extended vocabulary is usually associated with predictive (generative) metaphor

What about the sentence-level example, 'the economic agent is a utility maximizer'? Is this a metaphor? Knowing that economists extend economic theory by recognizing that 'situation x is just like situation y', a process of metaphorical extension, McCloskey would add, paraphrasing Becker's analytical innovations, 'the criminal is a small businessman' and 'the family is a little firm' (McCloskey, 1994: 328). Fragments of language, here dealing with aspects of economic agency, are still inadequate to establish meaning. There may be discourse communities in which such statements are taken literally, as perhaps in a crime-ridden district of Naples. The 'is' in the case of the economic agent can easily carry the force of a definition, reversing the order of terms does not lead to any significant degree of tension. (Would it if it simply said 'man is a utility maximizer' or would we wish to define 'man' on some other basis?) Reversing the sentence order in the case of the 'criminal' and 'the family', however, leads to dissimilar results: 'the small businessman is a criminal'! There is a surplus of meaning and acceptable, negotiated meaning is less certain. The metaphor in both these cases is disruptive so long as we keep in mind families and businessmen in general.

Economic metaphors such as Becker's, however, must be argued for, rather than assumed. Meanings are settled again, 'after' the innovation, by an explicit logic, using economic concepts derived, in his case, from the theory of the firm and from investment theory (Becker, 1993). The logic spells out the sense in which the analysis is or is not sustainable. Poets need not do this but Becker, in extending applications within economics, must. The focus shifts from descriptive to predictive power. When successful ideas are repeated and the association of words settles down (a new 'equilibrium'), the force of the metaphor is intentionally deadened. The full force of such extensions can thereafter only be understood 'before the event' (that is historically, textually) and within a context of economic argument beyond the level of the sentence. 'Dead' metaphor (cliché) is the anticipated outcome of knowledge but not the anticipated outcome of poetry.

For an understanding of the development of economic ideas, the notion of *extended* metaphor, either as a series of related metaphors, or as models and analogies, with implications that help sustain longer stretches of argument, is likely to be much more significant (Loewenberg, 1973: 32). 'Root metaphor', providing a basis for the sustained discussion of a topic from which supporting metaphors and a consistent language springs, highlights the generative role of metaphor. Pepper points to four philosophical root metaphors which have stood the test of time: formism (in which the root metaphor is 'similarity'), mechanism ('the machine'), organicism ('the organic process') and contextualism ('the historical event') (Pepper, 1942: 141). Conventional economics has been heavily influenced in theory development by an underlying notion of a mechanism of some sort, the precise mechanism altering according to particular mechanics. There can be little doubt that whole sets of language from the notion of 'the economic system' itself to particular aspects of microeconomic modelling ('the price mechanism', 'market forces', 'equilibrium') have been generated around a consistent root. Institutionalists should, in principle, use a set of concepts built around contextualism, though the language of institutional economics is likely to bear a strong family resemblance to conventional economics. Marshall hoped for an organic economics. Though his hope is still unrealized, trade in metaphor between economics and biology has been historically significant for both disciplines, and is still going on.

Root metaphors may be buried 'deep'. We may think, for example, of the 'magnificent dynamics' of classical economics in terms of economic growth. We could also think in terms of movement, bodies in motion or at rest. This move can lead towards a wider question, 'Who informed Smith's view of motion: Aristotle or Newton?', and so from there to the intellectual origins of 'the stationary state'. It is clear that, in attempting such an analysis, any 'digging' must be carried out on appropriate texts. Paradoxically, the 'roots' are on the 'surface' of discourse. Textual analysis has to be informed by issues raised by those interested in the rhetoric of economics, including issues of tropical recognition (mentioned earlier), narrative, point-of-view and cohesion (McCloskey, 1986; 1994; Brown, 1994). Once the 'roots' have been exposed, some sort of reconsideration may become appropriate. Such reflection is called for at moments of intellectual crisis. Thus the switch made by Keynes can be stylized as changing the question from 'Why is the automatic adjustment mechanism not working?', which suggests that the questioner is still being used by (in context) an inappropriate metaphor, to 'Is there such a mechanism?' In reframing, Keynes pointed to the cumulative rather than corrective aspect of market disturbance. The spiral structure of *The General Theory* is testimony to the difficulties involved in escaping from the influence of a pervasive metaphor and replacing its world view with a new one (Marzola and Silva, 1994).

Edgeworth, who was, like Keynes, a creative and visual thinker, 'saw', by metaphorical insight, the relationship between imprecise quantities in physics and imprecise quantities in economics and then developed the specific analogy: 'kinetic energy : potential energy :: expenditure : utility' (Henderson, 1993; Mirowski, 1995). As a result of such an interdisciplinary extension, spelled out also by other founding members of the neoclassical school, the lexis, argumentation and genres used in the economic community gradually changed. The move towards mathematical analogies, as well as a turn to 'scientific process' as the major metaphor for knowledge development, increases the pace of change. The humanities essay, found in the *Economics Journal* at the start of its life, gradually changed into (or was replaced by) the scientific research paper as published in the *Economic Journal* today (Dudley-Evans and Henderson, 1993). Whilst the original extension made (say) by Edgeworth is metaphorical, concepts such as 'utility maximization' or 'equilibrium' rarely have to be traced back to their foundations in order for us to develop an understanding of what is intended.

At the frontiers, researchers constantly look to see if they can borrow, by extension, ideas which are effective elsewhere. 'Human capital' is one such innovation. Taken literally, 'human capital' would point to 'slavery'. The linguistic transfer extended the insights of capital analysis to educational activity, switched education from 'consumption' to 'investment' and initiated studies in 'rate-of-return' analyses. The 'selfish gene', a predictive concept in biological research, is merely economic agency extended metaphorically to genetics. While these are illustrations of powerful generative metaphors, it is less clear that these can be specified in generic terms. Poetic insight is one way of specifying the initial selection process. In living metaphor, the original discourse, from which the idea is extended to the target discourse, remains relevant, at least in the early stage of the transference of ideas. Dead metaphors, in contrast, are embedded in a set of stable subject associations or definitions. There is clearly a cline, with the Becker examples, above, still somewhere in the active groups. A natural process is for useful metaphors to be repeated, to develop a consistent set of related words around them and hence to 'decay', however gradually. Of course, newcomers to the discipline may find dead metaphors coming awkwardly to life.

The evaluation of metaphor in the various ways of 'doing' economics is complex. Metaphor's communicative and heuristic role can be outlined by the use of text analyses. It would be surprising if it were substantially different from the use of metaphor in other reasoned discourse. A list of attributes would include: incisive communication, a capacity to reveal something new, access to a language which can then be extended to new areas of discussion, a method of linking complex ideas to familiar ones and an ability to develop a community of interest between author and readership (Crider and Cirillo, 1991).

Historically, the fruitfulness of past metaphors is partly revealed by the traces left in the language of present-day economics: for example, various 'watery' metaphors used to communicate ideas of 'equilibrium'. What about 'deeper' aspects of assessing generative and extended metaphors? Mirowski, for example, argues that neoclassical economics is flawed because it failed to achieve a complete mapping of nineteenth-century physics onto economics (Mirowski, 1989). This judgment must be approached with care. Hoover holds that, according to Mirowski, just about everything is metaphorical (Hoover, 1991). We need a theory of metaphor within which to evaluate such methodological claims.

Metaphor does not imply a complete mapping. Indeed, as the terms in a metaphor are not synonyms, as long as the metaphor remains alive a degree of tension must remain. The sense in which a mapping can or cannot be made is part of the research process. A complete fit would imply that economics is physics and so talk of metaphor would be irrelevant. Metaphors usually articulate positive aspects of 'fit' and suppress negative aspects. Articulation and suppression are significant parts of their success. Metaphors, in this sense, imply only partial success, a continuing tension, deadened, but not quite extinguished, by convention. If there is a constant need to return to the source discipline, in order to enhance understanding or to settle meaning, the metaphor has failed.

The most active metaphors are likely to be at the frontiers of the discipline. If models are extended metaphors or mixtures of metaphors and analogies then along with predictive success go questions concerning their 'truth value'. If metaphors are useful lies then clearly some reflection upon their 'truthfulness' as well as their usefulness may be required. Here there is probably a need for more systematic work on the methodological consequences of seeing models and analogies, including mathematical analogy, as extended metaphor. A philosophical rather than a literary or linguistic approach is probably required, though an advantage of an approach via 'poetry' is that is stresses the imaginative and innovative function of metaphor. A systematic dialogue between conventional methods of evaluating models and the pattern based upon metaphor and associated ideas, such as narrative, which integrates various aspects of current discussion is essential (McCloskey, 1990; Henderson, 1994).

WILLIE HENDERSON

Note
1.   This tells us that this use of 'clean' end 'dirty' is unique to the language of financial economics.

Bibliography

Becker, G. (1993), *Human Capital: a theoretical and empirical analysis*, 3rd edn, Chicago: University of Chicago Press.
Brown, V. (1994), 'The Economy as Text', in R.E. Backhouse (ed.), *New Directions in Economic Methodology*, London: Routledge.
Crider, C. and L. Cirillo, (1991), 'Systems of interpretation and the function of metaphor', *Journal for the Theory of Social Behaviour*, **22**, (2), 171–95.
Dudley-Evans, T. and W. Henderson, (1993), 'The Development of the Economics Article: 1891–1993', *Finlance: A Finnish Journal of Applied Linguistics*, **xii**, 159–80.
Henderson, W. (1982), 'Metaphor in Economics', *Economics*, **18**, 147–53.
Henderson, W. (1993), 'The Problem of Edgeworth's Style', in W. Henderson, T. Dudley-Evans and R. Backhouse (eds), *Economics as Language*, London: Routledge.
Henderson, W. (1994), 'Metaphor and Economics', in R.E. Backhouse (ed.), New Directions in Economic Methodology, London: Routledge.
Hoover, K.D. (1991), 'Mirowski's screed: a review of Philip Mirowski's *More Heat than Light: Economics as Social Physics, Physics as Nature's Economics*', *Methodus*, **3**, (1), 139–45.
Klamer, A. (1983), *Conversations with Economists: New Classical Economists and Opponents speak out on the Current Controversy in Macro-Economics*, Totawa, NJ: Rowman & Littlefield.
Loewenberg, I. (1973), 'Truth and Consequences of Metaphor', *Philosophy and Rhetoric*, **6**, (1), 30–46.
Marzola, A. and F. Silva (eds) (1994), *John Maynard Keynes: Language and Method*, trans. R. Davies, Aldershot: Edward Elgar.
McCloskey, D.N.(1983), 'The rhetoric of economics', *Journal of Economics Literature*, **321**, 434–61
McCloskey, D.N. (1986), *The Rhetoric of Economics*, Brighton: Wheatsheaf.
McCloskey, D.N. (1990), *If You're so Smart: The Narrative of Economic Expertise*, Chicago: University of Chicago Press.
McCloskey, D.N. (1994), 'How to do a Rhetorical Analysis, and Why', in R.E. Backhouse (ed.), *New Directions in Economic Methodology*, London: Routledge.
Mirowski, P. (1989), *More Heat than Light: Economics as Social Physics, Physics as Nature's Economics*, Cambridge: Cambridge University Press.
Mirowski, P. (1995), 'Marshalling the Unruly Atoms: understanding Edgeworth's career', in P. Mirowski, (ed.), *Edgeworth's Writings on Chance, Economic Hazard and Statistics*, Totawa, NJ: Rowan & Littlefield.
Patinkin, D. (1973), 'In search of the "wheel of wealth": On the origins of Frank Knight's circular flow diagram', *American Economic Review*, **63**, 1037–46.
Pepper, S. (1942), *World Hypotheses: A Study in Evidence*, Berkeley: University of California Press/London: Cambridge University Press.
Viner, J. (1937), *Studies in the Theory of International Trade*, London/New York: Allen & Unwin.

Methodological Individualism/Atomism

The doctrine of methodological individualism is widely accepted in economics and in other social sciences, yet the doctrine itself is seldom clearly formulated and in fact many different ideas fall under the individualist rubric.[1] Some of those ideas are eminently plausible, others are far less so. In each case the crucial issues are empirical ones, either about economic and social processes or about the effects of various research strategies on scientific progress. This entry outlines these issues, focusing on ontological, reductive, explanatory and heuristic formulations of the doctrine.

Methodological individualism draws much of its intuitive plausibility from its *ontological* formulations. Three common ontological theses are (1) that society is composed of and does not exist over and above individual human beings, (2) that social processes are completely determined by processes involving individuals, and (3) that all the economically or socially relevant properties of individual persons are monadic, that is are properties that do not involve either other individuals or social entities such as groups or institutions. A logically weaker version of (3) would allow non-monadic properties of individuals so long as they involved only non-essential or external relations. These three claims are logically independent: the truth of one does not entail the truth of any other.

The first two ontological claims have seemed like truisms. They perhaps are, but only on their least interesting formulation. Holists can grant that social entities are composed of and not separable from individuals, yet still claim that collective entities have an essential place in our ontology because of the role they play in explanation, just as biologist can grant that organisms are composed entirely of molecules and yet think that organisms are real entities. So this ontological principle takes on significant content only when conjoined with further claims about explanation and reduction. The second ontological claim is perhaps best put as a claim about supervenience (see entry, 'Supervenience'), that is, that once all the facts about individuals are set then so are the facts about social entities. This principle looks highly plausible on first sight, but again that is because it ultimately asserts very little. Once we drop the qualifier 'all' and substitute specific kinds of facts about individuals – biological, psychological and so on – the thesis is far from a truism. Moreover, as we will see below, these two ontological principles do not necessarily entail other, more important individualist claims about the reduction of social theories to individualist theories, about explanation or about research strategies. Much of the intuitive appeal of individualism may thus come from conflating the plausible but relatively trivial ontological versions of individualism with its much more substantive but contentious formulations about explanation, reduction and the like.

The third ontological claim is the root idea behind the related doctrine of *atomism*, whose denial is *organicism* (see entry, 'Organicism'). Atomism is a considerably more substantive doctrine; not surprisingly, it is not an obvious truth like those cited above. Our best evidence about what properties individuals have comes from our best theory about them, and thus the plausibility of atomism depends on the plausibility of other individual doctrines about reduction and explanation. If every explanation in terms of social entities can be captured by some individualist explanation, then arguably atomism is supported, for we need make no essential reference to non-individual properties. So this ontological doctrine depends on other versions of individualism discussed below.

Apart from claims about ontology, individualism is also frequently put forward as a claim about *theory reduction*, and in this form draws inspiration from the general positivist view that the sciences form a hierarchy that is unified by reducing the special sciences to their more general counterparts below them, such as sociology to psychology, psychology to biology, or biology to chemistry. The basic goal of theory reduction is to show one theory to be a special case of another. Doing that requires at least two things. First, the basic descriptive terms or predicates of the theory to be reduced must be shown to exhibit lawful coextensionality with some predicate(s) in the more fundamental theory. Such 'bridge laws' allow us to substitute terms of the reducing theory for terms of the theory to be eliminated. (Note, however, that this sameness of reference is a weaker condition than definitional synonymy, which is an unreasonable requirement for reduction: 'gene' may not have the same semantic content as 'DNA sequence', yet the two have the same referent.) The second requirement for reduction is that we be able, with the help of the bridge laws, to derive the true or well-confirmed laws, explanations and so on of the theory to be reduced from those of the more fundamental theory. These requirements for reduction represent the ideal case. In actual practice, reductions are a more messy affair, with some concepts and statements of the reduced theory being revised and still others eliminated altogether as ties are made to the reducing theory.

Thus, as a thesis about reduction, individualism claims that any adequate explanation in terms of social entities can be derived from a theory referring solely to individuals. This reductionist thesis can take different forms, depending on what individualist variables are invoked. For example, if the explanatory variables are those described by some psychological theory (excluding rational choice theory), the reductionist thesis will be one version of the somewhat ambiguous doctrine known as psychologism.

Supporters and critics have traditionally tried to show that theory reduction must be possible or impossible because of some general facts about the economic and social world. Thus holists have argued that reduction is impossible because individual behaviour is causally influenced by larger social processes. Individualists in turn frequently support reducibility by citing the plausible ontological principles mentioned above. Since society is made up solely of individuals and does not act independently of them, they reason that theories referring to social entities must be reducible (Watkins, 1973).

Neither argument succeeds. Macroeconomic processes might influence individual behaviour and yet that influence might itself be in turn capturable in individualist terms. Similarly, every economic process above the level of individuals might result from the action of individuals and yet our theory of individual behaviour might not have the power necessary to capture non-individualist explanations in individual terms. Theory reduction requires a one-to-one linking between each term to be reduced and some purely individualist description. Such linkages may be hard to find because the given macro state may be brought about in indefinitely many different ways by individual behaviour. This possible problem – generally called the 'multiple realizations' problem in the literature on reduction – is enough to show that the simple ontological theses do not *entail* reducibility (see Fodor, 1974). To use an example from outside economics, the terms 'chair' and 'antibody' describe physical entities, but we have little chance of reducing explanations in terms of them because there are indefinitely many ways to make chairs and millions of different structures that can serve as antibodies. A similar conclusion can also be reached by noting that even explanations that refer to individuals may not support reduction, because they explain partly in non-individualist terms. Thus an account of individual behaviour within corporations that described individuals in terms of their institutional roles or an account of consumer behaviour that invokes unreduced macroeconomic variables like aggregate income or government taxation would not provide a complete reduction; in the process of explaining individual behaviour, we would be using rather than eliminating information about social entities. Nothing about the ontological claims mentioned above guarantees that our best explanations of individual behaviour will not be like this. Again, reducibility is not entailed or even shown likely by the obvious ontological truths of individualism.

The upshot here is that individualism as a reductionist thesis is an empirical issue, one that will have to be decided case by case. The key issues will be whether in actual fact the possible problems mentioned above are real in practice: are economic phenomena of the same general kind brought about by very diverse types of individual behaviour? Do our best accounts of economic actors necessarily invoke variables from higher levels of organization? There is no reason to expect any single, universal answer, and thus an overall assessment here is impossible. At best we can provide some more specific examples of what the empirical debate will look like and the kinds of considerations that might tip the evidence one way or the other.

Three factors are likely to determine whether theory reductions are possible: the level of aggregation involved, the extent to which selective processes are invoked and the extent to which micro-level theories are truly individualist in character. When the explanations to be reduced are at a very high level of aggregation, the prospect that macro-level processes can result from diverse micro-level states is increased. For example, if there are any general causal macroeconomic patterns at the level of aggregate employment, income and the like, there may be good reason to think those patterns can be brought about by quite different combinations of market activities at lower levels of aggregation. Since theory reduction requires a lawlike, one-to-one mapping from predicates of the reduced theory to those of the reducing theory, these divergent ways in which macroeconomic patterns might come about argue against reducibility.

Selective processes – for example, the differential survival rates of corporations with different traits due to competition – raise obstacles to reduction because they may not 'see' or 'care' about individual-level detail. Thus, if we explain market phenomena by invoking profit-maximizing behaviour by corporations and justify the latter assumption on the grounds of economic selection, real obstacles may exist to reducing those explanations to individualist ones. A variety of different internal structures, incentive systems and so on may result in profit-maximizing corporations, as the variety of recent work on the firm would seem to suggest, since theories based on efficiency wages, implicit contracts, asymmetric information, transactions costs and so on can all be consistent with maximization at the corporate level. So long as selection is for profitability and not internal structure, we may expect diverse sets of individual behaviour producing macro-level behaviour. Since theory reduction requires that we equate-macro-level descriptions with some determinate set of individual behaviour, *reduction* seems unlikely.

Another key issue in debates over reducibility is the extent to which current microeconomic theories really are individualist in nature.[2] There is good reason to think that extant work is not and thus, whatever is involved in supplying 'microfoundations', those foundations are not individualist reductions. Explanations in terms of corporations and households are in terms of collective social entities, not individuals. Treating an aggregation of consumers or producers as a representative agent is again not explaining in terms of individuals. (One can always, of course, simply decide to call aggregate or collective social entities 'individuals', but doing so threatens to trivialize the issue, since individualism now becomes compatible with the unreduced appeal to classes, institutions and other standard holist explanatory devices.) Moreover, even when microeconomic accounts treat only individuals, those accounts still may not suffice for full reduction. Rational choice explanations generally presuppose, rather than explain, much institutional structure: for example, property rights or initial distributions of resources and preferences. For these reasons, current microeconomic theory may not provide individualist reductions. However, *partial* reductions – of the social to the relatively less aggregative or of parts of macro-level theories to individualist ones – may still be possible and arguably are warranted by successes in microeconomic theory.

Apart from claims about theory reduction, individualists may make claims about *explanation*, both claims about what suffices to explain and what is necessary. As a thesis about what suffices to explain, individualism asserts that, even if macro level theories cannot be reduced, still at least every macro event can be fully explained in individualist terms. This thesis is ambiguous and again may owe some of its appeal to conflating a plausible but less interesting interpretation with an implausible but interesting one. To see this it is important to distinguish explanations of tokens from explanations of types: 'the business cycle' is a type, 'the recession of 1973–4' is a token. The plausible thesis is that every macro event token has at least a partial explanation in individualist terms. The implausible thesis is that those explanations are complete or that every macro event type has an individualist explanation. The latter claim is dubious because it is really the reductionist thesis all over again, for it claims that we can link types of events, which is what reduction involves.

A much more interesting claim is that individualist theories suffice to explain fully, even if reduction fails. In other words, by explaining each token in individualist terms, we get a full explanation even though the type–type connections needed for reduction are not available. This thesis raises complex issues about explanation. If we think of explanation as providing causal information, an explanation is complete to the extent that it provides all the causal information. The key question then becomes whether a full account of the individual behaviour bringing about a given macro state suffices to capture all the causal information. There is reason to think it does not, for macro-level causal generalizations provide us with causal knowledge that is lost if we focus only on the specific individual actions involved. Without reduction, we are unable to tie the event in question to other *kinds* of macro-level events, thus preventing us from answering many standard causal questions.

The second way to understand explanatory versions of individuals is to focus on what is necessary to explain: to take individualism as a claim not about what *can* be done but about what *must* be done. Two versions of this thesis are common: one that says that *unreduced* macro-level theories are explanatorily inadequate and a second, weaker, thesis that claims *mechanisms* are necessary. The strong thesis that no macro-level theory explains is quite implausible. In science in general, macro-level causal explanations are common currency, and no one asserts that Kepler's laws cannot explain since they were advanced without and still do not have a quantum mechanical reduction. So there is no general principle of methodology that shows unreduced macro-level theories as inadequate. Thus, if such theories in economics are inadequate, it must be for reasons special to the discipline. For example, it might be that some macroeconomic aggregate variables are not the proper kind of things to stand in causal relations – averages come to mind (see Nelson, 1989) – but we know of no good argument that establishes that conclusion for all aggregative concepts in economics. Barring further arguments, it seems implausible to claim that macroeconomic explanations are inadequate simply because they are unreduced.

The demand that good social science must provide individualist *mechanisms* is intuitively both interesting and plausible. Some version of this demand was advocated by Popper (1966) and Agassi (1973), called by the latter, and more recently by Elster (1989), 'institutional individualism'. It is important to note that the demand for mechanisms (a) is not the same as a demand for reduction or even full explanation in individual terms and (b) can be taken as a claim either about what is necessary for confirmation or for explanation. Those who are most vocal in defence of this methodological imperative claim it is a general precept of good science (for example, Elster 1989). That is obviously wrong. A first problem is that 'the causal mechanism' is of dubious sense, since there are indefinitely many levels at which causal processes can be described. Moreover, the history and practice of science is full of cases of well confirmed and explanatory accounts that do not provide the underlying causal mechanism. Darwin, for example, explained the evolution of traits and species without a molecular biology of the gene and, in fact, did so with a mistaken theory of the mechanisms of inheritance.

The need for mechanisms is thus contingent and contextual. The importance of mechanisms in confirmation seems to depend on such things as (a) how much confidence we have in our aggregate account, (b) how specific are the presuppositions of the macro-level theory about underlying processes, and (c) how much confidence we have in our theory of the mechanisms. Demands for microfoundations in macroeconomics thus have to be evaluated in light of these questions and cannot be taken as an unqualified demand of good science. For example, assuming that New Keynesian models do not assume systematic irrationality but can instead result from a variety of different plausible individual behaviours (efficiency wages and so on) and assuming that those models fit well the aggregate data, precise microfoundations are probably not essential to confirmation. In fact, it is entirely possible that in some circumstances our confidence in macro-level theories might be sufficiently high and our understanding of underlying individual behaviour sufficiently poor that we could reasonably demand 'macro-foundations' for any account of individual behaviour.

The role of microfoundations in explanation are less clear because of unclarities in the notion of explanation itself. Current views about explanation frequently make pragmatic factors such as the interests of the audience, the problem situation of the time period and the state of background knowledge essential parts of what constitutes a good explanation (van Fraassen, 1980; Achinstein, 1983). That account would again make the demand for mechanisms, construed as a constraint on explanation, contingent and contextual. Thus it is hard to say anything convincing about the relative importance of individualist mechanisms in explanation without a much longer story about the state of economics in general. However, surely some relatively weak demand for mechanisms – one that allows mechanisms involving corporations, representative individuals and other such aggregate entities and does not make highly restrictive assumptions about rationality – is a plausible stricture on explanation, given the current context (see Janssen, 1993).

Finally, individualism can be taken as a *heuristic*: as a rough rule of thumb about how to produce good science. There are many possible different heuristics that could be labelled 'individualist', in effect one for each of the above versions of individualism. Thus we might recommend 'seek reductions' or 'seek mechanisms' or 'seek partial explanations of specific events' and so on. Evaluating such advice is complicated by a number of factors. Heuristics are presumably empirically based recommendations about what produces good science. That means we must both be clear about what the goals of good science are and be able to draw conclusions that hold across times and disciplines. It is probably unlikely that any single strategy promotes scientific growth in all contexts. Moreover, there is no guarantee that a roughly reductionist strategy will produce reductionist theories or that more holistic heuristics cannot lead to reductionist results. Vitalism, for example, was arguably a productive heuristic in early nineteenth-century biology when biochemistry was primitive; the success of the organismic approach ultimately made possible modern molecular biology.

It would thus be surprising if any strong general conclusions could be drawn about individualist heuristics in economics. Individualist heuristics – largely of the 'seek mechanisms' variety rather than 'seek reductions' – have been enormously powerful. Yet much of modern economics would not have been possible if the corporation had not been treated as a black box, with the underlying causes in terms of individual behaviour within corporations being more or less totally ignored. The successes of general equilibrium theory would not have been possible if complete individualist underpinnings had been demanded, for arguably making everyone a price taker leaves the market price an unexplained aggregate concept (see Janssen, 1993). And surely much of macroeconomics as we now know it would not exist if only individualist theories or theories with individualist mechanisms had been sought.

HAROLD KINCAID

Notes

1. For collections of articles defending and criticizing various versions of individualism, see Martin and McIntyre (1994) and O'Neill (1973). The general approach to individualism employed here is defended in Kincaid (1994, 1995, 1997). Blaug (1980) and Gordon (1991) have extensive discussion of methodological individualism in economics.
2. For more detailed arguments along these lines, see Nelson (1989), Janssen (1993) and Kincaid (1995, 1997).

References

Achinstein, Peter (1983), *The Nature of Explanation*, Oxford: Oxford University Press.
Agassi, J. (1973), 'Methodological Individualism', in J. O'Neill (ed.), *Modes of Individualism and Collectivism*, London: Heinemann.
Blaug, Mark (1980), *The Methodology of Economics: Or How Economists Explain*, Cambridge: Cambridge University Press.
Elster, Jon (1989), *Nuts and Bolts for the Social Sciences*, Cambridge: Cambridge University Press.
Fodor, J.A. (1974), 'Special Sciences (Or: The Disunity of Science As A Working Hypothesis)', *Synthèse*, **28**, 97–115.
Gordon, Scott (1991), *The History and Philosophy of Social Science*, London: Routledge.
Janssen, Maarten (1993), *Microfoundations*, London: Routledge.
Kincaid, Harold (1994), 'The Empirical Nature of the Individualism–Holism Dispute', *Synthèse*, **97**, 229–47.
Kincaid, Harold (1995), *Philosophical Foundations of the Social Sciences: Analysing Controversies in Social Research*, Cambridge: Cambridge University Press.
Kincaid, Harold (1997), *Individualism and the Unity of Science: Essays on Explanation, Reduction, and the Special Sciences*, Lanham, MD: Rowman & Littlefield.
Martin, Michael and Lee McIntyre (1994), *Readings in the Philosophy of the Social Sciences*, Cambridge, MA: MIT Press.
Nelson, Alan (1984), 'Some Issues Surrounding the Reduction of Macroeconomics to Microeconomics', *Philosophy of Science*, **51**, 573–94.
Nelson, Alan, (1989), 'Average Explanations', *Erkenntnis*, **30**, 23–42.
O'Neill, J. (ed.) (1973), *Modes of Individualism and Collectivism*, London: Heinemann.
Popper, Karl (1966), *The Open Society and Its Enemies*, New York: Harper & Row.
Van Fraassen, Bas (1980), *The Scientific Image*, Oxford: Oxford University Press.
Watkins, J.N. (1973), 'Methodological Individualism: A Reply', in O'Neill (ed.), *Modes of Individualism and Collectivism*, London: Heinemann.

Methodological Pluralism

Methodological pluralism is here equated with epistemologic pluralism, as representing an answer to the question of the number of appropriate paths or sets of criteria by which knowledge is attained. It must be distinguished from ontological pluralism, which raises a similar question as to the singularity of the ultimate nature or basis of existence, and from theoretical pluralism, which raises the question as to the number of meaningful theories which can coexist.

Methodological pluralism is readily but not necessarily combined with the view that the object of study, the economy itself, is a matter of social construction. Also epistemological (methodological), ontological and theoretical considerations are not mutually exclusive in practice. Although one can define each independently of the others, in practice, positions on one of them are frequently extended to the others. This is perhaps especially the case with the ontological assumptions and/or implications of epistemology. Moreover, complications arise from the inexorable operation of selective perception of 'order' and 'anarchy' in epistemological and ontological matters. Finally, not all the elements of the version of methodological pluralism presented here need be accepted; different versions would have different formulations – a situation consistent with methodological pluralism itself.

Methodological pluralism ultimately rests on a belief in the necessity of choice in the absence of a single conclusive final methodological or epistemological principle. Choice has to be made between alternative methodologies each of which has its own internal limitations, and there is no single unequivocal, conclusive metaprinciple on which to make that choice.

Methodological pluralism is uncomfortable for those who assume the existence of (1) a given reality, (2) one correct theory and/or (3) one correct methodology and who further assume (4) that our task to is find those singular things; that is, for those who seek determinacy and closure and are uncomfortable with open-endedness and ambiguity (such as, plurality of meaning). But even if everyone believed these assumptions they would still probably disagree as to their substantive content, with a resulting inexorable necessity of choice. The fact of the matter is that, according to methodological pluralism, whatever the status of those four assumptions, our definition of the economy ('economic reality'), economic theory and methodology are all socially constructed: *made*, not found.

Methodological pluralism affirms either that there are no methodological/epistemological absolutes or that no such absolutes have been demonstrated unequivocally; there is also the view that there are no metacriteria by which to choose between alternative methodologies. The position, therefore, affirms the existence and legitimacy of multiple methodological positions.

Induction and deduction, rationalism and empiricism, realism and nominalism, and similar antinomies are understood to be meaningful on their own terms but each is seen to have fundamental limits and to present no conclusive demonstration of the error of the other, such that no position is conclusively dispositive of the issues on which it takes a position. Logic may yield valid inferences or conclusions given the premises and system of reasoning, but a valid inference is not necessarily true. Neither can empirical testing yield a singular and conclusive Truth. Methodological pluralism does not deny the usefulness of the several positions constituting these antinomies, but maintains that no position can be summarily disregarded and that insight can be achieved on the basis of the matrix formed by knowledge generated potentially using each position in all antinomies, whatever individual preferences may be.

Methodological pluralism rejects any exclusivist prescriptivism which seeks to establish one approach to methodology as supreme or to give it a privileged position. This rejection is in favour of a credentialist approach which attempts to establish the specific bases on which particular claims to knowledge rest, without affirming that one set of credentials is *a priori* prescriptively superior to another.

The rationale of methodological pluralism is that, in the absence of metacriteria by which one methodology can be shown unequivocally to be superior to all others, analyses should not be rejected solely on the basis of methodological considerations. On the other hand, methodological anarchy is avoided by emphasizing, first, the identification of the precise nature, grounds and limits of particular methodologies; second, the importance of the *process* by which knowledge and the credentials of knowledge are pursued and knowledge worked out; and third, the process of *criticism* itself.

Methodological pluralism stresses not only the inconclusivity of the various methodologies but also that the object of study probably has many different facets to it, that it can be approached from different standpoints or perspectives, and that in fact different approaches coupled with different facets yield quite different theories and understanding. The possibility that the world is not heterogeneous, and that the multiplicity of facets may be illusory, is not denied. But methodological pluralism argues that decisions about such subjects cannot properly be made *a priori* without foreclosing the process of intelligent inquiry.

Methodological pluralism, with particular views about the status of individual methodologies and the putative character of the objects of study, also draws on the philosophy of language and the sociology of science. From the philosophy of language is derived the view that established linguistic usage is insufficient to ground conclusively statements of putative fact and epistemological procedure. Substantive statements tend to have both epistemological and discursive meaning, with the latter actually tending to predominate. From the sociology of science is derived the view that prescriptivist methodology tends to be conventional in character and to arise from the more or less temporary hegemony of particular sociological groups, including scientists and philosophers. Discursive meaning tends to be a matter of sociological situation and context. With regard to both the philosophy of language and sociology of science, emphasis is on social constructivism.

Apropos of the conduct of science, methodological pluralism affirms that science is not a singular, homogeneous enterprise: science, along with the logical empiricism or logical positivism which tends to be its epistemological rationalization, is comprised of several different methodological positions, so the concept or claim of 'science' does not obviate the case for methodological pluralism.

Methodological pluralism affirms that there are at least three kinds of work in which an economist can be engaged: (1) disciplinary work, pursuing the agenda of a particular paradigm or research programme – in economics, predominantly that of neoclassical economics; (2) subject matter work; and (3) problem-solving, or policy, work, pursuing knowledge of particular subjects and/or bringing that knowledge to bear on policy questions and seeking that knowledge from all relevant disciplines. Methodological pluralism also affirms that an economist may properly do *a priori* theory, quantitative and/or non-quantitative empiricism, history, and so on. Methodological pluralism affirms, too, that an economist may properly do static partial and/or general equilibrium theory or evolutionary economics. Within each of these modes of work there can be, and indeed are, varying methodological approaches – and there certainly are variances between them. It is also the case that no methodological procedure is or can be conducted in practice in absolute isolation from all others (for example, the choice is not between pure induction and pure deduction but between various procedural combinations of the two).

Methodological pluralism acknowledges several roles which theory can perform, and that different modes of practising economics (methodologies) need not perform all roles. These roles include (with variations within each category) explanation, description, prediction, hypothesis, confirmed hypothesis, definition of reality, providing a sense of economic order, understanding, a tool of analysis, mode of discourse (systematization of ideas, framework of discussion, organizing principle, mode of concentrating attention), facilitating manageability, an element in a logical–epistemological structure, prescription, a basis of social construction of reality, a basis of legitimation/criticism, a vehicle of ideology, wishful thinking, paradigm, a means of projection, social control, psychic balm, telling a story, giving economics the status of a science, and referring to neoclassical economics.

Methodological pluralism, so far from affirming a particular conception of economic truth and identifying the same with a particular practice of school of economics, holds that economics as a discipline is an organ of inquiry comprising a vast set of tools, instruments used in probing and telling stories about the economy. These tools include concepts, models, theories, assumptions and so on. They do not in and of themselves necessarily, if at all, define economic reality; rather, they are so many instruments available for use by economic analysts. Moreover, because no one theory can answer every question, and no one theory need give a comprehensive, complete answer to any particular question, tools are available for the selective use and modification of economists to suit their perceived needs of analysing the economy.

Methodological pluralism, in addition to denying hierarchical superiority to any particular methodology, emphasizes (a) the establishment rather than the invidious ranking of credentials; (b) the comprehension and recognition of methodological limits to substantive research; and (c) the process of inquiry, which is always laden with and channelled by metaphysical, discursive and sociological presuppositions.

Methodological pluralism tends to appeal to those economists who neither require nor 'find' absolutist and exclusivist epistemological foundations in order to pursue research. It also appeals to those who see any particular methodology, including any conception of 'science' (or any other conception of knowledge, such as theology), as socially constructed and open to challenge – and therefore to those who are prepared to accept methodology in general and science in particular not as finite givens but as matters of an open-ended (Darwinian) process – a process in which studied identification, juxtaposition and criticism of alternatives figure prominently.

WARREN J. SAMUELS

Bibliography

Caldwell, Bruce (1982), *Beyond Positivism: Economic Methodology in the Twentieth Century*, New York: George Allen & Unwin.

Dancy, Jonathan (1985), *Introduction to Contemporary Epistemology*, Cambridge, MA: Basil Blackwell.

Diesing, Paul (1971), *Patterns of Discovery in the Social Sciences*, Chicago: Aldine-Atherton.

Diesing, Paul (1991), *How Does Social Science Work? Reflections on Practice*, Pittsburgh: University of Pittsburgh Press.

Eisenberg, John A. (1992), *The Limits of Reason: Indeterminacy in Law, Education and Morality*, New Brunswick, NJ: Transaction.

Hutchison, Terence (1992), *Changing Aims in Economics*, Cambridge, MA: Basil Blackwell.

Laudan, Larry (1990), *Science and Relativism: Some Key Controversies in the Philosophy of Science*, Chicago: University of Chicago Press.

de Marchi, Neil and Mark Blaug (eds) (1991), *Appraising Economic Theories: Studies in the Methodology of Research Programs*, Brookfield, VT: Edward Elgar.

Medema, Steven G. and Warren J. Samuels (eds) (1996), *Foundations of Research in Economics: How Do Economists Do Economics?*, Brookfield, VT: Edward Elgar.

Raven, Diederick, Lieteke Van Vucht Tijssen and Jan de Wolf (eds) (1992), *Cognitive Relativism and Social Science*, New Brunswick, NJ: Transaction.

Rescher, Nicholas (1987), *Scientific Realism: A Critical Reappraisal*, Boston, MA: Reidel.

Rosenberg, Alexander (1992), *Economics – Mathematical Politics or Science of Diminishing Returns?*, Chicago: University of Chicago Press.

Roth, Paul (1987), *Meaning and Method in the Social Sciences: A Case for Methodological Pluralism*, Ithaca, NY: Cornell University Press

Samuels, Warren J. (1993), 'John R. Hicks and the History of Economics', in Warren J. Samuels, Jeff Biddle and Thomas W. Patchak-Schuster, *Economic Thought and Discourse in the 20th Century*, Brookfield, VT: Edward Elgar.

Samuels, Warren J. (1994), 'The Roles of Theory in Economics', in Philip Klein (ed.), *The Role of Theory in Economics*, Boston, MA: Kluwer Academic.

Weintraub, E. Roy (1991), *Stabilizing Dynamics: Constructing Economic Knowledge*, New York: Cambridge University Press.

Methodology of Scientific Research Programmes

In Imre Lakatos' methodology of scientific research programmes (MSRP), the subject under consideration is not an individual scientific theory but an entire network of interconnected theories dubbed a 'research programme' (Lakatos, 1978). A SRP is defined, according to Lakatos, by a 'hard core' surrounded by a 'protective belt'. The 'hard core' consists of a set of metaphysical assumptions accepted by anyone working within the programme plus a set of rules governing research within the programme; these rules are in turn divided into 'negative heuristics', directing researchers not to question the hard core of the programme, and 'positive heuristics', laying down guidelines for conducting research. The theories that constitute the bread and butter of the research programme make up the protective belt. A research programme, therefore, includes a well-defined procedure for applying hard core assumptions to the solution of selected problems with the aid of a theoretical structure as well as a strategy for dealing with anomalies so as to ensure the survival of the programme.

Some writers on the philosophy of science depict Lakatos' thinking as a dilution or even a betrayal of the ideas of Karl Popper, but others would argue that Lakatos is lots of Popper with a dash of Kuhn and that virtually everything that Lakatos ever said is found in Popper in some form or other. However, Lakatos' starting point, the idea that theories provide scientists with 'research programmes' that guide their daily practice, is Kuhnian. Being research *programmes*, scientific theories consist at their centre of metaphysical beliefs, 'paradigms', *Weltanschauungen* or Schumpeterian 'visions'. The idea that science cannot dispense with metaphysical beliefs, but that these are kept, so to speak, 'out of sight' is pure Popper. Surrounding the 'hard core' of empirically irrefutable propositions, Lakatos opines, is the 'protective belt' of scientific theories which always have predictive implications for the slice of reality with which they are concerned; apart from ironic language, this formulation is again just straight Popper.

The next idea is also no more than what is found in Popper, namely that scientific theories can only be appraised ex post and that such appraisals are never final because theories are in a constant dynamic process of change as the appearance of anomalies – unexplained phenomena – leads to continuous adjustments in the theoretical framework. These retrospective appraisals involve what Popper describes as 'assessing the degree of corroboration' of a theory, defined in turn as 'evaluating reports of past performance' (quoted in Blaug, 1992: 25). In the end, Popper argued that such reports were only qualitative in character and at best involved ordinal comparisons between two or more theories.

Now comes the genuinely new element in Lakatos that is not in Popper and which has attracted more controversy than any other feature of his methodology. For Popper, the 'evaluating report' of a theory consists of an assessment of its degree of testability, the severity of the tests it has undergone and the way it has stood up to these tests. All this is reduced by Lakatos to the stipulation that SRPs must be appraised in terms of their response to the appearance of anomalies. Programmes that are altered in the face of anomalies in such a way as to generate 'novel facts' are dubbed 'progressive' and programmes that fail to do this, that simply produce ad hoc excuses whenever a refutation is encountered, are dubbed 'degenerating'. Such appraisals are always provisional in the sense that nothing prevents a programme that has been degenerating for some time from becoming progressive again.

Even this characteristic Lakatosian idea was first formulated by Popper who restricted the use of face-saving, refutation-avoiding theoretical adjustments to ones that have 'excess empirical content', meaning new testable consequences. Lakatos at first adopted this definition of 'novel facts' but his followers soon weakened it to 'facts', possibly known beforehand as isolated instances, that are logically implied by a theory; in other words, what is ruled out are known facts which are first employed to construct a theory and then subsequently employed to support it (Hands, 1993: 43–4). Thus what we have in Lakatos is a somewhat less strict empirical criterion for 'progress of knowledge' in science than we get in Popper, but it is nevertheless extremely Popperian in flavour.

But there is absolutely nothing in Popper to warrant Lakatos' notion of a 'historiographical research programme' (HRP), a research programme for testing his own methodology. Lakatos conjectured that the history of science could be almost wholly written in terms of the 'rational' preference of scientists for progressive over degenerating SRPs. He called history so written 'internal history of science' and everything else 'external history', suggesting that the latter could be assigned to footnotes on the grounds that it would be swamped by the 'internal history' in the text (Blaug, 1992: 35–6). This claim is so strong that some have accused Lakatos of conflating historical appraisal and psychological acceptance (Hands, 1993: 61–2). But Lakatos always distinguished between the assertion that a SRP is progressive because it accurately predicts novel facts and the assertion that it is 'rational' for scientists to subscribe to that programme because it is progressive. The first is an issue in MSRP. The second is an issue in MHRP, the methodology of historiographical research programmes. The twain may meet but they need not.

Lakatos' MSRP has been criticized by economists at a number of levels. First, there is the criticism that the central concept of a research programme in Lakatos is both too narrow and too imprecise. Second, there is the objection that Lakatos' appraisal criterion, the successful prediction of novel facts, is too restrictive and would rule out much good economics. Finally, there is the rejection of Lakatos' MHRP as the rewriting of history so as to make it conform to Lakatosian strictures. Let us take these in turn.

We begin by noting that economists find it all to easy to recognize the Lakotosian concept of a SRP. The perfect example that immediately comes to mind is orthodox so-called 'neoclassical economics'. Its 'hard core' is clearly made up of rational economic agents maximizing utility subject to technical and institutional constraints plus the notion that all significant economic behaviour is summed up in the equilibrium solution of demand and supply equations. Its 'negative heuristics' include such prohibitions as 'do not construct theories in which agents act irrationally' and its 'positive heuristics' include such directives as 'classify all the relevant variables into the forces of demand and supply', 'assume identical agents possessing perfect information', and so on. The 'protective belt' is made up of such separate individual theories as the theory of consumer behaviour, the theory of the firm and the theory of international trade, but they are all held together by a common hard core and a common set of heuristics. Moreover, these theories in the protective belt will be judged by most economists in the light of their predictive record and, while commitment to neoclassical economics is no doubt influenced by a whole host of ideological and even sociological elements, ultimately it is the fact that neoclassical economics has proved to be both theoretically and empirically 'progressive' that has secured its professional dominance over rival SRPs. In short, neoclassical economics is a perfect example of Lakatos' SRP.

That notwithstanding, can we really view neoclassical economics as one SRP, ranged against Marxian economics, institutionalist economics, post-Keynesian economics and so on, or should we define human capital theory, Heckscher–Ohlin trade theory, the Chicago economics of the family, and so on, not just as sub-programmes of a larger SRP but as SRPs in their own right (Remenyi, 1979)? Similarly, is there a single neo-Walrasian SRP, including neo-Keynesian and new classical macroeconomics as one SRP, because they both adhere to methodological individualism as a research strategy, or should we classify them as separate SRPs because the former assumes fix-price and the second flex-price market clearing? And again, is monetarism Mark I *à la* Friedman really the same SRP as monetarism Mark II *à la* Lucas–Sargent since the former concedes that there is a short-run negatively inclined Phillips curve while the latter denies it (Backhouse, 1992; Hoover, 1991)? The point is not that we fail to find answers to these questions in Lakatos, but that the Lakatosian apparatus is so loosely described that we can fit it to any answer we care to find. Research programmes, at least in economics, frequently overlap, the implications of one programme feeding into another programme as a crucial input. Whether this is a serious criticism of Lakatos depends on one's point of view. Why should the role of overarching research programmes in one discipline perfectly match that of another?

Likewise, Lakatos' concept of SRPs has been criticized on the grounds that it may be difficult unambiguously to characterize the hard core of a programme. For example, is the hard core of neoclassical economics really that of individual optimizing behaviour, or is it that of rigorous mathematical modelling, or is it that of Pareto-efficient equilibrium outcomes? The arbitrariness of the answer suggests once more that SRPs in economics are not self-contained entities but also that the Lakatosian concept of a SRP is hopelessly imprecise. Against that it must be said that the Lakatosian separation of a 'hard core' from a 'protective belt' is partly a logical distinction. Once we agree that SRPs evolve, they must contain a flexible and an inflexible part if we are going to identify a changing research strategy as nevertheless the same essential strategy; the part that does not change may be labelled 'inflexible', 'unchanging' or 'hard core'. Perhaps that is all there is to Lakatos' categories.

That brings us to the second and more serious criticism of Lakatos, namely what Wade Hands (1993: 44–7) calls 'novel fact fetishism' as the criterion of 'progress of knowledge'. Lakatos' methodology of SRP enjoyed some esteem among economists in the late 1970s and 1980s as according with their view that sound economic theories are capable of accounting for out-of-sample data, thus demonstrating connections between events that had previously been thought unconnected. But a recent conference on economic methodology organized precisely to reassess that status of Lakatos' ideas in economics revealed a surprising wide-ranging hostility to it (de Marchi and Blaug, 1991: 500). Most of that hostility centred in fact on Lakatos' appraisal criterion, the dominant argument being that, while the history of economics frequently reveals 'analytical progress', it rarely demonstrates 'empirical progress'. By 'analytical progress' (or what Lakatos, 1978: 179 called 'heuristic progress') we mean the refinement of ideas and techniques, the clarification of terms, the honing of concepts and so forth. By 'empirical progress', we mean corroborated 'theoretical progress' *à la* Lakatos, that is, an improved grasp of the workings of the economic system as exemplified by more accurate predictions of the effects of changes in exogenous variables on the values of endogenous variables. There is no question that economics constantly exhibits analytical or heuristic progress but there is great doubt that it exhibits empirical progress, except intermittently. This being the case, the fear is that a Lakatosian appraisal of modern economics would leave little of it standing as a 'progressive' SRP. This may or may not be a fatal criticism, and it may be as much a criticism of modern economics as of Lakatos (de Marchi and Blaug, 1991: 504–10; Blaug, 1994), but the fact remains that the emphasis on novel facts as a criterion of appraisal remains one of the least developed aspects of MSRP.

That brings us to the third objection directed specifically against Lakatos' metamethodology for appraising methodologies. Lakatos proposed that historians of science should set down a 'rational reconstruction' of that history in the light of the methodology he or she is trying to appraise; he or she should then compare that reconstruction with the actual history because an acceptable methodology must be capable of endorsing the decisions made by practising scientists. In other words, a rational reconstruction must show that successful SRPs were 'progressive'; otherwise, the methodology that motivated that reconstruction is to be rejected as not capturing the 'rationality' of scientists.

Unfortunately, testing a methodology against the history of a discipline is almost as problematic as testing a theory against the empirical evidence for it. Moreover, the structure of incentives facing a scientist, the 'sociology' of the scientific profession, may be such as to distort the actual practice of scientists. There is no guarantee, therefore, that the history of a discipline will mirror an empirically oriented methodology. Be that as it may, the attraction of Lakatos' scheme is to clearly separate a positive and normative methodology, a study of what economists actually do as revealed by the history of economics, and the attempt to evaluate what economists do as enshrined in methodological precepts. No one in the philosophy of science has come closer than Lakatos in resolving the perennial tension that exists between these two separate but highly related activities.

Lakatos (1978) first defined his approach in 1970 in a paper entitled 'Falsification and the Methodology of Scientific Research Programmes' and further developed his ideas in 'History of Science and Its Rational Reconstruction', published in 1971. The first application of MSRP to economics came in 1972 and since then there have been some 25 case studies of Lakatos' methodology in economics (for a list, see de Marchi and Blaug, 1991: 29–30). In the final analysis, the utility of MSRP proves itself in these applications and the perusal of a few of these is more telling than all the general descriptions of MSRP or accounts of 'what Lakatos really meant'.

MARK BLAUG

References
Backhouse, R. (1992), 'Lakatos and Economics', *Perspectives on the History of Economic Thought*, vol. VIII, ed. S. Todd Lowry, Aldershot: Edward Elgar.
Blaug, M. (1992), *The Methodology of Economics*, 2nd edn, Cambridge: Cambridge University Press.
Blaug, M. (1994), 'Why I am Not a Constructivist, or Confessions of an Unrepentant Popperian', in R. Backhouse (ed.), *New Directions in Economic Methodology*, London: Routledge.
Hands, D. Wade. (1993), *Testing Rationality and Progress. Essays on the Popperian Tradition in Economic Methodology*, Lanham, MD: Rowman & Littlefield.
Hoover, K. (1991), 'Scientific Research Programme or Tribe? A Joint Appraisal of Lakatos and the New Classical Macroeconomics', in N. de Marchi and M. Blaug, (eds), *Appraising Economic Theories*.
Lakatos, I. (1978), *The Methodology of Scientific Research Programmes Philosophical Papers*, vol. 1, eds J. Worrall and G. Currie, Cambridge: Cambridge University Press.
De Marchi, N. and M. Blaug, (1991), *Appraising Economic Theories: Studies in the Methodology of Research Programmes*. Aldershot: Edward Elgar.
Remenyi, J.V. (1979), 'Core Demi-Core Interaction: Toward a General Theory of Disciplinary and Sub-disciplinary Growth', *History of Political Economy*, **11**, (1), Spring, 30–63.

Microfoundations

When discussing the issue of microfoundations of macroeconomics it is important to know what kind of foundations one is discussing and for what object foundations are being discussed. In other words, one has to know what the terms 'microeconomics' and 'macroeconomics' signify. Broadly speaking, two different sets of definitions can be distinguished in the literature (for some alternative definitions, see Machlup, 1963). Some economists (see, for example, Allen, 1967: 1; Henderson and Quandt, 1980: 2) regard microeconomics as the discipline investigating the behaviour of individual economic units, while they regard macroeconomics as the discipline studying relations between broad economic aggregates. Thus the quest for microfoundations can be understood as an attempt to base theorizing about aggregate relationships on the behaviour of individual agents. Some philosophers of economics, most notably Nelson (1984) and Rosenberg (1976), have taken this position when discussing some methodological issues concerning microfoundations.

The above division is, among other things, based upon the view that microeconomics confines itself to the explanation of the behaviour of individual units. However, it has also been argued (see, for example, Branson, 1979: 1; Nelson, 1989: 26) that microeconomics intends to provide explanations of aggregative phenomena such as relative prices and other market phenomena. Accordingly, both disciplines analyse *aggregate* phenomena. If this view is taken, the difference between the subjects can be understood along the following lines. Microeconomics is regarded as a method of doing aggregative economics in which (a) the actions of individual agents are regarded as the outcome of a constrained optimization problem and (b) the actions of individual agents form an equilibrium. Macroeconomics, on the other hand, is an interrelated set of concepts (like effective demand and involuntary unemployment) and theories that are not (yet) based on microeconomics. According to the second set of definitions, the quest for microfoundations of macroeconomics can best be understood as an investigation into the possibilities of rephrasing macroeconomic ideas in a microeconomic language or of making macroeconomics compatible with microeconomics.

The reasons for studying the possibilities of microfoundations also depend on which of the two sets of definitions are employed. If the first set is employed, the reason for studying micro-foundations lies in a form of the reductionist credo of *methodological individualism*. Roughly speaking, the argument for this view runs as follows: society consists of individuals who are the only subjects that make economic decisions; in order to explain what is going on in the economy as a whole one has to understand the individual decisions from which a particular situation originates.

If the second set is employed, the reason for studying microfoundations is more compatible with a 'unity of science' argument. This argument roughly runs as follows. Two distinctively separate disciplines such as microeconomics and macroeconomics can only coexist in a fruitful way if they have different domains of application. However, as the two disciplines in question both study aggregative phenomena, it is not clear when to apply one (and not the other). It is thus natural to study the compatibility of the two disciplines and, as microeconomics has a better developed analytical structure, the reasons for investigating the possibilities for microfoundations become clear.

A careful investigation of contributions that are commonly regarded as hallmarks in the economic microfoundations literature reveals that the second set of definitions (with its associated interpretation of what microfoundations actually establish) is more appropriate than the first set. A few brief examples are given here. Bénassy (1975) and Drèze (1975) show that an equilibrium exists in fix-price models in which rationing schemes bring about an allocation of commodities over individual agents. Moreover, they demonstrated that these fix-price models capture quite a number of ideas associated with Keynesian macroeconomics:

involuntary unemployment could be regarded as an equilibrium phenomenon in which optimizing households face a quantity constraint on the amount of labour they can supply. Also the Keynesian notions of effective demand and the multiplier were reformulated in their models. These fix-price models have microfoundations in the sense that they are based on decision-making individuals and a well-defined notion of (quantity constrained) equilibrium.

New classical economics attempts to explain macroeconomic phenomena as fluctuations in unemployment by means of models that are as close as possible to general equilibrium models. A seminal paper in this respect is Lucas (1972) which regards incomplete information about the aggregate money supply as the major cause of the cycle. Lucas constructs a model in which prices are market clearing and agents behave optimally given their expectations, which are also formed 'rationally'. As there are two sources of disturbance, the agents cannot infer from the market-clearing prices whether a shock results from a relative demand shift or a shift in the money supply. This is why, according to Lucas, monetary shocks may have real (cyclical) effects. The more recent real business cycle models (for example, Kydland and Prescott, 1982) are even closer to general equilibrium models as they regard changes in technology and/or preferences, the basic elements of general equilibrium, as the main cause of the cycle.

Cooper and John (1988) point out a common element in many contributions to new Keynesian economics. They argue that most of this literature departs in one way or the other from the perfect competition assumption. Under imperfect competition, an individual agent's optimal action depends on the actions undertaken by other agents. Inefficient, or 'Keynesian', equilibria may arise as a consequence of the fact that individual agents are not able to improve upon their situation if all other agents stick to their actions. There may be multiple equilibria that can be Pareto-ranked. Agents might find themselves then in a 'bad' equilibrium, but individually they have no means of changing their situation. They call this a 'coordination failure'.

The above examples show that equilibrium notions and 'rational' expectations are widely adopted in the microfoundations literature. To complete the argument that it is the unity of science argument that underlies the microfoundations literature and not an argument about methodological individualism, it needs to be shown that equilibrium notions and the notion of rational expectations are not based on (rational) individual behaviour. Janssen (1993) shows that, although equilibrium notions are not inconsistent with notions of (rational) individual behaviour, they are (generally speaking) not derived from them either. An economic equilibrium is usually defined as a set of individual actions (and possibly a price vector) such that, given the actions of the others (and the price vector), no individual agent can improve upon his situation. Although an equilibrium is defined in terms of individual actions, it is usually not clear how individual actions bring about the equilibrium (Arrow, 1959). So the conclusion must be that equilibrium notions are *extra*rational and *not* based on individual behaviour. (An exception must be made for recent evolutionary models, but these models fall outside the scope of the micro-foundations literature as it is typically conceived.) To see that the concept of rational expectations is also an equilibrium concept (and not derived from an explicit optimization scheme) one has to notice that economic outcomes depend on the actions of individuals and these in turn depend on their expectations. Thus the expectation an individual has to have so that it coincides with actual outcomes depends on the expectations of other individuals. This means that the same critique applies here.

It seems that intuition tells many economists that the notion of equilibrium can ultimately be derived from individual optimizing behaviour. If this intuition proves to be correct, the quest for microfoundations may be understood from the 'unity of science' perspective as well as from the methodological individualist perspective. The 'unity of science' that has been brought about by the microfoundations literature means that nowadays there is hardly any distinction between mainstream micro- and macroeconomic theory:

> The most interesting developments in macroeconomic theory seem to me describable as the reincorporation of aggregative problems such as inflation and the business cycle within the general framework of 'microeconomic' theory. If these developments succeed, the term 'macroeconomic' will simply disappear from use and the modifier 'micro' will be superfluous. We will simply speak, as did Smith, Ricardo, Marshall and Walras, of economic theory. (Lucas, 1987: 107–8)

A disappearance of the modifiers 'micro' and 'macro' will also imply that the term 'microfoundations' will stop being used.

It should be emphasized, however, that it is not the case that macroeconomics (or, more properly, economics) can be considered a branch of applied microeconomics as it existed at the beginning of the 1970s (Howitt, 1987). Important macroeconomic phenomena are inconsistent with the type of coordination that is assumed by the Walrasian equilibrium notion that prevailed in microeconomics at that time. As the above-mentioned literature suggests, the quest for microfoundations has also caused changes in the subject of microeconomics itself, in the sense that incomplete and asymmetric information, strategic behaviour, alternative equilibrium notions and adaptive behaviour play a dominant role nowadays. Paradoxically, the search for unification between micro- and macroeconomics has led to a situation in which some of the core assumptions are now shared by many economists at the expense of an enormous diversification of auxiliary assumptions.

MAARTEN C.W. JANSSEN

References
Allen, R.G.D. (1967), *Macroeconomic Theory*, London: Macmillan.
Arrow, K.J. (1959), 'Towards a Theory of Price Adjustments', in M. Abromovitz *et al.* (eds.), *The Allocation of Economic Resources*, Stanford: Stanford University Press.
Bénassy, J.-P. (1975), 'Neo-Keynesian Disequilibrium Theory in a Monetary Economy', *Review of Economic Studies*, **42**, 502–23.
Branson, W.H. (1979), *Macroeconomic Theory and Policy*, New York: Harper & Row.
Cooper, R. and A. John (1988), 'Coordinating Coordination Failures in Keynesian Models', *Quarterly Journal of Economics*, **103**, 441–63.
Drèze, J. (1975), 'Existence of an Equilibrium with Price Rigidity and Quantity Rationing', *International Economic Review*, **16**, 301–20.
Henderson, J. and R. Quandt (1980), *Microeconomic Theory: A Mathematical Approach*, New York: McGraw-Hill.
Howitt, P. (1987), 'Macroeconomics: Relations with Microeconomics', in J. Eatwell, M. Milgate and P. Newman (eds), *The New Palgrave. A Dictionary of Economics*, vol. 1, London: Macmillan.
Janssen, M. (1993), *Microfoundations: A critical inquiry*, London: Routledge.
Kydland, F. and E. Prescott (1982), 'Time to Build and Aggregate Fluctuations', *Econometrica*, **50**, 1345–70.
Lucas, R. (1972), 'Expectations and the Neutrality of Money', *Journal of Economic Theory*, **4**, 103–24.
Lucas, R. (1987), *Models of Business Cycles*, Oxford: Basil Blackwell.
Machlup, F. (1963), 'Micro- and Macro-Economics', *Essays on Economics Semantics*, London: Prentice-Hall.
Nelson, A. (1984), 'Some Issues Surrounding the Reduction from Macroeconomics to Microeconomics', *Philosophy of Science*, **51**, 573–94.
Nelson, A. (1989), 'Average Explanations', *Erkenntnis*, **30**, 23–42.
Rosenberg, A. (1976), 'On the Interanimation of Micro and Macroeconomics', *Philosophy of Social Sciences*, **6**, 35–53.
Weintraub, E.R. (1979), *Microfoundations*, Cambridge: Cambridge University Press.

Mill, John Stuart

John Stuart Mill (1806–73) was a precocious child, encouraged in his extraordinary early achievements by his father, James Mill. These intellectual exploits can be read in his admirable *Autobiography*.[1] Summaries John Stuart made at the age of 13 of their conversations on political economy during walks together formed the basis for his father's *Elements of Political Economy*, and John's first independent publication, on the theory of value, was written when he was still only 16. Though he is perhaps best known for his *System of Logic* (1843) and *The Principles of Political Economy* (1848), Mill's early essays on economic issues of the day, many of which appeared in the *London and Westminster* (later the *Westminster*) *Review* during the mid-1820s (vol. IV of the *Collected Works*), show plainly the same scepticism towards reasoning on a narrow observational basis as his methodological essay, 'On the Definition of Political Economy; and on the Method of Investigation Proper to It'.[2] More than that, they provide glimpses of Mill using, if not actually gathering, empirical data of the extensive sort that he would later argue are essential to forming the premises of sound deductions. Between these early empirico-deductive exercises and the writing of the methodological essay, Mill discovered the exemplar of economic reasoning, not in geometry but in the concurrence of causes (forces) model of mechanics. This became the guiding model of all his future economic analysis, and was the starting point for innumerable applications of economic thought in the political and social spheres. This short entry focuses on the methodological essay because of its centrality.

Mill's essay has become, as he hoped it might, 'classic and of authority'. It is probably the most quoted after Friedman's (1953). The two could not be more different, however. Friedman eschews all knowledge of true causes and settles for testing predictions as the sole available measure of a theory's worth. Mill, by contrast, insisted always on the importance, and the possibility, of knowing true causes. Indeed, his essay was written primarily to make a case for what he called *a priori*, or speculative, reasoning – reasoning from causes to expectations about effects – as the only practicable way to proceed in moral science.

The reverse – reasoning backwards from observed effects to their causes – is all but impossible, because, typically, multiple causes are at work, not all of them even known to us. Although causes work in political economy as they do in mechanics, each separately maintaining its effect even in causal interactions, and not as in chemistry where distinct effects disappear when causes interact (mechanical) causes nonetheless may neutralize each other. There simply is no way to identify reliably a complex of operating causes from any single combined effect, except in the case where we already know the causes that were at work in comparable, earlier experiences, and conditions are such that we can be sure also that no change of circumstances has occurred from the situations where these were first identified. Only in that case are regularities or low-level empirical generalizations of any use. For the rest, we must have resort to a prior knowledge of the causes. In this, as Cartwright argues (1994), Mill differs radically from Hume.

How is causal knowledge possible in political economy? Mill thought that laboratory experimentation in physics made causal analysis easier there than in moral science, where there are but few social experiments relative to the number of causal combinations we would like to try out, and these mostly of a sort thrown up rather than constructed and controlled by the observer. At the same time, in political economy we are able to conduct specific thought experiments and reason abstractly about these 'with as much certainty as in the most demonstrative parts of physics' (1967: 329). For the principal causes in the economic realm are 'The desires of man, and the nature of the conduct to which they prompt him' (ibid.), and these are 'within the reach of our observation' (ibid.). Self-knowledge, plus circumspect generalization, in other words, is all that is needed.

To expand on this somewhat, men and women desire to possess wealth (and prefer more to less), subject only to the 'perpetually antagonizing principles' of a desire for ease, and a preference for present over future enjoyment (ibid.: 321). By varying the wage rate one might arrive at a measure for the elasticity of labour supply response, and by altering the interest rate relative to the rate of time preference one might measure the responsiveness of time-related self-denial. Then, using the law of vector addition, which Mill accepted, one could arrive at the net quantitative effect of the two antagonizing, principles. Mill did not actually do that, though he reasoned constantly in his early essays on various issues of the day as if it were possible. When Jevons subsequently tried to measure empirical curves comprising series of (aggregate) supply–demand equalities but where supply only had shifted, he was seeking an empirical proxy for the final degree of utility.[3] Not this particular one, but exactly that sort of measure was what Mill imagined to be available to the mental experimenter. Cartwright correctly draws an analogy between Mill's thinking and the structural modelling of the early Cowles econometrics and of Tinbergen. With linear equational systems, assumed additive in the parameters, one has the exact equivalent of measures of the separate influence of independent variables conjoining to produce an effect (Cartwright, 1994: 106–7 and *passim*). The one important difference is that Cowles workers tended to think of their parameters as stable across circumstances, whereas Mill was inclined to think that causal accounts will tend to be singular. In any new situation, allowance must be made for an altered conjunction of causes (hence of net effects), including – significantly – 'disturbing causes' (Mill, 1967: 330) or causes not common to any large and identified class of cases and therefore not taken into account even in the mental experiment closest in nature to the case in question.

The gaps in our explanatory ability *a priori* caused by unknown, or as yet uncalculated, causes mean that allowances have to be made before the abstract results can be used for control purposes. This is what Mill dubbed the work of 'verification' which, however, forms no part of science, but rather part of its application. What remains unclear in Mill, however, is the extent to which he thought his mental 'estimates' of the 'powers' of the separate causes operating in political economy were stable – transferable across circumstances. If there are no trustworthy regularities in the real world, he is left with the option of constructing regularities by combining cases of his own invention (his mental experiments) which embody circumstances common to a great many (ideally, all) cases. This is what he referred to as the perfect or near-perfect abstract science of political economy (Mill, 1967: 329). A modern analogue, though it involves already assuming that the gap between abstract truth and application has been bridged, may be the actual situation in some parts of modern physics where such complete control is achievable that a single 'right' experimental outcome both precisely embodies and serves to establish well-specified theoretical convictions (Hacking, 1983; Cartwright, 1994: 94, 182; section 4 of ch. 2). His emphasis in the methodological essay on abstract truth notwithstanding, Mill too seems to have believed that abstract knowledge, supplemented by 'long and accurate observation', will give us the key to causally explaining many actual occurrences (Mill, 1967: 330, 332, 343; cf. 110, 111). There are two aspects to this conviction: first, a belief that most situations will be simple enough for us to be able to disentangle the complex of causes; which is to say that the important causes are in fact few (Mill lists just three for economics, plus a knowledge of production technology and population dynamics); second, a belief that these few main causes are stable, at least for a single country during particular periods of time and under particular sets of institutions. This emerges, then, as a conditional belief in the bridging possibility. Mill's willingness to discern periods of change and periods of stability in society, and the hopes he entertained for studies of the way the character of a people is formed (ethology), reflect the seriousness with which he took the need to find out when and where the bridging was in fact a real possibility.

Interestingly, there are moves within modern time series econometrics and macroeconomics to do away with structural models of the Cowles sort and instead to look only for subperiods of empirical stability within a series; but this is Millian faith in (temporary) stability without his faith in the explanatory value of underlying causes. Perhaps the most pressing methodological concern at this point in an already long history of interpretations of what Mill was about is to discover whether he believed more strongly in reform, which required control, or in altered causal interactions.

NEIL DE MARCHI

Notes
1. There is a modern *Collected Works*, including the *Autobiography*, volumes of letters and newspaper articles, as well as the better known writings, published by the University of Toronto Press under the general editorship of J.M. Robson.
2. The essay was first written in the autumn of 1831, revised in 1833 and shown to a few friends, published in the *London and Westminster Review*, 1836, republished as one of the *Essays on Some Unsettled Questions of Political Economy* in 1844, and formed the basis of Book VI of the *System of Logic*.
3. See White (1995).

References
Cartwright, Nancy (1994), *Nature's Capacities and Their Measurement*, Oxford: Oxford University Press.
Friedman, Milton (1953), 'The Methodology of Positive Economics', in *Essays in Positive Economics*, Chicago: University of Chicago Press.
Hacking. Ian (1983), *Representing and Intervening*, Cambridge: Cambridge University Press.
Mill, John Stuart (1967), 'On the Definition of Political Economy; and on the Method of Investigation Proper to It', *Essays on Economics and Society*, vol. IV of the *Collected Works of John Stuart Mill*, ed. J.M Robson, Toronto: University of Toronto Press.
White, Michael (1995), 'Perpetual Motion and Change: Statics and Dynamics in the Political Economy of W.S. Jevons', mimeo, Monash University.

Mitchell, Wesley Clair

Wesley Clair Mitchell was born in Illinois in 1874. He received his undergraduate and graduate training at the University of Chicago, where he began long friendships with Thorstein Veblen and John Dewey, both of whom influenced his methodological views. He received his PhD in economics in 1899. Mitchell spent most of his career at Columbia University, retiring in 1944. From 1920 to 1945, he was director of research for the National Bureau of Economic Research (NBER), which he helped to found.

Mitchell's considerable reputation among his contemporaries rested largely on his statistical research on business cycles, which includes his 1913 masterpiece, *Business Cycles*, Mitchell (1927) and Burns and Mitchell (1946). More revealing of his methodological views, however, are numerous articles and addresses in which Mitchell discussed the strengths and weaknesses of various schools of economics, promoted a greater role for statistical analysis in economics, and argued in favour of national economic planning based on sound economic research. These pieces, many of which are collected in Mitchell (1937), provide the main support for the traditional identification of Mitchell as a leading American institutionalist.

Mitchell, following Dewey, believed that the appropriate process of inquiry in both social and natural sciences involved a blend of induction and deduction, 'the patient process of observation and testing – always critical testing – of the relations between the working hypotheses and the processes observed' (Mitchell, in Burns, 1952: 96). There was no clear separation between theories and fact:

> The theories with which science works cannot be conceived as existing apart from the facts of human experience, and men can apprehend facts only in terms of the notions with which their minds are furnished. ... In an investigation of moment, both the theory and the facts are elaborated at various stages of the proceedings, each by the aid of the other, and later workers start with a fact–theory blend improved by the new contribution. (Mitchell, 1927: 59-60)

In describing his own work, he spoke of 'passing back and forth between hypothesis and observation, each modifying and enriching the other' (Mitchell, in Burns, 1952: 98).

Both the overall design of Mitchell's business cycle research programme and his pursuit of that programme in detail illustrate his view of the fact–theory relationship in the research process. Mitchell's business cycle books of 1913 and 1927 began with reviews of existing theories of business fluctuations, to 'provide working hypotheses to guide the selection of the data, and suggest ways of analyzing and combining them' (Mitchell, 1927: 3) As Schumpeter remarked, Mitchell 'looked upon [the theories] as so many statements of partial truths ... all of which had, on a common plane, to await trial in the court of the facts' (Burns, 1952: 334). But the goal was not to rule pre-existing theories true of false. Mitchell believed that the end process of his empirical analysis would be a rationalized account or 'analytical description' of a typical business cycle that synthesized, probably in modified form, several of the theories. Mitchell's 1913 book had included such an analytical description, and for the rest of his life he conducted further empirical research in the (unrealized) hope of producing an improved version of this description.

Hirsch (1967, 1976) describes how Mitchell, in the course of statistical research, engaged in an *a posteriori* method of theorizing. Careful statistical analysis would establish the existence of an empirical regularity; a tentative explanation of the empirical regularity would be fashioned; this explanation would suggest the existence of further regularities; and a search for these regularities would result in abandonment, modification or continued use of the hypothesis (see also Burns, 1952: 31). This approach can be seen in Mitchell's identification and explanation of a downward trend in the ratio of bank capital to bank liabilities and his attempt to reconcile the long-run and short-run relationships between the price level and the money supply (Mitchell, 1913: 350–56; 1927: 128–39).

Mitchell's bill of indictment against the classical and the emerging marginalist/neoclassical schools of economics also sheds light on his methodological views and shows the influence of Veblen. Mitchell argued that classical and early marginalist economists had erred by building their deductions on faulty assumptions about human psychology, assumptions arrived at through introspection rather than careful observation of human behaviour (Mitchell, 1937: 354–72). Further, what they assumed as innate psychological traits were actually malleable products of particular historical/institutional circumstances. Later variants of neoclassical value theory that dispensed with questions of psychology and took preference structures as given were little better. First, Mitchell doubted that people routinely made rational choices on the basis of stable preferences; second, this approach left out of value theory the fundamental question of the way preferences are formed (Mitchell, 1937: 407–8; 1927: 165).

Mitchell granted that neoclassical value theory could generate useful working hypotheses for the study of business activity, in which rational calculating behaviour was likely to be prevalent (Mitchell, 1937: 158), but he felt that theorists of the neoclassical tradition, like their classical predecessors, viewed their deductive creations, not as working hypotheses to be confronted with the data, but as ends in themselves. They showed little interest in subjecting the implications of their theories to rigorous empirical test and often employed theoretical concepts with no empirical counterparts, making their theories of limited use to those engaged in empirical investigation (ibid.: 25, 354–9). In general, what Mitchell objected to were 'deductions that rest upon assumptions that have not been, and perhaps cannot be, tested to determine their representative value, and without any attempt to test the results for conformity to fact' (Mitchell to A.B. Wolfe, 18 September 1938).

Mitchell's methodological views are of historical interest for at least two reasons. First, although Mitchell himself encouraged economists to avoid methodological controversy, his prominence in the profession and his pointed attacks on 'orthodox' economics led others to take his work and that of the NBER as representative of an institutionalist/empiricist or anti-theoretical position in the methodological debates of the period (Seckler, 1975: ch. 8). Best known of these is probably the 'measurement without theory' debate, in which Tjalling Koopmans criticized the Mitchell/NBER approach to empirical economics, arguing instead for a research programme combining neoclassical theory with statistical methods more explicitly grounded in probability theory (Mirowski, 1989). Second, as director of the NBER, Mitchell had the opportunity to influence a number of important economists of the next generation, including Arthur F. Burns, Simon Kuznets and Milton Friedman. Furthermore, the NBER outlived Mitchell and continued as an important promoter and source of support for empirical research in economics, although it has lost its identity as home of a distinctive heterodox approach to economics.

A more complete presentation and assessment of Mitchell's methodological views can be found in Rutherford (1987).

JEFF E. BIDDLE

References

Burns, Arthur F. (ed.) (1952), *Wesley Clair Mitchell: The Economic Scientist*, New York: National Bureau of Economic Research.

Burns, Arthur F. and Wesley C. Mitchell (1946), *Measuring Business Cycles*, New York: National Bureau of Economic Research.

Hirsch, Abraham (1967), 'Wesley Clair Mitchell, J. Laurence Laughlin and the Quantity Theory', *Journal of Political Economy*, 75, December, 822–43.

Hirsch, Abraham (1976), 'The a posteriori Method and the Creation of New Theory: W.C. Mitchell as a Case Study', *History of Political Economy*, 8, Summer, 195–206.

Mirowski, Philip (1989), 'The Measurement without Theory Controversy: Defeating Rival Research Programs by Accusing them of Naive Empiricism', *Economies and Societies*, 11, 65–87.

Mitchell, Wesley C. (1913), *Business Cycles*, Berkeley: University of California Press.

Mitchell, Wesley C. (1927), *Business Cycles: The Problem and its Setting*, New York: National Bureau of Economic Research.

Mitchell, Wesley C. (1937), *The Backward Art of Spending Money and other Essays*, New York: McGraw-Hill.

Rutherford, Malcolm (1987), 'Wesley Mitchell: Institutions and Quantitative Methods', *Eastern Economic Journal*, 12, January–March, 63–73.

Seckler, David (1975), *Thorstein Veblen and the Institutionalists*, Boulder: Colorado Associated University Press.

Models

Philosophy of science accounts of models can be organized around two rather different questions. One asks, 'What is a model?' and provides definitions as answers. The other asks, 'How do we get models and what role do they play?' and answers with categories and functions. Though modelling dominates the practice of modern economics, its treatment within conventional texts on economic methodology is exceedingly sparse. (Notable exceptions are Stewart, 1979, now rather dated, and Hausman 1992.) This account therefore explores a wider body of literature.

Older treatments in the mainstream philosophy of science defined models in terms of their logical and semantic connections with theories, where the latter are the real focus of interest. (The topic has also been beset by definitional changes which hinder attempts at simple exposition.) Thus the conventional account from the logical–positivist tradition defined theories as uninterpreted formal systems: sets of sentences in a formal language characterized by its syntactic structure (such as an axiomatized system). An interpretation constitutes a model of the theory if and only if all the sentences in the model are also true in the theory (the formal system). This account of models has not proved very useful in the philosophy of economics (though Hausman offers references to certain applications) and its shortcomings are fully exposed by Walsh in *The New Palgrave* (1987), using examples from general equilibrium analysis. Consequently, the alternative 'semantic view'' proposed by Suppes (1967), Suppe (1974) and van Fraassen (1980) redefined the theory as that set of models in any particular formulation which is true of the system. The semantic account thus has a flexibility to cover different representations not available in the syntactic account.

The more recent structuralist account applies the term 'models' to the logical structures that the scientific theory describes. By focusing on 'structures' as its unit of analysis rather than statements, the structuralists turned the focus away from the purely linguistic features of scientific theories towards the objects and relations the symbols of the theory are supposed to represent. (It is thus labelled a 'semantic' as opposed to a 'syntactic' approach.) In this structuralist approach, the basic mathematical structure of the objects and relations of the theory is characterized by its 'potential models'; 'models' of the theory must also satisfy the basic assumptions of the theory (such as equilibrium conditions). This 'model-theoretic' approach relies on logical analysis but it is not restricted to any one fixed formal framework. It has been developed and applied particularly in the philosophy of economics (see examples in Stegmüller *et al.*, 1982, Balzer and Hamminga, 1989) as a tool both for the logical analysis (or 'reconstruction') of economic theories and, with more intriguing results, for the comparison of theories which have often been thought rivals, if not incommensurable, by economists (for a nice example, see Janssen, 1989). A good account of the structuralist method in economics can be found in Hands (1985).

These philosophical definitions of models in relation to theories have proved grist for the philosophical mill, but do not properly address the problem of why economists might use or need the things that they call 'models'. What do 'scientific models' do? Both Giere (1984, for the natural sciences) and Hausman (1992, for economics) argue for a further development in the definition of models, one that they believe fits the normal usage of working scientists, and so can be used to interpret and understand the central role of models in scientific practice. Although they share concepts, Giere's terminology is probably preferable to Hausman's in being more descriptively exact and thus recognizable. Giere (1984) begins with his 'theoretical model', which is a set of statements defining a system. His 'theoretical hypothesis' asserts that this model is like (similar to) some specified real system(s). A model plus a general theoretical hypothesis constitutes a theory. In Hausman's 1992 account (from his table on 277), theories (equivalent to Giere's 'theoretical hypotheses') make empirically testable claims about the world (that a particular model is true of the world); whereas models (equivalent to Giere's 'theoretical models') on the other hand are either 'trivially' (analytically) true or 'neither true nor false' of the world, they are to be 'assessed mathematically or conceptually' and their point is conceptual exploration of theories.

This last point is the critical one for Hausman, who focuses his further analysis on the relationship between models and theories. This focus is one he shares with both the syntactic and semantic accounts, in which models are closely tied to theories and have to be true to their theories in one sense (logic) or another (meaning). For Hausman, however, we can learn from working with models; their function is to help form and explore theoretical concepts. While his description certainly captures some aspects in the practice of mathematical modelling in economics, his determination that the function of models is just about conceptual discovery may be too limited. Inasmuch as theoretical models incorporate characteristic elements of data or phenomena into their system, their usage in theory exploration inevitably involves elements of justification. Even his own case study of overlapping generations cites economic plausibility as one of the elements in choosing certain mathematical solutions. (See also Boumans, forthcoming, on the way business cycle theorists integrate data characteristics directly into their theoretical models.) Hausman has no account of the way models relate to the world, but then he explicitly states that his account refers to models in theoretical economics, not in econometrics (Hausman, 1992: 75).

For Giere (1988), in contrast to Hausman, any further discussion of theories is uninteresting: instead Giere discusses how models help us to learn about the world. His critical claim is that the theoretical hypothesis asserts that the relationship between the model and some real system is a relation of similarity, as opposed to the stricter isomorphism claimed by van Fraassen (1980). (This may be an important point for economics, given Gordon's (1991) claim there are a plethora of isomorphic models in the natural sciences, but very few in the social sciences.) By the insertion of a model between the set of statements which define the theory and the real world object, the required relation becomes one of similarity between two objects rather than a problem of correspondence relations or conditions between a set of statements and the world. Giere believes that models are a standard element in scientific practice and are used to explore the real world through the activities of identification and interpretation, both relying on similarity relations.

Giere's view of models forms part of his (1988) account of science as a 'cognitive process' (drawing ideas from psychology and artificial intelligence). Cognition relates both to the analogical account of models (see later) – how we move from what we do know into areas where we do not know something – and to important considerations of tacit knowledge in the use of models for scientific discovery and inference. These are relatively unexplored areas as far as the uses of economic models are concerned, though interesting recent work by historians points to their importance in other sciences (see Nersessian, 1990). So while both Giere and Hausman see models as doing major work in their sciences, and they share definitions, the role or function they each attribute to models is entirely different.

Another account of models, one which arose as a by-product from some other investigation, is the simulacrum account of models by Cartwright (1983). This account was designed in the context of her realist attack on the role of fundamental theories and the covering law account of explanation (the D–N account, in which, incidentally, models do not figure; see, for example, Hausman: appendix A3). In this account, as she describes it, the 'route from theory to reality is from theory to model, and then from model to phenomenological law. The phenomenological laws are indeed true of the objects in reality – or might be; but the fundamental laws are true only of objects in the model.' (Cartwright, 1983: 4) But this is not a description of the modelling process, rather it is the basis of her reconfigured account of explanation. The modelling process goes the other way, beginning with as accurate an account as possible of the behaviour of the phenomena. This is 'prepared' into a description, the model, which will match a mathematical representation coming from the theory. By such means the behaviour of phenomena (now the phenomenological laws) is brought under the fundamental laws. Models are the critical intermediary: they are at the same time models of theory and models of phenomena because the model is where these two elements are fitted together, but they are also relevant for intervention, because it is models (not theories) which are used as instruments for putting physics to work in the world (for example, to design, make and use lasers). This compares with Hausman, for whom models are instruments to find out about theories through conceptual exploration, and with Giere, for whom they are instruments to find out about the world through similarity relations.

In Cartwright's account, models are idealizations or approximations in the sense that they are only partially realistic accounts of the world, but the descriptions they offer are sufficient to describe certain aspects of the phenomena. They are also required to map onto the mathematical representation of the fundamental theory although, again, not necessarily in full. Models are therefore made up partly of genuine properties and causal relations, and partly of fictional ones. There are no case studies in economics adopting Cartwright's account of models, but it is possible that econometric models used for policy purposes might be characterized like this (the fitting together of theory elements and data elements into a representation which mixes fictions and fact, as discussed in Cartwright, 1983: 146–50, bears some resemblance to descriptions of econometric modelling in Morgan, 1990; Hoover, 1994) and Boumans (forthcoming) extends Cartwright's ideas in a study of business cycle modelling.

Idealization (of which Cartwright's models bear signs) can be seen as providing a broad account of modelling and has recently received considerable attention inside the philosophy of economics community. Although the idealization literature focuses on theorizing, in effect models appear inevitable in this procedure: models can be identified as the things you get as you idealize towards theory away from reality or concretize from idealized theory to the economic reality. Models are not of theory or of data or of phenomena (for example, see Suppes, 1962), rather they form a middle element between theory and the world, incorporating different degrees of both. The process of modelling becomes the main activity of both economic theorizing and economic application. This might seem like the simulacrum account, but is not quite the same, for in that account the two elements are explicitly fitted together, and the models have an independent status. In contrast, in this general literature on idealization, the models themselves appear curiously passive: they are points on the road between an origin and a destination and how they are used is not fully explored; they appear to have no separate function except those derived from their two end-posts: idealized theory and raw data. Such accounts offer definitions and descriptions of the process of modelling, but no analysis of their roles.

The advantage of the idealization notion of models is that it can, it seems, be shared to a considerable degree by both Marxist economists and neoclassical economics (see the papers in Hamminga and De Marchi, 1994 and, for an indication of difficulties in the comparison, Morgan, 1996). For those adopting dialectic methodologies, such a process envisages the essential elements remaining throughout the process of idealization, as more and more of the less essential elements are stripped away in the idealization process (or added back during concretization). For conventional neoclassical economists, the idealization process is portrayed as one of making more and further restrictive assumptions (or relaxing these). For econometrics, the notion acts rather naturally, as models move from data description (as with simple time-series models) to full-scale structural equations models. The practical details of the process can be conceived in very different ways and thus the modelling notion associated with the idealization literature has a great deal of flexibility. For example, it can be seen as having the character of a logical exercise (Maki), or as something broadly evolutionary (Walliser), or a dialectical practice (Nowak), or as adopting certain kinds of idealizing assumptions (de la Sienra, Reuten) (all in Hamminga and De Marchi, 1994, except for Reuten, forthcoming).

An alternative route to obtaining models is via the use of analogies. In this tradition, developed by Hesse (1966, see also Achinstein, 1964), an analogy from one field (a given set of features related together in a given system) is taken across to provide a model in the new field on the basis of certain positive features held in common. The negative (unshared) features are ignored, while the neutral features are explored as a source for creative theory building in the new field. Analogical models are therefore said by Hesse to function at the discovery end of scientific practice. (Recently this approach has been revived; for example, Psillos, 1995, gives cases from physics noting the importance of background theories, while Morgan, 1997a, uses cases from economics to discuss the role of the negative analogical features.) Analogical models rely on the similarity relation between two systems, a feature Hesse's account shares with that of Giere (1988), where similarity relations form the basis of models which function at the justification end of scientific practice as well as in discovery.

The use of analogical models *within* a subject field is in fact widespread within the sciences, and economics is no exception: different subfields within economics borrow models from each other (as in, for example, Becker's economics of the family or Lancaster's characteristics theory of demand), with varying degrees of success. Economics has also borrowed and lent to other sciences; most recently the interchange of analogical models has been between economics and evolutionary biology. In the nineteenth century, when the borrowing was between physics and economics, the trade is usually understood in terms of the transfer of ideas or of metaphors, rather than analogical models. There is, indeed, some similarity between analogies and metaphors, and McCloskey (1990) explicitly defines metaphors as the equivalent of the economists' models. This might be acceptable as a definition of a model: metaphor is defined as bringing 'two separate domains into cognitive and emotional relation by using language directly appropriate to the one as a lens for seeing the other' (McCloskey, 1990: 12, quoting Black, 1962) (note again the hint at the importance of the cognitive element), but it stops short of giving us an account of what work the model does, and how it functions.

One way to provide an account of the work models do within McCloskey's terms might be to say we need, not only the metaphor, but also the story you can tell with the model. McCloskey might agree here, for she suggests that, in terms of rhetoric, a metaphor plus a story is an allegory. Now we are getting there: this provides the kind of coverage we need for a full account of models, one which both defines them and describes how they are used. A story McCloskey defines as a 'presentation of a time-ordered or time-related experience that …

supplements, reorders, enhances, or interprets unnarrated life' (McCloskey, 1990: 12) In her account, metaphors and stories 'criticize' each other, perhaps limit each other, in a kind of balancing role. It seems plausible to modify this into something like the following: the metaphor introduces the model (as the analogy did in Hesse's account), but also constrains the story that can be told within it, while the story the economist wants to tell in turn limits the interpretation of the metaphor (see Morgan, 1997b). So, taking the definitions (above) of metaphors and stories together suggests that the function of models (allegories) would be to bring into focus, and help us to understand or interpret, the economic world and, perhaps, our economic theories.

Focusing on the storytelling element of models allows us to make a closing link, this time between the modified McCloskey position based on rhetorical analysis of economics and the older conventional definition of models as interpreted structures that we began with. This congruence occurs in one of the few philosophical accounts of models to have originated using economics as its guide. This is the notion of models as caricatures (Gibbard and Varian, 1978). The authors define an applied model as a story with a specified structure. By 'applied model' they mean a run-of-the-mill mathematical economics model as applied to casually observed everyday economic phenomena: this provides the subject for the story. The structure is given by the logical/mathematically expressed assumptions which are to be interpreted, and whose implications are deduced and then explored. Some applied models, they argue, count as approximations to the world, likened to a realistic drawing. More controversially, there are other such models which rely on deliberate distortions of known features: caricatures. To the extent that the distortion 'illuminates certain aspects of the world' and is relatively robust, we learn from the manifestly false model. As with McCloskey's rhetorical analysis, Gibbard and Varian are appealing to other theories of knowledge, this time based on visual ways of representing. There are clearly logical difficulties with their philosophical analysis of approximation models, for they argue that a successfully applied model gives grounds for believing in the approximate truth of the model's assumptions, even where you believed the assumptions false to begin with. Nevertheless, their account of caricature models is thought-provoking and resonates with the experience many economists have of the way models work in economics: that of learning something from the features of a model which is nevertheless a manifest distortion of economic reality.

We started with highly restrictive definitions of models which gave no account of the roles played by models in economics. We have ended with a variety of accounts, in which models appear to function as autonomous instruments that help us to learn about the world and our theories in a variety of ways, which are not yet fully explored and understood. Most accounts discussed here have also required that a model be true, in some sense or in some part, either to a theory or to the world, or both – but we no longer expect that the models will exactly reflect, in structure or form, either the theory or the world. Models thus have a shade of independence from one or both, which allows them to function autonomously (see Morrison and Morgan, forthcoming). This characterization also enables them to avoid the worst excesses of instrumentalism associated with the view that the model is only measured by its satisfactory predictions. (One needs to be careful here, however: any satisfying account of economic models must leave room for one of the most interesting developments in social science modelling, proposed in a series of essays on modelling complexity by Simon (for example, 1957). Such models do not attempt to replicate the world, but nor are they instrumental in the sense associated with Friedman, 1953; see Boumans, 1997.) Gordon's judgment is nicely expressed: 'The real test of a model, however, is whether it works effectively as a scientific instrument [of investigation], not the degree to which it replicates the real world' (Gordon, 1991: 108), to which should be added 'or the theory'.

MARY S. MORGAN

References

Achinstein, P. (1964), 'Models, Analogies and Theories', *Philosophy of Science*, **31**, (4), 328–50.
Balzer, W. and B. Hamminga (1989), *Philosophy of Economics*, Dordrecht: Kluwer.
Black, M. (1962), *Models and Metaphors*, Ithaca, NY: Cornell University Press.
Boumans, M. (1997), 'Lucas and Artificial Worlds', in J.B. Davis (ed.), *New Economics and Its Writing*, supplement to *History of Political Economy*, vol. 29, Durham: Duke University Press.
Boumans, M. (forthcoming) 'Built-In Justification', in M.S. Morgan and M. Morrison (eds), *Models as Mediators*, Cambridge: Cambridge University Press.
Cartwright, N. (1983), *How the Laws of Physics Lie*, Oxford: Clarendon Press.
Fraassen B.C. van (1980), *The Scientific Image*, Oxford: Clarendon Press.
Friedman, M. (1953), 'The Methodology of Positive Economics', *Essays in Positive Economics*, Chicago: University of Chicago Press.
Gibbard, A. and H.R. Varian (1978), 'Economic Models', *The Journal of Philosophy*, **75**, (11), 664–77.
Giere, R.N. (1984), *Understanding Scientific Reasoning*, 2nd edn, New York: Holt, Rinehart and Winston.
Giere, R.N. (1988), *Explaining Science: A Cognitive Approach*, Chicago: University of Chicago Press.
Gordon, S. (1991), *The History and Philosophy of Social Science*, London: Routledge.
Hamminga, B. and N. de Marchi (1994), *Idealization in Economics*, Amsterdam: Rodopi.
Hands, D.W. (1985), 'The Structuralist View of Economic Theories: A Review Essay', *Economics and Philosophy*, **1**, 303–35.
Hausman, D.M. (1992), *The Inexact and Separate Science of Economics*, Cambridge: Cambridge University Press.
Hesse, M.B. (1966), *Models and Analogies in Science*, Notre Dame: University of Notre Dame Press.
Hoover, K.D. (1994) 'Six Queries about Idealization in an Empirical Context', in B. Hamminga and N. de Marchi, *Idealization in Economics*, Amsterdam: Rodopi.
Janssen, M. (1989), 'Structuralist Reconstructions of Classical and Keynesian Macroeconomics', *Erkenntnis*, **30**, 165–81.
McCloskey, D.N. (1990), *If You're So Smart*, Chicago: University of Chicago Press.
Morgan, M.S. (1990), *The History of Econometric Ideas*, Cambridge: Cambridge University Press.
Morgan, M.S. (1996), 'Idealization and Modelling', a Review of Hamminga and De Marchi: *Idealization in Economics* (1994) in *Journal of Economic Methodology*, **3**, (1), 131–8.
Morgan, M.S. (1997a), 'The Technology of Analogical Models: Irving Fisher's Monetary Worlds', *Philosophy of Science*, **64**, S304–14.
Morgan, M.S. (1997b), 'Models, Stories and the Economic World', University of Amsterdam working paper.
Morrison, M.C. and M.S. Morgan (forthcoming), 'Models as Mediating Instruments', in M.S. Morgan and M. Morrison (eds), *Models as Mediators*, Cambridge: Cambridge University Press.
Nersessian, N.J. (1990), 'Methods of Conceptual Change in Science: Imagistic and Analogical Reasoning', *Philosophica*, **45**, (1), 33–52.
Psillos, S. (1995), 'The Cognitive Interplay between Theories and Models: The Case of 19th-Century Optics', in W.E. Herfel, W. Krajewski, I. Niiniluoto and R. Wojcicki (eds), *Theories and Models in Scientific Processes*, Amsterdam: Rodopi.
Reuten, G.R. (forthcoming), 'Knife Edge Caricature Modelling: The Case of Marx's Reproduction Schema', in M.S. Morgan and M. Morrison (eds), *Models as Mediators*, Cambridge: Cambridge University Press.
Simon, H. (1957), *Models of Man*, New York: Wiley.
Stegmüller, W., W. Balzer and W. Spohn (1982), *Philosophy of Economics*, Berlin: Springer-Verlag.
Stewart, I.M.T. (1979), *Reasoning and Method in Economics*, London: McGraw Hill.
Suppe, F. (1974), 'Theories and Phenomena', in W. Leinfellner and E. Kohler (eds), *Developments in the Methodology of Social Science*, Dordrecht: Reidel.
Suppes, P. (1962), 'Models of Data', in E. Nagel, P. Suppes and A. Tarski (eds), *Logic, Methodology and Philosophy of Science*, proceedings of 1960 International Congress, Stanford: Stanford University Press.
Suppes, P. (1967), 'What is a Scientific Theory?', in S. Morgenbesser (ed.), *Philosophy of Science Today*, New York: Basic Books.
Walsh, V. (1987), 'Models and Theories', in J. Eatwell, M. Milgate and P. Newman (eds), *The New Palgrave. A Dictionary of Economics*, London: Macmillan.

Monetarism

Introduction

The sufficient and necessary conditions for someone to be classified as a monetarist are (a) acceptance of at least a soft version of the quantity theory of money, (b) advocacy of a stable (though not necessarily fixed) growth rate of money, and (c) a belief that the economy is not in continuous Walrasian equilibrium. Other tenets held by most monetarists, such as belief in the stability of the private sector, support these three basic monetarist positions, but are not necessary for monetarism. The delineation of monetarism is vague because acceptance of the quantity theory and advocacy of stable monetary growth are both matters of degree. Nobody believes that the quantity theory explains 100 per cent of all changes in nominal income, and many monetarists would allow the growth rate of the money supply to vary somewhat.

The quantity theory

The quantity theory of money, already clearly stated by Cantillion and Hume in the eighteenth century, was reformulated by Milton Friedman in 1956 in a way influenced by Keynes. This revised formulation employs a portfolio approach to the demand for money and is applicable, not only to the long run, but also to the short run in which real income varies. Don Patinkin (in Robert Gordon, 1974) therefore contends that it is a Keynesian theory, not a quantity theory. This depends largely on whether one classifies a theory by its analytic mechanisms or by its conclusions.

The quantity theory maintains that the demand function for money is stable, and either that the arguments in the money demand function (other than income) are also stable, or that the elasticity of money demand with respect to them is low, so that disturbances in the money market, and hence changes in nominal income, are due primarily to changes in the money supply. These changes ultimately generate proportional changes in prices.

Criticisms of the quantity theory take two forms. One is to deny that the coefficients of the variables in the money demand function are stable. Another is to argue that these variables, particularly the interest rate, are themselves subject to major shocks, so that even if the demand *function* for money is stable, the demand for money is not. Hence changes in the demand for money, not changes in the supply of money, are the major explanation of changes in nominal income. Thus Keynes (1930) argued that focusing on saving and investment provides a more insightful explanation of changes in income than does the quantity theory.

The main issues in this debate are the stability of the demand function for money (or of velocity), the role of interest rates in this demand function, the explanation of the transmission process linking money to income, and the exogeneity of money. The interest elasticity of the demand for money creates two problems. First, as the money supply increases, the resulting temporary fall in interest rates raises the demand for money so that, with velocity falling, nominal income rises less than in proportion to the increase in the money supply. Quantity theorists point out that the rise in nominal income raises interest rates again and, as the interest rate returns to its previous level, so does velocity. Quantity theorists argue that this happens soon enough for the period during which interest rates and velocity are reduced to be relatively unimportant.

Second, the interest elasticity of money demand provides a way for 'Keynesian' variables to affect nominal income. For example, a rise in the marginal efficiency of investment raises the demand for loanable funds, and hence interest rates. The quantity theory therefore requires either that the net change in the 'Keynesian' variables (other than the money supply) is small, or that it has little effect on interest rates, or that the interest elasticity of demand for money is low, or a combination of these conditions. In accordance with their 'as if' methodology, monetarists have dealt with this problem mainly indirectly by pointing to the high correlation between money and income. If money is exogenous, this implies that at least one of the above conditions is met.

Monetarists do not deny that causation also runs from income to money, but contend that the main thrust is from money to income. Their most persuasive, although not their only argument is Milton Friedman and Anna Schwartz's (1963) masterly historical study that attributes specific changes in the US money supply to specific exogenous factors. On the causation issue, as on other issues, they rely on circumstantial evidence from several sources rather than on a single, conclusive argument.

Monetarists disagree among themselves about the transmission process. Following their 'as if' methodology, Friedman and Schwartz provide only a sketch of the way money impinges on the goods market, while agreeing that further work is needed. Their critics therefore object that they rely on 'mere correlations' and 'black box' economics, but that is questionable. Price theory tells us that, if the supply of an asset, such as money, increases its relative price falls. The debate here is partly methodological. Friedman and Schwartz, with their empirical orientation, allocate their time to developing wide-ranging empirical evidence, while their theory-oriented critics want the theory spelled out in detail. Frank Hahn (1971) even claims that Friedman lacks a monetary theory.

In contrast to Friedman, Karl Brunner and Allan Meltzer describe an elaborate transmission process based on wealth effects and relative price effects. This model is similar to some Keynesian models, and whether it yields monetarist or Keynesian conclusions depends on the values of certain coefficients. It has therefore been criticized for not being monetarist. But Brunner and Meltzer can respond that, although their theoretical model is neutral between Keynesian and monetarist theory, their empirical work shows that monetarist coefficients prevail. Moreover, their model, unlike standard Keynesian models, has separate markets for bonds and capital.

Some other aspects of monetarism
Monetarists, unlike many Keynesians, believe that the private sector is stable. It has proved remarkably difficult to present any credible evidence on this issue. Monetarists also maintain that it does not take long to reach a vertical Phillips curve. Moreover, they distrust large macroeconomic models, which are generally built on Keynesian foundations. They also attribute less importance than Keynesians to cost-push factors, because with a constant money stock cost-push pressures in one sector generate deflationary pressures elsewhere. A basic theme of monetarism is its emphasis on the long run. Monetarists generally, but not necessarily, favour market processes, and in Britain monetarism was adopted by the Conservative Party under Margaret Thatcher.

Policy recommendations
Monetarists usually oppose inflation more than Keynesians do. They also want the central bank to concentrate on a single variable, the money supply or the monetary base (currency plus reserves) and favour at least a stable, if not a fixed (or even zero) growth rate for that variable. These recommendations are founded on the beliefs that the private sector is stable, that the quantity theory is valid, that the Phillips curve is vertical in the not too long run, and that central banks are not effective stabilizers. If the private sector generates tolerable levels of unemployment

there is less justification for inflationary policies. With a vertical Phillips curve, inflation cannot permanently lower unemployment. If the central bank cannot manage the economy efficiently, it should be relieved of its stabilization task and instead given a single target that is easier to attain. The quantity theory implies that this should be some monetary or reserves aggregate. If the central bank is incapable of effective countercyclical stabilization, stable monetary growth is the natural policy.

One reason monetarists distrust central banks is that monetary policy operates with substantial and variable lags, while our ability to forecast is limited. Friedman (1953) showed that it does not take implausibly large forecast errors for countercyclical policy to be destabilizing. Second, Brunner and Meltzer (1989) and Friedman and Schwartz (1963) argue that the Federal Reserve (Fed) has often exhibited little economic understanding. Third, many monetarists advocate a public choice theory in which political pressures and bureaucratic self-interest distort central bank policy. Recently, concern about time inconsistency (that is, that central banks have an incentive to proclaim a strong commitment to low inflation and then to renege) has made the case against discretionary policy much more popular.

Monetarism and new classical theory
Initially, new classical theory was sometimes called 'monetarism, mark II' by its critics. That is wrong: monetarism is much more empirical, and much less concerned with rigorous choice-theoretic foundations. Thus Friedman as a Marshallian does not concern himself much with the question why agents hold money, but concentrates on predicting and explaining the amount they hold. Hence he does not clarify why he dichotomizes assets into money and non-money assets. Is money so important because it is liquid, because it is wealth, or is it a combination of the two? This matters for understanding why money is more important than Treasury bills or credit. Brunner and Meltzer also take a strong empiricist position, being unwilling to reject empirical regularities simply because we cannot explain them. All this differs sharply from the new classicals' Cartesianism.

Moreover, while some monetarists, such as Meltzer, treat expectations as rational, others, such as Friedman, use adaptive expectations. Monetarists reject instantaneous market clearing and adhere to a monetary, not a real, theory of fluctuations. One might even say that, apart from policy, compared to the challenge from new classical theory, the Keynesian–monetarist dispute is merely a family squabble.

The rise and decline of monetarism
After the publication of the *General Theory*, most economists ceased to take the quantity theory seriously until Friedman revived it in 1956. At least four, perhaps five, factors account for its subsequent success. One is current events. From the mid-1950s to the end of the 1970s, velocity in the United States grew at a stable rate and money demand functions gave good fits. Monetarist policy recommendations gained support as interest rates, the then preferred Keynesian target variable, led the Fed astray, as inflation became a much more serious problem, and as Fed policy appeared perverse. Second, the then prevailing version of Keynesian theory attributed much too little importance to the money supply, so that it was an easy target for monetarists. Third, monetarists published a stream of persuasive work, in particular Friedman and Schwartz's (1963) monetary history of the United States, their 1963 survey (reprinted in Friedman, 1969) of the evidence for the quantity theory, and Brunner and

Meltzer's demonstration of Fed confusion (reprinted in 1989). Though only arguably monetarist, Patinkin's (1956; 1965) elegant explication of the quantity theory also helped.

Fourth, in the mid-1950s, Keynesian theory consisted largely of deductions from introspection and of casual observation. Although some econometric work had been done, Keynesian theory seemed confirmed not so much by econometrics as by the commonsense plausibility of basic Keynesian assumptions, for example, that uncertainty makes investment erratic. But, as economists became influenced by Friedman's (1953) methodology, such casual evidence and appeals to the realism of assumptions carried less weight. When Friedman pointed out that the data show that, despite what casual reasoning might suggest, velocity was stable, it put Keynesians on the defensive. Abraham Hirsch and Neil de Marchi (1990) characterize Friedman's methodology by five principles: (1) take an 'outside' view instead of introspection; (2) begin with observations; (3) test frequently; (4) address concrete problems; (5) use the best available knowledge as the framework for empirical research. Except possibly for the last, which is a matter of dispute, these principles characterized the monetarist attack on the Keynesian hegemony. To a considerable extent monetarism came in on the coattails of Friedmanian positivism.

A possible fifth factor may have been that, by the mid-1950s, Keynesian theory had become stale. Many of the research opportunities it had initially presented had already been exploited and young economists were looking for new lands in which to achieve fame, if not fortune. Moreover, as is typical of an orthodoxy, Keynesian theory had accumulated some unexamined dogma, which made it vulnerable to attack. A good example is the importance attributed to the speculative demand for money, on virtually no evidence.

All that changed by the late 1980s. Velocity has become erratic, and it is widely believed that no usable money demand function now lives at peace with the data. The inflation rate has fallen, and the Fed seems more competent. Many promising monetarist research opportunities have been exhausted. Rational expectations theory replaced the adaptive expectations theory often used by monetarists. Methodological tastes have changed and rigorous choice-theoretic models are now preferred to the type of work that monetarists mostly do. But what could be even more important is that much of monetarist teaching has been absorbed by the prevailing orthodoxy, an orthodoxy that should perhaps be called the Keynesian–monetarist synthesis. The Keynesian–monetarist debate therefore fits into the Hegelian schema of thesis, antithesis and synthesis.

Monetarism and methodology: a recapitulation

As already discussed, one characteristic of monetarism is its positivistic methodology of evaluating theories by their predictions (and explanations) that Friedman (1953) and Brunner (1969) advocated. Hence monetarists focus relatively more on testing than on refining their theory. They test the quantity theory (often with straightforward techniques) against numerous sets of data covering long periods and many countries. While Brunner and Meltzer did build a price-theoretic model, Friedman and his students are, by and large, content to explain their findings by simple Marshallian theory.

Another methodological characteristic of monetarism is a scepticism about how much economists know. Friedman does not attempt to describe in detail the channels by which money affects income, in part because he does not think that we know them all. Monetarists therefore distrust large econometric models and also prefer to focus on the long run rather than on the more difficult to understand short run. Their reliance on simple tests performed on many data sets rather than on a single econometrically sophisticated test can also be explained that way.

Still another methodological characteristic of monetarism is a certain leaning towards institutionalism, expressed in its great concern with the behaviour of the monetary authorities and with the institutions that govern the money supply.

THOMAS MAYER

Bibliography
Brunner, Karl (1969), '"Assumptions" and the Cognitive Quality of Theories', *Synthèse*, **20**, 501–25.
Brunner, Karl and Allan Meltzer (1976), 'Reply – Monetarism: the Principal Areas of Agreement and the Work Remaining', in Jerome Stein (ed.), *Monetarism*, Amsterdam: North-Holland.
Brunner, Karl and Allan Meltzer (1989), *Monetary Economics*, Oxford: Oxford University Press.
Friedman, Milton (1953), *Essays in Positive Economics*, Chicago: University of Chicago Press.
Friedman, Milton (1956), *Studies in the Quantity Theory of Money*, Chicago: University of Chicago Press.
Friedman, Milton (1969), *The Optimum Quantity of Money*, Chicago: University of Chicago Press.
Friedman Milton and Anna Schwartz (1963), *A Monetary History of the United States, 1867–1960*, Chicago: University of Chicago Press.
Gordon, Robert (ed.) (1974), *Milton Friedman's Monetary Framework*, Chicago: University of Chicago Press.
Hahn, Frank (1971), 'Professor Friedman's Views on Money', *Economica*, **38**, February, 61–80.
Hirsch, Abraham and Neil de Marchi (1990), *Milton Friedman*, New York: Harvester Wheatsheaf.
Johnson, Harry (1971), 'The Keynesian Revolution and the Monetarist Counter-Revolution', *American Economic Review*, **61**, May, 1–23.
Keynes, John M. (1930), *A Treatise on Money*, London: Macmillan.
Keynes, John M. (1936), *The General Theory of Employment, Interest and Money*, London: Macmillan.
Laidler, David (1982), *Monetarist Perspectives*, Cambridge, MA: Harvard University Press.
Laidler, David (1991), 'Karl Brunner's Monetary Economics – An Appreciation', *Journal of Money, Credit and Banking*, **23**, November, 633–58.
Mayer, Thomas (1994), 'The Rhetoric of Monetarism', in Philip Klein (ed.), *The Role of Economic Theory*, Boston: Kluwer.
Mayer, Thomas, Martin Bronfenbrenner, Karl Brunner, Phillip Cagan, Benjamin Friedman, Helmut Frisch, Harry Johnson, David Laidler and Allan Meltzer (1978), *The Structure of Monetarism*, New York: W.W Norton.
Patinkin, Don (1956, 1965), *Money. Interest and Prices*, New York: Harper & Row.

Myrdal, Gunnar

In the present context, methodology is taken to mean a philosophy, or theory, of how to acquire knowledge through the employment of prescribed methods of investigation. The philosophy first chosen by Gunnar Myrdal (1898–1987) was that of the Enlightenment. He adopted this philosophy as his guiding light when he was a student in the *gymnasium* (high school). When he started his university studies in economics, he was especially impressed by the Enlightenment philosophers' emphasis on rationality. It was, therefore, logical for him to follow the example of his professors and become a practitioner of microeconomic theory. When the great depression reached the shores of Sweden in the early 1930s, Myrdal viewed its impact from the point of view of the more radical aspects of the Enlightenment. Hence he was shocked by the damage the depression did to the existing state of 'liberty, equality and brotherhood', as he put it. He was therefore motivated to search for the causes and remedies of unemployment. Thus he became a self-made macroeconomist and thereby a charter member of the Stockholm School. As an economist, Myrdal practised macroeconomics during the remainder of the depression decade at the same time that he became increasingly critical of the assumptions and methods of standard economic theory. Consequently, he was ready for another conversion.

The metastasis occurred in the course of a visit to the United States that Myrdal commenced in 1938 for the purpose of studying race relations there. When he viewed what was then called the 'Negro problem' from the point of view of the radical, egalitarian and semi-holistic philosophy of the Enlightenment, Myrdal became convinced that there were no economic, political or social aspects of the said problem, there was only *a* problem. Hence he adopted a holistic and multidisciplinary approach to his study, the results of which were published in *An American Dilemma*, in 1944. After World War II, Myrdal applied his holistic approach to the study of international economic integration and to inquiries into the nature and causes of underdevelopment in the former colonial areas of the world. The results of these investigations were embodied in *An International Economy* (1956), *Rich Lands and Poor: The Road to World Prosperity* (1958) and in the massive, three-volume *Asian Drama* (1968).

Characterizing himself as a 'philosophical idealist', Myrdal confessed that the 'desirability of political democracy and of equality of opportunity' constituted the Enlightenmentesque value premises that shaped his viewpoint in the above-mentioned studies, a viewpoint that, in its turn, determined his choice of approach, selection of problems, definition of concepts and gathering of data. Significantly, Myrdal imputed variants of his own value premises to the dominant social groups in each of those societies that he studied through that third period of his professional life which began in 1938.

In *An American Dilemma*, the variant is called 'the American Creed'. Tracing its roots to the philosophy of the Enlightenment, Myrdal pointed out that this credo was first expressed formally in the Declaration of Independence and that it has gradually taken the form of the white majority's belief in freedom, equality and justice. The black minority was a problem because of a conflict between the status awarded its members by the whites, on the one hand, and the ethos of the white population, on the other. According to Myrdal, the blacks in America were set apart because of the white majority's theory that the blacks constituted an inferior race. This notion came readily to Myrdal's mind when he observed contemporary American affairs through intellectual lenses that were ground and tinted in the mould of the Enlightenment.

In Myrdal's studies of development, the variant of his own value premises is called 'the modernization ideals'. As he explained it, these are the values of the influential elites in the underdeveloped countries. Again, the dominating ideals emanated from the Enlightenment and were introduced by some of the sons of the upper classes when they returned home upon the completion of their studies in European and American universities.

Myrdal devised a set of methods of inquiry for the purpose of explaining how the American Creed and the modernization ideals could become engines of socioeconomic advancement in those societies in which the said ethos was dominant. The origins of these methods may be described thus: when he viewed historical and contemporary data from the viewpoint of his value premises, Myrdal detected two related processes in the societies that he studied: circular or cumulative causation and backwash and spread effects. By cumulative causation he understood a process of interaction of economic and non-economic factors in a given community, interactions that might produce either vicious or virtuous circles of change. He conceived of backwash and spread effects as the results of interactions between a developed region and an underdeveloped region. The former effect is one that ensues when the developed region sucks resources out of the underdeveloped region to the benefit of the former and to the detriment of the latter. The spread effect, on the other hand, is an effect that follows when the developed region spawns growth and development in the currently underdeveloped region by means of its demand for the latter's products. Consequently, both regions benefit from this effect.

Given these concepts, it was a short step for Myrdal to develop methods for explaining how virtuous chain reactions of cumulative causation and spread effects could be ignited. One illustration of cumulative causation provided by Myrdal involves the relationships among black employment, black family incomes, standards of black nutrition and health, housing standards for blacks and the access of black youth to education. The method that he selected was the simple one of changing in succession each of these variables with a view to determining the most efficient push for bringing about a virtuous cumulative effect. Similarly, in order to demonstrate how a spread effect could be engendered, Myrdal built a model consisting of a developed and an underdeveloped region. He then assumed that the economic development in the former region took such a course that its demand for raw materials available in the latter region increased. Hence output, income and employment expanded in the underdeveloped region and a chain reaction was started in which industrial growth and diversification took place in both regions.

Myrdal's policy recommendations followed logically from his value premises and methods of investigation. For the United States, he recommended the abolition of legally mandated segregation in educational institutions, housing, restaurants and so on, as well as other types of civil rights legislation. Myrdal was confident that these and other methods of social engineering would bring the black population under the umbrella of the American Creed. His policy recommendations for underdeveloped regions may be summed up in two words: economic planning.

Apart from the hints provided above, is it possible to detect even traces of any coherent methodology in the works of Myrdal? At the risk of repeating what has already been stated, the following summary is offered as an answer to this question.

'Evaluations' are *the* fundamental element in what Myrdal called 'the main rules we should attempt to apply to social analysis'. By evaluations he understood the investigator's ideas about how reality ought to be. It is from this set of ideas that the scholar carves the value premise for his study: that is, the aforementioned viewpoint. The premise is a function of the investigator's class affiliation, upbringing, education, intellectual heritage, associations and experience.

Hence, as Myrdal never tired of reminding his readers, the social scientist's valuations enter into his choice of approach, his definition of concepts and his gathering of data. Myrdal viewed the processes in each of these segments as follows. The ends to be sought, and consequently the problems to be studied, are pinpointed in the approach. In the course of their definition, concepts are correlated and tied together to form a complex which Myrdal dubbed 'theory'. The bundled concepts define and determine the selection of data at the same time as they serve as the means for the transformation of the collected data into socioeconomic facts. The theory is the instrument by the use of which causal relations are established among the conceptualized facts. The conclusions that emanate from such an analysis provide the basis for policy recommendations designed to achieve the ends postulated in the approach. Myrdal concluded, therefore, that evaluations permeate the entire enterprise of social inquiry: from the selection of problems, through the analysis to which they are subjected, to the policy inferences drawn from the theoretical findings.

Finally, as pointed out earlier, Myrdal insisted that the social scientists' inquiry must be holistic in the sense that such scientists take account of, and integrate, demographic, economic, historical, cultural and sociopolitical factors and elements. In Philippe Adair's felicitous phrase, Myrdal's rules for social analysis may therefore be called 'methodological holism'. Hence it may not be unwarranted to conclude that Myrdal did indeed produce a detectable methodology.

HANS E. JENSEN

Bibliography

Angresano, James (1997), *The Political Economy of Gunnar Myrdal: An Institutional Basis for the Transformation Problem*, Cheltenham: Edward Elgar.

Dostaler, Gilles, Diane Ethier and Laurent Lepage (eds) (1992), *Gunnar Myrdal and His Works*, Montreal: Harvest House.

Myrdal, Gunnar (1944), *An American Dilemma: The Negro Problem and Modern Democracy*, New York: Harper and Brothers.

Myrdal, Gunnar (1956), *An International Economy: Problems and Prospects*, New York: Harper and Brothers.

Myrdal, Gunnar (1958a), *Value in Social Theory*, ed. Paul Streeten, New York: Harper and Brothers.

Myrdal, Gunnar (1958b), *Rich Lands and Poor: The Road to World Prosperity*, New York: Harper and Brothers; first published 1957 as *Economic Theory and Underdeveloped Regions*, London: Duckworth.

Myrdal, Gunnar (1960), *Beyond the Welfare State*, New Haven, CT: Yale University Press.

Myrdal, Gunnar (1968), *Asian Drama: An Inquiry into the Poverty of Nations*, 3 vols, New York: The Twentieth Century Fund.

Myrdal, Gunnar (1973), *Against the Stream: Critical Essays on Economics*, New York: Pantheon.

Natural kind

The notion of a natural kind was prominent in ancient Greek philosophy, and it has directly and indirectly had much influence on the interpretation of science ever since. A natural kind is a class of things that are grouped together in virtue of a shared nature.

'Shared nature' can be explicated in different ways. One might focus on the fact that we can recognize kinds and give them names in our everyday lives: dog, star, water and perhaps even chair. These abilities have suggested to some philosophers that each member of a natural kind shares a metaphysical essence that accounts for them. Another approach that is more directly suggested by scientific thinking is that members of a kind are naturally grouped because they are all governed by some scientific law. One might think, for example, that all samples of water form a natural kind because they all change state at 100°C in standard conditions. One might, finally, combine these approaches by understanding members of a natural kind as sharing something like an essence, where the essence is understood to be a scientifically characterized structural or microstructural property of the members. One might thus take having the structure, H_2O, as being the criterion for membership in the natural kind *water*, or having such-and-such DNA as the criterion for being in *dog*. Let us follow the seventeenth-century philosopher, John Locke, and call these scientifically determined properties 'real essences'.

The concept of the natural kind has proved to be a focal point for much debate in recent philosophy of science. Many have thought that the history of science shows that scientific theorizing is characterized by the search for laws which relate natural kinds to one another. Others, notably the philosopher W.V. Quine, have argued that one finds laws relating kinds when sciences are in their infancies. On this view, the natural kinds we pick out are vestiges of our prescientific world view which is based on how our perceptual systems have evolved. In mature sciences, this view has it that reference to kinds drops away as the structural properties of (what we might conveniently still call) real essences are discovered.

Each side of this debate has interesting consequences for the understanding of economics. If it is true that science is characterized by the discovery of lawlike relationships among natural kinds, we can ask what the natural kinds of economic science are and how much confidence we have in the corresponding laws. If, on the other hand, mature sciences dispense with kinds by eliminating reference to them in favour of microstructural real essences, then we can ask whether economics has successfully reached maturity.

The first alternative seems implausible for economics. Most of the lawlike relations among economics kinds seem little more than pre-theoretic truisms: 'bad money drives out good', or 'a change in preferences shifts the relationship between price and quantity demanded'. One does not need an economic science to arrive at these generalizations. Most theoretical work in economics instead seems aimed at the search for real essences: consider attempts to understand market phenomena in terms of optimizing behaviour, or to provide microfoundations for macroeconomic phenomena. But it is doubtful that economics kinds are analysable into real essences in the same way that 'water' or 'dog' might be so analysed.

One concern with such an analysis is that it seems to terminate in the psychology of individual economic behaviour; economies are, in the end, constituted by individual consumers and firms' owners and managers. This is problematic for two reasons. There are, first, considerable philosophical arguments for doubting the feasibility of the sort of cognitive psychological science needed to analyse economic kinds. These arguments themselves question whether the relevant psychological kinds – preference, choice, belief and so on – are sound.

And, second, if the doubts are overcome and the appropriate psychology is developed, it is unclear whether this theory will analyse economics, or instead conflict with it. The psychology of individual behaviour might, for example, be inconsistent with the theory of optimization, or have it that preferences are not stable enough even properly to define optimization.

A plausible reaction to these difficulties would be to regard them as artificial because they are based on philosophical conceptions of what a successful science must look like. If economics, and physics for that matter, appears problematic when viewed in terms of natural kinds, that might be regarded as a reason for reconsidering philosophical theories of the notion.

ALAN NELSON

Bibliography
Fodor, Jerry (1974), 'Special Sciences', *Synthèse*, 97–115.
Nelson, Alan (1990), 'Are Economic Kinds Natural?', *Minnesota Studies in the Philosophy of Science*, **14**, 102–35.
Quine, W.V. (1969), 'Natural Kinds', *Ontological Relativity*, New York: Columbia University Press.

Neurath, Otto

Otto Neurath (1882–1945) is well known as a founding member of the Vienna Circle, one of several points of origin of later logical empiricism. While Neurath's distinctive contribution to the philosophy of science is beginning to be recognized after long neglect, his economic thought remains relatively unexplored. A striking fact is thus obscured: Neurath is furthest from the 'positivist' economist one might be excused for expecting.

Returning to Vienna after his PhD in political economy with G. Schmoller and E. Meyer in Berlin in 1906, Neurath began publishing widely: from discussions of general scientific methodology to studies in history of science and social history; from empirical studies of legislative proposals and accounting methods to proposals for modern citizens' education and urban transport systems. In his own field, he had published by the time of his habilitation in Heidelberg in 1917, besides individual studies, a monograph on the economic history of antiquity and an introductory textbook of economics, and had co-edited a comprehensive anthology of the history of economic theory; most importantly, however, Neurath had developed 'war economics' as a separate discipline with new tools of analysis, which had led him to reconceptualize economics itself – away from both Austrian and Marxian value theories and the emerging neoclassical paradigm. Extended empirical research during the Balkan wars had suggested to him the exploration of the idea of a central administrative economy with planning in kind (a development documented in Neurath, 1919). After the war Neurath intervened in the debates on the nature and extent of the possible socialization of the postwar economy and participated in the Bavarian revolution. Barred from academia because of his conviction for these activities, Neurath increasingly turned, in the 'red Vienna' of the 1920s and early 1930s, to developing innovations in visual pedagogy (the ISOTYPE system of pictorial representation of statistical data) and pursuing his anti-foundationalist campaign in the philosophy of science, only occasionally restating his economic ideas.

As an Austrian, having taken his doctorate under leading figures of the Historical School, Neurath hit upon a unique solution to both the *Methoden-* and the *Werturteilsstreit*. Abstract deductive theory can be used to enlighten historical problems: the productivity of an economy (as opposed to the profitability of a firm) *was* assessable in terms that respected Max Weber's strictures on value-statements in science. Neurath rejected Menger's Aristotelianism, Schmoller's inductivism and Weber's ideal-types and adopted an instrumentalist conception of theory derived from Mach, Poincaré and Duhem; simultaneously, he sought to redirect economics from price theory to investigations of how socioeconomic institutions affect wealth understood as well-being, working towards a theory of relevant indicators and developing increasingly complex representations of the conditions under which a transfer of goods can be said to increase the welfare of those involved. Owing to the minimal assumptions of these calculi, only ordinal rankings were possible and even these were not always complete (Neurath, 1911). It follows that no unique welfare function is computable (Neurath, 1912). Moreover, without money as a universal value indicator there was no unit of calculation by reference to which different ensembles of transfers of goods could be measured for their optimality. An economy was understood as a function from 'life-conditions' (or 'life-situations') to 'life-moods', from objective natural and social conditions to subjective experience (Neurath, 1917); economics itself investigated 'correlations between life-orders and life-situations' (Neurath, 1935). All along, Neurath stressed that decisions between entire life-orders (systems of rules for goods transfers under given conditions) required judgments for which no scientific calculation could substitute.

This was the methodological background for Neurath's idea of socialization as the reorganization of the economy 'by society for society' by means of an economic plan. Roughly, a nation's entire economy was to be organized in terms of industry-wide producers' associations who received directives from a 'central economic administration' for the production of certain kinds and certain quantities of goods. This plan was based on a 'universal statistics' compiled from reports of the central bank and the industries, as well as economic control councils. It is important to distinguish the organizational from the calculatory aspect of his socialization models and to note the self-conscious but problematical lacuna of the political. A pioneer of the idea of command economy, Neurath's conception of it is distinct from the Soviet models, comparison with which it readily invites. To be stressed is the distinction, underlying his work but not always clearly enough stated, between directive and indicative planning. Directive planning sets the goals, the plan of an economy, which must be fulfilled; indicative planning explored what kinds of plans could be developed and provides models for orientation. Neurath's 'central economic administration' served both functions, but they can and need be separated, for this central agency did not act wholly autonomously. In its directive function it was subject to the political decision of the 'people's representatives' on which plan to realize; only its indicative function was wholly entrusted to this agency. Neurath left open the question of political power in his 'sociotechnical' schemes as lying outside his remit. Notably, however, he also left open how the different sectors of the economy were organized locally and did not require wholesale collectivization (Neurath, 1920). Neurath soon faced criticisms of the method of calculation-in-kind, raised by von Mises, Weber and von Hayek, that there cannot be rational economic calculation in the absence of the unit of money and the profit motive. Neurath remained remarkably unmoved on this point. Defending his conception against both Austrian Marxists and his neoclassical critics, he insisted that they themselves had to admit the insufficiency of monetary calculations for decisions concerning economic policy (Neurath, 1925; 1935). The multidimensionality of welfare could only be approximated by the further development of sets of indices for standards of living, sets which ultimately were envisaged also to account for the freedom experienced in these social orders (Neurath, 1937, 1942).

Professional economists – with the notable exception of Tinbergen – neglected Neurath's work. When viewed in conjunction with his concern for a new empirical base for an economics of welfare, however, it becomes clear that Neurath's resistance to the Mises–Weber–Hayek objection chimes with important present-day efforts: his 'rational economics' was to open up for investigation just what Sen's 'rational fools' are constitutionally incapable of taking account of. Neurath's scepticism about neoclassical welfare economics remains a healthy corrective to imperious claims, both conceptual and explanatory, for the priority of individual utility maximization.

THOMAS E. UEBEL

Bibliography
Cartwright, Nancy, Jordi Cat, Lola Fleck and Thomas E. Uebel (1996), *Otto Neurath: Philosophy between Science and Politics*, Cambridge: Cambridge University Press.
Neurath, Otto (1911), 'Nationalökonomie und Wertlehre, eine systematische Untersuchung', *Zeitschrift für Volkswirtschaft, Sozialpolitik und Verwaltung*, 20, trans. 'Political Economy and the Theory of Value', reprinted in Neurath (forthcoming).
Neurath, Otto (1912), 'Des Problem des Lustmaximums', trans. 'The Problem of the Pleasure Maximum', reprinted in Neurath (1973).
Neurath, Otto (1917), 'Des Begriffsgebäude der Wirtschaftslehre und seine Grundlagen', *Zeitschrift für die gesamte Staatswissenschaft*, **73**, trans. 'The Conceptual Structure of Economics and its Foundation', reprinted in Neurath (forthcoming).
Neurath, Otto (1919), *Durch die Kriegswirtschaft zur Naturalwirtschaft*, Munich: Callwey, excerpts trans. in Neurath (1973, and forthcoming).
Neurath, Otto (1920), 'Ein System der Sozialisierung', *Archiv für Sozialwissenschaft und Sozialpolitik*, **48**, trans. 'A System of Socialisation', reprinted in Neurath (forthcoming).
Neurath, Otto (1925), *Wirtschaftsplan und Naturalrechnung*, Berlin: Laub, trans. 'The Economic Plan and Calculation in Kind', reprinted in Neurath (forthcoming).
Neurath, Otto (1935), W*as bedeutet rationale Wirtschaftsbetrachtung?*, Vienna: Gerold & Co., trans. 'What is Meant by Rational Economic Theory?', in B. McGuinness (ed.), *Unifed Science*, Dordrecht: Kluwer, 1987.
Neurath, Otto (1937), 'Inventory of the Standard of Living', *Zeitschrift für Sozialforschung*, **6**, reprinted in Neurath (forthcoming).
Neurath, Otto (1942), 'International Planning for Freedom', reprinted in Neurath (1973).
Neurath, Otto (1973), *Empiricism and Sociology*, ed. M. Neurath and R.S. Cohen, Dordrecht: Reidel.
Neurath, Otto (forthcoming), *Economic Writings. A Selection*, ed. R.S. Cohen and T.E. Uebel, Dordrecht: Kluwer.
O'Neill, John (1995), 'In Partial Praise of a Positivist', *Radical Philosophy*, **74**.
Uebel, Thomas E. (ed.), (1991), *Rediscovering the Forgotten Vienna Circle. Austrian Studies on Otto Neurath*, Dordrecht: Kluwer

New Classical Macroeconomics, The

Principal doctrines
A clearly discernible school of economic thought since the early 1970s, the new classical macroeconomics is the product of a twofold reaction to the then reigning 'Keynesian' orthodoxy. On the one hand, it is the culmination of the drive to provide microfoundations for macroeconomics that began shortly after the publication of Keynes's *General Theory*; on the other hand, it is an answer to the perceived failure of econometric macro models and the demand-management policies based upon them to cure the ills of stagflation. More positively, the new classical macroeconomics is sometimes regarded as the natural successor to the monetarism of Milton Friedman and the Chicago School. While it is true that some prominent new classicals are products of the earlier Chicago School and that new classicals often accept monetarist policy prescriptions, the differences are profound. Where Friedman is a Marshallian

in the sense that he believes that economic theory should be the handmaiden to the pursuit of concrete, empirical truths, the new classicals are Walrasian, both in the sense that they believe that the Walrasian general equilibrium model closely approximates the actual behaviour of the economy and in the sense that they rank theoretical completeness and consistency higher than empirical efficacy in the hierarchy of methodological virtues.

The new classical assumptions that economic actors are fully rational and that economic information is efficiently processed rules out money illusion; the assumption that prices move rapidly to clear all markets rules out disequilibrium. The real allocation of goods and services depends only on real endowments, real production possibilities and the tastes of consumers for real goods. Without money illusion or disequilibrium, monetary and fiscal policies that act on nominal income do not have a handle on the real economy: macroeconomic policy can affect inflation, market interest rates and exchange rates, but cannot affect relative prices, real interest rates, real exchange rates, employment or real output.

The rational expectations hypothesis is commonly singled out as the most characteristic doctrine of the new classical school. It was originally formulated by John Muth in 1960, and Robert Lucas and Thomas Sargent introduced it into macroeconomics about 1970 as a way of avoiding the implication of the then prevailing extrapolative expectations models (for example, adaptive expectations) that economic agents made systematic and correctable errors in forming expectations. The rational expectations hypothesis asserts that economic agents form expectations consistent with the forecasts of the maintained model. The rational expectations hypothesis, in fact, is a subsidiary doctrine. The 'new' element in the new classical macroeconomics, which distinguishes it from monetarism and other related schools of neoclassical macroeconomics, is the insistence that only a disaggregative, Walrasian approach will do.

From the mid-1970s to the mid-1980s, the new classical macroeconomics intellectually dominated mainstream macroeconomics. Since the mid-1980s, however, the new classical macroeconomics has been challenged by a resurgent new Keynesian macroeconomics that stresses imperfect competition, (rational) failures of markets to clear and coordination failures.

The first substantial achievement of the new classical macroeconomics was to incorporate the rational expectations hypothesis into the expectations-augmented Phillips curve. Milton Friedman and Edmund Phelps had independently argued that output and unemployment would deviate from their natural rates only to the degree that workers mistook inflation for changing relative prices. Robert Lucas argued that the rational expectations hypothesis and flexible prices implied that such mistakes were unsystematic and fleeting. The new classical analysis of the Phillips curve led immediately to Thomas Sargent and Neil Wallace's (1975) celebrated 'policy-ineffectiveness proposition': aggregate monetary policy could not *systematically* alter real outcomes.

The Phillips curve represents an inverse relationship between inflation and unemployment. The rational-expectations-augmented Phillips curve suggests that this relationship will shift as expectations change in the face of rationally perceived changes in monetary policy. Lucas (1976) generalized this insight with the famous 'policy non-invariance (or Lucas) critique'. Lucas argued that econometrically-estimated relationships between aggregate economic data would not remain stable in the face of changing policies, because rational expectations introduce an unaccounted for interdependence between policy rules and underlying behavioural relations. The Lucas critique was at once an explanation of the inability of Keynesian macroeconometric models to predict the effects of changing policy and the foundation for a new classical research agenda. Henceforth, models would be acceptable only if they were grounded in the bedrock of tastes, endowments and technology, so that the microeconomics of general equilibrium and the interdependencies introduced by rational expectations could be accounted for. While the policy ineffectiveness proposition, based on the assumption of rapidly clearing markets and rapid adjustment of expectations, attacked the case for countercyclical demand policies, the policy ineffectiveness proposition, based on the interdependence of policy and public behaviour, attacked the usefulness of aggregate, macroeconometric models in evaluating policies.

Business cycles pose a problem for the new classical macroeconomics. Fluctuating output is compatible with continuous equilibrium and the rational-expectations-augmented Phillips curve only if the natural rate of output (employment) itself fluctuates. The new classicals universally turn to Robert Solow's neoclassical growth model to provide a propagation mechanism for business cycles. Such a model is always in equilibrium; but, if the capital stock is away from its steady-state growth path, the optimal path back to the steady state is slowly to raise or lower the capital stock. Output and employment fluctuate along with capital. Where new classical economists differ amongst themselves is over the source of the initial impulses that drive the capital stock away from its steadystate growth path.

Following on from their work on the Phillips curve, new classical economists (for example, Lucas, 1975) initially looked to monetary fluctuations as the source of business cycles. Observed prices reflect both inflation and relative prices. An increase in the supply of money raises inflation. Under rational expectations, workers and producers with limited information may mistake such inflation temporarily for a favourable increase in their real wages or product prices, and supply more labour and more output, and add to the capital stock. Because capital is long-lived, such unsystematic errors are transformed through the neoclassical growth model into systematic fluctuations of employment and output typical of the business cycle.

Accumulated failures to verify this 'monetary surprise' hypothesis empirically led to the dominance of 'real business cycle' models. In Finn Kydland and Edward Prescott's (1982) paradigm real business cycle model, technology shocks replace monetary shocks as the original source of cyclical fluctuations. Systematic fluctuations are amplified in this model through the incorporation of the fact that there is some construction time involved before capital becomes productive and through the assumption that labour possesses a high degree of intertemporal substitutability.

Methodological issues
The new classical macroeconomics raises many methodological issues. Some are shared with economics or neoclassical economics more broadly conceived. We can consider only those issues that are particularly pressing, even if not uniquely relevant, to the new classical macroeconomics.

Microfoundational issues
The new classical macroeconomics supports the reductionist programme of microfoundations for macroeconomics. Its commitment to methodological individualism is both critical (Keynesian and monetarist models are fundamentally defective because they deal in aggregates) and positive (macroeconomic models should be constructed on the basis of individual utility and profit maximization). Whether the commitment to microfoundations is only heuristic or whether it is epistemological (that is, a claim that it is the most effective way to learn about the macroeconomy) or ontological (a claim that only individual economic actors exist objectively) remains an open question.

In principle, new classical economists are willing to consider a variety of microfoundational approaches. They have, for example, been favourably inclined towards game-theoretic formulations, especially, in the analysis of the behaviour of policy makers. Nevertheless, in practice, the Walrasian model of perfectly competitive general equilibrium remains the centrepiece of their microfoundational programme. The only practicable method the new classicals have ever proposed to implement their programme is to model representative agents. In a representative agent model, one agent maximizes his utility or profit functions treating the economy-wide aggregate constraints as if they were his budget and production constraints. (Sometimes these models are generalized to a few types of agents, each representative of a large group in the economy.) Aggregation theory unequivocally demonstrates that the conditions under which a representative agent could represent the mass of individuals do not obtain. The representative agent does not, then, represent a successful implementation of the programme of microfoundations. At worst, the representative agent model is an evasion of the aggregation problem. The new classicals attack Keynesians and other advocates of aggregative macroeconomics for failing to provide microfoundations, and then provide models that begin with an unjustified assumption of successful aggregation, offering a simulacrum of microeconomics, rather than genuine microfoundations. At best, representative agent models are metaphors or idealizations of the macroeconomy.

Representative agent models are offered as solutions to the Lucas critique. Typically, they fail to pass the usual tests of statistical success when they are estimated econometrically. This is hardly surprising because of their idealized relationship to the actual economy. Kydland and Prescott, among others, have suggested that such idealized models may be useful nevertheless in quantitative policy analysis if they are accepted as stylized artefacts similar to wind tunnel models. This so-called 'calibration' methodology seeks models that mimic quantitatively a few key features of the economy. The calibration methodology appears consonant with philosophical accounts of idealization as a basis for scientific understanding, but it raises a critical problem common to idealization: if, by virtue of their idealization, models are born falsified, how can discriminating empirical tests be made of their success, absolutely or relative to competing idealized models?

Issues of rationality
The adjective in the 'rational expectations hypothesis' makes a clever rhetorical appeal. Few economists would wish to advocate *irrational* expectations. Beyond effective advertising, how the rational expectations hypothesis relates to larger conceptions of rationality remains an open question.

Internally to theoretical and econometric models, the technical role of rational expectations is to maintain consistency: the new classicals argue that the models should not ascribe to the agents that they model expectations that are different from the ones they would form as outsiders using the model to describe the economy. In other words, the model should not confer an informational advantage on the econometrician over the modelled agent. Such expectations must be unbiased: they must not produce systematic, remediable expectational errors. Lovell (1986) points out that there are other expectational schemes (such as, Edwin Mills' 'implicit expectations') that fulfil the criteria of consistency and unbiasedness yet differ from rational expectations.

External to the models themselves, three strategies have been used to justify the rational expectations hypothesis as the correct assumption to make about expectation formation in the actual economy. First is the straightforward one: people more or less understand the actual functioning of the economy and effectively calculate their expectations in a rational manner. This is clearly implausible. The economists who struggle to understand the economy professionally are also ordinary economic actors who are hypothesized to do as consumers and workers what they manifestly cannot do as economists. Such complex, detailed calculation is also uneconomical and would make sense only if information and its processing were virtually costless.

Second, the strongest justification for the rational expectations hypothesis is the conclusion of Abraham Lincoln's dictum: 'You can't fool all of the people all of the time.' People learn from their mistakes; even on a weak notion of rationality, one would not expect people to persist in systematic, and therefore correctable, error. This point is sometimes made in a homely way: one does not count on finding $100 bills on the sidewalk. It is not that they are never there; it is just that it is in people's interest to find them and appropriate them quickly. It is not clear from the large literature on learning processes that they necessarily converge to model-consistent expectations. Rather, it may be that adaptable rules of thumb and Herbert Simon's notion of bounded rationality better capture such processes. Sargent and other new classicals have shown some interest in bounded rationality. Sargent's interest, however, appears to be mainly in using the tools developed in the literature on bounded rationality to develop better ways of calculating traditional rational expectations equilibria in complicated models.

Critics have sometimes stigmatized the new classicals for believing that settled equilibria are the dominant feature of the economy. But this is not quite right. On Lucas' view, rational expectations are found only in stable environments in which unanticipated shocks can be reduced to Knightian insurable risk rather than uninsurable uncertainty. Such environments are not necessarily dominant, but given how little is known about learning processes, Lucas believes that sensible economic analysis can be applied only when they obtain.

Stable environments might nonetheless be characterized by rule-of-thumb behaviour. The new classicals typically ignore another clause of Lincoln's dictum: 'You can fool some of the people all of the time.' The literature on partial rationality shows that, when some agents have rational expectations and some agents have not, even those who have rational expectations do not act as they would if everyone had them (as a representative agent model presumes); rather they incorporate the actions of the rule-of-thumb agents into the rational forecasts. For example, it is rational to use one's knowledge of irrational stock market bubbles in forming one's own expectations for stock prices.

Third, the rational expectations hypothesis is often justified with Friedman's permissive instrumentalism: it may not be literally true, but models using it work well by treating it 'as if' it were true. As with other instrumentalist justifications, this has an occult quality. Furthermore, it is not clear that it is warranted by the empirical success in prediction of models incorporating rational expectations.

Policy issues

The Lucas critique questions the use of econometric models for policy analysis on the grounds that they do not reflect the true deep structure of economy. One class of responses to the Lucas critique has been to attempt to articulate that structure more precisely: both Lars Hansen and Thomas Sargent's programme of estimation of fully identified rational expectations, general equilibrium models and the calibration approach to real business cycle models embody this response. Identification is closely related to causality in the sense of Simon (see the entry

'Causality' in this volume). A principal difficulty, however, is that identification is based on *a priori* theory, but there are competing theories with equal *a priori* support that reflect alternative causal orders. How to discriminate between these competing theories is an unsettled problem in policy analysis.

Another strategy for dealing with the Lucas critique is to argue that genuine policy changes are so rare that the Lucas critique is practically irrelevant. Cooley and LeRoy, Sims and others have argued that the conception of a policy intervention as a change in a policy parameter that is then held fixed forever – the typical thought experiment proposed by the Lucas critique – is inconsistent with rational expectations. For if a policy parameter changes, individual agents should have formed probability distributions over the range of potential changes, so that what is observed is not a new policy but a stochastic realization of an unchanged policy.

This approach to the Lucas critique undercuts the role of the policy advisor. If policy makers and the public are seen as already behaving optimally, and if it is wrong to see them as choosing between alternative policy rules or alternative policy actions, what role is left for the policy adviser? The view that policy advice is part of a process that ratifies a pre-existing probability distribution among policy alternatives has been termed 'stochastic Calvinism', since it appears to underwrite a sort of predestination. Policy analysis in the new classical macroeconomics thus throws into high relief the paradoxes of omniscience that lie beneath much of neoclassical economics. Man is represented as freely choosing, but economic models purport to represent his choices as part of a closed system determinate up to a random error. The dissent of the Austrians and some other heterodox schools of economic thought (for example, institutionalism, new and old) from neoclassical economics and implicitly new classical macroeconomics is grounded in large measure in the belief that human choice cannot be understood through models that treat human action as positively predictable and that policy advice cannot make sense in models in which the only policy that can be implemented is one that is a realization from a probability distribution existing objectively in advance of any action on the part of the adviser.

The methodological questions that haunt the new classical macroeconomics are in no cases unique to it. In its emphasis on the connection between microeconomic decision making and the role of assumptions about knowledge in macroeconomics, the new classical macroeconomics nevertheless rendered those questions less spectral than they had previously been.

KEVIN D. HOOVER

Bibliography
Cooley, Thomas F. (ed.) (1994), *Frontiers of Business Cycle Research*, Princeton: Princeton University Press.
Haltiwanger, John and Michael Waldman (1985), 'Rational Expectations and the Limits of Rationality: An Analysis of Heterogeneity', *American Economic Review*, **75**, (3), 326–40.
Hartley, James E. (1997), *The Representative Agent in Macroeconomics*, London: Routledge.
Hoover, Kevin D. (1988), *The New Classical Macroeconomics: A Sceptical Inquiry*, Oxford: Blackwell.
Hoover, Kevin D. (1994), 'Six Queries About Idealization in an Empirical Context', *Poznan Studies in the Philosophy of the Sciences and the Humanities*, **38**, 43–53.
Hoover, Kevin D. (1995), 'Facts and Artifacts: Calibration and the Empirical Assessment of Real-Business-Cycle Models', *Oxford Economic Papers*, **47**, (1), 24–44.
Janssen, Maarten (1993), *Microfoundations*, London: Routledge.
Kirman, Alan (1992), 'Whom and What Does the Representative Individual Represent?', *Journal of Economic Perspectives*, **6**, (2), 117–36.
Kydland, Finn E. and Edward C. Prescott (1982), 'Time to Build and Aggregate Fluctuations', *Econometrica*, **50**, (6), 1345–69.
Lovell, Michael C. (1986), 'Tests of the Rational Expectations Hypothesis', *American Economic Review*, **76**, (1), 110–24.

Lucas, Robert E., Jr. (1975), 'An equilibrium model of the business cycle', *Journal of Political Economy*, **83**, (6), 1113–34; reprinted in Lucas (1981).

Lucas, Robert E., Jr. (1976), 'Econometric policy evaluation: a critique', in Karl Brunner and Allan H., Meltzer (eds), *The Phillips Curve and Labor Markets*, CRCS, vol. 1, Amsterdam: North-Holland; reprinted in Lucas (1981).

Lucas, Robert E., Jr. (1981), *Studies in Business Cycle Theory*, Oxford: Blackwell.

Lucas, Robert E., Jr. (1986), 'Adaptive Behavior and Economic Theory', Journal of Business, **59**, (4:2), S401–26.

Lucas, Robert E., Jr. (1987), *Models of Business Cycles*, Oxford: Blackwell.

Lucas, Robert E. Jr. and Thomas J Sargent (eds) (1981), *Rational Expectations and Econometric Practice*, London: George Allen & Unwin.

Sargent, Thomas J. (1993), *Bounded Rationality in Macroeconomics*, Oxford: Clarendon Press.

Sargent, Thomas J. and Neil Wallace (1975), '"Rational expectations", the optimal monetary instrument and the optimal money supply rule', *Journal of Political Economy*, **83**, (2), 241–54; reprinted in Lucas and Sargent (1981).

Novel facts

Amongst economists, the most widely-known exponent of the view that the successful prediction of novel facts is the 'ultimate test' of a scientific theory is Milton Friedman: 'The ultimate test of the validity of a theory is not conformity to the canons of formal logic but the ability to deduce facts that have not yet been observed, that are capable of being contradicted by observation, and that subsequent observation does not contradict' (Friedman, 1946: 631); 'The ultimate goal of a positive science is the development of a "theory" or "hypothesis" that yields valid and meaningful (i.e., not truistic) predictions about phenomena not yet observed' (Friedman, 1953: 7). Friedman qualifies this claim by observing that such predictions include not only (a) predictions made 'in advance' of events, but also (b) predictions of events that have not yet been observed, and (c) predictions of events that, though already observed, are unknown to the scientist making the prediction.

Friedman's position however, is not original, but can be traced back to Herschel (1830: 164–5, 203). Prediction of novel facts as a criterion for appraising scientific theories was also one of the issues involved in the argument between John Stuart Mill and William Whewell over the nature of scientific method:

> But it seems to be thought that an hypothesis of the sort in question is entitled to a more favourable reception, if, besides accounting for all the facts previously known, it has led to the anticipation and prediction of others which experience afterwards verified ... Such predictions and their fulfilment are, indeed, well calculated to impress the uninformed ['strike the ignorant vulgar' in early editions], whose faith in science rests solely on similar coincidences between its prophecies and what comes to pass. But it is strange that any considerable stress should be laid upon such a coincidence by persons of scientific attainment. (Mill, 1973: 500)

> However strange it may seem to [Mill], there is no doubt that the most scientific thinkers, far more than the ignorant vulgar, have allowed the coincidence of results predicted with fact afterwards observed, to produce the strongest effects on their conviction; and that all the best-established theories have obtained their permanent place in general acceptance in virtue of such coincidences, more than of any other evidence. ... If we can predict new facts which we have not seen, as well as explain those which we have seen, it must be because our explanation is not a mere formula of observed facts, but a truth of a deeper kind. (Whewell, 1860: 273)

Perhaps it is Mill's opposition that explains why the prediction of novel facts did not occur more frequently in the literature on economic methodology.

The reason why Herschel and Whewell (and possibly Friedman – see Hirsch and de Marchi, 1990) attached such importance to the prediction of novel facts is that they were concerned with the *discovery* of scientific ideas. They did not accept the distinction, emphasized by Popper, between the contexts of discovery and justification. Thus Herschel writes that in the process of induction every case 'present in our minds' will 'find itself duly *represented* in our final conclusion' (1830: 164). If cases are unknown to us, they constitute a valid test, for our theories cannot have been designed to accommodate them. Similarly, Whewell emphasizes the importance of invention and discovery in understanding science. This is closely linked to his criticism of Mill's theory of induction which, Whewell argued, could not provide new information – for this a new point of view, not merely a formula of observed facts, was required. Whewell's account of the problem is important because he distinguishes two types of prediction. The simplest is predicting facts of the same kind as those from which laws were derived (for example, having derived laws of refraction, we can predict the effects of new, previously untried, lenses). More dramatic are predictions of cases 'of a *kind different* from those which were contemplated in the formation of our hypothesis' (Whewell, 1858: 88, emphasis in original). Thus the theory of universal gravitation, designed to explain the perturbations of the moon and planets by the sun and by each other, 'also accounted for the fact, apparently dissimilar and remote, of the *Precession of the equinoxes*' (ibid.). This argument is extended by Whewell to a comparison of two theories:

> In like manner in Optics; the hypothesis of alternative Fits of easy Transmission and Reflection would explain the colours of thin plates, and indeed was devised and adjusted for that very purpose; but it could give no account of the phenomena of the fringes of shadows. But the doctrine of Interferences, constructed at first with reference to phenomena of the nature of the *Fringes*, explained also the *Colours of thin plates* better than the supposition of Fits invented for that very purpose. (Whewell, 1858: 88–9)

Amongst modern philosophers of science, such ideas on the importance of novel facts are most closely associated with Imre Lakatos, who used it as the appraisal criterion in his methodology of scientific research programmes. Discussion of Lakatos' methodology led to five definitions of novel facts (see Hands, 1991: 96–9):

1. temporal novelty – fact not known when the prediction is made;
2. heuristic novelty – fact not used in the construction of the theory;
3. background theory novelty (Musgrave) – fact not predicted by the best existing predecessor theory;
4. background theory novelty (Watkins) – fact has no counterpart among consequences of predecessor theories;
5. Novelty$_k$ – fact was unknown to the person who constructed the theory.

All five types of novel facts lend support to a theory for the reason put forward by Herschel and Whewell, though such support is less clear-cut with novel facts of types (2)–(5) than for facts that are temporally novel. For example, a fact may not have been used explicitly in the construction of a theory (it is absent from the list of assumptions) but if it was known to the scientist he or she may, consciously or subconsciously, have been influenced by it when choosing assumptions. Furthermore, given that scientists work in communities, their work will reflect presuppositions shared by those communities, and hence facts known to other members of those communities. Temporal novelty is subject to no such problems. Temporal novelty is a sufficient, though not necessary, condition for novelty in senses (2), (3) and (5): temporal novelty implies that the fact could not have influenced the scientist, either because she knew it, or because it influenced her work either subconsciously or through the presuppositions of the scientific community in which she was working.

There have been many attempts to find successful prediction of novel facts in economics. Some of the clearest examples are found in macroeconomics: for example, Friedman's prediction that the Phillips curve would break down, or Dornbusch's prediction that the consequences of monetary contraction in an economy with flexible exchange rate and mobile capital would be exchange rate overshooting (see Backhouse, 1991). Blaug (1990) has argued that economists were attracted to Keynesian economics because of its ability to predict novel facts, the main one being the existence of an expenditure multiplier greater than unity.

Against this is the argument that the case for economic theories rests on much more than simply the prediction of novel facts. Thus Hands has written:

> Why would we want to accept the position that the sole necessary condition for scientific progress is predicting novel facts not used in the construction of the theory? Surely humankind's greatest scientific accomplishments have amounted to more than this. ... Even if we can find a few novel facts here and there in the history of economics, and even if those novel facts seem to provide an occasional 'clincher', the history of great economics is so much more than a list of these novel facts. (Hands, 1990: 78)

Such arguments are particularly strong in microeconomics where, though novel facts can be found, many influential theories are devoid of concrete predictions. For example, though game theory is regarded by many economists as having led to such profound insights into a wide range of problems, it is so flexible that it leads to few definite predictions. The problem is that, if a theory produces no predictions, it is hard to know how the 'insights' or 'explanations' it offers can be tested.

The case for emphasizing the importance of novel facts fits well with a belief that the circumstances under which a theory was discovered can be relevant to its appraisal. If instead one accepts, with Popper, that the circumstances surrounding the discovery of a scientific idea must be irrelevant to the justification of that theory, and if one argues that philosophy of science is concerned only with the process of justification, novel facts lose their significance, for novelty refers to the context in which the theory was discovered. Lakatos could attach importance to novel facts because, in his methodology of scientific research programmes, theories were not appraised in isolation, but in the context of the research programme out of which they arose. Appraisal was, for him, a historical process. The case for novel facts also presupposes a concern with *empirical* progress. If one is satisfied merely that a line of inquiry demonstrates *theoretical* progress, there are, as Hands points out, other criteria to which more weight should be attached.

ROGER E. BACKHOUSE

References
Backhouse, Roger E. (1991) 'The neo-Walrasian research programme in macroeconomics', in N. de Marchi and M. Blaug (eds), *Appraising Economic Theories*.
Blaug, Mark (1990), 'Second thoughts on the Keynesian revolution', *Economic Theories, True or False? Essays in the History and Methodology of Economics*, Aldershot/Brookfield, VT: Edward Elgar.
Friedman, Milton (1946), 'Lange on price flexibility and employment: a methodological criticism', *American Economic Review*, **36**: 613–31.
Friedman, Milton (1953), 'The methodology of positive economics', *Essays in Positive Economics*, Chicago: University of Chicago Press.

Hands, D. Wade (1990), 'Second thoughts on "Second thoughts": reconsidering the Lakatosian progress of *The General Theory*', *Review of Political Economy*, **2**, (1), 69–81.

Hands, D. Wade (1991), 'The problem of excess content: economics, novelty and a long Popperian tale' and 'Reply to Hamminga and Mäki', in N. de Marchi and M. Blaug (eds), *Appraising Economic Theories*.

Herschel, J.F.W. (1830), *A Preliminary Discourse on the Study of Natural Philosophy*, London: Longman *et. al.*

Hirsch, Abraham and Neil de Marchi (1990) *Milton Friedman: Economics in Theory and Practice*, Brighton: Harvester Wheatsheaf.

De Marchi, Neil and Mark Blaug (eds) (1991), *Appraising Economic Theories: Studies in the Methodology of Research Programmes*, Aldershot/Brookfield, VT: Edward Elgar.

Mill, John Stuart (1973), *A System of Logic: Ratioclinative and Inductive. Collected Works of John Stuart Mill*, vol. VII, ed. J.M. Robson, Toronto/London: University of Toronto Press/Routledge & Kegan Paul.

Whewell, William (1858), *Novum Organon Renovatum*, London: John W. Parker and Son.

Whewell, William (1860), *On the Philosophy of Discovery: Chapters Historical and Critical*, London: John W. Parker and Son.

Ontology

Ontology, or metaphysics after the title given to Aristotle's 'first philosophy', is investigation of the nature, structure and constitution of reality. The term 'ontology' is cognate with the Latin *ens*, existing thing or entity, from the verb *esse* to be, so that ontology may also be characterized simply as investigation of that which exists. As such, ontology is distinct from other branches of philosophy, such as epistemology, which concerns the nature of knowledge, and logic, which concerns the nature of valid reasoning. Entity in the most basic sense includes individual things (or particulars), properties, relations, events, states of affairs, sets and so on, any of which, according to different philosophical views, may or may not be reducible to one another. For example, one might ask whether space and time should be thought of as particular types of individual things, within which we find more familiar types of individuals, or whether space and time should be thought of as (systems of) relations between individual things. Similarly, one might ask whether properties are reducible to sets of things, whether individual things are reducible to series of events, and so on.

In recent years, two positions regarding ontology have attracted the attention of economic methodologists. On the one hand, there are proponents of ontological realism, the view that the world is populated by real objects independent of our experience, and that these objects possess properties and enter into relations with one another independently of our understanding of them. On the other hand, there is the idealist view that the idea of objects with properties and relations independent of our experience and conception is incoherent, since any idea is a form of conception, and we cannot conceive what is independent of conception. This latter view seems to have recently enjoyed something of a revival among economic methodologists, but there are at least two good reasons to question it.

First, the expression 'our experience and conception' presupposes that there exist many individuals, who presumably possess properties and stand in various relations to one another largely independently of each other's experience and understanding. Thus it cannot be denied that some things exist independently of someone's conception. But if some things exist independently of someone's conception, it is possible that some things exist independently of anyone's conception and thus that ontological realism is true at some level. The eighteenth-century Irish idealist philosopher Berkeley saw the logic of this argument, and sought to escape it by assuming that God perceived everything (Berkeley, 1710). Modern philosophers, scientists and economic methodologists, however, tend to adopt a more secular perspective, accept the existence of many finite minds and are by and large ontological realist.

Second, the view that things do not exist independently of conception necessitates our explaining what exists in terms of what we may conceive. But we may conceive of many sorts of things as existing, including fabulous and imaginary things such as unicorns and green cheese moons. What, then, distinguishes conceiving that a particular tree we see before us exists from conceiving that a unicorn exists? Lacking the standard realist device of saying that the tree exists in conception and in an independent reality, but that the unicorn only exists in conception, the idealist must differentiate between kinds of existence appropriate to different kind of things. But this runs contrary to a widely held intuition that one can say that things either exist or they do not, in that the idealist must say that unicorns exist in one sense, but not in some other. A related problem in the history of pre-modern philosophy arises in connection with the ontological argument (compare Plantinga, 1965), in which the mediaeval scholastics argued that God's possessing the property of perfection, which we may conceive as necessary to the meaning of

God, proved that God exists. But that God's perfection may be conceived does not prove God exists in the sense that we believe that trees exist. Essentially, then, that the scholastics believed that conceiving God's perfection demonstrated God's existence turned on an ambiguity in the concept of existence.

In general, it seems fair to say that the majority of modern philosophers regard existence and conception as ontologically distinct and irreducible domains, and that they also subscribe to some form of ontological realism. Debate, nonetheless, has attached to the question of whether ontological investigation of any sort, realist or otherwise, is philosophically promising, and whether philosophers should restrict themselves to epistemology, logic and analysis as modes of inquiry. Thus Moore (1911) argued that neo-Hegelian idealism of Bradley and McTaggart violated the claims of common sense. Following the early Wittgenstein, the logical positivist Vienna Circle treated metaphysical (or ontological) propositions as meaningless. Carnap (1932) in particular asserted, 'The meaning of a statement lies in the method of its verification' and argued that, since metaphysical statements were incapable of verification, they were therefore meaningless. In response, Popper (1934) proposed that verifiability be replaced by falsifiability as a criterion of demarcation between science and metaphysics – not as a criterion of meaning – and then suggested that metaphysical ideas could be quite useful for science. Indeed, he went on to argue that theories may initially be metaphysical in nature and then later play heuristic roles in the formulation of scientific hypotheses: 'Atomism is an excellent example of a non-testable metaphysical theory whose influence upon science has exceeded that of many testable scientific theories' (Popper, 1983: 192). Against this, Quine, following Duhem in what has come to be known as the Duhem–Quine thesis, noted that falsifiability is not a successful demarcation criterion, denied that science and metaphysics could be sharply distinguished and warned of the danger of 'a blurring of the supposed boundary between speculative metaphysics and natural science' (Quine, 1951: 20). Better, in his view, to concentrate on science which alone provides genuine knowledge.

However, science and its empirical practices, as well as common sense, clearly all presuppose various ontological commitments, such as the idea that every event has a cause, the idea that our experiences are generated by things in the world and the idea that the world is populated by individuals with whom we interact in science and ordinary life. Thus, however difficult it may be to explain the nature of these commitments and their relation to science and common sense, that such commitments underlie our thinking seems adequate justification for their investigation. Moreover, though ontological or metaphysical propositions lack the status of being the sort of well-confirmed beliefs which scientific knowledge aspires to produce, metaphysics may still be regarded as a realm of belief in which distinct propositions may be rationally examined and disputed. An arguably more important posture towards ontology, then, concerns what attitude we ought to take towards the explanation of our ontological commitments. Should we be content to describe common sense and scientific views of the structure and nature of reality – a descriptivist metaphysics (Strawson, 1959) – or should we rather engage in a revisionary metaphysics that aims to develop a self-consistent ontological system?

These two projects are not always sharply distinguishable, but the former descriptivist project is sometimes associated with producing accounts of the most basic sorts or categories of entities (individual things or particulars, properties, relations, events, states of affairs and so on) presupposed in a science or discourse under investigation. Aristotle asked whether some things endure through time and through change in their properties and relations; that is, whether some things were substances. Thus in connection with neoclassical economics we might ask whether individuals are substances, or whether comparative statics analysis requires that they be treated as temporal series of momentary individuals with no essential connection. Relatedly, are firms substances that we may model as intentional beings, or are they nothing but bundles of properties and relations lacking any particular unity? Aristotle also distinguished between substances' essential and accidental properties, or between those properties required and not required for their existence. Economics might be said to encounter this distinction in the debate over whether mathematical formalization captures accidental rather than essential characteristics of individuals and firms, and thus whether formal theories are 'about' real world individuals.

The latter revisionist project may be associated with broad ontological views, such as realism, idealism, materialism, dualism, nominalism, holism and organicism. For example, materialism is the view that everything can be satisfactorily explained in naturalistic terms, where this implies, among other things, that mental states are brain states; or organicism is the view that the relations between things are internal, and as such explain their relata, or the things they relate. Often, however, individual philosophers subscribe to combinations of views, where how these views are structured and identified is a matter of prior views held about the nature of basic ontological categories. One might thus be a realist with respect to particulars, believing that they indeed exist as self-subsistent things, but be a nominalist or conceptualist with respect to their properties, believing that the predicates we use to characterize individual things do not refer to really existing properties. Alternatively, one might be a realist in the Platonist sense of believing that properties we predicate of things truly exist, and that things 'instantiate' or instance properties. Things, on this view, are always of a particular kind or sort.

Properties, characteristics, attributes, qualities, meanings and so on – perhaps the most disputed over and most complex of ontological categories – are generally referred to as universals by philosophers. Our interest in them as an ontological category derives in part from the fact that they constitute a subject matter from which knowledge is constructed, whether this is a matter of general epistemic relationships (such as when we ask about the relationship between income distribution and consumption) or a matter of our knowledge about particular things (such as when we ask about the income and consumption of particular individuals). Perhaps not surprisingly, then, ontological views often underlie epistemological ones. If one is a realist with respect to particular things yet a nominalist with respect to their properties, one is more likely to be empiricist in orientation. If one is a realist with respect to properties, since properties are generally not thought to be spatiotemporal in nature, one is more likely to invest less significance in empirical work and to be rationalist or formalist in orientation. Accordingly, methodological differences regarding how knowledge is organized and constructed often relate to differing opinions about the constituents of knowledge, which in turn link up with differing opinions about what is thought to be knowable according to what is thought to actually exist.

In economics, the question of what is thought to actually exist is central to one of the longest and most intractable ontological disputes. In classical political economy (and its subsequent revival), classes are said to exist, acquiring most clearly in Marx's thinking the status of agents over and above the collections (or sets) of individuals that make them up. In neoclassical economics, in contrast, individuals alone are thought to exist and act as agents, classes are not regarded as real, but constitute merely conceptual constructions. Methodological collectivism and methodological individualism, that is, are rooted in opposed ontological commitments that underlie entire research programmes and their associated epistemological strategies. Related disputes exist between old and new institutionalists and between proponents of individualist microfoundations for macroeconomics and proponents of an aggregative macroeconomics of a more holistic nature. In the latter dispute, those who propose individualist-reductionist accounts of macroeconomic relationships often reason that these relationships are theoretical constructions that must be explained in terms of the choices individuals make, the reason being that only individuals exist. Those who believe it is unnecessary to reduce aggregative relationships to individual action suppose that these relationships are real in and of themselves, and as such are objects of investigation.

Evaluation of these ontological positions by philosophers and economic methodologists involves what has been labelled above as descriptive metaphysics. Determining what sorts of agents or entities exist in economic life may be investigated in classic Aristotelian terms as a set of questions concerning whether one type of entity is reducible to or subsumed within another, and whether individuation and identity conditions are satisfied with respect to entities proposed as real. Ontological investigations of this sort are not likely to dispel classic oppositions in orientation between economists, but they may, as Popper suggested, permit formulation of scientific hypotheses regarding the nature and scope of economic agency that, if not directly testable, may nonetheless be subject to empirical and theoretical examination.

JOHN B. DAVIS

Bibliography

Berkeley, G. (1710), *A Treatise concerning the Principles of Human Knowledge*; reprinted 1982, ed. K. Winkler, Indianapolis: Hackett.
Carnap, R. (1932), 'The Elimination of Metaphysics through Logical Analysis of Language'; reprinted 1959 in *Logical Positivism*, ed. A.J. Ayer, New York: Free Press.
Moore, G.E. (1911), 'Defence of Common Sense'; reprinted 1959 in *Philosophical Papers*, London: Allen & Unwin.
Plantinga, A. (ed.) (1965), *The Ontological Argument*, New York: Doubleday.
Popper, K. (1934), *Logic of Scientific Discovery*; 6th rev. edn 1972 English trans., London: Hutchinson.
Popper, K. (1983), *Realism and the Aim of Science*, London: Hutchinson.
Quine, W.V.O. (1951), 'Two Dogmas of Empiricism', *From a Logical Point of View*, 2nd rev. edn, New York: Harper.
Ross, W.D. (1924), *Aristotle's Metaphysics*; rev. edn 1953, Oxford: Clarendon.
Strawson, P.F. (1959), *Individuals*, New York: Doubleday.

Operationalism

Operationalism was established as a philosophical term by Percy Bridgman's book, *The Logic of Modern Physics* in 1927, although historians have traced essentially similar uses of the term by other American physical scientists in the first decades of the twentieth century (Moyer, 1991: 381). In his seminal text, Bridgman defined the concept as follows (1961: 5):

> In general, we mean by any concept nothing more than a set of operations; the concept is synonymous with the corresponding set of operations. If the concept is physical, as of length, the operations are actual physical operations, those by which length is measured; or if the concept is mental, as of mathematical continuity, the operations are mental operations, namely those by which we determine whether a given aggregate of magnitudes is continuous.

Bridgman, although a Nobel Prize winner in physics, always prided himself upon a plain-spoken style, and in his book he made it seem as though his doctrine was little more than a restatement of the homespun wisdom that 'the true meaning of a term is to be observing what a man does with it, not what he says about it' (ibid.: 7). In order to conflate meaning with action in this manner, Bridgman admitted, 'We must demand that the set of operations equivalent to any concept be a unique set' (ibid.: 6). Among other implications, this suggested that, for the purposes of science, length measured by beams of light should be considered an effectively distinct entity or concept from length measured by means of rulers.

The most cogent objections to this version of operationalism were mooted immediately in reviews of the book, but were restated forcefully by the philosopher Adolf Grünbaum: 'If the rule of operationalist caution is strictly and consistently applied, physics must reduce to a mere record of isolated data, since the criterion does not warrant making extrapolations in *any* direction' (quoted in Moyer, 1991: 241). In a thoroughly operationalist world, strict correspondence between measurement operation and concept would result in concepts proliferating wildly out of control, far beyond any hope of synthesis. Further, the very act of identifying any two operations as effectively 'the same' (a problem highlighted more recently by the work of Harry Collins, 1985) would seem to be baseless.

The sources of Bridgman's operationalism can be traced to his early exposure to the empiricist critics Ernst Mach and J.B. Stallo, but there is also a notable strain of pragmatism associated with the teachings of William James at Harvard. Another important influence was Bridgman's prior intervention in disputes over 'dimensional analysis', which sought to place *a priori* restrictions upon the mathematical form of fundamental physical laws, largely as a consequence of imposing transitivity in definitions. While Bridgman was not himself a logical positivist, his work was championed in the 1930s by Herbert Feigl, and therefore it was not unusual for operationalism to become conflated with certain empiricist and positivist doctrines of the 1930s.

The historical background to Bridgman's methodological preferences in physics was significant, though lost in further debates when the doctrine was imported into the social sciences. Bridgman was very much a partisan of classical physics, finding the upheaval associated with general relativity and quantum mechanics antithetical to his own belief in the cumulative character of physics, as well as contradicting his own experimentalist's intuitions. Indeed, the *Logic* grew out of Bridgman's attempt to criticize Einstein's move from special to general relativity; he hoped that operationalism would serve to ensure that 'another change in our attitude, such as that due to Einstein, shall be forever impossible'. Obviously, things did not work out as planned, with Bridgman spending much of the rest of his career fighting rearguard battles against the empirical conundrums of quantum mechanics and the seemingly metaphysical core of thermodynamics (Walter, 1990). It is worth noting that Bridgman did attempt to backpedal from his earlier doctrines, writing as early as 1938 that 'my statement on page 5 of *The Logic of Modern Physics* that meanings are *synonymous with operations*, was obviously going too far when taken out of context' and 'I do not maintain that meaning involves nothing more than operations' (1955: 5, 4). Nevertheless, because his position remained unwaveringly revanchist, his philosophy was largely ignored by physicists after the late 1920s.

The situation was altogether different in biology and the social sciences. 'Operationalism' became the rallying cry of any number of social scientists, especially a group associated with Harvard in the 1930s. Although J.B. Watson's 'behaviouralism' preceded Bridgman's statement, the adoption of operationalism in the 1930s by such psychologists as S.S. Stevens and E. Boring (and in a less direct way by B.F. Skinner) set the tone for a generation of empiricist psychologists. The terminology also found its way into economics, first through the enthusiasm of Henry Schultz (Moyer, 1991: 393; Hands and Mirowski, 1997) and then, more importantly, through Paul Samuelson's *Foundations* (1965: 4, 173). There has been subsequently a substantial methodological literature disputing whether Samuelson either accurately or adequately represented Bridgman's version of operationalism, even though he does not explicitly cite Bridgman in his text. All Samuelson's explicit appeals to operational criteria equate the principle with 'meaningfulness' or 'a hypothesis about empirical data which could conceivably be refuted'; but the fact that he specified neither actual operational criteria nor conditions under which neoclassicism would be falsified in his view does not belie the profound extent to which Bridgman's themes infused his own early theoretical work.

Bridgman wrote in his *Logic*, 'I believe that many of the questions asked about social and philosophical subjects will be found to be meaningless when examined from the point of view of operations' (1961: 30) and this is exactly the rhetoric favoured by Samuelson in the 1930s and 1940s. More importantly, Bridgman's comments concerning the lack of 'physical reality' of electrical fields (ibid.: 57) and his programme for dispensing with differential equations in the empirical description of the field (ibid.: 115) read in retrospect as descriptions *avant la lettre* of the project of the theory of revealed preference, at least in its early phase. Samuelson first claimed that his theory of revealed preference would stand as a replacement for the differential equations of orthodox utility theory, grounding the theory of demand in a few operationally observable axioms. Later elaboration demonstrated that no such alternative grounding was practicable, as very nicely described in the book by Wong (1978); in response to these problems with revealed preference theory, Samuelson later dropped the operationalist rhetoric.

Samuelson's lifelong aversion to a fundamentally stochastic economics also echoes Bridgman's enduring distaste for a fundamentally stochastic physics, especially as it further undermined a strict operationalism. Various prejudices characteristic of Bridgman, such as a profound methodological individualism, a 'fear of social chaos concentrat[ing] attention on the means rather than the end' and a conviction that 'Science is about itself: meaning is no more than method' (Walter, 1990: 273, 264, 276) all found their counterparts in Samuelson. This combination of methodological prejudices was then spread far and wide by Samuelson's successful introductory textbook in the 1950s and 1960s. Hence operationalism as it was manifested in economics was not so much a single abstract doctrine about empiricism as it was a set of prejudices transmitted from one particular physicist to one very special economist. The fact that many other social disciplines were simultaneously adopting their own versions of operationalism in order to render their respective fields 'scientific', and that the sum total was temporarily conflated with logical positivism, only added to its appeal.

With the demise of behaviourism, operationalism is more or less a dead issue in the social sciences. Few philosophers and historians of science today believe it was anything beyond a tangential offshoot of the project of logical empiricism, little more than an artefact of one vintage of physics envy in the American academic context. Scepticism with regard to the stabilizing role of measurement is rife within the economics discipline. Yet, as with so many other defunct methodological doctrines, it does tenaciously hang on in certain pedagogical contexts.

PHILIP MIROWSKI

References
Bridgman, Percy (1955), *Reflections of a Physicist*, New York: Philosophical Library.
Bridgman, Percy (1961), *Logic of Modern Physics*, New York: Macmillan; first published 1927.
Collins, Harry (1985), *Changing Order*, London: Sage.
Hands, D. Wade and Philip Mirowski (1997), 'Harold Hotelling and the Neoclassical Dream', in D. Hausman *et al.* (eds), *Economics and Methodology*, London: Macmillan.

Moyer, Albert (1991), 'P.W. Bridgman's Operational Perspective on Physics', *Studies in the History and Philosophy of Science*, **22**, 237–5.
Samuelson, Paul (1965), *Foundations of Economic Analysis*, New York: Atheneum.
Walter, Maila (1990), *Science and Cultural Crisis*, Stanford: Stanford University Press.
Wong, Stanley (1978), *The Foundations of Paul Samuelson's Revealed Preference Theory*, London: Routledge.

Organicism

Organicism has generally meant different things to different individuals, and the term is often used without clarity. The problem is that, though there is a core conception to organicism that most share, other, sometimes loosely related, ideas are often associated with this core conception or thought to be implied by it. The shared core conception involves an ontological thesis concerning internal relations between things. Two things are internally related if their natures and/or activities depend fundamentally upon their relation to one another. Internal relations are contrasted with external relations between things where the natures and/or activities of things related to one another are relatively independent of the relations between them. Thus organicism is first and foremost a view about the essential connectedness of things in reality.

Some philosophers have gone on from this characterization of kinds of relations to make further claims about what basic entities populate the world. On an external relations view, the world is made up of self-contained things or atoms, the relations between which are explainable in terms of what we understand about the atoms (for example, Wittgenstein, 1922). On an internal relations view, the world is rather made up of relations, such that the things they relate, or their relata, are explainable in terms of what we understand about relations (for example, Bradley, 1930). From this perspective, organicism is to be contrasted with atomism. Note, however, that casting organicism and atomism in terms of competing views of the whole of reality takes us beyond our focus on the core conception of organicism as a form of relation between things, since there is nothing in the idea of how two things are related that necessarily refers us to the nature of reality as a whole. Indeed, one could believe that reality as a whole included internally and externally related things, and consequently it would be careless to suppose that making a case for one sort of relation in one context implies that that sort of relation must apply universally. The tendency to make claims about the nature of the whole of reality is nonetheless often associated with organicist views, perhaps because seeing the world as a collection of things does not as naturally suggest the idea of a totality as does seeing the world as relation. A view related to organicism in the narrow sense which adds further claims about the whole of reality is holism.

Holism may be framed in terms of principles that apply specifically to the whole of some set of things or activities, or are emergent at the level of the whole (Jackson and Pettit, 1992), but it is perhaps more commonly framed in terms of whole–part relationships. Holist whole–part analysis is a species of organicism when the relationship between the two determines the nature and/or activities of each, or when whole and parts are said to be internally related. For example, interactionist accounts of the way social structure and actor agents transform and recreate one another can be whole–part organicist views (Giddens, 1984; Bhaskar, 1979). But not infrequently, holist whole–part arguments tend to make parts depend only upon wholes, and not the reverse. An example is the Post Keynesian inversion of the neoclassical reductionist project of developing individualist microfoundations for macroeconomics, namely the alternative project of developing holist macrofoundations for microeconomics. Holism in this instance is not organicism, since the form of the relation between whole and part is not at issue, but rather whether whole or part has conceptual priority. Holism in this context is consequently better contrasted with reductionism. The related prescriptivist methodologies, methodological holism (sometimes collectivism) and methodological individualism, also counterpose holism and reductionism. Strictly speaking, these are not about organicism and atomism either, though confusion sometimes arises when methodological individualism is labelled 'atomistic individualism'.

Holist arguments, then, need to employ an internal relations analysis to be organicist. But holism may also be thought organicist when the whole is modelled on the idea of a living organism. In this instance, not only are the parts of an organism typically thought jointly instrumental to the life of the whole, thus suggesting the idea of their being organically connected, but the connotation possessed by the term 'organism' is sometimes conflated with the ontological internal relations idea. Living organisms and societies, of course, are complex entities, and metaphorical transfer of the idea of an organism to societies and economies must necessarily elide important differences between them. Nonetheless, some writers, such as Menger (1985), Veblen (1899b), Hobson (1914) and Hayek (1973), have favoured organic analogies as an alternative to reliance upon mechanical ones in social science. Organicism in this instance contrasts with mechanism, the view that organisms are no more than complex mechanisms and that the laws of matter and motion govern the phenomena of life.

Organicism in this tradition additionally emphasizes the idea that socioeconomic systems are evolutionary in nature. Menger argued that society could be regarded as an organism in the sense that its institutions evolved spontaneously as the unintended result of individual human actions. Society exhibits an organic unity in that its institutions relate to society as organs relate to organism. Veblen believed that economic interest guided a cumulative growth in society's conventions and methods of life, which he took to be the basis of its institutions. Evolutionary economics was 'a theory of a cumulative sequence of economic institutions stated in terms of the process itself' (Veblen, 1899b: 77). Hobson, influenced by Veblen, took the evolution of human wants and needs to be part of a wider process of organic development of society that was guided by a coordinating reason. This organic purpose or directive power expressed 'a collective consciousness and will ... capable of realising a collective vital end' (Hobson, 1914: 15). Hayek, in contrast, denied that social order implies conscious planning or deliberate design. Like Menger, Hayek held that the economy may be likened to an organism that evolves, but added that cultural evolution operates through change in rules of conduct that evolve when the groups who practise them are successful and displace those with other rules (Hayek, 1973: 18).

Putting aside holism, an altogether different phenomenon sometimes mistakenly taken to involve organic connection is interdependence. Individuals, for example, may be interdependent in the sense that one individual's activities are seen to elicit responses from other individuals that then alter the first individual's activities. This suggests a relatedness which appears to undermine the independence of the individuals so related, and which accordingly may be thought to imply organic connection between individuals. However, evidence of feedback mechanisms is compatible with the existence of external relations between interdependent things, as in Walrasian systems of interdependent agents. Individuals are unchanged in their essential nature as maximizing agents when prices, incomes and goods availability change, though such changes affect how individuals maximize. In effect, economic agents are defined prior to accounts of their interaction with one another. Interdependence would only imply organic connection if individuals' interaction transformed their behaviours. Some forms of game theory appear to verge on this stronger conclusion, as for example in Sugden's (1986) arguments that conventions emerge as evolutionarily behavioural stable strategies, though such a conclusion is controversial.

Finally, brief mention should be made of hysteresis and path-dependency analysis, historicism and process views. Hysteresis denotes the persistent influence of past events on the present, and pathdependent systems are ones which display a determinate, connected sequence of events. But, necessarily, both notions only emphasize the transformative effects the past has on the present, and clearly this unidirectional influence falls short of the two-directional internal relations idea of organic connection. Historicism is the idea that historical events are ultimately governed by general laws of history. Organicist thinking has been linked to such views, as in Hegel's (1930) notion that history is the progressive realization of *Geist* and in some versions of the inevitability of communism in Marxism, but in most cases historical events are expressions of historical laws which remain unconditioned themselves. Process views, which emphasize the category of becoming, have had a number of representatives in the history of philosophy, including Bergson and Whitehead. The idea of becoming as a unity of what is and is not logically depends upon the internal relations conception, but the idea's meaning as coming-to-be and passing-away also distinguishes it from the internal relations conception much as hysteresis/path-dependence and historicism are distinguished.

Organicism, then, is often difficult to identify, because many related but different views are said to be organicist. Accordingly, grand claims seem best avoided when using the concept, and attention seems better focused on more narrow tasks of characterizing specific examples of relations. This may be difficult to accomplish in evolutionary contexts where authors are committed to saying wholes may be likened to organisms, given their tendency sometimes to substitute the term 'organicist' for the term 'organic'. Nonetheless, it seems important that such a distinction be maintained, both to segregate the core internal relations conception and to allow more clear development of the notion that wholes may be understood as organisms. The former conception might thus be termed organicism and the latter termed the organic view.

JOHN B. DAVIS

References

Bhaskar, R. (1979), *The Possibility of Naturalism: A Philosophic Critique of the Contemporary Human Sciences*, Brighton: Harvester.

Bradley, F.H. (1930), *Appearance and Reality*, Oxford: Clarendon Press.

Giddens, A. (1984), *The Constitution of Society: Outline of the Theory of Structuration*, Cambridge: Polity.

Hayek, F. (1973), *Law, Legislation and Liberty. Vol. 1: Rules and Order*, London: Routledge & Kegan Paul.

Hegel, G. (1930), *Philosophy of History*, reprinted, New York: Dover, 1956.

Hobson, J. (1914), *Work and Wealth: A Human Valuation*, New York: Macmillan.

Menger, C. (1985), *Investigations into the Method of the Social Sciences with Special Reference to Economics*, New York: New York University Press.

Jackson, Frank and Philip Pettit (1992), 'In Defense of Explanatory Ecumenism', *Economics and Philosophy*, **8**, 11–21.

Sugden, R. (1986), *The Economics of Rights. Co-operation and Welfare*, Oxford: Basil Blackwell.

Veblen, T. (1899a), *The Theory of the Leisure Class: An Economic Study of Institutions*, New York: Macmillan.

Veblen, T. (1899b), 'Why is Economics Not an Evolutionary Science?', *Quarterly Journal of Economics*, **12**, (3), 373–97.

Wittgenstein, L. (1922), *Tractatus Logico-Philosophicus*, London: Kegan Paul.

Paradigm/Normal Science

The terms 'paradigm' and 'normal science' were introduced into the philosophy of science by Thomas S. Kuhn in *The Structure of Scientific Revolutions* (1962; 2nd edn 1970). Before Kuhn, the so-called 'received view' (strongly influenced by logical positivism, though not synonymous with it) focused on the logical structure of scientific theories and on the rules linking these theories to empirical evidence. In complete contrast, Kuhn started from the observations that science was undertaken in communities and that scientific communities are defined by shared paradigms. Research undertaken within settled scientific communities is normal science. Kuhn therefore claimed that to understand the history of science – and science itself – it was necessary to understand the nature and evolution of such communities. In other words, the logic of science could not be separated from the sociology of science, and neither of these could be understood apart from the history of science.

The paradigm that binds a scientific community together has two main elements for which Kuhn (1977) later used the terms 'disciplinary matrix' and 'exemplar'. A disciplinary matrix is the web of presuppositions and beliefs shared by a community of scientists. It determines which problems scientists consider worth addressing, the methods by which they are to be solved, beliefs about which phenomena should be taken as given, and so on. For example, within the disciplinary matrix of Newtonian mechanics, Newton's laws of motion are not questioned. Instead, scientists seek to apply them to new areas, to develop and improve them and to eliminate anomalies. Such research is essentially puzzle-solving, for the range of acceptable solutions is known in advance. Failure to find an acceptable solution reflects badly on the experimenter, not on Newton's laws. This is normal science. Normal science, however, requires more than simply a set of laws, for scientists need to learn how to use these laws to solve problems. This is the role of exemplars – concrete solutions to particular problems. In the course of their training, scientists learn to see resemblances between apparently diverse problems, solving new problems by relating them to previously solved ones (standard examples, the original meaning of the term 'paradigm').

Exemplars are fundamental to the structure of science because scientific communities (and periods of normal science) are normally established on the basis of specific scientific achievements, as with Aristotle's *Physica*, Newton's *Principia* or Lyell's *Geology*. Such works are both sufficiently unprecedented in their achievement to attract followers and sufficiently open-ended to leave numerous problems for followers to solve. Normal science, therefore, is the result of scientists' following the example set by a successful innovator.

But if normal science involves taking a disciplinary matrix of scientific laws, exemplars and other shared beliefs for granted, how does it change? How does science discover new and previously unsuspected phenomena? Kuhn's answer is that, from time to time, anomalies appear: scientists recognize that 'nature has somehow violated the paradigm-induced expectations that govern normal science' (Kuhn, 1970: 52–3). The result is that scientists readjust the paradigm until what was anomalous has become expected. Some anomalies, however, will resist such treatment. They will remain unsolved problems, possibly for many years. If these persistent anomalies concern minor, or peripheral, issues they will be ignored and normal science will continue. On the other hand, if they concern fundamental issues, central to the paradigm, they may result in a state of crisis – in a breakdown of the technical, puzzle-solving activity that characterises normal science. Scientists will flounder, looking around, seemingly at random, for solutions. Out of the many solutions offered, one will eventually become accepted, to become the new exemplar. On the basis of this exemplar, a new period of normal science, and a new disciplinary matrix, will be established. This is a scientific revolution.

Though *The Structure of Scientific Revolutions* constitutes an important landmark in the movement away from logical positivism (see Suppe, 1977), it shares the positivist concern with establishing the meaning of theoretical propositions. Scientific training – the socialized ability to relate new problems to shared exemplars – was for Kuhn a process whereby scientific terms acquired meaning. The use of exemplars enabled scientists to attach symbolic labels to nature without either definitions or correspondence rules. Thus when scientists (in a scientific revolution) switched to a new set of exemplars the meaning of scientific terms would typically change. It was thus his concern with the way the meaning of scientific terms is established, inherited from logical positivism, that led Kuhn to his conclusion, widely taken up by philosophers with more radical agendas than his, that there might be incommensurability across paradigms (see Kuhn, 1992).

Kuhn's ideas found a ready audience amongst radical economists and others opposed to mainstream economics. The concept of a paradigm shift could be used to explain the radical nature of the shift in economic analysis that such economists thought necessary, while the notion of incommensurability across paradigms made it easier to argue for a new type of economics that failed even to address many orthodox concerns (see, for example, Ward, 1972; Kregel, 1973). But Kuhn's ideas were also taken up by historians of economic thought, who found obvious parallels between Kuhn's ideas and the history of economic thought (for example, Coats, 1969). The 'marginal' and 'Keynesian' revolutions could be reinterpreted in Kuhnian terms; some of the books that have, at various times, dominated economic thinking – Smith's *Wealth of Nations*, Ricardo's *Principles*, Marshall's *Principles*, Keynes' *General Theory* – could be seen as Kuhnian exemplars.

On the whole, the attempt to test Kuhn's philosophy against the history of economic thought has not been that successful. First the story of economics is easy to tell in Kuhnian terms, and using his ideas raises many interesting questions (for example, the existence and role of anomalies and the existence of a crisis prior to the emergence of a new paradigm). It is, however, very difficult to identify specific paradigms in a satisfactory way: one can plausibly argue both that economics has been dominated by a single paradigm since the time of Adam Smith, this paradigm being refined and evolving ever since, and that events such as the marginal and Keynesian revolutions can be seen as Kuhnian paradigm switches. Second, Kuhn's vision of science as being dominated by a series of paradigms, each of which achieves a temporary monopoly, is inappropriate where basic frameworks remain contested. For many historians of economic thought, therefore, Lakatos' methodology of scientific research programmes, which analysed science in terms of continual competition between research programmes, offered a better way forward (for example, Blaug, 1976).

The current consensus is arguably that the concepts of paradigm and normal science do not provide precise, ready-made categories into which the history of economic thought fits neatly. There are many aspects of the structure of economics that either find no place in Kuhn's framework or are incompatible with it. But Kuhn has permanently altered our perspective on the history of science, the role of metaphysical presuppositions in science and the nature of scientific progress. It is no longer possible to neglect the social dimension of science.

ROGER E. BACKHOUSE

Bibliography
Blaug, Mark (1976), 'Kuhn versus Lakatos, or paradigms versus research programmes in the history of economics', in Spiro J. Latsis (ed.), *Method and Appraisal in Economics*, Cambridge: Cambridge University Press.
Coats, A.W. (1969), 'Is there a "Structure of scientific revolutions" in economics?,' *Kyklos*, **22**, 289–95; reprinted in A.W. Coats, *The Sociology and Professionalization of Economics: British and American Economic Essays, Volume II*, London: Routledge, 1993.
Hausman, Daniel M. (1994), 'Kuhn, Lakatos and the structure of science', in Roger E. Backhouse (ed.), *New Directions in Economic Methodology*, London/New York: Routledge.
Kregel, J.A. (1973), *The Reconstruction of Political Economy*, London: Macmillan.
Kuhn, T.S. (1970), *The Structure of Scientific Revolutions*, 2nd edn. Chicago: University of Chicago Press.
Kuhn, T. S. (1977), 'Second thoughts on paradigms', in Suppe (ed.), *The Structure of Scientific Theories*.
Kuhn, T.S. (1992), 'The trouble with the historical philosophy of science', Department of the History of Science, Harvard University.
Lakatos, Imre and Alan Musgrave (1970), *Criticism and the Growth of Knowledge*, Cambridge: Cambridge University Press.
Suppe, F. (ed.) (1977), *The Structure of Scientific Theories*, 2nd edn, Urbana: University of Illinois Press.
Ward, Benjamin (1972), *What's Wrong with Economics?* New York: Basic Books.

Pareto, Vilfredo

Born in Paris on 15 July 1848, Vilfredo Pareto (1848–1923), son of Marquis Raffaele Pareto (a civil engineer) and Marie Metenier (a French national), was four years old when his family moved to Italy. In November 1864, he enrolled at the University of Turin, where in 1867 he obtained his first degree in mathematics and physics and in 1870 graduated in engineering. After brief experience at the Railway Company of Florence, from 1873 he was deputy head and technical director of the San Giovanni Valdarno Iron Works Company. In December 1889, Pareto married the Countess Alessandrina Bakounine, an Italian of Russian origin, who left her husband for a young servant 10 years later (Pareto, however, did not remain single for long: in 1902, he set up home with a 22-year-old Frenchwoman, Jeanne Regis). In 1890, a crucial year for his life and career (for more details, see Busino, 1987), he was forced to resign from his position because of his bad speculations on the London iron market.

This episode allowed him to devote himself entirely to study and research for the rest of his life, with prompt and outstanding results: in 1893, he was appointed professor of political economy at the University of Lausanne, and in the following years he published his two most famous contributions to economic literature: the *Course d'économie politique* (2 vols, 1896 and 1897) and the *Manuale di economia politica* (1905; enlarged French edition, with the famous mathematical appendix, 1909).

Kirman (1987) concludes his entry on Pareto (as an economist) in *The New Palgrave* with the observation that, paradoxically, 'Pareto's work should place him clearly as one of the last [of the universal athletes], but the importance that has been attached to part of his mathematical economics is likely to condemn him unjustly to being described as one of the first of the "specialists".' No doubt this judgment applies, among other things, to Pareto's view on economic methodology. Indeed, like most of the greatest thinkers in the history of economics, Pareto (one of Schumpeter's (1951) 'great ten') frequently places his economic discourse in a wider context and never hesitates to state his own ethical, political, philosophical and methodological opinions.

Pareto was the successor of Walras to the chair at the University of Lausanne and is usually regarded as one of the founding members of the 'Lausanne School', but on most precepts of the school, as he himself acknowledges in a frequently cited letter to Maffeo Pantaleoni (Pareto, 1908), he held opinions quite different from (if not opposite to) Walras. In particular, concerning economic methodology, to Walras' advocacy of a rationalistic and deductivist approach to pure theory and passionate search for fruitful applications in favour of mankind, Pareto never ceased to oppose his strong positivist commitment to 'experimental' social science and agnostic disenchantment with the possibility of applying truly 'scientific' methods of inquiry to the solution of any relevant problem of practical economic policy. Their disagreement on the proper methodological foundations of pure economics is thus the first instance of that continuing debate on the methodology of (neoclassical) economic theory which even today seems to be far from a satisfactory conclusion.

As Blaug (1986: 184) notes succinctly, 'both the Course and the first two chapters of the Manual contain a remarkable discussion of the methodology of economics, which shows Pareto to have been better read in the then received literature on the philosophy of science than any other economist of the period'. As is also testified by a number of other methodological writings, Pareto's (1897; 1900; 1907; 1912; 1918; 1920) views on economic methodology come from three main sources of inspiration: (1) Comte's positivist philosophy of social sciences, (2) his own acquaintance, as an engineer, with the methodology of rational mechanics (implying, among other things, the absolute necessity but at the same time the plainly subsidiary role of mathematics), which he considered as the most crystalline instance of a 'truly scientific' method, and (3) Mill's advocacy of the method of successive approximations in order to preserve the empiricist character of economics.

Pareto (1912: 181) himself gives us a clear summary of the Comtean elements of his conception of 'modern Political Economy' and of his views on the role of mathematics in four brief statements

> First, political economy – like chemistry, or physics or astronomy – is conceived as a natural science. Therefore it must be studied in the light of the experimental method, and every effort must be taken to exclude the personal element. Second, the economist of today has no practical end in view. ... His work is merely to investigate the laws of phenomena, to discover uniformities in their workings. Third, political economy is but a part – and a small part – of the more general science of sociology. ... To complete our knowledge we must also consult other branches of social sciences. Fourth, one of the chief things to remark in economic phenomena is the mutual determination of their elements. To study this aspect, only one means so far has been discovered – the use of mathematics. But mathematics is only used in order to enable the economist to arrive at a conception of this mutual determination and of its effects on economic phenomena.

This is typical of many passages expressing the same concepts that we might easily find in the other works by Pareto previously mentioned. Of course no one, with the possible exception of Allais (1994: 293–4), who regards the result of a single experiment with fewer than 10 people involved as a conclusive test, nowadays would be prepared to maintain similar positions, but Pareto should be given credit for clearly and coherently spelling out the actual, even if unpleasant, implications of an old-fashioned but decidedly positivistic approach to economics (for a somewhat different judgment, based on a dubious reading of Pareto as a precursory advocate of 'operationally meaningful theorems' and a supportive evaluation of Samuelson's operationalism, see Tarascio, 1968). Indeed, subsequent famous attempts either to revive the empiricist tradition in economics, like those of Friedman (1953) or Samuelson (1963; 1964) or to find other kinds of methodological justifications for general equilibrium theory cannot be said to have reached much more impressive results concerning the methodological foundations of the discipline (see, for instance, Caldwell, 1994, part 2; Ingrao and Israel, 1990, respectively). In particular, Pareto deserves the credit for having forcefully pointed out:

> It is not that a work loses its experimental character if it starts from an abstraction to reach a representation of facts, but, in order to keep such a character, the abstraction concerned must remain a simple hypothesis that becomes true only after verification of the correspondence between the obtained results and the concrete facts. ... Consequently, mathematical economics ... loses the nature of logico-experimental science if it assumes the existence of utility independently of the facts to be explained, or if it takes the logical consequences of a hypothesis and wants to raise them to the rank of demonstration. (Translated from Pareto, 1918: 633)

All this does not mean, however, that he was unaware of the difficulties involved. In his 1917 jubilee address at the University of Lausanne, we find that such difficulties are openly recognized:

> At a certain point in my research in economics I found myself in a blind-alley. I was seeing the experimental truth but I was unable to attain it. ... It is beyond any doubt that quite often the conclusions of economic theories are not verified by experience, and we find ourselves embarrassed in the attempt to make them correspond. How to overcome this difficulty? Three possible reactions suggest themselves: (1) we may completely reject economic science, denying its very existence, as is actually done by the members of one very popular school. ... (2) We may surrender to such a lack of correspondence, claiming that we are not looking for what is, but for what ought to be. ... (3) Finally, as many examples provided by natural sciences teach us, we may wonder whether such a lack of correspondence can be ascribed to some other variables, not previously considered, that influence what we studied separately. (Translated from Pareto, 1920: 67-8)

It goes without saying that Pareto was strongly opposed to the first two and saw the third way out as the most promising (even if the most arduous). Precisely because of the difficulties he encountered in his attempts to apply to economics the method of successive approximations, at a certain point in his life, quite dissatisfied by the inevitable 'inexactness' (in the Millian sense) of the discipline, he gave up economics and devoted himself mainly to sociology (Pareto, 1916). In this field of research he maintained quite the same methodological approach, but (not surprisingly) he did not obtain the same outstanding reputation (at least judging from what remains in current textbooks) as he had previously gained as an economist. Obviously enough, his shift to sociology is not the message that we may find most appropriate today. Rather, what we may continue to appreciate in Pareto's methodological pronouncements is his honest acknowledgement (even more valuable because it came from a convinced supporter of nineteenth-century positivism) of the difficulties that are bound to be encountered by every empiricist proposal of methodological monism in economics.

ANDREA SALANTI

Reader's guide

Further references on the secondary literature may be found in Busino (1987), Kirman (1987) and Tarascio (1968). The recent English edition of de Petri Tonelli and Bousquet (1994) makes available to English-speaking readers two interesting essays on Pareto written by two of his disciples and friends. Pareto (1963–89, vol. XX; *Jubilé du Professeur V. Pareto – 1917*) includes a complete bibliography of Pareto's writings by G. Busino, together with a large bibliography of secondary literature up to the early 1970s by P. Tommissen. The problem, of course, is that in order to read Pareto (and most of the related secondary literature) one should be able to read French and Italian.

References

Allais, M. (1994), 'The fundamental cardinalist approach and its prospects', in M. Allais and O. Hagen (eds), *Cardinalism. A Fundamental Approach*, Dordrecht: Kluwer.

Blaug, M. (1986), 'Vilfredo Pareto', in *Great Economists before Keynes*, New York: Cambridge University Press.

Busino, A. (1987), 'Pareto, Vilfredo', in J. Eatwell, M. Milgate and P. Newman (eds), *The New Palgrave. A Dictionary of Economics*, vol. III: London: Macmillan.

Caldwell, B. (1994), *Beyond Positivism. Economic Methodology in the Twentieth Century*, rev. edn, London: Routledge.

Friedman, M. (1953), 'The Methodology of Positive Economics', *Essays in Positive Economics*, Chicago: University of Chicago Press.

Ingrao, B. and G. Israel (1990), *The Invisible Hand. Economic Equilibrium in the History of Science*, Cambridge, MA: MIT Press.

Kirman, A. (1987), 'Pareto as an economist', in J. Eatwell, M. Milgate and P. Newman (eds), *The New Palgrave. A Dictionary of Economics*, vol. III, London: Macmillan.

Pareto, V. (1896–97), *Cours d'économie politique,* 2 vols, Lausanne: Rouge; new edition edited by G.H. Bousquet and G. Busino in *Oeuvres complètes*, vol. I.

Pareto, V. (1897), 'The new theories in economics', *Journal of Political Economy*, 5, 485–502; reprinted in *Oeuvres complètes*, vol. XVI.

Pareto, V. (1900), 'Sul fenomeno economico. Lettera a Benedetto Croce', *Giornale degli Economisti*, 21, 139–62; reprinted in *Oeuvres complètes*, vol. XXVI.

Pareto, V. (1907), 'L'économie et la sociologic au point de vue scientifique', *Rivista di Scienza*, 293–312; Italian translation in *Oeuvres complétes*, vol. XXII.

Pareto, V. (1908), 'Letter to Maffeo Pantaleoni, 19 December', in *Lettere a Maffeo Pantaleoni. 1890–1923*, vol. III, ed. G. De Rosa, Rome: Edizioni di Storia e Letteratura; reprinted in *Oeuvres complètes*, vol. XXVIII/3.

Pareto, V. (1909), *Manuel d'économie politique*, Paris: Giard and Brière; reprinted in *Oeuvres complètes*, vol. VII; English translation: *Manual of Political Economy*, ed. A.S. Schwier and A.N. Page, New York: Kelley, 1971.

Pareto, V. (1912), 'Book review of G. Sensini. "La teoria della rendita" and P. Boven "Les applications mathématiques a l'économie politique"', *The Economic Journal*, 22, 467–9; reprinted in *Oeuvres complètes*, vol. XVI.

Pareto, V. (1916), *Trattato di sociologia generale*, 2 vols, Florence: Barbera; French 1919 edition reprinted in *Oeuvres complètes*, vol. XII; English translation: *The Mind Society*, 4 vols, trans. and ed. A. Livingston, New York: Harcourt Brace, 1935.

Pareto, V. (1918), 'Economia sperimentale', *Giornale degli Economisti*, 52, 1–18; reprinted in *Oeuvres complètes*, vol. XXVI.

Pareto, V. (1920), 'Discours pour le jubilé', Université de Lausanne, Jubilé du Professeur Vilfredo Pareto, 1917, Lausanne: Imprimerie Vaudoise; reprinted in *Oeuvres complètes*, vol. XX.

Pareto. V. (1963–89), *Oeuvres complètes de Vilfredo Pareto*, 30 vols, series directed by G. Busino, Genèva: Droz (all page references in the text refer to this series).

de Petri Tonelli A. and G.H. Bousquet (1994), *Vilfredo Pareto. Neoclassical Synthesis of Economics and Sociology*, London: Routledge.

Samuelson, P.A. (1963), 'Problems of methodology – Discussion', *American Economic Review, Proceedings*, 53, 231–6.

Samuelson, P.A. (1964), 'Theory and realism – A reply', *American Economic Review, Proceedings*, 54, 736–9.

Schumpeter, J.A. (1951), 'Vilfredo Pareto', in *Ten Great Economists from Marx to Keynes*, New York: Oxford University Press.

Tarascio, V.J. (1968), *Pareto's Methodological Approach to Economics*, Chapel Hill, NC: University of North Carolina Press.

Peirce, Charles Sanders

Charles Sanders Peirce (1839–1914) was the founder of pragmatism. Pragmatism was the distinctly American school of philosophy that was current in the late nineteenth and early twentieth centuries. Philosopher Philip Wiener writes that Peirce was 'the most versatile, profound and original philosopher that the Unites States has ever produced' (Wiener, 1958: ix). Other than founding pragmatism, Peirce made important contributions to mathematics, statistics, geodesy, symbolic logic and scientific inference. He also wrote about economics, but these writings mostly have been neglected. For most of his life, he worked for a government agency called the US Coast Survey. The first full-length biography of Peirce was completed by Joseph Brent in 1993. Brent's biography documents that Peirce spent most of his professional life trying to measure differences in the earth's gravity at various geographic locations in Europe and North America. Peirce continually appealed for additional funding to support research at new locations and the construction of a more accurate pendulum to reduce the inaccuracies introduced by the equipment. He considered himself a first-rate gravimetric researcher and was well known in Europe for his skill.

In his conception of pragmatism, Peirce sought to extend the experimental mind-set of science to all of life.[1] Such a mind-set was Peirce's prescription for making our thoughts and ideas clear (Peirce, 1878). Early in his career, he formulated the attitude in the following pragmatic maxim: 'Consider what effects, that might conceivably have practical bearings, we conceive the object of our conception to have. Then, our conception of these effects is the whole of our conception of the object' (Peirce, 1878: 31). The word 'pragmatism' comes from Kant's use of the term *pragmatisch* which connotes a relation to a definite human purpose (Dewey, 1949). For Peirce, this human purpose was the clarification of ideas with the critical attitudes of the experimental scientist. Economics played a role in this process of clarifying ideas. Economic considerations were to be used in narrowing the number of hypotheses to be considered for actual testing. But Peirce's emphasis on economics was neglected and probably had little impact on the subsequent development of pragmatism. William James, John Dewey and others were also important figures in the development of pragmatism as a philosophical movement.[2] At one point, pragmatism had become so popularized and altered from what Peirce had in mind that he renamed his philosophy 'pragmaticism':[3]

> So then, the writer, finding his bantling 'pragmatism' so promoted, feels that it is time to kiss his child good-by [*sic*] and relinquish it to its higher destiny; while to serve the precise purpose of expressing the original definition, he begs to announce the birth of the word 'pragmaticism', which is ugly enough to be safe from kidnappers. (Peirce, 1905: 255).

What Peirce wanted was to bring the mental habits of experimental laboratory science to philosophy. He wanted a method for finding agreement and establishing beliefs.[4] A method of agreement was as important as the content of the results of the method. Peirce's method evolved into a theory of inquiry and truth. The theory of inquiry encompassed logic, mathematics and statistics. Every statement was conceived as a relational logical proposition. Conclusions were to be drawn through a process of inference which was later called the hypothetico-deductive process. In the short run, the result of a process of inference was a provisional judgment. Truth was a longer-run consideration. In part, Peirce's conception of truth depended on realism. He assumed a realist view of the world which led him to a convergence theory of truth. In this convergence view, the methodologically drawn judgments of many genuinely informed individuals would lead asymptotically to a final opinion called the truth.[5]

Two other important aspects of Peirce's philosophy were his semiotics and his evolutionary cosmology (Hausman, 1974; 1993; Colapietro, 1989). Meaning was the result of an inferential process using a sign. A sign was an abstract concept which gained meaning in relation to another sign, and so on. Peirce (1897c) developed an elaborate theory and terminology of signs which is much too complex to explore in a brief overview. Peirce's (1897b) evolutionary cosmology attempted to explain some of the most fundamental philosophical questions, such as why is there something rather than nothing; is it reasonable to believe in God's existence; and what type of world is it in which processes of symbol construction, abstraction and meaning occur?

Questions like these led Peirce to offer a cosmology in which mind is more fundamental than matter, chance more fundamental than order, and evolution more basic that unchanging states (Sheriff, 1994).

Peirce's philosophical contributions continue to draw substantial interest from contemporary philosophers, social scientists and humanists. If anything, there has been a resurgence of interest in pragmatism both in Europe and in North America (Diggins, 1994). In part, this resurgence is due to the decline of logical positivism and its successor, the received view of the 1950s and 1960s. The resurgence is also due to an awareness that there are pragmatic philosophical problems inherent in the growth of knowledge literature of Popper, Kuhn, Lakatos and others and in the linguistic and deconstructionist approaches to science and epistemology. As a consequence, the philosophical problems raised by the pragmatists in the late nineteenth and early twentieth centuries are once again issues of importance.

While his contributions to philosophy, science and mathematics are well known, Peirce's essays and writings on economics are virtually unknown in the economics profession. Certainly, Peirce's contributions to other disciplines may be of interest to economists and could provide suggestions for redirecting and revising economic science. However, Peirce did write about economic subjects and problems. It is these long-neglected economic writings of Peirce which are summarized below. More specifically, Peirce's interest in economics took three separate but complementary directions. First, he had an abiding concern for creating a general mathematical political economy which focused on the theory of monopoly and a statement of the axiom of transitivity. Second, as part of his general evolutionism, he recognized the economic function of the conscious mind and of scientific theories. Third, he proposed a model of the economics of research as one of the major aspects of his theory of inference.

Until quite recently in the modern economics literature, the only place that Peirce's keen interest in economics was referenced was Baumol and Goldfeld's *Precursor's in Mathematical Economics: An Anthology*. The entry for Peirce is nothing more than a short letter. In the anthology, Baumol and Goldfeld (1968: 161–9) note that A.A. Cournot had published *Researches into the Mathematical Principles of the Theory of Wealth* in 1838. It was the most advanced work in mathematical economics in that period of time. What is found in Peirce's letter is comments on Cournot. The letter was written to the astronomer Simon Newcomb (Peirce, 1871a: 186–7). Newcomb also had an interest in political economy which resulted in a handbook in 1886 called *Principles of Political Economy* (Eisele, 1979b: 58). Peirce's letter contains a few simple equations concerning profit maximization under conditions of competition and monopoly using calculus. In the letter, he inferred that the results of profit maximization under conditions of competition and monopoly are dependent on whether there is unlimited competition or not. He concluded: 'This is all in Cournot' (Peirce, 1871a).

For Peirce, Cournot's project stimulated a vision for creating a mathematical political economy. The equations in Peirce's letter to Newcomb were intended to be a first step towards a mathematical political economy. Another economist who interested Peirce was David Ricardo (Eisele, 1979c). What interested Peirce was the logical structure of the theory of rent in Ricardo's *Principles* (Peirce, 1893; 1897c). Peirce thought that Ricardo's conceptualization of political economy made it amenable to mathematical representation. Besides Ricardo, Cournot and Newcomb, Peirce was aware of the economic contributions of Malthus, J.S. Mill, Charles Babbage and possibly Irving Fisher (Eisele, 1979c; 1979d; Peirce, 1871b; 1882). Additionally, Peirce's father, Benjamin Peirce, a professor of mathematics at Harvard and the foremost American mathematician of his time, also had a keen interest in a mathematical political economy. Apparently, Peirce and his father collaborated in giving at least one public lecture on mathematical political economy in 1871 (Eisele, 1979c: 253; Fisch, 1982: xxxv).

Peirce's theory of monopoly, which stems from his intrigue with Cournot's *Researches*, can be found in three different sources. One of these is the letter to Newcomb mentioned above. A second source is another letter, to an attorney, Abraham Conger (Peirce, 1873) in which Peirce again presents the mathematics of the profit-maximizing monopolist. The third source is a recently published manuscript titled 'On Political Economy' (Peirce, 1874) by the editors of the latest edition of Peirce's papers. This manuscript contains the basic calculus of the profit-maximizing monopolist. Then first-order conditions are formed and propositions are stated on the basis of the first-order conditions. It appears that Peirce is attempting what later became known as comparative static analysis. He also attempts to deal with discontinuities in the variables and to extend the analysis to more variables. In total, there are 19 equations which are argumentatively interconnected. Given the number of equations in this brief note, 'On Political Economy' is a dense piece of mathematical inquiry for its time (Wible, 1995).

While Peirce's model of monopoly is interesting because of its content and because of its sophistication in presenting the theory of monopoly inferentially and mathematically, the most extraordinary contribution of 'On Political Economy' comes near the end. The last quarter of the manuscript appears to be a separate fragment written on the same day as the model of monopoly. In this fragment, Peirce pens a short paragraph on the theory of demand. In the first sentence of this paragraph, he asserts that he will state the dependence of demand on price as a proposition. The second sentence summarizes marginal utility theory for a single individual. Peirce restates in words that an individual will choose an alternative which gives the greatest additional satisfaction or marginal utility. Then the last sentence reformulates marginal utility theory in logical form as the axiom of transitivity:

> The dependence of demand on price arises from this fundamental proposition. The desire of a person for anything has a quantity of one dimension, and a person having a choice will take that alternative which gives him the greatest satisfaction. In other words if a person prefers A to B and B to C he also prefers A to C. This is the first axiom of Political Economy. (Peirce, 1874: 176)

After formulating the axiom of transitivity, Peirce writes two more paragraphs that provide statements of the notions of substitutes and complements in demand and the idea of diminishing marginal utility.

Besides mathematical political economy and the theory of monopoly, the second major area of Peirce's interest in economics was the economic function of mind and scientific theories. A similar point of view can be found in John Dewey's philosophy (Wible, 1984). In the context of an uncertain, evolutionary world, Peirce recognized the economic function of conscious thought and of scientific theories. To be effective, thoughts and theories must distil meaning and information and represent them in an efficacious way. Peirce believed science to be an area of human thought where the economic function of the mind reached its most general form. Peirce (1896: 48) referred to the writings of the physicist Ernst Mach (1893; 1898) who developed this 'instrumental', economic view of consciousness and science much more elaborately than Peirce.[6]

The third and most developed aspect of Peirce's interest in economics was his economy of research. This culminated in his 'Note on the Theory of the Economy of Research' (1879). Here Peirce proposed an economic theory of research project selection in science. His theory is premised on the idea that resources can be used to increase the precision of measurement. The idea is that resources can be expended to reduce probable error in science. Probable error is a nineteenth-century term dealing with the precision of a statistical estimator in scientific inquiry. It is a precursor to the notion of a confidence interval. In the main body of the essay, Peirce focused on the allocation of additional resources to established, continuing research. Once the basic expenditures of a project had been made, Peirce maintained that additional expenditures would improve the accuracy of knowledge, but the benefits would begin to diminish:

> We thus see that when an investigation is commenced, after the initial expenses are once paid, at little cost we improve our knowledge, and improvement then is especially valuable; but as the investigation goes on, additions to our knowledge cost more and more, and, at the same time, are of less and less worth. ... All the sciences exhibit the same phenomenon, and so does life. (Peirce, 1879: 644)

In the 'Note on the Theory of the Economy of Research', Peirce followed a method of argument which any contemporary economist would recognize. He created a mathematical model of the choices facing the researcher. The model, which anticipated many developments in modern microeconomics, is presented in the hypothetico-deductive style of a modern economics journal article. Peirce theorized that the total utility of a series of research projects should be maximized subject to a limitation on total cost. Optimization in Peirce's model required the equalization of the ratios of marginal utility to marginal cost for all research projects being considered. The use of ratios circumvented the measurement problem associated with cardinal utility. Peirce presented a graphical portrayal of the special case when two projects were under consideration. His graph using the ratio of marginal utilities was more sophisticated than a similar graph by Jevons using diminishing marginal utility. The model is presented and described in some detail in Wible (1994).

Peirce's 'Note' was written relatively early in his career. After writing it, Peirce continued to make the economy of research an integral part of his theory of science. He repeatedly returned to this theme in his discussions of the nature of scientific inference. In a comment titled 'The Economy of Research', (1896), he restated the theory originally introduced in the 'Note'. Later, Peirce (1901) wrote a long essay approaching the length of a short monograph on the methodology of interpreting ancient manuscripts. In this essay, he asserted that 'economical considerations' played a fundamental role in his conception of the way such manuscripts should be interpreted. One of his last discussions of the economics of research was contained in his 1902 grant application to the Carnegie Institution. The purpose of the request was to pull together many of his disparate writings into a coherent set of memoirs which would form a unified system of logic; the economy of research was to have an important role in Peirce's unified logic (Peirce, 1902a; 1902b). But the grant was denied and Peirce's writings were left for others to organize and synthesize.

To date, Peirce has not had a significant impact on the economics profession.[7] However, his economics of inference and research project selection has inspired philosopher Nicholas Rescher (1976; 1978a; 1978b; 1989) to take a Peircean, economic perspective of science. Rescher (1978a: 72ff) maintains that an economic approach helps to deal with several disputes regarding aspects of induction. Among them are Carnap's total evidence requirement, Hempel's paradox of the ravens, Goodman's grue paradox and Popper's notion of falsification.

Peirce's economic writings may be pathbreaking for economics in a way that cannot be directly inferred from these writings. Fragmentary though they may be, Peirce's contributions to microeconomics, in conjunction with his other work in mathematics, logic, science and philosophy, can be pieced together to form a Peircean vision of economic science. This can be seen as an analytical evolutionary vision of economic processes with logic, microeconomics and a formal method of inference as important components. In spite of the prominence of neoclassical microeconomics in his economics, Peirce should not be characterized as a neoclassical economist. Peirce developed his own theory of evolution: both animate and inanimate entities evolve and change. Furthermore, human beings create abstract ideas as a way to create meaning and understanding. For Peirce, the construction and modification of ideas is also an evolutionary process which requires economic resources and a critical attitude similar to that found in science in order to test those ideas. To focus the issues more specifically, given the prominence of evolutionism and indeterminism in Peirce's thought, it is likely that Peirce would have been critical of the role of equilibrium in modern economic analysis and that he would have been sceptical of the notion of general equilibrium. Equilibrium appears to be an ex post reconstruction which ignores many of the evolutionary details and processes that enter into the construction of order and pattern in economic affairs. In other words, a Peircean vision of economics would reject what has become known as the Walrasian approach to economics. Reconstructing economics in a manner consistent with Peirce's evolutionism and his economic writings could provide a new way of conceiving of economic science. A Peircean reconstruction could be viewed as a way of rethinking the Marshallian approach to mainstream economics and as a conceptual framework for creating linkages with other evolutionary approaches to economics such as the institutionalist and the Austrian points of view.

JAMES R. WIBLE

Notes

1. One presentation of the ideas in pragmatism is Wiener (1949). For an overview of the relevance of Peirce and pragmatism to controversial issues in economics, see Kevin Hoover (1994).
2. For an overview of the philosophies of the major contributors to pragmatism see Thayer (1981).
3. Popular versions of pragmatism became confused with the businessman's attitude of adopting ideas which work and with utilitarianism.
4. For Peirce, a belief served to resolve real, irritating doubt, rather than the feigned doubt of Descartes.
5. Excellent philosophical treatises on Peirce's philosophy have been written by Murphey (1993), Hookaway (1985) and Anderson (1995).
6. Peirce's semeiotics and his theory of evolution may have implications for economics, but Peirce did not suggest such implications. See Dyer (1986).
7. An exception or two are the pieces by Lutz (1985) and Hill (1983) where they debate the impact of the ideas of Peirce, Dewey and James on social and institutional economics.

References

Anderson, D.R. (1995), *Strands of a System: The Philosophy of Charles Peirce*, West Lafayette, Indiana: Purdue University Press.

Baumol, W.J. and S.M. Goldfeld (1968), *Precursors in Mathematical Economics: An Anthology*, London: London School of Economics and Political Science.

Brent, Joseph (1993), *Charles Sanders Peirce: A Life*, Bloomington, IN: Indiana University Press.

Colapietro, V.M. (1989), *Peirce's Approach to the Self: A Semiotic Perspective on Human Subjectivity*, Albany: State University of New York Press.

Cournot, Augustin (1929), *Researches into the Mathematical Principles of the Theory of Wealth*, trans. N.T. Bacon, New York: Macmillan; first published 1838.

Cushen, W. Edward (1967), 'C.S. Peirce on Benefit–Cost Analysis of Scientific Activity', *Operations Research*, **XV**, 641.

Dewey, John (1949), 'The Pragmatism of Peirce', a supplementary essay in M.R. Cohen (ed.), *Chance, Love and Logic: Philosophical Essays by the Late Charles S. Peirce*, New York: Harcourt Brace.

Diggins, J.P. (1994), *The Promise of Pragmatism: Modernism and the Crisis of Knowledge and Authority*, Chicago: University of Chicago Press.

Dyer, Alan (1986), 'Semiotics, Economic Development and the Deconstruction of Economic Man', *Journal of Economic Issues*, **20**, 541–9.

Eisele, Carolyn (1979a), *Studies in the Mathematical Philosophy of Charles S. Peirce*, ed. R.M. Martin, New York: Mouton Publishers.

Eisele, Carolyn (1979b), 'The Correspondence with Simon Newcomb', in C. Eisele (1979a).

Eisele, Carolyn (1979c), 'The Mathematics of Economics', in C. Eisele (1979a).

Eisele, Carolyn (1979d), 'Introductions to *The New Elements of Mathematics*', in C. Eisele (1979a).

Fisch, Max (1982), 'The Decisive Year and Its Early Consequences', in E.C. Moore *et al.* (eds), *Writings of Charles S. Peirce: A Chronological Edition*, vol. 2, 1867–1871, Indianapolis: Indiana University Press.

Hausman, Carl (1974), 'Eros and Agape in Creative Evolution: A Peircean Insight', *Process Studies*, **4**, Spring, 11–25.

Hausman, Carl (1993), *Charles S. Peirce's Evolutionary Philosophy*, New York: Cambridge University Press.

Hill, L.E. (1983), 'The Pragmatic Alternative to Positive Economics', *Review of Social Economy*, **41**, April, 1–11.

Hookaway, Christopher (1985), *Peirce*, London: Routledge.

Hoover, Kevin D. (1994), 'Pragmatism, Pragmaticism and Economic Theory', in Roger Backhouse (ed.), *New Perspectives on Economic Methodology*, London: Routledge.

Lutz, Mark (1985), 'Pragmatism, Instrumental Value Theory and Social Economics', *Review of Social Economy*, **43**, October, 140–72.

Mach, Ernst (1898), 'The Economical Nature of Inquiry in Physics', *Popular Scientific Lectures of Mach*, 3rd rev. edn, trans. T.J. McCormack, Chicago: Open Court.

Mach, Ernst (1960), 'The Economy of Science', *The Science of Mechanics*, 6th American edn, La Salle, IL: Open Court; first published 1893.

Murphey, M.G. (1993), *The Development of Peirce's Philosophy*. Indianopolis: Hackett Publishing Co.

Peirce, C.S. (1871a), 'Letter to Simon Newcomb'; reprinted 1968 in W.J. Baumol and S.M. Goldfeld, *Precursors in Mathematical Economics*.

Peirce, C.S. (1871b), '[Charles Babbage]', *Nation*, **13**, November; reprinted 1982 in E.C. Moore *et al.* (eds), *Writings of Charles S. Peirce: A Chronological Edition*, vol. 2, 1867–1871, Indianapolis: Indiana University Press.

Peirce, C.S. (1873), 'Letter, Peirce to Abraham B. Conger'; reprinted 1982 in C.J. Kloesel, *et al.* (eds), *Writings of Charles S. Peirce: A Chronological Edition*, vol. 4, 1872–1878, Indianapolis: Indiana University Press.

Peirce, C.S. (1874), '[On Political Economy]'; reprinted 1982 in C.J. Kloesel, *et al.* (eds), *Writings of Charles S. Peirce: A Chronological Edition*, vol. 4, 1872–1878, Indianapolis: Indiana University Press.

Peirce, C.S. (1878), 'How to Make Our Ideas Clear'; reprinted 1955 in J. Buchler (ed.), *Philosophical Writings of Peirce*, New York: Dover Publications..

Peirce, C.S. (1879), 'Note on the Theory of the Economy of Research', *United States Coast Survey* for the fiscal year ending June 1876, US Government Printing Office, reprinted in *Operations Research*, **XV**, 1967 [1879], 642–8; also reprinted in *Collected Papers of Charles Sanders Peirce*, vol. VII, ed. A.W. Burks, Cambridge, 1958, 76–83; and in C.J.W. Kloesel (ed.), *Writings of Charles S. Peirce: A Chronological Edition*, vol. 4, 1879–1884, Indianapolis: Indiana University Press, 1986.

Peirce, C.S. (1882), 'Introductory Lecture on the Study of Logic'; reprinted 1986 in C.J.W. Kloesel (ed.), *Writings of Charles S. Peirce*, vol. 4, 1879–1884, Indianapolis: Indiana University Press.

Peirce, C.S. (1893), 'The Logic of Quantity'; reprinted 1960 in C. Hartshorne and P. Weiss (eds), *Collected Papers of Charles Sanders Peirce*, vol. IV, Cambridge, MA: Harvard University Press.

Peirce, C.S. (1896), 'The Economy of Research'; reprinted 1960 in C. Hartshorne and P. Weiss (eds), 'Lessons from the History of Science', *Collected Papers of Charles Sanders Peirce*, vol. I, Cambridge, MA: Harvard University Press.

Peirce, C.S. (1897a), 'Multitude and Number'; reprinted 1960 in C. Hartshorne and P. Weiss, (eds), *Collected Papers of Charles Sanders Peirce*, vol. IV, Cambridge, MA: Harvard University Press.

Peirce, C.S. (1897b), 'Synechism, Fallibilism and Evolution'; reprinted 1955 in J. Buchler (ed.), *Philosophical Writings of Peirce*, New York: Dover Publications.

Peirce, C.S. (1897c), 'Logic as Semiotic: The Theory of Signs'; reprinted 1955 in J. Buchler (ed.), *Philosophical Writings of Peirce*, New York: Dover Publications.

Peirce, C.S. (1901), 'On the Logic of Drawing History from Ancient Documents especially from Testimonies'; reprinted 1985 in C. Eisele (ed.), *Historical Perspectives on Peirce's Logic of Science*, Berlin: Mouton Publishers.

Peirce, C.S. (1902a), 'Carnegie Institution. Application for a Grant'; reprinted 1985 in C. Eisele (ed.), *Historical Perspectives on Peirce's Logic of Science*, Berlin: Mouton Publishers.

Peirce, C.S. (1902b), 'On the Economics of Research', Memoir No. 28 of 1902a, 1036–9, 1902b.

Peirce, C.S. (1905), 'The Essentials of Pragmatism'; reprinted 1955 in J. Buchler (ed.), *Philosophical Writings of Peirce*, New York: Dover Publications.

Rescher, Nicholas (1976), 'Peirce and the Economy of Research', *Philosophy of Science*, **43**, 71–98.

Rescher, Nicholas (1978a), *Peirce's Philosophy of Science*, Notre Dame: University of Notre Dame Press.

Rescher, Nicholas (1978b), *Scientific Progress: A Philosophical Essay on the Economics of the Natural Sciences*, Oxford: Basil Blackwell.
Rescher, Nicholas (1989), *Cognitive Economy: The Economic Dimension of the Theory of Knowledge*, Pittsburgh: University of Pittsburgh Press.
Sheriff, J.K. (1994), *Charles Peirce's Guess at the Riddle*, Bloomington: Indiana University Press.
Thayer, H.S. (1981), *Meaning and Action: A Critical History of Pragmatism*, Indianapolis: Hackett Publishing Co.
Wible, J.R. (1984). 'The Instrumentalisms of Dewey and Friedman', *Journal of Economic Issues*, **XVIII**, (4), 1049–70.
Wible, J.R. (1994), 'Charles Sanders Peirce's Economy of Research', *Journal of Economic Methodology*, **1**, 135–60.
Wible, J.R. (1995), 'Peirce's Mathematical Note "On Political Economy" and the Axiom of Transitivity', University of New Hampshire, paper given at History of Economics Society, June, Notre Dame.
Wiener, Philip P. (1949), *Evolution and the Founders of Pragmatism*, New York: Harper & Row.
Wiener, Philip P. (1958), 'Introduction', *Values in a Universe of Chance: Selected Writings of Charles S. Peirce*, Garden City, New York: Doubleday Anchor.

Plausibility

Plausibility is the fundamental epistemic property attributed by theoretical economists to economic theorems. Related terms that are used by economists in contexts of plausibility assignments are 'likelihood' and 'probability'. The terminology implies that the truth of these theorems is believed to some degree. This degree of credibility is, in the context of discussions in the theoretical economic literature, obtained from an analysis of the plausibility of the assumptions from which the theorem is derived. There is a logical transfer of plausibility from the assumptions to the theorem. Klant (1972) brought the role of plausibility to the forum of economic methodologists: 'Proofs in economic theory are partly based upon a discussion about the plausibility of assumptions in basic theories.' In sound economics, from his normative falsificationist point of view, he is giving plausibility a certain place: 'An appeal to plausibility may not give access to the station of destination, but it is valid for boarding at the station of departure' (ibid.: 187).

Plausibility transfer from assumptions to the theorems derived from them can be analysed starting from the standard logical structure of *propositions of economic theory* (PETs). The logical formula of a PET is the following:

$$V(C_1, ..., C_k \Rightarrow IT)$$

stating that a certain interesting theorem IT can be derived from conditions $C_1, ..., C_k$. This derivation presupposes a basic ontology or field V (specifying, for instance, whether there are 0, 1, 2 or an arbitrary number of consumers, producers, factors of production, commodities, countries and possibly objects specific for the special application the PET deals with). Examples of ITs are the law of demand and the factor price equalization theorem. A PET is a proof of such a theorem under certain conditions.

In theoretical economic research programmes, usual strategies for making progress are (1) field extension, (2) weakening of conditions, (3) clarifying the economic meaning of the conditions, often by finding deeper conditions from which conditions previously found to be sufficient can be proved, and (4) finding alternative conditions. There is also a hunt for *new* interesting theorems, that is, theorems that have a clear economic meaning, preferably policy implications, or theorems that unambiguously affirm or negate established opinions in the discipline.

The conditions $C_1, ..., C_k$ do not have an equal status in the economist's mind: at the one extreme, 'major' conditions express the economist's basic convictions about the behaviour and intentions of economic actors and the restrictions nature puts on them (for example, utility maximization and some general outline of what constraints on maximization should look like). At the other extreme, 'minor' conditions are of a merely technical nature, used only because they are thus far found to be necessary for deriving some interesting theorem, or useful for narrowing down a complex mathematical problem to manageable proportions (as with linear homogeneity, infinite divisibility of goods or infinitely small suppliers). These are the conditions that, if possible, the economist is especially ambitious to remove.

Since the main trend in this research programme strategy is weakening of conditions or, stated in terms of the Popper–Lakatos methodology, the *decrease* of their *content*, the PETs resulting from this strategy clearly cannot be, and are not, in fact, rationalized in terms of this methodology in which such a decrease of content is associated with degeneration, the opposite of progress in a research programme. Instead, *increasing the plausibility of the theorem* by means of increasing the plausibility of the conditions from which it is derived serves here among programme participants as the criterion for progress.

We may make the concept of plausibility more precise with the help of the Venn diagram below. The rectangle U represents the class of all logical possibilities (that is, all states of the world that can be described by the terms in which the theory is formulated; in the case of the PETs deriving the law of demand from considerations of utility maximization under constraints, for instance, this involves the set of all logically possible utility functions and all possible budget constraints). Now, for instance, the conditions $C_1, ..., C_k$ in the Hicks Allen PET identify a subset A of U as *sufficient* for the law of demand. Samuelson's revealed preference theory yields a PET in which the conditions for the law of demand are considerably weaker; that is, they identify a larger set B as sufficient for the theorem under scrutiny.

In the simple case where economists consider all logical possibilities in U to be equally plausible, Samuelson can be said to have raised the plausibility of IT, since the *a priori* chance

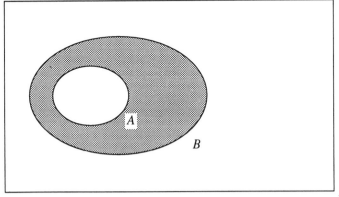

that real courses of events in the actual world are in *B* is clearly greater than the chance of their being in subset *A*. In reality, however, economists do not spread elementary plausibility assignments evenly over the rectangle, but assign different plausibilities to different logical possibilities in *U*. Some logical possibilities are left completely out of consideration, others are considered to be highly plausible. (Mathematically we may think here of a function mapping each logical possibility on a real number between zero and one; that is, graphically some plausibility plane above rectangle *U*, the integral of which equals 1.) But whatever may be the elementary plausibility distribution over *U* in some special discussion in some special research programme of theoretical economics, a weakening from *A* to *B* can never decrease plausibility and will increase it as soon as any non-zero plausibility is assigned to logical possibilities in the difference set *B/A* (shaded).

By way of corroboration of the hypothesis that the strategy of finding new PETs is rationalized as a strategy of raising the plausibility of the PET's interesting theorem, numerous quotations could be adduced in seminal articles in economic journals in which new PETs are presented (see, for example, Hamminga, 1983: 71–96, on international trade; Cools, 1993, on capital structure choice; Timmer, 1994, on the law of demand).

The following quotations may serve as key illustrations. In Stolper and Samuelson's (1941) seminal article on tariffs and trade: 'it is the purpose of the present investigation to show that under rather general assumptions definite conclusions can be derived concerning the absolute share of a factor' (1941: 62), 'One by one we have been able to drop our various restrictive assumptions with only slight modifications of results. … We have shown that there is a grain of truth in the pauper labour type of argument for protection' (ibid.: 72). For a textbook exposition of this type of rationalization, see for example, Södersten (1970): 'For many reasons it would be advantageous if we could use unspecified production functions. This means that, to derive the results we wanted, to prove certain theorems, we would need to assume only that a relationship exists between inputs and outputs, but we would not have to assume anything specific about the nature of this relationship.' An authoritative survey article by Chipman (1966) describes this cornerstone – so often overlooked by economic methodologists – of the methods of theoretical economics thus: 'But, as always happens in a theory as it develops, interest attaches to the quest for weaker conditions, in fact the weakest possible, or necessary conditions.'

BERT HAMMINGA

Bibliography
Chipman, J.S.(1966), 'A Survey of the Theory of International Trade: Part III, The Modern theory', *Econometrica*, **34**, 18–76.
Cools, K. (1993), *Capital Structure Choice: Confronting (Meta) theory, Empirical Tests and Executive Opinion*, Tilburg: Gianotten.
Hamminga, B. (1983), *Neoclassical Theory Structure and Theory Development*, Berlin: Springer.
Klant, J.J. (1972), *The Rules of the Game*, Cambridge: Cambridge University Press.
Nooteboom, B. (1986), 'Plausibility in Economics', *Economics and Philosophy*, **2**, 197–224.
Södersten, B. (1970), *International Economics*, London: Macmillan.
Stolper, W.S. and P.A. Samuelson (1941), 'Protection and Real Wages', *Review of Economics and Statistics*, **9**, 58–73.
Timmer, M. (1994), 'The Role of Plausibility in Economic Theory. Studying the Theory of Consumer Behaviour', mimeo, Eindhoven University.

Polanyi, Karl

Karl Polanyi was born in Vienna in 1886 and died in North America in 1964. He spent his formative years in Budapest. He is best remembered for his classic assessment of the political economy of modern capitalism, *The Great Transformation* (Polanyi, 1944) and a provocative essay drawn from it (Dalton, 1968: ch. 4). His work on the economic anthropology project at Columbia University in the 1950s has also been highly influential (Polanyi *et al.*, 1977; Polanyi and Rotstein, 1966; Polanyi, 1977; Stanfield, 1986).

Polanyi sought to explain the social change of modern capitalism in order to open the way for a vision of the future. His model of market capitalism is that of 'the double movement' in which the ever-increasing application of the market mentality to social life is met by a 'protective response' directed at limiting the socially dislocating effects of the self-regulating market system (Polanyi, 1944). The protective response has been very diverse. Governments have intervened to protect labour with legislation regulating the employment of children and women, working conditions and the length of the working day. Wide-ranging income maintenance programmes have been enacted, along with measures aimed at land use planning, resource conservation, pollution control and modern comprehensive environmental protection. Central banking, capital market regulations and aggregate demand management have been introduced in an effort to stabilize the macroeconomy. Regulatory agencies have been established to ensure consumer product safety and service standards for those providing care for the young and old. Trade unions and other voluntary associations such as civic, historical preservation or naturalist societies have played a major role. Even the modern corporation can be viewed as part of the protective response since its principal animus is the urge to stabilize and control the uncertain exigencies of the market mechanism.

The protective response essentially restores and protects reciprocity and redistribution as mechanisms for integrating the division of labour. This protection is necessary because the expansionary character of commodity production and the pecuniary myopia it breeds tend to destroy these social processes and the social bonds upon which they are premised and which they in turn foster. This pecuniary myopia obscures the protective response, which is in any case spontaneous, driven not by ideology but by social exigency. Spontaneous and obscure, ill-understood and haphazardly fashioned, the protective response adds to the political economic instability of modern life. Crisis becomes endemic.

In Polanyi's view, the task of imagining a better future cannot be accomplished until people escape the yoke of the 'obsolete market mentality' and recognize reciprocity and redistribution as necessary aspects of integrating the division of labour in the good society. His research in economic anthropology was aimed in this direction. By demonstrating that, generally speaking, pre-capitalist societies had no separate economic sphere with a distinct and explicit set of motives and functions, Polanyi sought to indicate the presence of socially embedded transactions that operate to integrate the division of labour in the 'substantive' or material economy.

The contrast of this substantive or material view of the economy to the 'formalist' mentality of modern economics was also an important part of Polanyi's effort to demystify modern economic thought. Mainstream economics is the theoretical expression and ideological justification of the self-regulating market economy (Stanfield, 1979: chs 2–5; 1986: ch. 2). It is ethnocentric, a cultural artefact of modern market society. The substantive view refers to the universal material aspect; all human societies have to reproduce themselves materially and to integrate the division of labour by an instituted process of transactions in order to do so. Exchange is only one such transactional process, in addition to reciprocity and redistribution. The formalist view is blind to these other two processes as integrative mechanisms. For example, redistributive transactions or transfers are seen as negative sum entities in that they produce no real income but bear administrative and disincentive costs in their operation. Hence the celebrated tradeoff between equity and efficiency that reveals the myopia of modern economics.

In a very real sense, the formalist view is unable to conceive the major political economic tendencies of the twentieth century. Socialism and the welfare state have arisen largely to counter the threat to society posed by the unregulated market economy. The leading issues of this trend are those of the place of economy in society. The formalist methodology treats the economy as an isolable social system with its own terrain and thus cannot conceive the issues that occur in the effects on society of a particular institutional configuration of economic activity. This problem of lives and livelihood was Polanyi's central concern, and it continues to configure the social and economic issues of modern society. Comprehension of this problematic will require a social or institutional economics, such as Polanyi suggested, that understands the material economy as it is placed in the historical social process.

JAMES R. STANFIELD

References

Dalton, G. (ed.) (1968), *Primitive, Archaic and Modern Economies: Essays of Karl Polanyi*, Garden City, NY: Doubleday.
Polanyi, K (1944), *The Great Transformation*, New York: Rinehart
Polanyi, K. (1977), *The Livelihood of Man*, ed. H.W. Pearson, New York: Academic Press.
Polanyi, K. in collaboration with A. Rotstein (1966), *Dahomey and the Slave Trade*, Seattle: University of Washington Press.
Polanyi, K., C.M. Arensberg and H.W. Pearson (eds) (1977), *Trade and Market in the Early Empires*, Chicago: Henry Regnery.
Stanfield, J.R. (1979), *Economic Thought and Social Change*, Carbondale: Southern Illinois University Press.
Stanfield, J.R. (1986), *The Economic Thought of Karl Polanyi*, London: Macmillan.

Popper, Karl

Professor Sir Karl Popper (born Vienna, 1902, died Croydon, England, 1994) has exercised a considerable influence over discussions about the methodology of economics, even though he has written little on the topic directly himself. His *Logik der Forschung* (1934) (translated as *The Logic of Scientific Discovery* in 1959) presented an account of scientific knowledge as fallible, and as developing through a process of conjectures and refutations. More specifically, he argued that, for a theory to be scientific, it had to be testable. He did not argue that non-scientific theories were meaningless and, indeed, in his later writings, he offered a theory of 'metaphysical research programmes' which discussed the role of non-testable programmatic ideas in the development of science, and of the way in which they and other non-testable ideas might be appraised (compare Shearmur, in Blaug and de Marchi, 1991). Popper's account was distinctive, in that he gave an account of that against which theories are tested as resting on an open-ended intersubjective consensus as to what is the case. (Indeed, in his view, objectivity is a social product, rather than, as it were, the product of an empty mind.)

In more recent terminology, one could say that Popper offered a non-foundationalist theory of the development of science, but one which, because he argued that we can appraise whether or not some new theory at least in principle constitutes progress as compared with earlier theories, is not relativistic. Popper's views are normative. While he was willing to take certain heroic episodes in the development of science as illustrative of his ideas, he did not claim to give a description of the development of science or the behaviour of scientists. Rather, he argued for his ideas as pertinent, given a particular conception of the aims of scientific activity, and he also argued for his favoured view of the aims of science – the idea that science should aim at true, contentful theories – as compared with other views.

Popper has also written on the methodology of social science. His *Poverty of Historicism* (1944–5) was directed against the view that the proper model for social science should be the discernment of long-term, unconditional trends. Instead, Popper stressed the conditional character of both prediction and explanation, and their dependence on both laws and initial conditions. In *The Poverty of Historicism*, and in some remarks on methodology in *The Open Society and Its Enemies* (1945), he espoused methodological individualism (although at the same time he stressed the socially situated character of human action). He argued that explanation in social science was typically concerned to discover knowledge of the unintended consequences of human action, which he suggested we should conceptualize in terms of minimal rationality on the basis of the logic of actors' situations. These ideas he has described as an attempt to generalize the approach of economics, so as to be applicable to the social sciences in general. In some of his earlier writings, he was a strong champion of explanation in the social sciences as involving universal laws, but he has also suggested that the assumption of rationality – the 'rationality principle' – can play the same formal role. (See, for his fullest account, 'Models, Instruments and Truth', in his *The Myth of the Framework*, 1994). And in some of his writings he has presented his views in ways that draw out their parallels to hermeneutics, notably to the ideas of Collingwood (for example, in his *Objective Knowledge*, 1972).

Popper had some somewhat diverse interests in economics. His uncle, Walter Schiff, was an economist, and Popper refers in passing to Boehm-Bawerk in his *Die beiden Grundprobleme der Erkenntnistheorie* (written 1930–33, published 1979). He became interested in some economic issues through his encounters with Marxism. His *Open Society*: ch. 21 includes some remarks on the trade cycle; it also includes some passing references to mathematical economics, a topic on which Hacohen (1994) has argued he would have heard presentations in seminars on the fringes of the Vienna Circle. Popper has described his ideas on the methodology of the social sciences as an 'attempt to generalize the method of theoretical economics', in which connection he refers specifically to Hayek's ideas (Popper, 1994: 151, 178), although Popper's generalization of this approach was very much in terms of his own ideas about epistemology and explanation. His ideas about scientific knowledge were favoured from early days by Haberler, who drew them to the attention of Hayek. They were subsequently found attractive by many who favoured empiricism, but did not identify with the more restrictive accounts of knowledge offered by logical positivism or logical empiricism. Popper's views also in some ways resembled those of Friedman and Machlup (although Popper was not in agreement with their instrumentalism), while his name was frequently invoked by those who saw prediction and testability as the basis upon which theories could claim legitimacy, but who knew little of the specifics of his ideas.

After World War II, Popper held a position at the London School of Economics. Some colleagues there, including Agassi, Klappholz and Watkins, developed his ideas and there was some (very limited) interaction with economists interested in methodological issues (see de Marchi in de Marchi (1988)). Popper's ideas also exercised considerable indirect influence through the work of his colleague Imre Lakatos, whose 'methodology of scientific research programmes' drew very extensively upon Popper. Popperian ideas, both directly and indirectly via Lakatos, have exercised a considerable influence, both on economists when they reflect self-consciously upon methodological issues, and also on specialized writers on the history and methodology of economics (for example, Birner, Blaug, Boland, Caldwell, Hands, Hutchison and Milford, and the earlier case studies of writers such as Weintraub). In more recent years, however, Popper's work has come under criticism. Some writers, such as Hausman (1992), have raised objections to the formal side of Popper's work. Others – in a way that would seem an indirect product of the influence of Kuhn – have argued for sociological and rhetorical approaches to the study of economics, but have, erroneously, presented this as if it had to be an alternative to Popper's concerns. Other writers again have repudiated Popper, as part of a more general repudiation of 'modernism'.

Popper's approach within philosophy is distinctive. While he has been treated as the patron saint of testability and empiricism, his philosophical views are complex and sophisticated, and themselves include many of the ideas to which people have had recourse in recent criticisms of empiricism. Those who find his approach attractive, however, are faced with the problem that economists do not seem very interested in testing their most basic ideas (although different schools of economists differ as to what they are willing to open to testing); and a concern with mathematical modelbuilding almost for its own sake would not score well with Popper's ideas on science, or with his own passionate concern that the social sciences should be of practical use to human beings. While those such as Caldwell and Koertge, who have stressed his ideas about situational logic as opposed to a narrow emphasis upon testability, are commending ideas which Popper himself developed as an attempt to generalize economic approaches.

JEREMY SHEARMUR

Bibliography
Blaug, Mark (1992), *The Methodology of Economics*, 2nd edn, Cambridge: Cambridge University Press.
Caldwell, Bruce (1982), *Beyond Positivism*, London: Allen & Unwin.
Caldwell, Bruce (1991), 'Clarifying Popper', *Journal of Economic Literature*, **29** (1), March, 1–33.
Hacohen, Malachi (1994), 'The Making of The Open Society', PhD Dissertation, Columbia University.
Hands, Wade (1985), 'Popper and Economic Methodology', *Economics and Philosophy*, **1**, April, 83–99.
Hausman, Daniel (1992), *The Inexact and Separate Science of Economics*, Cambridge: Cambridge University Press.
de Marchi, Neil (ed.) (1988), *The Popperian Legacy in Economics*, Cambridge/New York: Cambridge University Press.
de Marchi, Neil and Mark Blaug (eds) (1991), *Appraising Economic Theories: Studies in the Methodology of Research Programs*, Aldershot: Edward Elgar.
Popper, Karl (1944–5), *The Poverty of Historicism*, London: Routledge.
Popper, Karl (1945), *The Open Society and Its Enemies*, London: Routledge.
Popper, Karl (1959), *The Logic of Scientific Discovery*, London: Hutchinson.
Popper, Karl (1963), *Conjectures and Refutations*, London: Routledge.
Popper, Karl (1972), *Objective Knowledge*, Oxford: Clarendon Press.
Popper, Karl (1976), *Unended Quest*, London: Fontana.
Popper, Karl (1994), *The Myth of the Framework*, London: Routledge.

Positive–Normative Distinction, The

In Book III, Part 1, Section 1 of *A Treatise of Human Nature* (1739), David Hume claimed that all previous writers on ethics passed imperceptibly from observations about human affairs expressed with 'the usual copulation of propositions, *is* and *is not*' to conclusion 'connected with an *ought*, or an *ought not*': but, he argued, no one had ever given any good reasons for believing that 'this new relation can be a deduction from others, which are entirely different from it'. This passage is not unambiguous in meaning but it was traditionally interpreted to assert that it is illegitimate to deduce an '*is*' from an '*is*', implying that there is a class of statements of fact which are logically distinct from a class of statements of value and hence that the former cannot by themselves entail the latter. Max Black has aptly called this assertion 'Hume's Guillotine' (Hudson, 1969: 100) because it seems to cut off descriptive from prescriptive statements. To believe otherwise, to allege that ought-propositions are not essentially different from is-propositions, has ever since G.E. Moore's *Principia Ethica* (1903) been dubbed the 'naturalistic fallacy'.

Hume wrote in 1739. By 1836, the date of John Stuart Mill's (1967) pioneering essay 'On the Definition of Political Economy; and on the Method of Philosophical Investigation in that Science', followed in the same year by a discussion of the 'Limits of the Science' in Nassau Senior's *Outline of the Science of Political Economy*, the Humean distinction between is/ought propositions had been transmuted into the science/art distinction by steps which no one has ever traced in detail (but see Hutchison, 1964: ch. 1). The distinction was reiterated by John Elliot Cairnes, Henry Sidgwick, John Neville Keynes and Vilfredo Pareto later in the nineteenth century and by Max Weber in a series of influential papers written between 1903 and 1917; it seems to have been Neville Keynes who first employed the positive/normative in place of the science/arts distinction and by the time of Weber's essays this language had become commonplace. Nevertheless, it was Lionel Robbins' *Essay on the Nature and Significance of Economic Science* (1932) that finally made a dogma of the positive/normative distinction, a virtual hallmark of what it means to talk like an economist. Ironically enough, John Neville Keynes really proposed a triple distinction between a 'positive science' of economics that would establish uniformities, a 'normative science' of economics that would determine ideals and an 'art' of political economy that would formulate precepts (Hutchison, 1964: 36–7), but this tripartite classification never caught on.

Having distinguished positive from normative economics, mainstream economists without fail go on to insist that the distinction can be and should be clearly maintained in all economic discourse and particularly in applied economics. This has become, and still is, what might be called the fundamental tenet of 'orthodox' economic methodology: there is a well-defined area of 'positive economics' that is, at least in principle, value-free. While some well-known philosophers are critical of the standard is/ought distinction (see Hudson, 1969), it is the case that the positive/normative distinction is endorsed by most modern moral philosophers (MacIntyre, 1967: ch. 18). Nevertheless, the distinction between positive and normative economics has been frequently denied by radical economists and institutionalists, most conspicuously by Gunnar Myrdal, a Nobel laureate (Hutchison, 1964: 44–50; Wilber and Hoksbergen, 1984; Roy, 1989: chs 2–4; Blaug, 1992: 118–21; Proctor, 1991: ch. 13).

In considering that denial, it will be helpful to underline the various shades of meaning that have been assigned to the dichotomy between positive and normative economics. The following list is suggestive, not exhaustive (Machlup, 1978: 428–9).

Hume's Guillotine

is	ought
science	art
positive	normative
facts	values
description	prescription
explanation	recommendation
true/false	good/bad
empirical	ethical

laws	rules
objective	subjective
testable	non-testable
theory	policy
pure	applied

The simplest way to throw doubt on the doctrine of value-free positive economics is to note that all theoretical analysis must begin with the recognition of a significant problem that requires solution and 'significance' is not itself a fact but rather a value judgment; moreover, the mode of analysis that is undertaken and even the type of data that are gathered to support that analysis involve a further series of value judgments; finally, if the conclusions depend in any way on statistical inference, the level of statistical significance at which the so-called 'null hypothesis' is accepted or rejected is purely conventional and in this sense is again a value judgment. Thus positive economics begins and ends with norms and hence is not really different from normative economics.

So runs a leading argument against value-free economics. To assert the logical distinction between positive and normative economics therefore requires a further distinction between two types of value judgments, namely, what Ernst Nagel calls 'characterizing value judgments' and 'appraising value judgments' or what I prefer to call 'methodological value judgments' and 'normative value judgments' (Blaug, 1992: 114): the former involves the choice of subject matter to be investigated, the mode of investigation to be followed and the criteria for judging the validity of the findings, which are part and parcel of any inquiry whether in the social or in the natural science; the latter refers to evaluative assertions about states of the world, including the desirability of certain kinds of human behaviour and the social outcomes produced by that behaviour which can, at least in principle, be kept separate from existential assertions of facts. Such, at any rate, must be the contention of those who assert the *possibility* of value-free positive economics.

Having denied that positive economics is just a certain kind of normative economics, we must now consider whether normative economics is not after all very much the same as positive economics. Just as positive economics seems to involve two different types of value judgments, so normative economics also invokes two very different sorts of value judgments, namely, what Amartya Sen has called 'basic' or 'non-basic' value judgments (Blaug, 1992: 115–16). Basic or pure value judgments are those that apply under all conceivable circumstances and which are thus impervious to any factual beliefs; non-basic or impure value judgments, on the other hand, are held subject to definite factual beliefs about social causation or the relations between the relevant variables of the subject matter in question. It is doubtful that anyone is ever wholly committed to basic value judgments – 'all wars are wrong'; 'life is always sacred'; 'I value this for its own sake' – but there is certainly nothing in logic to preclude such value judgments. In any case, if most value judgments are non-basic or impure, it follows that virtually all propositions in normative economics rely on propositions in positive economics and, to that extent, Hume's Guillotine fails to cut cleanly. Nevertheless, this is a practical and not a principled argument against value-free economics and indeed might be employed to emphasize the importance of trying to separate positive from normative economics.

Enough has now been said to suggest that the positive/normative distinction has been bedevilled by the indiscriminate use of the term 'value judgments' to cover not just qualitative evaluative appraisals but also subjective assertions of facts and indeed any and all untestable metaphysical propositions that colour the pre-analytic vision of an economist. Thus interpersonal comparisons of utility are frequently dismissed as 'value judgments' when they are actually untestable statements of facts: they are true or false but to this day we know of no method of finding out which is the case (ibid.: 199). Likewise, the modern doctrine of Pareto optimality rests, among other things, on the fundamental postulate of consumer sovereignty – only self-chosen preferences count as yardsticks of welfare or, in popular parlance, an individual is the best judge of his or her welfare – and it has long been argued that consumer sovereignty is a value judgment *par excellence*, implying that Paretian welfare economics is fundamentally normative. However, Chris Archibald and Peter Hennipman have argued instead that the theorems of Paretian welfare economics are theorems in positive economics; on this view, the assumption of consumer sovereignty is not a value judgment but simply the assertion of the axiom that individual preferences are to be taken as given for purposes of assessing a potential Pareto improvement, without endorsing or approving of these preferences (ibid.: 124–6). Be that as it may, it demonstrates the difficulty of deciding just what is a value judgment and what precise role postulates that look like value judgments play in economic analysis. A final confusion in the definition of value judgments is the widespread belief that non-controversial, unanimously held value judgments, such as consumer sovereignty or the Paretian definition of an improvement in social welfare, are by virtue of that unanimity converted from value judgments into empirical judgments. This is simply a logical error, but it is nevertheless productive of much misunderstanding about value-free economics.

To sum up: the doctrine of value-free positive economics asserts, first of all, that the logical status of factual, descriptive is-statements is different in kind from that of normative, prescriptive ought-statements and, second, that the methodological judgments that are involved in reaching agreement on is-statements differ in important ways from those used to reach a consensus on normative value judgments, at least if these are basic value judgments; on the other hand, if normative value judgments are typically non-basic or impure, securing agreement on them involves a process identical to that involved in reaching agreement on positive questions of fact (see Taylor, 1961: chs 3, 9). The claim that economics can be value-free in this sense does not deny that ideological bias creeps into the very selection of the questions that economists investigate, that the inferences that are drawn from factual evidence are sometimes influenced by value-laden concepts and categories (rational choice, maximizing individuals, free competition and so forth) or even that the practical advice that economists offer is frequently loaded with concealed value judgment, the better to persuade rather than merely to advise. It is precisely for this reason that we must insist on the *possibility* of value-free positive economics, on clearly maintaining the positive–normative distinction as far as it can be maintained. If there are not at least some descriptive, factual assertions about economic uniformities that are value-free, it seems difficult to escape the conclusion that we have a licence in economics to assert just about anything that we please.

MARK BLAUG

References
Blaug, M. (1992), *The Methodology of Economics*, 2nd edn, Cambridge: Cambridge University Press.
Hudson, W.D. (ed.) (1969), *The Is–Ought Question. A Collection of Papers on the Central Problem in Moral Philosophy*, London: Macmillan.
Hutchison, T.W. (1964), *'Positive' Economics and Policy Objectives*, London: George Allen & Unwin.
Machlup, F. (1978), *Methodology of Economics and Other Social Sciences*, New York: Academic Press.

MacIntyre, A. (1967), *A Short History of Ethics: A History of Moral Philosophy From the Homeric Age to the Twentieth Century*, London: Routledge.

Mill, J.S. (1967), *Essays on Economics and Society. 1824–1845, Collected Works of John Stuart Mill*, vol. IV, ed. J.M. Robson, Toronto: University of Toronto Press.

Proctor, R.N. (1991), *Value-Free Science? Purity and Power in Modern Knowledge*, Cambridge, MA: Harvard University Press.

Roy, S. (1989), *Philosophy of Economics. On the Scope of Reason in Economic Inquiry*, London: Routledge.

Taylor, P.W. (1961), *Normative Discourse*, Englewood Cliffs, NJ: Prentice-Hall.

Wilber, C.K. and R. Hoksbergen (1984), 'Current Thinking on the Role of Value Judgements in Economic Science. A Survey', *Research in the History of Economic Thought and Methodology*, vol. II, ed. W.J. Samuels, Greenwich, CO: JAI Press.

Positivism

There was a time in intellectual history when the word 'positivism' had a very positive connotation. Positivism was viewed as a fresh and liberating philosophical movement, one that revelled in the rationality of science and the power of logical analysis; it was heralded as the philosophical programme that would hand the dark forces of metaphysics and superstition their final defeat. This situation has changed drastically during the last half-century. Positivism is no longer the venerated philosophical position it once was; in fact, the term is now used almost exclusively in a pejorative way.

While the descent of positivism is certainly an interesting story (see Suppe, 1977, or Caldwell, 1994), it is not a story that can be told effectively within the confines of a brief handbook entry. The objective here is far more modest, the goal being simply to summarize the main tenets of the positivist programme and then briefly to discuss its impact on the methodological writings of economists.

There have been three separate but related 'schools' of positivist philosophy. The first was the nineteenth-century positivism of Auguste Comte and Ernst Mach; the second was the logical positivism of the Vienna Circle in the 1930s; the third was the logical empiricism (or 'Received View') that constituted the dominant framework within Anglo-American philosophy of science during the middle of the twentieth century. Of these three philosophical schools, it was the logical positivism of the Vienna Circle that was most systematic and most cohesive in its perspective; far more than the other two versions, it was the Vienna Circle that most clearly defined 'positivism' as a unique and influential philosophical position. We will focus primarily on the logical positivism of the Vienna Circle, but will also consider a few of the ways in which the logical empiricists deviated from this earlier programme.

The term 'logical positivism' was first used by Blumberg and Feigel (1931) to label the philosophical movement that emerged from Moritz Schlick's Thursday evening discussion groups in Vienna in the late 1920s. The main participants in the Vienna Circle were Rudolph Carnap, Herbert Feigel, Philipp Frank, Hans Hahn, Victor Kraft, Karl Menger, Otto Neurath and Hans Reichenbach, although many others ultimately came to be associated with the Circle's general perspective. Some, like Ludwig Wittgenstein, Bertrand Russell and A.J. Ayer, were associated with the philosophical programme of the Vienna Circle but did not have much direct contact with the seminar itself. The manifesto of the Vienna Circle was the pamphlet, 'The Scientific Conception of the World: The Vienna Circle' (*Wissenschaftliche Weltauffassung, Der Wiener*

Kreis); this pamphlet was written primarily by Hahn, Neurath and Carnap, and it was presented to Schlick in October of 1929 when he returned from a visiting position at Stanford.

The two most important aspects of Vienna Circle's philosophical programme are captured by the term 'logical positivism': logicism and positivism. The Vienna Circle philosophers actively sought to combine the logic of Frege and Russell with the classical empiricist/positivist epistemology of Hume, Comte and Mach. Earlier empiricists, particularly Mill, had tried to reduce even formal disciplines like mathematics and logic to empirical science; while the logical positivists also considered such purely formal disciplines to be knowledge, they were a different type of knowledge from empirical science. Mathematical and logical propositions were *analytic*; they were true in all possible worlds, and thus represented a type of *a priori* – not *a posteriori* or empirical – knowledge. According to the logical positivists, the only type of genuine *synthetic* knowledge was empirical science. Science, unlike mathematics, was factual and empirical; its propositions were true only under certain specific conditions. For the Vienna Circle, there were only two kinds of meaningful discourse: the synthetic factual truth of empirical science and the purely formal analytic truth of logic and mathematics. All other types of discourse, including idealistic philosophy, theology and ethics, were simply 'metaphysics' and thus 'meaningless'.

The logical positivist view of science and metaphysics was sustained by the so-called 'verifiability criterion of meaningfulness'. In order for a (non-analytic) statement to be meaningful, it needed to be, at least in principle, verifiable; that is, it was necessary that observational evidence could be described which, if true, would conclusively establish the truth of the statement. This criterion, defended by Carnap in the *Aufbau* (1928), was later weakened (by Carnap himself) to the criterion of mere 'confirmability' or 'testability' (a doctrine that was weakened still further by the later logical empiricists). Despite this weakening, the verifiability criterion of meaningfulness, like the dismissal of metaphysics, became a core identifying characteristic of the positivist programme.

One continuing controversy within the Vienna Circle was the so-called 'protocol sentence debate'. In the *Aufbau*, Carnap had defended a version of empiricist foundationalism. According to Carnap, empirical observations formed the incorrigible foundations of knowledge, and all theoretical knowledge was built up systematically from sentences about these empirical observations. The sentences which formed the foundation for science were expressed in a purely observational language: the protocol language. Since scientific theories were merely redescriptions of observable phenomena in the protocol language – every statement in a scientific theory could be translated back into the protocol language by means of correspondence rules – the protocol language was the linchpin of this foundationalist programme. In response to criticism by Otto Neurath, Karl Popper and others, Carnap ultimately revised his view of the protocol language and moved more toward Neurath's 'physicalist' (roughly describable in the language of physical science) notion of the empirical basis of science. Since the physicalist language was dependent on the current state of scientific knowledge, this change significantly undercut the empiricist foundationalism of Carnap's original programme. There were many different responses to this initial blurring of the distinction between the language of theory and the language of observation – it led Neurath to a version of naturalism and Popper to a conventionalist view of the empirical basis of science – but, more importantly, it opened the door to the problems of theory-ladenness and underdetermination that ultimately helped contribute to the breakdown of the positivist programme in the latter half of the twentieth century.

The logical empiricist programme of philosophers such as Richard Braithwaite, Carl Hempel and Ernest Nagel was a continuation and gradual evolution of the logical positivist programme of the Vienna Circle. Two significant changes introduced by the logical empiricists were the movement away from induction towards a hypothetico-deductive view of the relationship between theory and evidence, and the reintroduction of explanation as a legitimate goal of scientific activity.

The hypothetico-deductive approach to the relationship between scientific theories and empirical evidence was a change from the inductivism of the early Vienna Circle. Rather than scientific theories being built up inductively from (theory-neutral) protocol statements, logical empiricists argued that the relationship between scientific theories and the empirical evidence that supported them was deductive in nature. The first step in testing a scientific theory was to deduce certain empirical predictions from the theory and its initial conditions. The second step was to check these predictions against the observational evidence; if the empirical predictions turned out to be true, the theory was confirmed, and if these predictions turned out to be false, the theory was disconfirmed. In either case, it was not induction, but rather the deductive consequences of a scientific theory, that were relevant to its empirical support. There were many reasons for the change to the hypothetico-deductive method, but one of the most important was that it seemed to help circumvent the Humean problem of induction. The argument was that, since the hypothetico-deductive method allowed scientific theories to be 'based on' empirical observations (deductively) without actually being 'built up from' those observations (inductively), it protected the positivist view of scientific theories from the traditional problems associated with the justification of induction and ampliative inference. The degree to which the hypothetico-deductive method actually solves (or even helps avoid) the problem of induction remains an open question, but, regardless of how one views the success of the hypothetico-deductive method, it is clearly related to the second major contribution of the logical empiricist programme: the deductive–nomological (or D–N) model of *scientific explanation*.

Recall that, according to classical empiricism and early logical positivism, scientific theories do not really 'explain' at all; the scientific domain is the domain of empirical observation and the purpose of scientific theories is to describe reliably those empirical observations. The commonsense view of science that it 'explains' what we observe in the world by uncovering underlying, not directly observable, causal mechanisms is alien to the empiricist view of science: in 'science there are no "depths"; there is surface everywhere' (Carnap *et al.*, 1929: 8). Despite their empirical and descriptive focus, even the logical positivists agreed that science does in fact explain, and one of the most persuasive arguments for adopting the scientific view of the world is how much better science explains what we observe than the explanations that were offered by earlier philosophical and religious views. Providing a model of scientific explanation that was broadly consistent with an empiricist view of scientific theories was one of the greatest accomplishments of logical empiricism. Their solution was the D–N model, initially presented by Hempel and Oppenheim in 1948. There is not room here to discuss the D–N model in detail, but the central thesis is relatively easy to state. According to the D–N model a particular observed event (say entity x exhibiting property y) is 'explained' by subsuming the event under a general law (say x is an instance of z, and all zs exhibit property y). In a D–N explanation the phenomena to be explained (the explanandum) is deduced (the 'deductive' part of the D–N) from the explanans, the explanation of the phenomena, which is composed of initial conditions and at least one general law (the 'nomological' part of the D–N).

The D–N model was the subject of a protracted debate in the 1950s and 1960s, and it has been severely criticized from a number of different points of view. Despite these criticisms, no alternative view of scientific explanation has emerged with enough support to be considered 'the' replacement for the D–N model; it thus remains the standard, if severely criticized, view of explanation within the philosophy of science. As a final comment on logical empiricism, notice how easily the D–N model of explanation connects up with the hypothetico-deductive method: the D–N model makes the deductive form of scientific explanation exactly the same as the hypothetico-deductive relationship between scientific theories and empirical data. This leads to another logical empiricist notion, the so-called 'symmetry thesis', that explanation and prediction have the same form; explanations come after events, and predictions come before, but the basic deductive structure is the same (that is, 'testing' and 'explaining' are two sides of the same scientific coin).

It is common in the literature on economic methodology to give Terence Hutchison (1938) credit (or condemnation) for introducing positivist ideas into economics. While this standard reading has an element of truth, it detracts a little from the power and influence of positivist ideas. Positivism, in any of its incarnations, was not a 'method' to be 'applied' to economics in some simple mechanical way. Positivism is a general philosophical vision about science, knowledge and metaphysics, not a formula for sifting out good from bad theories. Positivism provided a philosophical backdrop for the scientific form of life in the same way that religion and spirituality have provided a philosophical backdrop for other cultural traditions. While the cultural form that positivism helped congeal may be under some stress at the end of the twentieth century, it was positivism that provided the core notions of the factual and the universal that have formed the scaffolding for modern intellectual life. In this sense, all of the major 'schools' of twentieth-century economic methodology – from Hutchison, to Friedman (1953), to Samuelson's operationalism, to Popperian falsificationism – have been positivist-inspired. There have been other philosophical visions at work in economics – hermeneutics and essentialism in Austrian economics, and pragmatism in American institutionalism, to name just two – but they have always been associated with minority positions within the discipline (see Seligman, 1969). The philosophical backdrop of mainstream economics has always been a positivist vision of science and knowledge. This is not to say that the relationship between positivism and mainstream economics is devoid of tension, or that no other philosophical programme could provide an alternative backdrop, only that the vision (if not the practice) was positivist in origin.

D. WADE HANDS

Bibliography
Ayer, A.J. (ed.) (1959), *Logical Positivism*, New York: Free Press.
Blumberg, Albert E. and Herbert Feigel (1931), 'Logical Positivism: A New Movement in European Philosophy', *The Journal of Philosophy*, **28**, 281–96.
Caldwell, Bruce J. (1994), *Beyond Positivism: Economic Methodology in the Twentieth Century*, 2nd edn, London: Routledge.
Carnap, Rudolf (1928), *Der Logische Aufbau der Welt*, Berlin: Weltkreis-Verlag (translated as *The Logical Structure of the World*, Berkeley: University of California Press, 1969).
Carnap, Rudolf, Hans Hahn and Otto Neurath (1929), 'The Scientific Conception of the World: The Vienna Circle; (*Wissenschaftliche Weltauffassung, Der Wiener Kreis*); reprinted, Dordrecht: D. Reidel, 1973.
Friedman, Milton (1953), 'The Methodology of Positive Economics', *Essays in Positive Economics*, Chicago: University of Chicago Press.
Hempel, Carl G. (1965), *Aspects of Scientific Explanation*, New York: Free Press.

Hempel, Carl G. and Paul Oppenheim (1948), 'Studies in the Logic of Explanation', *Philosophy of Science*, **15**, 135–75; reprinted (with postscript) in Hempel (1965), *Aspects of Scientific Explanation*.

Hutchison, Terence (1938), *The Significance and Basic Postulates of Economic Theory*, London: Macmillan; reprinted, New York: Augustus M. Kelly, 1960.

Nagel, Ernest (1961), *The Structure of Science: Problems in the Logic of Scientific Explanation*, New York: Harcourt, Brace & World.

Seligman, Ben B. (1969), 'The Impact of Positivism on Economic Thought', *History of Political Economy*, **1**, 256–78.

Suppe, Frederick (1977), *The Structure of Scientific Theories*, 2nd edn, Urbana, IL: University of Illinois Press.

Post Keynesianism

The following is an attempt to articulate the methodological principles underpinning Post Keynesian economics, recognizing that thinking on these matters is still evolving. This methodology has much in common with other forms of political economy, but takes on its distinctive character as a result of a particular understanding of the economic process, or 'vision'. Post Keynesian methodology entails a range of methods of analysis – formal models, institutional analysis, historical analysis, econometrics, interface with other disciplines and so on – but this diversity of method is determined by a unifying methodology, which in turn is determined by a unifying ontology and epistemology. It is still a matter for dispute as to where the limits should be drawn on the range of methods to be included in Post Keynesian economics (that is, whether to classify particular approaches, or collections of methods, as Post Keynesian or not). But the development of consciousness in Post Keynesian economics of ontology and epistemology, and thus debate on their implications, are relatively recent. It is reasonable to expect that, as this consciousness becomes more widespread and matures, a greater degree of agreement will emerge as to the general character and scope of Post Keynesian methodology.

Post Keynesian economics has been characterized widely as realist (see Dow, 1990; Arestis, 1992; Lavoie, 1992; Lawson, 1994). Critical realism (most fully articulated in Lawson, 1997) entails a particular view of science as having the goal of increasing understanding of the causal structures underlying real processes; this contrasts with the positivist view of science as identifying event regularities. Thus, for example, a realist would focus on the processes underlying price setting, rather than statistical regularities, in order to understand inflation. Social structures in turn, according to the critical realist perspective, evolve within a system which is understood to be both organic and open in the sense that not all influences can be identified ex ante. This organicism is seen as following Keynes (1973a), although there is some dispute in the literature about Keynes' organicism (see Carabelli, 1995, for an account, with reference to these disputes, of the continuity of organicism in Keynes' thought). While it is possible (and epistemologically necessary) to segment analysis by employing different theories to focus on different processes within the system, these processes in reality are intertwined in a complex way and are open to unpredictable influences. Because such an imperfectly predictable shifting structure cannot in practice be formalized in a unified model, the scope for prediction is limited to tendencies (as in 'there is a tendency for inflation to increase markedly, although this may be counteracted by other tendencies which require attention'); event prediction (like the quantitative prediction of the rate of inflation) is not in general justifiable.

Because social (and thus economic) structures are understood to be organic and open, and our understanding of these structures and the way in which they evolve and interrelate is fundamentally limited, few predictions may be made on the premise of a given structure. It follows that most knowledge is held with uncertainty. Given the epistemological limitations imposed by the human condition, choices must be made as to which partial forms of knowledge to pursue; uncertainty can be reduced (if not eliminated) by increased knowledge. (It may also be increased if knowledge reveals new areas of ignorance.) The mainstream choice of aiming to identify those elements of knowledge which can be captured within given structural relationships is legitimate, in that imperfect knowledge in itself entails an absence of absolute epistemological standards as to how best to acquire knowledge. But the Post Keynesian understanding of the overwhelmingly organic nature of the economic system implies that the mainstream choice is unduly limiting. Rather, Post Keynesian economics aims for a range of (imperfect) knowledge which is not limited to given structures and yet which increases understanding of underlying structures, even if it does not yield definitive predictions. (There are mainstream economists who also gather knowledge in this broader range, but for whom this is not a methodological imperative; these economists work in the grey area between Post Keynesian economics and mainstream economics.)

This broader range of enquiry as to the underlying causal processes in an open system opens up the scope for employing diverse methods. Diversity of method, indeed, is the inevitable outcome of an epistemology which focuses on grounds for rational belief when knowledge is imperfect. According to Keynes (1973a; 1973b), belief is arrived at by means of a logic which, unlike classical logic, is suitable for application to open systems. (This logic is variously termed 'ordinary logic', following Keynes, or 'human logic', following Ramsey.) This logic is rationally supported by the nature and amount of relevant evidence and, in the absence of complete evidence, by convention. Since theories are logical structures, it is clearly of importance whether the logic being employed is human or classical logic. There are several important consequences of choosing to employ human logic for theorizing.

1. A primary characteristic of an open system (of knowledge or an economy) is that not all influences are known; there is no requirement to ground all theory in one set of axioms; where knowledge is imperfect, it is impossible to assign absolute truth value to any set of propositions, but particularly to a set of propositions which represent human choice as being deterministic.
2. Different partial theories will in general have different starting points, in order to identify particular processes; some variables will be treated as exogenous to some theories, while it is the purpose of other theories to examine the processes generating these variables; the exogenous/endogenous distinction is thus particular to the analysis at hand and accordingly does not have the same force as in mainstream theory, where the distinction has general application.
3. Equilibrium is not an organizing principle within open theoretical systems; it is employed rather in its partial sense, and as the destination of a tendency; but an open-system logic is employed because of the understanding of the economic process as involving evolution of behaviour and institutions, as well as both creativity and crisis, all involving irreversibilities in historical time: equilibrium in its conventional mainstream sense of simultaneous resolution in mechanical time, is therefore irrelevant.
4. Different forms of knowledge may be incommensurate; thus it is inconceivable that all knowledge may be combined, for example, in a formal mathematical system; to limit knowledge to one form, such as formal mathematics, is unnecessarily restrictive; similarly,

empirical evidence can take a range of forms (data series, questionnaire evidence, interview evidence and so on) which may not be susceptible to commensurate quantifiable measures.

5. No method is necessarily excluded on methodological grounds; thus some partial theories may start from *a priori* assumptions; other theories may start from stylized facts; some partial theories may be expressed mathematically, while others are expressed verbally; all that is ruled out on epistemological grounds is the assertion that a theory is anything other than partial. Methods may be excluded on ontological grounds, in that they are not suited to gathering knowledge of reality according to a particular ontological vision. Thus Lawson (1989) for example, argues against the use of econometrics.

It is this last feature of Post Keynesian methodology which has led to most misunderstanding. Caldwell (1989) characterizes Post Keynesian methodology as 'eclectic', 'pluralist' and 'heterogeneous', by which he means the embracing of diversity without a grounding in principle. First, as has been argued here, the diversity of methods employed within Post Keynesian economics is a direct consequence of a distinct ontology and epistemology. It is not the consequence of the immaturity of the school, or an inability to agree on a single method, as Caldwell implies. Post Keynesian methodology is founded on the belief that employing a range of methods is the best way to build up knowledge of an organic economic system.

Further, while the range of methods is not restricted on methodological grounds, it is restricted by the shared vision of the economic process, that is, by the content of Post Keynesian ontology. Post Keynesians share with other political economists (like neo-Austrians and institutionalists) the goal of understanding underlying economic processes, where knowledge is in general uncertain (see Lawson, 1994). Thus there would be broad agreement on most of the five points listed above. Nevertheless, the particular Post Keynesian vision of the economic process distinguishes it from other forms of political economy, and circumscribes the range of methods to be employed.

First, Post Keynesianism steers a middle course, in its understanding of the economic process, between the notion of natural order implicit in mainstream ontology and the individual-centred ontology of neo-Austrian economics (see de Carvalho, 1992). The economic process is seen as ordered to a considerable degree (because of institutions and conventional behaviour, rather than successful market coordination). Yet there is always the potential for disorder due to revisions of expectations under uncertainty, but more generally because the norm is a state of flux; institutions and behaviour have evolved to cope with this norm. Thus the main phases of the business cycle can be analysed according to relationships between investment, income, financial conditions and so on whose tendencies can be predicted; yet the precise cause and timing of turning points cannot be predicted. Importance is thus attached to discrete breaks in stable relationships, as when the state of confidence collapses, or as a result of creative behaviour. This differentiates the Post Keynesian vision from the more steadily evolutionary vision of the institutionalists, which focuses more on the institutional adaptation which attempts to preserve stability. Post Keynesian theory is presented as being general, in the sense that it offers a general analysis of modern capitalist economies, but, as an open system of thought, it is not general in the sense of providing the basis for generalised predictions (of the form, high interest rates discourage investment); the onus is on the economist to study particular contexts to see whether the conventional institutional/behavioural assumptions are applicable.

Second, Post Keynesianism involves a focus on production rather than exchange, because exchange relations are seen as being determined largely by production conditions. As a consequence, there is a marked reluctance to employ conventional supply and demand analysis, because of the interdependence between demand and supply conditions. Imperfect competition is regarded as the norm in product and factor markets. Product and factor prices are thus often analysed in terms of mark-up models; in some models the mark-up is taken to be determined exogenously, while other forms of analysis explore the determination of mark-up. Behavioural analysis is employed to investigate particular firms and industries in depth.

Third, money is seen as integral to the economic process, rather than as a separable variable (although some partial analyses are conducted in real terms). Money's primary economic role is as a unit of account, particularly as the denominator of wages and of debts. This role has economic importance because of uncertainty, from which the holding of money provides refuge. Thus money plays an active role in the economic process, but it cannot by its nature be controlled by the central banks of advanced monetary economies. (This topic provides another example of context-specific analysis: the appropriate theory will differ for different historical periods and types of banking system.) Closely related to Post Keynesian monetary theory is a growing literature on the determination of expectations under uncertainty according to rational principles (where rationality takes on a particular meaning and analysis within an open system of thought). This literature in turn affects the analysis of investment behaviour, which is regarded as a key causal variable.

Fourth, there is a significant emphasis on investigating the nature, causes and consequences of income distribution, reflecting a shared value judgment as to the importance of the issue. This focus of Post Keynesian theory derives from its ontology, involving a vision of the economic process where distribution plays an important part. There is a related interest in the concept of power, which is apparent in the inflation theory which focuses on struggle over income share, and in the analysis of industrial organization and market behaviour. Income distribution issues are most commonly expressed in the context of growth theories, where the focus is on long-run tendencies.

The last two points are of importance for the question of demarcating Post Keynesian economics from other schools of thought. Within the literatures which might be classified as Post Keynesian, the analysis of money and expectations tends to be divorced from the analysis of income distribution and growth, the latter being associated with neo-Ricardianism. There has been a range of analyses which have demonstrated successfully that the two strands of thought need not be incompatible. What is suggested by the fifth epistemological principle outlined above is that the two strands can be acceptable as partial analyses; they only fall foul of the principle if it is maintained that either constitutes a theory which is complete in itself. To the extent that neo-Ricardianism is presented as an exclusive theory, therefore, it cannot be regarded as part of Post Keynesianism (as when analysis of money and expectations is excluded as antithetical, rather than as segmentable).

As with other schools of thought, the notion of what constitutes the methodology of Post Keynesian analysis has often been left implicit; articulation has often focused more on proscribing mainstream methodology rather than prescribing Post Keynesian methodology. This outline, therefore, cannot be treated as definitive; much still remains to be articulated, and many of the statements made here may be controversial. But greatest clarity will be achieved if future articulations start with ontological and epistemological principles, since these map out the territory within which Post Keynesianism can settle on its preferred methodology.

SHEILA C. DOW

References

Arestis, P. (1992), *The Post-Keynesian Approach to Economics*, Aldershot: Edward Elgar.
Caldwell, B.J. (1989), 'Post-Keynesian Methodology: An Assessment', *Review of Political Economy*, **1**, (1).
Carabelli, A. (1995), 'Uncertainty and Measurement in Keynes: Probability and Organicness', in S.C. Dow and J. Hillard (eds), *Keynes, Knowledge and Uncertainty*, Aldershot: Edward Elgar.
de Carvalho, F.J.C. (1992), *Mr Keynes and the Post Keynesians*, Aldershot: Edward Elgar.
Dow, S.C. (1990), 'Post Keynesianism as Political Economy: A Methodological Discussion', *Review of Political Economy*, **2**, (3).
Keynes, J.M. (1973a), *A Treatise on Probability, Collected Writings*, vol. VIII, London: Macmillan for the Royal Economic Society.
Keynes, J.M. (1973b), *The General Theory of Employment. The General Theory and After*, Part II: *Defence and Development, Collected Writings*, vol. XIV, London: Macmillan for the Royal Economic Society.
Lavoie, M. (1992), *Foundations of Post Keynesian Analysis*, Aldershot: Edward Elgar.
Lawson, T. (1989), 'Realism and Instrumentalism in the Development of Econometrics', *Oxford Economic Papers*, (new series), **1**, (1).
Lawson, T. (1994), 'The Nature of Post Keynesianism and its Links to other Traditions', *Journal of Post Keynesian Economics*, **16**, (4).
Lawson, T. (1997), *Economics and Reality*, London: Routledge.

Poststructuralism

If postmodernism is the practice, then poststructuralism is the theory. Whereas postmodernism has been used loosely and alternately to describe a historical period, a form of critique, a 'condition', styles of writing, art, architecture and much else, poststructuralism has been used usually to designate something more precise: a philosophically informed, theoretical movement encompassing the traditional humanities, social sciences and even the natural sciences 'after' or 'beyond' structuralism. The emergence of poststructuralism as a theoretical movement dates from the 1960s and is most closely associated with the work of (primarily French) writers and thinkers such as Michel Foucault, Jacques Derrida, Jacques Lacan, Louis Althusser, Julia Kristeva, Jean-François Lyotard and Hélène Cixous.

The unmooring of poststructuralism from structuralist thought and writing has always been difficult to locate and describe (that is, as a decisive 'break'). One sign of this difficulty has been the tendency to place Foucault, Lacan, Althusser, Derrida and others in both the structuralist and poststructuralist camps, as can be seen in such collections as DeGeorge and DeGeorge (1972), Macksey and Donato (1972), and Sturrock (1979). While it is possible to see a continuum between these intellectual movements, some general differences between them can be noted as well.

Structuralism has a long history in the social sciences and the humanities. There are many variants of it, but in the recent past, and for the structuralism within and against which post-structuralism arose, structuralism has been associated, alternatively, with the 'linguistic' or 'semiotic' turn in social theory and with the idea that socially constituted and determining 'structures' are a first and/or ultimate 'cause' of human events. On the former point, structuralism was closely linked to the efforts of Roland Barthes to lay bare the system of signs that makes cultural and textual meanings possible. Barthes' semiotics owed much to the prior work of the philosopher Charles S. Peirce, as well as to the linguists Ferdinand de Saussure and Roman Jakobson. Barthes and other structuralists began to extend the analysis of the basic structures of language, meaning and signification to encompass most if not all cultural and social practices and occurrences. In this way, reading the world as a text – unearthing the meanings made possible by the complex play of signs – became a primary goal of much structuralist thought. The emphasis on semiotics and structures of meaning was an important corrective to older humanist traditions, which emphasized the primacy of human subjectivity and intentionality in the determination of cognition and sense.

Another key part of the structuralist movement was the belief that underlying the seemingly chaotic world of social relationships were 'elementary structures' of culture, whose discovery, it was hoped, would make clear the fundamental causes and limits of social life. This strand of thought was developed most by Claude Lévi-Strauss and his followers, though important strains of this idea were also found in Marx, Freud and others. Marx and Freud, in particular, were read to have introduced models of deep structural causality in the sphere of socioeconomic events and the human psyche, respectively. From the historical determination of the mode of production 'in the last instance' to the dominance of the unconscious in structuring the conscious, psychic make-up of humans, structuralists interpreted Marx and Freud as the forerunners to, if not the founders of, the structuralist movement. Again, a major aspect of structuralism, which would carry over into poststructuralism, was the refusal of human agency and free will as the wellspring of social relationships. Human subjectivity was shown, by structuralists, to be more of an effect than a primary cause of social practice. History, institutions, the mode of production, culture, structures of meaning, the unconscious and so forth were all promoted as likely candidates for the primary structural cause of social life.

The general spread of structuralist modes of thought in the 1960s affected economics, though it did so in combination with already well established quasi-structuralist traditions. As Amariglio *et al.* (1990) have argued, economists, particularly those working within Keynesian, Post Keynesian, institutionalist, radical and Marxist frameworks, had already paid close attention to the idea that institutions, social psychological structures, culture and the macroeconomy were the key determinants of economic events and behaviour. The critique of neoclassical thought and its pervasive 'humanism', in which the rational, intentional choices of economic agents are thought to provide the impetus for all consequent economic arrangements, was a defining feature of these different schools, as structural forms of determination were introduced to replace the rational subject at every level of analysis. The structuralism of the 1960s was especially important, not only for reinforcing these tendencies, but also for encouraging the rapid expansion of such subfields as economic development as well as whole schools of thought, such as radical political economy. Less important for economics was the linguistic turn, whose effects were delayed until the emergence of poststructuralism.

Poststructuralism grew up in the midst of the structuralist revolution of the 1960s, and its main practitioners were engaged in arguments that were set off largely by structuralism. Yet, despite the continuity in some of the positions, poststructuralism developed in the 1960s and thereafter as a modification of structuralism, at best, and, in most instances, as a critique of the same. While some of the defining themes of poststructuralism were introduced by structuralism, they soon took on a valence and direction that marked more of a break than a continuation.

The following are among the more familiar themes of poststructuralism and are listed in no particular order:

- a critique of 'scientism' in terms of the assertion of the fundamental discursivity of scientific thought, and a debunking of the notion of a singular scientific method;
- a rejection of post-Enlightenment 'classical epistemologies' (especially empiricism and rationalism) and a preference for anti-foundationalist, sometimes 'relativist', approaches to questions of knowledge as well as an appreciation of the plurality of knowledges;

- an emphasis on the fundamental 'undecidability' and uncertainty of meaning, and a celebration of notions of linguistic/discursive 'play' in all forms of textuality (which now includes 'the world');
- a refusal of 'teleology', by which was meant all notions of history and development that imply progression, regression or any particular trajectory known in advance of 'conjunctural' analysis; discontinuity, ruptures and specificity are preferred to general theories of historical movement;
- a strong anti-humanism, culminating in the rejection of all notions of subjectivity in which the existence of a universal and unified human 'I' is presumed, and its replacement with the notion of a 'decentred' subject;
- a critique of essentialism, the idea that things and beings have an essential nature, character or structure that pervades their entire historical existence and that can be 'discovered' by analytic investigation;
- a deep suspicion of 'totalizing' practices and 'master narratives' – that is, stories and social movements that tend to universalize, eternalize and generally bring under their explanatory or activist wing any and every event – and an opposite preference for particularity, microanalysis and politics, fragmentation and so forth;
- a rejection of determinism – particularly those forms of determinism that privilege, by specifying as an underlying 'cause', the mode of production, the economy, culture or any other social entity – and the substitution of other notions of multidirectional causation (or absence of causation altogether), such as the idea of 'overdetermination';
- the critique of 'representation', particularly the idea that images, words, discourses and so on 'represent', rather than partly construct, the entities that are presumed to lie underneath their surface or to which they refer, unable to find expression other than through a ventriloquism.

If there is an overarching motif linking together these different themes, it is the critique of what has been called 'modernism'. Though modernism has been understood differently by numerous contributors to poststructuralism (see Amariglio, 1990; McCloskey, 1985, for two economists' views on some of the central characteristics of modernism), what is held generally in common is a criticism, if not an opposition, to the dominant modes of thought and social organization operative at least in the west since the Enlightenment. In this way, poststructuralism – as a critique and a 'going beyond' of modernism – is often conflated with postmodernism.

If structuralism was appreciative of the contributions of Marx and Freud, poststructuralism has been more ambivalent about their legacies. Since, in some views, Marx and Freud are perhaps pre-eminent modernists (in their respective forms of determinism, essentialism, scientism, totalizing thought and much else), they have not been spared sharp critical analysis and even dismissal. While some theorists influential in the development of poststructuralism have been able to press Marx and Freud into service (Althusser, for example, borrows Freud's notion of 'overdetermination' to make the Marxian notion of dialectical causality resonate well with the poststructuralist critiques of essentialism and determinism – see Resnick and Wolff, 1987, for a discussion of this notion), for others, Friedrich Nietzsche's philosophical œuvre and his thoroughgoing perspectivism, his rejection of western epistemologies and moralities, and his appreciation of the pervasiveness of power in the determination of knowledge, including science, have been more of a guiding inspiration than either Marx or Freud (this is largely true, for example, of Foucault, Derrida, Lyotard and others). Nietzsche and Martin Heidegger, perhaps above others, have been cited as the principal forerunners of much poststructuralist thought, though attempts to cast more widely about for the sources of poststructuralism have tapped the writings of Ludwig Wittgenstein, John Dewey and other non-positivist philosophers and thinkers (see Rorty, 1979, for an appreciation of Wittgenstein and Dewey as originators of the poststructuralist critique of modernist epistemologies, especially as their work relates to the notion of scientific method and the creation of scientific knowledge).

Poststructuralism has been vastly influential since its dispersed beginnings out of structuralism. It has spanned many different fields of thought and has intersected with some of the most important intellectual trends and social movements since the 1960s. In particular, poststructuralism has been interwoven, at times, with feminism, multiculturalism, pluralism, queer theory and activism, post-colonial studies and revivals of Marxism. Poststructuralism has both gained ground within and has been added to by feminist (see Weedon, 1987), Marxist and other criticisms of the tyranny of scientific knowledge and the separation of the normative from the 'positive', of the purportedly dominant 'male, white, western' concept of subjectivity, of the naturalism and universalism of western thought and forms of socioeconomic organization, many of which are believed to spawn oppression and domination of women, minorities, non-westerners and other peoples, and much else.

Poststructuralism's entry into economic thought and method took place mostly in the late 1970s and early 1980s, as economics lagged behind many other disciplines, certainly in the social sciences, in receiving and considering the writings of Foucault, Althusser, Derrida, Lyotard and others (this is why economics is barely mentioned in Rosenau, 1992). Yet economics has been fertile ground for elaborating some of the key themes of poststructuralism, as it has added weight and new perspectives to existing attempts to provide economic theory with non-positivist philosophical foundations, non-neoclassical notions of rationality and agency, non-progressivist notions of the growth of economic knowledge over historical time, and so on and so forth. Though some elements of poststructuralist thought have perhaps found their way into the conscious awareness – if not the work – of those who make up the 'mainstream' of the profession, the predominant influence of poststructuralism to date has been in and on 'heterodox' approaches to economic theory, particularly those that have been critical of neoclassicism (though there are clearly exceptions to this). Likewise, poststructuralism has had more of an effect on such fields as economic methodology, history of economic thought, economic history and economic development (for one example of the latter, see Corbridge, 1990), fields whose main preoccupations are with the philosophical and methodological aspects of economic discourse, or whose primary focus has been on the historical process of modernization.

While it is difficult to place the exact time and date of poststructuralism's arrival in economics, it is possible to trace several different developments that have been extremely influential in the spread of poststructuralism. For most economists, poststructuralist thought, or at least some of its main themes, was first encountered in the emergence of the 'rhetoric of economic' approach pioneered by McCloskey (1985) and Klamer (Klamer *et al.*, 1988). McCloskey was among the first to identify the crisis in economic philosophy as the prevalence of 'modernism' and in particular the positivist view that economic discourse was (or should be) simply a 'mirror' of economic reality. McCloskey, Klamer, and others (such as Strassmann, 1993; Weintraub, 1988) borrowed from Rorty – if not the other poststructuralists – the view that scientific discourse is rhetorical, that is, structured by language and linguistic conventions that determine any discourse's sense and meaning and that give it its persuasiveness. Thus the superiority of one school or another in economic theory, argued the rhetoricians of economics, depended, not on its approximate closeness to a non-discursive, objective truth, discovered only by the 'correct' scientific method, but rather on its rhetorical force and flourish (three excellent collections reflecting the influence of the rhetoric approach and consequent developments in the literary analysis of economic discourse are Klamer *et al.*, 1988; Samuels, 1990; Henderson *et al.*, 1993).

The renewed interest in the fundamental discursivity of economic thought directed several economists to the writings of poststructuralists in addition to Rorty, especially Foucault, Derrida, Althusser and Lyotard (for an overview of some poststructuralist theories of discourse, see Macdonell, 1986). Part of this move can be attributed to the more developed literary analysis of some of these thinkers, as Derrida, in particular, had set off in the fields of literary and cultural theory a revolution in the reading of texts through his notion of 'deconstruction'. (A useful summary of the relationship between poststructuralism broadly defined and the particular significance of deconstruction is Norris, 1985.) In economics, Rossetti (1990), Amariglio (1990) and Ruccio (1991), among others, have employed the idea of deconstruction to show the necessarily contextual and discursive nature of economic knowledge as well as to uncover the instabilities, incoherences and undecidables implicit in a variety of economic discourses. Another motive for the move to Foucault and others has been the concern to highlight the play of power and authority in determining the content of an economic discourse and its reception in the profession. Thus, for Strassmann (1993), Milberg (1991), Milberg and Pietrykowski (1994), Amariglio *et al.* (1990), Samuels (1990) and others, the rhetoric of economics has needed to be supplemented with other poststructuralist writings to show the ways in which power and ideology have helped to organize the relations of dominance and subordination of economic discourses within the economics profession.

Another major source for the spread of poststructuralist thought in economics has been the post-Althusserian project in Marxian theory developed by Resnick and Wolff (1987) and many of their cohorts, such as Ruccio (1991), Callari (1985) and Garnett (1995). Before McCloskey's 1983 article on the rhetoric of economics in the *Journal of Economic Literature*, Resnick and Wolff had been rethinking Marxian economic theory along lines heavily influenced by Althusser, Foucault and other poststructuralists. Among the primary (postmodern) concerns of Resnick and Wolff and their colleagues have been specifying a distinctly Marxian (and non-empiricist or non-rationalist) theory of knowledge and a theory of causation for Marxian economics that avoids the problems of economic determinism and essentialism. As early as the mid-1970s, Resnick and Wolff had put forward a critique of scientific epistemologies heavily indebted to Althusser and other poststructuralists that anticipated much of the anti-scientism of McCloskey, Klamer and others, though Resnick and Wolff did not advance a primary interest in the literary/rhetorical construction of economic discourses. Recent work by Garnett (1995) on the discursive construction of Marxian theories of value and by Amariglio and Ruccio (forthcoming) on the notions of economy that proliferate in cultural and literary circles, for example, blend together these two strands of converging poststructuralist thought.

Some of the earliest work in economics that reflected a familiarity with poststructuralism was in the history of economic thought. There, as with Tribe's pathbreaking book (1978), Callari (1985), Brown (1993), Screpanti (1994) and others, poststructuralism's critique of teleological modes of historical presentation – in which only 'truth' survives and knowledge progresses – and its attack on the 'canonization' of 'great books' in the history of economic thought were brought to bear on traditional methods of the field. Borrowing not only from Thomas Kuhn's work on the revolutions in the history of scientific thought, but also from Foucault's 'archaeologies of knowledge', Gaston Bachelard's philosophy of science and other post-positivist philosophers of science, Tribe and the others called attention to the ruptures and discontinuities that have characterized the history of economics, as well as to the continuing battle among and between different economic discourses. The persistence of difference and struggle in economic discourse over time, in this typical poststructuralist view, is less a sign of the failure of the discipline to apply rigorous standards of economic proof in vanquishing one or another economic discourse than of the existence of mostly incommensurable (or at least alternative) notions of epistemology, truth, verification, method and so on, that constitute these discourses. The history of economic thought, then, is one that can best be viewed, not as the story of a battlefield where the false and erroneous have (or should have) fallen, but rather as a terrain of perhaps irreducible plurality (see Brown, 1993, for a description of this vision) where, only occasionally, differences are traversed and ruptures healed.

Poststructuralist notions of the 'decentred' or at least socially constituted and plural subject have also shown up in recent economic writing, largely in heterodox, non-neoclassical schools. Rational economic subjects and their preferences have long been the focus of anti-neoclassical critiques. What is new, perhaps, is the poststructuralist view (evinced, to different degrees and for different economic theories, in Hargreaves Heap, 1993; Amariglio, 1990; Burczak, 1994; Levin, 1995) that subjects (economic or otherwise) can be thought of as always fragmented, fundamentally uncertain, unstable, constituted by multiple and often conflicting narratives and without a central form of consciousness, desire, and/or cognition. The importance of this idea of subjectivity for contemporary economic theory is perhaps best seen in Mehta (1993), who, borrowing from Derrida, uses what she terms 'the deconstruction of univocal notions of meaning and subjectivity' to see how competing and discontinuous narratives give rise to multiple equilibria in bargaining game theoretic situations.

JACK AMARIGLIO

References

Amariglio, J. (1990), 'Economics as a Postmodern Discourse', in W. Samuels (ed.), *Economics as Discourse*, Boston: Kluwer Academic.

Amariglio, J. and D. Ruccio (forthcoming), 'Literary/Cultural "Economies", Economic Discourse and the Question of Marxism', in M. Woodmansee and M. Osteen (eds), *New Economic Criticism*, London: Routledge.

Amariglio, J., S. Resnick and R. Wolff (1990), 'Division and Difference in the "Discipline" of Economics', *Critical Inquiry*, **17**, (1), 108–37.

Brown, V. (1993), 'Decanonizing Discourses: Textual Analysis and the History of Economic Thought', in W. Henderson, T. Dudley-Evans and R. Backhouse (eds), *Economics and Language*, London: Routledge.

Burczak, T. (1994), 'The Postmodern Moments of F.A. Hayek's Economics', *Economics and Philosophy*, **10**, 31–58.

Callari, A. (1985), 'History, Epistemology and the Labor Theory of Value', in P. Zarembka (ed.), *Research in Political Economy*, vol. 9, Greenwich, CT: JAI Press.

Corbridge, S. (1990), 'Post-Marxism and Development Studies: Beyond the Impasse', *World Development*, **18**, (5), 623–39.

DeGeorge, R. and F. DeGeorge (eds) (1972), *The Structuralists: From Marx to Lévi-Strauss*, Garden City, New York: Anchor Books

Garnett, R. (1995), 'Marx's Value Theory: Modern or Postmodern?', *Rethinking Marxism*, **8**, (4), 40–60.

Hargreaves Heap, S. (1993), 'Post-Modernity and New Conceptions of Rationality in Economics', in B. Gerrard (ed.), *The Economics of Rationality*, London: Routledge.

Henderson, T., T. Dudley-Evans and R. Backhouse (eds) (1993), *Economics and Language*, London: Routledge.

Klamer, A., D. McCloskey and R. Solow (eds) (1988), *The Consequences of Economic Rhetoric*, Cambridge: Cambridge University Press.

Levin, L. (1995), 'Toward a Feminist, Post-Keynesian Theory of Investment', in E. Kuiper and J. Sap (eds), *Out of the Margin: Feminist Perspectives on Economics*, London: Routledge.

Macdonell, D. (1986), *Theories of Discourse: An Introduction*, Oxford: Basil Blackwell.

Macksey, R. and E. Donato (eds) (1972), *The Structuralist Controversy*, Baltimore: Johns Hopkins Press.

McCloskey, D. (1985), *The Rhetoric of Economics*, Madison: University of Wisconsin Press.
Mehta. J. (1993), 'Meaning in the Context of Bargaining Games – Narratives in Opposition', in W. Henderson, T. Dudley-Evans and R. Backhouse (eds), *Economics and Language*, London: Routledge.
Milberg. W. (1991), 'Marxism, Poststructuralism and the Discourse of Economists', *Rethinking Marxism*, **4**, (2): 93–104.
Milberg, W and B. Pietrykowski (1994), 'Objectivism, Relativism and the Importance of Rhetoric for Marxist Economics', *Review of Radical Political Economics*, **26**, (1), 85–109.
Norris, C. (1985), *The Contest of Faculties: Philosophy and Theory After Deconstruction*, London: Methuen.
Resnick, S. and R. Wolff (1987), *Knowledge and Class*, Chicago: University of Chicago Press.
Rorty, R. (1979), *Philosophy and the Mirror of Nature*, Princeton: Princeton University Press.
Rosenau, P.M. (1992), *Post-Modernism and the Social Sciences*, Princeton: Princeton University Press.
Rossetti, J. (1990), 'Deconstructing Robert Lucas', in W. Samuels (ed.), *Economics as Discourse*, Boston: Kluwer Academic.
Ruccio, D. (1991), 'Postmodernism and Economics', *Journal of Post Keynesian Economics*, **13**, (4), 495–510.
Samuels. W. (ed.) (1990), *Economics as Discourse: An Analysis of the Language of Economics*, Boston: Kluwer Academic.
Screpanti, E. (1994), 'Epistemic Relativism, the Postmodern Turn in Economic Philosophy, and the History of Economic Thought', *History of Economic Ideas*, **2**, 173–205.
Strassmann. D. (1993), 'Not a Free Market: The Rhetoric of Disciplinary Authority in Economics', in M. Ferber and J. Nelson (eds), *Beyond Economic Man*, Chicago: University of Chicago Press.
Sturrock, J. (ed.) (1979), *Structuralism and Since: From Lévi-Strauss to Derrida*, Oxford: Oxford University Press.
Tribe, K. (1978), *Land, Labour and Economic Discourse*, London: Routledge & Kegan Paul.
Weedon, C. (1987), *Feminist Practice and Poststructuralist Theory*, Oxford: Basil Blackwell.
Weintraub, E.R. (1988), 'On the Brittleness of the Orange Equilibrium', in A. Klamer, D. McCloskey and R. Solow (eds), *The Consequences of Economic Rhetoric*, Cambridge: Cambridge University Press.

Poznan Approach, The

The Poznan approach came to the English-speaking world via a paper by Nowak (1971). (The standard reference is now Nowak, 1980.) Related thoughts had been published by another Polish philosopher, Krajewski, whose classical reference now is Krajewski (1977). The approach is a method for describing the logical skeletons of theories based upon a view of the nature of scientific laws as *idealizations*. Scientific theories claim that scientific laws hold, albeit in worlds that nobody believes exist in reality. Canonic examples of counterfactual presuppositions for laws are complete absence of friction (in the law of falling bodies) and infinitely divisible commodities (in the law of demand). For a law q, the statement 'if p then q' ($p \rightarrow q$) is trivially true if it is commonly believed that the presupposition p is false, as is seen from case 3 of the truth table below.

	p	q	$p \rightarrow q$
1	true	true	true
2	true	false	false
3	false	true	true
4	false	false	true

The method of idealization and concretization consists of tracing the complete list $p_1, ..., p_k$ of idealizational presuppositions of the law q. The *initial* logical form of the law is (',' is to be read as 'and'):

$$(T_0)\, p_1, ..., p_k \rightarrow q$$

T_0 is called an *idealizational statement*, and $p_1, \ldots, p_k$ are called *ideal conditions* for the law q. Typically, scientists set out to drop the ideal conditions one by one, in each step modifying the law. Dropping p_1 thus leads to T_1:

$$(T_1) \qquad p_2, \ldots p_k \rightarrow m_1(q)$$

where $m_1(q)$ is a 'concretized' version of the law called the first modification of q. Scientists tend to make attempts to iterate this process. The successive steps can be written:

$$(T_2) \qquad p_3, \ldots, p_k \rightarrow m_2(q)$$
$$(T_3) \qquad p_4, \ldots, p_k \rightarrow m_3(q)$$
$$(\ldots)$$
$$(T_{k-1}) \qquad p_k \rightarrow m_{k-1}(q)$$
$$(T_k) \qquad m_k(q)$$

The version T_0 is called the *essential* version of the law. The kth modification of the law $m_k(q)$ would be a 'completely concrete' or 'phenomenal' version. Thus all conditionals with false antecedents turn out to differ in that some do and some do not give rise to sequences of conditionals whose antecedents contain fewer and fewer falsities as a result of which the conditionals become more and more realistic. The scientific ideal of reaching this phenomenal version is not considered to be realizable, but it could be approximated to some more or less satisfactory degree, measurable by plausible logical standards.

The structure of a scientific theory is given by a sequence of models Mk, Mk–1, ..., Mi, AMi, where Mk is the most abstract model equipped with k idealizing conditions, Mk–1 ... Mi being its subsequent concretizations; finally, AMi is an approximation of the least abstract of these models Mi to the empirical reality.

The order of the ideal conditions $p_1, \ldots, p_k$, determining the *agenda* of concretization, reflects the order of importance that the factors dealt with in these ideal conditions have in the theory the scientist is working at. This order is called the *essential structure* of the theory. In many cases the essential structure is only a partial ordering. Marx, for instance, in Volume III of *Capital*, describes six transformations, as follows (where '⇒' refers to a transformation from one concept to another:

$$\text{ival}(x) \Rightarrow \text{mval}(x) \Rightarrow \text{pri}_3(x)$$
$$\text{mval}(x) \Rightarrow \text{pri}_4(x) \qquad \text{pri}_3(x) \Rightarrow \text{pri}_4(x)$$
$$\text{mval}(x) \Rightarrow \text{pri}_5(x) \qquad \text{pri}_3(x) \Rightarrow \text{pri}_5(x)$$
$$\text{mval}(x) \Rightarrow \text{pri}_6(x) \qquad \text{pri}_3(x) \Rightarrow \text{pri}_6(x)$$
$$\text{mval}(x) \Rightarrow \text{pri}_7(x) \qquad \text{pri}_3(x) \Rightarrow \text{pri}_7(x)$$

The individual value of good x, ival(x), is obtained by taking into account only the 'most essential' force determining value: individual labour time. For market value, mval(x), the individual labour time of the other workers come in as a second force. For production price $\text{pri}_3(x)$, deviation from average capital intensity of the industry x comes in as a third force. But then pri_4, pri_5, pri_6 and pri_7 introduce deviations caused by non-average amounts of remaining fixed capital, merchant capital, differential land rent and absolute land rent, respectively. The modifications

pri_4, pri_5, pri_6, pri_7 could have been introduced in different order. Their effect is analysed relating to mval and pri_3, but not cumulatively, as was done with the sequence ival $\rightarrow$ mval $\rightarrow$ pri_3. Nowak (1980: 97) calls factor sets like those introduced with pri_4, pri_5, pri_6, pri_7 *equiessential*.

Nowak started out to employ and illustrate his method by reconstructing most of the transformations of the law of value in volume III of Marx's *Capital*, a particularly suitable example since Marx is, by economists' standards, exceptionally explicit and systematic in making his steps towards concretization of this law (Nowak, 1980: 3–38; for a complete reconstruction, see Hamminga, 1990). Once Nowak's method of reconstruction had become known among philosophers of science, it was applied to a great number of theories, not only in economics (Hamminga and De Marchi, 1994) but also successfully in the natural sciences. For a highly effective and illuminative example in physics, see Kuipers (1985). The method of idealization and concretization itself has been elaborated, expanded and made more realistic, dealing with concepts like *ceteris paribus* (Patryas, 1975; 1982), proto-idealizing (Brzezinski, 1985), stabilizing (Zielinska, 1981) and aggregating (Lastowski, 1988).

There is a remarkable analogy between the Poznan approach and the analysis of theoretical economics in terms of so called 'propositions of economic theory' (PET; see 'Plausibility' in the present volume), where the dropping and weakening of conditions for a theorem is motivated by the desire to argue in favour of the theorem's plausibility. The main difference is that in the PET approach the theorems are held to be proved from the conditions, whereas in the Poznan approach the law q is non-mathematically claimed to hold under the conditions. The difference is made most clear by imagining that somewhere a world could be found in which all ideal conditions would be satisfied. In the Poznan approach, the economist is assumed to be highly interested in seeing whether or not in this world the law q would hold. She would regard such observations as tests of her theory. In the PET approach, the PET is believed for mathematical reasons, which renders any alleged falsity of the theorem in that world an uninteresting error in the proper application of the concepts of the theory. Kuipers (1992) shows in what sense and to what extent both approaches are functional for refined truth approximation.

BERT HAMMINGA

Bibliography

Brzezinski, J. (1985), 'The protoidealizational model of the investigative process in psychology', in J. Brzezinski (ed.), *Consciousness: Psychological and Methodological Approaches*, Poznan Studies in the Philosophy of the Sciences and the Humanities, 8, Amsterdam: Rodopi.

Hamminga, B. (1989), 'Sneed versus Nowak: An Illustration in Economics', in W. Balzer, and B. Hamminga (eds), *Erkenntnis*, **30**, (1–2).

Hamminga, B. (1990), 'The Structure of Six Transformations in Marx's Capital', *Poznan Studies in the Philosophy of Science and the Humanities*, **16**, 89–111.

Hamminga, B. and N.B. de Marchi (eds) (1994), *Idealization IV: Idealization in Economics*, Amsterdam/Atlanta: Rodopi.

Krajewski, W. (1977), *Correspondence Principle and the Growth of Science*, Episteme 4, Dordrecht: Reidel.

Kuipers, T.A.F. (1985), 'The Paradigm of Concretization: the Law of van der Waals', in J. Brzezinski (ed.), *Consciousness: Psychological and Methodological Approaches*, Poznan Studies in the Philosophy of the Sciences and the Humanities, 8, Amsterdam: Rodopi.

Kuipers, T.A.F. (1992), 'Naive and Refined Truth Approximation', *Synthèse*, **93**, 299–341.

Lastowski, K. (1990), 'On Multi-level Scientific Theories', in J. Brzezinski, Fr. Coniglione, T.A.F. Kuipers and L. Nowak (eds), *Idealization II: Forms and Applications*, Poznan Studies in the Philosophy of the Sciences and the Humanities, **17**, Amsterdam: Rodopi.

Nowak, L. (1971), 'The problem of Explanation in Marx's Capital', *Quality and Quantity*, **V**, (1).

Nowak, L. (1980), *The Structure of Idealization*, Synthèse Library vol. 139, Dordrecht: Reidel.

Patryas, W. (1975), *An analysis of the caeteris paribus clause*, Poznan Studies in the Philosophy of the Sciences and the Humanities, 1, Amsterdam: Rodopi.

Patryas, W. (1982), 'The pluralistic approach to empirical testing and the special forms of experiment', in W. Krajewski (ed.), *Polish Essays in the Philosophy of the Natural Sciences*, Boston Studies in the Philosophy of Science, 68, Dordrecht: Reidel.
Zielinska, R. (1981), *Abstrakcja, Idealizacja, Vogolnienie* (Abstraction, Idealization and Generalization), Poznan: Poznan University Press.

Probability

Randomness is the epitome of the ineffable, and probability can be defined as the theory of the causes and consequences of the random. Definitions are treacherous in the realm of the random, however, since the very meaning of probability has been the subject of persistent unabated controversy. It has been suggested, following Carnap, that there are two intepretations of probability theory, one epistemic and the other ontological or 'objective'. While this is the division which seems to obsess most philosophers, it would not do for producing a taxonomy of the way the wider community of mathematicians, scientists and statisticians have proposed approaching the phenomenon of randomness. To that end, we will describe five major approaches to the theory of probability, which are (in rough chronological order of their appearance): classical, frequentist, logicist, subjectivist/personalist and complexity theories. Other, lesser approaches, such as Popper's propensity theory or the non-standard epistemic approach, are described in Howson (1995).

The origins of probability theory are conventionally dated from the Pascal/Fermat correspondence of 1654, which itself is a historical conundrum, since games of chance date back to antiquity. The earliest theory, which we will call *classical*, was focused more on equity than on chance, and more on expectation than on probability per se, primarily because it was derived from legal doctrines concerning the fair dissolution of partnerships. Its central tenet, the *principle of indifference*, states that all possible events should be assigned equal probabilities unless there is some reason to think otherwise. The rules of additivity of probabilities of mutually exclusive events and the multiplication rule for independence came built into this principle, and thus most of the rules of conventional discrete probability theory were worked out from this modest basis by the eighteenth century. In retrospect, philosophers regard the indifference principle as a flawed expression of epistemic ignorance, because true ignorance could potentially lead to any partition of the event state space and therefore would not restrict the numerical attribution of probabilities one whit. These and other objections led to the breakdown of classical probability theory and its widespread abandonment by about 1840.

The conception of probability which displaced the classical doctrine is known as the *frequentist* approach, often associated with the names Cournot and Venn, and formalized by Richard von Mises in the early twentieth century. Ian Hacking has argued that the frequentist conception was inspired by the establishment of national statistical bureaux in the decades after 1820. In this theory, probability is defined as the limit of a relative frequency of a subset of events to an infinite series of realizations of the relevant event population; these probability statements attribute an empirical property to the population (or in Misean terms, the *Kollectiv*), which is asserted to be a real property of its physical make-up. It is interesting to note that von Mises himself insisted that the frequentist conception was not applicable to the moral sciences, owing to the absence of events meeting the conditions of a *Kollectiv*, something conveniently forgotten by subsequent generations of frequentist economic theorists and econometricians. While the frequentist approach clearly wore its empiricist credentials on its sleeve, that very same commitment has proved to be its downfall; there are almost no modern probability theorists who are ardent adherents of the frequentist doctrine. The problem, put bluntly, is that 'No relative frequency probability statement, strictly speaking, says anything about any finite event, group of events or series' (Weatherford, 1982: 170). In other words, any calculated frequency is perfectly consistent with any probability attribution from zero to one. Combined with the injunction that there is no such thing as a probability of a 'singular' event, it would appear that definitive empirical attribution of numerical probabilities is a chimera; this sorry state persists even though most introductory statistics courses are taught in a frequentist idiom. Attempts, such as that of Popper, to rescue the spirit of frequentist probabilities have not been generally regarded as successful.

The next innovation in probability theory is widely credited to John Maynard Keynes, and is called the *logicist* approach. Here probability is regarded as a logical relationship between propositions, and not a property of things or events. Under the inspiration of Russell and Whitehead, a probability statement was defined as a logical connective between sentences given some specific evidence; yet a distinctive hallmark of the approach was to treat some classes of probabilities as having a certain *a priori* character. In Keynes' own version, individual probabilities would be two-valued (a numerical attribution accompanied by a measure of 'weight'), but in many instances, he suggested, would not be numerical at all. Since this structure did not conform to the conventional Kolmogorov axioms (defined below), it has been neglected in practice in most empirical and statistical implementations. Nevertheless, it did warrant favourable comment by Carnap, Jeffreys and others, and has been the subject of an extensive commentary in the literature of economic methodology by such authors as Anna Carabelli, Brad Bateman, Allin Cottrell and John Davis.

Perhaps the version of probability most popular amongst modern statisticians and philosophers is the *subjectivist* theory, which we will subdivide into utilitarian and personalist variants. The progenitor of the utilitarian school was Frank Ramsey, who developed his theory in explicit reaction to Keynes, while the innovator of the personalist variant was Bruno de Finetti. What these variants share is a conviction that probability statements can be reduced to idiosyncratic degrees of belief on the part of some individual, but that these ephemeral convictions are rendered operational or interpersonally measurable by means of some imposed consistency condition. Where they tend to diverge is in how the individual psychological states are to be conceptualized, and the specific means by which consistency is presumed to be imposed. For the utilitarian such as Leonard Savage, it is the 'laws of preference' which are primitive, and the 'laws of probability' which are derivative. For personalists like de Finetti, on the other hand, putative psychological regularities are not the source of the structure, but rather the algebraic structure of money provides the interpersonal basis, and the 'no Dutch book' condition imposes consistency. The salience of the Dutch book condition, which states that people will avoid sequences of bets which result in monetary loss with probability one, is a source of intense controversy in the subjectivist school, and is covered in Earman (1992) and Weatherford (1982). While subjectivists are often referred to as 'Bayesians', the use of Bayes' rule for inductive inference is neither a necessary nor a sufficient condition for belief in subjectivist probability.

The fifth and most recent school of probability theory, associated with the names of Kolmogorov and Chaitin, is the *complexity* school. It reveals the clear impact of information theory, recursive function theory and computational mathematics upon the continuing quest to extract the definition of probability from all subjective considerations. Here randomness is associated with the degree of the incompressibility of a string in some well-defined computational procedure. Complexity is generally defined as the length of a computer program (in 'bits') required to reproduce a given character string (also in bits), where the computer is itself taken to be an ideal Turing machine. If the string is so 'disordered' that the length of the computational description approaches the length of the string, the string is deemed 'random'. While the complexity approach has generated a lot of enthusiasm amongst scientists, it must be observed that, unlike the other four theories, it has yet to produce a consensus procedure on such a fundamental task as producing an algorithm for the attribution of numerical probabilities in specific cases.

From a purely mathematical point of view, most textbooks would assert that basic probability theory was successfully formalized and axiomatized by Andrei Kolmogorov in his *Grundbegriffe* of 1933 (von Plato, 1994: ch. 7). The conventional Kolmogorov axioms state:

$$P(\Omega) = 1, 0 \le P(X) \le 1, P(X \cup Y) = P(X) + P(Y)$$

if X, Y are independent. It is often suggested by non-philosophers that philosophical disputes over the meaning of probability are largely irrelevant, since all schools accept the Kolmogorov axioms as their foundation. As we have seen, this is not necessarily the case for the logicist and complexity schools and, indeed, some of the most interesting innovations in probability theory today do not treat probability as well-defined in the manner of the earlier Kolmogorov tradition. Moreover, Kolmogorov himself innovated the complexity approach in 1963 owing to some dissatisfaction with the empirical drawbacks associated with the earlier measure-theoretic formulation. Given these historical observations, the only safe generalization is that the concept of probability, so important to the prosecution of various natural and social sciences, itself still remains shrouded in obscurity. This should give pause to those economic theorists and econometricians who rest contented in the belief that economists have taken the 'probabilistic revolution' to heart.

PHILIP MIROWSKI

References
Earman, John (1992), *Bayes or Bust*, Cambridge: MIT Press.
Fine, Terrence (1973), *Theories of Probability*, New York: Academic Press.
Howson, Colin (1995), 'Theories of Probability', *British Journal for the Philosophy of Science*, **46**, 1–32.
von Plato, Jan (1994), *Creating Modern Probability*, Cambridge: Cambridge University Press.
Weatherford, Roy (1982), *Philosophical Foundations of Probability Theory*, London: Routledge & Kegan Paul.

Psychology and Economics

If psychology is the science that seeks to explain human behaviour, and economics is the science that deals with behaviour in the market-place or in the processes of allocating scarce resources (the two leading definitions of the subject), a literal-minded person might conclude that economics is a branch of psychology and would be quite astonished at how little communication there is between the two fields. The explanation for this separation lies in the vastly different views that are held in psychology and economics, respectively, about how human behaviour is best studied and described.

Neoclassical economics, which is today the mainstream (and sometimes almost the only stream) of economic theory, starts with strongly held and largely *a priori* notions about human economic behaviour, and explores these notions using methodologies that are quite different from the experimental methods used in psychology. Neoclassical economics assumes that people, at least in their market behaviour (and in the view of some economists, in all their behaviour), evaluate all choices by the utilities they expect to obtain from their outcomes and always choose the alternative that maximizes their expected utility. The utility function represents a consistent system of preferences, so that *C* will never be preferred to *A* if *A* is preferred to *B* and *B* to *C*. Economists then proceed to explore the logical consequences of this assumption theoretically, usually employing highly formal deductive methods and abstract mathematical models.

In the purest form of the theory, no additional constraints are placed on the content of the utility function beyond the consistency of choice and the transitivity of preferences. People may choose perdition, as long as that is what they prefer and provided that they do so consistently. In this form, the theory is quite weak, not permitting many predictions to be made about concrete situations, for it does not predict what people will value. In actual application of economic choice theory, however, much stronger assumptions are made: in most cases, it is assumed that what people are trying to maximize is their wealth, and business firms their profit or net worth. Moreover, until quite recent times, little account was taken of limits on the knowledge people might have about the consequences of their actions (including knowledge of the relevant future) or of limits on their ability to make sophisticated calculations of their economic advantage. This approach has produced a hypothetical picture of economic behaviour: how would the perfectly rational person behave – the person who consistently sought to maximize his or her utility and who had the knowledge and computational power to determine what actions would serve that end? This says almost nothing about the actual mechanisms of choice.

The neoclassical theory leaves little room for empirical tests of its assumptions, and in fact such tests have not played a major role in empirical work in economics. Instead, the great bulk of systematic empirical work has consisted in econometric studies that estimate the parameters of the theory when it is applied to specific situations (for example, how much the rate of interest will decline when the supply of capital is increased by some amount). Standard econometric methods introduce unobserved error terms into the models in just sufficient quantity for the equations to be able to be fitted unambiguously to the data (so-called 'just-identified' equation systems); but by the same token, the data then cannot refute the rational model represented by the equations. At best, the percentage of the variance in the data that is accounted for by the fitted equations can be reported and this percentage can be taken as a 'goodness of fit' measure.

Econometric studies also deal mostly with highly aggregated data, often totals of economic measures for a whole nation or a major area within it. Separate measures are also often available for separate industries, and less often for individual companies. The data are generally very coarse-grained and approximate, and usually reported only on an annual, or at best quarterly or monthly, basis. (Stock market prices and exchange rates are the chief exceptions.) Economists generally rely on publicly reported data, and are seldom in a position, except in the case of sampling polls that they conduct, to shape the quantities measured to the concepts of their theories. And finally, econometric studies are correlational studies of time series lacking the controls that enable the experimental sciences to distinguish causation from mere correlation reliably and to discover the mechanisms that underlie observed phenomena.

Not surprisingly, the application of this methodology, even on a large scale, has not severely tested, much less refuted, the assumptions of perfect rationality described above. Consequently, the choice of theories in economics (for example, the theories used in debates about national economic policies) is not much influenced by economic data. Attacks on the validity of a theory consist mainly of showing on logical grounds that it departs in some way from the assumption of perfect rationality. For example, Keynesian theory has been repeatedly criticized because it assumes that labour is (irrationally) more sensitive to money wages than to the real value of wages, and that rates of investment may be governed more by 'animal spirits' (Keynes' term) than by accurate prediction of the future (as in theories of rational expectations) and sophisticated calculation of the profitability of alternative choices. The empirical evidence either supporting or refuting either of these assumptions is very weak.

In recent years, this picture has been somewhat altered by a growing interest in what is usually called 'behavioural economics'. Behavioural economics is not so much a specific body of economic theory as a critique of neoclassical economic theory and methodology. First, it argues that the model of the perfectly rational decision maker is unacceptable, especially in view of extensive empirical evidence that human choice behaviour does not have the consistency predicted by the theory, and that human rationality is severely bounded by limits on knowledge and computational ability. Most of the empirical evidence that challenges the rationality assumptions has been gathered by researchers outside economics (such as Kahneman and Tversky in psychology) or on the fringes of economics (for example, Cyert, March and Simon in the study of organizations). Kahnemann and Tversky used standard experimental methods to show that people do not make consistent choices. For example, significantly fewer subjects opted for medical treatment when told that the chances of death from an operation were 30 per cent than when told that the chances of success were 70 per cent. Cyert, March and Simon, in developing a behavioural theory of the firm, made detailed field studies of the actual processes used by business firms in reaching important decisions and demonstrated how far these processes departed from those derived from the theory in terms of the numbers of alternatives examined, the kinds of computations that were carried out and the arguments that were advanced for the different alternatives.

At an even more specific level, the behavioural critique points out that cognitive psychology has produced, since World War II, a large and empirically tested body of theory about the way human beings actually go about solving problems and making decisions. This psychological research shows consistently that human decision makers, except in the simplest situations, do not attempt to optimize, but search for satisfactory alternatives: that is, alternatives that meet the decision makers' aspirations. Satisficing typically reduces by many orders of magnitude the amount of knowledge needed for making decisions and the complexity of the computations required. The search among alternatives is neither exhaustive nor random, but is highly selective, guided by rules of thumb, or heuristics. Moreover, these psychological theories show how such processes can lead to the discovery or design of new alternatives as well as choice among existing alternatives, adding an important new dimension to economic theory.

Psychological research has also shown the centrality of recognition processes, based principally on accumulation in memory of past experience, in experts' 'intuitive' handling of the situations that recur in their daily work. This body of research and the theory built from it show that decision processes cannot be understood without a great deal of empirical data about what the human actors know, what strategies they use in solving problems and what calculations they make. The available psychological models of problem solving and decision making could provide valuable components for models of economic decision making.

Within economics itself, the past decade has seen a rapid growth of another kind of empirical work: the use of experiments to study the operation of markets. Neoclassical theory predicts that, where competition prevails, a market will reach equilibrium at a price at which the quantity of a commodity supplied will equal the quantity demanded. There is considerable empirical evidence that markets do tend to equilibrate under many circumstances, and this observation has sometimes been taken as confirmation of the assumptions of perfect rationality of the market participants. With the growth of experimental economics (as the new methodology is called), the predictions that competitive markets will gradually approach equilibrium have most often been confirmed, but it has been found that equilibrium is often reached rapidly even when the economic actors are not acting with perfect rationality or anything approximating it. The most convincing demonstration of this has been obtained from simulated markets in which the agents are computer programs that make their decisions on the basis of very primitive rules that depart widely from the criterion of profit maximization and perfect knowledge.

If experimental economics continues to grow in popularity, if the critique that behavioural economics has made of neoclassical theory is attended to and if psychological theories of decision making are applied to economic questions, the ties between economics and psychology are bound to grow much closer than they have been in the past. At the most general level, the behavioural critique points out that the strong predictions of economic models do not derive from the rationality assumptions, but from a host of auxiliary assumptions about the institutional structures that surround particular kinds of decisions, and the kinds of knowledge and calculating capabilities the actors in these situations possess. These auxiliary assumptions (and the central rationality assumptions as well) need to be tested empirically, and not simply posited, as is a common practice now. Experimental economics and experimental psychology are the sources from which the needed empirical evidence can come.

The successes of experimental economics over the past decade or two have alerted increasing numbers of economists to this new (to economics) tool of empirical research, and substantial numbers of graduate students in economics are now being exposed to experimental methods as a part of their training in research. In economics graduate training there is still little attention to methods of studying behaviour in the field (for example, inside business firms) or to applying experimental techniques to phenomena other than markets. Perhaps the contrast in graduate training in the two fields gives us the sharpest picture of the relation between psychology and economics today. In psychology, the emphasis is upon the knowledge that has been gained from experiments, and upon the skills of planning and carrying out experiments. Theory is taught, of course, but always in close contact with the evidence that supports or limits it. In economics, the emphasis is upon the analysis of situations in terms of neoclassical theory, the mathematical formalisms that are required to carry out such analysis rigorously and econometric methods for estimating economic parameters from time series of a relatively aggregated sort.

The future prospect for productive relations between the two disciplines is bound up very closely with the debate between neoclassical economics and the behavioural approach. As increasing numbers of young economists become disillusioned about the power of formalized, deductive neoclassical theory to explain economic phenomena in the real world and to inform policy (there are many indications of this happening) and as increasing numbers of them are exposed to experimental methods and their products, we may expect the distance between the disciplines to shrink. Such a development would be further accelerated if economists became more closely aware of the tested positive theories of decision making that cognitive psychology now provides.

HERBERT A. SIMON

Bibliography
Baxter, J.L. (1993), *Behavioural Foundations of Economics*, London: Macmillan.
Cyert, R.M. and J.G. March (1963), *A Behavioral Theory of the Firm*, Englewood Cliffs, NJ: Prentice-Hall.
Hogarth. R.M. and M.W. Reder (1986), *Rational Choice: The contrast between economics and psychology*, Chicago: University of Chicago Press.
Kahneman, D. and A. Tversky (1973), 'On the psychology of prediction', *Psychological Review*, **80**, (4), July.
Simon, H.A. (1979), 'Rational decision making in business organizations', *American Economic Review*, **69**, (4), September.
Smith, V.L. (1991), *Papers in Experimental Economics*, New York: Cambridge University Press.
Thaler, R.H. (1991), *Quasi-rational Economics*, New York: Russell Sage Foundation.

Public Choice

Public choice is radically different from traditional political science. Essentially, it is the application of economic methods to politics. The difference in subject matter has meant that there are differences, in method even if these are not as striking as one might expect.

The theory of public choice, although it clearly resembles that in economics is far from identical. In a real sense, economics can be taken as advice to a public-spirited government as to what should be done. Public choice raises questions about whether the government is really public-spirited. This is not to allege that it is composed of wicked people, only that they are much like the rest of us. Like most of the rest of us they take a certain number of public spirited or charitable actions, but primarily they are interested in themselves. These are, of course, the same assumptions we make in economics, but economists do not normally directly apply them to government.

This self-interest is characteristic of politicians, bureaucrats and, most importantly, the voters. The question then arises as to what the point of public choice is. Improving the structure of government has the intriguing characteristic that there does not seem to be anybody who will be strongly motivated to do it. The government itself is more likely to be motivated to try to increase its rents than to improve its structure.

The bureaucrats' special interest groups and, for that matter, the voters are apt to be interested in their own special payoffs for the present. However, they all have, if they worry about their descendants, motives to improve the government. It is unlikely that a farmer who is interested in continuing to receive the special protections now granted would feel confident that his grandchildren would be benefited if they continued. Thus he might well be interested in abolishing them, say, 50 years from now.

There may have been such future motivation in the minds of the people who drew up the US constitution, but there are also some examples of special interests of the individual founding fathers: the provision added at the last moment increasing the number of representatives in the first Congress was apparently intended to guarantee that certain people at the convention would be elected to Congress.

A more likely way of limiting special privileges is to arrange things so that each individual, although losing his own privileges, gains even more through abolishing other privileges. On some occasions, this has worked. Further research in this area is obviously highly important and highly difficult. The methodological problem is one which we rarely have in economics. Normally in economics we look for matters which will benefit comparatively small groups of people. Trades in which people are injured along one dimension and benefited along another in a purely political context are virtually ignored in economics. This is particularly so of trades of the sort which involve a great many people who, although they act independently, must be counted and aggregated to have political effect. They must be considered in the new public choice area. Indeed, the whole subspeciality of constitutional economics deals primarily with this problem.

A great many people raise doubts about whether government personnel are really just like the rest of us. There is an immense literature, including an immense economic literature, which assumes that, if they know what is the right thing to do, they will do it. Many people think this is so and are deeply shocked when it is suggested that government civil servants, shall we say, are more interested in their careers than in the public interest. Of course, that is not to say that they are totally uninterested in the public interest. A good deal of statistical work in public choice, then, has been devoted to demonstrating that government officials are just as likely to be maximizing their own interests as anyone else. For example, the Forest Service is or was thought to be largely concerned with protecting the forests. Careful studies of its history seem to indicate that it is more interested in protecting the Forest Service budget than in protecting the forests; it engages in destructive cutting when the budget of the Forest Service will benefit.

All this requires, not only empirical work, but serious theoretical work. Economics has rarely dealt with conflict situations which are found all over public choice. Fortunately, it turns out that extending economic theory to conflict situations is not by any means impossible, although it is quite difficult. In both economics and public choice, the bulk of the work is what has been called 'normal science': in other words, a series of small steps forward. Every now and then we have very major steps, not necessarily Kuhn's scientific revolution, but big steps. The creation of public choice was an example, and work on rent seeking is another, but we cannot require that methodology guarantee such big steps forward. It is not generally possible to plan such things. What we do is to take the many small steps, and every now and then somebody will be inspired to take a big step.

The actual statistical methods used to test these things are once again not greatly different from those used in economics, but the public choice people have an additional advantage here. Since roughly the 1920s, political scientists have been using statistical tools to analyse various aspects of the voting process. Their statistical methods were originally quite bad, although some people, such as Key, were able to produce very good work in spite of the poverty of the available statistical methods. In recent years their statistics have been every bit as good as those of the economists, and in some areas better. Traditional political scientists examine rather different problems than do economists. In a way, their concern is what we might call the sociology of the voting process. William Riker used to give a lecture in which he accused political scientists of demonstrating that a Polish car worker, a member of the UAW and a resident of Detroit was likely to vote Democratic.

Basically, the difference between traditional political science in its modern statistical sense and public choice is the difference in the theory. Public choice scholars have the possibility of doing somewhat different types of statistical research than the ordinary economist, but this is not a revolutionary difference. In essence, there are a whole series of areas where public choice scholars have better data. For example, the number of people in each precinct in the state of Arizona who voted for Democratic congressmen in the last election is known. It is very rare that we have such detailed knowledge about customers in the market.

As a result, public choice scholars can engage in some types of research that cannot be done in economics. Of course, the fact that there is nothing equivalent to a price here means that economists can do research that political scientists cannot do. The public choice scholar can use both techniques and both bodies of data to advantage. When it comes to congressional or legislative votes, the problem is much more complicated, although the fact that the votes are quite frequently recorded does give public choice a statistical advantage. The problem is that the congressmen make trades with each other and these trades are not announced. Many of these gigantic long bills are approved in total by almost no congressmen, but the individual congressman has enough favourable provisions in it for him to be willing to take those that he does not favour.

Even if there is a separate vote on an amendment which deals only with a narrow issue, congressmen who actually oppose the amendment may vote for it because they have been promised something else in return. Since these bargains are not recorded anywhere, this means that the data on the congressmen's votes are not as helpful as one could hope, although information can and has been drawn out of them by people using statistical techniques and a very good intuitive knowledge of congressional activities. Here you have information of a type not available to the pure economist, but where use of the information requires that the individual be very sophisticated in his view of political process and have detailed knowledge about 535 rather devious people. Short of sneaking microphones into the committee rooms, there does not seem to be any perfect solution to this problem.

It is mainly in the theoretical development that public choice differs most from ordinary economics. It is different because, as a rule of thumb, individual decisions in political areas are, relatively, of little importance. Outcomes are determined by collective decisions of, more often than not, a majority. The majority is an aggregate of a large number of individual decisions, but the individual by himself has little weight. The rule as to what particular aggregate will get its way, that is, the specific voting procedure, is of great importance and is studied by public choice people with great intensity. Is the rule majority, reinforced majority or the 43 per cent which elected President Clinton in 1992?

For a considerable period of time, work here was paralysed by the mathematics of Kenneth Arrow which appeared to have demonstrated that all voting methods are subject to such severe paradoxes that the outcome really is not worthy of much respect. The present view would probably be that, although his proofs are mathematically impeccable, the actual empirical importance of the problem is quite small.

All told, then, the methodological problems in public choice are similar to those in economics, but different enough for considerable separate thought and separate study to be necessary to master them. It is true that public choice grew largely out of economics, although from the very beginning there were prominent political scientists involved. The first chairman of what became the Public Choice Society was a prominent political scientist. Public choice very definitely has a life of its own, but it is clearly related quite closely to economics and its methodology.

GORDON TULLOCK

References

Arrow, K.J. (1951), *Social Choice and Individual Values*, New York: John Wiley & Sons, rev. ed. 1963.
Buchanan, James M. and Tullock, G. (1975), 'Polluters' profits and political response: direct controls versus taxes', *American Economic Review*, March **65**, 139–47.
Niskanen, W.A. Jr. (1971), *Bureaucracy and Representative Government*, Chicago: Aldine-Atherton.
Tullock, G. (1983), *The Economics of Income Distribution*, Boston: Kluwer, rev. ed. 1997.
Mueller, Dennis (1997), *Perspectives on Public Choice*, Cambridge: Cambridge University Press.

Rational Choice

Most explanations and prescriptions in economics turn, at least in part, on an understanding of the origins of individual action. Since one way of understanding action is to construe it as 'rational', this puts models of rational action at the centre of economics. The best known of these models embodies an instrumental conception of reason. Individuals on this account have certain objectives (like the satisfaction of preferences or desires or 'passions') that motivate them to act and it is the calculating capacity of instrumental reason which tells them which action will best serve those aims. This hypothesis will probably be most familiar in the economic textbook form, where the degree of preferences satisfaction is often captured by a 'utility' function and agents are deemed rational because they choose actions to maximize 'utility' (that is, to satisfy best their preferences). Indeed, the model is sometimes referred to as the 'economic' theory of rational action, although it is more often called, somewhat misleadingly since there are other models, '*the* rational choice' model of action.

There can be no doubting the influence of the instrumental, maximizing model of action in economics and in the other social sciences. Nevertheless, the model is also the source of methodological controversy. The basic source of controversy is ontological and concerns whether this is really what reason and action consist of, and it gets very sharply focused when the model is allied with the commitment to methodological individualism to form the claim that all social life can or should be understood through the prism of individual preferences, beliefs and calculative rational actions based upon them. We will turn to the sharp version of this ontological controversy after a couple of brief comments. First, it may be sensible to say something about the modern axiomatic treatment of decision making and its relation to instrumental reasoning. The axiomatic approach associates rationality with choices that satisfy certain conditions (the so-called axioms). For instance one of these conditions/axioms of rational action is 'transitivity'. This requires that, if A is preferred to B and B is preferred to C, then A should be preferred to C. Other axioms require 'completeness' (that is, with any pair of actions, you can always say either which is preferred to the other or that you are indifferent between them); and so on (see 'Axiomatization' and 'Expected Utility Theory' in this volume).

The connection between these axioms and the instrumental hypothesis regarding rational action may not be immediately obvious. But first impressions can be deceptive. For example, it is easily shown that choices satisfying these axioms can he represented 'as if' they came from a process of maximizing a utility function (or expected utility in the more general case of choice under uncertainty. Of course, this result only establishes that one can, if one likes (and see 'Folk Psychology' for support on this), think of behaviour that is rational in the axiomatic sense using the instrumental language of preference satisfaction. However, the connection is even deeper. To appreciate this, consider what sense of rationality might underpin the axiom of transitivity.

One line on this question comes from noticing that *in*transitive choices can lead to poverty. Start, say, from a position where you hold A and have the following intransitive preferences regarding A, B and C: A is preferred to B, B to C and C to A. You would pay something to exchange the initial A for C (as C is preferred to A); with C, you will pay something to make an exchange with B (as B is preferred to C); and with B you will pay something to exchange with A (as A is preferred to B). Thus, at each stage of a cycle, which takes you back to holding A, you pay! Furthermore, if you continue to act on these intransitive preferences, the cycle can be repeated again and again, until you become impecunious. Since you cannot satisfy any preferences without some resources, it seems that someone who is concerned to satisfy preferences (that is, act instrumentally) must avoid intransitive choices. Thus an obvious sense of rationality which seems to be at play in support of the axiom of transitivity is the instrumental one.

Second, while the broad philosophical origins of this model are in Hume, who famously cast reason in the low position as the 'slave of the passions', it would be wrong to think of the maximizing model as embodying entirely the Humean view of agency. For example, Hume also makes much of the influence of custom on behaviour. Likewise, it is sometimes argued that a strictly Humean account of action actually allows for intransitive choices (see Sugden, 1991). Indeed, the move from acting on 'passions' to transitive choices appears to rely on an ability to compare passions which owes more to Bentham than Hume (see Hollis and Sugden, 1993).

At first glance, the instrumental model may not seem a very promising or rich motivational hypothesis for explaining the variety of social life. It seems to turn us into mere calculating machines and it is tempting to think that our behaviour is often more complicated and more noble than this model will allow. However, it is important to appreciate the strengths of the model. It can allow, for instance, for behaviour which is morally motivated, provided, of course, the morals are consequentialist, since actions here are to be judged by their outcomes. Indeed, the great strength of the hypothesis is that it says nothing about the origin or nature of our objectives. They can be altruistic as easily as they can be selfish, bad or plain boring. And the applications of the model are legion. From consumer theory where individuals maximize utility to produce demand curves, through the analysis of government policy which is motivated by the desire for re-election, to so-called rational choice or 'analytic' Marxism, the model has provided a host of insights. Furthermore, the model can generate surprisingly complex types of behaviour. It is not simply offering the banal explanation that someone did something because 'they wanted to do it'. In fact, although the objectives supply the motivation, the instrumental calculation of how to achieve it is often very tricky and it can produce surprisingly nuanced forms of behaviour. Two illustrations will make this clear.

The first relates to games (that is, settings where individuals knowingly interact with each other). When such games are repeated they can produce a distinctive sort of strategic behaviour where the individual acts in a way that conflicts with his short-term interest so as to generate a change in the beliefs of the other agent which secures benefits in the long run. An example is the monopolist who fights an entry in one market, even though it is more costly than agreeing to share the market, because this fuels a reputation for bellicosity which deters potential entrants in other markets. The second (sometimes referred to as 'self-command': see Schelling, 1984) is illustrated by the tale of Ulysses and the Sirens. Ulysses' instruction to his men (to tie him to the mast, to plug their ears and chart a course past the Sirens) was not immediately beneficial to Ulysses since it involved some discomfort, but it enabled him to listen later to the wonderful Siren voices without being drawn onto the rocks.

Nevertheless, it is difficult to believe that all social life can be adequately explained using this model; and yet this is the claim which comes from the alliance between this model and the commitment to methodological individualism (see 'Methodological Individualism/ Atomism'). To see how doubts might arise over such a claim, consider the difficulties associated with calculating many optimizing decisions. How can an individual calculate, say, what is the profit-maximizing investment when so much of the future affecting the viability of any investment project is shrouded in uncertainty (see 'Uncertainty')? Who for instance could have predicted an event like the collapse of the Berlin Wall? Yet this event dramatically altered some key interest and exchange rates which enter into many investment decisions. Or how does an individual really find out whether a Jaguar will better satisfy his or her preferences than a Honda? Such reflections feed the argument from Keynesian and other economists that it is impossible for instrumental reason to go to work when there is genuine uncertainty. There is simply not the information (or the brain does not have the calculating capacity, in Simon's (1982), version of a similar point, see 'Bounded Rationality') to enable the calculation of what to do for the best.

This is a brief introduction to one line of argument (see Hargreaves Heap, 1989, for a fuller discussion) which has echoes in contemporary game theory. Here there are growing doubts over whether common knowledge of instrumental rationality justifies the use of the Nash (and related perfect equilibrium) solution concept (see 'Game Theory'). Since this solution concept is used to narrow down the 'rational' courses of action in games, these doubts over its appropriateness serve to recreate at the heart of game theory the Keynesian problem of uncertainty over what are instrumentally rational actions. Indeed, even when these problems are set on one side, there remains significant uncertainty over what instrumental rationality entails in games that have multiple Nash equilibria (and these are especially common in games that are repeated) because the Nash refinement project has signally failed to develop well accepted principles for selecting between Nash equilibria (see Kreps, 1990).

To see this difficulty more concretely, consider the case where two motorists, travelling on different roads, are approaching the same intersection. What is the best action for an instrumental driver to take? Plausibly, it is best to slow down if the other speeds up and to speed up if the other slows down (since this avoids, respectively, a crash or an unnecessary delay). So it becomes crucial to form an expectation regarding what the other person will do. But here is the rub, because the other person is faced by exactly the same predicament. He or she will speed up or slow down according to what he or she thinks the first driver will do. So the action of each depends on their expectation of the other. Thus to answer the question of what we should expect, we find we must answer an equivalent awkward question on behalf of the other person, and so the problem does not disappear: it merely bounces back and forth between the two agents.

There are various possible responses to this problem and they illustrate some of the lines of the ontological debate over rational choice. One broad approach conjectures that people rely on rules of thumb in such conditions of uncertainty. When shared, these rules become the norms or conventions, which are more often thought to guide individual behaviour in sociology and anthropology. Thus there might be a norm or convention in the society which instructs the motorists in our example to 'give way to the right' and when each person at our intersection is guided by this norm, it solves the problem of expectations and action.

This move is unlikely to cause deep philosophical problems for the full-blown Humean, who has always acknowledged the powerful influence of custom and convention on human action. However, it may trouble the methodological individualist (and the typical mainstream economist) who aims to understand *all* important aspects of social life through individual intentions and instrumental calculation. The worry is simply that, while the presence of a convention may serve instrumental calculation and so be explained with reference to instrumental rationality, there are typically many conventions which could fit this bill. In our example of traffic at the interjection, why 'give way to the right' rather than 'give way to the left'? Once either is established as a norm, it pays an instrumental agent to follow it and, since it is not obvious that one will coordinate better than the other, it is difficult to see how instrumental considerations can explain why one norm is established rather than the other.

This may not seem a major explanatory shortcoming since in our example nothing much would appear to turn on the precise character of the convention (that is, whether to 'give way to the right' or 'give way to the left'). But in the 'crossroads of life' it is not hard to imagine conventions that might operate and which would have a powerful influence over the way the gains from coordination are distributed across the population. For instance, the operation of 'give way to men' rather 'give way to women' or 'give way to the old' rather than 'give way to the young' could affect significantly the character of a society and so it would become important to understand how a particular norm has been established.

The presence of norms will prove even more troubling to methodological individualism if they are given a Wittgensteinian spin. Here the following of rules is more akin to a new form of rational action because the rules can supply their own reasons for action. To be specific, the Wittgensteinian understanding of rules makes them not only regulative (serving as mere guides to actions which are motivated by antecedent preferences, as they are for Hume), but also constitutive of action (that is, they supply motives for action, just as the rules of chess supply reasons for moving a knight across the board which are separate from any plausible antecedent urge to shift bits of sculpted wood around a chequered board). Thus, under this interpretation of rule following, there is not just something unexplained with reference to individual intentions to worry the methodological individualist (the precise nature of the norm); there is the individual intentions themselves which have become worryingly dependent on rules which are social in origin.

While the introduction of something more than the individual *qua* individual is the basis of the first approach to the problem of indeterminacy or uncertainty, the second noteworthy line of attack builds changes directly into the model of the rational individual. The clearest philosophical warrant for this is Kant, but it is not a lead which economics, or indeed any of the social sciences, has been quick or enthusiastic to follow (see Hollis, 1987). Instead, in so far as economists have pursued this line, they have tended to rely on the quasi-mysterious/creative powers of the 'entrepreneur' and the skills of entrepreneurship to fill the gaps in the instrumental account of rational action (also see Hargreaves Heap, 1989, on expressive rationality).

This is only a quick sketch of what is an emerging ontological debate in economics over what constitutes rational action. It has been complemented in recent years by a vigorous experimental investigation of individual choice. So far, these experiments have concentrated on testing the instrumental model under conditions where the uncertainty is given by a well-defined probability distribution over outcomes. They reveal, beginning with the famous Allais paradox, a variety of systematic violations of expected utility theory (see Machina, 1987).

The ontological debate and the supporting experimental evidence are clearly important for any assessment of the explanatory power of the instrumental model. What is perhaps less obvious, or less well appreciated, is that the debate also matters for prescriptive statements in economics. The point is simple, but its precise form will depend on one's understanding of the relation between explanation and prescription. On one reading of this relation 'how things are' sets constraints on what can be prescribed (that is, one's prescriptions must 'work with the grain of human nature'). Accordingly the point is simply that the use of the instrumental model for making prescriptive statements is likely to be unreliable in so far as there are doubts over how well the model captures what actually makes people tick.

Alternatively, prescriptive statements can be regarded as applying with equal force to our own behaviour. So the instrumental model tells us how we ought to be and the fact that we may not behave like that now does not undermine the quality of that prescriptive advice. The problem for the instrumental model on this reading is that it often appears to offer no advice in situations where there is genuine uncertainty (as, for example, in the case of the motorists at the intersection). Thus the doubts over the capacity of the instrumental model to explain how people act resurfaces as worries over the ability of this model to offer concrete advice on how to behave in these settings.

SHAUN HARGREAVES HEAP

References

Hargreaves Heap, Shaun (1989), *Rationality in Economics*, Oxford: Basil Blackwell.
Hollis, Martin (1987), *The Cunning of Reason*, Cambridge: Cambridge University Press.
Hollis, Martin and Robert Sugden (1993), 'Rationality in action', *Mind*, **102**, 1–33.
Kreps, David (1990), *Game Theory and Economic Modeling*, New York: Oxford University Press.
Machina, Mark (1987), 'Choice under uncertainty: problems solved and unsolved', *Journal of Economic Perspectives*, **1**, 121–54.
Schelling, Thomas (1984), 'Self command in practice, in policy and in a theory of rational choice', *American Economic Review*, **74**, 1–11.
Simon, Herbert (1982), *Models of Bounded Rationality*, Cambridge, MA: MIT Press.
Sugden, Robert (1991), 'Rational choice: a survey of contributions from economics and philosophy', *Economic Journal*, **101**, 751–85.

Realism

When an economist talks about the 'realism of assumptions', he is not using the term 'realism' in any of its standard philosophical senses. Another difficulty that plagues the term is that it has a variety of legitimate philosophical meanings that are interrelated but do not reduce to each other. 'Realism' is used as the name for a variety of doctrines about things such as science, sense perception, universals, other minds, the past, mathematical objects, truth, moral values, possibilities and so on. This is expressed in the fact that the opponents of realists on these issues are not called uniformly by a single label. Depending on the issue at hand, the non-realists are said to subscribe to positions such as idealism, phenomenalism, empiricism, nominalism, conventionalism, instrumentalism, operationism, fictionalism, relativism and constructivism. This variety is also the reason why no shorthand definition – and no single non-disjunctive definition, whether short or long – of the term 'realism' can be provided. The following considers ontological, semantic and epistemological formulations of realism without pretending to be exhaustive.

As an *ontological* doctrine, realism has the general form of the statement, '*X* exists', or '*X*s are real'. '*X*' is a variable which may acquire different specifications. For each specification there corresponds a version of ontological realism. The most general and weakest variety of ontological realism is produced when '*X*' is replaced with 'the world'. No further specifications of the constituents and nature of the world is provided. This form of ontological realism does not include any ideas about the way the world exists, it only amounts to the idea *that* the world exists.

If we replace '*X*' with 'universals', we get doctrines such as *Platonic* or *Aristotelian realism* which state that universals exist; that is, it is universals (alone or also) that constitute the world. Not only (or not) the many particulars, such as round objects and business firms and rational men, but also (or only) roundness and firmhood and rationality and manhood exist. This is in fact the original usage of 'realism', used in connection with the debate over universals between the realists and their opponents, the nominalists. Nominalism may also be a form of realism: it replaces '*X*' with 'particulars' and states that there is nothing but particulars in the world.

If we replace '*X*' with 'medium-sized material entities' or 'objects of sense perception', we get standard forms of ontological *commonsense realism*. In general, realist theories in this category state that the perceivable commonsense world is real; in other words, that objects such as clouds and clocks, horses and houses, mountains and marmalade exist – that the objects that common sense takes to exist do exist in the objective way that common sense takes them to exist. The opponents of realism in the theory of perception include the idealists (to whom it is 'ideas' that constitute the world) and phenomenalists (who try to construe the world out of what they call 'sense data'). Commonsense realism can also be taken to comprise the idea that the mental entities in terms of which 'commonsense psychology' or 'folk psychology' conceptualizes our lives and behaviour exist. Accordingly, there is a fact of the matter regarding what we intend, want, believe, mean, hope and fear; that is, intentions, wants, beliefs and meanings exist (even in cases where what they appear to be about do not exist – such as mermaids and Rudolph the Reindeer). Eliminative materialists are among the opponents of commonsense realism about the mental.

If we replace '*X*' with 'the (often unobservable) entities as objects of (most or best, current or future) scientific theories' such as electrons, photons, quarks, electromagnetic fields, curved space–time, genes, viruses, brain states and so on, we get the ontological statement of *scientific realism*. The world as postulated in scientific theories now becomes the (or a) world that is real. The opponents of realism about the ontology of scientific theories are the fictionalists and (ontological) instrumentalists. In the case of radical physicalist scientific realism – according to which only entities postulated by physical sciences exist – the opponents also include those who advocate commonsense realism. More moderate forms of scientific realism may accommodate the existence of perceivable material entities of the commonsense world or even (at least some of) the mental entities of commonsense psychology.

There are other and more controversial versions, such as the one we get by replacing '*X*' with 'possible worlds', called *modal realism* by its advocates, such as David Lewis. According to this version, existence is not restricted to the actual world; the actual world is just one among many existing possible worlds.

An important question concerns the *quantifier* that the above forms of realism could use in relation to the entities that are claimed to exist. Such a quantifier indicates answers to the question 'how many?' such as 'all', 'no' and 'some'. No realist would like to claim that *all* posited universals, particulars, commonsense objects and/or scientific objects exist (this would imply that Father Christmas, centaurs and phlogiston are all as real as green tealeaves and DNA molecules). Many other realists commit themselves to the existence of at least some of these entities. Many scientific realists would say that *most* of the objects postulated in well-established scientific theories exist. However, none of these quantifiers is necessary for ontological realism; none of them should be included in the definition of realism. It is sufficient for realism about *X* to hold that *X* might exist, that the notion of *X* existing is a sensible and coherent notion. This raises the key issue concerning the appropriate concepts of existence.

Specification of the types and numbers of entities that are claimed to exist is not sufficient for a complete understanding of ontological realism. It is necessary to specify what is meant by the expressions 'exists' and 'is real'. The first decision to be made about this question concerns whether there is an ontological notion of 'exists' and 'is real' that is conceptually independent of epistemic considerations and of specific conceptual frameworks in which the specifications of 'X' appear; that is, whether in addition to a concept of 'existence within a framework' there is a sensible and 'X framework-independent' concept for expressing the idea that X exists (or does not exist). For example, the question may be whether the meaning of 'exist' in the statement, 'photons exist', may be understood independently of the meaning of the term 'photon' and of the specific theoretical frameworks in which 'photon' is embedded and of the epistemic claims we may feel to be justified in making about the existence of photons (such as 'the evidence suggests that photons exist'). If we claim that the very ontological notion of existence is in such a way independent, our notion is unproblematically a realist one. There are those, however, who claim to be realists but deny the framework-independent notion of 'exists' and 'is real'; they sometimes call themselves 'internal' or 'epistemic' realists, while 'external' or 'metaphysical' realism is preserved for those who subscribe to the independence thesis.

The second decision concerns the meaning of 'exists' and 'is real' more directly. The conventional specification is '*exists mind-independently*' or '*exists independently of the human mind*'. This formulation has the implication that it excludes realism about mental entities and entities dependent on the mental, such as persons, material artefacts, and social institutions construed in a dualist or non-eliminative physicalist fashion; it restricts the scope of realism to the material or physical world. What this entails is materialist or physicalist realism. Obviously, this formulation is not able to accommodate realism about social sciences postulating things such as intentions, expectations, roles, conventions or institutions; thus economics would be a hopeless case for such a realist. There are alternative specifications of 'exists' that could be thought to avoid the above implication, such as '*exists recognition-independently*' or '*exists inquiry-independently*' or '*exists independently of any particular act of representation of it*'. One may then argue that mental entities and/or social entities exist in one or more such senses and that these senses are genuinely realist ones.

'Realism' has increasingly also become a name for some *semantic* views, that is, views concerning such things as reference and truth. In the formulations above, the use of the notion of reference could not be avoided completely; for example, scientific realism as an ontological thesis about the existence of certain objects was defined in terms of theories being about those objects, that is, theories referring to them. The claim that scientific theories and the terms they include *refer to* real existents is part of the semantic thesis of scientific realism. The other part of semantic realism is the thesis that the sentences contained in scientific theories are genuine, *true or false*, statements about the real world and that they have a truth value irrespective of whether we are able to determine it. Some philosophers, such as Dummett, take bivalence – the principle that every proposition is either true or false – as a defining characteristic of realism. Standard forms of instrumentalism are among the opponents of realism so understood. For them, scientific theories are just calculation or inference devices with no semantic ties to reality; or if they have semantic properties – such as that of falsehood – these properties are taken to be irrelevant for our assessment of them. Various epistemic conceptions of truth, such as the idea of truth as warranted assertability or truth as idealized rational acceptability, challenge the notion that truth may escape even ideal knowers in ideal conditions; that truth is independent of our ways and chances of finding out about it. Pragmatisms of various sorts contain the negation of this realist idea. As against such views, realists hold the view that even a methodologically perfect theory, fully satisfying all the desiderata we can imagine, can still be mistaken.

These ideas are sometimes complemented by other views attributed to realism about science, such as that most current scientific theories are (at least approximately) true and/or that, as science develops, its theories get progressively nearer to the truth. However, these ideas are not required by the most basic and simple realist theses; realism might be correct even though most current science was wrong and even if science did not converge towards the truth. The same could be argued to be the case with a popular normative idea ascribed to realism about science, namely that science should pursue true accounts of the world.

'Realism' is also used in connection with a specific view of what truth is, namely the correspondence theory of truth. There are many versions of this theory, but they share the idea that it is somehow partly in virtue of the way the world is that sentences (statements, beliefs or utterances) are true or false – that truth is in this sense objective – and that truth amounts to a correspondence between the way the world is claimed to be and the way the world is. Correspondence theories differ from one another as to how they view the correspondence relation and the two poles linked by it. Many realists wish to link this view of truth with the very concept of realism. Many others dispute the connection. Some of them endorse the correspondence theory as a separate idea which is not implied by realism. Others again try to do without the correspondence theory, typically favouring redundancy or deflationary or minimalist views of truth instead; these views imply that, roughly speaking, to say that 'it is true that free trade tends to equalize factory prices' adds nothing to 'free trade tends to equalize factor prices'.

While the ontological meaning of 'realism' is the traditional and primary one, it can be and has been complemented by the epistemological point that the Xs that are claimed to exist are also knowable. Different forms of *epistemological realism* presuppose some versions of ontological realism and semantic realism and add to them the idea of being known or being knowable. Epistemological realism says of some existing X that facts about X are known or can be known, implying that knowers have epistemic access to X, that there is no veil separating the cognitive subject and the existing object. A variety of different forms of epistemological realism is possible, depending on how one analyses the very idea of knowledge, how the means of knowledge acquisition are conceived and what the relevant X is taken to be. Regarding the latter two matters, one can be a scientific epistemological realist, relying on what science now claims to be the case or on the potential capability of science to find out facts about the world, where both cases are based on a reliance on the cognitive power of the theoretical and empirical procedures (as well as the institutional organization) used by science.

Likewise, one can be a commonsense realist about perceptual knowledge. Traditionally, theories of perception have played a dominant role in realist epistemologies. Realist doctrines about perception are usually divided into two main categories, direct and indirect realism. *Direct realism* says that perception is directly about (is a direct awareness of) material objects which exist and that nothing else exists between perception and perceptible objects. *Naive realism*, usually unsupported by philosophers but postulated for purposes of criticism, is a version of direct realism which states that we perceive objects as they are; that is, that sense data or sensible qualities are the intrinsic properties of material objects and that these objects have all the properties they are perceived as having and that these properties are not affected by changes in perceivers and conditions of perception. *Indirect realism* states that perception is directly about mental representations (such as bodily sensations and after-images) and only indirectly about the external world and that both its direct and indirect objects exist. Versions of indirect realism include Locke's *representative realism* and a movement in the United States in the first decades of the twentieth century known as *critical realism* (Lovejoy, Santayana, R.W. Sellars and others). In a generalized form, the label 'critical realism' has been adopted by philosophers to indicate the view that there is a difference between that which is experienced and that which exists independently of being experienced. More generally, philosophers advocating such views emphasize the possibly distorting contribution of the knowing subject to the cognition.

This is related to the idea of fallibility. Fallibilism is the view that knowledge claims are in principle fallible (and possibly corrigible, revisable in the light of further evidence and arguments) so that full certitude is unattainable. Realists typically are fallibilists, opposing both dogmatism and radical scepticism. Even more, realism is often defined so as to presuppose fallibilism. This is entailed by the idea, mentioned above, that even an epistemically ideal theory or statement may be wrong.

It is a widely shared view among realist philosophers that the resolution of (or to put it less strongly: progress with respect to) issues about many themes mentioned above, such as what the world is made of, and what reference, truth and knowledge amount to, is up to future science. In other words, the specifications are understood as being *a posteriori* in regard to the progress of special sciences such as biology, cognitive science and, to anticipate boldly, economics. It is not the task of philosophy, in this opinion, to decide *a priori* what kinds of entities exist, what structure the world has, what relations our language has to the non-linguistic reality, what can be known and perceived, and so on. As an *a posteriori* exercise, philosophy produces claims that are fallible in the same sense that any other claims may be wrong.

Do realism and economics fit together? This is a question of interest to economists, economic methodologists, philosophers of science, politicians and lay public. The answer depends on what we mean by 'economics' and 'realism'. For example, we can take 'economics' to refer variously to any current form of economics or to economics as we would like it to be or economics as it might be – and the answer might vary accordingly. As for realism, we have not exhausted the full list in the foregoing, but we have come up with many forms of realism, and the answer obviously depends on the form(s) we choose. For example, if we opt for radical physicalist scientific realism, current economics will not fit. The outcome is the same if realism is taken to require that all components of economic theories be true.

However, a number of economists have been shown or can be shown to subscribe to one or another form of realism. These include J.H. von Thünen, J.S. Mill, Karl Marx, J.E. Cairnes, Carl Menger, Lionel Robbins, Nicholas Kaldor, Milton Friedman, Ronald Coase, George Richardson, Oliver Williamson and others. Even though there are important differences between them, they share the view that economic reality has an objectively (albeit not mind-independently) existing structure, and that economic theories, even though being partial and involving false elements, are able to truly represent some of the important aspects of this reality. There are some special features regarding realism about economics, such as commonsense realism playing a prominent role. This is because economic theories much of the time appear to be pretty much about the same objects that our commonsense understanding of the economy is about, such as households and business firms, money and prices, buying and selling, wants and expectations. Another feature, and an epistemologically significant one, is that the simplified and isolated settings theoretically brought about by economists usually cannot be reproduced empirically, thus making the empirical testing of truth claims particularly difficult. Fallibilism should therefore play an exceptionally prominent role in economics.

As an explicit research project, realism has been explored only recently in economic methodology. Two major realist projects have been those of Uskali Mäki (the first published statement appeared in 1982) and Tony Lawson (for example 1997). The differences between these two projects are many, but two 'meta-methodological' ones stand out immediately. One is that Lawson's project is largely an application of one philosophical system, that of Roy Bhaskar, while Mäki's is a matter of drawing from different philosophical sources as well as creating new conceptual tools that are hoped to reflect some of the peculiar features of economics. The other is that Lawson's project is supposed to have more or less direct critical implications about the poverty of what is called mainstream economics, while Mäki's project has been more neutral: the normative implications are expected to be more indirect and to require lots of factual premises that go beyond realism as a philosophical doctrine. Boylan and O'Gorman (1995) provide expositions and criticisms of these two projects. These projects do not exhaust all there is to the study of realism in the context of economics. Many other economic methodologists and philosophers of economics (such as Alex Rosenberg, Alan Nelson, Daniel Hausman, Don Ross, Nancy Cartwright and others) have contributed to the realist project without necessarily doing it explicitly under the banner of 'realism'.

USKALI MÄKI

Bibliography
Armstrong, David (1978), *Universals and Scientific Realism*, vols I–II, Cambridge.
Boylan, Tom and Paschal O'Gorman (1995),. *Beyond Rhetoric and Realism*, London: Routledge.
Devitt, Michael (1984), *Realism and Truth*, Princeton: Princeton University Press.
Lawson, Tony (1997), *Economics and Reality*, Cambridge: Cambridge University Press.
Leplin, Jarrett (ed.) (1984), *Scientific Realism*, Berkeley: University of California Press.
Mäki, Uskali (1989), 'On the problem of realism in economics', *Ricerche Economiche*, **43**, 176–98; reprinted in Bruce Caldwell (ed.), *The Philosophy and Methodology of Economics*, Aldershot: Edward Elgar, 1993.
Mäki, Uskali (1992), 'On the method of isolation in economics', *Idealization IV: Intelligibility in Science*, ed. Craig Dilworth, special issue of *Poznan Studies in the Philosophy of the Sciences and the Humanities*, **26**, 319–54.
Mäki, Uskali (1993), 'The market as an isolated causal process: A metaphysical ground for realism', in Bruce Caldwell and Stephan Boehm (eds), *Austrian Economics: Tensions and New Directions*, Dordrecht: Kluwer.
Mäki, Uskali (1996), 'Scientific realism and some peculiarities of economics', *Boston Studies in the Philosophy of Science*, **169**, 425–45.
Putnam, Hilary (1981), *Reason, Truth and History*, Cambridge: Cambridge University Press.
Searle, John (1995), *The Construction of Social Reality*, New York: Free Press.
Sellars, Wilfrid (1963), *Science, Perception and Reality*, London: Routledge & Kegan Paul.

Realisticness

Economists have the habit of arguing about the 'realism' of theories and their assumptions. In this usage, 'realism; is an attribute of economic theories: it refers to a property or a set of properties of theories and their constituent parts. In contrast to the usages of the term in philosophical literature, 'realism' that economists argue about does not refer to a philosophical view or thesis, such as a philosophical theory of scientific theories. In order to keep these two notions separate so as to examine how realism as a theory of theories is related to various attributes of those theories, it has been suggested in Mäki (1989) that another term be adopted to denote these attributes; this term is 'realisticness'.

The suggestion is that economists, and especially economic methodologists, should talk about the realisticness and unrealisticness of theories and assumptions rather than their 'realism'. The terminological separation of realism and realisticness is supposed to help us see, on the one hand, what different ideas about realism as a theory of theories imply concerning the realisticness and unrealisticness of these theories; and on the other, what different forms of realisticness and unrealisticness in different parts of theories imply concerning the philosophical interpretation of these theories in terms of realism as a theory of theories. One of the major findings reached on this basis has been that, with most forms and locations of realisticness, realism does not require realisticness. Realism and unrealisticness are compatible, provided unrealisticness is suitably understood and suitably located within theories.

Commentators customarily only focus on one specific pair of meanings of realisticness and unrealisticness, namely truth and falsehood. However, realisticness and unrealisticness appear also in many other forms in the ways in which economists characterize their theories. In his commentary on the assumptions issue in economics, the philosopher Ernest Nagel (1963) distinguished three ways in which a statement can be said to be unrealistic: it does not give an exhaustive description of some object; it is believed to be either false or highly improbable on the available evidence; and it contains theoretical terms in the sense of idealizations and therefore does not refer to anything actual. It is obvious that there are many more ways in which a theory or sentence may be said to be unrealistic or realistic. The following list goes beyond Nagel's classification by suggesting further divisions within his categories and by adding other forms. The list is incomplete, but it gives some representatives examples.

Referentiality
A term, assumption, or theory is realistic or unrealistic in that it either refers or does not refer to a real entity or a set of such entities. To refer to something is to 'pick out' this something from among the endless number of entities in the universe. There are alternative theories of the way reference is accomplished. Some link reference and description together, others do not. According to the latter, in referring to X one does not describe X as being like this or like that, as being this or that way. It is therefore possible to refer to consumers as real entities – and thus to be realistic in this referential sense – and yet attribute characteristics to them that they may not possess, such as transitive preferences. To refer to X is to be about X, not to assert true claims about X.

Observability
Being about some observable entity or set of entities is a special case of referential realisticness. On a popular view of so-called theoretical terms in science – such as, famously, 'electron' – these terms do not refer to anything observable, and thus they could be judged as being observationally unrealistic. Someone with strong empiricist preferences may then want to dispense with such terms in favour of observationally realistic theories; that is, theories phrased solely in terms of observational terms. Thus the theory of revealed preference purports to be about observable behaviour rather than about 'unobservable' preferences. One may also choose to extend the range of the observable by including anything encompassed by our ordinary 'commonsense' or 'folk' views of the world, such as wants and expectations. On this more general view, claims about preferences would be observationally realistic.

Truth
One of the conventional ways in which an assumption or theory may be taken to be realistic or unrealistic is for it to be true or false. In this case, we may talk about veristic realisticness and unrealisticness. If a theory states that the world is so-and-so, then the theory is true if the world really is so-and-so; otherwise it is false. If people's preferences are not transitive while it is assumed that they are, then the assumption is veristically unrealistic. A number of qualifications are needed in this sense of realisticness, owing to the complex nature of theories and the problematic notion of truth. To accommodate the fact that many claims are only more of less close to the truth, we may need a notion of closeness-to-the-truth, and adjust the concept of realisticness accordingly. Moreover, to take account of the fact that theories include

elements that play different epistemic roles, we may want to say that a given theory is veristically realistic even though it includes veristically unrealistic assumptions. It may be true about important aspects and false about unimportant aspects of the object under consideration. Finally, there is a variety of theories of what truth amounts to, and some of them suggest that truth can be defined in such epistemic and pragmatic terms as confirmation or plausibility or practical usefulness. They give rise to other concepts of realisticness; this implies that, in these cases, no separate concept of veristic realisticness is needed. However, if one wants to retain a non-epistemic and non-pragmatic concept of truth, such as truth as some sort of correspondence, then a separate concept of veristic realisticness can be maintained.

Partiality
The idea of being false is often confused with that of being partial. To distinguish between the two, the familiar distinction between nothing-but-the-truth and the-whole-truth may be invoked: violation of the former would lead to veristic unrealisticness, while violation of the latter leads to partiality. Partial representations are representations of only parts of the object under consideration. Marshallian models are more unrealistic than Walrasian models in that the latter include all markets of a given economy, while the former covers only a small fraction of them. Both exclude a number of items, from Jupiter's moons to the gender of the agents trading in the markets included. This is partiality in one sense, and all theories are partial in this sense: they isolate only a small slice of the world from the rest of reality. Marshallian and Walrasian models are equally unrealistic when they depict markets only in the abstract, without specifying any concrete, particular markets in real time and space. This is partiality in another sense: it is a matter of isolating types from tokens, universals from particulars, of including only the general aspects of certain items and excluding their time–space specific particularities. Consumer theory is abstract, thus partial, in that it does not speak about Mr van Dijk and Mrs Virtanen but rather consumers in the abstract. Partiality in both senses is ubiquitous. The issue of realisticness on this interpretation is how much of the world and which parts of the world have to be covered by the theory for it to do its intended job.

Success in empirical tests
Doing well in empirical tests is also to be kept distinct from being true. It is often taken not just as an *indication* of realisticness but also as a *form* of it. There are as many notions of realisticness (and unrealisticness) based on this general idea as there are more specific theories of what it is to do well in empirical tests. Such theories involve ideas about what a good test is like and what is actually tested in such a test (such as truth value or some pragmatic virtues). Such theories range from probabilistic to non-probabilistic accounts, from theories of instant assessment to more historical accounts, from Bayesian accounts to the bootstrap idea, from experimental to non-experimental and from inductivist to fully deductivist accounts. Consider two pairs of contrastive positions, familiar from debates on economic methodology. First, there is the contrast between confirmationist and falsificationist conceptions. While the former takes success to be a matter of being supported by empirical evidence, the latter conceives it as failure to be falsified by evidence in tests that seek refutation. (On the other hand, if in the latter case 'success' is understood as success in the pursuit of refutation, then 'success in empirical tests' has to be taken as defining unrealisticness rather than realisticness!) Second, there is the issue of the immediate target of testing a theory. The traditional division in the debates over economic theories is between those views which require the 'assumptions' of a theory – in particular concerning the behavioural dispositions of the actors – to be 'directly' tested, and

those that are content with testing only the predictive 'implications', concerning phenomena in the market or on the aggregate level. Many other more specific ideas about what appropriate testing amounts to could be cited. They can be taken to characterize different notions of realisticness with some family resemblance.

Plausibility

Sometimes, when economists say that a theory or assumption is realistic or unrealistic, they mean to say that it is plausible or implausible. When we say that a claim is plausible, we are not making an unambiguous assertion about that claim. We may take 'plausible' to mean the descriptive idea of 'believed by C' (where 'C' denotes some epistemic community) or the strong evaluative idea of 'worthy of belief' or the somewhat weaker evaluative idea of 'worthy of acceptance'. The concept of plausibility often invokes the connotation of appearance, thus making it even weaker; thus 'plausible' may be taken to mean ideas such as 'appearing to be true' or 'appearing to be worthy of belief' or 'appearing to be worthy of acceptance'. When an economist finds an assumption or theory plausible, she may think that, given her other (evidential and theoretical) beliefs or commitments, this theory or assumption has the chance of being true or believable: it is worthy at least of tentative acceptance and further exploration. It is the coherence with other believed or accepted statements that ascribes plausibility to a statement. An economist may find the assumption of rational expectations plausible because it fits the overall framework to which she is committed, while an ordinary consumer may find it implausible because it does not fit her commonsense conception of economic behaviour. This indicates that there is a strong flavour of subjectivity in this notion of realisticness.

Practical usefulness

An obvious sense of 'realisticness' is practical relevance or, more strongly, practical usefulness. Again, this idea is ambiguous; it may mean a number of things. An economic theory may be regarded as practically useful because it can be used to derive waterproof guidelines for fine-tuning a given economy with various policy instruments. Much more weakly, a theory may be taken to be practically useful in that it helps avoid large-scale mistakes regarding economic policy, perhaps by implying recommendations to refrain from action altogether. In the former case, a theory or its models have to be fairly detailed and comprehensive and predictively powerful, while in the latter case the theory may be a simple explanatory account of a few key properties of the economic order. In both cases, practical relevance and usefulness are defined in terms of the goals that the economist finds important. In the case of relevance, the issue is whether the theory has implications concerning these goals; in the case of usefulness, the issue is whether these implications in fact help attain these goals.

Once we have distinguished such forms of realisticness and unrealisticness, it can be shown that realism – as a philosophical theory of theories rather than a property of theories – is compatible with large doses of unrealisticness in many senses of unobservationality, falsehood, failure in tests, partiality, implausibility and practical uselessness.

USKALI MÄKI

Bibliography

Mäki, Uskali (1989), 'On the problem of realism in economics', *Richerce Economiche*, **43**, 176–98; reprinted in Bruce Caldwell (ed.), *The Philosophy and Methodology of Economics*, Aldershot: Edward Elgar, 1993.

Mäki, Uskali (1992), 'Friedman and realism' *Research in the History of Economic Thought and Methodology*, **10**, 171–95.
Mäki, Uskali (1994), 'Reorienting the assumptions issue', in Roger Backhouse (ed.), *New Directions in Economic Methodology*, London: Routledge.
Nagel, Ernest (1963), 'Assumptions in economic theory', *American Economic Review, Papers and Proceedings*, **53**, 211–19.

Reflexivity

> To include epistemological questions concerning the validity of sociological knowledge in the sociology of knowledge is somewhat like trying to push a bus in which we are riding. (Berger and Luckmann, 1966: 13)

The dictionary defines the word 'reflexive' as that which is 'directed back upon itself'. Examples would include the photographer who takes a picture of his own reflection in a mirror, or the physician who diagnoses her own illness. While such reflexivity occurs in a wide range of human activities from literature, to the arts, to the natural sciences, it seems to be particularly pervasive in the social sciences. After all, if a social scientist asserts that humans will necessarily believe certain things or behave in certain ways under particular circumstances, the social scientist making that assertion should also believe the same thing or behave in the same way under those same conditions. While reflexivity may be quite common in the human sciences, it is also clear that it is often not a serious problem. For example, neither the recognition that writing a paper about utility maximization can be described as the result of a utility-maximizing decision, nor the claim that the actions of a behavioural psychologist are actually conditioned responses, seems to be a particularly disturbing (or a very interesting) revelation. On the other hand, reflexivity is not always so benign; one place where reflexivity appears to be a serious problem is within the sociology of scientific knowledge (SSK).

While SSK encompasses a wide range of different approaches and different points of view, the common theme is that science, the behaviour of those within the scientific community, is a social phenomenon and should be studied in the same way that one would study any other social phenomenon; the beliefs and behaviours of scientists are to be explained in the same ways that one would explain the beliefs and behaviours of the members of any other society or culture. For example, the 'strong programme' within SSK explains the behaviour of scientists on the basis of 'social interests': either the interests of the scientists themselves or social interests defined in some wider (macrosociological) sense. This of course implies that scientific theories are caused by social processes and not, as traditional philosophy of science and most practising scientists would have us believe, by nature. While sociologists could remain agnostic about the veracity of scientific claims – in the same way an anthropologist who studies the religious practices of a particular tribe need not ask whether the god they worship really does exist or really does make the crops grow – such epistemic agnosticism is not standard practice within SSK. Standard practice is to debunk, or to unmask, the epistemic privilege of science; the routine attitude of those in SSK seems to be: 'Your theories are not the pristine reflection of nature that you claim; they are the (implicitly epistemically debased) products of social interests and culturally negotiated strategies (that is, the emperor has no clothes).' This deconstructive profile exposes SSK to a potentially damaging reflexive turn. If the output of the scientific community is a product of social forces at work within that community, then why should not this also be the case for the scientific community of those doing SSK? If theories are the result of social interests, why should not this also be true for the theory that says that theories are always the result of social interests? This performative self-contradiction is the *reflexivity problem* for the sociology of science.

There are many different responses to the reflexivity problem as it emerges within SSK. We will consider four of these, one from outside SSK and three from within, and then turn to the issue of how this problem might affect economic methodology. The most common response from outside SSK is the one that has traditionally been offered by philosophers of science – do not do SSK, do the philosophy of science! Philosophy of science has traditionally been a normative discipline (epistemically normative); it has considered the way that science ought to be done (in order to find truth, or to approach truth, or to demarcate itself from other activities, but what ought to be done in any case). While the Kuhnian revolution in the philosophy of science has raised serious questions about the relationship between this traditional normative stance and the actual historical practice of science, the traditional approach is formally protected from the reflexivity problem faced by sociological approaches to science. If philosophy of science is based on a uniquely philosophical, or epistemological, mode of analysis, one that is prior to (and has the authority to usher) the practice of scientists, its method is not indicted by what scientists do or do not do. The method of the philosophy of science is, according to this traditional view, not the method of science, and thus it is immune to the problem of reflexivity.

While reflexivity is recognized by almost everyone writing in SSK, various authors in the field have offered a wide range of different responses to the problem. We will just consider three of these responses, starting with the one suggested by the strong programme. The reaction of those within the strong programme has effectively been that SSK is based on legitimate empirical investigation and as such there is not really any problem when it discovers that certain natural scientists are not engaged in this same kind of empirical investigation. Sociologists must be willing to expose their own practices to a similar inquiry – 'otherwise sociology would be a standing refutation of its own theories' (Bloor, 1991: 7) – but this is not really a serious problem. The general response of those within the strong programme seems to be to nod knowingly in the direction of reflexivity and then simply go on back to work.

An alternative response is given by members of the so-called 'Bath School'. According to Harry Collins and Steven Yearley (1992a; 1992b) many of those involved in SSK have been engaged in a game of 'epistemological chicken': each new book or paper appearing in the literature has been more radical than its predecessor, leaving SSK with a version of radical relativism that 'has been destructive' (Collins and Yearley, 1992a; 323) of the original project. For Collins and Yearley, SSK should stick to its social science roots by practising social realism. Natural scientists believe in (and have ontologies inhabited by) things like quarks and genes; social scientists believe in (and have ontologies inhabited by) things like social interests and social processes. While the same causal mechanisms might be at work behind the actions of both sociologists and natural scientists, this should not have any effect on the core SSK project of uncovering those mechanisms that are relevant to the workings of natural science.

The final group we will consider comprises those in SSK who have dedicated the greatest number of pages to the issue of reflexivity. While there is not a convenient label for this group – perhaps it could be called the hyperreflexive school – its most visible representatives are clearly Malcolm Ashmore (1989) and Steve Woolgar (1988; 1992). These authors share a family resemblance to the French school of Bruno Latour and Michel Callon (Callon and Latour, 1992; Latour, 1993), but they are sufficiently different to be given separate billing on the issue of reflexivity The bottom line for Ashmore and Woolgar is that reflexivity is not a problem at all; it is an opportunity. It is the opportunity to push at the envelope of our discursive strategies, to abandon the stultifying framework of the monologue and the single author, to explore new literary forms and rhetorical tropes, to engage in the critical 'dynamic of iterative reconceptualization' (Woolgar, 1992: 333). Reflexivity is not a difficulty, it is a cause for celebration and an opportunity for liberation, and the variety of literary forms that appear in the work of these authors (from plays, to dialogues, to poems) are offered as testimony to this liberating effect. This is a very radical position and, needless to say, not all of those involved in SSK consider such hyperreflexivity to be particularly useful or interesting. Collins and Yearley, for example, summarize this view in the following way: 'Woolgar and the other reflexivists may stand steadfast in the path of the traffic, but a heroic description of the experience is misplaced. The traffic passes and they survive unscathed – but only because they have fallen down a hole in the road' (1992a: 308).

This entry closes with a brief consideration of some of the many ways in which the issue of reflexivity has affected economics and/or economic methodology. The first involves reflexivity in Marxian economics. If material conditions determine consciousness, how did Marx (or how can revolutionary intellectuals more generally) transcend (bourgeois) material conditions to produce a critique of capitalist society? While the history of Marxian analysis has provided a number of different responses to such questions, the most sustained discussion of reflexivity was provided by Karl Mannheim in *Ideology and Utopia* (1936). Mannheim argued that, because intellectuals form a separate class that is 'outside' the economic structure of society, the 'free intelligentsia', they are free of the interests of the ruling (or any other) class. Whether one finds this argument persuasive or not, Mannheim clearly recognized, and offered a response to, the problem of reflexivity as it emerged within the context of one particular type of economic theory.

The second issue concerns the direct application of SSK to the practice of economists. A number of authors have recently started to apply the general framework of SSK to the history of economic thought (Weintraub, 1991; Weintraub and Mirowski, 1994; Hands, 1994a, for example) and the issue of reflexivity surfaces immediately in such studies. If the theorizing of economists is best understood as a product of various social forces, should not the theorizing of the historians looking at those economists also be understood as a social product? Does this not have implications for the conduct and critical impact of such historical inquiries?

A third issue, closely related to the second, is reflexivity as it emerges within the relationship between economists and economic agents. Do economists behave like economic agents, or do economic agents behave like economists, and what implications do such questions have for the (supposedly general) theory of economic rationality? This issue was touched upon by economists like Hayek and Knight, but it has only recently begun to be seriously investigated in the context of contemporary economics. Esther-Mirjam Sent (1997) has provided a book-length discussion of such issues as they emerge within the context of rational expectations macroeconomics (Thomas Sargent's work in particular).

The final potential reflexivity problem has to do with the role of economics and economic metaphor in recent philosophy of science. There has been an increasing tendency for philosophers of science (and some economic methodologists) to employ economic argumentation, particularly the notion of the invisible hand, in their analysis of (even natural) science. This mode of argumentation seems to be (at least in part) a reaction to SSK; often in SSK the scientist-agents are self-interested in a way that generates (consistent with the debunking story) epistemically sullied behaviour, but if something like the invisible hand operates within the market-place of scientific ideas, perhaps this self-interested behaviour could still produce socially desirable (that is, epistemically efficient) outcomes (see Hands, 1994b). If one has a philosophical vision of scientific knowledge that is heavily dependent upon economics, the reflexivity problem would seem to emerge whenever one applies that view of science to the practice of economists. While there are many possible variations on this reflexive theme (see Hands, 1994c) the problem clearly indicates that reflexivity is not something that can be neglected by those interested in contemporary economic methodology.

D. WADE HANDS

Bibliography
Ashmore, Malcolm (1989), T*he Reflexive Thesis: Wrighting Sociology of Knowledge*, Chicago: University of Chicago Press.
Berger, Peter L. and Thomas Luckmann (1966), *The Social Construction of Reality*, New York: Anchor Books.
Bloor, David (1991), *Knowledge and Social Imagery*, 2nd edn, Chicago: University of Chicago Press.
Callon, Michel and Bruno Latour (1992), 'Don't Throw the Baby out with the Bath School' A Reply to Collins and Yearley', in A. Pickering (ed.), *Science as Practice and Culture*, Chicago: University of Chicago Press.
Collins, Harry M. and Steven Yearley (1992a), 'Epistemological Chicken,' in A. Pickering (ed.), *Science as Practice and Culture*, Chicago: University of Chicago Press.
Collins, Harry M. and Steven Yearley (1992b), 'Journey Into Space', in A. Pickering (ed.), *Science as Practice and Culture*, Chicago: University of Chicago Press.
Hands, D. Wade (1994a), 'Restabilizing Dynamics: Construction and Constraint in the History of Walrasian Stability Theory', *Economics and Philosophy*, **10**, 243–83.
Hands, D. Wade (1994b), 'Blurred Boundaries: Recent Changes in the Relationship Between Economics and the Philosophy of Science', *Studies in the History and Philosophy of Science*, **25**, 751–72.
Hands, D. Wade (1994c), 'The Sociology of Scientific Knowledge,' in R. Backhouse (ed.), *New Directions in Economic Methodology*, London: Routledge.
Jasanoff, Sheila, Gerald E. Markle, James C. Peterson and Trevor Pinch (eds) (1995), *Handbook of Science and Technology Studies*, Thousand Oaks, CA: Sage.
Latour, Bruno (1993), *We Have Never Been Modern*, Cambridge, MA: Harvard University Press.
Mannheim, Karl (1936), *Ideology and Utopia*, San Diego: Harcourt Brace Jovanovich.
Sent, Esther-Mirjam (1997), *Resisting Sargent*, Cambridge: Cambridge University Press.
Weintraub, E. Roy (1991), *Stabilizing Dynamics: Constructing Economic Knowledge*, Cambridge: Cambridge University Press.
Weintraub, E. Roy and Philip Mirowski (1994), 'The Pure and the Applied: Bourbakism Comes to Mathematical Economics', *Science in Context*, **7**, 245–72.
Woolgar, Steve (ed.) (1988), *Knowledge and Reflexivity*, London: Sage.
Woolgar, Steve (1992), 'Some Remarks About Positionism: A Reply to Collins and Yearley', in A. Pickering (ed.), *Science as Practice and Culture*, Chicago: University of Chicago Press.

Relativism

'Relativism' seems to be the derogatory term of choice in contemporary methodological debates. Authors from a wide range of different perspectives seem to view the discipline's recent forays into rhetoric, neopragmatism and the sociology of scientific knowledge as dangerous first (or perhaps last) steps down the slippery slope to dreaded relativism (Blaug, 1994, for example). So what is this relativism that so many seem to fear?

In simplest possible terms, relativism just means that the property in question can only be evaluated 'relative to' some relativizer, such as a particular group, culture, paradigm, system of values or historical period. Consider the example of 'moral relativism'. Moral relativism means that a particular moral code or system of moral rules is valid only relative to a specific group, culture, class, historical context and so on. If one believes that a moral code exists which is valid for all people, in all places and at all times, one is not a moral relativist – one is a moral absolutist. While moral and cultural relativism play an important role in the philosophy of social sciences like anthropology, it is not the type of relativism that is discussed in economic methodology. The relativism discussed (or used in denunciation) in economics is the relativism of contemporary science theory: ontological relativism and/or epistemological relativism.

Ontological relativism is the view that whatever *exists* is relative to an individual, a culture, a paradigm, a form of life and so on. Notice that there are potentially as many different versions of ontological relativism as there are groups and frameworks to relativize with respect to. Ontological relativism is sometimes claimed by advocates of 'social constructivist' views within the philosophy or (more commonly) the sociology of science. If the 'natural' world that scientists examine is socially constructed, if it is the product of the social and/or interest-conditioned practice of the scientific community in which such 'nature' emerges, then what exists is in a certain sense 'relative to' that scientific community. In some cases (for example, Collins 1985) the 'natural' world is (really, ontologically) constructed by, and thus relative to, the social conditions that constitute its existence. In other cases (for example, Rorty, 1979) the natural world may exist independently of the social process of knowledge production, but such an independent world, even if it exists, is irrelevant, since the only world that affects human practice is the mediated world of socially constructed knowledge.

Epistemological relativism is relativism about what we *know* (rather than relativism about what exists); epistemological relativism also comes in many forms. One reason for this diversity is the same as with other forms of relativism: the wide range of potential relativizers. Another, perhaps more important, reason for this diversity is the protean nature of epistemology itself. There are many different positions within mainstream epistemology – empiricist versus rationalist, foundationalist versus coherence and so on – and there are as many different types of epistemological relativism as there are epistemological positions. While such diversity clearly exists, it is not necessary to consider all (or even a large number) of these different versions of epistemological relativism. The reason we can neglect most of them is that they are not relevant to the literature on economic methodology. Almost all of the literature on economic methodology, Popperian as well as positivist, falls broadly into the epistemological tradition of empiricist foundationalism. This fact (whether or not such foundationalism is the proper way to interpret either Popper or positivism) allows us to simplify our discussion to relativism about empirical foundations. Not only is this variant of relativism the most important one in economic methodology (see Boylan and O'Gorman, 1995, for instance), it is also the type of relativism that is most frequently discussed in the recent philosophical literature (Hollis and Lukes, 1982; Laudan, 1990; Nola, 1988, for example).

According to empirical foundationalism, sense data (or sentences about sense data) form the incorrigible foundations for scientific knowledge. Scientific laws are universal generalizations derived from (inductively in positivist variants, deductively in Popperian) these incorrigible empirical foundations. This type of empirical foundationalism was radically undermined in the 1960s and 1970s by Thomas Kuhn (1970a) and others who argued that a purely observational language was not available (that all observations were theory-laden) and that in the absence of such a purely observational idiom it was not possible to compare directly the empirical implications of two different scientific theories (scientific theories were incommensurable). Kuhn argued that scientists in the same field share a collectively held paradigm and that the paradigm conditions, and potentially determines, the observations they make. Such an argument not only undermines empirical foundationalism, it also introduces the spectre of epistemological relativism: what a particular scientist 'sees' and thus 'knows' is 'relative to' the paradigm that they hold. Changing scientific theories involves a gestalt shift in the shared conceptual framework of the members of the scientific community, making new observations, like old observations, relative to the conceptual framework in effect at the particular time. Although Kuhn himself often denied being a relativist (Kuhn, 1970b), most philosophers of science (Doppelt, 1978, for instance) seem to accept such epistemological relativism as an obvious implication of his work. Many other historians, philosophers and sociologists of science have also come to similar (and often even more radical) relativistic conclusions over the last few decades; in fact, it is fair to say that the majority of the work in recent philosophy of science has been directed at trying, in various ways, to get around – or, in the case of certain sociologists of science, to revel in – this type of epistemological relativism.

Many authors have carried this relativistic critique of scientific knowledge over into the field of economic methodology. The theory-ladenness of observations and the incommensurability of scientific theories undermines empirical foundationalism within economic methodology just as effectively as it does in the philosophy of natural science (perhaps more effectively, given the nature of economic data and the simplistic versions of empiricism advocated by many economists). If all facts are theory-laden, then how can we ever objectively test an economic theory? If economic theories cannot be tested, if there are not good cognitive reasons for accepting one theory over another, is theory acceptance not purely a 'relative' affair?

While many economic methodologists seem to write as if we have only two choices – accept a traditional view (like Popperian falsificationism or positivism) or be doomed to relativism – these are not the only two options available in current philosophy of science and science studies. Within the philosophy of science, there are many different views that reject both foundationalism and relativism. For example, there are various versions of epistemological naturalism, some based on biology and others based on cognitive science, that retain the cognitive privilege of science (thus rejecting epistemological relativism) without resorting to a foundationalist view of scientific knowledge. Within the sociology of science, there are certain positions that try to avoid relativism by involving nature as a (constantly renegotiated) constraint on scientific practice, and there are others who adopt a non-relativist interpretation of social knowledge even though they seem to be relativist with respect to the knowledge claims of those in the physical sciences. The point is not to defend any one of these particular views, but rather to note that relativism, or getting around the relativist implications of Kuhn and others, is a major (perhaps the major) project in current science theory. Economic methodology is also beginning to free itself from the 'Popper–positivism or relativism' dichotomy, but progress seems to be very slow.

D. WADE HANDS

References

Blaug, M. (1994), 'Why I Am Not a Constructivist', in R.E. Backhouse (ed.), *New Directions in Economic Methodology*, London: Routledge.
Boylan, T.A. and P.F. O'Gorman (1995), *Beyond Rhetoric and Realism in Economics*, London: Routledge.
Collins, H. (1985), *Changing Order: Replication and Induction in Scientific Practice*, London Sage.
Doppelt, G. (1978), 'Kuhn's Epistemological Relativism: An Interpretation and Defense', *Inquiry*, **21**, 33–86.
Hollis, M. and S. Lukes (eds) (1982), *Rationality and Relativism*, Oxford: Blackwell.
Kuhn, T.S. (1970a), *The Structure of Scientific Revolutions*, 2nd edn, Chicago: University of Chicago Press.
Kuhn, T.S. (1970b), 'Reflections on My Critics', in I. Lakatos and A. Musgrave (eds), *Criticism and the Growth of Knowledge*, Cambridge: Cambridge University Press.
Laudan, L. (1990), *Science and Relativism*, Chicago: University of Chicago Press.
Nola, R. (ed), (1988), *Relativism and Realism in Science*, Amsterdam: Kluwer.
Rorty, R. (1979), *Philosophy and the Mirror of Nature*, Princeton: Princeton University Press.

Rhetoric

The study of rhetoric (often simply called 'rhetoric') is the study of the way people persuade each other. The rhetoric of economics focuses on economists as persuaders, and is concerned with the means whereby economists seek to persuade non-economists, students and (especially important) each other. It therefore encompasses an enormous range of topics, including economists' use of metaphor, the style of economics writing (for example, the style of the 'scientific paper'), the relationship between what economists write and the way they talk in seminars, the use of rhetorical devices such as appeals to authority or the use of mathematics, and the pedagogical devices found in textbooks.

As might be expected from this wide range of topics, the existing literature on the rhetoric of economics draws on a number of traditions including, amongst others, classical rhetoric (Aristotle), the American tradition of writing (Booth, 1974), discourse analysis (Bazerman, 1988; Myers, 1989), sociology of scientific knowledge (Knorr-Cetina, 1981), applied linguistics (Swales, 1990), literary criticism (Bakhtin, 1981; Fish, 1980) and philosophy and hermeneutics (Hesse, 1966; Ricoeur, 1977).

Though he was not the first to address such issues (see, for example, Henderson, 1982), the term 'rhetoric' was first popularized in discussions of economics by McCloskey (1983; 1986). Though he argued that paying attention to the rhetoric of economics would lead to greater understanding of what economists were doing, and enable them to communicate more effectively, he had a deeper reason for wishing to focus on rhetoric. Economists, he contended, were ensnared by positivism (which he often equated with modernism), a methodology that was unsound and had a harmful effect on the way they argued. They used the language of proof when they ought to be using the language of persuasion.

Underlying this thesis was an epistemological position close to that of Rorty's *Philosophy and the Mirror of Nature* (1980). This involves seeing economics as a conversation. In a conversation, methodological rules are inappropriate, the only appropriate rules being those that govern a good conversation: listening to others, not shouting, honesty. Methodological rules such as 'put forward only testable hypotheses' or 'abandon theories that have been falsified' are restricting and inappropriate. They harm the conversation.

McCloskey (1986) made his case not only with 'theoretical' arguments, but with a series of case studies showing that economists had not followed their positivist precepts, and analysing the way in which economists actually persuaded each other: Samuelson's use of mathematics to give authority to his arguments; Fogel's attempt to create a new audience, familiar with economics and history, by including arguments that would impress both historian and economist readers; Muth's scientistic style of writing on rational expectations; Solow's use of the master tropes (metaphor, metonymy, synecdoche and irony) in presenting the aggregate production function; and the complexity of the rhetoric involved in the use of statistical significance tests.

In *The Rhetoric of Economics*, McCloskey argued that economics uses 'literary' methods primarily through showing that their arguments relied on rhetorical devices such as analogy and metaphor. Economics models were to be seen as metaphors, deriving from this their persuasive power. In *If You're So Smart* (1990) he turned to story telling: in addition to using metaphors (like poets) they tell stories (like novelists). In the same way that economists are unaware that their models are metaphors, few of them realize they are telling stories. Economist's stories, like any other stories, can be analysed using categories taken from literary criticism, such as plot and genre. Thus economists' stories can be shown, just like folk-tales, to be made up of only a few types of action (such as entry, exit, price setting, orders, purchase, sale or valuation). Plots can be analysed like novels, in terms of whether they have satisfactory endings. Following Todorov (1977), McCloskey argued that much economics falls into the category of the 'marvellous', where the rules of reality are violated for the sake of the story (as when animals talk or carpets fly). Literary analogy sheds new light on the debate over whether assumptions should be realistic.

A different use of literary theory is found in Brown's (1994) use of Bakhtin's theory of voices in an attempt to resolve the long-standing puzzle over the relationship between Adam Smith's *Wealth of Nations* and his *Theory of Moral Sentiments*. Whereas the former is written in the monologic style of a scientific text, the latter was written in the dialogic style of a novel. This contract can be used to suggest that the moral arguments central to the *Theory of Moral Sentiments* have no place in the *Wealth of Nations*. A further use of literary theory is found in Gerrard's (1991) attempt to explain economists' failure to agree on the central message of Keynes' *General Theory*: following Ricoeur, Gerrard argues that important texts typically have a multiplicity of interpretations, and the failure of commentators to agree on a single interpretation point to the richness of Keynes' text. Lucas has, like the authors of literary works, been 'deconstructed' (Rossetti, 1990).

Rhetoric can also be approached through analysing different genres. Textbooks are a rich source for rhetorical analysis, for even small points can be used to rhetorical effect, in order to persuade the student reader to follow the argument. The 'paradox of value', for example, may be used, not simply to exemplify a technical point in economic theory, but to demonstrate the brilliance of microeconomic analysis or the superiority of the novice student's understanding to that of one of the greatest economists of all time (Swales, 1993). Even more important is the journal article, which has increasingly dominated academic economics. Journal articles have increasingly adopted the style of the 'scientific paper' (Dudley-Evans and Henderson, 1993), even to the extent that many journals impose a standard format: introduction, theory, data, results, conclusions. Dudley-Evans and Henderson (1990) have argued that changes in the way article introductions are written reflect changes in the relationship between author and intended reader: especially since the 1960s, introductions follow the pattern expected in an established discipline where readers are assumed to be professional economists. McCloskey (1991) has argued that the implied reader of economics articles has changed to support the scientific standing of the articles' authors, and that this is part of an (arrogant) scientistic attitude. Dudley-Evans (1993) found that the debate over Milton Friedman's monetary framework combined linguistic features commonly found in academic articles with other features, more frequently associated with spoken discourse (compare Klamer, 1984).

Rhetorical or linguistic analysis can also be applied to the contents of journal articles. Bloor and Bloor (1993), through analysing the 'hedging' strategies in a sample or articles, reached the conclusion that facts about the real world are not central to economics. Though argued on very different lines, this conclusion accords with Milberg's (1996) conclusion (on the basis of analysing articles on international economics) that claims to policy relevance are much more frequently made in theoretical than in empirical articles. As with Bloor and Bloor's conclusion, this is the opposite of what outsiders to the discipline would probably expect. McCloskey and Ziliak (1996) have sought to show how statistical significance tests are *in practice* used in ways that have no foundation in statistical theory. Goldfarb (1995) has shown that there is a bias towards the publication of 'interesting' econometric results, where the direction of this bias (towards positive or negative results) varies according to the stage of the debate at which studies are published: when there are no generally accepted answers, there is a bias in favour of positive results, but when these become accepted, this is replaced by a bias in favour of studies which undermine these results.

McCloskey's claim that the analysis of economic rhetoric can enhance our understanding of what is happening within economics and that this may improve the conversation amongst economists, and between economists and those whom they address, is uncontroversial. It is useful to have the rhetorical styles of various types of economics writing exposed, so that they can be understood more clearly. At a purely practical level, an understanding of the language of economics can be invaluable in teaching economics. Rhetorical analysis and tools of literary criticism have also been used to shed light on long-standing puzzles in the history of economic thought, such as the relation between Adam Smith's two major works (Brown, 1994), the impact of Keynes' *General Theory* (Marzola and Silva, 1994; Patinkin, 1990; Gerrard, 1991) or why Friedman and his critics failed to communicate more effectively (Backhouse, 1993a). Historians of economics have also been led to approach their tasks in new ways (for example, Weintraub, 1991).

McCloskey however, has gone much further than this, arguing that rhetoric should *displace* methodology, the latter being portrayed as restrictive and incoherent. As a rhetorical strategy, this was extremely effective – it provided a bold, clear, easily-understood message that attracted widespread support amongst a profession sceptical about methodology. If methodology is equated with the type of methodological remark that economists sometimes use to short-circuit discussion, McCloskey's arguments are persuasive. On the other hand, if methodology is seen as involving reasoned discussion about the methods used by economists, the principles underlying these methods and whether they enable economists to achieve various goals (whether practical or epistemic), rhetoric cannot be seen as an alternative to methodology. This has been pointed out by numerous critics of McCloskey's position (Caldwell and Coats, 1984; Rosenberg, 1988; Mäki, 1988; Mirowski, 1987; Backhouse, 1993b) who have criticized his characterization of modernism, his equation of rhetoric with anti-modernism and many other aspects of his argument. Rhetoric and methodology may approach economics from two different points of view, but are in no way incompatible.

ROGER E. BACKHOUSE

Bibliography

Backhouse, Roger E. (1993a), 'The debate over Milton Friedman's theoretical framework: an economist's view', in W. Henderson, T. Dudley-Evans and R.E. Backhouse (eds), *Economics and Language*.
Backhouse, Roger E. (1993b), 'Rhetoric and methodology', in Robert F. Hébert (ed.), *Perspectives on the History of Economic Thought*, vol. 9, Cheltenham/Lyme: Edward Elgar.
Bakhtin, M.M. (1981), *The Dialogic Imagination: Four Essays by M.M. Bakhtin*, Austin: University of Texas Press.
Bazerman, C. (1988), *Shaping Written Knowledge: The Genre and Activity of the Experimental Article in Science*, Madison: University of Wisconsin Press.
Bloor, Meriel and Tom Bloor (1993), 'How economists modify propositions', in W. Henderson, T. Dudley-Evans and R.E. Backhouse (eds), *Economics and Language*.
Booth, Wayne (1974), *Modern Dogma and the Rhetoric of Assent*, Notre Dame: University of Notre Dame Press.
Caldwell, Bruce and A.W. Coats (1984), 'The rhetoric of economics: a comment on McCloskey', *Journal of Economic Literature*, **22** (2), 575–8.
Dudley-Evans, Tony (1993), 'The debate over Milton Friedman's theoretical framework: an applied linguist's view', in W. Henderson, T. Dudley-Evans and R.E. Backhouse (eds), *Economics and Language*.
Dudley-Evans, Tony and Willie Henderson (1990), 'The organisation of article introductions: evidence of change in economics writing', in Tony Dudley-Evans and Willie Henderson (eds), *The Language of Economics: The Analysis of Economics Discourse*, ELT Documents, No. 134. London: Modern English Publications in association with the British Council.

Dudley-Evans, Tony and Willie Henderson (1993), 'Changes in the economics article', *Finlance: A Finnish Journal of Applied Linguistics*, **12**, 159–80.

Fish, Stanley (1980), *Is There a Text in This Class?* Cambridge, MA: Harvard University Press.

Gerrard, B. (1991), 'Keynes's *General Theory*: interpreting the interpretations', *Economic Journal*, **101**, 276–87.

Goldfarb, Robert (1995), 'The economist-as-audience needs a methodology of plausible inference', *Journal of Economic Methodology*, **2** (2), 201–22.

Henderson, Willie (1982), 'Metaphor in economics', *Economics*, **18** (4), 147–57.

Henderson, Willie, Tony Dudley-Evans and Roger Backhouse (eds) (1993), *Economics and Language*, London/New York: Routledge.

Hesse, Mary B. (1966), *Models and Analogies in Science*, Notre Dame: University of Notre Dame Press.

Klamer, Arjo (1984), *The New Classical Macroeconomics: Conversations with New Classical Macroeconomists and their Opponents*, Brighton: Harvester Wheatsheaf.

Klamer, Arjo, Donald N. McCloskey and Robert M. Solow (eds) (1988), *The Consequences of Economic Rhetoric*, Cambridge/New York: Cambridge University Press.

Knorr-Cetina, Karin (1981), *The Manufacture of Knowledge: an Essay on the Constructivist and Contextual Nature of Science*, Oxford: Pergamon Press.

Mäki, Uskali (1988), 'How to combine rhetoric and realism in the methodology of economics', *Economics and Philosophy*, **4** (1), 89–109.

Mäki, Uskali (1995), 'Diagnosing McCloskey', *Journal of Economic Literature*, **23** (3), 1300–1318.

Marzola, Alessandra and Francesco Silva (1994), *John Maynard Keynes: Language and Method*, Cheltenham/Lyme: Edward Elgar.

McCloskey, Donald N. (1983), 'The rhetoric of economics', *Journal of Economic Literature*, **31**, 434–61.

McCloskey, Donald N. (1986), *The Rhetoric of Economics*, Brighton: Harvester Wheatsheaf.

McCloskey, Donald N. (1990), *If You're So Smart: The Narrative of Economic Expertise*, Chicago/London: University of Chicago Press.

McCloskey, Donald N. (1991), 'Mere style in economics journals, 1920 to the present', *Economic Notes*, **20** (1), 135–58.

McCloskey, Donald N. (1994), *Rhetoric and Persuasion in Economics*, Cambridge/New York: Cambridge University Press.

McCloskey, Donald N. and Steven T. Ziliak (1996), 'The standard error of regressions', *Journal of Economic Literature*, **34**, (1), 97–114.

Milberg, William (1996), 'The rhetoric of policy relevance in international economics', *Journal of Economic Methodology*, **3** (2), 237–59.

Mirowski, Philip (1987), 'Shall I compare thee to a Minkowski–Ricardo–Leontief–Metzler matrix of the Mosak–Hicks type?', *Economics and Philosophy*, **3**, 67–96; reprinted 1988 in A. Klamer, D.N. McCloskey and R.M. Solow (eds), *The Consequences of Economic Rhetoric*.

Myers, Greg (1989), *Writing Biology: Texts in the Social Construction of Economic Knowledge*, Madison: University of Wisconsin Press.

Ricoeur, P. (1977), *The Rule of Metaphor*, trans. R. Czerny, Toronto/Buffalo: University of Toronto Press.

Rorty, Richard (1980), *Philosophy and the Mirror of Nature*, Oxford: Basil Blackwell.

Rosenberg, Alexander (1988), 'Economics is too important to be left to the rhetoricians', *Economics and Philosophy*, **4** (1), 129–49.

Rossetti, Jane (1990),'Deconstructing Robert Lucas', in Samuels (ed.), *Economics and Discourse*.

Samuels, Warren J. (ed.) (1990), *Economics and Discourse: an Analysis of the Language of Economics*, Boston, Dordrecht/London: Kluwer.

Swales, John M. (1990), *Genre Analysis*, Cambridge: Cambridge University Press.

Swales, John M. (1993), 'The paradox of value: six treatments in search of a reader', in W. Henderson, T. Dudley-Evans and R.E. Backhouse (eds), *Economics and Language*.

Todorov, Tzvetan (1977), *The Poetics of Prose*, trans. R. Howard, Ithaca: Cornell University Press.

Weintraub, E. Roy (1991), *Stabilizing Dynamics: Constructing Economic Knowledge*, Cambridge/New York: Cambridge University Press.

Ricardo, David

David Ricardo (1772–1823), political economist, pamphleteer, successful stockbroker, government loan contractor and member of Parliament, is known for his argument that capital accumulation in early nineteenth-century Britain brought inferior lands into cultivation, raising rents and lowering profits. His best known works, *An Essay on the Influence of a Low Price of Corn on the Profits of Stock* (1815) and *The Principles of Political Economy and Taxation* (three editions: 1817, 1819, 1821) used this argument to recommend repeal of the Corn Laws which restricted wheat imports. He also argued against Britain leaving the gold standard in the bullionist controversy, developed a labour value analysis, defended Say's Law and originated the principle of comparative advantage.

Ricardo's methodological reputation as an economist interested in abstract models without any direct application to immediate reality dates from his parliamentary opponent Henry Brougham's caricature of Ricardo as having dropped from another planet:

> his views were often, indeed, abundantly theoretical, sometimes too refined for his audience, occasionally extravagant from his propensity to follow a right principle into all of its consequences, without duly taking into account the condition of things to which he was applying it, as if a mechanician were to construct an engine without taking into account the resistance of the air in which it was to work, or the strength and the weight and the friction of the parts of which it was made. (*Works*, V: xxxiii)

The charge has often been repeated – though not by Cannan, who termed it a delusion (Cannan, 1917: 383) – and is perhaps best known from Schumpeter, who said that the Ricardian Vice was attempting to apply abstract reasoning to the solution of practical problems (Schumpeter, 1954: 473). However, the charge bears little critical scrutiny, since most of the main propositions of Ricardo's thought were closely tied to the policy disputes of his day, and in his propensity for abstract thought he hardly differs from many others in the history of economics.

Ricardo defined political economy as a science that investigated the laws regulating distribution of the social product. Whereas Smith and Malthus understood political economy as an inquiry into the nature and causes of wealth, Ricardo confined himself to an examination of the laws and tendencies that operate in economic life. To some extent, this merely involved an extension of the Smith–Malthus conception, since laws and tendencies presumably reflected cause-and-effect relationships that were thought constant and invariable. Yet it also reflected Ricardo's preference for putting aside transitory features of market economies to focus on those relationships which would prevail in the long run. Writing to Malthus in 1817, Ricardo had said: It appears to me that one great cause of our difference in opinion … is that you have always in mind the immediate and temporary effects of particular changes – whereas I put these immediate and temporary effects quite aside, and fix my whole attention on the permanent state of things which will result from them' (*Works*, VII: 120).

What, then, did Ricardo consider as laws and tendencies? Having said that political economy concerns the laws that govern distribution, Ricardo went on to refer in his chapter on rent to 'the laws which regulate the progress of rent', as compared to 'those which regulate the progress of profits' (ibid., I: 68), and then in his chapter on wages to 'the laws by which wages are regulated' (ibid., I: 105). These laws of political economy further depended on certain laws of nature, particularly Malthus's population principle and the law of diminishing returns in agriculture. By characterizing the former as laws, especially in relation to natural laws upon which they depended, Ricardo clearly held that the fundamental principles governing rent, wages and profits were unchanging and permanent. In contrast, tendencies were weaker principles that reflected relationships likely to prevail in the future. They might be thought of as 'contingent predictions' as de Marchi termed them (1970: 259), that is, as states of affairs that would obtain were certain conditions to hold. Thus Ricardo spoke of the tendency of rents to rise, the tendency of wages to fall as the necessaries of life became more dear and the tendency of profits to fall.

Tendencies are stronger than empirical generalizations based on past observation, in that tendencies presuppose the existence of laws that come into play under certain conditions. This gives tendencies a special significance with respect to prediction, since the existence of laws underlying tendencies provides grounds for thinking, *contra* Hume, that the future will indeed reflect the past. The structure of Ricardo's methodological thinking, then, was to provide credibility for his policy prescriptions by basing them on an analysis of the economy's tendencies, which in turn depended on there being laws of political economy, which themselves were embedded in natural laws. The fragility of this structure was demonstrated when Ricardo added a chapter on machinery introduction to the last edition of the *Principles* that showed labour supply was not strictly a function of the Malthusian population law. If labour were replaced by machinery when wage costs rose, rents need not rise or profits fall (Davis, 1989).

Ricardo's analysis of commodity values also emphasized relationships that were constant and enduring by making the labour required to obtain commodities the principal source of their exchange value. He regarded scarcity as only a temporary influence on commodity values, and market prices as departures from long-run labour values. Utility was essential to exchange value, but not its cause. This reflected not only his preference for attention to 'the permanent state of things', but also his desire to explain social relationships in terms of their foundations in nature. Since labour value as a measure of difficulty of production reflected the relationship of humanity to nature, a commodity's labour value was its 'natural price' (*Works*, I: 88–92). This conception has been retained and defended by some neo-Ricardian thinkers (for example, Pasinetti, 1993: 19).

JOHN B. DAVIS

References

Cannan, E. (1917), *A History of the Theories of Production and Distribution*, 3rd edn, London: P.S. King; first published 1893.
Davis, J. (1989), 'Distribution in Ricardo's Machinery Chapter', *History of Political Economy*, **21**, (3), 457–80.
De Marchi, N. (1970), 'The Empirical Content and Longevity of Ricardian Economics', *Economica*, **37**, 257–76.
Pasinetti, L. (1993), *Structural Economic Dynamics*, Cambridge: Cambridge University Press.
Ricardo, D. (1951–73), *The Works and Correspondence of David Ricardo*, ed. P. Sraffa and M. Dobb, 11 vols. Cambridge: Cambridge University Press.
Schumpeter, J. (1954), *History of Economic Analysis*, New York: Oxford University Press.

Robbins, Lionel

Lionel Robbins' *Essay on the Nature and Significance of Economic Science* (1935) is the most important and influential twentieth-century work on economic methodology before Friedman. It rested on three foundations. First, in conformity with the influence on Robbins of the Austrian writers and of Wicksteed, it sought to generalize the apparatus of economics to deal with non-material, as well as material, welfare; second, it sought emphatically to separate economics from ethics and to isolate the ethical judgments which economists smuggled into economics; third, it aimed to develop an apparatus destructive of the scientific pretensions of Pigovian welfare economics

Robbins' basic position was that economics – and economists – had achieved a very great deal in a century and a half and that it was the analytical – scientific – part of economics which was responsible for this achievement. It provided a logically coherent body of theory. His claims for the standing of economics were wide-ranging and, as has subsequently been observed, would have been highly acceptable to the profession. But in order for economics to achieve its proper position is was necessary to separate the 'scientific' apparatus from the value judgments which economists were prone to make. This desire to isolate value judgments derived to a considerable extent from the work of Max Weber, but it was applied specifically to reject interpersonal comparisons of utility, on the grounds that welfare was an entirely subjective matter of which there could be no objective measurement; this had its origins in the literature of Austrian economics, in particular the writings of Mises, Haberler (to whose 1927 work on the meaning of index numbers Robbins refers) and the later interpreters of Wieser, notably Mayer and Strigl. Economic activity was on the basis of *ordinal* rankings, by individuals, of different possible outcomes – and ordinal rankings did not permit cardinal comparison.

Given Robbins' satisfaction with the body of economic thought which he believed to have been developed as a result of the work of the English classical economists, and of Jevons, Wicksteed and the Austrians in particular, the question arises whether any of this body of theory required confrontation with data. It seems quite clear that Robbins rejected both the attempts to arrive inductively at empirical regularities and also the direct testing of economic theories. Secure in the direct line of criticism of induction stemming from Hume and continued by John Stuart Mill, Robbins was, in particular, very hostile towards the work of Wesley Mitchell. But although he later modified his language so as to introduce a degree of ambiguity concerning testing, it seems clear that, at least in his most important methodological work, he did not envisage the testing of economic theories, for the simple reason that economic theories were necessarily true if they were arrived at by reasoning correctly from plausible premises. The last point, however, is the point at which economic data enter the picture for Robbins. For, in line with the English classical concept of 'verification', Robbins believed that data could – and should – be used to test whether a theory was *applicable* to a particular situation. The correctness of assumptions was thus of key importance. It is in this sense that Cairnes, whose methodological writing (1875) undoubtedly influenced Robbins, considered the use of data legitimate; and it is in this sense that Robbins' own surprisingly extensive use of data in *The Great Depression* (1934) has to be viewed.

To avoid misunderstanding, it should be emphasized that Robbins, who wrote frequently on matters of economic policy, did not believe that *the economist* should abstain from value judgments. Indeed, Robbins employed them frequently, resting them on a utilitarian basis (Bentham was one of his great heroes). But *economics*, the logical apparatus employed by the economist, was distinct from the value judgments which the economist was free to employ when writing about policy. In particular, while Robbins was not opposed to income redistribution, such a policy went beyond what the purely scientific apparatus of economics could support. First, it made interpersonal comparisons (implicitly or explicitly) even though there was, as Robbins emphasized, no *scientific* way of resolving the matter when a Brahmin claimed to be capable of ten times more happiness than an untouchable. Second, redistribution involved a normative 'ought' for which there was no *scientific* basis.

Robbins' methodological position was at odds with much of present practice in economics. Although avoiding, through his acceptance of 'verification', the extreme apriorist position associated with Mises, he rejected the idea that, in the fluid world of an individualistic economic system, worthwhile estimates of empirical regularities could be obtained: his attack on the measurement of the elasticity of demand for herrings (Robbins, 1935: 107–12) is particularly famous. Such a position clearly enraged Beveridge, who used his farewell address as Director of LSE as the occasion for an attack upon it (Beveridge, 1937); and in a world in which technology has advanced far enough to enable virtually all economists to do quantitative work, such a position seems antiquated. Yet, at a deeper methodological level, Robbins' work raises serious questions about the way in which economics can hope to progress even if most economists, faced with a choice between shaky empirical results and the colossal data-free edifices which the resources of mathematical economics have enabled economists to construct, and which enable Sraffians and new classicists to talk past each other in a dialogue of the deaf, may feel that it is better to be roughly right than hugely irrelevant.

DENIS P. O'BRIEN

Bibliography
Beveridge, W. (1937), 'The Place of the Social Sciences in Human Knowledge', *Politica*, **2**, 459–79.
Blaug, M. (1980), *The Methodology of Economics*, Cambridge: Cambridge University Press.
Cairnes, J.E. (1875), *The Character and Logical Method of Political Economy*, London: Macmillan.
Haberler, G.v. (1927), *Der Sinn der Indexzahlen*, Tübingen: Mohr.
Hutchison, T.W. (1979), 'Robbins, Lionel', in D.L. Sills (ed.), *International Encyclopaedia of the Social Sciences*, vol. 18, biographical supplement, New York: Free Press.
Hutchison, T.W. (1981), *The Politics and Philosophy of Economics*, Oxford: Blackwell.
O'Brien, D.P. (1988), *Lionel Robbins*, London: Macmillan.
Robbins, L.C. (1934), *The Great Depression*, London: Macmillan.
Robbins, L.C. (1935), *An Essay on the Nature and Significance of Economic Science*, 2nd edn, London: Macmillan; first published 1932.

Robinson, Joan

Joan Robinson (1903–83) is best known for her contributions to Marshallian value theory in her first major work *Imperfect Competition* (1933), her involvement in the Keynesian revolution during the 1930s and her attempts to synthesize Keynesianism and classical long-period analysis in the Post Keynesian tradition. It is in the context of her interest in long-period analysis that her contributions to the capital theory controversies and questions of growth and accumulation in works such as *The Accumulation of Capital* (1956) can be situated. Throughout her extensive intellectual career, Robinson was consistently involved in thinking about the nature and methodology of economic knowledge, not only explicitly in works like *Economics is a serious subject* (1932), *Economic Philosophy* (1962), 'History versus Equilibrium' (1974) and 'Thinking about Thinking' (1979), but in all her theoretical writings.

Realism of Assumptions
Robinson's views on the methodology of economics changed substantially in the course of her long intellectual life. In her first published work, *Economics is a serious subject*, she systematically elaborated her methodological approach to economic analysis by making a distinction between approaches which emphasize tractable assumptions and ones that correspond to the real world. In the context of this methodological controversy, she put herself squarely in the camp of the 'optimistic economist' who pursues the development of a self-consistent theoretical system even if it gives unreal answers to unreal questions. Interestingly, however, *Economics is a Serious Subject* is subtitled *The Apologia of the Economist to the Mathematician, the Scientist and the Plain Man*, demonstrating her discomfort with this methodology even at

this early stage in her career. There is indeed a certain tension in this work since, on the one hand, she purported to defend economics against the objections of non-economists, while, on the other hand, she was quite sensitive, perhaps even sympathetic to and definitely apologetic about, the practical complaints of others.

Robinson started her *Economics of Imperfect Competition* in the same spirit as *Economics is a serious subject* by claiming it to be only 'a box of tools'. But even a year after her optimistic proclamations she had already gone beyond optimistically accepting the unrealism of economic assumptions. While her aim was still to build a logically self-consistent theory, she now also had the goal of basing the theory of value on the more realistic assumption of monopoly.

Short-period Equilibrium

Robinson's short-period analysis conducted mostly in the first half of her intellectual career was influenced by both Marshall and Keynes. From Marshall, Robinson developed an understanding of partial equilibrium analysis that could not be reconciled with Walrasian general equilibrium. For Marshall, a firm can be in equilibrium in the short period at a historically specific productive capacity and with a given set of expectations which may turn out to be wrong and/or inconsistent with those of others. What was useful in this kind of analysis for Robinson was its capacity for depicting partial equilibria which were often the closest we could come to explaining economic phenomena such as the formation of relative prices.

While retaining Marshall's notion of partial equilibrium as short-period and containing inconsistencies, however, Robinson abandoned his extension of the concept of equilibrium to a period in the future in which economic conditions were stationary. This is where Keynes comes into the picture in terms of the development of Robinson's short-period analysis, for it is Keynes' key argument 'that an unregulated economy contains no dynamic process that would tend, if left alone, to get into a position of general equilibrium' (Gram and Walsh, 1983: 521) which Robinson adopts in rejecting Marshall's claims for the possibilities of general equilibrium in the future.

Long-period equilibrium

After her intense involvement in the Keynesian revolution, Robinson moved on to develop an analysis of the dynamic long period to supplement Keynes' short-period analysis and to 'swallow up, as a special case, the long-run static theory in which the present generation of academic economists are educated' (Robinson: 1949: 155). In her famous 1953–4 article, 'The Production Function and the Theory of Capital', Robinson initiated the capital controversies by showing that, while it is legitimate to ignore the nature of capital in the short period when the capital stock is held constant, in the long period, with the capital stock changing, the question of how capital is measured and, more importantly, what its meaning is become especially relevant. Relatedly, in the context of the long period, she asked about processes of production and distribution, structures of reproduction and generation of surplus, and growth and accumulation in capitalist economies.

Robinson's long-period analysis culminated in 'History versus Equilibrium' and the methodological distinction she made between differences and changes in underlying economic variables, which for her was a distinction intimately linked with her view on the difference between logical and historical time. Specifically, in the simultaneous equation model of neoclassicism, general equilibrium is the outcome of a long-run process – a sequence of short-run equilibria at the end of which all markets clear – and as such needs a satisfactory analysis of how the economy can in fact get into equilibrium. Robinson observed, however, that this process moves in logical time in that it is only able to account for the differences and not the changes in the underlying variables. Moreover, this methodology is mechanical in its use of a space metaphor in order to describe a process through time: 'For mechanical movements in space, there is no distinction between approaching equilibrium from an arbitrary initial position and a perturbation due to displacement from an equilibrium that has long been established. In economic life, in which decisions are guided by expectations about the future, these two types of movement are totally different' (Robinson, 1974: 49).

The long-period method deemed useful by Robinson is one that starts in the steady state but quickly ends up in the short period in order to deal with the inevitable disequilibrium situations and uncertain expectations. This approach is in historical time, in that it identifies a set of variables with a 'particular set of values obtaining at a moment of time which are not, in general, in equilibrium with each other' and shows 'how their interactions may be expected to play themselves out' (Robinson, 1962b: 23). It is obvious that given this methodology, the theory would have to tell a whole new story 'about the behavior of the economy when it is out of equilibrium, including the effect of disappointed expectations on decisions being taken by its inhabitants' (Robinson, 1974: 52)

Thus Robinson pointed to major flaws in the concept of equilibrium. First, reliance on equilibrium not only disallows any admissions of uncertainty, it actually requires the existence of perfect foresight on the part of economic agents. Second, equilibrium implies the existence of stability, which Robinson saw as too mechanical to be applicable to economic life. Even if we assume that the economy starts out at an equilibrium that is subsequently disturbed because of a change in, say, tastes, the neoclassical story of the re-establishment of the new equilibrium is still too simplistic for Robinson, since it assumes a change in the pattern of production and demand devoid of any consideration of uncertainty. Robinson's preoccupation with historically specific issues meant that she viewed expectations as far more uncertain than do the neoclassicals, who see them in terms of calculated risk: 'As soon as the uncertainty of expectations that guide economic behavior is admitted, equilibrium drops out of the argument and history takes its place' (ibid.: 126). And history, is of course, a rather messy process which does not fit a sequence of discrete, well-defined and balanced episodes.

ZOHREH EMAMI

References
Gram, Harvey and Vivian Walsh (1983), 'Joan Robinson's Economics in Retrospect', *Journal of Economic Literature*, **21**, June, 518–50.
Robinson, Joan (1932), *Economics is a Serious Subject*, Cambridge: W. Heffer & Sons Ltd.
Robinson, Joan (1933), *Economics of Imperfect Competition*, London: Macmillan; 2nd edn, 1969.
Robinson, Joan, (1949), 'Mr Harrod's Dynamics', *Collected Economic Papers*, vol. I, Oxford: Basil Blackwell.
Robinson, Joan (1953–4), 'The Production Function and the Theory of Capital', *Collected Economic Papers*, vol II, Oxford: Basil Blackwell.
Robinson, Joan (1956), *The Accumulation of Capital*. London: Macmillan.
Robinson, Joan (1962a), *Economic Philosophy*, Chicago; Aldine Publishing Company.
Robinson, Joan (1962b), *An Essay on Marxian Economics*. 2nd edn, New York: St Martin's Press.
Robinson, Joan (1974), 'History versus Equilibrium', *Contributions to Modern Economics*, New York: Harcourt Brace Jovanovich.
Robinson, Joan (1979), 'Thinking about Thinking', *Collected Economic Papers*, vol. V, Cambridge, MA: MIT Press.

Rorty, Richard

Richard M. Rorty was born in New York City on 4 October 1931. He received his BA and MA degrees from the University of Chicago and went on to do graduate work at Yale, where he was awarded the PhD in 1956. After more than 20 years in Princeton's philosophy department, he became Professor of Humanities at the University of Virginia in 1982.

Although Rorty has written on a wide range of philosophical topics, the book that most clearly established his professional reputation was *Philosophy and the Mirror of Nature* (*PMN*) in 1979. This was a radical as well as influential work; it amounted to an all-out attack on what Rorty regards as the central dogma of the western philosophical tradition (at least since Kant). This central dogma is the 'mirror metaphor', the core notion that the human mind 'mirrors' the world. A corollary of the mirror metaphor is that 'knowledge' is simply a special class of representations: representations that are accurate or privileged. This perspective on mind and knowledge leads to a view of philosophy as an intellectual 'usher', as the mother-discipline that 'grounds' or provides 'foundations for' other parts of human culture such as science, art and ethics. This ushering role is particularly pronounced in positivist-inspired philosophy of science where the 'received view' attempts to provide standards for what is and what is not legitimate scientific (and possibly all) knowledge. Abandoning the mirror metaphor would fundamentally alter the role of philosophy in our intellectual culture. In Rorty's own words:

> If there are no privileged representations in the mirror, then it will no longer answer to the need for a touch stone for choice between justified and unjustified claims upon our belief. Unless some other such framework can be found, the abandonment of the image of the mirror leads us to abandon the notion of philosophy as a discipline which adjudicates the claims of science and religion, mathematics and poetry, reason and sentiment, allocating an appropriate place to each. (1979: 212)

Rorty's attack on the mirror metaphor is two-pronged; he engages in a direct assault on the philosophical mainstream, while simultaneously trying to charm the disenfranchised with his own alternative view. The direct assault is based on the repeated failure of the project of philosophy-as-epistemology to succeed on its own terms; quite simply, the discipline of philosophy has never been able to do that which it claims it has the right (and the responsibility) to do. The allies that Rorty recruits for this assault are numerous but perhaps not very surprising; they include Nietzsche, Heidegger, late Wittgenstein, Quine, Feyerabend, Kuhn and various authors from the sociology of scientific knowledge.

His own alternative view was called 'hermeneutics' in *PMN*, but he has used the term 'pragmatism' more consistently in later work. This pragmatist conception of knowledge draws inspiration from philosophers like Dewey and Gadamer (as well as from some of the authors employed in the direct assault) and it considers knowledge to be a matter of conversation and social practice rather than accurate representation. For Rorty, inquirers are inevitably situated and contextual; there is no transcendent philosophical position from which to judge all other positions. Criticism is possible under such conditions, but it is always criticism from within a particular situated perspective, and the resulting change will be piecemeal and relative to the local interests of those involved in the critical conversation. According to Rorty, we look for new and better ways of talking and acting, new and better ways of redescription, but these are never 'foundational': they do not represent a 'ground' or 'starting point' prior to, or outside of, all cultural traditions. Rorty's version of pragmatism does not view truth as correspondence but simply as Nietzsche's 'mobile army of metaphors' (Rorty, 1989: 17) and it also rejects the notion of science as a true representation of reality: 'modern science does not enable us to cope because it corresponds, it just plain enables us to cope' (Rorty, 1982: xvii). The result is a position that encourages us to 'drop the notion of the philosopher as knowing something about knowing which nobody else knows so well' and to 'drop the notion that his voice always has an overriding claim on the attention of the other participants in the conversation' (Rorty, 1979: 392).

Rorty's assault on the philosophical mainstream has an impact that goes far beyond the particular concerns of professional philosophers. The central thesis of *PMN* shakes the very foundation of western democratic capitalist societies. Our notions of freedom, of democracy and of scientific truth are all undermined by Rorty's position. If there is no place to stand outside culture in order to evaluate it, if all inquiry is situated and perspectival, and if natural science makes truth rather than discovers it, on what grounds is it possible to endorse our social, political and cognitive institutions? Most western intellectuals believe that the values of the Enlightenment and the institutions those values have helped create are 'better' than other values and other institutions, or at least they believe that our primary ground for criticizing institutions is the degree to which they fail to live up to the values of the Enlightenment. Rorty's position undermines any objective grounding we might have for these beliefs.

This problem, the problem of how to defend liberal values in a world without a 'first philosophy' or objective 'foundations', is the problem Rorty addresses in his book *Contingency, Irony, and Solidarity* (1989) and his autobiographical essay (1993). Although Rorty's response is many-faceted, one of the main themes is that his pragmatism actually extends Enlightenment values in a way that philosophy-as-epistemology does not. Philosophy-as-epistemology, particularly positivist philosophy of science, did not go all the way with the message of the Enlightenment; the message was to do without god, but positivism did not eliminate god, it simply substituted a new one: 'positivism preserved a god in its notion of Science (and its notion of "scientific philosophy"), the notion of a portion of culture where we touched something not ourselves, where we found Truth naked, relative to no description' (Rorty, 1982: xliii). Rorty's position is that we should 'try to get to the point where we no longer worship *anything*, where we treat *nothing* as a quasi-divinity, where we treat *everything* – our language, our conscience, or community – as a product of time and chance' (Rorty, 1989: 22).

Another aspect of Rorty's answer to the question of liberal values involves the separation of the private and the public self. His radical epistemological position is characterized by 'irony' and irony seems to be 'inherently a private matter' (ibid.: 87); as Rorty himself admits, even he 'cannot imagine a culture which socialized its youth in such a way as to make them continually dubious about their own process of socialization' (ibid.). Rorty advocates both private irony and liberal hope: private irony in accepting that one's final vocabulary is not any closer to the Truth than the final vocabulary of others, and liberal hope that such private recognition will bring about a social world that is less cruel and more consistent with our liberal values. For Rorty, the fundamental premise 'is that a belief can still regulate action, can still be thought worth dying for, among people who are quite aware that this belief is caused by nothing deeper than contingent historical circumstances' (ibid.: 189).

Given the radical nature of Rorty's position, it is hardly surprising that his work has generated a wide range of critical responses. It is fair to say that the philosophical community has taken Rorty to task on almost every aspect of his position (see the papers in Malachowski,

1990, and the discussion in Hall, 1994). Criticism has been particularly harsh in the areas of Rorty's interpretation of major schools of philosophy – such as pragmatism and hermeneutics – and his interpretation of major figures in the history of philosophy, such as Heidegger and Dewey (see Rorty, 1991b; 1994). His political philosophy has also come under attack from many different directions and it has generated at least one book-length critique (Bhaskar, 1991). Despite this critical literature, Rorty's voice continues to be heard and continues to be influential; the twentieth century ends with the 'end of philosophy' as a major topic for philosophical debate, and that is a debate that owes much to the work of Richard Rorty.

Rorty's work has contributed to methodological discussion in economics in a number of different ways; just three of these contributions will be mentioned in closing. First, and most broadly, it has contributed to a general anti-foundationalist (some would say postmodernist) mood in intellectual life. This impact, while undoubtedly significant, is sufficiently diffused for it to be impossible to measure in any meaningful way, but the bottom line is that fewer economic methodologists write about 'Truth' or 'Scientific Knowledge' in the way they wrote about such things a decade ago, and this change is at least in part due to Rorty's impact on contemporary philosophical discourse. Second, and much more specifically, Rorty has directly influenced the 'rhetoric of economics' programme of McCloskey (1985; 1994) and others. Rorty's critique of philosophy-as-usher and his pragmatic 'social conversation' alternative have both become essential components of the rhetorical approach to economics (see Davis, 1990). Finally, there is an economic element to Rorty's political philosophy, what he calls 'Postmodernist Bourgeois Liberalism' (1991a), and that economic element has become a topic of debate. Some, Bhaskar (1991) for instance, find too much bourgeois economics in Rorty's approach, while others, Posner (1993) for instance, find too little, but in either case it is yet another example of the expanding interaction between Rorty's philosophical position and the discipline of economics.

D. Wade Hands

References

Bhaskar, R. (1991), *Philosophy and the Idea of Freedom*, Oxford: Blackwell.
Davis, J.B. (1990), 'Rorty's Contribution to McCloskey's Understanding of Conversation as the Methodology of Economics', *Research in the History of Economic Thought and Methodology*, 73–85.
Hall, D.L. (1994), *Richard Rorty: Prophet and Poet of the New Pragmatism*, Albany: State University of New York Press.
Malachowski, A. (ed.) (1990), *Reading Rorty*, Oxford: Blackwell.
McCloskey, D.N. (1985), *The Rhetoric of Economics*, Madison: University of Wisconsin Press.
McCloskey, D.N. (1994), *Knowledge and Persuasion in Economics*, Cambridge: Cambridge University Press.
Posner, R.A. (1993), 'Richard Rorty's Politics', *Critical Review*, **7**, 33–49.
Rorty, R. (1979), *Philosophy and the Mirror of Nature*, Princeton: Princeton University Press.
Rorty, R. (1982), *Consequences of Pragmatism*, Minneapolis: University of Minnesota Press.
Rorty, R. (1989), *Contingency, Irony and Solidarity*, Cambridge: Cambridge University Press.
Rorty, R. (1991a), *Objectivity, Relativism and Truth: Philosophical Papers*, vol I, Cambridge: Cambridge University Press.
Rorty, R. (1991b), *Essays on Heidegger and Others: Philosophical Papers*, vol II, Cambridge: Cambridge University Press.
Rorty, R. (1993), 'Trotsky and the Wild Orchids', in M. Edmundson (ed.), *Wild Orchids and Trotsky: Messages from American Universities*, New York: Penguin.
Rorty, R. (1994), 'Dewey Between Hegel and Darwin', in D. Ross (ed.), *Modernist Impulses in the Human Sciences 1870–1930*, Baltimore: Johns Hopkins University Press.

Rule Following

The notion of *rule-following behaviour* is generally thought to be in conflict with the concept of *rational choice* that is at the core of theoretical economics. Whether the two are, indeed, incompatible outlooks on human behaviour depends, of course, on how they are interpreted. The concept of rational choice is surely incompatible with any notion of rule-following behaviour if its essence is seen in the claim that human beings respond, in a case-by-case manner, to the unique complexity of each and every single choice situation, and that they select from all possible choice alternatives the one that maximizes their utility. Conversely, the notion of rule following is surely incompatible with any concept of rational choice if it is meant to imply that human beings learn, in a process of socialization, to follow certain rules that they then continue to adhere to, unaffected by changes in incentives, that is in the payoffs of alternative behavioural options. Yet the concepts of rational choice and of rule following may well be compatible if, for instance, 'rational choice' means in essence that men are responsive to incentives and 'rule following' is meant to imply that men rely on behavioural patterns that they have found, in the past, to help to solve certain types of problems.

If man is, indeed, as Hayek (1973: 11) notes, 'as much a rule-following animal as a purpose-seeking one', an economics that aims at explaining social reality has to be based on a behavioural theory that can account for the rule following in human behaviour no less than for its purpose-seeking or rational choice aspects. Both within economics and in related fields, a number of theoretical approaches have been developed that all point in the direction of a behavioural theory that promises to accomplish this, which may be called a theory of *adaptive rationality* and *rule-following behaviour*. These approaches include the contributions by Hayek, Popper and others to what has become known as 'evolutionary epistemology', H. Simon's thoughts on bounded rationality, the work by J.H. Holland and others on complex adaptive systems, R. Heiner's theory of imperfect choice and others (for a discussion and for references, see Vanberg, 1993; 1994, chs. 1–3, 6). The common theoretical denominator of these approaches is the assumption that human beings do not, and cannot, respond to the full complexity of each and every particular problem situation they confront. Instead, they rely on simplifying mental models that reflect past experience and are adjusted in response to new experience. Such an assumption is in conflict with a rational choice approach that seeks to explain each *single act* as a maximizing response to the particular choice situation, yet it is compatible with other claims that are typically associated with rational choice theory, in particular the notion that human behaviour is self-interested and a function of its expected payoffs. Instead of supposing that single acts are 'rational' or adapted to specific situations, a theory of adaptive rationality supposes that – and seeks to explain why – a person's rules of behaviour are adapted to the kind of world she lives in.

The fundamental choice of theoretical orientation within economics that is at issue here has been pointed out by Hayek in his seminal 1937 article on 'Economics and Knowledge' (Hayek, 1948: 33–56). Hayek argues there, in effect, that economic theory can be developed along two different lines, depending on whether it takes its departure from a notion of objective or subjective rationality. An economic theory that starts from the concept of *objective* rationality implicitly supposes that there is no difference between the 'objective data' that the economic analyst talks about and the 'subjective data' that economic agents act upon. Economic actors are assumed to share the same, perfect knowledge that enables them to make optimal choices. The task that remains for economic theory is to work out the logical implications that can be derived with regard to the social outcomes of the interaction among such perfectly rational actors. Economic theory of this sort does not produce empirically testable conjectures about real human action in the observable social world.

The alternative research path that Hayek advocates starts from the assumption that economic actors are rational only in a *subjective* sense, that is, relative to what they actually know about the world. Their subjective knowledge need not correspond to the 'objective data', or be the same across economic actors, and between them and the observing analyst. It differs among different persons and it changes over time for the same persons. This means that differences and changes in knowledge become relevant for any effort in explaining people's behaviour. By implying, Hayek argues, that 'subjective data' correspond to the 'objective data', economists bypass the main questions, namely how people acquire knowledge of the world and how their subjective pieces of knowledge are adapted to each other and socially coordinated. The problem of how people learn about the world becomes paramount as soon as one acknowledges that 'the analysis of what people will do can start only from what is known to them' (Hayek, 1948: 44). Only by incorporating conjectures 'about how experience creates knowledge', Hayek concludes (ibid.: 47), can economists give their theories empirical content.

An economics that takes its departure from the notion of subjective rationality has to be based – this is Hayek's message – on a theory of how human beings learn to adapt to their environment and to cope with the problems they face. The approaches referred to above under the rubric of 'adaptive rationality' are relevant to theoretical economics because they are contributions to such a theory of learning and adaptation. And it is their conception of the learning process that is intrinsically linked to the notion of rule-following behaviour. In particular, both the theories of complex adaptive systems and of evolutionary epistemology show that the process of learning or knowledge acquisition and rule-following behaviour are but two sides of one coin.

The research programme of evolutionary epistemology to which Hayek (1952; 1978) and Popper (1972) have made major contributions revolves around the idea that all behaviour concerns problem solving, and that problem solving is always based on pre-existing 'conjectural knowledge', knowledge that could be translated into statements of the 'if–then' type: if confronted with a problem of type A, then a behavioural response of type X is appropriate. All organisms can, in this sense, be regarded as being endowed, at any time, with a more or less complex repertoire of behavioural conjectures or dispositions that make the organism inclined to interpret a problem situation that it encounters as belonging to a certain class of situations (perception as classification) and to respond by a certain type of problem-solving strategy that is conjectured to be successful. There is, as Hayek notes, a symmetry between rule-guided perception and rule-guided behaviour: 'dispositions towards kinds of movements can be regarded as adaptations to typical features of the environment, and the "recognition" of such features as the activation of the kind of disposition adapted to them' (Hayek, 1978: 41). The 'behavioral conjectures' can either be part of the organism's genetic make-up (reflecting the 'learning history' of the species) or acquired dispositions (reflecting the individual learning history of the particular organism). It is in the light of its repertoire of conjectures that an organism perceives the world (that is, perception is always theory-impregnated, interpretative) and that it responds to its environment. Learning or knowledge acquisition consists in the corrective adaptation of the behavioural repertoire to the problem environment through a process of trial-and-error elimination (Popper, 1972: 242). All learning proceeds, in this sense, from antecedent conjectures or expectations: 'Ontologically (that is, with regard to the development of the individual organism) we thus regress to the state of the expectations of a newborn child; phylogenetically (with regard to the evolution of the race, the phylum) we get to the state of expectations of unicellular organisms' (ibid.: 347).

An outlook at processes of learning and adaptation that is, indeed, quite similar to the evolutionary epistemology approach can be found in the *theory of complex adaptive systems* that has its main roots in cognitive science (Holland *et al.*, 1986). The question that this theory seeks to answer is how cognitive systems, that is systems that can process information from their environment, can learn about and adapt to their environment. Or, as Holland *et al.* (ibid.: 3) phrase the question: 'How can a cognitive system process environmental input and store knowledge so as to benefit from experience?' They answer this question in essentially the same way as evolutionary epistemology does. Adaptive systems are regarded as *rule-based systems* that operate on the basis of 'conjectural knowledge' or of dispositions that allow them to classify problem situations and to select 'appropriate' responses. And they are assumed to adapt their repertoire of dispositions to the contingencies of their environment in a process of trial-and-error elimination. Applied to the realm of economics, this theory is translated into a reinterpretation of 'rational action' as adaptive rule following. Economic actors are assumed to 'form mental models, or hypotheses, or subjective beliefs. ... Each agent will normally keep track of the performance of a private collection of such belief-models. ... Agents "learn" which of their hypotheses work, and from time to time they may discard poorly performing hypotheses and generate new "ideas" to put in their place' (Arthur, 1994: 407).

The theory of problem solving and of the growth of knowledge that evolutionary epistemology proposes can, as Popper (1972: 261) emphasizes, be equally 'applied to animal knowledge, pre-scientific knowledge, and to scientific knowledge'. The same can be said about the theory of complex adaptive systems. Both theories show why even the most 'mindless' rule-following behaviour can be said to be based on conjectural knowledge, and why even the most mindful rational choice can be said to be rule-guided. Both theories can provide economics with a model of human behaviour that captures much of what is generally regarded as the essential thrust of the rational choice paradigm, yet has the virtue of being grounded in empirical science.

The apparent adaptiveness of human behaviour, the fact that it is instrumental in a problem-solving sense, is, without doubt, a principal reason for the intuitive appeal of the rational choice model and for the economists' loyal adherence to it, in spite of accumulating criticism. The contrast between the received model of rational choice and the theory of adaptive, rule-following behaviour can also be described in terms of their respective accounts of the *adaptiveness* of human problem-solving behaviour. Rational choice theory postulates that economic actors are adapted; it does not explain where that capacity comes from. It defines rational action in a way that implies adaptiveness, and concerns itself with the logical implications of such a definition. By contrast, the theory of adaptive rule following seeks to explain how adaptiveness in human behaviour comes about by examining how human beings acquire the knowledge on which their attempts at problem solving are based. Adaptiveness in current behaviour is explained in a backward-looking manner, as a product of past experience. Such adaptiveness can only be adaptiveness to past environments and it is not claimed to guarantee success in current choice situations.

Viktor J. Vanberg

References
Arthur, W. Brian (1994), 'Inductive Reasoning and Bounded Rationality', *American Economic Review, Papers and Proceedings*, **84**, 406–11.

Hayek, F.A. (1948), 'Economics and Knowledge', *Individualism and Economic Order*, Chicago: University of Chicago Press.

Hayek, F.A. (1952), *The Sensory Order – An Inquiry into the Foundations of Theoretical Psychology*, Chicago: University of Chicago Press.

Hayek, F.A. (1973), *Law, Legislation and Liberty*, vol. 1: *Rules and Order*, London/Henley: Routledge & Kegan Paul.

Hayek, F.A. (1978), 'The Primacy of the Abstract', *New Studies in Philosophy, Politics, Economics and the History of Ideas*, Chicago: University of Chicago Press.

Holland, J.H., K.J., Holyoak, R.E. Nisbett and P.R. Thagard (1986), *Induction*, Cambridge, MA: MIT Press.

Popper, Karl R. (1972), *Objective Knowledge – An Evolutionary Approach*, Oxford: Clarendon Press.

Vanberg, Viktor (1993), 'Rational Choice, Rule-Following, and Institutions', in U. Mäki, B. Gustafson and Ch. Knudsen (eds), *Rationality, Institutions and Economic Methodology*, London/New York: Routledge.

Vanberg, Viktor (1994), *Rules and Choice in Economics*, London/New York: Routledge.

Schumpeterian Evolutionism

The work of Joseph Alois Schumpeter (1883–1950) on the capitalist economic system encompasses economic statics, economic dynamics and economic sociology. As the development of mind and thought, in his view, is concomitant with the development of a society, he also envisaged a series of studies on mind, thought and science, including the philosophy of science, the history of science and the sociology of science. According to this perspective, a set of substantive theories (economic statics, economic dynamics and economic sociology) is matched with another set of metatheories (philosophy of science, history of science and sociology of science) with a parallel structure. Each structure consists of three layers: static analysis, dynamic analysis and sociological analysis. Society and mind are in the process of evolving a bilateral relationship, especially through the link between economic sociology and the sociology of science. Schumpeter's two sets of studies may be called a three-layered, two-structure approach to mind and society, which was intended to replace Karl Marx's social theory based on the economic interpretation of history concerning the relationship between the substructure and the superstructure of a society. Schumpeter's universal social science and his evolutionism should be understood in this broad perspective.

Schumpeter's view of the research programme of a universal social science has been little known because Chapter 7 of the first edition of his *Theorie der wirtschaftlichen Entwicklung* (1912), in which he presented the idea of an all-encompassing social science, was omitted from subsequent editions. Nevertheless, the idea proved to be an organizing principle for his wide-ranging work and eventually contributed to his theory of evolution. His concept of a universal social science was animated by the intention of integrating theory and history, which constituted his response to the *Methodenstreit* between theorists and historians. In what follows, an exposition of the Schumpeterian system will concern, first, the relationship between economic statics and economic dynamics, second, the task of economic sociology to overcome the limitation of economic dynamics, and third, the relationship between the development of economy and thought as the subject of the history of economics, in which the sociology of science and the methodology of science converge.

Schumpeter's theory of economic development or economic dynamics is well known for its emphasis on entrepreneurial innovation in a capitalist economy, but it is only a part of Schumpeterian evolutionism. In his view, economic dynamics should be based on economic statics, that is, economic equilibrium analysis, on the one hand; and it should be combined with economic sociology, that is, an analysis of changes in the institutional framework of an economy, on the other.

Schumpeter's first book, *Das Wesen und der Hauptinhalt der theoretischen Nation-alökonomie* (1908), recapitulated the Walrasian version of economic statics by developing Ernst Mach's philosophy of science into an economic methodology of instrumentalism (see Shionoya, 1990). For Schumpeter, a general equilibrium in economic statics was the logic of an economy that formulated the consequences of the adaptive behaviour of economic agents responding to their exogenously given circumstances. He regarded economic statics as the Magna Carta of economic theory in the sense that economics should be established as an exact and autonomous science. Economic statics or the science of the economic equilibrating mechanism is applied to the process of circular flow, in which the economy repeats itself year after year, with its size and structure remaining constant under given conditions. According to Schumpeter, economic growth through an increase in population and capital can be explained by economic statics because these changes are exogenous. Although often misunderstood, economic statics, in his view, is not an abstract construction but a description of real forces in an economic process.

Schumpeter defined economic development by reference to three elements: its cause (innovation), its carrier (entrepreneur) and its means (bank credit). Economic development is the destruction of circular flow when entrepreneurs introduce innovations, including new products, new techniques, new markets, new sources of supply and new organizations. Bank credit provides entrepreneurs with new purchasing power, by which they wrest the means of production required for innovations from the circular flow of an economy. Schumpeter emphasized entrepreneurship because, he believed, the causes of economic changes were endogenous: change originated from within an economic system rather than from without an economy. His basic idea of evolutionism was that both the cause of changes in an economic system and the response mechanism to those changes must be endogenous; thus he regarded the entrepreneurial activity of innovation as the cause of economic development and the formulation of business cycles as the process of absorbing the impact of innovation with a response mechanism. He called the process of economic development 'creative destruction' and contrasted his dynamic conception of competition with the traditional one of neoclassical economics, which was concerned with the equilibrium mechanism of markets. However, since economic development is conceived as the destruction of equilibrium, it cannot be an object of scientific inquiry unless it is linked epistemologically with some mechanism of restoring order. Whatever destructive forces of innovation may emerge in the economy, markets can be relied on to adapt to them and absorb their effects in order to establish a new equilibrium. In this sense, Schumpeter emphasized that economic dynamics should be based on economic statics.

The entrepreneur is a special kind of a leader in the economic domain. The leader as the carrier of innovations in a particular area of social life is in marked contrast to the majority of people who only take adaptive or routine actions. Schumpeter believed that such a contrast exists not only in economics but also in science, the arts, politics, and so on. He applied the statics–dynamics dichotomy to various aspects of social life as the underlying idea of a universal social science. Schumpeter noted that the concepts of statics and dynamics were introduced into economics, not from mechanics, but from zoology via Henri de Blainville, Auguste Compte and J.S. Mill and that the idea of evolution depended on a zoological analogy, for a mechanical analogy does not apply to the development of an economy from within. He meant, for instance, that if a study of the organism of a dog is compared to statics, research on how dogs have come to exist at all in terms of concepts seen as selection, mutation or evolution would be rooted in dynamics.

Schumpeter's theory of economic development, however, presents a difficulty: even if an entrepreneur is regarded as being inside the economic system, the occurrence of the entrepreneurial activity of technological change cannot be explained endogenously by his theory; it remains in a 'black box' that is exogenous to the economic system. In other words, he could not account for the causes of innovations but only describe the various economic phenomena associated with them. Inquiries concerning the black box of innovations were left to Schumpeterian economists after World War II. Schumpeter himself found in economic sociology a way out of the difficulty.

When Schumpeter explained the nature of his theory of economic development, he referred to two great figures, Léon Walras and Karl Marx, to whom he had been indebted (Schumpeter, 1937). According to him, Walras provided 'a pure logic of the interdependence between economic quantities' and Marx 'a vision of economic evolution as a distinct process generated by the economic system itself'. Although he pretended that his idea was exactly the same as

Marx's vision of endogenous economic evolution, Schumpeter had to admit that the structure of his economic dynamics covered only a small part of Marx's ground. Schumpeter's theory of economic development conceived in terms of the economy alone is not sufficient to explicate the evolution of a capitalist society as a whole and is therefore no match for Marx's analysis of capitalism. Schumpeter thought that only in a wider perspective beyond economics was an endogenous explanation of the evolving capitalist system possible.

When Schumpeter limited himself to the economic domain, he defined capitalism as a set of three economic institutions: the market mechanism, private ownership and bank credit. When he took a broader view, however, he conceived of capitalism as a civilization that included the economic system, the political system, class structure, ways of thinking, value systems, science and the arts, lifestyles and so on. The evolution of capitalism, in his view, must be explained in terms of the changing relationship between the economic and non-economic domains.

After the publication of the 1912 book, Schumpeter shifted his interest to economic sociology and developed a theory of social classes (Schumpeter, 1951) that would serve as the focal point for linking the concept of leadership in various areas of social life with the overall concepts of civilization or the *Zeitgeist*, thus mediating bilateral interactions between the economic and non-economic domains. This is the skeleton of his economic sociology developed in *Capitalism, Socialism and Democracy* (1942) by the use of the two-structure approach in which he presented his famous thesis on the demise of capitalism in consequence of its success. According to him, the very success of capitalist economic development will produce non-economic factors that are inconsistent with it; these factors will in turn worsen the economic performance of capitalism. Although the economy can work effectively by itself, the impact of external factors that are influenced by the successful workings of capitalism will ultimately spoil it. Schumpeter did not say that the development of capitalism would automatically lead to socialism, but merely that the mental and physical conditions favourable for the political choice of socialism would be created.

Schumpeter's work includes contributions to the history of economics, especially his magnum opus, *History of Economic Analysis* (1954). Why was he drawn to it? For him, the development of economy and of economics – or, generally speaking, the development of society and of thought – were really aspects of one stream of events. The analysis of the relationship between these two concomitant developments formed the essential task of a universal, evolutionary social science in Schumpeter. The thesis of the future of capitalism can be construed as the analysis of the relationship between economic development and the *Zeitgeist*. As fur scientific thought, Schumpeter worked, first, on the philosophy of science (the rules of scientific procedure), second, on the history of science (the development of scientific apparatus) and third, on the sociology of science (the nature of scientific activity carried out in social circumstances). He anticipated the contemporary sociology of science in holding that the development of science is not brought about linearly according to the criteria prescribed by the philosophy of science, but rather in a zigzag fashion by clustering the innovations of scientific leaders who sometimes succeed in forming schools or paradigms in Kuhn's sense. A school, the phenomenon of a leader with a large following, is the subject matter of the sociology of science. Schumpeter defined the concept of the 'Classical Situation' as the achievement of substantial agreement on doctrines and methods after a long period of controversy. Vision, another feature of Schumpeter's sociology of science, is a preconception preceding the construction of theoretical models and often depends on the thought of previous scholars. In view of the fact that a new combination of past ideas sometimes leads to innovations in science, Schumpeter called this process of evolution 'the Filiation of Scientific Ideas'.

In an empirical analysis of capitalist development (Schumpeter, 1939), Schumpeter depended on the scheme of Kondratieff long waves; he distinguished three waves, starting from and ending at, the neighbourhood of equilibrium: the Industrial Revolution Kondratieff (1787–1842), the Bourgeois Kondratieff (1843–97) and the Neomercantilist Kondratieff (1898–). In a study of the history of economics (Schumpeter, 1954), on the other hand, he identified the periods of the Classical Situation as the acceptance of Adam Smith (1790), the maturity of the classical economics (1848) and the establishment of the neoclassical school (1890), occurring at roughly 50-year intervals. Although he observed that 'society and mind are two aspects of the same evolutionary process' (Schumpeter, 1954: 137), he did not fully develop the heuristic two-structure approach beyond his vision of failing capitalism. But this is a unique achievement of the synthesis between economic sociology and the sociology of knowledge.

YUICHI SHIONOYA

Bibliography
Schumpeter, Joseph Alois (1908), *Das Wesen und der Hauptinhalt der theoretischen Nationalökonomie*, Leipzig: Duncker & Humblot.
Schumpeter, Joseph Alois (1912), *Theorie der wirtschaftlichen Entwicklung*, Leipzig: Duncker & Humblot; 2nd rev. edn, 1926.
Schumpeter, Joseph Alois (1934), *The Theory of Economic Development* (abridged version of the German 2nd edn), trans. Redvers Opie, Cambridge, MA: Harvard University Press.
Schumpeter, Joseph Alois (1937), 'Preface' to Japanese Edition of *Theorie der wirtschaftlichen Entwicklung*; reprinted in R.V. Clemence (ed.), *Essays of J.A. Schumpeter*, Cambridge, MA: Addison-Wesley.
Schumpeter, Joseph Alois (1939), *Business Cycles*, 2 vols, New York: McGraw-Hill.
Schumpeter, Joseph Alois (1942), *Capitalism, Socialism and Democracy*, New York: Harper & Brothers.
Schumpeter, Joseph Alois (1951), *Imperialism and Social Classes*, trans. Heinz Norden, New York: Augustus M. Kelley.
Schumpeter, Joseph Alois (1954), *History of Economic Analysis*, New York: Oxford University Press.
Shionoya, Yuichi (1990), 'Instrumentalism in Schumpeter's Economic Methodology', *History of Political Economy*, **22**, (2).

Scientific Explanation

Successful science should *explain* the events we observe in the world. When an aeroplane crashes, one of our first goals is to find a scientific explanation of the event, an explanation that provides us with a scientific understanding of the reasons for the accident. The reasons for wanting such an explanation are manifold. For some, it involves litigation, assigning responsibility, guilt or innocence; for others, it is an issue of public safety, making certain that the conditions that caused the accident are understood so that they can be avoided in the future; for still others, it is theoretical (a test of a particular aeronautical or metallurgical theory); and for some it is simply a matter of idle curiosity. But whatever the motivation or possible use of the result, the goal is clearly a *scientific explanation* of the event.

While the explanatory role of science is part and parcel of our contemporary scientific culture, it is also an aspect of that culture that seems to be at odds with the basic presuppositions of empiricist epistemology. For strict empiricists like the early logical positivists, scientific theories are *purely descriptive*; the scientific domain is the domain of the purely empirical and the purpose of a scientific theory is (only) to generalize, and thus reliably describe, those empirical observations. The commonsense view of science (what is often called 'commonsense realism') that science should 'explain' what we observe in the world by uncovering deep, underlying, causal mechanisms was, for logical positivism, to open the explanatory door to metaphysics and occult forces. Explanation in terms of deep underlying mechanisms was alien to the spirit of empiricism; in 'science there are no "depths"; there is surface everywhere' (Carnap *et al.*, 1929: 8). Nonetheless, despite this ostensibly alien spirit, even the logical positivists agreed that science does in fact explain what we see in the world – that science tells us not only *what*, but *why* – and not only does science explain, but the power of its explanations (compared to theology, metaphysics or transcendental philosophy) is one of the great advantages of the scientific world view. It was a major accomplishment, perhaps *the* major accomplishment, of later positivists (the logical empiricists) to provide a model of scientific explanation that could comfortably combine the idea that science should provide causal explanations with the empiricist view of scientific theories. This accomplishment came with Hempel and Oppenheim's presentation of the *covering-law* or *deductive–nomological* (D–N) model in 1948. While this model of scientific explanation has been the target of continual (and often harsh) criticism during the intervening years, it remains *the* standard model of scientific explanation.

The basic idea of the D–N model is to subsume the particular event under (at least one) general law. More specifically, a particular observed event (say, entity x exhibiting property y) is 'explained' by subsuming the event under a general law (say, x is an instance of z, and all zs exhibit property y). An economic example might be to explain why a particular firm x raised the price of its product; the explanation might be that firm x is a monopoly that has experienced an increase in marginal cost, and all monopolistic firms will raise the price of their product when they experience an increase in marginal cost. In a D–N explanation the phenomenon to be explained (the explanandum) is deduced (the 'deductive' part of the D–N) from the explanans, the explanation of the phenomenon, which is composed of initial conditions and at least one general law (the 'nomological' part of the D–N). Schematically, then, a D–N explanation will take the following general form:

$$C_1, C_2, \ldots C_n$$
$$L_1, L_2, \ldots L_m \qquad \text{(explanans)}$$

$$E \qquad \text{(explanandum)}$$

where each C_i represents a sentence that describes an initial condition, each L_i represents a general law and E is the event to be explained.

Converting the previous economic example into this schematic form, we have:

$C_1 =$ x is a monopoly firm,
$C_2 =$ marginal cost increased,
$C_3 =$ no other relevant variables changed (*ceteris paribus* condition),
$L_1 =$ all monopoly firms raise their price when marginal cost increases (*ceteris paribus*),

Therefore firm x raised its price.

While space limitations prevent a detailed discussion of the massive literature that has grown up around the D–N model (see Salmon, 1989, for the definitive historical survey), it is useful to mention a few points of extension (first) and contention (second). First, the later elaborations of the D–N model weakened some of the restrictions about what was required for attaining the status of a scientific 'law'. In the original Hempel and Oppenheim paper, the general law(s) as well as the initial conditions had to be true; in later versions, the restrictions on the general laws were weakened to conditions such as 'confirmed', 'corroborated' or 'not known to be false'. Second, Hempel opened the model up to non-deterministic explanation by expanding the original D–N model to cover certain types of statistical explanations where the relevant law holds only with a certain (known) probability. Third, Hempel applied the model outside its traditional domain in natural science; he applied it to explanation in history (Hempel, 1942), certain types of functional explanations in biology and social science (Hempel, 1959) and, finally, and most importantly for economics, he applied it to explanations based on the rational choices of individual agents (Hempel, 1962; Ayer, 1967).

Not only did Hempel and his supporters expand the D–N model and apply it to a number of different fields of inquiry, the model also generated a substantial critical literature. It is fair to say that, during the 1950s and early 1960s, the topic of scientific explanation, with the D–N model always at the centre of the debate, became one of the most discussed topics in mainstream philosophy of science. Critics attacked the D–N model from the inside (suggesting minor changes but keeping the core arguments about deduction and general laws) as well as from the outside (arguing that the entire approach was flawed and suggesting alternative models of scientific explanation). One of the many internal points of contention was the so-called *symmetry thesis*. This thesis asserts that, since explanation (D–N) and prediction (hypothetico-deductive method) have the same deductive form, every explanation is also a prediction (and vice versa); explanations come after events, and predictions come before events, but the basic deductive form is the same. This implies, among other things, that 'testing' and 'explaining' are ultimately two sides of the same scientific coin. This led to a number of paradoxes (see Salmon, 1989: 46–50) including the flagpole paradox: since one can *predict* the height of a flagpole from the length of its shadow, one should also be able to *explain* the height of a flagpole by the length of its shadow.

In addition to such internal criticisms, a number of authors have offered their own alternative, non-D–N, models of scientific explanation. One example was Salmon's (1971) statistical relevance (S-R) model of explanation which he offered as a replacement for Hempel's own probabilistic model. While Salmon's S-R model was not aimed at the (deterministic) heart of the D–N approach, the same cannot be said for van Fraassen's (1980) alternative, 'pragmatic' model of explanation. In many ways, van Fraassen's approach to scientific knowledge – what he calls 'constructive empiricism' – harks back to the strict empiricism of the early positivists; for van Fraassen, the epistemic standard for scientific theories is 'empirical adequacy' (saving the phenomena) and empirical adequacy is a pure descriptive characteristic. But in addition to this epistemic criterion, scientific theories also play other, more pragmatic, roles and one of the most important of these pragmatic roles is scientific explanation. Kitcher's 'unification' approach to explanation offers an alternative to both van Fraassen's pragmatic approach and the D–N model (Kitcher, 1981; 1989). According to the unification account, the key aspect of explanatory power is the ability to use a similar type of argument, a particular kind of reasoning, in the derivation of a wide range of different phenomena. While van Fraassen's pragmatic approach and Kitcher's unification view are only two of the many alternatives that have been offered as replacements for the D–N model, these two seem to be the alternatives that have received the most discussion in the philosophical literature (see Kitcher and Salmon, 1989; Pitt, 1988). In recent years, with the breakdown of the received view and the bifurcation of science studies into the sociological and the philosophical, the debate about *the* proper characterization of scientific explanation has started to wane, but new approaches still continue to be offered, while the D–N model remains *the* reigning champion which no one has, as yet, decisively defeated.

This brings us to the question of economics. Are most explanations in economic science, proper D–N explanations? The discussion in Blaug's *Methodology of Economics* (1992) – a book which has the subtitle 'How Economists Explain' – seems to be fairly representative of what economic methodologists have written about the subject of explanation. Blaug discusses the D–N model (a model also endorsed by Karl Popper) and basically argues that, while it would be possible for economic explanations to comply with the D–N schema, they in fact almost never do. The problem is not with the deductive schema, nor with the initial conditions, but rather with the status of the scientific 'laws' in economics. The laws employed in the D–N model must be empirically tested – confirmed for Hempel, and have survived attempted falsification for Popper – and according to Blaug this testing does not generally take place in economics. It could, but it does not.

While Blaug's view of scientific explanations in economics is probably the majority view, there are certainly a number of other opinions. One argument for doubting whether economic explanations are legitimately of the D–N form is based on the fact that many economic explanations, particularly in microeconomics, are a variant of Popper's 'situational analysis' (SA) approach to social science, and there are a number of serious questions about the relationship between SA and the D–N model (see Hands, 1991). Secondly, there are arguments, particularly among certain Austrian and institutionalist economists, that economic explanations cannot be of (and we should not try to make them into) the D–N form, but rather they should be based on a more general 'pattern' model of explanation (see Hayek, 1967a; 1967b; Wilber and Harrison, 1978). Yet another group of economists argue for a version of philosophical realism and explicitly reject the D–N approach to explanation because of the model's ties to empiricist philosophy of science (Lawson, 1994, for example). Finally, there are a few authors, specifically Boylan and O'Gorman (1995), who reject the D–N model for van Fraassen-type reasons: it is simply not empiricist enough. The bottom line is that, in economic methodology, as in the philosophy of science more generally, the D–N model has many critics but it remains the standard characterization of scientific explanation.

D. WADE HANDS

Bibliography

Ayer, A.J. (1967), 'Man as a Subject for Science', in P. Laslett and W.G. Runciman (eds), *Philosophy, Politics and Society*, 3rd series, New York: Barnes & Nobel.

Blaug, Mark (1992), *The Methodology of Economics: Or How Economists Explain*, 2nd edn, Cambridge: Cambridge University Press.

Boylan, Thomas A. and Paschal F. O'Gorman (1995), *Beyond Rhetoric & Realism in Economics: Towards a Reformulation of Economic Methodology*, London Routledge.

Carnap, Rudolf, Hans Hahn and Otto Neurath (1929), 'The Scientific Conception of the World: The Vienna Circle (*Wissenschaftliche Weltauffassung, Der Wiener Kreis*)'; reprinted Dordrecht: D. Reidel, 1973.

Hands, D. Wade (1991), 'Popper, the Rationality Principle and Economic Explanation', in G.K. Shaw (ed.), *Economics, Culture and Education: Essays in Honour of Mark Blaug*, Aldershot: Edward Elgar.

Hayek, F.A. (1967a), 'Degrees of Explanation', *Studies in Philosophy Politics and Economics*, Chicago: University of Chicago Press.

Hayek, F.A. (1967b), 'The Theory of Complex Phenomena', *Studies in Philosophy, Politics and Economics*, Chicago: University of Chicago Press.

Hempel, Carl G. (1942), 'The Function of General Laws in History', *The Journal of Philosophy*, **39**, 35–48; reprinted with modification C.G. Hempel (1965), *Aspects of Scientific Explanation*.

Hempel, Carl G. (1959), 'The Logic of Functional Analysis', in L. Gross (ed.), *Symposium on Sociological Theory*, New York: Harper & Row; reprinted with some changes in C.G. Hempel (1965), *Aspects of Scientific Explanation*.
Hempel, Carl G. (1962), 'Rational Action', *Proceedings and Addresses of the American Philosophical Association*, **35**, 5–23.
Hempel, Carl G. (1965), *Aspects of Scientific Explanation*. New York: Free Press.
Hempel, Carl G. (1966), *Philosophy of Natural Science*, Englewood Cliffs, NJ: Prentice-Hall.
Hempel, Carl G. and Paul Oppenheim (1948), 'Studies in the Logic of Explanation', *Philosophy of Science*, **15**, 135–75; reprinted with postscript in C.G. Hempel (1965), *Aspects of Scientific Explanation*.
Kitcher, Philip (1981), 'Explanatory Unification,' *Philosophy of Science*, **48**, 507–31.
Kitcher, Philip (1989), 'Explanatory Unification and the Causal Structure of the World', in P. Kitcher and W.C. Salmon (eds), *Scientific Explanation*, Minneapolis: University of Minnesota Press.
Kitcher, Philip and Wesley C. Salmon, (eds) (1989), *Scientific Explanation*, Minneapolis: University of Minnesota Press.
Lawson, Tony (1994), 'A Realist Theory for Economics', in R.E. Backhouse (ed.), *New Directions in Economic Methodology*, London: Routledge.
Pitt, Joseph C. (1988), *Theories of Explanation*, Oxford: Oxford University Press.
Salmon, Wesley C. (1971), *Statistical Explanation and Statistical Relevance*, Pittsburgh: University of Pittsburgh Press.
Salmon, Wesley C. (1989), 'Four Decades of Scientific Explanation', in P. Kitcher and W.C. Salmon (eds), *Scientific Explanation*, Minneapolis: University of Minnesota Press.
van Fraassen, Bas (1980), *The Scientific Image*, Oxford: Clarendon Press.
Wilber, Charles and R. Harrison (1978), 'The Methodological Basis of institutional Economics: Pattern Model, Storytelling and Holism', *Journal of Economic Issues*, **12**, 61–89.

Selectionist Arguments

In economics, selectionist arguments involve an appeal to biological natural selection or other similar evolutionary processes to make claims about the efficiency, optimality or optimizing behaviour of specific economic elements or forms. One of the most famous and influential examples is Milton Friedman's (1953: 22) appeal to competitive 'natural selection' to justify the 'hypothesis' that firms are acting to maximize profits, whether or not firms and individuals deliberately do so. (See also Alchian, 1950; Penrose, 1952.) Friedman assumes that (a) market competition tends to ensure that the more efficient firms survive, and (c) the more efficient firms will be acting 'as if' they are maximizing profits. Before we consider these presuppositions let us address some further examples of selectionist arguments.

Douglass North (1981: 7) writes: 'competition in the face of ubiquitous scarcity dictates that the more efficient institutions ... will survive and the inefficient ones perish'. Also alluding to Darwinian 'natural selection', Michael Jensen and William Meckling (1979: 473) argue that codetermination or industrial democracy must be relatively inefficient: 'The fact that this system seldom arises out of voluntary arrangements among individuals strongly suggests that codetermination or industrial democracy is less efficient than the alternatives which grow up and survive in a competitive environment.' Similarly, Oliver Williamson uses selectionist arguments to support his contention that hierarchical firms are more efficient than cooperative or participatory alternatives. In several passages Williamson (1985: 22–3, 394) alludes to evolutionary processes of selection and asserts that, because hierarchical firms exist, they must be relatively efficient and more suited to survival.

Again the same presumption (a) is implicit in all these statements. In addition, Williamson also uses what might be regarded as a corollary of this: (b) if competitive markets exist and firms of a specific type are dominant, this type of firm is more efficient than other types, especially if the alternatives have been tried under such competitive conditions and they failed. Notably, Williamson is more concerned with what *causes* efficiency or optimizing behaviour than

Friedman. In Williamson's view, the relative efficiency of hierarchical firms is a result of its structure and the constraints it places on individual agents.

The three prominent selectionist claims may now be put in shorthand terms: (a) competition selects the relatively efficient, (b) under competition, existence implies relative efficiency, (c) the relatively efficient act 'as if' they are (profit) maximizers. In critically examining these three propositions, it may be tempting to approach this task by attacking the use of biological metaphors. There have been long periods when the use of biological analogies in the social sciences has been unpopular. The theorist may thus be enticed to dismiss the use of selectionist arguments simply as the unwarranted contamination of the social sciences by biology. However, such a dismissal is over-hasty. The selectionist arguments have to be examined in their own terms. Furthermore, arguments from modern biology can be used to show the limitations of propositions (a) to (c). Some such selection 'anomalies' will be discussed in the next three sections.

Error and fecundity
Biologists are aware of a number of cases where processes of natural selection do not lead to the emergence of relatively or increasingly fit organisms (see Hodgson, 1993: ch. 13). We will consider some of these cases and their relevance to economics.

In a loose sense, processes of natural selection can lead to some kind of improvement, because adaptation to the environment does occur. But it is a mistake to go further than this and assume that natural selection is necessarily a strong optimizing force. Adaptation is always relative to the environment and what is a favourable adaptation in one environment may not be so in another. Furthermore, natural selection is always an imperfect instrument, and it can sometimes lead to clearly suboptimal, even disastrous, outcomes. It is fallacious to assume that all adaptations are necessarily optimal or near-optimal.

Strictly, an evolutionary process involving selection cannot be an optimizing one because for evolution to work there must always be a variety of forms from which to select. Without such variety there would be no evolution. Furthermore, the obverse of selection is rejection, and the evolutionary process must thus involve ceaseless and systematic error making as well. As Stephen Jay Gould (1987: 14) puts it: 'imperfections are the primary proofs that evolution has occurred, since optimal designs erase all signposts of history'.

A second fundamental feature of 'natural selection' in biology that is widely ignored is that selection is not simply about the selection of the relatively fit and the extinction of the unfit. What really matters is reproductive success. Selection in leaving progeny is just as important as mortality selection. In economic systems the processes of institutional creation and reproduction are very different from sexual reproduction amongst organisms. However, an example will illustrate the relevance of fecundity as well as mortality in the economic sphere.

Consider the argument of Jensen, Meckling and Williamson that the greater density of hierarchical, non-cooperative or non-participatory firms in the real world must relate to their superior efficiency. It has been suggested that, whatever their relative efficiency when fully established, cooperative and democratic organisations are more difficult to get going than firms owned (initially) by single persons, single families or partnerships. This is because of the difficulties of forming collective organizations where individual benefits do not seem to justify the trouble and expense of organizing, or the difficulty of establishing collaboration between individuals where trust relations are not yet sufficiently established. As Nathan

Rosenberg and Luther Birdzell (1986: 316) point out, by comparison with cooperative enterprises, 'the promoter of an investor-owned enterprise can, by retaining part or all of the ownership interest, profit handsomely if the enterprise succeeds. So one might expect more investor-owned enterprises, small or large, to survive *simply because far more of them are likely to be born*' (emphasis added). Whatever their positive qualities once established, the reproduction by imitation of cooperatives is thus likely to be inhibited.

Consequently, there is good reason to doubt that the mere existence of a greater number of non-cooperative rather than cooperative firms would imply that the former is more efficient than the latter. It may be that cooperative firms are less numerous, not because they are less efficient, but simply because they are less likely to emerge than firms created on the basis of individual, family or partner ownership. If circumstances favour the birth of greater numbers of hierarchical firms then they may grow in size or number to swamp the non-hierarchical businesses, whatever the relative efficiencies.

Path dependence
Other types of selection anomaly are plentiful. Many involve the phenomenon known as path dependence. Path-dependent processes are now widely discussed in both biology and economics. Gould (1980; 1987; 1989) is widely known for his illustrations that biological evolution often depends on initial 'accidents' that somehow dispose it to take a suboptimal and often eccentric path. The study of non-linear dynamic systems by mathematical economists has also helped to put path dependence on the agenda. Studies of path dependence in economic history suggest that the development of the factory system and the modern capitalist firm was not simply a question of the evolutionary selection of the most efficient organizational configurations. For example, in a discussion of the formative years of the industrial revolution, Michael Everett and Alanson Minkler (1993) show in detail that labour-managed firms were at a substantial initial disadvantage compared with their capitalist counterparts, owing to the legal and financial environment, and that this could not be overcome later, whatever the relative efficiencies. Charles Sabel and Jonathan Zeitlin (1985) argue on the basis of historical evidence that in Europe there was an alternative path to industrialization based on small-scale firms and flexible specialization. Industrialization could have taken many possible pathways and occurred in different sequences. Ugo Pagano (1991: 327) considers the two-way and cumulative interaction of technology with property rights, pointing out: 'In this context, simple efficiency stories may well lose their meaning. Each outcome is likely to be path-dependent and inefficient interactions between property rights and technology are likely to characterise the history of economic systems.'

Contrary to his earlier view, North (1990) now accepts that path-dependent processes also apply to institutions, and therefore the surviving arrangements are not necessarily the most efficient. This involves a major change in his views, in notable contrast to Williamson. The kind of economic history which ignored path dependency and inefficient equilibria, and assumed that historical change involved a sequence of discrete steps to ever more efficient institutional arrangements, is now widely criticized (Binger and Hoffman, 1989).

Path dependency means that history matters. Changes in initial conditions and accidents can cause widely divergent outcomes. Development can be 'locked in' to restrictive outcomes or paths, as with the celebrated case of the survival of the relatively inefficient 'QWERTY' typewriter keyboard (David, 1985; Gould, 1987) and VHS video systems (Arthur, 1988). Path dependency clearly may arise in cases of 'multiple adaptive peaks' where there are several local optima. A journey to the global maximum may be ruled out by the distance involved and the depth of the valleys in between. The route followed and thus the peak obtained is again path-dependent: a result of history.

Context dependence

Another important class of 'anomaly' can be described as context dependence: where the selection environment is altered by the outcomes of the selection process itself. An important subset of cases of context dependence is when the selection environment is dependent on the frequency of the population. Consider the following example. Assume two types of firm, type A and type B. The population as a whole is a mix of type A and type B firms, with the associated culture and inter-firm relations. Given that a new entrant can be of either type, their profits can be given by one of the following formulae:

> Profit of type A entrant firm = 50 + (% of type B firms)
> Profit of type B entrant firm = (% of type B firms)

Such illustrative profit values can be justified in terms of the different types of organizational form and inter-firm relations, with positive externalities associated with firms of type B. Assume, first, that the initial (large) population is composed entirely of type A firms. In this case the profit for each type A new entrant will be 50, and of each type B new entrant will be 0. Clearly, type B firms are unlikely to become established if type A firms are dominant. However, if the initial population is composed entirely of type B firms then the profit for the first type A new entrant will be 150, and of each type B new entrant will be 100. Consequently, in this case, type A firms can successfully invade the type B population. In sum, type A firms are likely to become or remain dominant, whatever the starting position. This will happen even if average profits are greater in an industry composed entirely of type B firms than one composed entirely of type A. Assume that the above equations apply to all firms, and not simply new entrants. Then the average profits of a type A population will be 50 and of a type B population it will be 100. Yet type B firms are always at a relative disadvantage.

This hypothetical example of frequency dependence illustrates a number of general points. First, given that payoffs are dependent on the nature of the industry as a whole, the selected characteristics likewise depend on the overall environment. Indeed, research on cooperatives suggests that their success is highly dependent on the type of financial and cultural regime that prevails in the regional or national economy. Second, 'natural selection' does not necessarily favour the more efficient units, or always the optimal or near-optimal outcomes. The low density of cooperative or participatory firms in the real world should not be taken to mean that either individual firms of this type, or an industry dominated by them, are necessarily less efficient.

Note that, for the sake of the above discussion, efficiency has been conflated with profitability. This is not necessarily the case, but similar anomalies can occur if profit and efficiency are separate criteria. It should also be noted that profitability is not necessarily simply or positively correlated with the capacity to survive. In most evolutionary processes, including market competition, the probability of survival depends on a number of complex, interacting factors. Profitability may be taken as a proxy for efficiency, or for the probability of survival, only in the simplest of cases.

'Natural selection' of the profit maximizers?

In 1964, Sidney Winter published a major and extensive critique of Friedman's argument that profit maximizers would necessarily emerge in a competitive environment. Here it is possible to address a few aspects only. (See Hodgson, 1994, for a full discussion, with further references.) Winter finds several difficulties and ambiguities in Friedman's position. His major line of attack is to point out that for selection to work there must be some sustaining feature that ensures that the maximizers or near-maximizers that are 'selected' through competition will continue for some time in that mode of behaviour. For instance, if firm behaviour is random, as Friedman conjectures, there is no reason to assume that a firm that happens to be maximizing will continue to do so in the next period. Further, such randomness could mean that a firm on the brink of bankruptcy at one instant could by chance be a good profit maximizer in the next. Owing to the existence of selection anomalies, for instance, even if 'habitual reaction' is the actual determinant of firm behaviour, the selection of maximizers is not guaranteed.

For natural selection to work there must be heritable variation in fitness and this is missing from Friedman's account. He correctly presumes that the evolutionary selection process discriminates between firms on the basis of their manifest behaviour or – to use the corresponding biological term – the phenotype. However, for selection to work consistently in favour of some characteristics rather than others, this behaviour cannot be purely accidental. There has to be some equivalent to the genetic constitution or genotype, such as the routines or culture of the firm, which fixes, determines, moulds or constrains the phenotype in some way. To presume that maximization emerges from an evolutionary process means that routines giving rise to such behaviour are being selected through their superior capacity for survival. What is required is a degree of inertia in such routines so that selection can operate effectively. Although they are not nearly as permanent as the gene, organizations create and sustain structures and patterns of thought and action which have self-reinforcing and durable qualities.

Further, the more the relation between genotype and phenotype is determined and fixed, the more effective the evolutionary process will be in selecting particular characteristics through time. In these circumstances, by working on phenotypes, and causing the extinction of some and the prosperity and replication of others, the selection process can then be successful in indirectly altering the characteristics of the 'gene pool' of the group of firms. However, the phenotype is never determined by the genotype alone, and the phenotype is likely to be a function of the environment as well as of the genotype.

The genotype–phenotype distinction in biology suggests to Winter an analogous and important distinction in the socioeconomic sphere: between rules of action and action itself. As Tjalling Koopmans (1957: 140–41) remarked, if evolutionary selection is the basis for a belief in profit maximization, 'then we should postulate that basis itself and not the profit maximization which it implies in certain circumstances'.

Conclusion

The possibility of many plausible selection 'anomalies' in both biology and economics suggests that natural selection and competition do not always select the relatively efficient. Winter has dissected Friedman's argument and concluded that the assumption that the relatively efficient act 'as if' they are (profit) maximizers is justified only under a very limited set of conditions.

It is often taken for granted that survival means efficiency. However, as Edna Ullmann-Margalit (1978) shows, this is invalid. Strictly, in order to explain the existence of a structure it is neither necessary nor sufficient to show that it is efficient. Inefficient structures do happen to exist and survive, and many possible efficient structures will never actually be selected. Accordingly, selectionist arguments have to be severely qualified and buttressed by a detailed analysis of specific historical and causal processes. Their universal application is unwarranted. In the words of the old Gershwin song: 'It ain't necessarily so.'

GEOFFREY M. HODGSON

References
Alchian, Armen A. (1950), 'Uncertainty, Evolution and Economic Theory', *Journal of Political Economy*, **58**, June, 211–22.
Arthur, W. Brian (1988), 'Self-Reinforcing Mechanisms in Economics', in P. Anderson, K.J. Arrow and D. Pines (eds) (1988), *The Economy as an Evolving Complex System*, Reading, MA: Addison-Wesley.
Binger, Brian R. and Elizabeth Hoffman (1989), 'Institutional Persistence and Change: The Question of Efficiency', *Journal of Institutional and Theoretical Economics*, **145**, (1), March, 67–84.
David, Paul A. (1985), 'Clio and the Economics of QWERTY', *American Economic Review*, **75**, May, 332–7.
Everett, Michael J. and Alanson P. Minkler (1993), 'Evolution and Organizational Choice in 19th Century Britain', *Cambridge Journal of Economics*, **17**, (1), March, 51–62.
Friedman, Milton (1953), 'The Methodology of Positive Economics', *Essays in Positive Economics*, Chicago: University of Chicago Press.
Gould, Stephen Jay (1980), *The Panda's Thumb*, New York: W.W. Norton.
Gould, Stephen Jay (1987), 'The Panda's Thumb of Technology', *Natural History*, **1**, January, 14–23.
Gould, Stephen Jay (1989), *Wonderful Life: The Burgess Shale and the Nature of History*, London: Hutchinson Radius.
Hodgson, Geoffrey M. (1993), *Economics and Evolution: Bringing Life Back Into Economics*, Cambridge/Ann Arbor, MI: Polity Press/University of Michigan Press.
Hodgson, Geoffrey M. (1994), 'Optimisation and Evolution: Winter's Critique of Friedman Revisited', *Cambridge Journal of Economics*, **17**, (4), August, 413–30.
Jensen, Michael C. and William H. Meckling (1976), 'Theory of the Firm: Managerial Behavior, Agency Costs and Ownership Structure', *Journal of Financial Economics*, **3**, 305–60.
Koopmans, Tjalling C. (1957), *Three Essays on the State of Economic Science*, New York: McGraw-Hill.
North, Douglass C. (1981), *Structure and Change in Economic History*, New York: W.W. Norton.
North, Douglass C. (1990), *Institutions, Institutional Change and Economic Performance*, Cambridge: Cambridge University Press.
Pagano, Ugo (1991), 'Property Rights, Asset Specificity and the Division of Labour Under Alternative Capitalist Relations', *Cambridge Journal of Economics*, **15**, (3), September, 315–42.
Penrose, Edith T. (1952), 'Biological Analogies in the Theory of the Firm', *American Economic Review*, **42**, (4), December, 804–19.
Rosenberg, Nathan and Luther E. Birdzell, Jr, (1986), *How the West Grew Rich: The Economic Transformation of the Industrial World*, New York: Basic Books.
Sabel, Charles F. and Jonathan Zeitlin (1985), 'Historical Alternatives to Mass Production: Politics, Markets and Technology in Nineteenth Century Industrialization', *Past and Present*, no. 108, August, 132–76.
Ullmann-Margalit, Edna (1978), 'Invisible Hand Explanations', *Synthèse*, **39**, 263–91.
Williamson, Oliver E. (1985), *The Economic Institutions of Capitalism: Firms, Markets, Relational Contracting*, London: Macmillan.
Winter Jr, Sidney G. (1964), 'Economic "Natural Selection" and the Theory of the Firm', *Yale Economic Essays*, **4**, (1), 225–72.

Set Theoretic Structuralism

Set theoretic structuralism (SS) is a research programme in the philosophy of science which originated from work by Suppes, Sneed and Stegmüller. Sneed's 1971 book, inspired by Suppes' reconstructions of classical and relativistic particle mechanics, contains the first 'structuralist' exposition of a general model of scientific theories. This work was received and propagated especially by Stegmüller and his students during the following 20 years. Today, most contributors are located in and around Germany. Structuralists themselves do not use the label 'set theoretic'; they speak of the 'structuralist approach' to the philosophy of science or simply of the 'structuralist programme'. 'Set theoretic' is used here only in order to avoid confusion with 'French' structuralism. The structuralist view is closely related to the 'semantic' view of theories.

SS aims at modelling the structure and development, as well as the process of confrontation with data, and real systems, of scientific theories of various degrees of comprehensiveness. Its most characteristic features are, first, the commitment to reconstruct existing theories; second, the decision to do this in a particular frame of representation, namely in 'informal' set theory by means of set theoretic structures (whence the label); and third, its claim to provide a *general* model not restricted to the clarification of foundational issues of just one particular discipline. Similar to other approaches after the 1960s, it is also committed to take the history of science as one main source of data.

By means of reconstruction, 'theories' as they occur in the literature, in lectures, talks and notes, are transformed into 'idealized' objects, for which metatheoretical models can be constructed. In contrast to the 'rational reconstructions' of logical empiricism, reconstruction in SS is not meant to make science more 'rational'. Its purpose is purely descriptive: to make metatheoretic modelling possible. SS abstains from normative implications and recommendations for the scientists. It aims at the construction of models about its objects (theories, their development and application) in the way this is usually done in science.

Using informal set theory and set theoretic structures, SS aims at achieving precision without spending much effort on syntactical formalism, types and mathematical axioms. The particular format used in SS has proved as an efficient frame of representation for developed scientific theories which use non-trivial mathematical apparatus. Three features are salient. First, all syntactical requirements (description of a theory's vocabulary, sorts, types, terms and formulas) are either left implicit in an informally understood set theoretic background which presupposes acquaintance with basic set theoretic notation and concepts (set, subset, n-tuple, relation, function, Cartesian product like $C \times P$, power set $Po(A)$ of a set A) or are expressed set theoretically in a rather realistic manner by indicating which kinds of arguments are needed for the theory's relations, and which arguments go into, and which function values are produced by, the theory's functions. This frame is not committed to first-order predicate logic, it is very rich in expressive power and seems to be applicable to all theories that have emerged so far. Second, all mathematical axioms are left implicit, at least when they may be taken to be standard. The content of the axioms is represented in a structure only in terms of the set of mathematical objects which they characterize. The structures (models) of a theory using real numbers, for instance, are simply required to contain the set of real numbers in its standard meaning. The mathematical axioms needed to fix that meaning are not made explicit. Third, the theory's axioms are formulated as statements directly describing a system, or model, of the theory. No extra interpretation is needed.

An example will serve for illustration and as a point for further reference. According to Debreu, an economy consists of commodities, consumers, firms, endowments, fractions of profit, consumption sets, production plans and preferences. Talking realistically, an economic system is made up of these items, and of nothing else. Debreu's assumptions, used in order to prove the existence of equilibrium, state that preferences as well as consumption sets and production plans are 'theoretically nice' (convex, closed and so on). The central economic assumptions of feasibility, budget constraint, clearing of markets and maximization are thus hidden in the definition of a state of equilibrium whose existence is proved from those nice assumptions. By adding a state of equilibrium to the list of primitives and thus bringing the economic assumptions to the fore, in the frame of SS an economy satisfying these assumptions may be defined along Debreu's lines as follows; x is a *model of Debreu's theory* if there exist G, C, P, w, Θ, X, Y, $\geq$, eq and s, n such that

(A1) $x = (G, C, P, \mathbb{R}, \mathbb{N}, w, \Theta, X, Y, \geq, eq)$;

(A2) $\mathbb{R}$ is the set of real numbers and $\mathbb{N}$ the set of natural numbers 1, 2, 3, . . .;
(A3) (a) C is a finite, non-empty set; (b) G and P are the sets $\{1, . . ., s\}$, and $\{1, . . ., n\}$ of natural numbers; (c) $w : C \rightarrow \mathbb{R}^s$ (that is, w is a function from C to $\mathbb{R}^s$); (d) $\Theta : C \times P \rightarrow [0, 1]$; (e) $X : C \rightarrow Po(\mathbb{R}^s)$; (f) $Y : P \rightarrow Po(\mathbb{R}^s)$; (g) $\geq : C \rightarrow Po(\mathbb{R}^s \times \mathbb{R}^s)$; (h) there exist y, z and (a price vector) p such that $eq = (y, z, p)$ and $y : C \rightarrow \mathbb{R}^s$, $z : P \rightarrow \mathbb{R}^s$, $p \in \mathbb{R}^s$;
(A4) $\geq$, X and Y satisfy the above-mentioned nice conditions;
(A5) eq is a state of equilibrium (that is, y, z are feasible, y satisfies the budget constraint, $\Sigma y_i - \Sigma z_j = \Sigma w_i$, and y and $p . z$ are maximized).

C, G, P, w, Θ, X, Y, $\geq$ denote a set of consumers, a set of goods, a set of firms, endowment, fractions of profit, consumption sets, production plans and preferences, respectively; eq is a state of equilibrium consisting of particular consumption and production plans y, z and of a price vector p. Details may be looked up in Debreu. The mathematical sets $\mathbb{R}$ and $\mathbb{N}$ are called auxiliary base sets, and their characterization as given in standard mathematical textbooks is assumed as known. The conditions in (A3) fix the sorts and types of the primitives.

The basic metatheoretical model of SS captures the notion of a ('small') theory or a theory element. A theory element consists of six items: (1) a class M of *models* (defined in the way just illustrated), (2) a class M_p of *potential* models (which are like the models but need not satisfy the theory's cluster laws, like (A5) in the example), (3) a class M_{pp} of *partial potential models* (which look like truncated potential models in which the theory's 'theoretical terms' are omitted), (4) a set L of *internal* and *external links* which relate the theory's models to other models of the same theory (internal) or to models of other theories (external), (5) an apparatus U to handle approximation, and (6) a set I of *intended applications* containing those real systems to which the theory's practitioners intend to apply the theory. I is assumed to be a subset of M_{pp}. While M, M_p, M_{pp}, L and U can be set theoretically defined in the style of the example, I is determined pragmatically, by means of explicit paradigms and a vague relation of 'being similar to a paradigm'. The *empirical claim* that can be made with a theory element $T = (M, M_p, M_{pp}, L, U, I)$ is as follows: all intended applications can be approximately extended to models such that, in addition, all the links are satisfied. More comprehensive theories are modelled as *theory nets* and their development by *theory evolutions* (Balzer et al., 1987: ch. IV).

For the assessment of scientific progress SS has developed a cluster of notions of intertheoretic relations, most notably theoretization, specialization, reduction and approximative reduction. Theoretization roughly obtains when one theory takes over complete models of another one as 'parts' of its own models. In economics, this seems to be so for statistical theories (taking over not purely mathematically interpreted probability spaces) or for equilibrium theory (taking over models of utility theory or some theory about preferences). Specialization is the central relation obtaining in theory nets. Equilibrium theory exemplifies this structure of a theory net very nicely with Debreu's model as a basis which is specialized in various ways, for instance by introducing public enterprises, 'weightless' consumers and so on. Reduction of theory T to T' roughly consists of a relation between both theories' models such that each model of T gets related to a model of *T'*. Strict reduction in most cases is weakened to some approximative form. An economic example of approximative reduction is given by the proof that atomless models of the core 'contain' representations of sequences of finite, 'simple' models which – in some sense – shows that atomless models can be taken as limits of sequences of more realistic models.

SS claims that particular forms of theory nets and theory-evolutions can be used to make precise Thomas Kuhn's picture of 'normal science', and that the structuralist notions of (approximative) reduction can bridge the gap between theories which are incommensurably separated by a 'scientific revolution' in Kuhn's sense. These claims, however, are not regarded as central to SS. Some members of the group stress that, methodologically, SS is largely neutral and not committed to taking sides in discussions like that between Kuhn and Popperians.

In order to deal with questions of inaccuracy of fit, approximate application of a theory, and approximation of one theory by another one, SS has put much emphasis on the approximate nature of empirical theories. Topological notions like that of a uniform space or that of a pseudo-metric are used to cover 'distances' or mere 'similarities' among different structures. Moreover, the approximation apparatus *U* which belongs to each theory contains 'admissible blurs', that is, distinguished numbers or neighbourhoods pragmatically chosen to decide whether a degree of fit is satisfactory or not.

SS claims that metatheoretical models like the one described apply across different disciplines, in contrast to foundational studies which usually concentrate on one particular discipline. Originally, SS dealt with physical theories and their development but in the meantime the scope of reconstructed theories comprises several disciplines, from physics, chemistry and biology to economics, sociology and psychology, and even further, to the theory of literature and of accounting (Diederich *et al.*, 1989).

In the domain of theoretical economics, the above model and the extended notions of theory nets and theory evolutions face two problems. On the one hand, economic theorizing often proceeds purely mathematically (like Debreu's): no reference to concrete, real systems, to paradigms, is made; so the set of intended applications is difficult to determine. On the other hand, it is often unclear which terms are 'theoretical' in a given theory (the notion of equilibrium seems to be theoretical in Debreu's theory, but what about preferences?). While the second difficulty can be overcome by relaxing the notion of a theoretical term and regarding partial potential models simply as representing the data available (Stegmüller *et al.*, 1982: 16–40), the first one is salient in economics, and affords far-reaching amendments concerning the nature of idealization, and the relation between theoretical economics and econometrics which have not been achieved yet.

Contributions of SS to economics issues in English include the following. A comprehensive theory net of static equilibrium theory in the spirit of Debreu was reconstructed in Haendler (1980a), the more local case of pure exchange in Balzer (1982) with further criticism and discussions in Haslinger (1983), Balzer (1985) and Requate (1991). The empirical status of equilibrium theories is studied by Haendler in terms of reconstructions of the empirical claims of the aggregate market supply and demand functions approach (Haendler, 1980b) and by Balzer, who proposes a special form of empirical claims for economic theories, in Stegmüller *et al.* (1982). Haendler addresses problems of data and measurement in economics by means of a case study of the utility-maximizing regression approaches in Stegmüller *et al.* (1982); Balzer and Haendler reconstruct the method of ordinary least squares in the general structuralist format of a method of measurement in Balzer and Hamminga (1989); Diederich makes precise the structure and development of Marx's economic theory (Diederich, 1982; 1989); De la Sienra offers a more fine-grained reconstruction of Marxian theory (De la Sienra, 1992: chs 6, 7); (Hamminga, 1989) proposes a precise account of idealization as a relevant method for economics.

Macroeconomics, econometrics and institutional economics have not been dealt with.

WOLFGANG BALZER

References
Balzer, Wolfgang (1982), 'A Logical Reconstruction of Pure Exchange Economics', *Erkenntnis*, **17**.
Balzer, Wolfgang (1985), 'The Proper Reconstruction of Exchange Economics', *Erkenntnis*, **23**.
Balzer, W. and B. Hamminga (eds) (1989), *Philosophy of Economics*, Dordrecht: Kluwer.
Balzer, W., C.U. Moulines and J.D. Sneed (1987), *An Architectonic for Science*, Dordrecht: Reidel.
Debreu, Gerard (1959), *Theory of Value*, New York/London: Wiley.
De la Sienra, Adolfo G. (1992), *The Logical Foundations of the Marxian Theory of Value*, Dordrecht: Kluwer.
Diederich, Werner (1982), 'A Structuralist Reconstruction of Marx's Economics', in W. Stegmüller *et al.* (eds), *Philosophy of Economics*.
Diederich, Werner (1989), 'The Development of Marx's Economic Theory', in W. Balzer and B. Hamminga (eds), *Philosophy of Economics*.
Diederich, W., A. Ibarra and T. Mormann (1989), 'Bibliography of Structuralism', *Erkenntnis*, **30**.
Haendler, Ernst W. (1980a), 'The Logical Structure of Modern Neoclassical Static Microeconomic Equilibrium Theory', *Erkenntnis*, **15**.
Haendler, Ernst W. (1980b), 'The Role of Utility and of Statistical Concepts in Empirical Economic Theories', *Erkenntnis*, **15**.
Hamminga, Bert (1989), 'Sneed versus Nowak: An Illustration in Economics', in W. Balzer and B. Hamminga (eds), *Philosophy of Economics*.
Haslinger, Franz (1983), '"A Logical Reconstruction of Pure Exchange Economics": An Alternative View', *Erkenntnis*, **20**.
Requate, Till (1991), 'Once Again Pure Exchange Economics: A Critical View Towards the Structuralist Reconstructions by Balzer and Stegmüller', *Erkenntnis*, **34**.
Sneed, Joseph D. (1971), *The Logical Structure of Mathematical Physics*, Dordrecht: Reidel.
Stegmüller, W., W. Balzer and W. Spohn (eds) (1982), *Philosophy of Economics*, Berlin/Heidelberg/New York: Springer.

Shackle, G.L.S.

George Lennox Sharman Shackle (1903–92), British economist, methodologist and historian of economic ideas, was born in Cambridge and educated at Perse Preparatory School. He spent the first four years of his working life in a bank and, after a brief stint in a tobacco firm, 10 years as a schoolmaster. In 1931, he was awarded an external bachelor's degree from the University of London, majoring in Latin, French, Economics and Modern European History. His maiden article, on Keynes' *Treatise on Money* and Hayek's *Prices and Production*, appeared in the first issue of the *Review of Economic Studies* in 1933. This led to a Leverhulme research studentship at the LSE which he began in January 1935, working first on Austrian capital theory and then on Keynesian business cycle theory under the supervision of Hayek. He was awarded his doctorate in 1937 and published a revised version of his dissertation as *Expectations, Investment and Income* in 1938. By 1937, Shackle had moved to the Oxford Institute of Statistics as a research assistant to Henry Phelps Brown. Their work led to a number of joint papers for which, in conjunction with a paper on expectation and employment, he was awarded the Oxford DPhil in 1940. Shackle moved to Scotland to take up a lectureship at St Andrews in 1939, but was almost immediately summoned to the Admiralty with the outbreak of the war. He there served as a member of the team of economists in S Branch, moving to the Economic Section of the Cabinet Secretariat after the defeat of the Conservative Party in 1945. Shackle was appointed to a readership in Economic Theory at Leeds in 1950 and, shortly afterwards, to the Brunner Chair of Economic Science at Liverpool University in 1951. He retired from Liverpool as Emeritus Professor in 1969, but continued to publish extensively almost right up to his death in 1992.

Shackle's writings display a lifelong fascination with expectation in economic affairs and particularly with nature, representation and consequences of the fact that decision makers typically have only partial knowledge about the circumstances that will determine the outcome of their choices. Like Keynes, Shackle was strongly opposed to orthodox approaches to the problem of choice under uncertainty, such as representing the economic decision maker as some form of expected utility maximizer. And, as with Keynes, this opposition was based on his views about the inapplicability of standard probability concepts, and the relative frequency theory in particular, in economic decision making. It is possible to distil three main lines of argument in Shackle's critical writings on probability. First, he argues that significant economic decisions are generally not informed by a knowledge of frequencies since such choices are often 'crucial experiments', that is, so individual that they cannot be grouped with similar choices to form a reference class relative to which frequencies can be determined. Second, he argues that, even where relative frequencies are known, this knowledge cannot be used to assign probabilities to single outcomes because statements about frequencies, strictly speaking, apply to series of trails rather than single trails. Finally, Shackle is critical of the standard probability measure as a 'distributional uncertainty variable', that is, in so far as it presupposes a complete list of the possible events, outcomes or states of the world to which probabilities are to be assigned. Shackle argues that this assumption is unrealistic for many decision situations and that, by relaxing it and admitting a so-called 'residual hypothesis', it is possible to capture epistemic states not captured by subjective probability (Shackle, 1955).

Shackle (1949) provides a novel alternative to the expected utility model. At the heart of his approach is what he regarded as his single most important theoretical contribution: the notion of potential surprise. Let $s(h)$ be the (subjective) potential surprise or disbelief an agent assigns hypothesis h relative to his or her background knowledge k. The axioms of potential surprise are (Levi, 1979):

1. if $s(h/k) > 0$, $s(- h/k) = 0 =$ minimum degree of potential surprise;
2. if $k \vdash\neg h$, $s(h/k) = 1 =$ maximum degree of potential surprise;
3. if $s(h \vee g/k) = \min s(h/k), s(g/k))$;
4. if h_i $(i = 1, 2, \ldots n)$ is an exhaustive list of mutually exclusive hypotheses relative to k, then $s(h/k) = 0$ for at least one i.

Suppose h corresponds to the values of some continuous variable x (which may take negative values) such as the possible returns on some investment. Although the associated potential surprise function could in principle take any form, it is characteristically portrayed by Shackle as shown in Figure 1.

Shackle's decision theory may be sketched as follows. He begins by postulating an 'ascendancy' function $\phi = \phi(x, s)$, which is interpreted as an indicator of the power of particular (x, s) pairs to 'arrest the attention of the decision maker'. The ascendancy function has the following properties (where x is a loss it is represented by its absolute value):

$$\frac{\partial \phi}{\partial x} > 0 \quad \frac{\partial \phi}{\partial y} < 0$$

Given these and the appropriate second order conditions, the ascendancy function yields a family
of indifference curves such as those represented by the broken lines in Figure 2.

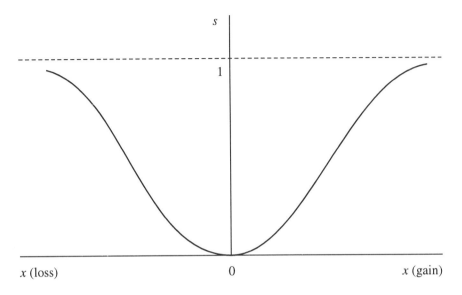

Figure 1

The ascendancy function is maximized over gain and loss separately, subject to the relevant
branch of the surprise function, this representing the decision maker's 'focusing' on the 'focus
value' (x, s) pairs at points a and b respectively (the valuation of a choice option, in Shackle's

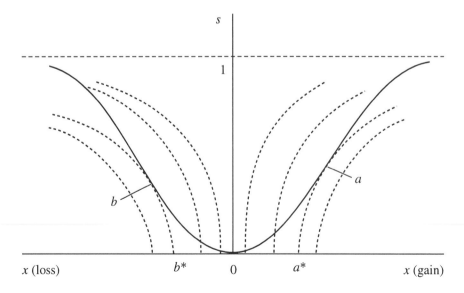

Figure 2

theory, is restricted to these two points, which is why it is sometimes referred to as the 'optimism–pessimism' approach). Focus values are standardized by substituting their zero-potential surprise equivalents in Figure 2, the standardized focus gain (SFG) value associated with a is $0a^*$ and the standardized focus loss (SFL) value associated with b, $0b^*$. Choice between different options is represented by way of a 'gambler preference' map, depicting different SFG/SFL combinations between which the decision maker is indifferent (with utility increasing in a north-west direction). In the case shown in Figure 3, for example, the SFG/SFL combination associated with option A is preferred to that associated with option B. For details, generalizations and an extensive survey of the critical literature on potential surprise and Shackle's decision theory, see Ford (1994).

Although the structure of Shackle's model is unorthodox from a decision-theoretic viewpoint, it is entirely orthodox in its reliance on the deductivist methodology of mainstream microeconomics. From the 1960s onwards, however, and although he continued to insist on the importance of the notion of potential surprise, Shackle came to reject deductivism as antithetical to the themes of expectation, uncertainty and choice in economic analysis. This rejection stems from a world picture that Shackle characterizes in opposition to theories that posit a deterministic world (where choice is illusory), a world of perfect foresight (where choice is empty) and a world without discernible order (where choice is powerless):

> We must assume a world where there is action and not merely the illusion of action: a world where history *comes into* being, not a world where the whole of history is complete and is merely revealed in successive stages to the human consciousness; a world where there are constraints upon the ways in which events can follow each other, yet where even a complete and perfect knowledge of these

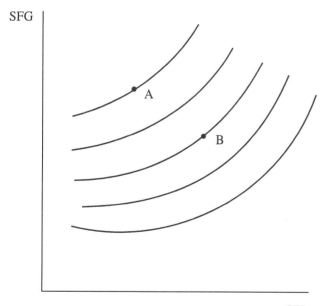

SFG

SFL

Figure 3

constraints would leave us ignorant of 'what will happen next'; a world where, in short, events are only partially shaped by what has gone on before. (Shackle, 1966: 74)

A key ingredient here is Shackle's 'inside time' perspective, the time *within* which we think, imagine and decide, as distinct from the 'outside' time *about* which we think as mathematicians, scientists or historians. Shackle portrays the flow of inside time as a succession of discrete 'solitary moments' in the mental life of the decision maker. Although he allows that thought is informed by experience and, when oriented towards practical action, constrained by what the decision maker regards as possible, he insists that it comprises what are essentially creative acts, undetermined by what went before. Thought, as expressed through choice and action, according to Shackle, therefore becomes a constant source of novelty and change in the social world.

An immediate methodological implication of Shackle's metaphysics is the impossibility of prediction in the social sciences (although he does not preclude entirely the 'projection of recent tendencies into the near future', what he calls 'inertial dynamics'). Related themes in his writings include his critique of general equilibrium theory, building on the point that the necessary pre-reconciliation of the choices of the agents in the economy is incompatible with the passage of time; his distrust of mathematics, probability concepts, quantification and aggregation for giving the relationships, magnitudes and aggregates of economic theory an unwarranted appearance of objectivity and immutability; and his concern that the deterministic 'whenever these conditions then that outcome' mode of reasoning associated with standard rational choice theory is unsuited to expressing the open and transient realm of thought and expectation. Shackle's positive methodological recommendations are less easily summarized, spread as they are over a large body of writings and often expressed obliquely in the form of commentaries on other authors. But he would perhaps have approved of having his contribution described as a continuation of the subversion of received economic theory he perceives in the development of Keynes' writings between the *Treatise on Money* and his 1937 *Quarterly Journal of Economics* defence of the *General Theory* (Shackle 1967; 1972; 1974). Shackle's preferred approach is probably best exemplified by his 'kaleidic' method: a discursive and impressionistic blend of descriptions or prevailing equilibria (understood not as optima, but as 'positions which do not contain within their structure an immediate source of movement') which are subjected to his subjectivistic brand of methodological individualism to show 'how in the nature of things, and in their own nature, these "equilibria" are vulnerable in the extreme to any expectation changing news' (Shackle, 1972: 437).

JOCHEN RUNDE

Bibliography
Ford, J.L. (1994), *G.L.S. Shackle: The Dissenting Economist's Economist*, Aldershot: Edward Elgar.
Harcourt, G.C. (1981), 'Notes on an economic querist: G.L.S. Shackle', *Journal of Post Keynesian Economics*, **4**, 136–44.
Levi, I. (1979), 'Support and Surprise: L.J. Cohen's View of Inductive Probability', *British Journal for the Philosophy of Science*, **30**, 279–92.
Shackle, G.L.S. (1938), *Expectations, Investment and Income*, Oxford: Oxford University Press.
Shackle, G.L.S. (1949), *Expectations in Economics*, Cambridge: Cambridge University Press.
Shackle, G.L.S. (1955), *Uncertainty in Economics and Other Reflections*, Cambridge: Cambridge University Press.
Shackle, G.L.S. (1966), 'Time, Nature and Decision', *The Nature of Economic Thought: Selected Papers 1955–1964*, Cambridge: Cambridge University Press.
Shackle, G.L.S. (1967), *The Years of High Theory: Invention and Tradition in Economic Thought, 1926–1939*, Cambridge: Cambridge University Press.
Shackle, G.L.S. (1972), *Epistemics and Economics: A Critique of Economic Doctrines*, Cambridge: Cambridge University Press.
Shackle, G.L.S. (1974), *Keynesian Kaleidics*, Edinburgh: Edinburgh University Press.

Simon, Herbert A.

Born on 15 June 1916 in Milwaukee, Wisconsin, Herbert Alexander Simon was the second son of Arthur Simon and Edna Merkel Simon. While he received an excellent general education at the Milwaukee public schools, Simon also found a stimulating intellectual environment at home. Admiration for his uncle, Harold Merkel, an economist and ardent formal debater, awakened in Simon a deep interest in the social sciences. Determined to analyse human behaviour in a scientific manner, he set out to become a mathematical social scientist. He earned a bachelor's degree in political science at the University of Chicago in 1936 and a PhD in 1943. After resigning from the Illinois Institute of Technology in 1949, Simon left Chicago for Pittsburgh, where he helped establish Carnegie Mellon University's new Graduate School of Industrial Administration. Since 1965, he has been Richard King Mellon professor of computer sciences and psychology at Carnegie Mellon University.

Starting off in political science and then moving through several disciplinary domains such as management theory, cognitive psychology, artificial intelligence and economics, Simon's whole academic career has been focused on analysing the foundations of human rationality. His positivist conviction that an understanding of rationality should be practical caused him to link management science to decision making, decision making to problem solving, and problem solving to artificial intelligence and economics. For Simon, the link was provided by the thesis that human rationality is bounded owing to limitations of knowledge and processing capability. The concepts he developed originally in management science led him into empirical studies of decision making. After discovering how to program computers to simulate human problem solving, he used these insights to make contributions to management science, cognitive psychology and artificial intelligence. He also sought to use this research to develop a computer-modelled theory of scientific discovery. Besides exploring the use of applied mathematics in economics, he examined the implications of his research on bounded rationality for economics.

Simon was driven by the conviction that neoclassical economists were not all that serious about describing the formal foundations of rationality, whereas he was. He criticized the four basic assumptions of neoclassical economics. First, the analysis started from the presupposition that each economic agent had a well-defined utility or profit function; second, all alternative strategies were known to the decision maker; third, neoclassical economics assumed that all the consequences that follow upon each of these strategies could be determined with certainty; finally, the comparative evaluation of these sets of consequences was assumed to be driven by a universal desire to maximize expected utility or expected profit. Simon believed that these four assumptions illustrated that the neoclassical orthodoxy gave too little attention to institutional constraints on economic behaviour and cognitive constraints on individual decisions.

Instead, Simon's bounded rationality programme proposed to include the whole range of limitations on human knowledge and human computation that prevent economic actors in the real world from behaving in ways that approximate the predictions of neoclassical theory. First, the bounded rationality programme assumes that decision makers were confronted by the need to optimize several, sometimes competing, goals. Second, instead of assuming a fixed set of alternatives among which the decision maker chose, Simon's theory of bounded rationality postulated a process for generating alternatives. He argued that, under most circumstances, it was not reasonable to talk about finding 'all the alternatives'. Third, he argued that individuals had difficulty coming up with original solutions to problems. The presence of uncertainty about the evaluation of the present and future consequences of alternative strategies led Simon to speculate that the mind mostly functions by applying approximate or 'cookbook' solutions to problems. Finally, instead of assuming the maximization of a utility function, Simon's bounded rationality theory postulated a satisficing strategy. It sought to identify, in theory and in actual behaviour, procedures for choosing that were computationally simpler and argued that individuals picked the first choice that met a pre-set acceptance criterion.

Starting from the conviction that there were external, social constraints and internal, cognitive limitations to decision making, Simon focused on the process rather than the outcome of decision making. Awareness of these constraints, according to Simon, caused people to use heuristics and to satisfice. Loosely articulated heuristics, or rules of thumb, Simon argued, governed the process of gathering information and choosing alternatives. According to Simon, these heuristics were employed generally because they had been proved successful in the past. Furthermore, they implied that the decision maker was searching merely for an adequate solution. That is, people satisficed, they accepted the first solution that was satisfactory according to a set of minimal criteria. These were laid down in goals that could be divided into independent subgoals (subtasks). This, then, allowed a problem to be broken down into subproblems and implied a hierarchy of decisions.

In 1978, some 30 years after he published his first research results, Simon received the Nobel Prize in Economics for his 'pioneering research into the decision-making processes in economic organizations'. The announcement made Simon feel 'a little like being struck by lightning' and caused consternation among many leading economists. While Simon's ideas seem to have taken little hold in any of the disciplinary fields that he traversed, he is at the same time the winner of many prestigious awards and has been a member of many policy-making bodies. What set him apart are his efforts to establish a social science that would be different from the natural sciences through the use of a different set of mathematical tools describing the processes rather than the state of the world.

Esther-Mirjam Sent

Bibliography
Egidi, M., R. Marris, H.A. Simon and R. Viale (eds) (1992), *Economics, Bounded Rationality and the Cognitive Revolution*, Brookfield, VT: Edward Elgar.
March, J.G. and H.A. Simon (1958), *Organizations*, New York: John Wiley.
Newell, A. and H.A. Simon (1972), *Human Problem Solving*, Englewood Cliffs, NJ: Prentice-Hall.
Simon, H.A. (1947), *Administrative Behavior*, New York: Macmillan.
Simon, H.A. (1957), *Models of Man*, New York: John Wiley.
Simon, H.A. (1960), *The New Science of Management Decision*, New York: Harper & Row.
Simon, H.A. (1969), *The Sciences of the Artificial*, Cambridge, MA: MIT Press.
Simon, H.A. (1977), *Models of Discovery*, Boston: D. Reidel.
Simon, H.A. (1982), *Models of Bounded Rationality*, 2 vols, Cambridge, MA: MIT Press.
Simon, H.A. (1991), *Models of My Life*, New York: Basic Books.

Simulation

To simulate something is to imitate its behaviour. Simulation is a procedure for modelling the behaviour of a system (a) in order to test a theory (the model) by comparing it with empirical data or (b) in order to make predictions that can be used for reaching decisions or creating designs.

In the first case, the theory is on trial; in the second case, the theory is presumably already validated, and its behaviour is simulated to achieve desired goals (such as to provide information for designing an aeroplane wing or for estimating the incidence of a proposed tax).

Simulation versus theorem proving

Simulation computes a detailed time path for a system, and thereby predicts the system's dynamic behaviour for specific initial and boundary conditions. The principal alternative to simulation is to prove general theorems: for example, theorems about the existence and locations of stable equilibria or limit cycles as functions of system parameters.

Classically, systems of differential or difference equations have been the most common formal means for representing theories. The preferred method for treating them was to solve them in closed form. Newton, by solving his equations of motion under the assumption of the gravitational law, could show that the path of any solitary planet must have the form of an ellipse, with equal areas swept out in equal times. These generalizations followed, once and for all, from theorems; it was unnecessary to trace out a planet's path, step by step for particular cases, as in simulation. General solutions in closed form contrast with simulation's case-by-case description of system behaviour.

Unfortunately, only a few classes of differential equation systems can be solved in closed form, and these usually only for special and simple boundary conditions. In economics, for example, strong theorems can often be proved if we assume perfect competition. One can then demonstrate the existence of stable equilibria and the fact that these equilibria produce Pareto-optimal allocations of resources. With even small departures from perfect equilibrium, the possibilities for proving such theorems vanish quickly. There is generally a tradeoff, therefore, between the simplicity/complexity of the systems that are modelled and the generality/specificity of the conclusions that can be drawn. To preserve the power of closed-form solutions of equation systems, the models must be limited to highly simplified and inexact approximations to reality. If one introduces much realism into the models, simulating their behaviour for specific initial conditions becomes almost the only available way of studying them.

Development of simulation methods

As long as computation was limited to paper and pencil tools, simulation did not play a large role in science. The growing availability of manual, then electrical, desk calculators and punched-card tabulating systems during the 1930s and 1940s brought about an increasing interest in simulation and, within economics, efforts were initiated to simulate, and hence predict, the behaviour of entire economies (in highly aggregated form, to be sure). With the appearance and rapid development of modern electronic digital computers, the interest in simulation mushroomed in virtually all the sciences, and continues to mushroom.

To use simulation for exploring increasingly realistic models, steps had to be taken to escape from the specificity of the knowledge gained from any single simulation run. Among the techniques now used for this purpose are sampling methods and sensitivity analysis.

Sampling

With more computing power, it became practicable to make numerous simulation runs to study system behaviour over different initial conditions and for different parameter values. If the sample paths are sufficiently dense, it is often safe to approximate the intervening paths by interpolation. Successive approximation can also sometimes be used to find the locations of maxima or minima when these cannot be calculated in closed form. Of course, the more complex the functions, the more likely that there will be local maxima and minima, so that care must be used to avoid stopping on a local hill and missing the distant mountain.

Sensitivity analysis
Closely related to the idea of sampling is the notion of testing how rapidly the functions of interest change as parameter values are altered. By sensitivity analysis, using simulation, we can study complex systems that approach in the limit systems solvable in closed form. The analysis can estimate what departures are allowable from the simple approximation before the closed-form analysis is invalidated.

Simulation combined with closed-form analysis
A powerful approach to systems of non-linear differential equations, say, is to carry out as much analysis as possible in closed form (usually qualitative analysis) and then to continue the exploration with simulations guided by what has been learned about the system's global properties. For example, Taylor's Series expansions of functions around local points will often disclose the general arrangement and stability of minima, maxima, and limit cycles, and determine the regions of state space governed by them. Simulations within each of these regions can often then provide a good picture of general system behaviour.

Numerical and symbolic simulation
Most classical methods for studying the behaviour of systems require them to be described in numerical form. In economics, by focusing on quantities of commodities, prices and perhaps 'utiles', the restriction to numbers was not, for a long time, felt to be a serious limitation on theories. With a growing interest after World War II in the actual processes for reaching economic (and other) decisions, and the actual methods for solving problems, numbers could no longer serve as the sole means of representation.

Here, too, the computer came to the rescue. It was soon recognized that a computer is not limited to numerical manipulations: it is a general symbol-manipulating device, capable of processing patterns of any form, whether they denote numbers, words, diagrams, pictures or anything else. For example, it can produce verbal protocols of its successive processing steps while performing tasks, just as human subjects often can when they are instructed to think aloud. With the development of artificial intelligence, more and more simulations modelled the verbal, diagrammatical and mathematical processes used by human beings in their reasoning.

Among the economic processes modelled and simulated in this way have been the decision processes of a bank officer managing a trust portfolio, of executives making investments for business firms, of a financial analyst interpreting a company's financial statements, of an executive analysing a business policy case, of students seeking employment, and others. In all of these, the simulations mingled numerical and non-numerical information and thought processes.

Human-Machine Simulation
In economics, and the human sciences generally, simulation is not limited to computer models. The business game, widely used as an instructional tool, is an example of a man-machine simulation in which the human participants simulate the decision-making behaviour of managers, while the computer simulates the consumers in the companies' markets. Of course

one could substitute human actors for the computer simulation of customers, in which case, we might not speak of the process as a simulation but as an experiment. The growing activity of experimental economics operates in both modes of experiment/simulation. The early experiments used human subjects (usually students in an economics course) who were given roles in a market game. The entire interaction took place without the need for computing devices. Today, it is more common to include a computer component in the market games, at least for the purpose of recording the transactions. But increasingly, some or all of the human players are being replaced by computer programs that simulate market traders.

What can be learned from such market experiments, with and without simulated traders? In their purely human versions, the participants simulate behaviour in various kinds of market situations, hence provide theories that can be extrapolated (with the usual cautions that accompany such extrapolations) to realworld markets. However, it is exceedingly difficult to obtain from human subjects data that reveal the detail of the information and thought processes they are using in reaching their trading decisions. By building hypotheses about these processes and incorporating the hypotheses in computer programs that can operate as traders, the observable human behaviour can be matched and theories of the human processes can be tested. In this way, much has already been learned about how much or how little information and sophistication is required of the traders in order for markets to operate at a high level of efficiency.

Complexity and chaos

In recent years, there has been a great burgeoning of interest in the behaviour of highly complex systems. Meteorology, economics, astrophysics, molecular biology and aeronautical engineering constitute a small sample of the domains of science and engineering that continually struggle with complexity and with the inadequacy of classical tools to deal with it.

The interest in complexity has been reinforced by the rediscovery of the phenomena of chaos: of fully determinate non-linear dynamic systems whose behaviour seems to incorporate a large element of chance. (The chaotic behaviour actually results, without the intrusion of chance, from the fact that very small differences in initial conditions can lead to rapidly diverging paths.) As a result, there is now considerable activity aimed at building computational methods for dealing with chaotic systems.

By the nature of chaos, the long-term behaviour of chaotic systems cannot be forecast accurately. The computational analysis of such systems must focus upon identifying and locating the regions in phase space within which they do, or do not, behave chaotically. The chaotic regions, called *strange attractors*, play a role similar to equilibrium points and limit cycles in non-chaotic systems. Recent research has shown that, by adding feedback controls to a chaotic system, it can sometimes be confined to a small region of the strange attractor, and thereby made amenable to prediction and control – a procedure that may have importance for the regulation of economic systems.

Other approaches to complexity

Complex systems, including economic systems, frequently possess a boxes-within-boxes structure (nearly complete decomposability), wherein subsystems have strong internal connections of their parts, but weaker connections to the other subsystems. Through the exploitation of this hierarchical architecture, the behaviour of each subsystem can be simulated separately for short time intervals, then a simpler model of the whole system, with aggregated components, can be simulated to reveal longer-term behaviour.

Systems that evolve under the forces of natural selection also often exhibit great complexity in their changes over time. This has stimulated an interest in simulations of the evolutionary processes themselves – so-called 'genetic algorithms'. In principle, such algorithms may be applied to the simulation of economic as well as biological systems, although it is too early to say what uses they may have in the understanding of the long-term dynamics of economies.

Prospects for simulation
As simulation tools have been used on a large scale for only a single human generation, and as the rapid growth in computing power shows no signs of abating, we may expect that simulation of complex systems, including economic systems, will continue to gain importance as a tool of analysis. The recent developments in symbolic simulation of human thought processes, experimental economics, the analysis of chaotic systems and simulation with genetic algorithms illustrate the wealth of ideas, both substantive and methodological, that is emerging from these applications of simulation.

HERBERT A. SIMON

Bibliography
Adelman, Irma (1968), 'Simulation: Economic Processes', *International Encyclopaedia of the Social Sciences*, vol. 14, New York: Free Press.
Cvitanovic, Predrag (1984), *Universality in Chaos*, Bristol: Adam Hilger.
Newell, Allen (1990), *Unified Theories of Cognition*, Cambridge, MA: Harvard University Press.
Newell, Allen and Herbert. A. Simon (1972), *Human Problem Solving*, Englewood Cliffs, NJ.: Prentice-Hall.
Smith, Vernon L. (1991), *Papers in Experimental Economics*, New York: Cambridge University Press.

Situational Analysis

'Situational analysis' and 'situational logic' are the terms used by the philosopher Karl Popper to identify a methodological approach whose use he advocates in the social sciences, an approach he claims is a generalization of the method of economic analysis. To undertake a situational analysis, the social scientist reconstructs the problem situation faced by an agent in such a manner that the action that the agent takes can be viewed as a reasonable response to the situation. It turns out that unpacking this brief characterization is a difficult task indeed; even Popper employed the concept in different ways over the years. We will approach the problem by tracing the development of the idea in his writings.

Early variants
Popper's earliest usage of the idea is in Sections 29 and 31 of *The Poverty of Historicism* (1957). In Section 29 Popper discusses:

> what may be called the method of logical or rational construction, or perhaps the 'zero method'. By this I mean the method of constructing a model on the assumption of complete rationality (and perhaps also on the assumption of the possession of complete information) on the part of all individuals concerned, and of estimating the deviation of the actual behavior of people from the model behavior, using the latter as a kind of zero-coordinate. An example of this method is the comparison of actual

behavior (under the influence of, say, traditional prejudice, etc.) and model behavior to be expected on the basis of 'the pure logic of choice', as described by the equations of economics. (Ibid: 141)

In this version, the actual behaviour of individuals is contrasted with the behaviour of perfectly rational (and perhaps perfectly informed) agents. There is no indication, however, of what one should do if (as should be expected, given the way that Popper sets things up) the actual behaviour is not the same as that predicted, given fully rational agents.

Section 31 is entitled 'Situational Logic in History'. Here Popper claims that 'the best historians' have 'more or less unconsciously' made use of the method of the logic of the situation (ibid.: 149), but again there is little elaboration of what this might mean.[1]

The 'logic of the situation' is mentioned twice in Popper's next major work, *The Open Society and Its Enemies* (1963). Here it is used as a weapon in the fight against *psychologism*, the idea that all social science explanations might some day be reduced to explanations that make reference only to psychological states. Here Popper for the first time introduces the notions of initial conditions and laws:

> most historical explanation makes tacit use, not so much of trivial sociological and psychological laws, but of what I have called, in Chapter 14, the *logic of the situation*; that is to say, besides the initial conditions describing personal interests, aims, and other situational factors, such as the information available to the person concerned, it tacitly assumes, as a kind of first approximation, the trivial general law that sane persons as a rule act more or less rationally. (Ibid., vol. 2: 265, emphasis in the original)

In his fuller discussion of the concept in Chapter 14 (ibid., vol. 2: 93–8), Popper makes a number of additional points. First, the main task of the social sciences is to analyse 'the unintended social repercussions of intentional human actions' (ibid.: 95), something that psychologism is unable to do.[2] An analysis of the logic of the situation can be helpful here, since 'our actions are to a very large extent explicable in terms of the situation in which they occur' (ibid.: 97). He further notes that the psychological part of such explanations 'is often very trivial, as compared with the detailed determination of his action by what we may call the *logic of the situation*' (ibid.: 97, emphasis in the original). Finally, it is here that Popper notes that 'situational logic … is, in fact, the method of economic analysis' (ibid.: 97).

It is evident from what has been said that Popper emphasized two distinct aspects of situational analysis in his early writings. In the earliest version, the full rationality of the agent is stressed, and the agent's actions are taken to be a sort of *benchmark* against which the actions of 'real individuals' might be measured. In the second variant, it is the *situation*, or the *constraints* faced by the agent, and not the agent's *rationality*, that receive all of the emphasis, and this because an agent's actions are 'to a very large extent explicable in terms of the situation'. In both approaches, Popper appears to assume that the social scientist *knows* what it is rational for the agent to do.

A further comment is necessary on Popper's joining together the notion of situational logic and the idea that the primary task of the social sciences is to explain the unintended consequences of human action. The two *can* be linked together. Carl Menger's *Principles of Economics* (1976) is an early, and arguably still the best, example. Menger showed how a variety of market institutions (such as markets themselves, competition and money) came into being as the result of self-seeking (rational) human action, but not as a result of any conscious (intentional) human design. Markets are unintended consequences of intentional human action.

We can see the role played by 'the unintended consequences of intentional human action' in Menger. But why does Popper introduce the idea? Its efficacy is clear enough: he uses it in arguing against psychologism in *The Open Society*. But he offers no rationale for it, nor does he state how to make the transition from intentional human action to unintended consequences, nor does he even tell us where the idea came from.[3] Popper continues to pay lip service to the idea of unintended consequences in his later articles but, since he never takes it any further than this, we will not give any further attention to it.

Later variants and Koertge's reformulation
In the 1960s Popper engaged in a dispute with some members of the Frankfurt School over the appropriate methods of the social sciences. In his contribution to a conference volume, Popper argued that the use of a deductive framework enhances the process of criticism (the process of 'conjecture and refutation') that characterizes the scientific method: 'The most important function of pure deductive logic is that of an organon of criticism' (1976: 98). It is within this context that he discusses situational logic:

> there exists a *purely objective* method in the social sciences that may well be called the method of *objective* understanding, or situational logic. ... Its method consists in analysing the social *situation* of acting men sufficiently to explain the action with the help of the situation, without any further help from psychology. Objective understanding consists in realizing that the action was objectively *appropriate to the situation.*
>
> ...
>
> The explanations of situational logic described here are rational, theoretical reconstructions. They are oversimplified and over schematized and consequently in general *false*. Nevertheless, they can possess a considerable truth content and they can, in a strictly logical sense, be good approximations to the truth ... Above all, however, situational analysis is rational, empirically criticizable, and capable of improvement. For we may, for instance, find a letter which shows us that the knowledge at the disposal of Charlemagne was different from what we assumed in our analysis. (Ibid.: 102–3, emphases in the original)

Popper stresses three points in his discussion. First, the method of situational analysis promotes objectivity: if the analyst knows what is appropriate to the situation, she gains objective understanding of the agent's actions. Next, his example suggests what should be done if the social scientist's prediction is not borne out: namely, re-examine the assumed situational constraints. In his example, new objective evidence (a letter) may allow us to modify our description of a situation. Finally, the method is itself criticizable.

In another paper, also first appearing in the 1960s, Popper states the procedure more generally. The rationality principle, which he says plays a role in the social sciences similar to that of universal laws in the natural sciences, is the claim that 'the various persons or agents involved act *adequately*, or *appropriately*; that is to say, in accordance with the situation' (1985: 359, emphasis in the original). Even though agents do not always act appropriately (his two favourite examples are a driver trying to fit a car into a space he knows is too small, or a person trying a key in a lock that he knows it does not fit), the rationality principle should never be rejected. When an agent does not act as predicted

> it is sound methodological policy to decide not to make the rationality principle accountable but the rest of the theory... The main argument in favor of this policy is that our model is far more interesting and informative, and far better testable, than the principle of the adequacy of our actions. (Ibid.: 362)

Though clearer than his earlier statements, there is still a certain vagueness in Popper's later explanations of how a situational analysis should be undertaken. In particular, for all his talk about the desirability of a deductive framework, none is provided. Noretta Koertge (1975: 440) remedies this deficiency with the following reformulation.

1. *Description of the situation*: agent A was in a situation of type C.
2. *Analysis of the situation*: in a situation of type C, the appropriate thing to do is X.
3. *Rationality principle*: agents always act appropriately to their situations.
4. *Explanandum*: (therefore) A did X.

An inconsistency between the methods of Popper$_n$ and Popper$_s$?

Wade Hands (1985) differentiated between the methodological writings of Popper$_n$ (*n* for 'natural science') and Popper$_s$ (*s* for social science) and asked whether the methods proposed by the 'two Poppers' are consistent. Specifically, Popper$_s$'s rule that one must never reject the rationality principle seems to contradict Popper$_n$'s rule that, when a theory is falsified, one must not employ an 'immunizing stratagem' to save it. Though Popper$_s$ had offered a number of 'good reasons' for never rejecting the rationality principle, such a blanket dictum appeared (from a Popper$_n$ perspective) to involve an immunizing stratagem of the highest order.

That a tension exists between Popper$_n$ and Popper$_s$ seems clear enough. According to Caldwell (1991), the exact nature of the conflict depends on the logical status of the rationality principle. There seem to be three possible interpretations of its status. One possibility is that the rationality principle is an unfalsifiable universal statement. This interpretation is most plausible when it is read as saying that 'agents always act appropriately to their situations *as they see them*'. The italicized clause signals to us that the 'description of the situation' incorporates the agent's aims, goals, expectations, beliefs, perceptions and so on – all of which are forever unobservable. But if all of these are included, no observed action need ever falsify the rationality hypothesis. Let us take Popper's own examples. A person who keeps trying to fit a car into a space that she believes (knows) is too small may actually be trying to scrape (carefully, hence the repeated efforts) the paint off the car that has parked too far over into her reserved space. The person jiggling the key that she believes (knows) will not fit may be trying to signal to an accomplice inside that the apartment owner is arriving and an escape should be made. One can always reformulate an apparently irrational act as a rational one by redescribing the agent's motives or information, or some other element in the description of the situation. Some of these may make reference to observables, as Popper's well-chosen example of Charlemagne's letter makes clear. But in social sciences that deal with intentional human action, other elements of the description will always include unobservables, and these can always be invoked to 'rationalize away' any apparent violation of the rationality principle.

If the rationality principle is unfalsifiable, two conclusions are possible. Either it is comparable to an analytic statement with no empirical content or it is simply a bit of metaphysics.

A second possibility is that the rationality principle is falsifiable. This would be the case, for example, if one viewed it as the equivalent of a general law for the social sciences. But if it is falsifiable, what have been the results of its testing? Popper's own conclusion is that there are 'good reasons' (1985: 362) to think that it is false. But if it is false, then (according to Popper$_n$) to retain it is to employ an immunizing stratagem. To see this, note the following argument, drawn from Caldwell (1991: 20):

1. Popper$_n$ maintained that the structure of scientific explanation is always the same: an explanandum is deduced from an explicans, which contains sentences describing initial conditions and at least one general law.
2. Popper$_n$ asserted that 'the *explicans* ought to be true although it will not, in general, be known to be true; in any case, it must not be known to be false' (1983: 132, emphasis in the original).
3. When theory revision is called for, the prime directive of Popper$_n$ is to avoid the use of immunizing stratagems, ad hoc adjustments of a theory undertaken to protect it from refutation.
4. There are good reasons to believe that the universal law used in the social sciences, the rationality principle, is false. (This violates condition (2).)
5. But Popper$_s$ insists that the rationality principle, though false, should never be rejected. Instead, the theory should be adjusted until the agent's actions can be shown to follow from the logic of the situation. (This violates condition (3).)[4]

A third option is to interpret the rationality principle neither as an unfalsifiable statement nor as a falsifiable (and falsified) one, but as a methodological principle that has been retained because it has been shown to be useful in the past. But Popper explicitly rejects this approach (1985: 361), possibly because to retain a principle on the basis of its usefulness would violate his famed anti-inductivism, or possibly because its use seems to suggest that the natural and social sciences follow different methods.

What, then, according to Popper, is the status of the rationality principle? In the paper in which he is supposed to be clarifying his position (Popper, 1985), he comes closest to endorsing the second of the three choices. Yet even there it is hard to tell what Popper thinks: in the course of four pages, he uses the following words in characterizing the rationality principle: 'an animating law', 'a principle', 'a zero principle', (ibid.: 359), 'does not play the role of an empirical explanatory theory', 'not empirically refutable', 'clearly false' (ibid.: 360), 'false', 'an empirical conjecture' (ibid.: 361), 'actually false but a good approximation to the truth' (ibid.: 362). As Watkins put it, 'Popper's own expositions of the RP are "appropriately vague"' (Watkins, quoted in Koertge, 1975: 441).

The link to economics

If there is a conflict between the prescriptions of Popper$_n$ and situational analysis, then (at least from an economist's perspective) it is so much the worse for Popper$_n$. Situational analysis should be very familiar territory for an economist. Standard microeconomic models employ rational agents whose actions ('choices') are determined in part by their situations (for example, constraints like 'endowments' and 'technology'). Changes in constraints cause changes in behaviour: this is the method of comparative statics. But even more than this, by modifying the description of the problem situation one can obtain a host of more recent alternative microeconomic models. For example, the satisficing model is obtained by modifying the assumed computational abilities of the agent. Alter the informational environment and one gets situations of adverse selection and moral hazard and, in response to them, various forms of monitoring, risk sharing, screening and signalling behaviours, each of them an 'appropriate' response to some specified informational environment. Alter the description of the situation again and one obtains transactions cost analysis. Not all of economics is microeconomics, and not all microexplanations are explanations of typical individual action, but virtually all microeconomic explanations of typical individual action are provided in terms of the logic of the situation. For better or worse, situational analysis is the method of mainstream microeconomic theory.

Why has the method of situational analysis proved to be so popular among economists? Three reasons might be mentioned. First, it is particularly well-suited as a framework for explaining intentional human action that takes place within specified environmental constraints. The mathematics of constrained optimization can be talked about within the framework, and so can the commonsensical notion that, when humans offer explanations of their behaviour, they do so in terms of 'reasons'. Situational analysis informs both the formalism and the intuition underlying explanation in terms of individual intentional action, and individual intentional action is at the foundation of neoclassical reasoning.

Second, it is an open-ended method of discovery. When we come across an action that we do not understand, situational analysis directs us to investigate our preconceptions about the agent and the environment in which the agent is acting. Sometimes such investigation leads to the discovery of new empirical data as Popper's example of a newly found Carolingian letter illustrated. Sometimes it may lead us to question our previous assumptions concerning the agent, as the satisficing model does, or about the informational environment, as the economics of information does. The multitude of possibilities keeps us searching; this would not occur if every unexpected action was attributed to the irrationality of the agent.

Third, the vagueness of its logical status helps to ensure the survivability of the rationality principle. It was noted that Popper was 'appropriately vague' about his formulation of the rationality principle. Economists appear to have followed the same procedure in their discussions of the 'neoclassical maximization hypothesis' or 'rationality assumption'.[5] And, as Popper$_n$ would emphasize, vague hypotheses are notoriously hard to refute.

Situational analysis is a powerful method of discovery. As the continued development of the neoclassical research programme demonstrates, it has also been a magnificently successful research heuristic. It has two main limitations. The first has to do with the question of empirical limitations. As noted earlier, intentional explanations perforce make reference to unobservables such as goals and expectations. It will always be possible to reconstruct a situation to yield the observed behaviour by invoking changes in motives, or in information, or in perceived transactions costs, or in some other unobservable variable. To the extent that this occurs without further attempts at independent testing, explanations are rendered ad hoc, which diminishes rather than enhances the process of criticism.[6] Second, situational analysis involves the relentless pursuit of the following legitimate research heuristic: 'Always reconstruct the problem situation in such a manner that the action actually taken by the agent can be viewed as a reasonable response to the situation.' It is a small but consequential step from here to the illegitimate presumption that all observed actions (or social outcomes, institutions and so on) are in fact reasonable reactions (or adaptations) to their environment.

BRUCE CALDWELL

Notes
1. 'Tolstoy, for example, when he describes how it was not decision but "necessity" which made the Russian army yield Moscow without a fight and withdraw to places where it could find food' (ibid.: 149) is Popper's illustration of the way an action can be determined by the logic of a situation.
2. The notion that individual action has unintended consequences is present in *The Poverty*, but it is not linked to the discussion of situational logic.
3. Mäki (1990) argues against the sufficiency of situational analysis arguments for the explanation of the unintended consequences of individual action.

4. Two key assumptions of the argument provided in the text are that the rationality principle (RP) is a part of the explicans, and that situational analysis is a method of explanation. In correspondence with the author, Professor Charles Christenson has argued that Popper did not intend the RP itself to be part of the explicans in an explanation using situational logic. He cites Popper's statement (1985: 360) that the RP 'does not play the role of an explanatory theory ... The empirical explanatory theories or hypotheses are our various models, our various situational analyses'. If this interpretation is correct, the apparent inconsistency between Popper$_n$ and Popper$_s$ is resolved. According to Professor Christenson's interpretation of Popper's position, the RP plays only the role of a heuristic device to be used in arriving at a model of the situation.
5. See Caldwell (1983) for more on the status of the maximization hypothesis.
6. Another common way of putting this idea is that unrestricted *ceteris paribus* clauses should be avoided.

References
Caldwell, Bruce (1983), 'The Neoclassical Maximization Hypothesis: Comment', *American Economic Review*, **73**, September, 824–7.
Caldwell, Bruce (1991), 'Clarifying Popper', *Journal of Economic Literature*, **29**, March, 1–33.
Hands, D.W. (1985), 'Karl Popper and Economic Methodology: A New Look', *Economics and Philosophy*, **1**, April, 83–99.
Koertge, Noretta (1975), 'Popper's Metaphysical Research Program for the Human Sciences', *Inquiry*, **18**, Winter, 437–62.
Mäki, Uskali (1990), 'Practical Syllogism, Entrepreneurship, and the Invisible Hand', in D. Lavoie (ed.), *Economics and Hermeneutics*, London: Routledge.
Menger, Carl (1976) *Principles of Economics*, trans. J. Dingwall and B. Hoselitz, New York: New York University Press.
Popper, Karl (1957), *The Poverty of Historicism*, Boston: Beacon Press.
Popper, Karl (1963), *The Open Society and Its Enemies*, Princeton: Princeton University Press.
Popper, Karl (1976), 'The Logic of the Social Sciences', in T. Adorno, H. Albert, R. Dahrendorf, J. Habermas, H. Pilot and K. Popper (eds), *The Positivist Dispute in German Sociology*, New York: Harper.
Popper, Karl (1983), *Realism and the Aim of Science: The Postscript to the* Logic of Scientific Discovery, ed. W.W. Bartley, Totowa, NJ: Rowman & Littlefield.
Popper, Karl (1985), 'The Rationality Principle', in D. Miller (ed.), *Popper Selections*, Princeton: Princeton University Press.
Watkins, J.W.N. (1958), 'Confirmable and Influential Metaphysics', *Mind*, **67**, July: 344–65.

Smith, Adam

Adam Smith (1723–90), Scottish moral philosopher and parent of modern economic thought, was born in Kirkcaldy. Little is known of his formative years prior to his university education at Glasgow University (1737–40) where he was greatly influenced by Francis Hutcheson. From Glasgow, Smith moved on to Balliol College, Oxford in 1740. He studied there for six years, years which were frustrating, for he found the intellectual energy he enjoyed so much at Glasgow to be entirely absent at Oxford. In search of intellectual growth during that period, Smith explored a vast literature including the work of David Hume. Hume and Smith were acquainted and through years of correspondence they became very close friends. Hutcheson and Hume are arguably the most significant influences in Smith's intellectual development.

Smith's professional career began in 1748 as a public lecturer in Edinburgh. On the basis of the reception of those lectures, in 1751 he was elected to the faculty of the University of Glasgow. It was during his tenure at Glasgow that he published *The Theory of Moral Sentiments* (1759). This treatise on ethics was very well received by his contemporaries and established Smith's reputation in Britain and on the continent. Smith-left his position at Glasgow in 1763 to become the tutor of the Duke of Buccleuch. From 1764 to 1767, Smith toured France with the duke. As compensation for his duties as tutor, Smith received a handsome lifetime annuity.

Financially secure, Smith returned to the quietude of his mother's home in Kirkcaldy to focus on his next big project, *An Inquiry into The Nature and Causes of The Wealth of Nations*. In 1773, Smith took his manuscript to London to have it published. Further work on the book delayed its publication until 1776. Smith then returned to Scotland, where he took a position at Edinburgh as commissioner of customs. He held that position until his death in 1790.

Smith's *Wealth of Nations* describes how a market system can provide a mechanism for the timely and smooth coordination of autonomous individuals' choices in an interdependent world, so as to produce the greatest possible wealth for the nation. This classical liberal vision of an invisible hand guiding the market system to an optimal outcome is widely acknowledged to be the vision on which the modern mainstream discourse in economics is based and which any alternative vision must address. There has been a suggestion since the mid-nineteenth century that there is an 'Adam Smith Problem': that there are different, inconsistent voices in *The Theory of Moral Sentiments* and *The Wealth of Nations*. I would suggest that there is no inconsistency: the *Theory* presents the social/psychological foundation for the beings who would inhabit the constructive liberal society imagined in the *Wealth*.

The foundation of the philosophical vision that Smith brings to all of his inquiries is the assumption that there is an order to nature, and that this order is the product of the design of a benevolent deity. Thus to represent (to model) the order of nature is to try to unveil its natural goodness. But, unlike contemporaries who believed the order of nature was discoverable and that, on the basis of this knowledge the existence of the deity was provable, Smith believed that such knowledge and thus such a proof were beyond the reach of human understanding. In Smith a sense of the limits of human understanding gave rise to intellectual humility rather than nihilism.

Smith believed that, while our senses allow us to experience the face of nature, we can never know its essence. We are at once a part of nature and at the same time its audience, but unlike an audience at a grand theatre of London or Paris where, after the show, we might be allowed backstage to see the 'machinery of the opera-house' that made such a grand spectacle possible, we are not 'admitted behind the scenes' of nature's grand spectacle (Smith, 1980: 42–3). We have no access to the principles of nature: either those that give things their nature or those that order the connections among these things. For Smith, then, inquiry is not about Truth – what is the deity's design – it is about imagination: what we believe that design is.

Human beings pursue this question, 'What is the order, the design, of nature?', because of a basic principle of human nature. We are distressed by what we cannot comfortably accommodate in our account of the unfolding play of nature. We sooth our imagination by constructing stories to explain what we see. The casual observer is generally satisfied with a story that allows the custom of a connection to stand as an explanation of an often observed chain of events. Smith cites, for example, the 'common artizans; such as dyers, brewers, [or] distillers' who daily watch their art unfold without ever wondering at the invisible chain of events that must link the sequence they observe. These constant, but casual observers 'cannot conceive what occasion there is for any connecting events to unite those appearances, which seem to [them] … to succeed each other very naturally' (ibid.: 44). It is only the more studied eye that wonders at the sequence and feels that there must be missing links in the common description of a chain of events derived from casual empiricism. This studied eye is the eye of a philosopher.

[A] philosopher … [spends] his whole life in the study of the connecting principles of nature … which, to more careless observers, seem very strictly cojoined. …

> Philosophy is the science of the connecting principles of nature … Philosophy, by representing the invisible chains which bind together all these disjointed objects, endeavours to introduce order into this chaos of jarring and discordant appearances. (Ibid.: 45–6)

For Smith the primary objective of philosophy is to explain what is or has been observed. A theory is likely to be recognized as an appealing representation of the invisible connecting chains of nature to the degree that it offers a simple and coherent explanation of what we observe in terms that are familiar to the audience. The broader the scope of that explanation, the more impressive the theory. Explanation, not prediction, is Smith's standard; for the weight of human experience lies in the past. To explain all that we have seen is more substantial than to explain new observations. But, as new observations are added to our experience, their relative weight increases and a theory's failure to explain this new scope of experience weighs heavily on that theory and encourages challengers.

All theories are provisional. Humankind's ability to observe improves over time, and so all theories ultimately lose their lustre as more detailed observation produces evidence inconsistent with that old vision. While this process of scientific evolution may be slowed by the intellectual inertia that comes from deference to authority and social investment with the implications of extant theory, Smith sees it as inexorable. Every theory fails, for each is only a construction of the imagination. Belief that one knows Truth is seductive, but Truth is beyond the reach of any theory. Closing his discussion of Sir Isaac Newton's work, Smith writes :

> even we, while we have been endeavouring to represent all philosophical systems as mere inventions of the imagination … have insensibly been drawn in, to make use of language expressing the connecting principles of this one, *as if* they were the real chains which nature makes use of to bind together her several operations. (Ibid.: 105, emphasis added)

Smith's work in his own area of inquiry, moral philosophy, reflects his philosophy of inquiry. He offers us an image of the course of human history and of the ideal (a limiting point) towards which that course is evolving. His vision of that process and that limiting point reflects his belief in the benevolence of the deity's design, for his story is one of an evolution of humankind (albeit not any particular society) that is progressive.

Smith envisions humankind as having evolved through four stages: hunting and gathering, pasturage, agriculture and commerce. Starting from a few psychological principles of human nature – that we have basic physical needs (such as, food and shelter, clothing) and that we are endowed with sentiments (such as self-love, justice and beneficence) – he represents the connecting principles that shape each stage and that lead to the rise and demise of various societies that carry humankind from stage to stage. Each stage represents a greater maturation of human potential. This maturation is the product of the coevolution of personal ethics, political justice and the division of labour with surpluses exchanged through markets. By chance of circumstance and serendipity, some societies develop a higher order of maturity. The limiting point is a liberal (commercial) society of independent, ethical individuals who live in perfect harmony and who realize, through their autonomous efforts, the greatest possible wealth for the nation.

Smith's standard of the credibility of his own presentation was its consistency with history as he understood it. One might call it scientific history, for his method was to intuit from history principles of being and of the connections among beings that could explain the course of history. His work has also been referred to as philosophical history. In Smith's day, the terms 'philosophy' and 'science' were closely related. Ultimately, his objective was to do for moral philosophy what Newton had done for natural philosophy, to present a compelling representation of the connecting principles that give rise to what we see – a story so convincing that, as with Newton's successors, his own successors would 'make use of language expressing the connecting principles of this one, as if they were the real chains which nature makes use of to bind together her several operations'. By that standard, Adam Smith has been both immensely successful and unsuccessful. The modern neoclassical economic discourse that he fathered has enshrined his invisible hand story; but it has also replaced the human foundation of Smith's story, the coevolution of individuals and society which develops ever more mature ethics, with an ahistorical and amoral *homo economicus*.

JERRY EVENSKY

Bibliography
Evensky, Jerry (1994), 'Setting the Scene: Adam Smith's Moral Philosophy', in Robin Paul Malloy and Jerry Evensky (eds), *Adam Smith and the Philosophy of Law and Economics*, Dordrecht: Kluwer Academic.
Lindgren, J. Ralph (1973), 'Inquiry', *The Social Philosophy of Adam Smith*, The Hague: Martinus Nijohff.
Skinner, Andrew (1979), 'Science and the Role of the Imagination', *A System of Social Science: Papers Relating to Adam Smith*, Oxford: Clarendon Press.
Smith, Adam (1980), 'The Principles Which Lead and Direct Philosophical Enquiries; Illustrated by the History of Astronomy', in W.P.D. Wightman and J.C. Bryce (eds), *Essays on Philosophical Subjects*, The Glasgow Edition of the Works and Correspondence of Adam Smith, Oxford: Oxford University Press.
Thompson, Herbert (1965), 'Adam Smith's Philosophy of Science', *Quarterly Journal of Economics*, **79**, (2).
Wightman, W.P.D. (1975), 'Adam Smith and the History of Ideas', in Andrew Skinner and Thomas Wilson (eds), *Essays on Adam Smith*, Oxford: Clarendon Press.

Socialist Calculation Debate, The

The opening round in what became known as the socialist calculation debate was fired by Ludwig von Mises in 1920, when the spectre of communism was once more haunting Europe, in his article 'Economic Calculation in the Socialist Commonwealth'. Mises' thesis was that rational economic calculation was impossible under socialism. His basic argument was that, in any but the simplest economy, economic calculation demands the use of a scalar common denominator for costing and valuation. In the capitalist economy, market prices provide such a common denominator. Mises assumed that, while there may exist a market for consumer goods in a socialist economy, there will not be a market for the means of production (as state property, the means of production will be *res extra commercium*), and neither will there be a labour market in anything like the capitalist sense. So market prices will not be available as a means of calculation. Mises briefly considered the classical Marxian alternative – the use of a direct calculus of labour time – but rejected this proposal, on three grounds. First, the summing of labour times ignores the phasing of the labour input over time (that is, the question of direct versus 'roundabout' production methods); second, a labour time calculus necessarily undervalues non-reproducible natural resources; and third, labour time is heterogeneous anyway: labours of differing skill and intensity can be reduced to a common denominator only by the use of market-determined wage rates.

Mises' argument was reprinted and elaborated upon by Hayek in his edited volume of 1935, *Collectivist Economic Planning*. Also reprinted there was Barone's 1908 essay, 'The Ministry of Production in the Collectivist State'. This piece was to play a paradoxical role in the debate. Barone had made the argument that a socialist planning ministry, in order to comply with the dictates of economic rationality, would have to duplicate the effects of competitive capitalism (in particular, to minimize cost of production and to set prices equal to marginal costs). Barone took this conclusion as a criticism of the socialist contention that a rational society would allocate resources on a basis quite different from the 'anarchic' market. But Lange (1938), in his famous response on behalf of socialism, turned this point against its author. What it showed was that the task facing the planning authority was essentially the same as that facing the market economy. In each case, the equations of general equilibrium had to be solved. If the market could do so, then so could the planners – if not directly, then via trial and error, by first setting a price vector then instructing the managers of socialist enterprises (a) to choose the production method that minimized average cost at those prices and (b) to produce output up to the point at which marginal cost equalled price. If the attempt to comply with these instructions gave rise to excess supplies and demands (as it well might) then the planning authority should adjust the price vector (raising the prices of goods in excess demand and cutting the prices of goods in excess supply) and try again. Yes, prices were necessary (as in Mises' argument) but these need not be real market prices: they might equally well be accounting prices set by the state. Besides, the state had an extra degree of freedom: it could choose the distribution of income and optimize the allocation of resources relative to that distribution, which might be quite different from that engendered by the market.

In the early postwar period, most commentators on the debate (notably Bergson (1948), Schumpeter and Samuelson) reckoned that the socialists had come off best. There was no reason why the socialist planners could not mimic a competitive equilibrium via a Lange-type procedure. During the 1980s, this account of the debate was sharply challenged. Lavoie (1985) gave the fullest statement of the revisionist position (see also Nove, 1983, for a rather different but also influential critique of the idea of socialist planning). Lavoie's claim was that the two sides in the debate had been talking past one another. Lange and others who made similar arguments (such as Dickinson, Lerner and Taylor), as well as the commentators mentioned above, took a Walrasian approach and were thinking in terms of attaining static general equilibrium, while the Austrians had a quite different problem in mind, namely that of dynamic adjustment (and discovery) in the face of continuously changing technological possibilities and preferences. According to Lavoie, Mises never denied that socialism would be able to perform acceptably under static conditions, but this was irrelevant to the real world. The whole Walrasian apparatus served at best to define the end-point of dynamic adjustment in a market economy, but this limit was never reached in a real capitalist economy and neither could it be reached under socialism. The formal equivalence argument stemming from Barone was therefore beside the point of the Austrian charge that socialism had no means of emulating the profit-seeking dynamic of capitalism.

Earlier commentators on the debate had seen Hayek as retreating from Mises' strong claim regarding the impossibility *in principle* of rational economic calculation under socialism, to the weaker objection that the planners could not solve the equations representing general equilibrium on a practical time scale. And they saw Lange's trial and error solution as an answer to that objection. According to Lavoie this was a misrepresentation. The 'computational' issue of solving a very large system of equations was strictly secondary. The true problem is not data processing, but rather the collection – even the *creation* – of information (on production possibilities and people's preferences). Such information cannot be regarded as 'given'; rather, it is generated in the process of rivalrous competition between capitalist entrepreneurs as they attempt to put into practice, and hence test the profitability of, their various incompatible plans for investment and production. As a reading of Hayek, this is supported by the latter's classic 1945 article, 'The Use of Knowledge in Society'. More clearly than in his work of the 1930s, this spells out a conception of the market economy as a system whereby 'not only a division of labor but also a coordinated utilization of resources based on an equally divided knowledge has become possible' (Hayek, 1945: 528). Individuals can make use of local knowledge available to them alone, while at the same time relying on price signals to tell them what they need to know about the actions of other market participants.

In recent years (against the background, of course, of the collapse of communism in the former Soviet Union) the Mises–Hayek–Lavoie argument has received both support and criticism. Joseph Stiglitz, working on the basis of what he calls the 'new information paradigm', has in effect seconded the Austrian claims regarding the problems of socialism, noting in addition, like Lavoie, that 'the failure of market socialism serves as much as a refutation of the standard neoclassical model as it does of the market socialist ideal' (Stiglitz, 1994: 2). This idea – that standard neoclassical economics cannot quite 'get at' and explicate the most important virtues of the market, and so can be seriously misleading as a guide to the design of economic systems – is also explored in Vaughn (1994).

Stiglitz's contribution is almost exclusively concerned with market socialism, and some responses to his arguments in this regard can be found in Bardhan and Roemer (1993). On the original point at issue between Mises and the Marxists (regarding the possibility and desirability of central planning), Stiglitz says only that 'Hayek had rightly criticized' the Marxian view, 'arguing that the central planner could never have the requisite information' (Stiglitz, 1994: 9). Cockshott and Cottrell (1993a; 1993b) have, however, defended planning against the Austrian arguments. They take issue with Mises' contention that a calculus of social labour time is incapable of taking the place of calculation via market prices, offering specific answers to his three arguments cited above. More generally, they argue that modern information technology (and theory) makes a substantial difference to the conclusions reached half a century ago, and they offer an account of reasons why the failure of the particular system of planning employed in the former Soviet Union need not invalidate the notion of planning in general.

ALLIN COTTRELL

References

Bardhan, P.K. and J.E. Roemer (1993), *Market Socialism: The Current Debate*, New York/Oxford: Oxford University Press.

Bergson, A. (1948), 'Socialist Economics', in H. Ellis (ed.), *A Survey of Contemporary Economics*, Homewood, IL: Richard Irwin.

Cockshott, W.P. and A Cottrell (1993a), 'Calculation, Complexity and Planning: The Socialist Calculation Debate Once Again', *Review of Political Economy*, **5**, (1): 73–112.

Cockshott, W.P. and A Cottrell (1993b), 'Socialist Planning After the Collapse of the Soviet Union', *Revue Européene des Sciences Sociales*, **XXXI**, (96), 167–85.

Hayek, F.A (ed.) (1935), *Collectivist Economic Planning*, London: Routledge & Kegan Paul.

Hayek, F.A. (1945), 'The Use of Knowledge in Society', *American Economic Review*, **35**, 519–30.

Lange, O. (1938), 'On the Economic Theory of Socialism', in B. Lippincott (ed.), *On the Economic Theory of Socialism*, New York: McGraw-Hill.

Lavoie, D. (1985), *Rivalry and Central Planning: The Socialist Calculation Debate Reconsidered*, Cambridge: Cambridge University Press.

Nove, Alec (1983), *The Economics of Feasible Socialism*, London: George Allen & Unwin.

Stiglitz, J.E. (1994), *Whither Socialism?*, Cambridge, MA: MIT Press.

Vaughn, K.I. (1994), *Austrian Economics in America: The Migration of a Tradition*, Cambridge: Cambridge University Press.

Sociology of Scientific Knowledge, The

In recent years, the sociology of scientific knowledge (SSK) has emerged as an influential new approach to understanding the scientific endeavour. Unlike traditional philosophy of science, where the focus is on the discovery of, and epistemic justification for, the rules that constitute the proper scientific method, SSK examines the behaviour of scientists sociologically, as an instance of a more general analysis of social behaviour. For SSK, the scientific community is in fact *a community* and as such the behaviour of its members is determined by the same factors that determine the behaviour of members of any other social or cultural community. While many specific approaches can be subsumed under the general SSK rubric, they all share two common features: an aversion to traditional philosophizing and a commitment to the idea that science is a social activity and must be understood as such.

While SSK draws its intellectual inspiration from a broad range of different sources, the most important is probably the various changes that have taken place within mainstream Anglo-American philosophy of science during the last 30 years or so. Initiated by the work of Thomas Kuhn (1970) and others, the philosophy of science has undergone a major transformation: the so-called 'received view' of logical empiricism, the mainstay of mid-twentieth century philosophy of science, has been entirely abandoned. No longer is science examined from a purely philosophical perspective; it is now investigated from a much wider range of historical and empirical viewpoints. The result of these changes has been the elaboration of a vision of science that is anti-foundational, fundamentally social, much less uniform and much more amenable to a naturalistic mode of inquiry. According to Kuhn, scientists are always in the grip of a collectively held paradigm that determines what they do and do not 'see'; observations are theory- or social context-laden and the objective 'facts' are no longer given the epistemic importance they once were. These changes have radically undermined the traditional philosophical approach to scientific knowledge and opened the door for other, more sociological, approaches that take the collective nature of scientific activity as their starting point.

SSK has also been influenced by earlier approaches to the sociology of science, such as the functionalism of Robert K. Merton (1973). Merton sought to uncover the particular cultural characteristics of, or social preconditions for, empirical science: those norms and social conventions that were unique to science and distinguished it from other cultural forms. His four defining characteristics of science – universalism, organized scepticism, disinterestedness and communism – served in a functional way to maintain the community and cultural integrity of science. Merton argued that science's unique cultural norms could be traced back to the values of ascetic Protestantism in the seventeenth century. Merton's work differs from most contemporary sociology of science in that he was concerned exclusively with the social and cultural conditions *for* science, those factors that contributed to its growth and development, and not with the social factors that might influence or determine the actual content of science. With respect to the content of science, Merton's sociology was quite consistent with the traditional vision of the 'received view'.

Most contemporary sociologists of science have a more radical vision of scientific knowledge than the one offered by Merton; for those in SSK, social factors not only influence the culture of science but they also influence (and for some even determine) the *content* of science. Social factors not only provide the cultural stage for the play of science, they also determine the scientists' lines. Since there are a number of different schools within contemporary SSK and each has its own particular interpretation of the main points of contention, we will only discuss the two most established programmes: first, the earliest and most articulated approach, the 'strong programme' of the Edinburgh School, and second, the more recent 'social constructivism' of the Bath School and others.

The strong programme is most clearly associated with the work of Barry Barnes (1974; 1977) and David Bloor (1991), although many other authors have been influenced by its general framework. The programme starts from a naturalistic approach to scientific knowledge: science, like everything else, is to be examined by the method of science. Scientists have beliefs; these beliefs are part of the natural world and, as part of the natural world, these beliefs are amenable to scientific investigation. The strong programme has been characterized by the following four methodological mandates (Bloor, 1991: 7).

1. causality: seek the causal conditions that bring about the beliefs of scientists;
2. impartiality: be impartial between true and false, or rational and irrational, beliefs;
3. symmetry: the same type of cause should be used to explain both true and false beliefs;
4. reflexivity: the explanations offered should also be applicable to the sociology of science.

While it is not listed as a defining tenet, the strong programme typically uses the (individual or group) 'interests' of scientists to explain scientific beliefs. The professional interests of the scientists are served by certain beliefs and those interests can therefore be used to provide a causal explanation for the beliefs that scientists hold. Since social interest rather than 'nature' (the explanation endorsed by the scientists themselves and traditional philosophy of science) is used to explain scientific beliefs, the strong programme radically challenges our conventional view of scientific knowledge. Needless to say, the strong programme is a bold and controversial approach to scientific knowledge and an extensive critical literature has grown up around it.

Another, more recent and less cohesive, approach to SSK is the 'laboratory studies' or 'social constructionist' approach of Karin Knorr Cetina (1981), Harry Collins (1985), Bruno Latour and Steve Woolgar (1979), Sharon Traweek (1988), and others. The basic idea behind laboratory studies is to observe directly the day-to-day practice of science at its actual (laboratory) site. The approach is anthropological or ethnological, and it requires the social scientist to spend a substantial amount of time doing fieldwork at the site of the scientific activity and to understand the particular details of the knowledge production process – in Steven Shapin's (1988) apt phrase, to 'follow scientists around'. Interests are often involved in constructionist studies of science, but they are more likely to be the microinterests of the individual scientists and their laboratory groups than the more general macrointerests that are often the focus of the strong programme. The laboratory studies approach is considered 'constructionist' or 'social constructionist' because it emphasizes the fundamentally contingent and contextual nature of the 'facts' and artefacts of science This constructionism does not deny that the material world (or the social world outside the lab) exists, or even that it offers certain resistances to scientific activities, but it does deny 'that the laws and propositions of science provide a literal description of material reality, *and hence can be accounted for in terms of this reality* rather than in terms of the mechanisms and processes of construction' (Knorr Cetina, 1995: 148, emphasis in original).

In some sense, the strong programme and social constructionism constitute the second round of SSK (Merton being the first) and they have in turn spawned a vast array of third round views. Some of these include the 'actor network' theory of Bruno Latour (1987) and Michel Callon *et al.* (1986); the 'mangle' of Andrew Pickering (1995); the 'hyper-reflexivity' of Malcolm

Ashmore (1989), Steve Woolgar (1988), and others; and the 'social realism' of Harry Collins and Steven Yearley (1992). We will not discuss the details of any of these later views here, but it should be pointed out that they are in many respects responses to the perceived problems of earlier work in SSK. While there are many such perceived problems (perceived from both inside and outside SSK) we will consider the three that have been given the most attention.

The first is the problem of *realism versus relativism*. If the beliefs of scientists are caused by their social interests (strong programme) or the contingent social context (constructivism), what is the role of nature, or the material world, in the formation of our scientific beliefs? Are all scientific beliefs equally valid or valid only relative to the particular community that has proposed them? Many of the later contributors – particularly Pickering and Collins – attempt to reconcile the relativism of SSK with some type of realism. The second bone of contention is *reflexivity*. If all scientific theories are the product of the interests of the scientists who propose them, then why should not interest also govern the beliefs of the sociologists doing the sociology of scientific knowledge? After a flurry of heated debate, this topic seems to have faded somewhat from the SSK literature during the last few years, but it still remains an issue. Finally, there is the issue of *SSK and traditional philosophy of science*. In particular, the question is whether SSK replaces the traditional (epistemically normative) study of scientific knowledge with a purely descriptive analysis of the practice of scientists, or simply provides a new set of answers to the traditional epistemic questions. In other words, is SSK revolutionary (totally replacing the traditional framework for the study of scientific knowledge) or is it simply reformist (providing new, perhaps radical, answers to the traditional questions)? All three of these issues continue to some degree to be debated in the rapidly expanding literature on SSK and related fields.

So SSK has expanded rapidly and it poses a number of interesting challenges to the traditional views within the philosophy of science and epistemology: what impact does this have on economics and economic methodology? We will close by considering the three issues that currently seem to be the main contact points between economics and SSK. First, there is the very general issue of the impact of SSK on the philosophy of science and thus, in turn, its impact on economic methodology. Traditionally, those writing in the field of economic methodology have simply borrowed (usually with a lag) from the 'shelf' of scientific philosophy and then applied, or attempted to apply, those philosophical views to the science of economics. SSK and the changes that have led up to the social turn in science studies have profoundly upset the shelf of scientific philosophy, and that will undoubtedly, in time, have an impact on what is written in the field of economic methodology. Second, there is a growing literature that *applies* SSK to the history of economic thought. In certain cases, economists have applied the work of a particular sociologist or school of science studies – Pickering in Davis (1997) and Hands (1994b), and Whitley in Coats (1993a; 1993b) – while in other cases historical work in economics has been broadly influenced by SSK without involving the direct application of any one particular school or approach: for instance, Mirowski (1989) and Weintraub (1991). Finally, there is the perhaps more subtle question of the extent to which SSK involves the application of economic ideas to the study of scientific knowledge. Certain programmes within SSK (such as the actor network theory) seem to employ an exchange and transaction metaphor in their analysis of science that sounds very much like the neoclassical notion of the competitive market (see McClellan, 1996), while other views (such as the early work of Latour and Woolgar) seem to characterize scientific activity in a way that is very close to the Marxist, or at least classical, model of capital accumulation (see Hands, 1994a; Mäki, 1992). These perspectives; on scientific knowledge certainly open up interesting new possibilities (and a potentially troublesome type of reflexivity) for both economists and those writing in the field of economic methodology. There are undoubtedly many other points of contact in addition to the three that have been mentioned, but these should be sufficient to demonstrate the breadth and the depth of the growing relationship between SSK and economics.

D. WADE HANDS

References
Ashmore, Malcolm (1989), *The Reflexive Thesis: Wrighting the Sociology of Knowledge*, Chicago: University of Chicago Press.
Barnes, Barry (1974), *Scientific Knowledge and Sociological Theory*, London: Routledge & Kegan Paul.
Barnes, Barry (1977), *Interests and the Growth of Knowledge*, London: Routledge & Kegan Paul
Bloor, David (1991), *Knowledge and Social Imagery*, 2nd edn, Chicago: University of Chicago Press.
Callon, Michel, John Law and Arie Rip (eds.) (1986), *Mapping the Dynamics of Science and Technology: Sociology of Science in the Real World*, London: Macmillan.
Coats, A.W. (1993a), 'The Sociology of Knowledge and the History of Economics', *The Sociology and Professionalization of Economics: British and American Economic Essays*, vol. II, London: Routledge.
Coats, A.W. (1993b), 'The Sociology of Science: Its Application to Economics', *The Sociology and Professionalization of Economics: British and American Economic Essays*, vol. II, London: Routledge.
Collins, Harry (1985), *Changing Order: Replication and Induction in Scientific Practice*, Beverly Hills, CA: Sage.
Collins, Harry and Steven Yearley (1992), 'Epistemological Chicken,' in A. Pickering (ed.), *Science as Practice and Culture*, Chicago: University of Chicago Press.
Davis, John B. (1997), 'New Economics and Its History: A Pickeringian View', *New Economics and Its Writing*. Durham, NC: Duke University Press.
Hands, D. Wade (1994a), 'The Sociology of Scientific Knowledge: Some Thoughts on the Possibilities,' in R.E. Backhouse (ed.), *New Directions in Economic Methodology*, London: Routledge.
Hands, D. Wade (1994b), 'Restabilizing Dynamics: Construction and Constraint in the History of Walrasian Stability Theory', *Economics and Philosophy*, **10**, 243–83.
Knorr Cetina, Karin (1981), *The Manufacture of Knowledge: An Essay on the Constructivist and Contextual Nature of Science*, New York: Pergamon.
Knorr Cetina, Karin (1995), 'Laboratory Studies: The Cultural Approach to the Study of Science', in S. Jasanoff, G.E. Markle, J.C. Petersen and T. Pinch (eds), *Handbook of Science and Technology Studies*, Thousand Oaks, CA: Sage.
Kuhn, Thomas S. (1970), *The Structure of Scientific Revolutions*, 2nd edn, Chicago: University of Chicago Press.
Latour, Bruno (1987), *Science in Action*, Cambridge, MA: Harvard University Press.
Latour, Bruno and Steve Woolgar (1979), *Laboratory Life: the Construction of Scientific Facts*, Beverly Hills, CA: Sage.
Mäki, Uskali (1992), 'Social Conditioning in Economics,' in N. de Marchi (ed.), *Post-Popperian Methodology of Economics*, Boston: Kluwer.
McClellan, Chris (1996), 'The Economic Consequences of Bruno Latour', *Social Epistemology*, **10**, 193–208.
Merton, Robert K. (1973), *The Sociology of Science: Theoretical and Empirical Investigations*, Chicago: University of Chicago Press.
Mirowski, Philip (1989), *More Heat Than Light*, Cambridge: Cambridge University Press.
Pickering, Andrew (1995), *The Mangle of Practice*, Chicago: University of Chicago Press.
Shapin, Steven (1988), 'Following Scientists Around', *Social Studies of Science*, **18**, 533–50.
Traweek, Sharon (1988), *Beamtimes and Lifetimes: the World of High Energy Physicists*, Cambridge, MA: Harvard University Press.
Weintraub, E. Roy (1991), *Stabilizing Dynamics: Constructing Economic Knowledge*, Cambridge: Cambridge University Press.
Woolgar, Steve (ed.) (1988), *Knowledge and Reflexivity: New Frontiers in the Sociology of Knowledge*, London: Sage.

Spontaneous Order

The concept of spontaneous order is an important framework in many fields of research in the natural and social sciences today, and it bears heavily on methodological problems related to economics in particular. In fact, all domains of scientific and philosophical research where it can be maintained intelligibly that an undesigned but nevertheless effective order has emerged through the interaction of the constituent parts of a given system and also through the interaction of this system as a whole with its environment fall under what is now often for preference called the 'paradigm of auto-organization'. This paradigm can be traced back to Leibniz (Dobuzinskis, 1989: 245) or even to the Spanish Jesuits of the Salamanca School of the sixteenth century (Lepage, 1983: 347), and a lot of scientific work has now been done from within its conceptual framework, such as Varela and Maturana's theory of 'autopoiesis', Heinz von Foerster's second-generation cybernetic models, Ilya Prigogine's thermodynamics of open systems and dissipative structures, and chaos theory. In economics, the concept of *social spontaneous order* is intimately linked with Friedrich Hayek's work, and Hayek has himself insisted on the effective kinship of such approaches (Hayek, 1979: 158). One can say that there is today in economics a full-fledged theory of spontaneous order (TSO) which articulates four distinct arguments.

The invisible hand thesis
The first argument can be labelled 'the invisible hand thesis' (Nozick, 1974: 18–22; but see also Nozick, 1994; Ullmann-Margalit, 1978; Rothschild, 1994; Brennan and Pettit, 1993). Hayek distinguishes sharply between *cosmos* and *taxis*. The first term is used to refer only to natural systems that have emerged from evolution by natural selection and to social systems that spontaneously arose during human history. The second term is used to refer uniquely to those systems which have been deliberately planned. Because the latter have been engineered, they are the only ones that can be legitimately considered human artefacts, for they can be said to be products of the will. But the former cannot, for they owe their existence to the fact that individuals use them, as systems of rules of conduct, to coordinate their personal plans. Thus they bring about spontaneous social order without individuals being aware of the process leading to it and without these having explicitly intended to enforce such a resulting order (Hayek, 1963; 1973: ch. 4).

This invisible hand thesis asserts that what is characteristic of social *institutions*, as opposed to *organizations* or forms of deliberate coordination of actions, is that they do not emerge out of individual awareness, deliberate decision or collective consent. As Hayek puts it, social spontaneous orders are just those that are 'the results of human action but not of human design' (Hayek, 1967c). This idea is in fact the convergent result of a long intellectual tradition inextricably intertwined with the reflexion on the nature and function of British common law. Each in turn, Bernard Mandeville, Adam Ferguson, David Hume, Josiah Tucker, Dugald Stewart, Thomas Reid and Adam Smith have contributed to the articulation of the general idea of spontaneous order. Hayek borrows from Adam Ferguson a formula which became widely known largely because of him: 'nations,' writes Ferguson, 'stumble upon establishments, which are indeed the result of human action, but not the execution of any human design' (Ferguson, 1767: 122; Hayek, 1967a).

The idea of a spontaneously emergent order is also at work in David Hume's *Treatise of Human Nature*, (Hume, 1967, Book III, Part I) where, arguing against Hobbes' constructivist rationalism, Hume gives a penetrating exposition of the way moral rules come into existence. But this very idea is perhaps fully grasped and exposed for the first time in Bernard Mandeville's famous *Fable of the Bees* (Mandeville, 1723), which presents itself at first glance as a vindication of egoism, self-interest and individual passion, but which is rather meant as a broad metaphorical argument showing how, because private vice sometimes produces public virtue, a coherent social order can unexpectedly result from innumerable independent actions. Hayek says of Mandeville that 'for the first time [he] developed all the classical paradigmata of the spontaneous growth of orderly social structures: of law and morals, of language, the market and money, and also the growth of technological knowledge' (Hayek, 1978: 253). Adam Smith's views on the workability of an efficient social and economic order are closely akin to those of Mandeville. Indeed, for Adam Smith, the observable division of labour is not 'originally the effect of any human wisdom, which foresees and intends the general opulence to which it gives occasion. It is the necessary, though very slow and gradual, consequence of a certain propensity in human nature which has in view no such extensive utility: the propensity to truck, barter and exchange one thing for another' (Smith, 1776: 25).

This classical tradition of economics was revived by the Austrian School of Economics which arose during the marginalist revolution. Carl Menger, the founder of that school, has had a tremendous methodological influence because of the role he played in the *Methodenstreit*, a crucial dispute in which he opposed Gustav Schmoller, head of the new German Historical School (Menger, 1883). Menger insisted that we conceive of economics as a fully theoretical or nomological science, fully comparable to Newtonian mechanics. He advocated for economics what he called the 'compositive–resolutive method', which holds that, while it may be legitimate to refer to societies as intricate wholes, such emergent aggregates must always be further analysed and explained in terms of lawful individual action. Menger argued that economics had to explain how thousands and thousands of individual actions could give rise to *organic* institutions like money, language, markets and legal systems. The aim of social science as a whole, according to Menger and his Austrian followers up to Hayek, was to discover the regularity patterns of those institutional realities, patterns related to the obvious empirical fact that those institutions all served the common human welfare without ever having been designed by any benefactor and, for that reason, without ever having been deliberately created by a common will. For Menger, money was without a doubt the paradigm example of an institution emerging as a spontaneous order. The explanations of such institutional regularities have been commonly characterized from Adam Smith onwards as 'invisible hand explanations', since they give justification for the existence of those processes by which 'man is led to promote an end which was not part of his intention' (Smith, 1776: 456). It can be said of the invisible hand thesis that it 'merely claims that a social order will emerge from the spontaneous actions of individuals without the necessity for an all-powerful central institution' (Barry, 1982: 146).

The thesis that society is not a super-brain
The second argument of TSO claims consequently that society as a whole has to be modelled as a system that has no proper centre of operation: the more numerous the interacting component parts of that dynamic system, the more cohesive, robust and productive will be the social order it implements. According to TSO, the quality of a social order, its efficiency and durability, are a direct function of the amount of reliable knowledge that millions of individuals living together are capable of using in making their own personal decisions. The more rapidly they can exchange reliable information between them, the more they can increase their understanding of the situation in which they find themselves and, for that matter, the more *coordination* they produce between themselves. This second ingredient of TSO is linked in Hayek's system of thought with considerations deriving from Michael Polanyi's philosophical reflexions.

Polanyi argues for the primacy of 'tacit knowledge' over propositional knowledge. He gives prime importance to practical knowledge over theoretical knowledge, and priority to personal knowledge over the bookish sort. This epistemological argument amounts to saying that, in all social sciences, one has to start from the fact that the building blocks of the structures whose functions we have to explain are human individuals possessing a certain amount of information which will cause them to act as they decide. But this knowledge is not representational for any individual. Rather, it presents itself as skills, acquaintances or other kinds of personal knowledge, that is, as diverse rule-governed practices that individuals master up to a certain degree, some being innate but many others being acquired through education or by cultural transmission. Most of this knowledge, formed by sets of unconsciously acquired rules of perception and action, is said to be 'tacit' because it is usually doomed to remain more or less inarticulate and not explicitly formulated.

The best example of this is perhaps linguistic knowledge. Most humans can speak a natural language and have mastered its grammatical rules more or less well, but few have studied these rules at a theoretical level (Hayek, 1967d: 45). The kind of knowledge TSO focuses on is incorporated into very different systems of rules of perception and conduct. But while the invisible hand thesis settles the question of how those rules are made to exist and how they come to constitute a social order, it does not say a word about the way those rules work in a given community. This is the problem which is being addressed with this second argument. For two distinct typical models are possible here: either those rules exist in a central organ which transmits the proper information from the centre to the periphery, or they exist by way of being dispersed among individuals forming a group. It is crucial to grasp 'the difference between an order which is brought about by the direction of a central organ such as the brain, and the formation of an order determined by the regularity of the actions towards each other of the elements of a structure' (Hayek, 1967b: 73). Michael Polanyi's dichotomy opposing monocentric to polycentric forms of order (Polanyi, 1969) is quite illuminating here. Finally, as Hayek insightfully remarks;

> such spontaneous orders as those of societies, although they will often produce results similar to those which could be produced by a brain, are thus organized on principles different from those which govern the relations between a brain and the organism which it directs. Although the brain may be organized on principles similar to those on which a society is organized, society is not a brain and must not be represented as a sort of super-brain, because in it the acting parts and those between which the relations determining the structure are established are the same, and the ordering task is not deputized to any part in which a model is preformed. (Hayek, 1967b: 74)

The cultural evolution assumption

The third component of TSO is the empirical conjecture that there exists a cultural evolution process at work in human history. The cultural evolution assumption evokes a process akin to the Darwinian natural selection of species, but of which the units are competing moral traditions. If, in order to explain anything about the functioning of the social order at any one time, one is to assume that sets of collective rules of perception and conduct like those alluded to are at work, one has to ask not only how those rules operate but first of all where they come from and why they keep functioning over time. The only legitimate answer to this crucial question seems to require that we take an evolutionary stance, even if one can challenge the idea that the mechanism implied here is really of the Darwinian kind (Rosenberg, 1992). What seems to be clear enough is that the rules of action followed by individuals in specific contexts have been selected for, and they have been enforced in virtue of, the effects that they have on the formation and subsequent upholding of the social order itself. TSO then necessarily has to incorporate an explanation of cultural evolution, that is, of the selection of the rules of perception and action of just those organized groups of human beings which predominantly survive and outgrow all the others.

Natural languages, common law and markets are for Hayek, as they were earlier for Menger, the best examples of such traditional rules. The origin of such institutions cannot be traced back to a decision of a single or collective mind. Markets in particular are not the kinds of things humans manage to create by way of central planning. Markets do not emerge as the constructive results of the rational actions of a designing mind. Markets are nothing but the process itself of coordination between individuals. Hayek insists:

> It is evident that this interplay of the rules of conduct and of the individuals with the actions of other individuals and the external circumstances in producing an overall order may be a highly complex affair. The whole task of social theory consists in little else but an effort to reconstruct the overall orders which are thus formed ... It [is] also clear that such a distinct theory of social structures can provide only an explanation of certain general and highly abstract features of the different types of structures ... Of theories of this type economic theory, the theory of the market order of free human societies, is so far the only one which has been developed over a long period. (Hayek, 1967a: 71–2)

The hypothesis of cultural evolution assumes that human groups are in competition with one another. Human groups throughout history have been seeking to adapt themselves in order to survive, reproduce and if possible grow, expand and spread abroad. What ties individuals together in such cultural groups is the practical rules they unconsciously follow, and one cannot explain the predominance of some groups except by appealing to cultural selection, that is, to the survival of the fittest. These sets of rules supervene on groups that get selected so that it can be said that the groups are selected *for* their rules (Hayek, 1988). This is why the most far-reaching methodological consequence of the adoption of TSO in economics is perhaps that it forces the theoretician to seek a diachronic rather than a synchronic understanding of the phenomena under study. Hayek makes it clear that

> the existence of structures with which the theory of complex phenomena is concerned can be made intelligible only by what the physicists would call a cosmology, that is, a theory of their evolution. ... The problem of how galaxies or solar systems are formed and what is their resulting structure is much more like the problems which the social sciences have to face than the problems of mechanics; and for the understanding of the methodological problems of the social sciences a study of the procedures of geology or biology is therefore much more instructive than that of physics. (Hayek, 1967b: 76)

The pre-eminence claim regarding the market economy

The presentation of TSO would not be fully articulated if we did not state the normative argument that is essentially tied to it. One can certainly try to maintain that no moral value judgment is really at stake here (Gray, 1986: 33–4, 118–25) but it is difficult not to see that TSO serves to support a pre-eminence claim regarding the market economy. It has already been said that Hayek opposes the form of order that results from an emergent evolutionary process to the one that is 'rationally constructed' by human beings, for example legislators. On that basis, TSO serves indeed to counter the arguments of 'constructivistic rationalism' (Hayek, 1973: 8–11; 1979: xii). TSO undeniably includes as one of its core elements the thesis that: market economies are superior as social orders to all centrally planned economies.

Preferring the term *catallaxy* to refer to market economy considered as a rule-based process, Hayek claims that this economic system has to be considered fully as a social spontaneous order because it is an evolutionary and undesigned process based on the price mechanism and the general rule of law. Consequently, the resulting social order is never intended as such or controlled by anyone, but it surely can be said that the consequences of the actions of each and every individual taking part in the process are necessarily accounted for in its aggregate result. TSO thus not only gives ground to an argument in favour of a free market economy but also gives reasons against the very essence of the welfare state, and especially the welfare state of the Keynesian brand (Hayek, 1995).

Basing himself on this shrewd analysis of catallaxy, Hayek puts forward the normative claim that it manifestly forms a social order which is far superior to any kind of state-governed social order. Hayek speaks here not only of an economic superiority in terms of efficiently allocated resources but also of an ethical and political superiority in terms of the quality of life that such a free market-based social order renders possible for the large majority of individuals. Hayek always maintained as a core thesis of his economic theory and of his political philosophy that a socialist economy, that is a social order generated by an interventionist state, will necessarily lead to such undesirable results as limits to human rights and liberty – it not, sooner or later, to complete serfdom (Hayek, 1944; 1988).

The error of constructivistic rationalism is to take it for granted that a designed economic order will be necessarily superior to an undesigned one because it will be formed by and based on reason. But, as Hayek points out, reason itself is the product of evolution and should not he seen as capable of planning and directing evolution. More than that, economic planning by itself does not create order if by 'order' we mean, with Hayek, 'a state of affairs in which a multiplicity of elements of various kinds are so related to each other that we may learn from our acquaintance with some spatial or temporal part of the whole to form correct expectations concerning the rest, or at least expectations that have a good chance of being correct. (Hayek, 1973: 36). Human reason, and especially the individual minds of a small group of people, as inspired, wise, knowledgeable and thoughtful as they may be, cannot by themselves achieve an order that would be better than the one from which rationality itself progressively emerged: 'On the contrary, by disturbing the regularities based on impersonal rules which are the product of evolutionary learning, rationalist social engineering results, if not in chaos, at least in unworkable or unnecessary coercive organizational structures' (Dobuzinskis, 1989: 243).

Hayek has stressed as a central fact that, in an undesigned or spontaneous social order, the economic knowledge globally available at one time is being used more efficiently than in a centrally planned social order. As John Gray puts it, a 'spontaneous social order can utilize *fragmented knowledge*, knowledge dispersed among millions of people, in a way a holistically planned order (if such there could be) cannot' (Grey, 1986: 28). Hayek was the first one to analyse from the economic point of view the use of knowledge in society (Hayek, 1937). This reflexion played a crucial role in Hayek's transformation during the mid-1930s (Caldwell, 1988).

Thus TSO ultimately presents itself as an epistemological refutation of socialism. Some will plead that TSO is value-neutral, the concept of order being a descriptive and not a normative one: 'It is in this way, as a value-free explanatory device, that I believe Hayek's idea of spontaneous order is to be understood. This interpretation foreswears the device of building into spontaneous-order explanations a definite moral content ... which would disallow an explanation of statism as a spontaneous formation' (Gray, 1986: 121). Of course, TSO quite evidently supports the idea of liberty, even if liberal order is not a necessary terminus or an ineluctable consequence of cultural evolution. But more to the point, TSO serves to support the general argument that a market economy is largely superior as a social order to any kind of planned economy. Catallaxy is held to be pre-eminent because it is more efficient, and it is said to be more efficient because it is alleged that no central political organism can adequately replace or even simulate the market pricing process. Hence a full-fledged spontaneous social order will always be economically preferable to a full-blown collectivist planned one. This is surely Hayek's understanding of what the whole socialist calculation debate was about (Hayek, 1935; 1940). TSO avowedly claims, not only on moral but first of all on logical and empirical grounds, that a resolutely interventionist state is bound to fail as the source of social and economic order: it will not only lead progressively to serfdom, but it will also ultimately cause the unavoidable collapse of the economy.

This fourth and last argument has to be considered not only as an integral part of TSO, at least from the Hayekian standpoint, but as its boldest claim. But it is also probably its most challengeable argument and it has indeed been submitted to criticism (for instance, Dobuzinskis, 1989; De Vlieghere, 1994; Steele, 1994). It seems that, if one adopts Hayek's evolutionary perspective, one cannot prove that a social order based on market processes is obviously superior: 'If anyone assumes an evolutionary point of view, where the individuals have a severely limited knowledge about the environment and their own rules of conduct, there is simply no room for saying that anything similar to optimality exists in Hayek's world' (Petroni, 1995: 119). Indeed, if social and economic orders are plainly contingent, that is, if they are the unintended and unforeseeable products of evolution in a struggle for the survival of the fittest traditions, the question of which is the optimal one is empirically undecidable because we cannot predict which one will outlast all others. If this holds, advocating that market economies and liberal orders as we now know them are, on an absolute scale, the best social traditions there can be is an untestable and thus a normative claim, and it should be considered as the expression of an ideological preference.

ROBERT NADEAU

Bibliography

Barry, Norman P. (1982), 'The Tradition of Spontaneous Order; Bibliographical Essay', *Literature of Liberty*, **V**, Summer, 7–58.

Brennan, G. and P. Pettit (1993), 'Hands Invisible and Intangible', *Synthèse*, **94**, 191–225.

Caldwell, Bruce J. (1988), 'Hayek's Transformation', *History of Political Economy*, **20**, (4), 513–41.

De Vlieghere, Martin (1994), 'A Reappraisal of Friedrich A. Hayek's Cultural Evolutionism', *Economics and Philosophy*, **10**, 285–304.

Dobuzinskis, Laurent (1989), 'The Complexities of Spontaneous Order', *Critical Review*, **3** (2), Spring, 241–66.

Ferguson, Adam (1767), *An Essay on Civil Society*, Edinburgh: Edinburgh University Press.

Gray, John (1986), *Hayek on Liberty*, 2nd edn, Oxford: Basil Blackwell.

Hayek, F.A. (ed.) (1935), *Collectivist Economic Planning: Critical Studies on the Possibilities of Socialism*, London: George Routledge & Sons; new edn, New York: Augustus M. Kelley, 1967.

Hayek, F.A. (1937), 'Economics and Knowledge', *Economica*, n.s., **4**, (13), 33–54; reprinted in F.A. Hayek (1948), *Individualism and Economic Order*.

Hayek, F.A. (1940), 'Socialist Calculation: The Competitive Solution', *Economica*, n.s., **7**, (26), 125–49; reprinted in F.A. Hayek (1948), *Individualism and Economic Order*.

Hayek, F.A. (1944), *The Road to Serfdom*, London: George Routledge & Sons/Chicago: University of Chicago Press.

Hayek, F.A. (1948), *Individualism and Economic Order*, Chicago: University of Chicago Press.

Hayek, F.A. (1963), 'Kinds of Order in Society', *New Individualist Review*, **3**, (2), 3–12; reprinted in K.S. Templeton Jr. (ed.), *The Politicization of Society*, Indianapolis: Liberty Press, 1979.

Hayek, F.A. (1967a), *Studies in Philosophy, Politics and Economics*, London: Routledge & Kegan Paul/Chicago: University of Chicago Press.

Hayek, F.A. (1967b), 'Notes on the Evolution of Systems of Rules of Conduct (The Interplay between Rules of Individual Conduct and the Social Order of Actions)', *Studies in Philosophy, Politics and Economics*.

Hayek, F.A. (1967c), 'The Results of Human Action but not of Human Design', *Studies in Philosophy, Politics and Economics*.

Hayek, F.A. (1967d), 'Rules, Perception and Intelligibility', *Studies in Philosophy, Politics and Economics*.

Hayek, F.A. (1973), *Law, Legislation and Liberty: A New Statement of the Liberal Principles of Justice and Political Economy*, vol. I, *Rules and Order*, London: Routledge & Kegan Paul/Chicago: University of Chicago Press.

Hayek, F.A. (1978), 'Dr Bernard Mandeville', *New Studies in Philosophy, Politics, Economics and the History of Ideas*, London: Routledge & Kegan Paul.

Hayek, F.A. (1979), *Law, Legislation and Liberty: A New Statement of the Liberal Principles of Justice and Political Economy*, vol. III: *The Political Order of a Free People*, Chicago: University of Chicago Press.

Hayek, F.A. (1988), *The Fatal Conceit. The Errors of Socialism. The Collected Works of F.A. Hayek*, vol. 1, ed. William W. Bartley, Chicago: University of Chicago Press.

Hayek, F.A. (1995), *Contra Keynes and Cambridge: Essays, Correspondence. The Collected Works of F.A. Hayek*, vol. 9, ed. Bruce J. Caldwell, Chicago: University of Chicago Press.

Hume, David (1739), *A Treatise of Human Nature*, ed. Sir Lewis A. Selby-Bigge; reprinted Oxford: Clarendon Press, 1967.

Lepage, Henri (1983), 'Le marché est-il rationnel? D'Adam Smith à F.A. Hayek', *Commentaire*, **6**, (22), 345–53.

Mandeville, Bernard (1723), *The Fable of the Bees*, new edition Harmondsworth: Pelican, 1970.

Menger, Carl (1883), *Problems of Economics and Sociology*, new edition published as *Investigations into the Method of the Social Sciences with Special Reference to Economics*, ed. Louis Schneider, New York/London: New York University Press, 1985.

Nozick, Robert (1974), *Anarchy, State and Utopia*, New York: Basic Books.

Nozick, Robert (1994), 'Invisible hand explanations', *American Economic Association Papers and Proceedings*, **84**, 314–18.

O'Driscoll, G.P., Jr. (1978), 'Spontaneous Order and the Coordination of Economic Activities', in L.M. Spadaro (ed.), *New Directions in Austrian Economics*, Kansas City: Sheed Andrews and McMeel.

Petroni, Angelo M. (1995), 'What is Right with Hayek's Ethical Theory', *Revue européenne des sciences sociales*, **33**, (100), 89–126.

Polanyi, Michael (1951), *The Logic of Liberty: Reflections and Rejoinders*, Chicago: University of Chicago Press.

Polanyi, Michael (1969), 'The Determinants of Social Action', in E. Streissler, G. Haberler, F.A. Lutz and F. Machlup (eds), *Roads to Freedom: Essays in Honour of Friedrich A. von Hayek*, London: Routledge & Kegan Paul.

Radzicki, Michael J. (1990), 'Institutional Dynamics, Deterministic Chaos and Self-Organizing Systems', *Journal of Economic Issues*, **24**, 57–102.

Rosenberg, A. (1992), 'Neo-classical Economics and Evolutionary Theory: Strange Bedfellows?', in D. Hull, M. Forbes and K. Okruhlik (eds), *PSA 1992, Proceedings of the 1992 Biennial Meeting of the Philosophy of Science Association*, vol. 1, *Contributed Papers*, East Lansing, MI: Philosophy of Science Association.

Rothschild, Emma (1994), 'Adam Smith and the Invisible Hand', *American Economic Association, Papers and Proceedings*, **84**, 319–22.

Smith, Adam (1776), *An Inquiry into the Nature and Causes of the Wealth of Nations*, The Glasgow Edition of the works and Correspondence of Adam Smith, vol. 2, ed. R.H. Campbell and A.S. Skinner, Oxford: Clarendon Press, 1976.

Steele, D.R. (1994), 'On the Internal Consistency of Hayek's Evolutionary Oriented Constitutional Economics, A Comment', *Journal des Économistes et des Études Humaines*, **5**, (1), 157–64.

Sugden, Robert (1989), 'Spontaneous Order', *Journal of Economic Perspectives*, **3**, (4), 85–97.

Ullmann-Margalit, E. (1978), 'Invisible Hand Explanations', *Synthèse*, **39**, 263–91.

Sraffa, Piero

The published writings of Piero Sraffa (1898–1983) contain no explicit statement of his methodological views. However, we can surmise that, as a close friend of Wittgenstein, he was conscious of methodological issues and was sensitive to the question of what constitutes a satisfactory explanation of observed phenomena. Some provisional remarks can be made on the basis of Sraffa's main scientific contributions.

Several elements of Sraffa's broad methodological stance can be gleaned from his earliest theoretical work, the 1925–6 critique of the Marshallian theory of supply. That critique was directed at the inability of Marshall's theory to provide a generally valid explanation of prices in a regime of competition. Sraffa showed that the theory could not accommodate important practical phenomena, such as increasing and diminishing returns, except under highly special assumptions. He concluded that Marshall's theory is capable of handling only the constant cost case, and that outside that case its practical usefulness is limited; see Mongiovi (1996) and Davis (1988) for discussions of Sraffa's critique of Marshall which emphasize its methodological ramifications.

Sraffa's choice of the Marshallian version of the marginalist theory as the object of his initial theoretical investigations is indicative of his methodological concerns. Marshallian partial analysis lends itself more readily than the general equilibrium formulation to the interpretation of empirical evidence and to the analysis of policy questions; Sraffa focused on the practically relevant version of the theory. In considering how economic theory might move beyond the 'first approximation' of constant costs, to take account of increasing and diminishing returns, Sraffa (1926: 541) explicitly dismissed the alternative of abandoning partial analysis in favour of a general equilibrium approach, on the grounds that 'the complexity of [the latter apparatus] prevents it from bearing fruit, at least in the present state of our knowledge'. Sraffa's views on this issue appear to owe something to the debates on method in the Italian economic literature of the last decade of the nineteenth century and the first two decades of the twentieth century. Though Italy avoided the standard dispute between advocates of a logico-deductive method and those of a historico-inductive approach, an Italian *Methodenstreit* arose over whether partial analysis or a general equilibrium approach was the more scientifically appropriate theoretical framework. Advocates of the Walrasian approach contended that partial analysis, though occasionally useful as an approximation, is nonetheless incapable of depicting reality because it ignores necessary and significant interdependencies. But the obvious difficulties associated with the practical application of general equilibrium theory led adherents of that approach either to avoid discussion of practical issues or to fall back on the partial method when writing on applied topics.

Sraffa appears to have shared with Marshall a mistrust of overly complex theoretical constructions; this mistrust may have contributed to Sraffa's attraction to the work of the classical economists and Marx. In his critique of Marshall, Sraffa exhibits an intuitive recognition that the classicals practised a method of logical separation in which the forces that regulate relative prices and the profit rate are analysed separately from the influences on wages, the level and composition of the economy's output, accumulation and the technical conditions of production.

This method has been clarified by Garegnani (1984), who identifies the analytical *core* of the classical theory as the set of logically necessary relationships that link prices, the real wage and the profit rate. These relations are captured in the equations contained in Parts I and II of Sraffa's *Production of Commodities by Means of Commodities* (1960). The classical theory takes as its fundamental data the size and composition of the social product, the technical conditions of production and the real wage (or, in Sraffa's formulation, the profit rate). If we impose the traditional condition of free competition, that profit rates must be equalized across sectors, relative prices and the unspecified distribution variable *must* coincide with the solution to Sraffa's equations. The data which establish the parameters of those equations, however, depend upon historical and institutional factors, and on the complex interaction of social and political forces; hence they are not required, as a matter of mathematical necessity, to take one set of values rather than another (though they may of course be constrained by technical features of the economic system). The different characters of the two types of theoretical problems – one involving exact and necessary formal relationships, the other concerned with aspects of the economic system that cannot be reduced to questions of formal logic – led the classicals to separate their explanations of outputs, accumulation, the real wage and the technique of production from the analysis of the forces that connect prices, the real wage and the profit rate.

This method of separating theoretical problems into two categories does not imply that problems belonging to the second category, and falling outside what we have called the core, are less interesting or less important than those which belong to the core; nor does the method deny the existence of recursive effects of changes in prices and distribution on the data themselves. On the contrary, the attention that Ricardo paid to the effects of accumulation on rents and the profit rate, or that Marx paid to economic crisis and to class conflict, suggests that the investigation of such issues is a crucial feature of the classical approach. But because these phenomena lack the property of logical necessity which characterizes the forces that regulate prices and the profit rate, they are analysed separately from those forces.

The often noted absence of demand functions from the analysis of price and distribution in *Production of Commodities* appears to be reflective of Sraffa's methodological views. He was evidently sceptical of subjectivist explanations and was drawn to the classicals and Marx because their theories were grounded in objective data as opposed to unobservable preferences; see Davis (1993) for an interesting discussion of Sraffa's views on demand.

Sraffa's critical writings share a feature that casts additional light on his methodological leanings. His critique of Marshall and his demonstration of the possibility of reswitching (1960) both call into question the generality of the propositions under attack: he showed that Marshall's theory of supply holds up only under conditions that are not typical of reality; similarly, the reswitching controversy brought out the fact that factor demand curves cannot be expected to be monotonically decreasing except under special circumstances (which, ironically, coincide with the conditions under which the labour theory of value is valid). Sraffa's criticisms undermine the practical usefulness of the marginalist tools by showing that they are applicable only in special cases. Thus the commonly held notion that Sraffa was concerned less with empirically relevant problems than with questions of abstract logic is a misconception, grounded in the spurious suggestion that these concerns are opposed to one another. In fact, Sraffa's logical argument demonstrates that a theory which claimed to have general relevance does not have it and is therefore inadequate to explain reality.

Sraffa's *Production of Commodities* is widely interpreted as an exercise in long-period comparative statics, and the solutions to his model are generally conceived as centres of gravitation around which actual variables are presumed to fluctuate. The mechanism which underlies this interpretation involves intersectoral capital flows, and the consequent adjustments in outputs and market prices, in response to profit rate differentials. This was certainly the method of the classical economists and Marx, whom Sraffa explicitly identifies as inspiring his own work. (It was also the method of the early marginalists, until the emergence of temporary and intertemporal general equilibrium theory after 1930.) But it should be noted that nowhere in *Production of Commodities* does Sraffa refer to a gravitation mechanism, and there is a possibility that Sraffa's methodological position was somewhat different from, and more cautious than, that of the classicals.

GARY MONGIOVI

Bibliography

Davis, J. (1988), 'Sraffa, Wittgenstein and Neoclassical Economics', *Cambridge Journal of Economics*, **12**, 29–36.
Davis, J. (1993), 'Sraffa, Interdependence and Demand: The Gramscian Influence', *Review of Political Economy*, **5**, 22–39.
Garegnani, P. (1984), 'Value and Distribution in the Classical Economists and Marx', *Oxford Economic Papers*, **36**, 291–325.
Mongiovi, G. (1996), 'Sraffa's Critique of Marshall: A Reassessment', *Cambridge Journal of Economics*, **20**, 207–24.

Sraffa, P. (1925), 'Sulle Relazioni fra Costo e Quantità Prodotta', *Annali di Economia*, **2**, 277–328.
Sraffa, P. (1926), 'The Laws of Returns under Competitive Conditions', *Economic Journal*, **36**, 535–50.
Sraffa, P. (1960), *Production of Commodities by Means of Commodities*, Cambridge: Cambridge University Press.

Supervenience

The notion of supervenience promises to be of some help in clarifying debates over methodological individualism, in providing a way of representing degrees of dependence between different domains or variables, and in avoiding some problems facing naturalized accounts of the normative. The concept originated in philosophical debates in ethics and in philosophy of mind to show how one domain of properties or descriptions might be irreducible to a second domain and yet dependent upon on it. G.E. Moore (1922), for example, thought that 'goodness' was not definable in non-moral terms Yet he thought that goodness depended on natural properties in that, if two entities shared all their natural properties, they must also share all their moral properties. In short, though he did not explicitly use the term, Moore was claiming that moral properties *supervene* on natural ones. However, Moore argued that this supervenience did not entail that moral terms were definable in natural terms, for there are indefinitely many different natural properties on which goodness supervenes. Similar uses have been made of supervenience in understanding the mental and the physical. Defenders of materialism or physicalism argue that, once all the physical facts are set, so too are all the mental facts. This allows them to describe a kind of dependence of the mental on the physical without having to defend the implausible assumption that mental terms can be defined in or reduced to physical terms. Supervenience thus is a notion that allows dependence between two domains that does not entail that the dependent domain is reducible.[1]

The notion of supervenience itself can be given a variety of more precise formulations, formulations that vary in their logical strength. The basic notion can be given equivalent formulations in terms of either properties or truths: (1) the family of properties S supervenes on the family of properties P just in case anything that shares all its P properties shares its S properties; or (2) the S truths supervene on the P truths just in case, when all the P truths are set, so are the S truths. Supervenience can be either weak or strong and global or local. Strong versus weak supervenience is determined by whether it is necessary for anything that shares its P properties to share its S properties. In the standard terminology for understanding modal claims, strong supervenience means that, in all possible worlds, fixing P fixes S. Weak supervenience only claims that this relation holds in the actual world. The global versus local distinction roughly depends on how large a batch of P properties or truths it takes to fix the S properties. If, for example, the meanings of a speaker's utterances depend essentially only on what is in the utterer's head, the meaning supervenes locally. If facts about the linguistic community also help to determine meaning, the dependence is not local but (relatively) global.

Supervenience has generally been most useful for two purposes: to describe a sense of dependence that does not entail theory reduction or one-to-one relations and as a way of explicating, by using its various versions, different kinds or degrees of dependence. Any uses in economics are likely to fall into these two camps. Most obviously, supervenience would seem to describe the relation between macro-level and micro-level explanations in economics. For example, if all the microeconomic facts are set, so too are the macroeconomic, or if all the facts about individual behaviour are set, so too are those about corporate behaviour. But such dependence does not entail reduction (see 'Methodological Individualism/Atomism' in this volume) and thus is compatible with an autonomous role for macro-level explanations.

Whether one set of facts supervenes on another or whether supervenience is global or local or strong or weak also gives us ways to explicate dependence or degrees thereof and thus might provide useful ways of explicating the relative importance of different phenomena or factors such as exogenous versus endogenous, path-dependent versus path-independent or individual versus institutional variables. For example, given sets of individual and social variables, we might represent their relative importance in determining the distribution of income by specifying which subsets of those variables fix the facts about income distribution (using global versus local supervenience); debates in economic history over the causal importance of various variables might be represented by specifying a set of possible government policies, for example, and then determining whether other variables of interest fix the economic outcome across the whole set or only some subset of policy variables (using strong versus weak supervenience).

In normative evaluations, supervenience may be of use as it was for Moore – namely, as a way of tying normative judgments to descriptive facts without a commitment to definitional equivalence. Since supervenience only requires that one set of facts be sufficient for another, it allows for a weaker form of dependence than the traditional search for individually necessary and jointly sufficient conditions, conditions which are notoriously hard to find in normative debates. Opting for the weaker relation of supervenience is one way to assert dependence without claiming to have identified the full set of necessary and sufficient conditions.

HAROLD KINCAID

Note
1. For discussions of the supervenience relation in its different forms, see Teller (1984) and Kim (1984).

Bibliography
Kim, Jaegwon (1984), 'Concepts of Supervenience', *Philosophy and Phenomenological Research*, **45**, 155–76.
Kincaid, Harold (1988), 'Supervenience and Explanation', *Synthèse*, **77**, 251–81.
Moore, G.E. (1922), *Philosophical Studies*, New York: Harcourt Brace.
Teller, Paul (1984), 'A Poor Man's Guide to Supervenience and Determination', *The Southern Journal of Philosophy*, **22**, Supplement, 137–63.

Survey Methods

It is widely alleged (McCloskey, 1983; Blinder, 1991; Shiller 1991) that economists do not like using questionnaire surveys as a basis for doing empirical work and do not make much use of such surveys. This widely held view provokes a range of methodological reactions. The majority position among economists and economic methodologists appears to be that economists' unwillingness to use surveys is well-founded. A minority position is that this is yet another unfortunate feature of the official methodologies and actual practices of economists.

While the claim is that economists do not make much use of questionnaire surveys, the facts are considerably more complicated. For instance, economists make extensive, though largely indirect, use of survey information on such things as income and unemployment. Here we review the historical debate that led to economists' distrust of surveys and we then consider kinds of data gathered in questionnaire surveys, methodological uses for these data and issues raised by these uses.

The historical distrust of surveys in economics

Economists' distrust of questionnaire surveys, especially opinion/perception surveys, goes back to the famous 'Lester–Machlup debates' of the 1940s. Lester (1946) interviewed employers, whose responses seemed at odds with profit maximization, leading Lester to question that assumption's correctness. Machlup (1946) denied the meaningfulness of these kinds of survey results. One reason was that *successful* entrepreneurs would no doubt have to obey these rules even if they did not recognize that they were doing so. This 'behave as if' argument is a major feature of Friedman's well-known 1953 article on methodology. Friedman indicates that Lester-type survey results are incapable of providing useful tests of economic theory. Shiller (1991) attributes the dislike for survey techniques directly to Friedman's article. He refers to: 'the damage that overliteral interpretation of Milton Friedman's theory of positive economics has wrought in the economics profession. Many people seem to have thought that Friedman's 'billiard player' analogy justifies omitting ever asking people about what they do' (Shiller, 1991: 97).

The historical debate seems to be dealing with 'how and why' surveys, surveys which ask people about *how* they behave (or would behave in changed circumstances) and *why* they behave (or would behave) that way. But many other kinds of survey data are used in economics; the debate's critique may not apply as persuasively to some of these current uses. Kinds of data collected and their possible uses are discussed below.

The range of information surveys can collect

Surveys can be used to gather a wide range of information, not just the 'how and why' information the Lester–Machlup debate focused on. The categories of information that can be collected include the following:

1. facts of past or current economic life;
2. predictions of future facts of economic life;
3. measurement of the value of goods and services not traded in the market;
4. the interviewee's description/explanation of his/her past and current behaviour;
5. predictions of future behaviour or behaviour under counterfactual conditions;
6. participant or observer opinions and ideas.

'How and why' direct surveys are the fourth and fifth categories above.

Examples of, and reasons for, extensive use

Despite the allegation that economists do not like using questionnaire surveys, certain kinds of surveys have been extensively used by economists. Which of the categories above are most extensively used by economists? Why might some of these categories appear relatively acceptable to economist users?

Category 1: 'just the facts'

Economists tend to make extensive use of survey data on the 'facts of past or current economic life'. Questionnaire surveys gather these 'facts': prices, quantities of goods bought and sold, incomes, expenditures, employment experience, revenues, costs and so forth. These 'facts' provide simple descriptions of economic activity, inputs into the measurement of economic parameters such as price elasticities of demand, and data for testing theoretical hypotheses.

Given the historical fuss in economics about using survey results, why are these survey results so widely accepted and used? One possible explanation is based on a distinction between the inherent 'believability' of different kinds of survey-generated information. Because these kinds of surveys merely require the recounting of facts presumed known by the respondent, they are accorded relatively high 'fact status' by economists.

Of course, such data are not without reliability problems. For example, respondents may lie or unwittingly provide false information. People overreport charitable contributions; self-reports of post-secondary school enrolment are overstated by students of low ability and low grades; and reported expenditures on alcoholic beverages in the US Survey of Consumer Expenditure are less than 40 per cent of actual expenditures.

Category 2: prediction of future facts
This category includes expectations about macro-level variables such as interest or unemployment rates and information on purchasing intentions of consumers or firms.

These data have many uses. Forecasting models using expectations about firm and macro-level variables obtained in surveys appear to predict output better than those based solely on past volumes of output and 'intentions to enlist' data have been used to improve forecasts of actual military enlistment behaviour.

Economists view these data as 'weaker' than 'just the facts' survey data, largely because there is no potential external check on their validity. But then why are they in relatively widespread use? An appealing answer is that they measure something, such as expectations, that economists believe may be important in the individual's decisions, and other more desirable measures are simply not currently available.

Category 3: measuring the value of goods and services not traded in the market
Perhaps the most striking growth in survey use is in measuring the value of goods or services not traded in the market and which are therefore 'unpriced'. The most widely used of these applications involves measuring benefits of environmental preservation or costs of environmental damages (Carson *et al.*, 1994, list over 1600 studies). In a typical contingent valuation (CV) survey, respondents are given background information on the projected environmental change, told how the change would be financed (for example, increased income or petrol taxes) and asked how much they would be willing to pay for the change.

Application of CV methods is controversial. (See the Symposium in the *Journal of Economic Perspectives*, Fall 1994.) Estimates of willingness to pay appear sensitive to questionnaire format (for example, open-ended versus dichotomous choice) and sequencing (for example, the amounts people are willing to pay to save seals or whales depends on whether one asks first about whales or seals). Do answers reflect 'true' valuations, strategic responses or just the 'warm glow' people receive from supporting a socially worthwhile cause? Recent experiments suggest that hypothetical questions result in very large overestimates of individuals' actual willingness to pay (Neill *et al.*, 1994; Cummings *et al.*, 1995).

On methodologically distinct uses of survey data
What distinct 'methodological activities' might survey data be used for? For example, the category 'facts of past or present economic life' might be used for such methodologically distinct

activities as measuring elasticities or testing a theory's predictions. It is helpful to distinguish among the following methodological uses:

1. hypothesis formation,
2. participant or observer evaluations/suggestions,
3. theory testing and 'anomaly generation',
4. measurement.

Hypothesis formation

Talking to people may 'turn up' things that the researcher otherwise would not have discovered. For example, Baker *et al.* (1988: 607) refer to

> the well-documented evidence that most people believe their performance is better than average. ... One [study] indicates that 58 per cent of a sample of white-collar ... workers rated their own performance as falling within the top 10 percent of their peers in similar jobs, 81 percent rated themselves in the top 20 percent ... Another study ... found [that] ... no one rated their performance below the 75th percentile.

If this finding turns out to be correct, it would seem to have sizeable implications for the efficiency of merit pay schemes. How could a researcher have discovered this phenomenon other than by hearing it from people?

Of course, what people say should not necessarily be taken at face value, but what they say may suggest important hypotheses to be investigated further by other methods.

Participant or observer evaluations/suggestions

One reasonable way to generate ideas for improving an organization's productivity is to ask its staff for suggestions. Suppose instead that one wants to evaluate the performance of a training programme or a service institution (say, a school). One useful piece of evidence may be assessments by clients of that programme or school. Weitzman and Kruse (1990) use attitude surveys of employees and managers of profit-sharing firms as one among many kinds of evidence to shed light on the relationship between profit sharing and productivity.

Theory testing and 'anomaly generation'

Lester's use of opinion/perception surveys to *test* theories aroused the ire of Machlup and Friedman. While this anti-survey line of argument seems to have gone largely unchallenged among economists, some serious observers do not accept it. For example, Alan Blinder (1991) proposes to 'test among' alternative theories of price rigidity by interviewing businessmen. Viscusi *et al.* (1987) use survey techniques to test predictions of expected utility theory with respect to risky products. They argue that their survey reflects 'a hypothetical market situation' replicating outcomes in a market with 'risk–dollar trade-offs' (ibid.: 470).

Another kind of evidence besides formal tests that bears on a theory's acceptability is the existence of anomalies. One way of unearthing possible anomalies is by listening to reports by individuals of their beliefs, preferences and so forth. The Viscusi *et al.* example above, which contains theory-testing elements, also generates evidence of anomalies in the form of large certainty premiums and so-called 'reference effects'.

Measurement

This category has a concrete and relatively narrow emphasis on something to be measured. The prediction and contingent valuation literatures discussed above fit into this category. The contingent valuation literature in particular seemed to have been spurred by a perceived need to *measure* the value of hypothetical outcomes in order better to evaluate investments intended to achieve these outcomes.

Conclusions

First, the historical debate pertains only to certain types of surveys, especially 'how and why' surveys. Second, actual behaviour of economists is less hostile towards surveys than some methodological discussions suggest. Economists make extensive use (sometimes uncritically) of other types of surveys, such as those gathering the 'facts' of economic life. Third, Blinder (1991) argues that the economist's preferred sorts of argument/evidence based on theory and econometrics 'have their limitations, too. Theoretical deductions are often untested or, worse yet, untestable. Econometric evidence is often equivocal and/or subject to methodological dispute.' Imperfect knowledge from interviews needs to be compared to imperfect knowledge obtainable from theoretical and econometric evidence. This 'compare the imperfections' theme, echoed by McCloskey (1983), has much to recommend it. The devil is in the details of the comparisons, however.

BRYAN L. BOULIER
ROBERT S. GOLDFARB

References

Baker, George, Michael Jensen and Kevin Murphy (1988), 'Compensation and Incentives: Practice Versus Theory', *The Journal of Finance*, **43**, July, 593–616.
Blinder, Alan (1991), 'Why Are Prices Sticky? Preliminary Results from an Interview Study', *American Economic Review*, **81**, May, 89–96.
Carson, Richard, T., Jennifer Wright, Nancy Carson, A. Albertini and N. Flores (1994), *Bibliography of Contingent Valuation Studies and Papers*, La Jolla, CA, Natural Resource Damage Assessment Inc.
Cummings, Ronald, G., Glenn Harrison and E. Elisabet Rustrøm (1995), 'Homegrown Values and Hypothetical Surveys: Is the Dichotomous Choice Approach Incentive-Compatible?', *American Economic Review*, **85**, March, 260–66.
Friedman, Milton (1953), 'The Methodology of Positive Economics', *Essays in Positive Economics*, Chicago: University of Chicago Press.
Lester, Richard (1946), 'Shortcomings of Marginal Analysis for Wage–Employment Problems', *American Economic Review*, **36**, March, 63–82.
Machlup, Fritz (1946), 'Marginal Analysis and Empirical Research', *American Economic Review*, **36**, September, 518–54.
McCloskey, Donald (1983), 'The Rhetoric of Economics', *Journal of Economic Literature*, **21**, June, 481–517.
Neill, Helen, Ronald Cummings, Phillip Ganderton, Glenn Harrison and Thomas McGucken (1994), 'Hypothetical Surveys and Real Economic Commitments', *Land Economics*, **70**, May, 145–54.
Shiller, Robert (1991), 'Discussion', *American Economic Review*, **81**, May, 97–8.
Viscusi, W. Kip, Wesley Magat and Joel Huber (1987), 'An Investigation of the Rationality of Consumer Valuations of Multiple Health Risks', *RAND Journal of Economics*, **18**, Winter, 465–79.
Weitzman, Martin and Douglas Kruse (1990), 'Profit Sharing and Productivity', in Alan Blinder (ed.), *Paying for Productivity*, Washington: Brookings Institution.

Tendencies

The social system, including the economy, is open in the sense that regularities of the form 'whenever event (type) *x* then event (type) *y*' are not pervasive. Indeed, strict event regularities of interest to science (including probabilistic ones) may not occur in the social realm at all. Economists who recognize and emphasize the openness of the social system usually designate the objects of scientific statements as *tendencies*. As such, the notion of a tendency is a central and fundamental one in economics. However, the term is also used by different economists in contrasting ways; there are competing conceptions of what tendency statements express. Not surprisingly, perhaps, conflicting usages often reflect competing conceptions of the nature of science and its goals. Some variants, however, can be seen as mutually compatible, with certain conceptions being special cases, or more restricted versions, of others.

A key distinction in the economics literature is between conceptions of tendency which (a) refer to some significant set (or patterning) of events or states of affairs, whether observed or conjectured; and (b) specify (typically non-empirical) items that are (or in relevant conditions would be) responsible for (which produce, condition or facilitate and so on) the events and states of affairs regarded as significant. Some usages in each category are listed in turn below.

Tendency as a trend in some phenomenon.
One common usage is for a broad movement or trend that is apparent in some phenomenon when viewed over time and/or space. It captures a change or development in something that is in evidence after abstracting from features regarded as non-systematic, short-run, local and so on. Any such development is often perceived as normal, fundamental, steady, enduring, underpinning or systematic. Examples are provided by claims of the sort that over the last hundred years there has been a tendency for UK industrial performance to fall increasingly behind that of its competitors; that prices tend to rise; that in many countries there is a tendency for income inequality to increase; that UK house prices tend to rise/fall as you move south.

Tendency as a high relative frequency
A second usage is to refer to the frequent recurrence of a given subset of a class of possible events. Examples are provided by assessments of the sort that in the UK wages tend to rise soon after increases in retail prices; or that I tend to win/lose at chess; or that there is a tendency for this coin to show heads more often than tails.

Tendency as a counterfactual course of events
In first two usages, the term 'tendency' captures the ex post patterning of some phenomenon. The openness of the relevant system is reflected in the acknowledgement that some phenomenon of interest is prominent but nevertheless not universal. An alternative usage of the term is to indicate that a particular set or patterning of events and so on *would* come about under certain conditions. This usage also usually reflects an implicit acknowledgement of the general openness of the relevant system by seeking to identify, and focusing attention upon, those special, but typically counterfactual, conditions in which some characteristic event pattern or course of action is conjectured to emerge unimpeded. An example is provided by Marshall: 'a law of social science, or a *Social Law*, is a statement of social tendencies; that is, a statement that a certain course of action may be expected under certain conditions from members of a social

group' (1986: 27). (For a more extensive analysis of Marshall's conception of tendency and science, see Pratten, 1996.)

Sometimes the term 'tendency' denotes less the idea of a specified outcome as the conjectured *movement* towards this particular outcome (under the relevant, typically counterfactual, conditions). An example of this usage appears to be provided by Hayek:

> In the light of our analysis of the meaning of a state of equilibrium it should be easy to say what is the real content of the assertion that a tendency towards equilibrium exists. It can hardly mean anything but that under certain conditions the knowledge and intentions of the different members of society are supposed to come more and more into agreement, or, to put the same thing in less general and less exact but more concrete terms, that the expectations of the people and particularly of the entrepreneurs will become more and more correct ... The only trouble is that we are pretty much in the dark about ... the *conditions* under which this tendency is supposed to exist. (Hayek, 1937: 44)

The second category of tendency, as something that is productive of, but typically irreducible to, events and states of affairs, is more interesting, in that it denotes aspects of reality which explain those events and states of affairs (including movements and trends) which actually (or under certain conditions are expected to) come about. Under this heading, various usages can be discerned once more, only a few of which can be indicated here.

Tendency as the continuing activity of a causal power
This first usage in this category is one which lies at the heart of the transcendental realist conception of science which has recently achieved some attention in economics (see 'Transcendental Realism', in the present volume), although its lineage in economics goes back to the classical period at least. An analysis of the nature of experimental practices and results (again see 'Transcendental Realism') suggests that the primary objects of science are not events and/or their (actual or imagined) constant conjunctions, but the structures, powers, mechanisms and so on that produce, facilitate or are in some way responsible for the actualities including events, at least some of which we do, or may, experience. Certain things, by virtue of their intrinsic structures, possess various powers. Such powers may or may not be exercised. When exercised, they may or may not be fulfilled because of the possible influence of countervailing factors. An acceptance of this general framework leads fairly naturally to the term 'tendency' being used to denote precisely this conception of a causal power that has been exercised, and so is in play, but *without necessarily being fulfilled*, that is without being straightforwardly manifest in any particular outcome. And a law statement refers to a tendency so understood (Lawson, 1994; 1997).

On this transcendental realist account of science, then, laws are analysed as powers of things which may be exercised without being actualized (or 'fully manifest' or 'fulfilled'). It is the idea of *continuing activity* (as distinct from enduring power per se) that the notion of a tendency is here designed to capture. The citation of a law statement presupposes a claim about the operation of a mechanism but not about the conditions in which it operates, and thus not about the results of its activity. It refers to something that acts *transfactually*: something that is really in play whatever the actual outcome; it is not a reference to results that would have emerged if conditions had been different (and in particular if a closed system had been obtained). The gravitational tendency acts on the object that I hold in my hand whatever I do with it; it does not merely act when I drop the object (whether inside or outside a vacuum).

This appears to be the conception of tendency which underpins Marx's general law of a 'tendency of the general rate of profit to fall'. Over a 30-year period prior to his writing, the economic conditions which Marx observed were such that, in his view, his 'general law' would have been operative. Yet it was not fully actualized. Marx thus turns to inquire into the forces which must be counteracting it:

> If we consider the enormous development of the productive forces of social labour in the last thirty years alone as compared with all preceding periods; if we consider, in particular, the enormous mass of fixed capital, aside from the actual machinery, which goes into the process of social reproduction as a whole, then the difficulty which has hitherto troubled the economist, namely to explain the falling rate of profit, gives place to its opposite, namely to explain why this fall is not greater and more rapid. There must be some counteracting influences at work, which cross and annul the effect of the general law, and which give it merely the characteristic of a tendency, for which reason we have referred to the fall of the general rate of profit as a tendency to fall.
>   The following are the most general counterbalancing forces: ... (Marx, 1974: ch. xiv)

Notice that in an open system, the actual outcome at some given point in space-time could, in principle, have been different. Although a situation which eventually materializes is determined (according to the perspective in question) by tendencies in play, there is no sense in which the outcome, prior to its realization, was inevitable. In the open economy, any actual situation will be the result of many different things that are going on, at least some of which might have been actively resisted (either though undermining their enabling conditions, transforming structures or initiating countervailing mechanisms). It is according to this conception that the following assessment by Keynes is most readily intelligible: 'we must not conclude that the mean position thus determined by "natural" tendencies, namely by those tendencies which are likely to persist, failing measures expressly designed to correct them, is, therefore, established by laws of necessity' (1973: 254).

Notice, too, that, at the conceptual level at least, the sort of counterfactual conjecture itemized earlier with reference to the first category of tendency, that is, the hypothesizing of a particular patterning of events under certain conditions, and typically *ceteris paribus*, can now be interpreted as a special case. For, on the transcendental realist view, a statement about a tendency which is unconditionally and transfactually in play may, in certain situations, license a subjunctive conditional about what would have happened at the level of the course of events if the system had been insulated from the activities of other mechanisms. However, even where such a consideration is appropriate, the full force and meaning of the statement, a comprehensive understanding of the situation, cannot be captured or conveyed in this manner. Rather, the practice of restricting the use of law statements to conditions wherein event regularities would come about, that is, to closed systems, is ultimately debilitating whatever interpretation is put on the term 'tendency'. For the focus of science is then exclusively on situations that are rare even in the natural realm (mainly those of experimental control) and more or less without counterpart in the social realm. To obtain a comprehensive and indeed practical understanding of the situation, tendency statements must be interpreted as categorical and indicative, as expressing a mechanism that is in play. For Marshall, in contrast, they appear sometimes to be interpreted as merely hypothetical:

> It is sometimes said that the laws of economics are 'hypothetical'. Of course, like every other science, it undertakes to study the effects that will be produced by certain causes, not absolutely, but subject to the condition that *other things are equal*, and the causes are able to work out their effects undisturbed.

> Almost every scientific doctrine, when carefully and formally stated, will be found to contain some proviso to the effect that other things are equal: the actions of the causes in question is supposed to be isolated; certain effects are attributed to them but only *on the hypothesis* that no cause is permitted to enter except those distinctly allowed for. (Marshall, 1986: 30)

If ex posteriori other things do turn out to be equal then, of course, such an undertaking as described by Marshall is hardly contentious. However, if such is not the case then the result is a restriction of focus to a possibly irrelevant counterfactual situation, to the neglect of enabling insights available, of a transfactual mechanism that may well be in play. Few, if any, autumn leaves descend according to the 'law of fall', yet a knowledge of (non-actual but nevertheless real) gravitational forces which act on the leaves unconditionally, that is, whether or not other things are equal, can be used, say, to send rockets (and leaves) to the moon.

Put another way, according to the conception in question the usage of a *ceteris paribus* clause, the qualification that other things are (or must be) equal, does not apply to a law's application, properly interpreted. If a mechanism is triggered, a tendency is in play, and a law can be cited, *un*conditionally. The satisfaction of the *ceteris paribus* clause, rather, is a condition for the actualization of the tendency designated in the statement. It acts as a reminder that the system in question may not be closed, that the tendency postulated in a law statement may not act in (relative) isolation and so be fulfilled. Once we use the category of tendencies to express continuing, transfactual activities of mechanisms, and not events that would come about if things were different, it is clear that, in principle, the *ceteris paribus* clause can be dispensed with entirely.

Tendency as indicating a cause that is always 'fulfilled'

If Marshall usually restricts the term 'tendency' to making hypothetical, conditional claims, that is, in elaborating the course of events that would come about if there were no countervailing or disturbing causes, Mill appears to be explicit in suggesting that such a restriction of focus is unnecessary:

> The error, when there is error, does *not* arise from generalizing too extensively; that is, from including too wide a range of particular cases in a single proposition. Doubtless, a man often asserts of an entire class what is only true of a part of it; but his error generally consists not in making too wide an assertion, but in making the wrong *kind* of assertion: he predicated an actual result, when he should only have predicated a *tendency* to that result – a power acting with certain intensity in that direction. With regard to *exceptions*, in any tolerably advanced science there is properly no such thing as an exception. What is thought to be an exception to a principle is always some other and distinct principle cutting into the former: some other force which impinges against the first force, and deflects it from its direction. There are not a *law* and an *exception* to that law – the law acting in ninety-nine cases, and the exception in one. There are two laws, each possibly acting in the whole hundred cases, and bringing about a common effect by their conjunct operation. If the force which, being the less conspicuous of the two, is called the disturbing force, prevails sufficiently over the other force in some one case, to constitute that case what is commonly called an exception, the same disturbing force probably acts as a modifying cause in many other cases which no one will call exceptions.
>
>   Thus if it were stated to be a law of nature, that all heavy bodies fall to the ground, it would probably be said that the resistance of the atmosphere, which prevents a balloon from falling, constitutes the balloon an exception to that pretended law of nature. But the real law is, that all bodies *tend* to fall; and to this there is no exception, not even the sun and moon: for even they, as every astronomer knows, tend towards the earth, with a force exactly equal to that with which the earth tends towards them (Mill, 1967: 387, 338)

But although Mill interprets tendencies as universal and unconditional, he still seems unduly influenced by a regard for the outcomes that *would* emerge under certain definite conditions. Specifically, on occasion at least, Mill appears to be suggesting that, for *each* causal tendency that is in play, an event regularity does always occur in some sense, or in some realm; that the overall result can be deduced as the collective effect, or 'sum', of numerous individual results, each of which derives from the condition of a fulfilment of some mechanism when acting in isolation:

> The general idea of the Composition of Causes has been seen to be, that though two or more laws interfere with one another, and apparently frustrate or modify one another's operation, yet in reality all are fulfilled, the collective effect being the exact sum of the effects of the causes taken separately ….
>
> All laws of causation are liable to be in this manner counteracted, and seemingly frustrated, by coming into conflict with other laws, the separate result of which is opposite to theirs, or more or less inconsistent with it. And hence, with almost every law, many instances in which it really is entirely fulfilled, do not, at first sight, appear to be cases of its operation at all ….
>
> To accommodate the expression of the law to the real phenomena, we must say, not that the object moves, but that it *tends* to move, in the direction and with the velocity specified. (1973: 443, 444)

On the transcendental realist understanding, in contrast, although each tendency has an effect and makes a difference, it is *not* the case that each is always fulfilled; this only happens in a system in which one set of tendencies is somehow effectively insulated from the action of others. On Mill's conception, it is as though, when Buridan's ass starved, it ate both of the bundles of hay.

Tendency as an enduring orientation

There is a further concept of a tendency which we have not so far considered, one that also turns on the ascription of powers to certain things, yet which is in principle distinct from those usages noted under b1) and b2). Indeed, if the conception elaborated under b1) effectively explains the focus identified under a3) it is the conception that we now turn to which most seems to explain the phenomena emphasized under a1) and a2). This conception, which is probably the one found most often in ordinary life, functions to indicate the *enduring orientation*, rather than the possibility of the *transfactual activity*, of some things; a power ready to be exercised. It depends upon distinguishing within the range of real possibilities for some thing or agency those which are characteristic or typical of it, as distinct from others of its kind. In this way it serves to individuate members of a class. Complex things, by virtue of their preformed structures, may be disposed to some but not others of the real possibilities open to them. Such things can possess powers in virtue of some sets of intrinsic structures, and exhibit tendencies (of the sort now in question) in virtue of the satisfaction of some enduring enabling conditions for the exercise of particular powers. Most humans possess the capacities to drink alcohol, suffer delusions and enjoy self-exaltation. But, respectively, alcoholics, paranoids and megalomaniacs *tend* to do such things.

Two issues of obvious interest to science arise once this conception of tendency is considered. To say that some thing possesses a tendency (of this sort) to act in a certain way is to indicate not only that (a) it has the capacity to do so, but also (b) important intrinsic enabling conditions for it to do so are satisfied, and (c) it will so act unless impeded by countervailing causes. One issue of interest to science, then, is to explain the relatively enduring orientation that differentiates the possession of a tendency from that of a power. Thus scientists are interested in the reasons behind the tendencies of any kleptomaniac or paranoid, whether or not such tendencies are fulfilled in any particular set of circumstances. A second issue of interest to science is to explain why it is sometimes the case that, in certain definite conditions appropriate to the fulfilment of such tendencies, they nevertheless remain unfulfilled; to identify the interfering causes responsible. Some tendencies are powers held off temporarily, and are immediately exercised when the obstructions to their exercise are released. Others require the positive stimulation of other mechanisms. Such *releasing* or *stimulating* conditions may be intrinsic or extrinsic to the thing possessing the tendency. Clearly, such considerations facilitate a variety of permutations of actually prevailing conditions, each of which might be associated with a different conception of tendency (see, for example, Bhaskar, 1993: 78), suggesting that, while a large number of conceptions of tendency are in evidence (only the most general and/or familiar of which are discussed here), an even larger number are in principle conceivable.

TONY LAWSON

References
Bhaskar, R. (1993), *Dialectic: the pulse of freedom*, London: Verso.
Hayek, F. (1937), 'Economics and Knowledge', *Economica*, February, 33–54.
Keynes, J.M. (1973), 'The Collected Works of John Maynard Keynes', vol. VII, *The General Theory of Employment, Interest and Money*, Royal Economic Society.
Lawson, T. (1994), 'A Realist Theory For Economics', in R. Backhouse, (ed.), *New Directions in Economic Methodology*, London: Routledge.
Lawson, T. (1997), *Economics and Reality*, London: Routledge.
Marshall. A. (1986), *Principles of Economics*, 8th edn, London: Macmillan.
Marx. K. (1974), *Capital: A Critique of Political Economy, Volume III: The Process of Capitalist Production as a Whole*, ed. F. Engels, London: Lawrence & Wishart.
Mill, J.S. (1967), *On the Definition of Political Economy and the Method of Investigation Proper To It*, in *Collected Works of John Stuart Mill, Volume IV: Essays on Economics and Society*, ed. J.M. Robinson, Toronto: University of Toronto Press
Mill, J.S. (1973), *Of Plurality of Causes; and of the Intermixture of Effects,* in *Collected Works of John Stuart Mill, Volume VII*, ed. J.M. Robinson. Toronto: University of Toronto Press.
Pratten, S. (1998), 'Marshall on Tendencies, Equilibrium and the Statical Method', *History of Political Economy*, Cambridge (forthcoming).

Time

Time complicates things. Our pasts are mansions of memories, and the future is a mist of uncertain expectations. The present is the border between an imperfectly discerned history and an unknowable future. Thus all humans blunder and err, experience surprise and lament regrets. Moreover, just as time complicates our lives, it also complicates economic analysis.

Most approaches to economic dynamics employ an analogy between the temporal ordering of events and the quantitative ordering of the real numbers. Early phenomena associate with small numbers and later ones with large. This method of treating time as congruent to a Euclidean dimension enables formal mathematical analysis of economic dynamics, but in identifying time with space also imposes non-trivial presuppositions.

Chief among these is an implicit incapacity inherently to distinguish future from past. Motion along a spatial dimension is essentially indistinguishable in either direction, so that conceiving time as space renders motion forward through time as basically identical with motion backward in time. Thus, although humans innately apprehend time's passage as unidirectional – they perceive a fundamental epistemic separation between what has been, and is therefore potentially knowably memorable, and what has not been, and is therefore inexorably unknowable and only imagined – rendering time as a dimension permits motion in either direction, thereby conflating past and future. That is, the method of modelling time as a dimension obscures its peculiar function as a one-way street.

Remembering time's epistemically imposed unidirectionality is especially important to microeconomic method. All choices necessarily face forward, for people decide between alternative opportunities, each of which is a currently imagined possible outcome in an uncertain and manipulable future. Although recollection of the past influences contemporary images of the future, at every instant the past is forever bygone and only hopes and fears for potential futures motivate decisions. This fundamental volitional dichotomy between past and future methodologically ought to inform all of microeconomics and any microfounded macroeconomics, yet is singularly lacking in the usual formal incorporation of time into economic models.

The logical-time method of modelling temporal sequences as spatial dimension typically takes one of two general forms. These models are either deterministic, in which the values of variables at each instant are determined solely by equations of motion and initial conditions, or are stochastic, in which case each period's state is subject to the effects of random exogenous shocks. The former focuses attention on the internal dynamics of the system to explain intertemporal variation, whereas the latter approach emphasizes the system's response to the external exigencies of a probabilistic fate.

Methods of deterministic dynamics model the economy's behaviour in terms expressed by equations (either difference or differential) of motion representing the mechanisms governing change, subject to initial conditions and particular parameter values. The most common example is the Walrasian tâtonnement, as expressed in

$$dp/dt = T(x(t)) \tag{1}$$

where p is the price vector, t is a real-valued variable representing time, $x(t)$ is the vector of market excess demands at time t, and T is a differential equation representing the system's tendency to change through time. Typically, $dp_1 dt$ preserves the sign of $x_1(t)$, and $T(0) = 0$. Within this context, market-clearing equilibrium becomes associated with dynamical stationary states, and it is natural to examine the conditions under which such equilibria exist, are unique and are globally attracting. The familiar neoclassical arguments concerning these properties are to be found in Arrow and Hahn (1971) and Katzner (1988). Attention focuses on equilibrium states, and change symptomizes disequilibrium. Events, however, never affect the foundations upon which equilibrium is determined, the equilibrium outcome or the mechanisms governing approach to it. This period's prices, production and consumption decisions and other experiences cannot fundamentally affect the conditions upon which future economic activity arises. They are embedded within, not formative of, the economic process.

Alternative insights arise in models of sequences of 'temporary' equilibria. See, for example, Hicks (1946) and Grandmont (1977). Here current market outcomes yield end-of-period conditions which determine the initial conditions for the succeeding period's markets. Questions concern not so much the approach towards equilibrium as the evolution of equilibrium through logical time. Nevertheless, although the state of a temporary equilibrium may not be stationary, the foundations of the economy are unalterably encased within the model's initial conditions and parameters.

Nevertheless, the dynamics of sequences of economic equilibria remain subject to complex motion. Even with apparently simple non-linear equations of motion, (such as the logistic) the system may exhibit intensely complicated motion in which aperiodicity and extreme sensitivity to initial conditions arise. The possibility for such 'chaotic' economic behaviour has been much examined in recent years (see, for example, Grandmont, 1985), but its empirical status is difficult to assess and remains ambiguous. See, for example, Brock (1987).

The most popular alternative to deterministic dynamics interprets variation as reaction to exogenous random shocks. According to this method, the system is modelled in terms of random variables for which deviations from equilibrium are probabilistically controlled, and intertemporal differences in the state of the economy are conceived as resulting from changes in external phenomena. Time's dominion shrinks to the temporary displacement of equilibrium from its 'permanent' unshocked state.

Particularly influential has been the assumption of 'Muthian' rationality. Presented as the case in which agents have gained access to the 'true' model of the economy so that all systematic variation is unerringly predicted, this condition manifests two properties. First, all residuals are distributed with mean equal to zero so that expected 'permanent' values are, on average, correct. Second, residuals are orthogonally distributed. Thus deviations from 'permanent' values are not autocorrelated so that the effects of exogenous shocks are felt immediately and only temporarily. Together, these properties have been extensively used in 'new classical' models, and are a favoured device for presenting the economy as internally well-behaved, but vulnerable to random external temporary disruption. Since the 'permanent' state of the system remains logically antecedent to actual events, however, systemic properties are immune to time's travails, and the truly historical complications of a system capable of transformation through time escapes this logical-time-only method. Indeed, since each instant is deliberately insulated from its neighbours, assuming the system occupies a rational expectations equilibrium denies any role to history and obliterates any place for time in the model. One simply substitutes stochasticity for dynamics.

Each of these attempts to incorporate time into economics methodologically suffers in contrast to 'historical' time. None conceptualizes future as essentially distinct from the past. None reflects the epistemological chasm dividing a perceivable yet unalterable past from an unknowable yet changeable future. None exposes history's unique embedding of expectation and opportunity within the moment. Indeed, Muthian rationality mandates that all periods appear essentially indistinguishable. Only 'permanent', that is, intertemporally unchanged, values really matter. Time's passage presents only transitory jiggles. Nothing lasting transpires; nothing can be learned. Past, present and future meld together in everything but name.

To capture time authentically requires alternative methods. Decisions must face temporally forward, towards an unknowable future of imagined possibilities. Ungoverned by knowledge, this future is subject to psychological whimsy. Consequently, the passage of time may yield surprises, and methodologically rich understandings of choice must possess the potential for surprise to transcend and transform the future and, indirectly, actions anchored in motives focused upon it. These considerations yield three methodological criteria which any bona fide historical-time economic analysis obeys.

First, time cannot be construed simply as a spatial dimension along which, except for its sign, motion in either direction is the same. As Joan Robinson observed (1971; 1980), at each instant, past and future must be conceived as essentially different and time's flow must be forever forward. Understanding time only in terms of its sequential character obscures this distinction between past and future in the illusion that motion, in either direction, along the real line mimics time's passage.

Second, each instant must fundamentally be unique. The past at distinct points is distinct, just as the future at distinct instants is necessarily distinct. Friday's future cannot be the same future as imagined on Monday. At the very least, opportunities and imagined possible outcomes at recognizably different periods must differ. No matter what else has happened or not happened, simply being older (and knowing it) makes an agent a different person than previously. Consequently, plans must be constantly revised, strategies renovated and behaviours adapted. On Monday I may have imagined Wednesday's weather, but by Friday this is no longer an object of imaginative expectation. Moreover, since everyone's opportunities always evolve with the passage of time, there can be no stationary economic state.

Third, time's flux requires change, and change may surprise. Surprise, however, is *prima facie* evidence of disequilibrium. Thus historical time economics must permit analysis away from equilibrium. Since mistakes do happen and surprise sometimes overtakes us all, historical analysis must not be chained to equilibria. Otherwise, the analysis methodologically suppresses the full richness of time's complications and methodologically obscures the full repertory of human behaviours and experience: what Shackle called 'kaleidics' (1969; 1974).

These considerations lead many post Keynesian and institutionalist economists to deep methodological scepticism towards mathematically formal economic dynamics. They insist that neither deterministic nor stochastic models capture the ineluctable, unavoidable efflorescence of imagination, expectation and opportunity as each instant transforms into its successor. An uncertain future lodges both novel adventures and feared catastrophes within the soul. Mere mathematical formalism, they argue, cannot adequately represent time's full impact on economic phenomena. Consequently, they opt for methods in which verbal description of historical processes replaces an abstract rigour reminiscent more of physical mechanics than of historical social transformation.

RANDALL BAUSOR

References

Arrow, Kenneth J. and F.H. Hahn (1971), *General Competitive Analysis*, San Francisco: Holden-Day.
Brock, William A. (1987), 'Distinguishing Random and Deterministic Systems: Abridged Version', in J.-M. Grandmont (ed.), *Nonlinear Economic Dynamics*, New York: Academic Press.
Grandmont, Jean-Michel (1977), 'Temporary Equilibrium Theory', *Econometrica*, **45**, 535–72.
Grandmont, Jean-Michel (1985), 'On Endogenous Competitive Business Cycles', *Econometrica*, **53**, 995–1096.
Hicks, J.R. (1946), *Value and Capital*, 2nd edn, Oxford: Clarendon Press.
Katzner, Donald W. (1988), *Walrasian Microeconomics. an Introduction to the Economic Theory of Market Behavior*, Reading, MA: Addison-Wesley.
Robinson, Joan (1970), *Economic Heresies*, New York: Basic Books.
Robinson, Joan (1980), 'Time in Economic Theory', *Kyklos*, **33**, 219–29.
Shackle, G.L.S. (1969), *Decision, Order and Time in Human Affairs*, Cambridge: Cambridge University Press.
Shackle, G.L.S. (1974), *Keynesian Kaleidics; the Evolution of a General Political Economy*, Edinburgh: Edinburgh University Press.

Tinbergen, Jan

Tinbergen (1903–94) studied physics from 1922 to 1926 at the University of Leiden (Holland) where Paul Ehrenfest was his most influential teacher. Tinbergen's strong social feelings and his concern for the unemployed led him to feel that he could be more useful as an economist

502   *The handbook of economic methodology*

than as a physicist. It was to guide Tinbergen away from theoretical physics to mathematical economics that Ehrenfest proposed the subject for his thesis, minimum problems in physics and economics in 1929. This subject was specially chosen because of the probable mathematical analogy between the relevant physical problems and certain economic problems. Ehrenfest himself had been occupied with it 10 years earlier. At the time, he had been struck by the possibility of developing an analogy between thermodynamics and economics. In Tinbergen's dissertation, the analogy was provided by Lagrange's dynamical equations.

By the 1930s, Tinbergen's method already had the distinctive shape that would not change during his lifetime. His aim was to know the implications, of certain changes in the social mechanism or in the conditions under which that mechanism works. To gain this desired understanding, observation was not enough: one should, in addition, make use of reasoning. Tinbergen distinguished two types of reasoning: deductive and inductive. He compared the first with economic reasoning and the second with statistical analysis.

In the beginning, the economic reasoning propositions had to be deduced from the economic principle of maximal satisfaction. Conceived in this way, economic problems were maximization problems and the mechanism could be described by Lagrange's equations. Tinbergen was able to deduce from the central principle four schemes: static competition, static monopoly, limited competition under static conditions (Cournot's scheme) and dynamic competition. Statistical analysis had to decide which scheme provided the best explanation of the empirical data.

Tinbergen applied these schemes to his investigations into the structure of various supplying industries: the potato flour industry, the coffee market and the markets of cotton, wheat and sugar (Tinbergen, 1933). He was interested in the supply side of the market because of the influence of supply regulation on the price. Tinbergen found that the dynamic scheme could best explain the supply policy of the (cartelized) coffee market, while Cournot's scheme provided the best interpretation of the supply curve of the potato flour market.

Tinbergen's main interest in economics was always economic policy: the determination of the optimum policy. To deal with this problem one had to dispose of some collective ophelimity function and calculate which policy would optimize this function. Although Tinbergen admitted that the determination of such a function was an almost impossible task, he always remained optimistic that in the future this problem would be solved (Tinbergen, 1935). One of the results of his thesis was that, with respect to purchasing power, which was to be optimized, the business cycle was not the optimal path. Therefore, in his later works, Tinbergen focused on identifying the causes of the business cycle and how to attain stabilization.

His method in analysing business cycles was to incorporate into his own business cycle schemes the explanations of the cycle he found in other literature. By 'schemes' he meant simple representations of reality. A scheme had to fulfil two conditions: first, it had to be as much as possible an economical representation and, second, it had to be easy to handle for calculations or other purposes. Tinbergen's ultimate purpose of business cycle research was to draw the lines of business cycle policy. The shift of the goal from explanation to policy corresponded with a change in name from 'scheme' to 'model'.

The first example of this kind, a model of the Dutch economy, was published by Tinbergen in a paper read to the Dutch Economic Association in 1936. The same year, Tinbergen was commissioned by the Economic Intelligence Service of the League of Nations to undertake statistical tests of the business cycle theories examined by Haberler for the League. Tinbergen worked at this task for two years and reported his results in two volumes, *Statistical Testing of Business-Cycle Theories*, published in 1939. The first volume contained an explanation of a method of econometric testing, and a demonstration of what could be achieved, in three case studies. The second volume contained a model of the United States.

Tinbergen was quite aware of the fact that economists did not agree upon which were the most important causes of a phenomenon like the business cycle. From Ehrenfest he had learned to formulate differences of opinion in a 'nobler' way than merely as conflicts. Ehrenfest's favourite formulation was cast in the general form: if $a > b$, scholar A is right, but if $a < b$, then scholar B is right. This method was exactly the method Tinbergen would follow in his work for the League of Nations: two opinions, as a rule, do not exclude each other. The question is in what degree each is correct, or how these two opinions are to be combined to have the best picture of reality (Tinbergen, 1988).

This method modifies the earlier one as follows. The dynamical equations were no longer obtained by maximizing or minimizing an ophelimity function and thus were no longer Lagrange's equations. The method essentially starts with (a) *a priori* considerations about what explanatory variables are to be included. This choice must be based on economic theory or common sense. In place of a simple general principle we thus have theories $T_1 \dots T_n$. The next steps are (b) to draw up a list of equations or relations the variables have to obey and (c) to test the validity of the equations, which implies the estimation of their coefficients, if any. As a consequence of (c) especially, we may have to revise (a) and (b) so as to arrive at a satisfactory degree of realism of the theory embodied in the model. The variables $x_1, x_2, x_3 \dots$ x_n represent the vectors which set up a multidimensional economic space. The problem for econometrics was to compute the coordinates of the state in which the system can be found.

The national econometric model developed according to this method and used for the analysis of economic problems can also be applied to policy problems (Tinbergen, 1956). The difference is that the role of variables is changed. In an analytical model, the exogenous variables are the data which fix the movement of the endogenous variables. In the political arena, the situation is the reverse: one wants endogenous variables, or at least some of them, to obtain prescribed values, namely the policy objectives. Some of the exogenous variables – the instruments – then become the unknowns because it has to be decided which values should be attached to them in order to obtain prescribed objectives. From this it follows that the number of instruments must always be equal to the number of objectives. If the number of objectives is smaller than the number of instruments, various combinations of instrument values could lead to the same results. But if the number of objectives is larger, the preference function of the 'policy maker' should be maximized.

Macroeconometric modelling also shaped Tinbergen's later work on development planning and his last work on international order and peace. Under certain conditions, the solution of a complex and large mathematical model is possible in a number of consecutive stages instead of through a simultaneous solution. Tinbergen used this mathematical theorem in the methodology of development planning by distinguishing three stages, a macro, middle and microstage (Tinbergen, 1967) and in his conceptualization of international order (Tinbergen *et al.*, 1976).

Tinbergen established a whole new methodology in economics framed by macroeconometric models of which he was a pioneer. By his methodology, he showed that economic science and economic policy were two sides of the same coin.

MARCEL BOUMANS

Bibliography
Boumans, M.J. (1992), '*A Case of Limited Physics Transfer, Jan Tinbergen's Resources for Re-shaping Economics*', Amsterdam: Thesis Publishers.
Klaassen, L.H., L.M. Koyck and H.J. Witteveen (eds) (1959), *Jan Tinbergen–Selected Papers*, Amsterdam: North-Holland.
Morgan, M.S. (1990), *The History of Econometric Ideas*, Cambridge: Cambridge University Press.
Thanawala, K. and J.B. Davis (eds) (1988), 'Jan Tinbergen's Contributions to Social Economics', *Review of Social Economy*, **XLVI**, 3.
Tinbergen, J. (1933), 'The Notions of Horizon and Expectancy in Dynamic Economics', *Econometrica*, **I**, 36–51.
Tinbergen, J. (1935), 'Annual Survey: Suggestions on Quantitative Business Cycle Theory', *Econometrica*, **III**, 241–308.
Tinbergen, J. (1936), 'An Economic Policy for 1936', paper given to the Dutch Economic Association, translated and reprinted in Klaassen et al. (1959).
Tinbergen, J. (1939), *Statistical Testing of Business-Cycle Theories*, Geneva: League of Nations.
Tinbergen, J. (1956), *Economic Policy: Principles and Design*, Amsterdam: North-Holland.
Tinbergen, J. (1967), *Development Planning*, London: Weidenfeld & Nicolson.
Tinbergen, J., A.J. Dolman and J. van Ettinger (1976), *Reshaping the International Order*, New York: Dutton.
Tinbergen, J. (1986), 'Recollections of Professional Experiences', in J.A. Kregel (ed.), *Recollections of Eminent Economists*, I, London: Macmillan.
de Wolff, P., F. Hartog, H.C. Bos and J.P. Pronk (1970), 'J. Tinbergen – R. Frisch', *De Economist*, **CXVIII**, 2.

Transcendental Realism

Any position can be designated a *realism* in the philosophical sense of the term that asserts the existence of some disputed kind of entity (such as black holes, quarks, class relations, the Loch Ness monster, utilities, probabilities, economic equilibria or truth). A *scientific realism* is a theory that the ultimate objects of scientific enquiry exist and act (mostly) quite independently of scientists and their practices (Bhaskar, 1978; Lawson, 1989; Mäki, 1989). A *transcendental realism* of the sort that has recently gained some attention within economics is primarily a metaphysical theory constituting an account of what the world must be like before it is investigated by science, and for scientific activities to be possible (Bhaskar, 1978; Lawson, 1994a; 1997). Such a realism neither turns on nor endorses any particular substantive theory. Once obtained, however, it may provide insight as to how science can be done. It may also facilitate an appropriate standard of comparison for those economists interested in a particular version of the question of naturalism: whether economics can be a science in the same sense as the sciences of nature.

Transcendental analysis

A transcendental realist metaphysics of science is so labelled because of the manner of its derivation. This takes the form of an enquiry into the conditions of the possibility of some central, especially significant or pervasive, activity or other feature of our experience; a manner of proceeding identified as 'transcendental' by Kant. If this label is accepted, it is important to acknowledge that there is nothing inherent in method in question which forces us to accept the individualist and/or idealist mode in which Kant framed his own enquiries. Several points warrant emphasis here. First, the features of experience to be accounted for (that is, the premises for the transcendental inference) may be normatively corrigible, essentially contested, historically transient and spatially highly restricted. Second, any human activity which is to be so accounted for may depend on an array of powers that people possess as physical, biological and social agents, and not merely those most directly implicated in thinking and perceiving. Third. the analysis itself, which in the manner of its premises will be normatively corrigible and socially contested, may give rise to realist, not idealist, and so epistemically relativist, not absolutist, results and to conclusions which may only be domain-specific.[1]

An important question, clearly, is how the premises for a transcendental enquiry are to be selected without implying an arbitrary, 'external', unjustified, or otherwise unpersuasive and/or unwarranted commitment to the epistemic (or other) worth of the practices described. Science, or research activity, never takes place in a philosophical vacuum; all science-related practices are sponsored by one or more prevailing philosophies of science. Transcendental enquiry thus takes the form of immanent critique. That is, the premises chosen for transcendental analysis must be not only acceptable to the investigator (if conditional synthetic *a priori* knowledge of possibilities for science is the aim) but also acceptable to, and accepted by (indeed, if possible, of paramount importance to) conceptions of philosophy currently dominant, or at least in contention. In other words, the premises of transcendental arguments will be descriptions of practices which influential, or potentially influential, science-oriented philosophies give prominence to, so that successful transcendental arguments will constitute transcendental refutations (or confirmations) of pre-existing accounts of science.

Thus conceived, transcendental analysis is ultimately a process of 'determinate negation'. The aim, basically, is to take a (dubious but influential) science-oriented philosophy which focuses on some more or less inadequately analysed activity; to render explicit the ontological, sociological and other presuppositions of the science-oriented philosophy, and hence to set it in the form of a science-oriented realism, sociology and so on; and to demonstrate that, when the activity in question is adequately analysed, it is seen to presuppose a transcendental realist conception incompatible with that of the science-oriented philosophy thus critiqued.

Experimental activity and a theory of ontology

The transcendental realism that has recently gained some attention in economics is derived by questioning how experiments and its results are possible (Bhaskar, 1978; 1989; Lawson, 1989; 1994a; 1997). The philosophical context is that experimentation is heavily sponsored by Kantians and empiricists. For such traditions, regularities of the form 'whenever event *x* then event *y*' are at least necessary (transcendental idealism) and perhaps sufficient (empiricism) conditions for causal laws (and other features of knowledge). And these traditions have seized upon the *experimental* establishment, knowledge and practical application of such 'laws' as being of fundamental epistemic significance in science. Bhaskar's initial input is to point out that, outside of astronomy at least, most of the constant conjunctions of events that are held by these traditional philosophies to be significant in science, in fact occur *only* under the restricted conditions of experimental control; they are not typically spontaneously occurring, but a product of human intervention. A second observation drawn upon is that results and insights obtained through experimental activity are, along with other forms of knowledge, nevertheless successfully applied outside the experimental situation. Put differently, constant conjunctions of events are in fact extremely rare, spatiotemporally restricted and usually artificially produced, while lawlike knowledge appears to be generally available and widely useful.

It is immediately clear that these observations raise fundamental problems for those post-Humean philosophies which tie laws, or 'significant results' in science, to constant conjunctions of events. For, if scientific laws, or significant results, only occur in such restricted conditions as experimental set-ups, this bears the (rather inhibiting) implication that science and its results are far from being universal, but are effectively fenced off from most of the goings-on in the world. In other words, most of the accepted results of science are not of the form 'whenever event *x* then event *y* always follows' after all, but are of the form 'whenever event *x* then event *y* always follows, as long as conditions *e* hold', where conditions *e* typically amount to a specification of the experimental situation. This also bears the rather counterintuitive implication that any actual regularity of events that a law of nature supposedly denotes generally does not occur independently of human intervention. In addition to such problems, and at least as seriously, the constant conjunctions view of laws leaves the question of what governs events outside the experimental situation unaddressed and, in doing so, it also leaves the observation that experimentally obtained results *are* successfully applied outside experimental situations without any valid explanation.

In order to explain this situation, it is necessary to abandon the view that the generalizations of nature consist of event regularities and to accept instead (something like) an account of the objects of the world, including those of science, as *structured*, that is, irreducible to the events of experience, and *intransitive*, that is, existing and acting independently of their being identified. From this (transcendental realist) perspective in question the world is constituted not only by events and states of affairs, and our experiences or perceptions of those actualities, but also by structures, powers, mechanisms and their tendencies that, although perhaps not directly observable, nevertheless exist, whether or not detected, and govern the actual events and so on that we do, or may, experience. Thus not only does the autumn leaf pass to the ground, and not only do we experience it as falling, but, according to this perspective, underlying such movement and governing it are real mechanisms such as gravity (or curved space) and so on. In the UK at present not only are cows dying prematurely, or showing signs of losing control of their bodily functions, and not only is their behaviour interpreted as 'madness' (the illness is widely known as 'mad cow disease') but, according to scientists implicitly acting on the perspective in question, this phenomenon is governed by some, albeit as yet less than fully understood, agent or causal mechanism – and the search is on to uncover it. In short, three overlapping, but ontologically distinct, domains of reality are distinguished, namely the *empirical* (experience and impression), the *actual* (actualities including events and states of affairs in addition to the empirical) and the *real* (structures, mechanisms, powers and tendencies, in addition to actual events and experiences).

Now according to the perspective here being put forward, not only is it the case that the three domains identified are ontologically distinct, but, crucially, they are unsynchronized, or out of phase, with one another. Thus, while experiences are out of phase with events, allowing the possibility of contrasting, as well as revisions to, experiences of a given event, so events are typically unsynchronized or out of phase with the mechanisms that govern them. On the latter structure/event non-correspondence, for example, autumn leaves are not in phase with the action of gravity for the reason that they are also subject to aerodynamic, thermal and other causes or tendencies.

According to this theory of reality, then, one which, following Bhaskar, we refer to simply as 'transcendental realism', it is easy enough to see that, or how, the experimental situation elaborated above can be rendered intelligible. For experimental activity can now be recognized as an attempt to intervene in order to *close* the system, that is, in order to insulate a particular mechanism of interest by holding off all other potentially counteracting mechanisms. The aim is to engineer a closed system in which a one-to-one correspondence can obtain between the way a mechanism acts and the events which eventually ensue. In other words, on this view, experimental activity can be rendered intelligible *not* as creating the rare situation in which an empirical law is put into effect, but as intervening in order to bring about those special circumstances under which a non-empirical law, a power, a tendency or mechanism and so on can be empirically identified. If the triggering conditions (where applicable) are activated, the mechanism in question is operative, whatever else is going on. On this transcendental realist view, for example, a leaf is subject to the gravitation tendency even as it lies on the ground or 'flies' off over roof tops and chimneys.

Knowledge

If the transcendental realist ontology just defended entails that knowledge is not merely given in experience, it must come about through the transformation of pre-existing knowledge-like material. In other words, it is necessary to acknowledge a *transitive* dimension to knowledge, or epistemology, to complement the intransitive dimension, or ontology, already established. It is necessary to recognize a dimension of transitive objects of knowledge, including facts, observations, theories. hypotheses, guesses, hunches, intuitions, speculations and anomalies, which facilitate, and come to be (actively) transformed through, the (laborious) social practice of science. Knowledge, in short, is a produced means of production (of further knowledge) while science must be recognized as a continuing transformative social activity. Knowledge is a social product, actively produced by means of antecedent social products, albeit on the basis of a continual engagement, or interaction. with its intransitive object.

Science

A rational account of scientific development quickly follows. The aim is the production of knowledge of mechanisms that, singly or in combination, produce the phenomena that we are interested in. Usually (in natural science), this will involve employing antecedently existing cognitive resources and operating on the basis of something like analogy and metaphor, in constructing a hypothesis, or 'model', of a mechanism which, if it were to exist and act in the postulated manner, would account for the phenomenon in question. The reality of the postulated mechanism (and usually there will be several hypotheses) must then be empirically assessed, of course. Once this is achieved, any explanation accepted must itself in principle be explained; and its explanation in turn explained; and so on. On this conception, then, science is distinguished by its *retroductive* mode of inference: the move from knowledge of some phenomenon existing at any one level of reality to the knowledge of mechanisms at a deeper level or stratum of reality by which the original phenomenon of interest was generated.

Critical realism

If, according to the account of transcendental realism described, the essence of science lies in the move, at any one level, from manifest phenomenon to structures which generated it, a questioning of the possibility of naturalism boils down to investigating the feasibility of making a comparable move in illuminating the objects of the social realm. A perspective derived by so questioning whether the study of social phenomena can be a science in this sense is that recently systematized as 'critical realism' (Arestis, 1999; Bhaskar, 1979; Boylan and O'Gorman, 1995; Dow, 1996; Fleetwood, 1995; Foss, 1994; Clive Lawson, 1993; Lawson, 1994a, 1994b, 1997; Peacock, 1993; Pratten, 1993; Rotheim, 1993; Runde, 1998; Sofianou, 1995). The starting point of this project is the observation that interesting event regularities have yet to be uncovered in the social realm and seem *a priori* unlikely to be so (especially given the reality of human choice, that each person could always have acted otherwise, along with the infeasibility of experimental control in the social realm). And the perspective in question has been developed through questioning whether there are specifically *social* structures (facilitating human agency) which a social science such as economics can uncover and for help to understand.

Any such assessment of the possibilities for a social science of economics so conceived necessitates a conception not only of specifically *social* structure but also of numerous aspects of human subjectivity more generally, together with some understanding of their interconnection. It is easy to see why. In an open and structured world, all possibilities for capable human agency depend upon whatever structures and mechanisms are in place. But any aspects of structure that can be designated *social* must (in order to be so designated) also depend in turn on human agency. Social rules, such as language systems, are like this. They both depend upon speech acts and are a condition of the latter's possibility. Clearly, the nature of this interdependency and related features warrant further elaboration. Space limitations preclude detailing here very many of the results sustained in critical realism (for an extended discussion, see Lawson, 1997). Rather, some of the more important insights are briefly sketched.

In opposition to individualists, on the one hand, and collectivists, on the other, critical realism emphasizes an essentially *relational* conception of the social. And in opposition to structuralists and subjectivists alike, critical realism supports a *transformational* conception of the agency/structure relation whereby neither element can be identified with, explained completely in terms of, or reduced to, the other. On the relational conception of the social, all social forms, structures and systems, such as the economy, the state, international organizations, trade unions and households, depend upon, or presuppose, social relations. And of particular interest are the internally related positions into which individuals essentially slot, with their associated, relationally defined, positioned practices, tasks, rights, obligations, prerogatives and so forth. On the transformational conception of social activity, the existence of social structure is the often unacknowledged but necessary condition for an individual act, as well as an often unintended, but inevitable, outcome of individual actions taken in total. Social structure, in short, is the unmotivated condition of our motivated productions, the non-created but drawn upon and reproduced/transformed condition for our daily economic/social activities.

On this critical realist conception, then, the objective of economics is to identify the structures governing some economic phenomenon of interest. Essentially, this entails identifying, understanding and explaining certain practices of relevance to the phenomenon in question; that is, identifying the unacknowledged conditions of these practices, unconscious motivations, tacit skills drawn up, as well as unintended consequences. While society and the economy are the skilled accomplishment of active agents, they remain to a degree opaque to the individuals upon whose activities they depend. The task of economics, then, is to describe the total process (whether or not adequately conceptualized by the agents involved) that must be going on for some manifest phenomenon of interest to be possible.

Notice that, because critical realism acknowledges the openness of the economic world and accepts as the primary aim of science the identification and elaboration of the deeper structures that govern surface phenomena, the central criterion of theory assessment must be explanatory power, not predictive accuracy (see, for example, Bhaskar, 1978; Collier, 1994; Lawson, 1994a; 1997). Notice too that, because critical realism recognizes both that significant event regularities are rarely in evidence in the economic sphere and that the aim of economic science is instead to uncover relatively enduring underlying structures, it holds that economic policy is properly concerned *not* with predictive control (with manipulating values of variables in the hope of controlling future events, with the attempted amelioration of states of economic affairs) but with emancipation, through the knowledgeable transformation of structures that govern and facilitate human action.

One final observation to make is that, because social structure is dependent upon human agency, it follows that it is open to transformation through changing human practices which in turn can be affected by *criticizing* the conceptions and understandings on which people act. This sensitivity of social forms to social criticism largely accounts for the labelling of the perspective in question as 'critical' realism. Of course, it is at least conceivable that competing social philosophies will emerge which both accept the transcendental realist account of science sketched above and recognize the dependency of social life on human conceptions (without being reducible to them) and so on critical reason. Although the position outlined here, then, takes the heading of 'critical realism', it warrants emphasis that there may be numerous conceptions eventually forthcoming which equally qualify for this ascription.[2]

TONY LAWSON

Notes

1. On this account of transcendental analysis, then, both premises and conclusions of philosophical argument necessarily constitute contingent claims. If in the manner suggested it turns out that philosophy can so establish synthetic *a priori* knowledge, it can only be in the relative or conditional sense just noted. That is philosophy (in the form of transcendental analysis) can get going on the basis *only* of prior conceptualizations, of definite ideas of determinate social forms and any results must be interpreted as conditional and expressed in hypothetical form. On this conception, then, transcendental inquiry neither exists independently of the various sciences and other social practices nor is it used to investigate a different world: philosophy treats the very same world as science. And it aims to reveal what our conceptions of certain practices of interest presuppose about that world. It represents, in short, an investigation that necessarily takes contingent historical premises and specific social conditions, and aims to produce hypothetical and conditional conclusions; an investigation which can never be foreclosed but is always open to elaboration and transformation. On this conception, there is no philosophy in general, only philosophy of particular, geo-historically determinate social forms.
2. And, indeed, the position sketched here has itself recently been further elaborated as 'dialectical critical realism'. Space limitations prevent a discussion of such developments, but see Bhaskar (1993).

References

Arestis, P. (1992), *The Post-Keynesianism Approach to Economics: An alternative analysis of economic theory and policy*, Aldershot: Edward Elgar.

Bhaskar, R. (1978), *A Realist Theory of Science*, 2nd edn, Harvester.

Bhaskar, R. (1989), *Reclaiming Reality*, London: Verso.

Bhaskar, R. (1993), *Dialectic*, London: Verso.

Bovlan, T.A. and P.F. O'Gorman (1995), *Beyond Rhetoric and Realism in Economics: towards a reformulation of economic methodology*, London: Routledge.

Collier, A. (1994), *Critical Realism: An Introduction to Roy Bhaskar's Philosophy*, London: Verso.

Dow, S.C. (1996), *Macroeconomic thought: a methodological approach*, rev. edn, Oxford/New York: Basil Blackwell.

Fleetwood, S. (1995), *Hayek's Political Economy: the socio-economics of order*, London: Routledge.

Foss, N.J. (1994) 'Realism and Evolutionary Economics', *Journal of Social and Evolutionary Systems*, 17, (1), 21–40.

Lawson, C. (1994), 'The transformation model of social activity and economic activity: a reinterpretation of the work of J.R. Commons', *Review of Political Economy*, 6, (2).

Lawson, T. (1989), 'Abstraction, Tendencies and Stylised Facts: A Realist Approach to Economic Analysis', *Cambridge Journal of Economics*, 13, (1), March, 59–78; reprinted in T. Lawson, G. Palma and J. Sender (eds), *Kaldor's Political Economy*, London/San Diego: Academic Press, 1989.

Lawson, T. (1994a), 'A Realist Theory for Economics', in R.E. Backhouse (ed.), *New Direction in Economic Methodology*, London/New York: Routledge.

Lawson, T. (1994b), 'Critical Realism and the Analysis of Choice, Explanation and Change', *Advances in Austrian Economics*, vol. 1.

Lawson, T. (1997), *Economics and Reality*, London: Routledge.

Mäki U. (1989), 'On the problem of realism in economics', *Recherche Economiche*, 43, 176–98.

Peacock, M. (1993), 'Hayek Realism and Spontaneous Order', *Journal for the Theory of Social Behaviour*, 23.

Pratten. S. (1993), 'Structure, Agency and Marx's Analysis of the Labour Process', *Review of Political Economy*, **5**, (4), 403–26.
Rotheim. R.J. (1993), 'On the Indeterminacy of Keynes's Monetary Theory of Value', *Review of Political Economy*, **5**, (2), 197, 216.
Runde. J. (1998), 'Assessing Causal Economic Explanations', *Oxford Economic Papers* (forthcoming).
Sofianou, E. (1995), 'Post-Modernism and the notion of Rationality in Economics', *Cambridge Journal of Economics*.

Truth, truthlikeness

Truth is a central concept of semantics (the study of the relations of language and reality), epistemology (the study of the possibility of knowledge) and methodology (the study of the best means of knowledge seeking). The various theories of truth reflect important divisions between philosophical schools. The concept of truthlikeness or verisimilitude, intended to express a gradation in the 'closeness to the truth', has become a crucial element within the philosophy of science in the debate between scientific realism and instrumentalism.

Different theories of truth have chosen various candidates for the bearers of truth. Sometimes it is beliefs that are classified as true or false, but is more natural to think that every meaningful, complete, indicative sentence has a truth value. (Questions and commands are excluded by this criterion.) In Alfred Tarski's semantic approach, which is mostly followed in modern logic, truth values are assigned by interpretation to the sentences of a formal or a natural language. However, if the sentence contains identical expressions, the truth value does not belong to the uttered sentence as such, but rather to the statement determined by the context or situation. For example, if John says to Mary: 'I love you', the conveyed statement is 'John loves Mary'. In some theories, truth value is associated with propositions, where the proposition that John loves Mary is an abstract entity, roughly speaking the common content of the equivalent English and German statements 'John loves Mary' and 'John liebt Mary'.

Theories of truth usually separate the concept of actual or material truth from logical truth (such as tautologies like 'It is raining or not raining') and analytic truth (consequences of definitions like 'All bachelors are unmarried'). While material truth concerns the actual world, logical truth is characterized, following Leibniz, by truth in all possible worlds. Both of these notions can be defined in Tarski's model theory, which treats truth as a relation between sentences and models (that is, possible worlds or possible situations). The most fundamental idea of material truth is expressed by the classical condition that, for example, the sentence 'Snow is white' is true if and only if snow is white. This condition is known as Tarski's T-equivalence: (T) Sentence 'p' is true if and only if p. The redundancy or disquotational theory of truth asserts that (T) alone is a sufficient account of the use of the truth-predicate. Another version of this minimalist approach is formulated by Horwich (1990) in terms of propositions: (T') The proposition that p is true if and only if p.

Condition (T) expresses an equivalence between object language, where the sentence 'p' is used, and metalanguage, where 'p' is named or mentioned. Therefore (T) alone does not capture the idea of the classical correspondence theory of truth, which takes truth to be a relation between language (or beliefs) and the world. According to this theory, a statement is true if and only if it corresponds to facts, that is, expresses a state of affairs which actually obtains in reality. The critics of the correspondence theory argue that no satisfactory account has been given of the key notions 'correspondence' and 'fact'. The best accounts in this direction develop the picture theory of Wittgenstein's *Tractatus* (1921): sentences are isomorphic representations of facts. Tarski's 1933 definition and its later refinement in model theory, which work for formal languages and syntactically well-defined fragments of natural language, build the truth values of complex sentences from the evaluation of simple atomic formulas (Tarski, 1956; Davidson, 1984). This definition is relative to an interpretation which fixes the reference or extension of the non-logical vocabulary (names, predicates, relations) in the given language. For example, the sentence 'John loves Mary' is true (relative to interpretation I) if the referents of the names 'John' and 'Mary' determined by I form a pair which belongs to the relation that is the interpretation by I of the verb 'loves'.

According to the coherence theory of truth, a judgment is true if it forms a coherent system with other judgments. If coherence here means only logical consistency, there are always several alternative coherent systems. In choosing the 'right' system, appeal is usually made to some epistemic principles, such as God's beliefs (Baruch Spinoza) or the ultimate opinion of the scientific community (Charles Peirce). In this form, the coherence theory is transformed into what Jurgen Habermas calls the consensus theory of truth: truth is the limit of ideal discourse in a community free from domination. Other epistemic definitions define truth in terms of verification (William James), warranted assertability (John Dewey), proof (Michael Dummett, 1978) and ideal acceptability (Hilary Putnam, 1981). As the verification of a belief involves the testing of its validity in practical action, the pragmatist account of truth associates truth with utility.

The correspondence approach is realist in the sense that statements are true or false independently of our beliefs or interests. Many truths are now unknown to us – and perhaps remain so for ever. Contrary to Dummett's semantic anti-realism, truth may be 'recognition-transcendent'. This realist concept of truth can then be used in the classical definition of knowledge as justified true belief. The epistemic definitions of truth instead characterize truth in epistemic or methodological terms: truth is the ultimate outcome of the best or ideal processes of knowledge seeking. The main problems in these accounts are to specify such ideal conditions (in a way which is easier to understand than the concept of the actual world) and to show that the proposed definition satisfies the T-equivalence.

Classical logic is two-valued: each statement is either true or false (relative to a given interpretation). Many-valued logics accept more than two truth values, but their philosophical content has remained controversial. In fuzzy logic, developed for statements with vague terms, there may be a continuum of degrees of truth between the extremes 0 and 1.

Truth has to be distinguished from the concept of epistemic probability (degree of belief in the truth of a hypothesis on given evidence). In the fallibilist tradition, the notion of truth is supplemented by the idea of 'truthlikeness'. The first attempt to define truthlikeness or verisimilitude was proposed by Karl Popper in 1960. According to his qualitative criterion, applicable to theories as deductive closed sets of statements, a theory A is more truthlike than theory B if and only if $B \cap T \subseteq A \cap T$ and $A \cap F \subseteq B \cap F$, where one of the set-inclusions is strict, and T and F are the sets of the true and false statements, respectively. Intuitively, A should have larger truth content than B, but smaller falsity content than B. If A and B are true, then the logically stronger of them is the more truthlike. However, David Miller and Pavel Tichý proved in 1974 that this definition does work in the intended way, since it cannot be used for comparing false theories: if A is more truthlike than B in Popper's sense, then A must be true.

Since 1975, a new approach to truthlikeness has been based upon the concept of similarity. The idea is that a distance between alternative states of affairs (or sentences describing them) is first defined. For numerical statements such a distance can be defined by means of the underlying metric, but other cases involve more complex technicalities. Then the distance of a theory from the truth depends on the distances from the truth of those states allowed by the theory. Let C_* be the truth, and let H be the disjunction of $C_1, C_2, \ldots, C_n$. Let d_{i*} be the distance of C_i from C_*. Then, in the approach of Tichý and Oddie, the distance of H from C_* is defined by the average function $\Sigma d_{i*}/n$ (Oddie, 1986). In Ilkka Niiniluoto's approach, it is defined by the weighted average of the minimum distance min d_{i*} and the (normalized) sum Σd_{i*} of all distances (Niiniluoto, 1987; Kuipers, 1987). Niiniluoto has also proposed a way of estimating the distance of H from the unknown truth C_* as the expected value of the degree of verisimilitude of a theory.

The concept of truthlikeness has been used for defending scientific realism. Instrumentalism usually takes notice of the idealizational nature of science, and concludes that theories lack truth values (Cartwright, 1983). Some methodological anti-realists admit that theories have a truth value, but regard it as irrelevant to science, which seeks only problem-solving capacity (Laudan, 1977) or empirical adequacy (van Fraassen, 1980). Against these alternatives, and without appeal to naive or dogmatic realism, a critical realist can claim that scientific theories are more or less truthlike descriptions of reality, rival false theories can refer to the same unknown theoretical entities in the world (as with the electron theories of Lorenz and Bohr) and science makes progress in so far as it succeeds in finding new theories that are more truthlike than their predecessors (Niiniluoto, 1984).

ILKKA NIINILUOTO

Reference
Cartwright, N. (1983), *How the Laws of Physics Lie*, Oxford: Oxford University Press.
Davidson, D. (1984), *Inquiries into Meaning and Truth*, Oxford: Oxford University Press.
Dummett, M. (1978), *Truth and Other Enigmas*, Oxford: Clarendon Press.
Horwich, P. (1990), *Truth*, Oxford: Blackwell.
Kuipers, T. (ed.) (1987), *What is Closer-to-the-Truth?*, Amsterdam: Rodopi.
Laudan, L. (1977), *Progress and Its Problems*, London: Routledge & Kegan Paul.
Niiniluoto, I. (1984), *Is Science Progressive?*, Dordrecht: D. Reidel.
Niiniluoto, I. (1987), *Truthlikeness*, Dordrecht: D. Reidel.
Oddie, G. (1986), *Likeness to Truth*, Dordrecht: D. Reidel.
Putnam, H. (1981), *Reason, Truth and History*, Cambridge: Cambridge University Press.
Tarski, A. (1980), *Logic, Semantics, and Metamathematics*, Oxford: Oxford University Press.
van Fraassen, B. (1980), *The Scientific Image*, Oxford: Clarendon Press.

Uncertainty, Keynesian/Knightian

Economists traditionally define uncertainty in opposition to risk. Decision making under risk is usually taken to refer to situations in which agents assign point probabilities to the outcomes of their actions (or the 'states of the world' that determine the consequences of their acts). Decision making under uncertainty refers to situations in which they do not.

The risk/uncertainty distinction is often attributed to Keynes (1973a) or Knight (1921), both of whom provide sophisticated treatments of the subject of rational conduct under uncertainty. The distinction is a natural one for them to make as, writing prior to the development of the personalist 'betting' approach to probability by de Finetti (1964), Ramsey (1978) and Savage (1954), they tend to think of the use of numerically definite probabilities as being restricted to cases in which it is possible to invoke the classical conception of probability or where agents have knowledge of statistical frequencies. Given that most economic decisions are not guided by probabilities determined on these lines, numerically definite probabilities then become the exception rather than the rule. We will concentrate on Keynes' account of the determination of numerical probabilities and then compare it briefly with Knight's, before moving on to their respective notions of uncertainty.

In his *Treatise on Probability*, Keynes analyses probability as a relation of partial entailment between the conclusion of an argument h and some set of evidential premises e. These relations are presented as logical entities, the apprehension of which warrants some rational degree of belief intermediate between certainty or maximum probability on the one hand (where h is a logical consequence of e) and impossibility or minimum probability on the other (where h stands in a contradictory relation with e). Relations of partial implication are written $h_1 | e_1$ (read 'h_1 relative to e_1') and the theory builds on binary comparisons of the form $h_1 | e_1 >^* h_2 | e_2$. The symbol $>^*$ denotes the relation 'at least as probable as' and yields to what we would now call a partially ordered set of probabilities (the relations $=^*$ and $>^*$ are defined in the normal way).

The conditions that must be met to arrive at numerically definite probabilities within this framework are as follows. First, the alternatives to which probabilities are to be assigned must be 'indivisible'. Keynes proposes a formal definition of indivisibility, the substance of which is that the alternatives must not be able to be split into subalternatives of the same form. Second, the alternatives must be judged to be equiprobable by appeal to the principle of indifference, that $h_i | e =^* h_j | e$, for all i, j. Given that the list of alternatives $h_1, h_2, ..., h_n$ is exhaustive and the h_is are mutually exclusive, it is then possible to assign numerical probabilities. Let $H = h_1 \vee h_2 \vee ... \vee h_m$ ($m \leq n$). The (Keynesian version of classical or *a priori*) probability of H is then $p(H/e) = m/n$. Further on in the *Treatise*, Keynes also allows that it may sometimes be possible to assign numerically definite probabilities on the basis of a knowledge of relative frequencies, and sketches an outline of the relative frequency theory of probability as a special case of his 'logical' theory (Keynes, 1973a: 109–14).

Like Keynes, Knight (1921: 224–5) finds it useful to distinguish between situations in which numerical probabilities can be determined on purely general principles (*a priori* probability) and where they are based on a knowledge of frequencies (statistical probability). Although there are some ambiguities in the way that Knight distinguishes between these two situations (Runde, 1998), the essential difference again appears to be that, whereas *a priori* probability assignments are based on the assumed equiprobability of outcomes, statistical probabilities are determined *ex posteriori* by the empirical method of 'counting instances'. Unlike Keynes, Knight does not propose formal criteria by which to adjudicate on the likeness of the instances (members of the reference class of trials relative to which statistical probabilities are determined) which are involved. He merely notes that successive throws of a fair die are 'alike' in a sense and degree that cannot be predicated on such things as different buildings exposed to fire hazard, and that the question of whether the instances in a particular case are 'like' enough to be treated as homogeneous trials is a matter for the individual to decide.

Both Keynes and Knight regard uncertainty as arising in situations in which it is not possible to determine *a priori* probabilities or where there are not enough 'like' instances to form a reference class relative to which numerically definite probabilities can be determined. It is possible to distinguish between two categories of 'Keynesian' uncertainty in terms of the framework outlined above. The first consists of cases in which it is possible to make qualitative comparisons of probability relations, comparisons which, in conjunction with certain specified rules, may then be used to derive further comparisons. The second category consists of cases in which it is not possible even to compare probability relations, perhaps because they are not comparable by $\geq^*$, or simply because they do not exist or are not known.

Knight describes the 'estimates' we make in situations of uncertainty as the product of our subconscious intuitions, although he allows that their formation may involve some sort and amount of analysis and synthesis. But he believes that judgments of probability are actually made in situations of uncertainty, and that these are sometimes even expressed by way of numbers in the interval [0, 1]. This has encouraged the view that Knightian 'estimates' may be likened to personal probabilities in the modern sense (Leroy and Singell, 1987), in which case Knightian 'uncertainty' would reduce to 'risk' in terms of the definitions proposed above. But Knight's estimates are in fact rather different from personal probabilities. In particular, he disagrees with what is now the orthodox personalist view 'that there is only one estimate, the subjective feeling of probability itself' (Knight, 1921: 227) and suggests that agents not only form the best estimate they can regarding the possible consequences of their actions, but also a second-order estimate of the probability that their first-order estimate is correct. His view appears to be that, although agents may well sometimes express their beliefs as numerical probabilities in situations of uncertainty, they generally do not have and, crucially, do not act 'as if' they have precise point probabilities at the back of their minds when making such statements.

This brings me to a further, non-probabilistic, measure Keynes introduces in the *Treatise*, of what he calls 'evidential weight'. The weight of evidence in respect of some conclusion is a measure of, in some sense, the amount or degree of completeness of the evidence bearing on it (Runde, 1990). The difference between evidential weight and probability is easily seen in the following example. The situation is one in which there are two urns, urn 1 known to contain 50 black balls and 50 white balls and urn 2 known to contain 100 balls, each of which may be either black or white. The problem is to determine the probability of drawing a white ball from the two urns, each taken in turn. Taken individually, in terms of Keynes' theory, there is no evidence in favour of a white ball being drawn from either urn that is not symmetrical with the evidence in favour of a black ball being drawn. He concludes that the probability of drawing white is 1/2 for both urns. However, there is a difference between the two cases, namely 'that the weight of the argument in favour of this conclusion is greater in the first case' (Keynes, 1973a: 82). Keynes suggests that, in using probability as a guide to conduct, and other things being equal, it is rational to prefer the probability with greater weight.

Again, Keynes regards the evidential weight of an argument as a magnitude that can only sometimes be compared with that of another, and is in fact quite hesitant about its importance in the *Treatise*. That said, the probability/weight distinction reappears and plays an important role in his later economic writings on investor confidence and liquidity preference (Runde, 1991, 1994). It is interesting that Knight (1921: 227–8) seems to be hinting at similar ideas in his distinction between the 'favourableness of' and 'confidence in' an opinion and his emphasis on the 'subjective feeling of confidence of the person making the prediction'. These issues re-emerge in Ellsberg's (1961) famous counterexamples to the personalist interpretation of probability associated with subjective expected utility theory. According to this theory, if an agent conforms to certain postulates of 'rational' choice, he may be regarded as if he assigns a unique probability function defined over all possible uncertain contingencies that will determine the consequences of his actions. Ellsberg offers some hypothetical experiments which suggest that differences in the amount of information regarding different choice situations may lead to behaviour that is inconsistent with these postulates. In the example presented above, for instance, most people profess indifference between betting on white or black in the case of either urn taken separately, implying $p(w_1) = p(b_1) = p(w_2) = p(b_2) = 1/2$. When asked whether they would prefer to bet on white from urn 1 or white from urn 2, however, they tend to prefer urn 1, implying $p(w_1) > p(w_2)$. This contradicts the previous choices and suggests that point probabilities may often not be an appropriate way to characterize partial beliefs (the links between Ellsberg and Keynes are discussed in Brady and Lee, 1989a; 1989b; Curley and Yates, 1989).

The discussion thus far has been restricted to uncertainty about or probabilities of possible outcomes that are sufficiently well defined for them to be the objects of partial belief. Shackle, in various writings, stresses the importance of uncertainty in the sense that possible choice outcomes might not even be conceived of at the time of decision (Shackle, 1961). Although they do not say much about uncertainty in this sense, this form of uncertainty is sometimes also attributed to Keynes or Knight. Shackle proposes a non-additive measure of *potential surprise* as an alternative to the standard probability measure in situations of uncertainty. Levi (1979) observes that the formal properties of this measure are the same as those of Cohen's (1977) measure of inductive probability, which is explicitly concerned with the dimension of appraisal Keynes calls 'the weight of evidence'.

Recent years have witnessed a growing number of attempts to capture ideas that could be described as Keynesian and Knightian in formal models. The notion of comparative (qualitative) probability has been extended by Fishburn (1986), for example, and 'ambiguous' probabilities, have been modelled by replacing point probabilities with convex sets of probabilities (Bewley, 1986; Levi, 1986) and by invoking subadditive probabilities (Gilboa, 1987; Schmeidler, 1989). Kelsey (1994) adapts Gilboa and Schmeidler's (1989) maxim expected utility model to elucidate Keynes' notion of evidential weight, and Fishburn (1993) offers an axiomatization of ambiguity. That said, the Savage (1954) conception of the rational agent, who chooses under risk according to the above criterion, continues to dominate modern economic theory. Heterodox schools of thought such as the Austrians (for example, O'Driscoll and Rizzo, 1985) and the Post Keynesians (for example, Davidson, 1991) have done most to emphasize the importance of uncertainty as opposed to risk, particularly with respect to investment and liquidity preference decisions. Many of these authors argue that taking uncertainty seriously has negative methodological implications for the formalist programme in economics, echoing Keynes' (1973b) remark that 'as soon as one is dealing with the influence of expectations and of transitory experience, one is, by the nature of things, outside of the realm of the formally exact'. Shackle (1972) provides a strong statement of this position from a subjectivist/idealist perspective, Lawson (1995) from the perspective of critical realism.

JOCHEN RUNDE

References

Bewley, T.F. (1986), 'Knightian Decision Theory: Part 1', *Cowles Foundation Discussion Paper*, no. 807.

Brady, M.E. and H.B. Lee (1989a), 'Dynamics of Choice Behaviour: The Logical Relation Between Linear Objective Probability and Nonlinear Subjective Probability', *Psychological Reports*, **64**, 91–7.

Brady, M.E. and H.B. Lee (1989b), 'Is there an Ellsberg–Fellner Paradox? A note on its Resolution', *Psychological Reports*, **64**, 1087–1090.

Cohen, L.J. (1977), *The Probable and the Provable*, Oxford: Clarendon Press.

Curley, S.P. and J.F. Yates (1989), 'An Empirical Evaluation of Descriptive Models of Ambiguity Reactions in Choice Situations', *Journal of Mathematical Psychology*, **33**, 397–427.

Davidson, P. (1991), 'Is Probability Theory Relevant for Uncertainty? A Post Keynesian Perspective', *Journal of Economic Perspectives*, **5**, 129–43.

Ellsberg, D. (1961), 'Risk, Ambiguity and the Savage Axioms', *Quarterly Journal of Economics*, **75**, 643–69.

de Finetti, B. (1964), 'Foresight: Its Logical Laws, Its Subjective Sources', translation of 'La prévision: ses lois logiques, ses sources subjectives', 1937), in H.E. Kyburg and H. Smokler (eds) *Studies in Subjective Probability*, New York: Wiley.

Fishburn, P.C. (1986), 'Interval Models for Comparative Probability on Finite Sets', *Journal of Mathematical Psychology*, **30**, 221–42.

Fishburn, P.C. (1993), 'The Axioms and Algebra of Ambiguity', *Theory and Decision*, **34**, 119–37.

Gilboa, I. (1987), 'Expected Utility with Purely Subjective Non-Additive Probabilities', *Journal of Mathematical Economics*, **16**, 65–88.

Gilboa, I. and D. Schmeidler (1989), 'Maxmin Expected Utility with a Non-Unique Prior', *Journal of Mathematical Economics*, **18**, 141–53.

Kelsey, D. (1994), 'Maxmin Expected Utility and Weight of Evidence', *Oxford Economic Papers*, **46**, 425–44.

Keynes, J.M. (1973a), *Treatise on Probability, The Collected Writings of John Maynard Keynes*, vol. VIII, London: Macmillan.

Keynes, J.M. (1973b), *The General Theory and After. Part II: Defence and Development. The Collected Writings of John Maynard Keynes*, vol. XIV, London: Macmillan.

Knight, F.H. (1921), *Risk, Uncertainty and Profit*, Chicago: Chicago University Press.

Lawson, T. (1995), 'Economics and Expectations', In S.C. Dow and J. Hillard (eds) *Keynes, Knowledge and Uncertainty*, Aldershot: Edward Elgar.

LeRoy, S.F. and L.D. Singell (1987), 'Knight on Risk and Uncertainty', *Journal of Political Economy*, **95**, 909–27.

Levi, I. (1979), 'Support and Surprise: L.J. Cohen's View of Inductive Probability', *British Journal for the Philosophy of Science*, **30**, 279–92.

Levi, I. (1986), *Hard Choices: Decision making under unresolved conflict*, Cambridge: Cambridge University Press.

O'Driscoll, G.P. and M.J. Rizzo (1985), *The Economics of Time and Ignorance*, Oxford: Basil Blackwell.

Ramsey, F.P. (1978), 'Truth and Probability', in D.H. Mellor (ed.), *Foundations: Essays in Philosophy, Logic, Mathematics and Economics*, London: Routledge & Kegan Paul.

Runde, J.H. (1990), 'Keynesian Uncertainty and the Weight of Arguments', *Economics and Philosophy*, **6**, 275–92.

Runde, J.H. (1991), 'Keynesian uncertainty and the instability of beliefs', *Review of Political Economy*, **3**, 125–45.

Runde, J.H. (1994), 'Keynesian Uncertainty and Liquidity Preference', *Cambridge Journal of Economics*, **18**, 129–44.

Runde, J.H. (1998), 'A note on Frank Knight's discussion of the meaning of risk and uncertainty', *Cambridge Journal of Economics* (forthcoming).

Savage, L.J. (1954), *The Foundations of Statistics*, New York: Wiley.

Schmeidler, D. (1989), 'Subjective Probability and Expected Utility Without Additivity', *Econometrica*, **57**, 571–87.

Shackle, G.L.S. (1961), *Decision, Order and Time in Human Affairs*, Cambridge: Cambridge University Press.

Shackle, G.L.S. (1972), *Epistemics and Economics: A critique of economic doctrines*, Cambridge: Cambridge University Press.

Utility

Introduction

Utility and concepts allied to it have been central in the development of neoclassical economics over the past 125 years and more. The utility-maximizing agent is the key building block and a shared characteristic of this set of theories. In an increasingly self-conscious and systematic way, during the three-quarters of a century preceding Samuelson's *Foundations of Economic Analysis* (1947), and then relentlessly ever since, individual utility maximization subject to a constraint has served as the unifying principle of neoclassical economics. Increasingly, this notion has been imported by other social sciences, especially sociology and political science, under the rubric of rational choice theory. However, over the past several decades at least, it has been becoming increasingly apparent that utility ideas have serious difficulties, in their application to economics and in general. While it is easier to understand the rise to dominance of utility ideas in economics, it may be more important at this time to reflect on the reasons for their probable decline.

Basic ideas and ascent

The concept of utility as a motivator of individual behaviour predates neoclassical economics (Hutchison, 1988). Nearly 350 years ago, Hobbes provided the foundational statement that the study of individual action should be patterned on the sciences, as 'voluntary motion' with motion towards an object being 'desire', and repulsion from it 'aversion'. All motives were reduced to this one single motion, in terms of which good and evil could then be defined: 'whatsoever is the object of any man's Appetite or Desire; that is it, which he for his part calleth Good: And the object of his Hate, and Aversion, Evill.' In addition, the basis for evaluating an action meant taking the sum of desire and aversion produced by it (Hobbes, 1991: ch. VI). Moreover, the individuals in question are 'as if but even now sprung out of the earth, and suddainly (*like* Mushromes) come to full maturity, without all kind of engagement to each other' (Hobbes, 1983: ch. VIII, 1). While particular issues such as the reference to good and evil have become transmuted, at least four features of these statements are notable and have far-reaching influence on utility theory. It is clear (1) that all reasons for action are reduced to a single scale; (2) that a tight link is made between individual welfare and choice; (3) that there is an aspiration in this conception to scientific status; and (4) that the agents in utility theory are isolated and have complete though unexplained preferences.

These features extend to Bentham's use of utility ideas, and with him become more closely associated with economics (Hutchison, 1956; Stark, 1952–4). For him, the utility is 'that principle which approves or disapproves of every action whatsoever, according to the tendency which it appears to have to augment or diminish the happiness of the party whose interest is in question' (Bentham, 1970, ch. 1, para. 2). Bentham was clear that utility was the only relevant criterion (ibid.: ch. 2, para. 14, note d). Perhaps what is most notable about Bentham's elaboration of utility ideas is his linking of the scientific aspiration mentioned in connection with Hobbes to the management of social life. In 'Pauper Management Improved', Bentham writes: 'Every circumstance by which the condition of an individual can be influenced, being remarked and inventoried, nothing … left to chance, caprice or unguided discretion, everything being surveyed and set down in dimension, number, weight, and measure …' (cited in Bahmueller, 1981: 83). This connection between utility ideas and their use in social evaluation and management is one of Bentham's lasting legacies. In Bentham's case it is made clear, in a way that has found no parallels since then, that a utility approach to social management entails a certain sort of political order; that is, in his case, it required a bureaucracy, schools, prisons, courts, voting reforms, a centralization of authority, and so on, to use the utility information about social states of affairs so as to improve upon them (Halevy, 1949).

In recent times, Benthamite pleasure and pain have been transformed into preference or want satisfaction and dissatisfaction. For most of the nineteenth century, social theorists meant by 'utility' usefulness, satisfaction or well-being; they thought that the utility of a person was measurable in the sense that weight or height is measurable (cardinal utility); and that utility could be compared across individuals, indeed added up to yield a measure of social well-being. At the end of the nineteenth century, and continuing into the twentieth century, the notion of utility changed in economic discourse. Now, a higher utility simply came to mean more preferred. Thus cardinal measurable utility was replaced by ordinal utility or, more simply, by a preference ranking. Interpersonal comparability was also denied by a number of authors, for instance by Jevons: 'Every mind is thus inscrutable to every other mind and no common denominator of feeling seems to be possible' (Jevons, 1970: 85). The links between preference and utility are well-established (see, for example, Varian, 1992: ch. 7) and no further attempt is made to distinguish them here.

Bentham's utility ideas provided the basis for the marginalists, Gossen, Jevons, Menger and Walras, three-quarters of a century later, to link utility firmly to economic analysis. While the marginalists focused on the use of marginal utility to underpin demand curves and the associated price theory, Robbins (1935: ch. 2) emphasized the aptness of the utility conception for framing what he asserted was any properly economic concept; that is, any problem involving limited means and unlimited but given wants. It is precisely this generality of application which has made the utility conception so fecund. From Robbins, it is a short step to Samuelson's *Foundations* and on down to this day. By now, every economist is familiar with the formulation of economic problems as individual utility maximization subject to constraint, along with the methodological injunction that this is the correct way to proceed. It is probably better to say (ignoring a small amount of methodological pluralism that exists within economics) that these notions *are* the modern economist's toolkit than it is to say that are *part* of that toolkit.

Yet the very popularity of utility ideas has been accompanied by a large number of nagging concerns and distinctions which by now threaten the basis of the validity of the concept itself. These are of two sorts. On the one hand, there are developments within economics itself which show that the utility ideas failed to give what was expected of them. In this sense, utility ideas have not been *sufficient* to establish the results of concern. On the other hand, there are developments stemming from methodological reflection within and without economics which suggest that utility notions themselves are deeply flawed. These latter developments indicate that utility ideas are not *necessary* to move forward in economics. If this reading of the status of utility ideas is correct, these problems – from the inside as well as from the outside, as it were – are what is making the continued and well-justified use of utility notions in economics so difficult. We now consider these issues in turn.

Utility and economics

Choice and welfare
An important distinction, though one which is not often made, in the use of utility in economics is that utility can motivate choice and it can also indicate the welfare of the agent making those choices (Sen, 1973). It is this dual aspect of utility which gives it its special importance. Choices made under constraints can then be interpreted as being the best possible for the agent concerned. Corresponding to these two motives, utility has played a two-sided role in neoclassical economics, with the two sides being closely tied together. As the motivator of choice, utility has served as the basis of demand theory. As an indicator of welfare, utility motivates welfare economics.

In both demand theory and in welfare theory, a further distinction separates individual and aggregate (social) realms of applicability. It is at the aggregate level that the negative results in both of these areas appear most strongly. It should be clear that while – as would be expected in a methodologically individualist discipline – the initial formulation of economic problems will necessarily begin at the individual level, nearly all of the applicability of the ideas developed will be sought at the aggregate level. So, on the demand side, clothing demand by a particular individual is rarely of interest as such, whereas the clothing demand in the aggregate is of interest. Similarly, to the extent that nearly any perturbation of the economic system will affect each individual differently, it is of interest to know what the overall or aggregate welfare effect happens to be.

Utility and demand

For a very long time it has been supposed that demand theory needs a basis in utility theory. Constrained maximization by agents results in choice, and the relation between such choice and relative prices (the demand curve or demand correspondence) can be obtained by varying prices. Indeed, the history of utility theory has often been portrayed (for example, Stigier, 1950; 1954) as a search for the appropriate way of coming up with such demand curves. One may ask two questions about such an approach: is utility theory necessary for demand theory; and is it sufficient?

To begin with the latter: demand curves have been derived for individual demands from a utility basis, and they obey certain regularity properties such as continuity, Walras' law and well-defined income and substitution effects (as is explained in textbooks such as Varian, 1992; Deaton and Muellbauer, 1980). In this sense, utility theory is *sufficient* for demand theory *at the level of individuals*. However, most applications of the theory – theoretical applications such as those for ascertaining uniqueness and stability, providing econometric identification and micro-foundations for macroeconomics, and so forth, as well as more practical applications, such as comparative static analyses of most policy matters – are carried out at the aggregate level, not at the individual level. Then it becomes crucially important to understand that utility theory does not possess the sufficiency property at the aggregate level. The results of Sonnenschein, Mantel and Debreu (called SMD theory) demonstrated that, save for Walras' law and continuity, the aggregate demands resulting from individual constrained maximization were arbitrary. That is, they were not further restricted by the individual-level assumptions on preferences, for instance. In particular, there were no well-defined income and substitution effects. Thus the utility hypothesis proved insufficient as a basis for aggregate demand theory. This has meant that no general progress beyond existence results could be made on the basis of individual utility maximization in the general equilibrium model on the uniqueness and stability of equilibrium, on comparative statics, on econometric identification and on the microfoundations of macroeconomics (Kirman, 1989; Rizvi, 1994). The usefulness of utility theory as a basis for demand analysis, then, is restricted to the individual level.

The *necessity* of utility theory for demand analysis is also doubtful. Not only have there been systematic accounts of the relation between quantity demanded and prices as empirical phenomena (as in the mercantilists Davenant, Law and King) even before the elaboration of utility ideas, but well-behaved aggregate demand curves, as theoretical constructs, can be derived with very little or no utility structure at the individual level. For instance, Becker (1962) was able to show an example in which aggregate demand was well-behaved although agents chose randomly (albeit uniformly – which is why this is only an example) within the budget plane. Becker's model can be seen as a special case of a general approach in which distributional assumptions at the aggregate level (such as increasing dispersion of preferences, or increasingly diverse demand at higher income levels) provide the regularity at the aggregate level (Grandmont, 1992; Hildenbrand, 1994). Perhaps the most striking result of this sort is Grandmont's demonstration that aggregate demand is well-behaved, given certain distributional restrictions, even if individual behaviour merely satisfies budget constraints (that is, has no utility background at all). The distribution-based approach itself can be seen as growing out of a probabilistic approach to social phenomena common at the turn of the nineteenth century, but forgotten in economics as the individual-based utility maximization school took hold, although it has been referred to from time to time (Rizvi, 1994) and has now been revived by Hildebrand, Grandmont and the European school (Rizvi, 1996).

In assessing the contributions of these authors who play down or eschew the role of utility in demand analysis, it is important to remember the traditional link that has heretofore been maintained between the choice and welfare aspects of utility. So, while a few writers simply assumed well-behaved demand held at the individual level and was not derived from utility maximization (for example, in Cassel, 1924), these approaches found no resonance in neoclassical economics and were not further developed, most likely because they severed the link between choice and welfare which is such a defining aspect of neoclassical economics. For, if demands are not derived from utility maximization, it is difficult to say anything about the welfare aspects, conceived in terms of utility, of the resulting outcomes in the economy. In other words, to proceed this way leaves welfare theory hanging in the air. A large part of the acceptability of the distributional approach to aggregate demand will rest, then, on the acceptability of its cutting demand analysis loose from utility and related notions of welfare. Let us therefore now turn to the links between utility and welfare as they have been traditionally sought in economics.

Social welfare
In Bentham's formulation of utility, the link between utility at the individual level and the utility of the society was made simply. Utilities were the excess of pleasures over pains for each individual, and utilities were added up across individuals to get an overall welfare measure. Yet this is not a measure or approach to social welfare that has persisted in economics. Around the turn of the nineteenth century, cardinal utility was replaced by ordinal utility. There are several reasons for this. The first is that, as the marginalist economists showed, ordinal utility was sufficient to derive well-behaved demand functions at the individual level. In this sense, and to the extent that individual demand analysis was your goal, supposing the cardinality of utility was superfluous: it could be done without. This left the issue of social welfare without basis, though, since it was not at all clear how to aggregate ordinal utilities (this issue is addressed below).

Another reason for the impetus towards ordinal utility was that cardinal utility had an unwelcome implication for some influential practitioners of economics. It was quickly realized that cardinal utility functions which were identical across individuals, together with the reasonable idea of the diminishing marginal utility of income, implied that an equal distribution of income maximized social welfare (the sum of individual utilities). This line of thinking culminated in Pigou (1932), in which one of the two main welfare propositions was just this argument that optimality is consistent with equality. In opposition to this, Robbins denied the interpersonal comparability of utility. When Robbins discusses interpersonal comparability (1935: ch. 6), he makes it clear that he is motivated by the application of diminishing marginal utility and identity of utility across individuals to the political ideas of equality (ibid.: 136–7). He faults, among others, Edgeworth and Cannan for 'justify[ing] the ways of economists to the Fabian Socialists' (ibid.: 136).

With ordinal utility not being comparable across individuals, the Benthamite adding-up approach to welfare is not conceivable. Indeed, at the time ordinal utility was coming to the fore, its promulgators did not pursue a measure of welfare at the aggregate level. Instead, Pareto efficiency emerged. A situation is Pareto-efficient if no one can be made better off without making someone else worse off. This concept serves as the basis for the two welfare theorems of general equilibrium theory which assert that competitive equilibria are Pareto-efficient and that each Pareto-efficient allocation could be achieved as a competitive equilibrium for some reallocation of initial endowments (Koopmans, 1957). In such careful, though not surprising, elaborations, it is never claimed that competitive equilibria somehow lead to an overall optimal state. This is precisely what cannot be done without an overall welfare measure such as Bentham's, or such as those which Arrow (1951) established could not be counted on to exist (this is discussed below). Nevertheless, until the present day (and beginning with the marginalists themselves: Jevons, 1965: 134; Walras, 1954: 125, 255) it is often claimed that neoclassical economics provides an 'invisible hand' result, showing market outcomes to be optimal. Wicksell commented aptly of these claims that 'with such a definition [as Pareto efficiency] it is almost self-evident that this so-called maximum obtains under free competition ... But this is not to say that the result of production and exchange will be satisfactory from a social point of view or will, even approximately, produce the greatest social advantage', so that, in his view, 'Pareto's doctrine contributes nothing' (Wicksell, 1934: 82–63).

Because of the change from cardinal to ordinal utility, together with the accompanying emphasis on non-comparability of utility, a gap was left concerning an overall measure of welfare. Pareto efficiency did not address this issue. Was there any analogy between well-behaved individual ordinal utility functions and something like that at the aggregate level? That is, did social welfare functions exist for the dual purposes of assessing current states of affairs and as guides to action? This sort of aggregation of preferences is clearly important to the analysis of such politco-economic issues as voting procedures and equity, but also to straightforwardly economic issues such as national and international gains from trade. The answer to this question is very definitely discouraging. This construct cannot be counted on to exist, save in extremely special situations. This is the content of the modern version of social choice theory, initiated by Arrow (1951). He showed that no aggregation procedure, of which majority voting is just one example, could simultaneously satisfy some fairly innocuous conditions of reasonableness and also be counted on to exist. Recent attempts to get around Arrow's theorem have not been successful (Sen, 1995).

One issue regarding overall social welfare functions has not been made explicit in the literature. One might ask, as did Bentham, what is this concept for and what institutional structure does its use imply? In his case, the concept assessed the prevailing state of affairs and was the basis for correct action on behalf of the polity. With social welfare functions, the relation between this dual role or evaluation and action, on the one hand, and the political structure required to use this information on the other, has become obscured. That is, while social welfare functions were desired and sought, it never was made explicit what they were desired for. Nevertheless, one might imagine a centralized decision authority (or, as Sen and Williams, 1982: 3, put it, a sovereign decision centre) which might make use of this information. In this way, the quest for social welfare functions suggests a particular conception of political life. In addition, once we go beyond Bentham and deny identical and cardinal utility, even assuming (against Arrow's theorem) that an overall social welfare measure exists, how could the information it employed (each individual preference ranking in the society) ever be located and aggregated appropriately and, again, by what institutions? This has not been addressed.

We can conclude that, while utility approaches to economics have had limited success at the individual level, they have met with disastrous results in aggregate economics, which is where positive results are most naturally desired. In both the fields of choice and in welfare, robust impossibility results (SMD theory and Arrow's theorem) block the way to further meaningful elaborations. As may be conjectured, Arrow's impossibility result, since it concerns aggregation and because utilities are related to individual demands, bears kinship to the SMD results on the arbitrariness of aggregate excess demand (Saari, 1992). A striking weakness of the utility approach, then, has been its inability to address macro-level or societal issues on the basis of an aggregation from individual behaviour.

Utility in general

Givenness of preferences
Utility (or preference) serves as the basis for welfare measurement. For it to be useful in this regard it is necessary for it to be invariable with respect to the things which it is being used to assess. The effect of advertising on preferences is a well-known species (Galbraith, 1958) in a large genus of exceptions to this requirement. Another is the observation that the growth of the market in traditional societies alters preferences in favour of market goods and against traditional pursuits (Hefner, 1983). In general, it is hard to reconcile a notion of endogenous preference formation or genesis of wants with the requirement that utilities measure welfare (Gintis, 1974). For these and related reasons, users of utility theory have often tried to avoid any discussion of preference formation by declaring it non-economic – not within the purview of the field (Friedman, 1962) – or by exhibiting a strong commitment simply to ruling out of court all appeals to changing preferences (Stigler and Becker, 1977). A problem with these reactions is that they so clearly avoid an obvious issue: where did preferences come from and how do they change? Yet the dilemma is unavoidable and deep-rooted, going all the way back to Hobbes' rational agents as 'mushrooms'.

Now this might be seen as a technical issue alone, but a number of authors have argued, in modern times beginning with Frankfurt (1971), that choosing among different systems of preferences (having second-order or metapreferences) is a characteristic of people. As they decide what sort of life to live, they are engaged in choosing among different sorts of preferences: searching for values, if you will (Sen, 1977; Hirschman, 1985). If there is truth in this characterization, and much philosophical literature argues for it (Macintyre, 1981; Taylor, 1989; Hurley, 1989), then preference change is fundamental to our being human agents, and is not only a technical matter impinging on the correct formulation of a welfare standard.

Utility analysis of social phenomena
Utility analysis conceives of individual agents as autonomous, as is made clear in Hobbes' statement quoted at the beginning of this entry. Thus addressing any social phenomena in this framework amounts to seeing them as arising through a confluence of individual interests and desires, most recently under the rubric of game theory. Harsanyi (1968) states this attitude towards social phenomena as the argument 'that social norms should not be used as basic explanatory variables in analyzing social behavior, but rather should themselves be explained in terms of people's individual objectives and interests' (Harsanyi, 1968: 321). It can be argued that this

view impoverishes our conception of social phenomena, since there is nothing which is irreducibly social. Another criticism that is often made is that a consequence of seeing all social institutions as arising as a result of their desiredness by individual agents is an impetus towards seeing them as being reflexively good (see Field, 1979; Mirowski, 1981).

Other philosophical criticisms
Utility has come under other significant criticism in philosophical discussion. Sen and Williams (1982) summarize a number of these objections. One of the problems that critics of utility themselves face is that utilitarianism's basic idea, that it is good to bring about what is wanted, seems at first sight so plausible. Yet this *prima facie* plausibility has been countered by in-depth objections. Thus the critics do not fault utility ideas as a whole, but merely object to their exclusive use. At the same time, some critics (such as Hampshire, 1982; Taylor, 1982) do not feel that an alternative with the same scope and ambition as utility theory is needed in the human sciences.

First, while individual rationality is choosing the right thing to do, this does not require using a *single* criterion, in this case utility, to make decisions. Instead, a number of values can contribute, and these may, in part, be incommensurable in terms of a single scale. Utility forces all interests, desires and goals to be on the same level, and commensurable in terms of utility, a process which has been called 'levelling' or 'reduction' (Taylor, 1989: ch. 1; Sen and Williams, 1982). Second, since utility requires conversion of all values into a single scale, it constitutes a narrow view of people. An individual is where desire and desire fulfilment (or pain and pleasure) take place, and no more. Such a view seems to neglect personal integrity and autonomy (Williams, in Smart and Williams, 1973). This is illustrated in Pareto's remark that the 'individual can disappear provided that he leaves us with a photograph of his tastes' (1971: 120). Third, utility conceptions assume welfarism (Sen, 1979) and consequentialism (Anscombe, 1958). Welfarism means valuing situations according to the welfare, satisfaction or utility they give. So while utility may be affected by a person's social attachments or intentions, for instance, these are not, in the utility approach, to be valued in themselves. Fourth, welfarism thus implies an identity between what is chosen and what is valued, and this has led many people to doubt that there is even a difference between these two things (as is noted by Scitovsky, 1976). Why would an agent not choose the best possible alternative available? One answer depends on a variety of secondary issues, which are relatively easily incorporated into the framework: the agent has insufficient information, or cannot calculate the best choice with available resources, and so forth. Other answers give more basic objections, such as weakness of will or multiple criteria of evaluation (see Elster, 1979; 1986). In addition, things may be desirable even if no one values them, or values them very little. This can arise from the fact that what is valued generally depends on experience, and so judgments given a particular realization of histories of experience imply no universal judgment. For instance, Scitovsky has pointed out that judgment concerning the consumption of culture may be biased negatively, since the appreciation of culture depends on the acquisition of consumption skills, which are partly based on the earlier consumption of culture (Scitovsky, 1976: 224–47, 273–8). And Kynch and Sen (1983) have discussed extensive evidence indicating choices made by some Indian women during famines which show a preference for their husbands and sons to the point that the survival of the women was in question. These two very different examples show that choice and welfare (or valuation) need not be identified as being different sides of the same coin. Finally, as concerns cardinal versions of the theory, things may be valuable since they give satisfaction, yet their value may not be measured by the amount of satisfaction they give. Fifth, consequentialism entails the idea that a correct action is one chosen on the basis of the situation arising from its consequences. Objections to this view have been much explored in philosophical discussion. Some actions may be seen as valuable or not, regardless of their consequences. We could value certain rights (Nozick, 1974), opportunities (Rawls, 1982) or capabilities (Sen, 1985) more highly than consequences, for example. Sixth, utilitarian ideas in particular seem to conflict with rights. If people decide about things in which others are also involved, and this tramples on the rights of others, then doing what gives greatest satisfaction is inconsistent with notions of liberalism. Sen (1970) explores this in the context of a conflict between right-based decisions and Pareto optimality. If, to avoid this situation, we 'edit' preferences to exclude those which impinge on others' rights, there is, at a minimum, the problem of a lack of correspondence between the edited version and actual behaviour.

Conclusion
Utility ideas in economics are pervasive, in theories of choice and of welfare, at the individual level and at the aggregate level. Their popularity has been promoted by the portability and simplicity of the basic idea of utility maximization subject to constraint. Yet the pervasiveness of utility-based modelling in economics and other social sciences is accompanied by basic foundational problems with the approach itself. First, there are deep results within economics showing that progress using utility ideas cannot be made along desirable lines. Second, these ideas are weighed down by heavy methodological objections. Thus there is a significant disjunction between the use of utility ideas and their justifications.

S. ABU TURAB RIZVI

References
Anscombe, G. Elizabeth M. (1958), 'Modern moral philosophy', *Philosophy*, **33**, 1–19.
Arrow, Kenneth J. (1951), *Social Choice and Individual Values*, New York: John Wiley.
Bahmueller, Charles F. (1981), *The National Charity Company: Jeremy Bentham's Silent Revolution*, Berkeley: University of California Press.
Bentham, Jeremy (1970), *An Introduction to the Principles of Morals and Legislation*, London: Athlone; originally published 1789.
Cassel, Gustav (1924), *The Theory of Social Economy*, London: T.F. Unwin.
Deaton, Angus and John Muellbauer (1980), *Economics and Consumer Behaviour*, Cambridge: Cambridge University Press.
Elster, Jon (1979), *Ulysses and the Sirens: Studies in Rationality and Irrationality*, Cambridge: Cambridge University Press.
Elster, Jon (ed.) (1986), *The Multiple Self*, Cambridge: Cambridge University Press.
Field, Alexander (1979), 'On the explanation of rules using rational choice models', *Journal of Economic Issues*, **13**.
Frankfurt, H. (1971), 'Freedom of the will and the concept of a person', *Journal of Philosophy*, **68**, 5–20.
Friedman, Milton (1962), *Price Theory A Provisional Text*, Chicago: Aldine.
Galbraith, John K. (1958), *The Affluent Society*, Boston: Houghton-Mifflin.
Gintis, Herbert (1974), 'Welfare criteria with endogenous preferences: the economics of education', *International Economic Review*, **15**, 415–30.
Grandmont, Jean-Michel (1992), 'Transformations of the commodity space, behavioral heterogeneity and the aggregation problem', *Journal of Economic Theory*, **57**, 1–35.
Halevy, Elie (1949), *The Growth of Philosophical Radicalism*, London: Faber & Faber; originally published 1928.
Hampshire, Stuart (1982), 'Morality and convention', in A.K. Sen and B. Williams (eds), *Utilitarianism and Beyond*.
Harsanyi, John C. (1968), 'Individualistic and Functionalistic Explanations in the Light of Game Theory: The Example of Social Status', in Imre Lakatos and Alan Musgrave (eds), *Problems in the Philosophy of Science*, Amsterdam: North-Holland.
Hefner, R.W. (1983), 'The problem of preference: economics and ritual change in Highland Java', *Man*, **17**, 323–41.
Hildenbrand, Werner (1994), *Market Demand*, Princeton: Princeton University Press.
Hirschman, Albert O. (1985), 'Against parsimony: three easy ways of complicating economic discourse', *Economics and Philosophy*, **1**, 7–25.

Hobbes, Thomas (1983), *De Cive*, Oxford: Clarendon; originally published (in Latin) 1642.

Hobbes, Thomas (1991), *Leviathan*, Cambridge: Cambridge University Press; originally published 1651.

Hurley, Susan L. (1989), *Natural Reasons: Personality and Polity*, Oxford: Oxford University Press.

Hutchison, Terence W. (1956), 'Bentham as an economist', *Economic Journal*.

Hutchison, Terence W. (1988), *Before Adam Smith: the Emergence of Political Economy, 1662–1776*, New York: Blackwell.

Jevons, W.S. (1970), *The Theory of Political Economy*, Harmondsworth: Penguin; first published 1871.

Kirman, Alan (1989), 'The intrinsic limits of modern economic theory: the emperor has no clothes', *Economic Journal*, **99**, 126–39.

Koopmans, Tjalling (1957), *Three Essays on the State of Economic Science*, New York: McGraw-Hill.

Kynch, Jocelyn and Amartya K. Sen (1983), 'Indian women: well-being and survival', *Cambridge Journal of Economics*, **7**, 363–80.

Macintyre, Alasdair C. (1981), *After Virtue: A Study in Moral Theory*, Notre Dame: University of Notre Dame Press.

Mirowski, Philip (1981), 'Is there a mathematical neoinstitutional economics?', *Journal of Economic Issues*, **15**, 593–613.

Pigou, Arthur C. (1932), *The Economics of Welfare*, 4th edn, London: Macmillan.

Rawls, John (1982), 'Social unity and primary goods', in A.K. Sen and B. Williams (eds), *Utilitarianism and Beyond*.

Rizvi, S. Abu Turab (1994), 'The microfoundations project in general equilibrium theory', *Cambridge Journal of Economics*, **18**, 357–77.

Rizvi, S. Abu Turab (1996), 'Arbitrariness and its consequences in contemporary economics', in John Davis (ed.), *History of Political Economy*, special issue: New economics and its writing, forthcoming.

Robbins, Lionel (1935), *An Essay on the Nature and Significance of Economic Science*. 2nd edn, London: Macmillan.

Saari, Donald J. (1992), 'The aggregate excess demand function and other aggregation procedures', *Journal of Economic Theory*, **2**, (3), July, 359–88.

Samuelson, Paul A. (1947), *Foundations of Economic Analysis*, Cambridge, MA: Harvard University Press.

Scitovsky, Tibor (1976), 'The joyless economy: an inquiry into human satisfaction and consumer dissatisfaction', New York: Oxford University Press.

Sen, Amartya K. (1970), 'The impossibility of a Paretian liberal', *Journal of Political Economy*, **78**, 152–7.

Sen, Amartya K. (1973), 'Behaviour and the concept of preference', *Economica*, **40**, 241–59.

Sen, Amartya K. (1977), 'Rational fools: a critique of the behavioural foundations of economic theory', *Philosophy and Public Affairs*, **6**, 317–44.

Sen, Amartya K. (1979), 'Utililtarianism and welfarism', *Journal of Philosophy*.

Sen, Amartya K. (1985), *Commodities and Capabilities*, Amsterdam: North-Holland.

Sen, Amartya K. (1995), 'How to judge voting schemes', *Journal of Economic Perspectives*, **9**, 91–8.

Sen, Amartya K. and Bernard Williams (eds) (1982), *Utilitarianism and Beyond*, Cambridge: Cambridge University Press.

Smart, John J.C. and Bernard Williams (1973), *Utilitarianism. For and Against*, Cambridge: Cambridge University Press.

Stark, W. (1952–4), *Jeremy Bentham's Economic Writings*, 3 vols, London: Allen & Unwin.

Stigler, George J. (1950), 'The Development of Utility Theory. I and II', *Journal of Political Economy*.

Stigler, George J. (1954), 'The Early History of Empirical Studies of Consumer Behavior', *Journal of Political Economy*, **62**, 95–113.

Stigler, George J., and Gary S. Becker (1977), 'De Gustibus non est Disputandum', *American Economic Review*, **67**.

Taylor, Charles (1982), 'The diversity of goods', in A.K. Sen and B. Williams (eds), *Utilitarianism and Beyond*.

Taylor, Charles (1989), *Sources of the Self: The Making of Modern Identity*, Cambridge: Cambridge University Press.

Varian, Hal R. (1992), *Microeconomic Analysis*, 3rd edn, New York: W.W. Norton.

Walras, Léon (1954), *Elements of Pure Economics: or The Theory of Social Wealth*, trans. William Jaffe, Homewood, IL: Richard D. Irwin; originally published 1874.

Wicksell, Knut (1934–5), *Lectures on Political Economy*. vol 1, *General Theory*, trans. Ernest Classen, New York: Macmillan

Williams, Bernard (1973), 'A critique of utilitarianism', in J.J.C. Smart and B. Williams, (eds), *Utilitarianism, For and Against*.

Van Fraassen, Bas

Bas van Fraassen, born 1941 and currently at Princeton University, is a central figure in modern philosophy of science. His major works include *An Introduction to the Philosophy of Time and Space* (1970), *The Scientific Image* (1980) and *Laws and Symmetry* (1989). However, it was with the publication of *The Scientific Image* that he launched his unique philosophy of science, called constructive empiricism. At that time, the power of logical positivism was in utter disarray and scientific realism was emerging as the dominant influence. While constructive empiricism fully accepted the scientific realist devastating attack on positivism, especially on its dualistic approach to the language of science and on its emphasis on a syntactical rather than a semantical approach to scientific models, it explicitly opposed the then emerging hegemony of scientific realism.

Many economists share with scientific realists the view that the primary aim of any scientific theory is to furnish the correct explanation of the scientific facts. Van Fraassen, however, emphatically rejects this view. Re-echoing Hanson, Hesse, Quine and numerous other modern philosophers of science, constructive empiricism maintains that all scientific description is theory-laden. A primary function of scientific theory is to furnish scientists with a sufficiently sophisticated language which enables them to describe the world as accurately as possible. Van Fraassen shifts the theoretical focus away from scientific explanation and onto scientific description. Theoretical or pure science is centrally concerned with describing the world and this has nothing to do with the quest for explanation.

Unlike the earlier positivists, however, constructive empiricism develops a pragmatic account of scientific explanation, which is explicitly opposed to that of scientific realism. In the spirit of the later Wittgenstein, constructive empiricism draws our attention to the vast varieties of explanations on offer, such as those of common sense, theology, superstition and science. What makes an explanation scientific, rather than, say, theological, is that one is using scientific, rather than theological, parameters in constructing one's explanation. In general, scientific explanations are answers to 'why' questions posed in specific contexts. In these specific contexts, certain contrasts are either implicitly assumed or explicitly stated. For instance, consider the question, why did the Irish unemployment figures reach 20 per cent in 1993? This question, when taken in context, takes on different meanings depending on the contrasts assumed. Given these different contrasts, different explanations, all acceptable, will be furnished. The explanation as to why this Irish unemployment figure was attained in 1993, rather than in 1983, will differ from the explanation as to why the Irish, rather than the Belgian, unemployment rate reached 20 per cent. Furthermore, according to van Fraassen, scientific explanation is even more complex for reasons which go beyond the role of assumed or explicitly stated contrasts. The contextualization of scientific explanation also entails that different scientific experts, political, historical, anthropological, geographical, economical and so forth, can each furnish different explanations for the Irish unemployment figures. They each appeal to their own specific domains of expertise in choosing their salient or relevant explanatory factors. This in turn adds to the multiplicity of acceptable scientific explanations. In this fashion, constructive empiricism severs the scientific realist links between theory and explanation. By focusing on the contextualization of scientific explanation, the latter is relocated in applied, rather than pure, science. When this constructive empiricist approach to explanation is applied to the philosophy of economics, van Fraassen is clearly opposed to contemporary realist account of economics, on the one hand, and the Popperian account, on the other.

Like numerous realists, van Fraassen accepts that any sentence in a scientific theory is either true or false and that it is true or false in virtue of the real world. Scientific realists, especially those influenced by the early Putnam, go further. These hold that any sentence of a mature scientific theory can be known to be true or approximately true. Van Fraassen, however, unequivocally refuses to take this final step. According to constructive empiricism, pure science is concerned with the construction of theories which are empirically adequate, that is, theories which furnish the truth about observable events and entities. By shifting the epistemic focus onto empirical adequacy, van Fraassen is drawing our attention to the empiricist position that scientific knowledge is limited to what is in principle observable, and thereby attempting to hold some middle ground between instrumentalism and scientific realism. This notion of empirical adequacy is central to constructive empiricism. It imposes a significant constraint on what portion of a mature theory can be accepted as true. Science needs theory to construct accurate descriptions of the observable world. To this end, it constructs theoretical models. These models, as well as furnishing descriptions of the observable world, will in all probability also postulate entities which are unobservable in principle. Any such model is epistemically acceptable on condition that it furnishes accurate descriptions of the observable world: the constructive empiricist suspends judgment on anything said about the unobservable in principle. This in turn precludes the use of any realist notion of explanatory power of a theory in terms of unobservable-in-principle entities generatively causing the observable events of the world. Scientific knowledge is limited to what is in principle observable. Thus van Fraassen shifts the methodological focus onto the construction of theory-laden models and the scientific quest for empirical adequacy.

Van Fraassen's constructive empiricism is acknowledged by Hesse, Hooker and others as the most sophisticated empiricist response to the numerous developments in the course of the philosophy of science over the last half-century. Largely, however, its sphere of influence has remained within the boundaries of the philosophy of the physical sciences. Since the early 1990s, some attempts have been made to apply constructive empiricism to the philosophy/methodology of economics. This application severs the various links between economic theory and economic explanation. Moreover, it takes the debate beyond the parameters set by recent rhetorical or postmodern approaches. In particular, contrary to McCloskey, it insists on significant distinctions between economic models and metaphors. Furthermore, it shifts the focus of pure economics onto the construction of empirically adequate theories. In this connection, Kaldor's critique of neoclassical economics is interpreted as demonstrating the empirical inadequacy of that theory.

PASCHAL F. O'GORMAN
THOMAS A. BOYLAN

Bibliography

Boylan, T.A. and P.F. O'Gorman (1991), 'Economic Theory and Explanation: A Constructive Empiricist Perspective', *Methodus*, **3**, 53–7.

Boylan, T.A. and P.F. O'Gorman (1991), 'The Critique of Equilibrium Theory in Economic Methodology: A Constructive Empiricist Perspective', *International Studies in the Philosophy of Science*, **5**, 3131–42.

Boylan, T.A. and P.F. O'Gorman (1992), 'Constructive Empiricism: A Reconstruction of Economic Methodology', *The Journal of Interdisciplinary Economics*, **4**, 145–60.

Boylan, T.A. and P.F. O'Gorman (1995), *Beyond Rhetoric and Realism in Economics: Towards a Reformation of Methodology*, London: Routledge.

Churchland, P.M. and C.A. Hooker (eds) (1985), *Images of Science*, Chicago: University of Chicago Press.

Lagueux, M. (1994), 'Friedman's "Instrumentalism" and Constructive Empiricism in Economics', *Theory and Decision*, **37**, 147–74.

van Fraassen, Bas (1970), *An Introduction to the Philosophy of Time and Space*, New York: Random House.

van Fraassen, Bas (1980), *The Scientific Image*, Oxford: Clarendon Press.

van Fraassen, Bas (1989), *Laws and Symmetry*, Oxford: Clarendon Press.

Veblen, Thorstein

Background, contributions and influences
Thorstein Veblen, the founder of American institutional economics, was born to Norwegian immigrants in 1857. The family settled in Minnesota, not far from Carleton College, where Veblen studied under J.B. Clark. He attended lectures by C.S. Peirce at Johns Hopkins but took his PhD in philosophy at Yale in 1884. Veblen returned to economics at Cornell in 1891, whence he accompanied J.L. Laughlin to the new University of Chicago in 1892; there he taught and edited the *Journal of Political Economy*. He also taught at Stanford, the University of Missouri and the New School for Social Research. Veblen died in 1929, leaving 10 books, among them the best-selling *Theory of the Leisure Class* (1899), *The Theory of Business Enterprise* (1904), *The Instinct of Workmanship* (1914), *The Place of Science in Modern Civilization* (1919) and *Absentee Ownership* (1923).

Veblen's iconoclasm made his academic tenure perpetually insecure, but he had many prominent students (including W.C. Mitchell) and was the best-known American economist of his day. In 1925, 225 leading economists asked for his appointment as president of the American Economics Association (he declined). Institutional economics, by then led by Mitchell, R.G. Tugwell and J.R. Commons, remained highly influential in the United States for a generation after Veblen's death and was central to the economic programmes of the New Deal.

In his economic theories, Veblen emphasized cultural habit and belief ('institutions') in economic behaviour, arguing that private property, status emulation and invidious distinctions supported the dominance of pecuniary manipulation and waste over industry and serviceability in market processes. Veblen produced a major pre-Keynesian account of the role of finance in business cycles and is unique among founders of schools of economic thought for his feminism. The main influences on Veblen include early anthropology, the evolutionism of Darwin and Spencer (whom he subverted) and American pragmatism. Socialists, including Marx and Bellamy, were also important.

Core methodological precepts and philosophy
Much of Veblen's methodological argument appears in *The Place of Science in Modern Civilization* (1919). The core precepts are anthropological and evolutionary. Economic interests and activities are viewed as aspects of, and only 'vaguely isolable' from, the larger web of cultural processes that make up individual lives and integrate social relations and events. Evolutionism signifies substantive cumulative change, historical open-endedness and the absence of a 'meliorative trend' in actual cultural conditions. The combined result recommends theories of endogenous cumulative cultural causation in which meanings, actions, their environment and outcomes are viewed as phases of cultural life that must be explained 'in terms of the process itself'. Social order is the precondition for and is reconstructed by the purposeful action of individuals. No significant causes are exogenous (except perhaps biology; see below), no outcomes constitute consummations, no trans-historical 'definitive normality' governs social orders, nor are individuals atomistic.

Veblen's rejection of 'animistic' natural law and rational individualism is expressed in his first publication (1884), where he found segregation of rational free will from natural determinism unable to justify human action. To be purposeful, human action must introduce non-deterministic, discretionary elements into material causation while 'adapted induction' – Peircean abduction, or the creative inference of order among diverse events – guided action.

Animism and teleology, the improper inferences that nature conformed to human purpose and intellectual powers, arose with abductive orderings despite the total uselessness of 'ultimate purposes' in everyday life. Veblen, following Darwin, displaced purpose from nature onto human thought and action in an open-ended universe. Following Peirce, he saw knowledge as the fallible, partial and provisional product of culturally conditioned inquiry.

Veblen highlighted the role of self-referential and self-reflexive interpretation within social processes, including social inquiry (Samuels, 1990). The 'fabric of institutions' tended to yield interpretations that conferred, reproduced and justified social privilege as the putative result of largely mythical contributions to social well-being. Such invidious institutional bias was more pronounced, however, in the more speculative and abstract regions of 'higher theoretical knowledge', such as orthodox economics, theology and literary studies. In the more mundane regions of 'work-day efficiency', a more 'matter-of-fact' apprehension of cause-and-effect relationships was enforced by greater proximity to 'material exigencies'. Thus Veblen based prospects for improved knowledge on the habits of thought fostered by the 'machine process', which he hoped would reduce the influence of status and myth in social thought.

The 'Veblenian dichotomy' differentiates social explanations and values based on impersonal cause-and-effect relationships ('efficacy') from attributions linked to personal status ('invidious distinction'). Veblen saw virtually all human powers as grounded in cultural resources and knowledge, and consequently viewed differential assessments of personal worth as the privileging of elite vantage points and the discounting of less exalted but often more matter-of-fact knowledge. Parochial misconceptions could be exposed, however, by studying actual causal sequences and by the reinterpretations involved in both social evolution and anthropological study. Veblen's *Theory of the Leisure Class* is notable as a semiotic reinterpretation of the cultural reproduction of invidious distinctions. His remarkable and exotic phraseology is itself a semiotic device used to dislodge conventional interpretations, making cherished beliefs and behavioural norms appear strange. The caveat concluding many of his most striking redescriptions, that he intended no disparagement, was at least half-serious. Veblen sought accurate, matter-of-fact accounts of actual social practices; set in new light, however, they could hardly be viewed as complacently as before.

Veblen emphasized the biological basis of social life as a rejection of mind–body dualisms, but refuted Spencer on biology in social evolution and behaviour. Biology was 'remote', largely exogenous; the 'proximate' causes of human behaviour lay in socially developed knowledge that grounded, expanded and channelled human capacities and potential. Veblen made no analogy between biological and cultural evolutionary mechanisms and criticized Marshall's focus on 'normal' selection mechanisms as 'Spencerian'.

Assessments

Veblen's emphasis on endogenous, cumulative cultural causation has little in common with current economic orthodoxy. Institutional complexity, by which a change in any portion of social arrangements necessarily implies some rearrangement of all other processes and systemic social meanings, belies the adequacy of equilibrium-based mathematical formalism and individualistic foundations in social analysis. Nor are institutionalized habits simply (or singular, isolable) routines, rules, structures or bounds within otherwise orthodox rationality, as often depicted in the 'new institutional economics' of Herbert Simons, Oliver Williamson or Richard Nelson and Sidney Winter.

Veblen's hopes that the matter-of-fact habits of thought of the engineers might assist the redirection of industry away from profit and emulatory display towards less invidious social ends have been labelled 'scientistic' (Mirowski, 1987). Mary Douglas (Douglas and Isherwood, 1981) has also criticized Veblen's accounts of conspicuous consumption as neglecting the almost universal social marking functions of cultural consumption patterns and the integrative role of social hierarchies. These criticisms may indicate inconsistencies in Veblen's use of the concept of culture in so far as he sometimes implied that culturally external standards for knowledge or equity were available. Veblen was aware that his own views bore the inescapable imprint of his historical milieu, however, and saw the extent of invidious distinction as an internal standard for social progress and a fulcrum for criticism within evolving processes of social inquiry. He challenged both the abstractions of Marshallian equilibrium theory and what he viewed as the atheoretical descriptive narratives of the German Historical School for lacking any such standard. They were thus useless to human foresight and met current change with teleological self-congratulation. Veblen's critical reinterpretations were, by contrast, intended to afford some purchase on cultural expansions of real human potential within processes of social change.

Other, perhaps more famous, criticisms of Veblen were offered by Theodor Adorno and Herbert Marcuse of the Frankfurt School. Adorno (1941) focused on Veblen's pragmatism as methodologically conservative, the captive of 'mere facts' and further saw Veblen as a disenchanted utopian 'adaptationist' whose critiques of 'high culture' amounted to anti-cultural, 'primitivist' aesthetic luddism. Adorno also viewed the combination of pragmatism with Darwinism as insufficiently cognizant of both dialectics and 'the law of value.' Veblen was not a primitivist, however; his criticisms of refined aesthetics and leisurely speculations concerned their exclusivity and derogation of less exalted perspectives in society. The stronger elements of Adorno's strictures have been better stated by Douglas and Mirowski.

Marcuse's (1941) criticisms of Veblen, centring on distinctions between technological and critical rationality, are more adequate. Marcuse applauded Veblen's recognition that the machine process imbued workers with the former, but noted that a uniformitarian debasement of critical powers also resulted. Technological egalitarianism had promoted social atomism and the subordination of human reason to centralized control of mechanical processes, particularly in the case of Nazi Germany. Marcuse's assessment of technological rationality can also be extended to the work of one of Veblen's followers, C.E. Ayres, who elevated Veblen's 'technological process' to the engine of social progress.

ANN L. JENNINGS

Bibliography

Adorno, Theodor (1941), 'Veblen's Attack on Culture,' *Studies in Philosophy and Social Science*, **9**, 389–413.

Douglas, Mary and Baron Isherwood (1981), *The World of Goods*, New York: Basic Books.

Dowd, Douglas (ed.) (1958), *Thorstein Veblen: A Critical Reappraisal*, Ithaca: Cornell University Press.

Jennings, Ann and William Waller (1994), 'Evolutionary Economics and Cultural Hermeneutics', *Journal of Economic Issues*, **28**, 997–1030.

Marcuse, Herbert (1941), 'Some Social Implications of Modern Technology', *Studies in Philosophy and Social Science*, **9**, 414–39.

Mirowski, Philip (1987), 'The Philosophical Basis of Institutional Economics', *Journal of Economic Issues*, **21**, 1001–38.

Samuels, Warren (1990), 'The Self-Referentiability of Thorstein Veblen's Theory of the Preconceptions of Economic Science', *Journal of Economic Issues*, **24**, 695–718.

Simich, J.L. and Rick Tilman (1980), 'Critical Theory and Institutional Economics: Frankfurt's Encounter with Veblen', *Journal of Economic Issues*, **14**, 631–48.

Veblen, Thorstein (1884), 'Kant's Critique of Judgment', reprinted in *Essays in Our Changing Order*, New York: Viking Press, 1934.

Veblen, Thorstein (1899), *The Theory of the Leisure Class*, New York: Macmillan.
Veblen, Thorstein (1904), *The Theory of Business Enterprise*, New York: Charles Scribner.
Veblen, Thorstein (1914), *The Instinct of Workmanship*, New York: Macmillan.
Veblen, Thorstein (1919), *The Place of Science in Modern Civilization*, New York: B.W. Huebsch.
Veblen, Thorstein (1923), *Absentee Ownership*, New York: B.W. Huebsch.

Verstehen

A well-established, originally German, tradition of thinking insists that social science needs to achieve not just *Erklaeren* or explanation but also *Verstehen* or understanding. The idea is that it is not enough for social science to find laws under which to make explanatory sense of the way people individually or collectively behave. It is also necessary for social science to facilitate the sort of understanding of people that we achieve in ordinary life when we come to have an empathetic sense of how others are feeling and reacting.

The *Verstehen* tradition has been very influential in sociology, particularly as a result of the influence of Max Weber, but it has also made an important impact in historical and anthropological circles. The point of view associated with the tradition offers an important challenge to ways of thinking that are well established in economics, though it has not been given much attention in the mainline literature. What it suggests is that the rational sort of explanation which predominates in economics may not be as powerful a method of understanding as is generally supposed.

Rational explanation of the broadly economic sort tries to make intentional sense of a person's attitudes and actions, representing their beliefs and desires as rational states of mind and representing their actions as the rational products of such states. We may postulate various obstacles to rationality in the course of offering such explanations, but the point of the exercise is generally to present the individual as a more or less rational subject: as a subject who, within the constraints of the obstacles postulated – and they can be quite severe – displays a rational pattern of attitude formation and decision making (Cherniak, 1986).

One of the best known regimentations and idealizations of rational explanation is given by the apparatus of Bayesian decision theory. According to such decision theory, there is a pattern in a rational person's responses which allows us to assign a probability function, which determines degrees of belief, and a utility function, which determines degrees of desire, and to see everything they do, and indeed every revision of probability they undergo, as rational in terms of those functions. The utility function gives a utility figure to every prospect and the probability function offers us suitably corresponding measures of probability: different versions of Bayesian theory introduce different measures (Eells, 1982). We find that, in every thing the person does, they maximize expected utility: the utility of the option chosen, computed as the sum of the utilities of its probabilistically weighted possible outcomes, is always greater than the utility of any alternative.

If we were able to make decision-theoretic sense of people in this way, we would surely have good explanations of their responses. We would be able to subsume those responses under regularities that count as ideals for a rational subject. We would be able to see each of the responses as being produced by the state of the agent's utility and probability functions and we would be able to see the sort of production involved as a process required in any suitably rational agent.

How might we fail to achieve *Verslehen* or understanding in the event – in truth, the unlikely event – of being able to give an idealized decision-theoretic account of a person's behaviour? There are different answers given in the hermeneutic approach that emphasizes *Verstehen*, each of them focusing on what is allegedly a different shortfall. A common version argues that such a high-powered, rational explanation can still fail to deliver understanding, because it may not be infused with any sense of empathy or fellow-feeling for the subject whose behaviour is explained. But the most persuasive version argues that the Bayesian explanation can fail to deliver understanding, because it may not make it possible to hold a conversation with the subject in question; it may not deliver the possibility of dialogical or interpersonal understanding.

When people hold conversations with one another, one of the things they each do is to raise questions about what explains and justifies the other's beliefs and choices. You say something with which I disagree and straightaway I go into interrogative mode. How can you say that? What possible reason is there for thinking that such and such? Or you do something, or announce the intention of doing something, that I find objectionable or think is stupid from your point of view and immediately I begin to challenge you. Can you really think that you are justified in taking such a step? How can you believe that such a course of action would be in your interests? When I challenge you in this way, I assume that, whatever the sources of your beliefs and desires, you are capable of recognizing and responding to considerations of evidence and valuation. You are not the sort of creature who will be unaffected by considerations to the effect that the brunt of the evidence supports such and such, or that such and such and so and so are inconsistent claims. You are not the sort of creature who will be unmoved by the thought that this or that action would be cruel or unjust or dishonest or that it would jeopardize your future interests. If I did think you would be unaffected or unmoved by such considerations then I would avoid wasting my time talking to you (Pettit and Smith, 1996).

The striking thing about many rational explanations, even the powerful Bayesian one mentioned, is that they need not give us any conversational or dialogical sense of the person whose behaviour is in question. That explanation represents the agent as rational, in an intuitive and highly precise sense of the term, but it does not represent the agent as ratiocinative: it does not represent them as a person who can recognize and respond to reasons of the sort illustrated. To be rational is to form beliefs and desires in such a way that a certain end pattern is satisfied: for example, the choices of the agent maximize expected utility. To be ratiocinative is to form beliefs and desires according to a certain process of reasoning or in a way that is open to the effects of such reasoning.

The fact that the Bayesian explanation does not give a sense of the agent as a reasoning or ratiocinative subject shows up in the fact that it is consistent with the complete absence of reasoning (Pettit, 1991). Consistently with displaying the patterns that sustain decision-theoretic explanations, Bayesian subjects might be just automata. They might enjoy such a superb design that, exposed to appropriate evidence, they revise their degrees of belief in the rational way and, presented with any range of options, they form degrees of desire, and choose according to strength of desire, in the rational way. They might never have to think about the import of the new evidence put before them, weighing its significance in a balance with more familiar facts. And they might never have to deliberate about the options which they face, trying to determine their relative attractions and trying to establish which is the most desirable.

Their decisions about what to do and their revisions of belief might materialize without any consciousness or surveillance on their part.

Suppose, then, that the agent in question does indeed reason and is indeed fitted for conversation; the agent is not an unconscious, autonomic paragon of rationality but a creature like one of us. Being consistent with the complete absence of reasoning, decision-theoretic explanation is silent on how things present themselves within the forum of that agent's attention. The explanation of a change of belief or a choice of action does not suggest, on any plausible reading, that the agent thinks explicitly in terms of their own probabilities and utilities; it is not clear how an agent would even know what these are, given the detail involved (Herman, 1986: ch. 9). And the explanation leaves it entirely dark as to how the agent reasons otherwise.

Suppose the agent passes from the full belief that if p, then q, and the partial belief that p to the partial belief that q. They cannot think: if p then q, p, therefore q; that mode of reasoning does not register the partiality of their beliefs that p and that q. So how do they think? With some notion of probability perhaps? Or with some quite different set of concepts under which what they register is not probability but something like degree of cultural acceptability or degree of authoritative endorsement? For all that the Bayesian explanation tells us, we have no idea.

Or suppose an agent has a degree of belief that there are such and such options relevant in a given choice, has certain degrees of belief that link those options with possible outcomes and has certain degrees of desire for the possible outcomes; and suppose that these rationally lead to a preference for one option: the agent forms a higher degree of desire for this option than for any others. How is the person supposed to have thought and deliberated about the choice that eventuates? Starting from a certain degree of desire that p, for example, they cannot think: p, therefore …; that mode of reasoning does not register the fact that the agent desires that p rather than believing that p. So how do they think? With some notion of attractiveness, where a prospect is attractive to degree x just in case it is desired to degree x? Or with a less subjective notion of desirability? Or in some more specific terms still: in terms that refer to modes of desirability such as kindness and justice and friendliness and the like? For all that Bayesian explanation tells us, we are left entirely in the dark.

Consider a case where an agent walks up to a beggar by the roadside and puts some money in his cap. The decision-theoretic mode of explanation would direct us to the agent's utilities for the different possible outcomes – probabilistically weighted – of that option and would present the option as superior in such terms to the alternatives. But it would not give us any idea as to how the agent is thinking; indeed, as we have seen, it would be compatible with the complete absence of thought. Everyday interpretation would score over the decision-theoretic story in this regard. It might say, for example, that the agent took pity on the beggar and gave him the first coin that came to hand; or that the agent was following the principle of always giving beggars a certain amount; or that the agent conceived it to be his duty to help a beggar a day and this was the lucky one; and so on. But in any case, it would draw attention to the sorts of things that imposed themselves, more or less consciously, on the agent's attention. It would give us a conversational *entrée* to his cast of mind.

Such interpretation invokes psychological states that produce the responses explained, as decision-theoretic explanation does. But it also lets us see the structure of the subject's thought, as we might put it. The human subject is no longer an arena within which degrees of belief and desire rationally come and go and rationally congeal, as occasion requires, in the formation of decisions; the human subject is no longer a black, rational box. By contrast with what rational, Bayesian explanation provides, this interpretation offers us an image of the subject as a ratiocinative, conversational animal. It gives us what is reasonably described as understanding, or *Verstehen*.

PHILIP PETTIT

Bibliography

Cherniak, Christopher (1986), *Minimal Rationality*, Cambridge, MA: MIT Press
Eells, Ellery (1982), *Rational Decision and Causality*, Cambridge: Cambridge University Press
Harman, Gilbert (1986), *Change in View*, Cambridge, MA: MIT Press.
Pettit, Philip (1991), 'Decision Theory and Folk Psychology', in Michael Bacharach and Susan Hurley (eds), *Foundations of Decision Theory*, Oxford: Blackwell.
Pettit, Philip (1993), *The Common Mind: An Essay on Psychology. Society and Politics*, New York: Oxford University Press.
Pettit, Philip and Michael Smith (1996), 'Freedom in Belief and Desire', *Journal of Philosophy*, **93**, 429–49.

Von Mises, Ludwig

Introduction

Ludwig von Mises views on economic theory, public policy and methodology invoke strong reaction. On the methodological front, he was often dismissed as the product of the pre-positive Neanderthal age. Paul Samuelson stated, 'I tremble for the reputation of my subject' when he read the 'exaggerated claims that used to be made in economics for the power of deduction and *a priori* reasoning' (1964: 736). More recently, Mark Blaug has regarded Mises' methodological writings as so 'cranky and idiosyncratic that we can only wonder they have been taken seriously by anyone' (1980: 93). On the other hand, F.A. Hayek argued forcefully that Mises was generally misunderstood with regard to economic theory, public policy and methodology, and this misunderstanding was a result of the fact that, with regard to the consistent development of the marginalist/subjectivist revolution, Mises ran ahead of his contemporaries (Hayek, 1952: 52, fn. 7).

No doubt, aspects of Mises' writings can be seriously questioned in the light of subsequent developments in economic theory and the philosophy of science, but it is important to get an accurate picture of what his system was before criticizing or revising it. Mises was working within a continental philosophical context, and the German language debates of the late nineteenth and early twentieth centuries concerning the epistemological status of the social sciences remained his point of reference throughout his long career. In fact, Mises was a post-positivist before positivism was in vogue within the economics profession. A re-examination of many of his positions with regard to methodology reveal a surprising complementarity with many arguments made by post-positivist philosophers. Many of the dismissals of Mises, for example those attributed to Samuelson and Blaug above, were the product of positivistic pretensions and must now be re-examined in light of the developments within the philosophy of science. In a strange way, Mises' methodological writings – while a product of an earlier age – were evaluated too early, at a time when a naive faith in the power of the positivistic conception of scientific knowledge was dominant in the social sciences. Contemporary scholars can return with benefit to Mises' writings from the point of view of the post-positivist philosophy of science and critically assess his writings anew.

Mises on methodology
Mises methodological writings can be found in four books, *Epistemological Problems of Economics* (1933), *Human Action* (1949), *Theory and History* (1957) and *The Ultimate Foundations of Economic Science* (1962), and a host of articles which are derivative of these book-length treatments. There is evidence that Mises considered *Theory and History* to be the most satisfactory statement of his position with regard to the social sciences, but probably his *Epistemological Problems of Economics* is the most academically sophisticated treatment of the subject. There is, however, no substantive difference in the basic argument that is put forward in these books. Mises' position can be divided into four propositions concerning the nature of the human sciences: methodological dualism, methodological individualism, apriorism and value-freedom. The common thread that holds these four propositions together is Mises' commitment to the subjectivism/marginalist (with the emphasis on subjectivism) research project in the human sciences.

Methodological dualism
Against the dominant trend of his time for the human sciences to imitate the experimental methodology of the natural science, Mises argued that the human sciences were separate and distinct. Whereas in the physical world the object of study consisted of the 'simple' phenomena of constant relationships, the human sciences studied 'complex' phenomena where there were no constant relationships. Moreover, whereas in the physical sciences causal relationships were difficult to establish, the human sciences could establish relationships of cause and effect. In essence, Mises argued, we know the final cause in human events – the purposes and plans. The task of economic theory was to elucidate genetic–causal explanations of market phenomena. The desires and beliefs of market participants initiate a process the outcome of which is the effect realized in the market (see Cowan, 1994)

   The immediate implication of Mises' argument that the model of the natural sciences was not applicable to the study of human actors would appear to be the denial of the ability of the social scientist to generate universal laws or principles in the realm of the complex phenomena of human society. Many of Mises' intellectual allies in the argument over scientific monism, such as Wilhelm Dilthey, adopted this position. The cultural sciences were distinct from physical sciences and the project of covering laws. Max Weber, the major influence on Mises besides the economics teachings of classical economics (Carl Menger and Eugen Böhm Bawerk), accepted the cultural science view and devised his ideal-type methodology for interpretative sociology in an attempt to provide a bridge between theory and history. Weber, though, denied the universalistic status of a covering law to his ideal-types. But Mises resisted this argument, and sought to demonstrate that, while the physical and culture sciences were distinct, the cultural sciences were capable of producing laws that possessed the same epistemological status as the laws of physics. Mises (with Menger) rejected historicism, yet with Dilthey, Wilhelm Windelband, Heinrich Rickert and Weber he also rejected monism. It is in this unique philosophical–social scientific context that Mises should be understood. He was part of the neo-Kantian movement, but was also influenced by the birth of phenomenology in the works of Edmund Husserl and the philosophical writings of Henri Bergson (see Ebeling, 1995). These continental philosophical developments, all of which denied that the study of the human realm could be dealt with by using the methods developed to explore the physical world, were enlisted by Mises in his defence of the theoretical sciences of human action. There was, these writers contended, something fundamentally different about the human realm that required different philosophical justification and different methods of procedure for critical appraisal.

Methodological individualism

The acceptance of the subject/marginalist project – and the denial of the positivist project for objective knowledge in the human sciences – meant that the task of the social sciences was distinct from the natural sciences. If the goal of the sciences of human action was to generate causal explanations of social interaction, the methods of analysis must be appropriate to the task. Mises did not deny the existence of collective entities, but rather sought the appropriate methods of enquiry which could render intelligible the being and becoming of collective entities in terms of the purposes and plans of individuals (see Mises, 1949: 42).

Mises argued that methodological individualism was the appropriate mode of analysis for the task at hand – intelligibility and meaning – because it was only at the level of the individual that the social observer could attribute meaning to social actions. Only individuals possess purposes and plans and act by arranging the means available to them to obtain the ends sought. It is individuals and their actions that give meaning to social institutions and thus render their import to human action intelligible.

Mises' methodological individualism, however, is not the atomistic individualism criticized as reductionist by many social theorists and philosophers. Man, in Mises' system of thought, is a socially constituted being. Neither isolated man nor some fiction of *homo oeconomicus* animates Mises' theory of human action. In fact, he explicitly denies both of these theoretical constructs. It is the social animal, born into an already existing intersubjective life-world and socially constituted by this world, that is the subject of enquiry for Mises. 'Economics,' Mises stated, deals with the real actions of real men. Its theorems refer neither to ideal nor to perfect men, neither to the phantom of a fabulous economic man (homo oeconomicus) nor to the statistical notion of an average man (homme moyen). Man with all his weaknesses and limitations, every man as he lives and acts, is the subject matter of catallactics' (1949: 651).

Apriorism

The most controversial of Mises' positions was his strict insistence on the *aprioristic* nature of theoretical knowledge in economics. However, his position should be less objectionable in wake of the post-positivistic critiques of Michael Polanyi and Thomas Kuhn. But for a proper assessment, the *a priori* proposition offered by Mises must be divided up into separate claims about knowledge in the sciences of human action. These claims can be put as follows: (a) that sound deductions from *a priori* axioms are apodictically true; (b) that all important facts are theory-laden in the social world: and (c) that theory cannot be empirically tested (as understood in the positivist tradition), but rather is to 'tested' through an examination of the logic of the theory and its *applicability* to historical situations. Most commentators on Mises only deal with (a) and a misreading of (c), and dismiss him from a positivistic perspective, but they do not deal with the arguments implied in (b) and a sophisticated reading of (c) which are quite consistent with themes in the post-positivistic philosophy of science literature.

Mises argued, with regard to (a), that the category of action was part of the structure of the human mind following Kant. Apodictic certainty did not mean scientific infallibilism (Mises is clear in his rejection of infallibilism: see (Mises 1949: 7, 68)), but rather philosophical 'sureness' in his logical deductions. If an argument begins with an *a priori* true statement, and the logical steps of the argument are sound, then the conclusions will be apodictically certain.

The theorist, however, could err in his deductions. In addition, the empirical subsidary assumptions that are employed in economic reasoning (such as the disutility of labour) could be factually incorrect, and thus conclusions drawn from a logically sound deduction would be false. In both instances, the theory would fail on its own terms.

Moreover, Mises – contrary to most interpretations – did not see his insistence on the *aprioristic* nature of economic reasoning as new to him but instead the method by which economic theorizing had always proceeded: 'We do not maintain that the theoretical science of human action should be aprioristic, but that it is and always has been so' (1949, 40). In other words, Mises was stressing that it was not philosophy coming from the outside of the discipline that was prescribing apriorism, but rather reflection on the history of the discipline and its methods and procedures (an argument which D.N. McCloskey would surely find refreshing). Nassau Senior, Destutt Tracy, J.B. Say, John Cairnes, Carl Menger, Lionel Robbins, Frank Knight and many others were apriorists of some sort or another. Economic theorems, these writers contended, were derived from 'self-evident' axioms. Reflection on common-sense behaviour, combined with the logical deductions that were implied, yielded (often counter-intuitive) propositions concerning human interaction in the market. That is the way economic theory had been done by classical and neoclassical economists for a hundred years or more. Positivism, on the other hand, was the attempt to import a philosophical doctrine derived from reflection on the nature of knowledge in another discipline into the knowledge acquisition process in the sciences of human action.

Thus to reject Mises' position was to reject the work that was produced by classical economists and neoclassical economists concerning the operation of market phenomena (including many basic theorems, such as the law of comparative costs, as they were traditionally derived). Samuelson, in the quotation given above, does in fact feel comfortable with that rejection, and so did many of the methodologists of the time, especially T.W Hutchison. If economics was truly to become a science, these authors contended, it must make a formalist (Samuelson) and positivist (Hutchison) turn. But their version of modernist epostemology has been seriously questioned recently by philosophers and many different heterodox groups within the economics profession.

Nevertheless, Mises is on questionable grounds with his extreme aprioristic stance, and especially the claims to apodictic certainty in his work in theoretical economics. It is not the claim that if a syllogism is valid and the premises are true then the conclusion will be true that bothers scholars. That basic claim is an accepted part of logic. But what is objected to is the claim by Mises that (a) he had discovered *a priori* true axioms, (b) these were the only possible *a priori* true axioms, (c) he had satisfactorily established that he had made no mistakes in his verbal logic, and (d) the fact that there was no empirical 'test' of his assertions was unproblematic (see Caldwell, 1984).

With regard to both the theory-laden claim and the issue of testing, Mises was on better ground and would find many supporters in the contemporary literature. The theory-laden claim, simply put, is a challenge to notions of pure inductionist view of knowledge. As Mises pointed out, in a fashion similar to arguments one hears from the German philosopher Hans-Georg Gadamer, historicism and empiricism 'were able to believe that facts can be understood without any theory only because they failed to recognize a theory is already contained in the very linguistic terms involved in every act of thought. To apply language, with its words and concepts to anything is at the same time to approach it with a theory' (1933: 28). The choice is never between theory or no theory, but one between articulated and defended theory or inarticulated and non-defended theory.

The theory-laden nature of the 'facts of the social sciences', to Mises, implied that we should strive to articulate our theory and defend it in a clear and logical fashion. But this did not mean that theory was immune from criticism or could not be 'tested'; nor did it deny the fundamental importance of empirical work for an understanding of the social world. In fact, in Mises' system, the entire purpose of theory was to aid the act of historical interpretation. He divided the realms of knowledge – conception (theory) and understanding (history) – due to the separate epistemological issues involved in both endeavours. But it is clear in his writings that historical understanding was the vital goal for which the theoretical construct of economics was to be employed. Theory was the servant of empirical work.

The 'test' of any theory, however, was not to be found in an appeal to facts. Facts, as such, were always theory-impregnated and thus could not serve as an unambiguous arbiter. That does not imply that theories cannot be subjected to rigorous intersubjective assessment. Refutation of any theory is an exercise in logic and scholarship. A theory which has been demonstrated to be logically flawed, that reveals ignorance of some fundamental facts and about the empirical magnitude of events can be rejected as either false or not applicable to the problem at hand.

Mises' point about the impossibility of unambiguous tests of a theory was not as philosophically astute as the Duhem–Quine thesis (which stated that the truth or falsity of a theoretical statement cannot be determined independently of a network of statements). Rather, Mises' position was a philosophical development of the argument for the necessity of theory in the social science – the pragmatic value of which Austrian economists had argued for against historicism for a generation before Mises took up the task of philosophical justification. However, the Mises and Duhem–Quine positions possess the same implication for the idea of the 'testability' of theoretical propositions in scientific work. Mises' methodological dualism, however, implied that positivism was the correct methodology for the natural sciences. The Duhem–Quine thesis challenges, as does the post-positivist philosophy of science literature in general, the strict applicability of positivism even in the most natural of natural sciences. In other words, it turns out that many of the objections Mises raised concerning the application of positivist standards of scientific knowledge in the social sciences are just as relevant to the natural sciences. Once the philosophical difficulties of the testing of scientific theories are recognized, Mises' methodological position no longer possesses the 'cranky and idiosyncratic' character that a positivist age attributed to his writings on the subject.

One final point that should be made clear is that Mises' endorsement of apriorism and deductive exercises did not give licence to any deductive enterprise. If that were the case, the Arrow–Hahn–Debreu world of competitive equilibrium would have to be recognized as one of the great achievements of economic theory. The point of Mises' system is that the procedure does not begin with an arbitrary choice of axioms, but rather with reflection on the essence of human action. An economic theorem, Mises argued, not connected to the foundation of real human purposes and plans (that is, intentionality) would be nothing more than a free-floating abstraction unconnected to the world we live in and thus irrelevant except as a mental exercise. The point of economics, to Mises, was to illuminate the real world with the aid of economic theorizing. Apriorism, as Mises understood the doctrine (in a somewhat ironic twist), ensured that economic theory was grounded in reality rather than an arbitrary set of theorems floating in mid-air.

Value-freedom

Precisely because of the complexity of issues involved in the sciences of human action and the epistemological problems with 'objectivity' in historical scholarship, Mises insisted on the strict value-freedom of the theoretical propositions of economics (see the discussion in Kirzner, 1994). This is another example of Mises offering an argument quite different from that of contemporaries who stressed value-freedom. Mises was a non-positivistic 'positive' economists. His argument, as we have seen, was not that the procedure of testing determined whether a statement was scientific or not. It was that scientific objectivity was a consequence of the radical subjectivism of ends in theoretical economics.

Economic theory could establish parameters on the utopias of public policy advocates: the economist could reveal the policy advocates' conceit, not by challenging the ends sought, but by examining the efficiency of the means chosen to obtain those ends. The ends of the policy advocate were taken as given, and the logic of economic analysis (especially opportunity cost reasoning) was to be employed to assess critically the choice of means. Economics thus provides a value-free tool for critical appraisal. Policy advocacy, Mises warned, was different and required the judgment of the citizen (the introduction of values).

Mises' strict adherence to classical liberalism is often taken as an inconsistency in his system. He was an outspoken opponent of most, if not all, political interventions in the market process, yet he was also an outspoken proponent of value-freedom. But this position is not internally inconsistent when closely examined because it focuses on the suitability of means and not at all on the ideological ends sought (though it may, like all arguments of its kind, be subject to the external critique of objectivity in science that is found often in the contemporary literature on the philosophy of science).

Conclusion

Mises' methodological writings demand reconsideration in the wake of subsequent developments in the philosophy of science, and can no longer be dismissed as mere relics of some unenlightened pre-positivist age. Furthermore, Mises' methodological writings can best be understood within the context of the philosophical and intellectual tradition within which he worked – the continental philosophies of neo-Kantianism, the phenomenology of the early Husserl, and the arguments for a distinct cultural science associated with Dilthey. In sifting the analytical contributions of the Austrian School of Economics through this philosophical blend, Mises developed a bold and enduring humanistic project for the study of man that invites our critical attention.

PETER J. BOETTKE

Acknowledgment

I would like to thank Mario Rizzo, Israel Kirzner, Bruce Caldwell, William Butos and the editors for comments on an earlier draft. The usual caveat applies.

References

Blaug, M. (1980), *The Methodology of Economics*, New York: Cambridge.
Boettke, P. (ed.) (1994) *The Elgar Companion to Austrian Economics, Aldershot*: Edward Elgar.
Caldwell, B. (1984), 'Praxeology and Its Critics: An Appraisal', *History of Political Economy*, **16**, (3).
Cowan, R. (1994), 'Causation and Generic Causation in Economics', in P. Boettke (ed.), *The Elgar Companion*.
Ebeling, R. (1995), 'Austrian Subjectivism and Phenomenological Foundations', in P. Boettke and M. Rizzo (eds), *Advances in Austrian Economics*, Vol. 2.
Hayek, F.A. (1979), *The Counter-Revolution of Science*, Indianapolis: Liberty Classics; first published 1952.

Kirzner, I. (1994), 'Value-Freedom', in P. Boettke (ed.), *The Elgar Companion*.
Mises, L. (1966), *Human Action*, Chicago: Henry Regnery; first published 1949.
Mises, L. (1979), *The Ultimate Foundations of Economic Science*, Kansas City: Sheed Andrews & McMeel; first published 1962.
Mises, L. (1981), The *Epistemological Problems of Economics*, New York: New York University Press; first published 1933.
Mises, L. (1984), *Theory and History*, Auburn, AL: Ludwig von Mises Institute; first published 1957.
Samuelson, P. (1964), *Economics*, 6th edition, New York: McGraw-Hill.

Walras, Léon

Leon Walras (1834–1910) was born in Evreux in France, and christened Marie Esprit Léon (see Walras, 1965a). After completing his education at the lycée level, he became in turn a writer, a journalist, a railway employee, and, in 1865, a managing director of a cooperative association bank. Subsequently, he contributed articles to the journal *Le Travail*, gave lectures on social economics and worked for another bank. He participated in a congress on taxation in Lausanne which led in 1870 to his being appointed professor of economics at the Academy (subsequently University) of Lausanne in Switzerland, where he remained until his retirement in 1892.

He published his most important writings in three volumes: the *Eleménts d'économie politique pure* (1874, 1877, 1889, 1896a, 1900, 1926, 1988), a book on economic theory; the *Etudes d'économie politique appliquée* (1898), a collection of essays on money, monopolies, credit, banking, the securities exchange and methodology; and the *Etudes d'économie sociale* (1896b), a collection of essays on normative economics, including notably his thoughts on taxation, property and ideal economic institutions. Walras was unable to obtain a university position in France, primarily because of his lack of formal credentials, but also because of opposition to his mathematization of economics and his policy views. Nevertheless, at the end of his life he was honoured by a jubilee at which many of France's leading economists congratulated him on his disinterested efforts to strengthen the scientific foundations of economics. He was the founder of the modern theory of general economic equilibrium, and methodology and methodological innovations in economic modelling were two of his deep and abiding interests. Indeed, the theory of general equilibrium that he developed is itself a method of analysis, an approach to the investigation of economic phenomena, a way of organizing economic facts and a method of tracing their interrelationships.

Influences

Léon Walras was influenced by a number of philosophical writers. He admired René Descartes's analytical approach and regarded mathematical economics as being in the same class of scientific achievements as his geometry (Walras, 1876: 367). Hugo Grotius' and Samuel von Pufendorf's conceptions of natural law strongly influenced Walras's father, Antoine Auguste Walras, a junior high school administrator and teacher, who was deeply interested in economics and whose philosophical outlook was accepted totally by Léon. Auguste's ideas on natural law influenced Léon to believe that there is an underlying economic order and that there are inherently true principles of economic justice that spring necessarily from the nature of things and of economic interrelationships. Etienne Vacherot (1809–97), who believed in the reconcilability of metaphysics and science and who argued that experiences are a synthesis of objective and subjective elements, was responsible for Walras' metaphysical ideas (Walras, 1898: 459–61) and also inspired his philosophy of the unjustness of taxation. Victor Cousin (1792–1867) transmitted Immanuel Kant's ideas to Walras, taught him that policies should be founded on a scientific basis, and disposed him to favour the doctrine of conciliation of socioeconomic interests.

Walras did not cultivate purely philosophical fields such as logic, epistemology or metaphysics. He was primarily interested in economics, in social doctrines with economic implications and in the classification of studies in the natural and social sciences, and most particularly in economics (Walras, 1874: 3–44; 1926: 3–40; 1988: 25–66). He drew many of his economic and methodological ideas from other economists, including his father. It was Auguste Walras who persuaded Léon to study economics, suggested that it should be a mathematical discipline, and generated Léon's interest in utility and scarcity. Auguste also convinced Léon that the state should own all land because it is not produced as the result of the activity of any economic agent and because its value is given to it by the growth of population and the economy. Léon Walras studied the mathematics of Isaac Newton and J.L. Lagrange (Walras, 1965a: 1) and was strongly influenced by the mathematical economics of A.-A. Cournot (Walras, 1965b, vol. 1: letters 253, 293). Walras also learned from John Stuart Mill and Jean-Baptiste Say. A.N. Isnard anticipated some aspects of Walras' model of exchange and probably provided him with some ideas on that topic. Louis Poinsot, in his *Eleménts de statique* (1803), developed a model of general equilibrium of the phenomena in a physical system which Walras declared was a powerful source of inspiration for his theory of general economic equilibrium (Walras, 1965b, vol. 3, letter 1483).

Classification of scientific studies

Walras believed that 'the right and the duty of the economist is, before all and with care, to construct the philosophy of science' (Walras, 1874: 10; 1926: 10; 1988: 32). All scientific disciplines, according to him, are concerned with pure science, which establishes facts and relationships. One branch of it is pure natural science, which establishes 'the facts and relationships having their origin in the play of the inevitable forces of nature' (Walras, 1879: 246). It results from the application of mathematics to such fields as physics, chemistry and vegetal and animal physiology (Walras, 1898: 452). The other is pure moral science, which observes 'the facts and relationships having their source in the exercise of the free will of men' and 'includes the history of human activity in all its forms' (Walras, 1879: 246). It results from the application of cœnonics, the theory of social behaviour, to psychology, history, sociology, geography, statistics (Walras, 1898: 266, 452), languages, literatures, religions, art, science, industry, morals, law, war and politics (Walras, 1879: 246).

All disciplines are also concerned with applied science, which prescribes rules of conduct. One branch of it is applied natural science, which furnishes 'rules for the conduct of persons with respect to impersonal things' (ibid.). In this 'rational and experimental' (Walras, 1898: 453) branch of study, what ought to be is considered from the viewpoint of expediency, usefulness and material well-being (ibid.: 452–3). Examples are agricultural technology, industrial technology and medicine (Walras, 1879: 246). The other branch is applied moral science, or applied ethics (Walras, 1898: 452–3), which furnishes rules 'for the conduct of persons with respect to each other' (Walras, 1879: 246). In this 'exclusively rational' (Walras, 1898: 453) branch of study, what ought to be is considered from the viewpoint of equity and justice in relation to the phenomena that result from the exercise of human will (Walras, 1874: 16–17; 1926: 16–17; 1988: 38–9). Examples are individual and social ethics (Walras, 1879: 246). Finally, Walras identified 'industry', the actual practice in the economy of the principles and rules of applied natural science, as distinct from the study of them, and 'mores', the actual practice of the principles and rules of applied moral science, namely the functioning of the institutions of property, the family, and government (Walras, 1898: 453, 458).

Classification of economic studies

Walras viewed economic studies as a special case of science in general, by which he meant that economics is like all scientific disciplines in being partitioned into the categories just discussed, and, in fact, he wrote many pages trying to establish parallels between his economics and the formulas of rational mechanics (see, for example, Walras, 1909; Walras, 1993: annexe

III). Applying his general scheme, he identified three economic subject matters (Walras, 1868, in Walras, 1896b: 31; Walras, 1874: 22; 1926: 20; 1988: 42–3). One is pure economic theory, which establishes what is true. This is the study of exchange and of value in exchange, or the theory of the determination of social wealth. It is the analysis of the workings of any part of the market economy. Walras described economic theory as a physicomathematical discipline (Walras, 1874: 32; 1926: 29; 1988: 53) early in his career, and as a psychicomathematical discipline in the mature phase of it (Walras, 1898: 464; and see Walras, 1909: 2). He classified his demonstrations that freely competitive markets ensure a relative maximum of welfare as part of pure theory.

The second subject matter is applied economics, an applied natural science which deals with the relationships between people, not as moral beings, but as workers undertaking tasks in accordance with their relationships with things, and which enunciates rules of what is useful (Walras, 1898: 453). To study that subject matter, Walras developed models of the situation that interested him and then deduced the conjectural future that would materialize in them as a consequence of the adoption of policies intended to achieve practical and expedient goals (see Walras, 1898). For example, the goal of maximizing the output of the economic system is useful; applied economics is concerned with how to achieve it.

The third subject matter is social economics, which deals with what is just. It is normative economics, undertaking the formulation and evaluation of normative principles with respect to the distribution of wealth, taxation and rules of property ownership, and determining how to achieve the associated goals. To study that subject matter, Walras used his economic theory to understand a problematic situation, relied on his normative views to formulate a goal regarding it and then made policy recommendations designed to achieve the goal (see Walras, 1896). The usefulness and justice of economic policies are different matters (Walras, 1874: 16; 1926: 16; 1988: 38; 1898: 458), as he explained in an illustration: If 'commodities are sold at high prices to the rich and cheaply to the poor ... there will be a great increase in effective utility', which would be expedient. Social economics, however, reveals that the goal to strive for is not simply maximum utility, but 'the maximum satisfaction *compatible with justice*. The fact that you may be hungrier than me does not confer upon you, in and of itself, the right to eat my dinner' (Walras, 1965b, vol. 2: letter 652). Walras developed an extensive programme of reformulation of economic institutions, incorporating therein his normative goals. These were designed to achieve his conception of economic justice by determining the proper functions of the individual and of the state and by solving the problem of the poverty of the working class. He recommended the purchase of all land by the state, state control of natural monopolies, a regime of free competition, a respect for individual ownership of non-land property and for private income, and the abolition of income taxes.

Walras' theoretical methods

In his economic theorizing, Walras adopted several principal methods. He constructed economic models, defining hypothetical situations in which a simulated economy operates as a functioning system. In the models, he assumed that some conditions that are variables in the real economy are constants. He postulated a system of institutions and procedures that give rise to a pricing process in each market. He used mathematics to express the dependency of variables upon those which determine them and to specify the interrelationships between all variables in his model. He defined microeconomic supply functions and aggregated them, and similarly for demand, and used the aggregate equations in a model of an entire system of interrelated markets. He assumed that the desire to maximize utility is the motivating force in each of his models and in that connection used the marginal method, portraying economic agents as finding their optimum situations by undertaking additional amounts of economic activity as long as the benefit of the additional activity exceeds its cost. Finally, he made simplifying assumptions, such as the assumption that all markets are organized and freely competitive.

Walras developed a method for the construction of his major models (see Walras, 1988). First, he specified their structural characteristics. These include their parameters, variables, types of commodities, participants and market institutions, organization, rules and physical features. Second, he examined the existence of equilibrium and described the equilibrium conditions of the model. For this purpose he used static equations, asserting that they have the equilibrium values of the variables in the model as their solutions. Third, he analysed the stability of the model; that is to say, its adjustment behaviour in disequilibrium whereby the variables converge to their equilibrium values. Fourth, he examined the comparative statics of the model by changing its parameters, tracing the consequences of each change by examining the adjustment processes and deducing the consequences for the equilibrium values of the variables.

Walras also adopted the method of progressive complexity of modelling of an economic system, which he believed that he did in such a way as to achieve progressively closer approximations to reality (Walras, 1877: 310; 1926: 369; 1988: 579). He began with analysing how prices and the volume of sales of commodities are determined if there are fixed total stocks of commodities; then he assumed that there is production of consumer commodities as well as exchange, and that there is also saving and the production of new capital goods; he then undertook a detailed analysis of fiat and commodity moneys, cash balances and the market for loans; and finally he considered the impact of some parametric changes on economic growth.

Thus Walras developed a comprehensive description of the aspects of science in general and applied it to the identification and classification of the branches of economic studies. Moreover, he developed theoretical methods that have become standard procedures in modern economic modelling.

DONALD A. WALKER

References

Walras, Léon (1868), *Recherche de l'idéal social. Leçons publiques faites à Paris. Première série (1867–68) Théorie générale de la société*, Paris: Guillaumin et Cie et Ag^cc Gén^le des Auteurs et Compositeurs; reprinted in Walras (1896b).

Walras, Léon (1874), *Eléments d'économie politique pure ou Théorie de la richesse sociale*, 1st edn, 1st part, Lausanne: L. Corbaz/Paris: Guillaumin/Bâle: H. Georg.

Walras, Léon (1876), 'Equations de l'échange', *Bulletin de la Société Vaudoise des Sciences Naturelles*, **14**, (76), October, 367–94; reprinted in Walras (1993).

Walras, Léon (1877), *Eléments d'économie politique pure ou Théorie de la richesse sociale*, 1st edn, 2nd part, Lausanne: L. Corbaz/Paris: Guillaumin/Bâle: H. Georg.

Walras, Léon (1879), 'De la culture et de l'enseignement des sciences morales et politiques', 2nd part, *Bibliothèque Universelle et Revue Suisse*, 84th year, 3rd period, **3**, (8), September, 223–51; reprinted in Walras (1987).

Walras, Léon (1889), *Eléments d'économie politique pure ou Théorie de la richesse sociale*, 2nd edn, Lausanne: F. Rouge/Paris: Guillaumin/Leipzig: Duncker and Humblot.

Walras, Léon (1896a), *Eléments d'économie politique pure ou Théorie de la richesse sociale*, 3rd edn, Lausanne: F. Rouge/Paris: Guillaumin/Leipzig: Duncker and Humblot.

Walras, Léon (1896b), *Etudes d'économie sociale (Théorie de la répartition de la richesse sociale)*, Lausanne: F. Rouge/Paris: F. Pichon.

Walras, Léon (1898), *Etudes d'économie politique appliquée (Théorie de la production de la richesse sociale)*, Lausanne: F. Rouge/Paris: F. Pichon.

Walras, Léon (1900), *Eléments d'économie politique pure ou Théorie de la richesse sociale*, Lausanne: F. Rouge/Paris: F. Pichon.

Walras, Léon (1909), 'Economique et mécanique', *Bulletin de la Société Vaudoise des Sciences Naturelles*, 5th series, **45**, (166), June, 313–27; reprinted in Walras (1987).
Walras, Léon (1926), *Eléments d'économie politique pure ou Théorie de la richesse sociale*, definitive edition, Paris: R. Pichon and R. Durand-Auzias/Lausanne: F. Rouge.
Walras, Léon (1965a), *Notice autobiographique*, in Walras (1965b, vol. 1, 1–15).
Walras, Léon (1965b), *Correspondence of Léon Walras and Related Papers*, 3 vols, ed. William Jaffé, Amsterdam: North-Holland.
Walras, Léon (1987), *Mélanges d'économie politique et sociale*, ed. Claude Hébert and Jean-Pierre Potier, vol. 7 of Auguste et Léon Walras, *Œuvres économiques complètes*, Paris: Economica.
Walras, Léon (1988), *Eléments d'économie politique pure ou Théorie de la richesse sociale*, comparative edition, prepared by Claude Mouchot, vol. 8 of Auguste et Léon Walras, *Œuvres économiques complètes*, Paris: Economica.
Walras, Léon (1993), *Théorie mathématique de la richesse sociale et autres écrits d'économic pure*, ed. Claude Monchot, vol. 11 of Auguste et Léon Walras, *Œuvres économiques complètes*, Paris: Economica.

Weber, Max

Weber (1864–1920) is generally regarded as one of the founders of modern sociology as well as a prominent member of the German Historical School of Economics. He was born in Erfurt, grew up in Berlin and studied in Heidelberg and Berlin. He worked as an economist during the early part of his career but became increasingly interested in sociology towards the end of his life. Owing to a nervous illness he only taught for brief periods: first economics in Freiburg (1894–6) and Heidelberg (1896–9) and later sociology in Vienna (1918) and Munich (1919–20). For an introduction to Weber's life and work, see Käsler (1988).

Weber's fame as a scholar is primarily connected with *The Protestant Ethic and the Spirit of Capitalism* [1904–5] (1988), even though he is also the author of a large number of other important works in methodology, economic sociology and economic history. Weber's writings in methodology are still often referred to (for a selection in English, see *The Methodology of the Social Sciences*, 1949). Sociologists as well as economic historians count *Economy and Society* (first published posthumously in 1921–2) and *General Economic History* (first published posthumously in 1923) among their classics. Much valuable information can also be found in Weber's brilliant history of Antiquity, *The Agrarian Sociology of Ancient Civilizations* [1909] (1976), and in his impressive 3-volume work on the relationship between religion and the economy in non-western religions, *The Economic Ethic of World Religions* [1915–20] (1951; 1952; 1958).

Even though Weber had been taught the historical kind of economics that dominated the universities in nineteenth century Germany, he was also interested in analytical economics of the British and Austrian type. In the 1890s, he became convinced that the *Methodenstreit* between historical economics and analytical economics could lead to a disaster for economics as a whole, and from then on he devoted a huge amount of energy to attempting to reconcile the two factions. Weber felt that there should ideally be a mixture of historical and analytical economics, and he called his own, preferred type of economics *social economics* (*Sozialökonomik*). When, in 1908, he was asked to edit a giant handbook of economics, he called it *Outline of Social Economics* and invited participants both from the analytical camp (such as Friedrich von Wieser and Joseph Schumpeter) and from historical economics (such as Karl Bücher and Werner Sombart) to participate. More than a dozen volumes finally appeared in Weber's series, though their impact was blunted by World War I and by Weber's premature death in 1920.

During the last two decades of his life, Weber wrote a series of essays on methodology that are still very much discussed in sociology and occasionally also in the other social sciences.

Two ideas that Weber fought hard to establish have been of particular interest to economists: that economics must under no circumstances be a partisan science (as Schmoller and some other German economists had wanted) and that the concepts in the social sciences are formed not only through abstraction but also through an accentuation of what is essential to the phenomena under study (Weber's famous concept of 'ideal type', which has been much debated in economics, especially by the Austrians). A few economists have also noted Weber's effective rebuttal of the position that economics should be based on psychology (Weber, [1908] 1975). Less attention has been paid to Weber's critique of the German Historical School, his concept of causality ('adequate causality') and how sociology should use the approach of *Verstehen* in their analysis of society, including economic phenomena.

The Protestant Ethic and the Spirit of Capitalism has been surrounded by acrimonious debate ever since its first publication in 1904–5 and there are no signs that the debate will abate or be resolved (see, for example, Marshall, 1982, for an account of the various standpoints). Weber's argument was subtle and easy to misunderstand. For modern capitalism to emerge, he argued, it was not only necessary for there to exist a number of modern economic institutions, there also had to be a change in society's basic attitude to entrepreneurship and profit making. Paradoxically, what helped to bring about this change in attitude and to legitimize profit making was religion – more precisely a certain kind of Protestantism that emerged in the sixteenth and seventeenth centuries and which Weber called 'ascetic Protestantism'. In Calvinism and similar sects, hard and methodical work was seen as a way to save one's soul (work as a 'vocation'); and for the average believer, wealth came to be seen as a sign that one had succeeded in pleasing God. Some time after profit making had become legitimate in society at large, Weber argued, the link to religion was broken – and modern capitalism was set free. Today we all have to live in 'the iron cage' of industrial work, to cite one of Weber's most famous metaphors.

General Economic History consists of a lecture series that Weber gave just before his death in 1920, and covers the western world from its beginning to the early nineteenth century. Much interest is focused on the rise of capitalism, and *General Economic History* is seen by some as a corrective of the ideas expressed earlier in *The Protestant Ethic* (see, for example, Collins, 1980). While in the latter work Weber only spoke of the impact of religion on the economy, in *General Economic History* he discusses a number of other factors that have helped bring about western capitalism, such as the rational state, modern accounting, the western city and technology. Weber's work also contains sketches of all the major economic institutions that have appeared in the west, including the guild, the factory and the commenda.

Economy and Society represents Weber's contribution to *Grundriss der Sozialökonomik*, but he unfortunately never got the time to complete it. In its more than 1400 pages the reader will find a full account of Weber's ideas on sociology, including his famous discussions of such topics as charisma and bureaucracy. In Chapter 2 of Part I ('Sociological Categories of Economic Action') the foundation is laid for economic sociology. Like most of Weber's works, *Economy and Society* is very demanding and can hardly be read from first to last page. It nonetheless contains a wealth of ideas on western society and its economy; and it is certainly worth the effort it takes to penetrate. Weber had an encyclopaedic mind and his work – including his essays on methodology – has passed the test of time much better than that of his contemporaries, such as Gustav Schmoller or Werner Sombart.

RICHARD SWEDBERG

Bibliography
Collins, Randall (1980), 'Weber's Last Theory of Capitalism: A Systematization', *American Sociological Review*, **45**, 925–42.
Käsler, Dirk (1988), *Max Weber: An Introduction to His Life and Work*, Trans. Philippa Hurd, Cambridge: Polity Press.
Marshall, Gordon (1982), *In Search of the Spirit of Capitalism: An Essay on Max Weber's Protestant Ethic Thesis*, London: Hutchison.
Weber, Max (1946), *From Max Weber*, ed. Hans H. Gerth and C. Wright Mills, New York: Oxford University Press. This fine anthology contains, among other things, the famous introduction to Weber's *The Economic Ethic of World Religions* ('The Social Psychology of World Religions').
Weber, Max (1949), *The Methodology of the Social Sciences*, trans. and ed. Edward Shild and Henry Finch, New York: Free Press; first published 1904–18.
Weber, Max (1951), *The Religion of China: Confucianism and Taoism*, trans. Hans H. Gerth, Glencoe, IL: Free Press; first published 1915. This is the first volume in *The Economic Ethic of World Religions*.
Weber, Max (1952), *Ancient Judaism*, trans. Hans H. Gerth and Don Martindale, New York: Free Press; first published 1917–20. This is the third volume in *The Economic Ethic of World Religions*.
Weber, Max (1958), *The Religion of India: The Sociology of Hinduism and Buddhism*, trans. Hans H. Gerth and Don Martindale, New York: Free Press; first published 1916–17. This is the second volume in *The Economic Ethic of World Religions*.
Weber, Max (1975), 'Marginal Utility Theory and the Fundamental Law of Psychophysics', *Social Science Quarterly*, **56**, 21–36; first published 1908.
Weber, Max (1976), *The Agrarian Sociology of Ancient Civilizations*, trans. R.I. Frank, London: Verso Books; first published 1909.
Weber, Max (1978), *Economy and Society: An Outline of Interpretative Sociology*, trans. Ephraim Fischoff *et al.*, 2 vols, Berkeley: University of California Press; first published 1921–2.
Weber, Max (1981), *General Economic History*, trans. Frank Knight, New Brunswick: Transaction; first published 1923.
Weber, Max (1988), *The Protestant Ethic and the Spirit of Capitalism*, trans. Talcott Parsons, Gloucester: Peter Smith; first published 1904–5.

Whewell, William

William Whewell (1794–1866) was educated at Trinity College, Cambridge, obtaining a BA degree in 1816 (he graduated Second Wrangler), an MA degree in 1819, and a Doctorate in divinity in 1844, and devoted his life to that college. In 1817, he was elected a Fellow of Trinity College and eventually became Master of that college in 1841. He held professorships in minerology and moral philosophy. Throughout his career, he championed educational reform at Cambridge. In 1837, his *History of the Inductive Sciences* was published, and three years later his *Philosophy of the Inductive Sciences* appeared. These marked him as the leading historian and philosopher of science in Britain of his time. He also published four mathematical economics papers in the *Transactions of the Cambridge Philosophical Society* and a small volume titled *Six Lectures on Political Economy*, which appeared in 1862.

Sydney Smith's biting remark that 'science was his forte, and omniscience his foible', exemplifies the recurrent references to Whewell as a 'polymath'. However, this misconstrues an essential characteristic of his intellectual life which was a continuing effort to synthesize a vast range of allegedly disparate material in the sciences and moral philosophy. Thus understanding Whewell's contributions to economics requires delving into his moral philosophy, his educational doctrine, his estimation on the place of economics in the hierarchy of the sciences and his views on the proper type of mathematics to apply to economics for the purposes that he intended.

Whewell launched a methodological attack on Ricardian deductive economics. Central to Whewell's philosophy of science is the theory that science develops by a careful step-by-step inductive process which uncovers an increasingly comprehensive system of laws that are both universal and necessary. The different stages of development created a hierarchy of sciences. For a discipline as underdeveloped as economics, adopting the deductive method was premature. The Ricardians began 'with some inference of facts'. However, 'instead of working their way cautiously and patiently from there to the narrow principles which immediately inclose a limited experience, and of advancing to wider generalities of more scientific simplicity only as they become masters of more such intermediate truths', they immediately leap 'from the most limited and broken observations to the most general axioms' (letter from Whewell to Richard Jones, 5 March 1829, in the Whewell Papers Collection, Trinity College Library, Cambridge, Add.Mss.c51[62]). Whewell insisted that 'Political economy ... must be a science of *induction* and not of *deduction*. It must *obtain* its principles by reasoning upwards from facts, before it can *apply* them by reasoning downward from axioms' (Whewell, 1831a: 52; italics in original).

Whewell employed mathematics in order 'to separate the moral axioms and assumptions on which the theories rest, from all other matter which may tend to obscure or confound them' (Whewell, 1829: 194). He claimed that his objective was 'to shew the *mode* of applying mathematics so as to extract difficulties of calculation from difficulties of moral reasoning' (letter from Whewell to Richard Jones, 5 March 1829, Whewell Papers Collection). The Ricardians, faulty method led them to commit three types of errors: 'They might have assumed their principles wrongly; they might have reasoned falsely from them in consequence of the complexity of the problem; or they might have neglected the disturbing causes which interfered with the effect of the principal forces' (Whewell, 1829: 194). Whewell's mathematics aimed specifically at the second of these three errors.

For Whewell, mathematics was more useful in the deductive process of deriving conclusions from scientific findings than it was in the inductive process of discovering scientific truth. In his second mathematical economics paper, he stated his conviction that the inductive method must replace Ricardian deduction in economics if economics was to be made scientific:

> The most profitable and philosophical speculations of Political Economy are ... those which are employed not in reasoning *from* principles, but *to* them: in extracting from a wide and patient survey of facts the laws according to which circumstances and conditions determine the progress of wealth, and the fortunes of men. Such laws will necessarily at first, and probably always, be too limited and too dependent on moral and social elements, to become the basis of mathematical calculation: and I am perfectly ready to admit, that the discovery of such laws, and the investigation of their consequences, is an employment of far higher philosophical dignity and importance than any office to which the Mathematician can aspire. (Whewell, 1831b: 196–7)

To appreciate Whewell's contributions to economics, and to mathematical economics in particular, they must be examined within the context of his comprehensive thought, in particular his theological ideas. For Whewell, science and religion do not conflict. Whewell's theological views led him to argue that the laws that regulate people in nature must have counterparts governing people in society. He found political economy particularly interesting because it treated people's interaction with nature (production) as well as their social interaction (exchange). In 1831, he claimed that 'Political economy stands near the boundary line of these two departments of objective and subjective sciences: many of its facts are external (statistical and commercial details), some internal (motives, happiness and virtue, sin and misery)' (Whewell, Whewell Papers Collection, Trinity College Library, Cambridge, R18.17[15]: 46, dated 2 July 1831, quoted in Yeo, 1993: 197). The chapter, 'Political Economy as an Inductive Science', in

Whewell's 1860 book, *On the Philosophy of Discovery*, elaborates this claim. With some reservations, he concluded that the philosophy of discovery employed in natural science might be applied to social science, though such methods would need 'to be greatly modified, or replaced by processes altogether different, when we would make advances in ethical, political, or social knowledge'. The 'observation of external facts of human, individual, and social conduct, and generalizations derived from such observations' are probably governed 'by laws like those which govern the physical sciences', and thus are amenable to the scientific method, which in nineteenth-century Britain meant inductive analysis. Specifically, 'the facts of political constitutions and social relations of communities of men, and the histories of such communities, afford large bodies of materials for political and social science'. Since the 'different forms of society, and the principal motives which operate upon men regarded in masses, may be classified as facts', we might develop 'bodies of knowledge which we may call *Sciences*. ... Among such bodies of knowledge, I may notice as a specimen, the science of *Political Economy*' (Whewell, 1860: 292–3). However, such an approach must probably be limited to such 'external facts' which were in the domain of 'objective science'. Such a method was much less likely to be fruitful when considering the 'internal facts' of the 'subjective science' aspects of political economy.

JAMES P. HENDERSON

Bibliography

Henderson, James P. (1990), 'Induction, Deduction and the Role of Mathematics: The Whewell Group vs. The Ricardian Economists', *Research in the History of Economic Thought and Methodology*, **7**, 1–36.

Henderson, James P. (1996), *Early Mathematical Economics: William Whewell and the British Case*, Rowman & Littlefield.

Hollander, Samuel (1983), 'William Whewell and John Stuart Mill on the Methodology of Political Economy', *Studies in History and Philosophy of Science*, **14**, 127–68.

de Marchi, Neil B. and R.P. Sturges (1973), 'Malthus and Ricardo's Inductivist Critics: Four Letters to William Whewell', *Economica*, **40**, 379–93.

Whewell Papers Collection, Trinity College Library, Cambridge.

Whewell, William (1829), 'Mathematical Exposition of Some Doctrines of Political Economy', *Transactions of the Cambridge Philosophical Society*, vol. III, part I, 192–230; reprinted New York: Augustus M. Kelley, 1971.

Whewell, William (1831a), 'Jones ... on the Distribution of Wealth and the Sources of Taxation', *The British Critic, Quarterly Theological Review, and Ecclesiastical Record*, **X**, (XIX), July, 41–61.

Whewell, William (1831b), 'Mathematical Exposition of Some of the Leading Doctrines in Mr. Ricardo's "Principles of Political Economy and Taxation"', *Transactions of the Cambridge Philosophical Society*, vol. IV, part I, 155–98; reprinted New York: Augustus M. Kelley, 1971.

Whewell, William (1850a), 'Mathematical Exposition of Some Doctrines of Political Economy, Second Memoir', *Transactions of the Cambridge Philosophical Society*, vol. IX, part I: 128–49; reprinted New York: Augustus M. Kelley, 1971.

Whewell, William (1850b), 'Mathematical Exposition of Certain Doctrines of Political Economy, Third Memoir', *Transactions of the Cambridge Philosophical Society*, vol. IX, part II: 1–7; reprinted New York: Augustus M. Kelley, 1971

Whewell, William (1860), *On the Philosophy of Discovery, Chapters Historical and Critical*, London: John W. Parker and Son.

Whewell, William (1862), *Six Lectures on Political Economy*, Cambridge: The University Press; reprinted New York: Augustus M. Kelley, 1967.

Yeo, Richard R. (1979), 'William Whewell, natural theology and the philosophy of science in mid-nineteenth century Britain', *Annals of Science*, **36**, 493–512.

Yeo, Richard R. (1986), 'Scientific Method and the Rhetoric of Science in Britain, 1830–1917', in J.A. Schuster and R.R. Yeo (eds), *The Politics and Rhetoric of Scientific Method*, Boston: Kluwer Academic Press.

Yeo, Richard R. (1991), 'William Whewell's Philosophy of Knowledge and its Reception', in Menachem Fisch and Simon Schaffer (eds), *William Whewell: A Composite Portrait*, Oxford: Oxford University Press.

Yeo, Richard R. (1993), *Defining Science: William Whewell, natural knowledge and public debate in early Victorian England*, Cambridge: Cambridge University Press.

Index

meaningfulness 375
'measurability controversy' 174–5, 176
mechanical materialism 287–8
Meckling, W. 443, 444
Meek, R.L. 243
Mehta, J. 387
Meltzer, A. 323–5
Menger, C. 46, 160, 220, 223–4, 260, 350, 374,
    463–4, 479, 481, 536–7
mental states 288, 345
mercantilism 70
Merkel, H. 457
Merton, R.K. 150, 474, 475
metacriteria 301
metaphor 289–94, 319–20
metaphorical criterion (biology) 162–4
metaphysics 344, 368, 375, 440
metapreferences 140
metatheory 66, 449–51
Metcalfe, J.S. 165
Methodenstreit 130–31, 265, 331, 436, 485, 544
methodological activities (survey data) 490–92
methodological analogy 9
methodological collectivism 345
methodological criterion (evolutionary
    economics) 161
methodological dualism 535–6, 539
methodological holism 229, 328, 350
methodological individualism 13, 14, 41, 69,
    158, 186, 224, 229, 294–300, 306, 308–10,
    335, 345, 350, 400–403, 456, 487, 536–7
  evolutionary economics and 161–2, 165, 250
methodological issues (new class
    macroeconomics) 335–8
methodological pluralism 79, 300–303
methodological principles (institutionalism)
    249–51
methodology
  Hayek 220–23
  Mises on 535–9
  monetarism and 325–6
  professionalism and 142–5
methodology of scientific research programmes
    (MSRP) 270, 271, 304–7, 369
Meyer, E. 331
Meyer, J.H. 132
microeconomics 134, 145, 147, 308, 310
microfoundations 158, 162, 224, 297, 299,
    307–10, 335–6, 519
Milberg, W. 244–5, 386, 420
Mill, J. 311
Mill John Stuart 18–20, 45–6, 55–6, 93, 101–3,
    154, 157, 194, 247, 260, 265–6, 268, 282,
    311–13, 339–40, 355, 359, 371, 425, 496–7,
    541

Miller, D. 16, 511
Miller, G. 75
Millerson, G. 142
Mills, E. 336
Minkler, A. 445
Mirowski, P. 78, 146, 148, 158, 236, 292, 293,
    315, 347, 415, 421, 476, 523, 530
mirror metaphor 429
misspecification testing 117–18, 119, 126–7,
    128–9
Mitchell, Wesley Clair 103, 134, 158, 251–2,
    313–15, 425, 528
Mizon, G.E. 113, 114
model realism 405
models 316–21
  conventionalism 79–83
modernism 79, 370, 384, 385, 419, 421
modus ponens 184
modus tollens 183–4
Mokyr, J. 162
monetarism 48, 322–6, 333
money
  illusion 334
  income 56
  quantity theory of 322–3, 325
  supply 48, 50, 221, 324, 326
Mongin, P. 175, 176–7, 280
Mongiovi, G. 485
monopolistic competition 199
monopoly 359, 360
Moore, G.E. 344, 371, 487, 488
moral hazard 466
moral philosophy 470–71, 546–7
moral principles 86
moral relativism 416–17
moral values 139–40, 481
Morgan, A. de 260
Morgan, C.L. 157
Morgan, M.S. 217–18, 219, 264, 318–19
Morgenstern, O. 30, 171–8, 195, 197, 220
Morishima, M. 14
Moseley, F. 285
Moss, S. 22
Moyer, A. 347
Muellbauer, J. 519
Mullineux, A. 62
multilateral trade 71–2
multiplier–accelerator 62
Munz, P. 169
Murphy, J.B. 165
Murray, P. 284, 286
Musgrave, A. 170, 186
Muth, J. 334, 500
Myers, G. 419
Myrdal, Gunnar 243–4, 326–8, 371